MODERN EUROPE

A History Since 1500

MODERN EUROPE

A HISTORY SINCE 1500

PAUL H. BEIK

AND

LAURENCE LAFORE

SWARTHMORE COLLEGE

A HOLT-DRYDEN BOOK

Henry Holt and Company, Inc., New York

PREFACE

TEACHERS ALWAYS HAVE their own methods and notions. They have, as well, hopes—of composing the perfect syllabus and the perfect lecture, of conducting the perfect discussion. Out of such methods and notions and hopes has grown this volume. It is certainly not the perfect textbook we would like it to be. We hope, however, that it is a practical one which blends the best of the traditional with new views and information.

Specifically, the book's organization embodies the conviction that it is helpful, perhaps necessary, to present topics in segments small and coherent enough to be understood one at a time. The most natural way of doing this is to divide European history by countries and dates, to begin with familiar realities instead of with complicated current interpretations. We have therefore used national histories as the first basis for our divisions into chapters, and terms of time as the basis for our grouping of chapters into sections. But the student must be led beyond the separateness of nations to the patterns of *European* development. We have therefore complemented national histories with general chapters dealing with different kinds of material—social, economic, intellectual, and diplomatic. And we have strongly emphasized the qualities of unity which have led people to speak of Europe as a civilization.

Within the organization as a whole we have been guided by the belief that chapters ought, if possible, to stand by themselves as separate essays. Flexibility in the planning of courses is the aim here; we hope that teachers will be able to omit or rearrange materials without cost in understanding.

Several other beliefs are reflected in this book. The regions of the east are treated here on about the same scale as those of the west, with attention to comparisons between them. It is hoped that this will enhance European history's already honorable role of acquainting American students with societies largely alien and yet related to their own. Correspondingly, we have grown more and more convinced of the importance of the rest of the world to the student of European history. Our book is a history of modern Europe, not of the modern world—but of a Europe recognizably part of the world. We have been at pains to find the ways in which European and world history are intertwined. We have also tried to do justice to the events of the decade and a half since World War II, by now so numerous as to demand ordering; and we have provided for recent years the same volume of detail and the same sort of analysis as for earlier eras. Finally, mention may be made of our hopes for the lexicon of terms in Appendix A. It is a list of words which appear frequently in historical explanations. It is not an attempt to sum up, define, or repeat the substance of our text. Our aim is to provide explanations which foster (not substitute for) thought about terms which are continually encountered and often misused.

If the period of preparation for writing this book coincides with our teaching careers, its actual composition has occupied some five years. During that time we have been enlightened and assisted by many people. Our debts are too large to be reported in detail, but our gratitude is particularly due to Professor Mary Albertson of Swarthmore College, who has for years encouraged our teaching and thinking about history; to Professors Henry Bertram Hill and George L. Mosse of the University of Wisconsin, Fritz Stern of Columbia University, and Robert F. Byrnes of Indiana University, who read and improved the manuscript, Professor Hill in full and the others in part; to Professors Edith Philips, Frank C. Pierson, and James A. Field, Jr. of Swarthmore, who were consulted concerning, respectively, intellectual, economic, and military history; to Professors Robert M. Walker and Hedley Rhys of the Swarthmore Fine Arts Department, who gave invaluable assistance in the selection of illustrations; to Mr. Carl Zigrosser, Curator of Prints and Vice Director of the Philadelphia Museum of Art, who suggested several of the illustrations; to Mr. Robert L. Patten, an undergraduate at Swarthmore, and to Mr. Paul H. Noyes and Miss Jean Herskovits, recent graduates, who made most helpful suggestions about various parts of the manuscript; and to Mr. Jan Hasbrouck of the European Edition of the *New York Herald Tribune,* who provided much of the material for Chapters 54 and 56. Our deepest gratitude and greatest respect are owing to Doris Beik, who contributed incredible amounts of time, patience, and expertness both to the substance of the book and to the many chores which attended its preparation.

Swarthmore, Pennsylvania   P.H.B.
February 20, 1959   L.L.

CONTENTS

PART TWO

THE OLD REGIME

1648–1789

PART THREE

REVOLUTIONARY AND CONSERVATIVE EUROPE
1789–1870

PART FOUR

PLEBEIAN AND IMPERIAL EUROPE
1870–1914

PART FIVE

THE FORFEITURE OF WORLD POWER
1914–1939

PART SIX

DIVIDED EUROPE
SINCE 1939

LIST OF MAPS

PART ONE

THE
BUILDING
OF THE
EUROPEAN
STATES

1500–1648

1

THE ASPECT OF EUROPE IN 1500

THE AGE SINCE 1500 is known by historians as the modern age. No single event marked the birth of the modern world; and to begin studying its history is not to begin the story of a civilization which was suddenly created whole and new, but to come upon actions already underway—or, more graphically, to board a moving train on a journey that it had already begun across a rapidly changing landscape.

The modern age might well be called the European age, for it has been shaped by the ideas and customs of the people of Europe. It is their product. But in 1500 their extraordinary achievements were largely in the future. Indeed, a few decades earlier many Europeans had imagined their civilization in danger. In May of 1453, Constantinople fell to the Turks, and when the news reached Rome there were many who heard it with dread, fearing that the center of western Christendom might shortly follow its sister-capital in the east into enthrallment by the Moslem conquerors. But Rome and the west were to stand. Henceforth the vitality of its Moslem rivals would decline while that of Christian Europe grew. There were evidences of European vigor on every hand. Already, in Mainz on the Rhine, Gutenberg was printing his Bibles and providing the west with a curiously powerful invention to spread its culture. The great explorations were already in progress, and forty years after the fall of Constantinople, Christopher Columbus was to find for Spain and Europe a new world. Henceforth, Europe, the heir of the Mediterranean cultures of classical times, was to face the west, drawing new riches and new power from the Atlantic lands.

But no listing of actions in progress could have foreshadowed the impending five centuries in which European civilization was to experience worldly and intellectual successes without precedent in history. Prodigiously virile, Europeans were to people empty continents, to release the forces of nature, to generate fantastic wealth, and to impose their culture throughout the planet.

THE PLACE AND THE PEOPLES

This Europe was a peninsula projecting westward from the massive Eurasian continent. It possessed no clear boundary to the east, although geographers have arbitrarily chosen the Ural Mountains north of the Caspian Sea. But "Europe" has always meant more than a measurable territory. It has been the interaction of the place and its peoples which earned for it in history a rank that geography denied it—the rank of "continent." In the Middle Ages European life may best be described as "Christendom", a cultural fusion of the western half of the Roman Empire with the peoples who conquered it and took its religion. In the late fifteenth century the consciousness of religious community was still strong, but in certain "European" activities, such as the formation of military alliances, the Moslem Turks were beginning to play a regular part (as the Russians, whose Christianity differed from that of Rome, were to do later on). Moreover, for some the meaning of "Europe" was to expand in future time: upward with the achievements of the European mind, and outward as those achievements were impressed on ever-widening portions of the globe.

We may begin, however, with the physical home from which these accomplishments sprang. Europe's most important features are its waters and mountains. Almost surrounded by ocean and seas, it has been enriched by the treasure and stimulated by the information brought home by its mariners. The great mountains near its center have divided Europe into separate cultural and geographical regions; from these mountains rise the great rivers flowing outward like spokes of a wheel—Po to the south, Danube to the east, Rhine to the north, Rhone to the west—watering the surrounding plains, and forming paths of commerce. South of the Alps, waterways cut through endless mountains and plateaux. The great crescent above the Mediterranean is a crumpled, difficult terrain, like Maine or California. In the valleys and along the coast from Spain to Asia Minor, the Mediterranean climate offers hot dry summers and warm rainy winters. North of the Alps the hills level off to plains which sweep, several hundred miles wide, along the whole northern coast. The land slopes down to sea-marshes and sand-islands along the North Sea, then sinks beneath the water to rise again in the hills and mountains of the British Isles and Scandinavian peninsula.

This large area is not geographically and historically a unit. Western Europe is France, the left bank of the Rhine, and the British Isles. To this region of broad plains, long rivers, green, rainy countryside in summer, and moist, mild winters, the Romans came by way of the Rhone valley. Central Europe—roughly, east of the Rhine and north of the Alps and Danube—the Romans did not colonize, except briefly along the Rhine and lower Danube. It is an inland region of more severe weather. East of a line from Denmark to the Adriatic, winters are long and bitter, summers short. Since no barriers except occasional marshes divide it from the Russian plains, it is difficult to distinguish Central from Eastern Europe in purely physical terms. It is enough here to notice the broad isthmus between the Baltic and Black seas, and with it two subregions: (1) the plain above the Sudeten and Carpathian mountains; and (2) below them Bohemia and the Danube basin. In studying modern history it is most convenient to consider the Mediterranean climatic zone along with the others, adding Spain and southern France to Western Europe, Italy to West Central Europe, and the Balkan peninsula to East Central Europe.

These regions in 1500 held a thinly scattered sixty to seventy million people. Or, better, "peoples," for Europe then as now was polyglot. Out of the confusion of migrant tribes who had crossed the Romans' Rhine-Danube frontier a thousand years before (and had themselves been intermittently shocked and rearranged by invasions across the steppes from Asia), there had settled finally most of the nationalities we know today.

The best introduction to the nationalities of Europe is to study the names on a language map. Although language is not a certain guide to nationality, the languages of Europe were the most persistent indicators of national associations through centuries of political change. On the map, certain primary language groups are readily discerned. First, the "Romance" languages, descendants of the Latin of the Romans. The most important Romance languages are French,

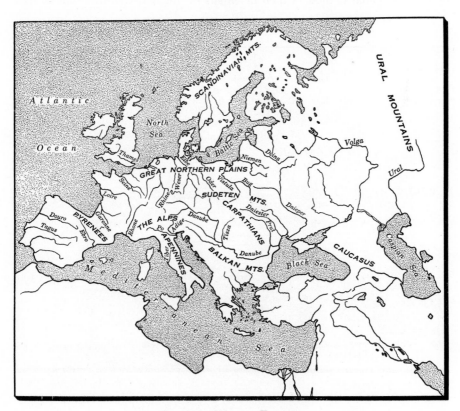

PHYSICAL MAP OF EUROPE

Italian, Spanish, and Portuguese, along with Catalan (spoken in northeastern Spain) and Rumanian, and various smaller dialects. Second, the Teutonic languages, of which the most important are German, Dutch, Danish, Swedish, and Norwegian. Third, the Slavic languages, which include Russian, Polish, Czech, Serb, Bulgar, and many others. Some of the less important languages of these groups have played large historical roles, when the people who spoke them (such as the Slavic Ukrainians) claimed or achieved political importance, or when, like the Romance Provençaux of southern France, they contributed to literature and thought. There are, moreover, very important languages which do not fall into these main groups. Greek is of a separate ancestry. So is the Finno-Ugric group, variations of which are spoken in Hungary, in Finland, and in Estonia and Lapland. So is the Celtic group, to which belong Welsh and Irish and the Scots' Gaelic; so are the Baltic languages of Lithuania and Latvia. English, the most important of all, is a hybrid, derived basically from Teutonic sources but altered and enriched by large accretions of Latin words and forms.

All these languages, except the Finno-Ugric, are descended from ancient sources in India and Persia. They are called, together, "Indo-European." By 1500 most of them were so far evolved along independent lines that each was completely incomprehensible to people who spoke another, but they had not yet assumed their present form. What is modern French was then the language of a small group of people in the Paris region. The rest of the French spoke dialects often more similar to those of their neighbors in "foreign" countries than to that

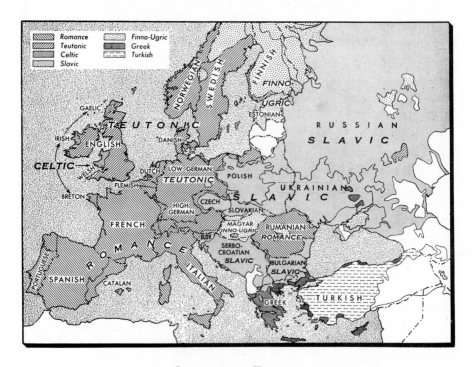

LANGUAGES OF EUROPE

of their capital city. Portuguese was still a Spanish dialect, and Dutch a German one.

These complexities of the European scene, bewildering at the first encounter, need not be absorbed all at once. It will help to simplify them if we start with a first estimate of how Europeans lived in 1500.

A SOCIETY AND ITS PAST

Most Europeans were peasants who farmed the land crudely in traditional ways. They lived in small isolated villages, the houses huddled together against winter cold and the peril of strangers. The villages varied physically from region to region: the plaster and tile of Italy, stone in France, timber and thatch in the far north. But all had certain things in common. The center of each was a church, and in every church of Western and Central Europe the Latin service was intoned and the Bishop of Rome was revered as the Vicar of Christ. From the village, usually dominated by a castle or manor house, peasant families went on foot to unfenced fields or to shared pasture or woodland. Usually one of the three main fields for crops lay fallow, regaining its fertility. In the other two the peasants worked separate strips, each family holding some of the good land and some of the bad. A peasant did not "own" the land, in our sense of the word, nor did he usually "rent" it. Most peasants had rights in the fields, forests, pastures, and villages, but so did the manor lord to whom they owed labor and payments and obedience.

It was a slow-moving existence, keyed to survival rather than to change. In the normal course of things a villager would not leave home, learn to read, raise a new crop, or see an object not made or grown within a few miles of his village.

The Europe of those days was not entirely rural, however, nor was it without commerce. Despite slow communication by cart or pack train along dirt roads or by boat on weed- and silt-infested rivers or by ocean-going ships which hugged the coasts; despite bandits and toll gates, meager surpluses and innumerable regulations, goods were exchanged. Trade had never wholly ceased even in the most troubled eras of the Middle Ages. By 1500 it had for centuries been on the increase. Differences of climate and landscape coupled with human needs had set in motion Swedish iron, Baltic lumber, English and Spanish wool, Flemish and Italian cloth, French wines, spices from the Orient, glassware, cutlery, and other artifacts. If most Europeans lived close to subsistence, a minority of the well-to-do was ready to buy. The Europe of the peasant villages was dotted with towns, some of them great seaports on the northern or Italian coasts, others linking the routes between. The towns were few, by our standards, and not large—perhaps two dozen had more than 40,000 residents—but they were the leaders. With the proceeds of banking and commerce, townsmen (burghers, bourgeois) grew rich and added their contributions to princely and religious sponsorship of the arts. Businessmen's houses abutted tranquilly on the spires of cathedrals and the cloisters of abbeys and the palaces of princes. Widening use of money affected the incomes and political power of kings and nobles. In those country districts most sensitive to commerce, dues in cash had long been replacing payment in goods and humiliating personal servitudes. In the towns old-fashioned skilled craftsmen with mainly local interests and a regulatory cast of mind were alarmed by the self-confidence of great merchants and bankers. The Church was affected too; since it was a major holder of property and of political power and guardian of learning and conduct, it was worried by the threat of change.

The old European society still held its contours. Each man was still expected to remain at the station in life where he had been born. A similar social hierarchy, in which each group had its own function, existed all over Europe: a "first estate" (clergy); "second estate" (nobles); "third estate" (townsmen and peasants).

European society, standing in 1500 on the threshold of unprecedented power, wealth, and glory, was already the heir to long ages of achievement. Greek

A VILLAGE IN SOUTHERN ENGLAND, little changed since 1500 except that the fields, instead of being farmed in strips, are today surrounded with the hedges which originated in the "enclosure movement" (described in Chapters 2 and 12). (Radio Times Hulton Picture Library, London)

culture had reached its height and spread over the Mediterranean world by the time of Christ; and Rome by 500 A.D. had conquered, extended, and then lost control of that world. The next five centuries, the so-called "dark ages," were characterized by the movement and settling down of peoples on both sides of the old frontier of the Roman empire. From the world of Rome three heirs emerged: an Arab empire from Spain to the Indian Ocean, devoted to Islam and the cult of Mohammed, preserving much of the learning and culture of classical civilization; Byzantium in the Balkans and Asia Minor, a direct descendant of the eastern half of the Roman Empire, with its political and religious (Greek Christian) capital at Constantinople; and the Europe of our story.

After the year 1000 Europe was finding new energy and inspiration. As life became more secure, better agriculture enriched it. Europeans were able to increase in numbers, plow more land, build cities, crusade eastward along the Baltic and Mediterranean and southward in Spain. Into the schools of law, medicine, and theology of the universities was increasingly reintroduced the science of the ancient world. Into the masonry of castles and cathedrals which still reign in unrivaled splendor above the European skyline went extraordinary artistic and engineering achievement. By about 1250, a convenient date with which to mark the end of what are usually called the High Middle Ages, representative assemblies had appeared and new business activity was stirring. Thereafter such an extension and adjustment of medieval methods occurred as to warrant the label "transition to modern times," though, to be sure, the assigning of periods to history is best thought of as an exercise of the imagination.

INTRODUCTION TO EUROPEAN POLITICS

On a political map of Europe in 1500 there may be recognized many of the states of our own century. England existed and so did France, Spain, and Portugal. In the north, Scandinavia—Norway, Sweden, and Denmark—was still united under Danish rule; at this time these peoples were no less homogeneous than the residents of various parts of France, although distinct national sentiments were already growing, especially in Sweden. The map of Central Europe was a jig-saw puzzle bearing the title Holy Roman Empire but suggestive of modern Germany. In the south the pieces of the puzzle were patterned around Italy's principal cities. Something resembling the modern Netherlands was visible, as was Switzerland. To the east the Ottoman Empire of the Turks, Hungary, and Poland-Lithuania were somewhat swollen versions of states with which we are familiar. Muscovy, built from the expansion of the Moscow principality, suggested Russia to come. Although not all of the nation states of contemporary Europe were there in 1500, there were visible indications of the form they would take. This is particularly clear if we compare the map with that of, for example, 1453, on which Spain will be found divided, Russia still fragmented and at least nominally under Mongol rule, France as yet unconsolidated by its kings, and archaic Burgundy perhaps the strongest power in western Europe.

This dramatic half century of consolidations is associated in most histories with the names and work of monarchs to whom we shall return later—Ferdinand and Isabella of Spain, Louis XI of France, Henry VII of England, Ivan the Great of Russia. Its progress is one of the justifications for calling the sixteenth century "modern", but in adopting this convenience, particularly with a map before us, we are in danger of being misled. The characteristic feature of modern states is "sovereignty"—complete and final independence. It is all too easy to look with twentieth-century eyes at this map; to see states as complete and separate entities, sovereign to the earth's core; to see all nationalities striving for the creation of their own states; and to see all rulers as aiming at the boundaries we have come to regard as "natural."

The reality of the life beneath the colors on the map was far more complex than might at first appear. To do that reality justice it is necessary, first, to discuss the question of nationalities.

Because Europe was always a melting pot of peoples we may best avoid such terms as "race." Breeds of men do exist, but their complexities defy our analysis. Nationalities, on the other hand, may be identified by their shared awareness of things learned in living together, usually language, sometimes religion, always distinctive customs of some sort, and consciousness of their difference from others. The centuries after the fall of Rome saw the formation of many such nationalities in Europe. Some, the French in the valleys of the Seine and Loire,

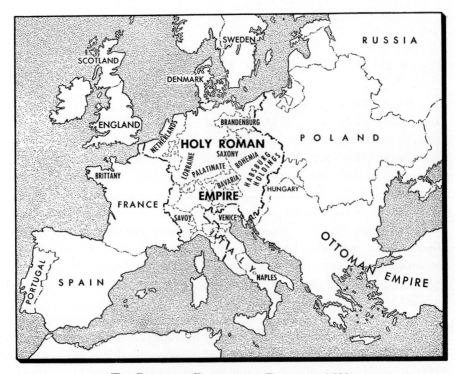

THE POLITICAL DIVISIONS OF EUROPE IN 1500

or the English along the Thames, or the Portuguese in the Atlantic lowlands of the Iberian peninsula, reached a high level of national consciousness. Others such as the Bulgars and Serbs, recently subjected to Turkish rule, possessed more dimly the sense of brotherhood.

A historian cannot now measure the national sentiments of those days, which varied with levels of culture and communication in the various regions. But we can emphasize that *nationality* depended on awareness, on psychology, not on blood inheritance or political independence.

In 1500 a sense of nationality existed in many, indeed in most, places, but in varying degrees of intensity. National sentiment poses one of the most difficult of the historian's problems. It is not easy, for example, to find evidence of what "France" meant to a Burgundian or a Parisian. "France" was coming to mean something, without doubt, but Burgundy and Paris meant something too, and the most that can be said is that a fusion of local with national loyalties was taking place. We can study the words (though their meaning has changed) of a gifted Italian like Machiavelli who was aware of the idea of "Italy" and of an Italian nationality, but what can we know of the sentiments of illiterate Venetians and Neapolitans?

Such questions are important because awareness of nationality, unquestionably on the rise in 1500, was to increase in intensity through succeeding centuries, first in Europe, and then throughout the world. One of the most potent political forces in our own times is national*ism,* which may be defined as a tendency to give one's highest loyalty to one's nationality and to require compatriots to do likewise, especially in moments of crisis. Precisely because we are so accustomed to nationalism in the full tide of its psychological power, we are in danger of imagining its appearance at too early a point in history. Probably the best safeguard against this error is to distinguish between nationalities and nationalism: nationalities (aware of national characteristics), which as we have seen were deeply rooted in the Europe of 1500; and national*ism* (intense loyalty to a nationality), which belonged to the future. If nationalism existed at all in 1500 it was the exception, not the rule.

In the Europe of 1500 political allegiance was still largely centered on human leaders. The idea of the state was still half-mixed with that of personal property. Populations were expected to be loyal to the duke or king in whose realm they lived. Such realms, indeed, were like family patrimonies which in war and diplomacy could pass from family to family with no thought to the inhabitants' wishes. Such a change of sovereign could happen to a Brittany or a Bohemia, even, as we shall see, to Spain. Unquestionably the dynastic ambitions of some rulers, like Louis XI of France, furthered national (as well as personal) aggrandizement. But their motives differed little from those of other monarchs who, like the Habsburgs, presided over a variety of national groups. National sentiments certainly existed in those days, and played a part in many events; but the most important interest of sovereigns was to win glory and lands for themselves and their heirs. The states of Europe were still primarily dynastic.

To grasp the importance of the unification by 1500 of such dynastic states as France, we must recognize the shortcomings of their competitors, large and small. There remained in the Christian community two large organizations recalling medieval aspirations toward political unity. One of them, the Catholic Church, still claimed the religious allegiance (and religion was broadly interpreted) of all Christians, rulers and ruled. In fact, however, the zone between religious and political supervision on the part of the church was subject to dispute.

A second international body, the Holy Roman Empire, shared with the Papacy the ancient tradition that all Christians owed dual allegiance to Pope and Emperor. The Holy Roman Emperors had once claimed to be superior to Christian kings. Since the fall of Constantinople to the Turks in 1453, the Empire's only rival to the imperial tradition of the original Rome was the little-known Ivan III of Muscovy, who had married the niece of the last Byzantine emperor. In actuality, however, the Holy Roman Empire had now shrunk to a central European organization of uncertain solidity. Of its more than three hundred members, most, though not all, were German-speaking duchies, archduchies, archbishoprics, free cities, and so on. But the Empire was not a national state, nor was the emperor an effective ruler over this network of interlocking loyalties. The Habsburgs had enough influence to maintain family possession of the imperial crown, traditionally bestowed by seven powerful princes known as electors, but like other rulers the Emperor gave most of his attention to his hereditary holdings, within and without the Empire. The Holy Roman Empire was thus in theory more, and in practice less, than a state.

At the other extreme from the Empire and Papacy were the many city-states like Venice, Florence, Milan, and the Papal States in the Italian peninsula, or the confederated trading cities—Lübeck, Hamburg, Bremen, Danzig, and so on—known as the Hanseatic League. Some of these, like the Hanseatic cities and Milan, were nominally under the Empire. Other places like the Netherlands cities Ghent, Bruges, Antwerp, Brussels, Liége, Utrecht, Delft, and Rotterdam were in theory dynastic holdings but in practice enjoyed a large measure of self-government.

The Swiss cantons, by virtue of their military power and practical independence from the Holy Roman Empire, may be called city-states. It is difficult to generalize about the city-states. Many of them, in the late Middle Ages, had reached a high level of prosperity and civilization. But probably, on the other hand, class and personal rivalries tended to be especially bitter in such small arenas. Even where this was not the case city-states could not match the power of the larger monarchies like France, England, and Muscovy, though they might excel in wealth and culture. Both the German and the Italian cities were to suffer relative economic declines as trade shifted, after the great discoveries, to the Atlantic seaboard. The city-states were less at home in sixteenth-century Europe than they had been in earlier ages. Like the imperial tradition embodied in the pretensions of the Church and the Holy Roman Empire, they were fading.

The future belonged to the dynastic, monarchical states which were coming into being by 1500. Europe by this time was reaching a cultural level which favored political units intermediate in size and coherency *between* the city-state or principality and the vague international structures of Church and Empire. This is not to say that there would be no further question of supernational domination. The Church and the Empire, aided by Habsburg ambition, were still to wield great force. Later, the French and the Germans, each on two occasions, and the Russians at least twice, were to spread alarm in Europe.

Anticipating these great dramas of international conflict, we may observe that there was to develop in the state system of independent and competing units a tendency often referred to as the "balance of power," by which the weaker joined forces against a power or powers which threatened their independence. Without as yet requiring a complete analysis of the system's complexities, three additional observations may prove useful. In the diplomacy of the Italian city-states in the half-century before 1500 may be found a kind of forecast in miniature of the European state system to come, for there with cold-blooded rationality ambitious rulers held each other in check until larger units from outside the system (France and Spain) entered the game and overran them. Secondly, in Europe as a whole a "state system" of this kind was long in forming but was to be most clearly visible after 1648. And in the third place, as we shall have occasion to observe, maneuvering for aggrandizement and survival has been constant throughout modern times, but other motives—for example, religious, economic, dynastic, and nationalistic aims—have varied with the evolution of societies and governments.

FORMS OF GOVERNMENT

The characteristic form of government in the developing nation-states was a strong monarchy, but this term, like the map of Europe, merely summarizes a complex situation. Monarchy, in the sense of the personal leadership of kings, was a tradition inherited from the days when the Germanic tribes overran the Roman Empire, perhaps inherited also from the Romans themselves. Kingship had altered its character during the Middle Ages, when a minimum of trade and travel had encouraged a tendency toward government on a small scale in each local community. Even in the later centuries, with the revival of towns, commerce, and communications, kings did not exercise authority directly over all of their subjects. Except in the king's home province, the actual governing (tax collecting, commanding soldiers, judging) was often done by his vassals, that is, by nobles with whom he had entered into agreements for mutual support. The nobles were powerful in their own regions, whose rights to their land were not clearly distinguished from their rights over the inhabitants. In return for their right to govern, they swore to support and defend the feudal monarchy. The business of government in these feudal times was scattered over a complicated network of property rights and personal relationships. Being king meant presiding over and respecting this network of rights. It did not mean having a monopoly of the functions which we would call governmental.

By the late fifteenth century, kings had for some time been increasing their

CARCASSONNE, FRANCE. A medieval walled city. (French Government Tourist Office)

authority in two principal ways. They had been consolidating their personal holdings, the royal domains over which they enjoyed direct political control, as Louis
XI of France did when he inherited Provence in 1481. They had also been extending the functions of royal government, reaching, whenever possible, into the
jurisdictions of their nobles, taking from them bit by bit the right to govern but
leaving them the right to properties, such as land and the dues of peasants. This
process, by which kings dismantled feudalism and built in its place absolute
monarchy, began in the late Middle Ages and continued through the early centuries of modern times. It is one of the great themes of European political history,
for out of the struggle between kings and aristocracies grew the machinery of
modern states and their characteristic constitutional forms.

There would come a time when absolute monarchy as a political force
would be replaced by other forms, but for the moment the tide of everyday living
conditions was running its way. The consolidation and stricter rule of larger territorial units brought many advantages. Probably the king's justice and policing
were better for business and agriculture than the feudal politics of an earlier age.
Although the "lower" orders did not, of course, vote feudalism out and absolute
monarchy in, their increasingly various activities did provide means by which
kings overcame the resistance of feudal nobles. Money for the royal treasury,
educated but subordinate and removable officials, knowledge of Roman law which
justified the king's actions by recalling a time when rulers were not bound by
feudal contracts—these were some of the means which the new age provided. The
list is not complete. One would have to mention the gunpowder and firearms
which kings could better afford than even their wealthiest subjects, the mercenary
armies, the overseas explorations, and with all these the relative economic decline,
at a time of rising commercial profits, of the military aristocracy whose incomes
were largely dependent on agriculture.

Among the means used by kings in their push toward absolute power was
royal control of church and military appointments, a useful patronage. Besides
influencing noble families by lucrative offices in the church or the royal service,
kings began to provide, in court ritual, a symbolic indication of royal supremacy.
Perhaps most important of all was the use, from the thirteenth century on, of
representative assemblies like the Estates General in France, the Cortes in Spain,
Parliament in England, and much later the Zemsky Sobor in Russia. Such assemblies, crudely representing the various occupations in society, could provide kings
with justifications for acts which seemed useful to the safety or welfare of the
whole people. In such assemblies kings could seek the collaboration of townsmen
against the nobles. Their mere existence posed the question of an authority for
the *whole* realm.

Most of the devices used by the king had their dangers from his viewpoint. Representative assemblies could divide and quarrel, or, more ominous still,
take a solid stand against the king's authority. Church appointments could lead
to quarrels with the Pope. Even court ritual, if it surrounded a weak ruler with
powerful nobles, could misdirect or paralyze absolutism. The European future
was big with these possibilities, but in 1500 absolutism as a political form was

still only half-grown. In later chapters we shall follow its fortunes in specific countries.

EUROPE'S PROSPECTS

All of the historic changes mentioned thus far—the formation of absolute monarchies, the consolidation of the kingdoms, the growing importance of nationality, the greater use of money, the spread of commerce, the beginnings of overseas explorations, the increasing weight of townsmen in a hierarchical society—all these, discernible now after five hundred years, were at the time lost in the welter of current events. Few men in any age have the genius to see the pattern of a new world taking shape within the familiar diversity of the old. If such men existed in the late fifteenth century, they must have glimpsed signs of a changing mood, of new tastes and ideas, besides the new social and political contours of Europe. There was a greater value being placed on earthly things, a changing notion of how life should be lived and of how death should be faced and salvation obtained. The mind of Europe was changing.

It is these changes which lead men to call the sixteenth century the first of the modern age, and we shall return to them in later chapters. They came about gradually, and were intricately connected with one another. Modern Europe, indeed, is merely the sum of a number of combinations of changes, each in turn mingling with others to produce a constant flow of further changes and further combinations.

For the sake of convenience, the course of events since 1500 will be divided, arbitrarily, into the following sections:

I. The Building of the European States, 1500–1648. This was the early modern stage, when the institutions and customs already recognizable in 1500 were solidifying.

II. The Old Regime, 1648–1789. During this stage the characteristic institutions of the early modern period achieved maturity and provoked a need and a demand for their drastic alteration.

III. Revolutionary and Conservative Europe, 1789–1870. In this age of drastic experimentation and remodeling of the political and economic life of Europeans, many of the problems of our own age were arising as those of early times were disappearing.

IV. Plebeian and Imperial Europe, 1870–1914. This was the age of European predominance in the world and of new power of the mass of the people at home and solicitude for their needs—and the age, too, when internal conflicts prepared the way for the serious weakening of Europe.

V. The Forfeiture of World Power, 1914–1939. This was the age when a great war broke the world domination of European nations and brought about conflicts and problems which threatened European civilization.

VI. Divided Europe: since 1939. The place of Europe in the contemporary world.

Europe on the eve of this journey—Europe of the fifteenth century—had already a rich accumulation of assets. The critical clarity and the sense of proportion of the Greeks were at work beside Roman respect for law and Roman administrative practices. Hebrew and Christian monotheism, Hebrew wrath at injustice and Christian compassion and respect for every person, were already ingredients of a European point of view. The science of the ancient world, saved and added to by Byzantium and the Arabs, was being supplemented by new inquiries. The processes of Reason were not alien to a Europe which had known the rigid intellectual disciplines of the medieval philosophers, who were called scholastics. Now Reason was being coupled more frequently with investigation of the facts of the everyday world. In feudal contracts and town charters and parliaments Europe had a reservoir of political experience to add to that of its kings and churchmen. In princely courts and urban guilds, universities, and vernacular languages, it had found talent and means of expression. The list would be too long if we tried to summarize the qualities which made Europe's prospects auspicious. For the moment it is enough to be reminded once more that we are entering a story in the midst of rapid action. Next we shall examine some of the forms of that action.

2

THE GEOGRAPHIC AND ECONOMIC EXPANSION OF EUROPE

In the previous chapter Europe was introduced in 1500. Now come the explorers, the merchants, the manufacturers, and the officials of the expanding material world. Later will come the men of art and thought and religion; and finally the soldiers and statesmen. This first group of chapters surveys the early modern period. The events described in each chapter were of course influenced by what will be narrated in others. But it is impossible to think of everything at once, and so different aspects of European life must be treated one at a time.

In the present chapter there will be five main sections. First will be told how Europe's medieval ways of making a living evolved into new and more productive forms. A general term, "capitalism," useful in summing up the characteristic economic activities in modern times, will be introduced. Next the great discoveries beyond the old Mediterranean world will be described. Here the term usually used is "expansion of Europe." Third and fourth, economic and social changes in Europe will be analyzed, bringing together several notions such as "commercial revolution," "sixteenth-century price rise," and "putting-out system" of manufacturing. Finally, the ideas and policies called "mercantilism" will be discussed.

THE RISE OF CAPITALISM

Many people still have a cartoon-like picture of medieval life being lived on self-sufficient manors in an economy where barter took the place of money. The texture of medieval society was of course more rich and varied than this. In the earliest centuries, say the sixth and seventh, much remained of Roman cities, coins, and country villas. It is true that in what people used to call the "dark ages," the eighth and ninth centuries, the supply of merchandise, merchants, and money declined as sea trade in the Mediterranean became unsafe. Cities shrank or disappeared, and something resembling self-sufficiency became the rule in each rural community. More than nine-tenths of Europeans knew little except life on the manor. With local variations, some form of economic and social organization like the manor prevailed from England to Russia. If one had to give a single name to the medieval economy, "manorial system" would be as good as any.

But medieval life was not static. Too much emphasis on the manor does injustice to the population growth and revival of trade and of town life which took place between the eleventh and the mid-thirteenth centuries. Whether or not one calls the medieval economy "manorial," it contained a considerable amount of trading and of manufacture of goods for sale. Exchange enriched life, although subsistence was still the major problem. Anxiety about subsistence was expressed in town and guild regulations aimed at assuring citizens access to the food and organized craftsmen access to the customers of the region. It was also reflected in the Catholic Church's teachings about business practices: usury was condemned and was defined simply as taking interest on a loan, for money was regarded as sterile, and he who demanded repayment of more than he lent was profiting by the misfortunes of others. Those who sold goods should charge only a just price, that is, the cost of production plus a fraction for the wage of anyone who had worked on the product. A Christian should not seek profits or try to amass wealth or get ahead in life. It was proper to earn only enough to maintain the station into which one was born. These were views appropriate to a time of scarcity. Imperceptibly, however, as the thirteenth century gave way to the fourteenth and fifteenth, the medieval economy changed, and with it some men's attitudes toward business enterprise.

By the mid-fourteenth century periodic fairs like those of Champagne, in France on the trade route between the Rhone Valley and the Low Countries, were giving way to permanent markets in cities. In the north the Hanseatic League of cities on the German and Polish rivers, the North Sea, and the Baltic, was matching the activities of the Italian cities like Venice and Genoa. Ocean-going ships were passing Gibraltar on their way to and from the English Channel and the North Sea. The Alpine passes, the Rhine, the cities in the Netherlands and Southern Germany, were busy. Throughout Europe, lesser towns were developing trade. Manufacturing was everywhere expanding, and new means of securing capital were developed. Merchants became money-changers and bankers, and dealt in a variety of credit and investment devices. The Church's prohibition of usury could be avoided by pretending that the lender was a partner. Shares were sold in joint-stock enterprises. Banks and merchants-turned-bankers accepted deposits and issued bills of exchange (promises to pay at a later date, perhaps at another place and in another currency) which facilitated transfers of funds. By the end of the fifteenth century there were many examples of capital (wealth invested to produce more wealth) being used in trade and banking and to some extent in industry. Europe was able to produce a surplus over and above the needs of subsistence. There were increasing numbers of men with capital, with knowledge of how to use it to produce more wealth, and with willingness to use these methods for profit in spite of the Church's traditional attitude toward business.

These attitudes and activities were not dominant in Europe's economy by 1500. They were important enough, however, to change the quality of life for many people, strong enough to change the direction of economic development. For this reason it is customary to attach the name "capitalism" to the new economic practices which made use of accumulations of capital in a new spirit. In other words the movement inside the medieval economy from at least 1200 to the point where our book begins in 1500 was toward capitalism.

Most people are familiar with this term, for we have been accustomed to thinking of it as the economic system of modern times. If asked to define it, we would probably make such a list as the following, embracing most of the characteristics of familiar economic life: (1) private ownership of the means of production; (2) profit as the motive which keeps men competing to organize production and supply the market; (3) exchange based on the use of money, which ties the whole economy together; (4) production for a market which will sell goods to consumers; (5) competition of producers and consumers in the market place, setting the prices of goods; (6) markets on a large as well as a small scale, serving many people and areas; (7) a distinction between the people who own and control the means of production, and those who are hired to work for wages.

If this list is descriptive of the workings of the economy during much of modern times, it is clearly not applicable to the economy of the Middle Ages. Yet many of the things on the list originated in the Middle Ages. It is worth noting that capitalism did not mature as a *system* of which men were *conscious* until long after 1500. But capital, techniques, and spirit, or, more crudely, money, methods, and mood, were already doing their momentous work in the period described in later sections of this chapter.

It is time now to turn to an experience which influenced every aspect of life in the new Europe and which was itself the consequence of the broadening economic horizons: the great discoveries.

THE GREAT DISCOVERIES

There is much that is known and also much that is mysterious about the discoveries which by the end of the seventeenth century had put Europeans in touch with all but a few corners of the world. We know what were men's desires and knowledge and plans. The mystery enters when one considers the immensity of what men were doing—setting Europe upon a path of conquest unlike anything the world had known since Roman times, and vastly larger than Rome's—and when one wonders what springs of energy and resolve made this expansion possible.

Europeans had found energy to strike out toward the East in the crusades in the late eleventh century. About 1300 the existence of a vast Mongol empire from China to Eastern Europe, including much of what later became Russia, facilitated the travel of a few Europeans into Asia. The Venetian Marco Polo (1254–1324?)[1] went to far-off Peking by way of Mongolia and returned by way of Sumatra, the coast of India, and Arabia. In the turbulent fourteenth and fifteenth centuries, however, Christian hopes of converting Asia, and even of trading there, were dimmed. Although legends remained, peaceful contacts decreased. The Ottoman Turks took over much of Asia Minor and the Balkans, threatening Constantinople and even Central Europe. From Europe's point of view a period of contraction followed its medieval expansion. But Europeans were meanwhile perfecting the means which were to take them to Asia and the Americas by sea and launch a second wave of expansion which was to last for four centuries.

It used to be thought that the Turkish conquests cut off the Europeans' purchases of oriental spices and gems and forced them to seek trade routes by ship around Africa and across the Atlantic. This view proved to be only a crude approximation. Actually the Mediterranean trade, particularly in the hands of the Venetians, continued to bring the wares of Arab traders to Europe. But the goods were annoyingly high-priced, and the monopolistic position of the Venetians was envied by the new monarchies in Western Europe. Moreover, Christian kings like those of Portugal and Spain had never ceased crusading against the Moslems, whom they hoped to outflank by reaching and joining forces with legendary (but non-existent) Christian kingdoms of the East.

Prince Henry "the Navigator" of Portugal (1394–1460) sent expeditions down the African coast, where gold, ivory, and slaves were found. Europeans by this time were learning to sail bigger ships, to use the compass for direction and the astrolabe for determining latitude (they were still unable to measure longitude or distance traveled). In 1487 Bartholomew Diaz in stormy weather rounded Africa's southern tip, which came to be called the Cape of Good Hope—hope of reaching India. And in 1497–1499 Vasco da Gama sailed to India and back, bringing home a cargo worth sixty times the cost of the expedition.

In the 1490's, only a few decades after the fall of Constantinople to the Turks, Europe was on the move again, for treasure, for the power of her growing states, for the spread of Christianity, and for scientific knowledge. In the East the Portuguese were building an empire of trading posts and forts widely flung along the African and Indian coasts, in China, and in the East Indies, and held together by sea power. In 1500 Pedro Cabral, ostensibly en route to India but possibly on the lookout for other lands, swung too wide around Africa and was blown to the

---

[1] Parenthetical dates after the name of a sovereign show the duration of his reign; parenthetical dates after the name of any other individual show the years of his birth and death.

bulge of South America, founding Portugal's dominion of Brazil. In 1509 near the island of Diu, west of India, nineteen Portuguese ships shot up, rammed, boarded, and dispersed about one hundred Egyptian and Indian vessels, ending the Moslem monopoly of trade in the Indian Ocean and demonstrating a European military superiority which was to have far-reaching consequences.

Portugal was rivalled by Spain, whose sponsorship of Christopher Columbus won a magnificent empire in the West. Spanish motives were like those of the Portuguese. The missionary zeal which was to lead to the conversion of most of the Latin Americans to Catholic Christianity was blended with national feeling, scientific curiosity, and an appetite for profits.

Christopher Columbus (1451 ? –1506) was probably a native of Genoa. He had worked in the Mediterranean, been to Iceland, and had made several trips down the African coast, and he was eager to demonstrate that India could be reached by sailing west. Although most educated people knew the earth to be round, especially since the Renaissance had revived the science of the ancients, there were disagreements about the distance that a ship would have to sail west to reach India. Columbus through the mediation of Spanish merchants won the support of Queen Isabella. He set sail with three ships, the largest of which was the *Santa Maria* of about 100 tons, 90 foot length and 20 foot beam. The first voyage lasted from August 3, 1492, to October 12, when the Bahamas were reached. Columbus had found the distance greater than he had expected and had been forced to mislead his crew. On this first voyage he discovered Cuba and Santo Domingo. He returned three more times, bringing colonists, and after exploring other islands reached the mainland of South America. It was another Italian explorer in Spanish service, Amerigo Vespucci, whose name stuck to the new continents after his reports had been used by a German geographer (1507).

And now discoveries and conquests followed in rapid succession. Ponce de León was in Florida in 1512. In the following year Balboa crossed the Isthmus of Panama and found the Pacific. Hernando Cortez in 1519 conquered the Aztec empire of Mexico, and Francisco Pizarro, also in the service of Spain, conquered the Incas of Peru between 1531 and 1533. In 1494 by the Treaty of Tordesillas, approved by the Pope, Spain and Portugal agreed on a line of demarcation cutting both the Atlantic and the Pacific, and dividing the unexplored world between them. As if to link the Portuguese and Spanish movements of exploration, a Portuguese in Spanish service, Ferdinand Magellan, set out in 1519, rounded the tip of South America (Straits of Magellan), and crossed the Pacific to the Philippines. Magellan was killed by natives of the Philippines but a part of his expedition reached home by the known route across the Indian Ocean and up the west coast of Africa (1522). It was now actually demonstrated that the earth was round.

Unlike the Portuguese empire in the Far East, the Spanish empire in the New World became one of production and of settlement. Spanish culture was to overlay the whole of Latin America, with the exception of Portuguese Brazil, which was in many respects similiar. Like the Portuguese, the Spaniards tried to maintain their empire against the ambitions of other powers. It brought them

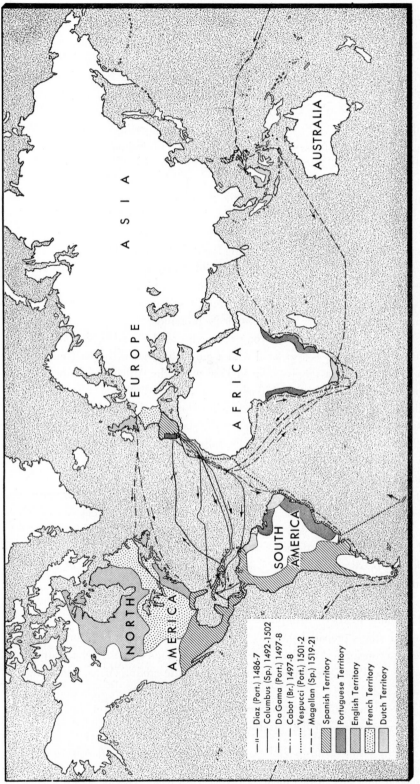

Diaz (Port.) 1486-7
Columbus (Sp.) 1492-1502
Da Gama (Port.) 1497-8
Cabot (Br.) 1497-8
Vespucci (Port.) 1501-2
Magellan (Sp.) 1519-21

Spanish Territory
Portuguese Territory
English Territory
French Territory
Dutch Territory

ASIA

EUROPE

AFRICA

NORTH
AMERICA

SOUTH
AMERICA

AUSTRALIA

THE EXPANSION OF EUROPE, 1500 TO 1800

much plunder as well as much trade, and encouraged Spain to play a great role in international politics in the sixteenth and early seventeenth centuries.

Spain and Portugal were a century ahead of their northern rivals in the building of colonial empires. Still, in the sixteenth century and the first half of the seventeenth, many exploits by Dutch, English, and French mariners and explorers laid for these nations the foundations of colonial empires.

In examining the Dutch case, it is important to remember that the Netherlands belonged to the Spanish crown but that the northern provinces were in revolt from the late sixteenth century until they finally gained their independence in 1648. Thus the Dutch began as part of the Spanish Empire, but made war upon it, and while so doing developed as a great trading and naval power in their own right. Much of what was to be the Dutch colonial empire was seized from the Portuguese while Portugal was annexed to Spain (1580–1640) and therefore fair game. The Dutch received trading privileges in Japan in 1609 and in Formosa in 1624. Henry Hudson, working for the Dutch, explored the river which bears his name (1609) and made possible the Dutch settlements at New Amsterdam and Fort Orange (Albany). These North American possessions were to be seized by England in the 1660's during a series of wars against the other great seventeenth-century sea power—the Netherlands.

In English history the strong monarchy of the Tudors spanned the sixteenth century and was associated with a growing national consciousness, which was perhaps never more alive than in 1588 when the Armada of Catholic Spain approached Plymouth with 130 ships carrying an invasion force of 19,000 soldiers. English firepower and gusty winds brought England victory over the greatest colonial and maritime power of the sixteenth century. Although Tudor England anticipated Britannia's future ruling of the seas by starting the Royal Navy and crowding its medium-sized, maneuverable ships with artillery, and although John and Sebastian Cabot in 1497–1498 reached Newfoundland, Nova Scotia, and the New England coast while sailing under the English flag, the sixteenth century is best characterized by Francis Drake's two decades of forays into Spanish waters "to kill Spaniards, sell negroes, sack gold ships." By 1607 and 1620 permanent settlements at Jamestown and Plymouth in the New World indicated the direction English colonial development was to take in the seventeenth and eighteenth centuries.

It was a Frenchman, Jacques Cartier, who sailed up the St. Lawrence in 1534, and another, Champlain, after whom the great lake was named. These men and others prepared the way for France to gain a foothold on the North American continent. Like the English and Dutch, the French also made attacks on Spanish and Portuguese America and on the route around Africa and along the coasts of India.[2]

No one with imagination can fail to see the long-term significance for Europe of this remarkable extension of its power. New products and profits

[2] In a full catalogue of European expansion from the fifteenth to the mid-seventeeth century, the eastern land boundaries of the continent would also have to be mentioned. In a later chapter the formation of Muscovite Russia and its drive eastward against the declining Mongol khanates will be described.

SHIPS IN A STORM by Peter Brueghel the Elder (about 1528–1569). Engraving by Frans Huys. A reflection of the growing overseas commerce of the Netherlands in the sixteenth century. (Courtesty of The Metropolitan Museum of Art, Dick Fund, 1928)

spurred the economy, and there were enormous social effects which (among other things) sharpened the differences between the Atlantic seaboard and Central and Eastern Europe. There were also great effects upon minds and outlooks. Knowledge of new worlds and peoples brought a sense of limitless frontiers. Fascination with the unknown engendered a sort of self-confidence in dealing with it, and a new acceptance of movement, advancement, progress. There was much to ponder in scientific, religious, and political realms. Such intellectual movements were slow-starting and reached their greatest force in a later period. Shakespeare's use of a magic island in the *Tempest*, and Thomas More's imaginative description of a new land in his *Utopia* are illustrations.

THE COMMERCIAL REVOLUTION

Like capitalism, the great discoveries help to account for all sorts of changes in the Europe of early modern times. Of these, one of which historians often speak is the "commercial revolution." This was the great shift in centers of trade from the Mediterranean to the Atlantic, coupled with an increase in the volume of European commerce between the fifteenth and the eighteenth centuries. This twofold "revolution" must be considered also in its relationship with other aspects of early modern Europe—the formation of strong, dynastic states, and the doctrine of mercantilism which began to guide economic decisions.

After the building of the Portuguese trading empire in the Far East and the Spanish conquests in the Western Hemisphere, dramatic new business opportunities opened up which outdistanced those of the Mediterranean past. Portuguese spices arrived at Lisbon and Spanish gold and silver at Seville or Cadiz, but they did not remain there. Neither Portugal nor Spain could provision their colonial empires. Other European traders brought them the goods with which to do so, and carried back spices and treasure to the ports along the Atlantic and North Sea. In the Netherlands Antwerp remained queen through the sixteenth century, as many as five hundred ships and three thousand wagons arriving there a day. The south German cities like Augsburg and Nuremberg turned away from Venice and toward the Atlantic and managed to stay prosperous, but the rest of Central Europe failed to advance as rapidly as the Atlantic powers. The Baltic, like the Mediterranean, suffered economic decline relative to the West. The Hanseatic cities faded. In the seventeeth and eighteenth centuries the tendency away from the Baltic and Mediterranean and toward the Atlantic was accentuated. When one realizes how immense were the social and indeed the political changes encouraged by the growth of commerce in the West, and the resulting contrast with Eastern Europe, one cannot begrudge the commercial revolution its dramatic title. From about 1600 Amsterdam rose at the expense of Antwerp, a victory aided by political and military events having to do with the successful Dutch struggle for independence from Spain. England and France, which in the later seventeenth century were to outdistance the Dutch, grew in wealth and power while Spain and Portugal declined. Mediterranean commerce and the prosperity of Italian cities did not so much decline as fail to grow rapidly in comparison with the more fortunate parts of the West.

Europe's trade grew even before the commercial revolution, because Europe was growing in population and wealth, and in the demands of its princely courts, cities, and mercenary armies. Within Europe there was a certain amount of specialization: art works and silks from Italy; cloth from the Netherlands, France, and England; silver from German mines; cereals, lumber, and livestock from the Baltic and Eastern Europe; and so on. Europe needed Asiatic products such as textiles and copper, and for the most part paid for them with precious metals. After the great discoveries the flow of gold and silver to the East continued, and the list of products from both sides became longer.

Europe now traded, too, with Africa and the New World. African slaves were landed in Virginia and Brazil. They were paid for in Africa by weapons, cloth, liquor, and various trinkets, and in America by gold, silver, sugar, and tobacco. This triangular trade made many European fortunes, especially in Portugal at first, for Portugal had an agreement (*asiento*) which gave it a monopoly in providing slaves for the Spanish Empire in the New World. English, Dutch, French, and Americans also profited from the slave ships. Europe, and ultimately the world at large, became familiar with many products from America. Tobacco and the habit of smoking furnish one example, corn another, the potato still another.

The commercial revolution was also an affair of techniques and business knowledge testifying to the maturing of capitalism. In the money markets of cities like Venice and Antwerp, later in Amsterdam and Paris and London, bank deposits, bills of exchange, insurance (at first a form of betting), and company shares (many owners made for larger enterprises) were multiplied and perfected. Lending at interest became commonplace, even in Catholic countries. The Protestant Reformation added greater freedom to profit-seeking, as well as the gospel of hard work and austere saving. Merchants branched out into banking. The sixteenth century was the great age of family enterprises in finance.

An outstanding example of a family bank was that of Jacob Fugger, "the Rich," of Augsburg (1459–1525), who inherited from his weaver ancestors a clothmaking and wholesaling business and capital worth several hundred thousand dollars in today's prices. Building a great international network of agencies, Jacob Fugger tapped Europe's growing wealth with loans to merchants, bishops, and cities, and with transfers of money, deposits, and the buying and selling of bills of exchange. Many times a millionaire by our standards, he became associated with the Habsburgs, lending them huge sums. In return he was favored with mining concessions and the right to make tax collections in Hungary, Germany, and the Netherlands. The Fuggers also lent money to the Holy See (Bishopric of Rome). Their agents were involved in the indulgences-selling campaign by which the Church was raising money at the start of the Protestant revolt. Through other agents they collected reports on the European political picture. They made friends among the nobility with gifts of gold rings, necklaces, and silks. The Habsburgs sheltered them from criticism of their business deals. These arrangements were characteristic. Kings and financiers of the early modern period grew up together.

By the seventeenth century, however, the great family banking enterprises of the Renaissance type were tending to give way to state-favored companies such as the Bank of Amsterdam (1609). States made their own economic regulations, permitted monopolies like the English and Dutch East India Companies, and issued securities rather like government bonds. The English Merchant Adventurers, recognized in 1564 as having a monopoly on the export of cloth, was an association of merchants with its own fleet and its own rules, but each merchant bought and sold for himself. The English East India Company, chartered in 1600, was like our modern corporations in that it was a joint stock company; that is, capital for conducting its business was obtained by selling shares of stock, and the business was managed by directors elected by stockholders. By such means did commercial capitalism advance.

ECONOMIC PROGRESS AND SOCIAL TENSIONS

In the period from 1500 to 1648, problems of getting together capital and managing enterprises were related to the problem of monetary supply. Money by itself was not necessarily capital, but a supply of coins was basic to the money economy of capitalism. In the second half of the fifteenth century there was a shortage of precious metals in Europe, and commerce was handicapped. The main remedy was provided by the gold and silver from Mexico after the 1520's and from Peru after the 1530's and especially after the silver mines of Potosí were discovered in 1545.

The Spanish treasure was of immense importance in European history. In the sixteenth century it made its way to the rest of Europe because the Spaniards bought goods with it. No amount of restrictive legislation was able to prevent these purchases, for Spain itself did not produce enough goods to satisfy its people at home and in the colonies. An estimated 200 tons of gold and 18,000 tons of silver were imported into Spain between 1503 and 1660. During this period the stock of precious metals in Europe probably tripled. The result of this enormous increase in the amount of money was, naturally, that money became cheaper—which is another way of saying that other goods became dearer. In short, prices rose. During the "sixteenth-century price rise" European prices increased by even more than 300 percent, for governments devalued their coins by putting less and less gold or silver into them, with the result that prices in terms of actual coins rose farther than prices in terms of gold and silver. In general, rises in wages tended to lag behind increases in prices. This reduced real wages; that is, the amount of goods that a laborer could buy with his wages.

The inflow of precious metal into Europe decreased after 1620 and fell off sharply after 1650. The long price rise slowed down by the 1620's. But Europe's economy had been provided with a supply of metallic money that spurred greatly the progress of the commercial revolution and of capitalism. Spain, which first and most directly felt the effects of the gold and silver, drew much of its strength from this precious flow. Without it Spain could not have played such a great role in European history, though treasure was not the only cause of its greatness. But Spain's domestic economic growth was probably slowed by the wealth which could so easily buy goods produced elsewhere.

Meanwhile statesmen in other parts of Europe pondered the lessons of the Spanish good fortune. Most of them failed to see the connection between precious metal and the European price rise, although a Frenchman, Jean Bodin, pointed it out in 1568. But countries with no colonies containing gold and silver, or no colonies at all, turned their attention to ways of attracting it through trade regulations. Especially after the mid-seventeenth century, when the supply dwindled, the competition of states and statesmen stimulated the development of economic policies which came to be called mercantilist.

Manufacturing was also affected. The Middle Ages had seen a great growth of craft guilds in the towns; in the early modern period they persisted. The guilds were organizations of small businessmen which kept down the number of master craftsmen in a given city and controlled the training of apprentices, the working conditions and wages of journeymen employed by the guildsmen in their shops, and the quality and prices of products. With the expansion of Europe and the commercial revolution there was a demand for larger quantities of such things as textiles, without so much regard to quality, provided the price and appearance were right. The guilds with their low output and higher quality would not rise to the occasion. They were fearful of the competition which might ensue if they allowed more journeymen to become masters, and they did their best to maintain the traditional standards of craftsmanship regardless of the needs and opportunities presented by the new age. But if the guilds controlled the towns, they were unable to manage the countryside, and here, in what is called the "putting-out system," or "home industry," or sometimes "cottage industry," enterprising capitalists organized production in their own way. There were also during the early modern period numerous examples of large-scale production in shipyards, mines, iron foundries and the like, where large amounts of capital were required and where there was reason to centralize production so that expensive hoists, pumps, and so on could be used by many workers. These large-scale enterprises remained the exception, not the rule.

Europe was still mainly agricultural. As 1600 approached, more intensive methods improved the output of food in some areas, notably in the Low Countries. Here farmers had learned how to raise enough fodder to keep livestock through the winter months, whereas in most other areas the lack of fodder made it necessary to slaughter the livestock every autumn. In most of Europe, techniques of food and livestock raising did not change much in the early modern period. In the absence of fertilizers, the ground still had to be allowed to lie fallow for a third or fourth of the time. Agricultural tools were poor. Except in harvest time there was too little for the country population to do. Most people were poorly nourished on their diet of soup and bread. Peasants (if they survived their first year, when half the newborn babies died) lived on an average twenty-five years; if they survived into their thirties or forties, they looked very old by our standards. Even the aristocracy seldom lasted beyond its fifties.

Agriculture remained primitive in the early modern period, but one should not conclude that capitalism was not having any influence on it. International and local markets really made a difference in people's relationships to each other even in rural areas. To take one famous example, in sixteenth-century England the demand for wool encouraged an "enclosure" movement which was to continue in various forms until the end of the eighteenth century; that is, men who were able to do so reserved land for their sheep-raising even when this meant interference with traditional village rights to share common lands, or with the raising of food crops.

In France, Belgium, Southern and Western Germany, and parts of Italy, enclosures were not so easy to make, for the peasantry had strong customary rights to their lands provided they continued to pay dues to the lord, or seigneur. In these regions capitalism favored those who were able to make favorable contracts. For example, many nobles were hard-hit by the sixteenth-century price rise because the dues they received had been fixed as unchangeable money payments which, in the inflation, would buy less and less. In general it was the "bourgeois"—the townsman—who made a good businessman, even in the countryside. Many of them were able to buy land from peasants and profit by renting to share-croppers or other tenants. Many bourgeois bought the lands of nobles and themselves became seigneurs. As for the peasants, some profited from the money economy while others, unskilled in marketing and weighted down with rents, dues, and taxes, lived poorly or even lost their land.

In Eastern Europe, for example in Germany east of the Elbe, in Poland, and increasingly in Russia, capitalism affected agriculture in a peculiar way. Here the fact that there were international markets for grain stimulated the landlords to produce a surplus by whatever means they could. The means they used was the serf system, which was worse in the seventeenth century than it had been in the sixteenth, and worse in the eighteenth century than in the seventeenth. The surplus produced by the backward methods of this unfree labor force was not great, and in time the serf system would prove uneconomical and politically dangerous. In the early modern period the serfdom of Eastern Europe, caused by many factors, managed to fit into Europe's growing capitalism and commercial revolution.

Europe in this early period was rather like some of the less developed parts of the world today. The population was rising, from about 53 million in 1300 to about 70 million in 1600 (excluding Russia). Much of this rise took place in the late fifteenth and sixteenth centuries as the growth of commerce helped bring food into areas of shortage and the growth of occupations such as home industry helped pay for provisions. Nevertheless, Europe in this period proved able to produce far more people than it could keep alive. Given the low technical efficiency of agriculture, there was never enough food to go around. Famines turned the diseases which were endemic, awaiting the lowered resistance of a scanty diet, into epidemics. Periods of population rise were followed by drops. Population kept pushing beyond subsistence and being cut back by nature.

Because agriculture was the occupation of the great majority of the people of Europe, it dominated the economy. Poor crops did not simply mean higher prices to compensate the farmer, for the peasants lived in a complicated network of payments in money and kind. Sometimes when they had made these payments they did not have enough left to eat. Famine in the country meant vagabonds on the roads, and an upsurge of crime. Unemployed in the country joined unemployed in the towns, for when food prices jumped, people ceased buying other things. Social peace was threatened. In the sixteenth century during the long price rise the real wages of laborers declined considerably. There was an increase of rebelliousness on the part of journeymen who were finding it harder and harder to become masters.

The master craftsmen (owners of small enterprises) of the guilds were themselves at odds with the rich and daring merchants who became bankers and putting-out manufacturers, but although they envied the financiers, the guildsmen were still comfortably situated in the growing towns. The existence of a strong middle class and the fact that they had money and abilities which could be used by the state were important influences on political history. On the other hand many peasants, inefficient farmers loaded with dues and taxes and unable to make wise decisions about marketing, were rebellious against both nobles and middle class.

ECONOMIC POLICIES

The foregoing economic and social material forecasts Europe's unusual place in world history, for it marks what some historians of economic development have called the "take-off" from a relatively static and uneventful economic life. The men of early modern Europe were not blind to the advantages to be gained from this process, nor to the maladjustments which accompanied it. Three possibilities for economic control are worth noticing.

As Europe emerged from medieval times there were two prinicpal means of regulating economic life. One was local, the other universal. The local, which consisted of the regulations of towns and guilds fearful of shortages, has been discussed. The universal regulatory agency was the Church of Rome. The Church, as a great international authority interpreting the meaning of life, held certain definite views of economic activity. The scholastic philosophers had taught that economic goods should be sought with moderation, not overrated; that they were only a means to maintain oneself on earth while serving spiritual life in preparation for the hereafter. Work was necessary but work to amass wealth attached too much importance to earthly existence. Lending money at interest was usury and was to be deplored.

With the coming of the Protestant Reformation (discussed in detail in

Chapter 4) certain changes in business ethics were apparent. John Calvin in particular accepted commerce, profits, and interest as proper if they did not threaten the dominance of religion in the lives of men. The manner of life which he and his followers preached called for hard work, thrift, and sobriety—just the kind of behavior which was suitable to a capitalist system. Calvinists everywhere, in Switzerland, France, Scotland, the Netherlands, and ultimately New England, made good businessmen who lived simply and ploughed back the profits into the business. Martin Luther was more old-fashioned about business than Calvin, but like most Protestants Luther taught the dignity of work, which justified businessmen in being as efficient as possible.

Impressed by such changes in attitude, certain historians and sociologists have seen in Protestantism one of the main influences on the rise of capitalism. The German sociologist Max Weber linked the capitalist spirit to Calvinism. The Englishman R. H. Tawney noted its relation to Puritanism. When these apparently causal connections were first noticed, it was difficult to evaluate them, but they seemed to be a brilliant contribution to the understanding of the modern world. In the discussion of the Weber thesis, however, thinkers about capitalism pointed out some of the facts which have been used earlier in this chapter. Capitalism arose in Catholic Europe long before the Protestant revolt and continued in Catholic sections of Europe such as Italy, Belgium, and South Germany without being noticeably handicapped by religion. The Catholic Church was proving itself capable of adjusting to new conditions of everyday life. Nevertheless it *was* easier for Calvinism and other Protestant points of view, which grew up in conditions of early capitalism, to compromise with the business mentality. The fact that they did so probably speeded the rise of the capitalist spirit.

Whatever one may think of the relation of the Reformation to capitalism, it did break the religious unity of Western Christendom. There was no longer to be one source of moral judgments in economic affairs. In this way the Reformation may have encouraged capitalism. It certainly contributed to a new kind of economic control characteristic of modern times, a control halfway between the localism of the cities and the universalism of the medieval church. This was "mercantilism," the set of economic policies and practices associated with the states of the early modern period.

If one thinks of the other characteristics of the sixteenth and seventeenth centuries, it is easy to understand mercantilism. The formation of strong states like England, France, and Spain, which were neither as big and loosely constructed as the Holy Roman Empire nor as small and vulnerable as the city states of Italy, had economic implications. It was natural for the rulers and even for some of their subjects to want unity in such things as coinage, weights and measures, customs and tolls, and taxation. Part of the job of creating a state consisted of taking over aspects of government formerly exercised by feudal lords, towns, guilds, provinces, and the Church. The process of unification involved decisions about economic matters. Government officials developed practices and policies in all sorts of economic affairs.

The outlook embodied in these policies is known as mercantilism. The mercantilistic rules were of bewildering variety, but their aim was simply the unity, wealth, and power of the state. Economic unity was an inevitable part of state-building. Wealth and power went together, but mercantilism was not the justification of the wealth-seeking of individuals or of a single class like the bourgeoisie. With the coming of mercantilism the state was accepted as properly intervening in economic matters where necessary for the general welfare. The general welfare included not merely the sense of unity and the pleasures of wealth but also the need for power in a Europe of competing states. In mercantilism, political and economic history join with the history of international relations.

The specific policies associated with mercantilism grew up naturally in the context of early modern times. States needed money to pay for mercenary armies and supplies. The European states naturally envied Spain's American treasures and turned to thinking of ways by which they, without mines of gold and silver, could attract money into their countries. "Bullionism" is a word applied to this desire for precious metals and to the policies which states adopted in order to secure them. Bullionism was a sort of early mercantilism. The chief difference was that mercantilism became more complicated and sophisticated, aiming not merely at precious metals (and bullionists did not always limit themselves to this aim) but also at agricultural and industrial production, a high population, sea power, colonies, and the avoidance of wasteful luxury and idleness. Like bullionism, mercantilism aimed at a favorable balance of trade (more exports than imports) and expected commerce to provide raw materials and to dispose of such products as it was useful for the country to sell.

The period from the mid-seventeenth to the end of the eighteenth century was to see mercantilism reach its height and become a more fully formulated doctrine, although it was not given a name until the eighteenth century. In this chapter about the early modern history of Europe we have seen how mercantilism as a means of economic regulation made its appearance along with national states, capitalism, the great discoveries, and the commercial revolution. The following chapters treat other aspects of the early modern age: the Renaissance, and then the Reformation.

3

THE RENAISSANCE

Europe's age of expansion was described in the preceding chapter. Much, though not quite all, of the span of time described there goes by another name, the Renaissance. In its broadest usage, defining a time when men's interests, attitudes, and actions could no longer be called "medieval," the Renaissance in Italy occurred in the late fourteenth century, all of the fifteenth, and some of the sixteenth. As it spread over France, England, and Germany, it started later and lasted longer—into the 1700's, according to some. Dates are not important; the most interesting questions about the Renaissance arise when one asks what it was that changed, what it was that "spread" in those years.

The idea of the Renaissance as an age distinctly different from the Middle Ages began to grow up during the period itself. The name was used first (so far as anyone knows) by a student of art history, to describe what he saw as a rapid transformation in the character of Italian art. This student, Giorgio Vasari, writing in 1550, used the word "rinascita," which is Italian for "rebirth," to describe the remarkable upsurge of excellence in painting which he thought had begun to take place many years before he wrote. Translators and commentators on his work used the equivalent German and French terms, "Wiedergeburt" and "Renaissance."

The notion of a revival of excellence, occurring sometime after 1250, was gradually broadened to include a great deal more than painting. Scholars began to discover a similar "rebirth," taking place at roughly the same time, in other fine arts, in writing, history, and scholarship. Eventually it came to be felt that rebirths had also taken place in science, religion, and politics, and in economic development. By the middle of the nineteenth century an eminent Swiss historian, Jacob Burckhardt, had produced the idea of a rebirth of all aspects of civilization which had transformed the life of the Italians and, indeed, the nature of society and of human beings. Other historians, before and after, discovered Rebirths in other parts of Europe, either occurring independently or as a result of the importation of Italian ideas. Modern scholars, fascinated by this idea, have discerned Rebirths not only in different places but at different times. Ideas and procedures which Burckhardt said were "typically Renaissance" have been found to exist long before the second half of the thirteenth century, and some historians have thought to discern a "twelfth-century Renaissance" and even a "Carolingian Renaissance," which pushed the beginnings back to the ninth century in the middle of what used to be called the Dark Ages.

This tendency to search through history for little-known Renaissances is confusing. What the searchers are saying is that the characteristics of the age known as *the* Renaissance were not without precedent and cause in earlier periods, and that the break between the Middle Ages and the Renaissance was less sharp and less complete than was once thought. But there is no doubt that something happened; that from sometime near the fourteenth century there began to emerge in Italy, and later in other places, *new attitudes, tastes and techniques.* The new ways are clearly distinguishable from the old. Moreover, they are identifiably similar in the different places and decades where *the* Renaissance flourished, and they represent a transformation, more or less total, which affected every phase of men's thinking and ways of doing things, and which formed the first state of the modern mind.

The principal question which must be asked about this transformation is: What was it a "rebirth" of, if anything? The answer, to earlier writers, was obvious: the rebirth was of excellence—of skills and understanding. And excellence, until recently, was always deemed to have reached its peak in classical times, in Greek and Roman civilization. It was natural for Vasari, and for those who followed, to associate the rebirth of excellence with the idea of the revival of a *kind* of achievement similar to that of the classical cultures, and (as a next step) to see the rebirth of the fourteenth, fifteenth, and sixteenth centuries as sparked by the growth of study and understanding of ancient art and thought. There thus developed a view of history which regarded the past as a kind of diurnal sequence—the blinding sunlight of Greece and Rome, followed by the night of the Dark Ages, followed in turn by the new dawn of the Renaissance. Recent students have greatly modified this view. They have reappraised with a more admiring eye the great achievements of medieval Europe. They have discerned the vital differences which made the Renaissance distinct from classical times. And they have seen in it, and especially in the years which followed it, the rise of achievements which are of a wholly different kind from, and certainly far in advance of, anything which Greece or Rome dreamt of. The more modern view is not, therefore, that of an alternation of light and darkness, but of development out of one kind of emphasis and talent into another.

The Renaissance was, however, undoubtedly classics-conscious to a degree never equalled since. In the fourteenth century, first-class minds devoted decades to imitating the standard language and verse forms of the Augustan Age of Rome, fifteen hundred years earlier, and cultivated people spoke and wrote to one another in classical Latin. One of the greatest of fifteenth-century Italian architects, Filippo Brunelleschi, spent long periods of time measuring the surviving buildings of ancient Rome with a tape measure. Brunelleschi was too imaginative a genius to engage in mere imitation: he was looking for an understanding of the art and engineering spirit of the Romans. But at its worst, in the hands of the average man of the Renaissance, the new civilization sometimes meant merely formal imitation of the old.

While creativeness was frequently couched in the form of classical scholarship, especially in the period before 1500, the inventiveness of the human mind operating amid the very unclassical remnants of medieval civilization led to ideas and art which were often very different from those of Greece or Rome. This new energy and outlook are what we now call the Renaissance, and what is frequently seen as the beginning of modern civilization. It is difficult and artificial to disentangle the various aspects of civilization and achievement, to assert separately what is "Renaissance" in economics, science, music or sculpture. For one of the characteristic ideals of the Renaissance was that a truly cultivated and virtuous man should be learned and adept in all branches of human achievement —the hero of the Renaissance was a man of universal comprehension, what the Italians called an *uomo universale*. Nonetheless, we can discover something of the character of the Renaissance, and its development, by looking separately at three fields of human endeavor transformed by it: philosophy and scholarship; statecraft; and certain fine arts, including painting and design. Scrutiny of these three fields reveals certain of what are usually regarded as the basic attitudes, tastes, and techniques of the early modern world.

PHILOSOPHY AND SCHOLARSHIP

The Renaissance is generally taken to connote a new view of mankind in relation to the physical universe and to God. It has frequently been asserted that this viewpoint was *secular*—concerned with worldly problems and pleasures and with the happiness of men in mortal life, as distinct from the *religious* view attributed to the Middle Ages, in which men were mainly preoccupied with their connection with the Deity and their salvation after death. This view of the Renaissance is entirely too simple. There was in the Renaissance some real skepticism about the existence of God and the importance of Christian virtues. The roots of later doubts about immortality and a personal God may be traced to the classical scholarship of the Renaissance. But the great majority of scholars and artists were at least formally orthodox, and many of them were intensely devout.

It is true, however, that by 1500 new and exciting ideas of the nature of the universe and man's place in it had developed, and a new view of Christian virtue tended more and more to displace the rather monastic ideals of medieval intellectuals. There were still, to be sure, a great many passionately devout and ascetic men in the Renaissance, even before the rise of Protestantism caused the pendulum to swing back toward austerity. In Florence, a notoriously worldly city, the Dominican monk and prophet, Girolamo Savonarola, captured control in the

MADONNA AND CHILD, twelfth-century wood carving. The figures are proportioned, not according to nature, but rather to an idea. The Madonna sits on a church-like chair with Romanesque columns. The Child, a miniature adult, makes the traditional sign of blessing. Drapery and posture suggest stability and dignity. (Metropolitan Museum of Art)

GRIEVING MADONNA by Tilman Riemenschneider. By the sixteenth century, when this statue was carved of linden wood, the Madonna was being portrayed less as a religious symbol, more as a human being. Unlike the Madonna above, here the head and hands suggest human emotion. This shift in perspective reflects a growing concern with earthly affairs. (Main-Fränkisches Museum, Wurzburg, Germany)

late fifteenth century and introduced a regime of extreme austerity and piety. And while Savonarola was eventually burned at the stake (1498), he for a time received ardent support in many quarters. Nor were the most worldly and sensuous of the artists, rulers, and philosophers by intention irreverent, though they carried to excess what so many people in the Renaissance felt: a new meaning in the ancient Christian virtue of joy.

This shift in emphasis involved mainly a new concern for the Christian ideals of joy and moderation at the expense of those of discipline and sacrifice. It is associated with a group of students who are called Humanists. Because they were not theologians but were primarily concerned with mortal rather than immortal life, it has sometimes been said that Humanists were leaders of the first secular—non-religious—movement in western civilization. Humanists were intellectuals who were concerned with the study of humanity and its achievements, its past, its place in the world—the branches of learning which even today are called Humane Letters, or the Humanities. The Humanists of the Renaissance found their greatest inspiration in the literature of Greece and Rome, the "classics."

Churchly persons, clergymen and Popes, were in the forefront of Humanism, and the Church itself showed its devotion to the new ideals by accepting, and even sponsoring, investigations into its history. The Vatican, long a center of scholarship, unflinchingly espoused impartiality in investigations and independence of judgment in interpretation. There were shocks in store, which the Church absorbed, but which may in the long run have influenced the growth of disillusionment and even skepticism. The most famous shocks were administered by Lorenzo Valla (1406–1457), who in many respects may be regarded as typical of Renaissance scholars.

Valla was one of a group of scholars whom Pope Nicholas V had gathered in the Vatican in the middle of the fifteenth century. Like similar groups of classical scholars in Venice, Florence, and elsewhere, this group devoted itself primarily to the study and interpretation of Greek writings. Valla, who was appointed Papal Secretary in 1455, proceeded further, however; he undertook historical investigations and as a result of one of them came up with the discovery that the Donation of Constantine was a forgery. The Donation of Constantine was one of the documentary bases for the primacy of the Bishopric of Rome and its temporal power, allegedly bestowed upon the Pope by the Emperor Constantine. Valla's examination of the text proved that the document had been forged many hundreds of years later. In addition to this discovery, he made others, in company with other scholars, concerning the Scriptures themselves. Some of the Bible was found to be variously translated, and other parts probably inaccurate. It was shown that the Apostles' Creed had not been written by the Apostles. Moreover, turning to the field of ethics, Valla wrote a treatise called *On Pleasure* in which he rejected the monastic ideal, asserting that moderation and disciplined enjoyment of life (in the tradition of the pagan Epicurean philosophers) were more truly Christian. The essence of goodness, Valla and many of his contemporaries believed, was in providing happiness in mortal life.

But Valla never doubted the dogma of the Church nor the validity of Christian theology, nor did the Church reject his writings. What he and other

Humanists were doing was really what the great medieval philosophers had done —reconciling the undoubted profundities and truths of the thinkers of pagan antiquity with the teachings of Christ.

This process of adaptation, extended gradually to include observations on the nature of physical matter as well as the dicta of classical philosophy, was carried to rather startling lengths by another of the Humanists, Pico della Mirandola, a prince and a priest, who lived from 1463 to 1494. Pico was a Florentine Humanist and a protégé of Lorenzo de Medici, the gorgeous despot of Florence and lavish patron of art. Pico was one of the most prodigiously learned men of his day. He represented the peak of learning in the group of students of Plato who formed what was called the Platonic Academy of Florence, and he proposed to catalog *all* human knowledge in one encyclopedic summary. This large venture did, indeed, get him into trouble when some of his statements were discovered to be contradictory to Christian beliefs, and Pico was accused of heresy. He was acquitted of the charge, however, (after a change of Popes) and returned from exile in triumph.

One of Pico's most illuminating thoughts was the view of the categories of living things, which achieved notoriety under the name of the Chain of Being. Christianity had previously preached that there were (aside from the Trinity and Angels) two distinct groups of living things, human beings, who have souls and thus are capable of salvation or damnation, and other forms of life, which are soulless and therefore incapable of morality. Pico devised the notion that there is no sharp distinction between Angels, Men, and Beasts, but merely a gradation in their capacity for goodness. He saw Man, as one modern scholar has observed, "stationed in the middle of the great chain of being, endowed with freedom either to degenerate to the brute or to ascend and 'be reborn into the higher forms which are divine.'"

This theory, so remote from the scholastic writings of the Middle Ages, led to bizarre interpretations. It is said that one priest buried a particularly virtuous dog in consecrated ground, on the chance that he might have a soul and be capable of salvation. But what this and similar ideas really indicated was pride and assurance in the power of man himself to create, to improve himself, and to do things which were in themselves worth doing, although few Humanists went to the length of Pietro Pomponazzi, who openly denied the immortality of the soul. Like the Florentine comedian, Giovanni Belli, who wrote

> I sing the first cause of all things corruptible and incorruptible . . . . .
> Who hath ordained various kinds of creatures for the services of man,
> Who hath endowed man with intellect to know Him and with will to love
>   Him . . . . .
> Join with me, light of my mind and freedom of my will, ...
> It is today man who sings Thy praises,

the Florentine philosophers were enchanted by the world, by men and by ideas. They were exuberant, and conceived their medieval ancestors to have been gloomy.

This mixing of theology and scholarship with joy emphasized the Grecian quality in Christianity, what scholars called Hellenism, as opposed to the Old

Testament's Judaism, which was stricter and gloomier. It was the essential character of the thinking of the Renaissance, but the frivolity which it sometimes led
to, and the philosophic processes which it encouraged, were presently to provoke
a new emphasis on strictness and simplicity and preoccupation with the world
to come, of which the Protestant Reformation was the most dramatic and far-
reaching symptom.

STATECRAFT

The Italian Renaissance was associated not only with Humanistic studies
but with a new idea of civil society and the nature of government. In no sphere
did its innovations contribute more to the development of modern men and their
institutions. To show the nature of the change which was taking place in 1500,
we must examine the medieval idea of government and the political history of
Italy.

The medieval idea of government had revolved around two basic notions:
the existence of Divine Law, which governed the universe and should govern
human behavior, and feudalism. In the Middle Ages, Divine Law occupied
approximately the place which the idea of liberty occupies today in civil government. Government and laws were seen primarily as an attempt to enable men to
lead lives which would prepare them for salvation and harmonize human actions
with divinely ordained precepts. Government was considered to be paternalistic—
to have responsibility like that of a father for his son, which in turn reflected the
relationship between God and mortals.

In earthly matters, medieval political institutions were what historians call
"feudal". The core of the system was military and political, but material possessions were also involved. In return, say, for the right to hold certain properties,
provide justice for the inhabitants, and collect dues from them, a lord would
promise to supply men and arms for the defense of the overlord who granted him
his powers. The arrangement was contractual: it depended upon a willingness
of both parties to abide by the agreement. Violation was considered to be against
Divine Law.

Where this system existed in its most perfect symmetry, in England and in
France, it worked out as a hierarchy of lords and overlords headed by a king, who
was supreme overlord. In Italy, however, feudalism had never developed to the
point of being a real, unified system. During most of the Middle Ages, Italy was
nominally controlled by the Holy Roman Emperor, whose principal seat of power
and usual residence was in Germany. The Holy Roman Emperor sometimes
regarded himself as the supreme feudal chief, like the king of France. But in fact
very special conditions made Italy quite different from France, caused its development into a series of small independent provinces each centered upon one city,
and paved the way for the Renaissance, to say nothing of the national disunity of
the country which persisted until a hundred years ago.

The most noticeable of the forces which impeded the establishment of an orderly feudal monarchy in Italy was the existence of the Pope, who was not only Bishop of Rome and supreme pontiff of Latin Christianity but was also political ruler of central Italy. To sum up a long and intricate history in a few sentences, the history of medieval Italy had been the history of a struggle for control between the Papacy and the Emperor. In this struggle, each contender naturally sought to develop friends and allies. Local potentates and towns formed into two bitterly divided and almost perpetually warring parties, the Guelphs (supporters of the Papacy) and the Ghibellines (supporters of the Emperors). The principal contenders were induced to grant extensive privileges to the towns in order to secure their support, and in the general chaos very highly developed and virtually independent municipal governments emerged. These governments made use of the general confusion to extend their territories by annexing the surrounding countryside and neighboring hostile communities. By 1300, northern Italy from Rome to the Alps was divided into city-states over which neither Pope nor Emperor exercised effective control.

The municipal governments were for the most part miniature republics. And since Italy was a busy manufacturing and merchandising center, the most influential people in the republics were generally the merchants and bankers, in contrast to the mainly agricultural countries beyond the Alps where landowners constituted the governing class.

THE ITALY OF THE RENAISSANCE TO 1600

The most important, powerful, and rich of the several hundred city-states were Milan, Florence, Genoa, and Venice. As time wore on these states tended to absorb the smaller ones which surrounded them—as did the States of the Church. By 1500, these five had come to control most of northern Italy. Another tendency, more relevant to the revolution in statecraft which was taking place, was the development of what has been called Despotism, the rule of the city-state by a single man, replacing the democracy or republicanism of the Middle Ages. As a rule the *signore,* or lord, as the despot was called, was invited to take over the rule of a republic temporarily, in order to provide more efficient government for quelling internal disputes among quarreling groups or to assist in the defense of the city in war. But once installed, *signori* were hard to dispose of, and by 1500 most of the despotisms had hardened into hereditary and absolute monarchies. In Florence the despots, the Medici family, ruled behind a thin veil of republican forms, preserved for reasons of tradition and convenience. In Milan, the Visconti and Sforza families successively established gorgeous but uncloaked tyrannies. The only Italian city-state which had retained its ancient constitution intact was the richest and most splendid of all, Venice, secured from invasion behind its watery ramparts.

The *signori* fashioned the revolution in attitudes toward government in Renaissance Italy. They had no claim to power in law or tradition; they were not, like the hereditary kings of the north, "legitimate." Moreover, most of them ruled as absolute sovereigns; their decision was law, their command subject to no review or protest. They were independent of feudal contract and of Divine Law alike. It was in their power to make of the state what they liked.

They chose, for the most part, to make it useful to its citizens, and glorious to behold. In the phrase of Burckhardt, the state came to be regarded not as a series of procedures divinely ordained but as "a work of art." In virtually every city-state the *signori* were lavish patrons of the arts, sponsors of scholarly endeavor, and themselves highly educated men. For the edification of the citizens, they spent money wildly on public works and festivities, and on wars for the glorification as well as the advantage of the city. They presided over, and sponsored and participated in, the most prolific flowering of the creative impulse in human history. And they fashioned for themselves ways of doing things—conducting foreign policy, collecting taxes, making wars, and regulating the lives of citizens—which were based entirely upon their own estimate of what was wise and not upon any ancient precept or custom. By the middle of the fifteenth century, the Italian cities were as remote from the form and theory of feudalism as it was possible for a state to be.

These developments found a theorist—or rather many of them, of whom one has remained famous—Niccolo Machiavelli (1469–1527), a Florentine diplomat and statesman. After he retired Machiavelli wrote a book called *The Prince,* based on his own political experiences and purporting to be a series of suggestions as to how a good *signore* should conduct himself. Writing at a time when the glories of the despots were disappearing in the maelstrom of foreign invasions which swirled through Italy at the end of the fifteenth century, he sought to discover how political stability could be restored to his country. Arguing mainly from examples in Roman history, he found the answer in the forcefulness and wisdom of the leader. His book became both a set of extremely realistic rules for the guidance of the prince and also a justification of the idea of the absolute state— in which one authority is ultimately responsible for the forming of policy, the making of decisions, and the shaping of institutions. Only in such a state could evil be controlled, patriotism incited, and defense assured.

By 1500, then, a new and essentially modern notion of statecraft was taking its place in the world. The notion had developed of policy consciously made, of institutions deliberately fashioned, of laws stemming from human decision, of an authority total in its power and wholly separate from contract, of loyalty deriving from the choice of the individual as a citizen and not from his obligation to God.

PAINTING AND ARCHITECTURE

It was in the field of the fine arts that the Italian Renaissance produced its most durable, most extensive, and most famous legacy to the ages that followed. The modern world's inheritance of ideas is invisible and immeasurable. Its inheritance of paintings, sculpture, and buildings is visible and solid. Just as the word "Renaissance" was first used in connection with the characteristic art of the period, so the average person today thinks first of painting when the word is mentioned.

The characteristics of Italian Renaissance art which are most striking are these: its enormous volume; its superb quality; its concern, theretofore unprecedented in Christian Europe, with the mortal world and with facts and pleasures unrelated to religion; its technical progress, particularly in architecture; and its inspiration—in theme in the case of painting, and in form as well as theme in sculpture and architecture—by Greek and Roman models.

The first two of these characteristics, volume and quality, are difficult to explain, since they relate to human tastes and genius, which are imponderable. But certain facts are obvious: art was fashionable; the will and resources for encouraging it were at hand; and a rich background of tradition was available to inspire it. Perhaps as a consequence, the most creative and ablest men in Italy were drawn toward art. It is now believed that the sponsorship of artists and scholars by the innumerable patrons of the Renaissance—governments, *signori*, businessmen and others—represented a form of investment. When times were bad—which they frequently were during the troubled decades of the Renaissance —princes and wealthy men with capital and leisure bought pictures and statues in the same way that an American today might buy government bonds. Art was durable and sometimes resalable. Moreover, its sponsorship and possession conferred prestige and a sense of virtue upon the patron.

The development of Renaissance art out of medieval art was gradual, and it came earlier than most Renaissance developments. Italian medieval art had never wholly lost the classical inspiration, nor had it been much influenced by the growth in the north of the wholly unclassical artistic development which we call

Gothic. Its emphases were, however, almost entirely religious, like those of the Gothic north. Out of the "primitive" styles of northern Italy—crude and flat, if vigorous—developed the fine and subtle genius of the Florentine, Giotto (1276?–1337), who is usually described as pre-Renaissance. His inspiration was still mainly medieval, and so were some of his techniques, but his paintings have a freedom and delicacy which set them sharply apart from the primitives. He gave to painting the most important single conception in its history, depth: he saw the surface on which he painted not as a something to be decorated with a design but as something to be transformed into a window through which scenes would be observed in three dimensions. From this conception stems almost all subsequent art.

After Giotto for two hundred years a torrent of paint was loosed in northern Italy. In each city or region a recognizably distinct "school" of painting developed—Venice became known for its emphasis upon color harmonies, for example, and Florence for its depth and composition. Each generation improved and perfected the methods of its predecessors. In 1500 Titian, Raphael, and Michelangelo were just beginning careers which were to constitute the supreme peak of what is called the High Renaissance of painting, the beginning of the sixteenth century. But the walls of Italian palaces, churches, and homes were already covered with the works of artists scarcely less admirable, less refined, and less famous.

It was not only in technique and conception that Renaissance art represented something new; it was also in subject. Religious themes continued to dominate, but they underwent a change. The traditional subjects—the lives of the Saints, the Annunciation, the Last Supper, the Crucifixion, the Resurrection and Ascension, the Assumption of the Virgin—were portrayed now not merely as inspirational symbols or ornaments for churches, but as pictures of life, to be enjoyed with little reference to their religious significance. For more and more artists, the traditional subjects were merely formal frameworks; into them, sometimes, in the guise of scriptural or saintly figures, painters inserted likenesses of their patrons, wives, and even mistresses. Without irreverence they showed intensely human Virgins and Martyrs.

Increasingly, artists departed altogether from religious themes. Portraits of living persons became common, divorced from allegory. Scenes of municipal glory—vast sea battles, installations of *signori,* and other strictly civic occasions—were frequent subjects. And, naturally enough, classical scenes were popular. Raphael (1483–1520), the most exquisitely pious of later Renaissance artists, painted scenes of Athenian life and classical mythology almost as frequently as he painted Madonnas.

Almost all of the painting of the fifteenth and sixteenth centuries, whether religious, classical, or contemporary in subject, showed its scenes and people in frankly contemporary costume and design. The Archangel Michael, for example, is almost invariably portrayed as a Renaissance soldier in full armor, and Biblical Bethlehem and Nazareth look like Italian towns of fifteen hundred years later.

In architecture the transformation of ideas and techniques was no less complete and the expenditure no less lavish, and here the derivation from classical forms was more tangible. At first the influence of the surviving buildings of Rome and Greece was rather haphazard. But admiration for the classics grew upon Renaissance architects. From faint indications in Giotto's plans for the cathedral tower at Florence to the most gigantic of Italian architectural efforts, Saint Peter's in Rome, the progress of classical influences may be traced. But even Saint Peter's, for the building of which the best artists of the day were summoned to Rome, for which the Papacy almost bankrupted itself, is still original in basic plan, if strongly Roman in detail.

For if architectual style in Italy increasingly showed an imitativeness, the inventiveness of architects did not. There was constant experimentation with new building forms. Arches and plinths were expanded to hitherto undreamed-of lengths, and enormous open spaces, windows, and domes were made possible. The vast cupola of Saint Peter's rests upon impeccably classical columns, but it represents a Renaissance achievement in engineering.

The classical influences, and the "secular" spirit of the Renaissance, showed in architecture as in painting. People built as many town halls, palaces, and residences as they built churches. Even the churches were frequently lacking in the spirit of intense religiosity which had permeated the Middle Ages. Religion, like everything else, was now housed in buildings which emphasized worldly achievements and tastes.

The architectural heritage of the Renaissance has proved remarkably enduring. The western world has never since been wholly freed from the admiration for classical models. In America, the White House and the Capitol are both essentially Renaissance buildings, borrowed from ancient Rome via sixteenth-century Italy and eighteenth-century England. So is the whole "style" of architecture called "Colonial," or "Georgian," so popular until recently for schools, post offices, and houses. Until the advent of modern architecture at the beginning of the twentieth century, the western world produced few architectural designs which represented any considerable departure from the inspiration of the Renaissance.

THE RENAISSANCE IN EUROPE

In speaking of the "spread" of the Renaissance in the sixteenth century it is often supposed that the cultural flowering in other regions was due to imitation of the shining example of Italy. Nowadays, however, historians see comparable developments in France, Germany, the Netherlands, England, and Spain in the period prior to their close association with Italy. To some extent each of these other countries began its own Renaissance.

Italian influences were, nonetheless, extremely important, especially in France and Spain. The Spanish rulers controlled much of Italy from the fifteenth century on, and were deeply enmeshed in Italian affairs. Toward the end of the fifteenth century (in an effort to get rid of Spanish interference) the Milanese invited French armies into Italy, and the French attempted to make their stay permanent. Frenchmen from Italy brought home not only ideas and art, but also artists. French palaces and churches flowered into elaborate imitations of Italian models. Classical columns were grafted onto specimens of the decadent French Gothic of the period and onto the grim monastic austerity of Spanish architecture. In northern Europe, Italy also spread its influence. In these more remote regions the vigor of the Renaissance more often showed itself in characteristic native forms, but the pervasiveness of Italian ideas is nowhere more clearly evidenced than in the fact that many of Shakespeare's plays are based on Italian models or set in Italian cities.

Let us look at Renaissance civilization outside of Italy, using the same three headings: philosophy, statecraft, and art.

The northern Renaissance thinkers, no less scholarly and intelligent than the Italians, differed from them in several major respects. They were also called Humanists, and they stressed many of the same subjects as the Italians. They were, however, more academic; most of them were connected with universities, in contrast to Italy where Humanists were almost invariably the protégés of princes and were not in touch with the Italian universities (which were, indeed, centers of a persistent medievalism in many cases). Northern Humanists were for the most part less bold and wayward in their philosophical interests; typically they were theologians, devoted to orthodox biblical scholarship.

The most famous man of the northern Renaissance was the Dutchman Erasmus (1466–1536). Like the Italian Humanists, he studied and sought to emulate classical models. Like them he preached moderation in the classical sense— an avoidance of extremes in living and in doctrine. But Erasmus, like many of the other northern Humanists, showed a sort of gravity which was frequently lacking among Italian scholars. For those who disagreed with him he showed a broad, cool tolerance, almost unprecedented in his age. He was not only devout, as they often were, but preoccupied with religious questions. He was concerned with the reform of the worldly and sometimes corrupt clergy (whom the Italian Humanists abetted), and with the inoculation of religion among the common people. He satirized and denounced the extravagance and sensuality which southern scholars and their patrons frequently practiced.

Erasmus was one of the most famous men of his age, and his writings and preachings carried great weight, particularly in the Church. But by drawing attention to its need for reform, and by laying almost exclusive emphasis upon the purely rational aspects of its dogmas, he contributed to the intellectual revolt against Rome, devout Catholic though he was.

A similar Humanistic churchman of the North was Sir Thomas More (1478–1535), an urbane and exceedingly cultivated English lawyer and philosopher, trained at Oxford and by Carthusian monks, who was executed by King Henry VIII and later canonized by the Roman Catholic Church as a martyr. Like so many men of the Renaissance, he combined many fields of activity, and he was no less prominent as a statesman—advisor to the king and speaker of the House of Commons—than as a scholar. His most famous work, *Utopia,* published

St. Peter's Cathedral, Rome (1606–1626). The great Michelangelo, who contributed the major elements of the design, used an unprecedented monumentality of scale. Note how tiny the man standing at the left seems. The classical proportions show the care with which Renaissance architects studied Roman models.

in 1516, sketches an imaginary island where an ideal human society flourishes, at once perfectly moral and perfectly enjoyable.

In the field of statecraft, the developments in the North were quite different on the surface from those in Italy. Here (with the exception of the free cities of Germany and the Netherlands) and in Spain as well, feudalism had developed. The political systems were based upon territorial lords presided over by kings. The kind of government which was workable in, say, Florence was obviously quite out of the question in France. Nevertheless, the Renaissance produced in the North some comparable developments.

In the first place the northern rulers, no less than the Italian *signori*, adopted the pose and role of "Renaissance princes." Francis I and Henry II in France, Henry VIII in England, Charles V in Germany and the Netherlands (all of whom ruled in the first half of the sixteenth century) thought of themselves in somewhat the same way as did a Medici in Florence. They prided themselves on their learning and on their patronage of art and letters. They sought to become "universal men," skilled in accomplishments as varied as diplomacy, chemistry, and wrestling. They were all immensely extravagant and enthusiastic in their construction of palaces. And they all surrounded themselves with a pomp which was intended not only to reflect their own glory but the glory of their country and of the enlightened age in which they lived.

Furthermore, despite the different organizations and problems of the northern states, their rulers were moving in the direction taken earlier by the *signori* of the Italian cities. There was a strong tendency—dating back to the early Middle Ages in some cases, but greatly speeded in pace after 1450—to augment the authority of the king and to diminish that of the nobility. This meant, in effect, a step toward replacing ancient "constitutions" with despotism. The feudal subcontracting of political authority was being done away with. The essential powers of lawmaking and administration, defense, and levying of taxes were being concentrated in the hands of agents of the Crown who exercised their powers through appointment, not through hereditary and independent right.

In most places ancient rights and institutions persisted, but sometimes only in form, as in Florence. In England by 1560 the Church had been brought under royal control, the important courts were all under royal authority, the political and military power of the nobility in their own territories had been largely destroyed. The old English diet, called the Parliament, although it retained its independence and was sometimes intractable, was often able to be lured or intimidated into doing the king's will.

It is perhaps excessive to refer to the development of the modern national, centralized state as a product of the Renaissance, and it is certainly misleading to draw very distinct parallels between a prince like Lorenzo de Medici and one like Henry VIII of England. But these tendencies, in some ways similar in northern Europe and in Italy, were the characteristic political developments of the *period* of the Renaissance.

In the realm of the arts and architecture (and of literature as well) the great development of the northern Renaissance did not really take place until later in the sixteenth century. Shakespeare (1564–1616) is often regarded as a son of the Renaissance, and so is the Spaniard Cervantes (1547–1616), both of them born after the most vigorous artistic impulses had slackened in Italy. But in the excellence of painting the North and Spain yield little—and the Netherlands nothing—to Italy. The painters of the late sixteenth and early seventeenth century in Holland and Flanders—Hals, Vermeer, Rubens, Bosch, and, greatest of all, Rembrandt—rank with Tintoretto, Raphael, Titian, and Michelangelo in the history of man's artistic achievement. And in some ways they deal with similar conceptions through similar techniques: the portraits and landscapes, the paintings of large municipal events, scenes from the classics or the scriptures. But in flavor, as in epoch, they are very different, even from the Italian painters of the High Renaissance; they belong to a culture, and for the most part to a religious setting, which is entirely remote from fifteenth or sixteenth century Italy. Perhaps the chief point which they share is an interest in artistic experiment and a regard for the pleasures of this life—textures, living people, money, learning, and color.

THE TRANSITION FROM
THE RENAISSANCE

The civilization which we describe as the Renaissance did not end. It did not, as the lives of Shakespeare and Rembrandt suggest, even decline. But its residence and its character changed, and the ideal of the Universal Man, the preoccupation with classical studies, the typical political structures, were transformed into something else.

Italy itself underwent many paralysing disasters, and with them changes of taste which did not, perhaps, indicate decline in creative powers, but which marked a new era of taste and forms. The invasions of the Spaniards and French, and later of the Germans, wrecked the political structure and bled the prosperity of Renaissance Italy. Confusion, fear, poverty, and insecurity spread, and simultaneously the ideas and techniques of artists began to change. The movement of "mannerism" slid toward the end of the sixteenth century into the movement called "baroque." Both of them were in some ways less robust if not less fecund and attractive than the earlier ages of Renaissance style. They tended toward the ornate and occasionally toward the frivolous. Baroque art and design, transported across the Alps, were to flourish in other countries, especially in Austria and southern Germany, in the following century. Unimaginably polished and graceful they were, but their inspiration and their canons of taste were different. Italy in the seventeenth century still produced more competent artists than any other region in the world, but they were no longer geniuses to rank with Michelangelo.

In Italy, as in the rest of Europe, the forces which worked to destroy the smug but robust ideal of the Renaissance man were partly religious. Against the worldliness and occasional corruption of both church and society serious minds revolted. It was appropriate that the storm of religious revival should have been occasioned by a German monk, Martin Luther, who was protesting against

Indulgences from penalties for sin sold by the Papacy in an effort to raise funds for the building of Saint Peter's. In the vast and devastating struggles which followed, the Renaissance ideal became impracticable. Catholics and Protestants alike for the most part chose, or were forced, to turn their attention again to considerations of theology and salvation. Wars between them ensued. In such an atmosphere the glowing self-assurance and enjoyment and urbanity of the Renaissance was doomed.

THE
REFORMATION

FOR MANY PEOPLE alive in the sixteenth century, the greatest event of their time was the religious upheaval which wrecked the unity of Christendom. Thereafter, for almost two hundred years, religious debate guided the mind and politics of Europe, and it has by no means disappeared in our own day.

The Protestant break with the Catholic Church is commonly called the Reformation; the subsequent rebuilding and revival of the Church of Rome is known as the Counter-Reformation. The terms are unfortunate, for they prejudice the story in advance, suggesting that Catholic ways were improved upon by the Protestants and that reform of the Catholic Church was the consequence of Protestant competition. People today still quarrel over terminology, and over the meaning of the revolt which occasioned the split. But it is possible to narrate the story of what happened and how vast its consequences were.

CHRISTIANITY

The Reformation was intricate and confusing. In studying its details it is easy to lose sight of the essential fact: Western Christendom lost its formal unity and broke into competing parts. The split was not a purely religious affair—on that everyone agrees—but before describing the web of contributing causes it is important to say something about the Christian religion.

Christianity had appeared within the vast edifice of the Roman Empire and had triumphed there amid the many cults brought together by the political unification of the Mediterranean world. In the "apostolic" period for a century after the birth of Jesus of Nazareth the records of his teachings were set down. The new religion continued to spread in spite of Roman persecution which at times used it as a scapegoat. It offered mutual respect and brotherhood and love, regardless of social class, giving new dignity to all humans. The Christians had high ideals of earthly conduct, and related them to the existence of a God whose plans gave meaning to earthly existence and held out hope of eternal happiness to the faithful. By 313 A.D. Christianity was tolerated in the Roman Empire, and by the end of the fourth century it had become the state religion. St. Augustine (354–430) was the great defender against heretics and outside critics. Gregory the Great, Pope from 590–604, was an outstanding organizer. The organization of the Church developed under the influence of the Roman Empire. Into Christian doctrine went many influences of the ancient world such as Greek philosophy (in part the contribution of St. Paul and his followers), oriental mysticism and asceticism, and Hebrew monotheism and longing for justice and righteousness.

The sacraments illustrate how Christian faith and works gave life meaning. There were seven sacraments through which priests guided Christians in awareness of daily needs and of the life to come. Baptism freed the child from original sin and brought him within the Christian community. Confirmation "confirmed" or made firm what baptism had started. Penance, which recognized that human imperfection persisted in spite of baptism and confirmation, was the sacrament by which the contrite sinner, after confession to a priest, undertook certain penalties such as prayers, pilgrimage, or acts of charity. Related to penance was the Eucharist, or Mass, or Last Supper, which repeated Christ's sacrifice in atonement for the sins of man: the communicant, by partaking of bread and wine transformed by the priest into the body and blood of Christ (a process known as transubstantiation), was placed in physical communion with God. The sacrament of Holy Orders was the ceremony by which a candidate became a priest. Matrimony and Extreme Unction were respectively the sacraments of marriage and the last rites administered when death was expected and the Christian was prepared for the life to come. Since the sacraments were vital to salvation, the withholding of them, known as excommunication, was a fearful penalty.

In the sacraments was embedded a philosophy of history which explained the relationship of the earth to heaven. Perfection in life on earth had been spoiled by the disobedience of Adam, who with his descendants had been expelled from the Garden of Eden and exposed to toil, suffering, and death. Faith in God had been kept alive, however, and God had sent his son Jesus to atone on the cross for the sins of mankind. Thereafter, those who believed in Jesus Christ could be saved from the consequences of Adam's sin and attain perfection in life everlasting. These truths were divinely revealed in the Holy Scriptures. In time other criteria of truth were recognized—logic, experience, even to some extent experimentation. Interpretation of the Scriptures themselves became more complicated, allowing for allegory, moral teachings, and prophecies. But the final explanation of truth remained a function of the Church.

By 1054, Christians had separated into Eastern Orthodox and Roman Catholic churches. The latter guided the west from ancient times to the 1500's. This millennium saw many changes in the Church as well as in European society. The Patristic period, to about 600 A.D., when the Church first triumphed and became organized, was followed by the several hundred years of the so-called "dark ages" during which it was hard to preserve learning and priestly asceticism. The Church Christianized the Germans, Slavs, and Scandinavians. In the centuries of mainly agrarian and decentralized society the Church survived by becoming a landowner and feudal power. Sometimes it was hard to tell bishops from nobles, priests from peasants, and Popes from kings. Much of the task of preserving Christian ideals was performed by the regular clergy, the monks of the monasteries, who were distinguished from the secular clergy who were in everyday contact with the public. Catholic faith and works were an essential part of the High Middle Ages, contributing much to the Truce of God, the Gothic cathedrals, the universities, the Crusades, and to constitutional and political theory.

The Popes, as Bishops of Rome where the apostles Peter and Paul had had their missions, became in a certain sense also the successors to the Roman emperors. Now chosen by a College of Cardinals, the Pope with his *curia,* or council, was like a universal monarch. Many were the disputes in which the Popes, who controlled a network of properties, church or canon laws, taxes, and officials in every country, declared their supremacy over all secular rulers.

No one can say precisely what the unlettered masses of Europe drew from their religion, but it is generally agreed that Christianity was a force pushing toward certain values and away from others. From its earliest days it emphasized the dignity of every individual in the eyes of God, and this was to be reflected in Western political thought. Although the Church was organized like a monarchy and in everyday life taught the people to be patient and obedient and not to expect too much of this world, Christianity did not lend itself to the building of an omnipotent state. Unlike Byzantium and, later, Russia, where the head of the state was also head of the church, Europe even its days of absolute monarchy was never to lose sight of the idea that all governments were limited by divine law.

Apart from politics, the Christian attitude toward the world was conditioned by the drama of salvation, of which the world was the stage. Man's place in nature was therefore central. The "worldly" experiences—pride, and pleasures of the senses—were not supposed to be overrated. There was in Christianity a strain of asceticism, of what would later be called "Puritanism," but Christianity did not teach flight from the world. The Church learned to work in the world and even tended to become soiled by it. Christian love meant appreciation of the divine in all the children of God, underneath the human failings. The Church was also aware of man living in imperfection, of his natural weakness and wickedness, of original sin, and yet also of man's part in the drama involving a future life. All sorts of people lived side by side within the spacious Church which housed the entire Western European society and was its principal link to ancient civilization as well as to life hereafter.

THE CHURCH IN THE
LATE MIDDLE AGES

The Church was placed under a strain by the developing social and political institutions of Europe. In the 14th and 15th centuries the new money economy raised questions of business ethics. The Church as a collector and spender of money came into severe competition with the newly consolidated states. The famous "Babylonian captivity" during which the Papacy, from 1309 to 1378, was kept at Avignon, surrounded by French territory, illustrates the danger from powerful monarchs. So does the "Great Schism" which followed, from 1378 to 1417, during which there was a Pope at Avignon supported by the French, and another at Rome. Such events could not fail to damage the Church's prestige. Whether they wished it or not, Christians were given a choice between spiritual leaders—and even *among* them, for there were at one time three Popes. Although the Babylonian captivity came to an end and the Schism was healed, the church did not quite recover its position.

The Renaissance in most of its aspects did not contribute directly to the Protestant revolt. True, the humanist Lorenzo Valla exposed in his studies the "Donation of Constantine." Erasmus, "Prince of the Humanists," satirized abuses in the clergy as he satirized everything else in his worldly and civilized manner. But the church took Valla's discovery in its stride. Humanists like Valla and Erasmus were not rebellious as they went their aristocratic and scholarly ways. The worldliness of the Renaissance—the sort of thing which made people value the literature of Greece and Rome—had effects on the Church which contributed *indirectly* to its loss of the spiritual guidance of Europe. The amours of Pope Alexander VI, the military adventures and extravagant patronage of the arts of Julius II, the indolence and improvidence of Leo X intensified the need for reform and thereby contributed to a dangerous situation.

A Catholic Reformation was under way before the Protestant break with Rome. In the fifteenth century a "conciliar movement" within the Church attempted to make regular Church council meetings into a kind of parliamentary government. Councils at Pisa (1409) and Constance (1414–1417) and elsewhere reviewed the Church's problems. Reform within the church was in the direction of firmness. The Papacy would not yield its absolute authority to the conciliar movement. Movements to tighten the moral standards of the clergy and to defend orthodoxy in doctrines were begun. These moves were strongest in Spain, where crusading against the Moors was still going on. The Spanish Inquisition founded in 1478 by Ferdinand and Isabella was, however, controlled by the Spanish rulers and was not always approved by the Popes, who since the thirteenth century had used a more relaxed Inquisition of their own to investigate and try heretics in emergencies.

The Church's reiteration of papal authority and doctrinal orthodoxy encountered heresies in the fourteenth and fifteenth centuries. These heresies were accompanied by national feeling and resentment at clerical abuses and wealth at a time when the poor were suffering from the economic dislocations of the age. The two outstanding examples of this religious and social mixture are John Wyclif (1328–1384), an Englishman, and John Hus (c. 1369–1415), a Czech. Wyclif's time was one of war, plague, and suffering among the common people, when Church abuses were dramatized by the start of the Great Schism. He wanted all men to have access to the Scriptures, and himself translated the Bible into English. He attacked transubstantiation. Through his "Lollard" followers, Wyclif's ideas, though condemned by the Church, remained alive in England until the Reformation.

Hus, a Bohemian priest who preached in the Czech language, took part in a struggle between Czech and German elements in the Church at the time of the schism. He too preached against Church abuses, and although he did not accept all the ideas of Wyclif he taught that the Bible was the supreme authority and minimized the role of the Church and clergy in salvation.

Wyclif and Hus are famous cases, but there were many lesser examples of restlessness and rebellion against abuses in the Church and, more important, against its doctrine of salvation. But there was much piety as the fifteenth century came to an end. It was a religious age still. This time, however, the Catholic Church failed to hold all Christians under its authority and within its doctrine.

MARTIN LUTHER AND THE COMING OF PROTESTANTISM

This failure of European Christians to settle their differences within a single church took place in the sixteenth century in the midst of many other distracting events. It took place also among the long-range developments which have already been mentioned: growing material wealth, with resultant economic appetites of kings and nobles, who interfered with the Church's sources of revenue; Renaissance worldliness and zest; renewed appreciation of the pagans of antiquity; independent-minded study of texts; growth of national feelings coupled in some cases with strong states; decline of the Holy Roman Empire and of that other "international" influence, the Latin language. This list of changes in European life is sometimes given as the "causes of the Reformation." Such secular influences were certainly important. Undoubtedly the Catholic Church was handicapped by its own worldly abuses as well as by the worldly ambitions of princes and their subjects.

It is less easy to account for the strictly religious side of Protestantism, around which worldly ambitions rallied. Viewed in long perspective, Catholics and Protestants agreed more than they disagreed about mankind's nature and need for salvation. Up to the mid-seventeenth century, and for most people long afterward, the questions of Christianity remained the all-important questions.

Here again, as at the start of this chapter, it is useful to remember that much depends on the point of view. To some historians the vast debate over religious questions in the sixteenth and early seventeenth centuries marks a slipping backward into the Middle Ages, an interruption of the forward march of reasonableness began in the Renaissance. To others, though they might take opposite sides in the Catholic-Protestant dispute, the intense religious concerns of early modern times mark a renewal of Christianity in the West. To complicate matters further, while Protestant historians have tended to celebrate the advance in culture which made the Reformation possible, Catholics have sometimes taken the view that the Reformation was part of a cultural decline.

The act of Martin Luther (1483–1546) in nailing ninety-five theses about "Indulgences" on the church door at Wittenberg (1517) may be taken as the symbolic beginning of the Reformation. The Indulgences to which Luther objected had grown up in connection with the sacrament of penance. If the penance given by the priest after confession was insufficient, the sinner, it was thought, would have to make up the difference in purgatory. The time in purgatory could, however, be shortened by the Pope, who could draw on the "treasury of merits" stored up by the good acts of Christ and the saints. In so doing, the Pope was granting an "Indulgence," and it is easy to see how disputes about this practice could arise. Technically, Indulgences were granted, not sold, and would do the sinner no good if he were not genuinely contrite.

In practice, people came to feel that they could buy Indulgences, for it was customary to make a monetary contribution when they were granted, and the Church encouraged this practice. The dispute in which Martin Luther became involved was the aftermath of a papal money-raising campaign partly destined for the construction of St. Peter's in Rome and partly to enable a German prince, Albert of Hohenzollern, to recover the 10,000 ducats he had borrowed to pay the Pope for his installation as archbishop of Mainz. The public were being given the impression that they could buy remission of their sins and the release of their friends from purgatory. Luther, who was a professor of divinity at Wittenberg, objected to the sending of German money to Rome and, more important, to the claim that the Pope could shorten terms in purgatory. Most important, Luther's deep personal convictions about salvation were outraged by what seemed to him to be a shallow and misleading treatment of the subject.

Luther was the son of a prosperous free peasant in Saxony, and originally intended to prepare himself for the law. Luther was sensitive and imaginative and even after he had become a monk he was oppressed by his own miserableness in the face of God's majesty. The gap seemed too great to be crossed by penance, for contrition and good works by men like himself seemed to Luther pitifully small. When he had turned to teaching, he came upon his answer in Christ on the cross saying "My God, my God, why hast Thou forsaken me?" For now he saw the miracle of Christ suffering the human condition when he was not obliged to; the miracle of God's gift of forgiveness when there was nothing man could do to earn it, nothing man could offer that would add to God's greatness. Luther did not consider his discovery original. He felt that he had at last understood the Apostle Paul and Saint Augustine. Salvation was God's gift, understandable only in terms of faith, not in terms of God's "reason" to grant it or man's capacity to earn it.

THE LAST SUPPER by Albrecht Dürer (1471–1528). A woodcut.

In the dispute over indulgences, Luther was soon forced to admit to himself and to the world that he really did not consider the Catholic priesthood and most of the sacraments necessary for salvation. This view, denying the importance of the Church's ministrations, struck at the whole foundation upon which the Church was built. In 1519 at Leipzig the theologian Eck confronted Luther with decisions of Popes and councils, but Luther rejected them. In his *Appeal to the Christian Nobility of the German Nation* (1520), he said in effect that all baptized Christians could be their own priests if they had faith and followed the Gospel. After Luther that same year had burned a Papal edict condemning his doctrines, he was given a hearing at the meeting of the German Diet at the city of Worms in 1521. There, in the presence of the newly elected Emperor Charles V of the Holy Roman Empire, he refused to back down. Nor would he in secret meetings compromise, as many of his German supporters and others among the liberal, Erasmian Catholics wished. Luther for his intransigence was outlawed and later excommunicated. The Edict of Worms prohibited his doctrines.

But Luther had powerful friends. On his way home from Worms he was kidnapped on orders of the Elector of Saxony and hidden in Wartburg castle, to keep him from harm. In his enforced leisure, with considerable talent and much feeling, he translated the New Testament into his native German. At Wittenberg and elsewhere his friends began to practice his principles, giving bread and wine to the laity in communion, holding church services in German, permitting priests and even monks to marry. Luther approved of these changes. In 1522 on his return to Wittenberg he took charge of the spreading Reformation and began to build a church independent of Rome. In the emergency he encouraged the German princes to act as bishops and adopt his church. Putting the new printing presses to work, he set himself to instruct the German people through hymns and religious tracts. The Reformation was the first great public debate which used the medium of print.

The German lands of the 1520's were ready for some kind of outburst. Political development had fallen behind the times, and the social structure was being upset by the money economy. The medieval Holy Roman Empire was no longer the universal monarchy its name implied; yet the Emperor was kept from transforming it into a strong German state by the jealousies of the territorial princes, who preferred to go on behaving like kings. The Pope himself feared the Habsburg Holy Roman Emperor and up to the last moment had intrigued against the election of the new emperor, Charles I of Spain, who became Charles V, Holy Roman Emperor, in 1519. The whole constitutional question had lain like a plague over late medieval Germany. Sick of political ineffectiveness, Germans were more conscious of their common culture, more critical of clerical and social abuses, more hostile to Rome.

When Luther stood his ground he proved to be a rallying point for national sentiment. He did not originally intend a break with the Church; rather he wished to reform the Church. In the struggle he appealed to German sentiments. In the end he appealed most of all to the German princes. The Lutheran inspiration in the hands of the lesser nobles and peasants and some townsmen threatened to run amuck. In the Knights' War of 1522 some of these lesser nobles (who were being impoverished by the rising prices of their purchases and the declining incomes from their tiny farms) seized upon Lutheranism and attempted to play robber baron with various bishoprics. They were checked by the greater princes, with Luther's approval.

In the Peasants' War of 1524–1525 social tension again burst into action. The peasants, like the knights, were the victims of the growth of the money economy, which led landlords to squeeze ever more tightly in the hope of greater revenues. Luther was no lover of exploitation, but he believed that the sword should never be wielded by private hands, even for religious reasons. When he saw the peasants looking to him for inspiration he was horrified, and urged the princes to stamp mercilessly on the conflagration. He was equally hostile when radical Protestant sects in the towns mingled religion with the quest for utopian social justice. The civil authorities were capable of keeping order among the sinners of this world, and should be left to do so. Luther was no crusader and no theocrat.

What, then, should his attitude be toward that most eminent civil authority, the Holy Roman Emperor? Charles V had not, in earlier times, been averse to reforms within the Church. Now, as nominal ruler of the Holy Empire (which in fact meant the German lands), he had a great opportunity to welcome the national consciousness which Luther's courage had aroused, and use it to make a strong German state. This would have involved disciplining the princes even as the rulers of France, Spain, and England were doing to their great nobles. Charles V might have done the same. But as ruler of Spain and other lands outside of Germany, he was not prepared to risk losing their vital support by grabbing for Germany. He was, after all, a Habsburg dynastic ruler, not a German nationalist. And he was a good Catholic. So, as events transpired, Charles V ended in one camp, Luther in the other. Charles' Diet had outlawed Luther; the latter had to fall in with the German princes in their assertion of rights against the Emperor. Thus Luther, who believed that church and state should cooperate, each in its proper sphere, made (in spite of himself) a powerful contribution to German political disunity.

Several events will indicate the working out of this drama on the German stage in the sixteenth century. First, it is important to realize that Charles V, for all his ability to throw Spanish soldiers into the German arena, suffered from bigness. His great international empire could not help being a threat to the security of everyone who aspired to independence. Not only the German princes but also France, and even the Pope as a political ruler in Italy, opposed him when they could. He had also to face the thrust from the East of a revived Turkish power under Suleiman the Magnificent (1520–1566), whose troops beseiged Vienna in September and October, 1529.

In 1529 the word "Protestant" was born. The preoccupied German Diet reiterated the Decree of Worms against Luther, and in practice allowed the schismatic churches to continue in regions where they could not for the moment be crushed. This interim solution was scarcely satisfactory to Luther's followers, and they "protested" the decision. In the following year, at the Diet of Augsburg, there was some attempt at reconciliation with the schismatics. Luther's friend

Melanchthon presented the most they could offer in the "Augsburg confession," but neither side would meet the other's terms. Interminable wars and negotiations dragged on. In the end the best solution that either side could get in Germany was the religious Peace of Augsburg in 1555, a settlement unsatisfactory on many counts but one which lasted in a state of worrisome deterioration until the Thirty Years War of 1618–1648.

The Peace of Augsburg adopted the principle of *cuius regio, eius religio* (whose region, his religion), which meant that the civil ruler was to decide the religion of the territory, with dissidents allowed to go elsewhere. Although it recognized the tearing of the "seamless robe of Christ" in Europe as a whole, it did not grant religious liberty, for the view was still held that society needed not just an official government but an official religion as well. The only choice allowed by Augsburg was between Catholicism and Lutheranism. The Calvinists, who by this time were flourishing in various parts of Europe, were granted no recognition.

THE REFORMED CHURCHES OF ZWINGLI AND CALVIN

In the half-independent provinces which made up Switzerland, Ulrich Zwingli and John Calvin had started a form of Protestantism somewhat different from Lutheranism. Their churches and those which they influenced are usually called the "reformed." The term "Calvinism" also applies to the beliefs of most of these churches, for Calvin's great influence shaped one of the main types of Protestantism—today represented in the United States by the Presbyterian and Congregationalist churches.

Ulrich Zwingli's life (1484–1531) shows that others in Europe besides Luther had been undergoing deep changes in their religious views. Zwingli was a parish priest who was also a humanistic disciple of Erasmus, and he arrived through scholarship at the destination which Luther reached by way of anguished personal experience. In 1519 he began to preach with the Gospel open before him, substituting, as it were, the original sources for the official Catholic doctrine. Like Luther, he rejected papal and conciliar authority, revised and simplified the sacraments and liturgy, repudiated clerical celibacy and monasticism, used the vernacular in church services, denied the efficacy of good works and indulgences and preached that salvation came through God's gift to the faithful. Zwingli was more inclined than Luther to take images out of the churches and esthetic sense-impressions out of the service. He was more inclined than Luther to make communion a simple rite, an outward sign of membership in the community of believers, with no "real presence" of Christ in the bread and wine. Unlike Luther, he tended to emphasize the power of the Church in the Church-state partnership.

Zwingli died in 1531. In 1536 John Calvin (1509–1564) published his *Institutes of the Christian Religion,* and five years after that, in 1541, Calvin set up his church in Geneva, which became the center of world Calvinism. Geneva was an independent city, recently liberated from the Duke of Savoy. John Calvin, a French Protestant refugee, was a humanist intellectual with a legal training and an orderly mind. Under his leadership Geneva, through banishment of unbelievers and the influx of the faithful, became the "city of the saints." Theoretically the church and state were parallel, but in practice Geneva tended to be ruled by the religious authorities.

Unlike Luther, who did not expect much improvement on the earthly plane, Calvin thought that men should serve God by making a Holy Commonwealth on earth. This demand for action was backed by a philosophy of history. God had chosen the Jews to set up this commonwealth, but they had failed. Then God had selected the Christian Church, but it had not done its duty. Now God expected the "elect" predestined for salvation to do the job. Calvin did not pretend to know who the elect were or claim that his church contained only the elect—that could have been determined only through knowing men's consciences —but he presumed that they would be among those who professed their faith openly, took part in the sacraments, and lived upright lives without drunkness, obscenity, dancing, gambling—the "Puritanism" with which we are familiar has a Calvinistic background. Calvin did not believe that men ought to brood over whether they were among the elect. They should get to work at their various callings, which was the proper way to honor God. This the Calvinists did with vigor, in Switzerland, France, Scotland, England and New England, in the Netherlands and parts of Germany, and even for a while in parts of Eastern Europe such as Poland and Hungary.

In France the Calvinists were called Huguenots (from the German *eidgenossen*, confederated, leagued together). During the reigns (1559–1589) of the three weak and heirless sons of Catherine de Médicis the French "religious wars" took place, complicated by political and dynastic considerations. In France as elsewhere the great nobles tended to resent the building of an absolute monarchy capable of replacing their feudal functions. As in Germany, religion was in part an excuse for political action. Although many of the Protestants were townsmen, some of the great nobles were Huguenots. Catherine de Médicis was not moved by religious considerations so much as by political. Her concern was to safeguard and extend the authority of the crown, and to this end she allowed herself Machiavellian means. In August, 1572, in a panic at possible Protestant revenge for a Catholic atrocity, she ordered a wholesale massacre of Protestants which came to be known as the massacre of St. Bartholomew. After the "war of the three Henrys" (one a Catholic cousin, one son of Catherine, one Huguenot Bourbon) the third (and only remaining) Henry not only inherited the throne but won it by force of arms. In order to insure the pacification of the country, he renounced his Protestant faith when he became King Henry IV (1589–1610), one of France's most beloved kings. By the Edict of Nantes in 1598, Henry guaranteed the Huguenots toleration and civil rights, and as a pledge of his sincerity turned over to them a number of fortified towns. This religious settlement lasted until 1685, although the fortified towns were taken from the Huguenots by Henry's successor.

Besides Switzerland and France, Scotland was strongly influenced by Calvinism. The Scottish Presbyterian Church was established in 1560 under the leadership of John Knox (1505?–1572), a former priest, at a time when Scotland was pulled this way and that between English and French influences. When a new ruler, Mary Stuart, Queen of Scots, arrived in 1561 there was a historic contest between the young Catholic Queen and the stern theologian. Mary's tangled affairs, and especially her marriage to the Earl of Bothwell shortly after he had murdered her husband, led to her defeat and overthrow (1567). The Presbyterian form of church government, which entailed rule by church elders, with no hierarchy of bishops to supervise the congregations, was established. It was to play an important part in Scottish and English history.

Calvinism took part in the competition of many sects and beliefs in the Netherlands, and emerged victorious in the seven Northern, or Dutch, provinces as they won their independence from Spain. The ten Southern provinces, which would one day be Belgium, retained the Catholic faith. In Poland, Hungary, and Transylvania, Calvinism took root for a time, and even found haven under the rule of the Ottoman Turks who, ironically, were more tolerant of Christian dissenters than were the Catholics in the Habsburg monarchy.

ENGLAND'S BREAK WITH ROME

England's part in the Reformation was in some respects a special one. In the fifteenth century it had had an experience of sectarianism and heresy with Wyclif and the Lollards, and of civil disorders in the Wars of the Roses (see Chapter 7). Moreover, like France and Spain, England was slowly "nationalizing" its portion of the Catholic Church. Henry VIII (1509–1547) championed the Church against Luther, and received from the Pope the title, Defender of the Faith (1521). Unfortunately for religious peace, however, the stability of the Tudor dynasty seemed threatened by the ruler's lack of a male heir. He and his wife, Catherine of Aragon, had only one child, Princess Mary. Five other children had been born to them but none had lived. For the sake of a stable succession, Henry turned to the Church for an annulment.

At this juncture, international politics entered the English picture. Pope Clement VII was embarrassed, but this was perhaps the least of his worries. Catherine, as it happened, was the aunt of Charles, King of Spain, who was also Charles V, Holy Roman Emperor. Charles V was nearby, powerful, and more than that, had invaded Italy. In 1527 Rome was looted by his troops and the Pope for a while made a prisoner. Pope Clement played for time as best he could, but these tactics failed to soothe Henry VIII, who took matters into his own hands. After consulting universities in England and on the continent, he received a divorce at the hands of the Archbishop of Canterbury, whom he had recently appointed, and married Anne Boleyn. When the Pope excommunicated him, Henry in 1534 secured from Parliament the Act of Supremacy which declared him to be Protector and Only Supreme Head of the Church and Clergy of England.

England was pious but strongly national in sentiments, and was inclined to resent interference from Rome and criticize at times some institutions such as the monasteries. There was no national outcry when the king, a superb politician, confiscated the monasteries, thereby improving his income and clearing the way for substantial rewards by sale and gift to those in the royal favor. In the main, Henry's program was schism without heresy. He was, indeed, the more anxious to appear orthodox in doctrine, and in 1539 arranged for Parliament to pass the Six Articles, reaffirming transubstantiation, penance, celibacy of the priesthood, and other Catholic practices.

After the death of Henry VIII, his ten-year-old son Edward VI (1547–1553) took the throne. His advisors favored first Lutheran, then Zwinglian and Calvinist religious tendencies, and Protestantism continued to develop. After Edward's death, Queen Mary (1553–1558), the daughter of Henry VIII and Catherine of Aragon, tried to shepherd the country back into the Catholic fold. Mary herself married Philip II of Spain, the great champion of Catholicism. After Mary's death, Queen Elizabeth I (1558–1603) encouraged the development of an Anglican Church (Church of England, Episcopal Church) distinct from both Catholicism and the current Protestant sects. The Thirty-nine Articles (1563) were its first doctrinal statement, Protestant but not very precise, the ambiguities admirably suited to a settlement which enabled as many people as possible to remain within the church. Organization and ritual remained very similar to the Roman Catholic. The shape of Anglican doctrine and institutions was debated and decided by Parliament, which represented many shades of religious opinion. Many people came to know and love the English Book of Common Prayer. Elizabethan England, unlike Luther's Germany and the France of the Three Henrys, had no religious wars, although various Protestant sects continued to develop. In the seventeeth century England was to have its time of troubles, much of which would consist of religious strife.

OTHER FORMS OF PROTESTANTISM

To illustrate the splintering within Protestantism, we may cite the Anabaptists, who appeared in Central Europe as the radical wing of Protestantism when Luther and Zwingli were first becoming known. "Anabaptism" means "re-baptism," and the term was used because of the adult baptism practiced by these groups, who had no single organization and were treated as outcasts all over Europe. The baptism of adults had very subversive political implications for those times. It meant that the church and the state were to have nothing to do with each other. The church was to contain only genuine believers, and not the general public. It was therefore foolish to baptize children before it was known which ones would qualify. The Anabaptists, as if transferring monasticism into everyday life, meant to keep the church from being contaminated by the world. They repudiated war and capital punishment, refused to carry weapons or take oaths or appeal to the law. They dressed plainly and pioneered in abstinence from alcoholic beverages. They were not revolutionary, and would obey the state except in matters affecting their moral standards.

But their missionary zeal was so intense as to frighten powerful and respectable people. In 1529 at the Diet of Speier, *both* the Protestants and Catholics agreed that the death penalty should be inflicted on the Anabaptists. (If this is hard to understand, it must be remembered that for most people in the sixteenth and seventeenth centuries, "no state church" was as unsettling a doctrine as "no state" would be to most people today.) The Anabaptists were therefore persecuted and butchered wherever they could be found. And it is small wonder that under this great provocation their policies of nonresistance occasionally faltered. Some groups of Anabaptists went in for socialist doctrines during the Peasant War in Germany. Some thought they knew the date for Christ's return in the near future. In 1534–1535 one group seized the city of Münster, in Westphalia, and tried to establish a society with no law, no marriage, no property. Anabaptism was stamped out in Germany, where it might otherwise have provided competition for Lutheranism, to the edification of the German public. Some Anabaptists survived in the Netherlands and Switzerland, where the movement was very strong at one time. But most of those who survived were pushed outward to the fringes of European society, to Poland, Moravia, Hungary, and even Russia, and ultimately to America. The followers of the Dutch Menno Simons became the Mennonites of Pennsylvania, Ohio, and elsewhere.

The Anabaptists show how Protestantism could lead to a radically new attitude toward church-state relationships, and also to a variety of interpretations once people began studying the Bible for themselves. There are, of course, many other illustrations. Thomas Münzer (1489–1525), who was denounced by Luther, expelled from Wittenberg, and put to death for participation in the peasant revolt, preached the forceful establishment of a new theocratic social order. He was sure also that the theocrats, the elect, were those who had a certain kind of emotional experience of regeneration. Münzer illustrates a tendency to emphasize the emotional side of Christianity, a tendency which was to turn up in some of the Protestant sects of later centuries.

On a much more sophisticated level was the mystical experience of being in touch with God. This too had always existed, but if given sufficient importance it would make unnecessary the whole theological and sacramental apparatus of both Catholics and Protestants, and indeed, of any organized religion. For this reason mystics seldom bothered to leave one church for another, and it is impossible to know how many of them existed within the various churches of the sixteenth century.

Oddly enough, mysticism was often combined with rationalism in the independent spirits of the Reformation period. Rational criticism of theological doctrines and documents—the sort of criticism which Humanists liked to undertake—could if carried far enough destroy all belief in systems, whether Catholic or Protestant. In extreme cases there was nothing left for the rationalist except the fact of mystical religious experience on an individual basis. In less extreme form, rationalistic criticism of Christian theology tended to simplify it beyond the points at which most Catholics and Protestants insised on stopping. The Trinity, and to a lesser extent the vicarious atonement, suffered at the hands of both mystics and rationalists. The Spaniard Servetus (1511–1553) is a famous example because he was burned at the stake by Calvin for attempting to revise the doctrine of the Trinity. The Italian Fausto Sozzini, known as Socinus (1539–1604), after whom the Socinian movement was named, was more fortunate. He took refuge in Poland, where in the sixteenth century there was much toleration and free discussion. The Socinian beliefs were Antitrinitarian and also critical of the doctrine of vicarious atonement. They are an example of the view which is today called Unitarian and which grew up in Eastern Europe and later in England and America largely through rationalistic criticisms of the doctrine of the Trinity.

One other Protestant tendency may be mentioned because of its lasting influence on church organization. Robert Browne (1550–1633), a clergyman of the Anglican Church, proposed that congregations should make their own "covenants" and choose their own ministers. Congregationalism was a system which lent itself readily to radical Protestant sects that refused to follow the rules of large church organizations and believed, like the Anabaptists, that the faithful should keep to themselves. In England the Separatists and Independents had their own congregations, and this method of church organization was transplanted to America.

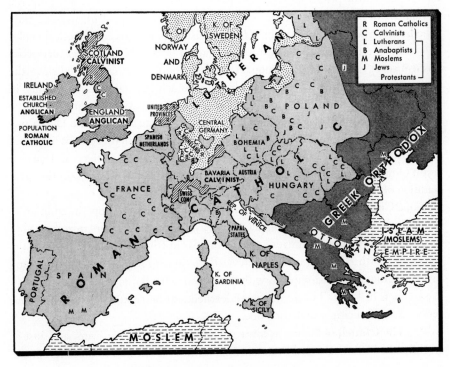

THE SPREAD OF PROTESTANTISM

THE CATHOLIC REFORMATION

It has been noted that Catholic efforts to reform the abuses within the Church were started before Luther posted his theses. The Catholic Reformation did not compromise with the Protestants and did not reunify Europe religiously. It did take a courageous stand in defense of the dogmas and organization of the Church, and it succeeded in fighting Protestantism to a standstill and in turning it back in some areas, so that Europe was more or less evenly divided.

The Catholic Reformation was carried out through the efforts of both religious and secular authorities. The Popes, especially from the time of Paul III (1534–1549), were not blind to the need for good appointments capable of purifying the hierarchy. A great church council, the Council of Trent (1545–1563), refused to compromise on dogma but began a long list of practical reforms. The Council was handicapped by national and dynastic rivalries, even among Catholics. The Protestants were invited but did not appear—it is probable that by the late 1540's compromise was out of the question on both sides.

The Council of Trent reaffirmed the Church's traditions as expounded by Thomas Aquinas, maintained the interpretation of Holy Scripture in the hands of the Church, condemned Protestant teaching about grace, justification by faith, the sacraments, purgatory, and indulgences. To correct pernicious practices, statutes were issued forbidding sale of church offices, making prelates reside in their dioceses, and ending the issuance of indulgences for money. Seminaries were established for the proper education of priests. A uniform catechism was prepared at Rome, and a new standard edition of the Latin Bible, the Vulgate, was published. Also, there was published the Index, a list of dangerous and heretical books.

In its reform efforts the Church was aided by the thirteenth-century ecclesiastical court called the Inquisition. A Spanish Inquisition had existed since the fifteenth-century efforts of the Spanish rulers to achieve religious uniformity in the peninsula. Both Inquisitions were used, sometimes with ferocity, as in the torture and execution of Protestants in the Low Countries during the Dutch war of independence. Probably more useful than the Inquisition, because it joined self-sacrifice and good example to organized effort, was the Society of Jesus, or Jesuit Order, founded by the Spanish soldier Ignatius Loyola in 1534, in the great tradition of the reforming orders of the Middle Ages. Dedicated to the service of Catholic Christianity and with a special vow of loyalty to the Pope in addition to those of poverty, chastity, and obedience, the Jesuit Order was organized on military lines. It saw service in every part of the world from India and China to the forests of North America, using whatever tools came to hand, fearlessness among savages, patience and discipline with European schoolboys, realistic counsel in the cabinets of kings. The Jesuits were learned and brave and relentless in their service to Catholicism and to the Pope.

The Church of Rome, as always, had to rely on secular arms, and just as worldly considerations aided Protestantism, so they also helped to block its spread. It would be unrealistic not to recognize the work of Catholic monarchs like

Charles V and Philip II of Spain, or Henry II of France, son of Francis I, and many others, some of whom failed, like Queen Mary of England and Mary Queen of Scots. Catholicism in France and Spain and Portugal undoubtedly profited from the concessions which the Church had made to their kings regarding appointments. In Spain and Portugal, much of the time in France, in Poland, and in Ireland, national sentiment was identified with the Roman Church, and Protestantism seemed politically subversive, a tool of powerful foreigners. The Habsburg lands and South Germany remained Catholic. The ten southern provinces of the Netherlands, mostly French-speaking and with different economic interests from the seven northern or Dutch provinces, found it easy to retain Catholicism as part of their way of life.

On the other hand the Scandinavians (Denmark, Sweden, and Norway) had motives of politics and national patriotism which turned them toward Lutheranism, as did Northern Germany. Politics and national sentiments helped win over the Dutch to Calvinism, the English to Anglicanism, and the Scots to Presbyterianism.

THE BALANCE SHEET TO 1648

The efforts of the Catholic Reformation were to continue into the seventeenth century and were to merge with the Thirty Years War (1618–1648), described in a later chapter. As we know now, the struggle between Protestants and Catholics ended in complete victory for neither side, and in spite of all the mighty efforts of the Thirty Years War the religious map of Europe was not to be greatly changed at its close.

How did the Reformation affect the political life of Europe? Kings and princes obviously benefited from the seizure of church properties. In many cases kings also added to their powers the right to decide the official religion, as was the case in Germany after the Peace of Augsburg. The tendency of state churches to be subservient to the civil power is known as "Erastianism." The Lutherans, ever since their founder turned against the peasant revolt, have been criticized for Erastianism, and some historians have gone so far as to see the roots of Hitlerism in the Reformation. Yet the Scandinavian countries embraced Lutheranism without losing their taste for freedom. And while sixteenth-century England was Erastian, England in the seventeenth century was to have many independent religious sects and two political revolutions. Thus while the Reformation increased the powers of rulers like Henry VIII or the Elector of Saxony, it is not enough to say that authority slipped from the grasp of the Catholic Church into the hands of secular rulers. The religious struggle helped the princes in the short run, but in the long run it probably contributed even more to the rise of self-government.

Several aspects of the Protestant-Catholic struggle were to contribute to the growth of self-government. Both sides, when they found themselves in the minority and subject to persecution, were driven to advocate the right of resistance to impious kings. Among Catholics the Jesuits, and among Protestants the Calvinists, took this step. The idea that there are principles more important than kings was not a new one, but the Reformation conflicts helped transfer it into the political arena. Among the Calvinists, theories of a "convenant" or contract between the ruler and the people were developed when it was felt that the ruler had to be opposed. Some of the radical dissenters later pioneered in democratic practices. Presbyterian church organization provided practice in self-government, and proved to be a thorn in the sides of kings such as the Stuarts of England and Scotland.

But the greatest influence of the Reformation struggles on politics is probably the simplest one. The heavens did not fall when men of diverse religious views inhabited the same Europe and in some cases the same countries. It was only a question of time before most educated people drew the conclusion that diversity of opinions is not a disease.

The contribution of the Reformation era to the rise of toleration was a long time reaching fruition. For at least a century and a half the effects of the Reformation were almost the exact opposite: fanaticism, feuding, bitter intolerance, persecution, hysteria, and witch-hunting. It is worth remembering that masses of people were involved in this great debate, which reached the common man as the Renaissance was never able to do. Protestants for the most part abandoned monasteries and convents, and even permitted the clergy to marry, but they transferred some of the monastic ideals to the way of life which we think of as "Puritan". The depth and breadth of the Reformation struggle did not, however, preclude the onward march of other influences. Increased interest in the business world with its growing opportunities probably contributed, along with fatigue and disgust with religious squabbles, to the rise of toleration. Meanwhile, in realms primarily interesting to the intellectuals, Renaissance humanism and scientific interests had been almost invisibly at work. For a time the great drama seemed to be overwhelmingly religious, yet the mixture of human interests was subtly changing. The ingredients seemed the same, but some were losing and others gaining in potency.

But to return to the purely religious, it is not unjust to think of the Reformation era as a religious renewal within Christendom. Luther's point of view may be compared with another which had been present all the time in a minority of onlookers. To these few, as to some later historians, the Reformation was a last upsurge of medieval piety. This was to be the view of the "age of science and enlightenment" which will be described in Chapter 21, and like the Catholics and Protestants, it is still with us today.

5

CHARLES V AND THE HOLY ROMAN EMPIRE

THE EMPEROR Charles V (1519–1556) stands with Charlemagne, Napoleon, and Hitler among those men who most nearly achieved the unification of Europe. He never succeeeded in subjecting France or England to his rule, and he probably never seriously aspired to the sovereignty of Christendom, but he dominated the first half of the sixteenth century, and the list of his territorial possessions is prodigious. He was ruler of Spain and of almost all that was known of America. He ruled or controlled most of Italy. He ruled Hungary and Bohemia, Burgundy and the Low Countries. He was overlord of the German princes, and bore the title, pregnant with memories and, as yet, possibilities, of Holy Roman Emperor.

This vast and varied collection of holdings possessed no unity. Charles's dominions were widely separated and entirely different from one another; his status, rights, and powers were different in each of them. They had come into the hands of one man through a series of accidents, military, political, and biological. At the end of his reign the empire—if such it may be called—was at his wish divided in two, and each of its halves slowly but steadily declined into impotence and eventual partition. Unlike the empire of Charlemagne, that of Charles V broke up without trace of tradition, but its existence dominated its own era and had profound and lasting effects upon its component parts and upon its opponents.

Charles, faced with the necessity of governing a dozen realms, of defending a hundred frontiers, had to concede and to compromise, to bleed one loyal province for resources with which to suppress sedition elsewhere, to allow one enemy to go unpunished while he pursued another. In the end his enemies joined in common cause against him and were largely victorious. Among the consequences to which his failure contributed was the future supremacy of France, which was to last for two hundred years; the decline of Spain into oblivion; the division and decay of Germany; and the spread of the Protestant movement. All of these and many other consequences of Charles's reign affected profoundly the substance of European civilization and its descendant societies in the Western Hemisphere.

THE INHERITANCE OF CHARLES V

The tracing of Charles's heritage is enormously intricate. The various marriages, deaths, wills, and conquests whereby the picture puzzle of his empire was fitted together over generations is of interest, however, not only because it eventuated in an extraordinary skyscraper of sovereignties but also because it was a sort of macrocosm, an example vastly expanded, of what was going on all over Europe. It was an age of dynasts—princes who consolidated alliances or expanded territories through marriage. The Habsburg family to which Charles belonged was merely the largest and most successful of dynastic operators.

The Habsburgs had originated as feudal lords on a small mountain near Basel, in what is today Switzerland. Over a period of hundreds of years, they had expanded their properties and eventually, in 1273, one of them had been selected as a compromise candidate for the Holy Roman Emperorship, to which office princes of the family were elected frequently thereafter. By the end of the fifteenth century, the family had shifted its center of gravity eastward. Its principal town, Vienna, and most of its holdings, were located in the eastern Alps and along the Danube.

The man who succeeded to the Habsburg lands and was elected to the imperial throne in 1493 was named Maximilian I, and he had had the good luck and wisdom to marry the richest heiress in Europe, the Princess Mary of Burgundy. Mary was the only child of a maverick empire-builder, Charles the Bold. Following her father's death, Mary's dominions had been ruthlessly gnawed away by his enemies, and the largest single section, the duchy of Burgundy, had gone to France. But there was quite enough left to satisfy any princely husband. There was the so-called Free County of Burgundy, the eastern part of the province, which lay within the borders of the Holy Roman Empire. And there were the seventeen provinces called the Low Countries, or Netherlands, which included the area of modern Benelux, the rich lands dominating the commerce and manufacturing of northern Europe, strategically located at the mouths of the great waterways, the Maas and the Rhine. These properties which Mary brought to the Habsburgs were far richer and more powerful than that family's own possessions along the Danube: Brussels, their principal city, became the chief residence of the Habsburgs in the next few generations. It was the birth-place of Mary's grandson, Charles V.

But even greater inheritances than the Low Countries were coming to Charles. Charles's father, the Archduke Philip, son of Mary and Maximilian, also made a brilliant marriage. The marriage was only politically brilliant (the lady was mad), but it brought the great Spanish empire to the Habsburgs. Philip was married to Juana—Joanna or Jane—the eldest surviving daughter of the king and queen of Spain. She was to be known in history as Jane the Insane of Spain.

The great and rich realms which this witless lady bestowed upon her notably witty son, Charles, were in themselves a new and complex creation. The Iberian peninsula had for centuries been on the political as well as the geographical periphery of Europe, shut off by mountains, divided into petty kingdoms engaged upon endless domestic wars punctuated by sporadic outbursts of determination to drive the infidel Moors from their land. In the second half of the fifteenth century, the peninsula had abruptly emerged from its gory obscurity into a position of political and religious leadership and intellectual brilliance. In 1469 the heirs of two of the major Iberian kingdoms, Ferdinand of Aragon and Isabella of Castile, had married. Such marriages had been common before, but this one provided a durable link between the two realms. In 1492 the Moslem kingdom of Granada was conquered, and all of Iberia except Portugal was brought under the control of the "Catholic Sovereigns" as the Pope permitted them to style themselves.

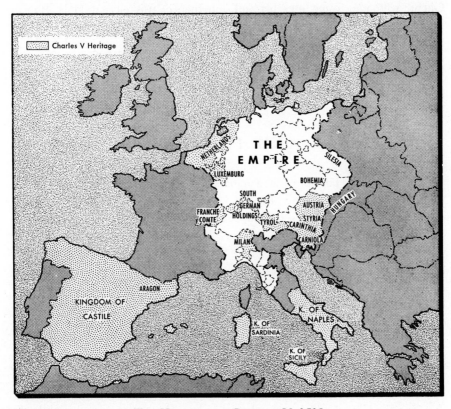

THE HERITAGE OF CHARLES V, 1519

To this newly united kingdom, Isabella had brought the plateau of Castile, whose main resource was its heroic, melancholy, and saintly population which for centuries had been devoted to warfare against the Moslem kings of Seville. Ferdinand brought a very different legacy. Aragon was Mediterranean, urbane and strongly mercantile. From Barcelona and Valencia, its principal cities, merchant ships sailed the Mediterranean and competed on even terms with the sailors of Venice or Genoa. In addition to the treasure and sophistication which came to Aragon through these connections, there had come an empire. The traders and navies of Barcelona had acquired the Balearic Islands and Sicily, and thence their influence had crept up the Italian mainland. Aragon, by the time Charles inherited it, was a major European power.

In 1492 the agent of Isabella of Castile, Christopher Columbus, discovered the group of semi-tropical islands several thousand miles west of Spain. Using these islands as bases, admirals and explorers from Castile extended their knowledge and domain to the American mainland, as recounted in Chapter 2, and by the time Charles succeeded his maternal grandparents, the Castilian crown had come into the possession of ill-defined but assuredly enormous and stupendously wealthy kingdoms in the Western Hemisphere.

In 1506 Charles's father Philip died. In 1516 his grandfather Ferdinand passed on, having expanded his possessions in 1512 to include Navarre and so establish Spain's frontiers on the crest of the Pyrenees. In 1519 the other grandfather, Maximilian, was at length interred. The nineteen-year-old prince from Ghent, who now came into his full inheritance, was elected Holy Roman Emperor. A path of unprecedented glory lay before him, and an empire which included more square miles than men had thought the earth comprised a generation earlier.

THE MAN AND THE GOVERNMENT

Charles of Habsburg was a remarkably good example of a Renaissance prince. As befitted the greatest of rulers, he was one of the best of men. Even his enemies confessed his virtues; he had, so far as the record goes, no vices. He was hard-working (he had to be) and serious. He was undoubtedly intelligent. He was magnanimous to his foes—perhaps to a fault—and open-handed with his friends. He was, like the other rulers of his family, sternly, even fanatically devoted to the welfare of the dynasty. Under God, his supreme duty was to the Habsburgs and their aggrandizement. But his first duty was to God; he was a devoted, if somewhat wordly, Catholic.

Being a man of the Renaissance, he shared the secular interests of its greatest sons, although he did not appreciate the intellectuality of the Humanists. He was bored by theology, and to the end of his life he was never able to understand what the Reformation was about or why men like Luther were so bent on changing the Church. There was about him something narrowly, thoughtlessly insular. He was a Belgian by birth and training, and a Belgian he remained. Spain he never understood and Germany he despised. The German language he reportedly regarded as unfit for civilized men; he spoke it only to his horse.

Spain was the most orthodox and devout of his kingdoms, and it was also the largest, most energetic, most easily defended and, taken with its gold-rich Amercian provinces, the wealthiest. It was natural that he should choose Spain as his base, as the capital kingdom of all his kingdoms.

For his purposes, this base of operations had its shortcomings. Spain was only recently unified. It preserved the jumbled and overlapping institutions of its medieval past, and also a remarkable diversity of population, including very large numbers of ex-Moslems and ex-Jews, only recently and (there was reason to believe) insincerely converted. Moreover, there survived the *Cortes* of the various Spanish kingdoms, medieval representative institutions jealous of their prerogatives. There also survived a large feudal nobility which had only recently lost its freedom to rule as it pleased, and, in addition, a large number of cities equipped with charters guaranteeing extensive liberties. The monarch, to be sure, had acquired a royal army and a royal civil service. He had secure though not abundant sources of revenue. He had control over the Church and its appointments and, most important, its investigating agency and court for trying heretics, the Inquisition.

These were powerful aids, but they were not powerful enough to dispel the monarch's fear of heterodoxy and diversity, nor were they sufficient to prevent an outbreak of conflict. He wanted the Spaniards' assistance in buying his election as Holy Roman Emperor and in waging wars in Germany, because he wanted to defend Europe against the Moslem Turks who were threatening it from the east. The Spaniards remained distrustful, and in 1520 they revolted. The revolt, called a Rising of the Communeros, was overcome, the disruptive elements destroyed, and Spain became more than ever the center and base for Charles's operations. But the revolt was an omen; it was a stab in the back at a time when his attention was occupied with crises in Germany. The rest of his career was to run in such torturing courses.

Spain was complex, and the royal power was only imperfectly established there. But Germany—the Holy Roman Empire—was far more complex, and the imperial authority was not established at all. The nobility of Spain was sullen, but disarmed. The nobility of Germany had all the arms there were.

The Holy Roman Empire was a very strange edifice. Its boundaries included all the German-speaking peoples of Europe, and many more peoples besides—Dutch, Belgians, Slovenes, Italians, Czechs. It in no way corresponded to the national monarchies in Spain, France or England. Its ruler, elected by seven electors, bore a title whose connection with Rome was now only sentimental— Charles's great-grandfather, Ferdinand II, had been the last of the Emperors to go to Italy to be crowned. The Emperor still claimed to be "the head and defender of all Christendom," and this claim Charles took very seriously, but it had little relation to his power in the Empire itself. No one was very clear what powers the Emperor was supposed to have over the German nobility. He was assisted in governing by an Imperial Diet, or parliament, which consisted of three houses containing representatives of the electors, the aristocracy, and the towns, but even the members of the Diet were not clear what their function was. For several hundred years, the nobles had run their affairs without serious interference from the Emperor or Diet, and they had found this situation much to their liking. Since the Emperor was himself also a local lord, with German possessions of his own, he understood the dislike of his colleagues for meddlesome interference from Frankfurt, the imperial capital.

At the time of Charles's election, there were seven major principalities in the Empire: in addition to his own duchy of Austria, Saxony, Hesse, Bavaria, Brandenburg, Bohemia and the Palatinate. There were in addition a dozen or more princes still weak but ambitious and very much on the make. The rulers of all these states were anxious to increase their domains. More especially, they were eager to augment their freedom from interference either from without (by the Emperor or the Diet) or from within (by their subjects).

But while the princes were growing more powerful and ambitious, the Emperor and the central government, if such it could be called, were also showing signs of activity. German national feeling, long quiescent, had been stirred by the fall of Constantinople and the advance of Turks through Hungary to their very borders. The Diet that had been convoked at the city of Worms in 1495 by Charles's grandfather, to raise an army against the Turks, had shown a quite unprecedented energy and enthusiasm. Not only had it raised the army, it had proceeded to enact various laws aimed at establishing a central administration for the Empire. The territory was divided into counties (*kreise*), each to be equipped with a representative of the Emperor.

It was clear that a struggle was to take place in Germany between the Emperor and the princes. It broke out with Charles's accession and lasted until his defeat and abdication. It was won overwhelmingly by the princes, and their victory was due in no small measure to their use of the issue of Protestantism.

INTERNATIONAL COMPLICATIONS

The major battles in the early years of Charles's reign were fought in Italy, against the King of France. The reason lies in the confusion of the Italian political situation and the weakness of the Italian states, which drew the great rulers of France and Spain into Italy as if by magnetic force. The intricacies must be greatly oversimplified. Charles had inherited, as part of the possessions of Aragon, the island of Sicily and the southern half of the Italian peninsula, which formed the kingdom of Naples. North of Naples lay the states of the Church. They were ruled by the cultivated Pope Julius II, who was busily engaged upon a costly program for the beautification of the Mother-Church of Christendom, Saint Peter's of Rome. The Popes had frequently looked to the Habsburgs for protection from the French, and Julius II was dependent on Habsburg power. Further north lay the city-states—Florence, Venice, Genoa, and a dozen others,

CHARLES V by Titian (1477–1576). Charles V was highly cultivated; he
understood and appreciated painting, and it is just that he should be
remembered mainly by Titian's picture—the greatest portrait by the
greatest portraitist of the time. It shows a handsome, regal, and intelligent
face, marred by the trademark (or deformity) of his family, the pro-
tuberant Habsburg lip. (Prado, Madrid. Photo by Anderson)

each burgeoning with flowers of artistic achievement unprecedented in both volume and quality (as described in Chapter 3) but each busily engaged in undermining its neighbors' security. Into this maelstrom had been drawn a few years earlier the ambitious kings of France. By the time of Charles's accession the French had gained control of powerful Milan, in the north, and had bought or blackmailed into alliance a number of the other city states. In northern Italy, French and Habsburg interests collided.

The principal opponent of Charles V in the earlier years was Francis I (1515–1547), like himself a noble and inventive prince of the Renaissance, ruler of the only political organization—the French monarchy—which could compete with the Habsburg agglomerations of power. These rulers fought each other in four separate wars—more properly, campaigns. Their ostensible issue, at least in the beginning, was the control of Italy. Charles's aspirations to possess this region derived partly from the ancient and shadowy dominion which his predecessors as Holy Roman Emperors had claimed to exercise and partly from his Aragonese inheritance. Francis, on the other hand, was heir to the conquests which his predecessors had undertaken in the decade or two preceding his coronation.

In the 1520's, immediately following his accession, Charles fought two wars against the French for the control of northern Italy. The outcome appeared to be overwhelmingly unfavorable to the French. At the most spectacular battle of the period, Pavia, in 1525, the French ruler was actually made a prisoner of war (an event rather common in the Middle Ages but rare in modern times, although a similar fate was to overtake Napoleon III in the nineteenth century). He was taken to Madrid and forced to sign a treaty in which France abandoned all claims to Italy and to the duchy of Burgundy, which had been incorporated into the territories of the French crown a generation earlier.

This treaty in 1526 marked the peak of Charles's successes. He had reduced his principal rival to impotence and acquired legal title to prizes which his forebears had long coveted. But the workings of a sort of natural law or mechanism prevented the consolidation of his gains. The other sovereigns of Europe, alarmed by the prospect of a Habsburg domination which might ultimately engulf their realms and independence, ganged up on him. The desire of other rulers to preserve a balance of power came into play. It was the balance of power which was eventually to defeat and destroy the Habsburg supremacy.

This phrase has come in the twentieth century to have connotations increasingly varied, vague, and even sinister. But in its simplest sense it describes hardly more than a situation which *must* exist in a world where there are a number of independent governments which value their independence. If, by one means or another, one of the governments achieves a position in which it threatens to acquire the means of conquering the others, then the others will in alarm unite in the common defense.

The sovereigns first affected by such alarm were Pope Clement VII (1523–1534) and the king of England, Henry VIII (1509–1547). After the Treaty of Madrid, they lent aid and encouragement to the French king who, upon reaching French soil after his release, immediately disavowed his solemn promises and renewed the struggle. Turning upon the weakest of the coalition which faced him, Charles—devout Catholic—attacked the Papacy with an army mainly recruited in Germany and consisting in part of Lutheran reformers. In 1527, Rome was occupied and sacked.

The only major Italian opponent was now reduced, and Charles was able to make the Peace of Cambrai, in 1529, with France. Having ensured, as he thought, his control of Italy, he agreed to surrender his claim to Burgundy. An accommodation with France was thus arrived at. Exuberant at what seemed to be the fulfillment of the thousand-year-old claims of the Emperors, Charles set up his court in the peninsula and had himself crowned at Bologna (1530), in the tradition of the medieval Emperors.

But Charles, in his efforts to give substance to the ancient dream of a Christian polity embracing most of Europe, was bucking the current of his times, and he found himself presently facing in Protestantism a menace entirely different from and more intractable than the arms of foreign kings. In the Italian distraction, he had neglected German affairs, and in 1530 the German disturbances revealed themselves as paralyzing.

As explained earlier, the German reform movement, widely misunderstood and underrated, had been condemned and outlawed in the 1520's by the highest authorities. Despite the formal measures against it, however, it had become grafted upon the political and national structure of Germany in a fashion that made it inextinguishable. It corresponded to two deep currents of German

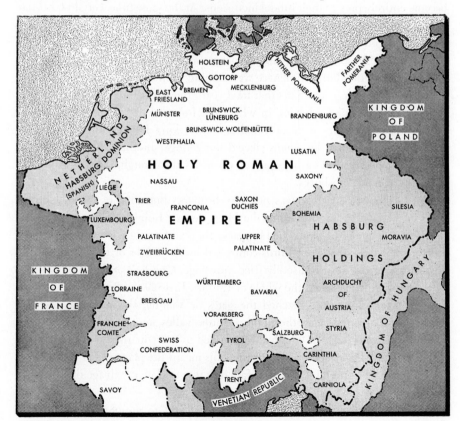

THE HOLY ROMAN EMPIRE IN THE 16TH CENTURY

development: the sense of national consciousness, which resented the dominance of uncongenial elements in its Church; and the striving of the German princes for increased independence from the suzerainty of the Emperor.

In the ensuing struggle the balance of power tilted against the Empire and the Papacy. The Protestant princes, publicly labeled heretics and outlaws, were threatening the disruption of Germany's civil institutions as well as its religious unity. By all the laws of past experience, a German civil war, bloody but brief, was in the making. It would almost certainly end in the victory of the Catholic overlord because he would be supported not only by the loyal princes but by foreign rulers such as the kings of France and England, both still Roman Catholic and also presumably solicitous of a fellow monarch's control of his nobility and subjects. But the balance of power, and chance, decreed otherwise. Germany's civil war was to continue, in forms either political or military, for a hundred and seventeen years. In a certain sense it was to continue indefinitely, for German unity, political and religious, was permanently compromised.

The first element to enter the situation and to distract Charles from the imposition of order in Germany was an assault by Islam. To understand the impact of this assault, two distinct factors must be held in mind. First, ever since the fall of Constantinople in 1453 Christendom had contemplated with horror, but usually with inaction, a mounting threat. The Turks were growing visibly stronger, and most people (when they thought about it) worried lest Europe become entirely prey to their infidel incursions. At the same time, certain Christian groups had succeeded in accommodating themselves to the Turks. Venice, and to some extent other Italian cities, had made commercial agreements with them, which were regarded by right-minded people as immoral and hazardous.

Second, the Turkish menace was shaping up in a way peculiarly unpleasant for the Habsburgs. In 1526 (that fatal year) there was fought on the plains of Hungary the Battle of Mohács, in which the forces of the united kingdoms of Bohemia and Hungary were defeated and their king killed by the Turks. To replace him the united kingdoms elected the younger brother of Charles V, the Archduke Ferdinand. The beleaguered countries thus sought, and received, the aid of the potent Habsburgs.

Ferdinand's heritage was not very brilliant. Bohemia, of mixed German and Czech population, lay within the Holy Roman Empire and had long been regarded as a vital part of it, but Hungary, alien and remote, lay without it, and was for some time about two-thirds controlled by the Turks or their puppets. To the defense of the new and sorely tried appanage, Charles's attention was called by an event which shocked the whole of Europe. In 1529 the Turks crossed what was left of Hungary and reached the gates of Vienna, the principal town of Austria, which commanded the upper Danube valley and south Germany. The menace was deflected, but Charles was obliged to avert its recurrence, and to do so had to secure the support of Germany. This meant the placating of the treasonous Lutherans, but his efforts to do so failed. It was too late to salvage the dream of a reunited western Christendom.

Furthermore, the conduct of France brought to nought his hope of reversing, or at least blunting, the Turkish expansion. In 1536, Francis I—operating with theological ruthlessness but in perfect consonance with the precepts of national power—entered into an alliance with the Sultan of Istanbul, Suleiman II, Charles's nemesis. Charles's strategic position was grave indeed. He was militarily threatened both in the west and the southeast by the Franco-Turkish alliance. And he was also engaged in extensive naval warfare in the Mediterranean, undertaken mainly at the behest of the Italian cities for which he had made himself responsible by his successes in the 1520's. Genoa in particular was critically affected by pirates who were the co-religionists and agents of the Sultan; against them and their nests in North Africa, the Genoese fought a magnificent naval campaign, under the command of their most eminent statesman and admiral, Andrea Doria. The naval warfare, culminating in the Battle of Patras Bay, in Greece, in 1532, temporarily cleared the sea and momentarily restored Christian rule in Tunisia, but it represented a further extension of Charles's concerns, and a further drain on his resources.

War between the Emperor and his enemies now became endemic. A truce was patched up in 1538, but it was followed almost at once by another naval campaign, this time against the Moslem Corsairs of Algeria. In 1542, another campaign against Francis I was undertaken; it ended two years later in a stalemate. So far, the desperate duel had proved indecisive. If Charles had not succeeded in dispelling the outside menaces or in subduing the Protestants, he had at least held his own and had tightened his grip on Italy. Now, however, his situation began to deteriorate, and with it his own personal assurance and competence.

Everywhere there was trouble. The Reformation was spreading, and was taking new and frightening forms. There was dissent in Italy itself. In the Burgundian provinces of the Netherlands, Charles's homeland, Lutheranism and even Calvinism had secured a foothold and were beginning to assume alarming proportions. The response of the government was the sternest possible repression. By 1530, the death penalty was being imposed on people who were shown to have *discussed* the new doctrines. In the mountainous Swiss provinces southwest of Vienna, which had won their freedom from direct Habsburg rule after a lengthy struggle, a center of Protestant infection was growing as the free cantons proved receptive to Lutheranism and spawned Calvinism.

Even in Spain, which (thanks in large measure to the reforming zeal of Cardinal Ximenes) never wavered in its orthodoxy, there were political difficulties. The Rising of the Communeros was not renewed, but there were complaints and obstructions against the levies which Charles regularly imposed to support his dominion elsewhere. The Spaniards, rigidly orthodox, were nonetheless unwilling to pay for the imposition of orthodoxy abroad.

It was in Germany, however, that the trouble became most severe. In 1546 the Protestant princes, judging the moment opportune to get rid of the imperial overlordship, made war upon the Catholics. Civil and religious conflict, for fourteen years postponed, now broke out. By this time there were more Lutheran princes than ever, and they had support from abroad. Francis I, most orthodox of Catholics, nonetheless found it essential to his struggle with Charles to give aid and support to the Lutherans. The princes, even those who remained Catholic, were not eager to see the Emperor triumphant. His success would presage the end of their virtual independence. The tide turned decisively against Charles V.

In 1552, following military reverses, he was forced to accept the Peace of Passau, which recognized at least limited rights for Lutherans and confirmed the extensive independence of the German princes. Immediately following, the French launched an assault in the west and succeeded in capturing three German cities which France was to hold thereafter, the "three bishoprics" of Metz, Toul, and Verdun, surrounded by the imperial duchy of Lorraine.

GERMANY AFTER CHARLES V'S ABDICATION

Charles, aging, disillusioned, and discouraged, now began to withdraw from the scene. In 1556 he renounced his power and retired to a monastery in Spain, to end his life in bitterness two years later. Realizing the impracticality of maintaining any measure of unity in his vast and varied realms, he divided them. To his son Philip went the lands he had inherited from his mother and grand-mother—Aragon and Castile, with their Italian and American possessions, and the Burgundian inheritance, which included the seventeen very troubled provinces of the Netherlands. To Ferdinand, already king of Hungary and Bo-hemia, and about to be elected Holy Roman Emperor, went the old Habsburg holdings on the Danube, Austria and the Tyrol, and adjacent counties south of the Alps. He expected that the two branches of his family would henceforth cooperate closely to maintain Habsburg glory and Catholicism.

In Germany, Charles's failure was profound. During his reign a number of factors had come together to confirm a development which had been in the making for centuries—the degeneration of Germany into a congeries of small states. The distractions of the Emperor, the interests of the French, the cleavages of the Protestant movement, had all combined with the previous weakness of the central government, the diversity of the Germanies, and the constitutional jealousies of the local authorities. Ironically, at the very moment when German national spirit had first stirred, German political organization had broken down; and broken down under the attacks of the very people who agitated in the name of German-ness against the foreignness of the Church and the Emperor.

It was almost a century after Charles's abdication that the total failure of central government was finally embodied in statutes—the treaties of West-phalia which ended the Thirty Years War in 1648. That century was occupied with the long, and painful, unweaving of the various threads in the German skein. The Germany of those years is better understood if certain facts, noted previously, are recalled.

In the first place, Germany was suffering a prolonged economic decline. Convulsed by domestic disorders, and shut off from the benefactions of the At-lantic trade, the great trading centers of Germany began to atrophy. Secondly, while the imperial claims of the Habsburgs were disintegrating, the consolidation of their own hereditary dominions proceeded unimpaired. By 1618, they had developed a home base in the provinces of what is today the Austrian Republic, with its capital at Vienna. Thirdly, as the authority of the central institutions waned, a furious struggle for advantage ensued among the petty princes, revolving mainly around religious and dynastic questions. Dynasties, prelates, and merchant oligarchies struggled to expand their holdings; alliances and power balances, marriages and wars, intrigues and plots, abounded.

Efforts to bring some kind of order into this bewildering picture were not lacking. The settlement of the religious issue was clearly the first thing called for and this Ferdinand, upon taking over the reins from his brother, immediately attempted. The Imperial and Catholic armies were in retreat, the Lutherans triumphant. Bowing desperately to the inevitable, Ferdinand agreed to the Peace of Augsburg in 1555, which, as explained in Chapter 4, allowed each prince to decide between Lutheranism and Catholicism as the religion of his principality.

The Peace of Augsburg did not solve any of the major problems of Germany, religious or constitutional. Diversity and decentralization, now established, led to perpetual conflict. Several features of the settlement gave rise to particular difficulty in the years that followed, especially the provisions concerning Church property.

It was agreed that Church properties in areas which had become Lutheran before 1552 should be acquired by the Lutherans, but nothing was said about holdings in the states of princes who were subsequently converted to Lutheranism (as was their unquestioned privilege). Endless wrangling, litigations, and wars ensued. Even more serious, however, was the position of the prince-bishops, of whom there were several dozen. These potentates ruled states like ordinary princes, but their control over them derived from their consecration as prelates of the See. Suppose a bishop wished to turn Lutheran—did he have a right to do so, like an ordinary prince, and then order the conversion of his subjects? And, should he do so, had he the right (releasing himself from celibacy) to marry and found an hereditary principality? The Peace of Augsburg specifically forbade such tergiversations, but the provision proved exceedingly difficult to enforce. Secular princes (particularly the Electors of Brandenburg, the most talented and ambitious ruling family in eastern Germany) tended to cause their relatives and even themselves to be elevated to bishoprics and then, by gradual stages, to Lutheranize them, claim inheritance to them, and ultimately annex them. Another problem was presented by the inheritance of a Catholic principality by a Lutheran heir. This was legal under the Peace of Augsburg, but the Emperor and the Catholic princes strove manfully to prevent it, especially where provinces of some importance were involved.

In the disarray which followed the Imperial humiliations of 1555, little was done to stem the southward march of Protestantism. Austria and Bohemia, Saxony and Bavaria, were riddled. Ferdinand, faced with constantly mounting problems during his ten years' reign, was helpless in the face of the incursions.

Under his successor, Maximilian II (1564–1576), and the latter's son and heir, Rudolf II (1576–1612), some of the ground lost to the Catholic cause was recovered. Although neither ruler was particularly able (Rudolf, indeed, was mentally unbalanced and under restraint in his later years), the situation was more favorable to the Catholic cause, and the rulers themselves more determined in this, if in few other matters.

An Inquisition was introduced and, after some wavering, conformity was decreed and rigidly enforced. In the German-speaking Habsburg provinces and in adjoining states of south Germany, the treatment proved effective relatively quickly. Moreover, the Counter-Reformation, strongly supported by Rudolf and the Catholic princes, extended further and further into Germany. Sometimes by choice, more often by force, large areas were returned to the fold.

The situation was poised for an outbreak of renewed war in Germany. The Counter-Reformation was so successful that by 1600 the two parties in Germany were more or less evenly matched. It no longer seemed as sure as it had a generation earlier that the power of the emperors was permanently broken or that Lutheranism was permanently secure. Moreover, the fifty years or more of incessant intriguing and unrest had built up interests and alliances and jealousies which were irreconcilable. When Rudolf died, hopelessly insane, in 1612, and was succeeded by his ineffectual son Mathias, the last and most terrible act of the German Reformation struggle, and of the constitutional struggle between local lords and Emperor, was about to begin. The Thirty Years War came in 1618.

6

PHILIP II AND THE
SPANISH EMPIRE

THE SIXTEENTH CENTURY is known to historians of Spain as *el siglo de oro,* the century of gold. The allusion is to two features of Spanish history in the years between the discovery of America and the death of King Philip III in 1621: the flow of precious metal from the American provinces of the Spanish crown, and the extraordinary flowering of the Spanish nation which took place at the same time.

This flowering appeared in all aspects of national achievement. It was as remarkable in literature as in art or philosophy, in constitutional development as in feats of military glory. It was most striking in the story of Spain's position in the world. The Spanish kings became the arbiters of Europe, the Spanish empire extended its borders ever more widely, and Spanish prestige and power stood at a peak not previously attained by a European nation-state. Spanish literature in the sixteenth century, particularly in its second half, attained a variety, volume, and excellence comparable to that of the Age of Pericles of Athens, to the Italian Renaissance, Elizabethan England, or the France of Louis XIV. It was one of the great ages and sites of human creativity.

The glory of Spain and its capacity to contribute widely to the enrichment of western civilization were huge but short-lived. By the end of the seventeenth century, little more than a hundred years after the moment when the Spanish sun shone with most blinding intensity over the western world, the country had been debased into poverty, stagnation, and impotence. Its empire was shrinking, its culture moribund, its dynasty degraded. Symbolically, the last king of the line of Philip II was a dwarf and an imbecile, Charles II, who died in 1700.

The causes for this extensive calamity have fascinated and puzzled historians ever since, and each age has produced a cluster of analyses to supplement or revise earlier explanations of the decay. It is a subject scarcely less written about than the comparable, if much slower and more grandiose, "decline and fall" of the Roman Empire. Most historians now would argue for an "eclectic" explanation, combining a variety of causes: the concealed weaknesses which existed in the organization of the Spanish empire at its most golden moment; the peculiarities of its constitutional system; the disastrous and to some extent fortuitous effects of religious and national uprisings in its far-flung provinces, particularly the Netherlands; the inadequacies of its monarchs; the draining of its resources to conquer, consolidate, and settle the New World; and the elusive but spectacular effects of the inflow of gold and the resulting economic inflation. But the problem is still capable of stirring controversy.

No less interest, and far more passion, has attached itself to the personality and career of the most eminent of the Spanish Habsburgs, King Philip II (1556–1598). Revered as a hero of supreme accomplishments and untarnished virtue by Spaniards, he assumed in his own lifetime for many foreigners, particularly for Englishmen and Dutchmen, the stature of a monster; and this reputation has in many circles survived into the twentieth century. The view of Philip as a villain was indeed extended to his country and his policies. It enveloped in odium the whole of Spanish history and the history of the Spanish empire in America, and to it has been given by more recent historians the name of the "Black Legend."

The vilification of Philip arose, one may suppose, mainly out of the political and religious animosities of his opponents. He was regarded by Protestants, in an age when a religious opponent was anti-Christ, as not merely a Catholic leader but as a cruel and tyrannical bigot as well, unwholesome and brutal. Stories for which there was no basis in fact—including the most famous, that he brought about the murder of his lunatic son and heir—received the widest currency in Protestant circles, and have been accepted by the naïve ever since. And to the strictly religious grounds for hatred there were added political and national rivalries and economic factors which further disseminated the Black Legend. It was mainly by Catholic Venetians engaged in a naval conflict with Spain that the story about Philip's murdering his son was spread.

The Golden Century has therefore been an age not only of glory for Spain but of controversy for historians and of extravagant prejudice for observers.

THE INHERITANCE AND CHARACTER
OF PHILIP II

When Emperor Charles V (who was Charles I of Spain) abdicated in 1556, having divided his staggering empire between his brother and his son, the more extensive and more valuable portions passed to the son, Philip II. In 1559 Philip arrived in Spain from the Netherlands to assume the most important part of his patrimony, the Spanish crown, and never again left the country. At that time the catalogue of his possessions was already vast, and it was to grow greater during his lifetime.

To his uncle Ferdinand I, already established in Bohemia and Hungary, had gone the troubled Germanies and the Imperial crown. To Philip went the seventeen provinces of the Netherlands, which comprise today Holland, Belgium, and Luxembourg; the duchy of Milan, commanding most of northern and central Italy, whose rulers, except for those of the Republic of Venice, were for the most part subject to Spanish influence; the kingdom of Naples, which included the Italian mainland south of Rome, together with Sicily and Sardinia; the kingdom of Aragon, including the prosperous east coast of Spain, with its empire in the Mediterranean Islands and along the northern coast of Africa; the kingdom of Castile, which by now included most of what remained of Spain, together with its empire in the Caribbean area, Mexico and Central America, all of South America except for Portuguese Brazil, and other holdings in Africa and the Pacific.

To these extensive possessions was to be added, in 1580, the kingdom of Portugal and its empire, which included not only Brazil but commercial and colonial interests in Africa and the Indian ocean. The king of Portugal had died without direct heirs, and Philip managed to secure his own election to the throne.

THE EMPIRE OF PHILIP II, AFTER THE DIVISION OF THE HABSBURG DOMAINS IN 1556

As a consequence the Iberian peninsula was united under a single crown, as were the two largest and oldest colonial empires.

The empire thus formed was in some respects diverse, varied, and vulnerable, but it did constitute a rough strategic and economic unity. Its various parts complemented one another economically. The rich manufactures and commerce of the Netherlands, northern Italy, and Spain itself, the agriculture of Spain, the treasure and potential markets of America, and the shipping and naval power which connected all these, fitted together into a sort of whole.

Socially and politically, however, the dominions matched less well. Different kinds of society bred different problems and institutions; different tongues and traditions gave rise to animosities. The rich burghers of the Netherlands were divided among themselves on many subjects, but as a whole their outlook was precisely the opposite of that of the Spaniards, whom they frequently detested. The Netherlanders' devotion to their own rather old-fashioned provincial "liberties" and to their own local aristocrats set them sharply apart from the Castilian tendency toward a modern governmental machine commanded by a royal dictator. In Aragon and parts of Italy, a not dissimilar jealousy about local rights and powers subsisted. In the vast and thinly settled expanses of America, ancient native cultures had to be governed, along with the predatory and energetic Spaniards who had subdued them. Each region had its own institutions, its administrative and constitutional traditions, its own views of the proper role of the king.

Castile itself was the core of Philip's empire. Upon his accession, it had benefited from a long period of prosperity and relative contentment during the favored days of Charles V's reign. Its industry and commerce had expanded. The inflow of gold from America had been sufficient to stimulate the economy without as yet raising prices beyond all reason. Moreover, the institutions of Castile had proved adequate to the needs of the day. Once the flames of the communeros (see p. 73) were quenched, few disturbances troubled Castile. The nobility and the towns, while jealous for their prerogatives, were for the most part content loyally to accept and implement the king's policies. The Castilian Diet, the *Cortes,* unlike that of neighboring Aragon, was frequently summoned, owing to its willingness to vote funds and commend royal policies.

Charles V had begun to build a modern administration. A series of royal councils, dealing with the major areas of government and corresponding (though very roughly) to modern executive departments, had been set up (the earliest had originated during the reign of Ferdinand and Isabella). The most important, dealing with general policy, was the Council of State. As consultative bodies, recommending policies and helping to put them into effect, the royal councils brought together experts without impairing the quickness of decision which was supposed to result from the king's supremacy. As in England, where sixteenth-century government took a similar form, the so-called "conciliar" system proved an adequate answer to the expanding problems of government.

The young man who was called upon to operate the large and intricate imperial mechanism after 1559 was Philip of Habsburg, son of Charles V, grandson of Jane the Insane, great-grandson of Ferdinand and Isabella. He was, like his father, a person of unusual accomplishments and virtues, he spoke many languages, he was widely read, he was incredibly hard-working and almost painfully conscientious, he was exceedingly devout, he was a fond father and a good husband to most of his numerous wives, he was generous with the poor, and he was a man inclined to moderation and tolerance.

He had, nonetheless, his peculiarities and shortcomings. Obstinate to the point of pig-headedness, he was at the same time dilatory. He was always postponing problems which, since he insisted upon settling all issues himself, even the most trivial, no one else could deal with. Perhaps his greatest failure as a king, and certainly one of the most powerful causes for the terrible aggravation of the problems with which he had to deal, was this personal handling of all problems. On one Latin document is a typical marginal note by Philip pointing out that "quasi," (spelt "quassi" in the paper) "should have but one s."

THE PROBLEMS OF PHILIP'S REIGN

It was natural that the list of difficulties which beset the empire should be very long. Like his father before him, the king found himself faced by interlocking difficulties; one hostile force or leader became involved with another, and each in turn with others. Philip's reign was not exactly a failure, since he achieved some of his objectives—notably, the salvaging of what was left of Catholic Europe, especially France, from Protestantism. Moreover, he built for the American lands a constitutional structure and link to Spain which was to survive, almost miraculously, for two centuries after his death—the most impressively long-lived empire since Rome's. He was, then, a more successful ruler than his father. By the time of Philip's death, however, the primacy and wealth of Spain had been expended, and his nation was doomed to two hundred years of mediocrity.

The situation which faced Philip on his accession foreshadowed some of his difficulties and triumphs. He inherited his father's interminable feud with France which, shortly afterward, took a peculiarly ominous form. The French king, Henry II, had engaged upon a program of encouraging European Protestantism, in order to embarrass the Habsburgs. Hostilities, in abeyance for a year, broke out in 1557 between this Catholic friend of heretics and the most powerful and ardent friend of Catholicism in Europe. This time the war proved at last decisive. Philip finished off his father's incessant struggle with the French monarchy at the battles of Saint Quentin and Gravelines, and in 1559 the Peace of Cateau-Cambrésis sealed the outcome of the duel. It was, in effect, a Spanish victory, for the French recognized Philip's title to the Netherlands—the remnant of his inheritance from French princes, the dukes of Burgundy—and delineated the frontier. France's threat to the peace of the two Habsburg monarchs abated, for Cateau-Cambrésis was to be followed by a civil war in France, and Philip was able to intervene on the side of the Catholic party.

Philip II was thus in 1559 the most important person in Europe. The forces which reduced him and his country from this position are complex. One may list, in an arbitrary order, the more majestic of these influences: first, difficulties in Spain, particularly suspected subversion by the Moorish population which had been conquered and converted to Christianity incompletely and within living memory; second, the conquest and consolidation of America; third, the periodic threat of France and England, sometimes separately and occasionally in partnership; fourth, and most intractable, the terrible and almost permanent rebellion in the Netherlands; and finally, the intricate economic problems arising both from the flow of precious metals from America and from the heavy costs of the perpetual wars and rebellions.

The first of these may be dealt with briefly. Since the conquest of Granada, the Moslem kingdom in southern Spain, and its annexation to Castile in 1492, the problem of the Moorish population had been exceedingly troublesome. Under Ferdinand and Isabella, the Moors had been forced to choose between Christianity and expulsion, and most of them had agreed to the former. The converted Islamites were called *Moriscos;* their Christianity was merely formal, and their allegiance to the Catholic crown dubious. Annoyed by *Morisco* distinctiveness, the orthodox Spaniards suspected them of heresy. Many of their ways scented of the outrageous, particularly their custom of taking baths, which was regarded as both unhygienic and un-Christian. More serious, they constituted a divisive and potentially disloyal element, wealthy and influential, in the Spanish State. In an age when both political and religious conformity were expected, the intimation of covert Moslemism suggested potential treason.

In 1567, Philip II was led to deal with this situation by an attempt at forcible integration called the *pragmatica,* a decree which forbade the display of native customs and dress, or the use of the Arabic language. The converted Moors responded with open, and bloody, revolution. The war in the south lasted for three terrible and precarious years, and ended with the loss of sixty thousand Spanish lives, a larger number of *Moriscos,* and the virtual devastation of Spain's richest province. The surviving Moors were treated with great rigor; murder, deportation and persecution were the order of the day, and all hope of reconciliation disappeared. The Moorish population, while reduced in numbers and wealth, persisted, to the number of several hundred thousand, periodically reduced by flights to Moslem Algiers. They continued recalcitrant, and efforts to appease and proselytize them failed. They tended, not unnaturally, to conspire with Spain's enemies—Turks, and later French and Dutchmen.

In 1609, eleven years after Philip II's death, his successors determined to deal with the matter in a bold and brutal fashion. In what most contemporaries regarded as the only possible solution, the *Moriscos* were expelled outright from Spain, forced to leave the country where their families had dwelt for many centuries. By this massive gesture the most persistent of Spain's domestic problems was solved, but at the cost of losing the most cultivated and productive portion of its dwindling population. It is widely believed that the expulsion of the Moors, however necessary to Spain's tranquility, was a blow to the health of society from which the country did not recover.

The problem of the Moors in Spain was especially serious, because they were potential allies of Spain's enemy, Turkey. Philip II inherited Charles V's war against the infidels, and it lasted for almost twenty years. The Moslem power still represented a powerful threat to Christian Europe. But in 1571, at the naval battle of Lepanto, the Turks were defeated by Philip's half-brother, Don John (or Juan) of Austria. The battle was decisive; the Turkish threat in the Mediterranean was dispelled forever. But the victory was one more cost charged up to the account of Spanish power and wealth.

THE SPANISH EMPIRE IN AMERICA

While these internal difficulties were being triumphantly resolved, if at large cost, a no less costly triumph, even more distracting to Spanish energies, was being won in the west, on the remote and barbarous transatlantic shores. During the sixteenth century territories vastly greater than the whole of Spain's European dominions were conquered, explored, settled, Christianized, and provided with stable government. These feats, which ensured the permanent dominance of Spanish language, culture, and traditions in the southern part of the Western Hemisphere, were the most extraordinary achievements of a European power in any era. The grandeur of the task which was accomplished is now almost impossible to conceive.

The real job in America was done by Spanish emigrants (exclusively from Castile, whose populace was regarded as more dependable religiously and politically than that of Aragon). These emigrants did the exploring, built the new towns, farmed the new land, mined the incredible mineral wealth and—over the constant protests of the crown—reduced the native Indian populations to semi-slavery. These accomplishments cost the mother-country very dear; the ablest and most enterprising portion of the Spanish population struck out for the New World. A population which was, to begin with, too meager for the support of its empire and its economy was thus progressively weakened.

Moreover, the Indies contributed in other ways to the undermining of Spain's wealth and power. The sea routes, long and vulnerable, were subject to constant depredation by the hostile navies or subjects of France, England, and Holland. The efforts involved in naval defense led to further burdens and losses, and to a grave constriction of Spanish commerce. This constriction accelerated a tendency on the part of the emigrants to develop manufactures of their own. The effect was a progressive reduction of American markets for Spain's goods. The government at Madrid strove to halt this process by banning manufactures in the New World, and by forbidding the Americans to trade with foreign countries, but such mercantilistic policies were ineffective. Spanish commerce with America continued to decline, and with it Spanish manufacturing, while the American kingdoms themselves expanded rapidly.

These relations between Spain and its western kingdoms illustrate the noble, and even romantic, motives which led to a path of glory, aggrandizement, and conversion of whole continents to Christianity at the cost of distracting and impoverishing the homeland.

THE STRUGGLE WITH ENGLAND

The creation of Spanish America was a costly glory. Spain's long conflict with England was not only costly but also inglorious. This passionate international rivalry arose from several factors. One was the tendency of the British to prey upon Spanish shipping, chiefly through government-sanctioned privateers such as Francis Drake, who was knighted by Queen Elizabeth. A second was the Dutch imbroglio (which is dealt with below). A third, and certainly not the least significant, was the religious conflict.

Philip II's second wife (his first had died very young) was Mary, Queen of England. She was an ardent Catholic. Had she borne Philip children, the crowns of Spain and England might have been united—not, one supposes, permanently—and England might have been restored to the Church of Rome. But Mary died without children in 1558 and was succeeded in London by her Anglican half-sister, Elizabeth I. In the meantime, she had excited strenuous opposition by her excess of orthodoxy and by the execution of large numbers of non-Catholics—a persecution against which the moderate Philip had on several occasions warned her.

English opinion tended, accordingly, to be anti-Spanish and anti-Catholic in large part. More and more Elizabeth began to sponsor European Protestantism, particularly in the Netherlands. Simultaneously English attacks on Spanish shipping multiplied. Philip, challenged in his principal role as the defender of Catholicism, and engaged in a life and death struggle in the Netherlands, was led to seek the destruction of Elizabeth's power. When he championed the claims of a pretender to the English throne, Mary Stuart, Queen of Scotland, relations deteriorated rapidly. By 1585, war was next to inevitable.

Philip was forced to evolve a scheme for the invasion of England. A vast Spanish fleet, equipped and based in Spain, was to attack the English coast and prepare for the landing of a Spanish army in the Netherlands. In 1588 the *Flota armada* (Armed Fleet) of 130 ships was dispatched against the island kingdom. Handicapped by bad weather and inadequate command, the great Armada was harassed and battered by much smaller English naval forces and, on August 8, off the coast of Flanders, routed by the English and Dutch. The Armada limped homeward around Scotland and Ireland with a total loss of sixty-three ships.

The defeat of the Armada was one of the crucial naval battles of modern times. Spanish power was weakened permanently. The whole European picture now altered; the Protestant cause now possessed an impregnable and devoted champion.

In order to understand this change in European politics, one must remember that before 1588 the duel had appeared in the light of a David-and-

Goliath struggle. England was small, poor, obscure, and beset with internal difficulties, while Spain was the transcendently powerful, rich, and triumphant arbiter of Europe. It is not surprising that the defeat of the Armada, eventually regarded as one of the brightest chapters in English history and as one of the darkest in Spanish, has come to symbolize a turning of the tide of Spain's greatness.

THE REBELLION IN THE NETHERLANDS

The seventeen provinces of the Low Countries, facing England across the narrow channel and forming a wedge between modern France and Germany (both of which have acquired parts of the territory held by the Low Countries in the sixteenth century) were a vital part of Philip II's empire. They were strategically located, densely populated, and extremely productive; their commerce dominated the northern sea routes, and their metropolis, Antwerp, was the most important port of Europe and possibly its largest city.

The struggle to retain control of these provinces lasted throughout Philip's reign. It involved a constant drain upon Spain's resources, and a constant invitation to intrigue by other rulers. Throughout the bruising struggle, the revenues and power of the Netherlands were largely subtracted from Philip's treasury. What should have been the most important contributor to his financial and political stability became his principal weakness. And in the end, while half of the Low Countries was saved for Spain and Catholicism, the war led to the creation of a vigorous and violently anti-Spanish nation, and to the impoverishment and impotence of the provinces which the Habsburgs still retained.

When Philip succeeded to the throne, he found wide unrest and grave problems already confronting him in his northern realm. There was serious question as to the terms of his power, and there was religious unrest, arising mainly out of the sternness of Charles V's repression of the Reformation. The majority of the Netherlanders were certainly Catholic, but a considerable number were Protestants, and there was (rare in Europe at the time) some disposition on the part of the Catholics to feel that their Protestant neighbors ought not to be interfered with. For Philip, as for his father or for almost any ruler of the century, this tendency toward religious diversity was intolerable. It had not yet occurred to anyone (and indeed it was probably not yet true) that religious and political loyalties were separable. Protestant subjects of a Catholic king were universally regarded as subversive.

The Netherlanders were themselves without national unity. Two distinct languages were spoken, a variant of French, called Walloon, in the southern provinces, and several variants of German (more different from it than Walloon from French), called Flemish or Dutch, in the northern. There were also areas which used the ancient language called Frisian, which is understandable to both Germans and English. But however diverse among themselves, Netherlanders united in an increasing distrust of Spaniards, and particularly of Spanish soldiers who came to enforce the tax exactions which Philip was obliged to impose. These "foreigners" who were sent by the king excited general animosity.

This animosity was heightened by the severe constitutional struggle, which reflected familiar sixteenth-century issues. The government of the Low Countries was, by standards of the day, exceedingly old-fashioned and unwieldly. Each province possessed "liberties" (enjoyed mainly by guilds and noblemen) of different sorts; each had its own institutions and diet, its own aristocracy, and its own strong sense of interest and identity. Extremely complicated and slow procedures were required for the enactment of laws and, especially, the imposition of taxes, in the jealous provinces. Similar local institutions existed in France, Spain and most other European regions, but in most of them by the middle of the sixteenth century a powerful king, in charge of policy and equipped with his own armed forces and staff of government servants, supported by his own councils of state, a kingdom-wide church, and at least a nascent sense of nationality, operated on top of the local institutions. Not so in the Netherlands. Charles V had sought to develop a centralized governmental system, but he had been unsuccessful.

The Netherlands, moreover, were doing extremely well with these outmoded institutions. In the face of the impulse of the alien king to tidy up their constitutions and impose some sort of symmetry, order, and central authority, they became indeed almost pathologically devoted to the old ways. And they early realized that Philip intended to reform the government in the direction of concentrating more authority in the central government—that is, in his own agent—at the expense of the provinces and the nobles.

The constitutional struggle, though it brought to the rebellion the sympathy of many of the nobility and gave it a legal basis, would probably not have led to insurrection had it not been for financial problems. It seemed appropriate that the enormous costs of the reign should be borne in large part by Philip's wealthiest domain, but the kinds of taxes proposed provoked great resentment.

The most influential member of the Netherlands aristocracy was William, Prince of Orange, a Protestant and a member of the old German house of Nassau. He had large estates in Belgium, and he had been a favorite of Charles V. Popular, intelligent, handsome, and gay, he had by his extreme discretion earned the name of William the Silent. Gradually William developed into a leader of all those who were discontented, whether persecuted Protestants, jealous aristocrats, or impoverished taxpayers. Already, beginning in 1567, he had led an insurrection aimed at forcing the king to accept the dictates of the Council of State. The Spanish ruler had responded by sending a considerable force of Spaniards under the command of the Duke of Alva to quell William's rising and to pacify the religious troubles which were rapidly increasing.

From 1572 on, the war was waged with great ferocity and, for a long time, without a decision. On one side were the Spanish regulars and part of the Catholic populace; on the other, the Protestants and many others, led by William and his fellow rebels, who called themselves The Beggars. Reprisals were massive and bloody, and there were deeds of great skill and heroism on both sides—the most famous of them the opening of the dikes by the rebels to drown the Spanish troops who were beseiging Leiden.

From the first, William had two powerful supports in his struggle against the most powerful monarch in Europe. The Beggars, including many sailors from the port cities, had a powerful navy and merchant fleet which could challenge, though not defeat, the Spaniards; and they had the occasional support of both England and France who were not averse to seeing Spain weakened.

As the war continued, the Spaniards gradually strengthened their hold on the south, through a more moderate and skillful policy, and William consolidated his position in the north, where the elements of a federal union began to take shape. In 1580, in a speech known as the Apology, William in effect proclaimed the independence of the provinces and, incidentally, retailed the crimes and misdeeds of Philip in a lurid, libelous fashion. In 1584, he was assassinated by a Spanish agent, and Spain's hopes of recovering the provinces rose again. But able successors to William appeared. Commerce and industry flourished, as did the Dutch navy. A remarkably prosperous and united republic arose in the seven northern provinces.

The war did not cease, however. The Spanish fatuously persisted in their efforts to recover the lost provinces, while tightening their hold on the ten remaining to them. Not until 1648 did they finally acknowledge the loss. Meanwhile the long struggle was yet another case of attrition of Spanish strength.

SPAIN'S ECONOMIC DIFFICULTIES

Enough has been said to indicate the drain upon Spanish resources which was involved in the various struggles and adventures which engaged Philip II and his successors. The base for these operations, the kingdom of Castile, was itself already faced with major economic difficulties. A mountainous inland country, it had limited resources agriculturally. And while its towns had flourished in the years of internal peace under Isabella and later Charles V, its manufacturing had not kept pace. Moreover, Charles's financial obligations, no less crushing than Philip's, had already imposed a heavy strain.

Under Philip, financial crises multiplied. Wilder and more ill-advised means for raising money were resorted to. Loans were floated of whose repayment there was not the slightest prospect. Imprudent privileges were freely sold. In 1574, and on several occasions later, the State resorted to the extraordinary measure of declaring itself bankrupt—which merely meant, in effect, that it cancelled most of its internal debts. The costs of self defense, of the constant wars, of the enormous panoply which the kings felt compelled to maintain in order to keep up appearances, and of the intricate and costly royal administration, eventually led, after Philip's death, to the devaluation of the Spanish currency and to a paper inflation which further debilitated the economy.

The principal source of revenue throughout the entire century which followed Philip II's accession was the importation of gold and silver from America. Of all the precious metal from the American kingdoms, one quarter came to the Crown—mostly as part of a legal levy of a fraction of all metal mined. The volume of imports of bullion increased steadily throughout the sixteenth century, though the royal share was never sufficient to cover the royal budget. It was a fabulous source of easy money, but the supply proved exhaustible. Deliveries of bullion to the treasury began to decline with the turn of the century; through the reign of Philip III (1598–1621) they continued to diminish. The financial difficulties of the Spanish government grew steadily worse. Extravagance and maladministration played their part, especially in the seventeenth century, but the physical falling off of American gold and silver production (and the increasing toll taken by Dutch, English, and French raiders, who could not be fended off because there were insufficient funds to maintain an adequate navy) was a major factor in the quasi-insolvency which perpetually beset the Spanish rulers.

American treasure had, however, more alarming effects than those caused by its diminishing volume after 1600. As explained in Chapter 2, it had far-reaching and peculiar effects on the Spanish economy. The rush of precious metals dramatically raised prices throughout the civilized world. But Spain, where the gold and silver came first and where some of it remained, experienced earlier and sharper price rises than the rest of Europe. The consequence was, of course, that Spanish goods were always somewhat more expensive than those of other areas,

ESCORIAL (1563–1584). Engraving by Pedro Peret after an elevation by Juan de Herrera. This huge building, half palace, half monastery, located thirty miles from Madrid, was commissioned by Philip II. It embodied the glories and riches of Spanish greatness and the intense religiosity of the Spanish monarchy.

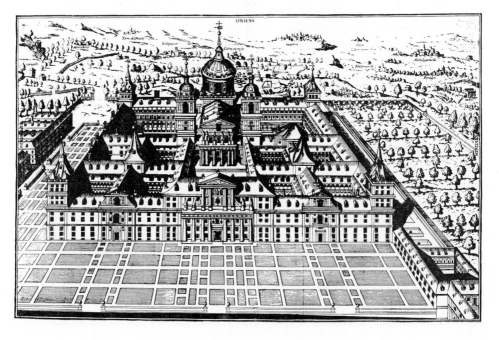

so foreign customers chose to buy elsewhere. The European export trade of Spain suffered accordingly.

Combined with the decline of the American markets, and with other factors such as the credit crisis which followed the government's bankruptcy, the effect on Spanish industry and commerce was baleful. The government, seeking to counter the disadvantages of high prices, tried to lower them by decree; the result was to drive manufacturers out of business. Agriculture was also suffering a crisis because the nobility found it more profitable, and easier, to use their land for sheep-raising and wool production than for crops.

The picture of the Spanish economy, then, is sufficient in itself to account for the precarious and declining status of Spain. It was overtaxed, its goods overpriced, its population low, its agriculture moribund, its manufacturing and commerce in retreat. These symptoms of an unhealthy economy were compounded by the great imperial venture, the almost worldwide thrust of Spanish ambitions, Spanish power and energy, and the Spanish dedication to the cause of Roman Catholic Christianity.

The three monarchs after Philip II—Philip III (1598–1621), Philip IV (1621–1665), and Charles II (1665–1700)—whose reigns span the seventeenth century, were vastly less competent than he. Surrounded by extravagance, increasingly tinged by an almost morbid ecclesiastical gloom as the century wore on, the courts and administrations fell more and more into the hands of incompetent favorites. The century was one of, at best, stagnation and, at worst, continual decline, although at times it sparkled with literary or artistic highlights of whom the most conspicuous was the painter Velasquez. Embroiled in all the great struggles of the period, Spain saw its expenses continue to mount; its revenues, productivity, and population decline. Holland's loss was admitted in 1648. Portugal regained its independence in 1640. A sort of Dark Age succeeded the Golden Century.

Later generations in Spain were, not surprisingly, to be preoccupied with the age of greatness, a fact which helped to make Spain the most conservative society in Europe. But admiration of the Golden Century is justified. In its years of towering grandeur, the Spanish nation shone with a superb brilliance. Under Philip II, it undertook or completed tasks seemingly beyond its capacities but nonetheless noble, imposing, and, in some cases, indispensable for the growth and expansion of Europe.

7

THE RISE AND
FALL OF STRONG
MONARCHY IN
ENGLAND

THE ENGLAND WHOSE THRONE Henry Tudor won at Bosworth Field in 1485 was a small and sparsely inhabited country which occupied the southern part of the island of Great Britain. From the Scottish border on the north to the Channel which separated it from France and the Netherlands on the south, England measured no more than three hundred miles. It was in the southern half, or less, that the bulk of its wealth and population—the "effective nation", so to speak—was settled. Here lay the centers of commerce and of such manufactures as there were, in the Channel ports and London. Here the king's power had already established modern order and central authority. Northern England, especially near the Scottish border, was in 1485 still almost like a foreign and archaic country.

Above the border was the wild and hostile Scottish kingdom, dominated in its mountainous solitude by its clans, with a language, civilization, and government entirely different from England's. To the west, another nation, Wales, also mountainous and exotic, had long since passed under the rule of the English crown. The Welsh had remained restive, but it was from them that the House of Tudor had sprung, and their conciliation was to be made easier by this fact. In the sea beyond Wales lay another appendage of the English crown, the island of Ireland, which also possessed its own language, institutions, and traditions, and a civilization as ancient and in some respects as advanced as England's. Ireland was imperfectly subdued, and retained a considerable measure of independence. It was not subject to English law or the English Parliament, and the ferocious independence of its population was to be a source of increasing embarrassment to the government at London for the next four hundred and fifty years.

The kingdom of England, to a greater extent perhaps than any of the continental countries in the fifteenth century, was conscious of its national unity and its national past; this consciousness was mainly limited to the people of the southeastern third of present-day Great Britain. A national language, already recognizable to modern readers, had become the common tongue, blending and replacing the Anglo-Saxon of the common people, the Norman French of the aristocracy, and to a considerable extent the Latin of scholarship and officialdom. For centuries a national law and government, growing unevenly stronger, had sheltered at least the south under a single political roof. The Tudor dynasty was to become the symbol and source of an allegiance based largely upon their identification with the interests of a newly matured self-knowledge of nationality.

HENRY VII, THE FIRST TUDOR RULER

In 1485, England was at the end of a long and wearing period of civil strife. Rival factions, the houses of Lancaster and York, had disputed the throne for a generation. But at Bosworth Field in 1485 Henry Tudor defeated in battle the last Yorkist king, Richard III (1483–1485), and succeeded him. An exceedingly able ruler, Henry faced exceedingly intricate problems of statecraft.

In the first place, he had a highly uncertain claim to the throne. Somewhat obscurely descended from a much earlier king, Edward III (1327–1377), he owed the crown to the support of the Lancastrian party, to his victory in the field, and to recognition by Parliament. His position remained for some years rather insecure, and he was beset by pretenders and imposters seeking to dethrone him. He faced, in the second place, an endemic financial problem. The country had been fought over, and much treasure expended in the preceding Wars of the Roses. Revenues were insufficient, and the administrative arrangements were inefficient and extravagant.

Henry VII ruled from 1485 to 1509. For a quarter of a century he molded England's institutions to meet the needs of the kingdom and put the country on its feet. Husbandry and commerce prospered. Order was ruthlessly maintained, foreign wars carefully avoided, the administration streamlined and brought under royal control. The power of the nobility to make trouble was broken. The budget was balanced, and indeed, for the first time in generations, showed a slight surplus.

The times were ripe for a strong king, and Henry showed considerable judgment and imagination in his policies. The Council, a body of royal advisors including most of the high officials of the realm, developed into an extremely efficient, businesslike, and powerful organization, advising the ruler and executing royal policy. The Council developed offshoots in the form of special courts —the most famous was called the Court of Star Chamber—which tried cases which did not fall under the jurisdiction of the common law, and where recalcitrant nobles could be fined or imprisoned without the usual safeguards of the judicial process.

The common law, however, survived along with the special courts developed by the king. It was a legal system peculiar to England, developed over a period of centuries in competition with the feudal law. Administered by royal officials, it offered surer, better, and cheaper justice to litigious subjects, and it had developed a curious and pervasive autonomy. Its rules were, in the last analysis, made by judges, but after centuries of custom it had come to have an almost mystical character. Great stock was later to be put in the supposed protections which it provided for the liberty of the subject, and it was eventually to be alleged that the king himself was subject to legal limitations arising out of the common law procedure. The common law stood in contrast to the Continental countries where feudal law was being replaced with legal systems patterned on Roman models, where the source of law was merely the command of the state authority.

Henry VII did not outwardly alter the ancient forms of English government, but he developed and strenghtened them. Parliament continued to exist, though it met infrequently. It consisted of important representatives of the nation —noblemen, bishops, abbots, and selected delegates from the counties (called "knights") and from the towns (called "burgesses"). These eminent persons were called together from time to time to offer advice and approve royal measures. It had become accepted as part of the basic law of the kingdom that the king could not impose new taxes without the consent of Parliament. By this time the representatives had begun to meet into two groups. One, the nobility and higher clergy of the kingdom, came to be called the House of Lords. The other, the knights and burgesses, came to be called the House of Commons. Henry only rarely summoned Parliament because there was no great need to impose new taxes or pass new laws. By his frugal policies, and by the popular technique of blackmailing noblemen into making him large gifts, he was able to "live on his own" without parliamentary grants.

HENRY VIII

The second prince of the House of Tudor was Henry VIII, who is notorious for his many marriages. His reign (1509–1547) was a momentous one. Henry was a Renaissance king. Unlike his father, he fancied extravagant displays at court, and he was a patron of the arts and of science. Well-educated, worldly, and sophisticated, like contemporary princes on the continent, he conceived of himself as a great leader in war. Most of the first fifteen years of his reign were spent in fruitless involvements in European affairs, mainly in a struggle with his brilliant contemporary, Francis I of France, and with France's ally, Scotland. At the time, at least, Henry's wars appeared unproductive and costly. It became necessary to debase the coinage, contributing eventually to the Europe-wide inflation of the sixteenth century, and to ask for more money from Parliament.

Henry VIII might have got into serious trouble with his Parliament and subjects had it not been for the distraction caused by momentous developments in the field of religion. In order to understand the English reformation, with its important constitutional results, it is important to realize that there was, by the time of Henry's reign, a long background of discontent with church affairs in England. There had always been resentment against the considerable payments from the Church in England to its mother-Church in Rome. There had been mounting dislike of "foreign" papal interference in English ecclesiastical affairs. There was popular feeling against the numerous and sometimes rather corrupt monastic and conventual foundations. Perhaps, as in Germany, the factor of nationality was among the most important: a consciousness of "Englishness" was beginning to develop and sometimes to verge upon intemperance. Of this consciousness Henry was a sponsor and champion, and the distant Papacy was placed in the position of appearing to be an enemy.

Henry VIII desired to divorce his queen, the Spanish princess Catherine of Aragon, because she had failed to provide him with a male heir. The story of his unsuccessful efforts to secure a papal annulment is told elsewhere (see Chapter 4). Henry was a determined man. Feeling that his chief minister and long-time friend, the orthodox Cardinal Wolsey, had been insufficiently ardent in pushing his case, Henry dismissed him. He then tried to threaten the Pope into submission to his wishes, and to this purpose he summoned a convocation of the Church (convocation was a sort of ecclesiastical parliament). With surprising readiness the churchmen performed his wishes. The king was proclaimed head of the English Church (although the supremacy of Rome was not explicitly rejected) and, later, he was given the power of approving or vetoing all its rules.

Henry also summoned Parliament and asked it to repeal the unpopular laws which constituted the real sources of papal influence in England. The payment of almost all money to Rome was stopped, and appeal from English church courts to Rome was banned. By 1533 most of the ties which had united England to Roman Catholicism had been severed by a willing, indeed enthusiastic, Parliament. The king now proceeded to have his case for annulment tried in English courts, which at once approved it. Catherine was put aside; Henry married an English lady, Anne Boleyn, and had her crowned queen. And in 1534, at his request, the Act of Supremacy was passed, recognizing Henry as Supreme Head of the Church of England. The Reformation, creating a church still Catholic in doctrine and liturgy but no longer Roman, was a fact. A number of opponents of the scheme, particularly Thomas More and John Fisher, the most eminent scholars of the English Renaissance, were martyred for their fidelity to Rome. A considerable pro-Roman rebellion, the Pilgrimage of Grace, broke out in the north in 1636, but generally speaking the country applauded the change, or at least accepted it.

The English Reformation was important in constitutional as well as religious history, for it bestowed upon the government (specifically upon the king and Parliament acting jointly) control over the whole religious life of the nation. And it gave to both crown and Parliament a new sphere of power.

They were quick to take advantage of it. In the years which followed the Act of Supremacy, the personnel of the church was purged and, more important, the numerous and vastly wealthy monasteries were dissolved, beginning in 1636. This revolutionary step had many effects. Most of the lands of the monastic foundations were sold or given to supporters of the crown, and thus passed into the hands of an enterprising group of *nouveaux riches* —often supplied with Tudor titles of nobility—who were to play an important part in English society ever afterward. It also provided temporary but considerable surcease to the perpetually money-short king. On the other hand, so long as Henry lived the Church remained entirely Catholic in its doctrine. The Lutheran and Calvinist heresies from the continent were as sternly repressed as was Papalism, and indeed the most influential advisor of Henry's later years, Thomas Cromwell, was executed, partly because of his tendency to Lutheranism.

Henry's marital career reflected the changing political interests of the court. Each of his six wives was intended to secure the alliance of either a foreign dynasty or a great English family. After the divorce from the Spanish Catherine, he married, successively, Anne Boleyn (beheaded for immorality 1536); Jane Seymour (died 1537); the German Anne of Cleves (divorced 1540), and Catherine Howard (beheaded 1542). His last wife, Catherine Parr, outlived him. Catherine of Aragon and Anne of Cleves were married for diplomatic reasons. The Boleyns, Seymours, and Howards were English families seeking influence at court. In a day when monarchs were permitted great latitude in the matter of mistresses, Henry's marriages indicate nothing about his private morals or psychology but rather the intricacy of the web of influence and intrigue in which a Renaissance monarch ruled.

EDWARD VI AND MARY I:
THE RELIGIOUS PENDULUM

Henry was succeeded by his three children in order. The first, his son Edward by his third wife, Jane Seymour, reigned from 1547 to 1553, dying while still a boy. The second, Mary, reigned from 1553 to 1558. She was the daughter of the first marriage to Catherine and was an ardent Catholic. The third, Elizabeth, daughter of Anne Boleyn, ascended the throne in 1558 and reigned until 1603.

The two short reigns witnessed some of the most troubled years of the century, and left behind them memories of instability and extremism which undoubtedly influenced the later acceptance of Elizabeth's strong government and moderation. Some of the difficulties in the reigns of Edward and Mary arose from economic affairs. An important export trade in woolen textiles had developed and expanded in the century before Henry VIII's death, replacing the old mode of agriculture which had been based on the fact that most of what was produced on a farm was also eaten there. This expansion of the wool trade, involving the possibility of large profits, had led enterprising landowners to try to increase wool output by buying up (or acquiring by less scrupulous means) farms and common lands hitherto used for crops, building hedges around them, dispossessing the peasants who had tilled them, and devoting them to sheep pastures. This so-called "enclosure" was painful; it caused distress and instability, and in the reign of Edward led to a peasant rising.

Another cause of the disturbances of the two short reigns was the incompetence of the rulers. Edward's inadequacy was due to youth; he was only sixteen when he died, and his reign was dominated by rather undesirable regents and place-seekers. Mary's inadequacy was due to a lack of judgment, an imprudent devotion to her Spanish husband (none other than Philip II; see Chapter 6), and exaggerated religiosity. It is only fair to add that she was faced with difficult problems and recalcitrant opponents who would have made her position painful no matter how skillful a ruler she had been.

The chief difficulty of these years arose from religion, and here England's situation reflected in many ways the general religious cleavages of Europe. The Church of England, as Henry VIII left it, was ill-defined and anomalous, an invitation both to Protestant reformers and to Roman Catholic restorers. In Edward's reign an effort was made to turn the Church Protestant. The first of the regents, the Duke of Somerset, introduced a few moderate changes. The services were henceforth conducted in English instead of Latin, Protestant ideas were tolerated, and a Prayer Book, conservative but not Catholic, was prepared. The second regent, the Duke of Northumberland, affected a violent Protestantism. Extremist Reformers were encouraged, and groups known as the "hot Gospellers" were permitted to destroy religious objects such as statues and stained glass. A thoroughly Protestant doctrine was established.

Just as these changes, distressing to many loyal Anglican priests and horrifying to all Roman Catholics, were inaugurated, the boy king died. He was succeeded by his Catholic half-sister Mary, under the terms of the will of Henry VIII. Northumberland, aware that he would be intensely unpopular with a Catholic court, tried to prevent her succession by proclaiming a distant cousin of the queen, Lady Jane Grey, as queen. This stratagem resulted merely in the execution of both Northumberland and the unfortunate Lady Jane.

Mary, supported against the pretender by the great majority of her people, soon alienated many of them. She induced a reluctant Parliament to undo not only the reforming measures of her brother's reign, but also those of her father's. The English Church was, legally at least, restored to the Roman fold, and dissent and heresy were strenuously attacked. Several hundred Protestants were beheaded (a rather mild repression by the standards of the time, but exceedingly unpopular in the country). Moreover, Mary had the ill fortune, at the end of her reign, to witness the loss to France of the continental port of Calais—the last vestige of the English crown's once vast empire in France, the last remaining fruit of England's glorious victory at Crécy a century and a half earlier. By the time of her death, dissension and strife were widespread; England was dangerously exposed to foreign enemies, and the troublesome problem of religion was more threatening than ever.

ELIZABETH I

The reign of Elizabeth, from 1558 to 1603, was epoch-making. At the time, as to most people since, it appeared a splendid and heroic era of history, in which religious peace was assured, orderly and efficient government restored, England's international position consolidated, its commerce and manufacturing vastly expanded and its worldwide empire begun, and English culture brought to a supreme peak of brilliance with Shakespeare and a horde of vigorous and imaginative writers and painters. But it was also a tense era, and the grandeur of both the ruler and the nation was a consequence of their robust and imaginative response to a series of alarming challenges, internal and external.

The success of Elizabeth in meeting these challenges may be mainly ascribed to her cautious and ingenious policies. She based her appeal, and her throne, upon a patriotic emotion, and she thoroughly understood the character and prejudices of her subjects. She shared many of their weaknesses—a tempestuous disposition, distrustful of foreigners and dissenters and sometimes brutal with the brutality of the age, along with fondness for over-indulgence in frivolities. But weaknesses shared are weaknesses forgiven, and Elizabeth remained popular.

Her settlement of the religious question is characteristic both of her faults and of her success. She approached religion from the purely practical standpoint of what would serve the interests of herself and the country, without reference to anything which she regarded as truth. From the beginning, her effort was to create a national church which, under her dominance, would reenforce royal power and enhance national unity. This meant, in effect, a national church which would include as wide a variety of opinions as possible. She moved toward this goal gradually and with the hearty support of the great majority of the members of Parliament, who were called upon to register her wishes in law. The queen's position of supremacy in the church was recognized. The papal connection restored by Mary was broken, an act which led eventually to Elizabeth's excommunication in 1570 (although for a while she coyly indicated to Catholic powers that she was considering a return to orthodoxy). A new prayer book, deliberately vague on the doctrinal points which excited the most controversy, was written. The purpose was to discourage peoples' finding salvation outside the Church, and those who persisted in doing so were sternly dealt with. This solution, while partial and temporary in its effectiveness, did bring religious peace (outside of Ireland) for most of the reign. It certainly provided England with a period of relative religious tranquility in an age when most continental powers were torn by religious war.

Foreign affairs were another sphere in which the queen displayed her somewhat unscrupulous talents. England was faced, from time to time, with encir-

Queen Elizabeth of England by William Rogers. Copper etching, done 1589. "Elizabeth Triumphant" is portrayed in regal ornament against a background which symbolizes England's sway on land and sea and reveals the extravagant pride and accomplishments of Englishmen in the late sixteenth century. (British Museum)

clement and possibly invasion, especially after Elizabeth's excommunication in 1570, when Rome announced the religious duty of all Catholics to seek her deposition. Scotland, France, Spain, and the Holy Roman Emperor were all, at one time or another, considering war upon her. Her great success in dealing with these terrible threats was her ability to string along with possible enemies until the last minute, dividing them from one another and, when they became irrevocably hostile, doing all in her power to weaken them. The most dramatic example of this, and the one which finally brought war, was her periodic assistance to the Protestant rebels against Spanish rule in the Netherlands (see Chapter 6). But especially in the early years her chief purpose, and success, was avoidance of both war and commitments.

The most trying circumstance in this lethal chess game was the fact that Elizabeth's heir to the English throne (for all her lengthy and numerous courtships with foreign princes, she never married and probably never intended to do so) was her cousin, Mary, Queen of Scotland. Mary Stuart was a devout Catholic and was recognized by many Catholics as England's proper ruler. Most of her Scottish subjects had been converted by John Knox (see Chapter 4) to a peculiarly rigid and anti-Catholic form of Calvinism. In 1568 Mary was chased out of Scotland after a series of scandals and uprisings, and took refuge in England. As Elizabeth's prisoner she was able to make less trouble, but she was a center of conspiracy and subversion. Eventually her name was inextricably linked with a Spanish-sponsored conspiracy of revolution, which was part of the general anti-Elizabeth campaign which the king of Spain was evolving. Mary was finally executed by the English in 1587 (an event that gave rise to a large body of extremely sentimental literature in following centuries).

The next year, despite the loss of this Catholic candidate for the English throne, Philip pushed on with a plan to unseat Elizabeth through invasion. His purpose was not purely religious; he found England's championship of the Protestant cause on the continent a threat to his own security, particularly in Holland, and he was driven reluctantly to the attempted trial of strength. It was a failure. The great Armada was defeated in the summer of 1588 (see Chapter 6). The battle of 1588 marked the end of all serious threats to England's safety and Elizabeth's security. It also opened up vast new opportunities for England's shipping, and brought an enormous increase in prestige and influence.

Like Henry VII, Elizabeth developed the royal power to a new peak, and like him, she did so without altering the formal institutions of the kingdom. Her authority derived in part from her efficiency as an administrator. In matters of finance, she was canny, frugal, and tactful. Few new taxes were necessary, and those that were adopted were clearly justified by national emergency (until near the end of her reign, when the foreign dangers had subsided). The principal instrument of government remained the Council, a body of advisors and administrators admirably organized, similar to the government agencies which were developing in France and Spain at the same time. The Council, acting both as agents of royal power and as a combined court, finance ministry, and executive power, carried out the queen's policies with great effect, and gave England the best government it had ever enjoyed.

Important measures put a curb on inflation; a series of statutes regulating prices, wages, and conditions of work and apprenticeship suppressed some of the more notable distresses of the laboring class and at the same time established rather rigid governmental control of the entire economy. A significant example was the Poor Law, in 1572, which placed the care of the poor (formerly a duty of the monastic orders) in the hands of taxpayers of the parishes. Companies were chartered to undertake the manufacture of various goods, or their commerce, or the exploration of new sea-lanes and foreign markets. The new privileges were sold by the crown; they increased royal revenues and were perfectly in harmony with the best mercantilist theories of the day (see Chapter 2).

The Elizabethan Age brought to completion a social and cultural revolution which had been in the making for generations. All of the Tudor policies conspired to foster the growth of a new class of wealthy people, bankers, merchants, manufacturers, and medium-sized landowners, upon whom the government relied increasingly for support, both financial and political, and who often staffed high government offices and ultimately became nobles. These people, frequently vigorous and imaginative, supported not only the Tudor monarchy and the expansion of England in the world, but also a new burst of art and literature. The Elizabethans were pushing, inquisitive, vigorous, and often crude, but they were supremely, if rather chaotically, creative. It was in the field of the theater that the greatest productions of the age were forthcoming. Not only Shakespeare, but Kyd, Marlowe, Fletcher and Beaumont, Dekker, and many others produced poetic dramas of the highest merit.

By the end of Elizabeth's life, the nation and the national heritage were not only secure but glorious.

THE TRIBULATIONS OF THE STUARTS

James VI of Scotland, son of Mary Queen of Scots and great-grandson of Henry VII, succeeded his cousin Elizabeth on the English throne as James I (1603–1625). The government of the Tudors had remained, in many respects, remarkably stable during the century of their reigns. After 1603 the constitution of England experienced that evolution which, continuing to the present day, has provided British institutions with the reputation for combined stability and flexibility which is one of their principal glories. But the changes in the hundred years after Elizabeth's death are of more than merely English importance. In the history, generally unhappy and frequently violent, of the House of Stuart, there emerged in England most of the political ideas and arrangements which have come to constitute the modern idea of liberty. Modern government in most of the western world is deeply indebted to English developments in the seventeenth century.

The most fundamental issue which the Stuart kings were called upon to solve was the distribution of authority between crown and Parliament. The theory of this distribution seemed to be clear enough: certain kinds of decisions and powers, known collectively as the Royal Prerogative, belonged exclusively to the king and to his appointed aides. The Prerogative included the conduct of foreign affairs and the command of the army and navy; the appointment of administrative officers and the control of administrative action; the enforcement of laws; and, somewhat less certainly, the management of the Church of England. The king also had the authority to collect and use certain fixed revenues which were his by ancient tradition—income from royal forests, feudal dues, import and export duties, and various other unalterable taxes. The sphere of Parliament, smaller and less well defined, was nonetheless universally conceded to be indispensable to good and legal government: the Lords and Commons must approve, as must the king, new laws or changes in the law, and they must approve new taxes or exceptional appropriations above the fixed sources of revenue. They might also petition and advise the crown, although under precisely what circumstances or on what subjects, and at whose initiative, was not clear.

This division between spheres where the king could do what he wanted and spheres where he and Parliament had to act jointly began to become less clear during the reign of James I. Each partner insisted that the other was overstepping the proper limits; each came, in the course of years, to try to obstruct the other. The result was a complete logjam in the process of government. It ended in civil war between king and Parliament.

Among the reasons why James I found himself perpetually embroiled in disputes with Parliament, and in the end lost much of the royal initiative and Prerogative to it, were the personality and background of the king himself. He was, to begin with, a foreigner raised in Scotland. He never exercised any of the patriotic appeal which the three great Tudors, whatever their faults of character, had always demonstrated. The Scottish Parliament was far less independent than the English, and the position of the crown far more autocratic. The Scottish legal system was mainly Roman, with its emphasis upon law imposed and defined by the state. James never liked, or understood, the sanctity with which Englishmen regarded the common law, which was widely regarded not as a command of the state but as a sort of Mystical Truth born of the very soil of the kingdom.

Moreover, James had developed certain personal views, highly academic and following the most advanced philosophical notions of the times, about the nature of kingship. He thought of kings as divinely appointed, and of subjects as having a religious obligation to obey. These views he had set forth in one of his numerous writings on political theory, *The True Law of Free Monarchies*. Unfortunately, he also tended to interject them, sometimes arrogantly, into his disputes with Parliament.

There were other and deeper reasons why the Stuarts got into trouble. The first was financial. As noted above, the crown had for generations enjoyed revenues from certain stipulated sources which needed no parliamentary approval. In theory, these revenues were sufficient to support the costs of government in normal times. Emergency funds could be raised only by summoning Parliament and asking it to authorize extraordinary taxes. Actually the sums available through "regular" revenues had never been adequate, and they were rapidly becoming less so as the years advanced—mainly because prices were rising. Even Elizabeth, notoriously frugal, had been forced in her later years to ask Parliament for increasingly large sums. She had met with some reluctance, but James, who got on the nerves of the legislators anyway, met with a blank wall. His position was extremely difficult, for Parliament seemed not to care whether the expenses of the government were met at all. James tried to survive by padding the regular sources of income with schemes doubtfully legal. There were forced loans and benevolences. Old fines, for half-forgotten misdemeanors, were newly imposed. A new order of honors, baronet (whose title did not carry the right to a seat in the House of Lords), was created, and membership was openly sold. By such unusual methods of expanding his income, James was spared the necessity of humble pleas to Parliament, but the delicate balance of his finances was wrecked by participation in the Thirty Years War on the Protestant side (see Chapter 9). The war was popular in the country and with the Commons, but the sums they voted were frankly inadequate. It seemed clear that the Commons were seeking to use their power of tax-voting to blackmail the king into surrendering his proper powers over foreign policy, thus (from James's view) upsetting the balance of the constitution.

There were larger, vaguer and even more ominous issues than finances between the early Stuarts and their Parliaments. Provincial landowners and business interests (many of which had gotten their start in life with the patronage of the early Tudors) increasingly felt that the power of the government ought to be sharply limited. They saw in Parliament a means of assuring the independence of local government against the centralizing tendencies of the London regime. This issue was developing in Elizabeth's reign, and would have continued even had James been more tactful. Put simply, the English administration had tended more and more to interfere with local government and meddle with local economic conditions, usually in the interests of the underprivileged although often with the purpose of securing economic stability. This paternalism the local interests, particularly the smaller landowners, intensely disliked. They were determined to frustrate the central government whenever possible, cloaking their position in elaborate talk about freedom from tyrannical rule and about the king's being subject to the law of the land.

The temptation to assert local and individual rights against the crown was strengthened, ironically, by the tranquility, prosperity, and security which the successful policies of the Tudors had achieved and those of James I had consolidated. In the sixteenth century, when England was threatened by internal cleavages and by foreign enemies, there was a natural willingness to rely on strong rule by the sovereign. But when the kingdom seemed impregnable and the internal rifts had subsided, landowners and politicians felt free to indulge in bullying the crown.

THE RELIGIOUS QUESTION

Perhaps the most conspicuous source of trouble between James I and his Parliaments—and public opinion—was religion. Here again the problem arose less from acts or omissions on the king's part than from changes in the country itself. The Elizabethan religious settlement had set up a form of worship strongly episcopal in form—that is, the Church was largely run by bishops, appointees of the crown—and deliberately ambiguous in doctrine, intended to provide a spiritual home for as many people as possible, whether Catholic or Protestant in inclination. Those who had found themselves unable to accept the settlement had been strenuously persecuted. But the great majority in England found the Church of England a satisfactory answer to their religious problems. In Ireland, however, the vast majority remained staunchly Roman Catholic, except for a Protestant stronghold in the northeastern corner where the government implanted large groups of Scottish settlers.

During the last years of Elizabeth's reign, however, a movement became noticeable which was to cause endless difficulty for her successors. This was a growth in the Protestant party. Generally speaking, these people were called Puritans. "Puritan" implied "purification" of the English churches of the taints of Catholicism—the lingering ambiguity in the Mass about transubstantiation, the remaining elements of priestly vestments. The name also suggested the "pure" way of life which the Protestants generally advocated—a sort of chaste and godly imitation of Calvin's Geneva.

As time went on, two groups of Puritans began to be discernible. There were first of all those who, strongly influenced by Scottish Calvinism, sought to reform the Church of England along Presbyterian lines, by eliminating all forms and doctrines reminiscent of Catholicism, and by replacing the government of bishops with that of elected presbyters. This group wished to maintain an established, if reformed, Church, and to enforce conformity to its teachings. A second group, much smaller, and later to be called Independents, sought religious toleration (for all except Catholics and Anglicans) and the effective suppression of a state church.

It is not wholly clear why these beliefs should have spread as rapidly as they did in the years that followed James' accession. One may guess that they were associated with the assertion of personal independence which attended the prosperity of businessmen and country landowners.

Both groups ran headlong into the crown. There were several reasons for the dislike which both James I and his successor Charles I felt for the Puritans. Most important, they were attacking the power and authority of the crown when they attacked the organization of the Anglican Church. The power of the bishops, who were really the king's agents, was an important part of royal authority. Against suggestions of church self-government, James reacted violently. He was no less violent, and considerably less justified by law and tradition, when he held that Parliament (where Puritans were more and more strongly represented) had no powers over the Church of England. It was, after all, an act of Parliament which had created that Church with the king as its "supreme governor"; presumably Parliament could alter what it had created.

With the accession of Charles I, who ruled from 1625 to 1649, the situation grew even more complicated. The new king was as rigidly Anglican as his father, but his wife was the French princess Henrietta Maria, a devout Catholic around whom gathered an unpopular little group of co-religionists at court. Moreover, Charles himself was the friend and patron of an eminent churchman, Bishop Laud. Laud was not inclined toward Rome, but he emphasized the Catholic character of the Church of England—what became known as High Church practices. He favored vestments for priests, candles on the altar, and the placing of the altar in the Chancel, instead of in the middle of the congregation. Moreover, and more serious, he was determined to impose uniformity in such matters upon all local churches, where liturgical practices differed greatly. He was denounced as an agent of tyranny, a papist, and a traitor.

All these controversies—personal, constitutional, economic, and religious —aroused violent passions which were increasingly reflected in Parliament.

THE PARLIAMENTS OF CHARLES I

Both Charles and James appeared to believe that the House of Commons was merely a collection of captious critics, and for the most part they strove to dispense with its services. During the two reigns, few Parliaments were called. Each one that was called provoked a quarrel. Each time, the king tried to clamp down on discussion of his Prerogative, and each time the Parliament declined to grant much-needed funds.

THE BRITISH ISLES IN THE 17TH CENTURY

By the time of Charles I's succession, the financial plight of the king was very serious. The crown jewels were pawned, royal lands were mortgaged and, in desperation, Charles resorted to a policy of forced loans. But the financial needs were not satisfied. A new Parliament, in 1628, met in an aggressive spirit. In return for voting new taxes, Parliament forced the king to accept a statement of principles called the Petition of Right. This document, frequently regarded as one of the cornerstones of political liberty, asserted the principle that the king was subject to the laws of the realm, like all other subjects. It forbade forced loans and arbitrary imprisonment; it outlawed the compulsory billeting of troops on citizens (to which Charles had resorted in the absence of money to pay for their lodgings); it forbade the king to proclaim martial law in time of peace.

Despite these concessions, the next Parliament, in 1629, was again recalcitrant in voting funds, and began to pass resolutions aiming at the king's ministers and accusing him of seeking to exercise autocratic power. The Parliament was dissolved, and for eleven years, making do with such funds as he could find, Charles did not call another. But the moment of constitutional conflict was merely postponed, for public opinion inclined more and more toward belief that the king, ruling without representation, was an autocrat, and the means he adopted for raising money irritated people and reenforced this impression. The issues concerning taxation, law, and liberty were now inextricably intertwined, and when Charles tried to impose an ancient (and theoretically proper) tax called "ship money," designed to support the navy, by taxing inland towns, a champion of freedom arose in the person of a landowner called John Hampden. Hampden, refusing to pay the tax, became a popular figure, and he was gifted with a talent for dramatizing issues. He presented his case as a choice between disobeying the king and accepting enslavement (which it certainly was not).

Charles managed to struggle along until 1637, when he committed an incredible folly. He ordered the Anglican prayer book (or something closely resembling it) to be imposed upon the Church of Scotland. The Scots revolted, hastily organized an army, and invaded England, defeating the underpaid and outnumbered royal forces. Charles was forced, in 1640, to call a Parliament, but as usual, it refused funds, and presented grievances. It was dissolved after three weeks—becoming known to history as the Short Parliament.

But money was still urgently needed, and later in the year 1640 Charles summoned his last Parliament—which was to sit, off and on, for twenty years. The Long Parliament, when it met, clearly had the upper hand. Under the leadership of the extremists, Hampden and Pym, it caused the arrest and execution of Laud and of Charles's principal minister, the Earl of Stratford. This fate led people to think twice before agreeing to serve the crown in high office.

For two years the Long Parliament sat, presiding over a period of mounting excitement and strife. The show-down came in 1642, when Nineteen Propositions were presented to the king, demanding that he surrender most of his power in religious and administrative affairs; demanding even that his children be placed under parliamentary control. Charles withdrew from London, raised an army, and started to march on the city to disperse Parliament by force.

CIVIL WAR

The English Civil War was fought by two hastily organized armies, one commanded by Charles and supported by many of the aristocracy and conservative squires and country folk, and the other commanded by Parliament and supported by the people of London, most Puritans, and most of the more prosperous and progressive commercial and manufacturing towns. The two most conspicuous issues were the religious one—the Anglican Church versus Presbyterianism and Puritanism—and the economic one—the question of who should control taxation. But there were more important issues at stake than these. The parliamentary cause had become one of personal liberty and of freedom from arbitrary government. The parliamentarians had appropriated English history, and the common law, to suggest that ancient English practices were on their side, and that these practices protected the "Rights of the Subject" from royal interference and the rights of Parliament to interfere in practically any field it chose.

The war was won, fairly and squarely, by Parliament. It controlled in the areas under its sway—generally, the South and East—the bulk of the liquid wealth of the country. It possessed most of the seaports and the navy and in effect blockaded the royalist areas; and it possessed a brilliant military leader, Oliver Cromwell, who succeeded in creating an extremely effective army.

The military history of the war was for several years one of see-sawing advantages, but the parliamentary forces gradually gained ground, with the assistance of the furious Scots. Eventually Charles was left with little territory and less army. By 1646 the king was defeated. He surrendered to the Scots, who turned him over to the parliamentary forces. An increasingly anti-royalist House of Commons eventually had him tried for treason and, in January, 1649, he was executed in London.

The defeat of the Cavaliers, as the royalist forces were called, had left the House of Commons the only effective political force in England. Most of the loyalists and Anglicans had withdrawn, or been expelled. The remaining members, however, were divided into two groups: Presbyterians who sought to convert the Church of England into a Presbyterian establishment and enforce conformity to it; and the Independents, mostly members of extreme Protestant sects, who found an enforced Presbyterianism as distasteful as enforced Anglicanism and insisted upon a separation of church and state. Moreover, outside Parliament, in the general excitement and disorder, new and alarming ideas were developing. The connection between religious rebellion and political freedom had led to the statement of extreme political ideas. Small but prophetic groups called Diggers and Levellers advanced the notion (distressing to men of substance, such as the Puritan leaders in Commons) that all men, regardless of their position in society, ought to be allowed to participate in government and to vote for members of Parliament. Some of them advocated distribution of the national wealth and the suppression of private property.

But it was neither divisions within, nor premature democracy and socialism without, which led to the dethronement of the House of Commons. The efficient army organized by Cromwell, called the New Model Army, in general represented the Independent position; and it was also eager for power and profit. Annoyed by the conduct of the Presbyterian majority in Parliament and its tendency to negotiate with Charles while he was a prisoner, the army took over. In 1648 the Presbyterians were expelled from Parliament by an army unit led by a Colonel Pride—thus "Pride's purge." The remaining Independents (a small minority of the original Long Parliament, called the "Rump"), supported by the army, became the government of England. In view of dangers and disorders, and the inclination of the extremists to try to enforce their views, a military dictatorship rapidly evolved. In 1649 England was a good deal further from freedom than it had ever been under the Stuart kings—but the fermentations of liberty had begun, and the cause for which the Civil War had been fought would one day triumph.

PROGRESS UNDER THE STUART KINGS

The constitutional struggles of the first half of the seventeenth century, culminating in the spectacular events of the Civil War, obscure national developments which were in the long run no less important. This was, beneath the political surface, an era of enormous expansion for England. James and Charles, if politically inept, nonetheless headed an administration which was wise and indefatigable in its pursuit of the national welfare. In this respect they were worthy successors to the Tudors.

The period saw, notably, the foundation of the British empire. It was an age of growing naval and commercial power, and of great explorations. In 1606, three years after he came to the throne, James chartered companies for the exploration and settlement of North America. In the next year the Jamestown colony, the first English settlement in America, was founded, and thirteen years later the Puritan emigrants reached New England. From these early settlements English influence and colonists spread rapidly, challenging the already ancient empire of Spain in the Western Hemisphere. In the same period the English trading centers in India—established in the last days of Elizabeth's reign—were expanding, competing successfully with other European posts and beginning a profitable trade. At home, while English manufactures and commerce were developing, the great literary and cultural flowering of Elizabethan England continued almost unabated.

These developments were, if anything, stimulated by the constitutional struggle and the war. The English nation, despite its domestic difficulties, was clearly capable of a vigor, and imagination, and an industry which were as well reflected in the development of the national resources as in the vigorous assertion of rights against the crown. A great power, shortly to become the greatest in the world, was in the making.

8

THE RISE OF
ABSOLUTE
MONARCHY IN
FRANCE

FRANCE IS A PLEASANT, temperate land with an oceanic climate and enough mountains and hills to provide variety without obstructing communications. The four main river basins, those of the Seine, the Loire, the Garonne, and the Rhone, cover 60 percent of France's area and are within easy reach of each other. In ancient times when France was Gaul the Romans passed easily from the Rhone to the Loire by chariot. The plateau and mountains to the west of the Rhone, the Massif Central, never provided much of an obstacle to political unity. France has distinct regions, although they overlap: the central plateau, the Paris basin, the Rhone and Saône valleys, the west from Normandy to Spain, and the Mediterranean coast. There was nothing in this geography which made political unity inevitable, but as history unfolded it was the rulers of the Ile-de-France region around Paris who unified the rest of the country. Or perhaps it would be better to say that they threw their net of royal controls over France's diversity, for it was not until the great Revolution of 1789 that French institutions became uniform.

France's position in Europe was always so central and so vulnerable that its population became thoroughly mixed. There is no French "race." Although Julius Caesar wrote about Gaul's natural frontiers as the Rhine, the Alps, and the Pyrenees, and this phrase was to be recalled in the seventeenth century by Frenchmen interested in expansion, the northeast was always open, geographically. Just as the Romans had come from the Mediterranean coast, so came the Germans from the east when Rome fell. Later the Normans and Bretons came by sea from Scandinavia and England. In time the English Channel and the Atlantic made further contributions when the Great Discoveries and the commercial revolution enriched French life as the Mediterranean was no longer able to do.

France's position gave it a part in the ancient world as well as a head start in the modern—Marseille was a Greek colony, Lyon a Roman capital, and the Romans called Paris "Lutetia" and made it a residence of the emperor. The combination of peoples and historic opportunities helped to create French culture, which mediated, as one writer puts it, between the Mediterranean and the north. But France was also in the midst of the European nations. The Rhine was no barrier. The fields of Flanders, moreover, were the tip of the great North European plain which began at the Urals where Russia merges with Asia. The boundaries in the southeast, between Frenchmen and Italians, were far from clear. Even the Pyrenees were low in the east and west. Much French energy was devoted to defense or conquest, and this left its mark on institutions from Caesar to Napoleon.

France had been made by the accumulation of provinces by its kings, in much the same way that the Habsburgs were in the process of building a world empire by inheritance and conquest of widely separated regions. But the French king's acquisitions were all adjacent to the motherland from which the royal house of Capet had sprung, the province of the Ile-de-France which surrounded Paris. This region gave its name to the king, to the country, and to the nation which inhabited it. One reason for the enduring greatness of France was the compactness of the dynastic holdings.

From the heartland of the Ile-de-France, royal power had spread outward during the Middle Ages. By 1500, the boundaries of the provinces which the French crown had accumulated were recognizably similar to those of France in our day. To the west and north were Normandy and Picardy, and to the west were Anjou and Maine, all four taken centuries earlier from the English. Southwest of the heartland was Touraine, and beyond it the great expanse of Guyenne, which had fallen finally to the French crown after the expulsion of the English only half a century before. To the south and southeast, stretching down to the Mediterranean, were Auvergne, Languedoc, and Provence. To the east and southeast were the great wine-growing provinces of Champagne, long a possession of the French crown, and of Burgundy, which had been won only decades earlier after the death on the battlefield of its ambitious duke, Charles the Bold.

All of these provinces had their own nobilities and many of them their own ancient institutions, separate from one another and until very recently united to the rest of the realm by no link more substantial than a common ruler. The kings had sought, with some success, to build over these varied provincial institutions a roof of royal power administered by royal agents. This process was to be the characteristic royal technique which led to the development of a strong central government and an absolute monarchy, which forms the main theme of this chapter.

In the sixteenth and early seventeenth centuries, France was already a big country. France had in the year 1500 some 15,000,000 people. In those days of slow communications, when the frontiers between nations and provinces consisted of forests or barren lands, the problem of ruling such numbers spread out in far-flung communities was immense. But once these people could be organized, even loosely, and made to pay taxes to a central government, there would be power as yet unprecedented in modern Europe, even in Spain's sixteenth-century magnificence. In the period before 1648 the French kings began to perform this feat. There were many setbacks—indeed there was a kind of rhythm of power, chaos, power, more chaos, more power. France did not yet play the dominant role in Europe in this early modern period. But in the story of this chapter will be seen the preparation for the age of French predominance which was to follow: the age of Louis XIV.

THE FRENCH MONARCHY BEFORE 1500

The growth of absolute monarchy in France is the outstanding example of a political tendency which was general in early modern times. Medieval politics might be described as a network of customary and contractual arrangements about various rights: rights to the functions which we would call governmental, as well as to the use and enjoyment of property. These medieval ways were not overthrown by any one assault, but the kings encroached upon them gradually by taking for their own agents the governmental functions of making laws, taxing, rendering justice, supporting permanent military forces, and organizing armies of officials. This process was to reach its height in the late seventeenth century in the "age of Louis XIV," but tendencies in this direction were visible in the late Middle Ages and had reached a rather high stage of development in the sixteenth century.

Many of the characteristics of European life contributed to the rise of absolutism. Growth of national patriotism was one. Awareness of common interests on a larger-than-local scale was spread by the king's officials as they did their work of justice or taxation. By the time of the commercial revolution the larger-than-local tendencies were clearly advantageous in the competition with other states. Moreover, the struggle of states with each other made strong central power necessary. A place like France was made up of so many units, each with its own rights and officials left over from the Middle Ages, that someone had to make them work together in time of peril. Given a higher civilization, perhaps, that "someone" might have been a representative body, a parliament, but in brute fact in most European countries it was the king and his officials who made the provinces, estates, towns, guilds, universities, clergy, peasants, nobles, journeymen, and so forth work together. And while doing so the kings deprived these groups bit by bit of their customary medieval political rights.

Another spur to absolutism was the Renaissance, which made fashionable the Roman Law concept that the ruler should have all the powers, legislative, executive, and judicial. The Renaissance ideal of the hero-leader, part lawgiver, part soldier, was a stimulant to royal imaginations. But social conditions were the most powerful forces working for the growth of absolute monarchy. Besides those already mentioned—the fact of war and the need to make diverse groups pull together in wartime—it is important to appreciate the role of kings in keeping order at home, even in peacetime, and to recall what the changeover to a money economy was doing to society.

A king who needed money to pay for armies, and dependable officials to collect the money, would rely on the ambitious class of townsmen rather than on nobles who were jealous of his power. The kings and the *bourgeoisie* were therefore able to do each other favors. But there were many kinds of bourgeois, and the king could do many kinds of favors, from military protection of guildsmen against rebellious journeymen, to concessions to moneylenders, to permission to bourgeois officials to buy offices and lands which made them nobles. Naturally the older nobles did not like this pressure from ambitious, social-climbing, middle-class people. They grew more scornful than ever of the *parvenus.* They accentuated more than ever their own noble characteristics, which, unfortunately for them, consisted to a large extent of lavish consumption of goods and services which they could ill afford. This process of social competition played into the hands of the king. The great nobles, potential political competitors and military rebels, were forced more and more to come to him for royal governorships, church offices for their younger sons, and various income-bearing sinecures. The king's control of church appointments was a valuable political asset to him. A French king like Francis I scarcely needed to embrace Lutheranism and seize the monasteries as long as he could appoint bishops and abbots.

All of these generalizations about the rise of absolute monarchy are drawn from French history, but the list may be used, with some adjustments, as an aid in understanding the political development of most European countries in early modern times. In the French case the process was at work over a long period of time. A few illustrations chosen from the High Middle Ages and the centuries of transition to modern times will indicate the trend of events.

The French King Philip II, or Philip Augustus (1180–1223), used royal officials called *baillis* (*sénéchaux* in the south) to dispense royal justice and collect taxes. The *baillis* were salaried civil servants, and one of the reasons they were needed was that an older class of officials, the *prévôts,* who had been rewarded with gifts of land, had become too closely indentified with local interests. In the reign of the famous "Saint Louis," Louis IX (1226–1270), the *baillis* in their turn were being watched by still other officials. This process by which kings, not trusting the nobility, hired officials who in time became like the nobles, and themselves had to be watched by other officials, is to be found in most European countries, including Russia, in early modern times. In France the *baillis* were still important in the sixteenth and seventeenth centuries in spite of the addition of other officials. As will be seen below, the most famous sixteenth- and seventeenth-century agents of absolutism were to be the *intendants.*

In the Middle Ages the king periodically summoned his great vassals as a king's court, or *curia regis,* to discuss important problems. For day-to-day advice he had the officers of his royal household, who looked after his supply of food, his house furnishings, his religious services, written records, and so on. These officials were nobles, and alongside their duties on the king's estate there grew up departments of the French state. But the kings always had good reason to fear that important nobles would be less obedient than lesser nobles and commoners, and besides, educated men—which most great nobles were not—could be used as experts and specialists in the branches of government business. Instead of the *curia regis* sitting occasionally as a court there grew up a permanent group of judges, the *parlement* (in French history this word means law court). Instead of relying on the officers of his household, the king more and more chose lesser nobles or commoners as ministers to handle state affairs. On great occasions when the support of the whole realm was needed, the kings developed the old *curia regis* into a kind of national representative body by adding to it representatives from the towns (14th century) and later representatives of the peasantry (16th century). This body first met in 1302 when Philip IV, called "the Fair" (1285–1314), felt the need of public support in his struggle with Pope Boniface VIII over the taxing of the clergy and other matters having to do with his eagerness to be as powerful a king of France as possible. The French representative body, called the Estates General because it came to represent the three "estates" of clergy, nobility, and commoners, was only consultative at first. If it had succeeded, like the English Parliament, in advancing beyond consultation, France would not have become an absolute monarchy.

Absolutism grew up in France as the crown became the institution around which was organized the fight against external interference and internal disorder. The crown also became the rallying point for an awakening national sentiment. This result was greatly influenced by France's exposed position on the continent and by the intensity of the struggle which was necessary to consolidate its territories. In the late Middle Ages the effort to eliminate the English kings from control of what is today southwest France led to a series of struggles which lasted from 1338 to 1453 and are known as "the hundred years war." One example from the later stages of that war will illustrate the chaotic nature of conditions in France and the way in which the crown outlasted its opponents.

At the time of Joan of Arc (1412–1431), the village girl who became the personification of French patriotism, conditions in the monarchy could scarcely have been worse. When Joan—later Saint Joan—heard Voices ordering her to save France, King Charles VII (1422–1461) was a weak, almost pitiful figure. The French nobility were divided, some siding with the English king, who claimed the throne of France and occupied most of the country. The Estates General was also internally split, and in the background lurked the danger of peasant uprisings. It was a genuine time of troubles. Yet in the long run—after Joan of Arc had inflicted several defeats on the English, been betrayed to them, and burned at the stake by the Inquisition in 1431—it was the monarchy which induced the Estates General to raise money, developed a modern army, took advantage of the national sentiment which Joan of Arc had helped to arouse, and finally drove out the English.

The son of Charles VII, Louis XI (1461–1483), the sly "spider" with his Machiavellian cunning, advanced absolutism to a still higher point and triumphed over the last dangerous vassal, Charles the Bold of Burgundy (1467–1477), who if things had turned out differently might have made northeastern France, along with the Low Countries, into a separate state. The successors of Louis XI, Charles VIII (1483–1498) and Louis XII (1498–1515), secured Brittany, marrying in turn its heiress-ruler. They were also attracted by the lure of Renaissance Italy.

THE EARLY SIXTEENTH CENTURY

The year 1500 found the French deeply involved in trying to conquer Italy, whose riches were to lure them for many decades into a hornets' nest of European power politics. The struggle was exhausting, but it hastened the coming of a new age in France, an age in which Italian ideas and culture were preeminent and which left a deep mark on French development. Francis I, who reigned from 1515 to 1547, is called the first Renaissance king of France. He was, like his predecessors, deeply involved in Italy, and deeply impressed by it as well. At the beginning of his reign, he won a thundering victory at Marignano, in 1515, but later encountered adversity. He was defeated and captured at Pavia in 1525 and taken as a prisoner to Madrid, where he was forced to sign away Burgundy and abandon his Italian claims. Back home and free to fight another day, he renounced these sacrifices as having been made under duress. The rest of his reign he passed in intermittent hot and cold wars against Charles V, against whom he did not scruple to ally with the Turks and the German Protestant princes.

The Italian adventure ended with the Treaty of Cateau-Cambrésis in 1559, when Henry II, Francis's successor, finally abandoned the claims to Italy and turned to a policy of alliance with Spain. But before they ended, the French occupations of Italy had given Frenchmen a chance to become acquainted with the Italian Renaissance, and to invite Italian artists and scholars across the Alps, to bring the Renaissance to France. In the era of Francis I great palaces in the new taste, the chateaux of the Loire were built, and the Louvre in Paris was remodeled. It was an era of a brilliant court, and of brilliant men of letters such as Rabelais. Like Henry VIII of England, Francis prided himself on encouraging culture in the manner of an Italian despot.

Francis I was better suited to his role of Renaissance patron of the arts than to that of Renaissance despot, but with the help of his mother and other advisors his reign saw absolutism entrenched a little more firmly. The institutions of the absolute monarchy were inching their way forward under the debonair Francis, and this process was continued by the servitors of the uninspired Henry II, who reigned from 1547 to 1559.

Political theorists of the time recognized that the king was responsible to God, and he was also supposed to respect customs and contracts and the funda-

VINCENNES (right). The don-jon, or principal tower. (Photo Viollet) These grim royal forti-fications, dating from the four-teenth century, contrast strongly with the Renaissance chateau at CHAMBORD (be-low), built by Francis I in the sixteenth century, illuminating the transition of the kings from military leaders to patrons of art and heads of a richer, more cultivated society. (French Government Tourist Office)

CHAMBORD – Le Château

mental laws of the kingdom, which consisted mainly of the rules of succession. He was also under oath, from the time of his coronation, to defend the Church against heresy. In actual fact the kings were now the masters in France. Even where provincial "estates" still voted on taxes, as in some of the more recently acquired provinces such as Burgundy and Provence, they did so as a privilege. The Parisian and provincial *parlements* and below them officials like the *baillis* provided the king's justice and worked at administration. The king had a mercenary army garrisoned at some three hundred strong points calculated to hold the country in respect. The rights of towns as of provinces were more and more whittled away by the king's officials. The Church was regarded as an ally of the monarchy. The Concordat of Bologna of 1516 gave the king the right to nominate bishops and abbots, a most useful patronage. The king's great vassals were being encouraged to become courtiers, while his officials reached past them to tax and judge their former subjects.

But French absolute monarchy in spite of its advances was still precariously based. Its officials were few for such a large and recently united country where customs were many and deeply rooted. A strong king could have his way while he was present, but much happened while his back was turned. Habits of personal loyalty and clan allegiance persisted. Great families like the Guises and Condés and Bourbons all had their hosts of clients among the lesser nobles and inhabitants of their native regions. Like the king they had patronage to dispense, and officials of their own who had bound their fates with their noble masters and who would fight and betray for them. Even the peasants still had most to gain from keeping in the good graces of the lords of the region whose influence was permanent and who still led them against trespassers and intruders in times of civil disturbance.

The great nobles considered themselves entitled to participate in government. They resented the king's use of educated commoners and lesser nobles in advisory and judicial capacities. Many of them considered themselves masters of the provinces in which they were hereditary governors—an office the king was doing his best to render inconsequential. When these men revolted, they brought into play the whole system of personal attachments and loyalties which was still such an important part of society. This is what happened during the sixteenth-century wars of religion.

THE WARS OF RELIGION

The religious wars in France lasted from 1562 to 1598. It is possible to count at least nine of them, with uneasy pauses between. In all, they amounted to a half-century of national uncertainty and weakness, a time of constitutional as well as religious troubles, as if the monarchy had grown too fast and overextended itself. Afterward French absolutism went forward again into its greatest age.

The wars were between Catholics and Calvinists. This struggle was genuine, but there was much more to the wars than their religious side. Much of the trouble was dynastic. Henry II, killed in an accident in 1559, left four sons, three of whom reigned weakly one after the other until 1589, by which time the fourth had died. These last kings of the Valois house need not be given much attention.

Francis II (1559–1560) was tubercular and unable to cope with affairs of state. His young wife, Mary Stuart, was the future Mary Queen of Scots. Charles IX (1560–1574) was only ten when he became king, and remained the tool of others. Henry III (1574–1589) had an odd brilliance and some eloquence but was too soft-willed to dominate what was by then an intense crisis. The times called for a great king, and indeed, one of France's best was waiting offstage, but he did not inherit the throne until 1589, and was unable to dominate the country until 1594. This was Henry IV, first of the Bourbons.

France's trouble was more than religious and dynastic. A half century of costly wars and careless financial management had left the kingdom without the means to keep up its military forces. This meant that the absolute monarchy was at the mercy of its subjects. When the private militias of the Catholics and Protestants began fighting, the government could not match them in strength and had to appease whichever was in the ascendancy. Intermittent efforts to solve the problem of money (and therefore law and order) through calling the Estates General did not succeed. The Estates General reflected the divisions in the kingdom. To make matters worse economic hardships, partly stemming from the fighting but also from developments such as the changing value of money, placed people under strain. Impoverished nobles, for example, and small guilds-men and artisans resentful of the more prosperous merchants, and peasants un-able to cope with fluctuating prices, took out some of their irritations in the civil wars. Such worldly and irreligious motives inspired both the Catholic and Protestant sides of the ordeal. Moreover, political theories multiplied as the crisis seemed to call for constructive thinking to solve it. There was a deluge of political pamphlets as the religious wars neared their end.

The mixture of religious and secular motives is most clearly seen in the Protestant movement, which reached its numerical peak in France about 1560. Authorities disagree concerning the number of Protestants in France, and the best one can do is to describe them as somewhat more than one third of the popu-lation at their high point. By this time the Catholic-Protestant split had taken on a regional character, the north and east remaining primarily Catholic, while whole districts in the south turned Protestant, from the nobility down to the peasants. The Reformed churches were defended and more or less dominated by great nobles like Condé and Coligny and the Bourbon King of Navarre, father of the future Henry IV. As Protestantism grew, and became regional, it presented serious problems, for Catholic properties were seized by Protestant noblemen and congregations. Both Protestants and Catholics appealed to the law. In self-defense the Protestants organized their own garrisons in the towns under their control, pleading loyalty to the crown, yet threatening to become a state within the state.

To the French monarchy this challenge was philosophical as well as military. The king was both defender of the faith and civil ruler. When some of his subjects severed their religious connection with him, his powers were reduced. If this reduction could be done once by the will of some of the king's subjects, it might be done again. Actually neither the Protestants nor the Catholics really believed in reducing the link between the state and religion. Each side wanted to win the war and exercise the state's responsibility for religious and moral welfare. Yet if the contest proved to be a draw, both sides would be faced with the unaccustomed challenge of mutual toleration, and the tradition of *one state, one religion* would be shattered.

The domination of certain regions by the Protestants, led by great nobles, amounted to the appearance in new form·of the fifteenth-century aristocratic revolts against royal authority. Unfortunately for the crown the Catholics also used their cause as an occasion for defying the king's authority. Thus did the dynastic and financial and military weakness of the monarchy coincide with religious and secular unrest.

The problems posed by Protestantism led to actual fighting by way of the king's council chamber. Because Francis II was sickly, the question of who should exercise his authority naturally arose. When Francis died in 1560 and the ten-year old Charles IX became king, this question was still more acute. The mother of these ineffectual kings, Catherine de Médicis, gladly rose to the occasion. She had been the neglected wife of Henry II, but now at last had a chance to use her talents for intrigue and domination. For thirty years, until her death in 1589, she did her best, as regent or as advisor to her sons, to maintain the authority of the crown. It was a limited objective, but at this time a most difficult one, and some historians have credited Catherine with trying to serve the general welfare. Therein lies the problem of judging Catherine's career and influence. For she was Machiavellian in her methods, had few moral or religious convictions, and was partly responsible for the St. Bartholomew massacre whose stain has never been effaced from her reputation.

The massacre of Protestants known as St. Bartholomew's Eve (1572) was not the only atrocity in the religious wars, but it was the greatest, and it will illustrate the tangled forces which were at work. Catherine de Médicis wanted neither the Catholics nor the Protestants to wield the king's authority. She tried to use both groups in the councils, and to manage them. Lacking force with which to suppress the Protestants, she appeased them, and as part of this program arranged the marriage of the king's sister Marguerite to the Protestant leader Henry of Navarre. This event, taking place in 1572, brought many Protestant leaders to Paris.

No massacre of these Protestants was planned in advance. Catherine, however, became alarmed at the influence of one Protestant, Coligny, over her son, King Charles IX, and arranged for Coligny's assassination. When the attempt failed, Catherine feared Protestant reprisals and took the preventive action of unleashing a wholesale massacre of Protestants. It spread from Paris to the provinces and lasted for two months.

St. Bartholomew did not wipe out Protestantism, which from this point on became more embittered and more radical politically. The southern provinces organized assemblies and claimed autonomy. Protestant theorists taught that the king's power was limited by the rights of the people. But the timid Henry III once again appeased the Protestants. In reply a Catholic League was formed under the leadership of Henry of Guise, the king's cousin. As civil war again flared, the Catholic League, in its aversion to the tolerant king, also began to attack his power. It entertained theories idealizing the traditional monarchy of the sixth century, when the king was not absolute and had to rule with the aid of his nobles. Both Protestants and Catholics were thus subversive from the point of view of absolutism.

Between the two extremes was a third party known as the "Politiques," who thought that the national interest demanded religious toleration. The most famous of them, Jean Bodin (1530–1596), defended the monarchical authority as it had developed in recent centuries, and rejected the theories of both Protestants and Catholics. The Estates General, which might conceivably have limited the monarchy at this juncture, took no determined action.

Public suffering grew worse under the weight of disorders and unwise taxes until the climax came in the so-called "war of the three Henry's." Upon the death of King Henry III's younger brother in 1584, the legitimate heir to Henry's throne became the Protestant leader Henry of Navarre. The third Henry (of Guise), leader of the Catholic League, objected and tried to change the succession to favor himself or some other Catholic. The ambitions of Philip II of Spain were also stirred, for his wife Elizabeth was Henry III's sister, and his daughter Isabella made claims to the French throne, especially when the Catholic League allowed Spanish soldiers to come to its support.

King Henry III, having no power of his own, had to call upon the power of either the Catholic or the Protestant side. He favored the Catholic Guise until the latter seemed on the point of taking all leadership and kingly dignity away from him; thereupon he had Guise murdered (1588). Shortly afterward he was himself murdered. Henry of Navarre (ruled 1589–1610), the first of the Bourbon branch of the French ruling family, was now king according to the law of succession, but not according to the Catholics and Spaniards who, among other things, held Paris.

The end of the story came as Henry IV, with courage and fine political sense, bargained and fought his way to victory. He had behind him the Protestants and the Catholic "Politiques," who agreed to liberty for Protestantism but insisted that Henry turn Catholic for the sake of political stability and the views of the majority. Against him was the Catholic League, backed by popular objections to a Protestant monarch and helped by Spanish soldiers sent by Philip II. For the sake of national unity Henry IV turned Catholic in 1593. In 1594 Paris fell to him. In 1598, by the Treaty of Vervins, the war with Spain was ended, and the Spanish restored all French territories which they had seized. The Edict of Nantes, in the same year, granted the Huguenots freedom of worship in specified districts, and guarantees of equal political rights. The most tangible guarantee which the Huguenots received was control of a number of fortified towns.

The religious wars played an important role in the eventual triumph of absolutism in France. Their example of internal confusion and foreign intervention encouraged acceptance of a strong king and a strong royal power.

THE REIGNS OF HENRY IV
AND LOUIS XIII

Henry IV was the best-liked and perhaps the ablest of the French kings. A man of action who had spent his youth in army camps, he was indifferent if not actually skeptical in religious matters, intelligent and adaptable, persuasive as well as brave. Not given to office work, he conducted the business of kingship while on the move. He understood men and events, but he was poor at matters which required study, such as finances. Such affairs he left in the hands of his lifelong companion the Protestant Maximilien de Béthune, better known as the Duke of Sully (1560–1641). Henry was himself a free spender, but required of Sully that he make economies in government and provide the savings which were necessary to the survival of royal authority. The king himself concentrated on foreign policy and the all-important reconciliation of the groups so lately at odds within France. He had to hold the Catholics in line, but he strictly controlled the French Church, using appointments for political purposes in the tradition of his predecessors. He was inclined, naturally enough, to conciliate the Protestants, overlooking the power of their fortified cities, which constituted a real problem in a state which was back on the road to absolutism.

Meanwhile Sully, as superintendent of finances, worked efficiently both as courtier and treasury watchdog. He was the real boss of the internal administration of the country. In the realm of finance he was forced to use what expedients were at hand, increasing some taxes while lowering others, selling offices, and above all economizing and reducing the government's debts with small sympathy for the state's creditors. He managed to put the finances in order, cut the debts, pile up savings, and render yearly accountings which became famous. Although convinced of the prime importance of agriculture, he was a mercantilist who also encouraged industries and undertook canal-digging and road-building.

Sully, in the name of Henry IV, drew up a "Great Design" for a European international organization based on toleration of Catholics, Lutherans, and Calvinists for each other, with international councils for the discussion of problems. He was among the earliest to envisage something like the United Nations. But Henry IV, being a practical statesman, could not forget the balance of power. The Great Design may have been intended to checkmate the Habsburgs, whose possessions in Spain, Austria, and the Netherlands Henry IV still considered a menace. Henry's reign was one of peace and recovery from the religious wars in France, but he was not likely to forget the recent Spanish intervention in his country's affairs, and he did what he could to turn back Spain's enveloping influence. Under cover of neutrality, he helped the Dutch revolt. He also hoped to cut Spanish communications by way of Italy with Austria and the Rhine. Henry encouraged the twelve-year truce between the Spanish and Dutch which was signed in 1609, but a year later tensions in Germany threatened the peace, and Henry prepared to head a coalition against Spain and Austria.

In that year, 1610, Henry IV was assassinated by a Catholic madman and thus passed from the scene by violence, as had his two competitors in the "war of the three Henry's." He had lived long enough to set the monarchy firmly in the way it was to take under Richelieu, Mazarin, and Louis XIV. He had not destroyed the opposition, however, and it turned up immediately, during the regency of his widow, Marie de Médicis.

Marie de Médicis took the direction of affairs because the heir to the throne, Louis XIII, was not quite ten years old. She was a vain and excitable woman, the prey to those around her and particularly to her favorites, the Florentine Concini and his wife Léonora. The officials left from the previous administration could not cope with these intriguers. Sully retired, and the royal authority was twisted this way and that as the great nobles wrested offices, privileges, and pensions from incompetent advisors of the Queen Mother. Sully's treasury was soon wasted, and the Estates General of 1614 failed either to seize command of the situation or to grant the Regent the funds she demanded. There were very serious reasons for disagreements in the Estates General, the last one to meet before the Great Revolution of 1789. It was an era of triumphant Counter-Reformation in Europe. In French Catholic circles, Jesuits looked to Rome for guidance, while Gallicans worked for the continued independence of the French Church. The Huguenots were potentially very dangerous because they had their own organization and military power and were concerned by the Catholic Reformation's forward strides.

In international relations France seemed trapped between Henry IV's anti-Habsburg line, which meant helping Protestants in the Netherlands and Germany and encouraging the Huguenots at home, with all the risks which such a policy entailed, and the opposite course of valuing Catholicism and religious unity above defense against the Habsburgs. The latter policy would have meant cutting down Huguenot power at home while accepting Spanish preponderance in Europe. The latter seemed to be the intent of Marie de Médicis when she arranged the marriage of Louis XIII to Anne of Austria and of Elizabeth of France to Don Philippe, son of Philip III of Spain. But some Frenchmen, while powerless as yet to alter this trend of affairs, nevertheless believed that France was in mortal danger if it failed to oppose Spanish power. Spain was dominant in the Western Mediterranean, in Belgium, in Portugal, and on the sea route to the Netherlands (except for the stubborn Dutch), and was linked dynastically to the Habsburgs of Austria and the Holy Roman Empire.

In 1617 Louis XIII, now sixteen years old, asserted himself. He had been growing up a pious, sober adolescent with a cold temperament very unlike that of his father, Henry IV. He had pride and ambition, however, and had resented the insolence of Concini, whom he now struck down with suprising suddenness. Marie de Médicis was set aside. The young king meant to rule, gloriously if possible. When the Thirty Years War broke out in 1618 and the powerful French Protestants became restive, Louis XIII assembled what force he could, to teach them discipline. But he failed. The great reign he wanted was not going to be easy unless gifted officials could be found. After seven years of indifferent success, in 1624 he found the man he needed, Cardinal Richelieu.

THE STATES GENERAL OF FRANCE, 1614 by Jan Ziarnko. Etching. This was the
last meeting of the Estates General until 1789. (National Gallery of Art: Rosen-
wald Collection)

RICHELIEU AND MAZARIN

Richelieu was a younger son in a family of lesser nobles—typical beginning of many a success story in the annals of absolute monarchy. He was headed for the army when he was unexpectedly appointed Bishop of Luçon after his older brother had vacated the see. There, from 1606 to 1614, Richelieu developed his Catholic orthodoxy, which was sincere, and his taste for administration, which was insatiable, until he went to Paris for the meeting of the Estates General of 1614. His first service, to the Queen Mother, won him a Cardinal's hat in 1622, but he had meanwhile been swept out of government service in 1617 with the rest of Marie de Médicis' clientèle. In 1624 Louis XIII appointed him to his Council, and after six months the King was convinced that Richelieu had a program compatible with his own need for obedience and military glory. Richelieu remained chief minister until his death in 1642, shortly before that of Louis XIII in 1643. There is a legend that Richelieu controlled the king, but in fact Louis XIII could have thrown him to the jealous aristocracy by a mere nod of the head. The reason that he did not do so is that Richelieu respected the crown's authority and was always careful to present the raw materials for a decision without usurping the right to make the decision itself. In spite of periods of bad feeling, the partnership lasted for eighteen years, during which Richelieu, knowing the king's suspiciousness and sensitivity, watched his potential rivals like a hawk, while Louis XIII recognized the minister's talents and let him work.

Richelieu's main interest was the foreign policy of France, but as is usually the case in times of crisis it was impossible to separate internal and external affairs. The Thirty Years War was exciting Catholics and Protestants in France, and the Huguenots were intensifying their fortification of La Rochelle and other points in a challenging manner. Richelieu in 1627–1628 laid siege to La Rochelle and defeated the Huguenots in a contest which would have been his undoing if he had lost it. Then he deprived them of their military and political privileges but confirmed the religious liberty granted by the Edict of Nantes. Richelieu would have preferred to have religious unity in France, but he was realistic enough to admit the century-old existence of the Huguenots, and he did not intend to make loyalty to the state depend on Catholicism.

Richelieu's personal position was now strong, but the great nobles were against him, for he represented royal absolutism. Every year had its conspiracies. Richelieu on his side was determined to teach the aristocracy to respect the king's officials. It was a contest between law and order and the turbulent bad habits which the nobility had learned during the religious wars.

Richelieu's struggle with the aristocracy came to a crisis from about 1630–1632. Richelieu broke the nobility as a political power by making it clear in specific cases that he could ruin individuals. In places where the nobles had sufficient military power to terrorize the countryside and resist the king's officials, he dismantled the chateaux. To the idea of a feudal monarchy in which the nobility had political power and privileges, he opposed that of an absolute monarchy run by the king's employees. He had no desire to wipe out the nobility—he was a noble himself—but he would not grant them political independence.

Until about 1632 the need to defeat opposition at home embarrassed Richelieu in his foreign policy, but he never lost sight of his main objective. That was to defeat the Habsburgs and restore the balance of power.

His determination to conclude the long duel, which had begun with Francis I and Charles V over a century before, led to confusions and paradoxes. Richelieu, a Catholic Cardinal, had defeated the Huguenots, but in the Thirty Years War he took the Protestant side. Catholic opponents argued that he was preventing the reconquest of Europe by Catholic Christianity and was therefore valuing the French state more highly than his religion. Richelieu and Father Joseph, a mysterious priest-diplomat who served him, were both competent theologians and sincere Catholics, but they denied that the cause of Christianity was being served by Catholic Spain and Catholic Austria, and they accused the Habsburg rulers of pursuing secular ends. To Richelieu the preservation of the French state in the balance of power was a service to the Church, for France was one of the greatest Catholic powers.

FRANCE IN 1648, WITH PROVINCES

Whether this view is regarded as sophistry or consistency, Richelieu placed the defeat of the Habsburgs, and particularly of Spain, first on his list of objectives. Until that job was done, France would have to live in peril and austerity. With the French nobles in hand again and the state machinery working, with the *intendants* whom Richelieu sent into the provinces as trouble-shooters in all branches of administration, the king's subjects could be made to support the war effort. There was suffering, and the overburdened peasants revolted so frequently and violently that Richelieu had to send regular troops against them. He had little sympathy for the lower classes. In most of these instances the peasants attacked mainly the government tax collectors, sparing the chateaux. Meanwhile the *parlements* and nobles grumbled and occasionally town workers rioted. France did not readily come to heel under absolutism; but since the various social classes did not cooperate in revolution, Richelieu could push forward his grand design. If he had had peace, like Henry IV in his last years, he would have been glad to turn to domestic progress, for he was a mercantilist in his ideas, and even during the war found time to lay down rules for the government of Canada and the new West Indies possessions. But he continued to put first things first, as he saw them, and although the people grumbled and finances were in a sorry state the worst was over when he died, worn out, in 1642.

When Louis XIII died a few months after his great minister's passing, the new king, Louis XIV (1643–1715) was only five. The Queen Mother, Anne of Austria, took the reins as regent, but she was impatient with the business of state and not good at it. Luckily Cardinal Mazarin was on hand, a former Italian diplomat whose talents Richelieu had perceived and put to work. Only recently naturalized (1639) and made a Cardinal (1641), Mazarin was graceful, intelligent, and tricky. The French, who came to hate him, have left many portraits of his unctuous humility, his acquisitiveness, and the roundabout tactics by which he avoided whenever possible the direct application of force. A foreigner scorned by the French aristocracy and ridiculed by the public, Mazarin captivated the lonely queen (who may even have married him secretly). He served the French state with devotion (1643–1661) and, by dividing the opposition, was able to carry Richelieu's war to a successful conclusion in the Peace of Westphalia (1648). After that, the French aristocracy, long held in check by the absolute monarchy, burst into turbulent rebellion, and it took all of Mazarin's cunning before order was restored and absolutism again advanced upon its victorious way.

9

THE THIRTY YEARS WAR

THE THIRTY YEARS WAR lies like a blight across the first half of the seventeenth century. Approaching it from earlier times, the historian sees advance warnings for a long time before the event—warnings as diverse as the unresolved differences of Catholics and Protestants at Augsburg in 1555, the unfinished duel between the Dutch and the Spanish, and a coalition of anti-Habsburg powers which Henry IV was planning the year of his death, 1610. And after the fatal year of the war's beginning, 1618, there persist within the conflict, which lasted until 1648, most of the themes which the reader has encountered since his first meeting with the Renaissance. In the period 1618–1648 these themes—in politics and international relations, for example—develop and mature, so that "modern Europe" after 1648 has more clearly defined characteristics, like the firmer lines of an adult face. The first and most important of these modern characteristics to mature in the period of the Thirty Years War was the system of relations among states.

THE EMERGENCE OF THE BALANCE
OF POWER, 1500–1618

The Thirty Years War provides an opportunity to review the direction which international affairs had been taking since 1500. Europe was made up of increasingly consolidated states. Usually it was a case of a king becoming master of his kingdom, as in France, but even in England, where an opposite tendency was in course and representative institutions were winning a permanent place, the central government was more firmly consolidated. Stronger states were stronger competitors. As feudal warfare declined *within* each realm, warfare continued *among* realms. Each state appeared to be maneuvering for advantage at the expense of others. The weaker insured their survival by banding together against the one most likely to swallow the rest. There arose the tendency to maintain the "balance of power," or an "equilibrium," but changing conditions led to constant shifts. In the period 1500-1648 this kind of "state system" was not consciously planned, but arose out of the conditions of the times without most men's having any philosophy about it. Efforts to seize and dominate were met by efforts to survive. To most contemporaries the Thirty Years War looked like nothing more than a struggle between Protestants and Catholics.

Theories of international affairs were slow in catching up with the facts. The idea of Europe, as summed up by the Catholic Church and the Holy Roman Empire, lingered all through the early modern period. Its defeat was not clear until 1648. But the word "empire" gradually changed in its associations, from the vision of European political and religious unity to the nightmare of one nation dominating the others. As early as 1500 the Holy Roman Empire had added to its title the words "of the German nation." The French king used the slogan "The king is emperor in his kingdom," which meant that he reported directly to God, and not through the Holy Roman Emperor. The medieval idea of a hierarchy of secular rulers with the Holy Roman Emperor at the top was giving way to the "modern" concept of free and independent states, all legally equal. Efforts to find in the Bible and in history a set of laws which would apply to every state in its dealings with others brought forth what is usually called the first text on international law, *On the Law of War and Peace* (1625), by the Dutch Humanist Hugo Grotius (1583-1645).

Within the system of European states, national sentiment played an increasing part, but it was by no means dominant in this early modern period. States were still considered to be the dynastic, or family, holdings of their rulers. The element of nationality helped some rulers (English, French, Spanish) to consolidate their states, but in other cases (Germans, Czechs) national sentiments worked against the process of consolidation. Religion, so important in international relations in this early modern period, would appear at first glance to have been stronger than dynastic and national loyalties. Germany was split by religion from Luther's time right through to the end of the Thirty Years War, and remained so. In France and England there were many who placed religion ahead of dynasty or nationality. In the end, however, the Reformation struggles contributed to the strengthening of national sentiments. Spanish patriotism was stronger for its sense of Catholic mission, English patriotism for the sense of common resistance to the Spanish and Catholic threat. France rallied behind the first Bourbon king, Henry IV (1589-1610), when he successfully put the nation above religious differences.

As the system of states took shape in the early modern period, their need for permanent representation in one another's capitals brought forth the profes-

MAN IN ARMOR by Sir Anthony Van Dyke (1599–1641). Van Dyke was born in Antwerp, but lived much of his life in England. Admirer of Titian, pupil of Rubens, he was a great portrait painter and an incomparable etcher. (Fogg Museum of Art, Harvard University)

sion of *diplomacy*. When not fighting, the new states were gauging each other's strength and building alliances. It was useful even to enemy states to be in contact with each other through their representatives called, generally, ambassadors. Side by side with official emissaries, secret agents worked for their rulers' objectives, exploiting religious conflicts, rivalries between kings and nobles, and moments of dynastic weakness like the French regencies. It was customary to intervene secretly or openly in other people's civil wars. It is especially noticeable how in this period loyalties to persons, to regions, to traditional feudal rights, and to religious ideals still competed with the growing determination of states to monopolize the loyalty of their subjects.

These tendencies have been seen at work in the various chapters devoted to particular countries. There is no need to recall the details, but it is useful to review some of the stages in the development of the state system prior to the Thirty Years War.

The miniature system of balance of power in Italy had been intruded upon by the French and Spanish at the end of the fifteenth century. It was the Spanish who stayed, and won control which lasted, in the south of Italy, at least, for three and a half centuries. A glance at the sixteenth-century map will recall the exploits of Charles V, Holy Roman Emperor and ruler of Spain, the Netherlands, the Habsburg lands grouped around Austria, and the Spanish holdings overseas. Charles sought to control Germany through his office as Holy Roman Emperor, and to rebuild the Burgundian realm in the Low Countries and along the borders of France. He succeeded only in maintaining the Spanish domination of Italy. In Germany and among other European powers he encountered resistance. It will be recalled that upon his abdication the Habsburg holdings were split. Charles's brother Ferdinand had already begun to manage the territories in Central Europe. Charles's son Philip II inherited the power in Spain, Italy, the Netherlands, and overseas. Henceforth there were "Spanish" and "Austrian" Habsburgs, although the two branches still cooperated and still thought of their dominions as composing a Catholic unity in Europe.

The map in the second half of the sixteenth century is marked with the enterprises of Philip II. There were projects for subduing the rebellious Dutch and piratical English and interfering in the French succession during the War of the Three Henrys. Also, from 1580 to 1640 Spain annexed Portugal and joined under its dominion the two great oceanic empires. Spanish naval power defeated the Turks in the Western Mediterranean and pursued them in the Indian Ocean. Almost all of Catholic Europe was still in Habsburg hands, except for France.

But as the seventeenth century opened the currents of early modern international relations—political consolidation, religion, the commercial revolution, nationality—were washing at the foundations of Habsburg greatness. Merchant and fighting ships of the English and Dutch denied command of the Atlantic and the Channel to the Spaniards. The northern powers—Sweden and Denmark—were ready to contest for the shores and shipping of the Baltic. The great land power of France was growing mightier. German princes burned with their own ambitions for dynastic state-building. To see these forces in motion it is best to arrange them as they pressed forward at the outbreak of the Thirty Years War.

THE ISSUES AND OUTBREAK OF THE THIRTY YEARS WAR

Philip II, who ruled from 1556 to 1598, and his successors, Philip III (1598–1621) and Philip IV (1621–1665), loomed very large in the eyes of their contemporaries, who did not appreciate Spain's weaknesses, and thought mainly in terms of Spanish gold, of the fighting reputation of Spanish soldiers, and of the militancy of Spanish Catholicism. Spain's truce with the rebellious Dutch (1609) was supposed to last until 1621. But it was a source of general uneasiness.

When it came to an end and the Spanish attacked again, would not the Protestant powers come to the aid of the Dutch? Moreover the French, unless they chose to sacrifice everything to Catholicism and let the Spanish take the lead in Europe, were bound to resist the Spanish Habsburgs. For the Spaniards, with the Atlantic and the Channel rendered unsafe by English and Dutch naval power but with the Western Mediterranean and most of Italy in their hands, could strike at the Netherlands only by negotiating or conquering their way from Italy along the eastern borders of France.

Along this route from Italy to the Netherlands lay the multitudinous German states presided over by the Holy Roman Emperor, who was an Austrian Habsburg. The Austrian Habsburg ruler during most of the Thirty Years War was to be Ferdinand II (1619–1637), much more a crusading Catholic than his immediate predecessors and a man whose imminent rise to power was a source of worry to Protestantism. Catholicism aside, the Austrian Habsburgs had their own political interests which were to play an even larger part in the Thirty Years War than Spanish efforts to haul the Dutch back into their fold. The constitutional future of Germany was still unsettled, and the old German issue of unity versus diversity was more alive than ever. Ferdinand II was seeking, like his ancestors, to make Germany not only Catholic but also a more centralized and uniform country under his rule as Holy Roman Emperor. That is to say, the office of Emperor would become powerful at the expense of the princes of Saxony, Bavaria, Brandenburg, and so on. These princes, if Ferdinand succeeded, would go the way the French nobles were going, and the Empire, instead of being a loose federation of what were really independent kingdoms, would become one kingdom, like France. There would be room for only one king, not many.

In the time of Martin Luther the German princes had been aware of this possibility, and they were no less so now. Some princes, like Catholic Maximilian of Bavaria, were to help the Emperor's Catholic crusade, fearing all the while lest its success lead to the political centralization of Germany. But most Protestant and some Catholic princes opposed him from the outset. The Emperor, as a Habsburg, turned to Spain for military and financial aid. The German princes, when they opposed the Emperor's religious or political program, tended to turn to the enemies of Spain, particularly to France. Germany—or, rather, the Germanies—seemed fated to become the battleground of Protestant and Catholic, Bourbon and Habsburg, Frenchman and Spaniard.

European Protestants in the early seventeenth century were apprehensive because of the forward strides of the Catholic Reformation, spearheaded by the Jesuits. To many it seemed conceivable that Catholicism would reconquer all Europe. The most militant defenders of Protestantism, moreover, were the Calvinists, whose existence had not been recognized by the Peace of Augsburg, the German religious settlement of 1555. There had been accumulating since Augsburg many disputes over secularization of former Catholic properties in Germany by Protestant princes—a course of events about which no agreement had been reached at Augsburg—and it was with dread that princes and Protestants

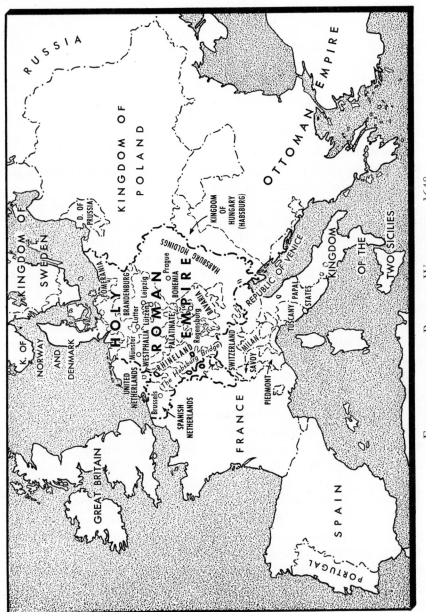

EUROPE AFTER THE PEACE OF WESTPHALIA, 1648

thought of the patronage which would be at the disposal of the Holy Roman Emperor if he should be able to annul these transfers.

Actual threats of fighting in Germany had loomed up from time to time. In 1608, in response to some land seizures by Catholic Bavaria, a Protestant Union was formed, led by the Elector Palatine, Frederick IV. His most important province (called the Rhenish Palatinate) lay at the confluence of the Rhine and Moselle, near the border between French-speaking and German-speaking peoples. In 1609 Maximilian of Bavaria headed a Catholic League. It was at this time that King Henry IV of France, on the eve of his assassination in 1610, was contemplating an anti-Habsburg coalition with some of the German Protestants. Frederick IV's Palatinate was a roadblock in the overland route which the Spanish would wish to take in their drive to reconquer the Dutch. Nothing came of this particular crisis, and both Frederick and Henry IV died in 1610, but the eyes of statesmen were fixed on the year 1621, the approaching end of the truce between Spain and the Dutch. Unexpectedly the war began in 1618 in Bohemia.

It happened that the last Habsburg ruler before Ferdinand II was his cousin Mathias (1612–1619), who was weak and childless and not very stern in enforcing Catholicism. Ferdinand II was not only chosen successor but made virtual ruler even before Mathias's death. The change of administration led to a tightening of anti-Protestant regulations in the Habsburg lands, including Bohemia. There, Czech patriotism and religious reform movements dating back to John Hus led to open revolt. In the course of the uprising two Habsburg officials were thrown from a window of the palace in Prague—the famous "defenestration" of May, 1618. The Bohemians continued their revolt, received aid from the Protestant Union, and chose Frederick V, the new Elector Palatine, to be their king in place of Ferdinand of Habsburg. Frederick, young and ambitious, accepted.

This was the start of the Thirty Years War, in which the issues discussed above were fought out. Maximilian of Bavaria, head of the Catholic League, came to the aid of Ferdinand against Frederick and the Protestants. The religious wars had begun again, and now there was more at stake than ever. Frederick's Palatinate lay in the path of the Spaniards whenever they chose to head down the Rhine toward the Netherlands. If Frederick fell, the liberties of the Dutch and the cause of Protestantism would be in peril, and so would the cause of all who feared Habsburg power in Europe. There was a third issue at stake, for if Habsburg power proved great enough, Ferdinand might draw upon it to settle the German constitutional question in favor of a centralized Empire headed by himself. If he succeeded, the German princes would have to cease behaving like kings and face the prospect of becoming nobles at the emperor's court. Thus religion, the balance of power in Europe, and the organization of Germany were the three main issues as the Thirty Years War opened. But they were not the only things being decided; such a struggle could not fail to leave its mark on European minds as well as on the European countryside. Great wars have a way of changing moods and attitudes among both leaders and led. And matters both political and religious which had nothing to do with the origins of the war soon came to be decisive elements in it.

THE STAGES IN THE THIRTY YEARS WAR

It is customary to distinguish four main stages in the Thirty Years War:

(1) The Bohemian Period, 1618–1625
(2) The Danish Period, 1625–1629
(3) The Swedish Period, 1630–1635
(4) The French Period, 1635–1648

These will be briefly narrated.

In the Bohemian period, the Habsburg ruler Ferdinand II rallied, after the first trying days when revolt seemed likely to spread from Bohemia into Austria and Hungary. He had the help of the Spanish, who invaded the Palatinate while its ruler Frederick was away in Bohemia, and of the Catholic League led by Maximilian of Bavaria, whose troops helped those of the Emperor win the Battle of the White Mountain (1620) in Bohemia. As a result of this battle the unfortunate young Elector Palatine, Frederick V, lost his new kingdom and was driven into exile. He became known as the "winter king," and with his strong-minded wife, daughter of James I of England, was to tour the courts of Protestant Europe for years in the hope of finding support for a comeback. Frederick's Palatinate and his office of Elector of the Holy Roman Empire were assigned to the Catholic Maximilian of Bavaria. Bohemia paid excessively for its rebellion. The Czech aristocracy was uprooted and dispersed, a German and international nobility was brought in to possess their lands and rule henceforth in the name of the Habsburgs over the Czech peasantry, and the Counter-Reformation was backed to the hilt. The treatment of Bohemia was one of history's most severe and effective disciplinary actions.

In this first phase of the war the cause of Protestantism was badly mauled, without much English, Dutch, or German Protestant interference. When Spain in 1621 opened war on the Dutch again, it was able to use the key Rhineland passage through the Palatinate. English and French aid to the Dutch was almost inconsequential. The Protestant states of North Germany had not come to the aid of the rebel "winter king" Frederick, whose cause was dubious and whose youth did not inspire confidence. The Emperor Ferdinand was able to advance not only Catholicism and the designs of the Spanish Habsburgs but also his own position in Germany. The Protestant states, if they had hoped by their policy of nonintervention to keep Spanish resources and influences out of German affairs, now had reason to regret their inactivity. Even Catholic Maximilian of Bavaria had reason, as a German prince, to share their misgivings.

In the second, or Danish, period of the war (1625–1629) Emperor Ferdinand reached new heights and overcame a second Protestant champion, but in so doing sharpened the issues of the organization of Germany and the relations of the Austrian and Spanish Habsburgs. In 1625 King Christian IV of Denmark entered the war. As a Protestant and as Duke of the German province of Holstein, he was concerned about German affairs. He was also jealous of Swedish power and eager to seize the mouths of the Elbe and Oder rivers (to the west and east of Denmark) and control the traffic there. Subsidized by the English and French, he was in his own right a power in northern Europe and was no mean antagonist for the Emperor. Ferdinand faced him with the aid of the Catholic League, but, not liking dependence on those German princes, found other and rather ominous means of defending himself.

There now entered the picture the great soldier of fortune, adventurer, and business genius Wallenstein (1583–1634). A Bohemian from a family with Hussite traditions but himself educated as a Catholic, Wallenstein was one of the beneficiaries of the land expropriation following the Battle of the White Mountain. Buying up properties for a song, he organized industries there, recruited and equipped soldiers, and became a military and financial power. Ambitious, with cloudy but grandiose aims, little concerned with orthodox religion but with visions of a great Central European Empire, he cared little for the traditional rights of the German princes. He entered the service of the Emperor.

Wallenstein, with the help of Bavarian troops, defeated Christian IV at the Battle of Lutter in 1626. He conquered Holstein, pushed ahead with his own army, and virtually clubbed the Danish ruler into submission. Christian IV, by the Peace of Lübeck (1629), escaped from the war with the loss of various German lands but with his homeland intact. Things might have gone worse but for his antagonists' lack of sea power and their fear of the intentions of the powerful Swedish King, Gustavus Adolphus. Emperor Ferdinand, riding high, was able to issue the Edict of Restitution (1629), which restored lands seized by the Protestants in violation of the Peace of Augsburg, and reiterated the ban of Calvinism. The edict, backed by the predatory execution of Wallenstein's mercenary troops, was a terrible blow to Protestantism and to the position of the Protestant princes.

But Emperor Ferdinand was faced with a difficult decision about Wallenstein, who was a dangerous man. To be sure, Wallenstein's resources and military power and disregard for tradition offered a chance to forge a Catholic, centralized Empire at the expense of the German princes, Catholic and Protestant alike. But would it be wise to play this game with so powerful an accomplice in the face of the Catholic princes' opposition? Respect for tradition, and for the wishes of such men as Maximilian of Bavaria, meant continuation of the loose organization of Germany, but promised a safe succession for Ferdinand's son. At the Electoral Assembly at Regensburg in 1630, the Emperor heeded the warnings of the Catholic League and dismissed Wallenstein.

Freed of the threat and promise represented by Wallenstein, Emperor Ferdinand was still the most powerful Holy Roman Emperor since Charles V. But without Wallenstein's resources he was more than ever dependent on his Spanish relatives. The Spanish aims were not identical with the Austrian. Ferdinand's collaboration with Spain may have been necessary, but it led to complications. When at Spain's wish he sent armies to Italy he antagonized the Pope, who was anxious to escape Habsburg domination. Papal opposition to the Holy Roman Emperor was an old story, but in this setting of seventeenth-century

European states and the balance of power it meant papal encouragement of France against Austria and Spain. France, of course, did not need papal consent before opposing the Habsburgs, but the Pope's attitude made its position easier. Cardinal Richelieu, the great French minister, was so anxious to check the encircling power of Spain that he helped arrange a truce between Poland and Gustavus Adolphus of Sweden, who was now able to enter the war.

Gustavus II Adolphus (1594–1632) came into the Thirty Years War like a meteor. He was soon dead on the battlefield, but it was his greatness which gives the name "Swedish period" to the years 1630–1635, and it was his moment face to face with Wallenstein which provides its highest drama. Gustavus, besides being a Protestant leader, was a born fighter and conqueror. He had concrete notions of controlling the Baltic and somewhat vaguer plans for a Protestant Germany which, had he not been cut down at the height of his fury, might have carried him to leadership of a great new kingdom. Richelieu of France, not yet ready himself to enter the combat openly, furnished Gustavus with money. The shock of the Swedish entrance into Germany in 1630 set up currents of reappraisal in all the German parties.

The Catholic princes, led by Maximilian of Bavaria, had brought about Wallenstein's dismissal but had become alarmed by the influence of Spain upon the Emperor. The approach of Gustavus forced Maximilian into line again behind Emperor Ferdinand. The latter faced decisions too. Against the Swedes he needed the support of the Protestant powers, Saxony and Brandenburg, but the price of this support would have been abandonment of the anti-Protestant Edict of Restitution. Ferdinand's Catholic conscience could not leap this barrier. Brandenburg and Saxony did not relish Swedish intervention in Germany, but to them the Edict of Restitution meant such large Imperial and Catholic aggrandizement that Ferdinand's refusal to abandon it drove them to the side of Sweden. Thus the stage was set for the drama of the "Swedish phase."

Gustavus Adolphus defeated the Catholic forces at Breitenfeld, near Leipzig, in 1631, and Protestants everywhere took heart. But instead of heading for Bohemia and Vienna as expected, he turned toward the Rhine. Gustavus did not mean to be trapped in Central Europe if the Emperor and the Protestant princes should choose to become reconciled. Then, after turning eastward again into Bavaria and defeating a Bavarian army, the Swedes mounted their threat to Austria. Emperor Ferdinand in his hour of need recalled Wallenstein, who now had more power than ever. The two antagonists maneuvered for some weeks and finally clashed head-on in the Battle of Lützen in November, 1632. It was a Swedish victory, but Gustavus was killed in the battle. His impact on German affairs was short-lived, but it had been sufficient to check Emperor Ferdinand's last chance to unify the country under his crown and faith. Sweden continued in the war with diminishing success. Its military power was to decrease through the rest of the century, while that of France rose.

For a moment Wallenstein with his vast resources and vague plans was the key figure on the European stage. Increasingly he became estranged from the Imperial court. What he stood for was uncertain, but the princes of the Catholic

League knew that he had little respect for them. And together with the Spanish party they intrigued for his removal from command. Wallenstein, playing a game of balance within Germany, negotiated secretly with the Protestants, and also with the Swedes and French. Ill and superstitious at this decisive juncture, he seems to have tried to force the Emperor to abandon the Spaniards and make peace. Some have called him a patriot working for the best interests of Germany. However that may be, he was prepared to take his army to the Protestant side if necessary, and he almost certainly had in mind substantial rewards for himself, perhaps the crown of Bohemia or some even higher prize. He was murdered in February, 1634. There is no evidence that the Emperor plotted his death, though he profited from it and rewarded the assassins.

The Swedish phase of the Thirty Years War came to an end in the Peace of Prague (1635) between the Emperor and the Protestant Elector of Saxony, a peace which Brandenburg and most other Protestant states accepted. Real concessions were made to the Lutherans as to freedom of worship and those Catholic lands secularized up to 1627. The Edict of Restitution was now a dead letter, and Saxony was to help the Emperor against Sweden. Ferdinand hoped that if the war continued all the Protestant German states would be on his side. The war did continue, into the "French phase" (1635–1648). Richelieu was bound, for the interests of France and the Bourbons, to keep alive the struggle against the Habsburgs. He now took the field openly at Sweden's side.

This last phase of the Thirty Years War was one of devastation punctuated by peace negotiations, as if everyone were too tired and yet too stubborn to bring the long affair to a conclusion. There were few decisive battles. The chief sufferers were the people of Germany over whose land the ravaging armies marched, playing out the last act of a drama which was becoming less religious and more national, and above all a naked contest over the balance of power between the Bourbons and the Habsburgs. In the new generation of leaders changing motives were visible. Ferdinand II was succeeded by his son, Ferdinand III (1637–1657), whose interest lay more and more in safeguarding his own hereditary dominions and less and less in controlling the Holy Roman Empire and Germany as a whole. Richelieu died in 1642, but his successor Mazarin continued the policy of implacable opposition to Spain and its German allies. In Brandenburg the Great Elector, Frederick William (1640–1688), showed equally secular and calculating talents on behalf of the Hohenzollern dynasty which would one day become the chief Habsburg rival in Central Europe.

In this final period of the war, certain outlines of the future became visible. Of these perhaps the most striking was the decline of Spain. No longer was Spain's alliance an asset to its Austrian dynastic connection. Spain's dwindling income from the New World, and failure to increase home production, were telling now; and the predominance which had alarmed other states since the days of Charles V and Philip II sank noticeably. The vital overland link to the Netherlands was broken by French entry into the war, and it was now clear that the Dutch would go free. Revolts at home and in Italy put Spain on the defensive. Meanwhile France forged ahead as the great generals Turenne and Condé devastated the Rhineland, previewing French aggressiveness in the age to come.

SEVENTEENTH-CENTURY WARFARE AND DESTRUCTION

Armies of the Thirty Years War were not greatly different from those of the sixteenth century. Hand arms such as pikes and halberds were giving way to muskets. Artillery was used on the battlefields as well as for sieges. Lightweight hand muskets for cavalry appeared: pistols. Soldiers were professionals recruited for pay and trained to maneuver with these weapons. As the case of Wallenstein illustrates, the formation of an army was often like a business venture. The general made a contract with the king above him and with the colonels below him, who in turn contracted with the captains. The officers, taken together, were rather like a joint stock company which for certain guaranteed sums agreed to recruit and train and equip a certain number of soldiers. These ventures could be very profitable when the man in charge had, like Wallenstein, extensive domains on which to produce food and clothing and weapons for sale to their armies.

From the point of view of the rulers who contracted for them, such armies were not altogether satisfactory. Quite apart from the question of reliability posed by the case of Wallenstein, good mercenary armies were very expensive. Troops of poorer quality were obtainable, for officers of all sorts from the many small German states were in the business, but such troops as these men could furnish were often so drunken and disorderly as to be almost useless. There were, of course, "national" armies from Spain and Sweden and France and Bavaria, recruited in much the same way but having a common national origin. Toward the end of the Thirty Years War the international and purely mercenary armies were tending to give way to the national ones, which were found to be more reliable; this was a tendency which had existed before the war began and was to continue after its conclusion. But as American students know, there were mercenary "Hessians" in the service of the English king, George III, as late as the American Revolution.

Whether or not officers and men were bound by ties of nationality to the ruler they served, they had to be paid, and it was inevitable that the kings with the greatest resources and best-organized administrations would have the most military power. The rise of mercantilism as a set of economic practices and policies designed to make a state unified, wealthy, and powerful should be recalled in its relation to military affairs. Mercantilism as an economic weapon in international relations was appreciated by government officials before it became acceptable to the general public. In the period of the Thirty Years War most nations lacked the experience and the trained personnel to apply mercantilist regulations efficiently. The relation, however, between international competition, economic regulations, and strong governments, was not overlooked by the shrewdest seventeenth century officials.

The peculiar destructiveness of the Thirty Years War resulted in part from the organization and manner of fighting of the armies. In the seventeenth century frontiers between states were still vague in many places. A country at war did not establish a "front" covering its whole frontier—there were not armies enough for this, and communications were too slow. Since the Renaissance the art of fortification had kept up with artillery sufficiently to make sieges long, and strongly fortified cities important. Seizure of such points was an essential part of campaigning. The strategy was to besiege such fortresses, then cut the enemy off from provisions and force him to give up and make peace. Unlike the later warfare of Napoleon, the object was not to destroy the enemy army and seize his capital. The capital was not as important as it would be in the later period of greater administrative centralization, and as for the army, it was almost impossible to force it to fight against its will. Because firearms were not yet long-range and accurate, it was difficult to damage a fleeing enemy. Fighting formations were painstakingly assumed through long hours of preparation, but marching formations were less difficult and more rapid of movement. Therefore if one side chose to stay in marching order and run away, rather than form in battle order and fight, it was usually able to do so. The great battles were almost always by mutual consent.

Given the advantages of defensive warfare and the financial value of mercenary troops to their officers, it is not surprising that there was more campaigning than fighting and that armies did not aim at each other's destruction except on crucial occasions. Usually the aim was to take prisoners for ransom and to occupy vital portions of the enemy's country. Whether at home or abroad, soldiers were a scourge to the countryside. At best, they lived at the expense of the inhabitants; at worst, they looted, raped, and destroyed. If the officers of mercenary troops were to stay, so to speak, "in business", they had to find their troops quarters and provisions and allow them certain liberties. Parts of Germany were so devastated by the passage of armies that the peasants were reduced to eating grass and the bark from trees. Life at times fell below the level of civilized existence, and wolves roamed. City life and trade in Germany were disrupted. Production fell off, and what had once been a flourishing culture of burghers and peasants became economically and culturally backward in comparison with Western Europe.

Germany's declining condition from the mid-seventeenth to the nineteenth century is an important part of Europe's story. But it would be a mistake to overdramatize the part played by the Thirty Years War. For all the tremendous damage done, certain qualifications must be made. All of Central Europe was handicapped economically in comparison with the West once the commercial revolution had shifted the trade centers to the Atlantic seaboard (see Chapter 2); this relative decline, with all that it implied for bourgeois culture and town activity, had already set in before the Thirty Years War began. Secondly, while the war was long, it was intermittent, and the armies were not everywhere at once. While some cities were being ransacked, others were prospering. Money and people disappeared from some regions to turn up in others. It used to be thought that the population of Germany fell from sixteen to about four millions, or about 75 percent, but it is probable that it was greater to begin with, perhaps twenty-one millions, and fell by only about 30 percent.

The Thirty Years War, coming on the heels of the commercial revolution and Germany's failure to share in the proceeds of overseas expansion, helped to harden the distinctions between classes in Germany. The peasantry, at first somewhat benefited by the drop in population, soon fell more than ever under the domination of the nobility. The Emperor's failure to dominate the Holy Roman Empire was equivalent to a victory for the princes and their courtiers in the many parts of Germany. Instead of one despot, far away, there were hundreds close at hand, and against them the peasantry was powerless. The townsmen, who with better luck might have developed a certain independence through wealth, were reduced to dependence as officials of the many little states. The sense of German nationality, which had been strong in Luther's time, was almost smothered in the atmosphere of provincialism. National art and culture declined. Art became identified with the courts of the many little princes who, in the following century, mimicked French culture. Thus, paradoxically, out of provincialism there developed for the upper classes a cosmopolitan culture out of touch with the majority of Germans. These hundreds of little rulers with their little courts, armies, and bureaucracies, and in time their miniature mercantilisms, became a picturesque burden which weighed heavily upon the German people. Their story, a tale of duplication of the costs and functions of government, will be told in a later chapter. It was one of the results of the Thirty Years War, along with Germany's part in the changed balance of power in Europe.

THE PEACE OF WESTPHALIA

The Thirty Years War dragged to an end amid bickerings over diplomatic formalities. Negotiations were begun as early as 1643. Eventually, in October, 1648, were concluded the Treaties of Westphalia, named after the district where the Emperor came to terms with the French, at the city of Münster, and with the Swedes, at Osnabrück.

The Westphalia Treaties were a landmark in European history. The Holy Roman Empire, which in the early stages of the Thirty Years War had seemed to be on the verge of unifying Germany and restoring all of it to Catholicism, achieved neither of these aims. In the rivalry between the Emperor and the princes, the princes were victorious: the Westphalia settlement recognized them as sovereigns in their own lands and competent to make treaties with each other and with foreign powers. Although in theory they were still restricted by a few obligations to the Empire, they were in practice independent rulers.

The Holy Roman Empire lived on in name until 1806, when the shock of Napoleon's power finally killed it. From the standpoint both of German constitutional history and of European international relations, 1648 marked its end more clearly than 1806. After 1648 the Habsburgs themselves paid more attention to the building of their dynastic holdings than they did to the Holy Roman Empire, now that they had failed to make it an effective state.

In its religious provisions the Peace of Westphalia confirmed this divisiveness. The authority of the rulers of the two hundred and more German states was increased by leaving in their hands the choice of the state religions. Germany remained divided between Protestants and Catholics. The main differences between Westphalia and Augsburg (1555) were that it was now possible to choose Calvinism as well as Lutheranism or Catholicism; and the date beyond which seizures of church lands were not recognized was set at 1624. Protestants and Catholics were to have equal representation in the imperial courts. Religious differences in northern and southern Germany helped make the Holy Roman Empire ineffective even as a confederation of states.

Territorially the Peace of Westphalia left the Habsburgs most of their lands but granted positive gains to their opponents. France, the coming great power in Europe, received most of Alsace and was confirmed in its possession (since 1552) of the frontier bishoprics and cities of Metz, Toul, and Verdun. Sweden received part of Pomerania (along the Baltic, at the mouth of the Oder River) and the Bishopric of Bremen at the mouth of the Elbe. Sweden had been a power to reckon with in the Thirty Years War, and would still be from time to time, but the future in north Germany belonged to others, and Sweden would not be able to hold these territories. Brandenburg, whose destinies had come into the capable hands of the Hohenzollern Frederick William, known as the Great Elector (1640–1688), received part of Pomerania and several bishoprics. The Palatinate was divided between Bavaria, where old Maximilian (1597–1651) was still in office, and the son of Elector Frederick the "winter king." Maximilian now became an Elector too. Switzerland and the United Netherlands were recognized as independent of the Holy Roman Empire. The southern, or Belgian, provinces of the Netherlands still belonged to Spain. Spain continued to fight France until 1659, when, by the Treaty of the Pyrenees, France received Roussillon (eastern end of Pyrenees) and several towns on the Belgian border. A Spanish princess was to marry Louis XIV, bringing with her a dowry but renouncing all claims to the Spanish throne. This marriage was to provide the French with future justifications for expansion.

France's emergence as the greatest continental power; Spain's decline; the turning of Austrian interests elsewhere; Dutch and Swiss independence; Sweden's temporary success; the hints of Hohenzollern ambition; these were all part of the changed international picture in 1648. But the most important single fact was the absence of a Germany able to act as a state. The many German princes might congratulate themselves after 1648 on their emergence as genuine rulers. The "German liberties" had been preserved, even extended. But, with the exception of Austria, the German states were too weak individually to act as great powers, and they were utterly incapable of working together. To complicate matters, Sweden and above all France were "German" powers by virtue of their possessions there, and were guarantors of the Westphalia settlement. This settlement—and the disunity of Germany—became the main concern of French policy in Europe. The spectacle of France and Spain fighting their battles on German soil during the late stages of the Thirty Years War was open to repetition. There was no "Germany" to defend its own integrity. The complicated pattern which was Central Europe went on existing because of the European balance of power— because the European states would not permit each other to swallow each other.

The Peace of Westphalia is often viewed as marking an epoch in European history, on the grounds that the religious wars came to an end and that from this point forward the system of states maintaining a balance of power was mature. These generalizations are half-truths. They are easy to remember, and useful, but they should serve to open discussion, not to close it. The tendency called "balance of power" was in operation before 1618, and religious motives were always intertwined with others. To be sure, in the century and a half from Westphalia to the French Revolution of 1789, Europe's wars were to take on a more openly competitive and material character. New ideals and philosophies had not yet arisen to replace religion. The successor to religion as a source of personal passion and national policy was to be the sense of nationality. But in the eighteenth century it had as yet little influence on the making of policy. And the ideals of self-government which would one day be associated with the French Revolutionary wars were still not formulated in the minds of most people. For a time yet, after Westphalia, the springs of war and diplomacy were to be the ambition and the glory of autocrats. Philosophers were to fashion a system extolling them, but the struggles in their name were fought without the passion which had inspirited the age of religious conflict or which was, after 1789, to inspirit the age of conflict over national aspirations and ideals of human freedom.

10

EAST CENTRAL EUROPE

We have been looking at Central Europe, and in the following chapter we shall go east into Russian history. What we are concerned with now is an area neither "central" nor "eastern" but between the two, a broad isthmus from the Baltic to the Black and Aegean seas. This is a region where complexity is the rule in human affairs, where since ancient times civilizations have clashed and intermingled. Western Europeans and Americans have had an understandable vagueness about its peoples and their role in European history.

THE PLACE AND ITS REPUTATION

East Central Europe is not very complicated physically. A convenient introduction to its topography is to find the Sudeten and Carpathian Mountains, then the long Danube river valley, then the Balkan mountains. East Central Europe may then be remembered as having three subregions: a Baltic section which is really part of the great plain of Northern Europe and Russia; the Danube valley, which is a kind of termination of the steppes of southern Russia; and the Balkan peninsula, a slice of the hilly Mediterranean world.

It is easy to see how both the Danube valley and the North European plain lent themselves to movements of migration and conquest in either direction. One passage is the Iron Gate, where the Danube passes between the Transylvanian Alps and the Balkan mountains; but there are other river valleys through the

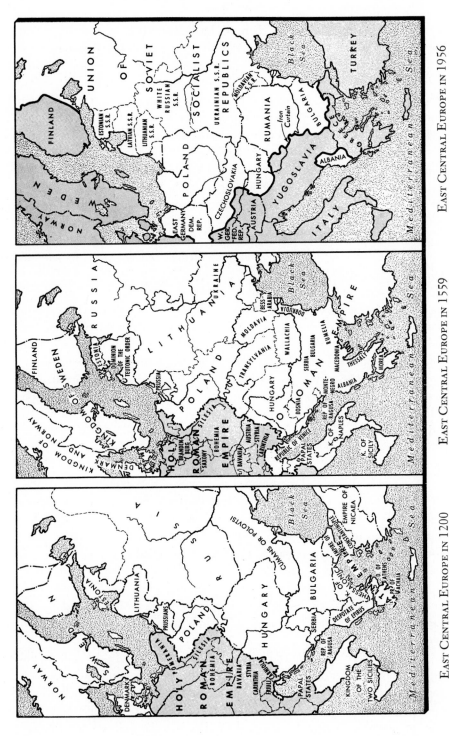

EAST CENTRAL EUROPE IN 1200   EAST CENTRAL EUROPE IN 1559   EAST CENTRAL EUROPE IN 1956

Balkans, suggesting how small a barrier these mountains have been to passage between Central Europe and Asia.

But the metaphor may be changed. East Central Europe has also at times been a shield for Western and Central Europe against eastern invaders, a fact which has weighed heavily on the peoples of the area, who had to bear the brunt of invasions. This has much to do with their poverty and with the undeveloped economy which has for a long time shown a strong contrast with that of Western Europe. The connection between the terrain, the wars, and the poverty of this region—and, as we shall see, its mixture of nationalities—is not always appreciated. The area is too often described as a "trouble spot," "tinder box," or "powder keg." Many people in the west carelessly blamed World War I on something called "Balkan politics." Most of Hitler's early triumphs took place here, including the attack on Poland. Six years later Russian armies had replaced the German. Actually most of the historic contestants in these lands have been outsiders. Residents of the area have seldom decided its fate. They have often tried to do so, but the odds have been against them; and some of their reputation for ferocity and political incapacity is the result of this fact.

The large number of nationalities in East Central Europe is its outstanding characteristic and is related to most of the area's other problems. As an introduction to their tangled stories, something may be said about the elbowing back and forth of peoples in the region between the Baltic and Aegean seas. Germanic peoples of Central Europe and the Slavs of Eastern Europe have been in competition since ancient times. No simple division of East Central Europe between Germans and Slavs was possible, for several reasons. There were other peoples in the area, such as the Finns in the north, the Greeks and Illyrians in the south, and the Dacians on the site of present-day Rumania. Secondly, the area was not left to the contention of Germans and Slavs, but invaded time and again from across the steppes out of Asia.

These invasions of nomadic cavalry accompanied by families and livestock are hard to explain. Often a people overpoweringly fierce to Europeans—the Magyars, for instance—were forced westward across the plains by pressure from a still more menacing group—in this example the Petchenegs. The original source of the difficulty lay in population or climatic conditions in Asia which sent nomadic peoples farther afield than usual and set them bumping into each other all the way across the grassy track into the Danube valley. From ancient times through the Middle Ages these Asiatic invaders beat like waves at East Central Europe, forced apart the Germanic and Slavic peoples, and left residues of their own groups.

But that is not yet the whole story. The rise and fall of principalities during these migrations and conflicts, especially in the Danubian and Balkan regions, tended to keep alive the multiplicity of nationalities. With greater stability, the lesser peoples might have been assimilated and East Central Europe might have come to resemble Western Europe. Instead, when the political map became simplified it was through the creation of multinational empires whose rulers cast their systems of government indifferently over all peoples, or actually encouraged diversity out of regard for the precept: *divide and rule.*

BACKGROUND OF MODERN HISTORY

In illustration of what has thus far been said about the entrance of nationalities upon the geographical scene, it is necessary to chart a few specific events.

Before the Year 500 A.D.

The frontier of the Roman empire lay along the Rhine and Danube rivers. The Romans had a vague knowledge of various peoples beyond this frontier, Germans and Slavs, for example. North of the Black sea the Greeks had planted a few trading settlements, and by its western shore in what is now Rumania the Romans ruled the province of Dacia.

In some of the most famous migrations the Germanic Goths of the second and third centuries A.D. moved southeast from the Vistula to the shores of the Black Sea. In the fourth and fifth centuries the Huns came across the steppes from Asia, pushed the Goths west (some of them into the Roman Empire), and themselves raided as far west as France. Their leader Attila, who died in 453, spent some of his last years in the Danube Valley; hence the name Hungary.

It is now generally agreed that the original European home of the Slavs was north of the Carpathians, but no certain evidence concerning their life on that site exists. The Slavs, in this period before 500 A.D., began moving in three directions: the Western Slavs along the Vistula, Elbe, and Oder rivers; the Eastern Slavs toward the Dnieper; the Southern Slavs toward the Adriatic Sea.

From 500 to 1000 A.D.

During this period Slavs and Germans were rivals in the Baltic, Danubian, and Balkan regions. Charlemagne, who revived the western half of the Roman empire and was crowned Emperor in the year 800, campaigned against the Slavs along the Elbe and Danube. Beginning in at least the sixth century, groups of Western and Southern Slavs were becoming differentiated. Some of the Western Slavs formed the independent Kingdom of Poland and the Dukedom, later Kingdom, of Bohemia, which at most times recognized the overlordship of the Holy Roman Emperor. In the late ninth century the Asiatic Magyars captured the Hungarian plain and separated the Western and Southern Slavs from each other.

Meanwhile the Byzantine empire, eastern half of the original Roman empire, had been hard-pressed—by the Arabs (Saracens) of the seventh and eighth centuries, for example. It was unable to bar the Balkan peninsula to various tribes of Southern Slavs, ancestors of the present-day Serbs, Croats, Slovenes, and Bulgarians. The original Bulgars were Asiatic nomads who by the eighth century conquered some of the Southern Slavs and were absorbed by them. The Kingdom of Hungary and the non-Slavic former Roman province of Dacia (think of present-day Rumania) cut off the Western from the Southern Slavs.

The Eastern Slavs, ancestors of the present-day Russians, had pushed northeast along the Russian rivers and among the Finns and Lithuanians of the northern forest zone. They were ruled by various conquerors from the steppes but learned to trade with Byzantium. In the ninth century, with the help of Norse soldier-traders, a state was formed. We shall say more about Russian history in the next chapter.

From 1000 to 1500 A.D.

Many of the events of this momentous era have a place in world history. It is convenient to think of one theme in particular. As Byzantine power in southeastern Europe declined, there appeared for a brief moment independent or autonomous Bulgarian, Serbian, Croatian, Greek, and Albanian political organizations, doomed to later submersion in the advancing Ottoman Empire which took over from Byzantium.

In this period Asiatic pressure of the old kind eased for a time, although the Kievan state in Russia, which was something of a barrier, was never able to control the steppes all the way to the Black Sea, and in the eleventh and twelfth centuries dangerous nomads were still active there. Moreover, the Seljuk Turks in the eleventh century threatened Byzantium and called forth a European reply in the Crusades, which began in 1095. Carrying on where the Seljuks had left off, the Ottoman Turks in the fourteenth century began seizing the Balkan peninsula and encircling Constantinople, which fell to them in 1453, bringing an end to the long history of the Eastern Roman empire. In the next seventy years the Ottomans completed the conquest of most of southeastern Europe.

During this whole eventful period, East Central Europe was also under pressure from the reviving West. In the thirteenth century the Venetians, in the Fourth Crusade, took Constantinople. As life became more stable in Central Europe, and German trade, cities, and population grew, the Germans renewed their push toward the east. From this period (twelfth to mid-fourteenth centuries) dates the difference between cultured and relatively free western Germany, and the despotic, frontier-like eastern parts. Austria was Germanized (Austria is the Latin for *Osterreich*, which in turn is German for "eastern realm") and the Teutonic Knights obtained lands in Pomerania (the Slavic *Pomorze*, meaning land along the sea, or the Baltic) and Prussia. Moreover Germans settled in Poland, Bohemia, and Transylvania.

Thus East Central Europe was under pressure from both sides, east and west. There was also, however, a difference between north and south, for as will be seen in a moment, Poland was developing into a great independent power.

CULTURAL FRONTIERS

East Central Europe at the end of the fifteenth century found itself heir to several conflicting traditions. In the first place the Christian church, like the Roman empire, had split into two parts. Although the final break did not come until 1054, there were at Rome and Constantinople by the ninth century competing centers of religious belief and organization. It was the fate of East Central

Europe to be divided in loyalty between the Roman Catholic (Latin) and Eastern (Greek) Orthodox confessions.

The Western Slavs (Poles, Czechs, Slovaks) were cut off from ready communication with Constantinople by the Magyar thrust into Hungary. They were thus more easily influenced by neighboring Germans to become Roman Catholics, using the Latin alphabet and falling under the influence of Western European culture. In time the Hungarians themselves became Roman Catholic, as did those South Slavs (Croats, Slovenes) who had contacts with Italy by way of the Adriatic. Of the other South Slavs, the Bulgarians were converted to Orthodoxy in the ninth century, and the Serbs by the twelfth. The Cyrillic alphabet was developed to record the sounds of Slavonic languages by the Greek missionary St. Cyril (d. 869), and was adopted by the Bulgarians, Serbs, and Russians. The Rumanians became Greek Orthodox but kept the Latin alphabet.

Generally speaking, this division within Christianity meant that educated people were subject to two different kinds of training. In the Greek Orthodox world the imperial tradition combined the offices of pope and emperor, so that supremacy over both church and state fell to the emperor. Roman Catholic tradition was different, distinguishing between "secular" and "priestly" authority. There were many other differences of outlook between the Byzantine and Roman traditions. The Greek and Roman halves of the ancient world had always had different characters, and as the Greek half slipped toward ultimate conquest by the Ottoman turks, and the Roman half participated in the development of young Europe, they grew further apart. After the fall of Constantinople, the shifting of Eastern Orthodox leadership into raw Muscovite Russia accentuated these differences. The presence of numerous Jews in Eastern Europe, and the Turkish conquest of the Southeast, which spread Islam, further complicated the religious picture; so did the founding of the Uniate, or "Greek Catholic" Church and the coming of Protestantism to East Central Europe, events which will be described later.

Besides the east-west division, this region of Europe inherited another, a north-south division, for some territories had been within the Roman empire and some had not. The former had a tradition of imperial authority, and also, in places, a superiority associated with having been for a long time part of the highly developed Mediterranean civilization. On the other hand, association with Danubian "Central Europe" rather than with the Turk-dominated Balkans came in time to imply superiority in the minds of such peoples as, for example, the Croats and Slovenes. And as medieval Europe developed, the Catholic states of Poland, Bohemia, and Hungary shared its cultural gains.

POLITICAL DIVISIONS BEFORE 1648

East Central Europe in the first century and a half of modern times was ruled by three multinational empires. In the southeast the Ottoman Empire poured over the peoples of the Balkans and Danube valley like a flood. Also at the height of its extent and splendor was the vast kingdom of Poland-Lithuania, whose territories reached from the Baltic to the Black Sea and from the Vistula to well beyond the Dnieper. The third empire was the dynastic state of the Habsburgs, whose inheritance of Hungary and Bohemia brought them into close and lasting contact with the affairs of East Central Europe. Russia by now was at last free of the Mongols, but it was still an inland country, cut off from the Black Sea by the Tartars in the Crimean peninsula, whose state became a satellite of the Ottoman Empire. In the far north, Finland was in the possession of Sweden, and the Baltic coastline was contested among Sweden, Denmark, and Poland. Russia lay in these years on the outer edge of European politics; but the other three empires were intricately and vitally involved in them.

THE OTTOMAN EXPANSION

The Ottoman Empire was a military despotism based on conquest. Since the Turks numerically and culturally were inferior to the peoples they conquered, their accomplishments seem all the more remarkable; like an army in occupied territory, they set up an administration, collected taxes, recruited soldiers, and made use of the knowledge, techniques, and labor of their subjects. Able soldiers from the first, they long maintained superiority by their readinesss to use muskets and artillery in quantity. On the sea they used galleys of the best construction. Not very technically minded themselves, they employed a cosmopolitan host of shipbuilders, metalworkers, gunsmiths, cartographers, and weavers. They captured or bought administrative and military talent as well as materials. The most famous of their institutions was the elite military force, the Janissaries, recruited every five years as a kind of human tax, by which Christians were required to contribute one in five of their sons, who were then brought up in the Moslem religion and trained as professional soldiers, forbidden to marry or to engage in commerce but otherwise well rewarded for their service.

Over their vast conquests the Turks threw an administrative network designed not to assimilate or convert but to keep order and supply the army, the fleets, and the treasury. At the top was the Sultan, a commander in chief chosen by the army from within the Osman (or Othman, or Ottoman) family. He was holder of all the titles of his conquered foes, including those of the last Arab caliph (the successor to Mohammed, a sort of Moslem pope) and of the Byzantine emperor (the successor, it could be claimed, to the emperors of Rome and Constantinople). He was both a political and a religious leader, outside and above the law, who could execute his own relatives for reasons of state. And he was the richest ruler in Europe, estimated to have twice the income of Charles V. This revenue came from taxes on the incomes of Moslems, head taxes paid by infidels, land taxes paid by everyone, tariffs, fines, tribute, and war booty. The beys and pashas who governed the provinces, or sandjacs, of the empire, were given a free hand provided they kept order and furnished their quotas of revenue and soldiers. Under them were many who held fiefs in return for various services to the state. This system permitted a minority of conquerors, by rewarding dependent agents, to govern a heterogeneous and expanding territory. Many of the generals and grand viziers (ministers) were refugee foreigners or converted captives.

By-passing Constantinople, the Turks had landed in Europe in the fourteenth century and begun to subjugate those South Slav states which had appeared as the power of Byzantium ebbed. In 1389 at the Battle of Kosovo they defeated the Serbian army, and four years later they captured the capital of Bulgaria. In the following century they were held off for a time by the Hungarians, but Constantinople fell in 1453 and the Ottoman armies went on to complete the conquest of Southeastern Europe. They reached the height of their power under Suleiman the Magnificent (1520–1566), with a right flank in Moldavia and Wallachia (present-day Rumania) and a left extended by way of Syria, Egypt, and North Africa as far as Tunis, and with sea power sufficient to sweep the Mediterranean and raid commerce as far as Spain. Suleiman, after taking Belgrade, the Serb capital, in 1521, advanced on the Danube to Mohács, where his artillery proved too much for the armies of Hungary and Bohemia. And then, in one of the most frightening moments in the history of Christian Europe, the Turks besieged Vienna in 1529, and sent cavalry up the Danube, as far as Ratisbon in present-day Germany. But they had reached the limits of their expansion, although they remained an endemic threat and laid siege to Vienna as late as 1683. Suleiman took Buda, the capital of Hungary, together with most of the country.

The success of the Turks resulted in part from divisions among the Christians. In the Balkans, the Rumanian provinces, and Hungary there were many peasants whose resentments against seigneurial dues, particularly labor dues, led them to welcome a change of masters. The European states failed to make a common stand against the Ottoman advances. Francis I of France and his successors used a Turkish alliance in their struggle to balance the power of the Habsburgs. Ferdinand of Habsburg, who had to help his brother Emperor Charles V against France and against the Protestants, appeased and paid tribute to the Sultan. Even the Hungarians were divided between those who accepted the leadership of the Habsburgs against the Turks, and those who wanted to drive out both Turks and Habsburgs with the help of the Poles. On the other hand, Europe doubtless benefited from divisions within the Islamic world, particularly the incessant territorial and religious conflicts between the Ottoman Empire and Persia.

The Turks in Southeastern Europe garrisoned the strategic passes and towns and ruled either through their own bureaucracy, as in Serbia, Bulgaria, and Hungary, or through autonomous tribute-paying princes, as in Transylvania, Moldavia, and Wallachia. In its period of greatness the Ottoman Empire had an efficient administration and showed considerable tolerance. Except for the former aristocrats, who were killed, exiled, or converted, the peoples of the Balkan peninsula did not find their lives greatly changed, particularly since they were now well behind the battle lines. The atmosphere of the Ottoman Empire was cosmopolitan and tolerant, in sharp contrast to that of Western Europe.

Hungary, however, became a frontier where both Habsburg and Turk taxed heavily in support of military operations. Matters other than the military were neglected. Buda (now Budapest), once a center of culture, was largely destroyed. In the long run, moreover, the parts of Southeastern Europe which remained under Turkish rule suffered not only the exploitation of a declining and increasingly corrupt officialdom but also the terrible loss of not keeping up with the rest of Europe. The Turks contributed little in the way of innovations, and when they were driven out in the nineteenth century they left behind peasant countries in varying degrees of poverty and ignorance.

HUNGARY AND BOHEMIA

The Habsburgs, about whose interests in Spain and the Holy Roman Empire we have already spoken, were not primarily interested in East Central Europe in the sixteenth and first half of the seventeenth centuries. During that period they were still vainly seeking to build, if not a European empire, at least a German one.

But they already had a foothold in East Central Europe. At the Battle of Mohács in 1526, Louis Jagiello, king of Hungary and Bohemia, was killed by the Turks. He was the brother-in-law of Ferdinand of Austria, brother of Emperor Charles V. By extraordinary good fortune the Habsburgs thus inherited the crowns of Hungary and Bohemia, and after 1648 they were to turn more and more in this direction.

Until that time their interest in the region was of necessity mainly directed to defense against the Turks, who occupied two thirds of Hungary, threatened Bohemia, and occasionally menaced Germany itself. Meanwhile they rivaled in power and glory not only the Turks, but also the Jagiello dynasty which ruled Poland-Lithuania. Habsburgs and Jagiellos were, like the Ottomans, state-builders and collectors of regions and peoples. Both were Catholic, and both had problems with religious minorities. But while the Habsburgs were moving in the direction of absolutism and centralization, the Jagiellos were successful, though decreasingly so, in conducting a representative government with constitutional guarantees jealously guarded by the nobility.

In the period with which we are dealing, the Habsburg program of empire-building, centralization, and religious uniformity was only partly successful in Hungary and Bohemia. Ferdinand of Austria was elected King of Hungary by one group of Hungarian gentry, while another favored a native Hungarian, John Zápolya, the leading noble of Transylvania. The Zápolya group fought a civil war against the supporters of the Habsburgs, whom they accused of importing centralized absolutism and German culture. Zápolya allied with the Turks, and had the sympathy of the Jagiello King Sigismund I of Poland (1506–1548), who had been unable to oppose Ferdinand's succession in Hungary. So Hungary, besides the Turkish and Habsburg portions, consisted of a third part, the Transylvanian territory inside the mountainous hook of the Carpathians and Transylvanian Alps. For the moment this area was under Turkish suzerainty, but autonomous, and would have liked to expel both Turks and Habsburgs from Hungary. Habsburg Hungary remained a narrow military frontier and no true test of the dynasty's capacity for constructing a strong, monarchical state. The self-governing tradition of the Hungarian Diet persisted, although damaged by its inability any longer to represent the whole Hungarian people.

Bohemia, where Ferdinand of Austria was elected by the gentry without opposition, was an ancient outpost of the Western Slavs, who here made up a distinctive nationality called Czech. It had long been associated with the Germans as part of the Holy Roman Empire. Many Germans settled there in the late Middle Ages, and by 1500 about a third of the Bohemians were German. There were anti-German feelings among the Czechs. The Hussite rebellion of the 15th century, following the execution of the religious reformer John Hus (1415), was a Czech national as well as a religious movement.

But with the election of Ferdinand of Austria in 1526, Bohemia entered upon nearly a century of comparative calm. The Hussite tradition was still alive, and during the Reformation Lutheranism grew. The Bohemian Estates opposed use of their troops against the Protestant princes of Germany. In spite of a certain amount of pressure from the Habsburg kings, political autonomy and religious freedom remained in Bohemia until the seventeenth century.

Tension mounted in the reign of the Emperor Mathias (1612–1619) and burst forth in 1618 in the opening clashes of the Thirty Years War. As we have seen, that war gathered together all the themes of European history in the first half of the seventeenth century. The Czech part in it was disastrous; their deposition of Mathias's successor, Ferdinand II, in the name of state-rights and religious freedom led to their defeat in the Battle of the White Mountain in 1620. In the repression which followed, the Czechs lost most of the rights of their Estates, Protestantism was outlawed, and the German language became official. Worse still, the Czechs lost their native leaders, for the Czech aristocracy was displaced by execution or exile and their property was used to endow a new ruling group of loyal and Catholic Habsburg supporters, cosmopolitan in point of view but for the most part German in culture. Bohemia, besides suffering the devastations of the Thirty Years War, was linked more tightly to the Hapsburgs and to the politics of Central Europe.

POLAND–LITHUANIA

Poland was having its golden age. The Kingdom of Poland and the Grand Duchy of Lithuania had been joined in 1386 by the marriage of a Polish queen, Jadwiga, to the Grand Duke of Lithuania, Jagiello, and by their marriage contract Jagiello and the Lithuanians became Christians. The dynastic connection was eventually expanded into a federation, with one bicameral diet of Senators and Deputies. The crown remained elective, and the Kingdom and Grand Duchy retained their separate, though similar, treasuries, law codes, and administrations. It was a tremendous country, able to maintain suzerainty over the Baltic lands of the Teutonic Order—Prussia and Livonia—when they were secularized and able to hold Muscovite Russia at bay beyond the Düna and the Dnieper. At times Poland counted the Black Sea principalities of the Crimea and Moldavia (in present-day Rumania) in its sphere of influence. At the height of its dynastic good fortune it succeeded in placing Jagellonian relatives on the thrones of Bohemia and Hungary. These last four regions, as we have seen, were lost by the time of the Thirty Years War, but Poland-Lithuania remained strong through the whole early modern period. After Westphalia it was to survive for another century, but would in its turn weaken, like the Ottoman and Holy Roman empires.

What held so large and diffuse a state as Poland-Lithuania together for so long, no one can with certainty say. We can at least try to avoid the common mistake of assuming that because it later disintegrated we need do nothing but search for weaknesses. Poland-Lithuania of early modern times was an elective monarchy whose ruler's powers were limted by a flourishing aristocracy of great landowners. There were many occasions when the *szlachta,* or nobles, had set the conditions of government. In the fifteenth century (c. 1404) regional dietines (assemblies) were established. In 1430 the elective character of the monarchy and the rights and privileges of the nobles were affirmed, one of the latter being that no one would be imprisoned without trial. In time the lawmaking powers of both the local dietines and the diet (Sejm) were confirmed. It was clearly established that "nothing new" would be decreed without the consent of both of the diet's chambers, the Senate grown out of the King's Council, and the Chamber of Deputies chosen by the local dietines. It is clear that Poland, like other monarchies emerging from the Middle Ages, experimented with institutions of self-government.

In the sixteenth and seventeenth centuries, in spite of repeated concessions to the *szlachta,* the kings were able to maintain their authority amid public support. It was a time when town life and commerce still flourished in Eastern Europe. The West, although winning an economic lead, particularly in overseas trade, was not as far ahead of Central and Eastern Europe as it was to be by the late seventeenth and eighteenth centuries. Moreover Poland-Lithuania, through its cultivated upper classes, shared in the artistic and intellectual experiences of the Renaissance, carrying them across the whole of East Central Europe. Unlike Hungary and Bohemia, it did not experience the disasters of the Ottoman conquest and the Thirty Years War. It would be unrealistic to forget the deep gulf between the aristocracy and the peasant majority, but clearly the political structure of the commonwealth was reinforced by a sense of community in the upper classes.

In religion the Poles and Lithuanians were Roman Catholics, while the large number of Ukrainians and White Russians (Byelorussians) in the realm were Eastern Orthodox.[1]

The Polish-Lithuanian government never stopped hoping to win the Ukrainians and White Russians for Rome (or at least away from the Great Russians). In 1439, when the position of the Byzantine Empire had become desperate because of the Turks, there had been held a Council of Florence at which representatives of the Eastern (Greek) Orthodox Church agreed to reunion with the Roman Catholic. This reunion was rejected by Basil II of Moscow, who in 1448 appointed another Metropolitan, cutting the ties to Constantinople. The Orthodox within Poland-Lithuania came to recognize this Metropolitan of Moscow as their leader, and the government of Poland-Lithuania acquiesced. After 1453, with Constantinople and its Greek Orthodox Church in the hands of the Turks, another attempt was made in 1596 to bring about "union" of the Orthodox White Russians and Ukrainians with Rome. This time some of the Orthodox were won over to a "Uniate" Church admitting Papal supremacy and Catholic doctrine but keeping the Eastern rites. Formation of the Uniate Church split the White Russians and Ukrainians[2] and aroused the hostility of Moscow and Constantinople. In the long run it was to contribute to the growth of Ukrainian nationalism, but this development belongs to a much later period.

In the sixteenth century Poland-Lithuania, like the rest of Europe, experienced the spread of Protestant doctrines in considerable variety. There was no repression. Catholicism was not forced on the people as it was to be in Bohemia during the Thirty Years War. But the Counter-Reformation had a high degree of spontaneity, and Catholicism, rather than Protestantism, was linked to national sentiment in the consciousness of the majority. Protestantism, to a large degree, died a natural death.

THE BALANCE OF POWER
IN EASTERN EUROPE

Poland-Lithuania in the period before Westphalia was not surrounded, as it was to be in the following century, by neighbors able to maintain greater military power by a superior organization of their resources. Indeed, it had amply demonstrated its ability to triumph over pressure from the outside. When the personal union of Poland and Lithuania took place in the fourteenth century there had already been for a century German penetration of the Baltic coastal

---

[1] That is, two of the three groups (Great Russians, Ukrainians, White Russians) usually called Eastern Slavs were in Poland-Lithuania at this time, leaving the third, the Great Russians, in the Muscovite state. The Ukrainians are sometimes called Little Russians. "Ukrainia" was originally applied to all frontier regions, but in time (by the nineteenth century) came to be used for this particular Dnieper frontier region.

[2] The split was to some extent on class lines, since the Uniate Church was more attractive to landlords than to the traditionalistic peasantry.

regions. There was a possibility that Poland, like Bohemia, might be brought into the Holy Roman Empire. Moreover, there were Tartar raids in the southeast, and from the east the Mongols and their growing vassal, the Moscow principality, provided further threats. Poland-Lithuania was able to resist these external pressures. In the east, Muscovite Russia in the sixteenth and early seventeenth centuries was gathering the Russian lands, and seemed a threat to expand into Lithuania and Livonia. But the Russian expansion, which will be described in the next chapter, had its cost in internal stress and strain. The Russian "time of troubles" between 1598 and 1613 saw so many internal disagreements that for a time the Polish king could intrigue for the Russian throne. Not until after the Thirty Years War was Russia again strong enough to menace Poland.

For Poland-Lithuania there was a dangerous moment when its line of Jagiello rulers came to an end in 1572. The monarchy was elective; with no more Jagiellos of the direct line to choose from, there was the possibility that a member of some other great European family might be seated on the throne of Poland-Lithuania, a development which would greatly alter the balance of power. Naturally the Habsburgs had their candidate, and even considered buying Russian support by the cession of Lithuania, thus anticipating the partitions of two centuries later. But in the sixteenth century Poland was not so easily disposed of, and indeed, the outcome of this affair is a good illustration of the diplomacy of balance of power. The Polish *szlachta* first chose Henry of Valois, of the anti-Habsburg ruling family of France. When Henry almost at once inherited the French crown, the Poles chose Anna, sister of the last Jagiello, and her husband Stefan Báhory (Batory in Poland), the anti-Habsburg ruler of Transylvania. Upon Batory's death without children in 1586 the Poles turned to a Swedish candidate of the House of Vasa, a move which promised continued Swedish-Polish cooperation against Russia in the Baltic. For Sweden, as the possessor of Finland, was anti-Russian. So as matters stood the problem of the Polish succession did not yet play into the hands of its neighbors. Although there were disagreements, the nobility of Poland-Lithuania were still able to make decisions which contributed to the survival of their country.

The other great military-diplomatic drive of the period we are covering was the advance of the Ottoman empire, already seen to have reached its height by the mid-seventeenth century. As a threat to Poland-Lithuania, the Ottoman expansion was most dangerous in the frontier region of the lower Dnieper, nowadays called the Ukraine. Here the troublemaker was the Khanate of the Crimea, which was under Turkish control. Polish rulers, vulnerable to raids into the Ukraine, were reluctant to oppose the Ottoman Empire openly, and meanwhile looked for ways to checkmate the Crimean Tartars.

For some time, in the dangerous lower Dnieper region, rough and ready communities of semi-independent Cossacks had been forming (*Kozack,* word of Turco-Tartar origin, meaning undisciplined person outside stable political organization). The Cossacks would have been extremely useful to Poland-Lithuania if they had been obedient; but they were reluctant to devote themselves to establishing a law and order which when successful would turn most of them into servile peasants. Thus while they sometimes raided the Crimea there were also occasions when they revolted against Poland, and there was always the possibility that with their Orthodox religion the Cossacks might decide to shift their loyalty and the area within their reach to the side of Muscovite Russia.

Apart from the crushing discipline administered to Bohemia, East Central Europe was relatively calm during the Thirty Years War. Catholic and Slav Poland was divided in sentiments concerning the Bohemian experience. Hungarian Protestants tried without success to help the Czechs and at the same time drive the Habsburgs from Hungary. France, which had long tried the diplomatic maneuver of persuading both Poles and Turks to fight simultaneously against the Habsburgs, did not succeed. Poland remained relatively disengaged and prosperous during the last years of the Thirty Years War. Its "time of troubles," and a great change in the balance of forces in Eastern Europe, were to come in the period after 1648.

11

STATE-BUILDING
IN MUSCOVY

THE YEARS from Columbus's first voyage to the end of the Thirty Years War almost coincide with the era when Muscovite Russia was built by Ivan the Great, Ivan the Terrible, and the first Romanovs, after the liberation from the Tartars. Russian independence may be dated from the year 1480, when Russian and Tartar armies faced each other across the river Ugra and the Tartars turned away without fighting. At the end of the era, the year 1682 was the first in the reign of Peter the Great, with whom the history of Imperial Russia is usually said to begin. The use of measures such as these—a battle which was not fought, and the inheritance by a ten-year-old boy of half a throne (for Peter was at first only co-czar)—shows what a game it is, after all, to periodize history. Yet the game has its rewards. It is convenient to know that during the European Middle Ages there was a surprisingly commercial and free Russian society whose capital was at Kiev, in what would later be called the Ukraine. It is useful to reflect that while Western Europe was being inspired by the Renaissance, Kievan Russia had fallen under the sway of Tartar (Mongol) conquerors from Asia. The "Muscovite" period after the liberation from the Tartars suggests the leadership of the Moscow princes. Behind the term "Imperial" usually applied to Russia from the last years of Peter the Great to the Revolution of 1917 lies the fact that Russian history was then more closely interwoven with European; symbolic of the change was Peter's wish to parade, as Emperor, in western military uniform instead of in the priestly robes of the Orthodox Czar. Crude though they are, the conventional periods serve as a useful introduction to the study of Russian history. These early centuries witnessed the birth, in lands and climate remote from the west, of the state and the traditions which in the twentieth century were to throw long shadows over the entire world.

EARLIEST TIMES AND THE
KIEVAN PERIOD

Russia derives its name from a very early period. No one has been able to prove whether the word "Rus" was Scandinavian or, as some say, Slav, but it is certain that the Norse trader-soldiers who traveled the rivers between Sweden and Constantinople were called Rus, Ros, or Rhos. It was they who, sometime before the legendary founding date 862, began to organize, rule, and defend the storehouse-fortresses which were the early Russian cities located on the trade routes—Kiev, Novgorod, Chernigov, Smolensk. According to legend the Slavs of Novgorod invited Scandinavians to govern and protect them. One Rurik came, with his brothers, and founded the dynasty from whose headquarters at Kiev most of the Russian cities were gathered into a state. It is more likely, however, that several Norse bands, after a century or more of intermittent conflicts and alliances with the Slavs, formed the Kievan state in response to danger from nomads of the steppes and in hopes of negotiating from strength with Constantinople. The Scandinavian manpower reservoir which dealt Europe so many blows in the ninth century also left its mark on Russia.

At a time when Western Europe was plagued by disorder and was building institutions later known as "medieval," and was reaching toward a certain level of security and well-being, Russia was doing the same. In the "Kievan" period (ninth to thirteenth centuries), there grew up a medieval Russia corresponding in time to Europe's "High Middle Ages" but with institutions of its own: Christian, like Europe, after 990, but separated from European culture by the Cyrillic alphabet and by the hostility of its Greek priests to Rome. The Kievan state was huge, though sparsely populated. In the eleventh century it covered a wide swath from the Baltic almost to the Black Sea and from the Upper Volga to the Carpathians and almost to the Vistula. Much of what later became Poland-Lithuania was in its sphere, origin of many future arguments among Russians, Ukranians, and Poles.

In its society and government the Kievan state was not like medieval Europe. It was founded on trade and cities and was more like a federation of city-states than like feudal Europe. Each prince lived in the chief town of his territory and, with his warrior companions (*druzhina*), engaged in commerce as well as in war. Only toward the end of the period—when Western and Central Europe were building up their cities, commerce, and money economy—did a decline in trade and monetary circulation turn the attention of Russian princes and their most successful servitors (*boyare*, in English: boyars) to possession and exploitation of the land. Thus Europe and Russia were moving in opposite directions, and this symmetry is to some extent understandable in terms of a shift in the channels of international trade. Commerce eventually dried up in the south, owing both to nomadic raids and to the weakening of Constantinople. Population began shifting to the northeast. The Russian state was far along in provincial self-sufficiency when it was overrun by the Tartars between 1236 and 1240, the year the city of Kiev was taken.

THE TARTAR DOMINATION

The Tartars were a branch of Mongolian tribesmen who had united in Central Asia in the early thirteenth century and, under Genghis Khan, had conquered North China and Turkestan. The Tartars cut several paths of destruction across Russia and briefly terrorized Central Europe before establishing a capital at Sarai, near the big bend of the lower Volga. Batu, their leader, was the grandson of Genghis Khan. He had inherited the right to conquer all lands between the Urals and the Dnieper. With him came his people, with wagons, women and children, and livestock, and settled in the southeast. Thus the area which we today would call European Russia came to be divided into three main parts: (1) the Khanate of the Golden Horde, Batu's empire in the southeast, nom-

CATHEDRAL OF SANCTA SOPHIA, NOVGOROD. Built 1045–1052.

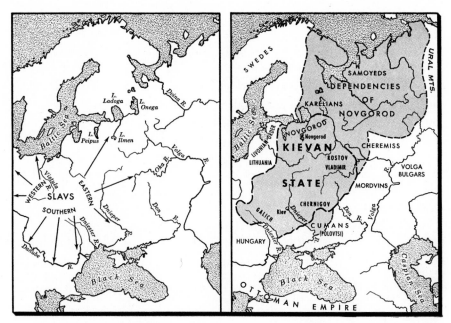

EARLY MOVEMENTS
OF THE SLAVS

THE KIEVAN STATE,
11TH TO MID-13TH CENTURY

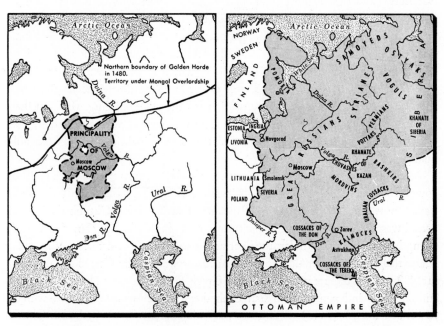

EXPANSION OF MOSCOW
PRINCIPALITY TO 1462

EXPANSION OF MUSCOVY
TO 1682

inally dependent on the Great Khan; (2) a vast northwest territory of Russian principalities paying tribute to the Khan at Sarai and periodically disciplined by swift punitive raids; and (3) in the west and southwest, on both sides of the Dnieper and Niemen rivers, stretching from the Baltic to the Black Sea, the independent Grand Duchy of Lithuania.

Lithuania, as we saw in the last chapter, was in 1386 joined with Poland into one of the great states of early modern times. It comprised much of what was formerly Kievan Russia, including the capital, Kiev itself. With the disintegration of the Kievan state into competing principalities, many of the Russian princes of west Russia (later called White Russia or Byelorussia), and of southwest Russia (later called the Ukraine), chose or could not resist the overlordship of Lithuania. This was one of the effects of the Tartar conquest, but also of the Kievan weakening which was under way before the Tartars came.

The influence of the Golden Horde's two centuries of suzerainty and exploitation in northeastern Russia is one of the great debatable historical questions, but we may conclude that it was substantial, though in many ways indirect. The Tartars' main interest in their Russian principalities concerned tribute and taxes, both of which they learned could be collected with least friction through the agency of the Russian princes. Politically, this system had the effects of encouraging several tendencies already in train at the time of the conquest. It helped increase absolute power in the hands of the princes, who were legally and materially powerless against their master at Sarai but who could use both his authority and his troops against their subjects. For example, the town assemblies (*veche*), became powerless in this period except in the far North. The Khan's despotic regime also set a legal and intellectual example, and the Russian princes engaged in a fierce cutthroat competition in which some of them succumbed to others who were more ruthless and more clever in their subservience to the Khan. There could scarcely be better preparation for the state-building Machiavellianism of the Moscow rulers who emerged from this contest with the richest, most powerful, and most expanded of the Russian principalities. They were able, finally, to defy the Khan himself.

Not all of the direct and indirect effects of the Tartar period were political, however. Christianity, which in the Kievan period had reached mainly the upper classes, now spread to the mass of Russians. The Orthodox Church during this period was the only all-Russian institution, and, paradoxically, gained greatly in strength and enjoyed, under the Tartars, greater independence of the state's power than at any other time in Russian history. After the Council of Florence in 1439, which temporarily placed the Greek Orthodox Church under Roman authority, an independent Russian Orthodox Church was established with its center at Moscow (1448). Even after the independent Greek Orthodox Church was revived following the conquest of Constantinople in 1453, the Russians refused to subordinate their church to its former patriarch.

Socially the period of Tartar domination gave Russia a push away from the relatively free society of Kievan times toward a society with more clearly defined social classes bound by state service. The town assemblies and indeed town life itself declined. The Tartars did not cut Russia off completely from the outside world; they acted as middlemen, and goods from Greece, Persia, India, and Russia passed through their hands. In most of Russia, however, agriculture became more and more predominant—as it was to remain until the twentieth century. These conditions, amid many local wars, Tartar disciplinary raids, famines, forest fires, and the Black Death, characterized Russian life in the period of the Tartar conquest.

THE FORMATION OF THE MOSCOW STATE

In Russian history the period which most closely parallels early modern Europe is that span of two centuries between the Mongols and Peter the Great. It was a period named after the city of Moscow, the new political center of the northeast. It was a period characterized by the success of Moscow princes in swallowing their lesser relatives and neighbors and defeating all efforts within their own courts to check their growing autocracy. And it was a period in which national unity grew at great social cost and was inspired and justified by new political theories and a heightened sense of nationality. It is convenient to remember this Muscovite period as divided into two parts by the Time of Troubles (1598–1613), which was a kind of breakdown resulting from the over-rapid growth of the Russian state and the authority of its rulers.

IVAN THE GREAT (New York Public Library, Prints Division)

Four czars, two famous and two less well known, reigned between the Tartar period and the Time of Troubles. The first was Ivan III (the Great), who ruled from 1462 to 1505. He was a severe, cautious man, with the cruelty and occasional violence of the time and place, who worked hard and had a sense of his own position as ruler of a great power. He only occasionally used the title "czar," which in Russian meant an independent ruler of highest authority (corresponding to the western caesar or kaiser), like the Byzantine emperor or the Mongol khan. But Ivan III was well aware of his dignity under that definition. Ten years after becoming Grand Duke of Moscow, he had married Sophie Paleologue, niece of the last Byzantine emperor. She brought with her to Moscow artists and tastes of the Renaissance and also the vague but powerful implication that her husband was heir to Byzantine authority. He had, indeed, already one attribute of Byzantine sovereignty, for he was protector of the Orthodox Church.

The Tartar empire was by then breaking up into separate khanates, which gave Ivan III the chance to play one against the other. He defied the Golden Horde in 1480 and refused to pay tribute. During his reign he had dealings with Rome, Venice, the Hanseatic towns, Denmark, Hungary, and other powers. The existence of the Russian state began to be apprehended in European capitals.

Ivan III lived to the age of sixty-six, an unusually long life for that period, and had an eventful reign, but he is best remembered in three situations which have an important bearing on the history of Russia. One was the shipping to Moscow of the "liberty bell," which was symbol of the free asembly of Novgorod, dissolved by Ivan as he annexed that northern outpost of self-government. The czar's method is worth noting. Besides executing one hundred and fifty of the most prominent Novgorodian boyars, he transferred some eight thousand influential families to Muscovy, replacing them with an equal number of Muscovite families. By placing all these people in new surroundings and making their new holdings *conditional* on service to him, the czar forestalled the resistance of sixteen thousand potential rebels. Ivan III was the first Muscovite ruler to use on a large scale this system of conditional holdings (*pomestie*) of "service" nobles. By such means, he ended his career with all but one or two of his competitors reduced to subservience.

On another occasion, in 1501, Ivan III received an envoy from Lithuania. He sent word by this envoy that Lithuania would have to return all those Russian lands annexed in the fourteenth and early fifteenth centuries. This amounted to saying that he was successor to the early Kievan rulers. Ivan III warred intermittently with Poland-Lithuania from 1492 to 1503 but made slight gains. The clash of interests between Russia and Poland-Lithuania was to be an abiding element in the balance of power in Eastern Europe.

In 1503, on the eve of a meeting of the ecclesiastical council, the czar considered confiscating church properties in Muscovy, as he had done a few years before in Novgorod. In the Orthodox Church at that time there were two competing points of view, that of the mystical followers of one Nil Sorsky and certain other hermit monks in northern Russia, and that of the Josephites, followers of an abbot called Joseph of Volokolamsk. The attitude of Nil Sorsky's trans-Volga hermits was that religion was inward, salvation to be gained through inner regeneration, and persuasion the only way to combat error. The church needed to be left free, but did not need the government's forceful backing or great wealth of its own. This was a point of view of which Ivan III was prepared to take advantage by seizing church properties. But the Josephites proved so strong that he decided not to oppose their belief that the church, to oppose error and perform social services, needed both property and the support of the state. In return they were convinced that it was the church's duty to support the state. The victory of the Josephites in the Russian Church meant support for the ruler's autocracy by the clergy.

The reign of Ivan the Great's son Basil III (1505–1533) was important chiefly for its continuation of the tendencies exhibited by his father. He annexed the last principalities which had retained any independence, warred against sporadic Tartar raids, and succeeded in taking Smolensk from the Lithuanians. In both theory and fact his reign witnessed the strengthening of autocracy. Writings of the clergy developed a fantastic genealogy by which the House of Rurik was said to be descended from the Roman Emperor Augustus by way of a supposed brother Prussus, of Prussia, from which Rurik emigrated to Novgorod.

At this time also was spread the messianic philosophy of history which was to play so great a part in Russian thought under the watchword of "the Third Rome." The mission of the ruler and church of Moscow was declared to be nothing less than the preservation of Christian life in its true form; for the first Rome, and the second, Constantinople, had perished through heresy. The third Rome, a political-religious harmony, was to be the last. The astonishing events of the fifteenth century—the fall of Constantinople (1453) after its compromise with the Catholic Church at the Council of Florence (1439), the establishment of an independent Orthodox Church in Russia (1448)[1], the liberation from the Tartars (1480), and all the stimulating controversies associated with the rise of the Moscow State and the fall of Novgorod—all these had stirred Russian imaginations and led them to look for explanations satisfying to their quickened sense of nationality.

Basil III, proud of the celestial sources of his authority, accentuated the social and political measures of his father's long reign. In completing the subjugation of other principalities, he used the same system of "removals" and multiplied the properties conditional on service. Where his father had at least listened to the objections of the council (duma) of his great nobles, Basil III decided everything for himself and took vengeance on the least opposition. There was developing an ominous situation with respect to the boyars which was to cause difficulties in later reigns. In the old Russia of many principalities, each prince had had his important servitors, or boyars, who had become landholders. As the number of principalities declined in the Tartar and early Muscovite periods, more and more princes themselves became boyars to their more successful neighbors. The end of the process was the Moscow state, with one ruler, now czar, surrounded by an abundance of boyars, great and small, many of them from former princely families. The princely boyars had two serious grievances. (1)

[1] The Metropolitan of Moscow became Patriarch of the Russian Church in 1589.

They wished, through the czar's council, to participate in the management of the state. And (2) they were determined, in their service to the czar, not to lose caste to families of lesser renown. The former wish was denied by the increasing independence of the czar, though the *duma* still existed, and the term "boyar" was coming to be restricted to its membership. The pride of caste was clumsily satisfied by a system of "precedence" by which genealogical seniority prevailed in the filling of positions in the army and administration. There was a contradiction here, however, which would one day cause trouble. The interest of the czar was loyalty and efficiency, which required free choice of officials. The interest of the nobles was in hereditary rank.

IVAN THE TERRIBLE

After the death of Basil III in 1533 there began the most notorious reign in Russian history, that of Ivan IV, known as Ivan the Dread (Ivan Grozny in Russian, often called Ivan the Terrible in English). His reign, lasting half a century from 1533 to 1584, may be viewed in two ways—from the point of view of dramatic and frequently horrifying human drama, or from that of evolving Russian institutions. The latter will perhaps be clearer after the story of human conflict has been recounted.

Ivan IV is more understandable today, in this century of preoccupation with psychology, than he was in times past. He was only a child of three when his father died, and thereafter grew up in the midst of the rather anarchic regency shared by his mother and the quarreling factions of the boyar duma. When he was eight his mother died in suspicious circumstances, probably poisoned. Ivan IV spent the rest of his youth being treated with servility in public but bullied and robbed in private by the great boyars. Between times, he withdrew to rest his oversensitive nature in bouts of theological and historical reading. He grew into a neurotic, impetuous, artistic young man. At seventeen he put an end to the regency of the boyars, married Anastasia Romanov, and was crowned czar in the first such coronation ceremony in Russian history (1547).

The first years of his reign were fairly calm and successful. The Empress Anastasia was beautiful and intelligent and, more important, had a calming influence on her husband's powerful but erratic personality. Ivan with the help of level-headed advisors extended the system of military service fiefs, created a new standing army, the Streltsy (in Russian, shooters), and took over the khanates of Kazan and Astrakhan on the middle and lower Volga—eastward expansion was characteristic of this reign; at its very end Russians crossed the Urals into Siberia. Ivan also strengthened his ascendency over the boyars by planning his reforms in collaboration with a much broader body, a bicameral Assembly of the Land (*Zemsky Sobor*), which first met in 1550. The *Zemsky Sobor*, comprising representatives of gentry and merchants as well as the boyar duma, the highest bishops, and various other officials, approved a new law code and a new system of local administration.

Trade with the West was increasing through the efforts of English merchants, who discovered a northern route to Russia through the White Sea. Ivan and his advisors wanted further cultural and commercial dealings with Western Europe, but disagreed on the method. Some of the czar's councillors favored war on the Khanate of the Crimea, to end Tartar raids and open a way to the Black Sea, but Ivan preferred a drive to the shores of the Baltic, where the Livonian Knights, Poland, and Sweden were entrenched. He therefore invaded Livonia in 1558, touching off a long, unsuccessful war with Poland-Lithuania and Sweden, which proved superior to Russia in military techniques. Russia was not to have its "window" on the Baltic until the time of a later czar, but Ivan IV, having safeguarded his eastern frontier, opened the question.

CATHEDRAL OF ST. BASIL, Moscow. Begun during the reign of Ivan IV (the Terrible).

One of the reasons for this failure was the unsettled condition of Russian internal affairs, which among other things had the effect of increasing the agitation of Ivan IV's mind. He had always been suspicious of those around him, understandably so in view of his youthful experiences. Under the strain of war and disagreement with his advisors, and especially after his wife's death in 1560 (which he attributed to poisoning, like his mother's), he began to suffer from a conviction of persecution which was to darken the rest of his life. He was especially perturbed by fears that the great boyars were betraying him, and began to imprison or execute the generals who lost battles. One such, his former friend Prince Kurbsky, went over to the Lithuanians rather than be disgraced for a military defeat. There followed a remarkable exchange of letters in which Kurbsky defended the traditional boyar right to serve another prince, while Ivan stated the case for his own absolute right to obedience.

In 1564 the czar reached such heights of suspiciousness that he executed a drastic but carefully prepared blow designed to break once and for all the power of the boyars by means of a new political police called the *oprichnina*—literally, "separate household", in practice a whole new administration staffed by black-clad *oprichniki*. During a seven-year reign of terror the *oprichniki* administered the whole central and northern part of Russia, confiscated boyar estates, which were then distributed in return for loyalty and service, and carried out a large-scale purge of the boyars and their sympathizers, including the Metropolitan of the Russian Orthodox Church. The terror was finally ended in 1572 after the boyars had been enfeebled and internal disunity threatened the safety of the country.

The *oprichnina* of Ivan IV had a meaning which it would be easy to overlook if one saw only the theatrical side of the czar's macabre ceremonials and the pathological traits of his personality. In the process of winning and governing wide territories, the new Muscovite state had to pay a high price in men, money, and freedom. The actual process of Russian territorial expansion was aided by, and in turn aided, the early czars' efforts to curtail the liberties of the aristocracy and build an administration responsible to themselves alone. Ivan IV's twisted personality carried to excess a struggle between czar and boyars. With better luck it might have taken a less bloody course, but violence was an enduring characteristic of Russian political life down to the eighteenth century.

In the fight between the crown and the great nobles, the common people of Russia tended to remain neutral, for they had no special sympathy for the aristocracy. But they could not escape the influences of war and civil strife. Many did move south to the recently conquered territory of Kazan, or if they were really desperate, to the free Cossack communities on the lower Dnieper and Don. By one of the ironies of history this search for freedom brought about an early step in the rise of serfdom. The exodus from Central Russia caused a labor shortage which was especially threatening to the small "service" holdings upon which the czars were dependent for rewarding their officials and army officers. The larger patrimonial properties of the boyars were less dependent on free tenants, for they were of longer standing, and usually had slaves. In the face of complaints from the new "service nobles," the czar began to proclaim certain years "prohibited," which meant that peasants could not move in those years. The first of an increasing number of prohibited years was 1581. From the sixteenth century, therefore, as Western Europe was emerging from serfdom, the Russian peasantry was becoming attached to the land, and the land was being used by the state to reward the service nobles. This process, like the political alignment of czar and service nobles against the boyars, was to last until the eighteenth century.

Ivan IV after the death of his first wife married again six times without, however, finding another empress as beneficial to his disposition as Anastasia Romanov. If he could have persuaded Queen Elizabeth of England to yield one of her relatives he would have married yet again, but Elizabeth was politely noncommittal. Russian prestige in Europe had to get along without a Tudor alliance. Two years before his death, Ivan in a disorderly rage accidentally killed his oldest son, who was also named Ivan and was apparently a healthy and normally intelligent heir to the throne. The remaining heirs were Theodore, weak in body and mind, and Dmitri, a child by the seventh marriage. Theodore became czar, and reigned from 1584 to 1598, but the real ruler during this period was Boris Godunov, the czar's brother-in-law. He was an able statesman who continued Ivan IV's policy of appealing to the interests of the lesser gentry and restricting the freedom of the peasants. In 1591 the czar's half-brother Dmitri was found mysteriously dead. Theodore himself died childless in 1598. In the struggle over the succession the accumulated grievances of the past century boiled forth in the Time of Troubles.

THE TIME OF TROUBLES

Some historians date the Time of Troubles from the tense days in 1598 when the populace wondered whether Theodore Romanov, a popular boyar who was second cousin to the late czar, or Boris Godunov, who had been the power behind the throne, would be their next ruler. Because the *Zemsky Sobor* chose Boris, who ruled until his death in 1605, the Time of Troubles has sometimes been dated from the later year. In any case Boris, during his reign, was never secure. Although he was something of a reformer, and receptive to Western European techniques and ideas, he was plagued by opposition and misfortune and became increasingly harsh, as if in imitation of Ivan the Terrible. The boyars resisted, bad harvests spread misery, the public grumbled, and at the time of his death Boris Godunov was being threatened by one of history's most unusual revolts.

Certain Russian boyars, in collaboration with Polish nobles and Jesuit priests who hoped to convert the Russians to Roman Catholicism, brought forward a young man of gentlemanly training who had been taught since childhood that he was the heir to the throne. He sincerely believed himself to be Dmitri, youngest son of Ivan the Terrible and half-brother and successor to Godunov's predecessor, Czar Theodore I. It was believed that Godunov, to advance his own career, had planned the murder of Dmitri in 1591 (which may have been true) and had brought about the assassination of the wrong boy (which was false). Backed by various Poles, Cossacks, peasants, and boyars, and having agreed secretly to embrace Catholicism, the false (but innocent) Dmitri invaded Russia from Poland in 1604. He had been promised the throne and the hand of Marina Mniszek, the alluring daughter of one of his Polish benefactors.

The death of Boris Godunov in 1605 coupled with a boyar revolt in Moscow turned this adventure into a temporary success which placed Dmitri and Marina on the Russian throne and opened an eight-year period of almost unbelievable turmoil. Before it was over Marina had backed the pretensions of a *second* false Dmitri, upon his downfall had run away with the chieftain of the Don Cossacks, and in due time attempted to place their son on the throne. Both the Poles and the Swedes had invaded Russia, and simultaneously Sigismund, King of Poland, and his son Vladislav, had laid claim to the Russian crown. Peasant armies, the population of Moscow, gentry, boyars, Tartars, and at least three Cossack armies of differing allegiances had joined in the struggle. This national calamity was finally brought to a close by the Orthodox Patriarch, an abbot, a Nizhni Novgorod merchant, and a patriotic boyar.

Restrictions of space forbid a narrative of these events, but it is possible, from the list of interests involved, to sort out the main forces at work. In spite of its unusual setting, Russia's crisis was similar to the growing pains of other early modern states. The most characteristically Russian features of the Time of Troubles were the absence of clearly defined rules of succession to the crown, and the peasant and Cossack revolts against encroachment upon their social position and liberties. These sources of friction added unexpected force to the boyars' resistance to advancing absolutism. As in other countries in such times of crisis, neighboring states intervened to press for their own territorial and dynastic advantages. Russia began to recover when national sentiment forged a semblance of unity against the foreign invaders, and the *Zemsky Sobor,* in 1613, was able finally to agree upon a compromise candidate, the young Michael Romanov. The Romanovs were to rule Russia until 1917.

THE EARLY ROMANOVS

Russia's recovery took place gradually under the first three Romanov rulers, Michael (1613–1645), his son Alexis I (1645–1676), and Alexis's oldest son Theodore III (1676–1682). The men themselves matter less to an understanding of Russian history than the changes which took place in boundaries, beliefs, social structure, and government. These constitute the last performance of old Muscovite Russia, but they foreshadow Peter the Great and the Imperial Age.

Although Russia was able in this period to reach neither the Black Sea nor the Baltic, it continued its eastward march with energy and success. There were no organized states to bar the way to its fur trappers and government agents in Siberia. By 1648 Cossacks stood on the shore of what would later be called Bering Strait, facing North America. In the decade of the 1640's Russians began to penetrate the Amur River basin, to be checked there in the 1680's by Chinese forces. In the south as a by-product of the Time of Troubles the Russian state had captured Marina Mniszek and her Cossack husband and son and made a protectorate of the territory of the Don Cossacks. The Cossacks on the lower Dnieper, who sypathized with the Ukrainian peasants in their Orthodox faith and in their resistance to the advance of serfdom, finally joined Russia against Poland (1654). After a thirteen-year struggle the Ukraine was divided between Poland and Russia, the former taking the right (west) bank except for the city of Kiev, and Russia taking the left (east) bank, plus Kiev.

In religion, this period of the early Romanovs was one of increasing sophistication, countered by old-fashioned resistance. The conflict took at least two forms. Renewed contacts with Greek scholarship and with the Ukraine led to a movement to correct errors in the prayer books and church ritual of the Orthodox Church. Led by the Patriarch Nikon, this return to original sources aroused the opposition of many people who revered the traditions which had grown up in the Russian Church, and who saw in the corrections a rejection of the whole Third Rome idea. The objectors, called Old Believers, were condemned by a Church Council in 1667 and thereafter persecuted, but their movement did not die out; it became a part of Russian religious life, particularly among the common people. There was a political and social side to this conflict, for Nikon's corrections were expected to make Russian Orthodoxy more attractive to the Ukrainians. On the other hand, many of the peasant and Cossack protests against the advance of serfdom became intermingled with the religious protests of Old Believers. Politically, the Patriarch Nikon upheld the doctrine that czar and patriarch should rule jointly, but czar Alexis would have none of this, and exiled him to a distant monastery.

In quite another sense changing beliefs also played a part in the history of this period. As in the stimulating days of Constantinople's fall and the liberation from the Tartars, Russian imaginations were stirred by the part their nation was playing in history. In the seventeeth century the deep social and political crisis which lay back of the Time of Troubles set men to thinking about their country's future. Now, owing to more numerous contacts with western technicians and merchants as well as with Greek and Latin scholarship, the idea of Europe as a source of improvements began to find expression in men's taste and opinions as well as in the arts and apparel of some of the upper classes. The note of westernization which was to ring so loudly in the reign of Peter the Great was already sounded in the period of the early Romanovs.

All groups in Russian society were expected to serve the state whose dramatic and sometimes disorderly growth was so evident in the Muscovite period. There were still old boyar families, of the kind assailed by Ivan the Terrible and later involved in the Time of Troubles, but their ranks had been thinned by these events, and many replacements had been brought up from the ranks of service nobles. Toward the end of the seventeenth century there was less difference between the holdings of the boyars and those of the newer service nobles, for the government began to allow holdings conditional on state service to be passed from father to son. On the other hand, except for the richest merchants and manufacturers, the townspeople whom we would today call "middle class" were required, like the peasants, to remain at home in their local communities. They were regarded as owing service in the form of taxes, which could best be collected if the government knew where everyone was.

The peasants of Russia were of two principal kinds: those attached to landlords' estates and increasingly under the landlords' authority and direction; and those "state peasants" who lived on state lands but were bound to their villages and required to pay taxes in labor and kind to the government. There were still slaves in Russia whose low estate the serfs had not yet reached. It was possible to take the view that everyone but the slaves was serving the state under a set of restrictions which suited his station in life.

The structure of Russian society continued to be modified by the advance of serfdom, interrupted by heroic and fruitlessly destructive rebellions. This advance was part of the process by which the state paid the officials who helped keep order and extend its boundaries. The best seventeenth-century illustration is the law code approved by the *Zemsky Sobor* in 1649, which removed all restrictions on the right of the gentry to pursue and capture runaway serfs. The outstanding seventeenth-century rebellion after the Time of Troubles was that of Stenka Razin from 1667–1671, which gathered together runaway serfs, national minorities, and other discontented groups. Preaching war on landlords and officials and a rude form of self-government, Razin gave the Russian upper classes a bad fright until he was finally defeated and captured by regular troops.

In summary, the period after the Time of Troubles may be thought of in two parts. At first there was a stage of convalescence in which the government and society appeared to be in harmony. The *Zemsky Sobor,* which had chosen Michael Romanov to be czar, deliberated over issues of foreign and domestic policy. The boyar duma shared administrative decisions with the czar. The Orthodox Church had played an honorable part in ending the Time of Troubles, and was now headed by the czar's father, the same Theodore Romanov who had once challenged Boris Godunov and had in consequence been forced to take holy orders. Philaret, as he was now called, raised the office of patriarch almost to the level of the office of czar, but with his doubly paternal influence favored harmonious relations with the *Zemsky Sobor.*

After the death of Michael Romanov in 1645 the social and political climate in Russia changed, and once again autocracy took up its march, encouraged by the social and religious disagreements already described. The *Zemsky Sobor* was not called in full session after 1654. The influence of the Patriarch suffered with Nikon's downfall. The boyar duma declined in importance. In 1682 the czar's obligation to give precedence in administrative and military appointments to members of the boyar aristocracy was abolished. That was also the year when Peter, one day to be called "the Great," first set foot on the steps of the throne.

PART TWO

THE OLD
REGIME

1648–1789

12

EUROPEAN SOCIETY AND ITS OVERSEAS INTERESTS

EUROPE FROM 1648 to 1789—from the Thirty Years War to the French Revolution—was still "early modern Europe." But it is also called "the old regime," and the group of chapters which makes up Part II of this history retains this conventional title. The apparent contradiction between the use of "early" and "old" to describe the same era is instructive—and it is no contradiction.

The "old regime" (in French, *ancien régime*) is a term which began to be used in Europe after the great French Revolution of 1789 had apparently swept away a whole society. Looking back at the pattern of their lives before 1789, people became aware of what they had taken for granted while it was all around them, a certain kind of political and social life decorated by certain ideas and arts now seemingly outmoded. Frenchmen began to refer to the period in their history before the revolution as the "old regime." In time, some historians found the term useful as a shorthand reference to the general contours of society and politics not just in France, but in Europe, not just in the eighteenth century, but in much of the seventeenth as well.

It is to this era that we turn after having described the years 1500–1648, the earliest phase of modern times. The period now entered, that of 1648–1789, was one of continuing growth, but the growth was for the most part within bounds already sketched. Absolute monarchy continued to be the most characteristic form of state, and mercantilism the most characteristic economic policy. Strict distinctions between nobles, bourgeois, and peasants still gave society in most places its basic structure. In international affairs, the balance of power still kept the system of independent states from falling before one all-conquering empire.

This preservation of the basic forms of "early modern times" explains the usefulness of the term "old regime." On the continent of Europe between 1648 and 1789 a certain way of organizing human affairs was more or less standard. It was in some places sufficiently perfected to inspire imitation. Versailles, the great palace of the French Sun King, Louis XIV, seemed the perfect expression of the political aspirations of the last few centuries; it became the symbol for the kind of society which the Russian Empress Catherine the Great was still trying to achieve a century later.

This section on Europe from 1648 to 1789 opens with the material basis and social organization of life on the continent. Europe's relations with the outside world are also described. Later chapters make the tour from region to region and state to state, to see how the efficiencies of absolutism and strong central government affected places with different problems, traditions, and stages of development.

EUROPE'S CONTINUING EXPANSION

Europe's position in the world improved immensely in the late seventeenth and eighteenth centuries. There were few spectacular discoveries, as in the previous period, although explorations continued. The whole world became known —not yet in detail, but in its broad outlines. For example the Russians by the mid-seventeenth century had reached the Pacific, seven thousand miles from Moscow. In 1725 Emperor Peter the Great as one of the last acts of an active career sent the Dane, Vitus Jonassen Bering, to explore the strait between Asia and America which came to bear his name. Russia, which in 1689 had agreed on a boundary with China, in the eighteenth century moved on into Alaska and probed southward on the American Pacific coast. The Spanish were extending their influence north from Mexico and south into Chile, and the French and English were making the rest of North America their own.

By the late eighteenth century the relative emptiness of the Pacific was being explored by men like the Frenchman Bougainville, whose book *Voyage autour du monde* (1771) became a best seller, and like the poor English boy who went to sea and became the famous scientific explorer Captain Cook (1728–1779). Besides mapping the coasts of Nova Scotia, Newfoundland, and Labrador, Cook explored both the north and south Pacific.

Two incidents of the eighteenth century illustrate an important point about European expansion in this period. The first was the capture by the Englishman Anson, voyaging from 1740 to 1744, of a Spanish galleon whose collection of maps revealed geographical secrets till then jealously guarded by Spain. The second was the order issued by Louis XVI of France during the War

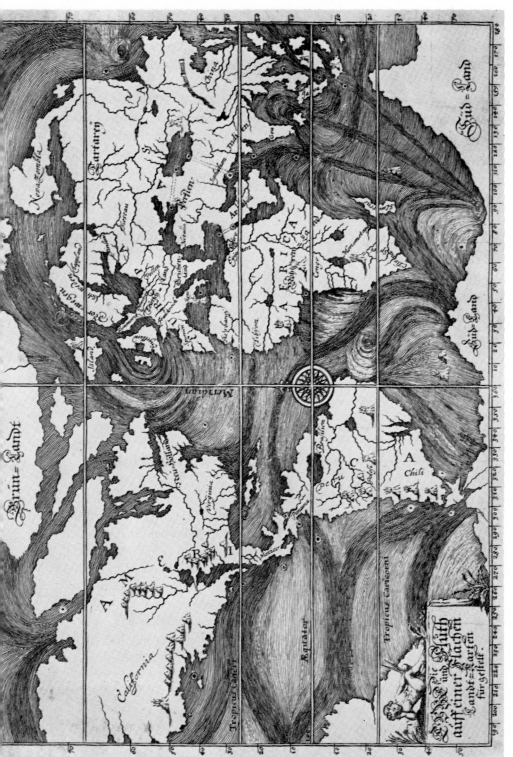

FIRST CHART OF OCEAN CURRENTS by Eberhard Werner Happel. In *Mundi Mirabilis Tripartiti*, 1708. (Library of Congress, Map Division)

of the American Revolution that the French navy should not molest Captain Cook, whose voyages were scientific work for the benefit of humanity. It is worth noticing that knowledge of the wider world was becoming scientific; that is, there was a real effort to make it *accurate* and *available* and therefore *cumulative*.

Europe had the military power to spread its influence abroad, and the needed curiosity and energy and acquisitiveness. There persisted what might metaphorically be called "crusading zeal." To it was joined the will of men and women to be free, particularly in the English-speaking colonies on the Atlantic seaboard. Except for the emigration to America, however, most of the European expansion of the late seventeenth and eighteenth centuries was less for settlement than for trading. It was the magnificent soaring of commerce which was the most significant single factor in Europe's expansion in this period.

In the long run this commerce was to build up Europe's wealth to a point where it could afford still more science and industry—much more than the rest of the world. Wealth created wealth. And in the nineteenth century the gap between Europe's economic and military power and that of the rest of the world was to be even wider than in the seventeenth and eighteenth. For the rest of the world, imitation of European ways was to become almost a matter of self-preservation. This was not yet true in the late seventeenth and eighteenth centuries, but the way was being prepared by the infusions of wealth from overseas, which were already bringing about a great transformation of European society.

A SUCCESSION OF EMPIRES

In this period the old colonial empires of the Portuguese and Spaniards were being seriously challenged by newcomers, especially Dutch, French, and English. Portugal never recovered from the Spanish conquest lasting from 1580 to 1640. Spain's enemies, particularly the Dutch and English, took advantage of this period to attack Portuguese trade and territories in the East Indies and India. Portugal managed, however, to keep Brazil, where gold was discovered in the 1680's and diamonds in the 1720's. Brazilian gold increased the world supply to such an extent that it pushed up eighteenth-century prices and, as in the case of sixteenth-century Spanish treasure, the gold found its way into the hands of more successful producing and trading peoples. Thus English gold coins became much more common in the eighteenth century.

Unlike the Portuguese, the Spanish empire in the late seventeenth and eighteenth centuries held together and even, in spots, expanded. The newer colonial powers, England, France, and the Netherlands, for the most part claimed territories which the Spanish had not occupied, such as the Atlantic coast of North America, Canada, and the Mississippi Valley. The English, French, and Dutch did, however, crowd into the Spanish West Indies, and even settled on

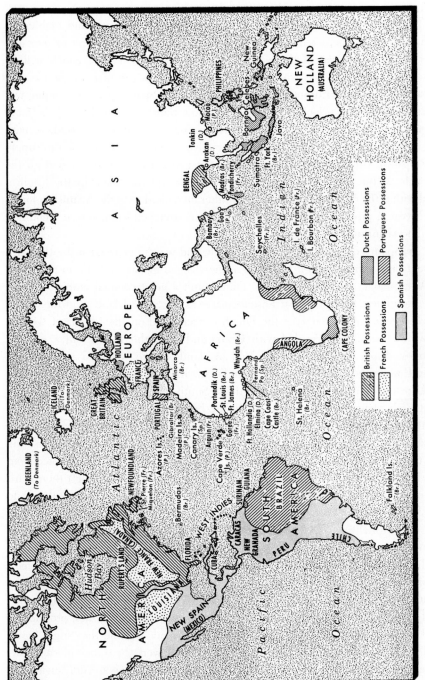

EUROPEAN EMPIRES IN 1763

the mainland of South America. The huge dominions were under constant challenge and survived largely because of the protection of Spain's powerful ally, France.

Spain's decline in Europe during the late seventeenth and eighteenth centuries was punctuated by many wars, and they tended to spread over the world. The great war of the Spanish Succession (1701–1714), which will be described elsewhere, was truly a "world war," perhaps the first, for besides the balance of power in Europe the gigantic prize of the Spanish colonial empire was at stake. For a time it looked as if France, whose Bourbon ruler, Louis XIV, managed to place his grandson on the Spanish throne, would enjoy the trade of both the Spanish and French empires. The lucrative *asiento* (the permission to supply the Spanish colonies with slaves) passed for a time from the Portuguese to the French. At the close of the war, however, the *asiento* was taken by the English, and with it the right to send one ship of other merchandise to the Spanish colonies each year, a privilege which English merchants stretched so far that it amounted to almost continuous trading.

Spain's onetime subjects, the Dutch, had won their freedom by the early seventeenth century and it had been acknowledged in law in 1648, in the Peace of Westphalia. In this century the Dutch built a great colonial empire, driving the Portuguese from such Far Eastern places as the Spice Islands and the Malay Archipelago. In the Far East the Dutch concentrated on the islands of what is now Indonesia. They traded with China and until the 1660's had a post on Formosa. From 1638 to 1854 they held an island close to Nagasaki and were the only Europeans allowed to trade with Japan. In 1652 the Dutch set up a post at Capetown on the southern tip of Africa. South Africa was to retain some of its Dutch characteristics in spite of its seizure by the English in 1806. The Dutch were great slave-traders in their day, and had other African stations for this purpose, along with the English, French and Portuguese. They failed to oust the Portuguese from Brazil in the 1640's and 1650's, and were themselves ousted from the Hudson River valley by the English in the 1660's. The Dutch left their mark all over the world from the Pacific (exploration of Tasmania, New Zealand) to the West Indies.

The richest part of the French colonial empire emerged from the seventeenth-century scramble in the Caribbean Sea, when French, Spanish, Dutch, and English all competed with each other and with the Carib Indians for possession of the islands. The Caribs were defeated and virtually extinguished by about 1660. On islands such as Guadeloupe and Martinique and Santo Domingo and others which changed hands often, French privileged companies, proprietors, and ultimately royal colonies flourished. These islands became the "sugar bowl" of France, where great plantations worked by slaves were the source of enormous revenues for the owners, the state, and the shippers and traders in rum, sugar, and slaves.

Compared to the West Indies, the rest of the French colonial empire was less profitable. French explorers, missionaries, trappers, and fur traders pushed up the St. Lawrence to the Great Lakes, and down the Mississippi, encircling the British colonies. LaSalle reached the mouth of the great river in 1682—thus Louisiana was named after Louis XIV. New Orleans was founded in 1718. The French empire of the forests and lakes and rivers in North America was carefully regulated and kept pure of heretics as far as that was possible in a distant land. Colbert, the great mercantilist minister of Louis XIV, sent out colonists, including boatloads of women, but in comparison with the English colonies in America, where there were religious and other refugees, the French territories were sparsely populated.

Colbert, too, founded the French East India Company in 1664, thereby giving a forward push to French colonizing in the Far East. Frenchmen had in 1626 set up posts on the islands of Madagascar and Reunion, way stations on the voyage to the Indies. The French established a few trading centers in India in the seventeenth century but had trouble holding them in the wars waged by Louis XIV, in which English sea power was almost always on the opposing side. In the eighteenth century, however, the French, along with the English, took advantage of one of the great changes in world history, the disintegration of the Mogul empire in India, which was losing its hold on the vast subcontinent. The situation was rather like the breakup of the Mongol or Tartar, empire which had covered Russia in the fourteenth and fifteenth centuries before breaking into rival principalities which the Russian czars could defeat. In India the French, with Pondicherry as a base, and with native troops (sepoys), were able to expand their inflence over numerous local rulers. In West Africa the French set up posts in the Senegal region and some on the Guinea coast, traded with the natives, and took part in the slave trade.

The English as traders, colonizers, and sea-fighters drew ahead of the Dutch in the seventeenth century, and throughout the eighteenth they engaged in a worldwide contest with the French which is sometimes called the Second Hundred Years War. Unlike the French and Spanish, the English permitted large-scale emigration of religious dissenters. In an age of social and economic dislocation at home, this policy brought Congregationalists to New England, French Huguenots to South Carolina, German sectarians to Pennsylvania, Presbyterians from Northern Ireland to various colonies, Quakers to Pennsylvania, and Catholics to Maryland, as well as thousands of slaves, indentured servants, and deported criminals.

The English colonies on the Atlantic seaboard varied in character from the small farms of New England to the great plantations of the South, and from the relatively Europeanized older coastal centers to the advancing frontier. In the West Indies, England competed with the Spanish, French, and Dutch, and secured several islands, for example Jamaica, captured in 1655. Like the French, the English islands were producers of tobacco and especially of sugar and were part of the circuit traveled by traders in slaves and rum. Like the others, England had a few African posts, but its greatest gains in the eighteenth century were in the Far East, where the East India Company traded in the Persian Gulf area and especially in India. The English founded a station at Madras in1639 and established themselves at Calcutta in 1690.

England's contest with France for colonial supremacy paralleled and was enmeshed in the main wars on the continent of Europe. In all the complexities of the changing European balance of power the steady antagonism of the English and French is one of the most visible strands. By the mid-seventeenth century the Portuguese and Spanish were on the defensive in the colonial field, while the English and Dutch were great rivals and fought a series of naval wars. But the menace of France both on the continent and abroad drove the English and Dutch together again as allies, as they had been against Spain. The Dutch in their turn were on the defensive by 1700. There remained the English and French.

The Anglo-French duel was fought in three main theaters: the Caribbean Sea, India, and North America. The series of wars continued throughout the eighteenth century, and did not come to an end until Napoleon's defeat in 1815. France was both a continental and an overseas power and in the long run was forced to put the continental policy first and suffered great colonial losses. Secure in its island position, England could afford to put first emphasis on colonial affairs while France, threatened by powerful neighbors, could not.

In 1713, in the Treaty of Utrecht which ended the War of the Spanish Succession, France recognized England's right to Newfoundland, Nova Scotia, and Hudson's Bay. In 1763 by the Treaty of Paris following the Seven Years War in Europe (known as the French and Indian War in America), the French lost Canada and Louisiana east of the Mississippi after having in the previous year ceded Louisiana west of the Mississippi to their ally Spain. And the Seven Years War also saw the climax of Anglo-French rivalry in India, which had become a duel between the sepoys and puppet rulers of the Frenchman Joseph François Dupleix (1697–1763), and those of the Englishman Robert Clive (1725–1774). Clive proved to have more skill at the game and he profited from the lack of support given Dupleix by the French government. By the Treaty of Paris in 1763 the English gave back Pondicherry, the seat of French power, which Clive had captured, but required the French to cease using trading posts as military bases. Thus it was the English who were to dominate India politically, not the French.

The French made a comeback in the American Revolution by helping the colonies against England (1778–1783), but had more satisfaction in weakening the British empire than in any specific gains of their own. In the wars of the French Revolutionary and Napoleonic period France fought England from 1793 to 1815 with only two short intermissions. Once more British sea power was decisive in the colonial field, while France's continental position and ambitions soaked up its interest and resources.

Having lost most of their first colonial empire, the French in the nineteenth century were to secure another in Africa and the Far East, and were thus to remain a great colonial power. The facility with which Europeans, enjoying a considerable advantage in economic and military power, could spread their influence is perhaps the greatest single factor in the history of the modern world. This European advantage was not merely the cause of colonization but was increasingly a *result* of it—a result of what colonization did to European society.

COMMERCE AND INDUSTRY

The economy of Europe from 1648 to 1789 was dominated by what is called the "commercial revolution," which in turn was largely the result of European overseas expansion. This does not mean that merchants were more numerous or more important to the economy than, say, peasants. Indeed, the Europe of the old regime remained primarily agricultural. But the part of the economy which grew the most was its commerce, and it was commerce, in turn, which brought the greatest changes to European industry, agriculture, and business methods. This is reflected in the term "commercial capitalism," which refers to the large amounts of capital invested in commerce. There were other forms of profit-seeking in the old regime, for example in banking and industry, and even agriculture. But in this period commerce led the way.

Even in the unreliable statistics of the day one can see the increase in quantity of trade. England's exports to its colonies rose by some 500 percent between 1689 and 1775, and imports from the colonies increased almost as much. The American Revolution proved to be only an interruption of this advantageous exchange. France, being a much larger country, had a greater overseas commerce than England. As the two raced through the eighteenth century the English rate of growth was somewhat faster, but both exceeded a 400 percent increase in total foreign trade.

The old seas around Europe were now more useful than ever, the Black Sea bearing increased quantities of grain from Russia, the Mediterranean serving its ancient purpose of transit from the caravans of the Near East, but the commercial revolution reached far beyond them. The world was shrinking.

Despite the opposition of English woolens manufacturers and French silkmakers, cotton cloth from India changed the clothing habits of Europeans. Italian luxury crafts, now overshadowed by the French, carried on business as usual, but aristocratic Europeans were growing accustomed to furniture of Brazilian rosewood and American mahogany, as well as to the silk and carpets of the Orient; and this was the age when porcelains from China were widely imported and imitated by Europeans. Into such cups (under which the Europeans placed the saucers instead of following the Chinese custom of putting them on top, to preserve the heat of the beverage) went the coffee, tea, and chocolate which were becoming European habits. The Russians and the English were rival pioneers in tea drinking. And there was the sugar from the West Indies, and molasses, and the rum which figured in the slave trade. As spices from the Far East, once so sought after, declined in fashion, tobacco rose. Furs from America and Siberia were no longer a novelty in eighteenth-century Europe.

And as European commerce with the rest of the world grew, its functions subdivided and multiplied. Merchants became specialized into wholesalers and retailers. Society was more complicated, and along all the crisscrossing lines of trade, reports and ideas about the world outside Europe made their way.

The overseas trade stacked up gold and silver in Europe, built up the coastal ports, particularly along the Atlantic, and deepened the older channels of commerce into the interior. The effects were greatest where commerce with the outside world was accompanied by production at home. Much gold from Brazil turned up in London because Portugal, like its neighbor Spain, did not produce many goods and had to import for itself and its colonies. Central and Eastern Europeans—Austrians, Prussians, Poles, and Russians—lacked the direct overseas contacts which Western Europe was developing, but in their way they too were affected. They wanted the amenities provided by Western Europe; to pay for them they forced their peasants to produce a grain surplus, which was shipped from places like Danzig and Riga and Russia's Black Sea ports late in the eighteenth century. Vast differences were growing up as a consequence of the commercial revolution, differences primarily between East and West, but also within Western Europe, like those between the Iberian Peninsula and the rest of the continent.

Industry in Europe was stimulated by the demand from colonial empires and overseas markets as well as the growing population at home. Commerce piled up the earnings which made possible new methods of supply. Through the seventeenth and early eighteenth centuries guild-choked towns with their carefully organized handicrafts dominated production. In general, it may be said that handicrafts and guilds remained the rule in Europe until the end of the old regime. In both France and England, however, demands for greater output encouraged the "putting-out" system. In the textile and metalware industries, "merchant manufacturers" took raw materials to be fashioned in workers' homes in the country, where guild regulations were absent and costs and taxes were lower. In some cities the guildsmen themselves were becoming toward the end of the eighteenth century virtual employees of the great merchants who marketed their product.

In a few cases in the west, notably in England, the demands of the great overseas commerce, the accumulation of capital, and the perfection of techniques of credit brought a leap from handicraft and "putting out" production to concentration of the labor force in factories, sometimes even with machines. Toward the end of the eighteenth century the motor of what would one day be called the "industrial revolution" was stuttering into motion.

There had long been large-scale enterprises in certain industries such as mining and shipbuilding and brewing and printing and metal smelting, in which mechanical devices and numerous workers were often called for. In the eighteenth century textile factories were growing larger as exports of textiles became a big business in France and England. The famous quartet of the old textbooks, Kay's flying shuttle (1733), Hargreaves's spinning jenny (c. 1765), Arkwright's water frame (1769), and Crompton's "mule" (c. 1779), illustrate the change, for the first two could easily enough be used by a workman in his home, but the last two needed water or other power and therefore pointed toward some kind of factory. The clumsy Newcomen steam engine (c. 1702) was used to pump water out of mines, but the more efficient one made by James Watt and first put to commercial use in 1776 is a better illustration of the revolution in power which was to build the world of our day.

CAPITALISM, MERCANTILISM, AND LAISSEZ FAIRE

Europe's overseas expansion, commercial revolution, and industrial methods were woven together. They were also interwoven with many governmental and private practices and even with movements of thought. The terms "capitalism," "mercantilism," and "laissez faire" are labels given to some of those practices and movements.

"Capitalism" (see p. 19) refers to various ways of organizing economic activity around the investment of capital, or wealth used to produce more wealth, in the hope of profit. Europe under the old regime became more and more "capitalistic," for there was more capital, and it was invested in an increasing variety of ways by more and more people. What is called "specialization"—the devoting of lives to a single occupation—was taking place. In spite of irritations and injustices, it was enriching life by multiplying occupations and therefore the nooks and crannies in society in which the individual might find his place.

In the areas most stimulated by such developments, gold and silver were supplemented by paper money and various forms of credit, for European business was thirsty for capital and means of exchange. Although the typical business was still a family firm or partnership, more and more companies were selling shares and holding out the promise of dividends. These and other paper titles to wealth were bought and sold, and bourses or exchanges to handle this form of trading grew larger and more sensitive to facts and rumors of facts. In the late seventeenth century Amsterdam was the financial center of Europe, but in the eighteenth London gradually overtook the Dutch city—a reflection of the changing fortunes of empire, trade, and industry. Indeed, the great banking companies tell the story of Europe's financial growth in their dates of founding: Bank of Amsterdam (1609); Bank of Hamburg (1619); Bank of Stockholm (1656); Bank of England (1694); Courant Bank of Denmark (1736); Royal Exchange and Note Bank of Berlin (1765); Russian Note Bank (1769).

Two of the most important innovations in finance came from the Netherlands, where the problems of money and banking were better understood than anywhere else in the seventeenth century. The Dutch, with their huge carrying trade and their extensive overseas connections, soon learned improved techniques for the transfer of money and for the development of credit, and their inventions in these fields made possible much of the later growth of corporations and banks.

The Bank of Amsterdam was the first bank in history which was both a commercial institution and a bank of deposit—that is, it not only received deposits and paid interest on them, but managed to lend the funds made available, at higher interest rates, to businessmen and governments. Its excellent management, and skillful observation, not only assured large profits but also revealed this fact: that, since depositors never all demand that their deposits be paid back at once, the bank may safely lend much larger sums than have been deposited in it. This represented the effective beginning of modern financing and made possible the vast growth of business and manufacturing later—since it enabled people with an idea for a manufactory which might prove profitable later to borrow *more money than existed* and repay it after the new production had begun to turn into profits. Financially, the Dutch discovered the secret of economic expansion: how to create wealth out of confidence.

And a second financial process, absolutely indispensable to the economic world which we know, was likewise perfected by the Dutch: insurance. Few individual businessmen could afford to take risks which might involve the wiping out of most of their investment, such as loss of ships through shipwreck. But it was realized in the middle of the seventeenth century that the total *percentage* of such losses was small, and that by charging a low insurance rate a large insurance company could still make a profit. This allowed an enormous expansion in the volume of business a single company dared undertake.

Another kind of activity which was promoted by the Netherlands' commercial activities and energies, was what we may call pure research. The expansion of scientific knowledge was not limited to the Dutch, but it was particularly noticeable among them in the seventeenth century. Geography, optics, mathematics, and, especially, navigation, all owe much to them. Such sciences were sponsored by businessmen who found them useful, and in turn they contributed greatly to the success of business.

In order to push these gradually accumulating economic advantages, the Republic—and especially the government of the province of Holland—sponsored commercial expansion. The government-chartered trading company, partially or mainly government-financed, which was to provide a pattern for commercial and colonial expansion in the eighteenth century, was perfected by the Dutch. In 1602, the Dutch East India Company was chartered. This was largely a state affair or, more precisely, a state within a state. Overseas it maintained its own armies and navies, operated the government of considerable areas in India and the East Indies, and enjoyed a monopoly on trade with the Orient. It was complemented, in 1621, by an Indies Company chartered to operate in similar ways in the Western Hemisphere. It was the Indies Company which explored the eastern seaboard of what is now the Central Atlantic states of America, founded New Amsterdam and Cape May, seized half of Brazil from the Portuguese, and established the still-extant Dutch possessions of Surinam in South America, and Curaçao in the Caribbean.

The Bank of England, founded in 1694, illustrates how other regions adopted techniques similar to those of the Dutch. After the triumph of Parliament in 1688, the government's ability to borrow money was greater because the lenders had confidence in Parliament, which was staffed by men very much like themselves. England's form of government became an asset in foreign policy as well, for England was better able to pay for its wars and subsidize its allies. The Bank of England was founded by a company of the government's creditors, who were allowed to accept deposits, borrow, lend, and issue notes which were legal tender. The Bank took over the management of the national debt, lent money to the government, and made itself useful by such services as transferring money abroad for the payment of the army and navy. It was not a monopoly. The Bank, besides helping the government helped business by providing currency and the means of making payments. In a larger sense it helped the development of the economy of England by attracting from their hiding places savings which were now usefully invested. As the falling interest rate testifies, it became less costly to borrow money.

The best illustration of how Western Europe was learning to use credit is the story of the "bubbles" of 1720. After the costly War of the Spanish Succession (1701–1714) the French government was concerned about its debts. A Scotsman, John Law (1671–1729), brought to France surprisingly advanced ideas about money. He regarded it as a medium of exchange, which should circulate rapidly if production was to be encouraged. Law won the attention of the Duke of Orléans, regent of France, and in 1716 was encouraged to found a private bank. In time Law's bank, which was backed financially by the government, became a royal bank whose notes were legal tender. Indeed, so many notes were issued that the amount of money in circulation was doubled, prices rose, and business was stimulated. With this paper money the government paid off many of its obligations. In 1717 Law founded a Compagnie d'Occident, also called the Mississippi Company, which was given the privilege of exploiting trade with Louisiana. Shares in this company could be bought with notes from Law's bank or with the state's old obligations. Thus the government's creditors tended to become shareholders in the Mississippi Company and the state's debt became linked to the enterprises of Law.

In 1720 the French government's continuing need for money helped bring about a further development in the situation. Law became Controller General of Finances. His trading company took over most of the other companies involved in French foreign trade, and in return for tax-collecting privileges Law was prepared to take over the government's debt and to simplify and reform the whole structure of taxation. At the heart of Law's scheme were useful ideas about paper money and about financing business through selling shares. But his projects, backed by the government, went too fast and too far. The supply of money, the government's debts, and the exploitation of France's colonial empire all became linked together because they were linked with Law's bank and trading company. Shares of the company were greatly in demand, and rose in value from 1000 to 10,000 *livres* each. In 1720, after this peak had been reached, it became apparent that the company's earnings could not keep up with the high cost of the shares. People sold as excitedly as they had bought. The value of company shares crashed down, dragging after them Law's bank. Law himself had to run away. Thus ended the "Mississippi Bubble." The French people for the rest of the eighteenth century remained suspicious of paper money and of large banks and of shares of stock—all of them devices which might have been useful in developing the French economy and helping reorganize the French finances.

In England the counterpart of Law's Mississippi Bubble was the South Sea Bubble. The South Sea Company was formed in 1710 to monopolize the trade with Spanish America, and in 1713 was given the *asiento* slave-trading monopoly. The government's creditors could receive stock in the company in exchange for their government obligations. As the company began to profit from speculative fever, partly imbibed from Law's French example, it took over more of the government's debt. Like the Mississippi Company's shares, those of the South Sea Company went up 1000 percent by the late summer of 1720 and then crashed. In England the South Sea enterprise was paralleled by a host of other companies, some of them of the most fantastic character (one company which sold stock in an enterprise to be announced later). The popping of bubbles in 1720 was heard far and wide, but although the English people suffered losses and had a fright, the South Sea Company and the government's creditors who had entered it were in part salvaged. The credit of the Bank of England was unshaken, and the public was not so heavily inoculated against shares of stock as the French of this era.

These adventures with banking and company shares illustrate the spirit and techniques of capitalism as well as the need to gather capital for investment.

Mercantilism was at its height in the period from the end of the Thirty Years War to the French Revolution. A collection of precepts and practices about how government intervention could best make countries unified, wealthy, and powerful, mercantilism was everywhere given official approval until toward the end of the period. Mercantilism may be thought of as the economic counterpart to the diplomatic, military, and colonial competition among European states. It should not be confused with capitalism. "Capitalism" is a word used to describe certain economic methods and incentives of those times. "Mercantilism" is simply the name for safeguards which statesmen and their advisors thought it wise to impose for the good of the state, society, and business itself. Mercantilism was a way of regulating economic activity under the growing capitalism of early modern times.

The greatest practitioner of mercantilism was without doubt Jean Baptiste Colbert, who served the French King Louis XIV from 1661 until 1683. Colbert was of middle-class origin, but his career was not an effort to make the state serve the middle classes but to make the middle classes and everyone else serve the state and the king. When Colbert pushed through the digging of the Languedoc Canal, which joined the Atlantic to the Mediterranean by connecting rivers which ran into each, he was encouraging France's wealth and power along with its commerce. His tariff legislation aimed at unifying the country economically and strengthening its position in the international struggle. Essential raw materials were to be imported if necessary, but in so far as possible important finished products should be made in France. Exports that would not weaken France were encouraged. A favorable balance of trade was to bring in gold and silver.

Colbert was concerned about the colonies, and built up the French navy and merchant marine and gave special privileges to chartered companies like the East India Company. He subsidized certain industries, and attempted to regulate the methods and the quality of industrial output, using for this purpose the guilds. Colbert was also concerned about agriculture and mining. Like most mercantilists, he thought that a large population was a sign of social well-being and a guarantee of national power.

It is difficult to assess the effectiveness of mercantilism as an economic policy. Each country developed its own set of measures characteristic of its needs.

The Dutch, for example, were a special case because their small homeland made it necessary for them to import the materials that they processed and re-exported. They were consequently inclined to permit much freedom to their merchants and shippers. English mercantilism leaned more and more toward regulation of shipping and foreign trade, with particular reference to the colonies, while at home economic controls and the influence of the guilds declined in effectiveness. The English colonial system, in attempting to fit the American colonies into a pattern of trade and production directed from London, ran into a crescendo of objections. Differing conceptions of colonial development and control grew into the American Revolution. But the "old colonial system" of the seventeenth and early eighteenth centuries did not prevent the building of English maritime and naval power nor, for that matter, of a vigorous and prospering set of colonies.

In places such as Austria, Prussia, and Russia the "enlightened despots" of the eighteenth century attempted economic development through state intervention patterned, more or less, after the classical French model. In the west, however, mercantilism began to be attacked by persons who said that goods would be more plentiful if the makers and sellers were free to use their own judgment (*laissez faire*, let alone—see Chapter 21). Officially, mercantilism remained the dominant point of view to the end of the period which we have called the old regime. And the lower middle classes in the west remained suspicious of free enterprise and distrustful of the powerful men who, late in the eighteenth century, were beginning to recommend it.

THE EUROPEAN COUNTRYSIDE

In spite of all the inroads made by merchants and townsmen, the European economy was still dominated by agriculture and European society by the owners of land. Hard times in the country meant hard times in the towns.

Almost everywhere in Europe the land was possessed or in some measure controlled by aristocratic lords—seigneurs, as they were called in France. Most seigneurs leased their own manorial domains to tenant farmers or had them cultivated by peasants who owed them labor service. The rest of the seigneur's land, apart from these personal domains, was distributed, usually in small strips, among the peasantry, whether free or serf. Most of these peasant holdings passed from generation to generation, as did the accompanying obligations to the seigneur.

By "feudal" dues that might be paid in goods, money, or labor, the peasants contributed to the upkeep of the aristocracy. The wastelands and woods and waters were shared by the peasants and the seigneur, but the latter kept for himself the right to destroy harmful animals and to hunt, and he sometimes also retained certain police powers and judicial duties which made him a power in the countryside.

There were sharp differences among the various regions of Europe. Generally speaking, the territory east of an imaginary line drawn from the Elbe River (left-hand side of Denmark) to the Adriatic Sea was characterized by serfdom and by a considerable number of large holdings of the most powerful of the aristocracy, although there were many smaller landholdings, whose proprietors are called, in English, squires. West of this Elbe-Adriatic line the peasants tended to be free and the holdings of the seigneurs smaller. Much of the countryside in France, Flanders, and parts of Italy and Spain, for example, consisted of small peasant holdings. These were not owned outright by the peasants, for they still paid dues to the seigneur, but the dues-payer was free to sell or bequeath his holding and the obligations which went with it. The serfs of Poland and Russia, much less fortunate, could themselves be sold.

In England from the mid-seventeenth to the late eighteenth century the countryside was changing, because of the "enclosures." Earlier there had been numerous small proprietors; now, more often, great proprietors collected rents from large commercial farmers. England by the late eighteenth century resembled Europe east of the Elbe in the high proportion of great estates, but in other respects it was quite different, for the people were all free, and an "agricultural revolution" was going on; that is, efforts were being made to increase output and profits by scientific cultivation.

The agricultural revolution, so-called, is a reminder that just as the European countryside varied from region to region, so also it changed through the passage of time. It is already obvious that the growth of great seaports in the west, linked to overseas markets and equipped with banks and merchant-manufacturers and numerous trading connections, was actually accentuating differences between Eastern and Western Europe. The demand for food made grain prices rise and farmland more valuable, the more so since a growing peasant population needed places to farm. But the growers of grain, though they might all be affected by the demands of traders and towns, reacted in various ways.

In England "enclosures" had been underway in the sixteenth century in the interests of wool growing. They were concentrations of fields by individual owners, who dispossessed the hereditary peasant tillers. In the eighteenth and early nineteenth centuries the use of fertilizers, the scientific breeding of beasts, and other methods of increasing output led more and more landowners to seek to "enclose" in order to raise crops and meat cattle on a larger scale. The small freeholder, deprived of the use of common lands and shouldered aside by consolidations, found independent farming more and more disappointing and tended to disappear into the ranks of farm or city laborers.

In France and western Germany, in contrast to England, the rise of population, prices, and land values in the eighteenth century bred infinite combinations of share-cropping, renting, dues-paying, and purchase on the part of the peasantry; but in general the holdings stayed small. The seigneurs continued to collect their dues. Some of them tried to increase their incomes by scientific agriculture and enclosures, and some by revival of forgotten dues (the "seigneurial reaction"), but the peasant clung to his land.

Everywhere, though first and foremost in Great Britain, "agricultural revolution" meant two things: first, a vast increase in the food supply; and second, a decline in subsistence farming and an increase in production for the wider market.

In the far reaches of the east, beyond the Elbe, Polish and Russian aristocrats (and indeed Prussian and Austrian ones as well) were no less eager to sell grain for money than their counterparts in the west. They wished to import to their manor houses the pianos and libraries and English governesses and French bindings which money could buy. The grain surplus was produced by a peasantry unable to defend itself, like the French, by paying dues in money and entering into innumerable deals for leasing or share-cropping the land; unable, also, to turn like the English to other occupations and perhaps to towns, leaving behind a skeleton force of hired farm laborers to make the earth produce. In Eastern Europe, lacking both freedom and science, the peasants produced in the old ways of their grandfathers, driven ever more deeply into servitude by the powerful aristocrats who owned them.

The impact of markets was thus very different in England, in Western Europe, and in the east, depending on the presence or absence of towns, industries, scientific agriculture, and, as will be seen in the following section, political traditions. In the east, serfdom grew worse till the end of the eighteenth century and there were great fruitless peasant rebellions like Razin's and Pugachev's, while in the west serfdom had almost disappeared. The great peasant revolt in France in 1789 was to come not from serfs but from ambitious small proprietors impatient of seigneurial dues. And in England there were few peasant troubles, so displaced were the smallholders from the countryside, and so influential the aristocratic landowners. But in England, as in other western countries, there were the beginnings of those urban lower classes who would one day be called the proletariat.

SOCIETY AND POLITICS

The Europe of the late seventeenth and eighteenth centuries wore for the last time its medieval costume and managed to the end of the era to retain the appearance of a continent ruled by kings and nobles, with the townsmen and peasants permitted to look on in admiration and provide material support. The persistence of a medieval appearance is misleading, however. Although the countryside looked much as it had for centuries, there were accumulating during this era the people, money, roads, ships, towns, and machines which were to make Europe astonishingly different in the nineteenth century.

For one thing, population was growing—no one knows quite why. Statistics are lacking, but good guesses can be made. England and Scotland had five to six million people in 1700 and by 1789 had nine million. France grew from about eighteen million in 1715 to perhaps twenty-five million in 1789. The German states grew, though aggrandizements make it difficult to judge the natural rate. For example Prussia under Frederick II, the Great (1740–1786) conquered its way from two and a half million to six million. Spain for all its economic backwardness grew from five million in 1700 to nine million in 1789. Russia, even more on the outer edge of European economic progress, but much expanded by conquests, grew from nine million in 1682 to thirty-six million in 1796.

Europe's increase was part of the great population growth which has come in the world since the eighteenth century. It is a historical fact explainable in some regions by the better order and improved agriculture which kept a greater percentage of the newly born alive, in other areas less easily explainable but none the less real. Population growth, along with the rise in prices, the hunger of the peasants for land, and the relatively stronger position of the *bourgeoisie* in the west, helps explain some of the tensions with which European political systems had to cope.

So the Europe which seemed to have everywhere the same kind of elite of aristocratic landholders, was everywhere changing beneath the surface. To pass from east to west or from west to east was truly to cross barriers of time as well as of space. In England a class of merchants and traders was becoming rich and self-confident, and was linked by connections of family and trade to the landed gentry and to the apparatus of the state. They were able to enjoy their place in society without bitterness against either the aristocracy or the government. In France, where a similar stimulus from overseas commerce greatly enlarged the wealth and self-confidence of the upper middle class, the latter became increasingly jealous of a nobility which held them at bay. In Central and Eastern Europe the middle class was less numerous, less self-confident, much more timid in its attitude toward the nobility and the state.

In England, younger sons did not inherit titles, and the peerage was small, and fluid, related by many ties of blood and business to the rest of society. After the "Glorious Revolution" of 1688, it had a predominant influence on the conduct of affairs. The French nobles, on the other hand, were disciplined by the absolute monarchy in the seventeenth century, but managed in the eighteenth to make a substantial comeback, not through formal changes in the government but through personal influence on weak kings and the monopolizing of offices in the aging bureaucracy. The aristocracy of Central and Eastern Europe oscillated between what might be called the French situation of the seventeenth century and the French situation of the eighteenth: they retained their privileged position and improved it whenever there were weak rulers. The case of Poland is a striking example of what could happen when the crown's authority declined, for in Poland the great nobles became supreme, but the country lacked sufficient central authority to defend its territory against cannibalistic neighbors.

The condition of the European peasantry was related to the political and social power of the nobles. In Russia and Poland the peasants were virtually unprotected by the state. In the absolute monarchy of late seventeenth century-France, the state refused to let the nobles take too large a percentage of the incomes of peasant taxpayers. In England the aristocracy won political power and used it to hasten the enclosures, but there was no real "peasant problem," for the society was developing rapidly enough to create new opportunities for the individual; however unsatisfactory their lot, the English poor never rose *en masse*.

The 1700's were, above all, a century of the aristocracy. From parliament-ary England all the way to autocratic Russia, the aristocracy in one way or another held an enviable economic and social position. Landed and usually titled aristo-crats now reached their peak, whatever the form of government. The significance of the aristocracy's position and the responsibilities and privileges which it en-tailed were not to become fully apparent until dramatized by challenges from the commoners in the late eighteenth and nineteenth centuries. For the moment, however, our purpose is to watch the development, country by country, of this "old order" which would one day be challenged.

13

FROM REVOLUTION TO STABILITY IN ENGLAND

THE MIDDLE YEARS of the seventeenth century were the most troubled years of modern English history. They were marked by civil war and by experimentation with a republic and with military dictatorship—the only breaks in the legal continuity of the British constitution since the Norman Conquest in 1066. The last years of the eighteenth century, while they did not lead to the overthrow of Britain's institutions, were hardly less anxious. The best part of the colonial empire had just been lost. Vast economic changes, which were to shape a wholly new society and indeed a new world, were under way, and revolutionary ideas were circulating. A great war for survival was beginning. The "constitution," the collection of laws and habits which determined procedures and the distribution of powers in English government, was increasingly unfitted to the needs of the day and increasingly unadaptable, and it was widely attacked. The old notions of the "liberties of Englishmen," which had meant security from arbitrary government by a tyrant, were taking on explosive new interpretations involving political rights and privileges for the ordinary citizen. But in the century which intervened between these anxious intervals an extraordinary measure of stability existed, extraordinary strides were taken toward a new and richer life for British subjects.

These various advances—toward stability, toward economic greatness, toward imperial power, and toward free institutions—form the major themes of England's history in the years between 1648 and 1789.

THE COMMONWEALTH AND PROTECTORATE, 1649–1660

King Charles I had taken up arms to subdue a Parliament which insisted upon various changes in English institutions, notably in its Anglican Church, and upon encroachments on the traditional powers of the crown, notably its right to appoint its own officials. Charles had been defeated in the field, by the "New Model Army" of Oliver Cromwell. The victors were in undoubted control of the country, but those victors were not the parliamentarians who had tormented the king and his father before him; they were, instead, the officers of the new army, and the army was controlled by Puritans.

The forces of freedom, as the Puritans and the army regarded themselves, now undertook a clean sweep of the old institutions. The king was hastily tried and, on January 30, 1649, executed in Whitehall, before his former palace. A republic was proclaimed. The House of Lords was abolished. Freedom of worship was decreed for all trinitarian Protestants—that is to say, everyone who was not a Roman Catholic, an Anglican, or a Unitarian. Recusant Ireland, staunchly Roman Catholic and royalist, was subdued with great ferocity. A third of the Irish population was killed and most land owners there saw their estates confiscated and turned over to Protestants, usually English army officers. This brutal policy created a not unnatural hostility among the Irish to their English masters, which had not abated by the twentieth century. Scotland, no less recalcitrant and scarcely less royalist, but Presbyterian instead of Roman Catholic, was also crushed, in a less gory fashion.

From these exploits Cromwell emerged as the unchallenged leader of the army and thus in unchallenged control of the British Isles. Four parliamentary bodies were in turn purged or dismissed by the army high command, which in the end installed Cromwell as a dictator. This reflected the division of the country. Royalists, Catholics, Unitarians, Presbyterians, antimilitarists, could never unite in support of any regime. Moreover, to the existing factions were now being added others of an even more irreconcilable sort. The general disruption of ancient institutions had brought forth several programs and parties which preached social equality—the abolition of power, privilege, and wealth for those who regarded themselves as specially equipped by experience and education to rule—and democracy. These groups, known as "Diggers" and "Levellers" were miniscule, but they were frightening. Unless a firm hand took hold of cloven England, it appeared that anarchy would necessarily ensue. As a consequence, the country acquiesed in, if it did not welcome, the iron rule of Cromwell as military dictator.

Another development which led the country to accept military dictatorship, and along with it the exremely unpopular tendency of the Puritan army to forbid wicked diversions—cockfighting, drunkenness, and the stage—was foreign war. A war against Spain, of a sort which had been endemically waged for almost a century, was now taken up seriously, and with the enthusiastic backing of almost the entire nation. The gratification of commercial, religious, and national ambitions at the expense of Spain's naval power and commerce added to British prestige and maritime authority, and helped to stabilize the regime.

But in 1658 Cromwell died, and the system which his compelling skill and character had maintained began to break down. His inadequate son Richard sought to replace him, but the accumulated discontents of the public would not abate. An army leader, General Monk, concluded what most of the rest of the nation had already concluded, that only a restoration of the ancient crown and constitution could unite the country. He seized the capital, dispossessed Richard Cromwell, dissolved what was left of the hastily assembled Long Parliament, and in effect invited the son of Charles I to return to England. Charles II, as he called himself, issued a tactful declaration promising religious toleration, forgiveness for most rebels, and payment of back salaries to the army, and then landed in England, on May 25, 1660. He was received by the nation with tumultuous enthusiasm and was installed on the throne. England's only experiment with republics, religious extremism, social revolution, and civil war had come to an end.

THE RESTORATION, 1660–1688

Most Englishmen—most Scotsmen and Irishmen too—were glad enough to welcome back their king and to see their affairs tranquilly conducted by him and by the restored Parliament representing the great nobles and wealthy men of the kingdom; they were not soon to forget the sufferings and perturbations caused by civil war. The reign of Charles II, from 1660 to 1685, was on the whole peaceful and, after the austerities of the Puritan era, prosperous and gay. England's empire, trade, and manufacturing expanded, and English civilization produced some of its most creative and urbane thinkers. The spirit of mercantile enterprise and scientific research mingled to produce—and pay for—the architectural triumphs of Christopher Wren, who redesigned the churches and public buildings of London after the Great Fire of 1666, which wrecked the heart of the city. Newton was discovering and formulating the law of gravitation. Thomas Hobbes—a mathematician—and John Locke—who began his career as a medical student—were examining the laws of society and government, and developing systematic political theories (see Chapter 21.) John Dryden was casting the polished forms in which English poetry and drama were to be written for a century. On the stage, the Restoration playwrights created a school of comedy (witty, sophisticated, and morally disreputable), which reflected the country's deep breath of relief at the lifting of the trammels of Puritanical censorship.

But the basic issues, constitutional and religious, persisted. The constitutional issue, which had plagued Cromwell not less than James I and Charles I, arose from the difficulty of allotting powers between king and Parliament.

Everyone agreed that the king should have complete control of certain powers, called the Royal Prerogative: he should choose his ministers, administer the laws of the realm, conduct foreign affairs, command the army and navy, and approve or disapprove acts of Parliament. Everyone also agreed that Parliament had the right to approve (or disapprove) new laws, and to raise new taxes. But there were problems. In certain matters, notably the organization of the Church, king and Parliament had at times both claimed the power to make the final disposition. Who was to judge between them? And suppose the king (fully within his rights) prosecuted a foreign policy, or appointed ministers, distasteful to the Parliament, and suppose the Parliament (fully within its rights) refused to vote taxes to implement the foreign policy or to pay the salaries of the unpopular appointees? People were coming in this period to distinguish between what was called the "executive" power (to execute laws) which belonged to the king, and the "legislative" power (to make the laws) which belonged to Parliament, and to applaud the idea of a balance between the two. But suppose the two, instead of staying in balance, were used to frustrate one another? This is what had happened in the reign of Charles I, and it was to happen again in England.

During the reign of Charles II, however, at least there was not quite a deadlock. Many of the king's policies were unpopular; he needed, for example, to cooperate closely with Catholic France. Charles, in turn, was exasperated by Parliament's tendency to keep him short of funds. He found even more exasperating the attempts of some parliamentarians to pass laws aimed at altering the royal succession—his heir and brother was a Roman Catholic, and widely disliked in Parliament. These attempts threatened, clearly, the independence if not the existence of the throne.

As a consequence, Charles II resorted to the practice of not calling parliaments, exactly as his father had, and to raising the money necessary for government by dubious evasions of Parliament's purse-string control. (He sold his own hand in marriage to the Portuguese; he sold Dunkirk to the French; he sold Bombay to a private company; he sold England's alliance in war to Louis XIV.) Charles II was more successful in these tactics than his father; but he merely postponed the renewal of the unavoidable conflict.

The religious issue, so closely connected with the constitutional, was at root different from it. The problem arose from the division of the British populace into numerous religious sects—Roman Catholics, Anglicans, Presbyterians (of several kinds), Baptists, Quakers, and others. Each of these felt that they had the only true path to salvation; most of them felt that their path should be forced upon everyone else.

Charles commenced his reign by promising toleration; but his first Parliament was strongly Anglican, and it insisted upon the extermination by law of dissent. It forced on Charles and his ministers a series of acts directed equally against Roman Catholic and Protestant dissenters, acts which have unfairly come to be known by the name of the minister who reluctantly agreed to them, the Clarendon Code. These laws, enacted at intervals through the 1660's, imposed uniform practices on all Anglican clergymen (Act of Uniformity); forbade groups of more than five people to worship in any save Anglican services

(Conventicle Act); and imposed other hardships and limitations upon dissenters. In 1672, the Test Act was passed to prevent non-Anglicans from holding public office.

These acts (which were enforced with very uneven severity) were extremely distasteful to Protestant dissenters, many of whom were persons of wealth and influence, particularly among the merchants who were doing well in the expanding international trade of England. But if they disliked the "High" Anglicanism of the Restoration, what they feared most was the possibility of a Roman Catholic sovereign and governor. It was these groups, and their sympathizers, who helped to precipitate the constitutional crisis by seeking laws to exclude the king's brother, the Roman Catholic James, from inheriting the throne.

By 1685, the exclusion campaign had resulted in the formation of two schools of thought among the politically influential and articulate people of England (a very small minority of the nation). One group, favoring exclusion, represented a cluster of opinions which also tended to favor toleration for Protestant dissenters, strict control of royal power, a policy favoring commercial expansion, increased authority for Parliament, and extensive guarantees of the "rights of the subject" against the government. While this section of political opinion, which came to be called "Whig," represented many different kinds of people, its greatest strength probably lay among the very wealthy and powerful merchants and noblemen who were the natural beneficiaries and legatees of any transfer of power from crown to Parliament.

In opposition developed a faction that came to be called "Tories." They opposed the exclusion of James from the throne not because they were sympathetic to Catholicism, which they for the most part were not, but because they disliked tampering with the independence and authority of the throne and of the Royal Prerogative. They tended, too, to dislike the pretensions of the great nobles who challenged the crown, and to support a powerful, rigid, and exclusive established Church. Generally speaking, the greatest strength of the Tories probably lay among squires and gentry—the smaller landowners—and country people, and in the Church.

THE REVOLUTION OF 1688

So matters stood when Charles II unexpectedly died, in 1685, and his brother James acceded to the throne as James II. Events now began to contribute to a gradual working out of the various conflicts which had troubled England since the death of Elizabeth. The most important contributor to this solution was James himself; he behaved in such a fashion that most of the influential groups in the kingdom were united in opposition to him, and a basis for national agreement on both constitutional and religious issues was found.

James was an able and virtuous man. But he was also a devout Roman Catholic. The English were alarmed by James's systematic attempts to relax the laws against his few Roman Catholic subjects and to install many of them in positions of authority. These attempts involved, moreover, acts of extremely doubtful legality. In addition to giving rise to suspicions that he intended to undo the Reformation, he suggested as well that he intended to behave unconstitutionally and to override the established laws of the land.

As a consequence of these developments, he was rapidly expelled from England. A group of members of Parliament invited his Protestant daughter Mary, and her husband William, the Stadholder of the Dutch Republic, to come to occupy the throne. The country welcomed them, and James and his Catholic son fled. What has been called the "Glorious Revolution," brief and bloodless, was complete.

The Glorious Revolution, ostensibly a merely conservative move to enforce the ancient constitution against a ruler suspected of subverting it, had extremely far-reaching effects, not all of a conservative nature. The laws which followed and defined the revolution provided the framework in which English government was to operate and, operating, develop and change down to the present time.

Perhaps most fundamental among the customs, principles, and statutes which are called the "Revolutionary Settlement" was the *fact* that Parliament had deposed a monarch and installed a new one in his place. A decade later, in 1701, Parliament did not hesitate to pass the Act of Settlement, which specified the royal succession by excluding any Catholic heir to the throne (or any heir married to a Catholic). From 1688 on, then, the king of England, though in name he ruled "by the Grace of God," clearly in practice ruled by "the Grace of Parliament."

The settlement also portended, but did not immediately signify, the control of Parliament over the king's choice of ministers and his conduct of policy. A long process was necessary before the exercise of the Royal Prerogative passed into the hands of ministers who could not maintain themselves in office without the approval of the majority of the two houses of Parliament. But the beginnings of this process were made in the reign of William and Mary, after 1688. The House of Commons made good its claim to almost exclusive control over money bills—that is, taxation. The Commons were henceforth in a position to blackmail the crown with threats of bankruptcy. The hereditary revenues of the crown, which had sufficed for the state expenses of Elizabeth and had been supposed to suffice for those of her successors, were now clearly inadequate to pay for the business of government. Parliament was called upon *habitually* for approval of taxes, something which had once been regarded as special and extraordinary. Thus, as taxation became the regular basis for government revenues, the body which was empowered to enact it became, permanently and increasingly, more powerful.

The "Revolutionary Settlement" included an important parliamentary act, called the Bill of Rights, which was passed in 1689. The Bill of Rights spelled out various restrictions on the executive power and defined liberties of individuals and other groups—more in the sense of preventing future encroachments upon traditional freedoms than in setting up new rights. Another act, the Triennial Act, of the same year, required that the king must summon Parliament at least every three years, thus preventing for the future experiments in personal rule like those of the two Charleses.

At the same time, an attempt was made to reach some satisfactory religious adjustment. The Toleration Act of 1689, which permitted all religious groups except Jews, Roman Catholics, and Unitarians to worship as they pleased, ushered in a new age of religious conciliation. There were still many controversies and incidents; and non-Anglicans were still in theory forbidden to hold public office, to attend English universities, or in various other ways to participate fully in national life. But even these restrictions were rather loosely enforced for the most part, except in Ireland where the great majority of the population remained Roman Catholic and where stern and brutal repression persisted. In England, non-Anglican Protestants had relatively wide freedom and were often enabled, by evasion of the law, to occupy public office and to follow political careers.

Roman Catholics continued to be rigidly excluded and were, during the eighteenth century, unpopular and badly treated by people and government alike. The average Englishman was bitterly and persistently prejudiced. The prejudice was in part the consequence of Roman Catholicism's association with foreign and unfriendly powers, Spain and especially France, whose king was harboring the family of the deposed James II and sometimes spoke of restoring him by armed force in England. Catholics were thus regarded as being automatically on the side of the enemy and therefore guilty of treason. But while the most important continental states were growing ever more rigidly and even bloodily insistent upon conformity to the state religion, England was moving gradually toward a religious toleration in which the vast majority of the population was allowed to practice differing creeds and rites without interference.

EIGHTEENTH-CENTURY STABILITY

These settlements and situations resulting from the Glorious Revolution of 1688 laid the foundations for a surprisingly stable England in the century that followed. But beneath the surface of a static constitution, changes of a far-reaching sort were invisibly molding newer forms and practices.

The most important changes affected the position of the monarch. In theory, his power and Prerogative remained unchanged. He was still head of the Church; he still appointed his own ministers, the bishops and most lesser officials, and still gave them orders; he still had the authority to carry on foreign affairs and fashion foreign policy; he still commanded the army and the navy; he could still veto acts of Parliament. But the practical meaning of these powers changed. Anne (1702–1714)—James II's daughter, and successor of William and Mary— was the last monarch to veto an act of Parliament. Her cousin and successor, the German Elector of Hanover, George I (1714–1727), met only occasionally with his ministers, preferring to allow them to settle things by consultation in his absence. George I and his son, George II (1727–1760), gradually accepted the practice of permitting one of the ministers to act as leader of the group and, when

ROYAL BRITISH ARMS. Heraldry, the art and science of "coats-of-arms," is believed to have originated in the Crusades, when knights were identified by the distinctive designs on their shields. Later, when shields were no longer used in warfare, coats-of-arms (or "armorial bearings" or, more simply, "arms") continued to be used as emblems of families. They became associated with high place or ancient lineage, the mark of aristocracy. The most important coat-of-arms was the sovereign's, and as modern states took form the king's arms came to be used as the emblem of the state. The use of the emblem, symbolizing the connected histories of dynasties and nations, survived the vicissitudes of changing regimes, the development of nationalism and democracy, and even in some cases the transition to republics.

The royal arms of Great Britain, shown above, is both the personal coat-of-arms of Queen Elizabeth II and the official device of the United Kingdom of Great Britain and Northern Ireland. The shield is divided into four sections, called "quarterings." The first and fourth "display" the three lions which are the arms of England; the second displays the framed red lion of Scotland; the third displays the harp of Ireland. Above the shield is the "crest," recalling the distinctive decoration which knights wore on their helmets, here consisting of the royal crown surmounted by a crowned lion. The shield is encircled with the oldest British order of knighthood, the Garter, with its motto "Honi Soit Qui Mal y Pense," and guarded by the crowned lion and the unicorn. Beneath it is the sovereign's personal motto, "Dieu et mon Droit."

a new set of ministers was appointed, to allow this leader a role—eventually the decisive role—in the selection of his colleagues. By the middle of the century, this minister was being called the "Prime Minister" and was, in effect, the executive head of the government.

The group of important officials who conferred most regularly together came gradually to be known as the cabinet, an institution which took on an increasingly regular and coherent form. And at the same time that the cabinet and Prime Minister were emerging as the body which really exercised the "Royal Prerogative," it was becoming clear that they were almost as fully subject to the choice and control of Parliament as of the king who theoretically appointed them. For Parliament, through its control of the revenues, could make the position of any cabinet and Prime Minister which it disliked exceedingly uncomfortable. Beginning just before the middle of the century, the king on several occasions found himself forced to accept the resignation of ministers whom he liked or (more striking) the appointment of ministers whom he disliked, at the insistence of Parliament. George III had the great William Pitt, whom he detested and feared, forced on him by parliamentary and public opinion.

By 1789, therefore, the power of the king to choose his own ministers was greatly reduced, and more and more he was forced to turn over the still undiminished body of royal powers to a cabinet which was coming to be something like an executive committee of Parliament. But this process was not recognized or accepted at the time. The king's prestige and influence were still very real. Even Parliament would hesitate on most occasions publicly to defy his wishes. The king appeared, at most times in the eighteenth century, to be able to get Parliament to do what he wanted. But this was true only so long as what he wanted coincided—as it usually did—with the views or inclinations of most of the Peers, Commons, and public.

In effect, by 1789 the control of government had passed into the hands of the Parliament, and the "separation of powers," the root of the great controversies of the seventeenth century, had begun to be supplanted by what later was called "parliamentary sovereignty." One reason why this process was not visible at the time, and not made manifest until much later in English history, was that the times were conservative: that is, few great changes in the structure of government or society were wanted or enacted. There were few great legislative controversies. The function of government was seen as being the improvement and execution of laws, not the use of law to remodel the nation. The eighteenth century was the great age of *administration*, as the nineteenth was to be the great age of *legislation*.

OLIGARCHY AND ARISTOCRACY

It is therefore of importance to look at the newly supreme Parliament and at the ruling classes which it represented, which set the tone and character of England in one of its most creative and successful centuries. The success was undoubtedly due at least in part to the talents and character of the oligarchy, and to the fact that it commanded the support or acquiescence of much of the country. It was also due to the way in which all the institutions of the state and most of the institutions of society were blended and articulated under its influence.

The Church of England, for example, served the needs of the aristocracy, and their rule. Its numerous offices, many of them extremely well salaried, provided incomes for sons of gentlemen and bait for politicians seeking to buy the support of influential fathers. Its bishops sat in the House of Lords and were all politically appointed. The Church, moreover, was useful in inculcating loyalty to crown and constitution among the poor. Like the universities, under the influence of the bland gentlemen who staffed it, the Church in the eighteenth century departed widely from any great devotion to its official and presumed purposes. It was highly secular in its character, and the preachings of its genteel prelates reflected the spirit of an age and class which regarded "enthusiasm," such as that which had dominated the preceding century, as both vulgar and dangerous.

The ruling class included, in the first place, the magnates. These men, usually holders of titles of nobility, owned thousands of acres scattered throughout the kingdom, and had far-flung interests, financial and political. They frequented London, and they were urban in their outlook. Controlling the House of Lords, they also controlled a good many seats in the House of Commons be-

ROOM FROM SUTTON SCARSDALE, Derbyshire. From one of England's great houses, built by the Fourth Earl of Scarsdale in 1724. (Philadelphia Museum of Art)

cause of their influence on elections in districts where they were the predominant landowners. To a man they were politically-minded, if not actually politicians. They staffed the high offices, and they influenced, if they did not always control, the king's policy. Many of the great names of eighteenth-century politics—Lord Carteret, the Pelham brothers, the Townshends, Lords Rockingham and Shelburne, Charles James Fox—were members of this class; most of the others—Pitt and Walpole, for example—were connected with it or protégés of its members.

The great nobles were cosmopolitan in their outlook and frequently imperial in their interests. They were also often skeptical and urbane in matters of religion. They were thus natural allies of the great merchants and particularly the great dissenting merchants and bankers of London and other large cities. They were prepared to push a spirited foreign and colonial policy, and to soften the edge of the remaining religious restrictions, and even to welcome into the nobility by royal bestowals of peerages persons who had, through finance or commerce, made their fortunes. In return the aristocrats asked only support of their own power, and freedom to borrow money—for their own personal or political needs—from the bankers. There was thus a sort of alliance between plutocracy and aristocracy which ended (as such alliances often do) by a blending of the two. Many a merchant and banker became a "gentleman," a landowner or peer welcomed in the highest society. "Trade," as Daniel Defoe remarked in the first half of the eighteenth century, "makes a gentlemen." The ruling class was very fluid and hospitable to self-made men.

A quite different group in the ruling class was the smaller landowners, the "squires" or country gentlemen. These were people of great local standing and influence, but generally without national connections and position. They went to London only rarely; their interests were provincial and agricultural. Typically, the squires were bluff, paternal, prejudiced, and excellent farmers. Unlike the great lords and magnates, they were provincial in their viewpoint. Some of them were actually illiterate; few of them had had anything like the cosmopolitan education and experiences of the noblemen. They tended to be conservative or even retrograde in their viewpoint, devoted to the Church and the crown and the "old ways," suspicious of foreigners, of foreign and imperial entanglements, and of townsmen and aristocrats.

In local government, the real power was wholly exercised by local landowners who held commissions as justices of the peace and, sitting together by counties, formed the local courts. These courts exercised far more than purely judicial functions. Most of the operations of local government—taxation, road building, the management of madhouses and other public institutions, the granting of liquor licenses, the administration of poor relief—were in their hands, and the landowning JP's were in effect local despots, usually if not always benevolent.

These men were permitted by the oligarchy to enjoy control over the local affairs which primarily concerned them while permitting the oligarchs undisputed preeminence in national policy and national affairs. The great magnates were the heirs of the "Whig" party which had grown up in the reign of Charles

II and which had taken credit for 1688, and they still often called themselves Whigs. The country gentlemen were the heirs of the Tories, and some of them were still called Tory. But there was little in the way of modern party politics in the eighteenth century. Divisions in Parliament in the eighteenth century were rarely if ever between Whigs and Tories, but rather between congeries of groups which surrounded individual leaders or patrons, generally with no principle or program dividing them, and little save political advantage motivating them.

Parliament, the Lords and Commons, contained representatives of these various groups in the ruling class. The Commons consisted of two kinds of representatives—those of the boroughs or towns, and those of the counties, or country areas. The county members were elected by everyone in the district who owned land appraised at a rental value of forty shillings, but in point of fact, since elections were public and since many voters were apathetic or subject to bribes or pressures, many of the country representatives were the agents (almost the appointees) of the aristocracy, or the squires. The towns chose their representatives in accordance with the terms of the town charters, and these varied greatly. A few were democratic; many were chosen by the city council; others by the principal landlords in the boroughs. But again the influence of the landowners and of the wealthy businessmen was predominant.

These practices and arrangements led to corruption and confusion on the surface; but under the surface there was genuine harmony of interests and

EIGHTEENTH-CENTURY COUNTRY HOUSE. This house, partly designed by Robert Adams, one of the great English architects of his time, was the "country seat" of a family of landowners of the sort that dominated rural life and in many cases public affairs in the eighteenth century in Britain. Its chaste and classical design, perfectly symmetrical and admirably proportioned, illustrates the taste of the day for reason, moderation, and formality; its size and beauty show the power and wealth of the aristocrats and squires who reigned over the countryside. (Radio Times Hulton Picture Library)

genuine stability. The old religious and constitutional issues which had proved so troublesome in the seventeenth century had largely disappeared.

The first two monarchs of the House of Hanover, George I and George II, were dull, unimaginative, and unambitious sovereigns, more interested in their German state of Hanover than in England, content to let their ministers cope with the intricacies of the British constitutional system. The ministers were first and foremost political managers—they had to be, to maintain favorable majorities in the House of Commons. The three principal figures of the reigns of the first two Georges, from 1714 to 1760, were the able, cynical, peaceable Robert Walpole (1676–1745), who is often called the first Prime Minister; the Duke of Newcastle (1693–1768), a wealthy political boss; and William Pitt the Elder (1708–1778), who later became the first Earl of Chatham.

There were only two major domestic disturbances in these years. Both were fomented by supporters of the House of Stuart, who looked upon the Protestant Hanoverians as having usurped the throne and rights of the Catholic Stuarts. In 1715, and again in 1745, Jacobite (from Jacobus, the Latin name for James) risings, originating in Scotland, briefly threatened the security of the Revolutionary Settlement and the Whig supremacy. But on neither occasion did the English people show much enthusiasm for their "legitimate" monarch. And after 1745, the dynastic issue died.

THE REIGN OF GEORGE III AND THE LOSS OF AMERICA

George II was succeeded by his grandson in 1760; the new reign—which was to last until 1820—saw drastic changes and troubles for Great Britain. The social and economic structure of the kingdom, already changing, was to throw the comfortable arrangements of the earlier Georges out of kilter. In the earlier years of George III's reign the most vital and disturbing changes were those produced by the king's constitutional notions and by the revolution of the North American colonies which became the United States of America.

George III was a more ambitious ruler than his predecessors, less concerned with the Hanoverian realms and more with Britain. He had decided views on how his British realms ought to be governed. He accepted without question the outline of the British constitution—he had no aspirations to be a despot. But he wanted to make the "separation of powers" in Britain count for something. Like many other people in Britain, he was worried about the growing menace of "factionalism." But his effort to create support for royal ministers of the king's choosing led merely to the creation of a new faction, the "King's Friends." Edmund Burke and Charles James Fox, the most accomplished orators of the day, inveighed against the royal appointments. The Whig leaders, led by Fox, gradually moved toward a program of curbing the crown. In 1780, Commons passed a famous resolution: "the power of the Crown has increased, is increasing, and ought to be diminished." The aristocracy which the Whigs represented feared the loss of the political dominance which they had built up since 1688.

The fate of George III's efforts to restore the king's freedom of action was determined by the American Revolution. The revolt of the colonies forced the brief installation of his principal critic, Fox, as Prime Minister, and in the end led to the long tenure of the younger William Pitt. Pitt enjoyed the confidence of both king and Commons. His historic function was to harmonize the relations between crown and Parliament.

The American colonies which revolted in 1776 were the most important part of the British empire, and their loss was the worst catastrophe to British prestige ever suffered. We need not describe here the long background of grievances and discontents which led to the revolt. Two aspects of the problem are, however, of particular concern. The first is the domestic quarrels which underlay the American Revolution, and the second is the involvement of the American war with international politics—with the relations of Britain and its great enemy, France.

From the point of view of many Whigs, the American colonists were simply Englishmen who were taking up arms against policies which were just as unwise and dangerous to Great Britain itself as to the colonies. Although there was really little truth in the argument, Burke and others believed that the Americans were fighting for "the liberties of Englishmen," against the advancing tyranny of George III. This argument became more and more popular as the war advanced and the British efforts to subdue the Yankees bogged down. It was an expensive war. It was conducted—badly—by ministers and generals who were sustained in power mainly by the crown's control of patronage against the will of most independent politicians. It came to be an unpopular war. And when the British military effort in America, hamstrung by the French, crumbled at Yorktown, the opposition attack triumphed in London. The king's choice as chief minister, Lord North, was forced to resign, and Whig ministers were forced upon the king in his place. A series of acts designed to remove the power of patronage from the crown was pushed through Parliament.

Although the long-term outcome of these events was not to become clear for a generation, two things were discernible at the time. Parliament, supported by some public opinion, had clipped the royal power. And the king's ministers must henceforth be acceptable to a Parliament which the crown could no longer control. The American Revolution confirmed and extended the victories of 1688.

The immediate effects of the war were, however, even more important in the international sphere than in the domestic. Great Britain had not only lost a campaign against its own citizens in the colonies; it had also lost a campaign against France. This was the low point in the Second Hundred Years War (see Chapters 12 and 18), and the most disastrous setback of British colonial history. The balance of power in the whole world, which had oscillated throughout the eighteenth century, was at stake, and swinging toward the French. The stage was set for the last, the longest, and the decisive encounter in the struggle, which came with the French Revolution.

THE CHANGING FACE OF BRITAIN

Three other kinds of change were taking place in the Britain of George III. One was population growth. Its exact extent is unknown—the first census was not taken until 1807—and the reasons for it are purely conjectural. But it certainly took place. In 1807 the population of the United Kingdom (including Ireland) was about ten million; a hundred years earlier, it had probably been five million. It was caused, apparently, by a decline of the death rate, particularly of infant mortality; and this in turn was probably due to improved scientific knowledge, particularly in the control of smallpox and in midwifery, and perhaps partly to a more humane treatment of bastards.

The second great economic change resulted from improvements in agriculture. Between 1650 and 1750 a whole series of new discoveries and usages had greatly increased agricultural output and changed the form and nature of life in the countryside. Much land was drained. Methods of fertilization, hitherto unknown, were perfected. The use of manure and of nitrogenous plants, the rotation of crops, the ploughing in of turnips, drill sowing (planting seeds in rows, instead of throwing them about the field by hand), scientific breeding of animals, the use of farm machinery—all of these contributed to a vast increase in the production of foodstuffs, especially wheat and meat. This enabled the countryside to feed itself; and it also produced an ample surplus for a population which was increasingly concentrated in the towns.

These changes in agricultural production involved changes in the life of the villages. Where for centuries villagers had cultivated their own tiny fields by primitive methods, large landowners now had the means to make "improvements"—to apply modern agricultural methods. They had the motives, too, for there were large profits to be made in farming now. Accordingly, the landowners more and more forced a breakup of the old village community. From Parliament they secured the passage of laws which extinguished the ancient rights to tillage and pasturage of the villagers, and permitted the "enclosure" of fields—that is, the making of big fields out of small ones, which permitted the application of the new methods and the multiplication of crops. Similar changes were making themselves felt in methods of manufacturing, particularly of textiles (see Chapters 12 and 25). The importance of the new manufacturing methods greatly exceeded the increase in production. As with the agricultural changes, they involved a great change in old ways of life which had subsisted without basic alteration for centuries.

By the end of the eighteenth century economic changes so large that historians later gave them the misleading name of "revolutions"—the Industrial Revolution and the Agricultural Revolution—were taking place. They were creating new groups in the population: factory-owners, capitalists, industrial workers, displaced villagers. New cities and new wealth were created. Machines were created and perfected. The enlarged surpluses and the eagerness for sales created a new kind of trade and commerce. To speed their goods to their markets businessmen demanded—and got—improvement of England's appalling highway system, and they sought alternate means of transport—canals, and, early in the nineteenth century, railways.

Each of these changes sparked others. New conditions, new problems, new demands, arose within the old framework of government. The haughty aristocrats and the hit-or-miss system of parliamentary representation found themselves challenged, in the 1780's, by occasional but ominous demands for a wider and fairer basis for parliamentary voting. The antique institutions of local government could no longer accomodate themselves to the needs of great provincial towns which were growing up. The old village system was disrupted. And the old regulations—of prices, taxes, wages, highways, by justices of the peace, fashioned in a simpler age—were becoming merely archaic annoyances in an era of swift development. England, as it approached the end of the century, was poised for change and faced with potential rifts and cleavages.

14

THE FRENCH
ABSOLUTE
MONARCHY
FROM HIGH NOON
TO EVENING

IN THE SEVENTEENTH CENTURY when England was unstable and revolutionary, France was looked upon as a model of political and social stability, Europe's wealthiest nation, the home of all that was best in European civilization. In the eighteenth century England's government long continued to be regarded as unsound, while on the continent "enlightened despotisms" based in part on memories of France's Louis XIV (1643–1715) became the rule.

But in France a change had come about by the eighteenth century. While the absolute monarchy was still in being in the reigns of Louis XV (1715–1774) and of Louis XVI from 1774 until the outbreak of revolution in 1789, a decline set in. Whereas a kind of harmony had existed in seventeenth-century France between the regime and its "intellectuals," the eighteenth-century French *philosophes* were highly critical of the government and society of their time. On the other hand England, toward the end of the eighteenth century, began at last to have a good press on the continent, as if in anticipation of the end of the old regime.

Louis XIV has been called the Sun King and is supposed to have said "I am the state." Inventive minds have pictured Louis XV as saying "After me, the deluge." Louis XVI, having said little or nothing, was drowned in the deluge: he was guillotined in January, 1793, precisely one hundred and fifty years after the accession of Louis XIV. In that period the French absolute monarchy had reached great heights of power and influence, seemed for a time to threaten Europe with domination, served as a model for many imitators. Then it declined in efficiency and aggressiveness. But the supreme influence of French literature and ideas in Europe persisted even after the harmony between government, society, and the arts had turned to dissonance, and revolution was preparing. And it was Frenchmen who most persuasively instructed their compatriots in the inadequacy of their government.

The French were fated to act out dramas of universal significance. First they showed the splendor and contradictions of absolute monarchy. Then, when that drama had ended in revolution, they were cast in the greater role of proving to Europe and mankind that a people can govern itself.

LOUIS XIV TRIUMPHS OVER THE FRONDE

Louis XIV was a boy of five when he inherited the throne in 1643. The great Cardinal Richelieu had died the year before. France was still involved in the Thirty Years War against the encircling Habsburgs of Spain and Austria. The new king's mother, Anne of Austria, became regent, and placed her trust in Richelieu's understudy, a flexible and resourceful churchman named Mazarin. It was a situation full of peril for a boy king, a woman regent, and a minister hated for his slyness and Italian origin, who nonetheless insisted on the crown's full authority, exercised by himself. Mazarin saw the Thirty Years War through to its conclusion in the Peace of Westphalia in 1648, which secured most of Alsace for France. The Austrian enemy was downed, but the war with Spain, still considered more formidable, continued. In 1648 powerful French interests balked at Mazarin's leadership, and there began a disorderly interruption in the forward march of absolute monarchy in France.

This was the Fronde (la fronde: sling, as in slingshot, suggesting riots), which lasted from 1648 to 1653. It began with legal objections in the king's chief law court, the Parlement of Paris, to taxation and lawmaking by a minister who seemed to be usurping the power of the crown—a usurpation the Parlement preferred to accomplish itself. The magistrates, powerful figures in the city, men of bourgeois origin whose families had purchased their offices, set themselves up as defenders of what they called constitutional traditions. Although they owed their positions to the French kings whose tools they had been, the moment seemed opportune to defend liberty and legality against the "despotism" of a minister whose personal ascendancy over the Queen Mother was enabling him to monopolize the power of the state. The Parlement found ancient precedent for limitations on royal power, and the Fronde began: a struggle between rival agencies of the government. But the Fronde proved to be more than a legal dispute, and was to have lasting effects on the French monarchy.

Because the *Parlement* was backed by the Paris populance, the city soon became unsafe for Mazarin and the defenders of absolutism. The court was obliged to move to suburban Saint-Germain (a humiliation which the boy Louis XIV never forgot). Mazarin was able to make a truce with the *Parlement* in the spring of 1649, but then the revolt was taken up by great noble families throughout France, whose still numerous clientele in their districts made them a formidable force. Mazarin was treated as an upstart and subjected to the vilest of pamphleteering attacks. From 1651 to early 1653 he left France and conducted from abroad the crown's campaign against the rebellion. Louis XIV came of age in 1651—French kings were allowed to rule at 13, in order to reduce the danger of regencies to a minimum. He remained loyal to Mazarin. The young king was able to return to Paris in 1652, but he brought with him lasting impressions of the political danger represented by the *Parlement* and the aristocracy, and antipathy to the notion that there could be legal curbs on the power of the crown and its servants.

The Fronde has suggested to some a parallel with the almost simultaneous Puritan Revolution in Engand, which saw Charles I executed in 1649. They were both civil wars in which the arbitrary powers of royal ministers were challenged. But the Fronde was not a revolution which reached very deep into French society. The *Parlement* and the aristocracy had little more than nostalgia for bygone days when Europe was younger and absolutism had not yet deprived the nobles of their political power. They were truly reactionary, whereas, for better or worse, the absolute monarchy represented by Richelieu and Mazarin was moving forward toward its greatest triumphs under Louis XIV. France was not England, but was a large continental country surrounded by potential enemies; a rich land, but one whose energies would be greater if harnessed and organized by a strong state. Under ideal conditions such a state might have been created by representatives of a self-governing community, but it is almost inconceivable that the French nobility of the mid-seventeenth century, or the nobles of the robe in the *parlements*—men whose titles originated in appointment to state offices—should have been able to organize such a state. The revolting parliamentarians of England had stronger roots.

THE FRENCH STATE UNDER LOUIS XIV

Once the Fronde was over, the French monarchy began to move into its days of greatest glory. The country was pacified. By 1659 the war against Spain was triumphantly ended with the acquisition of two precious provinces—Rousillon in the south and Artois in the north—and of a Spanish bride—the Infanta Maria Theresa—for the French king. And in 1661, Mazarin died and Louis XIV took into his own hands the conduct of French affairs.

Pictures of the French king at this time show him as a rather handsome young man, with brown eyes, a long imperious nose, and a regal bearing. Trained since childhood to accept his position as ruler, he was gracious but self-confident. Mazarin had supervised his formal education rather badly, but the king had learned much of Mazarin's diplomatic tact, and, for good reason, had come to be distrustful of most of the great nobles of his court. As for the *Parlement* of Paris, there is a story, dating from this period, of his entering their chambers, booted and spurred from the hunt, to order them never again to remonstrate, but to register his edicts in silence.

He was to be a king of only average intelligence, but of strong character, a hard worker of regular habits, much given to the public ceremonials which symbolized his authority. After Mazarin's death in 1661 he made it clear that he would be his own first minister, and entered upon a long career of daily council meetings wherein he proved his enjoyment of his "profession of kingship" and his ability to get the most out of the specialists who surrounded him. In his private life and pursuit of pleasure he was as regular and willful as in his work, and, soon tiring of Maria Theresa, enjoyed a succession of mistresses. Typically, his personal conduct was scandalous but not ignoble, and never undermined his growing authority and prestige. By 1661 he had already learned to keep the great nobles at a distance from high governmental posts. He had already disciplined the *Parlement* of Paris. He was never to call a meeting of the Estates General, the French representative body. He set to work with pleasure in meetings of his various councils, which crudely divided the regions of France and the tasks to be done. The looseness of the division of government functions meant that young

Louis xiv by Robert Nanteuil, French school (c. 1623–1678). Engraving. (Philadelphia Museum of Art)

men making their way upward in the king's service heard all sorts of problems discussed and had plenty of chances to learn. Such young men, usually called Masters of Requests, came for the most part from ordinary backgrounds. Louis XIV trusted men who were dependent on him for advancement, men like Colbert, the great economic administrator, and Louvois, the energetic minister of war. He wanted no doubts in anyone's mind as to who was the master.

In those early days the king's authority was never sure of extending outward to all parts of France. The country was tradition-laden, and diverse in its ways, with various sets of laws, weights and measures, and authorities. The governors of military districts were great nobles with local followings, and not always to be trusted. Some provinces were possessed of their own representative estates, and were thus called *pays d'états*, while others enjoyed no representation. The latter were called *pays d'élection*, not because there were elections in our sense of the word, but because assistants to certain tax collectors (Receivers General) were supplied by appointment (*élection*). The districts over which the Receivers General presided were called "generalities." They overlapped with military districts and judicial districts of the principal law courts, the *parlements*. Traditional regions, provinces with well-known names like Brittany, Provence, and Champagne, did not necessarily coincide with these more practical subdivisions of the kingdom. Municipalities and rural localities were even more various, and the tariffs, tolls, and economic regulations defied description.

If there is any key to what Louis XIV's state-building did, or tried to do, to this complicated heritage, it is to be found in two simple terms: *officiers* (office holders), and *commissaires* (commissioners). France, up to this time, had come to be administered more and more by *officiers*, men of bourgeois origin who had been sold offices because the government needed money and did not trust the nobles. Such men, once the monarchy's agents, and still trusted more than the feudal aristocracy, were the pulleys and wheels upon which Louis XIV in his councils depended. Yet, as the Fronde had proved, this mechanism of vested interests was not altogether reliable. More obedient and dependent men were needed, *commissaires* whose hopes made them look to the king for promotions.

Such men existed during Louis XIV's early years of personal rule. Masters of Requests who sat in council meetings and were sent on specific, limited missions, and *intendants* such as those who had been used by Richelieu and Mazarin, were available. Most of them were nobles of the robe, who had bought posts carrying nobility, but, unlike the older type, for example the nobles of the robe in the *parlements*, they were a kind of administrative nobility, eager for advancement to the top positions next to the king, with all the rewards which such service implied. Such *commissaires*, particularly the *intendants*, were made by Louis XIV into a regular force capable of overseeing continuously the work of government throughout France. Gradually, but without being destroyed, the old machinery of office-holders, royal governors, *parlements*, municipalities, and so on was *covered over* with a new network of authority. The new system did not insure immediate, automatic obedience to the will of the king in council; in those days of inked despatches carried in coaches or saddlebags, nothing could have. But to the extent that Louis XIV was an "absolute monarch" capable of regulating artisans through the guilds, dominating his towns and taxpaying peasants, and depriving his nobles of their antique control over the countryside, it was the "administrative monarchy" of *commissaires* that did the job.

A roof of absolutism was built over the surviving anarchy of the outmoded medieval administrative system. The resulting machine, intricate and asymmetric, was doomed to eventual breakdown. But this machine, working in a populous country, rich for those times, kept peace at home and channeled resources into economic and military conflicts abroad. The indefatigable Colbert, son of a merchant, was able to leave his own son wealth and honors and titles because he was Louis XIV's financial agent and economic organizer who provided the funds for the great palace at Versailles, the academies, art collections, fleets and armies. Louvois, the even more dynamic war minister, who did not blink at the necessity of giving orders to great aristocratic generals like Turenne and Condé, was equally indispensable. Under his leadership the military forces became the king's arm as they had never been before, with uniforms, drill, systems of promotion, and guaranteed obedience. It was a far cry from the hired armies of the religious wars, the Thirty Years War, and the Fronde.

But Louis XIV was the chief who listened to the recommendations of such men, and made the decisions. That he was able to do so was partly a matter of personality, partly of the times and environment in which that personality was formed. France had seen enough of disorder. Nobles of sword and robe had not provided the alternative—not in the religious wars, nor in the regencies, nor in the Fronde. After all the past disorders the peasants and *bourgeoisie* sought stability. Experience seemed to prove that one ruler was better than many. Among the middle classes and lesser nobles some of the ablest, seeking a way upward, placed their bets on the crown.

By the early 1680's, when he fixed his permanent residence at Versailles, the great palace newly built at the edge of a sleepy village ten miles from Paris, Louis XIV had reached the apogee of his power and grandeur. At Versailles the business of government was conducted in an aura of unprecedented splendor. Bureaucracy was enlivened with ceremonials symbolizing the king's—and France's —magnificence.

Versailles was designed to be the embodiment of the king's majesty and the nation's glory. But it was designed to be more: not only the most splendid building ever built, but also the handsomest. Its beauties reflected the best taste of the day, and the great artistry, and thus the creative genius, of the most creative of Europe's peoples. Further, the beauties represented the king's royal presence as master of ceremonies, the agent and midwife of the release and improvement of that genius. The palace became a visible symbol of French dominance in the arts and in diplomacy. Stocked with masterpieces and decorated in the heavy, comfortable "style Louis XIV" (carved and gilded portals and furniture, marble and mirrors and tapestries), it was backed by immense formal gardens, suggestive of order and discipline with their clipped hedges, geometric paths, their fountains and pools and roadways. Here in all seasons there were receptions, dinners, spectacles, and concerts to impress foreign diplomats. Here was the audience most coveted by writers, the patronage most sought by artists. The tastes of the court set the standards for the arts. Moreover, the arts reflected the times. Something of the same attitude—that the rules were known and would be followed by wise, and even by creative, men—was expressed in the design of buildings and fortifications, in painting and literature, as well as in statecraft. Technicalities aside, this is the essence of what has been called the "classicism" of seventeenth-century France. [1]

In addition to symbolizing French power and genius, Versailles had a definite political role. Here were the levers of power, directing diplomats and armies and *intendants* and mercantilistic requirements in guilds and seaports, and also the canons of elegance and good taste. To be a noble of consequence, now, one had to live at Versailles, under the king's eye. The aristocracy was being simultaneously bullied and bought out of its vested interest in government, supervised and pensioned off in continuing social eminence and privileges. If Louis XIV reserved the bureaucratic machine for career-hungry commoners and lesser nobles, he left the ceremonial offices for the old nobility. With a few military exceptions, he shouldered aside the aristocracy from the levers of power, but he heaped it with privileges, wealth, honors, and tax exemptions. It was a solution to the old problem of aristocratic rebelliousness, a halfway solution, but one which seemed to work. And the country accepted it. Louis XIV was popular during much of his reign, until the costs of his way of maintaining domestic tranquility, and most particularly, of his foreign wars, began to become apparent.

Every great system of government has its creed. In France the absolute monarchy had been analyzed and justified by political philosophers ever since the Renaissance. The revived legal theory of the Romans—the idea that the emperor makes the laws—served Louis XIV as it had his predecessors. In order to keep the Holy Roman Emperor from collecting this classical legacy it was said that "the king is emperor in his kingdom".

"Divine right of kings," another idea of those times, had a similar usefulness, for the king was said to be responsible directly to God; thus in secular affairs there was no place for papal interference. Bishop Bossuet (1627–1704), the great theorist of divine right and absolute monarchy, taught that the king had to rule through predictable channels which insured that the general welfare (and not just his will as a mere man) would be served. And the king was subject to God's law and answerable to God. What Bossuet's theory meant in everyday terms was that the king would always be under the influence of responsible advisors. The phrase "I am the state," attributed to Louis XIV, expresses more than vanity. In the deepest sense it calls attention to the idea that one authority has replaced the many conflicting authorities of decaying feudalism. The idea of the "general welfare" and of a monopoly of power and justice was still personified in a single

---

[1] In a short history of this kind there is little practical use in lists of names, but for those wishing to test the above generalization a beginning may be made by examining the cases of Descartes (1596-1650) and Pascal (1623-1662) in mathematics and philosophy, Bossuet (1627-1704) in religion and philosophy of history, Corneille (1606-1684), Racine (1639-1699), and Molière (1622-1673) in literature, and Poussin (1594-1665), Claude Lorrain (1600-1682), LeBrun (1619-1690), and Lenôtre (1613-1700) in the arts. For some observations about seventeenth-century science, see Chapter 21.

fallible human being. Men would one day learn to believe that a king was not needed as the agent of the general welfare. But that day was not yet.

Theory aside, what were the aims of the absolute monarchy as seen by its officials? One cannot with certainly say, but probably in an age which had seen so much disorder these men thought that the best way to help the people was to keep order; that in serving the state machine and the dynasty they were contributing to the common good. In the eyes of men like Colbert, Louis XIV's absolutism provided security and justice. Some of them may have seen on the horizon greater equality under the king's law, but they were practical men who had to accept the reality of the compromise with the nobility. And in practice, because of the dynasty's ambitions, personal and territorial, they had to try to meet the costs and repair the damages entailed by Louis XIV's wars.

Even at its apogee in the early 1680's, the France of Louis XIV had its unsolved problems. But in comparison with the rest of Europe or with what Europeans remembered of their past, France at that time presented a remarkable harmony. Government and society and beliefs and even the arts all seemed to fit together.

FRENCH SOCIETY IN THE AGE OF ABSOLUTISM

Louis XIV's administration never really altered the basic structure of society, which remained similar to that of earlier "feudal" times. It was more or less assumed that society had to be organized by professions; that the first estate, or clergy, looked after souls, that the second, or nobles, were the military and, to

VERSAILLES (French Government Tourist Office)

a decreasing extent, the governing officials, and the third estate, or commoners, fulfilled the functions of economic production and taxpaying. There were, of course, many subgroups, but society *was* organized by groups, not by individuals, and the king was arbiter over all groups and kept them working together presumably for the common good.

By taming of the French aristocracy, Louis XIV prevented them from reaching the sense of political responsibility which they might under other conditions have developed. And this method of keeping domestic peace was costly and unjust for the rest of the public, who had to pay the taxes. Moreover, the tax system, as a result of Louis's favoritism, was not as efficient as it needed to be if his expensive foreign policy was to be supported without mounting debts and financial expedients harmful to the French economy. In theory, the mercantilistic measures of Colbert (see Chapter 12) should have harmonized society and the economy with the state. But Colbert, who died in 1683, was never able to extract the maximum of usefulness from mercantilism. Louis XIV's wars were in part responsible for this failure, although in fairness to the king it should be noted that Colbert himself was not above making war on an economic rival. Even without war the privileged position of the nobility would sooner or later have posed political and financial problems.

The condition of the rest of French society is easier to understand once one has grasped the relationship between crown and nobility. The middle class, from great bankers and wholesale merchants down to small shopkeepers, made possible the building of an administrative organization independent of the nobility. But the middle class was controlled by the state, too. If they had had their way, middle-class people would probably have preferred to be protected against the nobles and against foreign competition, but otherwise to be left alone. The absolute monarchy and the mercantilistic economic policies permitted no such freedom.

The peasants still formed the great majority of the population. Their position in seventeenth-century France was scarcely enviable. The great weight of the taxes was upon them, and they paid for the court's grandeur out of the receipts from an agriculture which was not substantially improving its output. In France the king's authority was great enough to keep the nobility from enslaving the peasants as they did in Eastern Europe. In this way the absolute monarchy of the western type, able to rely on middle-class officials, made taxpaying citizens out of the peasants instead of serfs. Moreover, unlike the small farmers in England, where the aristocracy used their political power to further the enclosures, the French peasants managed to keep their small parcels of land. But they remained, for all that, third-class citizens. It is true that the king's peace in the countryside was better than the nobles' civil wars, but the social and economic domination of the nobility in the countryside remained long after their political domination was removed. The peasants of Louis XIV's era were at best its forgotten men. At worst, when foreign wars and taxes and poor harvests actually brought famine, they revolted and were suppressed by force.

In this society religion was in theory allied with the state. France was overwhelmingly Roman Catholic, and the Church was one of the main agencies of royal control. The priests and religious orders, besides caring for souls, managed charity and education. The Church kept intact the standards of conduct of the society. The great bishops, like Bossuet, expected to guide the king in the many realms where truth, like the canons of art, was known. In practice a commoner could still advance to the highest positions in the Church, but favoritism played a great part, and many of the upper clergy were members of the aristocracy. The Church had its own assemblies, controlled by the bishops; hence the clergy, though far from democratic, was closer to independence than any other group in French society.

Louis XIV, in spite of the liberties which had been granted the Huguenots by the Edict of Nantes in 1598, was entirely a man of his century in believing that a healthy society should have one set of religious and moral guides. What absolute monarchy sought and promised was unity—religious as well as political. In order to insure the loyalty of the Catholic clergy, he guarded jealously the rights of the Gallican Church; that is, of a more or less autonomous French national church in the appointment of whose officials he had much to say. The overlordship of the Papacy was wholly spiritual, not administrative. Many of the *bourgeoisie* were Gallican in their sentiments, and so were most nobles of the robe, whose families had purchased judicial and other offices carrying titles. Louis XIV would not allow the magistrates of the *parlements* to oppose him politically, but he encouraged their Gallicanism.

Toward the end of the reign, foreshadowing a struggle which would continue in the eighteenth century, the king opposed without entire success the religious movement known as Jansenism, which was popular with some nobles and with a great many of the *bourgeoisie*. Jansenists since the 1640's had been hoping to reform the Church from within. Like the Protestants they emphasized the individual's relationship with God. They warned that efforts to express religious truths in words were leading some people to concentrate on the words at the expense of the religious experience, others to escape from the mazes of theology into the requirements of excessive ceremonials, and still others to abandon religion altogether in favor of man-made moral systems. Jansenism, tirelessly opposed by the Jesuits, also violated the king's conviction of the need for religious unity. Although he jealously guarded "Gallican liberties" against the Pope's authority, he supported the Pope against the Jansenists.

The most striking example of Louis XIV's desire for "one faith" as well as for "one law" and "one king" was his revocation of the Edict of Nantes in 1685. This act denied the Huguenots the most elementary rights of citizens and forced thousands of economically and socially valuable families to flee to such places as Prussia and America. With the many wars, it cast gloom over the second half of the reign. In 1685 public intolerance was still very common all over Europe; the acceptance of the Huguenots in Prussia was an almost unique act of public policy connected with state-building. Catholics were still mistreated even in relatively tolerant England. Yet the French government in revoking the Edict of Nantes abandoned a position "in advance" of public opinion for one which was to be called "backward" by powerful leaders of opinion in the following century.

FRANCE AND EUROPE

France's influence in Europe in the age of Louis XIV rested on France's size and good order and apparent success in solving the problems of a complicated society. The French sun shone over Europe in many rays of statecraft and art and thought, with a warmth which continued long after the old king was dead. It did so because French society was capable of generating light as well as power.

Seen in this perspective, Louis XIV's wars are perhaps the least glorious part of France's story, but they were an integral part of a regime and policy which rested on glory. [2] The expansion of the French state, and its leadership in Europe, were as much a part of Louis' policy as its consolidation and enrichment. Louis XIV's first war was inherited—it was the Thirty Years War—and although the Austrians made peace in 1648, the conflict with Spain continued until the Peace of the Pyrenees in 1659. This early period of Louis XIV's career saw France gain Alsace in 1648, and Artois and Roussillon from Spain in 1659. In 1665 upon the death of his father-in-law he claimed the Spanish Netherlands in the name of his Spanish wife, but this challenge brought forth a response from the alert Dutch, who wanted no such youthful, powerful, and as yet undefeated neighbor as Louis XIV. The Dutch allied with England and Sweden and managed to limit the damage in the Spanish Netherlands to the loss of southern Flanders, which Louis XIV secured by the Treaty of Aix-la-Chapelle in 1668.

Louis XIV's next war was the "Dutch War" of 1672–1678, which was the last war in that early period when France's power and prestige were still growing and the young king seemed destined to have everything his way. In it, he added the force of his land power to that of English sea power. He allied with the English, and also with Sweden, and invaded Holland in 1672. But he was once again faced with the tendency of European powers to ally against anyone who was becoming too powerful. There were other men of his generation who were just as determined as he. William III in 1672 became Stadholder of the Netherlands (1672–1702) and entered upon the long duel with Louis XIV which was to be his life's work. William III managed to organize a formidable coalition consisting of the Emperor, Spain, and Brandenburg, and profited from the English return to neutrality when they saw the danger presented by French aggrandizement. Again the damage was limited; Louis XIV obtained only Franche-Comté—the Free County of Burgundy—in the Treaty of Nimwegen (Nimegue) in 1678. By means of "chambers of reunion" which studied (and favored) French claims to border territories, accompanied by military occupations, France edged toward the Rhine in the 1680's. Louis XIV after the Dutch War had reached the height of his power.

This, it will be recalled, was the period of the revocation of the Edict of Nantes (1685). Colbert (d. 1683), Louvois (d. 1691), and others of the team who had made the reign great were passing from the scene. It was also the period

[2] For a discussion of Louis XIV's wars in the perspective of European international relations, see Chapter 18.

when the influence of Madame de Maintenon, the mistress whom the king is thought to have married after the death of the Queen, began to make life at the court more pious and formal and rather oppressive. The King himself was still in his forties; he had many more years to reign, but they would be marked by opposition in Europe and by considerable strain and resentment at home. Louis XIV's fiftieth year, 1688, when England was embarked upon its "glorious revolution," saw the beginning of the costly wars which marred the second half of the reign.

Thereafter, war was almost continuous. The first was the War of the League of Augsburg (1688–1697). The League was in large part the work of William III, and was Europe's natural response to France's aggressions toward

THE EXPANSION OF FRANCE FROM 1648 TO 1789

the Rhine. The diplomatic and military situation was made more dramatic by the English revolution of 1688, which placed William III, with his wife, Mary, upon the throne of England. Louis XIV supported the deposed James II. The French armies were fairly successful—on the Rhine, in Italy, in the Netherlands—but peace was hastily concluded at Ryswick in 1697. Bigger game was in sight as the reign of the simple-minded, and childless, Charles II of Spain (1655–1700) drew to a close.

This unfortunate Charles II was the last of the line of Spanish Habsburgs, and he was also, as it happened, the brother-in-law of Louis XIV, who did not take very seriously his renunciation of the Spanish succession at the time of his marriage. Louis XIV's agents had prevailed upon Charles II to recognize as his heir the Duke of Anjou, Louis XIV's grandson, who upon the death of Charles in 1700 took the title Philip V and began the line of Spanish Bourbons. This solution to the problem of the Spanish succession was even more alarming to European statesmen than Louis XIV's previous drives toward the Rhine. Now all the Spanish possessions in Europe seemed to be falling into his hands, and with them the Spanish colonial empire and naval power. With the balance of power on the continent, on the seas, and in the New World leaning dizzily in France's favor, the other powers reacted by forming a coalition. In 1701 William III took the lead in creating the League of the Hague, which joined England, Holland, and the Empire and, soon afterward, Savoy and Portugal.

In spite of a number of victories on the Rhine and in Spain, France was hard-pressed in this war, and the sufferings of its people, particularly in the winter of 1709, were terrible. By 1710 Louis XIV was on the verge of abandoning most of the conquests of his reign, but he refused demands that he turn against his grandson, Philip V of Spain, and as the war continued the French king was saved by last-minute victories and by divisions among his enemies. The war was finally ended by the Treaties of Utrecht (1713), and Rastadt and Baden (1714), whose terms are summarized on pages 282–283.

The War of the Spanish Succession involved so many interests in Europe and overseas that it has sometimes been called the first of the "world wars." Certainly it merits an important place in the annals of the European balance of power (see chapter 18). In the French history which is the subject of this chapter the War of the Spanish Succession darkened the last years of the reign of Louis XIV and prepared the way for some of the dissatisfactions of the eighteenth century. France was not crippled, either at home or abroad, but a rich and beautiful country, the most advanced in Europe, had been led through an exhausting, deforming, and perilous war. The economy had been strained, the government's finances were a wreck, and it was generally believed that the population had declined. This was what the "age of Louis XIV" had turned into, and if the public as a whole was incapable of generalizing about the emptiness of dynastic ambitions, there was nevertheless much grumbling. Louis XIV had outlived most of his own generation and was now far from popular. His son and two of his grandsons had died, and it was his great-grandson, a small boy, who was heir to the throne and would later be known as Louis XV. The old king died in September, 1715.

LOUIS XIV'S SUCCESSORS

Between the death of Louis XIV and the outbreak of the French Revolution—the period usually regarded as "eighteenth-century France"—two more kings named Louis reigned: Louis XV (1715–1774) and Louis XVI (1774-1792).

Louis XV was only five and a half years old when his great-grandfather died and left him the crown. Once again France had a child king and a regency, this time the regency of the Duke of Orléans, and once again (as in the Fronde) there was a reaction against the preceding period of bureaucratic absolutism and an attempt on the part of the nobles to take a hand in government. The Orléans regency was accompanied by a revival of the *parlements,* who were once more allowed to remonstrate against the edicts of the king's officials, and by an experiment known as *polysynodie,* whereby councils of nobles were expected to help form the government's policies. There was a considerable relaxation of morals among the aristocracy, particularly in the Orléans circle. John Law's financial experiments (see Chapter 12) added to the atmosphere of excited liberation.

As on previous occasions in French history, however, the aristocratic effervescence of the Orléans period led nowhere. After Louis XV came of age (1722), he was influenced by a number of ministers, but finally settled on his old tutor, Fleury, a cautious, conservative man who served as first minister until his death in 1743. The absolute monarchy was on its way again, though it lacked the aggressiveness and creativeness of the previous century. After 1743 Louis XV acted as his own first minister. Although he was perhaps the most intelligent of the Bourbon kings, he was afflicted by a deadly, incurable boredom. And he was, in addition, rather timid about confronting his councils and asserting himself as chairman of the meeting. From the 1740's, for instance, he had a secret foreign policy of which even his ministers were uninformed.

While Louis was perhaps not as lazy as has been supposed, he did fail to unify and direct the government's policies, leaving the central control panel of the monarchy unattended. He allowed himself to be influenced by his mistresses, especially the Marquise de Pompadour, and later Madame du Barry, who had the power to relieve his boredom, with the result that the authority which was supposed to come from God actually passed through rather profane channels on its way to the administrative machine which ruled the people.

Louis XV, like his predecessor, saw France through a number of wars, but his foreign like his domestic policies were marked by less leadership and less grandiose goals than formerly. France's population and wealth were still growing. Potentially the country was as great a military power as ever, but Cardinal Fleury and Louis XV instead of forcing events tended to be drawn into wars against their will or at times and places chosen by others. Moreover, the clumsy tax system failed to secure for the state the benefits of the country's wealth. With a great colonial competition against England in full career, and with the growth of new powers like Prussia and Russia on the continent, France had need of firmer direction than the eighteenth-century monarchy provided.

Although it failed to secure the Polish throne for Stanislas Leszczynski, the king's father-in-law, the War of the Polish Succession (1733–1738) at least won Lorraine for Stanislas, and ultimately for France. The War of the Austrian Succession (1740–1748), in which France joined Prussia and Bavaria against Austria, was fought while Louis XV was in his thirties and still popular; the name *Bien-aimé* dates from his illness while campaigning. But nothing tangible was gained, either on the continent or overseas. When the fighting broke out again in the Seven Years War (1756–1763) the intricacies of policy-making at the French court had contributed to the famous "reversal of alliances" which placed France at Austria's side against Prussia, but, as usual, the overseas opponent was Britain, to whom France lost Canada and India.

By the end of the Seven Years War disappointments abroad together with heavy taxation and impending financial crisis at home were leading to a reappraisal of the governmental and social system. Public opinion was becoming a force; and although the monarchy itself was not called into question, its personalities and policies were coming to be examined in an ever bolder manner. Arguments over Jansenism and the influence of the Jesuits in the Church were now supplemented by the campaign of the *philosophes* for freedom of thought. Efforts of the king's ministers to modernize the administration, and particularly the system of taxes, encountered opposition which the king had not the will to overcome. The Duke of Choiseul, Louis XV's chief minister in his later years, tried between 1758 and 1770 to lift France back onto the road to military and diplomatic success. But Madame du Barry disliked him, and in the end he was disgraced. The *parlements* which Louis XIV had once silenced were appealing to public opinion against the edicts of the king's ministers, and were developing a doctrine that in the absence of the Estates General they were the representatives of the people and could veto legislation.

Many of the magistrates in the *parlements* were progressive in that they favored greater economic and civil liberty. As nobles of the robe, they tended to defend the privileges of the aristocracy. Politically, they contested the right of the king's ministers to unqualified obedience. Their obstructionism resulted in a kind of paralysis, for without being able to bring about reforms themselves, they convinced the public that reforms were necessary, and yet blocked those attempted by the king's ministers. Opposition on the part of the *parlements* finally led Louis XV in 1771 to consent to Chancellor Maupeou's reorganization of the judicial system, but this uncharacteristic firmness on the part of the old and now unpopular king was undone by his young and popular successor Louis XVI (1774–1792), who upon his accession recalled the *parlements*.

The new king, Louis XVI, was only twenty when he ascended the throne, accompanied by his young Austrian Habsburg wife, Marie Antoinette, who was nineteen. He was a heavy young man of only average intelligence, awkward, timid, and weak-willed. In him the public instinctively recognized an unpretentious man of good intentions, but at court his complete lack of social grace coupled with a tendency to overeat and to play crude practical jokes lost him the respect of the great nobles. Incapable of exerting leadership himself, he let the aristocracy persuade him to dismiss, one after another, the reforming ministers who seemed at first to promise so much for the new reign.

The first of these ministers, the *philosophe* Turgot, lasted from 1774 to 1776. He suppressed the notorious *corvée,* the labor service which the peasants had to contribute to the government, and replaced it with something like an income tax which nobles as well as commoners had to pay. He also abolished the guilds and tried to extend free circulation of grain; if he had had his way he would probably have worked against the tendency of the *parlements* and aristocracy to block legislation corrosive of their privileges.

After Turgot's dismissal the Swiss banker Necker was called in, and managed to bolster the government's credit sufficiently to pay for France's effort against England in the War of American Independence (1778–1783) without creating new taxes. His dismissal followed a too frank, though not altogether truthful description of the condition of the finances, his famous *Compte rendu* of 1781. Other ministers followed. They were all faced with the same needs for tax reform which had faced Turgot, and with the same inescapable need to reassess a social system which had congealed since the time of Louis XIV and on which the tax privileges of the aristocracy were based.

It was along this route that the Revolution of 1789 came to France. For a time, however, the reign of Louis XVI seemed a great success. The American War, although costly, seemed to be everything that one could wish for in the way of a triumph against the English enemy. It was perhaps a little odd for an absolute monarchy to favor the revolt of the American republicans, but this diplomacy, guided by Vergennes, was in the great tradition of the balance of power. No doubt Louis XIV would have done as much. Moreover, fresh currents of thought had long been stirring among the economists and *philosophes* of the eighteenth-century Enlightenment, and to these was added the inspiring example of the young people on the Atlantic seaboard fighting for its freedom. Louis XVI himself felt his lethargy somewhat lifted by the generous ideas of the age, and in 1787 gave back to the Protestant Huguenots their civil rights.

The old monarchy in France failed to evolve without violence past the point which our narrative has now reached. In the eighteenth century all aspects of French life—economy, society, beliefs, even international relations—had changed significantly since the days of Louis XIV. It was this growth which exerted more and more pressure on the old political institutions and presented a great challenge to those in positions of responsibility and power.

15

THE HABSBURGS
OF AUSTRIA

IN CENTRAL EUROPE, the century and a half from 1648 to 1789 witnessed a different kind of consolidation from that which was taking place in France. The map of the Holy Roman Empire in this period remained a patchwork of nearly independent states of all shapes and sizes. The Empire went on slumbering but developments within it portended a new course for all of Central and Eastern Europe. What must concern us first is the consolidation, roughly like that of France, of two large areas which lay on both sides of the borders of the Empire: the Austrian monarchy of the Habsburgs, and the Hohenzollern creation which came to be known as Prussia. Chapter 16 will be devoted to the Hohenzollerns and Prussia, and Chapters 19 and 20 will survey the changes in eastern Europe. In the present chapter we shall follow the Habsburgs as they turned their attention from the Holy Roman Empire to the solidification of their own dynastic domains.

THE HOLY ROMAN EMPIRE
AFTER WESTPHALIA

Twice before—in Luther's time, and at the outset of the Thirty Years War—the Habsburg dynasty had sought to make real the hope that the Holy Roman Empire might be organized into a viable state, its princes subordinated, and gathered under the banner of Catholicism. On each occasion the size of the task had defeated the aspiration. In the half-century after Westphalia, the Habsburgs continued to preside over the ghostly Empire, wearing its imperial crown and remaining without serious rivals within it until the successes of Prussia in the eighteenth century. But the Habsburgs after Westphalia concentrated on ruling their dynastic holdings.

In the first place the imperial title was elective, and although the Habsburgs were regularly chosen as emperors the elections were occasions for extracting from them guarantees of the "liberties" of the princes. Since the Treaty of Westphalia, many of the states within the Empire were, in effect, sovereign. Outsiders like the French and Swedish kings held possessions within the Empire, moreover, and as guarantors of the Westphalia treaties they could interfere in imperial affairs. Anything which the emperor did to aggrandize his power at the expense of the princes would arouse the chronic tendency of some of them to ally themselves with the emperor's enemies, especially France. Indeed, the jealously defended sovereignty of the princes was the choicest card in the diplomatic hand of the French kings, and it magnified the French opportunity to bid for predominance in Europe.

The Holy Roman Empire was, secondly, divided in its sentiments and way of life. Since the Reformation most of the northern states had been Protestant, and most of the western and southern ones Catholic; the Imperial Diet, since Westphalia, often divided on religious issues with each side having a veto over the other's proposals. Parts of the Empire, such as the Rhineland, were fairly highly developed economically, with numerous towns, a well-developed commercial and banking system, and small peasant holdings. In the east, town life had declined in importance since the sixteenth century, large estates were the rule, and the peasantry was tied to the land and subject to heavy payments in labor and kind. The *sizes* of the states in the Holy Roman Empire, as well as their location, gave them different interests. Some were ecclesiastical states, like the electorates of Cologne, Mainz, and Trier, some free cities, some margraviates (markgraf, count of the march), some landgraviates (land-graf, land count), some duchies, and so on, to the number of about three hundred, not counting the tiny independent manors of the knights of the Empire, which were numerous as the sands of the seashore.

In this story-book world of castles and vineyards, forests and peasant villages, once the home of robber barons and still a treasury of medieval complexity, diversity, dialects, music, and folklore, everything seemed possible except a single, all-embracing state. A swarm of noble families quarreled, allied, intermarried, and with the passing of the generations, dispersed or consolidated their inheritances. The stars in this firmament were the electors, traditionally seven (Cologne, Mainz, Trier, the Palatinate, Saxony, Brandenburg, Bohemia), with Bavaria added at Westphalia, and, toward the end of the seventeenth century, Hanover. The electors were often important enough to have contacts outside the Empire, and it is instructive to note some of their interests. Bavaria tended toward friendship with France against the Habsburgs. The Elector of Saxony became King of Poland in 1697 and for a long time played a part in the confused and tragic history of that country (see Chapter 20). In the eighteenth century the

Elector of Hanover became King of England, where he and his descendants, the "Hanoverians," reigned without losing touch with their German interests.

The old picturesque Germany had its good side. It was possible to live in the little states as if on vacation from politics. There was an engaging paternalism, a small-town intimacy, about many of the miniature governments. The multiplicity of capitals and potential patrons offered opportunities to artists, poets, and political job-hunters capable of moving from place to place.

But the hundred and fifty years after Westphalia were hard ones—sometimes humiliating ones—for the Germans. Recovery was slow from the economic ills which had accompanied the shift in the great centers of trade to the Atlantic seaboard, and from the miseries of the Thirty Years War. Not until the mid-eighteenth century was Central Europe in a state of economic convalescence; even then the increase in production was hampered by all sorts of man-made tangles, as though the people of the Holy Roman Empire were obliged to produce and exchange things through the interstices of a vast net.

The sovereignty of the little states was satisfying to the rulers, each of whom had his little Versailles, his little army, foreign policy, bureaucracy, and miniature mercantilism. In the last analysis, however, the diversity and fragmentation within the Holy Roman Empire was harmful. The little mercantilisms hampered trade. The duplication of palaces and armies and courts, while charming, bore heavily on a sluggish agricultural economy. Instead of accumulating and investing capital, gaining experience and self-confidence, like the western *bourgeoisie*, the German middle class remained officeholders beholden to the princes.

THE HOLY ROMAN EMPIRE AT THE BEGINNING OF THE 18TH CENTURY

Although negligible in the international balance of power, the armies kept order at home and could on occasion be rented out—thence the "Hessians" hired by Britain for use against the American colonists. Even in their patronage of the arts, for which many otherwise forgotten princes are deservedly famous, the numerous petty courts pursued the alien and austere ideals of French classicism to the detriment of the local, natural, and native German, which continued in the lower layers of society, scarcely noticed and certainly unhonored by the cosmopolitan aristocracy. Indeed, in the people themselves the sense of nationality which had been so strong at the time of Luther was as if drugged in the century after the Thirty Years War.

After the middle of the eighteenth century the Germanies produced an intellectual and literary revival of great cultural importance. Heralded by the music of Johann Sebastian Bach (1685–1750), the revival came like a sudden spring. Men like Lessing, Herder, Goethe, Schiller, and Kant, by writing memorable works in the German language, contributed to a cultural unity which transcended the political fragmentation of the area. It revived the sense of nationality and forecast political developments of a later age.

Meanwhile the solidification of areas *within* the old Empire into recognizable states went on apace. And of these the greatest, lying partly inside and partly outside of the imperial borders, was the Habsburg monarchy.

THE HABSBURG DOMINIONS IN 1648

Creation of a modern state in the Danubian basin was a remarkable feat. A small Alpine principality—having some outlying possessions, troubled by bitter religious dissent, by many distractions, by extreme diversity of population, and by constant attack from that most predatory of powers, the Ottoman empire—was converted into a large, powerful, stable, and well-run country in little more than a century and a half. The empire of the Habsburgs has no successors today, and its legal heir is the republic of Austria, very similar in importance and size to the negligible archduchy from which the great empire sprang. But while it lasted, the Austrian empire exerted vast influence upon the course of events in areas around it, and brought unity and progress to the jumbled peoples of central Europe. Its protracted and painful disintegration produced such fatal developments as World War I; and its disappearance, in 1918, left a void which was to be filled by Hitler and then by the Soviet Union.

The Habsburgs worked quickly in their state-building career. In 1648 the institutions and territories which they controlled did not in any way resemble the emerging, centralized absolutism of France. But in 1789, on the eve of the French Revolution, the Habsburg monarchy looked very much like the monarchies of England or France. Its borders were clearly defined. Its central government (sitting on top of feudal relics, provincial assemblies, and local liberties, as in France) was, as in France, autocratic. The regime was highly bureaucratic.

And, to a greater extent than France or England, its rulers had been toying with reforms and changes modeled on the most advanced and modern ideas of the day. But there were basic differences, which were to prove the undoing of the House of Habsburg and the cause of Danubian unity. When the monarchical superstructure was stripped from France, there lay revealed an extremely united and creative nation; while beneath the imposing superstructure of imperial Austria there lay a congeries of nations, provinces, and jealous regional ambitions, an archaic society, and a rickety but persistent system of antique local government.

To a remarkable extent, the Austrian empire was *nothing but* its monarchy.

In 1556 the greatest of the Habsburgs, Charles V, had abdicated, dividing his worldwide empire between his son, Philip II of Spain, and his brother Ferdinand. To the latter went the German, Hungarian, and Bohemian possessions, and the imperial title: he was elected Ferdinand I of the Holy Roman Empire, and he was the ancestor of all rulers of the Austrian dynasty until its dethronement in 1918. In 1648, besides Bohemia and Hungary, the holdings of the Austrian branch of the Habsburgs consisted of these territories: most of the present republic of Austria, which includes Vienna and the German-speaking Alpine provinces near it; Carniola to the south, now part of Yugoslavia; and the Adriatic province of Istria, with its important seaport of Trieste, now divided between Italy and Yugoslavia. To the west, the important Alpine county of Tyrol also belonged to the Habsburgs, but it had been granted as an *appanage* to a younger son, and it was not to be recovered for the older line until 1665. After that date it remained under the rule of Vienna until 1918, when it was divided with Italy.

These provinces were extremely varied, in 1648, as regards institutions, religion, and nationality. Each province possessed its ancient law and diet, with widely various liberties and customs. There were Protestant strongholds, particularly in Styria and Lower Austria. And while the great majority of the inhabitants were German, in Carniola, Styria, Carinthia, and Istria there were many Slavs, particularly among the peasantry. Istria and Tyrol both contained many Italian-speaking persons. There were few substantial links among the provinces; the only thing they had in common was their prince.

Bohemia and Hungary were more separate still. Bohemia, the lands of the Crown of Saint Wenceslas, was a group of provinces of mixed German and Slavic population: Bohemia proper, with the city of Prague which was in the seventeenth century the most frequent residence of the rulers; and the provinces of Lusatia, Silesia, and Moravia. Bohemia was ruled entirely separately from the Alpine and southern provinces, and it had more unified institutions. Although it was included in the Holy Roman Empire, it had always enjoyed a high degree of independent government. But by 1648 a catastrophe had overtaken the ancient kingdom (see p. 137). It had revolted against Habsburg Catholic rule in 1618, and precipitated the Thirty Years War. Bohemia had been rapidly reconquered by the Habsburgs, and the Battle of the White Mountain, in 1620, had extinguished the rebel power. After that, the most frightful revenge was visited upon the unfortunate kingdom. Protestantism was eliminated. The native aristocracy was replaced by reliable Catholic and pro-Habsburg Germans, a process not dissimilar to that which was to be carried on a few years later in Ireland by the English government which exterminated the native Irish, Catholic ruling class and replaced it with English, Protestant landowners.

The result was to deprive the native populations of their natural leaders and to substitute for a feudal nobility, with its ferocious aversion to royal absolutism, a nobility consisting of little more than agents of the central government. Moreover, Ferdinand II (1619–1637) succeeded in cajoling the Bohemian parliament into recognizing his family as hereditary rulers of Bohemia, replacing the old elective kingship. For the parliament, like the aristocracy, had become a rubber stamp of Catholic, central power in Bohemia. By 1648 Bohemia was more thoroughly subjected to the Habsburgs than any of their other dominions, and in Bohemia absolutism was already a practical if not a legal fact.

The kingdom to the south, Hungary, was larger, its situation was far more complicated, and its subjugation was slower and less complete. Two thirds of Hungary had fallen under Ottoman rule. A considerable portion of the nobility of Hungary (part of which was Protestant) actually preferred Ottoman rule, which was on the whole genial and tolerant, to that of the Catholic and centralizing Austrians. Under the overlordship of the Turks, the Hungarians were permitted not only to practice their Protestant faith, but also to set up almost completely independent governments.

There had arisen, in eastern, "Ottoman Hungary" in the early seventeenth century, a powerful substate called Transylvania. Under the leadership of an extremely able prince named Bethlen (Bethlehem) Gabor (1613–1629), Transylvania had developed beneath its Turkish suzerainty into a power of considerable importance. At the end of the Thirty Years War, Transylvania had better prospects of leadership in the Danubian plain than the Austrian Habsburgs. So strong, indeed, was the magnetic attraction of Calvinist Transylvania to the Habsburg-ruled nobles of western Hungary that Ferdinand II had been forced to recognize and tolerate the practice of Protestantism in Habsburg Hungary at the very time when he was seeking to exterminate it in Bohemia and to combat it in the rest of Germany. It was certainly not clear, in 1648, that the Habsburgs would be able to extend their control in Hungary, or even to make permanent their control in the third of the kingdom actually in their possession.

These varied holdings were separate; theoretically in all of them, and actually in all of them save Bohemia, the position of the Habsburgs was that of a medieval sovereign, not a modern autocrat. They ruled in each province by grace of ancient law and contract; in each their power was defined and circumscribed by ancient custom and usually by ancient representative institutions. Their rights were not even hereditary in some areas, notably in Hungary where the monarchy was still elective. Except in Bohemia, they faced a nobility fiercely devoted to its privileges. In most places they faced dissension from the religious orthodoxy of which they were the most ardent defenders in Europe.

In the next century and a half the Habsburgs consolidated and expanded their rule in the regions just described, and in others which they acquired during the period, and they abandoned all pretense or aspiration to the consolidation of their power in the Holy Roman Empire. The making of Austria was paid for by the abandonment of Germany. The Holy Roman Emperors were at last doing what they should have done five hundred years before if they were to follow the lead of England and France in the making of a modern state: they were abandoning their ecumenical claims, their Augustan inheritance of world suzerainty, and their impossibly far-flung jurisdictions, in order to develop a unified state stretching out from the core of the family possessions. Just as the small tenth-century duchy of France had given its name to a great kingdom, so much later did a small archduchy of Austria give its name to a great empire.

But the process remained incomplete. The Habsburgs had come too late on the scene to consolidate their recent and outlying acquisitions, and even in the old nucleus they never succeeded in creating a "nation". The title of the last of the Habsburg rulers, Charles I, who abdicated in 1918, suggests the processes of accretion whereby the empire was created, and the diversity and disunity of its parts:

> His Apostolic Imperial and Royal Majesty, Charles, by the Grace of God, Emperor of Austria and Apostolic King of Hungary, King of Bohemia, Dalmatia, Croatia, Slavonia, Galicia, Lodomeria, Illyria and Jerusalem; Archduke of Austria; Grand Duke of Tuscany and Cracow; Duke of Lorraine, Salzburg, Styria, Carinthia, Carniola, and Bukovina; Grand Prince of Transylvania; Margrave of Moravia; Duke of Upper Silesia and Lower Silesia, Modena, Parma, Plaisance and Guastalla, Auschwitz and Zator, Teschen, Friulia, Ragusa and Zara; Prince-Count of Habsburg and Tyrol, Nyborg, Goritz and Gradisca, Prince of Trent and Brixen, Margrave of Upper and Lower Lusatia and Istria; Count of Hohenembs, Feldkirch, Begrenz, and Sonnenburg; Lord of Trieste, Cattaro, and the Wendish March, Grand Voyvode of Serbia, *et cetera, et cetera, et cetera.*

THE CONSOLIDATION OF THE HABSBURG DOMINIONS

The making of Austria (the name was not officially applied to the Habsburg dominions as a whole until 1805) was favored by certain facts of the situation in central Europe. The overt aim of the Habsburgs was the wrecking of the power of the local nobility, and this aim brought them the support and sympathy of the peasant populations, who regarded the nobles as the most immediate and conspicuous of their many oppressors. The social struggle in these regions took many forms; one of them was religious, and the tendency of the Danubian landowners to become Protestant (a tendency much less noticeable among the simple people) was in part an effort to rid themselves of interference from their sovereigns. Further, the dynasty in the late seventeenth and early eighteenth centuries had fewer distractions than had its earlier generations. Spain and its empire were lost to them; the Holy Roman Empire was virtually abandoned as a theater for political power. It was both possible and necessary to cultivate their patrimonial holdings with greater assiduity. The Habsburg power benefited, moreover, from the slow decay of Ottoman power. Austria was the natural liberator and sole hope of such Central European Christians as preferred Christian to Turkish rule. And finally, the dynasty was blessed during these years with several exceedingly able rulers and first-rate servants, one of whom, Prince Eugene of Savoy, may well be termed the father of the Austrian empire.

There were essentially two phases in the making of Austria. The first involved the defeat of the Turks and the reconquest of Hungary, and the acquisition, later, of other territories, particularly in Poland. The second was the gradual consolidation of Habsburg control and the superimposing of imperial authority upon the variety of local institutions.

The defeat of the Turks and the reconquest of Hungary occupied, almost exactly, the second half of the seventeenth century. By 1699 Austria had attained very much the same frontier on the south that it was to have until 1918 and which was to be the northern boundary of Ottoman power until 1815. After that, Turkish power in the Balkan peninsula was to crumble, but it was not Austria that profited from its disintegration.

The campaigns against the Ottomans were complicated, as they always had been, by the disposition of the French to ally themselves with Constantinople in order to squeeze the Habsburgs between east and west. But from this encirclement the Austrians were now able to break out, owing partly to the preoccupation of the French with other enemies, to the internal weakening of the Turks, and to the generalship of Prince Eugene of Savoy. Moreover, after the collapse of the Protestant Calvinist state in Transylvania, in 1661, the eastern Hungarians turned more and more to Austria as the sole possible liberator. In 1664, the first decisive victory against the Ottoman forces was won at Saint Gotthard, and a slice of central Hungary and its subkingdom Croatia was abandoned to the Habsburgs by the Turks. In 1686, Buda, the principal city of Ottoman Hungary, was liberated and attached to the Habsburg kingdom. In 1697, the battle of Zenta led to the freeing of the entire Hungarian kingdom, under the brilliant leadership of Prince Eugene. The Treaty of Karlowitz, in 1699, signaled the final end of the Turkish threat to Central Europe. The highwater mark of that threat had come in 1683, when the Ottomans had reached the gates of Vienna and the capital had been rescued only by the timely—almost legendary—intervention of Austria's ally, King John Sobieski of Poland. After Karlowitz, the Habsburgs were safe, Hungary was in their hands, and the Ottoman empire commenced its long decline which was to end, like Austria's own, with destruction in World War I, in 1918.

The Islamic menace once eliminated, the House of Habsburg in the person of the energetic Leopold I (1657–1705) now turned its attention to the west again. It engaged in the long campaigns of the War of the Spanish Succession, in the first years of the eighteenth century, in an effort to place a member of the Habsburg family again on the vacant throne of Spain. The war ended in a draw. Louis XIV secured the throne of Spain for a Bourbon, but as compensation Austria acquired the remnants of Spain's European Empire: the Spanish Netherlands (which is modern Belgium); the duchy of Milan (the heart of the rich north of Italy), and the makings of a preponderant influence in the rest of the divided peninsula.

During the rest of the century the major external preoccupations of the Habsburgs were in German and Polish affairs. They lost the extremely rich and purely German province of Silesia to Prussia (see Chapter 16), but in the partitions of the Polish kingdom they gained its southern provinces. In the hundred and fifty years after 1648, the Habsburgs more than doubled the territories they controlled. The whole of Hungary (with its associated kingdom of Croatia), a third of Poland, much of northern Italy, and the distant but extremely rich Belgian province were all under Habsburg rule, which stretched (though with interruptions) from the Balkans and the borders of Russia to the Alps, the Mediterranean, the Adriatic, and the North Sea. It was one of the largest and richest monarchies in Europe.

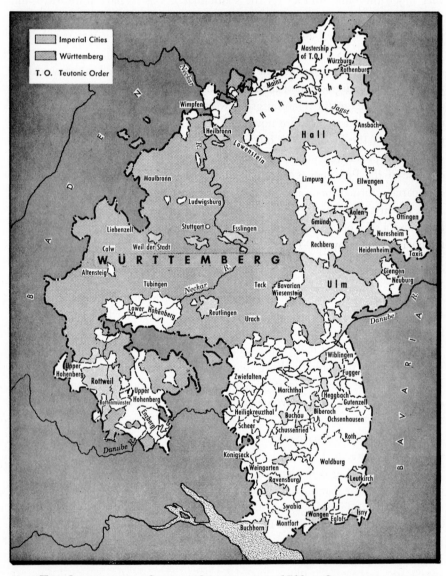

THE CONFUSION OF GERMAN GEOGRAPHY IN 1789: A SECTION OF THE
SOUTHWESTERN PART OF THE EMPIRE

INTERNAL CONSOLIDATION

So diverse and disjointed were its component parts, however, that legal sovereignty over them would have meant little had not the process of accumulating territories been accompanied by a process of consolidating the position of the dynasty and creating a modern state.

Various stages may be noted. Bohemia, by 1648, had been brought under direct control. So was Hungary as its territory was gradually liberated from Ottoman rule. Throughout the last decades of the century, the Hungarian nobility carried on a sporadic insurrection against the encroachments of the royal power from Vienna, but by 1687 the revolutionaries were defeated. In that year the Hungarian Diet finally voted to install the Habsburgs as hereditary (instead of elected) kings, although it provided that if there were no male heir Hungary might choose its own king, a provision which was later to lead to dramatic transactions.

Other steps were being taken to enhance the power and prestige of the dynasty. Just as in Tudor England and in Bourbon France the country nobility had been lured into the crown service by the attractions of court life, so in the Habsburg monarchy. Until the reign of Leopold I (1657–1705), the dynasty had had no fixed residence and no capital, being forced to govern through the ancient and established agencies in the various provinces.

Leopold undertook to change all this. Vienna became the permanent seat of the House of Habsburg and the capital of its scattered possessions. The court, like the contemporary Versailles, was made as splendid and as magnetic as possible, and the nobility, even from proudly independent Hungary, was drawn to its culture, luxury, and sinecures, finding them more attractive than the lonely life of a country noble. Most important of all, Leopold began to construct a royal service of his own. For the first time royal magistrates were appointed to try cases in all parts of the monarchy, and a general law for the various regions began to develop. There were centrally appointed administrations in strategic frontier provinces and a corps of centrally appointed army officers, although the defense of the realm was still the responsibility of purely local levies which could be used outside their own provinces only by the permission of the local authorities.

These were partial steps toward the erection of a modern state. The biggest steps in that direction came later, and the first of them resulted from the failure of Charles VI (1711–1740), Leopold's successor, to produce a male heir. He hoped to secure the succession of his daughter, the Archduchess Maria Theresa, to all his possessions, despite the fact that most of them had laws preventing the enthronement of a woman, and Hungary had specifically reserved the right to elect its own king if there was no male Habsburg to inherit. Charles also sought to secure the election as Holy Roman Emperor for Maria Theresa's husband, Francis, ruler of the small buffer duchy of Lorraine which lay within the Empire although surrounded by French territory.

To these ends, he sought before his death to secure the agreement of the diets and parliaments of each of his possessions, and of all foreign governments as well, to a document called the "Pragmatic Sanction,"[1] to whose acceptance he single-mindedly devoted most of his time for nine years (1713–1724). In the end he succeeded: all the provinces, and all foreign governments, agreed to respect the succession of his daughter. Some of the foreign governments, notably Prussia, later went back on their word, but the Habsburg provinces did not, and the Pragmatic Sanction amounted almost to a written constitution for all of the varied regions, uniting them into a single political entity under the perpetual sovereignty of Maria Theresa and her heirs of the dynasty which was, henceforth, to be known as the House of Habsburg-Lorraine. In the words of the Hungarian Diet's acceptance of the Pragmatic Sanction, all the countries of the Habsburg crown were henceforth to be "indivisibiliter et inseparabiliter"—indivisible and inseparable.

But for the Pragmatic Sanction Charles VI paid a price. In order to secure the adherence of certain provinces, he had to make concessions. Hungary had to be promised that the orders of the king could not take legal effect until they were approved by the Hungarian Diet, and similar though smaller concessions were made to the representative bodies of Croatia and Transylvania, and to the Free City of Fiume on the Adriatic, all of which were more or less self-governing provinces attached to the Hungarian crown. Hungary and its associated provinces were exempted from royal absolutism and maintained their separateness and their integrity. Many of the reforms and enactments of Maria Theresa and her successors were never applied to this kingdom which constituted nearly half of the realm.

An example, and an illuminating one, is to be found in the history of Austrian mercantilism. That doctrine, or policy, so popular in the west in the seventeenth and eighteenth centuries, had been aimed at creating an economic unity out of the various provinces of a kingdom. We have already noted the varying degrees of thoroughness and effectiveness with which mercantilism was adopted in the unified states of Britain, France, Spain, Portugal, and Holland. After the accession of Charles VI, it began to be applied to Austria. Little by little the various divisive commercial, financial, and manufacturing regimes of the separate provinces were broken down by the introduction of the *transito,* the right for any goods to be transported or sold in any of the Habsburg provinces without paying local duties or taxes. By 1775 the monarchy was a single economic unity: *except* that the *transito* and related practices were never introduced into Hungary. Hungary remained economically separate from the other Habsburg possessions.

On the other hand, some progress was being made in the direction of that other fundamental element of a modern state, a unified and centrally directed defense. Charles VI succeeded in getting Hungary to enter into what amounted

[1] A Pragmatic Sanction—from the Greek word for "a thing accomplished"—was originally a solemn decree with constitutional force in the Byzantine empire. There had been pragmatic sanctions before in Europe, always dealing with matters of the greatest consequence.

to a treaty of alliance with his other possessions, as part of the settlement of the Pragmatic Sanction. The provinces agreed to help defend one another, and they agreed, moreover, to a unified command.

THE REIGN OF MARIA THERESA

The young archduchess who, by grace of Pragmatic Sanction, succeeded her father on his numerous thrones in 1740 was a woman of enormous intelligence, wisdom, principle, firmness, and charm. She was certainly in most ways the equal of any of her contemporaries in ability, possibly excluding Frederick II of Prussia, and without doubt superior to all of them in moral stature.

She was, in some ways, an anachronism in the eighteenth century, that age in which Europe's rulers distinguished themselves for frivolity, philosophy, and irreligion. For Maria Theresa was exceedingly devout, serious to the point of solemnity, and resistant to the radical cosmologies of the Enlightenment. But politically she was progressive and adaptable; she understood as well as any one else of her age the requirements of successful absolutism, and she understood the need for the consolidation and modernization of the central governing power. Unlike many of her "enlightened" contemporaries, and especially unlike her son and successor, Joseph II, she understood the need for a patient and gradual approach, realizing that sudden changes in a highly conservative and rather primitive society would lead to difficulties, if not to failure. As was true with the other despots of her day, it never occurred to her that any tempering of autocracy was necessary or desirable: in the middle of the eighteenth century, it was still believed that representative institutions, laws restricting the power of the monarch, and chartered liberties, were old-fashioned handicaps to progress, and that a new and better world could be brought into existence only by the benevolent and unhindered action of an autocratic monarch operating through a modern state service.

Maria Theresa's reign began with a disaster which was also an opportunity. She had scarcely succeeded to her thrones when her neighbor, Frederick II of Prussia, on patently trumped up legal grounds, claimed and invaded the province of Silesia. This was immensely grave. Maria Theresa had at her disposal very inadequate defenses, and she had to depend upon the provincial authorities, particularly the Hungarians, to supply them. It was not at all sure that other foreign potentates, or even some of the diets of her own dominions, might not follow Frederick's lead, bringing about the disruption of the monarchy and her own dethronement. Moreover, Silesia was her richest province and, since it was purely German, one of her most reliables ones, which had no tradition of national separateness or independent institutions to lure it to sedition.

Maria Theresa lost most of Silesia—permanently, although she and her son intrigued for fifty years to recover it—as a result of the War of the Austrian

Succession (1740–1748) which followed Frederick's grab. From 1740 until 1945, when it became attached to present-day Poland, Silesia formed part of the Prussian state. But Maria Theresa did not lose her throne or her other dominions, and the exigencies of war permitted her to make reforms which might otherwise have been long delayed.

There were only two regiments of local levies available in Silesia to combat the Prussian aggression, and there was little financial or political opportunity for raising others. But Maria Theresa presented herself to the Hungarian Diet in

EMPRESS MARIA THERESA by Martin Mytens. In Schoenbrunn Palace, Vienna. (Austrian Information Service)

Budapest, pleading in a famous scene for aid to defend the threatened monarchy. The Hungarians—traditionally because they were charmed by her intensely feminine presence, and by the presentation of the future Joseph II, then an infant in his mother's arms—responded generously. They provided money and an army, and Frederick was successfully resisted, except in the lost province itself. Until 1749, the Empress continued to depend mainly on local levies for defense, despite the beginnings of a central military establishment in her father's reign. But in that year a full-fledged and united standing army under the sovereign's command was finally seen to be essential to the safety of each of the provinces separately as well as all of them together. After the middle of the century, the Habsburgs had a royal army like that of Spain or France.

Administrative and political organization followed. Aristocrats from all parts of the realm were encouraged more effectively than ever to come to Vienna. Meaningless but magnetic honors (including an altogether new one, the Hungarian Order of St. Stephen) were bestowed upon flattered Magyar gentlemen. A special school, called the Theresianum, was established in Vienna to train young Hungarian noblemen to the code of dynastic loyalty. More important, in 1748 the Hungarian and Bohemian Diets were persuaded to surrender their most important prerogative, the approving of new taxes.

On every front, the Empress (she is called an Empress because she was consort of the Holy Roman Emperor, Francis I) attacked the old decentralized and uncontrollable medieval institutions. Elementary schools were founded, controlled from Vienna, to teach Catholicism, loyalty, and the German language —which was replacing the native tongues of the common people and the Latin of the provincial aristocrats as a common means of communication. Replacing—or superimposed upon—the old aristocratic and local administration, was a well-organized public service (mainly recruited from German-speaking areas). The country (except for Hungary), was divided into administrative districts, each managed by an official in Vienna, and each with its own new officials and committees directing local affairs. For the first time laws made in Vienna were applied uniformly to all of the dominions of the crown. Belgium, Lombardy, and Hungary were less thoroughly subjected to this process of centralization than the other provinces, but they too felt the presence of the central government far more than ever before.

An elaborate system of law-making and law-enforcing agencies came into existence in Vienna. For the first time, "colleges"—which were at first committees, but soon became offices headed by a single minister—were set up, to take charge of particular aspects of public affairs: foreign policy, defense, commerce, justice, internal matters. The various ministers evolved policies and practices which equally affected all parts of the empire. This sort of arrangement, which is characteristic of every government in the world in our day, was only just beginning to take shape in France, Spain, and Britain. It was particularly significant in the Habsburg monarchy as a sign that a single "national" policy had superseded the separate provincial policies. Moreover, the civil service formed, out of its higher officials, an advisory council, the Staatsrat, which discussed national policies and made recommendations to the Empress, forming a sort of privy council which had, in some ways, some of the functions of a parliament.

By the time of Maria Theresa's death in 1780, it is proper to speak of "Austria" as a single state. It had a capital, an army, a privy council, a national policy and ministers and ministries to execute it, a civil service, a centrally controlled system of local government and education, a substantial measure of economic unity, a central fiscal system.

AN EXPERIMENT IN RADICAL ABSOLUTISM: JOSEPH II

Maria Theresa had borne sixteen children, few of whom displayed the statesmanlike qualities of their mother. Her second son, Leopold, was, to be sure, a brilliantly successful Grand Duke of Tuscany (a province which, after the extinction of the House of Medici had been given to Francis of Lorraine to compensate for the loss of his own duchy in France, and which he had willed to the second son). Her youngest daughter, Marie Antoinette, was to end her life on a French scaffold partly as a consequence of her refusal to follow her mother's wise advice on how a queen should act. Maria Theresa's oldest son, Joseph II, who reigned from 1780 to 1790, after sharing the conduct of affairs with her for several years, was learned, impetuous, and often unwise. Unlike his mother, he had swallowed whole the teachings of the Enlightenment. He was an ardent skeptic—an unbeliever in orthodox Christianity. He was an ardent friend of the common man, whose education and advancement he enthusiastically espoused. And he was an ardent enemy of all that was old-fashioned—bigotry, diversity, and medievalism. He wanted to turn his realm into a neat and symmetrical, progressive, highly uniform, well-educated, religiously tolerant, centralized autocracy: he was the most extreme of the Enlightened Despots. He summarized his own ideals of government: "The inner force, good laws, an honest judiciary, an orderly finance, an imposing military force, a ruler held in esteem are more worthy of a great European court than festivals, parades, expensive clothes, diamonds, golden halls, precious vessels and brilliant sleighing parties."

Joseph's major attacks were frontal ones, unlike those of his mother, to whose policies have been given the name of *douce violence*—gentle violence. His principal targets were the Roman Catholic Church, its intolerance of Protestants and Jews and its monopoly of education and charity; the provincial aristocracy and their peculiar rights over the peasantry of their estates; serfdom and inequality of individuals in general; estates and diets and the legal complexities of the several provinces; and linguistic and cultural diversity.

By autocratic decree, he abolished serfdom and extended equal rights to all his subjects, whatever their birth or class, to travel freely, to own property, to chose their profession, to marry whomever they wished, to worship as they pleased. He abolished the nobles' exemption from taxation and from the ordinary processes of civil law. He set up an entirely new system of royal courts, sup-

SCHOENBRUNN PALACE, VIENNA. The palace was begun in 1694 on the site of a former hunting lodge which had been destroyed in the Turkish wars. Empress Maria Theresa, who lived there with her husband and sixteen children, remodeled it in the Baroque manner in the 1740's. Later, Francis Joseph lived there during his long reign from 1848 to 1916. The park was laid out in the orderly French style of the eighteenth century. (Austrian Information Service)

planting in every kind of case the old local laws and judges. He conferred titles of nobility freely upon persons of humble birth, and even upon the hitherto semi-outcast Jews and gypsies. In an Edict of Toleration of 1781, at the very beginning of his reign, he extended complete freedom of worship to the fairly numerous but hitherto clandestine Protestant and Eastern Orthodox congregations. He restricted the power of the Pope and Vatican to issue decrees and bulls affecting Austria, and he regulated all Catholic religious practices. He dissolved about seven hundred monasteries and convents and brought all religious orders under direct control of the state. He sought to make the German language, and German culture, universal, introducing German aristans and peasants throughout all his polyglot realms. Even in Hungary, German was made the compulsory language of government offices. He abolished, or greatly restricted, the powers of all the old estates and diets. He suppressed the local "liberties" in all his dominions, so that all were equally subject to a uniform law and all laws were made in Vienna. Against the central government in its autocracy there were no longer any legal or constitutional safeguards for local rights, local practices, local self-government.

In economic affairs, Joseph was a mercantilist, but characteristically he adopted some of the liberal ideas of the Physiocrats (see Chapter 21), which were then the last word in economic thinking. He chartered an East India Company and attempted to build up the great ports of Ostend and Trieste as centers of world commerce. He encouraged and supported domestic industry. He pushed further the internal unification of the economy.

These reforms equaled, in speed and thoroughness, those which were to be carried through in the next decade by the French Revolution. Joseph II tried, as the French were to try, to sweep away the accumulation of centuries of habits and institutions; to create a society of individuals in place of a complicated society of groups having different functions and privileges. He attacked all the vested interests at once, the Church, the nobles, and the town corporations. But the peasantry became so unsettled by the concessions which were made to them that Joseph found it difficult to keep them in order. Reform from above threatened to turn into revolt from below. Regional dissatisfaction threatened to turn into secession. By 1789 the Hungarian estates were on the verge of an armed rising, and had to be placated, and those in Belgium were in open revolt. The forward march of his plans and projects was coming to a confused halt when he died, in 1790.

Not all of Joseph II's reforms were abandoned with his death. After all, his brother and successor, Leopold II (1790–1792), was also an enlightened despot, though a more tactful one. But Leopold was hard pressed. He had to grant the Hungarians new guarantees of their autonomy. He had to abandon the liberation of the serfs. He was able to divide the Belgian rebels and suppress them, but their dissatisfactions were to contribute to later conquest by the French revolutionaries. Not all of the abuses of selfdom returned to Austria and Bohemia, but after Leopold's death in 1792, the year the Habsburg monarchy went to war with revolutionary France, reaction settled in for a long stay.

In the century and a half since Westphalia, a remarkable work had been accomplished. A new European great power had been created out of the most unpromising materials and under the most difficult circumstances. But its composition was diverse, its institutions incomplete, its boundaries uncertain. Austria was destined in the nineteenth century to become stagnant; for its rulers were, like Joseph, unable to move in any direction without exciting opposition. The building of the Central European state had, perhaps, commenced too late. The unity which the Habsburgs brought to their empire was not to endure.

16

THE HOHENZOLLERNS OF PRUSSIA

BETWEEN THE THIRTY YEARS WAR and the French Revolution there arose in northern Germany a new great power. Emerging from the swarm of lesser dignitaries within the Holy Roman Empire, the Hohenzollern dynasty, by conquest and inheritance, assembled a number of scattered particles into a modern and efficient state. In 1648 the Hohenzollern Elector of Brandenburg was scarcely more than a face in the crowd of German princes. A century later his descendant, now king of Prussia, had defeated and despoiled the Habsburg overlord of Germany. Nowhere in the history of this period is there a comparable success story; nowhere a story which better exemplifies the dynastic state, the absolute monarchy, and the stratified society so characteristic of this period. And further, in the person of Frederick II, known as "the Great" (1740–1786), the Hohenzollern dynasty presents one of the best exemplars of the eighteenth-century phenomenon known as "enlightened despotism."

The great kingdom of Prussia, which was in the nineteenth century to sponsor and contrive the unification of Germany, was highly military, and its successes were in large part the result of ability to maintain a superior army and use it with skill. A French writer is said to have observed that whereas most states had armies, the Prussian army had a state. The Hohenzollern successes indeed illustrate the kinship of foreign and domestic affairs, of the army in the field and the society back of it. But war and diplomacy—inescapable conditions from which the Hohenzollerns drew much of their inspiration—are not the principal subject of this chapter. Here the emphasis is on the internal history which made the external successes possible.

THE NORTHEAST GERMAN FRONTIER

The family of Hohenzollern took its name from the medieval castle in which its ancestors, counts of Zollern, were living by the eleventh century. One branch of the family became burgraves of Nuremburg, princes of the Empire, and ultimately, in 1415, rulers of the March (or Mark) of Brandenburg, between the Elbe and Oder rivers in northeastern Germany, whose capital was a village called Berlin. It was a frontier district where since the thirteenth century German culture and the Christian church had been conquering the Slavs. By the time of the Hohenzollern arrival in Brandenburg, many free peasants had come from Western Europe, and numerous towns had been formed. Although the area was still underdeveloped in comparison with the west, the society was freer and more fluid, and the power of the nobility was balanced by the rights of the towns and of the free peasants.

Elsewhere on the northeast frontier a similar Germanic penetration had been transforming old Slavic areas into German marches. Besides Brandenburg, the places which were to concern the Hohenzollerns were Pomerania, a stretch of Baltic coast to the east of the Oder river, and Prussia, between the Vistula and Niemen rivers at the southeast corner of the Baltic.

German and Christian penetration of Pomerania in the High Middle Ages was on the whole rather peaceful, but in Prussia the case was different. The Prussians, a people related to the Latvians and Lithuanians, put up fierce resistance. In the thirteenth century the Teutonic Knights, one of the militant orders experienced in the Crusades, were given sovereignty over Prussia by the Pope and the Emperor. The Teutonic Knights used crusading methods, built castles to hold strategic points, established German towns, encouraged immigration from Western Europe, pacified the country, and built a state. Prussia was in some ways more advanced than Brandenburg and Pomerania, for the Teutonic Knights kept better order and had more funds. But in all three places at the close of the Middle Ages there was a considerable amount of political and personal freedom and a society which included free peasants and towns as well as nobles.

By the time the Hohenzollerns arrived in Brandenburg, eastern Germany was undergoing an agrarian crisis. In the late fourteenth and fifteenth centuries, economic and social growing pains affected all of Europe, but in the new and still raw northeast they had peculiar consequences. In the midst of feuds and wars—the Teutonic Knights, for example, lost western Prussia to the Poles—there were plagues, poor crops, famines, and depopulation. Towns faded away. Peasants deserted their villages. There were shortages of farm labor. As in most of Europe, nobles were suffering from the price rise and from the decline in value of their money dues. This, and the labor shortage, obliged them to farm the lands themselves instead of renting them or living off their dues. To assure a labor supply they began to restrict the freedom of the peasants. When prosperity returned in the sixteenth and early seventeenth centuries, Germany east of the Elbe was already taking on characteristics which were to contrast with Western Europe and were to persist, fatally, into the twentieth century: large estates; serfdom; production of grain for export.

Northeast Germany just before the Thirty Years War was relatively peaceful and prosperous, but the towns had not recovered their former vigor, and the peasants had been driven into serfdom in spite of their fruitless revolts. The chance to profit from grain exports to the west had led to an enclosure movement. The price of grain at Danzig had increased by 300 to 400 percent in the sixteenth century. Socially the nobles were stronger than they had ever been in the old frontier days; they had increasingly monopolized the land, the grain trade (to the detriment of the towns), and even such businesses as the brewing and sale of beer. The Reformation had made church lands a prey to princes and nobles. In its name the peasants had revolted in vain.

Until the Thirty Years War the princes who ruled such states as Brandenburg and Prussia were by no means absolute monarchs. The nobles, through their local estates (assemblies), protected their economic privileges and opposed policies which called for costly armaments or adventurous foreign policies which might have endangered the grain trade. The princes, themselves landed proprietors, were sympathetic to this point of view, and also allowed the nobles to maintain their privileges at the expense of the towns. This condition applied even in East Prussia, where in 1525 the Grand Master of the Teutonic Knights went over to Lutheranism and became hereditary duke. This man was a member of the Hohenzollern family.

The Hohenzollerns, as noted, had made a first big advance in 1415 when they had obtained the March of Brandenburg and had thus become margraves of that one-time frontier. To Brandenburg they wished to add Pomerania, on the Baltic coast to the north of them; and naturally after 1525 they hoped to obtain East Prussia, which upon its secularization fell into the hands of a younger branch of their family.

By carefully arranged marriages and treaties, these fruits and others began to fall into Hohenzollern hands in the early seventeenth century. In 1609 an inheritance cleared the way for possession of the duchy of Cleves, far to the west on the lower Rhine, and the counties of Mark and Ravensburg—strategically located territories which were to draw Hohenzollern attention into western Germany. In 1618 upon the extinction of the ducal family of East Prussia, that territory fell to the Hohenzollerns of the Brandenburg branch. East Prussia, however, was not held free and clear, but was a fief of Poland.

During the Thirty Years War the Hohenzollerns inherited a good claim to Pomerania, but owing to the presence of powerful Swedish forces were temporarily unable to collect. At that time Brandenburg-Prussia was too weak to do more than accede to the wishes of more vigorous friends and enemies whenever they were in the neighborhood. The Hohenzollerns did well to survive the Thirty Years War. When the fighting stopped they even managed, with French

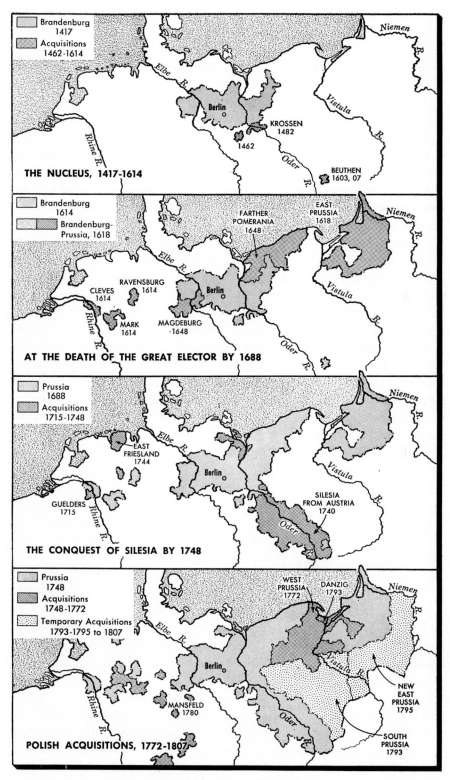

THE GROWTH OF PRUSSIA

support, to salvage their claim to some of Pomerania, and were given the less valuable eastern half (which at least joined Brandenburg to the Baltic.) For renouncing the rest of Pomerania they received three secularized bishoprics of Cammin, Halberstadt, and Minden, plus the succession to the archbishopric of Magdeburg on the west bank of the Elbe.

By 1648, therefore, the Hohenzollerns had collected territories to the east of Brandenburg (Prussia), to the north (Pomerania), and to the west (Cleves, Mark, Ravensburg, and Magdeburg). They had been drawn into conflicts which concerned Dutch independence on the lower Rhine, and Swedish, Danish and Polish ambitions for control of the Baltic, not to mention the friction of Germans and Slavs in Eastern Europe, and competition with other German states and with the Habsburg emperors. Brandenburg-Prussia had become the largest north German principality.

Brandenburg had long been one of the seven electorates of the Holy Roman Empire, although less influential than most of the others. Prussia, the eastern outpost of the Hohenzollerns, was not a part of the Holy Roman Empire, and was a Polish fief. West Prussia was in the hands of the Poles, and cut off East Prussia from Brandenburg and Pomerania.

Brandenburg was a poor country, sometimes referred to as the sand box of the Holy Roman Empire. The territories of the North European plain were not easily defended in the best of times. The decline of town life and the reluctance of the nobles and of the estates to support mercenary armies accounted for the Hohenzollern vulnerability through much of the Thirty Years War. Indeed, there was in the Hohenzollern situation a contrast between the dynastic success whose inheritances were drawing the family into the highest international affairs, and the lack of authority and state machinery with which to govern the family possessions.

FREDERICK WILLIAM THE GREAT ELECTOR

It was the work of Frederick William, Elector of Brandenburg from 1640 to 1688, which cut down the authority of the estates and built up an army and the beginnings of a common administration for all Hohenzollern lands. On this work rests his claim to the title "Great Elector," for the direction in which he steered the Prussian political and social system was not changed until the nineteenth century.

Frederick William was twenty years old when he succeeded his father. The Thirty Years War was still going on, but the army of Brandenburg-Prussia numbered only 4,650 men. There were times, before the end of the war, when the army fell to as few as 1,800 men. The estates of Brandenburg, like Frederick William, had been critical of his father's policies, and Frederick William at first governed with their collaboration. But in the long run his interest in the Hohenzollern territories from the Rhineland to the Baltic northeast brought him into conflict with the Brandenburg estates, and indeed with the parochial, parsimoni-ous, and pacific impulses of the local estates in all of his possessions.

The wars into which his dynastic and Protestant interests and the balance of power led him made Frederick William willing to concede much to the nobles who dominated the estates, provided they would furnish the money for his army. He did not intend to remain as helpless as he and his father had been during the Thirty Years War. In the crucial war of 1655–1660 between Sweden and Poland Frederick William made Machiavellian use of his resources and combined first with one side and then the other. This was perhaps the turning point in his reign. In the end he was able to get his sovereignty over Prussia confirmed by both Sweden and Poland.

To play this kind of game the Elector needed an army, and to get a bigger army he at first had to confirm the power of the estates, the privileges of the nobles, and their control over their peasants. For example, when dissolving the Brandenburg Diet of 1653 he acknowledged the privileges of the nobility and added new rights. The game was so important to him, however, that he went on to enlarge and provision his army regardless of the opinion of the estates. At last the existence of the army, along with the Elector's increased prestige, enabled him to get along without the support of the estates. He was no longer willing to tolerate their opposition. The wars required money. To get money, administrative changes and economic regulations were needed. What it all added up to politi-cally was more authority for the crown and more uniform instruments for the exercise of that authority in the scattered Hohenzollern lands.

In the reign of Frederick William, therefore, local estates were largely superseded by a Privy Council for the whole state. The Privy Council was made up mostly of nobles, but they were of necessity men with larger than local views. Frederick William employed some commoners, but frequently ennobled them in return for their service. They became assimilated to the old, landed nobility—there was no separate "nobility of the robe," as in France.

Out of the Privy Council, and soon independent of it, grew the *General-kriegskommissariat,* which might be loosely translated as "Department of War," with its *Generalkriegskasse,* which might be translated "War Treasury." The two keys to the importance of the *Generalkriegskommissariat* are these: (1) its officials, mainly nobles, were independent of local estates, and indeed of every-one except the ruler, and were active in breaking local privileges in all the various Hohenzollern territories; and (2) they did so many things that they have rightly been called the first Prussian bureaucracy. The officials of the *General-Kriegskommissariat* housed and supplied the army in all the diverse Hohenzollern lands, and collected taxes for that purpose. They came to regulate the whole economy upon which those taxes depended: imports and exports, the guilds, privileged companies, manufactures, the integration of the Huguenots after their admission following their expulsion from France in 1685, even certain naval and colonial enterprises that Frederick William undertook. The *General-kriegskasse* was the first central treasury of the Hohenzollern state (not count-ing the royal domains).

The thing to notice about all this is the effectiveness of a ruler who was also an energetic, ambitious man. This man's exercise of will power led to a series of decisions which, viewed from afar, look like the deliberate building of a state machine. There was probably less deliberation than improvisation in the work of Frederick William. Nevertheless, it was his leadership which built the army up to 30,000 men, even when, in order to do so, he had to defeat the estates and the local interests which they represented. It was his leadership which in place of the estates used the Privy Council and the *Generalkriegskasse* for all of his territories; which, moreover, increased government revenues to 3,382,000 talers from a population of only 1,000,000 by making them pay twice as much per head in this poor, sandy-soiled land as the people of Louis XIV's France did in their richer country.

This adventure of a dynastic ruler led beyond equipping soldiers and collecting taxes. Frederick William had spent part of his formative years in the Netherlands and (anticipating Peter the Great of Russia) wanted to have the benefits of more advanced European methods. The same kind of mercantilistic controls which have been encountered in west European history were employed in Prussia in an effort to produce more wealth for more taxes for more soldiers. But Prussia was an underdeveloped country, compared to Western Europe, with much less private capital. State efforts and the importance of the army as a customer were especially significant in economic life. And so were the subsidies which Prussia got from the Holy Roman Empire, as well as from the Netherlands, France, Spain, and Denmark at various times. The reception of some 20,000 Huguenot refugees after 1685 brought French enterprise and know-how in manufacturing and trade as well as French army officers and French family names. Frederick William also welcomed Swiss, Frisians (an ethnic group from the Netherlands), and Polish Jews. He gave such refugees land and building materials and temporary tax exemptions. As in Colbert's France, not all of the promotions of industry and the inspections and tax collections worked to perfection. Frederick William even tried, good mercantilist that he was, to found a colony in West Africa, but it failed and was later abandoned. But the Prussian bureaucracy was on the whole excellent, and many of the errors of the French experience were avoided—for example, the farming out of taxes.

THE JUNKERS AND THE STATE

In Prussian history one always encounters the word "*Junker*," which comes from *junger herr* (young gentleman). The word originally meant the kind of young man, son of a landowner, who entered military service, often as a simple soldier. There were many such in Frederick William's time, for there were many landed families who were not rich and whose younger sons looked to the state for employment in the army or civil service. This was especially important in northeast Germany where an underdeveloped economy made army and state service almost the only careers outside of farming. Later, the word was used to mean the class from which such young men were drawn, and in this sense the *Junkers* in Germany corresponded to the landed gentry of England. They were not necessarily titled noblemen, but they were people who controlled the land and with it the exercise of local political authority. The corresponding class in the Netherlands—the Jonkheers—gave its name to the New York city of Yonkers.

On their private estates where grain was grown for export the junker aristocracy had its way; the state did not enter here. "I am the state," the *Junker* might well have said. A kind of bargain was being struck in Frederick William's time which was to last for more than a century. The nobles were compensated for loss of their political liberties by being allowed to hold the peasants in serfdom and maintain a dominant economic and social position in spite of any claims the townsmen might make. In return, the nobles, in the army and bureaucracy, were learning to serve more than local and personal interests. They were learning the meaning of the idea of service to a "state" which was more than Brandenburg, or Pomerania, or Prussia. And this state was the Hohenzollern state, so that loyalty to the dynasty became a habit too. And it was to the Hohenzollerns and their state that Brandenburgers, Pomeranians, and Prussians of the nobility more and more looked for duty, honor, and profit.

It was a common sort of bargain—the sort that permitted the formation of a national policy, backed by a central administration, by the new state, without ruining the old landed classes. Comparable bargains were being attempted in France and elsewhere with varying degrees of success. It is often said that in Prussia this idea of obedience and service to the constituted authorities was helped by Lutheranism. In any case Lutheranism was among the things honored by the Prussian *Junker*. The Hohenzollern rulers had become Calvinists.

Nobody planned this pattern of behavior, but in practice the pattern became set in the reign of Frederick William: absolute monarchy, served by the nobles, who maintained a privileged position to the detriment of the towns and peasants. The *Junker* served the state and dynasty; these in turn respected the privileges of the *Junkers*.

The weight of this social system was heavy on the towns, which were harshly taxed and discriminated against to the profit of the *Junkers,* and especially on the serfs, whose condition steadily worsened. The sacrifice of the estates meant abandonment of representative political institutions. A measure of harmony and efficiency was indeed purchased at this price. Certainly there was harmony of state, army, and economy, for all were staffed by the same kind of men. Led by a dynasty which for another century produced able rulers, Prussia after the death of Frederick William in 1688 became one of the great powers.

THE HOHENZOLLERNS BECOME KINGS

The Great Elector died in the historic year 1688 when England was building parliamentary supremacy and Louis XIV was leading France into a nine-year drive toward the Rhine, his next-to-last great war. The Great Elector's successors profited, as he had, from troubled international conditions (thus merging Prussia's history with that of Europe) and demonstrated how a small, sparsely populated state could, through discipline, austerity, and guile, add to its holdings without actually fighting very much.

The Great Elector's son, Elector Frederick III (1688–1713) profited from the War of the Spanish Succession (1701–1714), Louis XIV's last offensive, by supporting the Habsburgs, who in turn allowed him to be crowned "King in Prussia." As King Frederick I, he ruled from 1701 to 1713. Becoming a king was no small achievement for a prince of the Holy Roman Empire, where, except for the special case of Bohemia, kings were not allowed. That is why Frederick became "King in Prussia," which was equivalent to "King outside the Holy Roman Empire," since Prussia was not a part of the Empire. But the very fact that the Hohenzollerns were building a central administration and army for all of their territories made this formality meaningless. In fact and in speech Kingdom of "Prussia" was to mean all of the Hohenzollern lands, and this kingdom spelled the doom of what was left of the Holy Roman Empire; it was more serious than the maneuvers of other German princes who became kings, for example the Elector of Saxony who became King of Poland (1697), or the Elector of Hanover who became King of England (1714). From now on there were two kings within the Holy Roman Empire, the Habsburg emperor who was also King of Bohemia, and the Hohenzollern King of Prussia. There were two great powers in Germany.

Another reign passed before the Hohenzollerns and Habsburgs clashed head-on. It was that of Frederick William I (1713–1740), who also added his bit to the family holdings (eastern Pomerania, 1720), but who is chiefly remembered for building the Prussian army from about 40,000 men to over 80,000, and for the careful, almost pacific foreign policy which hoarded all this force without using it and enabled the hard-working king to amass an enormous war chest. Frederick William I was an overworked, irritable man in uniform, the "sergeant king," who smoked and drank too much, demanded unreasoning obedience, supervised everything and everybody personally, and was contemptuous of literature and philosophy. He preferred tangible things—the tall soldiers who were his hobby, the military academy which he founded for the sons of *Junkers,* the cantonal system of recruiting which drew regiments from local districts and thus reinforced military discipline with the feudal authority of seigneurs over serfs.

Frederick William I continued the tradition of attracting foreigners to Prussia, and created hundreds of villages, settling Dutch and French refugees and equipping them with tools and seeds. The colonization which was at the root of Prussian history thus continued. But far from being the free society of earlier centuries, Prussia had become like a big army camp wherein everyone had a rank and a function. The *Junkers* had the privilege of monopolizing the ownership of lands classified as "noble"; and the best positions in the bureaucracy and army were reserved for them. The townsmen, unlike the self-confident *bourgeoisie* of France and England who were wealthy in money and in practical experience, owed their status to service in state-controlled enterprises or offices or universities, and almost always looked with deference toward the nobles, the military, and the state. And the peasant, whether as soldier or serf, was subordinate to his *Junker* master.

Prussia by 1740 numbered some 2,400,000 people. It was a society less fluid (as we would say today) than those which were taking shape on Europe's Atlantic seaboard. But in it there was discipline and work, and these generated great strength.

FREDERICK THE GREAT

Frederick William I is also remembered for brutal treatment of his son, the future Frederick II, who would one day be known as Frederick the Great (1740–1786). As a young man Frederick seemed to be the antithesis of his coarse father. He was physically delicate, sensitive to the arts, played the flute, and dreamed of being a great writer. The son's characteristics angered and probably frightened the father; the boy seemed too effeminate, too indifferent to the things that mattered, to keep up the dynasty's winning streak, now nearing the century mark.

Frederick William piled on discipline. His son resisted, and at the age of eighteen tried to run away. Frederick William caught him. There followed ten years of grinding discipline, as the young Frederick was put through a military and administrative apprenticeship in Hohenzollern rule. He survived it, thin-lipped, sharp-nosed, apparently cynical and contemptuous of humanity, but reading all the time, and writing in French, like a good apprentice of the eighteenth-century Enlightenment which was now under way.

In 1740 Frederick William I died, and before the year was out Frederick II, now twenty-eight, seemed to prove that his father's training had not been in vain. He struck forcefully for lands and glory, and he did so with more cynicism and imagination and daring than his father had ever displayed. In 1740 the Habsburg Emperor Charles VI died, leaving his lands to his twenty-three-year-old daughter Maria Theresa. His carefully prepared guarantee, the Pragmatic Sanction, declared the juridical unity of the lands and the legitimacy of their inheritance by a woman. Most of the European powers had accepted the Pragmatic Sanction, but many of them were ready to violate it, and Frederick II struck first. He wanted the rich province of Silesia, a part of the Kingdom of Bohemia lying in the upper Oder river valley and controlling its trade. Silesia would vastly increase the population of the Hohenzollern lands, and would guarantee Brandenburg against Austrian aggressions, since it was an ideal point from which to launch attacks on Bohemia. Frederick conquered the province by the spring of 1741.

In this so-called War of the Austrian Succession Frederick behaved like the Machiavelli against whose politics he had once written a youthful tract. He abandoned his allies in 1742 when Maria Theresa ceded him Silesia, rejoined them in 1744 when Austria seemed about to get the upper hand, and dropped out again in 1745. In 1748 the peace treaty of Aix-la-Chapelle confirmed his possession of Silesia, but nothing was really settled between Austria and Prussia, both headed by gifted rulers.

What Frederick had seized in his twenties he had to defend desperately in his forties, in the Seven Years War (1756–1763). Characteristically, he attacked first when he judged the Austrian comeback to be on the way, but this time the odds were impossible. Frederick proved forever his tenacity and military skill, maneuvering on interior lines between the Austrians, French, Russians, and Swedes. Fighting alone, since his English ally was inactive in Europe, he suffered terrible defeats and saw the enemy reach Berlin, but kept an army in the field and in the end was saved by the caution of his enemies and by a miraculous dynastic accident. Empress Elizabeth of Russia died (1762) and was succeeded by Peter III, an eccentric admirer of Frederick, who immediately ceased hostilities, thus ending the attack on Prussia from the east. At the Peace of Hubertusburg in 1763 Maria Theresa had to let Frederick keep Silesia.

This was not the last of Frederick's adventures in war and diplomacy, but while he maintained in the long years to his death in 1786 what many considered to be the best army in Europe, his reign after 1763 became more cautious, like those of his father and grandfather.

After the Seven Years War was won, he schemed with Catherine of Russia. They meant to weaken and partition Poland, and in 1772 this policy bore fruit in the "first partition," which brought Frederick the West Prussia which his ancestors had coveted. West Prussia with its 700,000 people joined East Prussia to Brandenburg. Austria and Russia were the other partitioners, and this was the occasion when Frederick is said to have remarked of Maria Theresa that "the more she wept, the more she took." In 1778–1779 and 1785 Frederick played the part of a satiated power and formed a coalition against the designs of Maria Theresa's "enlightened despot" son Joseph II, who wanted to take Bavaria.

FREDERICK THE GREAT AS AN ENLIGHTENED DESPOT

Frederick's fame was based on more than arms. He never lost his early taste for things intellectual, which made him read the works of the Enlightenment, now hitting its full stride as the century grew older. Montesquieu's *Spirit of the Laws* he called the Bible of the modern legislator. His favorite was Voltaire; in the years between Frederick's two big wars, Voltaire lived for a time at the Prussian court and received a pension for discussing Frederick's really meritorious literary output with him. Eventually they found this relationship impossible to maintain, but Voltaire publicized Frederick's "enlightened rule." Frederick really deserved his reputation as an intellectual.

Like the other enlightened despots, particularly his younger contemporaries Catherine of Russia and Joseph II of Austria, Frederick owed his reputation partly to the publicity furnished by men like Voltaire in an age when urban and literate public opinion in western Europe was for the first time assuming real proportions. The philosophers who wrote for this new audience went through a period, roughly from the 1740's to the 1770's, of placing their hopes for the future in absolute rulers like Frederick, Catherine, and Joseph. It was thought that these rulers would govern rationally; that is, in a manner approved by reasonable men like the *philosophes* themselves. Rulers like Frederick encouraged this hope by being cultivated persons whose sponsorship of philosophy and the arts was genuine, But they were of course not against improving their reputations abroad, where their foreign policies would benefit, and at home, where they would as a result be the more firmly seated on their thrones.

VOLTAIRE AND FREDERICK THE GREAT by Adolph von Menzel. Wood engraving from *Die Geschichte Friedrichs des Grossen*, 1840. Menzel (1815–1905) was a German painter famous for his illustrations in books of German history. (Courtesy of The Metropolitan Museum of Art, Dick Fund, 1935)

There was really a high coincidence, moreover, between what the philosophers recommended and what rulers like Frederick actually did. Even in less "enlightened" times (for example, those of Louis XIV in France and the Great Elector in Brandenburg-Prussia), circumstances had taught the rulers that uniformity and efficiency paid dividends in terms of power. Now, in the intense competition of eighteenth-century Europe, when events like Frederick's attack on Silesia could take place, there was more reason than ever to promote efficiency. In view of the new public opinion, and the faith of its leaders in "reason," absolute monarchy as an institution was on trial, and constrained to take on a progressive coloration. It was no longer impressive to educated people to point to traditional or hereditary rights; things were best justified by showing them to be "reasonable." To some extent the rulers themselves used this kind of claim; Frederick described himself as the first servant of the state. And although it is impossible to know his inner mind, Frederick probably believed it, for he was a thorough rationalist, disinclined to accept mysteries and myths. He was just as devoted to the Hohenzollern family and the Prussian state as his father and grandfather had been, but he would not have defended his legacy on the same grounds as they.

All these considerations played a part in Frederick's reputation as an enlightened despot. What Frederick actually did as a ruler was to a large extent a continuation and improvement of what his father had done. He worked hard for the welfare of the people without letting them choose their own idea of welfare, and probably without admitting even to himself that what was good for the dynasty and the state might not be good for the people. After the terrible devastation of the Seven Years War, with ruin everywhere and the population reduced by perhaps 20 percent, Frederick rebuilt the country and the army, encouraged immigration of colonists from other parts of Germany and Europe, and furnished seeds, livestock, and loans. By the 1770's Prussian grain exports hit a new high.

Frederick was a mercantilist in the late eighteenth-century style. He prohibited exports of vital raw materials and imports of luxuries. He used protective tariffs and subsidies and monopolies to stimulate production. He was a canal-digger (Vistula-Elbe), and a promoter of textiles, porcelain, and even shipping. In 1785 he signed a commercial treaty with the United States. Frederick permitted a high degree of intellectual freedom and religious toleration, which fitted well with the Hohenzollern policy of welcoming useful elements from other countries—thus he used Jesuit refugees from France in the teaching profession. He extended education to some degree, began to organize primary schools and some vocational training, and founded, no doubt more to his liking, the Berlin Academy. The Academy's findings were to be published in the universal language, French, just as Frederick's tariffs were revised by a French expert and his Potsdam palace was built by French architects and called *Sans Souci*. Frederick, like other enlightened despots of his time, planned to overhaul and publish the laws of his kingdom, but this project was not completed until after his death. He took a paternalistic interest in the welfare of the peasants, who were also the backbone of the military and economic resources of the country. He bullied them into growing and eating potatoes, reduced labor services and serfdom on his own domains, which amounted to 25 percent of the area of the country, and tried to curb brutality against the peasants elsewhere in the kingdom.

Frederick's performance over almost half a century was certainly dazzling. To his father's cult of work and detail he added his own brilliance, military and artistic. His was the broader view and the bolder action. Yet he trained no successor—at least the father was more far-sighted in that. For the Prussian state machinery, fine though it was, could not be expected to run by itself. Frederick in his lifetime never allowed it to do so, but interfered constantly and despotically.

Deeper still, Frederick's example poses the problem of enlightened despotism. His allegiance to the Enlightenment indicated reform in the name of the reasonable, indicated efficiency and justice at the expense of tradition. His actions to some degree took this direction, but only to a degree—they never passed the point where the old-fashioned state was being perfected without being basically changed. Frederick did not and perhaps could not step outside of the rules of the game laid down by his ancestor the Great Elector. He retained and strengthened the "bargain" with the *Junkers*. He did not attack serfdom, nor did he improve the status of the towns and middle class. Property and persons remained classified; society remained stratified. To change these relationships would have meant replanning the economy, the army, and the state itself. Unlike his young Austrian rival, Joseph II, Frederick refused to gamble on strengthening the monarchy by modernizing the society.

Frederick was enlightened despot enough to play the old game well, about as well as it could be played under the old rules. The peasantry—to take one example—were better off than in Poland and Russia, where the crown was not strong enough to restrain the aristocracy. Frederick's career was a personal triumph, with daring at the start (War of the Austrian Succession), courage in adversity (Seven Years War), and thereafter consolidation like that of his ancestors, without overlooking any opportunities (partition of Poland). When he died in 1786 he left the country in good condition (by the old standards), with a population of 6,000,000, and more territory, a good army, and a great reputation.

To have accomplished more would have required even greater efficiency and justice through such measures as the freeing of the serfs, the opening of careers to talent, and the repairing of the defects of absolutism in government. Frederick could not have made these changes without revising his life's work in a revolutionary manner. Nor was it given to Frederick's successors to inspire such reforms, or even to hold the line where he left it. Prussia's deluge was to come in the time of Napoleon.

17

THE NETHERLANDS, ITALY, AND SPAIN

DURING THE CENTURY AND A HALF which followed the Peace of Westphalia the great modern states grew to a point where they controlled the destinies of the continent. The new powers were big territorially, and growing bigger. All of them, by 1789, had effective central governments. In earlier times the greatest influence in Europe could be a monarch like Charles V whose power was based upon diverse and scattered provinces, but no longer.

Some parts of Europe were unable to meet the requirements of grandeur in the new age. We have seen how the Holy Roman Empire disintegrated, and we shall narrate in later chapters how the Ottoman empire weakened, and how Poland diminished in size and was ultimately extinguished. In Western and Southern Europe the decline of these three sovereignties was matched by the loss of power, influence, and independence of action in three regions which, earlier, had been in might and wealth among the leaders of Europe: the Dutch Republic, the Italian peninsula, and Spain.

In 1789, none of these regions still played a principal role in European politics. Spain was close to being a satellite of France, and Italy of Austria. The Republic of the Netherlands maintained a precarious independence between British and French competition. Relative to the other powers, all three were losing the economic competition. Relative to their own earlier creativity in the arts, all three were less productive.

There were, it is true, partial recoveries and revivals in all three regions during the period. Italy showed in the eighteenth century a remarkable if limited burst of intellectual and artistic activity, and some of its political parts, notably the Grand Duchy of Tuscany, underwent strenuous and salutary reforms. The

Dutch Republic was managing to maintain most of its wealth and much of its commercial and financial importance as, indeed, it has managed to do down to the present day. Spain, after a period of dramatic degradation, had begun an era of revival and reform in the third quarter of the eighteenth century.

THE DUTCH REPUBLIC

The Republic of the United Provinces of the Netherlands was a peculiar country. With Switzerland, Venice, Genoa, and some of the German Free Cities it shared the distinction of being a republic in the great age of European monarchies. It had gained its independence in its struggle to assure religious toleration and to preserve its ancient constitution and provincial liberties at a time when most successful states were moving toward religious uniformity and royal absolutism. But for all its old-fashioned origins, its economy was exceedingly modern; and upon the enterprise and profits of its citizens it built its greatness. And the pressures toward absolutism and religious uniformity were almost as strong in the Netherlands in the years that followed as they were in other parts of Europe. The country was divided between those who cherished the old ways and those who sought to embrace the new: its history in the seventeenth and eighteenth centuries is the history of conflict and oscillation between two ideals of government, neither of which could triumph permanently. In this unresolved struggle as much as anywhere else are to be found the difficulties and weaknesses of the republic.

The Peace of Westphalia, in 1648, brought independence but not surcease from internal anomalies. The composition of the republic was odd and amorphous. It was not a nation in any modern sense: its people were Low Germans, Frisians, and Flemings, most but not all of whom spoke a Low German dialect which was taking form as a separate literary language called Dutch. The Dutch were divided religiously among the predominant Calvinists, other and variously extreme forms of Protestants, and many Roman Catholics. The Netherland provinces, whose common destiny under successive Burgundians and Habsburg rulers had long been shared, were now divided. Only half of them were included in the republic. The southern ones (which form Belgium today), Catholic and in the end loyal to their Spanish sovereign, remained under Spanish rule.

Nor was the Dutch Republic symmetrical in its political structure. Its seven provinces, which occupied almost precisely the same territory as the present-day kingdom of the Netherlands, lay in the deltas of the great rivers from Central and Western Europe—Rhine, Meuse, and Scheldt—around the shores of the Zuider Zee, and in the sandy peninsulas and islets of the north, the area called Frisia. All of this territory was near salt water and a good deal was under it. Only the easternmost section was high and dry. The aqueous character of the Dutch terrain had advantages and disadvantages: in time of peril, it could be flooded against enemy soldiers, as William the Silent had shown in the war of liberation, and as was to be demonstrated later in wars against the French. It offered unequalled naval and mercantile advantages, with its many channels and harbors. The draining and protection of underwater areas sharpened the skills and alertness of the Dutch, who became through practice the best engineers, the best shipbuilders, and the best skaters in Europe. But it was precarious land, and although rich for horticulture and pasturage it was not suitable for crops like wheat.

Of the seven provinces, overwhelmingly the largest, richest, and most important was the province of Holland which gave its name, in the common usage of foreigners, to the whole country. Holland, with its great capital and harbor Amsterdam, was so superior in most respects to the other six provinces that the latter feared its dominance. Partly because of this fear, the development

THE NETHERLANDS IN THE 18TH CENTURY

of a strong government for the republic as a whole was tardy and incomplete.

There were other and deeper reasons, too. The war against Spain had been fought to secure the independence and privileges of the separate provinces; provincial self-government was equated with liberty. The States General, the central parliament and the only civil authority of the central government, consisted in effect of ambassadors from the provincial estates, or assemblies. And the provincial estates consisted usually of delegates from towns, corporations, and guilds, all whom had to be consulted before the States could take action.

This diversity and particularism were strongly defended by the local authorities and by most of the provinces. It was supported by the peasants, with their local loyalties, and by the nobility, with their ancient privileges. But if ever a country needed strong leadership and decisive action, it was the United Provinces, surrounded as it was by predatory enemies of every description. And certain forces did indeed tend to pull the country together in moments of crisis: fear and dislike of possible invaders; a common interest in defending their commerce and expanding it; and an almost mystical reverence for the House of Orange.

The House of Orange occupied, from the birth of the Dutch Republic, a very strange position which constantly varied in importance and character. Nowhere in modern European history is there anything like it. A younger line of the German princely family of Nassau had, in the early sixteenth century, taken up residence in Brussels, and inherited the southern French principality of Orange. Its scion, William the Silent, had led the Netherlands in the long, gruelling, and heroic struggle against the Spanish crown. William had been elected as stadholder—governor—of most (though not all) of the rebelling provinces. His heirs now and then occupied similar positions; all of them evoked some of the almost idolatrous loyalty which was directed toward the memory of William.

This persistent loyalty, among a people ferociously liberty-loving and republican, frequently led some groups in the Republic to urge the installation of the current prince of Orange as supreme stadholder of the whole republic, and even, on occasion, as king. These people from time to time gained the upper hand: they were known as Orangists. Their enthusiasm for strong central government reflected the tendencies of politics in the seventeenth and eighteenth centuries. But the attachment to the House of Orange was even deeper, and more sentimental, than a perception of expediencies. For in 1815 the family was to be installed on the throne of a newly established Dutch kingdom as a hereditary dynasty, and there its descendants quite happily reign today.

The Orangists were opposed by the Republicans, who sought to preserve the weak central government and the privileges of the provinces. From time to time the program of each party evolved to include other demands—religious toleration versus Calvinist uniformity was the most common. As long as the Dutch Republic lasted, the two parties lasted, in incessant and sometimes deadly conflict.

In the seventeenth century there had been a major crisis in the affairs of the Republic. The two parties, Orangists and Republicans, had permitted their internal struggle to become involved in the Thirty Years War. It was then the Orangists who won the dispute, and the House of Orange established something resembling a military dictatorship. But the end of the Thirty Years War, with its promise of international security, brought the temporary eclipse of the House of Orange. William II died in 1650; his heir was a posthumous son. The Republicans struck a medal commemorating William's death; the device read "The last hour of the Prince is the beginning of freedom." And so it proved—temporarily. The next twenty-five years were a great era for the Republicans.

The Republican platform was virtually put into effect. The office of stadholder was separated by law from those of Captain General and Admiral; in 1668 the stadholderate was abolished altogether in some of the provinces, led by Holland in 1667. The provincial estates were supreme again, and they were dominated by the wealthy merchants, who (as is so often the case with businessmen in political office) devoted themselves sedulously to the reduction of taxes. This parsimony stimulated the economy but starved the armed forces.

The textbook, as it were, of this phase of Dutch history was a book called *The True Interest of Holland,* written in 1661 by a man named Pieter Delacourt. It was a spirited defense of the notion of liberty, of a sort which was to become familiar in England by the end of the century. The notions of liberty which it set forth were a blend of the more modern idea of individual freedom under law, and the old-fashioned view of liberty as protection for the rights of ancient political authorities and provinces. Warmly espoused by Dutch and foreign republicans, the book was violently opposed by Orangists, particularly in the town of Leiden where an Orangist synod excluded its author from the sacraments of the Calvinist church.

If Delacourt was the theorist of Dutch Republicanism, its leader was John De Witt, the Grand Pensioner (Chief Minister) of the province of Holland. Once in effective control of the Republic, he played a role in his own country similar to that of Oliver Cromwell in England, whose protégé he had been in the 1650's. And his regime was destined for a similar fate.

The revival of Orangism began partly as a result of the jealousies of De Witt's fellow-burghers and of the embarrassing realization by smaller provinces that the "sovereignty" of the provinces led to the dominance of Holland over them. It profited too from the growth to maturity of the heir of William II; destined to become William III of Great Britain after 1688, he was a man of great determination and important connections. But mostly it arose from a classic cause: the threat of foreign war and the need for strong and united leadership. By 1670, William was being elected stadholder of some of the provinces, and his supporters were securing majorities in the estates of others. War with France threatened, and when it broke out in 1672, William became unquestioned leader and almost autocrat of the Republic. Holland restored its stadholderate and elected him to it, and he was made Captain General and Admiral. For the rest of his life—he died in 1702—his position was in practice indistinguishable from that of a divine-right monarch.

Comparable oscillations followed in the eighteenth century. After

William's death, the Orangist influence declined and that of the Republicans became predominant again. Under the impact of foreign danger there was again an Orangist revival in the 1740's, and in 1747 William IV was elected stadholder of *all* the provinces—the first time any of his family had achieved this distinction. But his triumph was followed by another decline in the fortunes of Dutch autocracy and by the growing agitation of the Republicans. On the eve of the French Revolution the power of Orange was once again threatened with extinction.

In the last half of the eighteenth century, the United Provinces failed to array sufficient strength to defend their freedom of action. By 1789, Dutch politics had become a political football game in which the quarterbacks were the French and British governments, the former backing the Republicans and the latter the Orangists. The devolution of authority was mainly due to the vast growth in power of these two neighbors. After 1714, when the rule of the southern Netherlands—Belgium—was transferred from Spain to Austria, Spain had ceased to be a major enemy of the Dutch. The new opponents were nearer, larger, and more threatening; to defend themselves from either, the Dutch were obliged to purchase the support of the other. The consequence was a steady loss of Dutch political power, commercial freedom, and overseas holdings, which began as early as the 1650's. Already in that decade, after serious naval defeats at the hands of the British, the Dutch had been forced to accept the harassments of the British Navigation Acts, which wrecked the indispensable Dutch policy of insisting on free commerce with all territories and freedom of the seas for all Dutch ships. The Dutch foothold in North America, New Amsterdam, was ceded to the English, who renamed it New York. The principal Dutch foothold in South America, central Brazil, was lost in the 1660's to the Portuguese, from whom the United Provinces had seized it. Dutch trading throughout the world was gradually surpassed by English and French.

If it was politics and power which led to the Dutch decline, it was in economics and naval warfare that the Republic's greatest achievements and contributions lay; and it was the enterprise and inventiveness of the Dutch which permitted them in their great days to achieve leadership. In the eighteenth century, even at its end, the United Provinces were still an important, if not quite a first-rate, commercial and naval power.

The core of economic power was the Dutch carrying trade; the Republic had built one of the great entrepots and markets of European trade. A very high percentage of exports from all Europe to non-European areas, and imports from them, passed through Amsterdam or the lesser Dutch towns. This trade led to other skills and occupations. The Dutch craftsmen became skilled at the processing of raw materials imported from overseas—Amsterdam remains today, for example, the center of the world's diamond-cutting trade and a major market for precious stones. Weaving, metal-work and furniture-making also flourished. But more than manufacturing or finishing, the Dutch trade led to the development of credit, banking, and research, described in Chapter 12, which were vital not only for the Netherlands' future but for that of all mankind.

The wealth and power of the Netherlands showed itself in the expansion of the merchant class. Nowhere in Europe in the seventeenth century were merchants so prominent and landowning noblemen so obscure; nowhere was a society so profoundly shaped by the materialistic but extremely well-educated class of haughty businessmen. It was these mercantile lords who promoted the great age of Dutch culture, the northern Renaissance and Baroque in the history of art. Nowhere did painting and portraiture achieve so high a level in the seventeenth century as in the Dutch towns, and the eminence of the painters was matched by that of architects, scientists, and philosophers. The list is very long: Vermeer and Rembrandt, Brueghel and Steen, are merely the best known names. Their variety was almost as striking as their genius: the chaste and geometrical skill of Vermeer, the sumptuous, mythological inspirations of Rubens, are again only the most striking of contrasting techniques.

In 1789, the Republic was still free, still rich, and still creative. But it was still free thanks solely to the rivalries of greater states, and specifically to the extreme aversion of the British to permitting French territories or influence to expand northward along the coast of the English Channel and the North Sea. When, a few years later, French power became suddenly invincible, the Dutch Republic disappeared. And while an independent Netherlands was to emerge again in 1815, the peculiar quality of the Republic, with its strange institutions, its economic hegemony, and its merchant civilization, was gone forever.

ITALY: THE LONG SLEEP

The difficulties of the Dutch Republic show the costs and profits of an effort to perpetuate fifteenth century political ideals in an age of absolutism. The situation of the Italian states illustrates the comparable costs of failing to create any modern state apparatus at all. The peninsula was mainly, by 1789, a series of colonies of larger and more unified powers. But while the political condition of the Italians seemed desperate, their culture and creativity were very much alive. In the nineteenth century, they were for the first time to turn their skills to the creation of a united and independent government in their peninsula and were to meet with dramatic success.

The hopelessness of their political state in 1789 did not seem to trouble the Italians—let alone anybody else. National unity, national power, national freedom, were not yet the ideals of peoples. Almost everyone regarded a divided Italy, and an Italy dominated by foreigners, as natural and suitable. The latter had existed, in 1789, for nearly three hundred years, and the former for about twelve hundred. Moreover, few Italians thought of themselves as forming a "nation." The cultural, economic, and even linguistic gulfs among the various parts of the peninsula seemed greater than, say, the differences between the state of Piedmont and the adjoining portions of France. A condition of political hopelessness is only a state of mind, not necessarily a tangible liability.

The domestic histories of the individual Italian states—governed or mis-

governed either by petty tyrants or by foreign potentates—are stale and unprofitable. The interest of Italian history in the seventeenth and eighteenth centuries lies, first, in its role as a stake in the international contests of the great
powers, and second, in its cultural developments. But a very brief summary of the
political divisions of Italy, and the changes in them, is important.

These two centuries of Italian history were, domestically, tranquil. There
were some wars, many changes of dynasties, rivalries and conflicts between the
governments. But the basic structure of the peninsula remained unchanged; in
1789 it resembled what it had been in 1648. Moreover, the great issues of the
rest of Europe scarcely touched Italy. There was no religious struggle. Owing
partly to the strict control of the very Catholic Spaniards in the age of the Reformation, Protestantism secured no foot-hold in Italy except in a few areas such
as Lombardy and Lucca, where it was rapidly repressed. Nor were the other
great issues of the day—the struggle to establish autocracy, the struggle to expand
overseas—relevant to Italy. Italian institutions were frozen in the rather stagnant

ITALY ABOUT 1740

patterns of the late sixteenth century; and the Italian states were neither vigorous enough nor large enough to embark upon the conquest of the world.

The political divisions of Italy were, in 1650, as follows. In the extreme northwest, in what is now Alpine France, was the Duchy of Savoy, with its dependent province of Piedmont, one of the two Italian states which throughout the period maintained real independence of foreign powers. South of it, on the Mediterranean coast, was the ancient and prosperous republic of Genoa, which also ruled, for most of the period, the island of Corsica, and which was strongly under Spanish influence. The plain of the Po river south of the Alps, the former Duchy of Milan (also called Lombardy), was in 1650 a Spanish province. In the northeast, the great Republic of Venice, with its hinterland, maintained like Savoy its independence of foreign dominance. South of these provinces, and scattered through the northern third of the peninsula, were more or less independent duchies and principalities, for the most part in 1650 still ruled by the descendants of their Renaissance despots: the Este family in Ferrara and Modena, the Farnese in Parma, the Medici in the larger Grand Duchy of Tuscany, the Gonzagas in Mantua, and several others. Most of the middle part of the peninsula comprised the States of the Church, in which the Popes ruled as autocrats. The southern third of the peninsula was occupied by the kingdom of Naples which, like the adjoining island kingdom of Sicily, was connected with the crown of Spain.

Changes which did not much affect the lives of the people took place in the sovereignty of these regions throughout the century and a half which concerns us. The Este family possessions were distributed between the States of the Church, which acquired Ferrara, and the Austrian dynasty, so that Modena passed to a Habsburg. In 1714, a large reorganization of Italian affairs took place to compensate Austria for its failure to place a Habsburg on the Spanish throne in the War of the Spanish Succession. Lombardy, Naples, and Sardinia passed to Austrian control, and Sicily and Genoa were ceded to the Duke of Savoy. But this settlement proved short-lived. Spanish ambition and ingenuity succeeded in recovering Naples for the Spanish royal family, and after 1735 a younger son of the Spanish Bourbon king ruled in southern Italy. In the meanwhile, in 1720, Austria and Savoy had exchanged Sardinia for Sicily. The Duke of Savoy took the title of King of Sardinia, and Sicily passed with Naples to the Spanish Bourbon prince, who took the title of King of the Two Sicilies.

Upon the extinction of the House of Farnese, another prince of the Spanish family was installed upon the throne of Parma. With the extinction of the House of Medici, the Emperor Francis I, the husband of Maria Theresa, was made Grand Duke of Tuscany. Thereafter, Tuscany was ruled by younger members of the Habsburg family.

In the middle of the century, the island of Corsica, long misgoverned by the Genoese republic, revolted; and for several decades a patriot government under the spirited leadership of General Paoli, established a free and independent regime. But in 1768, the rule of Corsica passed to France, which established itself as an overlord almost as oppressive as Genoa had been, and more efficient. The loss of Corsica was permanent: it is still part of France.

GRAND CANAL OF VENICE by Antonio Canaletto (1697–1768), most famous Italian painter of his time. Canaletto's charm and technical skill, unsupported by any great vigor or originality, exemplify Italian art after the great ages of the Renaissance and Baroque, just as the lovely scene shown here exemplifies the decline of Venice from a great power to a delightful playground. (Museum of Fine Arts of Houston)

By 1789, Austria was dominant in Italy. Lombardy was an Austrian province. Modena and Tuscany were ruled by Habsburgs. And in the other states, barring Piedmont-Sardinia and Venice, Austrian influence was supreme. Even with its Spanish kings, the policy of the Kingdom of the Two Sicilies was increasingly influenced by Vienna.

There are a few lessons to be learned from a brief survey of developments within some of these states. The most interesting and important state was unquestionably the Venetian Republic.

The constitution of Venice was the admiration of many throughout Europe who disliked absolutism—it was, logically, most enthusiastically admired and written about by the English, who at the end of the seventeenth century were looking for justifications of constitutional government. It provided, at least in theory, for the exercise of power by elected representatives of the propertied classes, mainly the great merchants, and resembled in some ways the constitution of the ancient Roman Republic. The chief officials of Venice were the elected *doges* (Venetian dialect for *dukes*). But the citizens were, with reason, extremely suspicious of their elected leaders, fearing that they nourished ambitions of becoming despots. They were also extremely sensitive to the threat of plots and subversion from foreigners and from the lower classes who did not share in the business of government. They thus surrounded the authority of the elected representatives with so many safeguards that political action became more and more difficult, and established so many measures against treason and so many forms of secret police control that enormous power came to be concentrated in the hands of the "security" authorities, and the liberties which the republic was intended to safeguard were frequently illusory.

The tendency to government by conspiracy—so noticeable in other parts of Italy as well—was usually attributed by historians of earlier generations to the moral decay induced by excessive wealth. There is, in fact, evidence of a decay in Venice, if not exactly of morality, at least of vigor and good sense. The Venetians, after the gorgeous artistic bursts of the sixteenth century, tended like other Italians more and more to mere decoration and display, and certainly to a somewhat languid luxuriation in comforts which made the extraordinary and beautiful city the most entrancing in Europe. It attracted noble and opulent vacationers from everywhere; it was the Palm Beach of its day. But the political effects of this transition to a sort of combined museum, amusement park, and night club were perhaps less important in causing than in reflecting the decline of vigor. The fact was that the source of Venetian power and energy, the Mediterranean trade, was declining.

Three circumstances weakened Venice: the expansion of Ottoman Turkey in the Levant; the competition of others, notably the Aragonese, for the Mediterranean trade; and the difficult necessity of defending the mainland holdings of the Republic (the province called Venetia which included such important cities as Padua and Verona) against powerful neighbors like Austria, France, and Spain.

The attacks of the Turks were the most tangible and most depressing of these problems. One by one, the eastern colonies of Venice, the outposts of

European Christianity, fell. Cyprus was lost; then, after a defense of twenty years, Crete was abandoned in 1669. Thereafter the Venetians sought to abstain from wars; the martial spirit ebbed, and the city became "the revel of the earth, the masque of Italy."

While the Venetian Republic was invisibly transforming itself into a decorative but fragile mummy, the monarchy of Savoy to the west was acquiring the life force of a real, if diminutive, European power. The House of Savoy, its homeland safely protected by the High Alps, governed efficiently, used its revenues wisely, juggled its alliances effectively, and set up a highly militarized state. The parallels with the activities of the Hohenzollern rulers in northern Germany are remarkable. There was a series of able and venturesome sovereigns, most spectacularly Victor Amadeus II (1675–1730), who freed the country from French control (much of his territory was French-speaking), expanded its boundaries, and gave it weight in European councils. His reign marked the end of French dominance in northern Italy, which had been sought and sometimes achieved for two centuries.

The other considerable state of northern Italy was the Grand Duchy of Tuscany, the heir of Renaissance Florence. Florence and the satellite city-states which made up Tuscany, like Siena, Pisa, and Leghorn, witnessed the same graceful decline as Venice. The military might was gone; the art became attenuated and often trivial. Civic zest and responsibility yielded to an acquiescence in absolute monarchy and indirect foreign domination. The last of the Medici, sometimes degenerate, sometimes artistic, were all flaccid. But after the Medici family died out Florence became in the second half of the eighteenth century the theater of a prophetic political experiment.

Leopold I, Grand Duke of Tuscany, was the son of Francis of Lorraine, who had become Tuscan ruler after the Medici extinction, and the brother of Emperor Joseph II of Austria. Like his brother (see Chapter 15) he sought, through the use of his absolute power, to remodel his realm along lines approved by the best modern political reformers. But Tuscany was smaller, more civilized, and more manageable than Austria, and Leopold was wiser; where the older brother failed, the younger succeeded. The influence of the priesthood was shaved away (Leopold, like Joseph, was a half-open skeptic); medieval taxation was reformed and equalized—even the property of the crown itself was made subject to taxation; commercial and guild restrictions on trade were abolished, and all regulation of the basic grain trade was ended; the universities of Siena and Pisa were modernized; extensive public works were undertaken. Most dramatic of all, the country was presented with a perfectly modern criminal code, based upon the advanced ideas of the Italian philosopher Beccaria, which abolished capital punishment and torture and inaugurated a system of trial and punishment which would seem satisfactory today. In 1790, when Leopold left Florence for Vienna, to succeed his brother on the Austrian throne, sleepy, archaic Tuscany had become the most up-to-date state in Europe, a prototype for twentieth-century political and legal organization.

No developments of comparable interest took place in most of the other Italian states. The smaller principalities, the States of the Church, the Kingdom of the Two Sicilies, mostly slept in the eighteenth century under the rule of uninventive autocrats. For the most part, the old institutions persisted unchanged. Naples and Sicily retained their old diets and their ancient liberties, marred and manipulated by political indolence and corruption. The States of the Church were widely regarded as the worst-governed provinces of Europe, and they were certainly the most conservative. Laymen could not hold office, and the priesthood showed little concern with economic problems. Agriculture and commerce decayed. The population declined. Rome itself became a small, and rather unhealthful, town.

An exception to this general languor, however, was to be found in Lombardy. After its transfer from Spain to Austria, in 1714, it at first continued to be governed by Spaniards employed by Vienna, and its condition was the most deplorable in Italy. But after 1750, the reforming impulse struck Vienna, and the Lombard administration became vigorous and drastic. The same sort of reforms as in Tuscany—fiscal, judicial, administrative, ecclesiastical, and economic—were pushed. New ideas were encouraged, and freedom of speech became practically effective. Milan was again an important cultural center; the best minds of the day taught and lectured there. And Lombardy prospered as it had not done for two hundred years.

By 1789, then, Italy presented a varied picture. Tuscany, Lombardy and Sardinia-Piedmont were moving ahead along roads of political reform and economic growth. In the center and the south, the economy was more backward and the political institutions more decadent than ever. But throughout Italy, although especially in the north, cultural life was persisting and reviving. In the seventeenth century, Italy had become the center of European music and had contributed to the world the new art form of the opera. Scarlatti, Picini, and Pergolesi were the cynosure of Europe, inventive and indeed revolutionary. In science, Italy shone in the eighteenth century. The first effective notions of electricity are associated with the names of Galvani, who taught at Bologna, and Volta, at Pavia, who invented the first battery. In public affairs, political theory, and economics, Italy was as productive of Enlightenment philosophers as France itself: Beccaria, Genovesi, Galiani, formulated recommendations for princes for the improvement of their realms with as much profundity and force as Voltaire or Montesquieu.

SPAIN: THE LATE RALLY

In 1789, Spain was still the largest country in the world. Or, more precisely, the Spanish crown still ruled more square miles and more subjects than any other. It still possessed some weight in European councils, a valuable commerce, the best coinage in the world, and a government which had just engaged in a drastic program of modernization. But Spain was weak, and growing weaker. Its weakness was to be fully revealed in the next thirty years. The revolutionary convulsions which were about to agitate Europe in 1789, and which were to lead to the obliteration of the weakened Dutch and Venetian Republics, were to cost enfeebled Spain most of its empire, much of its internal stability, and almost all of its prestige.

The decadence of Spanish power had long been manifest. Territorial losses since the days of Philip II, while gradual, had been extremely significant. The northern half of the Netherlands was lost by 1648, and the southern half in 1714. The Italian holdings also were mostly gone by 1714. Portugal and with it Brazil had been lost in 1640. The trans-Pyrenean provinces, most important of them Rousillon, were lost to France in 1659. Jamaica was lost in 1655 to England, and other Caribbean territories were one by one yielded to the navies of Britain, France, and the Dutch Republic; the Spanish monopoly, security of Spanish trade, the defenses of the Spanish mainland in America were breached and threatened.

This attrition of the imperial soil reflected problems which beset the homeland and forced a baleful procession of retreats and humiliations. It is difficult to sort out first causes. There was the overextension of Spanish power; neither the territory nor wealth nor technology nor manpower of Spain was fit to support its vast imperial undertakings. There was the Netherlands revolt, a costly drain and a more costly loss; there was the naval defeat, and the subsequent naval and piratical harassment by the British; there was the endemic financial crisis, which led to the endemic bankruptcy of the royal treasury; and there was the series of weak and even moronic monarchs who proved quite inadequate to the terrible responsibilities of absolute power.

In 1700 Charles II, the last of the Spanish Habsburgs, died. By then, the direst losses had already taken place. Spain was already notorious for the gloomy immobility of its government and the decay of its economy; and its empire was infamous for oppressive misrule. The population of Spain had fallen drastically. Spaniards who had remained in the homeland were to a very high degree unproductive. An extraordinarily large percentage of them were in the Church, particularly in the monastic orders, drawn by its great wealth and the promise of security and remunerative unemployment, no longer deterred by the rigors of a discipline that had become, in many orders, largely nominal. The aristocracy, forbidden by royal decree from engaging in manual labor or business, was proud, indolent, and uncreative. The peasantry, wrestling with a difficult and arid land, was inconvenienced by heavy burdens of taxation. The middle classes of the towns, their spirit and enterprise broken by repeated royal attacks upon their charters and their wealth, no longer counted for anything. And all these depredations had come about as a result of the efforts to construct a modern, centralized autocracy in the sixteenth century by breaking the power of the ancient rivals of the king's supremacy. The trouble was that the kings, once the door was open to their arbitrary rule, refused to go through it. Nothing was changed, and nothing improved, after the death of Philip II. In 1700, patriotic and intelligent Spaniards despaired about the plight of their country.

Charles II died without male heirs and (as is related elsewhere) a violent global struggle took place among the more vigorous European powers to secure his cobwebbed but priceless legacy. In the end, in 1714, the empire was divided among the participants in the struggle. To Austria, which had sought to install a Habsburg upon the throne, went the Belgian and Italian provinces. To the grandson of Louis XIV went the throne of Spain and its overseas possessions.

Under its new dynasty, Spain, widely and beneficently gallicized, became in international affairs the satellite and protégé of France. In the long Franco-British duel which followed, the "Family Compact," an alliance of the crowned cousins of Spain and France, assured that the two Bourbon powers should almost always ally against Great Britain, and other, incidental, enemies. Although Spain's freedom of diplomatic action was thus lost, its integrity was fairly well safeguarded. And the presence of the new dynasty and of French ideas brought an internal renascence within the kingdom and the government.

Philip V (1700–1746) and his successors used and expanded the autocratic powers which the recent Habsburg kings had failed to use. The first and most striking measures completed the destruction of the obsolescent nobility, which still controlled local government. The nobleman lost the power to sentence his tenants to death, and his authority in local government was turned over to elected councils. The legal ban upon the sale of noble estates was abolished. Throughout the empire, centrally appointed and controlled *intendants*, patterned on the French model, took over the effective business of governing from the old and often moribund local authorities. In 1707, Castilian law was introduced into all parts of the kingdom, replacing the congeries of old provincial laws and law courts. The old provincial *Cortes* (parliaments) were replaced with a single Spanish *Cortes*, which however was almost never called in the eighteenth century. Civil rights were extended to Jews, gypsies, and Protestants. In 1761, the independence of the Church was restricted by insistence upon the king's approval of all papal statements and bulls before they could be published in Spain. In 1767 the Jesuits were expelled from the country. From 1779 on, the power of the Inquisition was reduced.

In the field of economics, too, modern ideas were espoused and translated into policy. The extremely restrictive practices of Spanish mercantilism, which had closed the American kingdoms to trade with foreigners, were relaxed. Port after port was opened to at least limited trade—in 1778, 15 in Spain, and 25 in America. The monopolistic power of the guilds was attacked and eventually broken. Foreign artisans were imported. Manufactures were encouraged. An intelligent financial policy was at long last inaugurated and, in the 1740's the Spanish budget was balanced for the first time in three hundred years.

Many of these changes were due to the vigor and enthusiasm of Charles III (1759–1788), one of the most effective innovators among the enlightened despots. By the time of his death, Spain was equipped with economic institutions, an administrative and fiscal structure, and a legal system, in some ways in advance of France or England.

But rejoicing on the part of patriots in 1788 would have been premature. Many of the old weaknesses—notably, the poverty of Spanish soil and the paucity of Spanish manpower—were still present. And new and ominous handicaps were appearing. The House of Bourbon, in the persons of Charles III's son and grandson, was about to go to seed, as the House of Habsburg had done before it. The

ROYAL ARMS OF SPAIN. The coat-of-arms here shown is the ancient emblem
of the kingdom and dynasty of Spain. When Spain became a republic in
1931, it was changed to a republican device, but after General Franco's
victory in the Spanish Civil War (1939) the use of monarchical symbols
was revived. The shield indicates the union of the medieval kingdoms
which were brought together under a single ruler to form Spain: the first,
the castle of Castile; the second, the lion of Leon; the third, the red and
yellow stripes of Aragon; the fourth, the chain of Navarre. At the bottom
is the flower of Granada; and in the center a smaller shield (or "inescut-
cheon") with the lilies of France, added in 1700 when the Spanish throne
passed to Philip V, a prince of the French house of Bourbon. Since their
use was restored by General Franco, the royal arms have been displayed
against an eagle, symbol of empire, and with the addition of a yoke and
arrows, the badge of the Falange, the only legal party in contemporary
Spain.

routes of empire still required a naval defense which Spanish resources could not provide; once the protecting French navy was put out of action by the British, after the Trafalgar encounter of 1805, the Spanish colonies were defenseless against the ambitions of Britain or the aspirations of rebellious natives.

And there were more subtle contradictions. The American subjects had inveighed against laws which shut them off from the rich trade with foreigners and confined them to commerce with their impoverished mother country. Once those laws were repealed, foreign contacts multiplied and foreign ideas began to circulate in the colonies. Moreover, the whole tendency of Bourbon policy was to complete the work of centralizing the government. In America the attempt to *use,* vigorously, wisely, and beneficently, the absolute powers of the crown disrupted the salutary neglect of the Spanish colonies, and led to resentments and stirrings among the colonists. Already, by 1789, there were ominous writings and agitations pointing toward a separation of the American kingdoms—Mexico, Peru, New Granada, and La Plata.

Spain was both too small and too large for its century—its empire was too vast, its homeland too small. Militarily and economically it could not compel foreigners to respect it, or its own subjects to support it. Within a brief generation after 1789, the great edifice was to fall.

Spain achieved, if tardily, the kind of government which seemed necessary to success and progress in the eighteenth century—a streamlined, highly centralized, intelligent autocracy. The Dutch had the kind of economy which seemed necessary—an adventurous and expanding system of commerce, banking, and manufacturing. Italy had the background of wealth and intellect which seemed conducive to success. But all three were weak, and growing weaker. Spain was too large, the Dutch Republic too small, Italy too divided, to play an independent role in the struggle of the Titans. And all of them, once great and vigorous and pushing, seemed by 1789 to lack the inner compulsion which had made nations great in the last few centuries. In an age where nothing but power counted, they had lost the means and the will to power. Like the rest of Europe they were to be forced in the nineteenth century into the pattern embodied in and enforced by the new great powers.

18

DYNASTIC
DIPLOMACY
IN EUROPE AND
OVERSEAS

From 1648 to 1789 the idea of "Europe" took new forms in the minds of philosophers and kings. New enthusiasms replaced the old unifying factors such as the Roman Catholic Church, the Latin language, and the Holy Roman Empire, which had suffered badly in the Peace of Westphalia, in 1648. Educated men were aware that Europeans had much in common: classical traditions in the arts and literature, the scientific spirit, advancing techniques in government, trade and engineering, military methods, knowledge and experience gained in Europe's outward drive over the world. Christian ideals still reigned, though frequently disguised as faith in reason and progress. Outwardly European nations looked alike, with kings, landed aristocrats, towns, burghers, and peasants. Polite society was still cosmopolitan; local attachment and even patriotism were parochial and vulgar.

The court at Versailles and the French language and French taste set the tone. It was easy for writers such as Voltaire and Rousseau, great stars of the eighteenth-century Enlightenment, to dream of a Europe which was like one great nation, cherishing or soon to cherish similar values. The enlightened despots with their common respect for things French, their close relations with the *philosophes,* and their outwardly similar policies, contributed to the impression that European institutions were more alike than they were different. Even in Russia

Peter the Great (1682–1725) tried to Europeanize his country; and the great Catherine (1762–1796) insisted at the close of the era that Russia was a part of Europe.

Whatever the fancies of kings and intellectuals about "Europe," the theory and practice of international relations featured as never before the sovereignty of the state. It was a time of consolidation, of clearer frontier lines, of ending the overlapping allegiances which were leftovers from the Middle Ages. It was the era of dynastic states, most of them absolute monarchies. But sovereignty and consolidation did not depend on forms of government—the English and Poles considered their states just as absolutely independent as the absolute states of the Bourbons and Habsburgs. *Consolidation* was moving apace—in the scattered lands of the Hohenzollerns, in the scattered and even more diverse territories of the Habsburgs. States were being rounded off by territorial additions. It is not always possible to distinguish internal consolidation from external aggression. The dynastic character of the states led to all manner of succession disputes, with the result that the period abounds in wars of succession—Spanish, Polish, and Austrian. Religious motives are much less apparent in the warfare of this period. But whatever its reasons, war was universally accepted as a legitimate tool of policy. Pretexts were usually clothed with legal alibis, but the real law was the ambition of princes. The wars of this period were, moreover, the first to be fought with something resembling modern state structures.

The idea of a European equilibrium, bolstered now by analogies to physics in this science-conscious and "enlightened" age, was directed more toward survival than toward hopes of peace. There were dreams of peace—by the Englishman William Penn, the Frenchman Abbé de Saint-Pierre, and the German Immanuel Kant for example—but these were merely aspirations preparing the ground for a later age. Diplomacy worked on a mundane level, and international law was largely a codification of trifles, conveniences which were generally acceptable in the relations of armies, merchants, and diplomats. It never occurred to anyone that war itself could be illegal.

On the surface crowns glittered and aristocracies spoke French and intellectuals enjoyed a kind of international fellowship; beneath it the populations of European states went their separate ways, deeply committed to different traditions. The Europe of everyday life was far from being one commonwealth. True, Europe's economic and military supremacy was becoming sufficient to make contacts with the whole globe; and Europe had enough business, scientific, and political leadership to make the most of these forays. The home continent, however, in spite of the cosmopolitan dreams of the intellectuals, suffered grave divisions. The realities of power balanced states against each other. The aspirations of dynastic rulers, the requirements of survival, the growing competition for trade and colonies as well as for home provinces cultivated by taxpayers and potential soldiers—these forestalled united action with respect to the rest of the world. Graver still, while nationalities half slumbered, the time was coming when they would awaken to gaze at one another with hostile eyes. The span from 1648 to 1789 witnessed a quickening of national sentiments. The following period, announced by the French Revolution, would see Europe demonstrating to the world the excitement and danger of nationalism, but in the eighteenth century allegiances were still to sovereigns, not to nations.

THE BALANCE OF POWER BEFORE 1700

The major international developments in the second half of the seventeenth century—from the Peace of Westphalia to the beginning of the War of the Spanish Succession—were the wars which arose from the ambitions of Louis XIV. These wars reflected the new power of France and the determination of other European powers to "contain" France. No other government wished to see Louis XIV strong enough to dominate the continent—if that happened, every state and monarch would be endangered; the threat of a "universal empire," the perpetual threat to the liberties of diverse Europe, would materialize.

There is no certainty that Louis XIV seriously contemplated a "universal empire," but he definitely did contemplate certain changes in the boundaries of France. The most important of these was the extension of his kingdom to what came to be called its "natural frontiers," which meant the Rhine, the Alps, and the Pyrenees. At times, Louis cherished other and more grandiose schemes—notably the attachment of Spain and its empire to the French crown—but a frontier on the Rhine was the principal focus of his ambitions in the second half of the seventeenth century, and it made quite as much trouble in Europe as if he had openly pursued the goal of restoring the Roman Empire with himself as Caesar. It made so much trouble because of the strategic nature of the territories involved.

The provinces between France's northeastern frontier and the Rhine river (Belgium now, but then the Spanish Netherlands) occupied a crucial place in the European map. They were rich. They were a center of banking and commerce and manufacturing; control of them would have provided an enormous economic power over all of Europe. They lay, menacingly, across the straits from England, and he who controlled them could not only challenge England's island fortress but disrupt its commerce. They lay on the flank of the Dutch Republic, small, powerful, and sensitive. They lay at the end of the trade routes of all of Central Europe. And they commanded, militarily, the approaches to western Germany.

The vital interests of England, the Dutch Republic, all the German states, and Spain, would have been gravely threatened by French control of Belgium. And if England, the Dutch Republic, the German states, and Spain were enfeebled by French conquest of Belgium, then who in Europe would be able to prevent France's conquest of all of it? This is the real meaning of the balance of power in the later seventeenth century, and of the confusing and very limited wars which were almost unceasingly fought.

Louis XIV was not the only actor on the stage; secondary dramas were pitting other wills and ambitions against each other in various combinations. In this period the English and Dutch, both maritime peoples, clashed in three wars following the English Navigation Act of 1651.[1] Portugal, finally recognized as independent by Spain (1668), rebounded into a lasting alliance with England which, among other things, was to familiarize English palates with "Port" wine. The English and Portuguese expelled the hard-pressed Dutch from, respectively, New Amsterdam (New York), and Brazil. In the north of Europe, the Brandenburg of the Great Elector rivaled Sweden and Poland for the Baltic shore. And in the east, as we shall see, Austrians and Venetians set their faces once more against the Turks.

But Louis XIV set the pace, and it will be well to summarize, very briefly, his wars, as illustrations of the superficial confusion and the underlying logic of the international scene.

I. The War of Devolution (1667–1668). Louis XIV claimed (on spurious grounds) a number of key fortresses in the Spanish Netherlands. He was frustrated by the combined efforts of Spain, England, the Dutch Republic, and Sweden.

II. The Dutch War (1672–1678). Louis was better equipped with allies now. He had bought off Charles II of England (who badly needed money) as well as Sweden and some German princes, and attacked the Dutch Republic. But the Dutch defended themselves with ferocity, and English public opinion, which disliked the French alliance, forced England to withdraw. The war was long and complicated and there were engagements in western Germany as well as the Netherlands, and Brandenburg and Sweden took the occasion to attack each other. As in previous times the Habsburg Emperor and the Habsburg King of Spain opposed France. The French won little; at the Peace of Nimwegen in 1678–1679 they were awarded one Spanish province, the County of Burgundy (Franche-Comté) on what is now the Swiss border, and a few minor Belgian territories.

III. In 1680–1683, Central Europe was preoccupied with the Turks, who were making their last attack on Vienna. Louis XIV took the opportunity to pick up several Rhineland territories, mainly the Free City of Strasbourg. His method was a mixture of force and judicial procedure (Chambers of Reunion—impromptu courts supported by armed force which validated his legal claims to the areas).

IV. The War of the League of Augsburg (1688–1697). The League was the device of the Stadholder of the Dutch Republic, William III (by now William III of England as well), to organize all the states of France's borders to cut Louis XIV down to size. It was fought all over Europe and in America, where French and English colonists exchanged blows (King William's War), but it was inconclusive. At its end almost all the boundaries were put back to their 1689 lines, and France was once more "contained" behind the line of the Spanish Netherlands. (Treaty of Ryswick, 1697.)

Louis XIV, while he had gained military glory, the County of Burgundy,

[1] 1652–1654; 1665–1667; 1672–1674.

and the city of Strasbourg, had not won a Rhenish frontier. There had been some basic changes in Europe: the Dutch Republic had been greatly weakened, England strengthened, Spain revealed as militarily negligible. The stage was thus set for the great eighteenth-century duels between the British and the French.

THE WAR OF THE SPANISH SUCCESSION

Louis XIV's efforts to break out of the iron ring that the balance of power had forged around France came to a climax in the War of the Spanish Succession (1701–1714), which brought forth the biggest general peace settlement since Westphalia. There was not to be another of comparable extent until the Congress of Vienna (1814–1815) following the defeat of Napoleon.

The War of the Spanish Succession was a world war fought in America and India and on the seas as well as in Europe. Its breadth demonstrated that the European balance of power was now influenced by wealth and military power drawn from overseas. The time had passed when land and population in Europe proper were the only sources of power. From now on the European equilibrium was recognized to be related to strategic overseas bases, trade routes, and colonies. The War of the Spanish Succession was, like earlier wars, a struggle between Bourbon and Habsburg. It was also an episode in the rivalry between England and France for overseas influence, a "second Hundred Years War" which had begun at least in 1688 and was to continue in hot and cold forms until the defeat of Napoleon at Waterloo in 1815.

Almost every country had an interest in this war. Spain possessed the Spanish Netherlands, much of Italy, and the huge overseas empire comprising all of what we today call "Latin America" except Brazil. As the life of the last Spanish Habsburg, the incompetent Charles II (1665–1700), drew to a close, the French did not wish his cousins the Austrian Habsburgs to inherit Spain; that would recreate the Habsburg encirclement of the Bourbons of the time of Charles V. The Austrian Habsburgs opposed the transfer of Spanish resources to the Bourbons of France. And William III, Louis XIV's old opponent, now ruler in England as well as in the Netherlands, opposed France's acquisition of such enormous continental and overseas territories, with ports and ships enough to dismay even the combined English and Dutch.

Louis XIV was a cousin of the declining Charles II of Spain, and had married one of his sisters. This situation was duplicated by Emperor Leopold I, the Austrian Habsburg. Louis XIV's wife, like his mother, had renounced her Spanish inheritance, as Leopold's wife and mother had not, but it was tempting to renounce these renunciations. Charles II finally willed all his possessions to Louis XIV's five-year-old grandson, Philip of Anjou, with the stipulation that in case the French refused the legacy it should pass, intact, to the son of Emperor Leopold. Nowhere is there a clearer example of the way in which the idea of great nations being the personal property of their rulers still survived in Europe.

Charles II then precipitated the crisis by dying, in November, 1700. Thus the new century opened, as it was to close, with dismay at the possibility of French hegemony. Louis XIV, who had previously agreed to a partition treaty acceptable to the other powers, now defended his grandson's rights under the will. The boy king was accepted as Philip V by most of the Spaniards. William III, veteran antagonist of Louis XIV, fashioned a "Grand Alliance" in 1701, one of his last acts before his death in 1702.

Austria joined the Grand Alliance to keep the Bourbons from getting the whole Spanish inheritance, particularly the Italian parts of it. The Habsburgs pressed their own claims to the Spanish throne. Most of the states of Germany supported the Emperor. Bavaria, however, which always tended to be suspicious of Habsburg ascendancy in Germany, supported France. In Italy the Duchy of Savoy entered the war on the French side, but in 1703 switched to the Grand Alliance—the House of Savoy, like that of Hohenzollern, was to emerge from the war with a kingly title. Portugal sided with England and the Grand Alliance.

Most of the fighting took place outside of Spain. The English captured Gibraltar from Spain in 1704. The English general John Churchill, Duke of Marlborough, campaigned successfully in the Spanish Netherlands, and the English began what was to be a characteristic device, that of sending subsidies to their allies on the continent—English capitalist development and the credit of the state weighed in the balance of power. The outstanding Imperial general was Prince Eugene of Savoy, who campaigned successfully in Italy and the Rhineland. By 1708 the French had been driven from Italy and defeated in the Rhineland; the Allies were pressing from the Spanish Netherlands toward France. On the other hand, Philip V was solidly enthroned in Spain despite temporary Austrian and Portuguese incursions which had taken place. In the American colonies "Queen Anne's War," as it was called, saw British and colonial forces attack Canada with some success.

The strains of the war were so great that Louis XIV was willing to pay dearly for peace, but the Allies pressed him too hard for concessions, and the ordeal continued. France was still able to field an army and win occasional victories. When the Austrian pretender to the Spanish throne, Archduke Charles, became Austrian and Imperial ruler as well (Charles VI, 1711–1740), his allies lost their enthusiasm for his Spanish claim. In the end military stalemate and the changed attitudes of the powers made possible the Treaties of Utrecht in 1713.

To Great Britain (so-called since the union of England and Scotland in 1707) France ceded Newfoundland, Nova Scotia (Acadia), and recognition of its ownership of Hudson's Bay. Spain gave to Britain Gibraltar, Minorca, and the *asiento* privilege of trading with the Spanish colonies. France recognized the obligation to keep separate the crowns of France and Spain.

Holland received the Spanish Netherlands (for transfer to Austria), but was allowed to garrison strategic towns there against the eventuality of future French attack. Savoy received the island of Sicily and was henceforth recognized as a kingdom. Prussia was also recognized as a kingdom, and received minor territorial gains in western Germany. Portugal made some gains in South America.

When Emperor Charles concluded peace with France, for himself and the Empire, at Rastadt and Baden in 1714, Austria obtained the Spanish Nether-

lands and was confirmed in possession of Naples, Sardinia, and Milan. In 1720
Austria was to exchange Sardinia for Sicily, with the result that the Kingdom
of the Two Sicilies (Naples and Sicily) was in Austrian hands, while Sardinia
went to Savoy. The presence of an independent state and dynasty in an Italy
otherwise dominated by Austria was to count in the future balance of power.

Thus Spain acquired a new, Bourbon, dynasty and retained its overseas
empire, but was considerably reduced in Europe. France had lost a round in "the
Second Hundred Years War" with Britain, but was still the greatest European
power, and a great colonial power as well. The Habsburgs had lost Spain, but
the Austrian Habsburgs had gained in Italy and had acquired, in the "Austrian
Netherlands" (formerly the Spanish Netherlands—present-day Belgium), a buffer state between France and the Dutch Republic. Holland, though increasingly
overshadowed in size by its neighbors, had retained its independence and much
of its overseas empire. Most vital of all, *Britain had emerged as a great power
capable of intervening on the continent while also expanding overseas.* With
Gibraltar, Great Britain was a Mediterranean power for the first time. Savoy
(Piedmont) and Prussia had survived on the European checkerboard and their
rulers had been crowned as kings. The Westphalia settlement of 1648 had been
revised, but its basic meaning stood: more than ever, Europe was an ensemble of
competing, independent states. In Central Europe the Holy Roman Empire
counted for less, its individual units for more. In Western Europe the wealth
and power drawn from overseas connections were playing a greater part than ever.

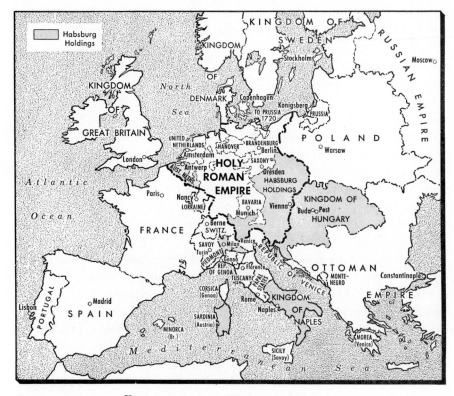

EUROPE AFTER THE TREATY OF UTRECHT

EIGHTEENTH-CENTURY WARFARE

After the War of the Spanish Succession military techniques went through a curious evolution. The key weapon was the ordinary soldier's gun, now no longer the seventeenth-century musket, but a piece of more manageable proportions, lighter, safer, and outfitted with a bayonet which made pikes and pikers obsolete. This gun, fired with hammer and flint, but still muzzle-loading, could produce a shot a minute in 1715 and by the middle of the century two or even three shots a minute. It greatly increased infantry fire power, which could cut down attacking horsemen in most circumstances, and thus transformed cavalry into an auxiliary of infantry.

Artillery in those days consisted of smooth-bore cannons of various sizes, muzzle-loading, with cannon balls of from four to thirty pounds. They were capable of firing about a mile, but they were very inaccurate; their effective range on the battle field was only a few hundred paces. Artillerymen could, however, send a light ball through six or eight human bodies. When defending against infantry they would send cannon balls ricocheting across a field, touching ground four or five times and doing terrible damage to whatever got in the way. But artillery, too, was only a supporting force for infantry; the pieces were too heavy to move readily; they were good defensively until overrun, but because of their immobility useless to a retreating army or to a pursuing one.

Eighteenth-century battle therefore revolved around the infantry soldier armed with his gun. In the early part of the century the generals tried to achieve a maximum of fire power by spreading their men as widely as possible and only about six ranks deep. The men, carefully trained, each in his usual place, would then march forward, firing in salvos; that is, the first rank would fire in unison, on command, then reload while those behind were firing. The objective was to sweep ahead with a wall of fire, and in open country this kind of advance or defense was indeed very potent. But the careful spacing and arrangement of the wide, shallow formations made the offense slower than the ordinary marching columns used by an army en route. Therefore, as in the seventeenth century, it was almost impossible to force battle on a reluctant enemy. This forced the continuation of the "strategy of accessories," that is, aiming at enemy communications, warehouses, and strategic fortifications rather than at the destruction of his army.

Frederick William I of Prussia (1713–1740) overcame some of the defects of early eighteenth-century practices in warfare by cutting the ranks of the fighting line to three and placing the men in each line closer together. These changes condensed the fire in more deadly fashion and made it easier for a marching column to turn sideways and become a fighting front three ranks deep. Three ranks were enough, the first on one knee, the second bent, the third upright, firing one after the other. Carefully drilled, they attacked in marching formation, firing salvos until the enemy either broke and ran, or was met with bayonets. The

Prussians of this era also used light artillery which could be dragged by infantry. Frederick the Great (1740–1786) increased still more the amount of artillery which could be moved along with the infantry, and trained his men for very rapid conversion from marching columns into the attacking line. Thus he emphasized fire power and speed. He also tried for deception by slanting his attacking regiments toward the weak spot in the enemy's position; Frederick made it look as if his regiments were side by side when actually the weaker ones were farther back and the stronger ones, with the reserves, were near the weak point of the enemy.

After the mid-eighteenth century Prussian methods were widely imitated, in spite of the discouraging amount of drill which they required. There was much theorizing about military methods, just as there was about everything else in the age of "enlightenment." A number of improvements were tried out on a small scale or suggested in writings like the French Count Guibert's *Essai général de tactique* (1772). The full significance of these proposals was not appreciated by most military men during the remainder of the old regime.

Guibert, for example, recommended that what soldiers had previously done against orders, and in desperation—firing at will, at a particular target, instead of concentrating on an effort to fire in unison—should be generally adopted. What was lost in precision was made up in aim, and the same was true of the marching which Guibert advised. He admitted that in open country, and especially on defense, a line offered more fire power than a column, but in some situations the forward speed and striking impact of a column was desirable. Since the middle of the century it had been found that skirmishers, sharpshooters who advanced with no particular order but took advantage of available cover, could protect an advancing army and, with their carefully placed fire, delay, confuse, and even damage an enemy. The combination of skirmishers with columns which could attack either head-on or after changing into the more traditional line, offered both defensive and offensive possibilities of new magnitude. Particularly with the new artillery which was developed in the eighteenth century into more precisely engineered, lighter weight, and more mobile weapons, armies greatly increased in offensive power. Maneuver and rapid concentration were theoretically increased by the creation of "divisions," each having its own cavalry and artillery.

In the relatively peaceful period from 1763 to the French Revolution, the generals did not have much opportunity to experiment, and the social system was not such as to favor promotions for the talented, but there were signs that the old stately warfare of the drill field was done for. Guibert's theories became better known, and were partially accepted by the French army. The farmers at Lexington and Concord demonstrated the value of skirmishers. With Napoleon, and even before him, with the armies of the Revolution, these possibilities would be realized in a new, aggressive warfare that would aim at destruction of the enemy army rather than at confiscation of its means of support.

In this kind of summary of the methods of war there is an antiseptic quality, a geometrical, chesslike, mathematical, abstractly beautiful quality which has little to do with the wars that people lived. The "science of war" was much loved and studied by educated men. The eighteenth century was the age of aristocratic *politesse* among its aristocratic officers. But this mutual respect did not extend to the mass of mankind. The brutality with which common soldiers and sailors were treated was taken for granted, and the brutalized condition of these men was widely regarded as incapacitating them for civilian life. Their brutality, in turn, toward the country through which they campaigned was even greater; and after them came the camp followers, the peddlers, thieves, and prostitutes in a swarm which further defiled the unfortunate region. Finally there was the battle itself, which, though infrequent, was a tremendous bloodletting. On land and at sea the story was the same; inadequate surgery, bandages, transport, inadequate antiseptics, and above all, absence of pain-killing drugs.

In the eighteenth century Europeans were drawing ahead of the rest of the world in the construction and use of weapons. It was not only in the sparsely settled North American continent that the English and French could direct their war against each other, with the Indians as mere allies, but even in India with its vast though divided population. The balance of power was not yet "global," as it would become when the indigenous peoples began to be able to stand up to the Europeans; but the European balance of power was reflected overseas, and was in turn influenced from overseas.

THE WAR OF THE POLISH SUCCESSION

While the War of the Spanish Succession was engaging Western Europe, Sweden, France's old ally of Thirty Years War days, was locked in a struggle with other northern powers which were in process of evicting it from its Baltic supremacy. This was the Great Northern War (1700–1721), described in Chapter 20. It was part of the decline of Sweden, Poland, and the Ottoman empire which took place in the eighteenth century, and it was also related to the rise of Prussia and, especially, to the entrance of Russia onto the European scene.

In the west, however, these auguries did not cause alarm. France had been held within bounds, and the Spanish empire in effect partitioned. Neither Spain nor Austria was satisfied with the partition, and for a number of years the Italian and Mediterranean region was the subject of minor wars and diplomatic maneuvers. France's uncertainties under the Orléans regency (see p. 225) contributed to these events, the upshot of which was that Spain once more won a foothold in Italy. The Austrian Habsburgs and the ambitious Savoy dynasty more than held their own in a process of territorial juggling which came to a conclusion in the War of the Polish Succession (1733–1735).

How did a quarrel over the Polish throne contribute to a readjustment in the Italian peninsula? The answer provides an almost classic example of the manner in which dynastic rivalries were settled without regard for the opinions of native populations.

Young Louis XV of France was married to the daughter of Stanislas Leszczynski, a deposed King of Poland. When the Polish throne fell vacant in 1733, Stanislas, with the help of French funds, was chosen by the Polish Diet, but was driven from the throne by the Austrians and Russians, who were backing another candidate (see Chapter 20). At the French court, family pride joined with the anti-Austrian tradition. Backed by Spain and Sardinia, France fought unsuccessfully in support of Stanislas; but the French were careful not to attack the Austrian Netherlands for fear of offending the British and Dutch. Most of the actual fighting was done in Italy.

The war came to an end with the Treaty of Vienna (1735, ratified in 1738): Stanislas Leszczynski abandoned his claim to the Polish throne, but kept the title of King and was given, for his lifetime, the Duchy of Lorraine, the westernmost state of the Holy Roman Empire. At his death, Lorraine was to pass to France. (It did so in 1766.) Austria ceded Novara, in Italy, to France's ally Sardinia, and the Kingdom of the Two Sicilies (Naples and Sicily) to France's ally, Spain, or rather to a Spanish Bourbon prince, Don Carlos. Don Carlos gave his rights in Parma and Tuscany to Duke Francis, son-in-law of the Austrian ruler and husband of the heir to the Austrian throne, Maria Theresa. *Francis had been Duke of Lorraine, which, as noted, was being transferred to Stanislas Leszczynski.* Thus the Austro-Russian victory concerning Poland was made palatable to France by a very substantial gain on its eastern frontier, and an exchange took place in Italy between the Spanish Bourbons and the Austrian Habsburgs, with France's ally Sardinia profiting somewhat as well.

France was from 1726 to 1743 under the direction of Cardinal Fleury, the former tutor of Louis XV, an elderly and peaceable man. Britain was from 1721 to 1742 under the leadership of Robert Walpole, also cautious and peaceful. During the 1730's France followed its traditional policy of supporting Turkey against the Austrians and Russians. The French were also carrying on a prosperous trade in India and the Near East, collecting profits from the sugar islands of the West Indies, and extending their influence in North America from Canada down the Mississippi Valley. French rivalry with Britain in the New World and in Asia was far from a dead letter. Moreover, there was also reason for conflict between the Spanish and British. It had not been the intention of the Spanish government to open its overseas empire to British trade; yet the British were consistently going beyond the limits permitted by the *asiento* (the slave trade and one ship a year of other goods) in a manner which still-mercantilist Spain, recovering from the War of the Spanish Succession, refused to tolerate. War actually broke out between Britain and Spain in 1739, the so-called "War of Jenkins' Ear," named after the British captain who aroused opinion by displaying in London what he claimed was his ear, amputated by the Spanish. It was more than likely that the French would be drawn into this new war for naval, commercial, and colonial supremacy.

THE WAR OF THE
AUSTRIAN SUCCESSION

Charles VI of Austria died, in October, 1740, and twenty-three year old Maria Theresa ascended the steps of the throne. According to the Pragmatic Sanction, the Habsburg lands were one, and this young woman was the rightful heir. The great powers had agreed, but now they prepared to take advantage of yet another "succession" question. Bavaria's Elector claimed the whole inheritance. The kings of Spain and Sardinia put in their claims too, as did the Elector of Saxony. But it was Frederick the Great, himself newly crowned, who made the first move, seizing the rich province of Silesia in the winter of 1740–1741.

This War of the Austrian Succession (1740–1748) was too complicated to be described in a brief space, but several points having to do with the European balance of power are worth special emphasis. A coalition of France, Bavaria, Spain, and Saxony joined Prussia in attempting to dismember the Habsburg monarchy. For France it was a serious decision dictated by the old anti-Habsburg tradition. In France, especially in court circles, there was less appreciation of commercial and overseas interests than there was in England. Moreover, for continental France there was still the lure of the Austrian (formerly Spanish) Netherlands, which now looked like easy pickings.

It was natural, therefore, for the British and Dutch to take the Austrian side. It was chiefly British subsidies and the ability of British sea power to hit French and Spanish shipping and, especially to blockade the sugar-rich West Indies, which dimmed French enthusiasm for the adventure. In the colonies this war, known as King George's War, was indecisive, although an expedition from New England did capture Louisburg on Cape Breton Island (1745) with the help of British warships, and in India the French under Dupleix captured Madras from the British (1746).

On the continent Maria Theresa was able to hold together her realms and break up the coalition which had formed against her. Frederick II of Prussia abandoned his allies in 1742 when he was ceded Silesia, but returned to the conflict in 1744–1745 when Austrian successes endangered his gains. In 1745 he withdrew again upon confirmation of his possession of Silesia. Never was there a more cold-blooded application of *raison d'état*. The Bavarian Elector managed to become Holy Roman Emperor (1742–1745), but upon his death Bavaria left the war, and the husband of Maria Theresa, Francis of Lorraine-Tuscany, became Holy Roman Emperor (1745–1765). In Italy there was a four-cornered fight of the Spanish, French, Sardinians, and Austrians. Toward the end of the war even Empress Elizabeth of Russia sent an army to the Rhine, in alliance with Austria.

The war stopped in 1748, with the Treaty of Aix-la-Chapelle, but it would be misleading to say that it was ended. Austria was unhappy about the loss of Silesia, although the Pragmatic Sanction was again recognized as valid.

Maria Theresa would have preferred losing Belgium and keeping Silesia; she was certainly not reconciled to the arrival of Prussia as a great power. Nor did Frederick II of Prussia have any illusions about his future security. The decisive fact was that Britain and France had had enough for the moment, although their quarrel was far from finished. Britain was, with the Dutch, determined to get Belgium back into Austrian hands, where it would be least menacing to the balance of power in Western Europe. Many French were astounded by Louis XV's willingness to make a treaty which returned France to its pre-war borders, but the effort of fighting on two fronts, the European and the colonial, was exhausting to France, and the prospect of losing the West Indies was not pleasant. Britain and France therefore gave up their conquests and waited for the next round, while forcing Maria Theresa to relinquish some Italian duchies to the Spanish prince Don Philip, and accept for the moment the terrible amputation of wealthy and populous Silesia.

THE SEVEN YEARS WAR

The next round was a big one, nothing less than the Seven Years War (1756–1763) in Europe, known as the French and Indian War in the colonies. This time the French continental position and involvements cost them dearly. The war began informally between the French and British in the American colonies in 1755, but as early as 1754 George Washington and Virginia troops had been driven by the French from their position on the Ohio river. In India Anglo-French competition among local potentates had been continuous, but the recall of the Frenchman Dupleix in 1754 prefaced British successes under the leadership of Robert Clive. The stakes were very high in India and America, but French European involvements, in which they scarcely ever had the initiative, led to the loss of almost their whole overseas empire.

What happened in Europe is a superb example of the workings of the balance of power, unclothed by motivations other than the most calculating self-interest. It was no secret to anyone that Maria Theresa and her gifted minister Kaunitz intended a comeback after the Austrian Succession War. Prince Kaunitz, who had been Austrian ambassador to France, understood the drift of affairs at the French court. There, influential people felt that the traditional "beat-Austria" policy was out of date. Kaunitz tempted the French with Belgium as a reward for abandoning Prussia. If France would take this step, Prussia might be isolated, for Empress Elizabeth of Russia had proved her anti-Prussian sentiments in the previous war, and Britain, Austria's former ally, was subsidizing Russia.

Britain was more concerned about the impending war with France than about Austrian plans for a comeback against Prussia. Britain needed an ally on the continent who could keep the French armies occupied, so that they would not be sent against Hanover, King George's personal possession and an important avenue of commerce. It would also be better for British prospects in the colonial war if France were thoroughly embroiled on the continent. Austria was now too preoccupied with designs against Prussia to be of much use to British policy. King George II therefore turned to Prussia, where he found Frederick II worried about Austrian designs and the Anglo-Russian alliance. In January, 1756, Britain concluded a treaty of neutrality with Prussia.

Thus took place the famous "diplomatic revolution." The French court, indignant at Prussia's new friendship with Britain, completed the rapprochement with Austria which had all along been a temptation, signing with Austria a defensive alliance in May, 1756. Russia, on the other hand, was indignant at Britain's new friendship with Prussia, and drew closer to Austria, as did Saxony and a number of the other German states. From the point of view of Frederick II the situation was growing very menacing, for he was surrounded by a potential enemy ring of Austria, Saxony, various other German states, France, and Russia, whereas he had on his side only Britain, Hanover, and one or two other German states (Hesse, Brunswick, Gotha).

Frederick decided to strike first in order to immobilize as many as possible of his enemies. He knew that France was not ready, and he still hoped that Russia would not enter the war at all. In quick succession in the fall of 1756 and spring of 1757 he struck down Saxony and invaded Bohemia. The first move was successful, the second not. After initial victories Frederick was driven from Bohemia. The coalition of France, Austria, the Empire, and Russia solidified around him, and Sweden joined it in hope of winning Pomerania.

Prussia was saved by Frederick's genius and perseverance. He struck at his enemies one after another before they could join forces, won great victories but lost battles too; kept a force in the field, but weakened, finally, and found himself unable to prevent Russian and Austrian concentration against him. But he was preserved by more than his own doggedness. The French were distracted by the overseas conflict with Britain, and the Austrian alliance was not popular in France. The French generals were not as inefficient as they might have been, considering the favoritism at court, but there were jealousies among them, and after initial successes in Hanover they allowed themselves to be contained by the Anglo-Hanoverian army. Even so, the Austrians and Russians might have crushed Frederick if they had worked together better, but they were slow to act; Austria was not altogether happy about Russia's advance into Central Europe.

But the greatest good fortune for Frederick, the "Miracle of the House of Brandenburg," was a dynastic accident in Russia, where the death of Empress Elizabeth (January, 1762) brought to the throne Peter III, an admirer of Frederick. Peter at once made a truce with Prussia, followed it by a peace treaty restoring all Prussian territory, and followed that by a military alliance. Peter III was deposed and murdered (June-July, 1762), but his successor, Catherine II, did not renew the war against Frederick, who was now able to devote his attention to settling accounts with Austria. Sweden had followed Russia out of the war. It was plain that Britain and France would soon make peace and that French support for Austria could not longer be hoped for. This being the case, Austria and Prussia made peace in the Treaty of Hubertusburg in February, 1763, with Prussia retaining Silesia, her material and symbolic guarantee of great-power status.

A few days before the Treaty of Hubertusburg, Britain, France, Spain, and Portugal signed the Treaty of Paris. Portugal in the Seven Years War had stood by England, while Spain, in 1761, had made a second "family compact" with France, just in time to lose Cuba and the Philippines to Britain. In the peace Spain recovered these territories, but lost Minorca and Florida to Britain. France, in compensation, ceded Louisiana west of the Mississippi to Spain.

France itself entered the peace conference with diminished assets. The British and colonials had taken Fort Duquesne (now Pittsburgh) from them in 1758, and in the north had captured Louisburg on Cape Breton Island (1758), and Quebec (1759). With the surrender of Montreal to the British in 1760, Canada changed hands. Meanwhile British sea power had enabled them to capture one West Indies island after another. In India the British had assured their supremacy in the Battle of Plassy as early as 1757. Throughout the war the French had sent few reinforcements abroad. But the British, led by William Pitt, had made a real colonial and naval effort, in full awareness that in subsidizing Prussia and keeping France busy on the continent they were investing wisely. Britain could finance this investment, for its political system had public confidence and the state could borrow money. In France, on the contrary, the war had put a terrible strain on the tax system.

In the Treaty of Paris, France turned over to Britain all of its claims to Nova Scotia, Canada, Cape Breton, and that part of Louisiana which was east of the Mississippi, except the island of Orleans. France ceded to Spain the parts of Louisiana west of the Mississippi. France retained fishing rights off Newfoundland, and was given the islands of St. Pierre and Miquelon. More important, the British restored Guadeloupe, Martinique, and other West Indies islands which they had seized—these were properties of immense value, and it was fortunate for the French that powerful British interests did not want the competition which the French sugar islands would have provided if taken into the British Empire. In India France was now finished as a political power, although it was allowed to retain a few commercial installations.

These changes were of importance in world history. Henceforth Britain was to organize the political life of India, and to preside over this vast subcontinent until its independence. Britain's own wealth and power were to be greatly increased by the connection, and British views on foreign policy were to be influenced accordingly; for example, its opinions of the Ottoman empire and of Russia were to be guided by concern for the "life line to India." In America some French influence was to remain, but for the most part the lands north of Mexico became part of the English-speaking community.

LAST YEARS OF THE OLD REGIME

In Europe the Treaties of Hubertusburg and Paris affirmed the "arrival" of Prussia as a great power, but Prussia was none the less exhausted by the effort.

The policy of Frederick II became thereafter one of peaceful absorption of his past gains. Austria had been weakened by the loss of Silesia and by the appearance of Prussia as a rival power in Germany, but the Habsburg monarchy was still a very large state in process of consolidation. The balance of power in the Empire was now closely interwoven with the balance of power in Europe; the Emperor's clients were counterbalanced by those of Prussia, and neither Prussia not Austria could substantially change its position without arousing the powers outside the Empire.

In the period from the Seven Years War to the French Revolution, both Austria and Prussia had to reconcile themselves to the presence of another great power in Eastern Europe, the Russia of Catherine the Great. (The developments in Eastern Europe will be described in Chapter 20.) In the first partition of Poland (1772), Prussia, Russia, and Austria maintained the balance among themselves by each taking pieces of Poland. Later (1793–1795) Poland was completely swallowed by these same three powers, whose "balance" was thereby maintained, but at the sacrifice of one of the units in the European balance of power. Apart from the partition of Poland, then, the period from the Seven Years War to the French Revolution saw little drama in Central Europe. There was one distraction. Joseph II tried to seize Bavaria, but Frederick II of Prussia aroused enough other German princes against him to make him back down. The very minor war of the Bavarian succession, in 1778, was the last of the dynastic wars. It ended with no losses and no gains, an epitaph to the eighteenth-century balance of power.

In spite of their mutual rivalries Austria, Prussia, and Russia advanced themselves in the period from 1763 to 1789. They were, relative to the older, established powers of the west—France, Britain, and Spain—increasing in weight in the European balance as a whole. The partitions of Poland made Austria, Prussia, and Russia accomplices who had an interest in preserving their gains. They were to be a triple alliance which opposed France through the period of the French Revolution and Napoleon, and they were to form a bloc through most of the nineteenth century.

France, in the period from 1763 to 1789, was unsuccessful in preventing this turn of affairs in Eastern Europe, made at the expense of its traditional allies Turkey and Poland and Sweden. One reason was that France in this period turned its main efforts toward the British. But it was still the richest, most powerful country in Europe, with a homeland unscathed by the Seven Years War. Coming into possession of Lorraine in 1766 upon the death of Stanislas Leszczyński acquiring Corsica from Genoa in 1768, France was still the leader of the continent.

Britain, moreover, was in difficulties. After the Seven Years War, it faced problems of imperial organization. Taxation and economic regulations caused disputes with the colonies about where the authority lay; principles were appealed to. In time, with the British colonies in full revolt, France moved from undercover encouragement to open support of them (1778–1783). The "Second Hundred Years War" was on again, and history, which had already seen Cardinal Richelieu allied with Protestant Sweden, and Louis XIV with the infidel Turk, now provided the spectacle of the absolute monarch Louis XVI aiding the American revolutionaries. Spain joined France in 1779, and the Dutch also made war on the British from 1780. This time the French evened the score. In the Peace of Versailles (1783), the French made only minor gains, but were pleased at having assured American independence and given a major setback to the British empire.

In the 1780's the old regime was drawing to a close. No one foresaw that the French Revolution would liberate forces which would alter the balance of power in Europe more than the drives of Louis XIV had ever done. European diplomacy had for many decades celebrated *raison d'état* without much regard for conflicts of ideas. Since the Thirty Years War religious themes had played less part in international relations. Dynastic quarrels had continued, for most of the states of the period were dynastic. Certainly no respect had been shown for the wishes of the subjects bartered back and forth at the peace conferences. But the dynasties had shown no respect for each other, either. They had, indeed, stopped at almost nothing; their intense competition had encouraged lying, theft, assassination, and even the encouragement of revolutions against each other. The coming era would again see wars of ideals, with revolutionary and counter-revolutionary philosophies overlying arguments for war and peace. When France appeared weakened by its revolution in 1789, the other powers would at first consider only that a competitor was down, and might possibly be partitioned. But before long it would become apparent that they themselves faced the revolutionary threat, and that their people might demand self-government. The age of dynasts was ending. The age of peoples was about to begin.

19

RUSSIA FROM PETER I TO CATHERINE II

Russia from the end of the Thirty Years War to the French Revolution came to resemble in many respects the states of Western and Central Europe. It could be argued that in this period more than in any other Russia was becoming a part of Europe, as Peter the Great (1682–1725) seemed to will at its start, and as Catherine the Great (1762–1796) plainly insisted at its close. Certainly the Russian court and aristocracy were more like their western counterparts, notably the French, than they had been in the dread days of Ivan IV in the sixteenth century. Russia now took more part than ever before in European diplomacy. Its borders reached the Baltic and Black Seas, and it sent troops into Central Europe. It can be argued that in this "old regime", when Europe was still mainly agricultural and the west had not yet rushed ahead with mighty industrial strides, in this age of absolutism tempered by the wishes of aristocracy, this age of dynastic states and largely mercenary armies, of landed wealth and upper class cosmopolitanism and lower class provincialism, Russia was made of the same stuff as Europe.

But in many ways Russia remained very different from the west. The rise of the commercial middle class in the west during the old regime, the decline of serfdom there and the growth of cities, the greater proportion in the west of aristocrats who could be called cosmopolitan, of persons who could read, of town folk, the lower proportion of serfs—in all these respects the west was profoundly different from Russia. By such standards Russia was more like Central than like

Western Europe, but was still unique, with its own visage behind the mask of westernization. In the early Imperial Age, from Peter to Catherine, we can see the effects of closer contacts with the west, and also reminders of old Muscovy.

THE EFFORTS OF PETER THE GREAT

Russia's Imperial Age did not begin when the boy Peter became czar. It was not formally announced until 1721, when the czar proclaimed himself Emperor. Thereafter, the Russian rulers were all technically called by the western title of Emperor, though in common usage the old style of "czar" continued. As the boy Peter grew into the seasoned Emperor, many things happened to amaze and horrify the Russians and make Europe aware of the new power in the east. Peter's reign can best be understood if several stages are distinguished.

The first of these stages, Peter's childhood, is steeped in family rivalries. The boy's mother had been Natalie Naryshkin, second wife of Czar Alexis. Peter's half-brothers Theodore and Ivan, and his half-sister Sophia, were children of the first marriage to Maria Miloslavsky. Out of these circumstances grew the childhood which turned Peter's tastes away from Russian traditions and toward things new and western—a direction, to be sure, which they might in any case have taken, for the times were ripe.

Half-brother Theodore succeeded Alexis and reigned from 1676 to 1682, gentle, well-educated, and ill. The Miloslavsky clan was in the ascendancy, and upon Theodore's death managed to remain there through the efforts of the strong-willed Sophia. With the help of the military force of Streltsy, by then disorderly and independent-minded, Sophia overcame Peter's backers and had herself proclaimed regent and the two boys co-czars: Ivan, her timid, unhealthy fifteen-year-old brother, and vigorous, big-boned, ten-year-old Peter. Sophia was herself twenty-five, ambitious and energetic, with somewhat westernized tastes, like her father Alexis. She ruled until 1689 with the collaboration of Basil Golitsyn, one of the best-educated men of his day, strong in theories about enlightened reforms but somewhat impractical—a contrast to the czar that Peter would be, whose partial measures, strongly willed, were to carry him so far.

Peter's mother and the Naryshkins were out of favor. The ex-queen and Peter lived in a village near Moscow, had little to do with the court, and were befriended by churchmen who disapproved of Sophia's western tastes. Peter's mother sympathized with the church's traditionalism, but the boy himself, free of court ritual, picked his own friends and lived an undisciplined and soon a dissolute life. Much of his time was spent among the Europeans of the "German suburb," a quarter of Moscow in which foreigners were still obliged to reside. Much of his inexhaustible energy was turned toward western techniques, especially shipbuilding, and to playing soldier with two regiments which he formed from companions of the lesser nobility. It was, for that time and place, a progressive education, but Peter was not thinking of progress or reform, but of amusement. As he and his friends grew older, the military games grew more real.

In 1689 the regent Sophia, probably alarmed by this reality, thought the time had come for transforming herself and Golitsyn into permanent rulers. She began to sound out the Streltsy about the project, but seventeen-year-old Peter, warned that his life was in danger, mobilized enough military support of his own to send Sophia to a convent and Golitsyn into exile. Then he went back to his military games, leaving the government to his mother, and neglecting the young wife she found for him. With scarcely a transition the play maneuvers became war. In 1695–1696 he campaigned against the Turks and took the fortress of Azov at the mouth of the Don. He found himself poorly prepared and unsuccessful at first, but in the face of failure multiplied his efforts and won. In this campaign Peter's boyhood Guards regiments saw action, along with a fleet specially constructed upriver from Azov.

At this point in Peter's career he began to rule, but his assumption of responsibility was gradual, touching at first only military affairs. After the death of his mother in 1694 Peter left most affairs of state to councillors. His half-brother Ivan died in 1696, never having asserted himself.

During and after the Azov campaign Peter was primarily interested in building a fleet; after sending men abroad to study navigation and shipbuilding he went abroad himself with a diplomatic mission, in a transparent disguise, visiting Brandenburg, Holland, England, and Austria in 1697–1698. The trip, which left a trail of anecdotes about the coarse-mannered giant and his work in shipyards and shops, finished what the German suburb had started in freeing Peter from the old Muscovite mentality. He was as yet interested only in technical and military matters, however. Peter's political and social innovations were to come as a by-product of his military needs. He was to be a practical-minded, tinkering czar, who devised repairs when circumstances demanded them.

PETER THE GREAT

Perhaps the best way to summarize the stages of Peter's adult rule is to mention the war which was his real teacher, and its relation to his efforts at domestic reform. Like Ivan the Terrible before him, who had turned from his eastern conquests to encounter the superior military skill and organization of the Pole Stephen Batory, Peter met superior skill and organization in the hands of Charles XII of Sweden. Viewed in the large, Russia's participation in the Great Northern War (1700–1721) is part of the story of Sweden's decline as a great power when its Baltic neighbors became strong enough to challenge its supremacy. Russia's experience during those years shows a loosely organized and old-fashioned society at grips with a more highly developed one. Peter had no one state as his model, no five-year plans. He went from one decision to the next, his limited objectives committing him to ever greater ones. Only toward the end of his career did he become aware that the logic of necessity resembled a systematic program of westernization.

Peter's attention was attracted to the Baltic during his first European trip. In the west he found little interest in continuing the war against Turkey. The European states were preoccupied with the Bourbon-Habsburg duel, and most of them were occupied with arranging peace with the Ottoman empire (Congress of Karlowitz, 1699). In Northern Europe there was another preoccupation, however. Danish and Polish diplomats were eager to take advantage of the death of powerful Charles XI of Sweden, who had been succeeded by a sixteen-year-old boy, Charles XII. The moment seemed opportune for driving the Swedes back from the shores of the Baltic. Peter made his own peace with the Turks (1700) and prepared to take up again the westward drive at which Ivan the Terrible had failed.

Charles XII was more of a surprise to Peter and his allies than Peter himself had been to the regent Sophia. He proved to be a military genius with a zest for battle, able to unbalance his opponents and hit them one by one with Sweden's experienced army, which was backed by a small but tightly organized state. Charles knocked Denmark out of the war at once, then with a force of 8,000 humiliated Peter and his 35,000 Russians at Narva (1700), then turned and drove into Poland. This first stage of the Northern War signaled the end of Peter's youth. Disconsolate, his reputation ruined, he soon replied with more activity than ever. Saved by Charles XII's involvement in Poland, he pushed out to the Gulf of Finland. There he founded St. Petersburg (the Leningrad of today) in 1703, facing the west and his opponent's city of Stockholm. St. Petersburg was symbolic of more than Peter's determination to reach the Baltic. It became for him a new German Suburb, the most European of Russian cities, the antithesis to Moscow's traditionalism. He was to move the seat of government there between 1714 and 1718. The building of St. Petersburg also suggests the despotism with which Peter ruled, for it was built by forced labor in a desolate swamp originally intended for a naval base; Peter simply ordered his officials to go there and provide themselves with dwellings suitable to their station. St. Petersburg continued on a large scale the visible changes which Peter on his return from Europe had required of those around him: shaving off beards, the appearance of women at social gatherings, adoption of European styles of clothing and manners. Peter's city, named after his patron saint, would always be a reminder of his disrespect for the old Russia symbolized by Moscow, and for the split in Russian society brought about by his Europeanization of the upper classes.

The first period of the Northern War lasted until 1709, when Peter finally beat Charles XII at Poltava in the Ukraine. It was a period of improvising efforts which kept armies in the field but stirred resentments. Peter no longer had to worry about the Streltsy—they had caused trouble both on the eve of his departure for Europe and while he was away, and he had disbanded them, replacing them with the Guards grown out of his former youth regiments. He did have to subdue numerous revolts, for during this period his demands on the Russians disrupted the old ways of doing things without providing any workable substitutes. In 1707 and 1708 a revolt among the Don Cossacks led by Kondrati Bulavin spread to neighboring serfs, and in 1709 Charles XII invaded the Ukraine in the expectation that the Cossack leader Mazeppa would raise a great Ukrainian rebellion. This support did not materialize, and Charles XII and Mazeppa were defeated by Peter at Poltava and escaped southward into the Ottoman empire.

During the next period of the war, from Poltava to the death of Charles XII in 1718, Peter reorganized some branches of government in the hope that he could find better ways of supplying his army; the stage of improvisation was over, but the systematic reforms were not yet effective. He blundered, too, much as Charles XII had done in the Ukraine. Charles had persuaded his hosts the

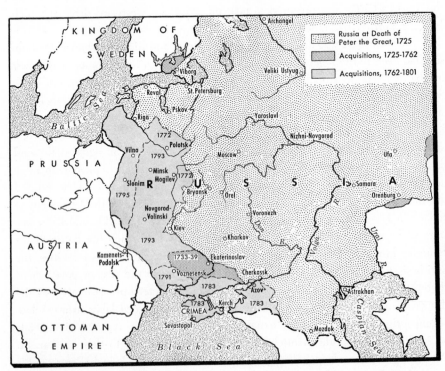

GROWTH OF THE RUSSIAN EMPIRE FROM THE DEATH OF PETER THE GREAT
TO THE DEATH OF CATHERINE THE GREAT

Turks to enter the war against Russia. Peter, hoping like later Russian rulers to arouse the Orthodox population of the Danubian area against the Turks, struck toward what is today Rumania. No revolt aided his efforts, however, and he was surrounded by a huge Ottoman army and forced to cede Azov, his first conquest, in order to gain peace with the Turks (1711). His prestige, rebuilt by Poltava, once more seemed ruined.

But as the war shifted to the Baltic Peter's navy began to win victories, and from the Aaland Islands was able to threaten Stockholm. By the time Charles XII was killed in action in late 1718 a coalition of Russia, Saxony, Prussia, Denmark, and Hanover had all but won the war, and Sweden was looking for peace terms. So was Peter, for his efforts at systematic reform at home had led to chaos. Moreover, his diplomatic efforts were not bringing satisfaction. The great powers were suspicious of the parvenu. England and Holland were hostile to Russian expansion at sea, and Austria and France to its expansion on land. Only small states on the make, like Prussia, saw advantage in Russian friendship. Peter made a second trip to Europe in 1716–1717 and this time visited Paris, an old ambition of his. But though the Russian giant was received with courtesy at the French court, he was unable to break the French friendship with Sweden.

From 1718 to his death in 1725 Peter's career was one of mixed triumph and tragedy. There were many occasions to celebrate, and yet, as we shall see below, everything seemed to have turned out badly. During this period his foreign policy paid its dividends in the Treaty of Nystadt (1721), which gave Russia Ingria, Estonia, Livonia, and part of Karelia—in other words the Baltic provinces from St. Petersburg to Riga. Here was the "window to Europe" which was to mean so much to Russian commerce and culture and to the European balance of power. Peter's new Senate celebrated by giving him the titles "Emperor" and "Great." In a brief war with Persia in 1722–1723 Peter won some Caspian shoreline, including Baku, but this gain was to be temporary. Substantial progress in the south had to await the reign of Catherine at the end of the century.

STATE AND SOCIETY IN PETER'S TIME

As a reformer of institutions, Peter the Great reached his full stature in the period from about 1718 to 1722. He had never stopped collecting ideas, but now he was able to put projects into practice with some success and was more the statesman, less the improvisor. He even realized—he who had once thought only of more troops and guns—that to have a strong army one had to safeguard the welfare of the society behind it. To be sure, he found such ideas expressed in the projects of his advisors, but his use of them shows that behind his restless activity and domineering absolutism there was at least a consciousness of what a state might be.

Peter's last years and the attitude of his contemporaries toward him will be seen in better perspective if the main outlines of his reform legislation are first given. Historians used to think that the debatable point was merely what was good or bad; they assumed that it was all the work of Peter's will. Now, with the benefit of further research, the continuity between Peter's problems and responses to problems, and the problems and responses of his predecessors, can be seen. What Peter did was to make westernization a deliberate policy, not for reasons of philosophy or political theory but because he wanted the benefit of western techniques. He copied Swedish administrative organization and European mercantilistic practices in an effort to make Russia stronger. Russia needed Europe if it was to hold its own with Europe. Yet in seeking techniques Peter opened the way to moral and political judgments. He established printing presses because he wanted books on engineering, but in time there were to be books of literary and social criticism.

Peter's political and social changes stemmed from the embattled condition in which he found himself when Russia attacked Sweden. He had already replaced the Streltsy, who had opposed him, with his own Guards, who henceforth were the defenders and enforcers of his whole program. The army was based on conscription instead of on the old system—part service nobles, part mercenary soldiers. For advisors Peter no longer used the boyar duma of his father's time. He sought the technical help of men from all stations of life. His administration was headed by a Senate (1711), which supervised the work of the Colleges (1718) which were departments of government copied after those of Sweden. Formerly Russia's governmental business had been crudely divided among offices (*prikazi*) partly according to subject matter and partly according to geographical divisions. The *prikazi* were now abolished, and under every College there were the administrative divisions of Russia, which were provinces (*gubernias*) (1708) with their subdivisions, again copied from the Swedes.

The *Zemsky Sobor,* or Assembly of the Land, which had been used so much by the early Romanovs, was now abandoned. If there had been any doubt after the Time of Troubles that Russia would move toward absolute monarchy again, that doubt was now at an end. The Orthodox Church, once under men like Philaret and Nikon, was not given another Patriarch after 1700. In 1721 Peter placed the administration of church affairs in a department called the Holy Synod, which was a government department like the others. In spite of his ribald celebrations burlesquing the Church, the Emperor was not irreligious, but he intended to be responsible to no one but God. The subordination of the Church was a great step forward for autocracy, but it tended to lessen the respect of the people for organized religion, and perhaps in the long run to help undermine the old society.

Many of these changes came about while Peter was looking for better ways to recruit men and provide for their upkeep. By 1725 two thirds of Russia's budget was being spent for the army and navy. Formerly the czars had used a tax on households, a system which encouraged several families to live together to evade the tax. Peter introduced a head tax (1718) on all "male souls" except for landholders and clergy; since those subject to the tax had to register, it was henceforth very difficult for any individual to escape the state's notice. Ultimately (1723) no distinction was made between various degrees of servile status. The partly free became the unfree. Serfdom was more deeply entrenched than ever.

Peter's "soul tax," coming after all sorts of indirect taxation and desperate measures such as currency inflation and payment of state employees in state-produced
goods, saw him through his wars, but it was a heavy burden on the peasantry.
Henceforth there was no substantial distinction between serfs and slaves in Russia.

It was not Peter's intention to discriminate against the peasantry, but he
in fact sacrificed them to their masters. With his eyes fixed on military and diplomatic objectives, the Emperor required everyone without exception to serve the
state, and thereby brought to a high point in Russian history a tendency which
had begun at least as far back as Ivan the Terrible. Peter created more service
nobles than ever and did his best to catch all who tried to dodge their obligations.
For all practical purposes, the distinction between patrimonial (votchina) and
service (pomestie) holdings was abolished by making the latter hereditary, a
move which amounted to a gift of land and peasants to the service nobles. He
created in 1722 a Table of Ranks, civilian and military, with fourteen grades,
the higher of which carried noble rank. In an effort to establish a firm economic base for the nobility he established entail, hoping to put an end to the
practice of subdividing estates into economically meaningless inheritances. If
continued, this change might have created a landed aristocracy comparable to
England's, but it went too strongly against Russian traditions and was cancelled
(1731) after Peter's death. One of the political weaknesses of the Russian nobility
—their tendency to be numerous and poor—therefore went unchecked. Peter
also for a time allowed peasants to escape their masters by enlisting in the army,
but gave this up, probably under pressure from the landowners.

Townsmen were organized by means of guilds and franchises for merchants and artisans. In his mercantilistic efforts to encourage production by
monopolies and privileges such as the right to use serfs in factories and mines,
Peter favored some of the people whom we would call "middle class", but generally speaking the status of townsmen was not much changed. His insistence
that everyone serve the state; his provision of the Table of Ranks, with promotion for service; and his willingness to employ experts of whatever nationality and
social origin—these measures leave the impression that Peter was working toward
a fluid society with careers open to talent. In fact he was merely holding together
by his autocracy and domineering personality a grandiose system which clumsily
responded to his demands. The price was high in suffering and opposition, and
when he was gone the system crumbled.

PETER'S LAST YEARS AND PLACE
IN HISTORY

Opposition might well be the theme of the last years of Peter the Great.
He had succeeded, but he had gone ahead by main force, leaving behind the
great majority of his countrymen. Over old Russia he had laid the restraints of
a governmental system which was part European, part a continuation of the

Moscow state. He had brought in techniques and manners which, momentous though they were, had not penetrated beyond the upper classes, who remained a thin top layer increasingly divorced from the mass. Even among these, there was always opposition. Peter had his way, but, as one historian puts it, he had built a bureaucracy, and beyond it was a hostile Russia. To his more moderate critics he was a man who had willed too much; too ambitious and costly a foreign policy, too many burdens, a capital too perilously located, an army and fleet too big for a country in no real danger. To some he was Anti-Christ, far worse than the Patriarch Nikon in his flouting of the unique traditions of Holy Russia.

Whether Peter was a ruler ahead of his time or one who guided his

CHURCH OF THE IMPERIAL PALACE, PETERHOF. Founded by Peter the Great in 1711, the town of Peterhof, eighteen miles from Petrograd, was the site of an imperial palace modeled after Versailles. This church, by Rastrelli, combines Byzantine cupolas typical of the Middle East with a Georgian façade copied from Western Europe. (Metropolitan Museum of Art)

country onto the wrong track was a problem which was to become one of the great issues dividing Russian intellectuals. Peter himself in his last years lived in a kind of isolation and had no one with whom to plan Russia's future. His first wife he had sent into a convent. Their son Alexis disliked everything Peter stood for, and became without being able to help himself the center of all kinds of opposition: of churchmen, of old boyar families, of persons shocked at Peter's private life and at the conduct of the parvenus he had favored, of landowners resentful of the state service which kept them from managing their estates.

Peter had married again and in so doing had transformed into Empress Catherine the captured Livonian servant girl who had been his mistress. Both Peter and his aloof and hostile son Alexis had small sons named Peter, born the same year. Alexis was willing to renounce the throne, and even ran away to Austria and Italy, but his father knew there was no security for his program unless Alexis died or changed his views. His agents enticed Alexis back to Russia with promises that he would be left alone, but Peter could not believe that Alexis had not aided or would not aid the rebels, and finally (1718) tried and tortured him. Alexis died before the death sentence could be carried out. Peter the Great's other son, the infant Peter, died the following year. In 1722 the Emperor proclaimed his right to name his successor, but could not make up his mind until it was too late. Dying (1725), he was unable to speak, and when he tried to write he succeeded only in finishing two words "leave all . . ."

THE ARISTOCRATIC REVIVAL

After Peter was gone his system was put to a severe test. A disturbing factor was the instability of the succession which, unlike western monarchies, did not work according to fixed, invariable rules.

Between 1725 and 1727 the sovereign was Catherine I, Peter's second wife. She was kept in power by the Guards, who came with drums beating to settle the issue between Peter's tough cronies such as Alexander Menshikov, and the old aristocratic families who wanted to get rid of them. Catherine was the candidate of the Menshikov group. She was tactful and quick-witted, but knew nothing of government. During her reign a small group of upper nobility began, by compromising with Menshikov, to control the state. They continued to do so through the reign of Peter II, Peter the Great's twelve-year-old grandson, from 1727 to 1730, for they had arranged his succession. When Peter II died suddenly from smallpox, the issue of whether a small aristocratic oligarchy was to rule Russia came to the fore.

The next ruler, Anna Ivanovna (1730–1740) was, as her name indicated, the daughter of Ivan, the Ivan V who had been co-czar with Peter the Great in his youth. Anna was the candidate of the oligarchy of upper nobility headed by the Dolgoruky and Golitsyn families and was brought from widowed obscurity on the Baltic coast on condition that she share her power with this small group.

Once in St. Petersburg she was clever enough to realize that the majority of poorer nobles did not want the government run by a few prominent families. With their backing she tore up the "Conditions" under which she had accepted the crown, and ruled as an absolute monarch. So passed a first faint suggestion that the Russian autocracy might be limited by its great nobles. But there was to be no Magna Carta in Russia. Some of the lesser nobility may have wanted a limited monarchy, but most of them were concerned with two objectives: forestalling a monarchy limited by only a few great families; and release from some of the more irksome obligations of state service.

Anna met both of these demands and at the same time maintained an autocracy characterized by concessions to nobles in general and by a reign of terror against any particular noble families which displeased her. She was a misanthropic, sharp-witted woman, plagued by boredom and continually surrounded by all sorts of dwarfs and court jesters, animals and guns to shoot the animals with, and Baltic German soldiers and officials, on whom she relied for security. During her reign Peter I's rules of entail were dropped, sons of nobles were allowed to become military or civilian officers without coming up through the ranks, one son in each noble family was relieved of the service obligation so that he could manage the family estates, and the period of service for nobles was reduced from life to twenty-five years. Peter the Great's system of fusing the nobility and the bureaucracy began to weaken.

Anna's reign staved off limitations on absolutism by exploiting jealousies within the nobility and by concessions to the nobles as a group. But she was a despot from whom nobody, whatever his rank, was safe, and her concessions to the nobility failed to satisfy them. There was a clash of interest over the peasants, who served both nobles and state and had to give one less if the other took more. Anna and her German bureaucrats meant to go just so far and no farther in making concessions to the nobility, but the latter wanted full emancipation from obligations to the state. They were, in addition, resentful of Anna's sumptuous but vulgar court and of the predominance of Germans like her lover Biron. To maintain Biron and her other favorites in power, Anna provided that her nephew Ivan, great-grandson of Peter the Great's feeble co-czar, should succeed her as Ivan VI. He was a baby in a cradle when Anna died in 1740, and the German favorites quarreled over the regency, but this reign lasted only to 1741, for once again the Guards took a hand. The unfortunate child was to grow up a prisoner.

Elizabeth Petrovna (1741–1762), daughter of Peter the Great, was then thirty-two, beautiful and intelligent, with her father's restless energy and capacity for sudden anger and cruelty as well as generosity. A contemporary of Frederick the Great and Maria Theresa, she gave the appearance of an Enlightened Despot. Many of the reforms associated with the reign later of the great Catherine II were begun in Elizabeth's day. St. Petersburg began to imitate Versailles. The German influence gave way to French, and the taste for French language, literature, and fashions which was for so long to characterize Russian aristocrats became established. Elizabeth abolished most internal tariffs and tolls, and appointed a commission to codify the laws. Most of the acts of her reign were, however, the work of her officials. The Empress herself lacked her father's taste for government.

She loved travel, clothes, luxury, and people; was harsh with personal enemies but lenient to political ones; was sincerely religious; and lacked all curiosity about affairs of state. Although great changes were taking place in the European balance of power, it was a period of domestic tranquility for Russia, partly owing to Elizabeth's great concessions to the aristocracy. For example, nobles could now be carried on the books of regiments from childhood, accumulating credits which greatly shortened their terms of service. Peter the Great had allowed some non-nobles to own serfs, but by 1762 the nobility's monopoly of the use of serf labor had been reestablished. Elizabeth's reign did much to transform the Russian nobles from state servants to provincial landowners with complete power over their serfs and over local administration.

Elizabeth's successor, Peter III, was her nephew and a grandson of Peter the Great. In 1762 he was thirty-four years old. After he had reigned for six months he was overthrown by the Guards regiments, and a week later he was murdered. His wife, the former German princess Sophia of Anhalt-Zerbst, rode at the head of the Guards when Peter was arrested. She was to be Empress Catherine II, known as the Great, who ruled from 1762 to 1796.

Peter III was victim of the last and most striking of the palace revolutions of the eighteenth century. His downfall did not result from any effort to reverse the stream of concessions to the nobility, for he ended altogether its obligatory service to the state except in times of emergency. He did indeed alienate the Church, for he confiscated its lands, as neither Ivan the Terrible nor Peter the Great had done. He aroused some opposition by withdrawing Russia from the Seven Years War, thereby reversing the foreign policy of his predecessor Elizabeth and giving her enemy Frederick of Prussia, whom he greatly admired, a new lease on life. More serious was the feeling among Russians that Peter III was foreign in his interests. He proposed to use Russian troops in alliance with Prussia to win Schleswig for his native Holstein. Worst of all, he alienated the Guards by reorganizing them in the Prussian manner. Peter's flouting of Russian tastes and interests, and his bullying of the force which all through the century had been king-makers, played into the hands of his estranged and ambitious wife.

CATHERINE THE GREAT

Catherine's titles to greatness were intelligence, realism, and force of character. Without these qualities her reign would have been no more than another illustration of the instability of the Russian crown and of the resurgence of the nobility in the eighteenth century, and her tenure might have been brief. She was, after all, a woman, a foreigner whose Russian remained imperfect, a convert to Orthodoxy, and the occupant of a throne to which she had no legal right. Married at fifteen to the boorish Peter, who soon showed a preference for others, she consoled herself with love affairs and with wide reading, particularly

CATHERINE THE GREAT

of the French philosophers, and sharpened her political sense on the intrigues at the court of Empress Elizabeth. Her son Paul was considered by many to have a better right to the crown. If not he, then the deposed child-Emperor Ivan VI, grown up in captivity, had prior claim. Orders that Ivan be killed if he tried to escape were carried out in 1764.

Catherine turned what might have been a brief adventure into a long and significant reign by proving that she had enough judgment and determination to act as her own first minister. True, she was influenced by the lovers whose succession became almost an official institution. But her will furnished the continuity to her reign, and its over-all pattern was her work.

Catherine II won fame as a ruler who had not only read the works of the *philosophes* and corresponded with the authors but wished to put their enlightened ideas into practice. She was too realistic to try to live up to this part of her reputation. She was genuinely what we would call an "intellectual", and in addition to an immense correspondence wrote histories, comedies, essays, and polemics which have since filled twelve bulky volumes. She was aware that her great reputation throughout Europe, to a large extent built by her friends the *philosophes,* solidified her position at home and helped her foreign policy. She may have become disillusioned with some of her early hopes as she learned more about Russia, but it is doubtful that she was ever naive enough to expect in her lifetime to eradicate such evils as serfdom. Catherine's claim to greatness cannot rest on practice of what she preached. Her great accomplishments were her personal triumph, the prestige and authority she restored to the Russian crown, and the significant part she played in European diplomacy.

Catherine's foreign policy will be considered elsewhere. Here it is enough to call attention to the territories she won. During this period Russia at last became firmly entrenched on the Black Sea coast, including the Crimea, and on the steppes above. But more than that, by initiating the partitions of Poland Catherine advanced far to the west and brought Russia into European politics to an extent undreamed of by previous generations.

These gains were largely the result of two periods of heightened activity, 1768–1774, in which a war with Turkey helped bring about the first partition of Poland; and 1787–1795, in which Russia fought Turkey and Sweden part of the time and helped cut up the remains of Poland in two more partitions. Before each of these periods of heightened activity in the foreign field there were years in which important changes were made or contemplated at home.

The first years of Catherine's reign, from 1762 to 1767, when she was new to her office and not yet secure in the country, have a kind of unity. Her first actions were tentative. In 1764 she placed the church's lands in a government department called the College of Economy, and began to use these resources for the state's needs. In this move she had the backing of most of the nobility, although they would have preferred that the lands be transferred to them. In 1763 she allowed more discretion to provincial governors, a forecast of later changes in local government. In the same year she appointed a commission to study Peter's manifesto freeing the nobility from service obligations, but it was not supposed that Catherine would dare reverse this grant, and the nobility awaited her further dispositions without nervousness, and indeed with anticipation.

The outstanding feature of this first period of Catherine's reign was her Legislative Commission, which was elected in 1766 and allowed in 1767–1768 to meet and discuss codification of the laws and all the great issues of social policy which lay behind such a project. The whole enterprise was given wide publicity at home and abroad. Catherine herself wrote a preliminary *Instruction* of some twenty chapters embodying what she took to be the basic principles upon which a code of laws should be erected. It was the high point of her career as a philosopher-queen, the culmination of her youthful years of reading advanced thinkers. To it she was to owe her reputation for wanting to recast Russia in a new mold. Drawn mainly from Montesquieu's *Spirit of the Laws*, the "prayer book of monarchs", as she described it, and from Beccaria's study on crime and punishment, the *Instruction* was stiffly censored by her advisors before it reached the public. True to Montesquieu's thought, she argued that in a large country like Russia absolute monarchy was the best form of government. Russia was a "European" country and should have the best European principles. An absolute monarchy would provide a rule of law, but not a despotism. Catherine apparently did not contemplate emancipation of the serfs, even in the censored parts of her *Instruction*, but she wanted principles defining the relationships of serfs to masters. She condemned torture and inhumane punishments.

Catherine's Legislative Commission was an anticlimax after her *Instruction*. It was an impressive assembly, the most representative of any called in Russia since the last full Assembly of the Land. Some five hundred sixty-four delegates brought with them fifteen hundred sets of instructions from their constituents, who were nobles, townsmen, government officials, Cossacks, and state peasants (there were no serfs or clergy). The nobles were outnumbered almost four to one, a fact which seemed to indicate that the Empress did not mean to be their tool. Nevertheless the Legislative Commission accomplished nothing tangible, and after meeting for two years was dismissed just as a war against the Ottoman empire ushered in a period of great military and diplomatic activity. In its failure, or apparent failure, most historians have sought the key to Catherine's reign. Was she really a dreamer of reforms, awakened by this fiasco to the reality of a divided country in which the demands of the lower classes were flatly refused by the nobility?

Such a proposition contains a fair, but incomplete, appraisal of the Legislative Commission's discussions. The Empress was no dreamer. Neither Catherine, with the shining generalizations of her *Instruction,* nor the majority of the deputies, was fitted to codify old laws, much less prepare a new code. Catherine's gains from the whole affair, whether or not she was disappointed, were substantial. She, a new ruler with a precarious eminence, got immense publicity at home and abroad. Whoever opposed her now was opposing a ruler who had consulted the influential segments of state and society. It is probable that Catherine knew from the beginning that she could not tamper with the privileges of the nobles and the institution of serfdom. She was not, in any case, to do so; and for the rest of her reign she had the justification that the Legislative Commission had not done so either.

After the outbreak of war with the Ottoman empire in 1768 the Legislative Commission was adjourned, never to meet again, and the Empress, her hold on the throne strengthened, gave most of her attention to military-diplomatic affairs. These built substantially her claim to successful leadership, for the first partition of Poland (1772) and the Treaty of Kuchuk Kainarji with Turkey (1774) provided great gains. As the first period of intensive activity in foreign affairs drew to a close, however, there occurred a reminder that acceptance of the status quo at home had its price. In 1773 and 1774 there broke out on the Yaik river (thereafter renamed the Ural), north of the Caspian Sea, one of those great revolts which had become periodic since autocracy and serfdom had begun to reach the frontiers.

The revolt was led by Emelyan Pugachev, a Don Cossack who claimed to be Czar Peter III. He was a veteran of the Seven Years War and the Turkish War who became rebellious against the military authorities and kept escaping from their jails. Serfdom during Catherine's reign was getting worse than ever, (as is suggested by the decree of 1767 that peasants could no longer complain to the authorities against their masters). In the Yaik and lower Volga areas the same old explosive mixture used by Stenka Razin a century before was still intact, strengthened not only by serfdom but by the continued differentiation between well-to-do and poorer Cossacks and by government intolerance of national minorities like the Kalmucks and Bashkirs and of religious dissenters like the Old Believers and Moslems. Pugachev's revolt ran a course similar to that of Razin. He preached abolition of serfdom, partition of the land, freedom of religion. He took the villages and besieged the larger garrison towns, and stirred up so much rebellion that all over Russia manor houses had to mount special guards. In the enflamed Volga region troops scarcely dared to venture into the countryside which the guerrillas knew so much better than they did. Pugachev by late 1773 had about 15,000 men and had even captured some artillery, but the ending of the war against Turkey in the following year freed the government's hands and frightened away his supporters. Finally Pugachev was betrayed by one of his accomplices for a reward of 20,000 rubles, arrested, and executed in Moscow. This particular fire went out, but the inflammable materials were still there in the Russian villages.

CONSOLIDATION OF THE AUTOCRACY

Catherine's reforms in the decade following the Pugachev revolt solidified the Russian state to a point unknown since Peter the Great. Local government, which had proved inefficient against the rebels, was changed in 1775 by making provinces smaller and subdividing them into districts. Officers of the provinces were appointed. Those of the districts were elected by the local nobility. The state acknowledged some responsibility for health, education, and social work in the provinces. In 1785 the cities of Russia were given a charter allowing each city a council (duma) chosen by six carefully distinguished classes of electors. In the same year the Charter of the Nobility recognized them as an Estate with its own organization and special rights. They were exempt from compulsory state service, free from direct taxation, exempt from corporal punishment, and recognized as absolute owners of their lands and as hereditary nobles who could be tried only by their peers. At the same time nobles of each province and district were organized into corporate bodies electing their own marshals. These organizations were to look after the genealogical records of the nobility, perform certain health and educational services for their own kind, and choose certain officials of local government.

These changes reflect Catherine's conception of Russia as a European monarchy which should have distinct orders with their separate functions, like the estates in France. On a more practical plane they reflect her acceptance of the social changes which had been coming since the time of Peter the Great. Peter had tried to fuse the bureaucracy and the aristocracy, but since his time the Russian nobles had escaped from state service. Catherine's reign saw them going home to the country. For the first time there was a large provincial aristocracy which remained on its estates in summer and inhabited the provincial towns in winter. Catherine's legislation associated them with the state through local government, and recognized their special privileges as a particular order in a society made up of orders. Actually the elements of self-government in the rural districts and in the cities remained subordinate to the officials appointed from Catherine's court. Catherine would not have dared attack the privileges of the nobility. In a sense her reign was an alliance of crown and nobles. On the other hand, she did not intend to let them govern. She would associate them with the government as its agents, but she meant to maintain and solidify absolute monarchy.

This intention is the more evident in matters concerning the central government. Here no systematic reforms took place. Catherine spoke of a rule of law, with regular procedures, but she and her favorites never tied their hands with guarantees that they would always proceed in the same manner. Catherine in 1768 and 1769 began to use an advisory council, but it could not act without her, and its position was never made clear. She gave the Senate founded by Peter the Great direct control over the new local government institutions and gradually eliminated the collegiate departments of state, but she held back many affairs of importance from consideration by the Senate. Catherine evidently distrusted any agency through which the nobility might set precedents restraining her power.

And in outward display as well as internal administration, she was a true autocrat. She maintained a brilliant court saturated with French literary and artistic influences, bought the libraries of Diderot and Voltaire, transformed St. Petersburg with new building and landscaping, and rewarded with an imperial extravagance all who served her. From the state domains she gave away lands peopled by more than 800,000 peasants, who now became serfs. During her reign serfdom was, in addition, extended to parts of the Ukraine where it had not previously existed.

In the face of all this lavishness and success, which was crowned by new triumphs in foreign affairs toward the end of the reign, there grew up in St. Petersburg an upper aristocracy eager to participate in the patronage, willing to serve the absolute monarchy, and disdainful of their provincial cousins. Catherine's reign is often called the golden age of the Russian nobility, and deservedly so. It was also the golden age of the autocracy, thanks to the Empress's shrewdness in placating the nobility as an order and enticing the most eminent among them into her service.

RUSSIA ON THE EVE OF THE FRENCH REVOLUTION

Imperial Russia by the end of Catherine's reign was one of the great powers of Europe. There had been thirteen million Russians at the death of Peter the Great. In 1796, the year of Catherine's death, these had increased to approximately twenty-nine million; with the populations of conquered territories the total was thirty-six million. People were now able to move from the less desirable lands of the forest zone down to the rich black soil region of the steppe.

Russian farming techniques did not change much during the eighteenth century, for too much depended on the limited knowledge and stubborn father-to-son traditions of the peasants. There was an increase in commerce and in the use of money, however, and many of the peasants of the poorer agricultural region in the north began to work full or part-time at household industry. The black soil region produced enough surplus to make up the deficit in northern Russia and to export some grain abroad, but most farm products were still consumed by the villages which produced them. Since the failure of Peter the Great's attempt to forbid the splitting up of estates, the Russian nobility had become increasingly numerous as manors were increasingly subdivided by inheritances. Most of the nobles were smallholders who thought in terms of consumption rather than of production of a surplus for sale. A few great landowners, particularly in the south, were interested in production for sale abroad or in the other parts of Russia. About half of the Russian peasants were serfs belonging to one or another kind of landholder; the other half were state peasants whose villages had no private owner but who owed dues and taxes to some branch of the state or to members of the imperial family.

As the reign of Catherine the Great demonstrates, Russia at the end of the eighteenth century had enough resources and military power to play a great part in European politics. Mining and manufacturing, although crude, continued to grow throughout the century under the stimulus provided by large government orders and rising population. Since there was no free labor to speak of, most of the work was done by the home industry of peasants in the poorer agricultural districts, by factories established on manors, or by the "ascribed peasants" ordered by the government to work for some favored miner or manufacturer.

Russian commerce grew throughout the eighteenth century in spite of an almost total absence of good roads, which meant reliance on river boats in summer and sleds in winter. Outlets to the Baltic and Black Seas helped foreign trade, especially exports of foodstuffs and raw materials. A few great nobles and merchants were interested in the foreign markets, and liked to think in terms of liberal economic ideas. The great majority of the nobles were small holders who were not business-minded; they insisted on enjoying all their newfound privileges and all the advantages of the serf system. Most merchants were bearded, traditionalistic Muscovites, suspicious of new ideas, who led socially isolated lives in a zone between the nobles and the peasants. Catherine the Great's alliance with the nobility is easier to understand if one keeps in mind the prejudices of the great majority of the nobles and the inadequacy of the townsmen as an alternative social force upon which to lean. The Empress's position was reflected in her economic policies, for she talked like the French physiocrats who favored the free play of economic forces, but in practice mixed mercantilism with laissez faire. Above all, she was willing to freeze society into estates with special privileges. This attitude harmonized better with the prejudices of the majority of nobles and merchants than it did with the ideas of individualism and occupational freedom which were leading the West toward an economic revolution.

Catherine's Russia with its "European" pretensions was as solidly constructed as she could make it, using both materials left her by earlier rulers, and her own best judgment as to which ideals of the Enlightenment were applicable. Her predecessors had left her certain problems to cope with: the advance of serfdom, the resurgence of the nobility, the growing contacts with Europe. Catherine tried to build a good absolute monarchy according to the standards of the eighteenth century, and gave priority to filling out its territorial contours by war and diplomacy. Somewhat like Frederick the Great, she brought close to perfection a kind of statesmanship which would no longer be adequate in the century to come. When the labor of serfs was no longer able to keep Russia abreast of Western Europe, Catherine's political system, into which serfdom had been built, would be in serious trouble.

The problem was not, in any case, one which Catherine wanted discussed. When Alexander Radischev in 1790 printed his *Journey from St. Petersburg to Moscow* describing and denouncing the evils of serfdom, Catherine burned the book and exiled the author to Siberia. By then the French Revolution had broken out, and the Empress was becoming alarmed at the subversive turn which the Enlightenment, so long praised by her, seemed to have taken in France.

20

THE STATES OF EAST
CENTRAL EUROPE

RUSSIA'S GROWTH to the status of a great power affected the balance among all the states of Europe. The new power of Russia was partly made possible by changes in the health of its neighbors and the decline of their power to resist its advances. Russia's story is thus best understood when it is related to the story of East Central Europe; correspondingly the destiny of that whole area between the Baltic and the Black Seas was determined by events to the east and west, among Turks and Russians and Germans.

The period from Westphalia to the French Revolution saw the turning point in the relations between the Ottoman empire and Europe. By 1700 the question was no longer what the Turks would do to Europe, but what Europe would do to the Ottoman empire and who would benefit most from its decline. The "Eastern Question," the question of how to manage the area occupied by the feeble Turkish power, was to have a major part in European politics until World War I. The Ottoman perils were comparable to those produced by the decay of the Holy Roman Empire and the magnetic attraction that its defenselessness exerted on more vigorous neighbors.

Of more immediate importance was another "Eastern Question." The kingdom of Poland was now having its Time of Troubles, and by 1795 would disappear completely—the Poland that before 1600 had been the chief Slavic power, the eastern outpost of European culture beyond which lay only crude Muscovite Russia. At the very time when the French Revolution was disrupting Western Europe, Poland's cannibalistic neighbors in the east were strengthening themselves by devouring its territory. This development greatly changed the balance of power in Europe as a whole. Together with the events of the French

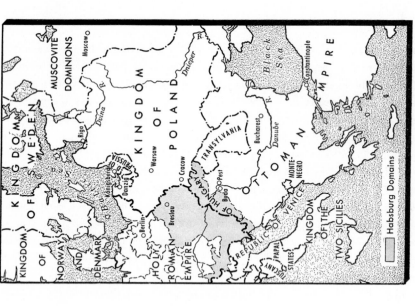

EAST CENTRAL EUROPE IN 1770

EAST CENTRAL EUROPE IN 1648

Habsburg Domains

Revolution—France's resurgence and the impact of its victories in Italy and Germany—the shift of fortunes in the east was a real turning point in the history of Europe.

Between Westphalia and the French Revolution, Sweden as well as Turkey and Poland declined. Sweden had been a great power during Russia's Time of Troubles (1598–1613) and the Thirty Years War (1618–1648), and even as late as the Great Northern War (1700–1721) in which Charles XII opposed Peter the Great. But by 1800 Sweden had been forced to give way to the advances of Russia and Prussia to the Baltic shore.

The greatest change in East Central and Eastern Europe between 1648 and the French Revolution was therefore the substitution of Russian, Prussian, and Austrian control for Turkish, Polish, and Swedish. Perhaps the best way to begin is to look for internal reasons for the decline of the Ottoman empire, Poland, and Sweden.

THE WEAKENING OF THE OTTOMAN EMPIRE

There were many landmarks in the rise of the Ottoman empire; perhaps its conquest of Constantinople in 1453 and its unsuccessful siege of Vienna in 1529 are the best remembered. After the reign of Suleiman the Magnificent (1522–1566) the expansive force of the Turkish system declined. Although Europeans did not appreciate it until late in the following century, the defects in the Ottoman empire were beginning to outweigh its strengths. First came an equilibrium between Turkish and European power, then European superiority. The inability of Europe to subordinate its own quarrels to a drive against the Turks postponed the consequences of Turkish weakness, and awareness of it. Europeans of the early seventeenth century, preoccupied by the Thirty Years War (1618–1648), had the habit of thinking in terms of a "Turkish menace", and it was no surprise to them when a new Turkish drive in 1676 took Crete from Venice, simultaneously rivaled Russia and Poland for control of the Ukraine, and in 1683 drove into Central Europe and besieged Vienna.

Gradually, however, it became apparent that the Turks did not have their old power. The Habsburgs, after receiving aid in the second siege of Vienna from the great Polish King John Sobieski, drove the Turks from most of Hungary. The Poles and Russians divided the Ukraine, Peter the Great took Azov in 1696, and the Venetians took parts of Greece. At the end of the seventeenth century the Treaties of Karlowitz (1699), which confirmed the Turkish losses, became another landmark, this time signifying the end of the "menace" and the realization on the part of Europeans that the roles of hunter and hunted might be reversed.

Actually the Ottoman empire of the seventeenth century had not been as much of a threat as it appeared to be, for its activities were only the result of temporary revivals under the leadership of Sultan Murad IV (1623–1640) and later of an energetic family, the Koeprili, who controlled the grand viziership most of the time between 1656 and 1702. This leadership was able for a time to halt the decay in the Ottoman system of government and administration but not to make fundamental reforms in its shambling institutions. What had in earlier times been a system capable of generating enough energy to conquer Asia Minor, the Balkans, and North Africa, was now settling into a low-voltage empire. Much of its effectiveness had always depended on the personal qualities of the sultans, who were like chiefs of an army victoriously encamped in a conquered country. Each sultan's replacement came from within his harem, in the person of a son chosen by him. This heir, who could not be certain of his good fortune in advance, grew up in the midst of the intrigues of the harem, and was subject to double peril. If not chosen sultan he would, with his brothers and half-brothers, almost certainly be killed by the successful candidate. Mohammed III, for example, in 1595 killed nineteen brothers and half-brothers. Whether chosen or not, the boys who grew up in the harem atmosphere, where intensely competing women tried to select and control a future sultan, tended to be spoiled in advance for a life of active leadership of the state.

Poor leadership was especially serious in the Ottoman empire because it was a despotism lacking governmental machinery able to maintain its own efficiency. Like the Russian czars with their service nobles who were given lands and peasants in return for helping expand and govern the state, the Turkish sultans had rewarded the agents of their power. Their system was more extreme than the Russian service noble system (which was probably copied from it). In the case of the Turks, most state officials were slaves, whose efficiency was ensured by their dependence as well as by their rewards. They had everything to lose and nothing to gain by relaxing their efforts or resisting the ruler. With the degeneration of the sultans, however, and their neglect of their duties, their network of power began to deteriorate in all its parts. Military and governmental offices began to become hereditary, and competitiveness and efficiency vanished from their holders. The army and state became both more expensive and less effective. To maintain this ever more stodgy machine, it became necessary to enforce greater sacrifices on the subjects by means of decreasingly effective instruments of government. In terms of everyday life this decrease of efficiency, combined with an increase of exploitation, meant heavier taxes, depreciation of the currency, the sale of offices, further decline in efficiency and income, and so on. The vicious circle was interrupted by occasional energetic action on the part of a sultan or vizier who would temporarily make the state's servants fearful and efficient again. When such a reform was not in progress the outlying parts of the Ottoman empire tended to move onto the road toward independent statehood.

As the Ottoman empire lost its momentum and ceased expanding, it no longer gained by conquest the skilled Europeans and the military and other equipment which had been part of its spoils in earlier centuries. It was still possible, of course, to secure European technicians, and the Turks were noted for their willingness to employ persons of ability, regardless of origin or religion. European techniques, however, were not readily transplanted to Turkish soil. Ottoman culture did not lend itself to innovations. The sacred law of Islam, as expounded by the jurists of the empire, had a conservative influence on the lives and mentality of the faithful. Politically and diplomatically, too, the cessation of expansion handicapped the Turks. Their ways of governing were better suited to conquest than to cold war, and it is probable that the decline in efficiency which has already been described was a result as well as a cause of their loss of momentum.

POLAND'S DIFFICULTIES

The decline of Poland-Lithuania is comparable to that of the Ottoman empire only in two respects. One is timing. We must not assume that because Poland was defeated and partitioned at the end of the eighteenth century, its doom was ordained by irremediable defects centuries earlier. As already noted (see Chapter 10), fifteenth- and sixteenth-century Poland was both huge and effective as a political and military organization. As in the case of the Ottoman empire, there were no *outward* signs of decay until after the Thirty Years War.

In one other respect the decline of Poland may be compared with that of Turkey. In spite of what is at first glance a contrast—the despotism of the sultan versus the powerlessness of the Polish king, hedged as he was by constitutional limitations—both states suffered in their decline from what might be called, for lack of a better term, dangerous decentralization. Just as the sultans, through the decaying efficiency of the machinery of state, had to contend with increasing independence and insubordination on the part of provincial rulers, so were the Polish kings faced with almost total loss of influence over the great nobles, or magnates, who controlled the various regions of the kingdom. The comparison is a very general one. But it calls attention to the most important element in the competitive state system of the seventeenth and eighteenth centuries: governmental institutions capable of mobilizing the energies of a people, of tapping the resources of a society without killing the goose that laid the golden eggs. This was the essential characteristic which the Turkish despotism and the Polish elective monarchy failed to achieve. At least they failed to achieve it to a degree sufficient for competing with such neighbors as Russia and Prussia, the Habsburg monarchy, France, and England.

Poland after 1648 entered a long period of warfare and internal disintegration which in the national tradition is called "the deluge." For the rest of the century it was almost continually at war, first with its own Ukrainian Cossacks and then with one or another of its neighbors. In the eighteenth century the wars continued, with occasional breathing spaces. As the Polish territory shrank in size, its government became more often the instrument of other peoples' foreign policies and ambitions. Its kings, elected by the szlachta, or nobles, who were some 6 or 7 percent of the population, were bound by the contracts they had made with the factions which had supported them. In many cases they were also embarrassed by the backing of some foreign power. Their impotence was matched by that of the diet, also elected by the nobility. The king could do nothing with-out consent of the diet, and the diet could do nothing if a single deputy said no. This famous *liberum veto* permitted any faction, or even individual, to block legislation, and was sufficient to break up ("explode") the diet. Local "dietines" of impoverished nobles, clients of a few powerful magnates, held the real power. In cases of national crisis there had grown up the custom that a "confederation" of nobles, voting by majority, could take upon itself the salvation of the state. This practice lent itself to action by self-appointed bands who presumed to speak in the name of the general welfare and often clashed with other "confederations" or served the interests of foreign backers.

In the face of such obstacles Poland in the late seventeenth and eighteenth centuries scarcely possessed a machinery of state. The army dwindled, the arsenals were empty, and the king's revenues were laughable. The great magnates, with their followings of szlachta, had their own military forces and did not hesitate to augment them with foreign aid. Paying no taxes themselves, the nobles stood between the public authority and the great mass of serfs, some 70 percent of the eleven million inhabitants. Since the end of the fifteenth century the peasantry had been restricted in their movements, and by the eighteenth they were deep in servitude, forced to work their masters' fields or pay them seigneurial dues. By these arrangements, unrestricted by the state, the nobles survived and the mag-nates produced grain in surpluses for sale abroad. Since the late sixteenth century the Polish nobles had enforced a policy of free trade for the objects which they imported through their foreign grain brokers, with the result that Polish manu-factures, handicrafts, and native merchants suffered ruinous competition, and town life was elementary. Most of the inhabitants of Polish towns were either Jews or Germans—Jews who had pioneered eastward to escape the intolerance of medieval Europe since the thirteenth century, and Germans who in the same period had been encouraged to bring their own patterns of municipal organiza-tion and settle in Poland. Town life in earlier times had flourished, before the collapse of the Byzantine empire and the commercial revolution had diverted trade from the Black and Mediterranean seas. After the sixteenth century, towns ceased to develop as the dominance in Polish society shifted overwhelmingly to the nobles, who despised the Germanic and Jewish town culture as alien.

In the sixteenth century the educated of Poland had enjoyed three great stimuli: the influence of the Renaissance, the religious controversies of the Refor-mation, and the efforts of the nobles to keep Poland from going the way of abso-lutism or falling into the hands of a few magnates. In the seventeenth and eighteenth centuries the situation changed, to the detriment of Polish culture. Except for a minority of wealthy, cosmopolitan noble families whose estates were like little kingdoms, the Polish people tended to lose contact with Western Europe. Although intolerance in religious matters was slow to arise and did not reach very great heights, Catholicism became identified with the Polish nation-ality, and Protestantism and Orthodoxy with such opponents as the Swedes and Russians. Large numbers of Orthodox remained in the eastern regions, for the White Russian (Ruthenian, Byelorussian) and the Ukrainian peasantry tended to keep their faith, while their landlords were becoming Polonized and Catholic. Differences of religion and nationality combined with the economic and social irritations of serfdom to ignite such movements as the great Cossack rebellion of 1648, which touched off the Polish time of troubles. As this civil war turned into a three-cornered contest of Poland, Russia, and Turkey for control of the Ukraine, and as the Poles and Russians finally divided it (1667, 1686), Russification on one side of the Dnieper was matched by Polonization on the other.

The decline of religious toleration and Humanist contacts with the west was therefore matched by a decline in Poland's effectiveness as a federation of peoples. The decline in town life was matched by the increasing weight of serfdom. The decline in the crown's effectiveness in maintaining national unity was accompanied by the triumphs of the nobility over all other interests. Poland's political development was almost the reverse of that of France, Prussia, and Austria, where the kings built up absolute monarchies while leaving the nobles social privileges. It was also very unlike that of England, where Parliament limited the crown's authority without destroying the state's effectiveness. Poland's difficulty was not that its constitution was unworkable from the start. In the sixteenth century the *liberum veto* had existed but served to make the majority in the diet offer compromises which the minority usually accepted. The earlier "confederations" were used in times of real crisis, and did not lose sight of the general welfare. Poland's tragedy stemmed from the failure of the constitution to continue its evolution after the middle of the seventeenth century. And this failure in turn was part of the general social and cultural crisis and of the incessant warfare which aggravated it.

THE DECLINE OF SWEDEN AS A GREAT POWER

Sweden's inability to maintain itself as a great power in the seventeenth and eighteenth centuries is perhaps less surprising than its climb to eminence in the first place. Sweden had only a million inhabitants, but their energies had been well directed. Trade with the rest of Europe had turned to advantage Swedish forests, grain fields, mines of iron and copper, and metallurgical industry. Sweden had shared in Europe's economic progress and political advancement. Its big maritime commerce stimulated naval power and a vigorous town life. Nobles and middle class had developed a taste for the arts and sciences. The peasantry was personally free and well-to-do. Able kings had organized a tight administration—one which Peter the Great tried to copy—and freed themselves from interference by the nobility and the Estates. Sweden, in spite of its small population, was able to play a decisive part in the Thirty Years War and to extend its holdings around the Baltic until it virtually controlled that sea.

From Gustavus Adolphus, of Thirty Years War fame, to Charles XII, the opponent of Peter the Great, Sweden's progressive society and efficient government were able to support a foreign policy aimed at domination of Finland, Ingria, Estonia, Livonia, and much of Pomerania, all of them provinces facing Sweden across the Baltic. However, with the solidification of Russia and Prussia, whose location and resources made them strong competitors on the Baltic shores, Sweden's defense of its predominance in that sea became too much of a strain. Charles XII's erratic genius enabled him to defeat Russia, Poland, and Saxony before his spectacular failure at Poltava in the Ukraine (see p. 298), but his career was more than Sweden could afford. The nation was tired of military levies which depopulated the countryside, of war debts and taxes, of inflation, of the decline of commerce. Although the peasantry still supported absolutism, many of the nobles, middle class people, and Lutheran clergy now wished to limit the monarchy. The long absences of Charles XII prepared the way for a revolt which took place in 1719, the year after his death, when the diet took charge of the succession and enthroned Ulrica Eleanor, a sister of Charles XII, and forced her to accept a constitution.

Thereafter, until 1772, the diet, representative of nobles, *bourgeoisie*, clergy, and peasants, held the legislative power and controlled the executive, a committee appointed by itself. This representative system, coming at a time when Sweden's Baltic empire was shrinking, led to intense competition by the poorer nobility for government posts. Such men were drawn into factions led by the great seigneurs who really governed the country. These aristocratic parties became identified with foreign backers, the "Bonnets" with England, then Russia after 1763, the "Hats" with France. Sweden was becoming like Poland, for the triumph of the aristocracy was threatening the national unity and interest. Catherine of Russia and Frederick of Prussia saw the symptoms and approved. In 1763, they agreed secretly that the constitution of Sweden, like that of Poland, must be preserved. The kiss of death was implanted upon the unfortunate Swedes and their decrepit constitution.

But Sweden did not die. Unlike Poland, it recovered sufficiently to maintain its independence and to play a part in European politics. Its circumstances were sadly reduced, however. After the death of Charles XII in 1718, it lost most of the holdings on the south side of the Gulf of Finland and the Baltic.

Sweden's recovery is one of the bits of testimony which the eighteenth century provides of the usefulness and dangers of enlightened despotism. In 1772, Gustavus III became king and, supported by the public and the army, pushed aside the oligarchy which the constitution of 1719 had favored. Gustavus chose his own ministers and with them seized the executive power from the Diet, leaving to it only rights over confirmation of tax laws and declarations of war. He provided Sweden with most of the typical reforms of enlightened despots— primary education, free trade in grain, an Academy, a new fleet and army, freedom of worship for immigrants, abolition of torture. But in the end, he fell victim to the aristocracy and its weakness for outside help. In the midst of a war against Russia, Gustavus had to face an aristocratic revolt that was backed by Catherine II (1788). He restored order at home, though at the cost of abandoning the war against Russia. In 1792 he was stabbed to death by aristocratic conspirators in the course of a masked ball. But he had lived long enough and worked hard enough to rescue his country. Sweden was spared for a happier future than Poland's.

POLAND'S SEVENTEENTH-CENTURY TIME OF TROUBLES

Generalizations about the decline of Sweden, Poland, and Turkey in the late seventeenth and eighteenth centuries help to show what it took to maintain a strong state in that period. They also illustrate the interaction between internal history and international relations. A narrative of the outstanding turns of fortune in Eastern Europe is needed if these illustrations are to be clear. The most convenient procedure is to begin with Poland's troubles in the second half of the seventeenth century, showing their relation to the ambitions which stirred in the surrounding powers.

Poland's "deluge" began with the revolt, in 1648, of the Ukrainian Cossacks under the leadership of Bogdan Khmelnitsky. His search for allies led him to the Crimean Tartars and to their overlord, the Ottoman empire, which under the energetic Koeprili viziers was on the eve of its last great surge of aggression. The Turks, however, were not alone in wishing to take advantage of the Ukrainian rebellion. In 1654 Russia made an agreement with the Cossacks and in return for a transfer of their allegiance, attacked Poland. The following year Sweden invaded Poland in an effort to dismember it along with the Russians, who were taking Smolensk. In 1656, the Hohenzollern Frederick William, the Great Elector, renounced the allegiance of his vassal duchy of East Prussia to its Polish overlord and joined the attack. Even the Prince of Transylvania, who was a vassal of the Ottoman empire, took part in the general assault on Poland.

But Poland's hour had not yet struck. There was still enough national resilience and sufficient disagreement among Poland's neighbors to permit a revival. The Russians, who had not yet reached the Baltic and wished to do so at Sweden's expense, were alarmed at Sweden's successes in Poland. Russia made a truce with the Poles. The Habsburg monarchy, alarmed by the backing which Protestant Europe, including Cromwell's England, seemed prepared to give to the Swedes, came to Poland's aid. Denmark joined the alliance, taking this opportunity to attack its old rival, Sweden. Under pressure from the Habsburgs, the Hohenzollern Elector of Brandenburg was induced to switch from the Swedish to the Polish side, in return for freeing the Hohenzollerns' East Prussia from Polish overlordship.

For the moment, disaster passed Poland by. The Swedes were driven from the Polish coast, and after their king died they were willing to make peace. Poland was saved, but in the Treaty of Oliwa, in 1660, the real gainer was Brandenburg-Prussia, strengthened in both the Baltic region and in the Holy Roman Empire.

Trouble continued. In addition to the devastation caused in Poland by the recent war, a civil war which broke out from 1664–1666 did nothing to strengthen the royal authority. In Poland's weakened condition it agreed in 1667 to the Armistice of Andruszowo, dividing the Ukraine with Russia and ceding Russia Smolensk. The settlement was declared permanent in 1686. Henceforth the Ukraine was to be Russified on the eastern side of the Dnieper and in the city of Kiev, Russia's only acquisition on the western bank; and the Poles were to do their best to Polonize the western Ukraine.

In spite of the losses to Sweden, Prussia, and Russia, and the civil war, Poland's cup was not yet full. After 1666 the Turks did their best to seize the Polish Ukraine. The stage was being set for the last great Turkish advance under the leadership of the Koeprilis. But in the face of this menace Poland revived under the leadership of one of its most famous kings, John III, or John Sobieski (1674–1696).

Sobieski was elected in the midst of his military activities against the Turks, but in his early years as king he allowed himself to hope for recovery of East Prussia from the Hohenzollerns. Sobieski's wife was French, and the foreign office of Louis XIV wanted to add Poland to France's list of Eastern European allies, along with Sweden and the Ottoman Empire. Now that Sweden and Poland had made peace it seemed for a time that they could cooperate against Brandenburg. These prospects became much dimmer when the Brandenburg elector, Frederick William, defeated the Swedes and joined the French camp himself. Sobieski turned in disgust from his dealings with Louis XIV. He made an alliance with Austria against the prospective Turkish attack. In 1683, when the Turks besieged Vienna, he appeared with an army of 25,000 men and personally led the cavalry charge which proved to be the turning point of the battle.

Thereafter, in league with Austria, Venice, and the Pope, Poland continued to war against the Turks. The Habsburgs profited most, for they drove the Turks out of Hungary and for the first time took entire possession of an inheritance for which they had been waiting since the Turkish victory at Mohács in 1526. Poland under Sobieski was less successful in trying to take Moldavia, part of present-day Rumania. With the Treaties of Karlowitz in 1699 the long war against the Ottoman empire finally came to an end. The Turks acknowledged their loss of Hungary to the Habsburgs, and lesser territories to the Venetians and Poles. Karlowitz marks a turning point in Eastern Europe. Thereafter, Poland and Turkey, both threatened by Russia, tended to draw together. Already Peter the Great had taken Azov from the Turks (1696), and he was soon to interfere in the Polish election following the death of Sobieski in that same year.

The election of Augustus of Saxony as the Polish king in 1697 was the first of a series decided by foreign pressure. Poland, which had recovered somewhat under Sobieski, was to be the pawn of foreign interests. At the close of the seventeenth century France would still have liked to bring Poland into its system of allies, along with Sweden and Turkey. It is impossible to say what the results of the election of a French candidate to the Polish kingship would have been. Perhaps a French alliance and the influence of French absolutism might have worked for Poland's survival. However, Russian and Austrian pressure prevailed in favor of the Elector of Saxony, whose policies encouraged Russian growth.

EIGHTEENTH-CENTURY WARS AND DIPLOMACY

Eastern Europe's wars from 1700 to 1763 were, for the most part, the same wars as those which concerned the west. An exception was the Great Northern War of 1700–1721, which took place at about the time of the War of the Spanish Succession. The War of the Austrian Succession (1740–1748) and Seven Years War (1756–1763) involved both east and west. They have, however, a somewhat different silhouette when seen from the eastern side of Europe.

The Great Northern War was primarily the victory of a rising Russia which took Ingria and the Baltic Provinces from a declining Sweden and so won a "window on the west." Peter was unsuccessful against the Turks, however, and was indeed forced to give up Azov, but his hope of arousing the Orthodox within the European territories of the Turks foreshadows the later "Eastern Question." More important at this time was Russia's interference in Poland, which Peter treated as a protectorate, marching through Polish territory, supporting the worst abuses of the constitution, and acting as arbiter beween King Augustus II and a rival backed by Charles XII of Sweden, Stanislas Leszczynski. Just as some aspects of the Great Northern War indicate the decline of Sweden and Turkey, so does Poland's role foreshadow its future partition.

Most of the other powers did not welcome Russia's entrance into European politics. The French, English, and Dutch looked without enthusiasm at the prospect of a Russian fleet in the Baltic. The Habsburgs disliked the growth of Russian influence in Germany and Poland. The ambitious Hohenzollerns, who proclaimed themselves Kings in Prussia in 1701, were closest to having a common interest with Russia in the defeat of Sweden and the enfeeblement of Poland. Peter I of Russia and Frederick William I of Brandenburg-Prussia agreed secretly to interfere in defense of the religious liberties of minorities (Lutherans, Orthodox) in Poland, and to defend the liberties (and defects) of the Polish constitution. In the Great Northern War Poland seemed to be victorious over an old enemy, Sweden, but the Russians won greater gains than the Poles, and their aggrandizement constituted a new peril for Poland.

When Augustus II died in 1733 there was a chance for Poland to throw off Russian tutelage, and with it the influence of Prussia and Austria as well. The majority in the Polish Diet supported their countryman Stanislas Leszczynski who since his last, Swedish-backed, attempt at the throne had become the father-in-law of Louis XV of France. It was to the interest of France and of all who opposed the Russian-Prussian-Austrian line-up in Eastern Europe to back Stanislas. The War of the Polish Succession which ensued with its bizarre intricacies is described in Chapter 18. Here may be remarked two features of the situation, which were to remain axioms of European diplomacy ever afterward. Poland, encircled by Russia and Prussia, was thrown into dependence on France. And Russia and Prussia were drawn into voracious collaboration by their appetite for Poland. The situation in 1733 was extraordinarily similar to that which produced World War II in 1939. In the War of the Polish Succession Austria and Russia, with Prussia's approval, forced on the Poles King Augustus III, son of the previous King and like him Elector of Saxony.

In 1740, the year the War of the Austrian Succession started, the situation in Eastern Europe was complicated by the deaths of the Habsburg Charles VI, of Frederick William I of Prussia, and of Anna, Empress of Russia. The year marks a change in Prussia from the careful acquisitiveness of Frederick William I to the bold aggressions of Frederick II. Frederick, besides seizing Silesia, would have liked an opportunity to take the Polish lands west of East Prussia.

Russian foreign policy, as directed by Empress Anna and her German favorites, had been pro-Austrian, and continued to be so during the brief regency which followed her death. As a consequence France took two anti-Russian measures. In 1741 France encouraged Sweden to try a comeback against Russia, an enterprise which lasted a year and lost Sweden parts of Finland. France, also in 1741, hoping to turn Russia against Austria and toward France, urged the coup by which Elizabeth took power in Russia. Elizabeth, although she ousted Anna's German favorites, kept to the pro-Austrian foreign policy of her predecessor. She considered Prussia under Frederick II to be a dangerous rival, and toward the end of the War of the Austrian Succession accepted English subsidies and sent troops to the Rhine, where their presence probably hastened France's decision to make peace. One of Elizabeth's motives was doubtless her intention to continue treating Poland as a Russian protectorate, rather than share it with Frederick of Prussia.

The diplomatic revolution which took place just before the outbreak of the Seven Years War (1756–1763) was related to the balance of power in Eastern Europe. France had for a long time attempted to unite Sweden, Poland, and Turkey against its rival, the Habsburg monarchy, and had also encouraged Prussia against the Habsburgs. With the decline in importance of Sweden, Poland, and Turkey, however, and with the increase in power of Prussia and Russia, France reconsidered. The French switch to Austria was a recognition of these new conditions, although it perhaps would not have taken place without the Anglo-Prussian alliance. No longer fearing a Prussian attack on the English royal family's domain of Hanover, the English no longer needed Russia, where Empress Elizabeth was in any case determined to remain pro-Austrian and anti-Prussian. Thus Russia in the Seven Years War found itself helping France as well as Austria when Russian troops marched through Poland and attacked Frederick of Prussia.

Frederick the Great, who had not expected active Russian participation at the side of Austria, now found himself in mortal danger. As the war progressed, England and France, concerned with domestic affairs and above all with their overseas rivalry, did little to help their respective allies. On the continent it appeared that the Russian power would be decisive. The two rising powers of Eastern Europe, Prussia and Russia, were at odds, and there was good reason to expect that Prussia's career would be cut short by the Russian opposition of Empress Elizabeth.

Prussia was saved by Elizabeth's death in 1762 and by the dynastic accident that her chosen successor, Peter III, was an admirer of Frederick and was determined to return to Peter the Great's policy of cooperation with Prussia. Peter III took Russia out of the war, and Frederick won it. The Habsburgs, bereft of Silesia, turned more than ever to consolidating their administration in Bohemia and Hungary. Poland for the time seemed closer to being a satellite of Russia alone than to partition by three neighbors. Russian troops remained in Poland until the death of King Augustus III in 1763. True, Peter III was murdered in 1762 and replaced by his wife, Catherine II, on the Russian throne, but Catherine did not reverse his pro-Prussian foreign policy; she merely toned it down. She cooperated with Frederick in interfering in the Polish election in 1764 and in a few years came to an agreement with him about the partitioning of Poland.

THE PARTITIONS OF POLAND

Poland's fate in the partitions of 1772, 1793, and 1795 is to be seen against the background of the late eighteenth century developments which made it possible. The western powers France and England were preoccupied, first with their colonial struggle and then with the French Revolution. In the east, Russia took advantage of the reduced circumstances of both the Ottoman empire and Poland. Catherine the Great's career in foreign affairs was largely devoted to these two states, although she also liked to pose as leader of Europe in defense of neutral rights against British sea power, in defense of the constitution of Germany, and in opposition to the French Revolution. Catherine collaborated primarily with Prussia against the Poles, and with Austria against the Turks.

The first partition of Poland illustrates Catherine's alternation of the Polish and Turkish themes. When the Empress first seized her throne she began a policy of close collaboration with Prussia which lasted until the 1780's. Catherine and Frederick were of course suspicious of each other, but Frederick badly needed an ally, and Catherine, once she decided she could not hope to have Poland all to herself, needed an accomplice. She and Frederick agreed to preserve the religious rights of minorities and the constitutional liberties in Poland (to interfere, in other words, in favor of Protestants, Orthodox, and the liberum veto). In 1764 they saw to it that Catherine's former lover, Stanislas Poniatowski, was elected King of Poland as Stanislas Augustus (1764–1795). Austria, beaten by Prussia and deserted by Russia in the recent Seven Years War, did not like this solution,

LE GATEAU DES ROIS (1773) by Jean Michel Moreau the Younger, French school (1741–1814). Engraving. Frederick II of Prussia holds the sword. At the left is Catherine II of Russia. Austria is represented by Maria Theresa's son Joseph, whose crown is awry. (Philadelphia Museum of Art)

nor did Turkey, a prospective victim itself, nor did France, with good reason suspicious of the two new aggressive powers in Eastern Europe. But the objectors did not cooperate with each other, whereas Russia and Prussia made an alliance; and so Poniatowski remained.

Poniatowski, however, turned out to be a Polish patriot who took his kingship seriously and encouraged the national revival which was under way.

Poland appeared to be on the road to constitutional reform and an independent foreign policy, but Russia interfered in 1768 and forced the diet to guarantee the old fundamental laws with the elective kingship and the *liberum veto*. Between 1768 and 1772 Polish patriots of the Confederation of Bar resisted this interference, but they were also at odds with the king, with whose program they disagreed, and since they received little aid from abroad they were finally defeated. One of their leaders, Casimir Pulaski, became famous in exile for taking part in the American Revolution.

Meanwhile the attention of Catherine II, which had been largely on Polish affairs since Poniatowski's election, turned toward the Turks, with whom a war broke out in 1768. The first partition of Poland took place in 1772 while this war was still going on.

The Russians were very successful against the Turks, but their successes led to diplomatic difficulties because the Austrians became alarmed at the prospect of Russian penetration of the Balkans. Moreover Prussia, the ally of Russia, disliked the prospect of (1) a partition of Turkey in which it could not participate (because of geography), and (2) a Russian war against Austria, in which it would have to participate. Poland provided a means of satisfying the appetites of all three countries, and thus preserving the balance among them, and that is how the Partition of Poland in 1772 came about in the midst of the Turkish war.

Austria took the province of Galicia in southern Poland. Prussia joined East Prussia to Brandenburg by taking Polish Pomerania. The Russian borders were advanced along the Dvina and the Dnieper. The partition was forced upon the Polish diet.

Meanwhile the Turkish war continued to a successful conclusion. Russia as a result of its agreement with Austria was not able to take the Danubian provinces (later Rumania), but by the treaty of Kuchuk Kainarji in 1774 gained concessions which had great significance for the future. The Crimea was declared independent of Turkey, as a preliminary step to Russia's annexing it (1783). Russia gained a strip of Black Sea coast and the right to send merchant ships through the Bosporus. Russia also won the right to protect Christians within the Ottoman empire and was thereafter in a strong position to pose as defender of the Balkan Slavs or to interfere in Turkish affairs when the occasion suited.

The second and third partitions of Poland took place in 1793 and 1795. In the 1780's Emperor Joseph II's ambitions in the Balkans drew the Habsburg monarchy into closer relations with Russia, where Catherine and her advisor Potemkin were working on a so-called "Greek project" for partitioning the Ottoman empire. These ambitions led to Catherine's second Russo-Turk war, between 1787 and 1792, and to the Treaty of Jassy which extended the Russian holdings on the shores of the Black Sea. Austria entered this war on Russia's side in 1788 and left it in 1791, following Joseph's death.

In Sweden, where Gustavus III since 1772 had built a form of enlightened absolutism, there was uneasiness over Russian expansion. Sweden attempted a comeback against Russia in 1788–1790 and managed for a time to threaten St. Petersburg and keep the Russian fleet from again going to the Mediterranean theater. Catherine encouraged an aristocratic revolt against Gustavus in 1788, but the Swedish king suppressed it. The Russo-Swedish war was a draw.

In Poland, 1788 was the year of the "Great Diet" which was that nation's next to last bid for independence. Since before the first partition of 1772, Polish patriots had been working to modernize the country's institutions and win an independent foreign policy. King Stanislas Augustus had seen most of his early efforts checkmated by Russia. But as the crisis deepened, the level of political discussion rose, and in the Great Diet of 1788–1792 the obstacle of the *liberum veto* was avoided by meeting as a "confederation" where the majority ruled. By this means the diet revised the constitution of Poland along lines suggested by the English and American constitutions and the debates of the French National Assembly. The monarchy was made hereditary to avoid the evils of elections. The *liberum veto* was abolished. Representation and civil rights were granted to the burghers of the towns. The Great Diet had little for the peasants except promises of better treatment; although some reformers wanted to end serfdom and build a more progressive society, they had to keep the support of the gentry if they were to drive foreign influences from Poland.

Like the effort of Sweden, the Polish revival came during Catherine's second war with Turkey. The Poles sought to detach Prussia from Russia while building up an army of their own. In 1790 they made an alliance with Prussia. In 1791 they completed their constitution. But in 1792 Russia made peace with Turkey and invaded Poland on the pretext of defending the traditional constitu-

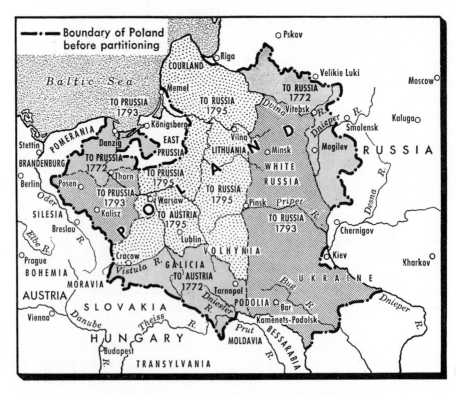

THE PARTITIONS OF POLAND, 1772–1795

tion against subversive principles. Prussia accepted this interpretation, abandoned Poland, and prepared to take part in another partition. Although Thaddeus Kosciuszko, already famous for participation in the American Revolution, led a resistance movement, the King of Poland lost his nerve and joined the small "confederation" of Polish conservatives which Russia was backing. This appeasement failed, and in 1793 a second partition of Poland extended the Russian and Prussian shares. This time Austria got nothing.

In 1794 Kosciuszko made a final effort to free Poland. Hoping for aid from the revolutionary French, he appealed to peasants and townsmen, and managed to hold Warsaw and Vilna for six months. But Prussian and Russian armies put down the insurrection. In 1795 the remains of Poland were partitioned among Russia, Prussia, and Austria. Stanislas Poniatowski died in exile in St. Petersburg. In 1797 the three partitioning powers agreed in secret never again to use the name Poland.

Revolutionary France had been unable to help the Poles. Indeed, the Polish independence movement helped the French Revolution by distracting the great powers which were at war with France. The partitions of Poland preserved the balance of power among Austria, Prussia, and Russia. But they increased the importance of these three eastern states relative to the other powers of Europe. The former great powers of East Central Europe, Sweden, Poland, and Turkey, had now been replaced by Prussia, Austria, and Russia. The many peoples of East Central Europe were now ruled by these three, except for the surviving Swedish and Turkish holdings in the extreme north and south. The stage was set for the nationalistic uprisings of the nineteenth century.

21

THE AGE OF
SCIENCE AND
ENLIGHTENMENT

Usually the whole seventeenth century is thought of as an age of great scientific discoveries, "the century of genius," as it has been called. By the second half of the century the cumulative effects of scientific thinking were impressive, especially in physics and astronomy, but also in other fields including political theory. After 1700 these accomplishments were to continue and be still more widely admired.

With the growth of European wealth and leisure, science and the arts were in the eighteenth century less dependent upon royal and aristocratic patronage. Thanks to a growing market and a new public opinion, artists and thinkers had more chance of independence, though their audiences were still small compared to those of the late nineteenth and twentieth centuries. The peculiar combination of eighteenth-century circumstances—the wider audience, the spread of science into all fields of social science, a growing self-confidence on the part of European thinkers—made possible what is called the Enlightenment, or Age of Reason. To the Humanism of an earlier time were added seventeenth-century science and an eighteenth-century celebration of man's powers. This, in crude approximation, is what was happening to European intellectual life before the French Revolution interposed and before the growing revolt against the Age of Reason shaped a successor, which has been called the Romantic Age.

SEVENTEENTH-CENTURY SCIENCE

Science is an attitude of mind and a technique of investigation. For a time it put Europe ahead of the rest of the world; indeed it gave to European civilization a distinctive flavor and a new kind of faith. Without science one cannot understand Europe's predominance in the modern world, or the social transformations and struggles which have helped Europe to lose that predominance.

Science is hard to define. One of the best introductions is the statement of the American psychologist William James. "I have to forge every sentence in the teeth of irreducible and stubborn facts." *Principles* that correspond with the *facts*—this is the key. There had always been philosophers in search of principles, and there had always been so-called practical men chiefly preoccupied with the facts of everyday life. What modern science did was to join the two, to look for principles through study of the facts. In the sixteenth, seventeenth, and eighteenth centuries an increasing band of educated people became interested in this search, either as practitioners or spectators. Their growth in numbers and influence was a revolution in thought as fundamental as any in the Renaissance or the Reformation.

The story of how this intellectual revolution took place bit by bit while the eyes of most people were turned elsewhere—toward the classics, or Luther's quarrel with Rome, or the overseas explorations, or the Thirty Years War—is too detailed to tell here. A few points may be attempted, however, and a few illustrations given. Speaking very generally of all sciences, with specific reference to none, one may note that the scientific method which grew up in early modern times had at least five elements:

(1) Observation of nature
(2) Use of exact mathematical measurement
(3) Inductive thinking; that is, finding a principle which ties together specific cases: going from facts to principles
(4) Deductive thinking; that is, reasoning *from* principles: "If such and such is true, it follows that . . ."
(5) Experiment; for example, if you observe and measure, and then think you see a principle which accounts for the facts (induction), you can deduce what will happen if the principle is true (applies to all cases), and you can try it. Others can check on you by trying it for themselves.

Until men developed faith that nature was everywhere the same and always worked according to the same principles—in other words that it had a *system*—the process indicated above could not be attempted. Moreover, men had to think it worth while to find out about nature's system. They had also to believe themselves capable of doing so.

No one knows exactly why the scientific method and the state of mind which enabled men to use it arose in Europe rather than, for example, in China. Many parts of European history may be relevant. The Middle Ages, for example, were hampered by the belief that nature was not uniform; that the heavens and earth were made of different "stuff" and, having different degrees of perfection, worked by different rules. In any case, what mattered about objects was not their size or weight, but their purpose in the scheme of things, and medieval men believed that their authorities such as the Bible, or Aristotle, had detailed knowledge of that scheme. One should not, however, make the mistake of calling medieval Europeans nonrational. Scholastic philosophy was very rational, not to say disputatious, and its deductive logic was better preparation for modern science than no logic at all.

The Renaissance did not contribute directly to a great outburst of scientific activity. Humanism, in spite of its care and independent-mindedness in the scholarly analysis of classical texts, was only distantly related to natural science. If the Renaissance is thought of, broadly, as a period of history, the growing complexity of European life with its cities and ships and banking houses and arsenals did produce a store of practical experience. Experience meant facts, and the harnessing of principles to facts was probably aided by the growing interest in the things of this world. While Renaissance attitudes were not automatically scientific and were indeed to some extent antiscientific, Renaissance worldliness and rebellion against medieval authority may have helped to create a climate favorable to science. Not quite as much can be said of the Reformation, which produced the rebellion with less of the worldliness. The Renaissance and Reformation did not, in any case, put science in the place of the authorities which they challenged. But while they were running their course the charms of everyday life were growing with the commercial revolution, state-building, and other secular experiences. And meanwhile a few great scientists were storing up principles illustrating the orderliness of a nature knowable to man.

The most striking example of how scientific theory is cumulative is furnished by the history of astronomy. Here the system of the Egyptian-born Greek scientist, Ptolemy, who had lived in the second century A.D., was overthrown by the system of the sixteenth-century Pole, Copernicus (1473–1543), whose theory was elaborated and checked by the observation of other men.

Ptolemy's theory of why the motions of the heavenly bodies looked the way they do to observers on earth was not unscientific, although it turned out to be inadequate. He assumed the earth to be stationary and the planets to be in motion around it. The solar system which he constructed (theory) was able to account for the motions observable in the heavens (facts), but was terribly complicated. Copernicus, following other critics, found it easier to make a model of the solar system (theory) if he assumed that the earth itself moved around the sun. This heliocentric (sun-centered) theory checked with the facts (observations of motions of heavenly bodies) available to Copernicus, and was confirmed with slight modifications by the observations of such men as the Dane Tycho Brahe (1546–1601) and the German Johannes Kepler (1571–1630). The Italian Galileo (1564–1642) used a telescope to find mountains on the moon and satellites encircling the planet Jupiter. Galileo was tried by the Church for publicizing the heliocentric system, and had to recant, though it is said that he muttered "and yet the earth does move." Galileo also made important contributions to the subject of dynamics; that is, to the study of motion and the forces which produce it.

At first, one might not appreciate the connection between astronomy and Galileo's measurement of the speed of a falling body, or of a ball rolling down an incline. But in fact the laws of motion which Galileo was demonstrating in small earthly examples were to be shown by Isaac Newton to apply in the heavens as well as on earth.

Galileo, for example, refuted Aristotle's venerable notion that a body in motion needed something pushing it. Galileo demonstrated what would later be called "inertia": that a body will continue in a state of rest or motion, which-ever it happens to be in, unless acted upon by some outside force (such as friction in the case of a rolling ball.) When the great Englishman Isaac Newton (1642–1727), who was born in the year of Galileo's death, demonstrated mathematically his great generalization about what holds the solar system together, he used Galileo's principles of dynamics.

For if the moon does not travel off into space never to return, but on the contrary follows a curved path around the earth, something must be pulling it—keeping it from following a straight line as the rolling ball would if not deflected. The same idea applies to the motion of the planets around the sun. Something must keep them from departing in a straight line. The answer, gravitation, as Newton described it, was simply a regularity in nature, a relationship between the masses of bodies and their distances from each other, but it was the greatest regularity yet discovered. It was applicable in the skies and on earth; and it had been demonstrated by a mathematics partly invented by Newton himself (the calculus), and used data provided by the accumulated observations of scientists in many countries.

The international and cooperative character of science not only helped it advance but also made for reliability. All scientific principles, new and old, were exposed to checking by anyone who might wish to do so.

Newton's work stood off all challenges for two centuries. When excep-tions to the law were found in the twentieth century, they opened new paths for research. Modern science has been cumulative and has enlisted the cooperation of different generations. Seventeenth-century science was appreciated by only a minority, even among educated people. The seventeenth century had its prophets, however. Francis Bacon (1561–1626), an English official of the reign of James I, recommended experimentation and inductive thinking and saw the promise of scientific discoveries in transforming civilized life. René Descartes (1596–1650), a French mathematician and philosopher, popularized a method of truth-seeking which called for rejection of all but the most self-evident premises, such as his celebrated "I think, therefore I am," from which further propositions could be deduced. He also taught the value of empirical (starting with the facts) scientific investigation, and experiments, and held out hope that the physical uni-verse could be studied like a great machine understandable through mathe-matics. Descartes, like Newton, did not attack traditional religion, but this cautious attitude probably made men feel freer to search out the secrets of physical nature. In the seventeenth century the social and cooperative traits of science were recognized by the formation of societies like the English Royal

Society for Improving Natural Knowledge (1662) and the French Académie des Sciences (1666) sponsored by Colbert.

The effort to reconcile principles with facts and to investigate with independence of mind touched many fields. In 1628, for example, the English physician William Harvey (1578–1657) exploded an old belief by demonstrating that the human heart is a pump which circulates the blood. In the less material realms of legal practice, historical scholarship, and Biblical criticism, rules of evidence and accurate chronology were developed. Decline of belief in witchcraft in the late seventeenth and eighteenth centuries was aided by changed attitudes toward facts and evidence. Books like the *Law of War and Peace* (1625) by the Dutchman Huig de Groot (Grotius) (1583–1645) illustrate the search for "natural" and "reasonable" standards of conduct in international relations.

Perhaps the best illustrations of the spread of scientific and rational thinking into social science are provided by the political philosophers Thomas Hobbes and John Locke. Hobbes (1588–1679), first of the great English political theorists, took a materialistic and rather mechanical view of people. They were selfish competitors whose ideas came from their sensations and whose lives in a state of nature tended to be "solitary, nasty, brutish, and short." Men could escape this anarchy only by making a contract with each other to submit to a sovereign as long as he was capable of keeping order and protecting them. These ideas, expressed in Hobbes' famous *Leviathan* (1651), reflect somewhat his disgust with the English civil war; but conservative though he was, Hobbes saw government as coming originally from the needs and will of the people, not from any divine right of kings.

Following the "Glorious Revolution" of 1688 another great English theorist, John Locke (1632–1704), published several books which showed how the growing scientific and rationalistic tendencies could be used to serve toleration and resistance to tyranny. Locke interpreted the triumph of Parliament over James II, and the signing of the Bill of Rights of 1689, as natural and reasonable. To Locke the state of nature was not the jungle situation pictured by Hobbes. Men had *natural* rights to life, liberty, and property. When they made a social contract, they did so the better to safeguard these rights against persons (like absolute monarchs) who might flout the law of nature. Thus the state was created to respect and defend the law of nature. If the state itself interfered with the natural rights of individuals, men could resist it. It is easy to understand how Americans like Thomas Jefferson would one day appeal to the writings of Locke in justifying their own revolution. But Locke was also to be remembered in other ways illustrative of the influence of science and rationalism. His belief that ideas were formed from sense impressions was to have a long career in philosophy and psychology. His defense of private property as a mixture of one's labor with a part of nature was used by generations of moralists and turned up later in Karl Marx's labor theory of value. Great Frenchmen whom we are about to meet in the eighteenth-century Enlightenment were deeply influenced by Locke's constitutionalism and political theory.

By the close of the seventeenth century educated Europeans had undergone some severe mental shocks. The tight little universe of their ancestors had been exploded by inquiring minds. Man had lost his place on the center of the stage and was adrift on a minor planet in a mysterious universe. Still, it was man's intelligence which had found this out, and there were signs that the forces of the universe could be harnessed and used. As one historian put it, earth used to be dark but the heavens were light; now the heavens were dark, but earth could be made light. This stage on the way to the faith of the eighteenth-century Enlightenment was well expressed by the quarrel at the end of the seventeenth century called, in France, the "ancients and the moderns," and in England the "battle of the books." Was there any hope that the golden age of the Greeks and Romans could ever be surpassed? To pose the question at all was to be aware that Europeans were showing considerable promise. In the eighteenth-century Enlightenment, the verdict was to be awarded overwhelmingly to the moderns.

THE ENLIGHTENMENT:
ORIGINS AND IDEALS

One convenient way to describe the Enlightenment is to say that men made confident by the accomplishments of seventeenth-century science attempted to apply the scientific method to all fields, to politics, economics, psychology, and ethics. Gifted popularizers spread awareness of science among more people. Many men tried to apply science to human problems. A great formula, Reason-Nature-Progress, provides another entry to the subject-matter and mood of the Enlightenment. Man, by applying his Reason and discovering the laws of Nature, could achieve Progress.

The German philosopher Kant wrote in 1784 that "Enlightenment is the liberation of man from his self-caused state of minority. Minority is the incapacity of using one's understanding without the direction of another . . . Dare to use your own understanding! is thus the motto of the Enlightenment." The American historian Crane Brinton sums up the Enlightenment in its most aggressive form when he describes it as "the belief that all human beings can attain here on this earth a state of perfection hitherto in the West thought to be possible only for Christians in a state of grace, and for them only after death."

A review of the Enlightenment's roots in other historic experiences should help to account for this high confidence. Renaissance humanism had expressed a quickened interest in man's secular life, in the "human." Humanists from the fifteenth to the seventeenth centuries had in varying degrees thrown off medieval canons of interest and taste. They had expressed their inclinations by studying and admiring the classics of the ancient world (thus the classicism in the arts of early modern times). Some of them, such as the cultivated and skeptical French essayist Montaigne (1533–1592), had become tolerant epicureans who believed that life should be enjoyed without forcing one's opinions upon others. This kind of attitude was humane without holding out great hopes for humanity as a whole. When, however, seventeenth-century science gave Humanism a new weapon, a new kind of rationalism which could find out the laws of nature, the stage was set for the Enlightenment.

Other experiences also contributed. The Great Discoveries, besides adding to the comforts of Europe and shaking up society with the rise in prices, made Europeans aware of the many customs of other peoples, thus offering a lesson in comparative cultures. If skepticism was thereby increased, there were also men capable of imagining, under peoples' differences, a great common denominator of basic "natural" institutions and needs. Meanwhile the Protestant Reformation was shaking Europe; from the point of view of some Humanists and most skeptics and partisans of the new scientific rationalism, it was leading backward into barren theological quarrels. In its own way, however, the Reformation contributed to the Enlightenment. In the long run the sight of competing truths (and the realization that life went on in spite of the break-up of the medieval unity of doctrine) contributed to skepticism and toleration. Eventually the example of such countries as England and the Netherlands, prospering in spite of religious disunity, and the English production of thinkers such as Newton and Locke, proved an inspiration to continental writers ambitious for freedom of expression.

Related to the historic background of the Enlightenment is the environment in which it took place. Concentrating for the moment on France alone, we may remember that the rise of a middle class, still small, but rich, provided both a market for books and young men aspiring to education and literary fame. With their sympathizers in the nobility and lower orders, the *bourgeoisie* dominated the towns and the new "public opinion" so characteristic of the eighteenth century. French *philosophes,* popularizers and searchers for practical applications of the new vogue of Reason and Nature, expressed in their optimism the euphoria of a century in which the upper classes, at least, knew increasing well-being. The *philosophes* expressed, also, the "good conscience" of the *bourgeoisie* and of their noble sympathizers who recognized that middle-class people, although barred from the highest offices and honors in the state, were contributing much to France's prosperity and intellectual progress. As the century advanced, it became more and more difficult, and eventually impossible, to censor the works of these men. But while the censorship by state and church remained effective—until about 1770—it contributed to some of the qualities of the Enlightenment; to the tendency to generalize in order to escape punishment for specific criticisms; to the use of satire and ridicule instead of direct attack.

Of all the varied and complicated ideas of the Enlightenment, we can consider only a few.

Nature, for example, could mean the great design of the universe whose contours had been disclosed by Newton's mathematical science. In general, the men of the Enlightenment, unlike those of the nineteenth century, did not think of the grand Natural Order as evolving. Some men groped toward evolutionary theories, but most educated and half-educated persons thought of the Natural Order as a kind of great clock, having motion but basically unchanging. It was this mechanism which man's Reason could understand. Reason might also show natural laws to be psychological, like Locke's theory that ideas come

DECORATION OF THE THEATER AT VERSAILLES FOR THE PRESENTATION OF THE COMEDY BALLET "PRINCESSE DE NAVARRE" by Charles Nicholas Cochin. Engraving (1746). The play was by Voltaire, the music by Jean-Philippe Rameau. The theater was especially constructed for the occasion. (Philadelphia Museum of Art)

from arrangements of sensations imprinted by experience on the *tabula rasa* (blank page) of the mind. Or natural laws might be the inescapable truths of economics demonstrated by the Physiocrats or by Adam Smith, whose work will be discussed below.

Reason itself did not always have the same meaning. To some, it meant the analytical separation of familiar ideas into their component parts, probing as closely as possible to the original sensations indicated by Locke. To others, Reason meant the drawing of inferences from assembled data, as Bacon had recommended. To still others, Reason was scientific method in its full panoply of induction, deduction, mathematical measurement, and experimentation. Toward the end of the era Rousseau excited innumerable readers by showing that the heart has its reasons, more indicative of Nature's wishes, perhaps, than all the arguments of philosophy. To many, Nature came to mean simple country life, away from the oversophisticated and "unnatural" cities, or better still, frontier life like that lived in the American colonies.

Reason and Nature, although variously used, were consistently useful weapons for attacking the old regime. It was easy to label "unreasonable" and "unnatural" the practices one disliked, and old, complicated Europe was full of arrangements whose only recommendation seemed to be their longevity. Mere age, or tradition, to the *philosophes* was no justification at all. More often than not, they viewed history as a record of unreasonableness, a museum of absurdities. The eighteenth century has often been called "unhistorical" because men wrote history didactically, to illustrate their convictions, instead of for its own sake; yet there were advances. Voltaire, for instance, enriched the subject matter of history by including social and intellectual material.

Free inquiry and toleration were articles of faith in the Enlightenment, not only because it was inhumane and useless to bully people into conforming without inner conviction, but also because progress would be more rapid if more minds were at work on mankind's problems. The *philosophes* were confident that freedom would lead to agreement, not anarchy: since nature was one, reasonable men would sooner or later come to the same opinion on any subject. Man and nature being everywhere basically the same, the *philosophes* were cosmopolitan in their outlook, emphasizing the underlying humanity of Europeans, American Indians, Chinese, and so on, rather than national and cultural differences. This cosmopolitanism in thought was paralleled by a cosmopolitanism of fact in the minority of educated Europeans, and especially in the nobles of the eighteenth century, who everywhere tended to speak French, have similar classical educations and gentlemanly manners, and be familiar with the stock of ideas which we have been describing. In spite of the Pope's interdictions, lodges of Freemasons appeared all over Europe and enrolled the most distinguished of members —Montesquieu, Voltaire, the Holy Roman Emperor Francis I, husband of Maria Theresa, Frederick the Great of Prussia. Claiming descent from organizations of actual medieval masons—the kind who built the cathedrals—the eighteenth-century Freemasons became an international order of deistic (see p. 339) rationalists dedicated to social and moral improvement.

THE ENLIGHTENMENT: APPLICATIONS

Many of the points of view characteristic of the Enlightenment are best seen as practical applications of the Reason-Nature-Progress formula. In religion, for example, a "natural religion" was arrived at by imagining all the world's peoples and their religions arrayed together and by taking from these the basic principles of belief in God, a life after death (usually), and a few simple moral principles. Surely a "deism" appearing so universally and insistently must be "natural," and by the same token all the theological and ceremonial complications of the particular religions must be superfluous. If one did not like this Grand Tour method of thinking about religion, there was always the argument that the great Newtonian design of the universe must have a designer. Clearly God, in this capacity, no longer interfered in the machine's workings; there were no miracles. Especially in the latter part of the eighteenth century, some *philosophes,* like Holbach, became atheists because they were contented to leave the machine's origin unexplained and to admire its workings and man's cleverness in analyzing them. Atheists like Holbach were few in number and indeed atheists, deists, and all *philosophes* and educated people together were a minority.

Among the great public, traditional Christianity went its way, unaware of Voltairian wit or Holbachian disbelief. The industries and slums of the nineteenth century probably did more to dissolve traditional religious practices than the pamphlets of the eighteenth. Yet it was no small matter that the portion of society which we today would call the "intellectuals" were deserting Christianity in its traditional form and denying its right to guide man's aspirations and control his acts.

The characteristic social science of the Enlightenment was based mainly on John Locke's psychology of the *tabula rasa.* As the basis for morals and politics, this psychology had many implications. All humans were equal at birth; none knew anything. If they later became geniuses or brutes, surely the environment was at fault. Change the environment (attack the old regime) and you can improve mankind! Part of the environment, and the part needing most immediate attention, was the school; but in the last analysis the whole society was a school which would have to be good if there were to be good people. But "goodness" was to this characteristic eighteenth-century psychology an affair of the senses, of this world, of happiness. Ideas were said to be obtained through the senses and then rearranged into larger concepts, including those of good and bad, which were like recollections of pleasure and pain. Goodness for a whole community was that which gave the most pleasure at the lowest cost in pain: the greatest good of the greatest number. This "utilitarian" principle, taught by Helvetius and others in France, and later popularized in England by Jeremy Bentham, had a fine cutting edge when set against old institutions.

Utilitarianism did not have a monopoly on enlightened minds of the

eighteenth century, but it had the advantage of being somewhat more sophisticated than the older "natural rights" doctrine, which held that certain truths
were self-evident to any reasonable mind. Many eighteenth-century people continued to assume that the wavelength from nature's moral requirements was
precisely attuned for good reception in the minds of reasonable men. The Scottish philosopher David Hume (1711–1776) was exceptionally astute—certainly
more so than most men of the Enlightenment— when he pointed out that man's
reason, contemplating the facts of nature, could know the consequences of certain acts without any hint from nature as to whether they were right or wrong.
Man would still have to choose, to *want* and *will* one course of action or another,
and he would probably do best to be guided by custom. But Hume was an exception in an age whose intellectuals leaned mainly toward Natural Rights or
Utilitarianism. That age was nearing its end when (in opposition to uncritical
emphasis on reason) Jean Jacques Rousseau (1712–1778) began to celebrate the
naturalness of feelings and sentiments, and the German philosopher Kant (1724–
1804), influenced by both Hume and Rousseau, said that man's moral nature and
the nature and existence of God were not subject to the proofs of physical science.

In economic thinking the Enlightenment is chiefly remembered for two
outstanding efforts, the first modern "schools" of economics (if one defines
mercantilism not as a "school" but as merely a collection of policy recommendations). These were the Physiocrats, whose greatest influence was in the 1760's
in France, and the work of Adam Smith, the Scottish moral philosopher and
economist whose *Wealth of Nations* was published in 1776. Before describing
these efforts it is important to realize that they were not bolts from the blue. In
the eighteenth century, mercantilism was facing a growing murmur of criticisms, especially in France and England. The term *laissez faire,* which meant
"leave alone," came to be used to express the point of view that if one did not
interfere, nature would regulate sufficiently.

Physiocracy, which meant "rule of nature," was led by François Quesnay
(1694–1774), court doctor of Louis XV, and by Du Pont de Nemours (1739–
1817). Its most typical expressions—Quesnay's *Tableau économique* (1758) and
Du Pont's *Physiocratie* (1768) argued that there was a natural order in human
society, built on natural rights of property and liberty. The best form of government was absolute monarchy, but the king was not a despot: he did not *make*
the laws but merely presided over persons who, like himself, recognized their existence. It was possible to build a good society on these laws, whose workings were
mathematically demonstrable. The key to economics was the circulation of
wealth among the parts of society. Land was the only producer of new wealth—of
a "net product" or remainder after all expenses of production were paid. Everyone but the proprietors of land was in effect like a wage earner paid out of the
proprietors' net product in a complex process of circulating wealth. Regulations
hindering free choice of occupation, conduct of business or agriculture, or shipment of goods, would cut into the efficiency of the system. Individuals were best
able to judge their own interests, and the public interest was the sum of individual
interests.

Adam Smith's *Wealth of Nations* (1776) was similar to Physiocracy in its emphasis on freedom and individualism in economics. Smith analyzed the processes of production and exchange of goods. In his famous example of the pin factory he showed how "division of labor," that is, each worker specializing in a part of the manufacturing process, could produce many times the number of pins made by individual artisans each making whole pins. Division of labor also applied to regions and nations, each doing what it could do best, but the success of such a system required freedom of trade and exchange if the benefits of increased productivity by this method were to be obtained. Smith went further toward economic individualism than his predecessors or contemporaries. He was, however, a moderate, practical man, who realized that as long as nations were military competitors some mercantilistic restrictions would have to be kept. He was by no means an apologist for employers against laborers, and deplored the tendency of manufacturers to exploit their workers and form combinations in restraint of trade. A typical man of the Enlightenment, Smith remained optimistic and humanitarian. It was his followers of the early nineteenth century, the "classical economists," who worked out the implications of *laissez faire* in a manner which made economics into the "dismal science"—dismal at least from the point of view of the numerous poor, condemned by "economic laws" to remain so.

In spite of the onslaughts of the economic liberals of the eighteenth century, mercantilism, the doctrine of a state-regulated economy, survived in practice and even in the writings of some economists. In economic thinking, however, as in psychology and moral philosophy, the Enlightenment contributed much to a rising tide of individualism. Where the medieval period had emphasized regulations in the name of religion and town life, and early modern times had emphasized safeguards erected by the state, the currents of the Enlightenment were running strongly toward trusting social control to the hands of individuals.

Educated people of the eighteenth century had in their minds a picture of how society must have formed. Somewhere in the distant past men must have realized that they were better off together than alone. Whether men had ever actually gathered together to make a contract made little difference. Whether one believed in natural rights or utilitarianism, there lay back of society and government the interest of individuals and therefore their consent.

Moreover the individuals could in most respects be presumed to be equal. Whether one accepted Locke's psychology of the *tabula rasa* or was contented with self-evident priciples that any reasonable person could not help seeing, all humans were equal in the eyes of nature. Nature meant *all* to be happy, not just a few aristocrats: this was one of the most revolutionary notions spawned by the Enlightenment.

The equality of persons before the law was not, however, incompatible with the ambitions of rulers like Frederick the Great and Joseph II of Austria and Catherine II of Russia. As long as equality did not mean self-government, it was to the advantage of "enlightened despots" to reduce everyone, including the great nobles, to uniform subjection in the name of efficiency and justice. Equality did not mean anything so radical as the sharing of wealth or the desirability of equal social status for everyone. Except for a few dreamers like Morelly and Mably in France or Spence and Ogilvie in England, eighteenth-century men were solidly and overwhelmingly in favor of private property either as a natural right or as a utilitarian necessity. Property was sacred either because (as Locke said) a man in mixing his labor with the earth's fruits imparted to them something of himself, or because (as the Physiocrats said) population grew too big for man to survive by just gathering nature's spontaneous productions, and to stimulate cultivation it became necessary to divide up the land. Along with private property the educated person of the eighteenth century accepted social differences—not necessarily hereditary ones, for few would have denied equality of opportunity— but differences based on the need for all kinds of work. Listen to Voltaire: "It is impossible in our unfortunate world for men to live in society without being divided into two classes: one the rich who command; the other the poor who serve; and these two are subdivided into a thousand; and these thousand still have various nuances."

Educated people who shared the ordinary enthusiasms of the age were inclined to attach little importance to political forms provided civil liberties were respected. Although the theoretical possibility of republican, aristocratic, and monarchical governments was recognized, most men took monarchy for granted. It was considered good form to express admiration for republics, adding that these virtuous governments were best adapted to small states like Geneva or the Greek cities of the ancient world. The three most famous writers of the century, Montesquieu, Voltaire, and Rousseau, all supported monarchy in practice, while allowing themselves brilliant digressions about other forms of government. Monarchy, however, could mean different things to different men. It is instructive to compare Montesquieu, Voltaire, and Rousseau, realizing that a brief treatment must be simplified and must refer mainly to their political views.

THREE GIANTS OF THE ENLIGHTENMENT

Montesquieu (1689–1755) was a "nobleman of the robe" who inherited a seat in the *parlement* of Bordeaux. He carried this background and training with him when he later turned to travel and writing and became France's foremost eighteenth-century social scientist. His book *The Spirit of the Laws* (1748) had everything to make it influential: style, erudition, scientific detachment, and a rich collection of examples which showed the kinds of government and the influence of geography and climate on human institutions. The work had its critics, but in the long run it pleased almost everyone and was used by the defenders of absolute monarchy and old-regime society as well as by liberal admirers of the English government.

Montesquieu praised the English constitution, which he (mistakenly) supposed to be based on a separation of "executive, legislative, and judicial powers." He was a great liberal who wished to show how governments could avoid arbitrary actions and the pitfalls of despotism or democracy (arbitrariness by the one or the many). Yet he was also, paradoxically, a great conservative who wished to acknowledge and preserve the best that was present in old-regime France. He did not recommend that France copy England. France had a constitution of her own bequeathed her by history. The government was an absolute monarchy and the king was sovereign. In practice however—and this was the *spirit* of the laws—the French king had full executive power, shared the legislative power with the *parlements,* and left the judicial power in the latter's hands. The French nobles of sword and robe, rightfully endowed with privileges which had a historic sanction, acted as *intermediaries* between king and people, protecting each from the arbitrariness of the other. The privileges of the nobles, clergy, *parlements,* provinces, and towns served this function. Every government had its principle, and the principle of monarchy was *honor*—the self-respect and independent-mindedness nurtured by historic privileges.

Montesquieu subscribed in the main to the thesis, popular among nobles of the late seventeenth and eighteenth centuries, that the distinctions enjoyed by the French nobility dated back to their ancestors, the conquering Franks, who had come from the forests of Germany bringing with them the habits of liberty. Thus unwittingly he contributed to later nineteenth- and twentieth-century racial doctrines which attributed political superiority to "Nordic" and "Aryan" blood and institutions. Far more important, however, was his impact on his own times through his immense popularity, which gave prestige to the resistance of the *parlements* to the king's officials. He influenced European and American liberals who adopted his liking for the separating and balancing of governmental powers. In addition, his work provided inspiration during the revolutionary period for conservatives like Edmund Burke who liked to emphasize the evolution of complex arrangements through the generations.

Voltaire (1694–1778) was a supremely talented bourgeois whose real name was François Marie Arouet. He was a professional writer, one of the first to make a fortune from the new reading public. Author of poetry, dramas, history, literary criticism, popular science, fiction, and innumerable pamphlets on subjects of current interest, he became internationally famous, knew the great, corresponded with Catherine of Russia, visited Frederick II of Prussia, and enjoyed offices and favors bestowed by the French court. He was an indefatigable craftsman with a clear, precise style and complete mastery of the art of ridicule. When he was young he was beaten up by the lackeys of a nobleman whom he had insulted, and on another occasion served a term in the Bastille for his impudence to the authorities. He visited England and admired its liberties; when someone alluded to the corruption of some members of Parliament he is said to have remarked that nobody bothers to buy *us—we* don't count that much. He was an irrepressible champion of human freedom and toleration and more than once staked his reputation in specific cases, as when he fought to clear the name of Jean Calas, a Protestant executed for supposedly murdering his son in order to keep him from becoming a Catholic.

Voltaire's greatest target was the Church as it then existed. His slogan *Ecrasez l'infâme!* (Crush the infamous thing!) was directed at intolerance, cruelty, and censorship in the name of religion. More than anyone in his century he was the father of the anticlericalism which was to play such a large part in nineteenth- and twentieth-century French politics. Yet Voltaire, like most men of the Enlightenment, thought that traditional religion was important in the lives of the lower classes. He did not even propose separation of church and state; he merely wanted a state religion properly supervised to insure toleration and respect for individual rights. For himself and other intellectuals Voltaire asked only "natural religion" of a deistic sort.

In political theory Voltaire is usually classified with the Physiocrats and other partisans of an "enlightened despotism" which would let the king retain absolute authority provided he used it only to make people conform to natural laws. Certainly this bourgeois rationalist, although he approved of Montesquieu's search for liberty, would have none of the great political scientist's historical and traditionalistic justifications of the privileges of the old regime. Voltaire lived so long and was such an old hand at keeping out of unnecessary trouble that it is hard to know whether in his last years he still believed enlightened despotism possible in France. He certainly did his share of praising England, but he probably paid little attention to the machinery of the English government. Certainly during most of his lifetime Voltaire would have settled for an absolute monarchy which presided over a free and open society, the ideal for which the French middle class waited in vain.

Jean Jacques Rousseau (1712–1778) was a prophet of democracy whose ideas were to be exploited by modern dictatorships. He was the father of progressive education. He translated the slogans of the Enlightenment into sentimental terms which the common people could appreciate, and was the first great writer of that Romantic movement which was to be in vogue after the French Revolution and the Napoleonic Wars. Rousseau was all of these without intending to be any —his influence went far beyond any positive programs he recommended. He himself was a timid and suspicious person who found it difficult to adapt to any circumstances except solitude. Yet after running away from his native Geneva at the age of sixteen he managed to find patrons and admirers from one end of Europe to the other. In spite of severe personal maladjustments, Rousseau used the genius of his sensitivity and uninhibited imagination to express feelings which a great many of his contemporaries shared. His rhythmic oratorical style captivated his generation.

At first Rousseau seemed to be an adventurer simply trying to attract attention. He wrote, in the midst of the Enlightenment, that the advance of the arts and sciences was not making men better but, on the contrary, was accompanied by increasing corruption (*Discourse on the Arts and Sciences*, 1750). Men in a state of nature had been noble and happy, but when they tried to perfect their condition they formed society, divided up the land, and began building institutions for the preservation of inequality, competition, wickedness, and wars (*Discourse on the Origin and Bases of Inequality*, 1754). Rousseau seemed to be against the Reason and Progress of the Enlightenment, keeping only the Nature, but further writings showed him attempting no return to savagery but merely seeking the natural in the midst of civilization. *Émile* (1762) told the story of a young man's education which encouraged and guided without distorting natural impulses. It was becoming clear that Rousseau's way of consulting Nature on fundamental questions was not just to reason but to seek an inner light, a conscience. The twenty-year-old Emile learns that philosophers may quarrel in matters of religion but if he looks sincerely for his innermost convictions he cannot but see that there is a God and another life. If he consults his conscience he will know right from wrong. Rousseau did not abandon Reason, but he was convinced that deep down in every man, beneath the selfish will inspired by his passions of the moment, there was a "general will," an understanding of "what man can demand of his fellow man and what his fellow man has a right to demand of him." This general will was the same for all men. It was a single destination which everyone could reach if selfishness and distractions were put aside. It was possible for men who lived right and consulted their consciences under proper conditions to agree with each other.

Rousseau used the general will in his *Social Contract* (1762), the work on political theory in which he tried to explain how men could have states and governments and still be free. He was still worrying about the growth of unnatural, oppressive institutions and habits. "Man is born free, yet everywhere he is in chains." Granted that civilization could not be abandoned, how could one be "natural" within civilization? If men made a contract with each other to form a community ruled by the general will, they would still be free; for the general will was what was natural and right, what everyone wanted. As long as the law was merely an expression of the general will, everyone without exception could be said to be consenting to the law. Rousseau's theory was democratic because no matter what the form of government, the social contract and the general will made it the people's government. Rousseau admitted that he was only theorizing, and that only in a very small state in a condition of unusual virtue could the people assemble to make the laws themselves with a probability that the laws so made would express the general will. Even so, the theory implied condemnation of any laws by any government, no matter how imposing, if the people's interests were flouted. But on the other hand it was going to be possible, as history would demonstrate more than once, for a minority, or even a single dictator, to claim knowledge of the general will and oppress the people in its name.

Montesquieu, Voltaire, and Rousseau are outstanding examples of the various ways of being Enlightened in the eighteenth century. There are other illustrations, of course, chief among them being the "Encyclopedists," contributors to the great collective effort which was the seventeen volumes of the *Encyclopedia* (1751 ff.) edited by Diderot and d'Alembert. Most of the French *philosophes* contributed to this great "reasoned dictionary" proudly summing up mankind's accumulated knowledge. The *Encyclopedia*, devoted to scientific, historical, and technical subjects, was not aimed at political ends. It is a good illustration of the indirect way in which the Enlightenment undermined the old regime. By self-confidently proclaiming man's abilities, by announcing principles that justified criticism in any field to which man might wish to turn his mind, by simply existing in the midst of traditional beliefs and practices, the writings of the Enlightenment served as a kind of declaration of independence. The intellectual origins of the French Revolution did not consist of reasoned appeals for insur-

ALLEGORICAL FRONTISPIECE OF "L'ENCYCLOPEDIE" by Charles Nicholas
Cochin. Engraving by B. L. Prevost. (Philadelphia Museum of Art)

rection, but the writings of the Enlightenment, loaded with assumptions about men's rights and abilities, served notice to the men in power that they had to promote progress or let someone else try.

CONCLUSIONS

The various parts of Europe and the New World experienced the intellectual fashions of the age in differing ways. In England the ideas of John Locke amounted to a defense of the existing order, while in France or elsewhere these same ideas were revolutionary in their implications. If England in the eighteenth century enjoyed a complacency which was to last until the unsettling effects of the French Revolution and the early Industrial Revolution, Scotland could produce the skepticism of a David Hume and the constructive criticisms of an Adam Smith. German thinkers were still in a stage characterized by the great poet-philosopher Wolfgang Goethe's (1749–1832) patronage by the Duke of Weimar. German thought tended to be abstract and academic, but Kant and Goethe illustrate the moral preoccupations of that time and place. In America men like Jefferson and Franklin were products of the French and English Enlightenments. The American Revolution was to be made in the name of the principles of the Enlightenment; when the historic rights of Englishmen appeared to be more useful to the mother country than to the colonies, the Americans turned to more abstract and less historical principles.

The Enlightenment differed not only in place but also in time. In France the first half of the eighteenth century was still characterized by rather theoretical, deductive thinking and by the absence of a wide public to whom writers could appeal. In the middle of the century, from about 1740 to 1760, "empiricism"— using facts on which to build theories—became more popular, and people valued the collection and evaluation of facts much more than previously. The public was interested in all sorts of practical problems having to do with government and society. This central part of the century also witnessed a triumph of toleration and the discrediting of the Church as a censoring agency and exclusive guide to right living. There was a larger public now, and although there were scarcely any appeals for an overthrow of the government the latter's actions were certainly no longer considered to be above criticism. Radicalism took the form of intensified curiosity and refusal to place any subject beyond the reach of inquisitiveness. There was also an increased tendency to carry principles to their logical conclusions, as when the Physiocrats worked out the implications of their premises about economics and the Utilitarians worked out those of John Locke's psychology.

After the 1760's sentiment was added to the stock of popular eighteenth-century attitudes. Especially to followers of Rousseau, to be "natural" was not merely to be reasonable but in the last analysis to trust one's feelings—about family, country, right and wrong. Men who were unspoiled because they lived in simple surroundings and were neither too rich nor too poor could be trusted to react impulsively in the "natural" way to the problems life presented. Although there were profound differences of outlook in the generation that went into the French Revolution, both reason and sentiment could be used to condemn the old society. Both were to help build the nineteenth-century outlook on life.

The Enlightenment, like the humanistic studies of the Renaissance, was the property of the few. In the eighteenth century the majority of the people continued to follow old customs of thought and action or to find new enthusiasms alien to the tastes of the aristocracy of birth and wealth and intellect. It would be a mistake to forget the popular religious movements such as Methodism in England or Pietism in Germany, or the continued strength of Catholicism in France in the face of all the barbs of the *philosophes*. But the Enlightenment touched more people than Renaissance Humanism ever had. Its ideas in simplified form left the drawing rooms for the street corners. It was a step toward the broader public opinion of the nineteenth century and the mass opinions of the twentieth.

The nineteenth and twentieth centuries, moved by the French Revolutionary and Napoleonic upheavals and the material and social changes of industrialism, were to look back at the Enlightenment and see shortcomings. It became commonplace to point to the opinions of the *philosophes* and call them oversimplified, obsessed with Reason to a point where they neglected the irrational elements in the human make-up, overanalytical, blind to the power and creativeness of slow evolutionary change and to the complexities of societies thus evolved. These assertions carry much truth, but it would be unhistorical to expect the men of the eighteenth century to behave like those who had shared the experiences of the nineteenth and twentieth.

Professor Carl Becker in the interlude between two world wars observed that the Enlightenment had not broken completely with the past. In his *Heavenly City of the Eighteenth Century Philosophers,* Becker argued brilliantly that the men of the Enlightenment, with their religion of humanitarianism, wrote their own version of the Christian story, preserving many essentially Christian values. Here too there is much truth. It is probable, however, that the Enlightenment involved a greater revision of Europe's traditional outlook than anything in the Renaissance or Reformation; that the Enlightenment, with its deification of man, took the longest step yet taken toward the mixture of pride and dismay with which we of the contemporary world examine our condition.

PART THREE

REVOLU-
TIONARY
AND
CONSERVA-
TIVE
EUROPE

1789–1870

22

THE FALL OF
THE FRENCH
MONARCHY

THE FRENCH REVOLUTION belongs to world history because it posed and tried to answer universal questions about society and politics. It belongs to European history because at the end of the eighteenth century Europe was ready to face the same problems, or would soon be forced to do so. It belongs to the French nation because, in spite of its universal and epochal significance, it was uniquely theirs. No people ever repeated the French Revolution; none ever passed through the same sequence—material and intellectual and emotional. Nor is the France of today conceivable except against this background.

But it would be a mistake to think that all revolutionary ideas and practices at the end of the eighteenth century originated in France. In the broadest perspective the French Revolution was part of a great movement toward self-government and a freer society which was to triumph in western Europe and America by the mid-nineteenth century. The French experience was not the "cause" of this enormous evolution in ideals and practices. It was the most force-ful, dramatic, and influential expression of a movement which, before the famous outburst in France, appeared independently and with local variations in the American colonies, Switzerland, the Netherlands, Ireland, and parts of Italy.

Historians are still trying to disentangle the French from the native and autonomous influences in appraising this great revolutionary era in European history. This much is clear: that political and social ideals were changing more rapidly in Western Europe than in Central and Eastern Europe and similarly underdeveloped parts of southern Italy and Spain; that America, despite the breadth of the Atlantic, shared in the developments occurring in western Europe; and that these political developments were somehow related to the growth of a more complicated commercial and industrial society.

The French Revolution "toured the world." In Europe in the nineteenth century, every country had to honor the principles of 1789 or find means to oppose them. Eventually they reached as far as China, Equatorial Africa, and Latin America. They are still recognizably at work today, even in those areas which are most ferociously striving for independence from European control. Much of this influence is directly traceable to the dramatic events of the revolutionary era. In every instance, however, it is vital to study revolutionary movements in their native setting, as we shall do in the case of the French Revolution.

CAUSES OF THE REVOLUTION

In the words of a great historian, the French Revolution came about because of an "ever increasing divorce between law and reality, between institutions and moral standards, between the letter and the spirit."[1]

In the old regime the law was the absolute monarchy. The king was supposed to be too powerful and rich to be tempted by anything except glory for himself and his people. He was therefore the ideal defender of the general welfare against special interests. In reality, although many of the king's actions were indeed directed toward the general welfare, he was surrounded by special interests, particularly those of the nobility. He was to a high degree their prisoner.

France's kings had once built a machinery of state which had enabled them to take the government away from the nobles. Leaving the aristocracy material and social privileges, they drew upon the brains and wealth of the commoners to modernize the state and its policies in a manner calculated to encourage the aspirations of all groups in society. France shared in the advancing wealth and culture of Western Europe, and grew mighty, but the machinery of state failed to keep pace. The very growth of the country—in population, wealth, knowledge, self-confidence—called for improvements which only the state could provide: for taxes and tariffs which did not discourage agriculture and other forms of business; for one system of weights and measures; for greater uniformity and predictability in the national policies. The monarchy, if it had been able to meet this challenge, would have become what is usually called an "enlightened despotism" and would have profited both in power and in popularity. Absolute in theory, in fact the king was faced with powerful aristocratic resistance whenever he allowed reforming ministers to tamper with the safeguards of the old society.

Socially, the old regime in France presents to the eye an intricate network of groups related to each other and to the state. The legal divisions were the three

[1] Albert Mathiez, *La Révolution française*, I, 1.

"estates," clergy, nobility, and commoners. But each estate had many levels, and on every level there were organized groups like the guilds, the municipalities, the provincial estates, the peasant villages, the assemblies of the clergy, and the professional bodies of attorneys and judges. Within this complicated edifice, each group had its chartered or traditional liberties, each its *esprit de corps*. In theory, individuals derived their rights and liberties through membership in a group or class. In practice the rights of the individual depended on the ability of the group to defend its members. Over all the king presided, acting as a kind of umpire, responding to pressures from their various assemblies and officials. It was a system of complexity and of theoretical symmetry, providing a place, and privileges, for everyone according to his profession and service to society. But inequality was built into this system, and social and economic changes were creating contrasts between theory and fact. The new wealth and self-confidence of many commoners, the yearning for equality, the land-hunger of the peasants—all the accumulations of a century of change placed a strain on the old formal categories of persons. It was as if within the antique groupings based on birth and profession a new society were struggling to be set free, a society with ranks based largely on wealth and ability.

The more or less official economic philosophy of France was still mercantilism, which justified government intervention on behalf of the state's unity, wealth, and power, and for the welfare of the public. Many government officials were being won over to ideas of economic freedom, however, as they came to appreciate the energy of the businessmen, the most successful of whom were convinced that the government was wisest which interfered least with the public's good judgment of its own interests. Among the lesser artisans and shopkeepers, fear of competition was often more characteristic than the self-confidence of the great merchant manufacturers and wholesalers, but probably the general economic advance of the eighteenth century was accompanied by a mood of optimism. Among educated people the slogans of the Enlightenment about man's ability to progress through understanding nature's laws acted as a stimulant and seemed justified by the century's economic and cultural advances.

The attack on the old regime is often associated with the writers of the Enlightenment. The French Revolution was not the work of the Enlightenment in any crude sense, for none of the influential *philosophes* plotted or recommended revolt, but in a deeper sense they did help to subvert the old order. Their ideas encouraged a spirit of curiosity, of self-confidence, of lack of reverence for authority and tradition; to that extent the Enlightenment helped bring about the revolution. For the most part its influence was indirect. It encouraged men to feel that there was nothing inappropriate about discussing taxes and treaties and the expenditures of the court at Versailles. But the Enlightenment was a direct assault on the view of man as essentially childish and needful of the supervision of kings and priests. As such it played a part whenever everyday disputes about taxation or other government policies reached a pitch requiring appeal to fundamental principles.

There are many myths about the French Revolution. One of them is that the people arose spontaneously, in dire economic need, against their oppressors.

Another is that not misery, but prosperity, caused the revolution—it is sometimes said that a middle class already triumphant in everything but politics took over the rule of France.

On the whole, true, the eighteenth century was one of prosperity for France. In comparison with the nobles, who also prospered, the middle class took a commanding lead numerically, financially, in service to the economy, and in their contribution to the state, even though they were increasingly barred from higher offices in the government and church. They did not plot the revolution. Indeed, having much to lose, they entered it with a certain trepidation. Nevertheless, when the monarchy proved incapable of modernizing its policies and policy-making, many middle-class leaders were at hand, prepared by the professions and by local and business experience. Familiar with the ideas of the Enlightenment and sharing its optimism, they were confident, in some cases overconfident. Without doubt the economic development of the country had contributed to this state of affairs, and therefore to the revolution.

It is also true, however, that the economy took a turn for the worse in the late 1770's and that a downward drift of agricultural prices, lasting into 1790, spread fear and suspicion in many ways. Most important was the hardship of the peasants who were a majority of the nation. Whatever their position, whether landholders subject to seigneurial dues, or tenants, or share-croppers, or a combination of these, most of the peasants found themselves with smaller profits out of which to pay their obligations to the state, the church, and the seigneur. The rising population resulted in greater demand for land, which forced rents upward; and dues-collecting nobles, trying by every means to increase their incomes, tightened the screws. Because at this stage the French economy was dominated by agriculture, industry and commerce suffered from the inability of the peasants to buy. Occasional poor harvests, as in 1788, led to shortages. These caused swift temporary increases in the prices of farm products, but most peasants, after feeding their own large families, had little left to sell, and only the minority of large landholders profited.

The peasants did not plot the revolution or begin it, but their desire for more land, their hostility toward the seigneurs, and their impatience at seigneurial dues made them potentially dangerous. Agricultural and business depression led to unemployment and to the presence of vagabonds on the roads and in the towns and built up nervousness about the safety of livestock, barns, and crops. Rumors spread in villages and marketplaces. The very sight of grain wagons moving toward areas of shortage gave rise to talk of speculators and government connivance. More literate and politically minded people, especially in the towns, could easily blame the government and its officials for discomforts whose origin was really too complicated for their understanding. The weight of taxes *seemed* to stem from extravagance at Versailles, and the business slump *seemed* to be the work of foolish or corrupt ministers who had negotiated the low-tariff Eden Treaty (1786) with England.

French aid to the revolting American colonies shows the web of circumstances which lay back of the French Revolution. Great Britain, the time-honored antagonist in the struggle for overseas commerce and empire, was defeated. In the years between the American and French revolutions the threat of French bankruptcy was in part a result of France's heavy outlays in the War of American Independence. But this financial problem, which was the fuse igniting the revolution, was the result of a political rather than a military or diplomatic failing. France was big enough and rich enough to pay for its wars; if it could not do so, the fault lay with a government unwilling or unable to clean and sharpen its taxes and levy them on the real wealth of the country. However, the origins of the shortage of revenue were also economic, for the reduced farm and business income of the last decade of the old regime made the taxes (and the church's tithe and the dues of the seigneur) seem more burdensome than they had seemed before, when in reality they were not greatly changed.

The efforts to reform the finances led to quarrels in which people were talking about taxes but really thinking about the threat or promise of doing away with the old society of hereditary privileges. Such quarrels had to be settled in the political arena. All this took place against the background of the popular ideas of the Enlightenment, made manifest by the Americans with their Declaration of Independence, their state constitutions, and their philosophical diplomat Benjamin Franklin. But it took place also at a time when depression had accentuated the long-term grievances within the society and made people more than ordinarily irritable.

OUTBREAK: 1787–1789

All of the influences described above came together with unusual force in the period 1787–1789. The revolution was already under way.

The Controller General, the brilliant, persuasive Calonne, who had been in office since 1783, was finally forced by the treasury's needs to prepare a reform program which struck at the exemptions of the nobility. Anticipating opposition from the courts of law or *parlements,* which were staffed by nobles of the robe and had taken upon themselves the functions of a supreme court, Calonne got the king to call an Assembly of Notables (1787). He hoped to overawe the *parlements* in a very formal assembly of representatives of the royal family, nobility, administration, and Catholic Church. But the notables, in which the aristocracy predominated, were unwilling to play Calonne's game or that of his successors, and the struggle with the *parlements* continued for another year, with both sides appealing to public opinion.

In May, 1788, the king's ministers tried to save absolute monarchy by replacing the *parlements* with a court which would confine itself to judging cases and not try to veto the king's laws. In the resulting dispute the *parlements,* now boasting that they represented the sovereign people in the absence of the Estates General, were the victors. Now on the verge of bankruptcy, the king yielded and in July and August, 1788, arranged for the calling of the Estates General. He also appointed as minister the popular Swiss middle-class banker, Necker. Absolutism, with scarcely anyone except paid pamphleteers to defend it, had been defeated by the champions of the aristocracy, who at this stage enjoyed public support.

Once it became clear that absolutism was to be replaced by representative government, the method of representation became vitally important. By the autumn of 1788 the public was aware that the Estates General for which the *parlements* had been calling was the old institution last convened in 1614 which gave representation separately to the three estates, and required their agreement if anything was to be done. On the other hand, the *parlements* and the aristocracy were vividly aware that vote "by order" in the Estates General—approval by each estate voting separately—must be maintained. Otherwise, a majority in that body might be formed to combat the nobles' privileges. It was more than a question of procedure, more even than a question of politics alone. The leaders of the nobility were willing to make concessions but they feared that unless the nobility, in alliance with the clergy, kept control of the new representative institutions they would become a persecuted minority. In the eyes of the Third Estate, however, the nobles meant to make France an oligarchy, replacing one-man rule with the rule of a privileged few. If that course were taken, the old society never would be reformed as the leaders of the Third Estate wished: with ability, and the wealth which they considered a sign of ability, opening doors to power as easily as did inherited titles.

In the winter of 1788–1789 this issue was so sharply drawn that a great shift in public opinion took place. The *parlements,* especially the leading one at Paris, became unpopular, and so did the aristocracy generally. Instead of an alliance of aristocrats and people against an absolute king, the struggle became one of the Third Estate against the aristocrats, with the king vacillating.

Louis XVI, whose talents lay in the direction of handicrafts and hunting, was well-meaning in a phlegmatic way and had an immense credit of good will with the public. But he was not personally respected by those who knew him best, the aristocrats at Versailles; he was a weak man, easily persuaded, yet sly. If he had been a strong leader, or even a loyal employer of men more able than he, the revolution might have been kept under control by judicious concessions. Probably a forceful announcement requiring the aristocracy of birth to share political and other distinctions with the new aristocracy of wealth would have been sufficient to keep the revolution from swinging to extremes, especially if this move had been coupled with genuine concessions to the peasantry. Louis XVI was not the man to accomplish such a feat, however, and although the popular Necker would have applauded it, he was too vulnerable—a foreigner, a Protestant, a commoner, and in the eyes of the court a financial speculator—to take the lead himself. The queen, Marie Antoinette, daughter of Maria Theresa and sister of the Habsburg ruler Joseph II, had perhaps at one time had the potentials of greatness, but she had been spoiled by an irresponsible environment and an unhappy marriage and had little political understanding to guide her strong will.

Because of the absence of decisive leadership the whole winter of 1788–1789 was a time of uncertainty and drift. In December, 1788, the number of deputies who were to represent the commoners in the Estates General was doubled, but nothing was said about granting vote "by head" or "by order"—the crucial issue, for unless each deputy had a vote the number of deputies would make no difference. There was nothing to prevent people's hopes from becoming danger-ously high, and little to reassure the fearful. A flood of some four to five thousand pamphlets, which completely engulfed the censorship, showed that literate people had advanced beyond the quarrel between the absolute monarchy and the aristoc-racy. The latter's claim that it was the traditional defender against tyranny was discredited. The pamphleteers tended to scorn tradition and to argue from abstract principles. Many wrote as if France had no constitutional tradition—a sharp break with the theory that France had an ancient constitution which gave the nobles the right to restrain the crown. Abbé Sieyès, author of the most famous tract of the times, *What is the Third Estate?*, took the view that the Third Estate was the nation, whose deputies had a right to make any kind of constitution they chose. The popularity of demands for a Bill of Rights was a sign that many people con-sidered the individual, and not the organized groups of the old regime, to be the basic unit of society.

The election of deputies to the Estates General early in 1789 further stimulated the public. Almost all Frenchmen had a chance to vote. All electoral assemblies prepared *cahiers*, or instructions, for their deputies to the Estates Gen-eral. This remarkable public-opinion poll showed that almost everyone, clergy and nobles included, wanted the king and Estates General to work together, both in the writing of constitutional laws and guarantees of freedom and in the regular business of voting taxes. But concerning the future role of the privileged orders there was ominous disagreement. Moreover, the fact that the views of the illiter-ate peasantry had to be reported and condensed by persons who could write prob-ably obscured the potential threat from the lower orders. [2]

FOUR REVOLUTIONS OF 1789

By the time of the formal opening of the Estates General at Versailles on May 5, 1789, the aristocracy had prevailed over the crown. But the nobility's triumph against the king had stirred up suspicion and fear of the nobility. An avalanche was starting. The decade after 1789 was to witness a whole series of revolutions, in which every group and layer of French society played a part at some time. The year 1789, like an overture, introduced the main themes.

The opening of the Estates General was a disappointment, for it led only to further delay. Neither the "Patriot Party" in the Third Estate nor the leaders of the nobles and clergy would concede on the voting question. The king and Necker still hesitated. Tension mounted until, in June, in a series of swift moves, action began.

On June 17 the deputies of the Third Estate declared themselves to be the National Assembly, by which they meant that as representatives of the sovereign people they could make a constitution, whatever the king and the aristocracy

[2] Assemblies of the nobles and clergy elected their deputies directly, each assembly writing its *cahier*. Deputies of the Third Estate were chosen indirectly. First, electoral assemblies met, bringing the original *cahiers*. Then the members of these electoral assemblies chose the deputies and prepared the "general" *cahiers*.

might do. The king's advisors responded that the Third Estate's action of June 17 was unlawful but that the king would present a program at a royal session of the Estates General in a few days. On June 20, finding their hall closed, the Third Estate met in an indoor tennis court and signed the famous "Tennis Court Oath" to the effect that the National Assembly would not disband until it had written and put into operation a constitution. This act of disobedience was formally rebuked by the king in person in the royal session of June 23, a joint meeting of the deputies of the three estates. Louis XVI, surrounded by armed force, presented a compromise program to the deputies and then ordered them to disperse and henceforth to meet properly as the Estates General.

This royal program amounted to acceptance of the aristocratic revolution of 1788 but not of the "lawyers' revolution" of June 17 and 20, 1789. The king promised personal liberty, provincial assemblies, and tax reforms, but he insisted that when considering anything touching on feudal dues or the constitutional and social privileges of the first two orders, the Estates General must meet and vote "by order" and not "by head." It was clear that the king had finally sided with the aristocracy. After Louis XVI and the first two estates had left the hall, the deputies of the Third refused to depart, as ordered. They thereby reaffirmed their existence as a National Assembly. On June 27 the king began to fear possible intervention by crowds from Paris, and he ordered the clergy and nobles (some of whom had already done so) to join the National Assembly. Thus under pressure the "lawyers' revolution" was accepted.

Louis XVI did not relish his defeat by the Third Estate's representatives in the National Assembly. He called up troops, almost certainly with the intention of dissolving that body. It was a move which came naturally to a king, and certainly the assembly could offer no resistance of its own, but these were not ordinary times. There was great tension in the whole of France, with the most contradictory feelings of hope and dread, brotherhood and social rivalry, equality and the urge to be led—if only some Necker, some Louis XVI, even, would clearly show the way. This was a dangerous time to call up troops: depression; unemployment; vagabonds; fears for property; the excitement of electing deputies and writing *cahiers*; the high expectations; all these had combined to create an explosive situation. Already there was more than ordinary lawlessness. Grain shipments were being attacked. Merchants did not feel safe amid grumblings about high prices. Peasants were not waiting for action from Versailles but were refusing to pay dues and taxes and were cutting wood in the forests and trespassing in places where they were not supposed to go. The troops themselves were not reliable, for the soldiers of those days had to buy their own food, and felt the economic pinch. Moreover, the non-commissioned officers were blocked from advancement by the aristocratic system. Seldom had so many people shared similar feelings of nervous hope, fear of deception, and the will to strike back at those who might thwart them.

When Louis XVI called up troops an insurrection occurred, on July 14, 1789. The Bastille, a powerful old fort used as a jail, was seized by the Parisians with the help of military units. Not only in Paris, but all over France, new municipal governments were formed, which armed themselves with a new military force, the National Guard, the middle class's answer both to counter-revolution from above and the threat to order and property from below. Louis XVI saw his troops fraternize with the insurgents. He had to give in, and, for his acquiescence, accept the applause of Parisian crowds. The National Assembly was saved by the mob violence in Paris. The revolution of the lawyers could go on, but they now carried a debt to this popular revolution of the multitude.

The National Assembly continued its work. The most angry and fearful of the aristocracy, led by the king's brother, the Count of Artois, left France. And the insurgency of the peasants, which had begun as early as June, continued unchecked. This "fourth revolution," following the revolutions of the aristocrats, the lawyers, and the populace of Paris on July 14, continued into August. As if answering some inner call, peasants in widely separated parts of the country pillaged manor houses, destroyed records of servitude, and most important of all, stopped paying taxes and dues. In late July and early August the actions of the peasants were dramatized by a hysteria known as the "great fear." It was a fear of "brigands" paid by aristocrats which arose from half a dozen insignificant incidents in different localities and spread like grass fires through the countryside. In defense against this imagined threat, the peasants resorted to greater violence, burning chateaux and sometimes murdering the agents of the owners.

Peasant lawlessness was not so easily harnessed by the revolutionaries as the popular upheavals in the cities. The National Assembly stood at a crossroads.

SIEGE OF THE BASTILLE ON JULY 14, 1789. CAPTURED IN TWO HOURS AND A HALF BY THE BOURGEOIS OF PARIS AND THE BRAVE FRENCH GUARDS by F. N. Sellier. Engraving, 1789. (Courtesy of Bibliothèque Nationale, Paris, Cabinet des Estampes)

If it restored order with the help of the king and the aristocrats, its members might find themselves at the mercy of the latter, who would hold them responsible for unleashing the disorders. If, on the other hand, they accepted the radicalism of the peasants as part of the revolution, they would alienate the liberal nobles and clergy and lose the chance to keep the leadership in the hands of a coalition of moderates.

The dilemma was avoided on the night of August 4 in a momentous session of the National Assembly. Liberal nobles took the lead in destroying "the feudal regime" by abolishing the feudal rights and tax immunities of the nobility and clergy, including church tithes, feudal dues and personal servitudes, and the special privileges of provinces and towns. The "night of August 4" was both a drastic modernization and a planned maneuver designed to placate the peasants while preserving the more defensible property rights in the countryside. It was also meant to demonstrate that the moderates were capable of leading and controlling the revolution. In the more sober sessions of August 5 to 11 the important body of seigneurial dues based on contracts and not on personal servitude was made subject to redemption. This solution hardly satisfied the peasants.

Having tried to cope with the peasant problem, the Assembly completed, late in August, its Declaration of the Rights of Man and of the Citizen, a vital part of the constitution. "Liberty, property, security, and the right to resist oppression" were declared to be natural inalienable rights. The most conservative deputies opposed the publication of this Declaration on the ground that it was dishonest and dangerous to talk to the people about abstract principles which they could not understand, and which would overturn society if the uneducated tried to apply them literally. The makers of the Declaration of Rights went ahead because they were realistic enough to want the lower classes aroused against the old regime, and idealistic enough to believe that once the unfair restrictions of that era were removed everyone would benefit, whether rich or poor.

Louis XVI was still in the way, for he refused to sanction either the Declaration of Rights or the legislation of August 5 to 11. The question arose: could the king veto the fundamental laws by which the Assembly was constituting the new order? One view was expressed by the more conservative deputies who wished to diminish the conflict of the middle class with the nobles and higher clergy, and to maintain a moderate coalition. Led by Mounier, these "Anglophiles" wanted something resembling the British House of Lords and wanted the king to have an absolute veto over the legislation passed by the two chambers of the legislature. The more radical members of the assembly, led by Barnave, Duport, and the Lameth brothers, opposed the "Anglophile" system as giving too much power to the king and the aristocrats. Efforts at compromise between the two groups failed. In September the Assembly voted against the "Anglophiles," but Louis XVI persisted in his position. The question remained whether anything the Assembly voted was valid without his consent. As in July and August the issue was finally decided by force.

During his deadlock with the Assembly, Louis ordered an army regiment to Versailles. Its arrival, coupled with the continuing economic crisis in Paris, had a psychological result similar to that of July 14. The suggestion of some of the radical deputies of the National Assembly was enough to bring a mob to Versailles. Lafayette, the hero of the American Revolution, and the National Guard of which he was commander, followed somewhat tardily from Paris. The demonstration succeeded in making Louis XVI agree to the August decrees and the Declaration of Rights, together with special measures for provisioning Paris, but a mob broke into the palace in the early morning of October 6th, massacred some of the king's bodyguards, and probably would have killed Marie Antoinette if she had not left her apartment in the nick of time. Later in the day the demonstrators insisted upon the royal family's returning with them to Paris—outwardly a sign of popular affection. But in the background were leaders who meant to keep Louis XVI from being used by counter-revolutionaries. Shortly afterward the National Assembly followed.

The "October days" had important constitutional, party, and social implications. It was now settled that the king could not block the work of the Assembly, which would henceforth interpret the will of the sovereign people. The hope for a moderate, "Anglophile" solution of the constitutional and social problems was shattered. Mounier deserted the National Assembly and later left the country, and the emigration of frightened or outraged conservatives quickened its pace. The king and queen (who had themselves considered flight before the October days) were now in effect prisoners, and the National Assembly was at the mercy of Paris. The debt of the politicians to the lower classes, which had once more intervened to push the revolution onward, was greater than ever. October provided the last of the great "days" of 1789, but the pattern of the revolution was now set: successive groups of revolutionary leaders would have to cope with growing counter-revolution on their right while their potential successors on the left exploited the irritations and disappointment of the populace.

THE WORK OF THE
NATIONAL ASSEMBLY

From the "October days" of 1789 to the closing of the National Assembly at the end of September, 1791, the revolution moved forward slowly, as if it had learned to be calm. There was one dramatic event, the escape of the king and queen and their recapture at Varennes (June 20–21, 1791), and this was followed by tension and brief violence on the Champ-de-Mars (July 17). Then the revolution appeared to be over when the captive Louis XVI took his oath to the National Assembly's constitution (September 14, 1791) and the Legislative Assembly provided by that constitution held its first session (October 1).

This period from October, 1789, to October, 1791, seemed mainly one of committee reports—on the constitution and on France's current problems—debated and voted upon by the Assembly. But under the deceptive parliamentary droning, interrupted by occasional sharp protests and explanations, France was being peacefully rebuilt into the form which it has had ever since. Few people suspected that turbulence, terror, and war still lay ahead, to be followed by the dictator, Napoleon. The explanation for this turn of events is most often sought in a later period, after the National Assembly had ceased to exist. There is, however, a rhythm in the two years after October, 1789, which repeats in slower tempo the motion of early 1789: revolutionary advance, royal resistance, and radical response checked by moderate leadership.

Before narrating the contests of parties and factions, let us summarize briefly, in tabular form, the Assembly's main reforms.

CIVIL RIGHTS FOR ALL . . . Freedom of speech and press; religious toleration; safeguards against jailing without trial and trial without a lawyer; abolition of the remains of serfdom, and of monastic vows (considered to be the signing away of one's liberty).

POLITICAL RIGHTS . . . Not for all, since voting was considered to be the responsibility of persons of "capacity," measured for the most part by payment of taxes (direct taxes amounting to three days' earnings). This excluded from voting (and from the National Guard) about 3,000,-000 "passive citizens" (persons with civil but not political rights), and left about 4,300,000 "active citizens" (a rather broad suffrage).

INDIRECT ELECTIONS . . . Active citizens chose "electors of the second degree," who then chose deputies to the Legislative Assembly. Electors and deputies both had to own considerable property to qualify. After the king's attempted flight in 1791, an upsurge of democratic sentiment forced the removal of the property qualification for deputies, but as a safeguard, that of second-degree electors was doubled. (The Assembly's caution about the populace is also shown by its failure to submit the Constitution of 1791 to popular ratification, and by the difficulties which it put in the way of amendment.)

CURBING THE KING . . . In theory the constitution had separation of executive, legislative, and judicial powers. On paper the king's power was considerable, but in practice the National Assembly (and after it the Legislative Assembly) reduced it considerably. The king could appoint his own ministers, and had a suspensive veto which could delay legislation for two legislatures (4 years). But the king could not dissolve the Legislative Assembly, and the distrust in which he was held by the deputies led them to usurp many of the prerogatives of his ministers by substituting the work of their own committees. They also investigated and bullied the king's chosen ministers.

THE DEPARTMENTS . . . These were new administrative divisions in France, 83 in number, which replaced the old provinces, generalities, and so on. Their subdivisions were districts and cantons. They were governed by elected officials (chosen by active citizens and second-degree electors). This reorganization was a very radical attack on the old diversity of rights and sentimental attachments. It tore up the local governments of the old regime by the roots, and cleared the way for nationalistic feelings.

CONFISCATION OF CHURCH PROPERTIES . . . The revolutionaries considered private property to be sacred, including the absolute monarchy's debts (owed to their constituents, of course), and they agreed to indemnify many persons deprived of offices or of certain kinds of seigneurial dues. They argued, however, that the Church's properties were not "private." In confiscating them, the state took on heavy obligations in education, poor relief, and payment of the salaries of priests.

THE ASSIGNATS . . . Selling of the Church's former holdings in order to repay the government's creditors could not take place at once. Many properties thrown on the market would have lowered the price. *Assignats* were at first interest-bearing bonds exchangeable for nationalized property. As revolutionary conditions continued to make tax collections difficult and borrowing uncertain, the *assignats* were made into paper money which could be used by the government and the government's creditors (to pay *their* creditors). The *assignats* were issued in larger and larger quantities as the revolution continued. They served the revolution by (1) paying current expenses; (2) making it more radical (as prices rose, consumers became irritable); (3) revolutionizing property-holdings (as the *assignats* depreciated, business activity was stimulated; there was much speculation, and much property changed hands—people were quick to see the advantage of buying "national property" with a down payment and the balance in installments of depreciating *assignats*).

OTHER ECONOMIC LEGISLATION . . . Abolition of seigneurial dues, as well as special categories of land reserved for nobles, internal tariffs and tolls, monopolies, guilds,—these abolitions pointed toward a free economy run by individuals, as did the Chapelier Law (1791) forbidding employers' associations and labor unions. But the lower classes did not share the optimism of the higher *bourgeoisie* and clung to certain notions of collective action and state intervention. This difference in outlook was to play a part in politics later in the revolution.

CIVIL CONSTITUTION OF THE CLERGY (1790) . . . The Church's organization was brought into line with the new administrative subdivisions of France. Bishops and priests were to be elected, and were to be paid salaries by the state. The Pope's religious authority was recognized, but not his administrative jurisdiction. The revolutionaries expected to use Church facilities for the nation's purposes (as interpreted by its representatives). They assumed that society needed religion to hold it together, and had no intention of separating Church and state. Pius VI in 1791 condemned the principles of the revolution and the Civil Constitution of the Clergy.

LOYALTY OATH . . . In November, 1790, an oath of allegiance to the constitution (including the Civil Constitution of the Clergy) was required of all clergy. Only seven bishops and about half the parish priests took the oath. The recalcitrant, "non-juring" clergy became a counter-revolutionary influence, providing mass support and moral justifications for the counter-revolution. Louis XVI's opposition to the revolution was strengthened, and the basis was laid for radical anti-clericalism on the part of the revolutionaries.

With these huge changes, the French Revolution made a double appeal, humanitarian and practical. Under the banner of universal principles proclaimed in the Declaration of Rights it attacked hated abuses. In its work of clearing the ground for an individualistic society it aroused innumerable hopes for personal advancement and invited to its side the strong and the able. The double incentive provided by the revolution's principles and by the social shakeup was to last through the decade of the 1790's and into the reign of Napoleon, arming France with a spirit and resources which no other country could match.

Between 1789 and 1791 the National Assembly still contained a few aristocrats who heckled the majority for going beyond what the French people had ordered in the *cahiers*. There were still some moderate admirers of the English constitution (Anglophiles), but they had no popular following. The most influential deputies attended the Jacobin Club. This most famous of the revolutionary clubs was to change character as the revolution progressed. In 1789–1790, with the Anglophiles withdrawn, it was dominated, like the National Assembly, by the followers of Lafayette, and (after October, 1790) by the somewhat more radical Lameth brothers and their friends Barnave and Duport. The "Fayettists" and "Lamethists" agreed on fundamentals. Both distrusted the king and the aristocracy too much to agree with the Anglophiles in 1789. Both believed that the political power which had been taken from the king and aristocracy should be kept in the hands of responsible, propertied people. Although they disagreed on details, the work of the National Assembly was their work.

In the Assembly and at the Jacobin Club there were a few deputies who,

FRANCE IN PROVINCES, 1789

like the very radical Maximilien Robespierre, insisted on the people's right to govern themselves regardless of wealth. There were few republicans, however. Robespierre and most of the people who preached a democratic franchise still favored the monarchy.

Louis XVI had been forced into one concession after another since 1788, when he first agreed to the Estates General. His strange apathy and willingness to agree to measures which he disliked puzzled foreign observers. What they did not realize was that Louis XVI and Marie Antoinette felt that it was not necessary to keep promises made under duress. The queen, especially, felt that history would judge them, and that their children's patrimony was at stake. The only solution seemed to be to escape, to regain the initiative, to discredit the Assembly and win back the leadership which Louis XVI had lost. Meanwhile it was necessary to hide their true thoughts.

The queen's Machiavellian policy was encouraged by a man who was for a time so powerful in the National Assembly that he was almost a party by himself. This was Honoré Gabriel Riqueti, Marquis de Mirabeau, one of the giants of the revolution. He was a noble with a scandalous past and a gift of oratory, who had become a leader of the Third Estate. Mirabeau saw that the old order of absolutism and special privileges had to go, and that whoever stood in the way of this forward march would be crushed by it. He tried to save the king by having him lead the revolution toward the inevitable changes. In this way the king would retain influence enough to head off rule by an aristocratic oligarchy or the omnipotence of a representative assembly. It was the latter, as things turned out, which

FRANCE IN DEPARTMENTS, 1791

Mirabeau found himself opposing. He tried to preserve the king's authority as a brake against the Assembly, tried vainly to save the absolute veto and the king's right to sanction the constitution. In November, 1789, the Assembly, fearing his demagogic influence and distrusting his ambition, tried to legislate him out of office, by excluding all of its own members from the ministry.

Mirabeau became the secret advisor to the king and queen from April, 1790, to his death in April, 1791. He played a double role of radical in the Assembly's public debates and counter-revolutionary in his confidential memoranda, for which he was paid handsomely. He recommended a network of secret agents to undermine the Assembly's reputation throughout France. Meanwhile the court was to dissemble, rebuild the popularity of the royal pair until the time was ripe to appeal to the nation against the National Assembly. If necessary the king and queen were to escape and lead the national party in a civil war.

Marie Antoinette accepted Mirabeau's advice to the extent that it agreed with her own plans. She loathed him and meant only to keep him from becoming an opponent. She had her own project for flight, about which Mirabeau knew nothing. The plan was to escape to the eastern frontier, where they would be under the protection of a loyal general. At this sign of the king's determination to resume leadership in France, his allies, including the queen's brother, Leopold of the Habsburg Monarchy and Holy Roman Empire, would meet in an armed congress. Louis XVI would mediate between the great powers and the French nation, at the expense of the National Assembly. On June 20, 1791, the royal family, disguised as the servants and children of a Russian baroness, stole out of Paris. Louis XVI's brother, the Count of Provence, also left by another route. Provence joined the *émigrés* and became their leader, but Louis XVI's party was stopped at the village of Varennes in eastern France on June 21.

The king's flight and capture jeopardized the whole carefully contrived structure upon which the National Assembly had been working for two years. Louis was brought back into Paris between lines of silent onlookers. The people were under no illusions about the danger they had been in. It was perfectly clear that the king had tried to check the Revolution, possibly by foreign intervention and civil war. The National Assembly suspended Louis XVI from his duties, and France was for a time virtually a republic. But what was to become of the constitution if its chief executive was a traitor? Faced with the prospect of another constitutional convention—which this time might make a democracy or even a republic—the National Assembly drew back. It began to spread the fiction that Louis XVI had been kidnapped, although on his departure he had left behind a damaging condemnation of the Assembly's acts. The moderate Fayettists and Lamethists now drew together in defense of their work. When a crowd gathered on July 17 on the Champ-de-Mars around a petition for removal of Louis XVI, the National Guard "restored order," in the process killing a number of people and wounding others. The Constitution of 1791, as it came to be called, was hurried into operation. When Louis XVI swore to uphold it (September 14) and the National Assembly disbanded (September 30) the revolution seemed to be at an end.

THE DOWNFALL OF MONARCHY

The Constitution of 1791, which had taken more than two years to make, survived less than one. The Legislative Assembly for which it provided met on October 1, 1791. On August 10, 1792, there took place another of those memorable insurrections with which the revolutionary decade was punctuated. Shortly afterward, France became a republic.

The short life of the Legislative Assembly cannot really be explained by the events of that one year; they were part of a rapidly moving stream. Everyone was being carried rapidly along.

Louis XVI and Marie Antoinette, haunted by the spectre of republicanism, continued to negotiate secretly for the intervention of the great powers. Lafayette and Barnave and their associates—the so-called "Feuillant Club" who had come together in defense of the Constitution of 1791 after the fiasco of the king's flight—secretly wished to return to a more moderate regime. They would now have welcomed the Anglophile solution which they had opposed in 1789. Members of the National Assembly had been excluded from the Legislative Assembly, but representatives of the Feuillant point of view at first dominated the latter, and others were appointed by Louis XVI as ministers. Barnave, like Mirabeau before him, secretly advised the queen.

On the left of the Legislative Assembly were the members of the Jacobin Club (from which the Feuillants had withdrawn). Most of them were younger than the Feuillant leaders, and of lower social origin, many of them professional or business men. They were coming to form something new, a class of professional politicians. The more radical followed Maximilien Robespierre, who was still in Paris though not in the Assembly. The more moderate followed Jacques Brissot, whose name came to be used for the group (thus "Brissotins," later "Girondins" because the leaders came from the Gironde in southwest France). In general the Brissotins wished to force the revolution ahead until they could take power. They were sincerely idealistic and had a missionary zeal about spreading the principles of 1789 to all Europe. They even believed that war would not be a misfortune if it solidified the country behind the revolution and made Louis XVI and his wife show, once and for all, whose side they were on. Robespierre was almost alone in warning that war, if it came before the consolidation of the revolution at home, would bring calamities which might lead to dictatorship.

War was declared on the Habsburg Monarchy in April, 1792. It was ostensibly occasioned by disputes over relatively trivial matters. Marie Antoinette's brother, the Emperor Leopold, was far from eager to crusade against the French Revolution. Most of the European monarchs of this time were too busy with their own plans, and too distrustful of each other, to do more than talk of uniting against revolutionary France. Another partition of Poland was impending. But the war came because a number of important people did not object to such an outcome. On the Austrian side, Leopold's death led to the succession of

Francis II, who took a firmer line against the mounting French pressure. In France, the minister Dumouriez, an adventurer closely associated with the Brissotins but possessed of ambitious plans of his own, was convinced that to avoid a partition of France, Austria must be isolated and beaten and its Belgian provinces separated from it. He also had the idea of strengthening the crown through war. When a series of French demands on Austria received no satisfaction France declared war on April 20. Prussia joined Austria in the war.

In France the war was accepted by the king and queen in the hope of regaining royal initiative through the king's role as mediator between the French people and the powers of Europe. They expected defeat, and worked for it, counting on the jealousies among the European powers to save the country from dismemberment. This was a dangerous, and treasonable, gamble. The queen continued to communicate with the enemy. Lafayette, leader of the militant wing of the Feuillants, took a command at the front but kept an eye on the situation in Paris and waited for a chance to use his army there. But his popularity was gone and he was suspect, both to the Legislative Assembly which he wanted to dissolve and to the queen, who counted to the last on outside help and rejected his project for the royal family's escape. In the end he became an *émigré* by giving himself into the custody of the enemy.

The French armies, disorganized by the revolution, at first fared badly. Defeats in Belgium coupled with inflation at home created the same kind of desperate apprehension which had characterized the great "days" of 1789. Passive citizens could no longer be kept out of section (ward) meetings and the National Guard in Paris. On June 20, 1792, the anniversary of the Tennis Court Oath, a great crowd visited the Legislative Assembly and then moved on to the Tuileries Palace, where they forced Louis XVI to meet with them for several hours. The king and queen were rightly suspected of negotiating with the enemy, but on June 20 Louis was phlegmatically courageous and nothing came of the popular demonstration except a temporary wave of indignation on the part of moderates throughout France. The Jacobins began to split into the two groups which would eventually become opponents after the monarchy's downfall: the Robespierrists, who wanted the king set aside but did not yet demand a republic; and the Brissotins (later, Girondins), who were hesitating now, considering the possibility that the existing regime might be saved with themselves in the important posts.

Paris decided the issue by one of those insurrections sparked by public fear of danger, and organized by the radical leaders of the Paris sections. On July 28 the public learned about the Brunswick Manifesto, in which the enemy commander stated that the allies were coming to restore the king, and threatened the city with destruction if it resisted. This caused great popular resentment in France. Two days later Paris was reinforced by the arrival of troops from Marseilles, who popularized Rouget de Lisle's revolutionary song, the "Marseillaise," which was to become the national anthem of republican France. In the midst of dread that the king was ready to seize the capital until the *émigrés* and Austrians and Prussians might arrive, the insurrection of August 10 took place. On the night before, delegates from the Paris sections displaced the legal municipal authority and formed a new revolutionary city government. On the 10th the troops from the departments, together with forces from the Paris sections, marched on the Palace of the Tuileries. They were fired upon, and in response massacred about six hundred of the Swiss Guards protecting the king. Louis XVI and the royal family escaped to the building where the Legislative Assembly sat.

There followed an uneasy period punctuated by violence. Where was the government of France? The Legislative Assembly, its Feuillant members discredited or in flight, was under the control of the Brissotins, or Girondins. It suspended the king, thus postponing the issue of the abolition of the monarchy. A National Convention was ordered elected (by universal manhood suffrage) to decide the fate of the king and the Constitution of 1791. Meanwhile the Paris Commune with its new revolutionary government held the police and military power.

The Convention, duly elected, met on September 20. In the intervening weeks much had happened. The Commune of Paris, under the leadership of Georges Danton, had aroused the city and called out troops to stem the advance of the Prussians. The first important victory for revolutionary arms was won at Valmy as the Convention assembled. There had been more violence, amounting to hysteria, in Paris—unchecked crowds had murdered with summary justice some twelve hundred unfortunates from the prison convoys and overcrowded jails. More than half were ordinary convicts, innocent of any political offense. Many of the rest were priests who had refused to accept the Civil Constitution of the Clergy. The "September massacres" ran their course without effective interference from the confused jurisdiction of the Legislative Assembly and the city government. There is no reliable evidence that the massacres were systematically planned. They were apparently the work of a minority obsessed with a defensive and punitive urge.

August 10, 1792, which brought down the monarchy, was a catastrophic finish to the maneuvers of the king and queen, a shock to Europe, and an awe-inspiring event even to the most determined of the revolutionaries. It marked the failure of France's attempt to make the transition from absolutism to representative government without taking the plunge all the way to a democracy for which it was scarcely prepared.

23

THE FIRST FRENCH
REPUBLIC

August 10, 1792, date of the insurrection which overthrew the French monarchy, is sometimes called the "second revolution." The name is a tribute to the seriousness of the event. In the midst of war, isolated in a Europe still dominated by monarchies and aristocracies, the French tried to rule themselves in a democratic republic. More exactly, an inspired minority of revolutionaries from the ancient, complex, and gifted French middle class tried, against overwhelming odds, to set up a democratic republic. In the Reign of Terror they surmounted the worst crisis of the Revolution, but they were unable to do more than plant the seeds of a republican and democratic tradition in France.

They were overthrown in 1794, and an effort was made to establish a more moderate representative republic. But the moderates were unable to remain true to their principles in the face of continuing warfare and social antagonisms, and after 1797 France was virtually a dictatorship. In 1799 the *coup d'état* of Napoleon Bonaparte brought to a close the decade of revolution.

THE STRUGGLE IN THE CONVENTION

The National Convention which first met on September 20, 1792, was to last until October 26, 1795. Its main purpose was the making of constitutional laws. It lasted so long because it had to govern and defend the country and, in addition, its members fell to quarreling over the shape of the new society.

The Convention passed through three stages: (1) September 20, 1792, to June 2, 1793, during which the Girondins and Jacobins struggled for control;

(2) June 2, 1793, to July 27, 1794, characterized by a crisis in the revolution and the Reign of Terror which arose from the crisis; (3) July 27, 1794, to the end of the Convention on October 26, 1795, a return to moderation usually called the Thermidorian Reaction. The first of these three phases is the subject of this section.

The Convention in its first few days declared the monarchy abolished and announced that a new calendar had come into effect with the republic. It was the year I. The revolutionary calendar expressed an ideal—of national order and freedom from the confusions of the past—and an emotion—a new era was beginning in the history of the world. But the new era was full of problems, and the deputies were soon quarreling over ways and means.

Of the Convention's 749 deputies, the Girondins, many of them nationally known, had enjoyed an advantage in the elections and were the largest cohesive group. Led by Brissot and men like him, with the best orators and most influential newspapers at their disposal, they were in a position to profit from the successful prosecution of the war during the rest of the year. The Girondins had associations with businessmen all over France and had the support of many local officials chosen under the 1791 constitution. Believers in economic liberty, they were the hope of most upper middle class people, who had not wanted the republic and yearned above all for stability.

On the left of the Convention, in the high seats which gave them their name, sat the deputies of the Mountain, the Montagnards. They were dominated by the Paris delegation led by such men as the austere democrat Robespierre and the sarcastic journalist Marat, with the help of new members like young Saint-Just. They were now in control of the Jacobin Club. In social background and training they were not very different from the Girondins, and like them thought primarily in political terms, hoping in their case to form as soon as possible a workable democratic republic. They were believers in private property, and most of them favored economic liberalism. They were indebted to the lower classes of Paris for the forward push given the revolution on August 10, a move whose necessity the deputies of the Mountain accepted with greater readiness than the Girondins. The Montagnards were less sympathetic to the propertied classes than the Girondins, and more idealistic about the common man. They were not exclusively identified with the lower classes, however. They felt themselves to be national leaders, and although inclined to enlist the support of the sans-culottes when the revolution was in danger, they did not mean to be their tools.

The term "sans-culottes" (literally "without knee breeches," the genteel costume, as opposed to the long trousers of the commoners) refers to artisans, small shopkeepers, journeymen, workmen—in general what we today would call lower middle class as well as manual laborers. They are not to be thought of as a class-conscious "proletariat." As at all times in history, people were aware of social differences, but there was more awareness of differences between commoners and former nobles than of differences within the Third Estate. It would take a generation or two of living in the poor housing around nineteenth-century factories to make a proletariat. In the Paris of the French Revolution workingmen and lower-middle-class people were not yet very different from one another.

FRENCH COATS-OF-ARMS: ROYAL, IMPERIAL, AND REPUBLICAN Unlike
many countries which have changed their forms of government, France
did not incorporate the old badge of royalty into its new coat-of-arms.
Both the republic and Napoleon introduced entirely new coats-of-arms
for the nation, indicating the complete break with the past which the
French Revolution embodied.

The royal arms (above) consisted simply of three golden lilies
(fleurs-de-lis) on a blue field, surmounted by the royal crown and surrounded by the chain and badge of the knightly order founded and
bestowed by French kings, the Order of the Holy Ghost.

The republican arms (top right), the official badge of contemporary France, is a shield flanked by the colors of the Revolution, and the
fasci, the symbol of authority in the ancient Roman Republic.

The imperial arms (bottom right) recalled the Roman Empire,
just as the fasci recalled the Roman Republic, in the late eighteenth century enthusiasm for classical ideas. The imperial eagle was similar to those
borne by Roman armies.

Although the fleur-de-lis, regarded as the symbol of tyranny and
inequality, has no official place in modern France, it continues to be used
unofficially as a symbol.

Nevertheless the interests of the sans-culottes were more local and limited than those of the members of the Convention. The sans-culottes were more concerned about the cost of living than about political theory. Their interests were direct and personal—in price fixing, in executions of traitors, in the need to form a revolutionary army and make the rich pay for it, in the importance of punishing speculators. Their leaders were obscure priests like Jacques Roux or neighborhood politicians who spoke in the unrefined language of the poorer quarters. In time journalists who copied Marat and aspiring political leaders like Hébert adopted these plebeian manners and learned to appeal to the interests of the populace, but for a long time Robespierre and the Mountain were their only spokesmen in the Convention. The Mountain during the first months had no detailed economic and social program and represented the demands of sans-culottes of Paris only imperfectly.

In the Convention the Center or Plain, its members sometimes insultingly called the Marsh Toads, held the balance between Girondins and Mountain. The Plain contained cautious men like Sieyès and some like Carnot (later famous for building the army) who were to rally to the Mountain during the Reign of Terror. Most of the Plain were moderates who believed in the revolution and were determined to defend it against internal and external enemies, men with no liking for bloodshed and dictatorial methods, men who preferred economic liberty to government action and distrusted the sans-culottes and their demands. Nevertheless, the men of the Plain were advanced revolutionaries in comparison with the French population as a whole, which from fear or indifference had for the most part stayed away from the polls when the Convention was elected. The Plain was aware that most Frenchmen were glad to enjoy the benefits of the revolution but that if the revolution was to be saved the minority of active revolutionaries would have to work together.

To the end of 1792 the Girondins profited from military victories and expansion. French armies under the reputedly Girondin General Dumouriez drove the Austrians into Belgium while other forces took Savoy and Nice and still others advanced into the Rhineland. France in its Constitution of 1791 had renounced wars of conquest and interference with the liberty of others, and had reaffirmed these ideals at the start of the war (Statement of April 14, 1792). But now expansion began with enthusiasm. In the Decree of November 19, 1792, the Convention promised "fraternity and aid to all peoples who wish to recover their liberty." By the end of the year Nice and parts of the Rhineland and the Low Countries had joined France, presumably of their own free will. The other countries of Europe began to draw together. This idealistic expansion began to seem more dangerous than the old-fashioned kind practiced by Louis XIV.

The trial and execution of Louis XVI outraged opinion in Europe. Louis was indicted before the Convention on December 11, 1792. From the 14th to the 17th the Convention received and voted on three questions. Is he guilty of conspiracy against public liberty and general security? The answer was overwhelmingly "Yes," for after the discovery of a secret cupboard of documents in the Tuileries palace there could be no doubt concerning his arrangements with foreign powers. Should there be a popular referendum upholding or rejecting the Con-

DEATH OF LOUIS XVI Engraving by Helman, after Monnet. (New York Public Library, Spencer Collection)

vention's judgment? The answer was "No" by a substantial majority. What should be the penalty? The answer was "Execution" by a vote of 387 to 334. Of the majority of 53, however, 26 had qualifications. By another vote in which the majority was 70 it was decided to execute the defendant, and the guillotining of Louis XVI took place on January 21, 1793, in the Place de la Révolution, now the Place de la Concorde. France received the shocking news without rebelling, but with profound emotion. Now, more than on August 10, the die was cast. Between the revolution and Europe, between those who like the stern Robespierre had argued that no compromise was possible and those who like many of the Girondins had misgivings about going forward, the decision had been made. In the last analysis it had been made by the Plain, who had rejected the Girondin point of view.

The formation of a coalition of European powers against France was hastened by the execution, but such a coalition was already in the making. Britain could not permit its old rival to control the Low Countries, springboard of invasion and trading entrance to Central Europe. Moreover the Convention's proclamations were a provocation to the restive Irish, and Jacobinism had the look of international subversion. The French ambassador was asked to leave Britain. France replied with a declaration of war on the British and Dutch, accusing the latter of being a satellite of Britain and Prussia. By the end of the year William Pitt's diplomacy had gathered an anti-French alliance, known as the First Coalition, including Austria, Prussia, Sardinia, the Netherlands, and for practical purposes, Spain, upon which France had also declared war. To the east, Russia remained neutral except for the hostile words of the great Catherine, busy with the second partition of Poland and contemplating a third.

As the spring of 1793 advanced, the Austrians and Prussians began at last to win victories. The northward push of Dumouriez was checked in March by two resounding defeats, and he deserted to the enemy, leaving behind rumors of profiteering and corruption. This was a blow to the Girondins, but only one of many, for they were the war party, and the war was reaping defeats, hardships, and rebellion. Food shortages and depreciating *assignats* brought price rises which were aggravated by counterfeiting and speculation. A conscription law of February, 1793, anticipating the principle of service which was to be adopted sooner or later by all modern states, touched off a royalist and clerical rebellion in the west. In the midst of recriminations between Girondins and Jacobins a report of the predominantly Girondin constitutional committee chaired by the *philosophe* Condorcet was shelved. Circumstances were calling for positive action, but the liberal economic doctrine of the Girondins made them hesitate. Their fear of Paris, its clubs and sections and its Jacobin deputies, led them into political blunders. Instead of reassuring the public, the Girondins unsuccessfully attacked leaders of the Mountain, in particular Marat, and tried to move the Convention out of Paris. The crisis temperature rose. All over France there was occurring a fight for control of local neighborhood meetings.

As this crisis developed in March and April, 1793, the deputies of the Mountain, with increasing cooperation from the Plain, began to pass emergency legislation. In March a revolutionary tribunal to try political offenders, urged by

Danton, was approved over the opposition of the Girondins. In April a Committee of Public Safety was formed, and Deputies on Mission were authorized to enforce the Convention's will in the departments. Also in April the Mountain came out for the economic controls demanded by the sans-culottes. On May 4 the first Law of the Maximum was passed. It attempted to control the price of grain, and, although ineffective, set an example of price fixing which was to be extended later.

In supporting such legislation the deputies of the Mountain were meeting the emergency at the cost of their long-term convictions about economic liberalism. Politically they were yielding to the pressure of the Jacobin Clubs, which in turn reflected the demands of the more radical section (ward — electoral district) meetings of Paris. Although the sections wanted the overthrow of the Girondins and their ousting from the Convention, the Mountain resisted this pressure. It was a delicate situation, for the local Paris politicians were jealous of the Mountain deputies even when the latter were appeasing them. There was real danger that an insurrection in the city would put an end to the Convention and bring about a civil war between Paris and the departments, an event which could only help the counter-revolution.

Between May 30 and June 2, 1793, such an insurrection did take place. Local demagogues seized control of the city government and National Guard. They led a crowd which surrounded the Convention and forced the arrest of the leading Girondin deputies. The Mountain deputies were placed in the position of accepting, guiding, and profiting from this violation of the sanctity of the national representative body. Popular sovereignty was assuming a most virulent form. The moderate members of the Plain, while unable to resist, did not forgive the Mountain for taking power in this way. The Girondin leaders soon escaped to the provinces to stir up revolt. The crisis associated with the war was thus deepened, and with the summer of 1793 it was clear that the sans-culottes and their leaders were still far from satisfied.

THE REIGN OF TERROR

With the Girondins gone, the most radical period of the Convention's history began. In fairness, it should be noted that the Mountain did not plunge at once into the Reign of Terror. Strictly speaking, the Terror began on September 5, 1793, one year after the "September massacres." The Terror lasted until July 27, 1794 (9 Thermidor by the revolutionary calendar), date of the overthrow of Robespierre.

In order to understand the Terror it is necessary to look first at the crisis of the summer of 1793. In addition to a "federalist revolt" in the provinces, stirred up by the ousted Girondins, the Convention still had on its hands a royalist uprising in the Vendée, the financial crisis, the food shortages and high cost of living, and the foreign war which was once again threatening France with invasion.

All of these problems reacted upon Paris, where the sans-culottes were being whipped up by rather shortsighted leaders, called *Enragés,* who threatened to bring on another "day" at the expense, this time, of the leaders of the Mountain. The *Enragés* were obscure neighborhood leaders, some genuinely concerned with the condition of the poorer people in Paris, some merely ambitious. Such men were perhaps dimly class-conscious, but had no broad interpretation of events. They considered themselves "practical" and, being better able than the Convention's leaders to express in the crude language of the street corners the irritations of the common man, became serious rivals of the Mountain for leadership of the sans-culottes.

Leaders in the Convention, like Robespierre, knew that the republic could not live without the support of the sans-culottes, and were realistic enough to make concessions to the latter's rudimentary ideas of social justice. But they also knew that the support of the bulk of the middle class and peasants all over France was likewise essential. The Convention was all that was left of a national government. It was the symbol of the unity of the sovereign French people in support of the revolution. If it fell before another onslaught of the poorer sections of Paris, something resembling anarchy would take its place and France's fate might be decided by counter-revolutionists and foreign invaders.

In the face of all these threats steps were taken to allay the most serious discontents. At the same time there began to form a government capable of disciplining as well as appeasing the Convention's dangerously turbulent allies. A brief and very democratic "Jacobin" constitution was hastily prepared in June, 1793, ratified by the votes of about 2,000,000 citizens throughout the country, and promulgated on August 10. It was clearly intended to refute Girondin accusations that the Mountain and Paris aimed at a dictatorship over the rest of France. Whether or not it was more than a political maneuver, the constitution was not put into effect, for such action would have meant the end of the Convention, and nationwide, democratic elections in the midst of foreign and civil war. Instead, a new Committee of Public Safety was formed, and Robespierre because of his reputation for uprightness was named to it on July 27, 1793. Émigré lands were sold in small lots, to satisfy the poorer peasants, and all surviving seigneurial dues were abolished without compensation. On August 23 the *levée en masse* was decreed: a complete mobilization of the nation, the first such act in modern times. Persons of all ages were subject to service where needed, and the government was directed to establish manufactures of arms and to requisition the necessary workmen and materials.

The assassination of the radical journalist and deputy Marat in his bath on July 13, by a young royalist girl named Charlotte Corday, left Robespierre the outstanding figure on the left. Under his leadership the Committee of Public Safety succeeded in July and August in crushing the federalist revolt, and took the offensive against the *Enragés.* But the danger from Paris was not over.

Some of the Parisians politicians, led by the journalist Hébert, set themselves up as the heirs of Marat in radical journalism, and of the *Enragés* in making social demands calculated to please the lower classes. Their chance came at the end of the summer, when a bread shortage gave rise to talk of speculators in high places. Moreover, the angry public heard news of a plot to liberate Marie Antoinette, and then news of the surrender of Toulon to the British. In these circumstances it was easy for the Hébertists to arouse the Jacobins, the Paris Commune, and the sections, and organize a great manifestation on September 5, which forced the Convention to declare Terror the "order of the day," and adopt many of the measures which the sans-culottes had been demanding. The Law of Suspects (September 17) provided a program of jailing suspect persons (rather vaguely defined) on the initiative of local committees. A new Law of the Maximum (September 29) ordered a nationwide attempt to fix prices and wages. On October 10 the official setting aside of the Jacobin constitution took place when it was declared that an emergency existed and that the government was "revolutionary." The Committee of Public Safety was to head the emergency government, giving periodic accounts to the Convention.

The Reign of Terror was several things. It was a war government at a time when ordinary constitutional methods would be slow and perhaps undo the unity that was needed in the face of the enemy. Secondly, the Reign of Terror was a means of satisfying the people's emotional response to the crisis. The government had to act against traitors and high prices to keep the people from acting independently and lawlessly. In the third place the Terror was a means of controlling the public. There was more than the problem of defending the Convention. There was also the enforcement of sacrifices once the system of price controls, taxes, forced loans, and recruiting was under way. In the fourth place the Terror was, in the eyes of some people, an opportunity to win permanent social benefits for the lower classes. Because of disagreements about how this would be done and how long it would take, a fifth characteristic of the Terror was to come into play: the use of the Terror by the Terrorists against each other.

The members of the Committee of Public Safety were not all of the same view. Carnot, the military organizer, was a moderate. Billaud-Varenne and Collot d'Herbois were radical Hébertist members of the Convention who were added to the committee after the September crisis. Robespierre and his young colleague Saint-Just were advanced and puritanical democrats who believed in social equality. Much of the committee's work was administrative, and Carnot in particular has been praised for his service to the country. But the work of the politicians Robespierre and Saint-Just was necessary to the preservation of the Committee in the Convention and of the Convention in its precarious Parisian environment.

By the end of 1793 the federalist revolt was dead. The English had been expelled from Toulon with the help of a soldier named Bonaparte. The Vendée rebellion was seriously weakened. By hard work, and through their Deputies on Mission, who sometimes behaved with despotic cruelty; through the Revolutionary Tribunal, the network of Jacobin clubs, and increasing controls over sectional meetings and local governments, the Convention committees pacified the country. By more hard work armies were recruited and generals found, sometimes purged, and replaced. The armies were equipped and fed. By means of the vast shaky edifice of price and wage controls a temporary slackening in the runaway inflation was achieved.

The armies began to move forward, directed by a core of professionals but practicing new ideas of movement and mass attack released by the fearful shake-up in personnel. By June and July, 1794, they were invading the Belgian Netherlands and crossing the Rhine.

Besides dealing with the military and political crisis the Convention, amazingly enough, continued to build for the future, planning for free public education, the Louvre Museum of Art, the Museum of Natural History, the National Library, National Archives, the metric system, the abolition of Negro slavery, the postal service, public relief, encouragement to artists and scientists. A measure of their optimism is the revolutionary calendar completed on November 24, 1793, with metric weeks of ten days, and months with poetic names, like Germinal (budding), Thermidor (heat), Vendémiaire (vintage), Prairial (meadows), Ventôse (wind), Brumaire (fog). The calendar was untraditional and un-Christian, and completed the previously decreed inauguration of a new era of mankind, which had begun with the fall of the monarchy in 1792.

It was in the spring of 1794 that the Terror government began to break up under the weight of its burdens and the strain of its disagreements. For the moderate Plain of the Convention, and indeed most of the deputies of the Mountain, the great and clumsy control mechanism provided by the General Maximum on prices and wages was a temporary wartime measure to be abandoned in favor of a free economy as soon as possible. Similarly, the suspicion and vindictiveness with which former nobles and rich *bourgeois* had been treated, appeared harmful to the revolution, for the services of able men, whatever their origin, were needed. Yet to the sans-culottes, government regulations and attacks on the upper classes had held out a promise of social betterment which they and their defenders could not bear to give up. The problem of religion also caused trouble, for the extremism of some of the Parisian political leaders threatened the principle of freedom of worship. An atheistic Festival of Reason celebrated at Notre Dame, the Cathedral of Paris, in November of 1793 threatened to alienate friendly neutrals as well as Catholics throughout France.

These differences of opinion became in the winter of 1793–1794 the rallying points for factions within the Mountain itself. The "Indulgents" attacked the Hébertists and, by implication, the policies of the Committee of Public Safety, for extremism and interference with liberty. Led by Danton, the Indulgents hoped to break the alliance of the Committee of Public Safety with the sans-culottes as a preliminary to a change of government which would enable Danton to take office, end the Terror, and make peace with the great powers. Danton and his friends were motivated by a desire for repose and amnesty from the strenuous "virtue" of the Terror, which equated profiteering with treason. Their arguments had a strong appeal. The majority of the Convention had little sympathy for the moralistic, reforming, egalitarian democracy which was clearly Robespierre's aim.

Robespierre, as the most influential of the politicians of the Committee of Public Safety, was determined to yield neither to the Hébertist extremism nor to the back-to-normalcy movement of the Indulgents. Although his colleagues on the two great committees of Public Safety and General Security were of various tendencies, they managed to repress their personal animosities and differences of

view until the worst of the crisis was over. The dictatorship was exercised collectively by the committees, and increasingly by the Committee of Public Safety
at the expense of that of General Security. In the spring of 1794 the Committee
of Public Safety, although irritable from overwork, managed to hold together
long enough to stave off bids for power by the Hébertists and Dantonists.

The campaign against the Hébertists took place on two fronts. In the
Ventôse decrees (February 26, March 3) the Committee tried to assure itself of
the allegiance of the sans-culottes and poorer peasants with the prospect that a
great survey of the property confiscated from public enemies would lead to free
distribution to needy patriots. On March 13 the Hébertists, who were working
for another insurrection, were arrested on grounds of conspiracy and treason,
quickly tried, and on March 24 guillotined.

Danton's associates had been under investigation, and no sooner had the
Hébertists been arrested than a batch of Dantonists was indicted for corrupt
financial dealings. Most of them were certainly guilty, but the Committees of
Public Safety and General Security were after bigger game. Danton himself and
the journalist Desmoulins, it was decided, were endangering the whole winter's
efforts by preaching reconciliation at home and abroad just at the start of the
spring military offensives, which were to win a chance of negotiation from
strength and therefore of real peace. The trial and execution of the Dantonists
for corruption and complicity in a foreign plot took place from April 2 to 5, 1794.
Although few doubted what research has since demonstrated—the considerable
financial corruption in this group—the main reason for their elimination was
the political threat which their policies represented.

The factions to left and right were gone, but the Terror accelerated. On
June 10 was passed the notorious Law of 22 Prairial, which removed many of the
safeguards to individual liberty in the procedure of the Revolutionary Tribunal
at Paris, including the Convention's right to decide the treatment of its own
members. In June and July, 1794, some 1,300 people were guillotined, a figure
greater than the total in Paris in the past year. Since this was a time of victories
in the foreign war and relaxation of the economic controls, the question was
bound to arise: why all this severity? Those who yearned for peace and business
as usual—and they were the majority of the Convention—could see no sense to it.
Those who had associations with Hébertist extremism or Dantonist corruption
were frightened by it. The Robespierrist ideal of an egalitarian republic held together by the public spirit of its citizens, an ideal which had seemed so noble while
France was in danger and needed sacrifices, now emerged as a minority view
placed in power by a crisis. Its champions, the organizers of victory, looked like
fanatics now that victory was in sight. Even the civic religion which Robespierre
supported as a counter-attraction to the Hébertists' atheistic de-Christianizing was
at best proof to the Convention and the public of the puritanical reforming
character of their government and at worst made Robespierre appear to be
ambitious for personal dictatorship.

Robespierre's function as defender of the Committee of Public Safety
in the Convention and in the Jacobin Club had made him a symbol of the revolutionary government. His aloof manner and his suspicion of anyone who op-

posed the government made him seem like a dictator when in fact he neither presided over the committee nor acted without the agreement of his colleagues. The Committee had held together against the threats of the Hébertists and Dantonists as persons, but they proved unable to agree on the policy questions posed by these groups. It was a crucial moment when the war should perhaps have been ended before the increasing national bitterness of the French toward other peoples, and the temptation to exploit conquered territory, made a negotiated peace impossible. By this time the majority of the French people were hostile to the emergency regime with its terror and regulations. The committee members themselves were worn out by a long year of crisis and overwork, and their personal dislikes and suspicions came to the fore and broke into violent disputes which could not be kept secret from the public. They still had the dictatorship, still drove the machine, but did not know where to turn it.

In July, 1794, came the collapse—from within. It was the disagreements within the Great Committee which released the fear and indignation in the other committees and in the Convention. Robespierre, with the majority against him, came to the end of his resources. Perhaps realizing the hopelessness of his position—an egalitarian democrat in a huge country not ready to practice this ideal government and wanting only to go about its business—he withdrew for a while from the Committee and from the Convention. When he returned, it was to appeal to the Convention over the heads of his fellow committee members, in a threatening and bankrupt speech on July 26 which could promise only more discipline, more purges, more sacrifices.

The Convention was hostile but mute, and Robespierre, knowing he had failed, repeated his speech at the Jacobin Club that night and returned to face the Convention the next day. There he was shouted down by prearranged outbursts from those who feared him most. He and his closest associates were arrested and jailed. The sans-culottes released the Robespierrists from jail that night, but leaderless and without real enthusiasm, the brief insurrection dwindled away as Robespierre and his friends hesitated to attack the Convention in whose name they had always ruled. When a force from the Convention arrested them, Robespierre tried to shoot himself but succeeded only in wounding his jaw. Next day, July 28 (10 Thermidor), he and his associates were guillotined. The men who had struck down Robespierre had not intended to end the Terror, but they soon found themselves swamped in a wave of genuine relief. It was a popular reaction, but toward what?

THE THERMIDORIAN REACTION
AND THE DIRECTORY

The "Thermidorian Reaction" is the term which has come to be applied to the remainder of the life of the Convention after the fall of Robespierre. On the calendar it lasted until October 26, 1795, when the Convention's work of making a constitution was done and a new government, usually called the "Directory," after the name of its executive, was installed. The Thermidorian Reaction and the Directory may be thought of together, for after the summer of 1794 the revolution tried to return toward the moderate positions of 1789–1792. The effort failed.

To the middle class people who were trying to stabilize a not-too-radical republic, royalism on the one hand and Jacobinism on the other provided perpetual nightmares. In earlier days the revolutionists had confronted the right with the backing of an aroused people. With what would they arm themselves now that they no longer dared appeal to the lower classes? Fearing both royalism and Jacobinism, and still involved in a foreign war, they tried to bring the revolution to an end. They honestly tackled some of its thorny problems, but they interfered at crucial times with elections, and relied increasingly on the support of the army. They prepared the way for dictatorship.

The military campaign of 1794, over which Dantonists, Robespierrists, and others had quarreled before 9 Thermidor, turned out well for the French. In July Belgium was invaded and Tuscany and Spain were knocked out of the enemy coalition. In the autumn, while the Thermidorian Reaction was under way, French armies advanced into Holland and toward the Rhine, threatening Prussian territory. Prussia sued for peace, which was concluded at Basel in April of 1795. Meanwhile, during an unusually cold winter, French cavalry had captured the Dutch fleet which was caught in the ice in the Texel river (January, 1795). The French also took Amsterdam, and in May, 1795 (Treaty of the Hague) Holland became a republic allied to France. In July, 1795, an attempted British and royalist landing at Quiberon Bay in Brittany was a failure and the hopes of French émigrés fell. With Prussia and Russia distracted by Poland, which was about to be partitioned for the third time, only England and Austria remained to oppose the French. The First Coalition was breaking up as the Convention drew to a close in the fall of 1795.

While the French armies were winning victories during the last months of the convention, the Thermidorian Reaction dismantled the machinery of the Terror, reasserted the control of the Convention over its committees, welcomed back the surviving Girondin deputies, and put an end to the Revolutionary Tribunal and the Jacobin clubs. There was a period of "white terror" during which gangs of jeunesse dorée (gilded youth) expressed the changed mood by beating and jailing sans-culottes and Jacobin sympathizers, and numerous former terrorists were executed. Meanwhile victims of the Reign of Terror were released, or their survivors compensated, and émigrés began to return. A revival of religion redounded to the benefit of the Catholic faith. The Convention in September, 1795, virtually separated church and state.

The removal of price controls, the continued inflation, unemployment, and bitter weather made the winter of 1794–1795 a hard one for the lower classes, and they responded with uprisings in April and May of 1795 (12 Germinal, 1 Prairial). Lacking in leadership, these protests failed to overthrow the Convention or turn it from its decision to abandon the Jacobin Constitution of 1793 in favor of an entirely new one.

The Constitution of the Year III (1795) was a moderate republican document designed to avoid the errors of the past and to place in power the propertied and educated members of the community. Suffrage was very broad, but the vote was indirect and the electors chosen by the citizens had to be rather substantial property-holders. The electoral assemblies chose a bicameral legislature which consisted of a Council of Five Hundred which passed resolutions. These became laws when the Council of Elders (250 members) ratified them. The executive consisted of five Directors chosen by the Elders from a list prepared by the Five Hundred. One of the Directors was to be replaced each year. The Thermidorian Convention claimed that it was replacing crisis, or revolutionary, government with a normal constitutional regime. In reality it dared not do so, and in a supplementary decree required that two thirds of the membership of the first legislature should consist of members of the Convention. Although this "two-thirds decree" was ratified in France at large along with the constitution, it was defeated in Paris, and the "perpetuals" of the Thermidorian Convention came in for much abuse. On October 5, 1795 (13 Vendémiaire), the Convention was saved from another Parisian insurrection, this time royalist, by a "whiff of grapeshot" from Napoleon's carefully placed artillery. As the Directory got under way at the end of the month its reputation as a normal constitutional regime was already soiled.

The Directory managed to function as a liberal and moderate government until 1797. Until then, it faced some of its necessary though unpleasant tasks, such as repudiation of paper money, and appeared to be on the way to ending the war. For a moment in 1796 communism, in the shape of the "Conspiracy of the Equals" led by François-Emile Babeuf, appeared on the scene. For years royalists and conservatives of all kinds had been predicting that the drive toward equality would end in an attack on private property itself. Babeuf and a few of his associates made this prediction come true. Disappointed with mere civil and political equality, they thought in terms of socialistic distribution of goods, and hoped to reach their goal through the dictatorship of a minority. They represented, however, no real danger to the Directory. Most of Babeuf's followers were Jacobins who wanted only a return to the Constitution of 1793. There were government agents among them, and the movement was easily crushed. Babeuf and many of his following were arrested in 1796 and tried in 1797. Babeuf himself was guillotined.

Meanwhile, in March, 1796, the young officer Napoleon Bonaparte got his first big command. He was only twenty-seven but the revolutionary turnover in the army had given him his chance and he had shown his skill against the British at Toulon in 1793 and later with troops on the Italian front. In 1795 he had been stricken from the list of generals for making excuses to avoid taking part in the Vendée civil war, but the Convention's need for protection after the two-thirds decree had given his luck a fortunate turn. After 13 Vendémiaire he was made commander of the Army of the Interior, and was the officer who closed the radical clubs at the time of the Babeuvist agitation. In March, 1796, he was placed in command of the Army of Italy, which was expected to play a subordinate part in the reopened campaign against Austria in the summer of that year.

The main offensive and permanent territorial gain were intended to be on the Rhine. If possible the Army of Italy was to seize lands with which to bargain when Austria was forced to agree to French annexation of the Rhineland, its "natural frontier."

THE TURNING POINT OF 1797

At this point in the story three elements—Napoleon's genius, the Directory's foreign policy, and internal French politics—must be seen as parts of one picture. Napoleon won spectacular victories in Italy, forced peace upon Sardinia and other Italian states, and made the war pay by extracting art treasures and cash indemnities from his defeated opponents. Some of the spoils he sent to the Directory, some he kept for himself, and some he distributed to his troops. He was becoming independent of the supervision of the Directory. The commissioners sent to watch him lacked the power of punishment which the representatives of the Committee of Public Safety had had during the Reign of Terror. Further, the Directory's need for self-supporting armies, and the loyalty of Napoleon's troops to him, made civilian control next to impossible. In the spring of 1797 Napoleon campaigned successfully against the Austrians and made an armistice with them on his own terms. He then went ahead with the creation of satellite "Ligurian" and "Cisalpine" republics in northern Italy, and in addition seized the ancient Republic of Venice.

Napoleon's independent behavior and the Directory's inclination to tolerate it had momentous consequences. French foreign policy in the first year and a half of the Directory was balanced on a knife edge between making peace with England and Austria and pursuing tempting conquests which would make peace impossible for an indefinite period. In general the royalists and social conservatives leaned toward peace, even if it meant abandoning the conquests of the revolutionary armies. The moderate revolutionaries of the Directory, and indeed the French armies, would not have consented to such an outcome. But the revolutionaries were not of one mind as to peace terms. If they could make peace on the continent they thought they could eventually force Britain to terms. But they were not in full agreement concerning how many of their conquests to retain. Retention of the "natural frontiers" (Rhine, Alps, Pyrenees) about which there had been much discussion since the beginning of the war would mean the annexation of at least Belgium and the Rhineland, with compensations elsewhere for Austria and Prussia. Such a solution was perhaps possible, though difficult, but if France attempted permanent conquests beyond its natural frontiers it could scarcely expect to bring the war to a close.

There was no certainty that the Directory could resist the temptations of expansionism, even in the absence of Napoleon. Certainly it did not try to check his independent behavior in Italy and Austria, which envisaged French expansion *beyond* the natural frontiers. For Napoleon, besides securing recognition of

The Conquests of Revolutionary France, 1792–1799

Belgium and the left bank of the Rhine as French territories, made Austria renounce its claims in Italy, and recognize France's satellite Cisalpine Republic there. Austria was to be compensated on the right bank of the Rhine and was to be given Venice, which Napoleon had conquered. This trafficking in provinces was the point to which the French revolutionary liberation of peoples had sunk! The terms were signed and the Austrians and French made peace for the first time since 1792, near the little village of Campo Formio, in Venetian territory, on October 17, 1797.

Campo Formio was a peace treaty with Austria, but it was not likely to last. Simultaneously French-English peace negotiations, which had been taking place at Lille, took a turn for the worse. The prospect of peace was disappearing. On his return from Italy at the end of 1797, Napoleon was put in command of the "Army of England," and studied plans for an invasion. That proving too dangerous, he was off in May, 1798, to invade Egypt (as a blow at British India), while at home the jubilant French government decorated itself with a necklace of satellite republics: the Cisalpine (Lombardy, in part); the Roman (Papal States); the Helvetic (Swiss Cantons); the Batavian (Holland); the Parthenopean (Naples). Owing to this gluttonous policy and to Napoleon's invasion of Egypt, a Second Coalition began to form against France. By early 1799 it consisted of Turkey, England, Russia, Naples, and Austria. France began to lose battles. Once again the republic seemed in danger.

France's expansionist foreign policy, which was to help put an end to the Directory in 1799, was partly the result of internal politics. The Directory was dependent on the military for its security against opposition at home. On the eve of the Treaty of Campo Formio in 1797 there occurred an event reminiscent of the troubles that followed the two-thirds decree. The Directors purged the Legislature and annulled some 200 elections, in what has come to be known as the Coup of 18 Fructidor (4 September, 1797). In this way they nullified a royalist and conservative victory at the polls. All Europe had been awaiting the outcome of these elections. The royalists, who stood for peace, were being subsidized by the British, who were in the midst of peace talks with the French at Lille while Napoleon negotiated with the Austrians in Italy. The Directory's flagrant falsification of the Fructidor election results was protected by troops sent by Napoleon to Paris. Under the circumstances it was scarcely to be expected that the Directors would be able to unmake the diplomatic commitments which Napoleon was so boldly completing. The balance tipped away from peace toward expansionism.

After 1797 the Directory was really a dictatorship which refused to allow the establishment of peacetime political conditions. A second coup d'état took place on May 11, 1798 (22 Floréal). This time the Directory found substitutes for many Jacobins who had been chosen in the elections. On June 18, 1799 (30 Prairial) they were prepared to purge the legislature again, for when military and naval setbacks were suffered the public, as in the past, turned toward leftists who advocated extreme measures. This time the legislature took action first, and purged the Directory. The atmosphere became ominously like that of 1793, with royalist and Catholic outbreaks intensified in the Vendée and the menace of invasion by the foreign coalition. A Law of Hostages was passed (12 July) by the newly radical legislature. Although the French armies began to win victories again, the very passing of the danger made the situation seem intolerable to the moderate revolutionaries. How long could this go on, this uncertaintly in which some sudden turn of events might throw the country into Royalist counter-revolution or a new Reign of Terror? And if it was not to go on, what firm mooring post was there to which a moderate regime might be attached?

Past appeals of the Thermidorian Convention and the Directory to the army gave the answer. The longer the war continued, and the farther from home it was fought, the greater became the sense of comradeship in the army and the reliance of the men on their officers. Along with the blatant new rich emerging from years of upheaval and inflation and the presence of a new generation of youth disillusioned with politics and eager to get ahead in the world, this new power and pride in the army was one of the social changes conspicuous under the Directory.

Of all the generals, Napoleon had the greatest reputation. He had reached Egypt in June, 1798, and taken Alexandria and Cairo, but had been cut off from home by the English Admiral Nelson's victory over the French fleet at Aboukir Bay. As the Second Coalition formed and the French conquests in Europe began to be lost, Napoleon saw that both his personal fortunes and the ultimate fate of the Egyptian expedition depended on the outcome of events in France and Europe. Secretly and without permission from the French government, he abandoned his Egyptian army and with a small flotilla managed to evade the British and land in the South of France in October, 1799. His journey to Paris became a triumphal march, so popular was he and so unpopular the Directory. In Paris both the Jacobins and the moderates hoped for his support. He decided to ally with the moderates, led by Sieyès.

Abbé Sieyès was the man who gave the theoretical answer to the problem of a firm mooring for a moderate regime. He was that same Sieyès of 1789, of the famous pamphlet *What is the Third Estate?*, which had taught the National Assembly and subsequent bodies to act in the name of the sovereign people. Abbé Sieyès had later shown the deputies how to take some of the sting out of popular sovereignty by distinguishing between "active" and "passive" citizens. Nevertheless, the revolution had gone considerably to the left of Sieyès, and he had remained very quiet as a member of the Plain in the Convention during the Terror. The Thermidorians had not followed his advice in making the Constitution of 1795, but he had been a member of the Council of Five Hundred and had become a Director in June, 1799—a Trojan horse, for he wished to change the regime.

Sieyès possessed very complicated conceptions of political science. He had been from the beginning of the revolution a theoretician of representative government. When he became alarmed at the royalist and Jacobin threats which free elections posed to the Directory, Sieyès did not abandon the sovereignty of the people, but altered his theory of representation to emphasize the *capacity* of the representatives rather than their choice by the people. There would still be elections, but the public was only to choose lists of *eligibles*. From these lists the men already in power would select the most reliable persons to fill the representative bodies of the government. It was a formal and legal way of doing what the Thermidorian Convention by the two-thirds rule, and the Directory, by the coups of Fructidor, 1797, and Floréal, 1798, had been doing: co-opting new members for the legislature.

This was the essence of the Sieyès plan of 1799 for drawing the fangs of popular sovereignty. There was still the danger that a military dictatorship would ensue if the plotters relied on a general. Sieyès and his friends knew that they were taking a risk of Napoleon's becoming dictator, but saw no attractive alternative, and took the chance, hoping that Napoleon, who was still only thirty, could be surrounded and guided by older men.

The *coup d'état* of 18–19 Brumaire (November 9–10, 1799) did not establish a military dictatorship, though contrary to plan it was necessary to appeal to the troops to make it succeed. On the pretext of a Jacobin plot a hasty meeting of the Council of Elders was called on 18 Brumaire. The Elders moved the legislature to suburban Saint-Cloud and placed Napoleon in command of the troops in Paris. Of the five Directors, who should have been behaving like an executive authority, Sieyès and two others resigned and the remaining two were placed in protective custody. On 19 Brumaire at Saint-Cloud the Council of Five Hundred almost spoiled the plan by shouting down Napoleon and calling for his arrest. His brother Lucien rescued him from the hall with the help of troops, and after that the two succeeded in convincing the troops that the legislature should be dispersed. That night enough deputies of the two chambers were convoked to give a legal appearance to the affair by naming Sieyès, another ex-director, and Napoleon as provisional "consuls," and appointing two constitutional commissions, one from each house.

Between November 10 and December 14, 1799, the period of the Provisional Consulate, a constitution was prepared along lines proposed by Sieyès. It became clear, however, that Napoleon was too intelligent and vigorous to be "contained" by the precautions of Sieyès. What was intended as a means of assuring the rule of an oligarchy of moderate revolutionaries became the vehicle of Napoleon's dictatorship. This Constitution of the Year VIII, which will be described later, was ratified in February, 1800, after it had been in effect for more than two months. Long since, the makers of the coup had filled out the new Senate, which named the members of the Tribunate and Legislature. Napoleon had persuaded the constitutional commissions to approve the naming of himself as First Consul. Sieyès, who had been unable to withstand Napoleon's seizure of power, was "rewarded" with the presidency of the Senate and a substantial estate. The public, caring little for constitutional subtleties, correctly saw Bonaparte's aquiline face mirrored in the constitution but ratified it 3,000,000 to 1,500. Napoleon himself knew that only accomplishments could keep him in power.

24

EUROPE'S DUEL
WITH NAPOLEON

THE CAREER OF Napoleon Bonaparte is an adventure story, one of the most astounding of all time. It is also the story of France, for without the great forces of the French nation, which he had the good fortune to encounter at the right moment, Napoleon might have lived out his days in sullen obscurity, an undiscovered genius. Napoleon's story is also Europe's.

France's position in Europe was never more powerful than in Napoleon's time. This would have been the case even if he had never been born. It was (almost) the largest nation in numbers, and incomparably the strongest. France provided the instrument upon which Napoleon played, and any effort to pass judgment on him must assess the uses to which he put these splendid assets. But France was not a passive instrument. It was possessed of a thousand sentiments and urges which Napoleon had done nothing to create, and which he could perhaps guide but never repress. Napoleon's career is a supreme example of individual will and temperament at grips with great collective forces.

Europe on the eve of the shock and rearrangement which Napoleon was to bring to it had not yet given itself single-mindedly to the defeat of France. Playing skillfully upon its divisions, Napoleon almost unified Europe by conquest. In the end he left it more deeply divided than before, as the nations which opposed him became more vividly aware of their own identities. Yet in international relations there was more of a sense of "Europe" among the powers when Napoleon was finally defeated than there had been before he made his challenge.

The story of Napoleon in France and Europe is also the story of a war of ideas—often overlooked when attention is focussed on battles and coalitions. The French Revolution, even when supposedly tamed by Napoleon's will, never ceased to represent a political threat to the European rulers, and a social threat to the European aristocracies. And defenders of tradition continued to be affronted by the spiritual pride and messianic pretensions of the French Revolution. This conflict of ideals was more lasting than Napoleon, and more lasting than the coalition which finally defeated him.

THE CONSULATE

Napoleon had come to power by overthrowing the feeble Directory and issuing the Constitution of the Year VIII, which laid the groundwork for one man's rule in the name of all.

The constitution was democratic in appearance, for there was universal manhood suffrage, but the voters chose only lists of local men eligible for public office, not the officers themselves. The local eligibles chose some of their number for a department list of eligibles, who in turn chose a national list. From the national list a Senate (which came into being with the constitution and filled out its own membership) would choose the members of two houses of the legislature: the Tribunate, to discuss projects of law proposed by the government; and the Legislature, to accept or reject the projects without discussion after hearing explanations from the Tribunate and the executive. The Senate was also to name three Consuls who were the executive power—hence the name "Consulate" for the republican government from 1799–1804. The Consuls had ten-year terms. It was the First Consul who had all the real powers, including appointment and dismissal of members of the Council of State, and ministers, ambassadors, and military commanders, as well as the members of the local administration. There was no Declaration of Rights in the constitution, but under "general provisions" it was made clear that gains of the revolution such as transfers of property were to be preserved.

Napoleon is said to have remarked approvingly that this constitution was "short and obscure." It set up a screen of apparently representative institutions behind which an oligarchy could work undisturbed. The lists of notables, never completed as planned, were a means of suppressing elections without appearing to do so. The assemblies were not chosen by the people, but by the conspirators of 18 Brumaire—they were "notables" called in for consultation, like the Assembly of Notables of the old regime. The French people were still sovereign in theory but they were no longer consulted.

The men in positions of power were still the revolutionaries. Napoleon could not do everything himself. Those who staffed the French government, from the great office-holders of Paris down to the departmental and local dignitaries were the men of 1789, of the Constitution of 1791, of the Thermidorian Reaction and the Directory: middle class people, for the most part, who still believed in the principles of the Revolution; people with a certain amount of education. They were a minority, but they were more numerous than the aristocracy whose overthrow had given them their chance to run things in their communities. Although they had not been consulted about the inauguration of the Constitution of the Year VIII, they were tired of instability and were willing to accept the new regime if it could spare them a choice between complete reaction and another Reign of Terror. They were to administer France for Napoleon, and indeed, with minor changes, were to administer France through all its nineteenth-century regimes.

If France had remained a democracy after 1799, men of this kind would have made the laws and exercised some control over the executive. As things worked out, the revolutionaries lost control of the executive.

The real question was whether Napoleon could dominate his fellow conspirators of Brumaire. The legislative chambers, and even the Council of State, put up some resistance at first, for they did not want his dictation, and accepted it only as a necessary evil. Napoleon growled that he could throw them to the Jacobins—a reminder that they had not stabilized the situation in France in ten years of trying and that now it was his turn.

Napoleon's real title to authority could only be success in governing, and he plunged at once into enormous bouts of work in his study in the Tuileries. He had a fine, clear mind and an unusual grasp of details, but what was rare about him was the combination of these assets with a powerful imagination verging on the visionary, and complete lack of awe in the face of large difficulties or ancient traditions. He relished solving problems—and the exercise of power—as others relished popularity and riches. When he met with his Council of State— men of experience in various posts during the Revolution and in some cases before—he held his own with them, discussed with them, learned from them, in what was surely one of the most astounding seminars of all time. If he had had ideals to place above his own career, and respect for others and a sense of service to humanity, he might have proved to be a stabilizing influence in European history. As it was, his star led him for a few years to serve France's best interests, before it drew him away into a hopeless duel with Europe.

THE REFORMS

These first years, from 1800 to 1804, saw accomplishments which would be unbelievable if the ground had not been prepared by ten years of assemblies, commissions, and half-finished projects. Napoleon drove his team of revolutionary politicians and old regime officials hard. Tax collections were reformed and centralized. The Bank of France was founded (1800) by a kind of alliance with the bankers, who handled government money and were allowed to monopolize the issuing of banknotes. The local administration of departments, districts, and communes, with prefects, sub-prefects, and mayors, all named from above, gave France the firm administrative structure which was to outlast all subsequent revolutions. Assemblies on all levels, named from above, gave scope for moderate revolutionaries and returned émigrés who were loyal to the regime. The police were reorganized. The system of courts was recast to harmonize with the local governments. The interior of France was pacified by a combination of ferocity and persuasion. Troops were ordered to shoot rebels caught with weapons in their hands, but loyal Catholics were allowed to use the churches again. Royalists were encouraged to return to France.

Napoleon also had to convince everyone that his foreign enemies were not capable of overthrowing him. In the spring of 1800 this meant another fight with Austria. While the public was predicting his downfall if he lost, Napoleon plunged into Italy and in the middle of June won the battle of Marengo. The Austrians retreated and signed an armistice which was turned into surrender in December when General Moreau defeated them at Hohenlinden. By the ensuing Treaty of Lunéville in February, 1801, Austria ceded the left bank of the Rhine to France. The Cisalpine Republic was extended by the addition of Papal territories. Soon Piedmont was annexed to France.

Through the year 1801 and into 1802 Napoleon was engaged in trying to turn war into victorious peace. Early in 1801 he began preparing for an invasion of England, induced Spain to prepare to attack Britain's ally, Portugal, and roused the opinion of other nations against Britain's highhanded actions on the seas. The British decided to negotiate. In the preliminaries signed in October, 1801, and in the Peace of Amiens of March 25, 1802, the terms were very favorable to France, for the British returned to them Egypt, Elba, and other conquests, and received little in return except an opportunity to test Napoleon's intentions. Europe was at peace for the first time since 1792.

Meanwhile Napoleon had been completing his hold on France. In December of 1800 when a royalist bomb missed him on his way to the opera, he took occasion to punish the left along with the right. In rural districts the brigandage which had accompanied royalist and Catholic resistance was wiped out, an accomplishment which won Napoleon the gratitude of the farmers. In July, 1801, in a Concordat signed with Pope Pius VII, the schism in the French church was ended. Salaries were still to be paid by the state, as provided in the revolutionary Civil Constitution of the Clergy, and the Church recognized the nationalization of its property during the Revolution, a move which reassured the purchasers. Bishops were to be appointed by the First Consul and anointed by the Pope. In 1802, without consulting the Pope, Napoleon added the Organic Articles which reasserted the state's controls over the clergy and its publications. Protestant churches were also regulated, and their pastors also received salaries from the state. The Concordat was an immense stride toward ending Catholic opposition within France. Napoleon, without being religious himself, thought that the aid of religion was necessary to maintain order and console the people in the face of inevitable inequalities of wealth. Pope Pius, although he hated to disavow the faithful clergy who had opposed the Revolution and to displease the émigrés and the Catholic princes, could not resist the temptation to reestablish the Church's position in France.

Napoleon's republican colleagues in the army and legislative assemblies relished neither his apparent softness toward the Church and émigrés nor his tough policy in dealing with Jacobins and brigands. Napoleon had to be careful of the military. He discreetly removed or transferred his most dangerous opponents. By 1802 he was in a strong enough position to consolidate his dictatorship. When the time came for renewal of one fifth of the legislative assemblies, he had the Senate replace the more rebellious members with more docile men. Thereafter he broke the Tribunate into sections and made their discussions secret. In 1807 he was to abolish it altogether. In May, 1802, following the Peace of Amiens, the question arose of a reward for the First Consul. Napoleon took the Senate's modest proposal of reelection for ten years and transformed it into a plebiscite which approved him as Consul for life. Thereupon he dictated a new constitution, into which he inserted the right to name his own successor along with much greater powers for the First Consul, including the right to revise the constitution with the consent of the Senate, and control over the membership of the Senate. Henceforth, the assemblies, and even the Council of State, became less and less significant, and Napoleon ruled with the collaboration of the Senate, whose leading members he richly endowed.

Napoleon's Civil Code, later known as the Code Napoléon, had been in preparation since 1800, and indeed long before that, for the revolutionary assemblies had tried to give France a single set of laws in place of the customary law of the north, the written law of the south, and the countless local variations and exceptions. After Napoleon's position was consolidated in 1802, discussions of the final codification took place in 1803, and the Civil Code was promulgated in March, 1804. It was a lasting expression of what the Revolution had done to everyday life in France, and of how these changes were interpreted by Napoleon. It was also a revolutionary influence when it was exported along with French armies to the various parts of Europe. The Code confirmed the disappearance of the old regime's society of hereditary ranks and the establishment of an individualistic society in which personal liberty, equality before the law, the secular character of the state, freedom of conscience, and freedom of labor were assured. Private property was also guaranteed, and great care was taken to ensure proper titles and transfers. Some of the extremely idealistic aspects of the revolutionary legislation were toned down. The rights of children to equal inheritances were somewhat curtailed in order to increase the authority of the father. The divorce laws, which had been relaxed in the interests of individual freedom, were tightened again in the interest of preserving the family, which Napoleon considered to be the basic unit in society. Husbands were given extensive powers in the administration of the property of their wives, and could imprison rebellious children for six months without trial. Employers and their property were safeguarded against employees. In wage disputes the word of the employer had precedence over that of the worker. As under the revolutionary governments, labor unions were illegal. Slavery, considered indispensable to the economy of the colonies, was reestablished. But these exceptions, which catch the twentieth-century eye, should not be allowed to obscure the fact that the Code, applied to any old regime society, in France or elsewhere, was basically egalitarian and individualistic. It embodied the civic reforms of the French Revolution, which Napoleon preserved while making a mockery of representative government.

NAPOLEON IN HIS STUDY by Jacques Louis David. French school, 1748–1825. (National Gallery of Art, Washington, D.C., Samuel H. Kress Collection, Loan)

ESTABLISHMENT OF THE EMPIRE

By the time the Code was finished in 1804, Napoleon was at war again. The Peace of Amiens had served him well in domestic politics, but he made no effort to prolong it. By temperament, he was inclined toward further adventures. His restless imagination was teeming with other projects. He toyed with the idea of developing Louisiana, before selling it to the United States in 1803. His envoys were probing Egypt and India, he was still expanding in Italy, and he had made a satellite out of Switzerland. In the Germanies since 1801 a momentous reorganization had been going on as a result of the French annexations on the left bank of the Rhine. The more important proprietors of left bank territories were being compensated on the right bank at the expense of dozens of principalities and small ecclesiastical states. The Holy Roman Empire was clearly on its deathbed. The fundamental decisions about the reshuffle were being made in Paris.

The British made no effort to avoid hostilities. They saw the inevitability of war and hoped to have on their side some of the German states and possibly Russia, whose young Czar Alexander disliked French interest in the Near East. Refusing to evacuate the island of Malta, as required by the Treaty of Amiens, the British denounced Napoleon's infractions of that treaty, and sent in April, 1803, an ultimatum about his behavior. War came in May. This time it was to last until 1814.

The war, as always, renewed the hopes of royalists and *émigrés*. There were also plots among several of Napoleon's generals, but the public remained loyal. When there was a report that the Duke of Enghien, a prince of the Bourbon family, was involved in a plan to invade France, Napoleon had him kidnapped on neutral German soil and brought to Paris and shot. At about the same time several royalist conspirators and the opposition generals Pichegru and Moreau were arrested. The royalists were guillotined. Moreau, the victor of Hohenlinden, was banished. Pichegru was found strangled in his cell. Although the educated and well-to-do were scandalized by these events, the great majority of the French were undisturbed. Indeed, the war encouraged loyalty to the leader, and he made the most of this moment.

In May, 1804, in a plebiscite ordered by the tame Senate, Napoleon was made Emperor. The imperial constitution embodied few changes, for he was already dictator. Napoleon brought Pope Pius VII to Paris in December, 1804, for a coronation ceremony in which, like a son of Charlemagne, he placed the crown on his own head—symbolic gesture, but it was significant that the Pope was there at all. His presence suggested that the plebiscite of the sovereign people had been insufficient for the legitimacy which the new Emperor sought. No one can say what the French people thought of the spectacle in the Cathedral of Notre Dame. Certainly they wanted order and the social gains of the revolution. There is little evidence that they wished to follow where Napoleon's star was leading—toward imperial grandeur and perpetual war.

THE CONQUEST OF EUROPE

The war with Great Britain was uneventful at first, for neither the great land power nor the great sea power could strike very effectively at the other. Napoleon occupied Hanover, the German home of the British royal house, and, in 1804, assembled 1,700 invasion barges along Dover Strait. Spain and the south German states became his allies. Britain's partners included, by the summer of 1805, Russia, Sweden, Naples, and Austria. Prussia in a fateful decision remained neutral. Napoleon never had to face all the great powers simultaneously until 1813.

Spain's presence in the war gave France an opportunity to use the combined Spanish and French fleets in an invasion plan. A great project was formulated by which the main British naval force under Lord Nelson would be lured away on a wild goose chase, enabling French and Spanish squadrons from scattered European ports to concentrate in the English Channel long enough to protect the invasion barges. The plan worked in part, as the French Admiral Villeneuve sailed to the West Indies and back with Nelson on his heels. But the Franco-Spanish fleet moved too slowly, and Villeneuve overcautiously put in at Cadiz until Napoleon, abandoning the Channel project, ordered him to an attack on Naples. Villeneuve and the Spanish, numbering thirty-three ships, were attacked boldly on October 21, 1805, by Nelson's twenty-five ships in two columns, which caught them off Cape Trafalgar and sank or captured eighteen ships. Nelson was mortally wounded in the battle, but British command of the seas in the coming years was assured.

In August, 1805, Napoleon turned away from the Channel and headed for Central Europe. This decision coincided with Austria's belligerency. Napoleon later claimed that all the Channel preparations had been a feint. In any case he defeated the Austrians at Ulm in October and the combined Austrians and Russians at Austerlitz in December, 1805. By the end of the year he had concluded the Treaty of Pressburg which virtually ejected Austria from both Germany and Italy. Prussia was forced into an alliance with France, and the furious Alexander withdrew the Russian army.

The instrument with which these military miracles were performed was still the conscript army invented by the Revolution. It was not a highly trained force. Recruits learned the arts of war from veterans on the way to the front, as they had during the Revolution. Discipline was loose, and officers often knew little more than the men, but there was swift advancement for enterprise and audacity, and underneath the disorder, good morale. A strong cavalry and artillery had been built, but weapons had changed little since the old regime. This campaign of 1805 was typical of many to come. Napoleon set the army in motion with two or three days' supply of bread, enough arms and ammunition, but inadequate clothing. They requisitioned while marching rapidly forward and counted on quick victory to place the enemy's country at their disposal. Napoleon's was not a creative military mind, but he was a superb practitioner of the new warfare which had begun to take shape in the last years of the old regime and had been perfected during the Revolution. He moved rapidly in a dispersed formation which quickly located the enemy. Skirmishers probed ahead and hid the real power of the advancing columns, which concentrated rapidly on the weak spot when it was found or created by artillery fire. The objective was destruction of the opposing force, and not the taking of fortresses; pitiless pursuit usually followed the battles. For a long time Napoleon's rapidity and punch confused and disorganized his slower, more traditional opponents.

After the campaign of 1805 Napoleon's "Grand Empire" began to take shape. A formidable structure of French-controlled territories was being assembled. Austrian territories were given to Napoleon's allies in south Germany. Württemberg and Bavaria became kingdoms, and in July, 1806, a Confederation of the Rhine was formed by sixteen states, clients of Napoleon. A month later the Habsburg Holy Roman Emperor, Francis II, gave up the imperial title. The German reorganization involved what was to be a lasting simplification of the complicated map, for about three hundred and fifty knights who had been vassals of the Holy Roman Emperor and were practically tiny sovereigns were "mediatized," that is, made into subjects of the rulers whose territories surrounded theirs. Meanwhile Napoleon's relatives were donning crowns: his brother Louis in Holland, his brother Joseph in Naples. Napoleon now controlled all of Italy except the Papal States, and had taken the Dalmatian coast (present-day Yugoslavia). He began to speak of Charlemagne as his "illustrious predecessor." His opponent Pitt could well say before dying in January, 1806: "Roll up the map of Europe: it will not be wanted these ten years."

Another coalition of Napoleon's enemies rose and fell rapidly in 1806 and 1807, and left the Grand Empire grander than before. This time Prussia led the assault. Displeased by the Confederation of the Rhine, irritated by Napoleon's coolness to Prussia's pet project of a North German Confederation, and clumsily treated by Napoleon, who now appeared to be about to betray Prussia by depriving it of recently acquired Hanover, the vacillating Frederick William III was finally won over by the war party. Russia was asked for aid, and in October, 1806, war against France began. Before the month was out Napoleon had crushed the principal Prussian army at Jena and had occupied Berlin.

Frustrated by British sea power from invading the islands, he now sought to strangle them economically. It was from Berlin in November, 1806, that he launched the vast "continental system," a combined blockade of Britain and closure of the continent to British goods (see the following section). Prussia's final disposition was postponed as the Russians and remaining Prussians advanced. The battle of Eylau in East Prussia in February, 1807, was a narrow victory for Napoleon, but inconclusive, and it was not until June, after a hard northern winter, that a reinforced French army defeated the Russians at Friedland and occupied the ground as far as the Niemen River. There, on a raft, in the month of July, Napoleon and Czar Alexander sized each other up and became allies. The resulting Treaty of Tilsit ended the coalition and united the continent of Europe against Britain.

Tilsit enlarged the Napoleonic Grand Empire by taking from Prussia its

Polish lands, which became the Grand Duchy of Warsaw (under the King of Saxony, a French puppet), and several western provinces, which became the Kingdom of Westphalia under Napoleon's brother Jerome. What remained of Prussia—about half of the former territory—had to join the economic warfare against Britain, reduce its army to 42,000 men, and, as arranged in a later treaty, support a French occupation until a large indemnity was paid. The terms of Tilsit called for French benevolence toward Russian expansion at the expense of the Ottoman empire. Under circumstances which soon came to pass, Russia was to enter the continental system and the war on France's side. But Tilsit was only a temporary accommodation between the two giants, neither of whom could afford to let the other's dreams of aggrandizement come true.

Napoleon continued to go from success to dazzling success. But clouds were gathering. Portugal was occupied (November, 1807), and then Spain, where in May, 1808, Napoleon forced the abdication of both Charles IV and his rebellious son Ferdinand. From the French point of view, Spain was backward, badly governed, and ripe for a dash of enlightened reform. Napoleon, never one to appreciate other people's feelings, installed there his brother Joseph as King. Patriotic Spaniards rose in rebellion, and Joseph was driven from Madrid in less than two weeks. Europe took heart, and the British sent an expeditionary force to Portugal.

Napoleon went south in person to put out the Spanish fire, but before he left, a significant scene was played at Erfurt, Germany, in September, 1808. In order to be sure of his allies during his absence, Napoleon met with Czar Alexander and renewed his promises of friendship. The Czar was noncommittal. Talleyrand, the opportunistic bishop who had joined the revolutionaries in 1789 and was one of Napoleon's diplomatic advisors, assured Alexander privately that Napoleon's ambitions and France's interests no longer coincided. Worse, he told Metternich, Austria's chief minister for foreign affairs, of the coolness between Russia and France.

Although Napoleon went to Spain and successfully retook Madrid in December, 1808, the Austrians took advantage of his absence. Before he could crush either the Spanish or the English forces, he had to return to face another European coalition. Fortunately for Napoleon, the Austrians rushed into combat without waiting for British reinforcements on the continent. Prussia, where reforms begun by Baron Stein and others were under way (see Chapter 31), did not yet risk turning on the French. Napoleon was able, at Wagram in July, 1809, to defeat the Austrians, but this time he was far from annihilating them. When Russia and Prussia failed to help them, the Austrians made peace at Vienna (October, 1809), yielding more territories.

Characteristically, Napoleon pushed his advantage over the Habsburgs to the utmost. After divorcing Empress Josephine, who had borne him no children, in April, 1810, he married Marie Louise, daughter of Emperor Francis of Austria. But this was not the least effective of a long line of Habsburg marriages for diplomatic purposes. As Metternich had foreseen, it helped finish off the Tilsit alliance with Russia. As no one could have foreseen, the marriage preoccupied Napoleon and contributed to his failure to go to Spain in 1810 and finish the war there, as everyone expected him to do. By 1811 he was too close to war with Russia, and had to leave Spain unsubdued. In March of 1811 a son, the King of Rome, was born to the new dynasty.

THE EMPIRE AT ITS HEIGHT

A map of Europe in 1812 shows an enormous France, reaching far beyond the "natural frontiers" of Rhine, Alps, and Pyrenees—along the coast to Denmark on the north and well into the Italian peninsula in the southeast. Not counting the Illyrian Provinces on the Adriatic coast, which were also directly ruled from Paris, this greater France contained forty-four million people and was organized in 130 departments (as compared with the original 83 of the Revolution). Around the borders of the France of 1812 clustered its satellites: Spain; the states of western and northern Germany grouped in the Confederation of the Rhine; Switzerland; the Kingdom of Italy; the Kingdom of Naples; and the Grand Duchy of Warsaw. Then there were Napoleon's reluctant allies: the Empire of Austria, now landlocked; the truncated Kingdom of Prussia; and the Kingdom of Denmark-Norway. Free Europe consisted, in the west, of Britain and Portugal, although Spain was fighting for its liberty and half free. In the east Sweden, Russia, and

THE GRAND EMPIRE OF NAPOLEON ABOUT 1812

the Ottoman empire were independent. Alexander's Russia was still nominally Napoleon's ally.

The French government and court after 1810 became increasingly reactionary. This last phase of the French empire has been called a "Bourbon restoration without the Bourbons." The old nobility had long been courted by the regime. Now it began to be favored. An imperial nobility had been founded in 1808 with hereditary titles. Napoleon gave all sorts of estates, pensions, and decorations such as the Legion of Honor in an effort to solidify his regime, but in the main the old nobility remained scornful and the new ungrateful. Those who had gained the most from Napoleon, including the rich *bourgeoisie,* were in the best position to understand and resent the absence of political freedom. Among educated people it became fashionable again to like the English and the English government.

The common people, workers and peasants, had been the most loyal to Napoleon. Beginning about 1812, the weight of wars and taxes, and especially the military conscription, turned them against the emperor, but during most of his reign they were satisfied as long as food prices were reasonable and there was work, which was true during most of the period. The ordinary citizen was not in a position to notice that Napoleon was becoming more despotic, less inclined to listen to advice, and more inclined to rely on force. The public knew about the censorship of the press and theater, the use of police spies and informers, and the return of *lettres de cachet* permitting arbitrary arrests, but these things did not touch the lives of most people, and Napoleon was intelligent enough to keep it so.

Napoleon never ceased working hard. The Civil Code was supplemented by others, such as the Code of Commerce of 1807 and the Penal Code of 1810. Finances were a problem. There was too little confidence in the duration of the regime for the rich to wish to lend it money, but Napoleon had several treasuries which he filled from his campaigns, as well as from taxes.

The Continental System, inaugurated by the Berlin Decree in 1806, and developed further by the Milan Decree of 1807, and by later interpretations, was an enlargement of the kind of economic warfare which the Revolution had already undertaken. It became a gigantic mercantilistic venture, and developed from its original aim, which was to close the continent to British goods and bring bankruptcy and discouragement to the British government, into a great system of regulation of the European economy. In the latter phase, which dated from 1809, trade was permitted with the British, but the French government tried through a system of licensing to regulate its nature and volume and direction.

The earlier phase of the Continental System was able to hurt British business, especially in 1808, but the British made an enormous and successful effort to send goods to the continent, even at a loss, and they were helped by the opening of the Latin American market even before Napoleon's armies overran Portugal and Spain. The government of Great Britain continued to have the confidence of the public and to be able to borrow. The British were, moreover, already in the foothills of the mountainous development which was to be known as the Industrial Revolution.

In its later phase, when it became a kind of plan for European trade, the

Continental System suffered from its vastness and from absence of any truly dominating conception. In general agriculture was left alone, industry sporadically regulated, and commerce controlled. France was favored over the other continental countries, but in France manufacturers and farmers were better off than merchants. Some merchants—such as those dealing with Central Europe—were better off than others—such as those hurt by the British blockade. The Continental System stimulated some inventions and new products, but it contributed much to the spreading of the war and to the downfall of Napoleon.

Napoleon sought to regulate thought and the arts. They for the most part eluded him, but he was able to shape certain institutions of modern France. His Concordat with the Catholic Church was to last into the twentieth century, but although he took Rome and made the Pope a prisoner in France, he was unable to subordinate the Church. Indeed, his bullying of it, coupled with the religious revival, helped rehabilitate the Church in the eyes of the public. Napoleon gave France the University—a public corporation having the monopoly of education. Private schools were still permitted, subject to inspection, but the principle of public education was established. Napoleon cared most about the secondary schools, through which he hoped to train the ablest youth in the service of his regime.

Historians and biographers have often asked the question: What kind of Europe did Napoleon mean to build? In the eyes of some he was driven by circumstances not of his own making; he was a defender of the revolutionary principles against Europe's kings, or of France's "natural frontiers" already conquered by the Revolution. According to this view, he was forced into conquest after conquest—from one defensive ring of satellites to a second ring to defend the first, and so on to the collapse. This thesis has a difficulty: Napoleon, as we have seen, could more easily have achieved security by not insisting on the occupation of places beyond the natural frontiers and vital to other great powers—as Italy was to Austria, or Holland to Britain. The opposite to this thesis of "perpetual defense" is the thesis of Napoleon as conqueror and maker of history. He has appeared to some as lured by the mysterious East—Egypt, Constantinople, India—and to others as trying to finish the "second Hundred Years War" with Britain for colonial supremacy. A variation of this theme is the view, doing scant justice to the Napoleonic imagination, that he was mainly trying to make thrones for his relatives. Others have seen him as trying to recreate a Roman empire. It has even been suggested that he was out of touch with reality, that is, mad, and no one who has read them can forget Albert Guérard's lines on the subject: "Insane asylums are filled with world conquerors. The cream of the jest is that Napoleon too labored under the delusion that he was Napoleon—and lo! he *was* Napoleon."[1]

Reality was evolving rapidly before the eyes of Napoleon's generation, and no one was better placed than he to be dazzled by the spectacle, but he was not insane. He was an empire builder. The Roman Empire and the vocabulary of ancient history were very familiar to his generation, but the past which was most firmly fixed in Napoleon's finely tooled brain was the Enlightenment. He was

[1] *Napoleon I, A Great Life in Brief* (New York, Knopf, 1956), 69.

an eighteenth-century cosmopolitan and a believer in efficiency and uniformity, rationally ordered. He has been called an enlightened despot, but this description fails in one respect. Try as he would to legitimize his position, he was no dynast but a new kind of despot where claim to rule was based on popular sovereignty. So far as he could, he planted the efficiencies and uniformities of the Revolution, and in some places—parts of northern Italy, for example—they took root. Where he took the Civil Code, embodying these efficiencies, he meant it to stay. He wanted to imprint French civilization and culture upon all Europe, but at least three great obstacles undid him.

In the first place, needing the aristocracies in vassal countries to form courts and administrations, he made them, and often the kings as well, his allies. Thereby he forestalled the kind of revolution which had taken place in France before his rise to power.

In the second place, this kind of revolution would not in any case have taken place, at least not in France's way, for the other parts of Europe were not France, and were in different stages of development. To the extent that Napoleon and his soldiers and his Code shook up Europe—and they shook it violently—they set in motion forces stronger than mere imitation of France. The countries of Europe responded to French expansionism with nationalistic ambitions of their own. They were not merely irritated by French levies of troops and money and art treasures; they saw the benefits of French administrative unity and wanted unity of their own making and with their own traditions: *national* unity. This was a great and unintended result of Napoleon's career, for he was not a nationalist, not even a French nationalist, but an eighteenth-century cosmopolitan.

In the third place, one may guess that Napoleon would not have known when to stop. Although he was a superb calculator, his temperament and imagination led him to value the game above the results, and this was the quality which led him on until he was beaten.

THE DOWNFALL

Napoleon had created the Grand Empire and the Continental System and embarked on a process of organizing Europe. When he had run into opposition he had crushed it by force. He had not been able to crush Britain, or Spain, or Portugal, but from his point of view these setbacks were temporary. Between 1810 and 1812, Russian antagonism to France and Russian abandonment of the Continental System became so flagrant that Napoleon determined to have it out with Russia before solving his other problems. He knew very well how hazardous an invasion of Russia would be, and he hoped to bring Alexander to heel—that is, back into his European system in a subordinate position—without this throw of the dice. But Napoleon was a great despot and a great gambler, and when Alexander, after repeated threats, refused to submit, Napoleon set out to prove himself the master. He was not thinking of France's welfare but of the game of organizing Europe in which he was involved, and in which he refused to throw in his hand.

Alexander knew that he was slated by Napoleon for a subordinate position. The Czar had already shown his courage in forcing the unpopular Tilsit breathing spell upon the Russian aristocracy, who considered Napoleon to be anti-Christ vomited forth by the French Revolution. Alexander was a strange personality, vain, inscrutable, sentimentally liberal, but fired with the importance of Russia's mission and his own office. He would not withdraw from the deadlock of wills.

Neither side could surprise the other. Alexander might have attacked first, in Central Europe, if he had been able to enlist the Poles of the Grand Duchy of Warsaw, Napoleon's satellites, and convince Austria and Prussia that the time was ripe. But the Poles wanted no Russian troops crossing their lands, and Austria and Prussia were bullied into an alliance with Napoleon. On the other hand, Napoleon failed in a last-minute attempt to make peace with Great Britain, and found Russia's traditional enemies Sweden and Turkey unwilling to participate in the attack. (Talleyrand had advised the Russians to conciliate them.) When Alexander persisted in refusing to negotiate until Napoleon had evacuated Prussia and his advanced Baltic positions, the French emperor crossed the Niemen, in June, 1812, with some 600,000 men.

Napoleon's Russian campaign was on such a scale that from the first it dwarfed the participants. In the emptiness of Russia the French searched for an opponent to defeat and found none. Alexander and most of his advisors wanted to oppose the invader, but the size of Napoleon's forces left them no choice but retreat, and so, in spite of themselves, the Russians called on their strongest allies, space and winter. The French did not try to live off the country in Russia as they had in other campaigns, but their supply system failed. Men—and horses—were suffering and dying before the taking of Smolensk in mid-August. Napoleon hesitated, considered setting up winter quarters, then went on in search of the big, decisive battle. At Borodino, sixty miles west of Moscow, the Russians made a stand on September 7, 1812. The battle was terrible and inconclusive, with the French losing 30,000 men and the Russians 40,000. A week later Napoleon entered Moscow, and that night the city started burning, no one knows how. Napoleon waited until mid-October for a sign from Alexander, and then ordered retreat. There could be no question of wintering in the half-ruined city when the surrounding country remained unsubdued. On the way out of Russia the trail of stragglers, fallen soldiers, and abandoned weapons and loot grew longer. In December, after passing through cold of seventeen degrees below zero, and fighting rear-guard actions against the Russians, some 100,000 men emerged in separate groups from Russia, leaving behind 500,000 dead or prisoners.

The Grand Army, which had been the backbone of Napoleon's power to organize Europe, was shattered beyond reconstruction. Napoleon sped straight to Paris to raise fresh troops and hold the Empire and his allies to their duties, but it was impossible to reproduce the splendid amalgam of veterans and new recruits which had held its proportions since the time of Robespierre. More serious still, Europe at last united against its reformer and tormentor. Prussian troops defected as the French came out of Russia, and in March, 1813, Prussia declared war on Napoleon. The Austrians were slower to move, for Metternich was distrustful of Prussia and afraid of a Russian advance into Europe. In an effort to achieve some kind of equilibrium among the great powers, Metternich tried to get Napoleon to settle for France's boundaries of 1801. But Napoleon was not one to compromise, and he negotiated only in the hope of gaining more from the delay than his opponents. In the end the Allies, joined by Austria, proved to be the gainers, and in October, 1813, they defeated Napoleon in a decisive battle near Leipzig. South Germany went over to them. More than 100,000 French remained trapped in various German towns. The Austrians overran Italy, except Naples, where Murat came to terms with them. Meanwhile, in Spain, Wellington drove Joseph from Madrid.

The end came for Napoleon in 1814, after he had made a stand in France. The Allies still hesitated, troubled by memories of French resistance to invasion in 1792. Metternich still wanted to make peace before the Russians and Prussians could profit unduly. But the allied armies entered France in December, 1813, and the following spring, after a brilliant winning streak on the part of Napoleon and his young recruits, the allied armies by-passed him and took Paris at the end of March. Napoleon, at Fontainebleau to the southeast of the capital, wanted to continue fighting, but his marshals refused, and early in April Napoleon abdicated. On April 11 the Allies did him the honor of making a special treaty, endowing him with the small island of Elba, off the Italian coast, and an income, with provision for the support of his relatives. On the night of April 12, the Emperor tried to kill himself, but the poison which he had carried to Moscow and back had lost its potency. He said farewell to his troops on April 20, and early in May arrived at the island which was supposed to be his future kingdom.

THE EUROPEAN SETTLEMENT

From all the diplomacy at the close of the Napoleonic wars, one large fact stands out. The balance of power in Europe was restored. The hegemony of France was brought to an end. Yet France was not partitioned, and was able to participate in the making of the general European settlement.

While the great powers were still fighting Napoleon, they made the Treaty of Chaumont, in March, 1814. It registered the determination of Britain, Austria, Prussia, and Russia not to separate until they had finished the war with Napoleon, and pledged that the four powers would keep watch on France for twenty years and, if necessary, furnish troops to defend the peace settlements.

The peace settlement with France was made first. The restoration of the Bourbon dynasty in the person of Louis XVIII, brother of Louis XVI, had been arranged by Talleyrand with the assent of Napoleon's Senate and Legislative Corps at the time Paris was taken by the Allies. The British, and Alexander of Russia, favored this solution, and Metternich accepted it. Frenchmen accepted the Bourbon restoration and the peace treaty passively, caring only that the privileges of the old regime should not be brought back. The actual terms of peace between the Allies and the new French government were fixed in the Treaty of Paris of May 30, 1814. France was allowed to retain the boundaries of 1792, a very favorable settlement, for by that date France had already taken Avignon and parts of Savoy, Germany, and Belgium. Great Britain restored most, but not all, of the French colonies.

The settlements which concerned the rest of Europe were made at the Congress of Vienna, which met from September, 1814, to June, 1815. It was a congress of kings and diplomats, very much an affair of the aristocracy, celebrating at last its triumph over the principles of the French Revolution. Alexander of Russia was there in person with a team of advisors. Metternich was the chief negotiator for Austria, Hardenberg and Humboldt for Prussia, Castlereagh and Wellington for Great Britain, and Talleyrand for France. The important decisions were made by the great powers in committee meetings. The full congress never really met, and the lesser powers were reduced to lobbying. Among the great powers, the Prussians tended to follow the lead of Alexander of Russia. Metternich and Castlereagh cooperated. Talleyrand, representing Louis XVIII of France, stressed "legitimacy" in order to ensure that France's voice would be heard in spite of the defeat of Napoleon.

In January, 1815, when there was a deadlock between Russia and Prussia, on the one hand, and Austria and Great Britain, on the other, Talleyrand was able to tip the balance toward the latter two, and gain allies. But in spite of Talleyrand's cleverness the coalition which had defeated Napoleon was not broken, and many of their decisions were aimed at containing France in the future.

Most of the changes provided for by the Act of the Congress of Vienna, signed on June 8, 1815, were territorial.

(1) In Central Europe the Holy Roman Empire was not revived, nor were most of the small states which had been suppressed during the Napoleonic era. "The Germanies" remained greatly simplified, but the hopes of the few articulate liberals and nationalists were dashed. The diplomats at Vienna did not accept the principle that peoples should decide their own political allegiances, but treated territories as dynastic properties. A Germanic Confederation of thirty-nine states, very loose in its structure, was created. The details of the German settlement are discussed in Chapter 31.

(2) The Italian peninsula remained divided and was dominated by the Habsburgs, who received Lombardy and Venetia (as well as the Dalmatian coast —Napoleon's Illyrian Provinces—on the other side of the Adriatic). Most of the duchies in the north were restored to their former rulers, as were the Papal States and the Kingdom of Sardinia, which received Genoa. The Kingdom of the Two Sicilies was returned to its Bourbon rulers after the ousting of Murat from Naples in the spring of 1815. Empress Marie Louise was given Parma and other small territories. Napoleon was for a time Emperor of Elba.

(3) Poland remained partitioned among Austria, Prussia, and Russia in spite of Alexander's desire to keep the whole of Napoleon's Grand Duchy of Warsaw as a satellite of his own. After the dispute in January, 1815, which has

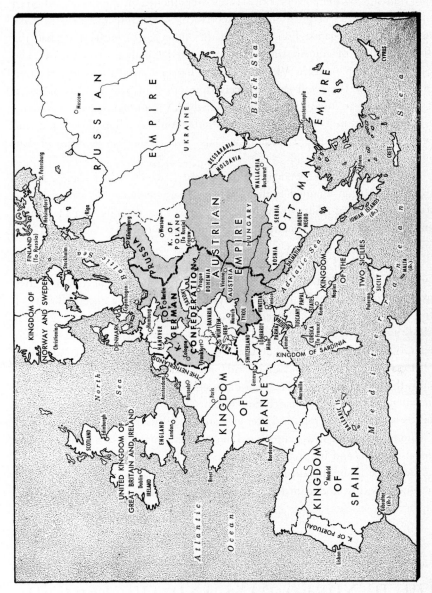

EUROPE AFTER THE CONGRESS OF VIENNA, 1815

already been mentioned, parts of the Grand Duchy were returned to Austria and Prussia. Alexander kept the rest, and made it into a Polish Kingdom with himself as king, but with its own Polish language, army, and institutions.

(4) In the reshuffling of territories an effort was made to establish an equilibrium among the powers. Prussia was strengthened on the Baltic and given Rhineland territories of great future importance. They were intended to make Prussia a bulwark against France, but in the nineteenth century they had the unforeseen effect of contributing to Prussian predominance in Germany. The Russian-Prussian plan at the Vienna Congress had envisaged Prussian possession of Saxony, but in the event Prussia received only half of Saxony. Austria ceded the former Austrian Netherlands (Belgium) which (as another means of containing France in future) was joined to the Netherlands as a kingdom under the House of Orange. Piedmont-Sardinia was also strengthened as a means of containing France.

(5) In the north Sweden retained Norway, which it had obtained early in 1814, and Russia retained Finland. Great Britain retained Helgoland in the North Sea, as well as Malta in the Mediterranean, a protectorate over the Ionian Islands (off Greece), and many French and Dutch colonies. George III was recognized as King of Hanover.

(6) It should be noted, finally that France's fate was not in question, having been decided in the Treaty of Paris before the Congress of Vienna. After Napoleon's comeback in the Hundred Days (related below), a Second Treaty of Paris (November 20, 1815) obliged France to cede small territories to the Netherlands, Prussia, Bavaria, and Sardinia (in general the boundary of 1790), pay an indemnity, and submit to partial occupation. A Quadruple Alliance of November 20, 1815 saw Austria, Prussia, Russia, and Great Britain agree to meet periodically to study the execution of the Treaty of Paris, and, if need be, contribute forces for its maintenance. A Holy Alliance proposed by Alexander and signed by Austria and Prussia on September 26, and later by many other European rulers, was a much less definite document which attempted to establish Christian standards for international relations and internal government. To some extent it expressed a mood of conservative internationalism which was to play a part in the history of the nineteenth century and contribute to differences between east and west (see Chapter 33).

THE HUNDRED DAYS AND THE LEGEND

In France during the winter of 1814–1815 it began to appear that the moderate tone of the restoration would be ruined by the intransigence of the returning aristocrats and the concessions which Louis XVIII felt obliged to make to them. Public indifference to the king and his Charter (see p. 464) began to give way to anger when it was feared that the social gains of the Revolution might be lost. Old revolutionaries like Fouché, Napoleon's former police chief, and various army officers were casting around for a substitute for the Bourbons when suddenly it was learned that Napoleon was in France again.

The Emperor had not been paid the pension promised by Louis XVIII and probably knew that there was talk at Vienna of moving him to the more distant island of Saint Helena in the South Atlantic. Even without these incentives he was not one to pass up a chance for action. Slipping into France on March 1, 1815, with a few hundred men, he reached Grenoble, in the Alps, by way of back roads and was acclaimed by the garrison, whose royalist officers were forced to run away. On March 10 he reached industrial Lyon and encountered popular enthusiasm. Marshal Ney, sent to arrest him, joined him a few days later. On the evening of March 20, Napoleon rode unopposed into Paris, and was escorted to the Tuileries Palace, from which Louis XVIII had left for the border the day before. It was a kind of miracle, and France applauded the drama, but in the end no good came of this escapade.

Napoleon had begun his comeback with talk of insurrection against the returned nobles and priests, but he was no revolutionary and he rapidly changed his tune when he saw that it might stir up disorder. He meant to return as an absolute ruler but found that to satisfy the influential politicians whom he had once bullied he had to grant at least as much of a constitution as Louis XVIII's Charter. This he did in the Additional Act to the Constitutions of the Empire, promulgated June 1. It was a document which satisfied neither the liberals, who tried at once to revise it, nor Napoleon, who probably would have changed or abolished it if he had won the battle of Waterloo on June 18.

Waterloo was the English Duke of Wellington's headquarters in Belgium, toward which Napoleon advanced as rapidly as possible in an effort to seize the left bank of the Rhine and destroy the coalition's armies before they could assemble. There had been no need for a new coalition when the news of Napoleon's return reached the Congress of Vienna. The old one held fast, outlawed Napoleon (March 13), and prepared to destroy him. The Emperor managed to round up about 700,000 men for all kinds of duty, and take 126,000 of them immediately into Belgium. Wellington and the Prussian General Blücher had almost twice as many. Napoleon tried to finish off Blücher first, on June 16, and almost did so, but the Prussians escaped. Then on June 18 he turned against Wellington, who was on the plateau of Mont-Saint-Jean. Wellington simply held out, using maximum fire power against the French columns, as he had learned to do in Spain. Napoleon, who was not at his best, made scarcely any effort to maneuver, but kept attacking. The French army finally broke when Napoleon's last reserve, the Old Guard, failed to dent the enemy, and the English, reinforced by Blücher, counterattacked. The French lost 30,000 men and 7,500 prisoners.

Napoleon abdicated on June 22. Louis XVIII returned promptly to Paris with Wellington's army. On July 3 Napoleon reached the port of Rochefort, between Nantes and Bordeaux, while, on July 8, Louis XVIII reestablished himself in Paris.

Napoleon had considered going to the United States, but he was in some danger of arrest by Louis XVIII's agents, and on July 15 surrendered to the captain of a British warship. He was interned on the island of Saint Helena in the

South Atlantic, several hundred miles off the African coast. He died on May 5, 1821, and the event passed almost unnoticed in Europe, so distant is the recent past. But within a few years his name became a legend. Napoleon's own contribution to this legend—not the least of his victories—was made as he dictated his memoirs at Saint Helena. He made over his career and, as he talked, became the apostle of the Revolution and the martyr of democracy, and created the myth of himself as the liberator, not the conqueror, of peoples.

25

REVOLUTIONARY ECONOMIC AND SOCIAL CHANGES

THE ECONOMIC CHANGES in the century after the French Revolution came so fast, and so contorted the societies they struck, that historians have given to them the name of "Industrial Revolution." Most of these changes were in the making in earlier days. Now the previous accumulation of invention and experience exploded in a burst of new wealth and new institutions which remade the millennial shape of the world.

The breakthrough began with varied advances. For one thing there was an explosion of population. Whereas the number of people in the world tripled from the mid-eighteenth to the mid-twentieth century, the population of Europe in that same period increased fivefold. In Europe there was, with the growth in numbers, a change in what might be called the "quality of the people," owing to improved diet for the most part, and to better medical care. But there were during the nineteenth century generations of under-nourished and stunted people, and in spite of the remarkable population growth, the mortality rate in the new industrial towns remained high.

People not only multiplied; they moved. This was an era when cities swelled to something resembling their present proportions. London between 1800 and 1880 grew from 950,000 to over 4,700,000 people. Paris in the same period grew from 600,000 to over 2,700,000, Vienna from 247,000 to over a million, Berlin from 172,000 to 1,300,000, and Moscow from 250,000 to 612,000.

It was an age of railways, supplementing the canals whose building was a great feat of the late eighteenth and early nineteenth centuries. The first commercial steam railroad opened in northern England in the 1820's. At the very end of our period, in 1869, the Suez Canal was opened, enormously shortening the route from Europe to the Far East. This was the era of the first trans-Atlantic steamship lines (Cunard, 1840) and of the telegraph (1832), the steel plow (1837), the first bicycle (1839), the trans-Atlantic cable (1865–66), the typewriter (1868), and the oil industry (1859).

All this meant the greatest dislocations in lives of people, dislocations which they neither welcomed nor in many cases understood, and which were as shaking to the established order as the French Revolution or the Reformation. The efforts of men to find new homes, new ways of organizing their lives, new political and social means of expressing and redressing their grievances, gave to every affected region a character of ferment and dismay in these years.

THE INDUSTRIAL REVOLUTION

The Industrial Revolution is a term which refers both to the use of machines in industry, and to the social setting in which their growing use took place. If one thought only of the mechanical side, one would mean by industrial revolution (a) the adoption of machines, and (b) the applying of power to these machines in order to make them run. Even this narrow definition does not make it possible to say with precision exactly when an industrial revolution began. The use of machinery and even of power-driven machinery was not unknown in early modern times. Moreover, the amount of power-driven machinery in operation in, say, Britain or France, was not very great until several decades of the nineteenth century had passed. It is therefore misleading to date the beginning of the Industrial Revolution with such tags as the invention of the steam engine or spinning jenny. One can only say that between the mid-eighteeth century and the early nineteenth the use of such power as steam engines and of such devices as textile machines increased gradually until their effects on output and on the lives of large numbers of people were noticeable.

A sizeable increase in the capacity of industry and a noticeable change in the lives of large numbers of people may indeed be called a revolution, even though these changes came over a long period of time. There was more to the increase of output, however, than mere mechanical invention. These new enterprises had to be organized. There had to be planning and investment and the employment of labor. There had to be raw materials and markets as well as the capital, the wage-workers, and the machines. Indeed, there had to be a certain almost mystical element, a faith in progress, a disposition to calculate and risk, certain habits of mind conducive to the search for profits, before all these men and materials could be brought together. In the broadest sense, therefore, the Industrial "Revolution" may be said to have included these social and psychological and economic elements as well as the purely mechanical.

A good way to appreciate the importance of the Industrial Revolution is to think about the still "underdeveloped" parts of the world today. These places—parts of Asia, Africa, and Latin America, for example—are underdeveloped precisely because they have not increased their production of raw materials and manufactured goods through the investment of large amounts of capital in modern methods, usually requiring machines. Low productivity means that their populations, often large, are not well provided with cheap clothing, food, and housing, not to mention cultural facilities such as schools and universities. In a greatly simplified fashion one may sum up the problem of these places by saying that their people work inefficiently through lack of knowledge and insufficiently through lack of opportunities. To get better results it would be necessary to have better tools and more cunning workmen, but this cannot be achieved without the building of machines and the training of a skilled labor force. It is terribly difficult to take this step forward because the people's labor is barely enough to keep them alive; there is almost nothing left over to devote to improvements. To start the chain reaction of economic development it is necessary to add something new. For example, the gift or loan of a sum of money might enable the country to import machinery. In either case the capital, the accumulated wealth capable of producing more wealth, would have to come from somewhere: from belt-tightening inside the country, or from aid from abroad.

Now if we think about the *first* industrial revolution, that of Great Britain, we can see that here, too, the capital, workers, raw materials, will power, and knowledge had to come from somewhere. In the case of Britain there was no advanced country to be copied or to borrow capital from. But capital in the form of money had been accumulating because of the commercial revolution. England's assets were great. As a trading nation and sea power it had almost limitless potential markets. Indeed it is customary to say that the demands of commerce stimulated and dominated industry in early modern times.

Labor for the new industries was at hand. The population increase, with Irish immigration, provided human material for the towns. In his beliefs and motives, as in mechanical inventiveness, the Englishman was well fitted for manufacturing. He was less handicapped by political interference, for although Britain knew mercantilist regulations, there was not the extensive bureaucratic state machine of a continental power. In Britain the business community had closer links to the landed aristocracy and to the government than did the continental businessmen. The English proved to have conveniently located supplies of coal and iron with which to outfit themselves for the new age. They went ahead most rapidly in the textile industry, where they had great experience and where the making of cottons was not hampered by much previous regulation. Then the iron and coal industries expanded until in 1851 about half of the industrial employment in Britain was accounted for by the textile, iron, and coal industries. The British output of coal increased from 16,000,000 tons in 1815 to 50,000,000 in 1848 and to 80,000,000 in 1860. Britain's output of iron increased from 1,000,000 tons in 1835 to 2,000,000 tons in 1848.

The development of industry spread rapidly to the continent. There were, of course, differences in the ways in which the various western countries—England, France, and Belgium in particular—embraced the new industry. These differences, however, are less significant than the differences between the industrial and non-industrial regions—Western Europe and parts of Central Europe on the one hand, and Eastern Europe on the other. In earlier times the west with its commerce, its merchant class, and overseas interests had contrasted with the less complicated landlord and serf society in the east. Now, in the nineteenth century, the west invented and financed its way to new levels of wealth and power, while the east and some of the central part of Europe lagged behind; and the contrast became far sharper than before. These differences in development were not merely differences in rate of growth but *became differences in the social and economic structures* which were built. Countries like Germany, Austria, and Russia industrialized later, on different social foundations, and with awareness of some of the lessons already learned in the west. They had both the advantages and the disadvantages of a late start. It is scarcely possible to overestimate the importance of these different economic experiences in the social and political histories of the countries involved. The difference in economic developments had much to do with the cause and course of the two world wars. It had still more to do with the contemporary division of Europe into free and Communist spheres. The eastern line of freedom in Europe today is, roughly, the eastern edge of industrialism in the nineteenth century.

In Britain the rate of output had substantially increased by the 1830's, owing to machines. Henceforth and unceasingly the economic transformation of the country had great effects upon the places where people lived and worked and upon their attitudes. France, a much bigger and richer and more populous country at the time of the Great Revolution, long continued to produce more than Britain but was slower in adopting machinery and in investing private capital in the new industrial enterprises. France during the period of the July Monarchy, from 1830 to 1848, was in the early stages of industrialism which Britain was by that time leaving behind. Like early Victorian Britain, the July Monarchy was a period of considerable social ferment, as men sought to make sense out of their new economic experiences. But in France the period of the Second Empire, from 1852 to 1870, saw a more spectacular forward drive toward large cities, large factories, large banks, enlarged industrial production. Before its collapse in the Franco-Prussian War of 1870 the Second Empire was to see the economy changed from one dominated mainly by agriculture, as in the years before 1789, into one in which factories and farms were more nearly balanced. In Western Europe Belgium rivaled France in industrial development. In Central Europe an "industrial revolution" did not really occur until the second half of the nineteenth century. In Austria and Prussia, in such cities as Vienna and Prague and Berlin, there was, to be sure, some industrialization before 1848. In Germany the greatest spurt of industrialization started soon after the country was united by Bismarck during the Franco-Prussian War. In Italy and Russia and Spain a similar though smaller industrial thrust may be found by the 1890's.

HANLEY, England. Factories mixed with slums. (Photo Ewing Galloway)

THE AGRICULTURAL REVOLUTION

In essence the Agricultural Revolution consisted, like its industrial companion, of an increase in productivity—that is, in efficiency. Many of the reasons for this improvement were the same for agriculture as for industry. Both, for example, were undoubtedly influenced by the expansion of Europe and by the wider markets which it brought. Both were also influenced by the improved methods of transportation inside Europe and within each European country. One could, indeed, speak of a "transportation revolution," for the improvements in the speed, safety, and reliability, as well as the greater availability and lower costs of transportation had a great deal to do with all of the economic changes of the nineteenth century. For example, better transportation meant that goods, both agricultural and industrial, could be made available to more distant places. Thus markets instead of being purely local and regional tended to become national and international. Farmers, like manufacturers, gradually learned the advantages and dangers of the wider markets. The lure of more customers and the threat of more competitors excited the able and brought forth new means of production.

The great enclosure movement in eighteenth-century England increased output by consolidating hitherto separated plots of ground. This ground was now cultivated in more efficient ways, for example with better plows, with manures, and by planting seeds in rows instead of merely scattering them. Enclosures put an end to the indiscriminate breeding of livestock in common pastures and made possible selective breeding, a change which greatly increased the size and value of the animals. The use of "crop rotation" in place of letting a portion of the land lie fallow meant an increase of 25 to 50 percent in the amount of land in use. Regional specialization in crops intended for sale which were specially suited to local conditions also improved agricultural output.

The English Agricultural Revolution was by no means typical of Europe as a whole. England became famous for the consolidation of landed properties into large holdings. Nineteenth-century England with all its wonderful industrial and political experimentation was a country whose rural countryside was owned by a very small proportion of its population. We are familiar with the fact that in Eastern Europe—in East Prussia, Poland, and Russia—there were also large estates. In Eastern Europe, however, there was not much industrialization until late in the nineteenth century. East of the Elbe there were large estates, but there were small farms too, and many of the large estates were for working purposes divided up into the small holdings of the peasant tenants who farmed them. This was especially true in Russia. In France and in western Germany as in earlier centuries the countryside was characterized by the predominance of small peasant farms. The great difference in the nineteenth century was that in France, in Belgium, in the Rhineland, and to some extent in Holland and some northern parts of Italy, the era of the French Revolution had left the peasantry as outright owners, no longer subject to seigneurial dues as in the old regime. This achievement created the "peasant democracy" so important in nineteenth-century French politics. It also meant that economically these lands were now fully liberated from medieval impediments and could enter the capitalist system, each proprietor farming as he pleased. But it should also be noted that small farms, such as those in France, were not necessarily efficient farms, and that agricultural methods did not advance rapidly in the nineteenth century.

In Central and Eastern Europe the move toward capitalism in agriculture also came in the nineteenth century, but slowly. In Prussia after the humiliating defeat by Napoleon in 1806 it was easier for reformers like Baron Stein to get a hearing. It now seemed desirable to modernize Prussian society in order to emulate the economic progress and military power of the French. The reform measures associated with the name of Stein and with the year 1807 emancipated the serfs, abolished servile dues of feudal origin, and encouraged enclosure. The peasants had to compensate the landlords, usually by giving up some of their lands in order to keep the rest. In contrast to England, Prussian enclosures did not sweep away the small farms of the peasants, but usually meant only consolidation of the gentry's scattered fields, leaving the peasants with their holdings. To some extent the peasants' interests were safeguarded when common pastures and woods were disposed of. Land could now be placed on the market and purchased by anyone, and persons were free to choose their occupations—in other words, economic considerations were no longer to be checkmated by questions of rank.

These Prussian reforms did not all come at once, but dragged on for almost a half-century. The Prussian territories in eastern Germany retained some labor services and dues of various kinds on the part of the peasants, whose inferior economic and social status was by no means ended in 1807. After the defeat of Napoleon there was a slowdown amounting almost to postponement of the contemplated changes, and it was only in 1850, after the great Europe-wide revolutions of 1848, that the abolition of seigneurial dues and services was completed. The social and economic power of the Prussian aristocracy was consolidated rather than broken. In the 1860's the eastern regions of Prussia had a predominance of large estates, but still had a peasantry with small holdings; the management of estates by Junker landowners was aided by the presence of this labor force. Unlike the great landowners of Britain, who mostly drew their incomes from renting to capitalist farmers, the *Junkers* tended to manage their own estates. In the western parts of the Prussian state—the Rhineland, for example—agriculture was mainly carried on by peasants who owned their small holdings, as in France.

In the Habsburg monarchy the eighteenth-century effort of the enlightened despot Joseph II to abolish serfdom had proved abortive; emancipation did not take place until the revolutions of 1848. The peasants then became small holders freed from labor service (*robot*), but the great Austrian and Hungarian landlords and gentry retained their holdings. In the years that followed, the poorer peasants found that they had to work for wages on the great estates, or rent land, since their own farms were too small to support them. There was a tendency for the lesser peasant farmers to sell out and move to the towns, where they became part of the labor force as industrialization progressed. The Habsburg monarchy remained for the most part an area of large estates, although there were regional differences. In Russia, whose agricultural problems will be treated in a later chapter, serfdom remained through the first half of the nineteenth century and became a drag on the rest of the economy—even a threat to social stability. Serfdom was abolished in the 1860's.

There was, then, no "Agricultural Revolution" in much of Central and Eastern Europe in the period we are considering. But greater agricultural efficiency and productivity were sought and attained as markets widened, and as the impulse to sell farm products in order to buy manufactured goods spread into the back country, following the canals and railroads. Even in Russia this pressure was felt, and a minority of efficient landowners were able to satisfy it. In East Prussia and the Habsburg lands there was more success in producing surpluses for the market. The point to be noted is the opportunity and desire to make profits out of farming, as the great English capitalist farmers had done, rather than the degree of success in doing so.

Farming in all of Europe was becoming by 1870 a business, producing surpluses, for sale at a profit, rather than just producing things to keep the farmer fed and clad.

COMMERCE AND CAPITALISM

In early modern times the Commercial Revolution had set the pace for the development of capitalistic techniques. It had accumulated capital in some areas and prepared the way for the Industrial Revolution by opening up prospects of wider markets. As the eighteenth century gave way to the nineteenth, commerce continued its role of catalyst to the economic development of Europe. The widening of markets made available to the whole world products which used to be of purely local interest. The addition of these resources, plus the specialization which came about as each region concentrated on what it could do best, increased total production. Quality of products became better and more standardized. There was also greater uniformity in prices. Good and bad times were shared by wider areas.

The growth of national and international markets is an idea easy to recognize but difficult to understand, for a market for one commodity was not the same as a market for another. It was easier, for example, to send grain to distant places than to ship butter and eggs. But more and more goods were being produced in bulk and sent to more distant consumers with each decade. There were, moreover, inventions in marketing as well as in manufacturing. Peddlers and annual fairs were becoming less important, as were artisans who retailed their own products. The weekly market, where people bought and sold, now faced competition from permanent retail stores, which had been few, except in large towns. After the middle of the century department stores began to appear.

Such things as the department store are reminders that not all inventions were mechanical. Among the most vital innovations in business were those in finance. Now that there were so many more ways to put money to work it was natural that ways of gathering capital should be perfected. The capital for Europe's economic development had come from many sources: rent and profits from land; related enterprises such as mining; taxes levied by governments (which then subsidized enterprises); banking; and above all profits from commerce. The more complicated the Industrial Revolution became, the more capital was needed to launch new enterprises. Stock companies were improved by such devices as the issuing of preferred stock (guaranteeing priority in the distribution of dividends from the company's earnings). In the first half of the nineteenth century stock exchanges became separated from commodity exchanges. The most significant new device for gathering money together was "limited liability": the practice of holding an investor responsible for the company's debts only to the amount which he had invested. Limited liability, which made for much greater security for investors, came to England in the 1850's, to France in the 1860's, and to Germany in the 1870's. Until this era, most companies were partnerships where all the owners were responsible for all debt. The limited liability company—or corporation as it was called in America—revolutionized many aspects of society. It meant that the small investor could buy stock without risking his entire fortune; private savings could be used to enrich the saver and also to feed capital into the expanding businesses. The growth of corporations also meant that it was possible to raise the huge sums which were needed for larger and more complex machines —limited liability, and the knowledge of corporation management which came with it, was indeed the indispensable condition for the huge industrial establishments that were necessary to exploit modern technology. When we think of General Motors or du Pont, with their hundreds of thousands of stockholders and their vast and ramified enterprises, it is hard to realize that only a hundred years ago it was still not legally possible in most countries to form a corporation.

Another device which depended on the law as well as on human inventiveness was a supply of money which was generally acceptable and relatively steady in value. In spite of early disasters, such as befell John Law's use of paper currency in the early eighteenth century, paper money become common in the late eighteenth and nineteenth century. The experience of the French *assignats* of the great Revolution proved that dangers from inflation were as menacing as ever. However, the issuing of paper money by banks regulated by governments made it possible to solve the problem during the nineteenth century. The Bank of England gradually secured a monopoly on the issue of banknotes, and by the middle of the century the Bank of France did likewise. There remained problems about how to back the paper currency, whether with a substantial portion of precious metal (gold and silver, but more usually gold, as the century progressed), or with the more flexible device of securities such as the promissory notes of businessmen. The credit furnished by banks to businessmen increased the amount of currency in circulation. Private banks were most often family affairs in the first half of the century, but tended to give way to stock banks, which were most common after 1850.

BUSINESS FLUCTUATIONS

Along with the revolutionary economic changes which came in the nineteenth century there appeared the first modern "depression." The term needs qualification. There had been economic dislocations for as long as men could remember. There had certainly been economic "depressions" in the eighteenth century—for example, the one which contributed to the outbreak of revolution in 1789. In the nineteenth century men began to notice the regular reappearance of these conditions. It began to be seen, moreover, that poor sales and unemployment were not necessarily the result of bad harvests, wars, or ill-advised economic regulations, but might possibly be the products of something within the economic system itself. As the nineteenth century grew older in relative peace and with more economic freedom than previous centuries had enjoyed, business ups and downs grew more, rather than less, impressive. In the growing complexities of industrialism and international trade there were many elements—money and credit, inventions, and new marketing methods, for example—which could stimulate or depress business activity. Operating continuously, combinations of these factors gave the economy of the more highly developed parts of Europe, and then of other regions in an ever widening area of interdependence, a wavelike motion. Economists in the twentieth century, looking back as far as available statistics permitted, called this motion the "business cycle," but disagreed concerning its fundamental causes.

These changes in the economic weather had many connections with political events and with human welfare. Economists have considered the popular notion of a "depression" to be descriptive of one part of the cycle, which as a whole was thought to consist of (1) a prosperity phase in which business activity and employment increased, (2) a recession phase when they declined from their better-than-average condition toward an average, (3) a depression phase when business activity and employment declined below average conditions, and (4) a recovery phase when they took a turn for the better and climbed toward the average again. This kind of description was based on what is essentially an historical study of what economists call "time series"; that is, of the fluctuations, through months and years, of such things as pig iron production, interest rates, employment figures, and so on. Naturally the cyclical motions which were found within the economy depended on what time series were studied. Economists tried to distinguish between "external factors" like wars, foreign tariffs, or bad harvests, which influenced the economy from the outside, and other factors within the economy itself, like an increase in bank loans, or the invention of a cheaper way to market some product.

The period after 1815 contained a number of business slumps of an increasingly international character. There were crises in 1816–1818, 1825–1832, 1836–1839, and 1846–1850. These periodic business slowdowns were all in greater or less degree related to poor harvests in a Europe still predominantly agricultural. The poor harvests would mean high food prices, which would make the public spend more for food and less for other things. As a result, business suffered, workers were laid off or put on part-time, and buying power was still further decreased. When harvests were so poor that the peasants had little to sell, and therefore could afford to buy little, the slowing down of peasant purchases added to the difficulties. Social antagonisms and resentments were worsened by these conditions. If elements of political strain and conflicts of belief were also present, revolutionary situations might result. The student of European history must remember this combination of circumstances when he considers the Revolution of July, 1830, in France, the Reform Bill of 1832 in England, and the revolutions of February and March, 1848, in many parts of Europe.

Of course there were other economic factors that agriculture involved in these economic crises, which apply, generally, to Western and Central Europe. One example was the tendency of Europeans to invest (or speculate) optimistically before each crisis: in the 1820's in South American companies and American cotton; in the 1830's in North American land and economic enterprises; in the 1840's in railways. From 1815 until about 1850, there was also a steady downward drift of prices, which aggravated crises and caused trouble for farmers and merchants.

The twenty years after the middle of the century were a period mainly of rising prices and prosperity. Prices in the fifties and sixties were stimulated by the availability of more gold (much of it from the '49 Gold Rush in California), for increased volumes of money always tended to drive prices up. The availability of more capital, the more rapid circulation of money, and the demand for goods in wars—the Crimean (1854–1856), American Civil War (1861–1865), Wars of Italian and German Unification (1859, 1864, 1866) and Franco-Prussian War (1870)—were also stimulants.

There was a serious international slump in 1857 which is often called the first purely "business" depression (as opposed to those brought on by agricultural failure or external factors). Stocks fell in value, banks failed, prices went down, and there was unemployment. But revival soon set in with the demands of continued railroad building, the transformation from wooden to iron ships and from sail to steam, and the application of the new Bessemer process for making steel. There was another slump from 1866–1868, but then prosperity returned with the help of the construction and opening of the Suez Canal (1869), the increase in international trade, and at the end of our period, the Franco-Prussian War.

For the historian, a knowledge of business ups and downs is essential to an understanding of the histories of individual countries. For example, the age of the Second Empire in France (1852–1870) was on the whole a bustling, prosperous period, and the same era in Britain was likewise one of general social harmony and Victorian prosperity. From the speculations of economists the student of history may derive a sense of the nature of change which will help him to understand that there was not a single "industrial revolution" but a series of changes in engineering and business techniques, and how these acted on employment, wages, prices, interest rates, and so on, reacting on each other to bring about other changes and at the same time shake every aspect of society.

NATIONAL ECONOMIC POLICIES

Europe's links to the rest of the world multiplied the number of ships, warehouses, bank accounts, exports, and imports. This multiplication was to be most striking after 1870, but it grew with the Industrial Revolution. As early as the early forties Britain had, in round numbers, 23,000 ships, France 14,000, the German states 6,000, Norway-Sweden 5,000 and the Netherlands, 1,200. Britain's imports and exports roughly doubled in the first half of the nineteenth century. Between 1840 and 1880 world trade increased fivefold. In 1840 Britain's trade accounted for about 32 percent of the world's total, in 1860 about 25 per cent, and in 1880 about 23 percent. The reason for the decline in Britain's share was not that the nation failed to increase its exports and imports, but that other countries, as they developed economically, increased their share or entered international trading for the first time. An important cause and consequence of this growing world trade was a change in the policies of governments toward foreign commerce.

In the eighteenth century, when mercantilist ideas still dominated commercial policy, high tariffs were the rule in Europe—and smuggling was an important part of international trade. We have seen how theories of the Enlightenment linked economics to nature and recommended that the "natural" be allowed to prevail. Adam Smith's *Wealth of Nations* of 1776 was the most famous example of an attack on mercantilist interference with "natural laws" of economics. The Franco-British Eden Treaty, ten years later, greatly reduced tariffs between the two countries, but the French Revolution raised them again, both because of the influence of businessmen on government in France and as a method of economic warfare. Napoleon's Continental System and the British Orders in Council continued what the Revolution had begun, by trying to weaken the enemy through prohibitions or licensed control of trade and shipping. After Waterloo the British were of two minds about tariffs. On the one hand, merchants and some manufacturers with advanced methods wanted to lower tariffs and increase trade; on the other, the agricultural interests of the aristocracy wanted protection for grains, and some manufacturers still feared continental competition. The Corn Law of 1815 and later versions such as the Duke of Wellington's "sliding scale" law of 1828 gave agriculture the protection which it sought. At first the free trade movement—for example a petition of London merchants in 1820—went unheeded.

Finally Britain led the way toward free trade; other nations resisted and then followed only tardily and briefly. William Huskisson, President of the Board of Trade from 1823–27, worked for lower tariffs and abolition of the most irksome features of the Navigation Acts which regulated shipping to and from Britain. Robert Peel, Prime Minister from 1841 to 1846, put through an income tax to make up for loss of tariff revenue; this permitted tariffs to be greatly reduced in the budgets of 1842 and 1845. Peel's most famous tariff reform was repeal of the Corn Laws in 1846, putting an end to duties on grain imports and thus to protection of domestic grain prices, to the satisfaction of business and consumer interests and to the dissatisfaction of aristocratic landowners. Another step in Britain's abandonment of mercantilistic regulations was the abolition in 1849 of the last remnants of the Navigation Acts. Britain's position as a leading shipper and manufacturer, with little to fear from continental competitors and much to gain from free competition, supported this economic liberalism. Able to undersell most competitors, and with a powerful navy and merchant marine to assure necessary imports even in wartime, Great Britain found it advantageous to preach and practice theories of free trade and international division of labor which to other nations appeared impractical.

In the first half of the nineteenth century the continental powers were all protectionist, refusing to follow Britain, with whom they could not compete industrially in most products. France maintained high protective tariffs until 1860, favored its own shipping and shipbuilding in a mercantilist manner, and monopolized the trade and products of its colonies. Belgium, Holland, Austria, the Italian states, and Russia all maintained high tariffs. Beginning in 1818, Prussia organized the *Zollverein,* a tariff union of German states, but although these states now formed one free trade area they maintained protective tariffs against outsiders. It was a German, Friedrich List, in his *National System of Political Economy* (1841), who summed up the protectionist arguments on behalf of underdeveloped states which needed to encourage production and encourage infant industries, so that they as nations might grow militarily and economically strong, as Britain already was. There were, on the continent, liberal economists who genuinely believed in free trade, but circumstances in the first half of the century did not favor their cause and they never enjoyed the public hearing that the British free traders did.

But after 1850 free trade and laissez-faire economics grew more fashionable on the continent. They were associated with the spread of political liberalism —Liberals, approaching power, tended to espouse British economic doctrine as well as British political institutions. And the business cycle helped. In its phase of general prosperity in the 1850's and 1860's, it made people feel that the old protections and regulations were unnecessary. The liberal theorists, backed by merchants and some manufacturers and farmers who did not fear British goods or Russian grain, began to get a hearing. Count Camillo Cavour of Piedmont, who was to be the unifier of Italy, secured lower tariffs and the repeal of the navigation acts in his country as a means toward modernizing its economy. The greatest single forward step toward free trade came in 1860, when the French Emperor Napoleon III, who had been won over to some of the ideas of economic liberalism, made a commercial treaty with Britain which lowered tariff rates on goods passing between the two countries. Usually called the Cobden Treaty, after Richard Cobden, an English free trader who negotiated it, the agreement was in part a political move to win British friendship. In the next few years, however, France continued to lower tariffs through agreements with many other countries. Since Britain was doing the same thing, there was a general lowering of tariffs in Europe. For a time it seemed that a free trade era was coming, to make good the liberal dream of international division of labor, each nation marketing what it could produce most efficiently and cheaply, with everyone profiting from the general exchange. But this era was also one of railroad and factory building, which increased output and need for markets. Moreover, with an eye to the problem of military security, governments still sought assured supplies of strategic materials.

By the late 1870's the competing industrial nations were raising tariffs again. Free trade and international specialization receded into the realm of theory without having been tried in full. Partly under the influence of depression and partly in uneasy military, economic, and nationalistic competition with each other, the nations revived their interest in colonial empires. Europe's economic development was still to be guided and interpreted by its sovereign states, not by an international, liberal idea.

SOCIAL CLASSES AND HUMAN MISERY

Great Britain's census showed in 1859 that half of its population was then living in towns—a situation not to come in the United States until 1920. By 1881, two thirds of the British were in towns; by the 1950's, nine tenths. A social transformation accompanied the technical and managerial innovations and the rise in productivity which we call the Industrial Revolution. Changes were less extensive in France, and still less in Central and Eastern Europe in the period we are considering. But even where it was absent this social transformation played a significant part in history, for the persistence of a rural society in the east deepened the contrast between it and the complicated, powerful, dynamic. west.

Economic development always had the effect of multiplying occupations and complicating society in some ways, although simplifying it in others. In rural England the enclosures were a kind of simplification. So, in a sense, were the dreary uniformities of urban slums and factory buildings; they at least provided a similar environment for large numbers of people whose common experience gave them a family resemblance and whose similar condition and outlook made them a new class distinguishable from the artisan workers and the poor of former times. And the workers were not the only new class. In large measure in the western countries, the nineteenth century was dominated by the "middle class," the wealthy townsmen who now took their place alongside the older aristocracy of birth and landed wealth. This change was scarcely under way, however, before their positions were challenged from below by the proletariat created by the Industrial Revolution. The townsmen soon found themselves "in the middle" in quite a different sense, between the older aristocrats with whom they were trying to win social and legal equality, and the new working-class people who were demanding equality with them. We shall see in the next chapter how nineteenth-century social philosophies were influenced by this problem. We shall see in studying national histories how the challenge of the middle and lower classes to the old order and to each other influenced politics.

"Social classes" are crude measures of the many realities and notions which blossomed from the factories and department stores and banks and railroads of the nineteenth century. The idea of social classes was not new, but in the nineteenth century it entered deeply into the world's habits of thought. At first it was merely a description of characteristics which came with the rapid economic development. But soon, instead of being an aid to description it came to be used as if it described something as definite and real as a tree. So it was used by some of the most influential thinkers of the nineteenth century, and so it is still used today. People came to think of themselves as belonging to a particular class and as having the same interests as other members of it, just as they had long thought of themselves as members of a church. "Class consciousness" and "class conflict" became potent forces.

There were undoubtedly realities which often coincided with the use of the word "class." But "classes" were always very complicated, and efforts to simplify them were misleading. As Marxian socialists found out in Russia much later, it was hard to fit peasants into their picture of history as determined by the conflict of classes. It was often hard, after 1850, to draw a sharp line between "aristocrats" (many of whom owned factories) and "bourgeois," many of whom owned land. It was hard to place lawyers and doctors and teachers. It was difficult to see how small shopkeepers could belong to the same "middle" class as great bankers or industrialists. What was the "class" of a ruined nobleman who went to work as a butler, or of a butler who made a fortune on the stockmarket? The more highly developed societies were most fruitful of variety in ways of life and attitudes toward life, and tended to defy rigid class analysis.

Another, and related, question debated by historians but also possessed of political implications concerns the effects of the Agricultural and Industrial Revolutions on the country and city people who bore their greatest weight, the former because of enclosures, the latter because of long hours and low wages and other conditions associated with early, unregulated industrialism. There were social critics of all sorts—aristocratic traditionalists, religious humanitarians, democrats, socialists, and so on—who protested against the effects of the Industrial Revolution while it was going on. The most famous early historian to do so was Arnold Toynbee, whose Oxford lectures, published in 1884, popularized the term "Industrial Revolution." Toynbee emphasized the rapidity of economic changes from the mid-eighteenth to the mid-nineteenth century and the human degradation and social antagonisms which accompanied these changes. Later researches have shown that the Industrial Revolution began earlier and took longer than Toynbee thought. Attention to earlier history has shown that the living conditions of country and town workers before the Industrial Revolution were on the whole just as bad as those in the new factory towns.

Later historians have shown that events like the Napoleonic wars and business fluctuations contributed to much of the human misery associated with the early Industrial Revolution in Britain. Workers were not especially dissatisfied when they were employed, although certainly the early industrialists, often operating on a shoestring, kept wages down. Studies of real wages have shown that the whole society, workers included, gained from the increase in wealth produced by the Industrial Revolution. The value of such increasing production is keenly appreciated today because of the dramatic problems posed by the under-developed parts of the world, of which Europeans and Americans used to be ignorant while they took their own economic progress for granted.

Nevertheless, most of the qualifications about the early Industrial Revolution explain more fully, rather than denying, the miseries and dislocations of the early generations of urban workers. These people, even though materially no worse off than their kind had been before, paid with their uprootedness and demoralization a heavy contribution to Britain's economic progress. In France and elsewhere, there were similar human costs. Europe did not rise painlessly to its position of world supremacy. Europe showed how to multiply wealth and power, a lesson which promised survival and even possible well-being for the swarming world population. But part of the cost was misery and the legacy of social conflict of which Communism in the twentieth century is one symptom.

26

NINETEENTH-CENTURY THEORIES OF SOCIETY

THE PERIOD FROM 1789 to 1870 was extremely rich in theories about how society should be organized. Most of the ideas and vocabulary used in twentieth century public affairs were launched in this period. Although not all of these expressions were new, and although some of them have since changed their meanings, there is nevertheless a very contemporary ring to the social theories described in this chapter, compared with those of earlier times. One reason is that many of the problems which were posed in the 1789–1870 era are still unsolved.

INFLUENCES ON NINETEENTH-CENTURY THOUGHT

Some of the essential qualities in nineteenth-century thinking were continuations of the Enlightenment's tendencies toward rationalism and science, on the one hand, and toward optimism and humanitarian concerns, on the other. The French Revolution and its Napoleonic aftermath also influenced nineteenth-century theories and attitudes. Quite apart from the spread of such principles as liberty, equality, fraternity, and individualism, for which the Revolution is best known, it taught lessons in social science by placing the society of the old regime on trial, by examining it in detail with all Europe looking on. To eighteenth-century rationalists the old regime's complexity and asymmetry appeared ridiculous. But many people who witnessed the dismantling of the old regime learned to respect society as a living, evolving thing—and therefore to respect tradition. There was a stronger incentive to study and theorize about society. History as a subject, and the use of historical method, became fashionable.

The Revolution held other surprises, moreover. In it human nature revealed unexpected resources of savagery and fanaticism. Reason pushed to extremes became unreasonable. Men who were determined to make their own history had revealed their impotence in the face of historic forces. The dangers of demagogues and of revolt by the lower classes became obvious to a degree unknown since ancient times. Toward the end of the revolution there appeared a religious revival which was noticeable in many countries. It was to last through much of the nineteenth century and was partly a reaction to the turmoil and extremism of the revolutionary age.

In the history of the nineteenth century the years from 1815 to 1848 are usually called the "Metternich era," after the Austrian minister who had presided over the Congress of Vienna and now seemed to preside over calm, reactionary Europe. Europe's fatigue after the Napoleonic wars, and the fear of further revolutions were influences on nineteenth-century thought. Although there were outbreaks in 1820 and 1830, officially all was decorum. Europe had returned to sanity and stability, and civilization had been preserved from the revolutionary plague of 1789–1815. Yet beneath this outward calm the mood of a great many people was one of uneasiness and urgency. The old regime was gone, and even most conservatives agreed that it could never be brought back. In spite of the desperate experimentation of the revolutionary era, no substitute had been found. The Metternich era was thus characterized by opposite kinds of thought: by an aversion to all change and at the same time by great uneasiness and by the impulse to search for new solutions. Not only political solutions: social solutions were also sought, for the century was one of economic and social transformation. Even drastic solutions to problems in the arts were ardently searched for, now that the classicism of the eighteenth-century fathers was no longer tolerable to the post-revolutionary sons.

The Metternich era came to an end in 1848 with a series of revolutions which passed across Europe like a rolling of drums. All of the social philosophies described in this chapter played a part in those revolutions. Their events are best described in the context of the histories of the several countries, but their existence may be recorded here as an intellectual event of significance for all Europe. As in the French Revolution of 1789, everyone was watching 1848 with strong hope or distaste, depending on his point of view. Everyone tended also to draw conclusions about the future of the liberalism and nationalism which seemed for a moment victorious and were then defeated—and about the conservatism which seemed defeated and was then victorious. Some few saw hope and many experienced dread at the flashes of democracy and socialism which appeared here and there for a brief moment.

The Revolutions of 1848 brought a change of mood in Europe. In a very general way it may be said that the era of uneasiness and search and variety which had characterized social thinking during the Metternich era gave way to one of consolidation, as the main problems were worked out by a generation of outstanding statesmen. There was also, after 1848, a turning away from esteem for imagination and speculation and ideal solutions, toward greater concern for practicality and visible results.

Compared with eighteenth-century social theories, those of the nineteenth, whether conservative or radical, tended increasingly to seek and claim scientific validity. There was more emphasis than ever before on evidence as opposed to intuition. This confidence in scientific method applied to social problems found its prophet in Auguste Comte (1798–1857), the French philosopher and mathematician who is usually called the father of sociology. He was an heir of the Enlightenment who tried to go beyond it to "positive" knowledge based on observation (his philosophy: "positivism"). We shall see below how other social theorists tried to be as scientific as possible.

Comte surveyed human knowledge throughout history and found it passing through three stages. Men had explained phenomena first by theology (as in

FREEDOM OF THE PRESS by Honoré Daumier.
The subtitle—"Ne vous y frottez pas" (Don't meddle with it)—is borne out by the strength of the workingman in the foreground, defender of freedom, and by the figures in the background: Charles X of France, attended by the kings of England and Austria after his overthrow in the July Revolution of 1830; and in the left background the new French king, Louis Philippe, with his characteristic umbrella, being urged toward strong measures by the prosecutor, but cautioned by the liberal Guizot. The drawing was published in the French monthly La Caricature in March, 1834. (Courtesy of Robert M. Walker, Swarthmore, Pa.)

the Middle Ages), then by metaphysics (as in the Enlightenment), and finally by observing relationships and constructing sciences (the positive stage, his own time). Comte was ahead of many of his contemporaries, but he illustrates here the growing nineteenth-century tendency to think historically. He believed that the positive sciences had evolved from the more general to the more concrete and complex, each depending on the preceding one: mathematics, astronomy, physics, chemistry, biology, sociology. Comte illustrates here another of the nineteenth century's key ideas, the idea of evolution, which may be found in many forms such as history and geology before its most famous appearance in Charles Darwin's theory of the biological evolution of species in 1859.

Time and place made a difference in what people were thinking and feeling. In Russia young men were sent to Siberia for the mildest kind of political speculation. In the absolutist climate almost everything passed for subversion, and the slightest whisper of an idea echoed in the silence. Social critics were able to express themselves only in novels and book reviews. At the other end of Europe, in Great Britain, Karl Marx, who was in rebellion against the whole nineteenth-century society, was studying and writing freely at the British Museum. Ideas were somewhat less explosive in Great Britain than across the Channel, but even on the continent, as the failure of the Revolutions of 1848 showed, ideas were not as powerful as the conservatives had feared and the liberals had hoped.

ROMANTICISM AND REALISM

Of the many nineteenth-century "isms," two which were not social philosophies, but were large and vague and controversial, were "romanticism" and "realism." Just what they were has been much discussed; so much discussed that it is necessary to have some familiarity with them.

Use of the word "romanticism" arose from the observation, largely among historians of the arts, that there was "something" which made for a family resemblance among the productions of artists of the period from the 1770's to about 1850. English poets such as William Wordsworth, John Keats, and Percy Bysshe Shelley had much in common with each other and with continental poets such as the great Frenchman Victor Hugo. Furthermore, poetry of the era seemed to resemble much contemporary painting, such as that of Eugène Delacroix (French, 1798–1863), and music, such as that of Hector Berlioz (French, 1803–1869) or of Franz Schubert (Austrian, 1797–1828) or of the great Ludwig van Beethoven (German, 1770–1827). There seemed, moreover, to be traces of the same quality in such widely different fields as the novel, philosophy, social and political theories, and landscape gardening.

What were these common features of the art and intellect of the early nineteenth century? Most obvious was the revolt against the rigid, classical forms of the eighteenth century. Then, symmetry, balance, and discipline had been the ideal. What was natural had been deplored as barbaric and what was emotional, as bestial. Starting in the late eighteenth century there developed a new admiration for nature and emotion and a new freedom of expression. The rigid conventional rhyme schemes and meters of poetry were abandoned. The classic theater gave way to sprawling plays of love and hatred, heroism and horror. Instead of trying to subdue nature by clipping trees into geometric forms, gardeners installed dead trees of bizarre shape on their lawns, to give a wild effect. Instead of designing rigidly symmetrical houses with Roman columns, architects built imitation medieval abbeys. In prose, wit and satire, polish and precision, were replaced as ideals by sentiment and emotional power.

Cultural historians have often chased after the will-of-the-wisp which would explain everything in a given era, from the design of furniture to the methods of warfare. The many efforts to account for romanticism furnish one of the best examples of this yearning. What could possibly make so many different artifacts seem alike? In the case of romanticism there have been some who saw the key in a revolt against the rationalism of the eighteenth century, others who saw it in efforts to escape from the drab nineteenth-century world of business offices and factory chimneys, others who described romanticism as merely a revival of things medieval, still others who preferred a psychological explanation drawing upon the resources of the unconscious.

The problem of romanticism calls attention to the fact that mood, as well as thought, plays a part in what is usually called intellectual history. It was perhaps not so much specific convictions about art or politics that created the resemblance among so many of the products of the first half of the nineteenth century. It was perhaps a common awareness—which later generations were in danger of overlooking—of what lay behind: the passing of an old era, and its style of life and expression, in the great revolutionary upheaval; a sense of both accomplishment and loss; and above all a need to create in all fields to replace what was gone, and to value qualities of energy and originality which served creation. We may note also that some of the awareness of unsolved problems, and the sense of wonder at human complexity began at least as early as Rousseau, before the old regime had collapsed.

The word "realism" is one which, like "romanticism," has been generalized beyond mere use in describing the arts. In the arts, by the middle of the century, the exuberance of earlier decades had produced many experiments, some of which disgusted the younger generation seeking its own ways of expression. One of the paths which the young were eager to follow after 1850 led toward the eliminating of evidence of the artist's personal feelings from the work, and toward describing "things-as-they-are." Although romanticism did not come to a sudden halt in 1850, the taste of artists tended to guide them away from the highly emotional, imaginative subjects, often distant in time or place, which had pleased the earlier generation. The French writer Gustave Flaubert (1821–1880) now took enormous pains, working and reworking his text, to give the impression of everyday life. The French painters Gustave Courbet (1819–1877) and Jean François Millet (1815–1875) illustrate the same tendency, which was, like romanticism, international.

In so far as the word realism can be applied in a general way to the mood and attitudes of Europeans after 1850, it refers to the evidence we have already mentioned in connection with the failure of the Revolutions of 1848. In politics and international relations a German word is often applied: *Realpolitik,* meaning attention to realities, to the facts of power, to the possible, to results, rather than unswerving but futile loyalty to ideals, principles, and traditions. In the period from 1850 to 1870, as we shall see, the great practitioners Louis Napoleon, Cavour, and Bismarck made a kind of breakthrough in Europe, achieving their objectives at the cost of principles confused, and corners cut.

There are also some grounds for applying the word realism to philosophy, where "tough-minded" and materialistic emphasis on the world of sense experience was gaining ground. Philosophies emphasizing the reality of *will,* such as that of the German Arthur Schopenhauer (1788–1860), author of *The World as Will and Idea,* became more popular. Schopenhauer taught that ideas were merely tools used by an underlying life force. In addition, the prestige of science continued to grow. The publication of Darwin's *Origin of the Species* in 1859 was to lead to a contest for public influence between scientists and clergymen.

With realism, as with romanticism, the parallels between widely separated activities should not be taken too seriously. Some of the generalizations which historians have turned up will, however, be seen to apply to the social theories which are our main concern.

CONSERVATISM

The word "conservative," describing a political and social attitude, was used by the brilliant counter-revolutionary French writer François René de Chateaubriand (1768–1848) and the other founders of a magazine called the *Conservateur* (1818). The term had already been used during the French Revolution by the counter-revolutionary theorist Louis de Bonald (1754–1840) and was to be used again beginning in the 1830's to describe the Tory party in Great Britain. Like Edmund Burke (1729–1797), whose *Reflections on the Revolution in France* (1790) had made him the idol of British conservatives, these men and others were awakened by the French Revolution to an acute consciousness of values which they had earlier taken for granted. They found that they loved the intricate old society that was put on trial by the revolutionaries, and they learned to defend it—something they had never had to do before.

The early opponents of the revolution were not as busy with the conduct of day-to-day affairs as were the revolutionaries, and were able to construct what became the foundations of nineteenth-century conservatism. They learned to condemn rationalism and the Enlightenment (of which most of them had once partaken) as hollow and frivolous and responsible for turning men's heads and causing the revolution. They considered themselves, by contrast, to be scientific, on the ground that they were generalizing only from concrete, historical facts. Men like De Bonald and Chateaubriand and their comrade-in-arms Joseph de

Maistre (1753–1821) claimed to have founded a "science of society." They were among the first sociologists.

On the other hand, these men were at war and did not scruple to use any likely weapon. Religion was such a weapon, and the conservative counter-revolutionaries exploited it, most of them sincerely, some not. The essence of their argument and the part which proved most lasting was that religion was needed to hold society together. The Enlightenment, they said, had flouted this truth and started a disintegration of the social bonds. Joseph de Maistre went so far as to say that the revolution was France's punishment by God for its hospitality to the Enlightenment. In later life, under the Restoration, De Maistre argued that there could be no good society without the supremacy of the Pope. Most conservatives, while less extreme than De Maistre, believed that men were essentially weak, childish, and defective beings who needed the guidance of paternal institutions, both religious and political. In religious terms, they thought that men were depraved, steeped in original sin. Burke in particular was eloquent on the subject of how little could be accomplished by a single generation, which he compared to "the flies of a summer." Both Burke and De Maistre defended prejudices as useful guides to most people. Metternich, the symbol of European conservatism between 1815 and 1848, called the typical rationalistic revolutionary the "presumptuous man," who thought that constitutions could be made by writing them on slips of paper, and that they were transferrable from one country to another.

Politically, the conservatives were of various kinds. Edmund Burke and the English conservatives were loyal to parliamentary government and civil liberties. De Maistre and De Bonald developed elaborate justifications of absolute monarchy. Metternich served an absolute monarch who would pay no attention to his extremely modest suggestions for reform. There were others with various shades of opinion, some wishing, like Metternich, that the monarch would consult historic estates comparable to the French Estates General, others willing to go as far as the British system, others even further in the direction of representing property along with "tradition" (which in this case meant landowners), as the British were to do in 1832.

The important point about most of these conservatives was that, whatever the form of government they defended, they were devoted to all or a large part of the old eighteenth-century society and its remnants. What they stressed in their theories was the "organic" and "corporate" nature of society, that is, a living society made up of functioning groups. In other words society was a kind of living animal, not just a collection of individuals. Individuals could and should be classified according to their functions in society. Whether conservatives held out for absolutism or favored some representative system of government, they were most of them trying to stem the avalanche toward individualism and democracy which endangered their ideal of a good society.

There were various forms of compromise in nineteenth-century Europe. The English aristocracy had long since learned to live with the merchants, and now it compromised with the industrialists. In France, as we shall see, the corresponding relationships were less harmonious. But nineteenth-century conservatives, even in Britain, opposed any tendencies toward exclusive government control by the middle class with its characteristic liberal theories. They preferred, like Benjamin Disraeli, the great Conservative Prime Minister of 1874–1880, to seek the support of the lower classes through legislation in their favor.

This kind of appeal, if carried to extremes, might depart from conservatism altogether. Napoleon I had carried his odd combination of absolutism with democracy to such an extreme. He was neither conservative nor radical in the usual sense of those terms. His nephew Napoleon III, French Emperor from 1852–1870, was a similar kind of "Caesar." Bismarck, the unifier of Germany in the 1860's, exhibited some similar traits of blending conservative ideals and appeals to the masses. In the history of political traditions, this kind of strong government based on a popular appeal has been variously named. In cases where such a regime retained many elements of tradition, it may properly be called "conservative," but where the traditional was sacrificed to a plebeian and revolutionary appeal it is common to use the term "Caesarism" or "Bonapartism."

LIBERALISM

The word "liberal," like the word "conservative," appeared out of the revolutionary and Napoleonic whirlwind when people were being forced into explicit formulations of their beliefs. The first liberals to call themselves by the name were Spanish constitutionalists, enemies of Napoleon. The term later became general and was used to describe a point of view found in almost all countries.

Liberalism is a collection of beliefs and also an emotional attitude toward liberty. Those whose attitudes and doctrines won them the name "liberals" were people who believed that liberty was an end in itself; that is, a thing of great worth for its own sake, indeed an indispensable quality of man. They also believed that liberty was a means to other desirable ends, for example the increase of wealth and the rational conduct of government.

The belief in liberty as an end was the product of centuries of experience. It perhaps had its origins in the Judeo-Christian view of the dignity of man. It early made its home among upholders of tradition. For many people, and not only in the aristocracies, there was self-respect and honor in defending, not liberty in the abstract, but particular rights, such as the right of a landowner to collect dues from tenants, or the right of citizens not to have taxes imposed without their approval. Indeed, liberty in early modern times meant different liberties for different individuals and groups, and was inseparable from a society where each person had a legally defined position. This was still what conservatives meant by liberty in the nineteenth century. But since the Enlightenment a compelling idea had spread outward from the revolutionary epicenters of Philadelphia and Paris: that liberty was cosmic and absolute and inhered in human beings: "that all men are created equal, that they are endowed by their Creator with certain unalienable Rights . . ."

Liberty as a means to other ends also had a long history. Both Catholics and Protestants had sought to safeguard, against kings, the paths of human beings to salvation. In material things the exhilarating successes of Europeans bred confidence in businessmen and intellectuals and impatience with mercantilist and other regulations which hampered the free movements of individuals. The Enlightenment's slogans of "nature" and "reason" were very effective in attacking such limitations. The first historic function of the liberal creed was this destructive one. In the late eighteenth and early nineteenth century men rather naïvely believed that clearing the ground was enough, and they set about dismantling the old regime.

"Liberal" and "liberalism" are words which have changed their meanings in American usage in the last fifty years. In the early nineteenth century in Europe, liberalism was quite definite. It stood for a political and economic program which involved a minimum of state interference. Socially it meant "careers open to talent," and intellectually it meant a free competition of ideas. In international relations, it came to mean freedom for peoples, including colonies as well as nations, to manage their own affairs, and it was hoped that this, along with low tariffs and a minimum of colonial competition, would reduce the danger of war. By the late nineteenth century, however, liberals had begun to perceive that not all of these policies conduced to liberty. If the government did not regulate wages, hours, and working conditions, for example, the working man might have his liberty encroached upon by tyrannical employers. In their pursuit of their ideal of liberty many people began to advocate government action to protect individual welfare. Though they thus backed precisely the opposite of what early nineteenth-century liberals had backed, they still called themselves liberals —and so they are called in America today. This later chapter in the history of liberalism, once it is known to exist, need not concern us here.

The chief ideas of liberals at the end of the eighteenth century were based on optimism about man and his prospects. There was—as the conservatives charged— a certain element of pride and overconfidence in the assumption that reason was strong, that the laws of nature were knowable, and that progress would not be spoiled by defects in human nature, which was not evil unless made so by the environment. In defense of the liberals it must be said that their optimism reflected European achievements that were far from hollow. Their irritation with the crutches and braces of an earlier day was natural when strength had grown. If man was neither an invalid nor a perpetual child, then the guardianship upon which the conservatives insisted could only serve the aristocratic guardians themselves. The liberals—not exclusively middle-class people, but all of them willing to acknowledge the achievements of the middle class—were inclined to scoff at the conservative warnings as old wives' tales advanced, whether cynically or not, in defense of privileges.

The social philosophy of liberalism was launched in the name of the individual, who was seen as the basic unit of society. Not the interests of traditional groups of "guardians" like the nobles or clergy, but rather the interests of every individual, should be calculated when the good of society was being sought. "The greatest good of the greatest number," the utilitarian formula of Jeremy

Bentham, was the measure used by the most rationalistic liberals, but all of them assumed the sacredness of the individual on some grounds or other. In nature's eyes all were equal in rights. They must become so in law: free to compete in any profession, which meant the dissolution of clusters of privileged nobles in the political and military seats of power. There should be a society where individuals rose if they had talent and energy, sank if they had not.

The great logical gap in the liberal position, as the conservatives pointed out, was their insistence on hereditary property. Was not this also a privilege, and if property in an honorable title or a hereditary office could be denied sanctity, might not the proletarians who had nothing but their labor to offer in the market-place insist upon equal opportunities with the sons of the wealthy? The French Revolution had briefly lifted the veil which hid this alarming possibility, and nineteenth-century socialism was to do its best to tear it aside. But the liberals were firm in their faith that property was different. Personal property was accumulated work, as Locke had written: a mixing of something personal with the goods of nature so that the product became as sacred as the individual himself. The conservatives might issue dire warnings that property was indivisible, and that properties such as titles and seigneurial dues were inseparable from other forms. The liberals held fast to their Lockean faith. They believed that it was enough to free the society from legal privileges of birth. In the greater wealth and opportunities which would thereby be produced, everyone would share.

To insure this kind of progress economic liberalism demanded freedom for the workings of "natural" economic laws—which was another way of saying that without special privileges all would prosper. The Enlightenment had given the world the Physiocrats and Adam Smith. Following Smith came the classical economists of early nineteenth-century Britain. Like Smith, they were rigorous and intellectually honest in their reasoning. They were "scientific-minded." Unexpectedly, some of their conclusions seemed to turn against the optimism of the Enlightenment. Economics became "the gloomy science," and they were accused of being mouthpieces for the selfish interests of the new middle class business community.

Two illustrations—perhaps the most famous examples—of the way in which liberal economic thought arrived at rather heartless conclusions may be noted. They are the population theory of Thomas Malthus (1766–1834), an English clergyman, and the "iron law of wages" of David Ricardo (1772–1823), an English banker and member of Parliament.

Malthus in 1798 wrote that population was growing faster than the food supply, and was bound by nature to do so, since its progress advanced in geometrical ratio (2-4-8-16 etc.), whereas the food supply advanced only arithmetically (1-2-3-4-5 etc.). It followed that population was kept in line with food only through periodic waves of pestilence or other natural disasters, unless limited by unnatural means such as vice (including birth control), or natural and morally acceptable means such as continence and late marriages. Malthus, who was a liberal economist of note quite apart from his population theory, found himself in the unwelcome position of having, in effect, to tell the poor that their poverty was chiefly their own fault, curable only by self-control.

Ricardo's "iron law" had a similar ring, and helps to make Malthus's conclusion explicit. Suppose one were to argue in favor of taking from the rich and giving to the poor. The Ricardian analysis of this would be twofold. (1) Population, as shown by Malthus, tends to rise when food is plentiful. Therefore a transfer of wealth to the poor would soon defeat its own purpose, for the poor would multiply. And (2) in such an experiment the "rich," being deprived of capital with which to start new enterprises and enlarge old ones, would be hampered in their role of providing employment. If one thinks of the effects of these two conditions on wages, one sees that by a kind of "iron law" they tend always to return to a level of subsistence. For when wages rise, the workers, being better off, tend to produce more job-seekers, whose competition with each other in the long run brings wages down. Interference with private accumulations of capital, by taxing the rich to bring benefits to the poor, would have the same effect, for it would reduce the capital available, decrease the number of jobs, and make the competition for them more severe. On the other hand if the life of the workers is made too difficult by the lowering of wages, the drop in the population will make workers scarce and drive wages back up to subsistence again. The "iron" in Ricardo's "iron law of wages" was its inevitability. No amount of government interference or interference by labor unions could apparently change it. There was "iron" too in the hardness of the "law" for the working class.

These are elementary examples of liberal economic analysis, but they show that the problem of safeguarding wealth so that it could be used as investment for new production was a central concern of the classical economists. They were men of their times: they were impressed by the population upswing which was under way in Europe, by the problem of securing capital, by the problems of wages and rent, and by the tariffs and other trammels of government regulation of the economy which mercantilist policies had produced. Like liberals generally, they were thinking in rather abstract terms, treating individuals as units in a market system and not as human beings. They invented an "economic man," the basic unit of society, and in so doing abstracted from the everyday life of traditional and humanitarian concern. But they were real economists in that they reasoned from what they took to be valid assumptions about the way economic life worked, and thereby threw light as best they could on the welter of reality.

Not all liberals were economic theorists. Most businessmen and politicians who would be classified as liberals were possessed of general attitudes rather than of tightly reasoned proofs of the benefits of free trade and free competition and the harmfulness of tariffs, factory acts, labor unions, and subsidies to the poor. It was natural for merchants to oppose the privileged companies of mercantilism's heyday such as the British East India Company, and for factory owners to oppose state regulation of products, wages, and working conditions. The so-called "Manchester School" in nineteenth-century Britain consisted of men like Richard Cobden and John Bright who held liberal economic ideas characteristic of Manchester and other industrial cities, and tried to get Parliament to legislate according to these ideas. The Anti-Corn Law League, for example, founded at Manchester in 1839, not only helped bring about repeal of the protectionist British

Corn Laws in 1846 but also did much to implant the doctrines of free trade in the minds of the British public.

What liberals wanted, then, was a "passive, policeman state," which kept order and defended property but did little else, since private enterprise was better suited to the needs of society as expressed through the market. This liberal's dream of a state had the advantage of costing little and charging little for taxes. One of the reasons why it was economical was that it would not need large military forces because it would be peaceably inclined. Since people would be free traders, there would be no desire to seize more colonies and indeed little desire to defend those already possessed, because colonies were an expense. In the best of all possible free-trading worlds everyone would trade with everyone else's colonies.

The economic side of liberalism here merges with the political side. Without being completely ready to abandon colonial empires (though some went to this extreme), liberals nevertheless advocated freedom for colonies as for all nationalities and individuals. Colonies should at least have self-government. Ties of sentiment and mutual benefit rather than force should bind them to the mother country. The liberal supposed that if all nations were reasonable about free trade, colonies, and national self-determination, there would be little need for warfare and for the expensive, warlike states of past centuries. The liberal was not a pacifist but his interests led him elsewhere than toward war, and he tended to think all enlightened people must share his interests and take his direction.

In domestic politics the way to keep the government from doing the excessive, the unexpected, and the unfair was to guarantee that it represented the interests of the society. Absolute monarchy, however enlightened, could not provide this guarantee. Some form of representation was necessary, either through a traditional unwritten constitution like that of Britain or through a written document like that of the United States. In either case civil rights and political freedom would be guaranteed, without which liberty as an end in itself and a means to progress would be in jeopardy.

The problem of representation raised the problem of democracy—in the sense of rule by all the people—as it had in the classic example of the French Revolution. Most nineteenth-century liberals were not democrats. They believed that continued progress would eventually enlighten the masses of mankind to a point where they could be allowed to vote, but for the present only persons of "capacity" should vote or hold office. The most convenient rule of thumb for political capacity was the ownership of property, since property more often than not indicated some measure of education and responsibility. Not all liberals agreed with this test of political capacity. In general, however, nineteenth-century liberals found themselves between conservative traditionalists who defended hereditary rights of persons and regions to political representation, and radical democrats who held that everyone—or at least every male—had an interest in the community, and should vote.

European liberals in the first half of the nineteenth century were more often monarchists than republicans, and more inclined to favor the parliamentary system of Britain than the presidential system of the United States, with its separation of powers. Republics were few, and were long associated in people's minds with ancient history or with the radicalism of the French revolutions of 1789 and 1848. On the other hand representative government made great strides in the nineteenth century, and the question of the choice of representatives was a crucial one, since it brought into play class antagonisms and attitudes concerning man's nature and the possibility of progress.

DEMOCRACY

Democracy as an idea went back to the Greeks and was less of a novelty than liberalism. In practical politics, however, democracy lagged behind liberalism in nineteenth-century Europe. Although there had been occasional democratic programs such as those of the English Levellers of Cromwell's time and the Girondins and Mountain of the French Revolution, only after 1870 did democratic forms of representation begin to spread over Europe. Even then the idea spread more rapidly than the practical realization. Indeed, this has been the case with democracy in the twentieth century as well.

It was theoretically possible for liberals to become democrats, but until late in the century most of them did not. Most democrats were liberals, but most liberals feared to be democrats. They feared that rule of the majority would mean oppression of the minority, particularly since the majority consisted of the ignorant and poor. The French Revolution was fresh in people's minds as an example of how liberalism-turned-democratic might fall into demagoguery and dictatorship. Napoleon with his plebiscites had professed to be a democrat. Before long there was another Napoleon in France, Napoleon III, whose empire (1852–1870) professed to be democratic. It was clear that the democratic principles of a people's self-rule could be corrosive of liberty.

Nevertheless there were forces at work which were advancing the cause of democracy. Strongest of all were the examples already set in England and France of resistance to kings and aristocracies. No doubt these examples by themselves would not have carried things so far or so fast, but the excitement and unrest of nineteenth-century economic and social development stimulated further change. What the well-born had won from the king, what the rich had won from the well-born, the people would win from the rich. It was a simple idea, but in the long run irresistible unless the egalitarian ideas of past revolutions could somehow be spirited away. This was the avalanche feared everywhere in Europe since 1789 and met with varying amounts of wisdom in the various countries.

Before 1870, however, democratic theoreticians were far in advance of practical organizers. In Britain the work of Wilkes, Tom Paine, and the men of the French Revolutionary era was carried on by the utilitarian philosopher and reformer Jeremy Bentham (1748–1832). The English philosophical radicals—Bentham, James Mill (1773–1836), and others—were originally interested mainly in abolishing or correcting the absurd, outdated penal and other laws, but when they found the aristocratic conservatives blocking their best efforts they went over to democracy (about 1808). It seemed reasonable, after all, that those whose greatest good was in question should be consulted in their greatest number.

The Benthamite Radicals were believers in the economic liberalism of Adam Smith and the classical economists, and many of their followers went on to support the Manchester School and the Anti-Corn Law League. But there was a possible conflict between Smith's "unseen hand" (the automatic reconciliation of individual interests) and Bentham's utilitarian formula "the greatest good of the greatest number." As the century advanced, some of the Radicals began to question laissez faire. John Stuart Mill (1806–1873), son of James Mill and one of the most famous democratic liberals of the nineteenth century, is the outstanding example. John Stuart Mill refined earlier utilitarianism by recognizing that there was more to values than easily calculable pleasures and pains. He was a democrat who was aware of the dangers to liberty in a society dominated by the masses, but he hoped that the democratic political process would itself educate the people. While recognizing that some legislation did more harm than good, Mill thought that there might well be utility in social legislation redistributing the wealth. There was always in utilitarianism the logical possibility that the greatest good of the greatest number might be achieved by state action. Mill was a pioneer who went further than most liberals of his time when he explored this possibility.

Other examples of democratic programs and actions were the Chartists in Great Britain from 1838 to 1848 and the republicans on the continent. The "People's Charter" was political, demanding manhood suffrage, equal electoral districts, removal of property qualifications for members of Parliament, payment of members of Parliament, secret ballot, and annual general elections. The Chartists, during the trying era when the Industrial Revolution was still new and raw and the labor movement in Britain had not yet found its most practical course, counted on political democracy to achieve social justice. Chartism failed in the 1840's, but in time most of its program became law.

Republicanism on the continent carried memories of the great French Revolution in its radical republican phase of 1792–1794. Although forced underground, republicanism persisted among intellectuals, students, soldiers, lower middle class shopkeepers, and artisans, and took root in the new factory proletariat as it slowly formed, but it was a minority view distrusted by the majority of the French as bloodthirsty and fanatical. Like Chartism in England, it was a political movement with strong social overtones, but it was more than a political and social program; it was what the French call a *mystique*, a mixture of creed and sentiment, and it glorified the sovereign people, Reason, the Great Revolution, the nation, liberty and equality, and political democracy, scorned kings, priests, and aristocrats and looked forward to the next revolution, in which the people's representatives, sitting in a unicameral assembly as in 1792, would set things right.

There was still a quality of crusading internationalism about the republicanism of the early nineteenth century, and there were republican secret societies in Germany and Italy as well as in France. This kind of internationalism did not rule out intensely nationalistic sentiments. The conspiratorial republicanism of the early nineteenth century was not identified with any particular social class, or with socialism.

Like the liberals, the republicans in Europe knew a moment of hope in the Revolutions of 1848, but they were much too radical for the taste of the liberals, and the two failed to work together harmoniously.

There were on the continent few theorists of democracy to equal the great French political scientist and historian Alexis de Tocqueville (1805–1859), who wrote *Democracy in America* (1835–1840) and *The Old Regime and the Revolution* (1856). De Tocqueville was rather like a French John Stuart Mill who became a democratic liberal in spite of the dangers of majority rule because he saw in people's yearning for equality and social justice the inevitability of democracy.

SOCIALISM

The word "socialism," like the words "conservative" and "liberal," appeared in the discussions of the post-revolutionary period. In its early history, "socialism" merely meant any theory which subordinated the individual to society. Later, it came to be used more specifically, by most people, to mean state ownership of land and capital, and in particular the "scientific socialism" of Karl Marx (1818–1883).

Certainly in this, of all historic periods, the tides of opinion were running most strongly against state control of the economy. Yet precisely for that reason socialism appeared. It was a minority report of protest, partly moral and humanitarian, partly economic. The idea of common ownership, known since the ancients, was less important in this movement than the emphasis on cooperation and the antagonism to unregulated competition.

Although modern socialism was born in the stress and strain of Europe's rapid nineteenth-century economic development, it was indebted to the great French Revolution for its egalitarianism and rationalism as well as for the example of revolution itself, and of state interference with economic matters. The Revolution also set the precedent of a minority dictatorship acting in the name of the whole people, and provided an example of internationalism and missionary zeal. During the French Revolution, most of these conclusions were reached by François Emile ("Gracchus") Babeuf, who organized the "conspiracy of the Equals" in 1796. Few of his contemporaries were attracted by Babeuf's ideas. The French Revolution took place in a world still largely agricultural, with virtually no class of wage earners conscious of themselves as differing in interests from the *bourgeoisie*.

By the 1830's and 1840's, however, such a class was in existence in Western Europe, living and working apart, visibly a problem to itself and to others. The classical economists themselves admitted the existence of class antagonism. Conservative traditions of paternalism and *noblesse oblige* moved some people to demand social legislation, and there were religious protests against the inhumanity practiced against wage earners. Socialists were therefore not alone in their protest. Indeed, in the first half of the nineteenth century they were part of a great chorus of discussion about the condition of man in society. This was a time of experimental thinking.

Socialists, as they first appeared, were independent of each other and sometimes unknown to each other. They scarcely agreed on any detail—not on the organization of work, nor on the role of property, nor on the role of the state, nor on the psychology and needs of the individual man. Almost all of these early socialists counted on modest experiments and persuasion, rather than on forceful revolution. If their means differed from those of the liberals, their premises were often similar, and their concern for the individual equally sincere. On the other hand, they resembled the conservatives in their emphasis on society and on groups.

Before generalizing further it will be useful to mention a few of the early socialists.

Claude Henri de Bouvroy, duc de Saint-Simon (1760–1825), was a French noble who fought in the American Revolution, gave up his title during the French Revolution, made and lost a fortune, and became the prophet of what he called the "new Christianity." He thought that from the study of history a science of society could be constructed. Saint-Simon wanted to advance beyond the limitations of the Enlightenment's reasoning to a more positive knowledge. He favored applying science to production and was a prophet of industrialism, but he hoped to persuade mankind that everyone should work cooperatively, with leadership and the greatest rewards going to those with the greatest abilities and accomplishments.

François Marie Charles Fourier (1772–1837) was an eccentric middle-class Frenchman who felt out of place in competitive business and turned to planning a more harmonious society. He concluded that no matter what their inherited characteristics, men and women could be happy in planned communities where each worked at a succession of jobs according to his capacity and was rewarded according to his contribution of capital, labor, and skill. Fourier led a solitary life, but through his writings he won disciples in Europe and America.

Robert Owen (1771–1858) was a self-made man, owner-manager of the New Lanark Mills in Scotland. After proving in his own business that enlightened labor policies were practical and actually increased his profits, he became a public figure who was drawn into discussions of pauperism and unemployment. Irritated by opposition from churchmen and other well-established dignitaries, he became more radical and advocated a number of schemes for the remaking of society, among them cooperative societies for production and distribution, a system of labor exchanges, a giant labor union, and socialistic communities of producers. Unlike Fourier, he believed that character and personality were formed by environment. Owen had a large public in England, and in the United States founded the unsuccessful socialistic community of New Harmony, Indiana (1824).

Louis Blanc (1811–1882) was a French democrat, historian, and politician who took part in the February Revolution of 1848 and in the Provisional Government of the Second Republic, which followed. As a critic of laissez-faire capitalism, he had proposed, in *The Organization of Labor* (1840), a plan of "national workshops" founded by the state and managed by associations of workingmen. His arresting slogan was: "from each according to his abilities; to each according to his needs." The actual workshops founded in 1848 fell far short of his hopes and were soon abolished; their suppression touched off the "bloody June days"—one of the first examples in the age of industry of "class warfare."

Pierre Joseph Proudhon (1809–1865) was a Frenchman of plebeian origin and loyalties, fiercely independent, who became famous for a pamphlet, *What is Property?* (1840), in which he answered, "Property is theft." Among the admirers of this essay was Karl Marx. In later life Proudhon, who hated both political and religious authority, repudiated communism and state direction in all forms. He hoped that workingmen would be able to emancipate themselves from capitalism without falling under state control, and to this end he advocated a system called "mutualism," by which workers would make and exchange goods for themselves.

These brief sketches indicate the variety in socialist thinking in its early years. Two main tendencies are worth noting: one toward the state as agency for social betterment; the other away from the state, toward anarchism. Socialism, in the broad sense of cooperative production and distribution, is present in both schools: where the "statist" wants a socialist society capped by a strong state, the anarchist is content with the society alone. Of the two schools, the anarchist is more optimistic, relying on the ability of men to cooperate spontaneously. Anarchists continue the theoretical dismantling of the state already begun by the economic liberals; the statists reverse the process.

Socialists in the period before 1848 were for the most part isolated thinkers, linked neither to labor movements nor, before the 1840's, to the democratic movement. After the wave of revolutions in 1848, in which it played only a small part, socialism was apparently in decline. Until about 1864 the triumphant reaction, coupled with economic prosperity, all but silenced the socialist leaders. On the other hand the formation of labor unions, less theoretical and radical, made real advances during this time of "realism." After the mid-1860's socialism revived and came into closer touch with labor. The first International Workingmen's Association was founded in 1864.

This is not the place to discuss the International, where a bitter struggle took place between the anarchist and statist tendencies within socialism. By this time Marxism was getting under way as a movement. Although Karl Marx's ideas were fully formed within the period covered by this chapter, and indeed illustrate the chapter's main themes, Marx is best introduced along with Marxism as a movement, which falls for the most part in the period after 1870 (see Chapter 34).

NATIONALISM

Nationalism is related to the social philosophies already mentioned, and has special importance of its own as one of the most powerful movers of men. The distinction between nationa*lity* and nationa*lism* is worth repeating here. Nationality is usually taken to mean the possession of certain qualities in common, such as language, culture, a sense of sharing the same history, and sometimes a common religion. The nationalities of Europe were very old. Nationalism is used to mean overpowering loyalty to a nationality such as that which the French exhibited in the midst of their revolutionary fervor. Nationalism was not old, for men's supreme loyalties had, except for brief periods of exaltation such as the defense of France by Joan of Arc, been elsewhere.

It took a great advance in sophistication on the part of Europeans before they could be nationalists. This is a statement which today has almost the quality of a paradox, for today nationalism's shortcomings are and have long been all too evident. It should not be forgotten, however, that with all its faults nationalism required of a nationality both a highly developed knowledge of itself and disillusion with other targets for supreme loyalty, such as kings or local chieftains. It required, for example, that the French should be loyal to such an abstract ideal as the destiny of the French nation. The "French nation" was harder to focus on than the king or a leading provincial family to which one's ancestors had always been loyal. The French of 1789 were able to do so because of a rise in the general level of culture.

The maturing of nationalism meant that leaders would have to associate themselves with their peoples' aspirations. It did not mean, as conservatives feared, that there would have to be democratic governments. This conservative fear, as we have seen, was partly practical (since the French Revolutionists were nationalistic) and partly theoretical (since there was a logical connection between nationalism and popular sovereignty). Conservatives were to learn after 1850, and especially after 1870, that peoples' aspirations could be appealed to by all kinds of potential leaders, conservatives included. Liberals and radical democrats, in the period we are considering, continued to be nationalistic. There were signs before 1870, however, that the extreme left, the socialists, were deserting the "nation" for the "class", and were becoming internationalists. This threat was to prove more theoretical than actual.

Nationalism before 1870 was not, in all parts of Europe, what might be called "mature." In the Revolutions of 1848 many Germans and Italians showed themselves to be nationalistic, but even here one cannot be certain how deeply nationalism had penetrated beneath the educated middle classes. In 1848 the Hungarians showed themselves to be nationalistic, and there were many nationalistic leaders among the Czechs of Bohemia and some of the other Slavic peoples, such as the Croats, within the Habsburg monarchy. The rank and file of these subject nationalities were not yet nationalistic, however, because they were too ignorant to attach any special importance to their own cultural traditions. The revolutionary year 1848 has been called the "springtime of peoples," but for many of the peasant peoples of East Central Europe it was very early spring indeed.

In general, nationalism came to these peoples after the middle of the century. As in the west, it appeared first among the more educated, who, partly in imitation of the west, sought information about their cultures and prepared dictionaries, histories, and collections of folklore. This cultivation of the sense of nationality was partly the result of economic development. When the growth of cities concentrated people of one nationality in districts of their own, with their own newspapers, schools, and professional class, the nationality began to develop its own educated leaders. Formerly the cities of the Austrian empire had been so overwhelmingly German in culture that the subject peoples lost their most intelligent youth as they mastered the German language and culture in order to get ahead in the world.

To the extent that economic development helped spread nationalism into East Central Europe by increasing the number of city-dwellers and the variety of jobs, it was repeating a process which had taken place in the west. But in East Central Europe there was the great difference that the upper and lower classes tended to be of different nationalities. Thus as nationalities on the lower levels became more aware of themselves, nationalism tended to become a political movement of emancipation with overtones of class antagonism.

Romanticism, too, had its relationship to nationalism. The new vogue for history and the new respectability of tradition encouraged literary and philological as well as historical researches which strengthened the sense of nationality. This is how, for example, the fairy stories collected by the Grimm brothers, William and Jacob, contributed to the rise of German nationalism. In romanticism the fondness for the emotional and exotic as well as for the particular, as opposed to the classical search for universal characteristics, helped strengthen national traditions.

In the era of romanticism, emphasis on *groups*, as having a kind of organic reality or life of their own, contributed to the treatment of national cultures as if they were individuals. This tendency was especially strong in Germany, where as early as 1784 Johann Gottfried Herder (1744–1803) published a *Philosophy of the History of Mankind* teaching that each people had its own special genius (*Volksgeist*), and should develop in its own way. As German nationalism flowered among intellectuals during and after the Napoleonic wars, the strengthening of this idea of *Volksgeist* furnished a contrast to the competing "Jacobin" nationalism of the French, which emphasized the sovereign people as a collection of freely associated individuals.

Historians have sometimes attributed to German nationalism—and indeed to romanticism—an exclusively conservative character, but these generalizations are misleading. There were both conservative and liberal German nationalists, as there were both conservative and liberal romanticists. Nationalism gave itself exclusively to no special political form or idea. By providing the national state with a fund of passionate loyalty, it hugely increased the power of governments of all sorts. It made the modern state the most powerful institution the world has ever known.

27

GREAT BRITAIN IN
THE AGE OF
INDUSTRY

In 1789 GREAT BRITAIN WAS ENGAGED with France in the long duel which had begun when the decline of Spanish and Dutch power left France and England without peers. This duel continued for another generation, the last, most perilous phase
of the century-long struggle. Already Britain had suffered the grave loss of the
thirteen colonies in North America. It had yet to face and survive the French
victories over all the European powers, which would bring French armies triumphant to Lisbon, Rome, and Moscow. By a skillful management of Great Britain's
most useful resources—the wealth of its homeland, the multiplicity of its colonies, the power of its navy, and the alarms of its allies—victory in the ancient feud
was won. Not until the maturing of Germany after 1870 would there be another
such menace to British grandeur and safety.

The victory over France, and Britain's nineteenth-century role as pace-
setter of the western world, were accompanied by durable changes within the
nation itself. The constitutional arrangements of the eighteenth century, which
had proved so successful in bringing internal stability, were beginning to be
outmoded by 1789. The adjustment of them to a new age was accomplished in
the following century with imagination and tranquility. There were many conflicts and tensions, but the almost complete transformation of British institutions
between 1789 and 1870 involved no such gory dislocations as had the last period
of great constitutional change, in the seventeenh century. By 1870, the outlines
of British political organization in an age of democracy were perfectly clear, and
they have not substantially altered since.

Nor were the great changes of this age merely political. More than ever before economic and social life were also changing. The people who possessed the bulk of British wealth in 1700 were for the most part different kinds of people from those who possessed it in 1900. The nature of the wealth had changed. The nature of the working class had changed. The distribution of wealth had changed. And, most of all, its volume had vastly increased, bringing a different kind of society. By 1870, there was sufficient visible wealth in the United Kingdom to lead the less fortunate and independent of its citizens to demand provision for their security and comfort. By 1870 something which the world had never known before, an industrial society, had come into being; and its coming had produced an intellectual and social ferment unprecedented since the upheavals of the Reformation. But British adjustment to this unknown world was scarcely less successful than was the adaptation of its constitution.

In 1870 Great Britain reached a high peak of power and riches, at the mid-point in the reign of Queen Victoria (1837–1901), who gave her name to the era.

THE ERA OF THE FRENCH REVOLUTION

Alone among the European powers, Great Britain emerged from the twenty-five years of European revolution and war, from 1789 to 1815, with its territory untouched by the French armies. The effects of the volcanic disturbances beyond the Channel were nonetheless great in almost every sphere of British life.

When the French Revolution began, Great Britain was in some ways as unsettled as any European country. Six years earlier it had been forced to accept the Treaty of Paris which recognized the independence of the United States and signalized the first time the British had lost a naval war or suffered major losses in a peace treaty in at least two hundred years. The War of American Independence had been costly in many respects. But there were deeper and truer causes for perturbation than the American Revolution. The effects of economic and social change in the eighteenth century were making themselves felt. There was widespread dissatisfaction with both the political and administrative arrangements of the country. The parliamentary franchise was denounced in some circles partly because it was illogical and partly because it excluded from a role in government so large a percentage of the population. The law and the law courts, the glory of British jurists, were being attacked as cruel, slow, intricate, unreasonable. Businessmen and farmers fretted at the high cost and inconvenience of the antiquated system of local government and economic controls, particularly the obligation of paying increasingly heavy taxes to provide relief for paupers, under the old Elizabethan Poor Laws.

To such complaints and demands a number of the gentlemen of the ruling class were prepared to listen with sympathy in 1789. The Prime Minister, William Pitt the Younger, was very up-to-date in his views. He sympathized with the demands for overhauling the economic structure of Britain to free the growing manufacturing class from the trammels of ancient regulations and taxes. He was sympathetic to the need for liberating religious dissenters from the civil disabilities —including the inability to vote or hold office—which dated from the Clarendon Code of the previous century. He was sympathetic to the need for parliamentary reform—that is, for making the arrangements concerning who could vote more orderly and perhaps providing representation for new cities and towns. Other men in high places, like the Duke of Devonshire and Charles James Fox, the elegant and impetuous leader of the Whigs, went further than Pitt, and lent their names to organizations which favored reform of various kinds—of the chaotic municipal governments, of the criminal code, of parliamentary franchises, of the paternalistic commercial and economic regulations. These proposals were all along lines suggested by the reforming continental philosophers or by native theorists like Adam Smith.

One of the principal effects of the French Revolution upon Great Britain was to frighten almost all respectable folk into opposing any changes of these kinds—or of any kind at all. By 1793, when Britain was forced into war against revolutionary French, the dangers of reform had become manifest across the Channel. The moral had been forcefully explained in Edmund Burke's extremely influential book, *Reflections on the French Revolution* (1790). Burke, an ardent defender of liberty against the crown, of the Rights of the Subject, and even of the American colonies in their struggle, suggested that any considerable change in a constitution would lead to violence, and eventually to dictatorship. By late 1792 a new tyranny seemed to have seized France, the tyranny of mobs and dictators. And this tyranny was not only oppressive but aggressive: it was engaged in attacks upon its neighbors. It was Burke's persuasive argument, wholly consistent with his earlier views, that any attack on the supremacy of law, any drastic change in legal institutions, leads to an abridgement of liberty.

The respectable people in Britain were frightened by the red menace from France and also by their domestic reformers, who, since they sympathized with the politics of the enemy, found that their political views were being viewed as treasonable. Reforming ideas were met, by Pitt and the government, with increasingly stern repressive measures. In 1794 the most important safeguard of civil liberties, *habeas corpus*, was suspended. Persons suspected of revolutionary inclinations were arrested, imprisoned, and transported. A sort of spy hysteria, aggravated by the very unfavorable course of the war against France, prevailed.

The rise of Napoleon in France, bringing an open dictatorship and an end to stimulating experiments with advanced political ideas, made France lose its attractiveness for British reformers. But the excesses in France had left a lasting fear of change among respectable people. For another thing, the disruptions caused by economic change and wartime stringencies brought social discontent which seemed to require new repressions and a more spirited defense of the existing order than ever.

The wars of the French Revolution and Napoleon had important economic effects. The need for supplying the army and navy as well as Britain's allies on the continent and overseas, and the opening up of Spanish America to

British commerce, spurred manufacturers to venture capital and to experiment with new methods in the hope of quick profits. In the 1790's, for example, raw cotton imports almost doubled, showing the growth of the cotton textile industry. France (which up until 1791 had shared almost equally with Britain the effects of the Industrial Revolution) found its economy blockaded and strained, and fell behind.

But despite this long-run progress, the war years were at various times and in various ways extremely burdensome in Britain. Taxes and prices rose drastically, as they frequently do in wartime, and the national debt mounted to staggering sums. The budget rose more than 600 percent from 1793 to 1813. The normal continental markets were frequently disrupted. The United States, the most important British market abroad, was closed from 1807 to 1809 and from 1812 to 1815. And the development of new manufacturing methods was causing "technological unemployment." Men were thrown out of work by machines which could do their work faster and cheaper. All this resulted in hardships in many sections of the economy. To these hardships, workingmen reacted in various ways. Some sought to save themselves, or improve their situation, by organizing into groups—unions, or "combinations," to bring pressure on employers for improvements in wages. Others, desperate like the Midlands weavers, began a movement which eventually became widespread, of wrecking the machines which were causing their unemployment. This movement, called "Luddism," was violent and frightening.

Nor did peace, which came in 1815, bring any surcease from unrest; on the contrary, it aggravated it. Peace was followed by a deep depression which lasted about five years. The problems of rapid growth were replaced by problems of unused resources. The victims now were the businessmen, the bankers, and particularly the landowners, who not only found the market for their wheat diminished but also found cheap foreign foodstuffs competing on the British market and threatening the aristocracy with ruin. The respectable classes were more edgy than ever. They faced, in addition to their own troubles, an ever greater flood of social reform movements, some even revolutionary, on the part of what were repulsively known as "the lower orders." Among them were the Philanthropists, the first organized socialists in England, and an alarming group called Blanketeers who threatened something in the nature of a hunger march on London, wrapped in blankets against the disagreeable weather.

In all the years from 1790 to 1820 no real effort was made to remedy any of the causes, political or economic, for these disorders. The answer of the government was usually repressive; and the government was more securely than ever in the hands of the landed aristocrats, in whom the fresh blood of William Pitt appeared to have curdled. In 1799–1800 the Combination Acts had been passed, which outlawed labor unions and indeed all forms of organized action by employees. In 1819, after a riot in Manchester known as the Peterloo Massacre, the government was induced to pass the Six Acts, which suspended freedom of assembly and a number of other popular rights. And repressive acts were matched by laws intended to safeguard the interests of the ruling landowners. In 1815 the Corn Laws were passed, which placed a very high duty upon imported wheat.

This presumably guaranteed the landowners' profits, but it incidentally raised the price of bread in a time of falling wages and of unemployment.

THE GENESIS OF REFORM

In reply to this situation, ever-growing numbers of people demanded reform. "Reform" was not entirely a political and economic movement. The name covered an extremely various set of demands, religious, literary, legal, and social. It concerned gentlemen who favored free trade, gentlemen who favored better morals, gentlemen who favored more flexible poetic forms, as well as workers who wanted bread or the franchise. The political reformers made little headway before 1820. Even moderate proposals for the reform of the criminal code (there were by now over two hundred capital offenses listed in it, including the wearing of a black mask) failed in Parliament. The one triumph of the political reformers was the election of one of their number, Sir Francis Burdett, to the House of Commons in 1807—the first reformer in Westminster.

But in other fields progress was made. Religious reform was the first to take effect. The very devout and influential William Wilberforce, who hoped to achieve what he called "the reform of manners," was campaigning for a more enthusiastic and fervent religious life, and he was gaining ground. The humanitarian concerns of a new form of Anglicanism called Evangelical led him to work against the iniquitous Slave Trade, which was in fact outlawed in 1807. Along with the Evangelicals, the rather similar Methodists, who broke in this period from the Church of England, were succeeding in their efforts to make Englishmen take religion personally and passionately. By 1820 a tidal change in popular attitudes toward theology and morals was in the making. The impressive movement toward what we call "Victorian morality," and toward missionary work and passionate piety, was turning the kingdom away from the polite abstractions of the eighteenth-century Church.

The religious revival foreshadowed and in some ways exemplified the wave of reform which broke over Great Britain after 1820. Then there came an age of drastic revision of everything, reflecting the extensive changes which were destroying eighteenth-century society. Men began—in Britain as elsewhere —to lose their confidence in old truths and cosmologies. The staggering experience of the age of revolutions just past, the spirit of free inquiry generated by the philosophers of the previous century, the changes brought about by industry, the growth of scientific knowledge which often seemed to discredit old beliefs, the growth of the population, all these combined to make people reexamine the fundamentals of their society and of their creeds.

This was part of the whole European pattern of new ideas which is described in Chapter 26. Here we have to mention those features of it which were peculiar to Britain and to show their connection with what actually happened there. The most strikingly British feature of the new ideas was the fact that so many of them were religious in source and aim. The nineteenth century in Britain—and America, too—was remarkable for the fervor of its theologians and moralists. And it was even more remarkable for the explosion of tangible reforms, mostly carried out by parliamentary enactment, in the structure of society. Never before had law-making been so widely regarded, or used, as an instrument for altering a civilization. This use of legislation reflected the social and political ideas which flowered in the nineteenth century. The programs were very various, and many of them merely quixotic, such as the socialist dreams of the Anglican novelist Charles Kingsley, who envisaged an English industrial Utopia constructed on the model of medieval monasteries. But there is a thread of consistency in what was actually done. This thread bears a closer resemblance to the theories of the two late eighteenth- and early nineteenth-century writers, Jeremy Bentham and Adam Smith, than to any of the other social philosophers. While few things that were done were strictly Smithian or strictly Benthamite, their writings often provided the texts for the interminable lectures on political economy to which the Commons and the public were treated in the years between 1820 and 1870.

Taken together, the doctrines of Smith and Bentham, and their followers, added up to a body of ideas which was, and is, known loosely as "liberalism." In essence, the purpose of "liberalism" and liberals was to rebuild the economic organization, the class structure, and the form of government of eighteenth-century Britain. The thoroughness with which such reformers sought to uproot the old order caused them to be called "radical reformers," (from the Latin *radix*, root) or simply radicals. It was their view that if men had liberty, that is, if they were left alone as much as possible and their actions regulated only when they threatened the security or liberty of another individual, they would act in a way calculated to improve their own lot and, with it, that of everyone else.

Adam Smith particularly disliked tariffs. He also disliked the price fixing powers which were confided to local authorities. His followers inveighed against the Poor Laws, which were by 1820 placing a heavy burden on taxpayers for the support of the paupers, many of whom, it was alleged, refused to work because they knew they could be supported on relief. What Smith wanted was a Free Economy, and after his death a whole new generation of economists elaborated and popularized his ideals. The center of the movement for a free economy— *laissez faire*—was the most important of the new industrial towns, Manchester, and the body of economists who grew up to support it is sometimes called the Manchester School.

In working-class quarters, educated and vigorous leaders were beginning to appear. Some of them had influential friends and a measure of political influence. In such places radicalism, or liberalism, was very successful. Labor and capital were often united in their dislike of the old, aristocratic government and society of Britain. Even among people who disliked Utilitarianism and Manchester economics, even among people who were themselves aristocrats and conservatives, there were those who espoused some sorts of reform doctrines. Some of the most important ones were willing to go along with Reform for reasons of party politics. These members of the ruling class, many Whigs and some Tories, felt that concessions to the swelling demands for change must be met to avoid revolution, or at least in order to capture votes and popular support. And it was these politicians who, after 1820, initiated the great sweep of reforms which was peacefully to destroy the old order in Britain.

The most basic reform that was being demanded was a widening and regularization of the parliamentary franchise, and this cause was cautiously taken up by some Whig leaders, mainly Lord Grey and Lord Brougham, just before 1820. Their proposals failed. But even Tories were growing hospitable to lesser changes. Certainly after 1822 the Tory cabinets were composed more and more of men who favored and carried through reform in many spheres. The Tories could not approach the reform of the franchise, however, because any substantial increase in the number of voters would (it was feared) threaten the control of the landed ruling class. But they could and did begin to attack some of the other targets of reformist and radical zeal.

From 1822 to 1830, mainly under the leadership of George Canning, who was in office, first as Foreign Minister and then Prime Minister, from 1822 to 1827, a group of remarkable ministers carried out a group of remarkable changes. Sir Robert Peel rewrote the criminal code (along lines suggested by writers of the Enlightenment) to simplify it and eliminate most of the capital offenses. To provide a new deterrent in place of the death penalty, he installed the first police force in London, whose members are still called "Bobbies," after him. Other ministers undertook reforms in their various departments. The Navigation Laws were amended, practically into extinction, and a new age of almost free trade between British colonies and the rest of the world began. The Combination Acts of 1800, which outlawed labor unions, were repealed. And most striking of all was the repeal in 1828 and 1829 of the laws which prevented Catholics and Protestant Dissenters from holding public office or sitting in Parliament.

Such changes in the decade of the 1820's showed that the people who controlled Parliament, all but the crustiest of Tories, were ready to admit the need for sweeping changes. Public opinion and the pressure of changing facts were overpowering.

THE GREAT REFORM BILL OF 1832

There was one line upon which many respectable folk and almost all Tories stood, which was the parliamentary franchise. Conservative people feared that if the new factory owners, or the new urban middle classes, or the new industrial working class, or the old rural working class, were in a position to control the House of Commons, all the old safeguards would be swept away. The Corn Laws, the peerage, the monarchy, the Church, all the old ways of doing things and all the old social and economic order which (they said) had led Britain to greatness in the past, might be endangered by a wave of irresponsible popular leaders.

But parliamentary reform was becoming a more and more popular cause, and the leaders of the Whig opposition more and more were inclined to espouse it, partly because they were afraid of a revolution, partly because they thought they could win elections with "reform" as a Whig program. And they were right. In 1830, the Whigs ran on a program of reform, and they won. As one contemporary observed, the fact that the reformers could win a majority with the old franchise proved that it was not so inflexible as the reformers claimed. The Tory ministers resigned, in accordance with now established constitutional custom, and a Whig cabinet under Lord Grey took office. It prepared and presented a bill for the reform of the parliamentary franchise which appeared so drastic as to shock the Tories out of their wits and to be received in radical quarters with numbed delight.

What the First Reform Bill (as it is called) provided was roughly this. The qualifications for voters in boroughs (incorporated towns) were to be made uniform, in contrast to the extremely varied requirements which until then had existed. Everyone who owned or occupied real estate which had an annual rental value of ten pounds (a fairly high value) would have the right to vote. In the counties—in order to allay the fear of the landowners that their traditional predominance would be swamped by the votes of their own tenants—the qualification remained basically unchanged, with the vote permitted to the "forty shilling freeholder" (a man who owned land with a rentable value of forty shillings) and extended to a few substantial tenants. Perhaps more important than changes in voting requirements, the distribution of electoral districts was changed. The new industrial towns, like Manchester, were given representation in the Commons, and some of the old "rotten" and "pocket" boroughs lost their seats. The electoral map now corresponded roughly with the changed map of British population: the newly enriched and rapidly growing areas of the Midlands caught up with the old, static agricultural south in parliamentary representation.

The bill was pushed through Parliament after a struggle of more than a year. There were several obstacles to be overcome, of which the most important

HOUSES OF PARLIAMENT. Planned by the architect Sir Charles Barry and begun in the 1840's, this is one of the most successful examples of the nineteenth-century revival of medieval Gothic architecture. (Photo Viollet)

was the House of Lords. The Lords at first voted down the bill. The Whig ministry dissolved the House of Commons and fought another victorious election campaign, to convince the Peers that the nation was strongly for the bill. The Lords still balked. The ministry resigned, and the Tories tried to form a cabinet and failed, since they could secure no support from the majority in the Commons. At this juncture there were popular riots and demonstrations in London. The king—William IV—recalled the Whig ministers, and they forced him to promise to create enough new peerages to form a pro-Reform majority in the Lords. The threat was enough; rather than see their membership diluted by several hundred new Whig noblemen, the Lords capitulated and the bill was passed.

Four aspects of the successful campaign for the passage of the bill are worthy of notice, for they portended many future developments. The first was the willingness of the great Whig aristocrats to espouse a constitutional change which they regarded, at best, as a repellent expedient. The second was the pressure of public opinion. Radical, middle-class, and working-class leaders put on a campaign to pressure the Lords and the Tories. There was what would today be called "propaganda," and there were contrived riots, slogans, and parades, mostly engineered by the politically adept master-tailor Francis Place, the principal working-class leader of the radical movement. Third, it had been admitted by the ruling groups that the basis of representation could and should be arranged to correspond to changes in society and the economy—which was a deep issue between the reformers and those who opposed them. Fourth, the Lords had been outmaneuvered by the threat to use the king's power to create peerages. This last was the most pregnant feature of the crisis. What it meant was that the House of Lords could, in the last analysis, be forced to do whatever the ministry wanted. It meant, too, that the king was controlled by the ministry. And the inability of the Tories to form a minority ministry showed that the ministry was controlled by the majority in the House of Commons. There was no branch of the British government which was not subject to the wishes of the legislative majority. There was no longer any "separation of powers." The House of Commons, if it wished to assert itself, was supreme. And the pattern for the British constitution as it has existed ever since was complete.

In the event, the Reform Act, so much applauded and so much feared, had fewer immediate concrete effects than anyone had supposed it would. The electorate was expanded by several hundred thousand, many of them well-to-do factory owners in the Midlands, and a small group of members of the first Reformed Parliament called themselves Radicals and expressed extremely Benthamite viewpoints. Both parties, and particularly the shaken Tories, found it expedient to begin building party organizations and framing platforms to appeal to the voters, instead of conducting themselves as parliamentary cliques without announced principles or views on large issues; something like modern political parties began to take shape. But, for a few years at least, it looked as if very little had changed. There was no sudden influx of "the manufacturing interest" into Westminster; the composition of the House of Commons remained much as it had always been. The country was not submerged in demands for democracy.

What did happen, however, was that a Whig party committed to a philosophy of reform, and ardently pushed by the Radicals, was installed in power for the next eight years, and it undertook a program of moderate but basic overhauling of many branches of British society. These reforms, which occasioned less debate and much less alarm than the Reform Bill itself, had very far-reaching effects. They laid down the lines which almost all British legislation was to follow in its course of remolding the country and in adapting it to the industrial age. The importance of the Reform Bill is what it made possible by its very example: a long process of peaceful, gradual change by legal means in the structure of the kingdom.

THE "CONDITION OF ENGLAND"

The reforms of the middle and late 1830's were all influenced, and some were inspired, by the reformers' urge to tidy up the face of England. The English Parliament now did the same kinds of things, peacefully and gradually, which an Enlightened Despot like Joseph II had tried to do in Austria and which the French Revolution had done by violence in France. The following is a very partial, but illustrative, list.

The Corporations—that is, municipal government—were reformed in 1835. The quaint and archaic variety of town governments, most of them based on charters as much as five hundred years old, was swept away. Municipal councils, with very wide powers, elected by the vote of all taxpayers were set up; this amounted almost to democracy in local affairs. This created very powerful, and uniform, local governments in which radicals, businessmen, and even working-class people could experiment and act. The cities of Britain became laboratories for change and class-rooms for politics.

The Poor Law was amended, in 1834. The old Poor Law had provided that the parish—that is, the local community—was responsible for the relief of suffering and the prevention of starvation through relief. But the system had become anachronistic and extraordinarily expensive. The new economic thought argued that the relief of suffering made sloth attractive to the poor. The new political thought argued that all administration ought to be concentrated in the hands of a small, cheap group of expert administrators, not left to the amateur country gentlemen of the parishes. The new Poor Law therefore did two things. It made relief as unattractive as possible, and as inexpensive to the taxpayer as possible, by requiring the poor to live in poor houses (which were truly appalling in their unattractiveness) in order to get aid. And it concentrated the administration of the Work Houses (as they were chillingly called) in the hands of a central board of professional men. It was the subject of innumerable tearjerking novels and bitter broadsides; and it tended to open a breach between the taxpaying middle classes and their erstwhile allies among the workingmen. But it was a long step toward changing the eighteenth-century way of life and taking control of local affairs out of the hands of the local gentry.

The Factory Act of 1833, on the other hand, seemed to work the other way. It was an attempt—typical of the nondoctrinaire kind of program which the Whigs sponsored—to succor the victims of industrialization. It was very limited in its intent—it forbade children under nine to work in factories, and limited the hours when older children might work—and it was rather casually enforced. But it was the precedent for further demands and more effective laws later.

Slavery was abolished in all British territory, including the Caribbean sugar islands, in 1834.

The Church of England was reformed in 1837. Its vast revenues were redistributed by Parliament, and the many abuses which had grown up in their administration were ended.

These and many other reforms, some of them carried out by Tories who returned to power in 1841, were piecemeal, partial, and often unsatisfactory. But they showed that Parliament was supreme, and it was using its supremacy to destroy the vestiges of the eighteenth-century system and to adjust British institutions to a new age with a vastly larger population and an entirely different economy.

The most important single step in this process was taken in 1846, by a Tory Prime Minister, Sir Robert Peel. This was the repeal of the Corn Laws, which had come to be regarded as the symbol and source of the persisting power of the landed aristocracy and gentry, since these laws protected their principal source of income, wheat, from foreign competition. The repeal was prepared, and effected, by the kind of organization which had proved effective in 1832, a national campaign supported by meetings, demonstrations, and propaganda. This time the effort was vastly greater and more sophisticated. It was the work, mainly, of the Anti-Corn Law League, led by Richard Cobden and John Bright. Both were factory owners, evangelical Christians, and humanitarians. Both disliked the aristocracy and sought to improve the lot of both manufacturers and working people by lowering the price of wheat and, therefore, bread. Both were typical liberals who believed on principle in free trade, international peace, low taxes, and letting people alone.

Landowners and other conservatives who cherished the role of the aristocracy in the British constitution fought hard, but unsuccessfully, to save the Corn Laws. In 1845 and 1846 there was a famine in Ireland, greatly aggravated by the high price of grain. In 1846, Sir Robert Peel introduced and carried—mostly with Whig and Radical votes—the repeal of the Corn Laws. The last great bulwark of the British landed aristocracy went down.

THE GOLDEN AGE

In 1846, with its "old regime" undermined, Great Britain seemed on the verge of still greater changes. In 1848 came the great outbreaks on the continent, whose varied manifestations of violence left behind varied problems, experiments and fears. But in 1848 only the slightest tremors of the European earthquake were felt in Britain, and in the years that followed there was a tranquil though rapid growth of riches and serenity. We must now describe the development of the remarkable stability after the storms of the Age of Reform.

Peel had split the Tory party. The old intransigent aristocrats and their followers cast him off for apostasy, and his followers formed a separate faction called Peelites, or "Free Trade Tories." There were now four parties in the House of Commons—Tories, Peelites, Whigs, and Radicals, not to mention the Irish, who usually voted as a unit and frequently held the balance of power. The political history of the 1850's and 1860's is intricate and obscure. There were many government changes, coalitions, and minority cabinets. But the basic fact was this: those who espoused the liberal ideal—most Peelites, all Radicals, some Whigs —gradually merged into a new party, called Liberal, which took shape formally after 1860. This party not only transformed Britain in its own liberal image; it also forced the Tories to transform themselves in much the same image, with minor and romantic variations. And it presided over a Golden Age of growth and power. The old, confining forms of the eighteenth century were now gone, and the kingdom moved forward to its proudest epoch.

The kind of change which took place between 1846 and 1870 was varied and was carried out with many confusions and partial retreats. But while the narrative of the enactment of these later reforms is confusing, the total picture is clear enough. Deliberately taken out of chronological order, and arranged in logical order, a partial list of the most significant reforms appears as follows:

1. The Second Reform Bill was passed in 1867. It extended the vote to almost every taxpaying resident of the towns. It was largely the work of the imaginative new Conservative, Benjamin Disraeli, who was leading the party away from the stigma of the Corn Laws and the stamp of the landed classes, just as Grey a generation earlier had led the Whigs away from the stereotype of eighteenth-century magnates.

The effect of the Second Reform Bill was much larger and more immediate than that of the first. The working class vote was now a reality, and increasingly after 1867 the political parties competed for it by promising favors to the humbler classes. Its effect was, moreover, greatly intensified by the institution of the secret ballot (by a Liberal government) in 1872, which helped to eliminate the influence and pressures of the wealthy on the impoverished voter. With the secret ballot, bribery was discouraged because no one could tell whether the bought voter had stayed bought.

2. The reform of the administration and the creation of a professional civil, military, and naval service with entrance by examination and promotion by merit, moved slowly. The army, navy, and civil service were preeminently the stronghold of the aristocracy, and tradition and vested interests deterred its ejection long after municipal government and Parliament itself had become "careers open to talent." The armed forces, particularly, were resistant to change. The administration of Great Britain was gradually opened to wider and wider circles. But the form of the examination, and the atmosphere within the services, prevented their democratization: success in the civil service or the armed forces

was still largely reserved for graduates of the older universities and men of background and connections.

3. In 1871, the laws limiting degrees from Oxford and Cambridge to Anglicans were repealed. This had some social importance, for while nearly all genteel folk were Anglicans, many middle- and working-class people were not. More important, new institutions of higher learning were being founded—in London in the 1820's, in Durham in 1833, and elsewhere thereafter. The "provincial" universities lacked the prestige of Oxford and Cambridge, but their graduates were beginning to appear in responsible government positions.

4. The Ten Hours Act of 1847 was an act of Parliament which in effect limited to ten hours the length of time per day that an industrial worker might work at his machine. It was one—the most important—of a series of laws which sought to ameliorate working conditions without affecting the profits of the employer too seriously. Other, comparable acts controlled conditions in the mines (which were particularly barbaric) and child labor, and provided for public health authorities to attempt to improve sanitary conditions in the industrial slums. These acts all represented a tremendous effort by assorted humanitarian movements and working class organizations, and most of them violated some of the precepts of strict "Manchester economics." Taken together, they form a pallid preliminary to what we call "social legislation" in the twentieth century. But they showed that even Parliament, which before 1867 represented exclusively men of wealth, was flexible and responsive in some slight degree to the needs of the working class.

5. In William Gladstone's great Budget of 1860, when he was Chancellor of the Exchequer in Lord Palmerston's Liberal Government, almost all the remaining traces of mercantilism, state economic regulation, and tariffs were abolished, completing the process which had begun in the 1820's. Britain was now a Free Trade country, admitting foreign products without tax duty. It could afford to be—its industrial supremacy was so great that few foreign manufactures could compete in the home market. 1860 marks the beginning of a Free Trade tradition which was not to end until 1931.

VICTORIAN SOCIETY

In almost every aspect of British life the years from 1832 to 1870 were ones of enormous movement and animation. The population was still growing—growing faster than ever, indeed. In 1801 it was (excluding Ireland), 10,500,000; in 1861 it was 23,000,000. The figures on population growth would have been far more dramatic still had they included emigrants: that is, Britons who—mainly by choice—had left their homes to go overseas. This number was vast, although incalculable.

And with the urban population growing the great industrial centers gave a new dimension to the word "city." With the growth of new cities which were no longer merely trading centers but bases of large factories, there came new

St. Pancras Station, London. Engraving. The station, built from 1863 to 1876, exemplifies the new architecture of the age of steel. (*Building News*, March 26, 1869)

problems. The industrial poor lived in unparalleled squalor and ugliness, and the mere concentration of population multiplied problems of public order and morality. Philanthropic, responsible and energetic men and women began to devote themselves to the plight of the urban masses. The industrial workers, and the paupers, had a "good press" in the great social novels of the age, like Dickens' *Oliver Twist* or *David Copperfield,* and Mrs. Gaskell's *Mary Barton.* There were institutes for workingmen's education and training, there were institutes to facilitate emigration, and there were endless charitable foundations to supervise the welfare of the workingmen's eternal souls. And there were, more dramatically, efforts by the working classes to help themselves. Trade unions flourished. In 1844 the first consumers' cooperative was founded.

The working classes were far from contented, to be sure, especially during periods of unemployment or low wages. They imbibed some of the social revolutionary ideas which many continental Europeans and a few Britons were formulating—Marx, Engels, Saint Simon, and the Scottish socialist Robert Owen. In the late 1830's and mid 1840's, which were periods of economic depression, there developed the working class movement called "Chartism," which verged on the revolutionary. The Chartists demanded the enactment of a "Peoples' Charter," which in effect demanded democratic government and popular representation. For some these were ends in themselves; for more, they were merely the means whereby the ordinary man, once having political power, could use it to reform society and economic institutions in his own favor. In 1839 and again in 1848 there were Chartist conventions, accompanied by some rather ominous shows of violence. But Chartism died after 1848, leaving little in the way of revolutionary disorders in Great Britain. The peaceability of the common man has been the most striking feature and most precious asset of the country ever since.

The disappearance of Chartism and revolutionary impulses was probably the consequence of the rapidly improving economic condition and wage rises after about 1850. It was also, one may suppose, due to the fact that Parliament, and many private organizations, were taking up the cause of the workingman in such legislation as the Ten Hours Act. Some have suggested as an explanation of the disappearance of revolutionary agitations among the British "proletariat" their widespread devotion to various forms of evangelical Christianity, which diverted their energies into religious instead of political channels. It is impossible to say with certainty what was the true reason for the absence of a class-conscious revolutionary movement in Britain in the later nineteenth century, but to the above explanations one must add the fact that the reforms so far achieved showed British working people what it was possible to accomplish by peaceful and constitutional means. Flexibility is a very great aid in allaying demands for violent change.

With its population, and the wealth of its manufactories, were growing Britain's foreign trade and overseas empire. After the losses of the American Revolution, new territories were being acquired, organized and settled. The period before 1870, the period of liberal triumph, was, however, a period when the empire provoked little enthusiasm. Liberals regarded colonial empires as expensive, troublesome, and, in some manner, immoral. But despite this relative lack of interest in the empire, and despite the deliberate loosening of the mother country's control over Canada, nobody in Great Britain of any consequence proposed abandoning any of the colonial territories, and their expansion continued apace.

More striking than the growth of the empire was the growth of British trade. British imports in the opening years of the century averaged £ 28 million a year. By mid-century the yearly average (1846–50) had risen to £ 72 million. Exports for the same dates rose from £ 33 million to £ 60 million. It was this extraordinary development, made possible by British industry, which in turn made possible the rising standard of living and of wealth in Britain. There was ample foreign money to pay for imported luxuries as well as for necessities. And what was left over was invested—often at high interest rates—in foreign enterprises. It was British capital which, for example, built the railway system of the United States and much of its industry. It was British capital which developed the Argentine beef and cattle industry, and poured into Mexican mines. The British had, between 1815 and 1875, invested overseas an estimated £ 500 million; and it was supplemented by a vast expansion of the British merchant marine.

There was no country in the world which could approach this measure of wealth and industry, this foreign investment, this commerce, and this empire. And the British were conscious and proud of their achievement. The Exhibition of 1851, the first world's fair, which marked the beginning of the Golden Age, showed the country's satisfaction—indeed, its smug satisfaction—in its unparalleled technology and riches. In certain lines of artistic endeavor, mainly the novel, it could take almost equal pride in its primacy. The long story which had begun with the arrival of Caesar's legions on the British shore had at last reached its climax. Liberal Britain, proud, free, and prosperous, seemed to reign over the nineteenth century.

28

FOUR FRENCH
REGIMES

In 1815 the twenty-five years of revolution and war, of bloodshed and exhilaration, of conquest and defeat, were at last over for the French. They had performed great feats of energy, imagination, and prowess. They had remade their own nation; they had, indeed, remade Europe.

One might expect the story of post-Napoleonic France to be an anticlimax. Instead, one enters a strange era where the most diverse people and views were struggling to live side by side. Nothing, it seemed, was lost or forgotten; every past cause had its partisans. True, there was a kind of hush in the early years when the monarchy and the nobles came back, and the art of saying nothing about certain topics became almost a political philosophy. By the 1830's and 1840's, however, there had grown up such a richness of views about political and social questions that the notions of the Enlightenment seemed innocent and old-fashioned. And the proliferation of ideas in France has never abated. As if the Great Revolution and Napoleon had not provided enough change, there came other revolutions, including the "industrial." Although England was first to become the workshop of the world, France led in social and political ferment and became the laboratory of revolutions.

This made French history colorful, and helped make French culture rich and varied, but it had its tragic side. The word "instability," once applied to seventeenth-century England, became attached to France—irrevocably, it seemed. But here an immediate caution is necessary. Beneath the comings and goings of rulers French society was amazingly stable, almost too stable in some respects. The Great Revolution had caused a vast simplification, as if the tangled forest of the old regime had been pruned and ordered like a French garden. Napoleon's strong hand had set in motion the ordered round of maintenance, by ministries and local officials and courts. If the throne room where policies were made was periodically raided, refurnished and repeopled, the administrative kitchens and workrooms remained unaltered. In society itself the relationships of groups and classes seemed, after 1815, to have found a balance, dynamic and restless but remarkably lasting.

These elements of stability must be remembered as we narrate the changes in nineteenth-century France. Here are the regimes to be described, in the order of their appearance:

I. The Restoration, 1814–1830, ended by the July Revolution of 1830;

II. The July Monarchy, 1830–1848, ended by the February Revolution of 1848;

III. The Second Republic, 1848–1852, ended by the *coup d'état* of Louis Napoleon (Napoleon III, nephew of Napoleon I);

IV. The Second Empire, 1852–1870, brought down by the Franco-Prussian War of 1870.

THE RESTORATION, 1814–1830

There were in fact two Restorations. The first one, in 1814, "restored" the Bourbon dynasty in the person of Louis XVIII, who was Louis XVI's younger brother. Louis XVI's son had died in prison in 1795. Louis XVIII had "reigned" since then, even though he was for those two decades a wandering and rather shabby exile.

Most of the French people were indifferent to the Bourbons by the time of Napoleon's defeat, if they had not forgotten them altogether. Only middle-aged people could still remember the old regime. The first Restoration, in 1814, was the work of Talleyrand and the Imperial officials, including the members of Napoleon's Senate, who wished to make peace with the great powers as painlessly as possible without disturbing things (particularly their own positions) in France. After Napoleon's dramatic "Hundred Days" in the spring of 1815 it was clear that the French people, who had not mourned the departure of Louis XVIII, were not ecstatic over his return "in the baggage train of the Allies." The Allied army of occupation settled down on the Champs Elysées, the hillside which after their departure in 1818 was to become a famous avenue. Louis XVIII, who in his years of exile had survived many humiliations, prepared to live down the Hundred Days.

Louis XVIII was a fat, lazy, intelligent, and sly man, who in his youth had shown sympathy for the liberal ideas of 1789. During his long exile he had behaved correctly, maintaining with imperturbable dignity, first the rights of his nephew, then his own. He was flexible and opportunistic enough to adapt himself to the conditions which he found in France upon his return. In 1814 he refused in theory to recognize anyone's right to place constitutional limitations upon his absolute power. But by freely "granting" a Charter he accepted, for practical purposes, a constitutional regime. By recognizing civil liberties, the Napoleonic code, the Concordat of 1801 with the Catholic Church, the abolition of seigneurial dues, and the shifts in ownership of property, he accepted the Great Revolution. Probably no government could have lasted in France without making these concessions.

The Restoration did not mean the return of the old regime. At the same time Louis XVIII kept up appearances by maintaining that he ruled by divine right. His ministers were responsible only to him, and not to the two houses of the legislature, the Peers (some hereditary, some appointed for life), and the Chamber of Deputies elected by voters with a very high property qualification. The king initiated and sanctioned legislation. Louis XVIII brought back the white flag in place of the revolutionary tricolor, and was called King of France (the pre-1789 title) rather than King of the French, the title forced on Louis XVI in 1791, which was regarded as less suggestive of Divine Right.

Superficially the Restoration with its Charter resembled the English political system following the Restoration of 1660. The parallel was noticed at the time, and applauded by many moderates. It was misleading. The economy and ideas and society of nineteenth-century France were very different from those of seventeenth-century England. The French were not nearly so happy to see Louis XVIII as the English were to see Charles II; the Great Revolution had created a much wider chasm between the old and the new France than had the Puritan Revolution between the old and the new England. In England landed and mercantile wealthy got on well together, and the Lords, of the House of Lords, were few and very rich. The French nobles, although some of them retained or recovered their lands, were not a true aristocracy of wealth and social influence capable of winning respect for a French House of Lords.

To become like the English system Louis XVIII's constitutional settlement would have had to guard zealously its vagueness while evolving through a long period of tranquillity until the hatreds of the Great Revolution were muffled by time. This indeed, is what the French moderate liberals hoped for. But it was not to be.

Under the Restoration there were no political parties in the modern sense of the term, but there were groups of political opinions. The three most important points of view were those of the Ultras (for ultra-royalists), the Constitutionals (or Doctrinaires), and the Independents (or Liberals). The Ultras, led by the Count of Artois, the king's brother, were those most sympathetic to the nobles and to the society of the old regime, and most hostile to the parvenu *bourgeoisie* and to the Great Revolution and the ideas of the Enlightenment. The Constitutionals (Doctrinaires) accepted the constitutional settlement provided by the Bourbon restoration and the Charter, and also the principal reforms of the Great Revolution. The Independents (or Liberals) were also defenders of the Enlightenment and of the revolutionary gains, but they did not think that the Charter was a sufficient guarantee. They disagreed among themselves, however, concerning what to substitute. Many of them wanted a monarchy on the English model and the enthronement of Louis Philippe, Duke of Orléans, the King's cousin, who had a reputation for liberalism. Among the Independents, some were Bonapartists. There were not many avowed Republicans to be found in the period of the Restoration; republicanism was too frightening a reminder of the Reign of Terror. The fires of Jacobinism and democracy still smouldered beneath the surface of the Restoration, but the principal contest was between representatives of the old regime and champions of the revolutionary bourgeoisie.

This contest with its accompanying fears and polemics did not keep France from being well administered, thanks to the bureaucratic legacies of the Revolution and Napoleon. The finances were in good order (a far cry from 1789), the occupation by the Allies was ended (1818), and France again negotiated on an equal basis with the great powers. In 1830 French forces crossed the Mediterranean to take Algeria from the Ottoman empire. It was a first step toward a second colonial empire after the overseas disasters of the eighteenth century and of the revolutionary and Napoleonic era.

At home, however, the Restoration failed to achieve the basic condition of permanence, to reconcile the old aristocracy and the new revolutionary and Napoleonic elite, who were mainly bourgeois. Louis XVIII said that he did not wish to be king of two nations. From 1816 to 1820 Louis tried to work with the more moderate Constitutionals. The Ultras turned to the king's brother, Artois, and the Liberals tended to set their hopes on his cousin, the Duke of Orléans. In 1820 a fanatic murdered the Duke of Berry, Artois' son. In the indignation called forth by the murder, Louis XVIII lost control of the legislature and was forced to appoint ministers who would work with the Ultras. Until his own death in 1824 the tired old king was unable to put France back on the road to fusion and moderation.

Artois became King Charles X in 1824, and reigned until 1830 in true ultraroyalist fashion. The former émigrés were compensated for their revolutionary losses to the tune of about a billion francs, a move not perhaps unjust in itself but infuriating to the middle class holders of government securities, whose interest payments were cut at the same time. A Law against Sacrilege ordered ferocious punishments for insults to the rites of the Church; although not enforced, it infuriated the still anti-clerical bourgeoisie. Increasingly it seemed that Charles X and his advisors meant to bring back the old regime. Especially after 1827, when the king lost control of the Chamber of Deputies, the situation became extremely dangerous. Charles X and his Ultra friends were a small minority out of touch with the true sentiments of the nation. Once again, as in 1789, the gap between law and fact, appearance and reality, was perilously wide, for the great majority in France had never ceased to be loyal to the principles and gains of the Great Revolution.

In 1830 revolution again struck France. It was a year in which political defects were accentuated by economic depression spreading from agriculture into the towns and workshops. As in 1789 the intransigence of the right spurred rebelliousness on the left. Charles X, having lost control of the legislature to the opposition, carefully reviewed what he took to be the lessons of 1789 and made a disastrous decision. Ripping aside the veil of obscurity which had grown up around the Charter, he insisted upon his right to have ministers whom the legislature detested. To his narrow mind, legislative control of the ministers was a crippling blow at the crown itself. Foolishly and courageously, he cast aside his opportunity to place the crown above partisan politics. In the ensuing battle the crown was struck from his head.

In March, 1830, the Chamber of Deputies expressed its concern over the king's stubborn support of his minister Polignac, an absolutist visionary whose presence seemed to indicate an approaching coup against the Charter. Charles X dissolved the Chamber, and when another, even more liberal, was elected, he dissolved that one too. This act was one of four famous ordinances, which also suspended freedom of the press, changed the electoral procedure, and ordered new elections. The ordinances were in some respects a violation of the Charter and were taken by the public as an affirmation of the king's right and determination to violate it at will.

This was a challenge which could not be ignored. Instead, the king's orders were ignored—by the liberal press, by students, by employers who closed their shops and turned their employees into the streets, and finally, by the political leaders of the opposition. Since much of the army was in Algeria, and the bourgeois National Guard had recently been dissolved for impudence (1827), Charles X's forces were unable to restore order in Paris. Too late he withdrew the ordinances, then tried to abdicate in favor of his grandson, the ten-year-old Count of Chambord. It was no use. With Paris out of control, the soldiers unable to subdue the public demonstrations (and some of them showing sympathy for the demonstrators), Charles X found the odds too great, and with his family set off for London. This time he was not to return.

In Paris there were some moments of anxiety at the close of the "three glorious days" (July 27, 28, 29) which had dethroned Charles X. The French had reason to know that a revolution, once started, could run to extremes. The liberals who had opposed Charles X—deputies, journalists like Thiers, bankers like Laffitte, literary men like Dumas, dignitaries like Lafayette—knew that they had to impose a settlement rapidly or run the risk of Jacobinism. Fearing a repetition of the Great Revolution, when the lower classes had turned against him and the other moderates, Lafayette rebuffed the advances of the Republicans and appeared on the balcony of the City Hall with Louis Philippe, Duke of Orléans, whom he wrapped in the tricolor flag of the Great Revolution. Before the republicans could gather their wits, the legislature which Charles X had tried in vain to dissolve had made Orléans into Louis Philippe, "King of the French" (no longer "King of France," for that venerable title recalled the centuries of absolutism), and accepted a few revisions of the Charter. The July Monarchy (1830–1848), headed by the Orléans branch of the Bourbon family, owed its being to a revolution but was the work of no constituent assembly and was sanctioned by no referendum. Its bourgeois founders preferred not to think of what might have happened if the people had been consulted.

THE FIGHT ON THE BARRICADES by Eugène Delacroix (1798–1863). Drawing inspired by the revolution of 1830. (Courtesy of the Fogg Art Museum, Harvard University, Grenville Lindall Winthrop Collection)

THE JULY MONARCHY, 1830–1848

The flavor of the July Monarchy was strong and peculiar. The new king was at pains to appear as liberal as possible. In place of the gilded pomps of his cousins' reigns, he constructed an "up-to-date" and middle class *décor* for the French state. He carried an umbrella in public: no one could see the heir of Louis XIV with an umbrella without realizing how vast a gulf divided this monarchy from the old regime. The umbrella became the symbol of the state, derided by some and applauded by some. The king was a good family man and a good businessman, like any French bourgeois. He had five sons, and enormous wealth. This "beef stew of a home-loving monarchy," Chateaubriand called the regime. The people in power were also bourgeois. There was still a very limited suffrage; the minister Guizot recommended to the opponents of the property qualifications for voting: "Go get rich." French industry grew and was coddled by tariffs, but there was no legislation to protect the working men and women. All kinds of social theories and movements flowered beneath the stagnant, respectable surface of politics.

The constitutional basis of the regime was still the Charter, hastily revised by the Chamber of Deputies in August, 1830. The Chamber had no constituent power, but the deputies took it upon themselves to behave like a constitutional convention. There was still a Chamber of Peers, but it was no longer hereditary—they were now appointed for life from among persons of "capacity."

Louis Philippe was a brave and intelligent man who had once fought in the army of the Great Revolution. Later he too had known years of emigration, and his father had been guillotined by the Jacobins. He had no great faith in the capacity of the people to manage their own affairs. Moreover, like a good merchant, he preferred thrifty peace to costly glory. He was sincere in his desire to be the "Napoleon of peace," but this virtue did not endear him to the many French who had hoped that July, 1830, would be the prelude to a French comeback on the international scene, undoing the humiliations of Waterloo and the Congress of Vienna. In Louis Philippe's peaceableness there was, moreover, a hidden wish to demonstrate to the other royal families of Europe that although he owed his throne to revolution he was no bloodthirsty Jacobin. He and his closest associates did not like to think of the regime as a product of revolution; they preferred to regard 1830 as a mere adjustment in the Bourbon dynasty.

The early years of the July Monarchy were disorderly because of the agitation of republicans, the spread of secret societies, the barbs of the free press, and the violent insurrections of workingmen, especially at Lyons in 1831 and at Paris and Lyons in 1834. There were even attempts on the life of the king. In the government ministers came and went, but the police maintained control of the situation and repressed the revolts with severity. In 1835, the "September Laws" put a rein on the press and speeded the trials of insurgents.

Louis Philippe did not at once dominate the situation. He was faced in the Chamber of Deputies with two principal points of view, usually called the

Party of Resistance and the Party of Movement. The Party of Resistance, led by the historian François Guizot (1787–1874), took the view that nothing more should be changed now that the repairs of 1830 had been made. The Party of Movement, led by Adolphe Thiers (1797–1877), an ambitious young journalist and historian, wanted the regime to evolve toward more clearly defined parliamentary government—nothing very radical, to be sure, but with a somewhat broader suffrage and more influence of the legislature on the ministers. It also favored a more dynamic foreign policy aimed at reasserting France's independence of the 1815 settlement and helping other peoples to do likewise.

Louis Philippe preferred Resistance to Movement, and by 1840 had learned to keep ministers of the former group in power. Although the revised Charter did not guarantee the responsibility of ministers to the legislature, Louis Philippe and Guizot did not attempt to undo the tradition of ministerial responsibility which had been nurtured by the July Revolution and by the early years of the July Monarchy. Guizot maintained his majority in the Chamber through patronage and manipulated elections, and in particular through a system of "functionary deputies;" that is, legislators who were also civil servants and who therefore tended to be subservient to the executive. Behind Guizot was the king, who exercised a real personal authority. In Guizot's words: "the throne is not an empty chair." From 1840 to the February Revolution of 1848 the Party of Movement and other critics were unable to crack this system, although complaints about functionary deputies and demands for extension of the suffrage multiplied.

Other critics there were, for the game of constitutional, parliamentary government was a very restricted one. The *pays legal*—the "legal country," which had the vote—was only a small part of the French nation. On the right, the Legitimist supporters of Charles X (d. 1836) and of his grandson, the Count of Chambord, were, as we now know, partisans of a cause without a future, but they were bitter and articulate. Largely nobles and upper clergy, they represented "high society" but had little real social power in this France of peasants and bourgeois and (now, at last) proletarian workers in the cities.

To the left, on quite another social level, were the republicans, heirs of the Jacobins, who were largely though not exclusively lower middle class and working people who had no voice in the regime of July and did not consider it theirs. This was an era when many among the French lower classes looked hopefully to *political* democracy for the solution of their *social* problems. There were numerous secret or half-secret republican organizations such as the Friends of the People, or the Society of the Rights of Man and of the Citizen. There were socialists in France, but they were still mainly intellectuals. In general it is accurate to say that as yet socialism and the labor movement had not united. Labor unions were illegal (as they had been since 1791), although societies of journeymen, some of them very ancient, persisted, and workers sometimes agitated and rebelled in spite of the law.

Bonapartism, too, was a political force working quite outside the parliamentary regime of the July Monarchy. Its originator, Napoleon I, had died in 1821 on the island of Saint Helena after successfully setting afoot his greatest triumph, the legend that he was a democratic liberator of peoples in France and

Europe. Napoleon's son had died in Austrian custody in 1832, but his nephew, the son of Louis Bonaparte, was at work on one of the most amazing careers in the nineteenth century. This young man, the future Emperor Napoleon III, was not taken very seriously by Louis Philippe and his advisors. He failed in two comic-opera attempts to overthrow the French government, coups at Strasbourg (1836) and Boulogne (1840); after this last escapade, he was interned in the fortress of Ham, about sixty miles north of Paris, from which he escaped in 1846. From time to time he brought out pamphlets which showed him to be a social critic holding fashionable ideas: *Napoleonic Ideas* (1839); *The Extinction of Pauperism* (1844).

The legend concerning his uncle was not for the moment strong enough to bring this young man to power; indeed Louis Philippe did not hesitate to use the legend himself to glamorize his extremely stuffy regime. The statue of Napoleon was replaced at the top of the Vendôme column; his body was brought to the Invalides with mock ceremony in 1840. But this orgy of Bonapartism was a mistake. It kept the name of Napoleon in French minds. And so long as there were peasants and old soldiers to keep alive stories of the old days, and dissatisfied republicans to contrast former glories with the present rule of the rich, Bonapartism represented a danger.

The deeper danger to the July Monarchy came from what would today be called "immobilism." Louis Philippe and Guizot assumed that their regime was stable because it was founded on the most substantial propertied interests in the country. They thought that they were avoiding the mistakes of Louis XVI and of Charles X, who favored the old aristocracy and allowed people of great economic power to be excluded from political power. This point of view was correct as far as it went, but French society kept on changing, while the political regime did not. The population was growing slowly but steadily—by 1840 it was about thirty-three million. The economy was still dominated by agriculture, whose methods were not changing much, but there were now canals and a few railroads and steamboats. The towns were growing; Paris and Lyons nearly doubled between 1800 and 1850. In the same period the number of steam engines used in industry grew from a few dozen to about five thousand. The Industrial Revolution was setting in, not dramatically, but with definite effects on life and thought. With the growing towns the old trades, the little shops, the artisans, increased along with the new factories, so that the old kind of urban society was mixed with the new. But there was more concentration of workers now, in shops and poor districts; there was more talk among similar men and women, more class consciousness and social antagonism. In the July Monarchy money was "tight"—that is, interest rates were high and capital scarce. Family connections meant a lot among the new industrialists, for a modern banking system was still in its infancy. Competition was stiff, in spite of the regime's protective tariffs. Wages were kept low. This was the classic early industrial period with all its evils: child and woman laborers, long hours, miserable housing, the worker's sanctuary in the wine shop, and the de-Christianization and "proletarization" of a part of the people. There were not enough churches to go around, and in the crowded industrial slums the worker felt orphaned; he had no sense of a place in society which belonged to him. The workers were a small part of the country still, for agricultural France moved slowly into the industrial age. But what was true in the eighteenth century was still true, and more dangerous now: hard times on the farms meant a recession in industry as purchases declined, and this in turn meant unrest in the towns.

Louis Philippe and his government were overthrown in February, 1848. No doubt they could have survived if a few timely adjustments had been made. The peasantry and well-to-do middle class were not revolutionary, and were not inclined to jeopardize their gains of 1789–1815. The February Revolution of 1848 was sudden and apparently unnecessary. It looked like an accident, but it was more a suprise than an accident. Having retained a very narrow base of wholehearted support in a large and complex country, Louis Philippe and Guizot remained inflexible a little too long. The king, by identifying himself too firmly with the Party of Resistance, went down with that party.

The February Revolution of 1848 was unplanned, unplotted, unforeseen in its consequences. In much of Europe there had been poor harvests in 1845, 1846, and 1847—the same which rotted the potatoes in Ireland and contributed to repeal of the Corn Laws in Britain. In France (where potatoes had also become part of the diet) the high prices of food cut down purchases of other things, hurt the textile industry, tightened credit, slowed railway construction, affected iron and steel and coal. Unemployed job-seekers crowded into Paris. The business slump began to lift in late 1847 and early 1848, but it left in its wake idle men and depleted savings and a backlog of pawned possessions. Psychologically the short-term irritations on top of accumulated dissatisfactions brought together all kinds of opposition to the regime. As in 1789 persons in power were blamed for uncomprehended economic and social trends. The natural defenders of the monarchy—especially the bourgeois National Guard—were divided in their sympathies.

There had been since 1847 a campaign of banquets—respectable and even expensive meetings at which the moderate critics, the Party of Movement, aired their grievances. Suggested by similar meetings of the Chartists in Britain, these affairs were in no sense intended to be revolutionary, and when Guizot objected in February, 1848, the sponsors prepared to disband with only verbal protests. But Guizot's ban proved to be the match which ignited an explosive mixture. Public attention was attracted, and a parade led to rioting which was put down by the police and army. Next day the government called out the army and National Guard to preserve order and prevent barricades, but some of the National Guard took it upon themselves to protect the public and its barricades from the troops. Louis Philippe was by now ready to dismiss Guizot, but when nervous troops guarding Guizot's house fired on the crowd, killing some twenty people (February 23), it was too late. As in 1830, the Monarchy lost control of the city of Paris. Louis Philippe, not wanting a civil war on his conscience, abdicated in favor of his grandson and left for England, like Charles X eighteen years earlier.

THE SECOND REPUBLIC, 1848–1852

Once more the continuity of French political development was broken and the door opened to the unknown. This time the moderate middle class did not succeed in shutting it as quickly as in 1830. If 1848 began like 1830, it ended quite differently, with a Bonaparte in control, after the middle and lower classes had frightened and alienated each other. In 1830, the revolution had been captured and controlled. Now it was to run its course.

As Louis Philippe departed, his little grandson, the Count of Paris, was presented by his mother to the Chamber of Deputies, but the Paris crowds had also entered the hall. Under their influence, a republic was proclaimed. Led by the poet Alphonse de Lamartine (1790–1869), a provisional government of moderate republicans was formed. Meanwhile, at the City Hall, center of revolutionary Paris, popular pressure supported the utopian socialist Louis Blanc and a program of radical social reforms. The result was a compromise provisional government in which Blanc had a place. Far-reaching guarantees were made: the right to work; national workshops for the numerous unemployed who had flocked to the city; and a commission to inquire into the conditions of labor. These measures were strong medicine to the mid-nineteenth century *bourgeoisie*. They were an illustration of how much more radical Paris had become than peasant and middle class France. This split was soon dramatized by the election (in April, 1848) of a constitutent assembly, chosen by universal manhood suffrage. This assembly was dominated by moderate republicans, with strong minorities of radicals, Legitimists, and Orleanists. The Paris radicals won no support outside the city.

In June, 1848, the National Assembly, determined to scotch what they took to be a subversive threat from the national workshops (which had grown huge and expensive), ordered them dissolved. Tragedy resulted. In the "bloody June days" (23rd–26th), the workers resisted on the barricades in the bitterest kind of fighting: civil and class war. At a cost of several thousand deaths, General Cavaignac, the Minister of War, with regular troops and the bourgeois National Guard, and reinforcements from the provinces, swept the city. This time France defeated Paris, but the gap between the middle class and peasants, on the one hand, and the workers, on the other, became a chasm. Mass deportations and a crackdown on the press and clubs followed. The moderates then made a republican constitution, but their golden mean was tarnished.

The constitution makers worked until November 4, 1848. It cannot be said that they displayed statesmanship of a high order, but they were indeed faced with great difficulties. After the June days, how could the defeated be won over to a republic which had crushed them, and how could the partisans of stability be given satisfactory guarantees? The constitution makers felt committed to granting the vote to all adult men, but apart from that they had many choices to make; the French past was by now rich with political experiments, and there were other democratic models, like the American, to draw upon. What they decided upon was a mixture—a rather bold mixture designed to insure governmental strength while appeasing those who aspired to social reform.

Their Declaration of Rights proclaimed liberty, equality, and fraternity, invoked God, and promised rights of employment, relief for the needy, and education. The legislative power was vested in a unicameral chamber, chosen directly by manhood suffrage. This body was daringly balanced by a president, also directly elected by manhood suffrage, for a term of four years. He could choose his own ministers—from the legislature, if he wished—but he was not eligible for reelection until he had been out of office for four years. Would the popularly elected legislature and the popularly elected president contest each other's authority? It was expected that they would, and that their competition would be a healthy one.

These hopes were to be disappointed, chiefly because the wounds in French society were so deep, the aspirations so complex, the republicanism so shallow. Almost at once the democratic suffrage boomeranged. In December, 1848, the pretender to the imperial throne, Louis Napoleon Bonaparte, was elected President of the Republic. In May, 1849, the new legislature was elected, and proved to have a royalist majority. Thus a *Bonapartist* president was required to get along with a *royalist* legislature if the Second *Republic* was to be a success. It was too much to expect, and indeed, the French public did not count on this miracle but watched with indifference or apprehension the inevitable contest.

Louis Napoleon was underestimated by his opponents. His short stature, insignificant appearance, and vague expressionless countenance seemed to offset the powerful Napoleonic legend to which he was heir. He was, however, a supremely capable politician, an adventurer to be sure, but a man of considerable vision. He had what the Bourbons lacked, imagination, which revealed to him what would appeal to the broad masses of the French people. And he could be all things to all men, a conciliator of conflicting points of view. One of his first acts as president was one of his most typical: the sending of French troops to overturn the Roman republic of Mazzini and restore the Pope. It was a move desired by the moderates in France, who more than ever felt the need of the Church as a guarantor of order; yet at the same time Louis Napoleon tried to impress the glory-hungry radicals with the reassertion of France's decisive force in European affairs and with the usefulness of the move in keeping reactionary Austria out of Italy. In domestic affairs Louis Napoleon seemed, to the poor, an alternative to the rule of the rich, and, to the rich, an alternative to socialism.

Louis Napoleon wished and intended to become an emperor, but he could not at once overturn the republican regime. He proceeded cautiously, first making it clear that he intended to control the ministry and not allow a cabinet responsible to the legislature to lead the way toward parliamentary government. His whole tendency was in another direction, as he made clear in announcing that his "name was a program." It was, of course, the Bonapartist program, which did not feature parliamentary institutions but instead presented a leader as the democratic people's agent who knew their will and would carry it out. Between 1848 and 1851 Louis Napoleon, in public appearances and carefully prepared outbursts of frankness, developed the Bonapartist themes of "Caesarist democracy" and national glory, while adding to them two elements appropriate to the mid-nineteenth century. First, he gave the impression that glory could be achieved without war. Second, without sacrificing his reassuring role as the policeman who could maintain order, he succeeded in suggesting his enthusiasm for material progress and social justice for the poor.

The Assembly, on the other hand, was revealing itself as reactionary. By the Falloux Law of March, 1850, the Church was allowed to reenter the field of secondary education, whence the anti-clerical July Monarchy had ousted it. By the electoral law of May, 1850, about three million workmen were deprived of the vote by a three-years' residence requirement. In this latter case particularly the president played a double game, for he quietly encouraged the Assembly in a move which he intended to use against them later.

Louis Napoleon's *coup d'état* against the legislature came in December, 1851, after he had made sure of his control of the key army officers. A month earlier the assembly had walked into his trap by refusing his request that they repeal the undemocratic electoral law of 1850. In the early morning of December 2, the anniversary of the coronation of Napoleon I and of the Battle of Austerlitz, regular troops filled Paris, the drums of the National Guard were found broken, the leading legislators were arrested, and people on their way to work found posters on the walls announcing that the president had dissolved the assembly, was restoring the democratic vote, and would ask the people's permission to draw up a new constitution. There was little resistance, but what there was proved that the new regime was prepared to crush dissent without mercy. In the plebiscite which followed, Louis Napoleon's dictatorship was overwhelmingly endorsed. The Second Republic was dead.

In January, 1852, the new constitution was ready. Louis Napoleon became president for a ten-year term; but he served less than a year. In November, 1852, there was another plebiscite. The French people were invited to approve a restoration of the empire, and President Bonaparte became, at last, Emperor Napoleon III.

THE SECOND EMPIRE, 1852–1870

France's Second Empire was not at all like the first, despite a sedulous imitation of Napoleonic forms and ceremony. This was an altogether different era, and the mood in France and Europe had changed. It was a practical era, exhilarating and expansive. There were bigger cities than ever before, and there was more international trade, with more railroads and steamships. It was France's turn to take giant strides. The Second Empire presided over the onward rush of the nineteenth-century economic growth. By comparison, the empire of Napoleon I seems to belong to an antique and classic age.

Louis Napoleon was very much alive to this movement around him, and his interests reflected it. Progress fascinated him, along with the stirrings of nationalities and the complexities of the social question. He was a promoter, trying to appease and harmonize many appetites with a somewhat vague prospectus for France and Europe. He seemed to embody and preside over the gas-lit, materialistic Europe where Charles Darwin was setting down the notion of biological evolution, while Karl Marx was attempting to chart the direction of economic and social growth.

The imperial court reflected the taste of the age and the success story of the emperor; it was gaudy, vulgar, extremely parvenu. The personalities were "new men," some of them a little unsavory. Empress Eugénie was a handsome young Spanish countess, strongly Catholic in faith and authoritarian in political outlook. The influential Duke of Morny, Louis Napoleon's half-brother, was the illegitimate son of an illegitimate son of Talleyrand, and was a brilliant adventurer, financial speculator, and connoisseur of the arts. Walewski, illegitimate son of Countess Walewska and Napoleon I, was a link with the past glories of the Grand Duchy of Warsaw, and was heaped with dignities. Baron Georges Haussmann, Prefect of the Seine, was a tough and high-handed businessman who rebuilt Paris. The ancient medieval streets were systematically demolished, and replaced by the splendid monotony of great boulevards—which the army could command with cannon in case of riots.

In many ways France took on its contemporary appearance during the Second Empire. It was not simply a question of bigger towns, and of railroad and factory building. Until the middle of the century the French economy had been dominated by agriculture, so that poor crops meant industrial depression, but thereafter the machines seemed to maintain their rhythm and seek outlets for their products—many of them abroad. The French countryside was more of a stabilizing influence on society than it had been in the eighteenth century, or early nineteenth. One reason why the machines could keep running even when the farmers bought less was that banking was coming of age, with its loans to businessmen. This was an era, too, when the sale of stock as a means of amassing capital became both legal and popular. It is no wonder that factories employing workers by the tens and hundreds increased in number, and that the old putting-out system fell off, although the number of small enterprises in France remained large. Now the cities, and above all, Paris, to which all of the great railroad lines ran, drained off the aspiring young from the countryside in a manner which had been impossible before the advent of industry.

Paris, by 1870, had almost two million of France's thirty-six million people. The metropolis now had around its rim radical working class districts, and in its center new banks and offices and merchandising palaces, the world's first department stores—Bon Marché, Printemps, Belle Jardinière, and Samaritaine. The beauty and culture of the capital had long been celebrated. Now it dominated so completely the intellectual and material life of the country that it threatened to drain away from the provinces the best minds and most active energies.

Napoleon III was anything but a narrow-minded bourgeois of the July Monarchy type. The list of his initiatives is impressive. The remaking of Paris was as close to his heart as to Haussmann's, and consisted not just of boulevards and the flamboyant Opera, but of modernization of the sewer system and water supply, completion of the Louvre and Tuileries palaces, and construction of a great general hospital and of a central market place. In his time the railroads were consolidated into six regional systems, with financial guarantees by the state and responsibilities to the public. Not only was the limited liability corporation legalized. Great credit institutions were founded—Crédit Foncier for building and loan activities, Crédit Mobilier for financing ports, railroads, and public utilities, and others, most of which lasted into the twentieth century. Louis Napoleon believed in planning and government spending. He insisted, rather stubbornly, on the Cobden treaty (1860) with Britain, by which the two countries lowered tariffs and inaugurated a brief period of almost free trade in Europe. Many were the French businessmen who did not forgive him for throwing open the doors to the cold air of competition. He paid court to the workers by permitting them, from 1864, to strike. He subsidized cooperatives.

By his admirers Louis Napoleon has been given much of the credit for France's growth and prosperity under the Second Empire. There is no doubt that he was sympathetic to many new ideas and did more than merely profit from the upturn of the business cycle in the 1850's. It is equally true that in this period France and all Western Europe were sharing the benefits of nineteenth-century progress and were more closely intertwined with the world economy. Despite the continuing hardships of wage earners, diet and health were improving in France, and the mortality rate for children was falling. On the other hand this period of material improvement saw a decline in the French birthrate.

Louis Napoleon was a true Bonapartist during the period of the "despotic Empire," from 1852 to 1860: an autocrat who ruled in the name of the sovereign people, supposedly as their best representative. He named his own ministers, responsible to him alone, his Council of State for preparing legislation, and his Senate (for life) which interpreted the laws. He had in effect the whole executive power. The legislature was, to be sure, elected by manhood suffrage, but official pressure for favored candidates and against their opponents was so strong that the regime had at first no worries in this quarter. Moreover, the legislature could do nothing except vote on laws presented to it from on high. The Legitimist and Orleanist opposition could only watch and wait as the emperor monopolized the role of defender of social order. The republicans were uncowed but for the moment impotent.

Although the regime was a dictatorship with democratic trimmings, it must be distinguished from the totalitarian dictatorships of the twentieth century. Louis Napoleon never dreamed of trying to control the beliefs and supervise the daily lives of his subjects. Indeed, compared with even the democratic states of today the Second Empire had very little government. Louis Napoleon was, nevertheless, a dictator who had profited from social antagonisms and was trying by a combination of force and appeasement to reconcile conflicting interests. In time he became prey to the very financial and industrial complexities which gave zest to the era.

This is not the place to mention Napoleon III's diplomacy except as it played a part in domestic history. From his days as President of the Second Republic, he inherited a situation in which French troops guarded the Pope's political authority in Rome, a situation satisfactory to certain Catholic and conservative circles but displeasing to republicans and to many liberals. The Crimean War (1854–56) in which France and England, joined by the Italian state of Sardinia, made war on Russia in defense of Turkey was, on the face of it, a resounding triumph. The peace conference at Paris in 1856 symbolized France's recovery from Waterloo and the Congress of Vienna. The birth of the Prince Imperial in the same year seemed to leave nothing to be desired. The empire was at its apogee. Thereafter, failures in foreign affairs shadowed its glitter.

In 1858 the Italian conspirator Orsini failed in an attempt to assassinate Napoleon III, and from his prison appealed to the Emperor to free Italy. Louis Napoleon, the insurgent of former times, had not forgotten Italy, and indeed had a feeling of inevitability about national unifications which prompted him to be on their side. Later in 1858 he met secretly with Cavour, the Premier of Piedmont, and agreed to help in a war against Austria. The details of what happened next are told in the chapter on Italian unification. Louis Napoleon campaigned in Lombardy, where French and Sardinian arms won the Battles of Magenta and Solferino in June, 1859. But the French emperor was not happy with this bloodshed—he endured other people's sufferings less well than the first Napoleon—and the Austrians were far from beaten. Moreover there was danger that Prussia might attack France if offered sufficient incentives by Austria, and in Italy popular risings were threatening the authority of the Pope, as in 1848. Louis Napoleon made a separate peace with Austria at Villafranca in July, 1859, but the fire he had helped to ignite blazed on. By 1861 a Kingdom of Italy had been formed, and France had acquiesced in the joining of most of the peninsula together to form it, but French soldiers were still guarding a truncated Papal State. Napoleon III had received Nice and Savoy as a price for his aid to Piedmont, but he had gained the enmity of the Italians, the Austrians, the French Catholics (who were concerned about the Pope), and the French liberals and radicals (whose hopes for Italy had not been entirely fulfilled).

In the late summer of 1859 Louis Napoleon returned officially triumphant from his Italian campaign and granted an amnesty to his political opponents. But the nineteenth-century currents were running faster now, and he was to have trouble navigating through the next decade. As if foreseeing this trouble, he suddenly in 1860 and 1861 decreed concessions which liberalized the Empire. The legislature was now permitted freer discussion, and government officials were to defend projects of law in their presence. The debates of the Legislative Assembly and Senate were to be made public. Thus began what is sometimes called the "Liberal Empire," which was to last until 1869. The emperor continued to try to manage the elections, but with decreasing success. He vacillated over the possibilities: further concessions, or a return to autocracy? The concessions won. In 1867 the right of the Legislative Assembly to criticize the government was permitted, and the Senate was treated less like a judicial body and more like an upper house—a House of Lords—than it had yet been. Still to no avail: the elections of 1869 increased the opposition, to a powerful minority. Outside of the legislature the republicans were growing stronger, especially in the cities. Inside, a "Liberal Union" of various kinds of opposition waxed and grew bold. A "Third Party" of liberals watched with interest the emperor's drift toward a parliamentary regime and were prepared to work with him if he would cover the last lap. His immediate entourage was divided. Some, including the empress, deplored the liberalism as weakness, and wished for a return to pure Bonapartism, to the man on horseback. Empress Eugénie, who idolized Marie Antoinette, began to treat her husband like Louis XVI.

The reason for this political vacillation was that by the decade of the 'sixties opposition groups were accumulating in a formidable way: the businessmen who disliked the low tariffs; the Catholics who would not forgive him for Italy; the Legitimists, Orleanists, and republicans (the latter even began to infiltrate the legislature); labor, which preferred the First International to Louis Napoleon's welfare state.

But that was not all. Fortune ceased to smile on his foreign ventures. Taking advantage of the American Civil War and the failure of the revolutionary Juarez government in Mexico to pay its debts, the emperor tried to found another empire in the New World. His troops reached Mexico City (1863), but his protégé, Archduke Maximilian, brother of Francis Joseph of Austria, was executed by the Mexicans (1867) after the United States got its hands free and Napoleon had to withdraw his troops. Other foreign ventures—in Africa and Asia—were more successful, but on the European scene he was alone now. Britain distrusted him, and he could do nothing to help France's traditional friends, the Poles, when they revolted against Russia in 1863. Then between 1864 and 1867 a new menace rose in the East: Bismarck, who defeated the Danes and then the Austrians and formed a North German Confederation (1867). France's policy had long been to keep Germany divided, but Napoleon III, calculating the trends, thought he could play the arbiter, patronize national sentiments in Germany as he had in Italy, and collect his commission in the Rhineland, Luxemburg, or Belgium. He underestimated Prussia's power and Austria's weakness, and overestimated Bismarck's willingness to pay for his neutrality. France felt frustrated when no compensation was forthcoming. Louis Napoleon's reign was now associated with humiliation. But he might still have held his throne if his last maneuvers had not been undone by war.

In retrospect there is little wonder that the emperor, in his final years, tried to rise above the struggle and, by relinquishing authority, to cease being the target when things went wrong. He was, through the 1860's, prematurely aged and increasingly plagued by illness. Clearheaded, but weakened in will, he lost personal ambition and aimed at the year 1874, when his son could be declared of age. It was not an impossible objective, and in 1869 and 1870 he came close to attaining it, for in those years the Empire reached its third or "parliamentary" stage. The Senate and Legislative Assembly became a two-house legislature, rather like the English, and the ministers became a cabinet, responsible, by implication, to this legislature. Émile Ollivier, leader of the "Third Party," was made Prime Minister. Napoleon III was clearly prepared to reign, rather than rule. But, ambiguous to the last, he had the whole affair approved by a national plebiscite. In this still-Bonapartist poll, the people voted "yes" by 7,360,000 to 1,570,000: an apparent endorsement of the regime, though he lost in all the big towns, and hostile observers noted (1) that the vote meant merely that his concessions were accepted, and (2) that persistent use of the plebiscite was a Bonapartist sword hanging over the parliamentary system.

But there was to be no time for such contradictions to work themselves out. The plebiscite took place in May, 1870. In June Prince Leopold of Hohenzollern-Sigmaringen consented to his own candidature for the vacant Spanish throne. He was a distant relative of King William I of Prussia. In July the French foreign minister, Gramont, demanded that the Prussian government not permit this candidacy, which threatened France with Hohenzollern encirclement. King William was not bellicose, and the candidacy was withdrawn. Gramont and the French government now demanded of King William guarantees that the candidacy would never be renewed. William, who was vacationing at a place called Ems, told the French ambassador, Benedetti, that he could not discuss such a capitulation. In Berlin Bismarck, the German chancellor, reduced the king's telegram to him from Ems just enough to make it appear that King William had been insulted and had broken off relations.

In other times this whole episode might have amounted to little. The Prussian king, the ailing French emperor, most of the German people, and most of rural France did not want a war. On the other hand, there had been strained diplomatic relations since 1867, and France had been trying, without much success, to create an alliance with Austria and Italy. There was a feeling that war was inevitable, and some German nationalist groups were noisily demanding it. Some people in France, eager to see upstart Prussia put in its place, also wanted to fight. Some people, including the empress, thought a victory would strengthen the dynasty. France had suffered a diplomatic defeat in failing to get the King of Prussia to agree that the candidacy should never be renewed. Opinion in Paris was outraged and bellicose. France declared war in July, 1870.

This outcome resulted from the nationalistic intoxication and lack of realism of most of the French politicians and press, and of the most vocal elements in the public. All kinds of people, Legitimists, Orleanists, Republicans, and Bonapartists thought that it would be dishonorable—that it would amount to appeasement—if Bismarck's string of triumphs were not halted. They did not doubt that France was capable, by military means if necessary, of accomplishing this task. The emperor perhaps wondered, but he bore the name Napoleon and was thinking of his son's inheritance, and besides, he was too sick to dominate the situation. The French army had some progressive reforms under way, but was not nearly as well prepared as the Prussian.

The war was a disaster. An entire French army, Marshal Bazaine's, allowed itself to be shut up by the Germans in Metz. Louis Napoleon, in personal command of his troops, should have fallen back in defense of Paris, but the empress wired that if he retreated all would be up with the dynasty. He made a stand at Sedan. The Prussians won. The French emperor surrendered (September 2, 1870) and was taken prisoner.

The news from Sedan reached Paris on September 4. The empress heard it in the Tuileries Palace, and followed Charles X and Louis Philippe to London and exile. At the Hôtel de Ville a republic was proclaimed. It was France's third.

29

THE AUSTRIAN
LABYRINTH

THE NINETEENTH CENTURY was the century of rising nationalism in Europe. In the two chapters following this one will be described the consolidation of an Italy and a Germany, each of them a national state with a strong government capable of expressing the "national will" of a people. The old cosmopolitan Europe was rapidly disappearing. Europe, at least Northern and Western Europe, was being organized on a new basis, of highly developed, highly separate national states.

The principal victim of Italian and German unity was the empire of the Habsburgs. The Austrian state was, in the nineteenth century, an anomaly. It had succeeded in creating for itself an imposing structure, centrally controlled and efficiently administered, but this structure, unlike the other great states of Europe, did not coincide with any national group. Austrian territory contained some twenty recognizable nationalities, and Austrian influence in 1815 extended south over what was to become Italy and north through what was to become Germany. When Italy and Germany became states, Austria suffered. And when the peoples of the Ottoman empire which lay to the south and southeast of Austria became aspirants to national freedom, in the late nineteenth and twentieth centuries, Austria tottered and expired. There was no room, it seemed, for an international empire in the kind of Europe which was being built.

The fact that the empire survived at all was a tribute to the excellence of its administration and to the attachment of most of its subjects to the venerable house which ruled it. Despite all the difficulties, and all the shifts and ineptitudes of the policy-makers, Austria prospered in these years. Compared to the regions to the east and south, in the Russian and Ottoman empires, it was rich, progressive, and well-governed. By 1870, its peasants were free and many of them were land-owners. There existed equality before the law, representative assemblies, and religious freedom. The educational system was good and it was extremely fecund in the life of the mind. Nowhere in Europe, save France itself, were there so many writers, musicians, and artists of high caliber as in Vienna. The national aspirations of the polyglot populations were not yet so mature as to obscure the vital fact of Austrian history: that the Habsburg monarchy brought to the diverse and divided provinces and peoples of Central Europe a degree of order and security to which there were no alternatives but anarchy or domination by an outside power.

THE ERA OF THE FRENCH REVOLUTION

Of the considerable states of Europe, barring Great Britain, the Habsburg monarchy was perhaps the least affected internally by the French Revolution and the Napoleonic era. Parts of Italy and Germany were remade from the bottom up, almost as thoroughly as France. Spain was temporarily equipped with a liberal constitution and a revolutionary administrative system. Prussia, vanquished and overwhelmed, was forced to embark upon its own program of drastic reform in order to save itself. Sweden was provided with a French revolutionary general as king. Even Russia felt the effects not only of a French army of invasion but of a whimsical emperor who dallied from time to time with his own version of revolutionary idealism. But Austria survived with its internal administration unchanged and its rulers untouched by the ardors of the age of tumult. The Habsburg monarchy was, in the end, the principal architect of the reconstruction of a conservative Europe.

So far as its form of government and its domestic arrangements went, the Habsburg empire in 1815 had changed almost not at all from 1789. But the age of tumult affected, profoundly and permanently, its frontiers and its destinies. The periodic wars which it waged against Napoleon each resulted in large revisions of its territories. And French revolutionary ideas of liberalism and nationalism, carried to some of its provinces by French armies and French writers, shaped the future of the conservative and polyglot state.

The intricate narrative of Austria's role in the Napoleonic wars may be briefly summarized, noting only those phases and developments which had lasting importance.

The reforming Joseph II died in 1790 and was succeeded by his brother, the model enlightened despot of Tuscany, Leopold II. Leopold's reign was too brief—he died in 1792—to permit any great successes, and in any case, he was preoccupied with the explosion in France, an imminent partition of Poland, and the liquidation of a Belgian rebellion and a Turkish war which Joseph had left him. He was succeeded by his son, Francis, who was to live until 1835, and was to reign over the age of tumult and the age of reaction. One of Francis's first projects was war on revolutionary France.

The first phase of the war against France lasted until 1797. It ended in a serious but not disastrous peace for Austria, the Peace of Campo Formio. By this treaty, Francis ceded to the French the Austrian Netherlands—what is today Belgium—and the Italian province of Lombardy, both of which his ancestors had acquired from Spain in 1714. Austria agreed to French annexation of a large part of the left bank of the Rhine, a region which it had long been the Habsburgs' role to protect from France. In compensation Austria received part of the Republic of Venice and certain German territories.

Two years later, Austria joined with Britain and Russia in an effort to eject the French from Italy and Germany. But, under the leadership of Napoleon, France recovered. In 1800, at the battles of Marengo and Hohenlinden, and again in 1805, at the great battle of Austerlitz, Napoleon defeated the Allies. A peace was signed at Pressburg, in 1805. The cost to the Habsburgs was very high: Venice was ceded to the newly formed kingdom of Italy and the home province of Tyrol, in the Alps, to Napoleon's ally Bavaria. Moreover, Napoleon's control in Germany was extended. He had already commenced the process of reorganizing the map of the Holy Roman Empire. Now, in 1806, Francis abandoned his imperial title.

So ended the titular claim of the Habsburgs to dominance in all Germany. And there ended, too, the style and institution which had given to the Habsburgs and their predecessors the name of Caesar, a shadowy link to the glories of ancient Rome, and an even more shadowy claim to suzerainty over all of Europe's monarchs. The last trace, long unreal, of Europe's dream of unity disappeared. But while the end of the Holy Roman Empire meant the extinction of the Habsburg pretensions to German or European primacy, which Napoleon—a much truer son of Augustus—now arrogated, it equally meant the defining of "Austria" as a European state. The prudent Francis had already, in 1804, taken the precaution of having himself proclaimed "Emperor of Austria"—*Kaiser* (or caesar) *Österreichs*—so after 1806 he was still an emperor, along with Napoleon and Alexander of Russia. The title meant something different—merely head of a large state which was one of many states, not a uniquely august sovereign mystically superior to other sovereigns. "Austria," a word which now acquired for the first time a precise territorial meaning, seemed on paper to be like France or Great Britain or Spain. But it was not. Francis II of the Holy Roman Empire had been transformed into Francis I of Austria, but the position of the Habsburgs and the character of Austria were still different from that of any other European dynasty or state. Austria was still a collection of heterogeneous provinces and nationalities.

In 1809, Austria again declared war on Napoleon. Defeat followed almost at once, at the battle of Wagram. In the Peace of Vienna, Austria was forced to cede its southwestern provinces, Carniola, Istria, and Dalmatia on the Adriatic, which were annexed to the French empire, and lost other lands to France's allies, involving a loss of three and a half million subjects. And Francis I was obliged to agree to the marriage of his young daughter, the Archduchess Marie Louise, to Napoleon, who (having divorced the unfortunate Josephine) thus gained a bride who brought him social distinction as a member of Europe's oldest and most splendid dynasty and who might be expected to give him an heir. An uneasy and (from the Austrian viewpoint) distasteful cordiality now united the imperial courts of Paris and Vienna, and the revolutionary despot of Europe was allied by marriage and treaty to the most ancient, most powerful, and stuffiest of his erstwhile rivals.

The situation lasted for three more years, during which Napoleon invaded Russia and reached Moscow. But the turning point had come; he was forced to retreat from Russia and to face not only advancing Russians but a reinvigorated Prussia. And in 1813, Francis I once again declared war upon the man who was now his son-in-law. In October, 1813, the Austrians, Russians, and Prussians met and defeated the French at Leipzig, and six months later the Allies were in Paris. The Napoleonic empire died; the age of tumult drew to its close. Austrian armies reentered Venice, Milan, Trieste, and Innsbruck. The nightmare of wars and revolutions, of confiscations and depositions, was over. Nothing was changed, or so it seemed to some in central Europe. Only the Holy Roman Empire was conceded to be extinct: it is possible to contemplate reviving a corpse, but not a ghost.

At the Congress of Vienna, after peace had been made with a subdued France, the pieces of Europe were put together again. Austria counted for much in the restored balance of power, again holding Lombardy, Venetia, the Illyrian provinces, the Tyrol, and Galicia, plus the presidency of the German Confederation. Austrian leadership in Italy was admitted, while in the simplified post-Napoleonic Germany only Prussia could pretend to equality. France was contained, Russia appeased, nationalism and liberalism shut up in their Pandora's box. A world safe for Habsburgs was constructed.

But during the years of Napoleon's ascendancy, much had happened to imperil the "Habsburg mission"—a phrase much used but not clearly defined, which, if it meant anything, meant protecting peace, order, unity, and Christian civilization in Central Europe. For one thing, the Italians and Germans had both been stimulated to dreams of national freedom and national greatness. For another, the peoples of the Illyrian Province, which Napoleon had constructed out of Austria's Slavic lands on the Adriatic, had had for the first time in their history a government of their own and been exposed to ideals of national freedom. And for a third, the *notion* of a people's government, free of aristocrats and landlords, free of the inequalities and anomalies of the old regime, free of the tyranny of one nation over another, had been implanted and spread throughout Europe—not only in Germany and Italy, but in the dark and backward corners of Eastern Europe, among the tangled peasant societies of Hungary and Transylvania, in Ottoman and Habsburg lands where dwelt forgotten peoples like the Bulgars, the Ruthenes, the Slovaks, the Croats, and the Rumanians, who had not entered the political history of Europe for a millennium.

THE AGE OF METTERNICH

The making of the peace of 1815 had been in large part the work of Austria's minister Prince Metternich, who was to be the greatest figure of the age that followed. Metternich was an aristocrat, a member of a family of imperial knights with lands on the Rhine. He was frankly a conservative. With monarchy, with the old cosmopolitan organization of Europe, with the settled hierarchical society of the old regime, he associated peace and civilization. He was an exceedingly loyal servant of Austria and its imperial master, Francis I. He fashioned the "Vienna System" to secure peace and order and security for Austria and Europe, and did his best to maintain it from 1815 to 1848. Within the empire, he tried to maintain without *basic* alteration the system of government which had been inherited from Joseph II and Leopold II—absolutism tempered by benevolence and reform.

The most urgent need for Austria was a peaceful Europe and the repression of Jacobin and nationalist agitations, and to this end Metternich devoted the most important part of his work. Although he was chancellor—prime minister—for part of his life, his greatest success was in foreign affairs and this was the sphere in which he was allowed to operate without interference by the emperor and rival ministers. What he tried to do in Europe was to secure *international* action whenever the Treaty of Vienna was threatened, to enforce its provisions and its spirit, and this involved the suppression of revolutions which imperiled the security of monarchs or frontiers. The story of the "Vienna System" is told elsewhere. Here it must suffice to note that until 1848, he was largely successful in preserving the structure of Europe which had been provided by the peacemakers of Vienna. The world remained safe for Habsburgs.

Inside Austria, the situation was almost equally stable, but much less satisfactory. It was clear that improvements were necessary, and some were undertaken, but they were neither wise nor adequate.

The principal obstacle to political progress in Austria was the emperor. Francis I was a serious, hard-working ruler. But he was unfit to operate the system which had been devised by Maria Theresa and Joseph II. This system, as it had grown up in the eighteenth century, was essentially a bureaucracy superimposed upon the old substructure of provincial and aristocratic local governments, and inspired by a powerful and imaginative autocrat. Francis was far from imaginative; he was himself, by temperament, a sort of bureaucrat, unable to perform the function of leadership which the empire demanded of him. He inclined to narrowness and suspicion, and he was inclined to rely more upon police—his were the best and most officious in Europe—than upon policy. The censorship and the spy system were the principal mainstays of the state.

The structure of central government had been raised at the expense of the class which was the traditional enemy of absolute monarchy, the aristocracy. But after the French Revolution, the old rivalry of monarch and aristocrat tended to disappear; they were drawn into alliance by their common fear of the common man. After 1815, Metternich and Francis undertook to revive the old centers of aristocratic power which had been so carefully and arduously suppressed. Provincial diets were restored or installed. In them the local noblemen found a forum for debate and an instrument for safeguarding their surviving privileges. The former enemy became, thus, a principal prop of the monarchy. With the Catholic Church, the army, and the police, the aristocracy formed the main support of the empire.

The policy was on the whole successful, at least in many provinces, and most dramatically in Hungary and the Polish areas. Both the Hungarians and Poles, members of ancient nations with splendid histories, might have been expected to be subversive. But both of them were rigidly stratified, dominated by very old-fashioned landed magnates. And (characteristic of the Habsburg monarchy) the magnates were not only apprehensive of *social* and *economic* demands by their peasants; they were also in some cases apprehensive of *national* demands. For many of the estates controlled by Polish and Hungarian magnates were inhabited by Ruthene or Rumanian or Serb peasants. Against the double threat of social change and national aspirations, the Polish and Magyar landlords were happy to have the support of the central government. They exchanged their own loyalty for that support, and for the right to manage their own local affairs in their own archaic fashion. In Galicia, the Polish province, this sort of bargain was very effective, for Austrian Poland remained loyal to the Habsburgs as long as the empire lasted.

The empire of Metternich's day was thus actually moving backward in its social and constitutional arrangements. Francis I, addressing the professors of the Laibach college in 1821, revealed his bent toward stagnancy: "Hold to the old," the emperor told the academicians, "for it is good, and our ancestors found it to be good, so why should not we? There are now new ideas going about, which I never can nor will approve. Avoid these and keep to what is positive. For I need no scholars, but worthy citizens. . . . He who serves me must teach what I order. He who cannot do so, or who comes with new ideas, can go, or I shall remove him."

In one respect, conservatism paid off in Austria. This was in the field of economic policy. By the 1820's many European states—led by Great Britain and Prussia—were at last abandoning the economic and commercial system which had been inspired by mercantilism. Austria, logically, clung to mercantilist ideas, and particularly to the ideas of state-sponsored development of the economy, in an age when laissez-faire notions were being adopted elsewhere. The result was a good deal of government attention to railroads: the Habsburg monarchy led Central Europe, at least, in the development of its railway system. Another important state project was the creation, at Trieste, of a first-class modern port for the empire, which was connected by rail with the major centers. Manufacturing lagged far behind Britain or France, to be sure, but it was already developing, under government sponsorship, around the two major imperial cities, Vienna and Prague. Moreover, fiscal policies and administration were ably conducted in these years, and taxes were low. As a consequence, the economic condition of the empire was good, and progressive. But economic and social progress only highlighted the political stagnation, and they helped to augment the very groups—such as the liberal middle classes in Vienna—who were most intransigently opposed to Habsburg autocracy.

If conservatism meant economic progress, it meant political stagnation, which was partly the consequence of Austria's peculiar and anachronistic composition. The balance of classes and nationalities was so delicate that change threatened to upset it. But it was in part the result of the character of Francis I. The problem of an inadequate autocrat in an absolute monarchy had plagued other countries, particularly the France of Louis XVI. In Austria, the difficulty was emphasized when Francis died, in 1835, and was succeeded by his son Ferdinand I, who was unfortunately an imbecile. There was now, in effect, no autocrat at all, not even an inadequate one. The conduct of the emperorship was confided to a committee, which consisted mainly of an archduke—one deliberately chosen because he was too languid to interfere much—and Metternich and another minister, Kolowrat. The stagnation was perpetuated. For thirteen years after Francis's death, even less was done than before. Autocracy was visibly withering on the vine of the Habsburgs' biological incompetence. Then, in 1848, the monarchy was shocked into a period of experimentation with reform.

THE HABSBURG LANDS IN 1847

The events of the year 1848—or, more precisely, of the eighteen months from February, 1848, to July, 1849—were among the most staggering of modern European history. Europe—the Europe of the "Vienna System"—exploded. Nowhere were these events more startling or more confusing than in the Austrian empire, nowhere did more drastic changes loom up, nowhere was the restoration of the old order more surprising.

The revolutions failed in Austria as elsewhere, but the situation was

PEOPLES OF THE AUSTRIAN EMPIRE

changed. Such alarming energies had been unleashed and such violent dissatisfaction voiced that everyone realized changes were necessary. Experiments were made and unmade in the years that followed; not until the end of our period, just before 1870, was a new stability achieved and a new stagnation inaugurated. By then, very extensive and peculiar alterations had taken place, and Austria had been ejected from both Germany and Italy. The stagnation after 1867, like the restoration after 1848, was due in large part to the total inability of radicals or reformers to agree on any program of change. The Habsburg monarchy was always being saved by its own weaknesses and divisions.

It is worthwhile to review briefly those weaknesses on the eve of 1848, and this can best be done by a survey of the empire. The following were its principal components.

I. The German areas. The provinces, around and to the west of Vienna, which today constitute approximately the Austrian Republic, were the heartland of the empire. Their populations were German, Catholic, and loyal, their culture and economy advanced. But they presented certain domestic and international problems. There were profound political differences in the rural populations between noblemen and tenant-peasants. There were differences, too, between the conservatives and the nationalistic liberals, who flourished in the cities. And most of all there were in the German provinces differences of attitude toward the question of Germany and of Austria's role in it. Some German-Austrians wanted a united Germany including the *whole* Habsburg empire and dominated by Vienna. (Few other Germans wanted this.) Others wanted to be integrated into a Germany which would not include the non-German provinces of Austria. Most Austrian-Germans, however, did not want to see Vienna made a provincial town and German control pass to the north Germans. Still others—perhaps a majority—wanted Germany to remain disunited, with Habsburg influence in it still strong, but wanted an Austrian Empire brought under complete control of its German population, with the other nationalities reduced to colonial status and eventually Germanized. These differing attitudes, along with differing views as to the sort of reform which was needed in Vienna itself, in the end reduced the German-Austrian revolutionaries to impotence.

II. Northern Italy. Although the Austrian provinces of Lombardy and Venetia (united as a "kingdom," and equipped with a viceroy after 1815) were among the best governed parts of disunited Italy, the Lombards and Venetians were the most intractably subversive of the empire's population. The Italians, by 1848 at least, almost to a man wanted out, and took the first chance they found to get out. But in 1848 and 1849 there was no military force in Italy sufficient to defeat the Austrian army and ensure the liberation of Lombardy and Venetia; so the aspirations were frustrated. The purely Italian kingdom of Piedmont tried, but it failed to win against Austria.

III. Hungary. Hungary was an ancient kingdom, and had preserved under Habsburg rule more self-government and more traces of its ancient constitution than any other part of the Empire. But the Kingdom of Hungary was itself very various, and within it were ample materials for a Habsburg policy of divide and rule. The major difficulties *within* Hungary were as follows:

A. The population was not by any means a united nation. The Magyars, the principal nationality, dominated the country and aspired to make it a national state, but they were a minority. In addition to them, there were: Slovaks in the north (a Slavic peasant people who were beginning to become aware of their national identity; a written language had just been invented for them); Croats and Serbs (also Slavic) in the south and southwest; Rumanians and "Saxons," the latter descendants of early German settlers, in the east and southeast.

B. Both Transylvania (Magyar-Rumanian-Saxon) and Croatia (Croat-Serb) had provincial governments of their own within Hungary. The Magyars mostly controlled that of Transylvania, but the Croat diet was in the hands of Croat-speaking noblemen, who regarded the Habsburgs as their principal safeguard against Magyar domination, and who were extremly suspicious of any policy of independence or centralization in Hungary.

C. Within the purely Magyar sections, there were social and political disputes. The great magnates were mostly supporters of the Habsburgs, but the local gentry (a class closely resembling the Prussian *Junkers* or the English squires) were eager above all to preserve the local governments, which were controlled by them, and their own medieval rights over tenant-peasants, from reform or control by Vienna. The gentry were the core of Hungarian movements for national independence and for self-government and liberal institutions. The Magyar peasants were an unknown quantity, wholly excluded from any political role.

IV. Bohemia. A movement for revival of the Slavic Bohemian (Czech) language was beginning, but it had not progressed much beyond the point of frightening the German-speaking populations of Bohemia. The Czech enthusiasts were divided between those who wanted the ancient Bohemian kingdom revived (consisting of Bohemia, Moravia, and the surviving bits of Austrian Silesia) as a governing unit under the Habsburg crown, and those who wanted complete independence and far-reaching social reforms. The Germans (something under half the population of Bohemia) were divided between those who wanted a revival of "historic" Bohemia, but under German dominance, those who wanted the whole country run directly from Vienna, those who wanted it integrated into an entirely new German national state, those who wanted liberal reforms for the Austrian empire as a whole.

V. Galicia. Polish landlords dominated the province, but Polish and Ruthene peasants agitated for social and agrarian reform.

One source of discontent, which was nearly empire-wide, should be noted. This was the *robot,* a tax paid by peasants to their landlords which had come to be a symbol of servitude. An important part of the risings in 1848 was a peasant insurrection designed to free the peasantry from these obligations and, in some cases, to bring about peasant ownership on the French and west German model. This agrarian revolution affected the other revolutions which took place, but it was basically separate from them. And it differed from the others in that it was largely successful. Although peasants in most parts of the empire did not secure ownership of their land, they did secure release from the *robot* and become free citizens. This was the most important and lasting of the changes which took place in Austria in 1848.

1848

The year 1848 saw revolution in all continental Europe outside of Russia. Now at last the liberalism and nationalism which had been born of the French Revolution were adolescent, and in their young exuberance strove to overthrow the rule of paternal conservatism. The causes were everywhere similar: exasperation with the static and stuffy regimes of the Metternich system; exhilaration in the example of France, where a Second Republic had been easily established; and discontent which followed from the general business depression of 1847–1848. The latter influences brought to crisis the first.

Everywhere, in France and Italy and Austria and the German states, the symptoms and course of the revolutions were similar. There were mobs in the streets agitating against the dynasties; there were popular risings against foreign overlords; there were lists of demands for constitutional change—representative parliaments, responsible ministries, equality of citizens, and bills of rights. There were more sweeping demands for *social* changes—abolition of aristocracy, separation of church and state—by groups called radicals. There was, here and there, working class agitation, tinged with socialism, against businessmen and private property.

In Austria the revolutions showed all these symptoms blended in a peculiarly complicated and explosive mixture.

The events of 1848–1849 may be summarized briefly. No amount of brevity, however, can eliminate the intricacy and confusion. It must be borne in mind that to some extent the course of the revolutions in Austria affected, and was affected by, the German nationalist movement of the same years, which ended with a German parliament fruitlessly debating a constitution for a united Germany at Frankfurt.

The trouble, sparked by news of the February revolution in Paris, became serious first in Hungary. There were riots in Budapest by extreme radicals, which frightened the conservative gentlemen of the diet and pushed them to extreme measures. They responded, in their alarm, to the advice of the Hungarian liberal leader, Louis Kossuth, who demanded and got a program of drastic reform in the "March Laws," which the diet enacted and which were the basis for political aspirations in Hungary until 1918. All constitutional links with the rest of the empire were severed, except for an officer called the palatine—or viceroy—who was to represent the emperor. Later, even this link was abandoned and outright independence was proclaimed. A very liberal constitution was set up, with a complete national government and a parliament elected by men of wealth, controlling a responsible ministry. The principal trouble with this program, aside from the fact that it destroyed the unity of the empire, was that it was an exclusively Magyar and largely a Magyar-gentry government which was to be set up. It was therefore ardently opposed in Vienna and in Croatia as well.

Prague next caught the infection. A revolutionary group was set up demanding self-government for the kingdom of Bohemia. Then, on March 13, it spread to Vienna. There were riots, outbreaks of street fighting, and the diet of the Province of Lower Austria (which sat in Vienna) demanded Metternich's resignation. He resigned, and authority in the capital passed to a students' committee. On March 18, the Lombards rose, and Austrian troops were withdrawn from Milan, where an Italian nationalist regime seized power. A republic was next established in Venice.

The court of Vienna was desperate. A series of ministers was appointed; each resigned in the face of more street demonstrations. The March Laws in Hungary were recognized and accepted. A liberal constitution for the rest of the empire was hastily written and promulgated, on April 25. The Viennese liberals disdained reform from the top, and the court (still nominally controlled by the imbecile emperor Ferdinand but actually run by his sister-in-law) agreed to calling an elected Constituent Assembly. On May 17, the imperial family withdrew from Vienna to the Tyrolean capital of Innsbruck (where nobody had yet revolted). A Committee of Public Safety, composed of extremists, seized control in Vienna.

In the meanwhile, the Croats had begun to revolt against the new Hungarian constitution, and were in this encouraged by the court at Innsbruck. An anti-Hungarian Croat general was appointed governor of Croatia and charged with suppressing the new government of Hungary, although the court had already recognized it as legal.

Events in Bohemia were also developing confusedly. The Czech national group which was in control was becoming frightened of German nationalism. Observing the formation of the German national assembly at Frankfurt, which solemnly voted the incorporation of Bohemia into a German state, the Czechs turned strongly pro-Habsburg. Only by working for autonomy in an independent Austria could they prevent the drowning of the Czech populations in a new Germany, they thought. Their most eminent leader, Alfred Palacky, now coined the famous phrase: "If Austria did not exist, somebody would have to invent it." The Habsburgs at Innsbruck welcomed this position, naturally, and found themselves in the strange and unnerving position of backing two "oppressed" Slavic national movements, Croats and Czechs, against the two "master-races" of the empire, Germans and Magyars, who were at the moment threatening the monarchy's existence.

The situation now began to alter, however. First of all, the military situation in Italy improved, thanks to the generalship of the loyal Radetzky, who commanded the Austrian army. Supported by reenforcements from Vienna, Radetzky defeated the Sardinians at Custozza in July and brought northern Italy under control. Meanwhile, in June, violent street riots had taken place in Prague, led by extremist students who opposed the Czech leaders' acceptance of Habsburg rule. These were put down by the imperial garrison under the spirited generalship of Prince Windischgrätz, who then found himself in control of the city. The moderate Czechs and Germans put their hope in the Constituent Assembly, which met in Vienna in July, 1848.

A legal governing body now existed, and most of the revolutionaries were prepared to await its decisions. The imperial family felt it safe to return to the capital in July, and a new ministry took office, led by the Viennese liberal Alexander Bach. The Constituent Assembly turned out to be more moderate than anyone expected. The really radical regions, Lombardy and Hungary, were not represented, since civil wars were still going on in them. The delegations from Galicia were controlled by Polish landlords. Since the German and some Bohemian provinces were mainly represented by peasants or gentry, the liberals from the towns were greatly outnumbered. The Assembly, divided by national aspirations and not very radical, made only one real and significant reform, contributed by its peasant members: the Act of Emancipation, of September 7, 1848, abolished the *robot* and all other medieval dues and obligations. The hereditary rights of landlords to control local government and act as local judges were also abolished —the remnants of feudalism were thus extinguished. Complete freedom of movement and legal equality were extended to all peasants.

But the Constituent Assembly did not get very far in drawing up a constitution. It was distracted by the Hungarians, who by now had proclaimed their complete independence, and by a rising in Vienna in October (of people who wanted to join in a German national state, which they thought was taking shape at Frankfurt), which chased the Constituent Assembly out of the capital to Moravia. The government ordered Windischgrätz to occupy the capital, which he succeeded in doing.

By now, the court was pulling itself together to assume leadership. The imbecile Ferdinand was persuaded to abdicate, to be succeeded by an eighteen-year-old nephew, who had an approximately normal intelligence and who became emperor under the name of Francis Joseph I. A new prime minister, Prince Schwarzenberg, a brother-in-law of Windischgrätz, who was sufficiently liberal to be acceptable to the Assembly and sufficiently firm and loyal to be acceptable to the court, was appointed. The government moved back to Vienna, although the Assembly continued to sit in Moravia, pursuing its lengthy debates. But as the situation settled down, with Italy reconquered and with plans made for the suppression of independent Hungary, the government felt strong enough to dissolve the Assembly altogether. It did so, in March of 1849, to the accompaniment of a new constitution of its own, which however never went into effect. Order, and autocracy, were now restored in all the provinces except Hungary.

The Hungarians, although opposed by an Austrian army and by the resistance of their own non-Magyar subjects, fought vigorously to defend their own national state. An altogether new factor, however, brought about their defeat. The emperor of Russia, alarmed by the persistence of revolution in Austria and eager to put the Austrian government in his debt, offered to send Russian troops to assist in the suppression of the revolutionary regime at Budapest. The offer was accepted. The Russians entered Hungary in June, 1849. The government capitulated. Kossuth and some of the other leaders fled. Most of them were executed. Vienna breathed easily again. So did the czar, and so did the non-Magyar groups in Croatia and Transylvania. Hungarian radicalism and Hungarian independence were ended.

By the end of 1849, the revolutionary movement throughout Austria had been suppressed. The Habsburg throne was safe, the dangers of partition had been averted, and the empire was at the disposal of the emperor and his ministers in Vienna, to do with as they chose. What they chose, at the initiative of Bach and Schwarzenberg, was the restoration of autocracy and the complete centralization of the empire. The old provinces and their rights were eliminated. Hungary's special privileges were extinguished. Taken together with the abolition of the landlords' rights under the emancipation law, this meant the completion of the work of transforming Austria into a unitary, uniform state governed by an imperial bureaucracy. The work of Joseph II was at last complete. But it was to prove short-lived.

The revolutions in Austria had followed the general pattern of those in Germany, in Italy, in France: an initial explosion, a few months of revolutionary success, and finally a gradual reaction. The reasons for the success of the conservatives were, in Austria as elsewhere, mainly these: the loyalty of the armies; the divisions among the revolutionaries; their inexperience and naïveté; and their inability to call forth the irresistible power of the masses. In the German states, the king of Prussia and his sacred army and aristocracy were back in power slightly harassed by a constitution. The effort to create a German state had come to nothing. In France, an increasingly conservative republic, presided over by a prince and supported by the army, was in power. In Italy, the Pope was back in Rome and the Habsburgs were back in Milan and Venice. In Austria, the façade of Metternich's system was rebuilt. But the deeper changes in Austria were abiding, for the nature of the Austrian state had changed.

EXPERIMENTS AND DEFEATS: 1849–1867

If the new absolutism of 1849 had been achieved by Joseph II in the eighteenth century, it might have served as the basis for a unified Austrian state in the nineteenth. Now it came too late, for national ambitions were exacerbated

IMPERIAL ARMS OF AUSTRIA The House of Habsburg, and the Austrian empire, had as their coat-of-arms the double-headed eagle. This ancient symbol of empire (which was also adopted by imperial Russia) was orginally the emblem of the Roman Empire in the East, at Byzantium. It was used by the Holy Roman Emperors to indicate their connection with ancient Rome and their claims to superiority over all other rulers. During the centuries when the Habsburgs were elected Holy Roman Emperors it became associated with the dynasty and survived on its coat-of-arms after the dissolution of the Holy Roman Empire in 1806 and the transformation of the Habsburgs into emperors of Austria.

The eagle bears on its chest a shield divided in three parts. On the first is the rampant lion which was the arms of the Habsburg family. The center part is red with a white bar, the arms of the archduchy of Austria which became the main seat of Habsburg power—the same device is used by the Austrian Republic today. The third section, with three eagles on a diagonal bar, is the arms of Lorraine, whose duke married Maria Theresa, the last Habsburg heiress.

and national consciousness had grown to alarming proportions. And the new absolutism was confronted with all sorts of liberal demands for representative government. The national ambitions and the liberal demands were too strong for Francis Joseph to maintain the victory which had been won, and scarcely had the revolutions been suppressed than a period began of experimentation with constitutional change.

The first of these was the installation of "radical autocracy" and centralization by Bach. The second, inaugurated as Bach's influence was replaced by that of a new minister, Kübeck, was the December Patent, of 1851, supposedly a new constitution but actually merely a confirmation of the absolute power of the emperor. But for the next few years, the principal authority was not Francis Joseph, but Schwarzenberg. Schwarzenberg and Metternich (who now had returned from exile) dominated the advisory Imperial Council which the Patent set up, in imitation of the similar institution of Maria Theresa. The policy which they followed was tinged with at least economic liberalism—the earlier mercantilist policies were abandoned, and state-sponsored enterprises like railroads were turned over to private ownership in the best laissez-faire fashion, but nothing else of consequence in domestic affairs was changed. The "police state" was tighter than ever. In foreign affairs, a strong and aggressive policy was adopted. It was felt that if Austrian military power and diplomatic prestige could be maintained, the internal situation could be stabilized.

But this was exactly what could not be done. There was rising agitation in Germany for a German state, and in Italy for an Italian state, both of which would mean a serious loss of influence and prestige for Austria. And in 1859, war broke out in Italy. In this year, Austria did not face merely the minor forces of the insurrected populace and the Piedmontese army, as it had in 1848. Instead, it faced a large French army, led by Napoleon III to liberate northern Italy from Austrian rule. The Austrians were defeated at Magenta and Solferino, and they signed the Treaty of Villafranca. By it, they lost Lombardy to Piedmont. Worse, many of the other Italian states now united with Piedmont to form the kingdom of Italy. The preoccupation of the Germanic emperors with Italy, which had begun some eight hundred years earlier, was now at last ended. A major pawn and sphere of influence was lost to the Habsburgs; their attempt to assert military power and diplomatic prestige had failed.

The Italian war and the unification of Italy had far-reaching effects. The people who had been most influential for the last ten years, the German bureaucrats who wished to run the empire as a centralized bureaucracy, were now largely discredited. Francis Joseph turned to another group, the aristocracy. And, in accordance with aristocratic wishes and traditions, he promulgated the next great experiment, the October Diploma, in October, 1860. For the first time it was avowed that the monarchy was "constitutional." The provincial diets, resurrected in the 1820's and suppressed in 1848, were revived and given extensive powers. They were to elect members of a new Imperial Council, the *Reichsrat*, which was to have limited legislative powers. A certain amount of freedom of the press, and of speech, was provided, although not safeguarded. The diets (elected in such a way as to give the aristocracy predominance) were to be the real centers of power; Austria was to be, in substance, federalized.

The October Diploma satisfied no one. It was particularly disliked by liberals, who were strongly averse both to decentralization and to aristocrats. And it was repugnant to the Hungarians, since it reduced each part of Hungary to the same position as each of the German provinces, and the old Kingdom of Hungary lost its boundaries and its identity. The Diploma had a short life. The emperor was led to summon another minister, von Schmerling, to revise it, and in February, 1861, it was replaced by the February Patent.

The February Patent reversed the tendency toward federalism, or decentralization. The provincial diets were preserved, but shorn of most of their powers. Much larger powers were now confided in the empire-wide *Reichsrat,* which was rebuilt in the outward likeness of the British Parliament, with a House of Lords and a House of Commons. The members of the latter were to be elected by the diets, from their own membership, and the diets were to be elected by a peculiar system, comparable in principle to that of the Prussian *Landtag.* Four *curias,* or groups of voters were established: one of landowners; one of other qualified voters in rural areas; one of chambers of commerce; one of other qualified voters in cities. Each *curia* elected a different number of representatives—the landowning *curia* choosing a disproportionately large number. The system was very carefully worked out to secure in each province a preponderant electoral influence for the groups which were thought to be most loyal to the monarchy—mainly Germans and, in non-German provinces, the higher aristocracy.

Like the October Diploma, the February Patent was repugnant to the Magyars of Hungary, and they resisted the regime which it instituted. The Vienna government responded by abolishing the powers of the county councils, which were in Hungary the stronghold of the Magyar gentry who had fought for liberalism and independence in 1849. As a consequence, Hungarian discontent mounted rapidly in the years that followed. In other provinces, too, there was trouble. The Bohemians were sullenly resistant to the revival of centralization. So were the diets of Croatia and Transylvania, both of which had to be dissolved by the imperial government. There was mounting hostility in all quarters to the Schemerling system, and in 1865 he was dismissed, and his place taken by a Moravian nobleman named Belcredi. Belcredi attempted to appease the Hungarians. Transylvania was returned to Hungary; county self-government was restored. The concessions were not enough to satisfy the Magyar nationalists, but negotiations were begun.

This was the situation when the second international disaster in a decade overtook Austria. In 1859, it had lost Lombardy and its influence in most of Italy. In 1866, Austrian leadership in Germany was destroyed. In the summer of that year, war broke out between Prussia and Austria. At the great Battle of Sadowa, on July 3, 1866, the Prussians surrounded and routed the Austrian armies.

Peace was hastily signed at Prague on August 23. The Prussians had no wish to destroy or divide Austria; they merely wished to eject it once and for all from the affairs of the rest of Germany. As a consequence, there was no loss of territory, no humiliation, no triumphal Prussian entry into Vienna. The war cost Austria nothing save the province of Venetia, which went to Prussia's ally, Italy, to help complete the unification of Italy. Nothing save that, and its position as a German power—its prestige and greatness and stability.

The Habsburg monarchy was now, despite its vast size and wealth, purely a Central European—a Danubian—power. Its anchors in the south and north were gone. The dynasty was now merely a German-speaking royal house which happened to rule over twenty million people, most of whom were non-Germans. Excluded from Italy and Germany, the Habsburg monarchy was forced to orient itself to the south and east, to become a Balkan power, to base itself upon a Danubian foundation, if the Habsburgs were to survive as a major force in Europe, or to survive at all.

This meant that Hungary could no longer be treated as an appendage. After 1866, Hungary was the core and center of the Habsburg monarchy, and it had to be pacified at any cost. It thus became necessary, after Sadowa, to give in to all the Hungarian demands, short of those for absolute independence. The negotiations which had already been started with the Hungarian liberal leaders, Déak and Andrassy, were continued, and a remarkable "compromise" was presently worked out, negotiated by a new minister, Beust. In December, 1867, new constitutional laws were promulgated. They created the Dual Monarchy, a constitutional arrangement unique in history.

The Dual Monarchy comprehended, in effect, two states: a kingdom of Hungary and an empire of Austria, and the country was known collectively as Austria-Hungary. Francis Joseph was henceforth known as "king-emperor," and was addressed as "imperial and royal majesty." Each state was complete: each had its own constitution, its own parliament, its own ministry, its own postal system, its own financial system, its own bureaucracy. Each had control of its own commercial policy: the customs and monetary union of the two countries was covered in a separate agreement which was to be renewed periodically.

But Austria and Hungary were not entirely separate. They shared a monarch and a ruling family. They also shared a sort of common parliament, made up of delegations from the separate parliaments and empowered to discuss and make laws on diplomacy, military affairs, and certain financial problems. There were three "common ministers" responsible to these delegations: for foreign affairs, for war, and for finance. These three cabinet posts were correspondingly absent in the separate cabinets of Austria and Hungary.

The two halves of the Monarchy were very different. The Austrian half, with its rather decentralized government, was—administratively at least—a federation of provinces. Its constitution was essentially the February Patent, amplified by a bill of rights. The Hungarian half was highly centralized. Both halves included many nationalities: in Austria, Germans, Italians, Czechs, Poles, Ruthenes, Slovenes; in Hungary, Magyars, Croats, Serbs, Rumanians, Slovaks, Saxons. In Austria the dominant people, Germans, constituted about a third of the population; in Hungary, the dominant Magyars about forty percent. But while Austria was frankly and genially cosmopolitan, Hungary was a unitary state and the ruling Magyars were eager to make it a "national state." Into the constitutional laws of 1867 there had been written provisions to protect the integrity and liberties of Croatia, which was incorporated within the Hungarian half, but these provisions were eventually to be disregarded.

At the end of our period, therefore, the Habsburgs had solved their problems of what to do with a polyglot empire by dividing it in two. Thus they could count on the more or less reliable loyalties of the Magyars and the Germans, the two most numerous peoples. The dynasty was preserved. But in the years that followed, Austria was to prove increasingly ungovernable by parliamentary means, and the discontent of the peoples of Hungary against the rule of the Magyars and the landowners was to mount. A workable compromise had been found, but it was harassed by national discontents which proved, a half a century later, to be the undoing of the Habsburg realm.

30

THE MAKING OF
THE ITALIAN STATE

ENGLAND AND FRANCE had become nations in the Middle Ages, Spain and the Netherlands on the threshold of modern times. Russia had emerged from the eastern mists by the seventeenth century. Austria and Prussia had taken shape in the eighteenth. At the beginning of the nineteenth century, the Italians and Germans remained divided among many governments; before its close, they had been united, completing the constellation of Europe's great powers. Their formation took place in an age when Europe was less fluid and when the form of the modern state was already set, and when nationalism had become popularly associated with governments. Italy and Germany were, therefore, not only the last examples in Europe of the making of major powers; they were also the first, and the model examples of the making of free nations. The freeing of Italy from political division and foreign domination followed a pattern which has been perceptible ever since, in places like Yugoslavia, India, Egypt, and Ghana: it was a nation-state made (at least in theory) by and for its people, not merely as a product of the ambition of a dynasty.

The particular aspiration of the people which the making of Italy satisfied was their sense of *Italianness*, and the corresponding sense that, being Italians, it was important to have a state whose boundaries included all Italians and which was free of foreign influences. This was a revolutionary notion in Europe, but (although most conservative people in the nineteenth century associated it with "Jacobinism" and regarded it with due hatred) it had its precedents. The ambitions of French kings since the fifteenth century had been accompanied by invocations of a mystical but compelling abstraction, "France," whose vague connotations evoked exuberance several centuries before *La Marseillaise* was

498

composed. "I glory," George III observed in the 1760's, "in the name of Briton." Already in 1789 Spaniards and Dutch—and North Americans—had learned to associate themselves with the glories of their state.

Italy might have seemed, in 1789, a rather unlikely site for a triumph of state-building based upon popular ideas of nationality. It had not been unified politically since the days of the Roman empire some fifteen hundred years before. It was in 1789, as it had been for three hundred years, largely dominated by powerful governments outside of the peninsula. Its local rulers were jealous of their small independence, and one of them, the Pope of Rome, could call for the defense of his freedom upon the conscience of half the Christian world. There was a wide discrepancy of origins and cultures among the peoples of Italy, most of whom did not even speak a common language. Cultivated persons (a tiny percentage) mostly spoke literary Italian, which was the Florentine dialect popularized and spread by writers since Petrarch first wrote in it. But such people usually spoke French with equal fluency. The rest of the country spoke local dialects (including, in some cases, Greek) which were mutually incomprehensible.

Moreover, the condition of the several parts was extraordinarily various. By 1789 the north, notably the independent kingdom of Sardinia-Piedmont, the Austrian province of Lombardy (the old duchy of Milan), and the Grand Duchy of Tuscany, were moving rapidly ahead with economic development and modern administrative systems. But central and southern Italy were backward and stagnant. The Kingdom of the Two Sicilies, especially, was unreformed and appeared unreformable. Sunk in illiteracy, poverty, and misgovernment, it had failed to respond to the effort of its kings. Half the land in the Two Sicilies was held by the Church and the other half by a retrograde nobility which composed one sixtieth of the population. The peasantry lived in sloth and squalor, frequently in caves, and paid all the taxes. They also paid archaic manorial obligations to the lords, including the obligation to allow the nobleman to choose peasant daughters as concubines and to collect regular deliveries of manure and rain water. There was no right of appeal from baronial to royal courts, a condition which had ended in northern Italy and most of Western and even Central Europe centuries earlier.

Nor was there in the peninsula in 1789 any very deep awareness of "Italianness," although there was ample abhorrence of foreign influences where they predominated—mainly Austrian in the north and Spanish in the south. The cultural and economic foundations for a deep sense of nationality were almost entirely lacking, and there was no political foundation for it at all. Not since Machiavelli in the sixteenth century had anyone spoken of "Italy" except as a geographical expression, like "Europe" itself.

But in the eighty years which followed, Italy was to be equipped with an almost excessive sense of nationality and with a highly centralized government. There was to be a blending of old-fashioned dynastic intrigues with the nationalistic enthusiasms of intellectuals, ably presented to the populace. The first and most evocative stages of this construction were accomplished, like so much else in the age, by the French Revolution and Napoleon.

THE FRENCH REVOLUTION
AND ITS AFTERMATH

For three hundred years the kings of France had been trying at intervals to conquer Italy. They had not succeeded in establishing more than temporary control over small areas. Republican France succeeded where the kings had failed, with dizzying speed. The war began in 1792; by 1799, after violent and confused campaigns, the French fiat ran from the Alps to Naples.

War in Italy had been prepared by French revolutionary penetration—what a hundred and fifty years later would be called a Fifth Column. After 1789, French agents and propaganda circulated in all the Italian states, preaching the blessings of liberty and the attractions of subversion. Even aristocrats dallied with extreme ideas along lines suggested by the philosophers of the Enlightenment with which Italy bristled.

By 1801 Napoleon had completed the French conquest of Italy. The order which Napoleon installed gradually took shape as a threefold division of the peninsula. In the north, Lombardy, the duchies, the eastern section of the papal states, and Venice were united to form a "Kingdom of Italy"—a name which was an omen. Piedmont, Genoa, Tuscany, and Rome were directly annexed to France. In the south, Naples became a French satellite ruled first by Napoleon's brother Joseph and later by his brother-in-law Joachim Murat. This state of things lasted until Napoleon's downfall and the victory of the Allies led to the almost complete reconstruction of the old regime, in 1815.

In the dozen or more years that "Napoleonic Italy" survived, however, very large changes took place, and these proved to be irreversible. There had been invasions and wholesale rearrangements of Italy before, but none had ever seriously affected the routine administration or the social structure of the country. Now, in large parts of the peninsula, the revolutionary system of France was installed, in the Kingdom of Italy and the Kingdom of Naples as well as the areas which had been annexed to France. Special privilege, local law, feudal obligations, manorial rights, all were swept aside. A modern centralized administration was established. Post offices, police forces, highway maintenance, tax policy, were operated from Paris, Milan, or Naples by a corps of bureaucrats supported by the French army. The legal position and way of life of the average person were drastically changed. Church lands and monastic foundations were vastly reduced. The Church lost its primacy in education and its rights to a separate court system of its own. Beneath—or above—all these changes ran the juridical reform, the application of the Code Napoléon—a legal system suitable for a modern society in which all men were equal before the law. It was the very antithesis of the old regime in Italy.

These were the stimulants which Napoleonic Italy provided to the activities of the next generation of Italians. But there were also goads, as there were wherever Napoleonic armies circulated outside of France. The Italians were not only edified by structural reforms; they were outraged by the depredations of foreign troops and the humiliation of seeing their land overrun by Frenchmen. Energetic and forward-looking Italians were learning that there were wholesome alternatives to the ramshackle and divided principalities of the old regime, but if they had little enthusiasm for their old rulers, they had none at all for the French invader.

They responded by organizing secret terrorist societies, to strike at the intruders, and discovered that for this kind of underground activity their people had a talent unparalleled in Europe. The societies proliferated, the most important of them being the *Carbonari* (the "charcoal burners"), who harassed the occupier and agitated for constitutions which would provide legal and popular control over the modern administration which the enemy had brought them.

By 1815, Napoleon was at last defeated and his satellite regimes in Italy had fallen. Austrian armies reoccupied the peninsula, bringing with them a following of displaced monarchs. Everything was turned back, so far as possible, to the situation of 1792. In Piedmont-Sardinia, indeed, the king upon his return decreed that every law and enactment passed since that date was invalid. The result was chaotic, and illustrative of the unreality of the restored Italian rulers. And against this wave of reaction, and its Austrian sponsors, the secret societies continued to agitate as strongly as ever they had against France. Their aim was a Jacobin Italy,—free of Napoleonic militarism and French dominance, as well as of old-regime reaction and Austrian dominance. In the days of frustration which followed, the genius of the secret societies kept alive the political aspirations of the Italian people and spread the gospels of revolutionary freedom and nationalism among them.

THE GENERATION OF FRUSTRATION:
1815–1848

The geography of Italy after Napoleon's fall was almost, but not quite, what it had been before 1792. Expediency and the self-interest of the powers required the rearrangement of some boundaries. In the south, the Neapolitan Bourbons reigned as before in the Kingdom of Naples, now again called the Kingdom of the Two Sicilies. In the center, the Pope reigned as before in the States of the Church. In the north, younger lines of the House of Habsburg reigned as before in Tuscany and Modena. But the republics of Genoa and Venice no longer existed: Piedmont-Sardinia had annexed the former, to acquire a seacoast and the second largest port on the Mediterranean, and the Austrian empire had added Venice to its Italian possessions. The tiny duchy of Parma had been bestowed, as a consolation prize for the throne of imperial France, upon Napoleon's wife, the former Archduchess Marie Louise, with the provision that upon her death it should revert to its previous dynasty, a branch of the Spanish Bourbons.

With these changes, the map of Italy resembled from 1815 to 1859 the map of Italy in the eighteenth century. Nor was there, in these years, any lasting change in the institutions of the region, with the exception of the kingdom of Piedmont-Sardinia, which will be discussed below. In 1859 autocracy, blended in some cases with feudalism and in others with theocracy, still persisted. Most of the princes showed no willingness to adopt reforms, even within the limits of absolute monarchy. Tuscany was the best governed of the Italian states: it had inherited the admirable system of its eighteenth-century enlightened despot, the Grand Duke Leopold. But in none of them except Piedmont was there anything in the way of imaginative or experimental leadership.

It was this curious immobility, perhaps, which encouraged the spread of revolutionary discontent in the thirty-three years after Napoleon's downfall. Good government, and a sense of movement toward something better, might have allayed the frustrations of the old regime. But whether it would have or not, one thing is amply clear: when the crises came, prematurely in 1848 and decisively in 1859, almost no one in Italy was prepared to fight on behalf of the old regime.

It is difficult to say just who were the militant fighters for change, or how numerous. The leaders are, of course, known today and revered by Italians, but their followers are less easily identified. There were the secret societies; there was the class known vaguely as "intellectuals" who were, almost to a man, agitators for change. There were the "middle classes," the progressive merchants and bankers of the north, who responded to the ideals of liberalism. But it is not clear how numerous they were.

If the extent of militant discontent was uncertain—Metternich, the Austrian chancellor, always believed that it was negligible and superficial—its character and aims were unclear and conflicting. The discontented were united on only one thing: the desirability of freeing Italy from foreign, that is, Austrian, control. Beyond that they agreed on nothing. No one was sure what "Italy" meant. Did it include the entire peninsula, and should good patriots strive for a united state? The answers were various. Most people thought in terms of a northern Italian state, including Lombardy, Venetia, Tuscany, the duchies, Piedmont, and part of the States of the Church. But very few thought it possible or desirable to extinguish the Papal States altogether, and even fewer envisaged the integration of the southern Kingdom of the Two Sicilies into an "Italy."

Nor did anybody agree on the way the freed territories should be organized. A good many of the most conspicuous agitators were Jacobin republicans of the most extreme sort. The most important of these were Garibaldi and Mazzini.

Mazzini was a northerner, a Genoese, a middle-class intellectual strongly influenced by the writers of the Enlightenment. He was a member of the *Carbonari*, imprisoned for terrorism in 1831 by the government of Piedmont and then exiled. He spent most of his exile in England, and his extensive political writings reflect a blending of British utopianism with French doctrinaire liberalism. He was an ardent republican, rejecting all the compromise proposals for a federated or monarchical Italy, including the one which eventually prevailed. He was, too, a free-thinker, regarding the Church and its doctrines with contempt. But he was, in his way, a mystic and a messiah whose message carried greater conviction for its intensity. Preaching republicanism and revolution first, he preached a united Italy second, and this second purpose met a warmer response. To the ideal of Italian unity he brought literary skill, passion, and deep humanitarian impulse which swayed his followers and readers into supposing that a love of mankind was somehow intimately connected with the existence of an Italian state.

Garibaldi was an altogether different sort of agitator. He was a tough soldier, a fighter in the brigand tradition. He was no philosopher and no doctrinaire. A republican by reflex, he was willing to sacrifice his political views to his ferocious patriotism.

There were other agitators during these years, of a more respectable and moderate kind. One of them, Gioberti, a priest and a Piedmontese politician, urged a federation of the Italian princes under the presidency of the Pope. It was a program unpopular among people who saw the Pope as one of the major targets of a reform movement, but it was accompanied by an infectious doctrine, the moral and intellectual superiority of Italians. Italy was in the end unified at the expense of the Church, not under its leadership, but Gioberti's dissemination of nationalistic ideas contributed vastly to the enthusiasm for an Italian state.

From 1831 on, writers like the great Massimo d'Azeglio were publicizing the evils of misrule in the States of the Church. Mazzini was organizing a movement, called Young Italy, and distributing an underground newspaper of that name. (In several parts of Italy, no newspapers at all were permitted by the authorities.) A quiet but ardent wave of organized opposition to the existing order was gradually spreading. It was met on every hand with the sternest repression; where local authorities appeared too lenient in their treatment of unrest and agitators, Metternich's agents were sent down to encourage them to greater strictness. The Austrian government was in a better position to know about sedition in Italy than everybody else, for all Italian mail passed through Vienna, where it was censored.

By the middle 1840's, the peninsula resembled a full kettle on the verge of boiling, with its lid held firmly in place by the hand of the Austrians. Ebullience amounting to obsession was noticeable everywhere, in trade journals and historical novels (including the major Italian literary masterpiece of the nineteenth century, Manzoni's *The Betrothed*), in plays and poems. All of these appealed openly or covertly to patriotic sentiment, and they drew a braver response each year. An animation, almost a violence, marked Italy's intellectual life; Italian intellectuals were becoming monomaniacs. The era which is proudly known in Italian history as the *Risorgimento*—the Resurgence—had begun.

These writers and workers in the cause, and many more, contributed powerfully to its fulfillment, and Garibaldi was to be responsible for the inclusion of southern Italy in the new kingdom. But the principal authors of Italy were not agitators but one of its kings and one of its ministers, Victor Emmanuel II and Count Cavour, of the kingdom of Piedmont-Sardinia. Their work did not commence until after the dramatic events of 1848, and we must next turn to the story of risings and revolutions which led up to that decisive year.

1848

Among the atomized parts of Italy, the kingdom of Piedmont-Sardinia was no less autocratic and no less repressive than the others in the years between 1815 and 1848. But its rulers displayed two characteristics which set it sharply apart from the other states: jealously independent of Austria, they were the only truly independent Italian princes; and within the limits of absolute monarchy they tried to develop the economy and prosperity of their small kingdom. These two aspects of Piedmontese policy suggested to many patriots that an Italian state, when one finally came into existence, might well be led and indeed constructed by Piedmont. The movement for "Italy" was urgently in need of responsible leadership; the attempt to achieve the goal by popular uprising had failed, and the force and dignity of a government and a dynasty were more and more clearly required. By exploiting the independence of Piedmont, and converting it into a sort of political and economic base of operations for the making of Italy, Piedmont's dynasty, the House of Savoy, secured for itself the crown of a great power, over which its descendants reigned until 1946. So was symbolized a combination of the old process of expansion and the new, the dynastic and the popular.

The kingdom of Piedmont was, however, negligible in power when compared to its great neighbors Austria and France. It consisted mainly of the upper Po valley—Piedmont proper—a rich and fertile region with a progressive agriculture, sourrounded by mountainous appendages. To the west and north lay Alpine Savoy, the cradle of the dynasty; to the south, rugged Liguria, with the great seaport of Genoa almost isolated by mountains from Piedmont, and the precipitous Italian Riviera extending south to La Spezia, another major port. Across the Tyrrhenian Sea was the remote, disease-ridden, and impoverished island of

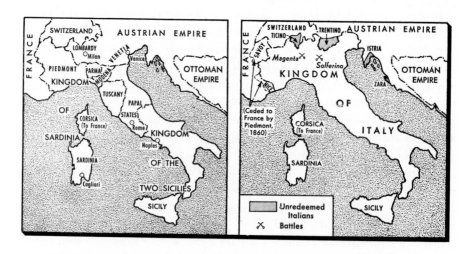

ITALY IN 1848   ITALY IN 1870

Sardinia. Obviously the king of so unpromising a country as Piedmont could not broadcast whatever ambitions he might possess to lead Italy to freedom.

He did not broadcast them, but King Charles Albert let it be known that he possessed such ambitions, and a vague movement or party gradually took shape among the fervent agitators and the more moderate reformers. They were called the *Albertisti,* and they looked to Piedmont, not to Rome (like Gioberti) or to a republic (like Mazzini) for guidance and hope. Interviewed by the Roman leader of the *Risorgimento,* d'Azeglio, Charles Albert gave a pledge: "Tell [the patriots] to keep quiet and not move, for at present there is nothing to be done: but they may be certain that if the opportunity comes, my life, the life of my sons, my resources, my wealth, my army, shall all be given for the cause of Italy." No one yet knew—or at least no one was yet agreed—on precisely what "the cause of Italy" might be. But at least it had a gallant sponsor.

The opportunity of which Charles Albert spoke began, strangely enough, as a result of a change of Popes. In 1846, Gregory XVI died and Pius IX was enthroned. Pius IX was regarded as being mildly reformist, and he gratified patriotic opinion by an unprecedented concession, a general pardon for all the numerous political offenders in his prisons. Then a new law was decreed permitting the appearance of newspapers and the formation of a people's Civic Guard. The effect of these reforms in the most conservative of the Italian states was electric. Pius became the popular hero of the hour, and there were parades and demonstrations in his honor all over Italy. The ice jam of Italian reaction seemed to be breaking at last; the authorities could hardly forbid demonstrations, however liberal and unwelcome, in the Pope's honor. As an alternative, the princes made concessions. Tuscany received a press (incredibly, Florence had not previously had any newspapers). There were reforms in Parma and Modena.

1848 was the year of revolutions, the "springtime of peoples" in Europe, and the Italians were first in the field, with a revolt in Sicily in January, which spread to Naples and forced the granting of a constitution on February 10. Tuscany followed with a constitution on February 17. Then came news of the February Revolution in Paris (February 22–24). Charles Albert of Piedmont-Sardinia, hurried by popular clamor, was next, with his constitution of March 4. It was modeled on the French constitution of 1830, and it was impeccably liberal, providing for a parliament elected by the well-to-do classes and an impressive Bill of Rights. Known as *Il Statuto,* the Piedmontese constitution of 1848 was to be the most honored document in Italian history. It was destined to become the constitution of the Kingdom of Italy, and, with changes, suspensions, and redraftings, it was to be the model and foundation of the constitution of the Italian Republic today.

Meanwhile, reform was changing to revolution throughout Italy and Europe. The March Revolutions had started in Budapest and Vienna (March 3 and March 12). Pope Pius granted constitutional concessions on March 14. The next day, in faraway Berlin, the Prussians rioted. On March 22 Austrian Venice proclaimed itself an independent republic, and the flag of Saint Mark floated once more over the city. The princes at Modena and Parma, finding constitutions and concessions insufficient, fled their countries. The Austrian garrisons were too weak to quell the spreading disorders. The "Five Days" uprising (March 18–22) drove them from Milan, and Lombard freedom was proclaimed. In Rome, a harassed Pius IX was led to utter the fateful invocation: *God Bless Italy.* If "Italy" could be blessed by the Pope, then it must exist, and throughout the peninsula patriots at long last set about its creation. A truly popular, undoubtedly eager, and deeply national movement had thrown the old order into disarray and toward destruction.

With the revolution in Vienna, Metternich had fled to England. But, unfortunately for the zealous Italian patriots, Austrian power was by no means broken. The Habsburgs had the good fortune to possess a commander of their Italian army, Prince Radetzky, who was skillful, loyal, and sensible. Although the Austrians had withdrawn from Milan, they were neither defeated nor disorganized. And against them the hastily summoned levies of patriotic amateurs could not hope to prevail. Neither could the armies of Charles Albert.

The king of Piedmont was in an extremely difficult position. Indecision in espousing the leadership of the patriot forces would cost him and Piedmont control of them; but militancy would bring him into war with Austria. He dared not hesitate for long. On March 22, 1848, as the Milanese drove Radetzky from their city, the Piedmontese declared war, crossed the frontier into Lombardy, and occupied most of the province. The Austrians withdrew, after trivial encounters, to reorganize, and for two months a military stalemate ensued. During these months, an "Italy" of sorts came into existence. The duchies—Modena, Parma, and Lucca—under their revolutionary governments, hastily voted to unite with Piedmont. It seemed to be only a matter of time before Austrian power, with revolution at its rear as well as its front, would collapse, and a united kingdom of the North—or possibly even a united Italy—could be formed.

The Austrians, however, were far from beaten. Radetzky was an abler general than Charles Albert, and his forces were better prepared. Reenforcements were at last forthcoming from Vienna, where order was being restored and a new, conservative government established. In late July, 1848, the Piedmontese and Austrian armies met in a decisive battle at the village of Custozza, near Verona, and the Piedmontese were badly beaten in the field. They fell back, evacuated Milan, and returned to their own soil. The Austrians rapidly reoccupied Lombardy and the duchies. The kingdom of North Italy ceased to exist.

Charles Albert surrendered to the Austrians and abdicated his throne. The victorious Austrians, within a matter of weeks, had reoccupied Venice and Florence, and the Habsburg double eagle waved in Milan. Everywhere the dukes and grand dukes were back. The great effort of a people to construct its own free nation had failed decisively.

Decisively, but not completely. There remained, in Turin, a new and energetic king of Piedmont and a still more energetic future minister, Count Cavour. There remained, too, *Il Statuto.* And there remained from 1848 the commitment of the House of Savoy to the leadership of a new Italy, and the exhilarating memory of Charles Albert's sacrifice of his throne and army in the cause.

CAVOUR AND THE MAKING OF ITALY

The Piedmontese statesman who now emerged and became—with his king, Victor Emmanuel II (1849–1878)—the maker of Italy, was wise enough to perceive two things: that the Piedmontese state must be developed into a model attractive to patriots, liberal enough to attract extremists but conservative enough not to repel moderates, strong militarily and economically, stable and well-governed; secondly, that Austria could never be expelled by Italians alone—the aid of powerful foreigners was necessary to the triumph of the cause. And Cavour was so skillful as a statesman that he was able to achieve these two purposes within a short span of ten years.

Camillo di Cavour (1810–1861) was a man of paradoxes: tough and shrewd, but passionate in his ideals; impetuous but cunning; tactful but recalcitrant; flexible, even opportunistic, but rigid in his purposes. The reforms which he undertook—loyally backed by Victor Emmanuel—and pushed through parliament converted Piedmont in ten years into the very pattern of a liberal state, free, progressive, and moderate, which made it seem Utopia to patriots of moderate inclinations. First, he believed in and efficiently operated a constitutional government and a bicameral legislature. There was, it should be noted, nothing *democratic* about Piedmontese liberalism—in that it contrasted strongly to the ideals of Garibaldi or Mazzini. The vote was restricted to a few tens of thousands of wealthy citizens, the parliament was composed of extremely substantial men, many of them noblemen, and the ministers were not explicitly declared "responsible" to the parliament, but were chosen and dismissed by the king. But the parliament established a tradition of orderly government, within an atmosphere of legally protected civil rights, which was both impressive and infectious.

Secondly, Cavour was a model liberal in his nationalism. He believed—and here he could agree with his rivals Mazzini and Garibaldi—that freedom meant not only freedom from autocracy but national freedom as well, freedom for all people of a nation to be governed by an independent government staffed and presided over by their own co-nationals.

Third, Cavour was a liberal in that he believed in equality before the law, in the abolition of old noble and manorial privileges, and in a centralized state where the *only* political authority should be exercised by agents of the central government acting in accordance with the decision of a national legislature and king.

Fourth, Cavour was a liberal in economic matters. He believed in, and installed, free enterprise and free trade. Like most nineteenth-century liberals, he tried (not with much success) to balance the budget and make the Piedmontese currency sound. Piedomontese commerce responded to these stimuli. In the 1850's the country was visibly progressing toward a modern and expanding economy.

Fifth, Cavour was, like many liberals, especially in Roman Catholic countries, anti-clerical. Like many other Italian nationalists of his age, he saw the Church as a bulwark of the old regime and an obstruction to the making of Italy, for Pius IX had been alarmed by the events of 1848; Rome now viewed nationalist ideas with distress, and the States of the Church were more conservative in their government than ever. Immediately after 1848, Piedmont embarked upon an anti-clerical policy, which led to the wholesale reduction of the numbers and influence of the clergy. The canon-law courts were abolished, the number of monastic orders reduced. The kingdom thus emphasized its hostility to the old regime and invited the support of radical opinion throughout the peninsula.

Cavour's domestic accomplishments were equalled, and even surpassed, by his handling of international affairs. It was clear from the beginning that outside help was necessary and that it must come from France and Great Britain. The latter could hardly be expected to play an active role in the ejection of Austria, but the British predilection for foreigners struggling to free themselves from oppression might, if supplemented by careful Piedmontese diplomacy, result in at least an attitude of benevolence toward the creation of Italy. From France much more was necessary. France—now ruled by Napoleon III—must furnish military assistance. But Napoleon III had promised his people peace. He had no special quarrel with Austria. And he was extremely pro-clerical in his policy, depending upon the support of the Church in France. Since 1848, French troops had been garrisoned in Rome, protecting the Pope from the republicans of the States of the Church. Napoleon III was not a very promising source of assistance.

The steps by which Cavour lured the emperor into a major European war for an objective which in no way served the interests of the Bonapartes or of France are long, obsure, and intricate. The major step was to get Napoleon III to commit himself to a war against Austria. He eventually did so, partly because of the persuasiveness of the Piedmontese prime minister, and partly because of his own somewhat whimsical sympathy for the ideals of "nationalism." He thought it would be suitable—harmonious—symmetrical—to have an Italy, and he thought it might be useful to have an Italy grateful to France and an Austria weakened and chastised. He thought that a few military victories would do his prestige no harm. And, most important, he believed (and Cavour cautiously let him believe) that the Italy they were talking about was the old kingdom of North Italy. Napoleon expected his war to end with a threefold division of the peninsula, the northern state, the States of the Church, and the Kingdom of Naples, and he expected that French influence would replace Austrian in all three.

Once Napoleon accepted the principle of a war against Austria, bargaining over details followed. In 1858 at a secret conference at Plombières, a spa in eastern France, Cavour and the emperor agreed upon an alliance. France would come to Piedmont's assistance if the latter found itself attacked by Austria. They also agreed that, in exchange, Piedmont should cede the partly French-speaking province of Nizza (the present city of Nice and its surroundings) and the duchy of Savoy to France. And Piedmont should also cede the king's eighteen-year-old daughter, Princess Clothilde, as bride for the Emperor's cousin, the disreputable thirty-seven-year-old Prince Napoleon. The emperor had some reason to think that he had made a good bargain, that he was replacing Austria as the overlord of Italy and getting paid for it. Things did not turn out that way.

The next thing for Cavour to do was to get Austria to attack him. To achieve this, he embarked upon a policy of provocation, the most important items of which were a large increase in army appropriations and the construction of several frontier fortresses, accompanied by sinister growls. The Austrians, who were under no illusions about the state of Italy by now, knew that the obliteration of Piedmont was the only thing that could save the old regime. They obliged by attacking Piedmont on April 26, 1859.

A great many things now began to happen all at once all over Italy, just as they had in 1848. As in that year, there were independent revolutions in most of the states at the same time as Austrian and Piedmontese troops were fighting a conventional war in the north. But this time there was one big difference: there were a hundred thousand French soldiers on the Piedmontese side.

On June 4, 1859, a decisive battle was fought at a village called Magenta. Austria was badly trounced, and the name of the village was immediately made part of the French language as jubilant Paris dressmakers applied it to a new shade of red which was supposed to resemble the color of the blood of the fallen heroes. Two weeks later, another victory was won at Solferino, near Mantua. The Lombard defenses were destroyed, the Austrian army routed.

At this point, the peculiar personality of Napoleon III, and his dubious sense of timing, intervened. Things were happening which he had not counted on. There had been revolutions—again—in Florence, Parma, Modena, and in some of the cities of the States of the Church. In these towns, liberal governments had been set up, and all of them had announced their intention of annexing themselves to Piedmont. The boundaries of "Italy" threatened to expand far, far beyond the intentions of the emperor. Moreover, Napoleon had been having his first prolonged experience on the battlefield, and if the Parisian dressmakers liked the color of blood, he did not. He was appalled by the carnage at Magenta and Solferino, and eager to end the bloodshed and the loss of his own Frenchmen. Without consulting the Piedmontese, he sent an emissary to the Austrian emperor and hastily negotiated the Peace of Villafranca, which was signed on the eleventh of July, 1859. By its terms, Lombardy was to be ceded to Piedmont, but Venice was to remain Austrian. Napoleon then went home, to be received as a hero in Paris.

Cavour was more than disappointed. He was certain he was betrayed. He had Lombardy, but Venice was withheld; his ally had failed him. He angrily resigned his office. All, however, was not lost, and Cavour shortly returned to power to bring triumph out of disaster. The Piedmontese, braving the threats of both Austria and France, accepted the wishes of the provisional governments in the duchies, in Tuscany and in the north Papal provinces, and they were attached to Piedmont. To safeguard these acquisitions, however, French approval was necessary. France would agree to the annexations in northern and central Italy (barring Venice) if Piedmont ceded Nice and Savoy. Reluctantly, the Piedmontese agreed. Plebiscites were arranged in all the areas concerned—Savoy, Nice, Parma, Modena, Tuscany and the northern Papal provinces. Those in Savoy and Nice were palpably fraudulent, but they met the legal requirements. The transfer was completed.

In the spring of 1860 it was still not clear what "Italy" was to be. An uneasy Bourbon still ruled in the Two Sicilies, and whether the Two Sicilies was really Italian was still an open question. The Pope, supported by the French garrison, still governed Rome and its province. It was hard to see how the center of Catholic Christendom could ever be safely attacked and integrated into Italy. Austria still ruled in Venice, and nobody was going to attack Austria again on behalf of Italy.

The first of these problems was solved, in an unexpected and dramatic way, by Garibaldi. The old radical fighter, covertly supported by Cavour, organized an old-fashioned filibuster against Sicily. He landed there with a thousand determined irregulars early in May of 1860, with the sympathy of the British navy, which covered his landings, and with military backing from Turin. On May 27, his little force defeated the royal army and entered Palermo, the Sicilian capital. In August he crossed the straits to the mainland and reached Naples. The king and queen fled, and their fleet and part of their army mutinied. By the end of August, most of the kingdom was in Garibaldi's hands.

Cavour hastily sent troops south. The eastern provinces of the Papal States—not Rome—were occupied, and the King of Italy and his army confronted Garibaldi on Neapolitan territory. The latter, in one of the great gestures of modern times, turned over to the king the country he had conquered. The tricolor of the House of Savoy now flew the length of the peninsula. The parliament, transferred from Turin to Florence, welcomed the southern deputies. "Italy" had become the Kingdom of Italy.

There remained outside of the kingdom a number of regions inhabited by Italians—"unredeemed Italy," they were called. The two most important were the provinces of Latium and Venetia, with their great capitals, Rome—the historic center of Italy—and Venice.

After 1860, the Austrian empire's army and prestige were badly battered. Austria was prey to indecision about its future organization, and was challenged in German affairs by its powerful German rival, Prussia. In 1866, Prussia attacked Austria. Piedmont, which for six years had been awaiting its chance to seize Venice, allied itself with Prussia. The Austrians succeeded—as they always succeeded—in defeating the Italians, but they were badly beaten by the Prussians. By the peace treaty, the Habsburg monarchy was forced to disgorge Venetia, which was immediately attached to the Kingdom of Italy.

The acquisition of Rome was impeded by two things, the sensitivity of Catholics throughout the world on the subject of the "temporal power," and the French garrison. The Temporal Power was now sadly reduced; the Kingdom of Italy had seized all of the States of the Church except Rome and Latium, the small province around it. But these were still enough to make the Pope a territorial sovereign, a status which was regarded by most of the Catholic world as indispensable to the independence and prestige of the Church.

The French troops offered a more material obstacle. They were there because domestic French political considerations made it essential for Napoleon III to appear in the guise of the Protector of the Church. But this substantial military force was withdrawn in 1870, during the Franco-Prussian War. The

Papal army, which was left, was impotent before the forces of the kingdom, which entered Rome in September.

The Catholic powers of Europe raised no protest against the Italian coup; they were occupied with the large issues of the Franco-Prussian War. But Pius IX protested. The Italian government made an effort to reach agreement. The parliament passed the Law of Papal Guarantees, by which the Vatican palaces and churches were to remain outside of the Kingdom of Italy, the Holy Father was to receive an annual grant, and the rights of the Church were to be respected. The Pope refused this offer from the government which had despoiled the Papacy. The pontifical throne was turned to the wall, and the Holy Father was declared to be the prisoner of the Italian state. The Temporal Power, usurped by the "cisalpine kingdom" (Pius IX, who had first used the word Italy in a political sense in 1848, now refused to utter it), was proclaimed essential to the welfare of Christianity and the independence of the Church.

Disregarding these plaints, and the outrage of the Catholic world, the government was transferred to Rome from Florence in June, 1871; the House of Savoy took up residence in the former Papal palace of the Quirinale. Once more, after fourteen hundred years, Rome became the capital city of a united Italy. The greatest force in nineteenth-century Europe, popular nationalism, had won a splendid victory.

31

THE MAKING OF
THE GERMAN
EMPIRE

MANY CHANGES had taken place in the Germanies in the centuries between the
Reformation and the outbreak of the French Revolution. Violence had been done
to the land by the long ordeal of the Thirty Years War, and to frontiers and
institutions by the incessant sparring for position of princes. The Hohenzollerns
had risen to contest the Habsburg influence. The Enlightenment had stirred
German intellectuals. Yet through all of these events the way of life changed
little within the boundaries of the old Holy Roman Empire, and the heterogeneity
which was Central Europe's fate and personality remained.

Between 1789 and 1870 Central Europe, from the Rhine east to the
Vistula, was transformed. On maps, diversity turned into unity. Germans awoke
to their Germanness, and fashioned a German state. A region which had been the
perennial victim of outside interference and internal schism became the strongest
power on the continent.

Within this imposing transformation in Central Europe a significant continuity is noticeable, however. German society, in spite of changes in the parts,
retained as a whole its traditional contours. Moreover, the dominant role in the
German drama was played by one remarkably stable institution, the Prussian
monarchy. The shocks to which it was subjected only temporarily changed its
nature, which remained true to its previous history and to its eighteenth-century
character. The Hohenzollern kings and their ministers continued to pursue with
great effectiveness their traditional policies of increasing the territories of the

state, enhancing the efficiency of the administration, strengthening the army, and resisting the meddling of all who sought to disrupt the power of the crown and army or the prosperity of the small group of squires upon which the kings depended for loyalty, solace, and support. In view of this remarkable stability and resilience, it was not surprising that Prussia should emerge, at the end of the period, the dominant power in Germany—a Germany in which the new and the old were curiously intermingled.

GERMANY IN 1789

The Holy Roman Empire still existed. The laurels of Augustus, Charle-magne, and the Hohenstauffen, now eighteen centuries old, were sadly withered, but a Caesar was still chosen by electors and crowned at Frankfurt-am-Main (see Chapter 15). As Holy Roman Emperor, he was supposed to command the allegiance of his fellow princes in Germany, but in point of fact the title was an empty one. The imperial institutions, while in some ways still impressive, were a skeleton. The real power in Germany lay entirely in the hands of the princes whose suzerain the emperor only theoretically was.

To most people raised in rationalist traditions, the German states in 1789 presented a picture of awful asymmetry. Within the boundaries of the Empire there were three hundred or more different states. They were of all sorts, sizes, and shapes. The largest, and the most powerful, was Austria. Then, proceeding down-ward in size and importance, there were the lands of the king of Prussia (scat-tered here and there throughout Germany) and of the electors of Saxony, Han-over, and Bavaria. Then came a fantastic assortment of grand-duchies, duchies, and principalities, archbishoprics, bishoprics, and provostships, free cities and towns; and finally the diminutive holdings of the knights. Some of these "states" were no more than large farms. Others were fairly respectable modern countries, like Saxony or Hanover. But in matters of law, currency, taxes, weights and measures, there was, naturally, chaos. The cost was high in duplication of courts, armies, and officials, in economic stagnation fostered by miniature tariff systems, in military weakness aggravated by internal rivalries.

It should be remembered that while many of these same conditions had been alleviated in France by the rise of a unifying absolutism, in some respects a not entirely dissimilar situation still existed in France on the eve of the great revolution. *Political* disunity in Germany was less conspicuous in a time when *administrative* disunity was still general, even in France. But the needs of the times, and the tides of opinion, were running strongly against such conditions. Some parts of Europe, such as Tuscany and Portugal and Prussia itself, had been greatly tidied up by their enlightened despots in the past few years. And against the administrative disorder of France the French nation had already begun its large and dramatic assault.

Strong forces, however, worked to preserve the anachronism east of the

Rhine. One was external pressure. The powers of Europe, and the stronger states within the Holy Roman Empire, would not allow each other to swallow the lesser and thereby upset the religious and military balance. Then, too, there was inertia—people were genuinely attached to the old order and to their local dynasties and institutions. The little German courts, generally dowdy and dull, were sometimes the cradles of brilliant intellectual life. Many of the great names of late eighteenth-century Germany were nourished by the patron-princes of tiny states—most famous was the Duke of Saxe-Weimar, at whose miniscule imitation of Versailles the genius of Goethe had flowered. If most states were autocratic, aristocratic, and oppressive, some were oases of freedom and close personal relations between ruler and ruled. Furthermore, the Germans were still mainly farmers, and much of the country was remote from the world of international trade in goods and ideas. Through the hills and mountains of the south, on the sandy plains of the east, and in the fertile, rolling country of central Germany, peasants and landlords tended to live out their lives undisturbed by any consideration more abstract than the weather.

In its diversity and ripe age the Holy Roman Empire in 1789 appeared impervious to anything short of an earthquake of continental proportions. This is precisely what was provided by the French Revolution.

THE FRENCH REVOLUTION
AND NAPOLEON

Into this scene, archaic and generally peaceful, erupted the armies of the French republic, and later of Napoleon.

The war broke out in 1792, when revolutionary France abolished the medieval rights and privileges of German princes who held lands in Alsace and Lorraine, on its eastern border. Tension had been mounting between the German states and France before that time, for the German rulers were deeply alarmed by the course of the revolution and their concern was fostered by the *émigré* French noblemen who had taken refuge in their courts. In general the main struggle was carried on by the Austrians and Prussians, who were fighting the French at intervals throughout the next twenty-three years. The smaller rulers, playing their traditional game of catch-as-catch-can, allied with all parties to the war, or remained neutral.

What happened, in its simplest form, was that France on several occasions invaded Germany, annexed parts of it and occupied other parts. Beginning in 1801, when all the German regions west of the Rhine were added to France, the smallest of the German states, the knightly and churchly principalities, began to disappear. They were obliterated in the Rhineland regions, where the holdings of knights were most numerous, and where Napoleon created a confederation of the larger states, the Confederation of the Rhine. To the east, other princes took the occasion to seize knightly or ecclesiastical states. Most of the free cities also disappeared into the territories of more powerful princes. By 1806, the whole strange character of the Holy Roman Empire had been so altered that what had been vestigial became preposterous. In that year, the Emperor Francis II renounced the title of Holy Roman Emperor. The most ancient secular dignity in Europe disappeared.

In the areas of Germany which were annexed to France, revolutionary institutions were imposed wholesale—the modern, centralized administration, the Napoleonic Code, the abolition of legal class distinctions, the destruction of seigneurial rights and dues, the dispossession of the Church from its property. To other areas in Germany revolutionary ideas and institutions were carried, in less pure form, by Napoleon's army. This wholesale remodeling of the German states took place in an odd form in Prussia. The Hohenzollern kingdom was brought to the lowest point in its fortunes after the military disaster at Jena in 1806. Its territories were reduced by more than half, its military power was broken. But the Prussians demonstrated their usual resilience, and in the end they emerged from the Napoleonic era stronger than ever. This recovery was in part due to the decisions of the peace-makers after Napoleon's downfall, but part of it was due to the efforts of the Prussians themselves, while the wars were still in progress. A very talented group of statesmen in the state service in Berlin were responsible for reforms which equipped Prussia with a new army and new institutions.

The most eminent was Baron Stein, who became chief minister after Jena. He saw clearly the need for reorganizing Prussia if the kingdom were to survive in an age of revolution. In 1807, he supported a law which abolished serfdom in Prussia. It ended other archaic prohibitions as well, which had forbidden city-dwellers to buy land, or noblemen to engage in business. Later, labor services which the peasant was obliged to perform for his lord were also partly abolished. Simultaneously, military reforms were being carried out by two army leaders, Scharnhorst and Gneisenau. Promotion by merit was introduced, along with improved training for officers. Universal military service for all male citizens was introduced in 1814. Another of the reforms of the period of regeneration was the founding in 1809 of the University of Berlin, whose professors contributed to a growing spirit of national pride. One of them was the philosopher Fichte, originally from Saxony, who delivered, in 1807–1808, a series of *Addresses to the German Nation* which celebrated the uniqueness and value of the German nationality.

Germany, in the late eighteenth century, had been proving itself capable of producing a characteristic thought and culture of its own. The French cultural domination which had been so pervasive in Europe since the era of Louis XIV was coming to an end. This German movement represented a form of romanticism, as opposed to the classicism and rationalism associated with the preceding century of French cultural predominance. German romanticists, while differing on many points, stressed history, evolutionary growth, and the organic nature of societies, and so lent their ideas to the construction of conservative political philosophies. They also gave impetus to studies of language, literature, folk tales, popular music, and other manifestations of the culture of peoples, from which it was but a step to a celebration of nationality like Fichte's, and thence to nationalism.

Throughout Germany, the French invader had provoked an opposing pride in nationality, which played its part in Napoleon's defeat. Prussia was reinvigorated. In the west, new institutions and ideas had taken root. The Holy Roman Empire was gone forever. A new Germany had been born, and was soon to grow to maturity.

THE CONGRESS OF VIENNA

Napoleon was at length defeated and exiled, and the chiefs of state of the Allied countries which had destroyed him charted at the Congress of Vienna a new form for Germany. None of their representatives in 1814–1815 had the slightest inclination to restore the situation as it had been before 1789. The dispossessed princelings swarmed like flies at Vienna, but the Allies brushed them aside. Instead, the following considerations dictated the decisions about what to do with Germany.

(1) The most essential aim of the peace negotiations was to achieve peace, and this meant in the first instance the restraint of future French impulses to conquer Europe. It was necessary to have a first-rate military power on France's eastern frontier, to contain French aggression. To achieve this, most of the German territory west of the Rhine was given to Prussia, overwhelmingly the strongest military power in northern Germany. Prussia could thus garrison and defend the western German frontier. There were some people who wondered about the wisdom of giving Prussia so strong a foothold in the west and so vastly expanding its territory. There were some conservatives in Prussia who disliked the addition of western populations who might alter and submerge the essential Prussianness of the country, but they were not heeded.

(2) It was not, however, merely France which might threaten the peace. There was the possibility of scuffles among the German states themselves, and between German states and Russia. The sorting out of ambitions and claims among the victorious powers was even more difficult than the containment of France. Prussia, for example, wanted to annex Saxony, whose king had been a close ally of Napoleon. Prussia was willing to go along with Russia's taking of the Grand Duchy of Warsaw, with compensation to Prussia in Saxony and to Austria in Italy. In the end, after much maneuvering by Austria, Britain, and France, Russia got only part of Poland, and Prussia only part of Saxony.

(3) The interests of Austria, the most powerful of German states and the most influential of the victorious Allies, must be safeguarded and enhanced. The Austrians, whose territories were predominantly inhabited by non-Germans, were not anxious to see the new German national spirit reflected in any kind of centralized state for Germany, and in this they were naturally supported by the other German rulers. On the other hand, it seemed necessary to placate the new national consciousness by replacing the Holy Roman Empire with some more plausible over-all German organization (which could also serve as a forum

for Austrian leadership). Accordingly, a German Confederation was created, with its seat at Frankfurt. It was in some ways similar to the old Empire. The diet consisted of representatives of the various governments. There were no arrangements for defense, trade, or federal courts. There was an article calling for representative assemblies in the member states, but this provision was to be largely ignored. But the Confederation differed markedly from the Holy Roman Empire. The number of constituent states was much smaller, and all of them were secular—the ecclesiastical principalities had disappeared. The head of the Confederation was no longer an emperor (the title of caesar, or kaiser, having been preempted by the Austrian rulers to describe their own hereditary position) but a president. The president, however, was to be the Austrian kaiser; The head of the Habsburg family, instead of being Archduke of Austria and Holy Roman Emperor, was now called Emperor of Austria and President of the German Confederation.

(4) The French Revolution had meant, for the leaders of Europe, nothing but wars and bloodshed, and they naturally thought of revolutionary ideas as leading to trouble. They accordingly agreed to do everything they could to prevent the sort of free conditions in Germany which would permit revolutionary agitation to get started again. This meant, in practice, the restoration of absolute monarchy and a stern repression of subversive ideas wherever they appeared.

So Germany entered the postwar world greatly changed from 1789. The Confederation resembled the shadowy Holy Roman Empire but was secular and less complicated. There was now a vastly expanded Prussian kingdom, whose future seemed to lie to the west instead of to the east as in the eighteenth century. There were sensibly expanded smaller kingdoms of Bavaria and Württemberg. There were thirty-eight states instead of three hundred twenty-four. There were, at least in western Germany, large areas with advanced legal and administative systems; in a few regions the landlord class had been dispossessed and its lands distributed to the peasants. There was, in spite of the Vienna settlement, a lively consciousness in some circles of the advantages of free institutions. And in many circles there was eagerness to create a more effective political union of Germans.

Almost the only things which were not changed were the predominance of the House of Habsburg in German affairs and the essential structure and character of the kingdom of Prussia.

YEARS OF REPRESSION: 1815–1848

For thirty-two years after the Congress of Vienna, no substantial alteration took place in this structure. The princes, with few exceptions, ruled with the vigorous determination of maintaining absolute monarchy and the existing order. In this they were heavily backed by the chancellor of Austria, Metternich, whose advice, warnings, and counsel were an inspiration and bulwark to the princes in their conservative policies.

Metternich's main concern continued to be, as it had been at Vienna, the prevention of any recurrence of revolutionary agitation which might threaten law and order and peace. From his point of view Jacobinism—political ideas and movements connected with revolutionary France—was the foremost threat to stability in Europe and in the multinational Habsburg monarchy. Accordingly, its appearance in Germany (as in Europe generally) was regarded as a subject for international concern and action. At international congresses held at Troppau and Laibach in 1820–1821, for example, the German princes were exhorted (and agreed) to suppress such political movements, and the kind of civil liberties which permitted them to develop. Among the most alarming ideas from the point of view of Metternich and the princes were those which aimed at the creation of a unified German state. German nationalism, they thought, could never achieve its purposes without a drastic and violent reorganization of every institution and boundary in Germany—the very sort of thing which would create new disorders and probably new wars. So when the students of various German universities began organizing fraternities (*Burschenschaften*), whose principal purpose was to encourage German nationalism, Metternich lectured the Prussian king upon their dangers and secured agreement in the diet of the Confederation to the issuance in 1819 of the Carlsbad Decrees which, in the name of internal security, abrogated academic freedom and placed severe restrictions upon all universities.

The more intelligent of the princes were not wholly inflexible; they realized that a pig-headed reaction might produce the very results they most feared. Several of them during this period found it prudent to issue constitutions, among them the kings of Bavaria, Württemberg, and Hanover, and the Grand Duke of Baden. Generally speaking, however, from 1815 to 1848 no major changes were made in political institutions and new ideas of all sorts were hounded and repressed—or rather: hounded but not repressed. The revolutions of 1830 in France and Belgium were accompanied by unrest and disorders in some of the German states, but the diet of the German Confederation, pressured by Austria and Prussia, responded with rules against political associations and public festivals. In the 1840's, however, the climate in Germany changed. There was a new king in Prussia, Frederick William IV, who dallied with a brand of fashionably romantic conservatism, and who was emotional and optimistic and seemed to be a German nationalist. In the eighteen-forties, moreover, railroads and bigger towns and the building of factories began to transform Germany. There was as yet nothing like the British Industrial Revolution, and Germany was still overwhelmingly rural. But there was a change—enough to produce a few big capitalist manufacturers and the beginnings of a proletariat in the growing towns. Along with the moderate liberalism of the middle class businessmen, university professors, and civil servants, there was a shading off into democratic and republican and even socialist ideas. Karl Marx, who had been born in 1818, was a young radical from Rhenish Prussia.

One major change did take place. The Prussian ministers, even at the height of the conservative reaction, were showing their concern for eliminating some of the more offensive features of disunity, and they sponsored a series of customs unions, called the *Zollverein*.

The *Zollverein* was a work of Prussian initiative in a field where the diet was supposed to act and did not. It became in fact a step toward German unity, but was not begun for political purposes. In 1818 Prussia unified its own sixty-seven tariff areas. Between 1819 and 1834 most of the other German states joined. Prussia became the spokesman for the tariff union and the negotiator with other countries as well as the leader in a move toward common coinage and commercial law for the members. Austrian efforts to join the *Zollverein* came to nothing. It became apparent that Prussian efficiency and leadership had gained prestige, and that the Prussians meant to keep the Austrians out. Commercially, a Germany already was coming into existence.

A partial economic union of conservative princes of course gave no satisfaction either to those who were sentimentally eager for a German national state, or to those who disliked the illiberal institutions of the princes, or to those (still very few) who disliked the hierarchical structure of German society and longed for a day of social equality for all and special protection for working class people.

1848

In 1848 a second shattering period of revolution struck Germany, as it did most of Europe. No state and no institution of Germany remained untouched. But the period of turmoil was brief—one or two years. This revolutionary period, unlike that after 1789, ended without any very great outward change in the structure of the country. Almost everything seemed to have been put back where it was. But the consequences of 1848, while subtle, were by no means negligible. The liberal reforms inaugurated by Napoleon in western Germany were completed. There was disillusionment and in many cases emigration of people who had hoped that a united and democratic Germany could be brought into existence by spontaneous popular action against the princes. A third change, much less noticeable at the time but important later, was the creation of a rough pattern for a federal Germany. The belief also grew that Prussia must be the leader in German unification and that this end might have to be achieved through the permanent exclusion of those parts of Germany which lay within the Austrian empire. Another change, which appeared very important to people in 1850, was the existence of a Prussian constitution providing for representative government. This seemed to augur the growth of a Prussia radically changed into a liberal monarchy. But this change was to prove illusory.

The revolutions of 1848 in Germany are exceedingly intricate, and a narrative account of them is impossible. There were, in effect, several dozen revolutions, each of which influenced the others. Most of the separate German states experienced uprisings of some sort. There was in addition a *national* German uprising which sought not to reform existing institutions but to create new ones for the whole country.

The largest and most complicated of the revolutions in the separate states took place in Austria (see Chapter 29). It was matched by a much simpler revolution in Prussia, the course of which can be dealt with briefly. At the beginning of March, in the Prussian Rhineland areas, most accessible to the stirring news from Paris, disturbances occurred among working class groups. There was a general economic depression in Europe in 1848, whose hardships contributed powerfully to the revolutionary temper. Unrest spread in the capital. Crowds rioted. The king, Frederick William IV, was urged by some of his advisors, as well as by popular clamor, to dismiss his conservative ministry and to grant a constitution. Thoroughly alarmed, he acceded on March 18 to the demands of the deputations of the people. A Prussian parliament was to be called, and a ministry of liberals was installed.

The history of the Prussian revolution now ends, and counter-revolution —to be protracted over many years—begins. The authority of the liberal ministry was never very great, and many of the earlier supporters of the revolution had become alarmed by the extremely articulate (although very few) red socialists who threatened to use the political changes as an entering wedge for social revolution. Moreover, the country people remained in general conservative—the revolution had been made in Berlin and the Rhineland cities. The army and the aristocracy, never wavering in their loyalty to the old order, exercised their influence on the crown to lure Frederick William into withdrawing from his rash promises of reform.

The Prussian National Assembly actually met and drew up a constitution—more conservative than had been expected. But while it was in the formative process, the liberal ministers were dismissed, and the monarchy, army, and bureaucracy began to take over the exercise of power. The constitution provided for a two-house legislature, whose lower house, the *Landtag*, was to be elected by a broad franchise. But scarcely had the constitution been composed when the authorities felt strong enough to enforce its amendment. Under the amended franchise, from 1850 until 1918, the "popular" chamber of the Prussian parliament was elected on the basis of the "three-class system." To oversimplify a very complicated system of indirect elections, this meant that the voting public was divided into three groups, according to the amount of taxes they paid. That group (a very small number of very well-to-do subjects) which paid one third of the taxes elected one third of the deputies. The group which paid the second third of the taxes elected the second third of the *Landtag*. The great mass of the people, who paid the last third, also elected a third of the deputies. The wealthy were thus greatly overrepresented in the lower chamber.

The *Landtag*, in spite of its curious franchise arrangements, nonetheless usually contained a large plurality of liberals. More serious a handicap to parliamentary government than the franchise, at least at the time, was the uncertainty as to its powers. It was assumed at first that the *Landtag* majority could control the policies of the government-appointed ministers. In the end it turned out that they could not, as will be shown later.

In most of the other German states, a similar course of events took place. Liberal ministries were appointed in all the major capitals, and constitutions were promulgated in places where they did not exist. They were extensively liberalized in other places. Moreover, in most of the western and southern states, a measure of social readjustment took place, notably in the abolition of seigneurial rights and the distribution of land to peasants in places where this had not already been done in the Napoleonic period. The distribution was often made on rather onerous terms for the peasant, but in every case it proved permanent. Indeed, a great many of the constitutional and social changes in Baden, Württemberg, and Bavaria, the three big south German states, proved permanent. From 1848 on, to 1918, these states—along with various others in other parts of Germany—proceeded steadily along the path toward democratic institutions. By 1900 the government of, for example, Bavaria resembled that of Great Britain or Belgium very closely in most of its major elements. This development was in sharp contrast to the situation in Austria or Prussia.

The *national* German revolution was destined for a drearier end than that of the German states, even of Prussia where at least a form of constitutionalism survived. The movement to replace the old Confederation with a united Germany in 1848–1849 broke down completely. Its breakdown was significant, for it left a vacuum in Germany which had to be filled from some other source than the efforts of liberal politicians. It was the only effort in German history at the creation of a national government by popular action and not by sovereigns, dictators, or armies. Its failure marked the end of genuine popular initiative in any sphere of German political life for many years.

At the height of the revolutionary agitation in the separate states, a self-appointed council of citizens met in Frankfurt, the ancient imperial capital, and drew up plans for an election of an all-German parliament. Such was the revolutionary ferment at the moment that the state governments cooperated with this election, which was held on May 1, 1848. The National Assembly so elected consisted of a heavy majority of intellectuals and amateur politicians. It met on May 18 and set about the business of drawing up a constitution for a united Germany.

The work was naturally lengthy, since there was no real precedent and no agreement among the members. On all the various decisions which had to be made, there was extensive disagreement. The most important of these issues were as follows.

(1) The relative role of Austria and Prussia. Austria, being only partly German, could not be included *in toto* in a German state, and most Austrians objected to the proposal that the empire be divided in order to accommodate the new nation. On the other hand, most of the other deputies were unwilling to envisage a Germany with the Austrians excluded and without the traditional leading German dynasty, the House of Habsburg. This complexity is dealt with in Chapter 29.

(2) The position of peripheral lands, traditionally included in "Ger-

many" but not occupied exclusively by Germans. Such areas as Prussian Poland, Austrian Bohemia, Luxemburg, and the Danish duchies of Schleswig and Holstein, caused difficulties. Some deputies hesitated to impose a German national state upon the Poles, Danes, or Czechs; others, highly expansionist, insisted upon it.

(3) The structure of the new state. Was it to be, as the more advanced liberals demanded, democratic and parliamentary? Or was it to be conservative?

On these points, and many others, the deputies at Frankfurt wrangled endlessly. At long last, a document was painfully produced. It was roughly patterned on the federal constitution of the United States and provided for a democratically elected parliament. The federal union was to be headed by a German emperor. A number of state governments accepted the draft (not including Austria), and the deputies elected the king of Prussia as emperor on March 28, 1849.

Frederick William was now restored to most of his former poise and power, and he was in no way inclined to do business with the revolutionaries at Frankfurt. He regarded their proceedings as illegal and was, like most of the other princes, appalled at the idea of a Germany which excluded the House of Habsburg. He coldly informed the delegation which offered him the imperial crown that he could not accept a position offered by popular vote unhallowed by dynastic approval.

With this blow, the Frankfurt parliament began to break up. The Prussians proposed a more conservative plan for unity, but under Austrian (and Russian) influence it was abandoned at a meeting of the Austrians and Prussians at Olmütz in 1850. The old diet was restored, and German aspirations were unsatisfied. For a while at least the old order persisted throughout Germany.

But national enthusiasm had received a great spark, even though liberalism had suffered a defeat. While the particular form and method in which unity was sought in 1849 had failed, the German appetite for unity was merely whetted. And nationalism of a more flamboyant kind, expansionist and exuberant, had had a wide public hearing in the speeches of the chauvinist politicians at Frankfurt. From now on it became apparent that some form of national state was widely demanded and, for economic and administrative reasons, needed. The clock which had been wound up in the Napoleonic age could not now be set back.

THE RISE OF BISMARCK

For a decade after the revolutions of 1848, no progress toward unification took place. After 1860, however, the situation began to change rapidly. Frederick William, overcome by his morbid indecisiveness, had gone mad in 1857, and in 1861 he died and was succeeded by his brother, William I. William was not one of the leading intellects in his country, but he was entirely sane, and he possessed firmness of character and a sense of realities in about equal quantities. Moreover, his accession coincided with the unification of Italy. This was important in Germany for two reasons: for one thing, it greatly stimulated the appetite of the nationalists; more important, it was accomplished by the defeat and routing of Austrian armies and the loss of Habsburg influence in Italy. The result was a decline of prestige for the Habsburg monarchy—and a simultaneous tendency for Vienna's statesmen to concentrate on setting their internal affairs in order and for other German governments to pay less attention to Austrian wishes in German affairs.

Moreover, a major political crisis was beginning to develop in Prussia which was to end with the preservation of the traditional authority of the Prussian state over its parliament and to provide the kingdom with a leader of extraordinary character and skill. A difference of opinion over military organization and the budget arose in 1861. The government and the army and the crown were determined to increase the size and power of the standing army and to eliminate the people's militia, which they regarded as militarily inadequate and politically dangerous. The parliament, which contained a majority of liberal and progressive deputies, was equally determined to assert its power to control the finances of the state and to impose its policy on the army and the king. A constitutional deadlock ensued.

It was broken in 1862 by the king's appointment of Otto von Bismarck as prime minister. Bismarck, already forty-seven years old, was an experienced Prussian diplomat, and was in some respects a representative member of the eastern Prussian gentry, the *Junkers*. He had a reputation for obstinate conservatism, and his appointment was regarded by German and Prussian liberals almost as a declaration of war. Moreover, his first action appeared to justify his reputation. He merely announced that the measures decided by the army and government, and opposed by the parliament, would be carried out. The necessary taxes were decreed and collected. The wishes of the *Landtag*, the Chamber of Deputies, were disregarded.

The Prussian Government was now returned to its traditional path: authority and prestige were concentrated in the hands of the king— and of the army, and the civil service, which, being recruited in large part from the old eastern gentry, were as loyal as they were efficient. The constitution, while still on the books, was a shadowy fiction. As a consequence, German nationalists were faced with a dilemma. Many of them were liberal—they wanted a German state which would be constitutional and parliamentary, with the rights of the individual protected and glorified. But a German state, it was increasingly clear, could be achieved only with Prussian leadership, and Prussia was the reverse of a constitutional and parliamentary government now. But no one could deny that it was an efficient and vigorous government, nor that it enjoyed the loyalty of most of its subjects. And few patriotic Germans, no matter where they lived, could resist a feeling of pride in Prussia's great tradition or in the skill of its armies. They were prepared to acclaim Bismarck, Prussia's prime minister, when he embarked upon the unification of Germany.

THE WARS OF UNIFICATION

It is not clear, and it never will be, whether Bismarck at the beginning of his premiership had in mind a blueprint for the empire which was to be created. It is possible to interpret his actions in the 1860's—and later— in terms either of an almost superhuman and clairvoyant Plan or of opportunistic juggling with no very clear idea of the ultimate outcome, or even of the next stage of action. But whichever viewpoint is espoused, the events of the years 1863 to 1870 remain exceedingly confusing. Indeed, it may be said that Bismarck made them as confusing as possible in order to baffle his opponents. All sorts of things happened at once. But certain considerations remained clear. It was necessary to secure and maintain a level of German national enthusiasm which would cause liberals to forget their grievances about Bismarck's highhandedness. It was also necessary to give some indication to the politically articulate among Germany's lower classes that they would gain from the changes that were taking place. It was no less necessary to secure as much support as possible from Prussian conservatives by assuring them that no basic change would take place in the institutions of Prussia. Outside, it was necessary to eliminate Austria as a competitor for leadership in German affairs. It was necessary to insure that foreigners would not meddle in Germany, as they had been meddling for years whenever the German situation began to change. To achieve this end, France and Russia, the chief meddlers, must be conciliated and held off.

THE UNIFICATION OF GERMANY, 1866–1871

In 1863, a revolution against Russian rule took place in the Polish provinces of Russia. Bismarck, motivated not only by a desire to win the Russians
but also by a natural dislike of Polish nationalism (Prussia contained many
square miles of ex-Polish territory) abetted and congratulated the czar on his
success in repelling the insurrection. He thereby annoyed all the liberals in
Europe but won the undying friendship of the Russian government.

In 1864, the Liberal party of Denmark forced the Danish king to try to
modernize and centralize the institutions of the country. This involved abolishing the semi-independent regimes in two of his provinces, Schleswig and Holstein, which were largely German-speaking, and making them an integral part
of the Danish state. The diet of the Confederation, and public opinion in Germany, urged action to prevent the Danish king's abolishing the separate status
of "the Duchies." The Austrian and Prussian governments decided to cooperate
in defending the interests of the Germans. Denmark was defeated in the brief
war of 1864, and the duchies were detached from the Danish crown altogether.
They were to be made into German states, and pending their final disposition
they were to be jointly administered by Austria and Prussia.

The Austrians and Prussians disagreed on the settlement of the duchies,
and each power accused the other of unsuitable and illegal action in the affairs
of the provinces. Bismarck was planning a showdown between the two great
German powers whose co-existence in German affairs had been for so long a
time so grave a barrier to German unity. Once more, he was at pains to secure
freedom from outside trouble. He went to France and had a little talk with
Napoleon III in 1865, in which he received a pledge that France would not
intervene in German affairs in return for a rather vague promise of support for
French annexation of the Grand Duchy of Luxemburg. With the Italians he
next negotiated a secret agreement that, in case of an Austro-Prussian war the
Italian army would attack Austria and would receive, in the event of victory, the
much longed-for province of Venetia.

Tensions in Schleswig-Holstein were mounting rapidly. The Austrians,
convinced that Bismarck was intending to annex the duchies to Prussia, requested
the other German states for military aid in a campaign to force Prussia to obey the
law of the Confederation. Most of the German states, also alarmed by Bismarck's
activities, agreed. With some difficulty, Bismarck and his generals convinced
William I that the time had come for a showdown with Austria. In June of 1866,
the peculiar conflict called the Seven Weeks War broke out between Prussia
and most of its fellow-members in the German Confederation.

In the course of the fighting Prussia showed how rapidly its army had
outdistanced those of all the other German countries. By a skillful use of modern
weapons and modern means of transport, and by its admirable generalship, the
Prussian army inflicted a decisive defeat on the Austrians at the Battle of Sadowa
on July 3. Austria, harassed by the Italians, was quite unable to contemplate
further hostilities; without its support, the other German states were helpless.
On August 23, at Prague, a peace treaty was signed. The Italians got Venetia,
but the Prussians took no territory from the vanquished major enemy. Instead,
Prussian territorial ambitions were satisfied by a wholesale gobbling up of the

smaller north German states which had fought against Prussia in fulfillment of their obligations under the Confederation. Several minor cities and duchies were annexed, and so was the second largest north German state, the Kingdom of Hanover. Prussia was now overwhelmingly the biggest country in Germany, and its territories stretched unbroken from the Russian border and the Baltic to the North Sea, Holland, and the French frontier.

Prussian opinion was frenziedly enthusiastic. Nationalistic feeling, at least in the north, ran higher than ever before. Bismarck took the occasion to make a final peace with the affronted liberals, sulking since 1863; he apologized to the *Landtag* for his highhanded action in that year, and the *Landtag* in return by an overwhelming majority voted to forgive him his past faults, and by implication to support him unreservedly in the future.

Now that Austria was disposed of, excluded at last from German affairs, Bismarck could set about unifying the nation. The old Confederation was at last dead. A constitution for a north German state was drawn up. Since there was little left in north Germany except Prussia (plus the satellite kingdom of Saxony, the free cities of Hamburg, Bremen, and Lübeck, and a few grand duchies and principalities which ranged from the unimportant to the invisible), the North German Confederation, as it was called, was almost entirely a Prussian affair. The king of Prussia was to be president; the all-powerful head of the administration, the chancellor, was to be the president's personal appointee. The powerful upper house represented the federated states, on the basis of relative size; Prussia, naturally, swamped the others. The lower house, the *Reichstag*, with powers of budgetary control and with the right to approve or disapprove all projects for laws, was to be elected by universal manhood suffrage—so winning the support of democrats and progressives and counterbalancing the particularism of the princes. It was a dazzling concession to advanced opinion, although it never led to the development of the democratic Reichstag as the controlling element of the federation.

The new confederation came into existence in 1867. A German state, wholly dominated by Prussia but leaving the component members with their dynasties and constitutions unchanged, now existed. There remained outside of it, in addition to Austria, the three south German states: the kingdoms of Bavaria and Württemberg and the Grand Duchy of Baden. Each of them had strong local traditions and a considerable feeling for independence, and Bavaria was staunchly Catholic, in contrast to the Confederation, which included a large majority of Lutherans, and which was dominated by the staunchly Protestant Prussian king and aristocracy. It was difficult to see how these southern states could either be absorbed into the confederation or could maintain themselves outside of it.

The problem of the "completion" of Germany was solved by an event which was largely extraneous—a war with France. The background of the Franco-Prussian War of 1870 has been described in Chapter 28. From the German side, the causes lay mainly in the extravagant German national pride and exuberance which were now flowering. The policy of Napoleon III appeared to Germans to be aggressive and offensive. It was believed that the French were preparing for

Otto von Bismarck

a campaign to prevent the completion of German unity and were, to this end, conspiring with the sulking Austrians.

In the summer of 1870, the throne of Spain having become vacant as a consequence of a revolution, a Spanish congress offered it to a remote cousin of William I of Prussia. In the sequel Bismarck's highly edited version of the "Ems Despatch" prompted the French to declare war, July 19 (see p. 479).

It is not clear why Bismarck deliberately undertook to tamper with the Ems telegram in a way almost bound to lead to war. Later, he argued that he had planned the whole thing in order to bring the south German states into the war at the side of Prussia and thus induce them, in the heat of a patriotic war effort, to enter the Confederation. There is no evidence that this assertion is true, and some that it is not, but that indeed was the way events turned out. Once the war had begun, in the anti-French fervor which engulfed all Germans Bavaria, Württemberg, and Baden joined in. Once fighting, it was easier for them to accept the idea of a permanent union with Prussia, and their adherence to the Confederation was negotiated quickly and without serious difficulties. A few concessions were made to Bavarian national pride—Bavaria was to retain its own army and its own postage stamps. The name of the North German Confederation was changed to German Empire, and the title of its head, the King of Prussia, changed from President to German Emperor. While the war was still in progress, on January 18, 1871, in the Hall of Mirrors at Louis XIV's palace of Versailles, the German Empire was proclaimed.

A Germany now, at last, existed, and most of the ambitions of the German nationalists and businessmen who had sought it were satisfied. There was a common market, a common currency, and a government empowered to bring into existence a common banking system and commercial code. For liberals and democrats there was a parliament elected by universal manhood suffrage. For Prussian conservatives, there was the predominance of Prussian influence and the Prussian army, and the presidency of the Prussian king. For particularists, there were the surviving dynasties and constitutions of the separate states within the framework of the federal government. Outside still lay Austria, as well as extensive German-speaking groups in Switzerland and along the Baltic coast and elsewhere, but the great majority of Germans had a common government and could look forward with enthusiasm to sharing a common destiny.

32

RUSSIA
FROM PAUL I
TO ALEXANDER II

RUSSIAN HISTORY in the nineteenth century is dramatic in a special way. To the casual student, it means little more than Napoleon's invasion in 1812, the Crimean War in 1854–1856, and, finally, the emancipation of the serfs in 1861. A little additional investigation brings to light that there were four czars from the death of Catherine the Great in 1796 to the assassination of Alexander II in 1881. Catherine's son Paul I (1796–1801) had a short, gloomy reign and was murdered in 1801. His son Alexander I (1801–1825) had a long, dramatic career which included fighting Napoleon and going as a conquering hero to Paris. His much younger brother Nicholas I (1825–1855) was a very conservative czar whose reign opened with the Decembrist Revolt (which he put down) and came to an end in the midst of the Crimean War. Alexander II (1855–1881), son of Nicholas, was the "liberator czar" who freed the serfs and yet was hunted like an animal by a secret society which finally killed him with a bomb in 1881.

These few bits of information would indicate that each generation had its drama, but there is greater drama in the challenge which Europe made to Russia. Europe was about to surge ahead rapidly into industrialization, to experiment with representative political institutions, to discuss all sorts of new ideas. Yet the drama of Russia's nineteenth-century condition was not simply a challenge to "catch up." Russians, even those of the revolutionary left, saw the shortcomings of Europe. Even among unbelievers, the old Orthodox sense of uniqueness and mission remained. Russia must do more than catch up. It must show the way. A sense of enormous potentialities and practical impotence frustrated nineteenth-century Russia. Western Europe with its wealth, its liberalism, its democracy, its socialism, was a provocation to Russians to affirm what they were and what they meant to be.

PAUL I AND ALEXANDER I

When the great Catherine died in 1796, her son Paul was forty-three, and bitter. He was an educated man, who had traveled in Europe and had ideas for reforming Russia, but for years he had felt his life slipping away, wasted, while his mother usurped the throne. Catherine, he felt, should have turned over the rule of Russia to him when he came of age. When she did not, he brooded in semi-retirement on his estates near Saint Petersburg, drilling troops Prussian style as his murdered father (Peter III, d. 1762) had done before him. Paul's reign (1796–1801) was in some ways like that of an enlightened despot. He thought government was for the welfare of the people, as interpreted by himself and served by an absolute monarchy. He hated the French Revolution, and had no intention of abolishing either serfdom or the privileges of the nobility. But he was determined, like Peter the Great before him, to make the nobility serve the state; and he tried to set limits to the abuse of serfs by their masters.

In spite of his good intentions, Paul was in fact a despot whose whims became increasingly incalculable and unpredictable. Increasingly aware of opposition, he became pathologically suspicious, and multiplied the insecurity of those around him. Finally in 1801 some officers of the Guards murdered him. His son Alexander was made czar.

Alexander was an enigmatic but well-mannered young man of twenty-four. He had been placed in his teens under the guidance of a progressive Swiss tutor, La Harpe, and had formed an affection for the ideas of the Enlightenment. But there was another influence in his life, his father's sternness and Prussian drills. Alexander was marked for life with the ideal of becoming a great reformer, but never ceased returning to the image of himself as a great conquering general. In his lifetime, he had the opportunity to play both roles.

Alexander, in the first years of his reign, sought peace abroad, and at home he brought to an end his father's censorship and terror. Gathering around him a "committee of friends," men interested in reforms, he seemed about to give the still youthful century a brilliant beginning. The Friends were aware of the evils of autocracy and serfdom, and were Anglophile in their political leanings, but hesitated to recommend anything drastic to the czar, who was also influenced by circles in the nobility and the army. Moreover, Alexander was soon caught up in the great currents of international relations. When Napoleon turned eastward from his preparations for invasion of Britain, Alexander entered the coalition against France (1805–1807) and along with Austria and Prussia was beaten in the swift series of moves which took Napoleon into East Prussia. The czar was determined that for the moment the war should not continue on Russian soil, and after the meeting with Napoleon on the raft in the Niemen he became Napoleon's ally (Treaty of Tilsit, 1807).

From 1807 to 1812 the alliance with France worked poorly and turned into a truce in which both sides prepared for conflict. Alexander's hands were not free, for besides keeping constant watch on Napoleon's reorganization of Central Europe, particularly the Grand Duchy of Warsaw, Russia fought both Sweden and the Ottoman empire. The czar was lured by territorial gains (Finland, 1809; Bessarabia, 1812). During those years, however, Alexander encouraged the planning of Michael Speransky, who hoped to turn Russia into a constitutional monarchy. Alexander even accepted Speransky's project in principle, but once again the international crisis forestalled all but minor changes in the organization of the Russian government. Speransky was unpopular with the Russian aristocracy, and it would take a bold historian indeed to argue that Alexander even in quieter times would have put the Speransky plan into practice. In fact Alexander in 1812 allowed Speransky to be condemned, unjustly, for treason, and exiled him. In 1816 he pardoned Speransky, whom he knew to be innocent, and in 1821 Speransky returned to Saint Petersburg, but never again to the innermost circle.

Napoleon's invasion of Russia in 1812 was, from the Russian point of view, a stirring though terrible national experience. The farther Napoleon penetrated, the stiffer became the resistance of the population. After the French retreat, the Russian government and aristocracy owed a debt to the people which long remained unpaid. From Alexander's point of view the invasion and its failure had a providential, almost religious character. The czar was firm in his determination to resist, and showed strength of character in his refusal to negotiate while the French emperor was in Moscow. The awful grandeur of the burning city and the wasting of the Napoleonic forces during their retreat out of Russia strengthened the sense of nationality in a whole generation of Russians. These events were certainly a turning point in the life of the czar, who, against the judgment of his generals, decided to pursue Napoleon and appear in Europe as the savior and organizer of the continent. In the triumph of the march to Paris and the great peace conference at Vienna, Alexander continued his liberal role, but the role of all-conquering czar was evident as well. He tried to dominate his allies as a super-sovereign. Sometimes he seemed to fancy himself as successor to Napoleon, and to seek the overlordship of Europe. Only the combined efforts of Metternich, Castlereagh, and Talleyrand prevented his acquisition of all Poland.

In the decade of life which remained to him, Alexander continued his dual character, covering it over with increasing vagueness. He was, personally, a part of the religious and anti-Jacobin current which engulfed much of Russian, and European, upper-class society in the years after the French Revolution. A Baroness Krüdener, with whom the czar had a number of interviews in 1815, was one of many mystical religious leaders who may have influenced him. As he grew older he retired more and more into his Orthodox faith. Alexander's sponsorship of the Holy Alliance of European powers (1815) was in part the product of a religious impulse (see Chapter 33).

Politically, Alexander continued to vacillate. There are many examples of the liberal posture. In 1818 he praised constitutional government in Poland,

and spoke of extending it to Russia. From time to time he even referred to hopes of freeing the serfs. He was aware that the young army officers who had seen Paris were carriers of liberal ideas, but he did not repress them. In practice, however, Alexander became increasingly reactionary. Speransky's antithesis, the autocratic administrator Arakcheyev, was put in charge of a system of self-supporting "military colonies" in 1816: army units which farmed and drilled, and whose whole life and that of their children was under military discipline. After 1820, when Alexander confronted rebelliousness in his Semenovsky Guards regiment as well as revolutions in Naples and Spain, he admitted to Metternich that the Austrian Chancellor was right and that he had been wrong in encouraging liberalism. After 1820 Alexander evidently subscribed to the view popular among conservatives in Europe that the mass of mankind would only fall under the sway of demagogues if they tried to govern themselves. He died in 1825, after taking part in the major experiences of his time.

NICHOLAS I

Nineteen years separated Alexander in age from his brother Nicholas I (1825–1855). Nicholas was born in 1796, the year Catherine the Great died. He grew up in the period of reaction which followed the French Revolution and came of age in the triumph over Napoleon, and he was never troubled by liberal doubts. There was in him nothing of Alexander's complicated personality. He was a militaristic czar who loved drill, uniforms, and bureaucratic detail. Poorly educated, he traveled to England and was not impressed. What he liked he found in Prussia. His conception of the office which came to him at twenty-nine was that he was placed on the throne by God and was duty-bound to discipline his people like a father, like an army officer.

Nicholas ascended the throne over the bodies of the "Decembrists." December was the month when Alexander I died, leaving the throne to Nicholas. The latter's older brother Constantine was still alive, but he had married a commoner and preferred to live in Poland. Constantine had abdicated his succession rights in 1822, but only a few people had been told, and Nicholas himself was not among them. The announcement of Nicholas's succession was therefore a surprise, and an occasion for revolt. Certain liberal officers in Saint Petersburg, the "Decembrists," hoping to win over the rest of the troops in the capital, demanded "Constantine and Constitution," but their call went unheeded by most of the troops, by the nobility, and by the rest of society. Nicholas I, nevertheless, began his reign with an immediate and dramatic problem posed by the liberalism of Western Europe, where many of the officers had campaigned in the days of Napoleon; and his first act after repressing the Decembrists was to preside personally over the investigation of their subversive beliefs and plans.

With a mixture of brutality and moral suasion which would today be called brainwashing, Nicholas extracted from the Decembrists the catalogue of their beliefs. What he learned was perhaps as significant in his career as Catherine the Great's Legislative Commission had been in hers. Five of the 121 men arrested were hanged; the others were exiled to Siberia or condemned to lesser punishments. The czar became more than ever an enemy of liberalism; he was to become a symbol of repression in Europe as well as in Russia.

But the reign was not without efforts at reform. It was a bureaucratic reign full of commissions for the investigation of problems. One, led by Speransky (whom Nicholas had forced to serve on the court which judged the Decembrists), codified the laws by 1833. At least ten commissions studied the question of serfdom without finding any solution. Nicholas knew that there were problems, and wished to solve them, but he was also convinced that the responsibility was all his, and that every precaution should be taken to avoid exciting the minds of the Russian people. Consequently he went to great lengths to avoid discussion, and even gave false names to some of his committees. The censorship which had begun in the last years of Alexander's reign was made severe. An official creed of "autocracy, orthodoxy, and Russian nationality" was meant to emphasize Russian traditions, but in practice meant intolerance of religious and political dissenters, and of Poles, Lithuanians, and Jews. Nicholas actually tried to limit education to the children of officials and nobles. The population in his view needed only simple instruction which would not excite them.

To such a ruler the events of nineteenth-century Europe could only be a provocation. Nicholas had scarcely disposed of the Decembrists when the revolutions of 1830 disturbed Western and Central Europe. He would gladly have intervened in France and Belgium during the revolutions of 1830, but the other Holy Alliance powers, Austria and Prussia, were hesitant, and Russia had to cope with a revolution in Poland. Poland was deprived of its constitution, its legislature, and its army. The University of Warsaw was closed, and Russian became the language to be used by governing officials. In the course of the much more alarming 1848 conflagration Nicholas emerged as the principal defender of European reaction. When Austrian troops failed to subdue the Hungarian revolutionaries in 1849 Nicholas moved in 150,000 men from Poland and suppressed the Hungarians with ferocity. Russian pressure also contributed to Prussia's decision to disperse the Frankfurt Assembly, and forced a reluctant Frederick William IV of Prussia to accept restoration of the German Confederation. Russia had become the "gendarme of Europe."

But the role of Nicholas was more than that of gendarme. History had bequeathed him, and he gladly accepted, the expansionism of Peter, Catherine, and Alexander, and also the grandiose dream of Russia's mission of defending the Slavs and Orthodox Christians outside the empire. Outside the empire meant, in Nicholas' time, *inside* the Ottoman empire. It was the fate of Nicholas to lead an unreformed and increasingly backward Russia in the international competition known as the "Eastern Question;" that is, the question of who would benefit from the decline of Turkish power.

In the 1820's Nicolas I fought the Ottoman Empire and Persia and gained territory and influence in what later would be called Rumania and in the area between the Black and Caspian seas. He helped the Greeks win freedom from the

Turks (1829–1830), but the other powers prevented him from establishing Russion predominance there. In the 1830's he threatened to make a satellite out of the Ottoman empire, but between 1839 and 1841 the other European states insisted on participating in Turkish questions along with Russia. In the 1840's he tried to arrange with England for a partition of the Ottoman empire. After the revolutions of 1848 had appeared to reaffirm the solidarity of Austria, Prussia, and Russia, he again stepped forward as protector of the Orthodox faithful within the Ottoman empire, aiming at ultimate conquest of Constantinople and the Straits. This time war resulted, with Turkey in 1853, and with England and France and Sardinia in 1854–1856.

The Crimean War (so-called because the Allies invaded the Crimean peninsula, on the north side of the Black Sea, where they besieged Sevastopol for 349 days) revealed Russia's feet of clay. The gigantic gendarme of the east was simply unable to organize an effective defense. The pen-dipping bureaucratic officialdom failed to provision the armies. Worse yet, the condition of the peasantry had become such as to cause a mounting crescendo of serf revolts. In spite of violent nationalistic pride in the upper classes, a real crisis in the regime seemed to be brewing. Austria and Prussia were no help, for although they remained neutral they had opposed Russian expansionism and were closer to supporting the Allies than to aiding Russia. This was the distressing situation when Nicholas died, in March, 1855.

ALEXANDER II

Alexander II (1855–1881) was thirty-seven when he became czar in the middle of the Crimean War, a big man, like his father, but otherwise dissimilar. He was well-tutored and traveled, and had trained for the job of ruling Russia; over-trained, perhaps, for he early tired of military affairs. He was intelligent but easy-going, a well-meaning, passive man, humanitarian but rather lazy. Russian policies were converging in a manner which threatened both international and domestic disaster. Alexander had enough intelligence and will to rise to the occasion, make peace before it was too late (1856), and emancipate the serfs (1861). Caught up by the tides of expectation characteristic of a new reign Russia seemed embarked upon a new era. Reforms came thick and fast for a while, until Alexander had earned for himself the reputation, before history, of a great emancipator. But he was really not a reformer so much as a man who shored up the old autocracy and society by timely concessions. In some ways Alexander's career was a turning point more potential than actual—a might-have-been. The old Russia reasserted itself in foreign and domestic policy, but a new Russia was trying to assert itself too, and in 1881 this contradiction cost Alexander II his life.

An inventory of the events which gave Alexander's reign its contours begins with the emancipation of the landowners' serfs (1861) and state peasants (1864)—a subject to be treated below. The Poles were given more autonomy in 1861, and the universities of Russia greater freedom in 1863. The judicial system was improved in 1864, and the following year the censorship was relaxed. The most significant of Alexander's reforms, after the emancipation of the serfs, was the founding (1864) of district and provincial assemblies (zemstvo—local assembly). The zemstvo reform was both conservative and potentially very progressive. It was conservative because (1) the peasants, although self-governing in their own communities (*mirs*) were like second-class, segregated citizens, living under their own customary civil law; (2) the peasant representation in the district or provincial zemstvo was overshadowed by the representation of the much less numerous nobles and townsmen; and (3) the zemstvo was allowed to act only on a restricted list of concerns such as education, public health, and agricultural improvement. On the other hand the zemstvo reform was potentially progressive because it was a form of representative government which in time gathered around it liberal nobles and technical workers. These would have been pleased to see the system capped by a system of national representation, a duma, or representative body for all Russia.

That this latter step was not taken at once, along with the emancipation of the serfs, was a source of disappointment to Russian liberals, but Alexander II did not wish to curtail the absolute monarchy or to change more than was absolutely necessary. A number of events strengthened this determination on the part of the czar. In Poland from 1863 to 1865 a patriotic and nationalistic rebellion against Russian domination had to be suppressed by force. Russian nationalism responded, weakening liberal impulses, which now seemed responsible for the disorders. Yet the limited nature of Alexander's reforms accentuated radicalism among students and intellectuals. This in turn seemed to vindicate the conservatives who said that concessions only promised to start an avalanche toward democracy and socialism comparable to that which seemed to be taking place in Europe.

During most of the 1860's and 1870's the regime of Alexander II became more conservative. An effort was made to weed out liberal influences from primary and secondary education and, with little success, from the universities. Government officials propagated an "official nationalism" emphasizing the dangers of foreign influences and the importance of the throne, the Orthodox Church, and the predominance of native Russian values. The zemstvo liberals were told to say no more about the desirability of a national representative body.

Alexander's later years were not entirely devoted to reaction. A muncipal-government reform paralleling that of the zemstvos was passed in 1870. In 1874 an army reform established the principle of universal military service for all classes, with rather liberal exemptions for educated people, and eliminated some of the worst abuses in the recruiting and treatment of soldiers. Toward the end of his reign Alexander realized that concessions to popular opinion were necessary. A wave of political assassinations was aimed at government officials, including the emperor himself, who had a narrow escape in 1880 when his dining room was blown up on a day when he was late to dinner. Alexander and an advisor, Count

Michael Loris-Melikov, embarked in 1880 on a program of conciliating public opinion. The program was climaxed by the so-called "Loris-Melikov constitution", which was really not a constitutional change, but a device for consulting representatives from the zemstvos and city dumas. Alexander was prepared to put these proposals into practice when he was assassinated by the terrorists in March, 1881.

Russian foreign policy in Alexander's reign began with the Crimean defeat which obliged Russia (Treaty of Paris, 1856) to accept the neutralization of the Black Sea, territorial losses, and internationalization of the defense of Christians within the Ottoman empire. The defeat had come about not only because of Russian weakness but also because of the failure of the three conservative eastern empires of Holy Alliance days to stand together. Austria, in spite of its indebtedness for Russian aid in putting down the Hungarian revolution in 1849, had thrown its diplomatic weight on the side of France and England out of fear of Russian expansion into the Balkans; and Prussia had been closer to the Austrian position than to the Russian.

It appeared for the moment that the Russian drive to Constantinople had been stopped. But expansion toward the east, in Central Asia and Siberia, continued. Russian pressure extracted from China trading rights and territory between the Pacific and the Amur river. Vladivostok was founded in 1860, and opportunely, the opening of the Suez Canal in 1869 reduced the sea voyage from Odessa, on the Black Sea, to Vladivostok, to about forty-five days. In 1867 Alaska was sold to the United States for $7,200,000. In 1875 Russia was recognized by the Japanese as owner of Sakhalin Island.

In European affairs Bismarckian Prussia in the 1860's moved close to Russia while preparing to beat Austria and France. In 1871, with England isolated and France defeated, Russia was able to denounce the Black Sea clauses which had demilitarized that sea to its disadvantage. Russia's renewed drive toward Constantinople in the 1870's will be discussed in a later chapter.

THE ECONOMIC LAG

In 1800 there were about 40,000,000 inhabitants of the Russian empire. By 1850, after more annexations and a steady natural increase, there were 68,000,-000. The urban population in 1850 was about 3,400,000, or 5 percent, but the term "urban" for the slumbering, mud-caked provincial towns of most of Russia is a misnomer. Most Russians were peasants, divided not quite evenly between serfs belonging to landlords and those who were the property of the state or of the royal family. All the Russians, whether nobles, peasants, or burghers, were classified in ranks and categories, and might confidently expect to be treated according to these usually hereditary positions.

The Russian economy was not stagnant, but in comparison with that of

Western Europe it was certainly sluggish. Its backbone was agriculture, which rested on the backs of the serfs. There were a great many country estates in Russia, and a great many nobles and country gentry who owned them. Most estates were small and unprofitable. In 1859 three fourths of the estates had fewer than 100 male serfs each, and 40 percent had fewer than 20 male serfs each. The number of estates is misleading, however, for in 1859 some 100,000 nobles owned approximately 30 percent of the land in Russia (at a time when the total population had passed 70,000,000).

Most of the Russian estates were not producing enough surplus to satisfy their owners or contribute to the prosperity of the country. Only a tiny portion of Russian trade represented grain exports, and there was surprisingly little trade even within Russia in the first half of the nineteenth century. Most of the products of Russian agriculture were consumed by the large and inefficient labor force which grew them. To change farming methods would have required enterprise and capital; but most of the landowners lacked enterprise, and their capital consisted largely of the very serfs upon whose old-fashioned tools and ideas they relied for the farming of their lands.

Owing to Russia's increased contacts with Europe and the general tendency to buy more things for money, the country gentry attempted to wring more income from their properties. Finding themselves unable to farm efficiently, they fell back on ways they knew; that is, they squeezed the maximum out of the labor service (*barshchina*) or dues (*obrok*) of their serfs. They also borrowed money, until by 1860 about 62 percent of the serfs were mortgaged, and so was about 53 percent of the value of the estates. From the peasant's point of view heavier dues along with more mouths to feed were making life excessively austere. It is not surprising that during the reign of Nicholas I the number of serf uprisings grew from about 14 per year in the first decade to about 35 per year in the last ten years.

While Western Europe was in the first big drive of industrialization, Russian industry slumbered. Since the time of Peter the Great the state's military requirements had produced a large demand for goods. In an agriculture-dominated economy the need had been met in part by state manufactures and privileged private concerns using whole villages of "possessionary" serfs as the labor force. Manorial manufactures in which owners used their serfs, particularly in winter, to weave and perform other simple tasks, were in decline in the nineteenth century. The putting-out system, particularly in the north where the soil was poor, was an important form of manufacturing. It provided many peasants with incomes with which to pay their *obrok* dues to their masters. A good many serfs learned to manage little manufacturing enterprises of their own, employing labor and making profits sufficient to pay large *obrok* dues and still prosper. Some of them managed to buy their freedom. Russia by these methods had held its own up to Catherine's time and had entered European history with success, but in the nineteenth century Europe pulled ahead. To take one example, in 1800 Russian production of pig iron was about the same as that of Britain, but by 1850 Britain's was ten times as great as Russia's. In the Crimean War the Russian railroad network was only one fifth as large as that of France.

THE EMANCIPATION OF THE SERFS

When Alexander was crowned in 1855, it was clear enough that something had to be done to check peasant rebelliousness before it became catastrophic. It was not nearly so clear that the nobility could be made to support a reasonable program. A minority of wealthy and progressive landowners was eager to put an end to what was, for them, an inefficient and old-fashioned way of providing labor on their farms. But most of the landowners, largely small holders, were less enlightened. However backward and socially dangerous serfdom was for Russia, to them it was a familiar and, until something better came along, an advantageous system. Alexander, maintaining as much secrecy as possible, set to work with committees in 1856, then sought discussion by provincial committees of nobles, then finally signed the manifesto in 1861.

The diversity of Russia, as well as the fears of the landowners and the dangerous expectations of the peasants, raised problems. In the regions where the land was good, it was to the interest of the landowners to keep as much as possible and to free the serfs with little or no land, so that they would become wage laborers. On the other hand, it was clearly not possible to deprive the peasants of land altogether; in the absence of industries to employ them such a move would be impracticable. Moreover, if the former serf-owners were to have capital, they would need to sell some of the land to their liberated serfs. Also, in justice to the Russian upper classes, it should be added that there existed in the consciousness of some of them strong Slavophile (see below) and humanitarian sentiments which opposed breaking up the peasant communities (*mirs*) and casting helpless individuals adrift in a competitive world.

In provinces where the land was poor, the interest of the serf-owners was to sell as much of the land to the peasants as possible. Here, the loss faced by the serf-owners was not so much the land, which they had been accustomed to leave in the serfs' possession anyway, as the dues (*obrok*) payments of the serfs, many of whom worked at handicrafts on the side in order to make these payments. Since it was decided in principle that the serfs would not be charged for their personal liberation, but only for the land which they retained, it was necessary to cover loss of *obrok* income by overvaluing the land which was sold to the peasants. The land which the serfs retained was also overvalued in the richer, black soil provinces, but in these the amount of acreage retained by the former serf-owners was much greater.

The emancipation therefore provided something for the landlord, something for the peasant, and something for the state. The landlords, where they wished to continue farming, were assured of capital from the emancipation because the serfs bought some land. The state paid the landlord at once, and the peasants were to pay the state in installments. The landlords were also guaranteed a labor supply, for in general the peasants received less land than they had been accustomed to farming on their own account, and could be expected to supplement their incomes by working for those landlords who wished to remain in the business of farming. The peasants, for their part, received their freedom, with some land (subject to the redemption payments).

In order to preserve the life of the *mir*, protect the less able peasants from their fellows, and insure the collection of the redemptions by the state, the peasants were not given the land as individuals, but were sold it collectively. Thus the land, and the responsibility for paying redemptions and ordinary taxes, went to the *mirs*, a good number of which continued the practice of "repartitional tenure"; that is, of periodically redistributing the plots among families according to their changed numbers (and therefore changed needs and tax responsibilities). As for the state's benefits from all these changes, they were expected to consist of improved welfare among the inhabitants, and therefore of greater social stability.

The state, or crown, peasants (those without individual masters, but subject to *obrok* payments to the state) received, after 1866, a treatment similar to that of the serf-owners' peasants, except that, in general, they were sold more land.

This has been an abridged description of what was in reality a very complicated operation which stretched out over many years. Historians have, understandably, held conflicting views concerning the wisdom and effectiveness of the liberation policies. We shall describe in a later chapter the fate which the future held in store for both the peasants and their former owners. But it was clear from the beginning that the results were in some ways unsatisfactory. The amount of the redemption payments required of the peasants was higher than the market value of the land which they received. Even so, the landlords as a class did not get the capital which they needed, since, by 1860, over half of the value of their estates, and about two thirds of their serfs, had been mortgaged. Most of the Russian estate owners were not, in any case, trained in the management of capital; many sold out within a few years, and still more fell back on arrangements with the peasants similar to those in effect in pre-reform days. From the peasants' point of view the fact that they had less land to farm on their own, and more payments to make (redemptions plus ordinary taxes), meant that most of them were soon back in relationships of share-cropping or spare-time wage earning with their former masters. The emancipation of the serfs performed no miracles for Russian agriculture or for Russian rural life.

The emancipation has sometimes been compared to the French Revolution in that all Russians attained the stature of citizens. It would not do to overlook the importance of this idea; a nation in which one part of the population *owned* the other part did indeed transform itself in the direction of common citizenship. We have seen how it was necessary for Alexander's bureaucracy to plan a whole new system of local government in order to take this fact into account. On the other hand, it would be an error to overlook the enormous differences between Frenchmen's equality before the law and the continued existence in Russia of different legal classes with different rights and obligations. Another claim often made is this: that the preservation of the *mir* was a continued training of the Russian peasants in socialism, and so paved the way for communism. This last is a dubious generalization of the kind which is virtually impossible to prove or disprove so many years after the fact. We shall see in a later chapter that the preservation of the *mir* did have consequences, but no one will ever know how alternative programs of emancipation would have worked.

THE INTELLIGENTSIA

Russia was falling behind Europe in the first half of the nineteenth century. There were Russian minds to deplore this fact and voices to propose remedies. Most of the time after the early, hopeful days of Alexander I and his Committee of Friends, and particularly after the great crisis of 1812, censorship of the press and universities was tight. In this as in so many matters, Alexander was equivocal, but Nicholas with his "autocracy, orthodoxy, and Russian nationality," the official doctrine, was a real inquisitor. Not for nothing were his first months as emperor spent in probing the minds of the Decembrists whose conspiracy had rung up the curtain for his reign. Nicholas himself expected his secret police to keep him informed of his subjects' foibles, and meant to supervise their beliefs as well as their conduct. For publishing a "Philosophical Letter" about Russia's shortcomings in comparison with Western Europe (1836), Peter Chaadayev was declared insane. In 1849, when Fedor Dostoevski and his friends in the Petrashevsky circle were arrested for alleged subversive activities, the future author of *Crime and Punishment* was sentenced to death by firing squad; he was reprieved only as he awaited the shot. Dostoevski did not know that a gruesome joke was being played, and experienced the genuine sentiments of a condemned man. There followed a genuine sentence of four years of hard labor in Siberia, though nothing more serious had been proved against the Petrashevsky group than discussion of the ideas of the French utopian socialist Fourier.

Dostoevski (1821–1881) was the son of an army surgeon, a rather low calling in those days. Vissarion Belinsky (1810–1848), the gifted literary critic whose premature death probably forestalled arrest for his radical social views, was the son of an impoverished navy surgeon. Nicholas Gogol (1809–1852), author of the famous satirical novel *Dead Souls,* was the son of a small landowner, possessor of several hundred serfs. Alexander Herzen (1812–1870), publisher (in London) of the first uncensored Russian journal, *The Bell* (1857 ff.), which had reverberations inside Russia, was the illegitimate son of a Russian aristocrat, but inherited his father's considerable wealth, and left Russia in 1847. Herzen was a great publicist, first among the "conscience-stricken gentry" and, like Belinsky, a "westerner" and a forerunner of Russian socialism. Their careers illustrate how, in spite of censorship, an "intelligentsia" was forming.

The Russian intelligentsia were what we today would call "intellectuals," but they were persons of varying backgrounds with no particular status in society and often with no particular formal education. Like the French *philosophes* of the eighteenth century, they played the role of social critics without having any unified program for change. Some of the intelligentsia were officials who would have been satisfied with enlightened reforms by the state machine. Some were traditionalists enamored of an imaginary past, while others were inspired by English, French, or German remedies from the great debates which were sweeping Western Europe. Almost all of them, whether they realized it or not, bore the imprint of the Orthodox mentality inherited from the Russian religious past, a habit of mind which tended to exalt the Russian mission to show the way to humanity. In earlier times most of the educated people in Russia had been nobles. The Decembrists who revolted against Nicholas I in 1825 were a curious mixture of Anglophiles and admirers of French radicalism, but they were young noblemen of the kind who had been exposed in the Napoleonic wars to ideas from the west. The Decembrists have aptly been called the last of the palace revolutionaries and the first of the nineteenth-century revolutionaries. As the examples given above illustrate, the intelligentsia by the time of Nicholas was no longer confined to nobility, but was spreading its membership to lower ranks.

In one vital respect the intelligentsia of the nineteenth century in Russia differed greatly from the French *philosophes,* who had been sustained by a rich and increasingly powerful middle class. The Russians were almost isolated in society, trapped, as it were, between a hostile bureaucratic absolutism and a mass of traditionalistic peasants unable and unwilling to listen to them. This fact, and the awful contrast between their awareness of needs and potentialities on the one hand and rude actualities on the other, drove the Russian intelligentsia toward extremes of anger and despair.

In the 1830's and 1840's influences from the west continued to penetrate Russia. Many young Russian intellectuals were influenced by Hegel's evolutionary philosophy, which from one point of view appeared to justify the present state of affairs but could easily be turned, as Marx turned it in Europe, to predictions of further evolution toward a new kind of society. Russians took readily to western socialistic thought. They were eager to avoid the mistakes of Europe, such as the heartlessness of *laissez faire* during the early Industrial Revolution.

In the 1830's and 1840's the "Westernizers," who wished Russia to profit from the best which the west had to offer, were opposed by the Slavophiles, who emphasized the values of traditions which Russia already had. The Slavophiles were not, as one might at first think, opposed to reform and progress. They were romantics who appreciated the grand, complex processes of historic change, and who sought guidance in Russia's past. Looking to remote periods before Peter the Great, they saw Russia as a community of the faithful, cooperating in such institutions as the peasant community, or *mir,* and the Assembly of the Land, or *Zemsky Sobor,* for all of Russia. They were reformers who were against serfdom and believed that the building of the bureaucratic autocracy since Peter the Great, and the introduction of European values since the Enlightenment, had turned Russia in the wrong direction. They were highly critical of Europe for what they felt was its destructive and selfish individualism and competitiveness. To the religious, class, and nationalistic rivalries of Europe they contrasted Orthodox and Slavic culture, in which they found an emphasis on brotherhood and on feelings of oneness and harmony (*sobornost,* sense of community). They were themselves nationalists, but not such warlike imperialists as their followers in later generations.

THE RUSSIAN CONSCIENCE

The emancipation of the serfs was an intellectual event in Russian history as well as a social one. The high hopes and discussion between 1855 and 1861 were an important experience. Disappointment with 1861 was also important. Not only the peasants felt let down. The liberals could not fail to note that the reform was handed down from above. True, the zemstvo reform of local government was to be an abiding influence toward liberalism, but the contradiction between representative institutions on the local level and autocracy at the center remained.

We have seen how the Polish rebellion of 1863 aroused Russian nationalism and aided conservatism. Nicholas Danilevsky's *Russia and Europe* (1869) argued that the superior Slavic culture should be kept pure and that it was Russia's mission to defeat Europe and rule over all of Slavic East Central Europe and Constantinople. This kind of Pan-Slavism was to play a part in Russia's foreign policy in the period after 1870. Its roots were similar to those of the Slavophilism already mentioned, but the Pan-Slavists added the notions of inevitable conflict and expansion by force.

In Russia the young people who came of age after the Crimean War and the emancipation of the serfs expressed in various ways their impatience with the present and their faith in Russia's future. Already, to the young men in Ivan Turgenev's novel *Fathers and Sons* (1861) their elders, cultivated Westernizers or Slavophiles of the 1840's who had survived into the new age, seemed ineffectual and even foolish. Bazarov, the protagonist of this novel, represented a new type which was to flourish after 1860: the nihilist. To the older generation this rude young man (illustrative of the fact that more and more of the intelligentsia were henceforth to come from the lower orders) seemed to believe in nothing, to scorn esthetic, philosophical, religious, and political values, and even to be contemptuous of common politeness and decency in human relations. But it was an extreme form of idealism which motivated the nihilists. They were concerned with liberating the human personality, and they wished to avoid all those influences which, in the past, seemed to have enchained it, including even such things as family sentiments. Their God was positivistic science—fact-finding; it was the only dogma to which they dared entrust themselves. Nihilism, an extreme form of individualism, did not for very long captivate the youth in Russia, who took more readily to those other enthusiasms of the late 1860's and 1870's, anarchism and Populism.

Anarchism and the name Michael Bakunin (1814–1876) were intertwined in Europe as well as in Russia in the nineteenth century. It was Bakunin, the Russian aristocrat and believer in "anarchism, collectivism, and atheism" who in the revolutions of 1848 tried to organize a Slavic federation and who quarreled with Marx in the First International from 1868 to 1872. Bakunin's anarchistic opposition to the state was natural enough for a Russian radical, and his determination to destroy the existing society in order to free men to achieve a new brotherhood reminds us of the Nihilists, but Bakunin came to distrust scientists and intellectuals and to rely on the leadership of small secret groups of conspirators. Secrecy and violence and direction by an elite of revolutionaries who, being few in number, and professionals, would not get caught, were tempting tactics in czarist Russia. Bakunin and his followers in some ways foreshadow the Bolsheviks, but it would be a mistake to draw too close a parallel, for the Bolsheviks were to have an elaborate historical and social analysis and, moreover, were to try to achieve socialism (which Bakunin also wanted) through the agency of state power.

Although there were anarchists in Russia until after the revolution of 1917, the main road taken by the Russian revolutionary movement passed by way of the movement known as Populism (Narod—people; Narodnichestvo—Populism). The Populist movement flourished in the 1870's. In its early stages it was associated with the agrarian socialist ideas of Peter Lavrov, whose Historical Letters appeared in 1868–1869. Lavrov, an army officier and mathematician, expressed feelings characteristic of many of the intelligentsia, caught between a hostile state and an uncomprehending people. Uneasy, aware of the privileges which had given them education, the Populists yearned to join hands with the peasantry, to lift them up, and at the same time to learn their secret. Like the Slavophiles, the Populists revered Russian traditions, not the newer tradition of autocracy since Peter the Great but the more spontaneous, cooperative, social brotherhood which the peasants had kept alive in the mir. They wished to lead the peasants upward away from poverty and ignorance, avoiding the pitfalls of European capitalism.

Out of Populism were to come the main strands of the Russian socialist movements of the twentieth century. These developments, and their relation to the last decade of the reign of Alexander II, will be continued in a later chapter.

33

THE CONCERT OF EUROPE AND ITS BREAKDOWN, 1815–1870

IN THE NINETEENTH-CENTURY WORLD which finally permitted itself to breathe freely after the Congress of Vienna, two fundamentals of the eighteenth-century international order were still intact: the system of independent, sovereign states, and the balance of power. Their preservation against the aggressions of Napoleonic France had been the crowning achievement of the war just ended, and became the preoccupation of statesmen worrying about the new age. Within the system of states, however, the nineteenth century was to see new tendencies. The member states themselves were to change. Representative governments and the power of public opinion—or at least the threat of such—became general. Decisions about foreign policy began in some measure to be complicated by public pressures. The interests of wealthy men, whether enfranchised or not, whose money came from manufacturing, not land, began to play a greater part in foreign policies. Even working class people might, through their riots and their press, exert influence.

Mixtures of belief and sentiment which animated people far outside the select realm of the governing class played an important role. Of such mixtures, the sentiment of nationalism was the most conspicuous, but liberalism too had its demands in international relations. Freedom for peoples, and a tendency to oppose colonial empires—these were tenets of nationalists and idealists. Conservative fears also had a combative role to play in international relations—a role which could not have been predicted in the eighteenth century when the views now called conservative had had such a monopoly on policy-making that no one had even bothered to name them. Technological novelties affected the motives and strategies of nations. Some of the world's islands were half forgotten when sailing ships disappeared from the seas. Others grew in importance as naval bases and coaling stations.

During much of the period from 1815 to 1870 fatigue from the great wars, fear of further social upheaval, and concern about rapid economic and social changes in domestic affairs combined to work for peace. The search for stability was a far cry from the predatory rivalries of the enlightened despots of the second half of the eighteenth century.

The Congress of Vienna, in its search for stability, made a contribution which had almost as profound an influence on the future as the ideas of the French Revolution. This was the fashioning of ideas and institutions for the maintenance of peace among independent nations. Never before had statesmen so seriously considered the difficulties of assuring stability in a world whose structure was founded on two conflicting values: the "sovereignty" of states, which meant that there could be no restriction on the right of a government to do whatever it wished; and the need for peace and security for those same states, which meant that aggression must somehow be curbed. The attempt to reconcile these two led to an elaborate definition of international law by the peacemakers, and this definition has struck very deep roots in the world.

The peacemakers set forth two ideas. Both of them had ancient origins in

PARTITION OF FRANCE BY THE ALLIES AT THE CONGRESS OF VIENNA. French school, colored etching, about 1814. The misleading title suggests the artist's patriotism, his apprehension, and his failure to foresee how well France would fare at the great congress. (Philadelphia Museum of Art)

Christian morality and European custom, but they added up to something new. The first idea was that the existing international order of things was morally inviolable: that it was a crime against the public law of Europe for one nation to attack another, or to alter on its own authority the existing body of treaties, rights, obligations, and boundary settlements. If a sovereign after 1815 acted as sovereigns had habitually acted before, and seized a province of a neighbor, it was immoral and unlawful. The second idea was that the supervision of the public law of Europe, and permission to change it, must lie with the great powers collectively, who had a primary obligation and interest in the delicate arrangements of the state structure. If, for example, one of the states created at Vienna wished to divide itself in two, then the approval of the great powers was necessary—such a situation in fact arose in 1830 when the Belgians revolted against their inclusion in the kingdom of the Netherlands. The great powers, acting in concert, were to form a sort of governing executive for the world, and to this agency was given the name, Concert of Europe.

These two ideas proved exceedingly tenacious in later history. The Concert of Europe remained part of the mechanism of European diplomacy until World War I in 1914. After that, broadened to include some representative small powers and to include governments outside Europe, it was written into the League of Nations in the interwar period. In our day, it is embodied in the Security Council of the United Nations, whose form and functions are almost precisely analogous to those conceived of for the Concert of Europe in Metternich's day. Similarly with the notion of a "public law" which sanctified treaties and boundaries and which outlawed assaults by governments against the existing order: deeply rooted in the past, this conception became more deeply rooted still after 1815. While it has been breached as often as it has been observed, its violators ever since have found it expedient to cloak their infractions with words which accept the precepts of the public law.

The peacemakers of 1815 tried to put their theoretical formulations into practicable form by a system of international conferences, at which "the Concert of Europe"—France, Great Britain, Austria, Prussia and Russia—could assure order. This meant, first, enforcing the Vienna treaties and, second, adopting a common policy toward new threats to peace. The principal instrument of these arrangements was the Quadruple Alliance, signed in the autumn of 1815 by Britain, Prussia, Russia and Austria. The fifth great power, France, was permitted to adhere as soon as it had shown that it was no longer disposed to dally with aggressive Napoleons or subversive revolutions. The signers of the alliance met, as will be told below, at frequent intervals to supervise the European situation.

There was also signed in 1815 something called the "Holy Alliance." This was intended to include *all* the European governments and it was the invention of Alexander of Russia. The czar was increasingly preoccupied with the mingled concerns of God and absolute monarchy, and the Holy Alliance was designed to provide the postwar world and the Concert of Europe with a religious foundation. It merely stipulated that the rulers should follow Christian principles in dealing with each other and with their own subjects, but there was a strong implication that the rulers' obligation to God involved the rejection of constitutions. The

Europe in 1815

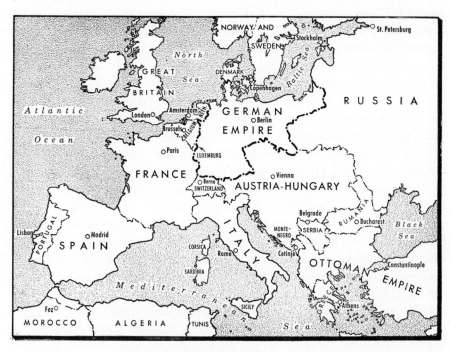

Europe in 1871

text was kept secret—for which reason the British government declined to sign it, on the grounds that the British constitution forebade the sovereign to enter into treaties of which his cabinet could not be informed. Most other rulers signed it without taking it very seriously. But public opinion, learning of its existence and its terms, tended to imagine that it was a plot of autocrats against freedom, and the Holy Alliance shortly acquired a very bad reputation indeed.

Nor was this reputation, unjustified in the letter of the treaty, wholly unjustified by the spirit of its signers. In proposing a Holy Alliance which would law down principles for a Concert of Europe, Alexander was merely carrying things to a logical conclusion, for then as now the idea of Concert implied agreement on at least a few fundamentals. The difficulty, then as now, lay in finding principles upon which the great powers could agree. In Alexander's circle, as in Metternich's, the Revolutionary and Napoleonic wars had generated the conviction that liberalism and nationalism meant international conflict. Self-government and pride of nationality, they thought, reinforced each other. Worse, they created political instability which led straight to external aggression—witness the case of Napoleon. It followed that peace depended on the maintenance of conservative governments. This was the kind of thinking which lay back of the Holy Alliance during the early nineteenth century, and implied a right of intervention.

The name "confederation of Europe" has been given to the era from 1815 to 1830, when the governments, led by the Austrian chancellor, Metternich, maintained some measure of cooperation and when international congresses continued to meet fairly regularly to deal with threats to peace. But two weaknesses soon appeared. In the first place, the community of political ideals began to break down. Autocratic conservatism, however congenial to Prussia, Austria, and Russia, was not a practicable goal in Britain or France. The British, in particular, even the most conservative of them, began to have grave doubts about the feasibility or value of an international system which was based upon the repression of liberty. It was one thing to join hands with czars and kaisers to destroy the Jacobin ogre, but it was quite another to send troops to Spain to restore the king's autocracy and suppress a constitution which was not very dissimilar to Britain's own. A difference of interpretation appeared: in Vienna and Petersburg, it was supposed that any revolution of any sort anywhere threatened peace and must be repressed by international action. In London, revolutions against odious tyrants were not regarded as sinister. They were, indeed, applauded.

A more important rift underlay this growing gap between east and west. Differences in national interests recrudesced, and made international cooperation difficult even among autocrats. When a revolution against Turkish rule broke out in Greece, for example, the Russians were so extremely anxious to foster a Christian friend against the traditional Moslem enemy that they were perfectly willing to overlook the fact that it was a revolution and to support the Greeks. By 1830, with fears of Jacobinism and general war receding, national interest had begun to replace international solidarity as the guiding consideration of foreign policy.

But for several years, the "confederation of Europe" worked with remarkable efficiency to maintain peace, and it is worth examining some of its achievements.

1815–1830: THE CONGRESS SYSTEM

Following the Congress of Vienna the first important meeting was at Aix-la-Chapelle in 1818, when France completed payment of the indemnity charged for Napoleon's escapade of the Hundred Days. The powers removed their troops from French soil, and France was admitted to the alliance of the great powers, making it the Quintuple Alliance. The original four continued to watch France's behavior, however. By this time the revolution which was sweeping Latin America posed the problem of whether the European powers should help Spain recover its colonies. At Aix-la-Chapelle this issue was sidetracked by the British, who wanted to go on trading with the newly formed Latin American states. Liberal revolts in Spain and Naples soon raised the question of intervention in general, which was discussed at the Congresses of Troppau and Laibach in 1820 and 1821. In the Troppau protocol, Metternich proposed the principle that the powers of Europe were justified in intervening against revolutions. Russia and Prussia agreed, but Britain refused to adhere. Austrian troops intervened to restore absolutism in Naples and in Piedmont, where a liberal revolt had also occurred. A Spanish revolution was put down by French troops following the sanctioning of this assignment by the Congress of Verona in 1822. Again the British objected.

The case of the Spanish colonies threatened to come up again following the suppression of the revolution in Spain itself. In 1823 the British Foreign Secretary Canning decided to consult with the United States State Department, for the United States relished neither European intervention in the Western Hemisphere nor the possible closing of the Latin American markets. President Monroe, before anything came of the Anglo-American conversations, made (1823) a public announcement of United States policy—the Monroe Doctrine: United States would not intervene in the affairs of Europe, and would continue to recognize the legitimacy of the remaining European colonies in the new world, but would henceforth oppose further extension of European influence. The United States in issuing the Monroe Doctrine acted independently of Britain, but was fortunate in having British sea power and diplomacy at its side. Canning discouraged French ideas of intervention in Spain's favor, and in 1825 Great Britain recognized the Latin American republics.

The case of Greek independence illustrates the fact that the eastern powers did not always stand together for conservative causes or follow Metternich's lead. The Greek revolution, which broke out against Turkish suzerainty in 1821, was a bloody, stubborn, and prolonged struggle. It was also a sore temptation to Czar Alexander I of Russia, who might have used aid to Orthodox Christians as an excuse for Russian expansion into the Ottoman empire. But Alexander, although he vacillated, resisted the temptation and remained formally in agreement with Metternich, who did not recognize the right of the Greeks to revolt. Western Europe at the time was obsessed by interest in classical culture, and the Greeks, their history, and their cause were fashionable, especially after the romantic poet

Lord Byron lost his life fighting for Greek freedom. After Alexander's death in 1825, Nicholas I of Russia took up the Greek cause and in 1826 and 1827 agreed with Britain and France that the Ottoman empire should be persuaded to give Greece self-government. In 1827, as a gesture of persuasion, the combined British, French, and Russian squadrons at Navarino destroyed the Turkish navy. War between Russia and the Ottoman empire followed in 1828–1829 and led to the Treaty of Adrianople (1829) by which Greece was granted autonomy.

But the Greek revolution was brought in the end under the control of the Concert of Europe. An international conference at London in 1830 declared Greece to be independent, and in 1832 another international decision gave Greece its first king, Otto I, a son of the king of Bavaria, whose principal qualification was a taste for classical sculpture.

There was more to Greek independence than a sentimental concern for the homeland of Plato and Sophocles, however. It marked the formal opening of a long contest among the European powers for influence and security in the Middle East. In this endemic Eastern Question, the perennial antagonists were Russia—intent on continuing its expansion toward Constantinople—and Great Britain—intent on preventing the establishment of a major power in the eastern Mediterranean, astride the overland route to India. It was to *balance* the Russians that the British had taken part at Navarino. For the most part, British policy aimed at shoring up the enfeebled Ottoman empire against Russian assaults. The British were extremely sensitive to the possibility that Russia might get control of the Straits, or approach them by extending their influence in the Balkans. The Russians did indeed win recognition of autonomy for Serbia and the Rumanian principalities which they hoped would become client states.

To complicate matters further, France and Russia worked closely together during the Greek affair, and afterward, when France took Algeria in 1830, Russian diplomatic support encouraged the French to ignore the protests of the British. This complication illustrates the bizarre ways in which the Eastern Question affected western politics.

1830–1848: DISHARMONY
IN THE CONCERT

The period from 1830 to 1848 opened with dramatic revolutions in France, Belgium, and Poland, and lesser disturbances in Italy and Germany. When the July Revolution in France evicted Charles X, it was expected that French foreign policy would change to crusading again in an attempt to arouse the peoples of Europe against the settlements of 1815. In spite of the liberal exaltation of French public opinion, Louis Philippe, the new king, turned out to be pacific. He maneuvered some troops in protest against Austrian repressions in Italy, and vainly suggested mediation as the Russians crushed the Polish rebellion, but France did not try to revolutionize Europe. In Belgium, however, French intervention had lasting results.

The Belgians inhabited what before 1789 had been the Austrian Nether-lands. They revolted against their enforced union with the Dutch. Partly French-speaking, Catholic, and more industrial than their commercial neighbors, they disliked their inclusion in the enlarged buffer state against France which had been created by the Congress of Vienna. The British and French both supported their attempt to win independence, and stood against the eastern powers. Austria, Prussia, and Russia would perhaps have intervened in support of the Vienna settlement had not Russia been preoccupied with the Poles. Once it became clear that Louis Philippe did not dare to push France's traditional aim of trying to annex Belgium, Britain and France cooperated in a London conference of ambassa-dors (November, 1830) which proclaimed Belgian independence. There was some friction over the choice of a king. Leopold of Coburg, the widower of a British princess and the future husband of a French one, was eventually agreed on, and Britain allowed French armies to drive the armies of the Dutch king, William I, from Belgium. The Dutch did not accept the separation until 1839, when Belgium was proclaimed independent and perpetually neutral by the powers.

The Belgian crisis had split the liberal west from the conservative east. It had ended in an international agreement to revise the Vienna treaties, but only because the eastern powers had no choice but to accept the results of Franco-British policy. International cooperation had ceased to work, and the balance of power was replacing it again.

Between Britain and France there ensued several years of *entente cordiale*, foreshadowing the "cordial understanding" which was to precede World War I. The two countries both had parliamentary governments of a moderate sort, and strong middle classes, and industrial revolutions in process. The royal families were congenial, and the sending of the aged Talleyrand as ambassador to London seemed to indicate that much past bitterness was forgotten. But this division of Europe was not to last. There was friction between France and Great Britain— in Mediterranean affairs, over Spanish and Portuguese questions, over colonial outposts, over the French protective tariff. From the mid-thirties Louis Philippe turned more and more toward the conservative monarchies in the east. After Belgian independence, the attention of diplomats reverted to the "Eastern Ques-tion." The weakness of the Ottoman empire aroused Russian acquisitiveness and British and French alarm lest the straits leading from the Aegean into the Black Sea should fall into Russian hands. On these occasions the concert of the European powers still functioned.

As Ottoman strength declined, the control of the sultan over the outlying parts of the empire loosened. The powerful Pasha of Egypt, Mohammed Ali, became a threat to his master the sultan. Mohammed Ali demanded Syria as a reward for his aid at the time of the Greek revolution. The sultan refused. Mo-hammed Ali attacked in 1832–1833 and was on the point of overthrowing the sultan. To the alarm of Britain and France, Russia sent aid to the sultan. After great tension—for British and French fleets were ready to intervene—Turkey was obliged to sign with Russia the Treaty of Unkiar Skelessi (July, 1833) which in effect made Russia the protector of its ally the Ottoman empire.

This kind of protection of the Ottoman empire was far too close to ownership, or at least new management, to please the British and French—or the Turks. The sultan, aware of Russian ambitions, observed when he signed Unkiar Skelessi, that he was grasping at Russian protection "the way a drowning man grasps at a snake." The western powers were bound to do their best to "internationalize" the Turkish problem—that is, not let Russia handle it exclusively. On the other hand Russia, a few weeks after the Treaty of Unkiar Skelessi, tried to line up support by renewing the ties of the Holy Alliance binding Russia, Austria, and Prussia. An uneasy balance now prevailed in the Levant.

In 1839 the struggle between the sultan and Mohammed Ali, always surrounded by clouds of diplomacy, mushroomed into another international crisis. The sultan, in the midst of trying to drive his vassal out of Syria, died. His youthful successor did not seem capable of preventing Mohammed Ali from taking over a good part of the Ottoman empire, and this time all five great powers intervened to regulate the affairs of the empire. Ultimately (1841) Mohammed Ali, prodded by a British expeditionary force in Lebanon, was pushed back into Egypt as hereditary ruler under nominal Ottoman sovereignty. There he subsided. His heirs were to reign in Cairo until the expulsion of King Farouk in the 1950's. The height of the crisis, however, occurred in 1840 when France, traditionally interested in Egypt, found itself alone in defending Mohammed Ali when the other great powers had decided to coerce him (Treaty of London, July, 1840). Isolated, and with Austria, Prussia, Russia, and even Britain on the other side, France had to back down, change ministers, and accept the verdict of the European Concert. National interests and ambitions had disrupted the alignment of the "Liberal Bloc," just as it had previously disrupted the Concert of Europe.

In the Eastern Question there was always another round. The 1840 crisis had seen an international solution to the Turkish problem, rather than a purely Russian one. In 1841 Russia was forced back from its exclusive position at the Straits. By a Straits Convention signed by the five great powers, the Straits (Bosporus and Dardanelles) were closed in peacetime to the warships of all powers except the Ottoman empire. From the Russian point of view the decision was a good one in that it denied other people's navies access to the Black Sea; but on the other hand it also bottled Russian warships up in the Black Sea. But Russia, like France in the previous year, had to defer to the decision of the Concert of Europe.

Russian expansion southward had been checked by international supervision of the Eastern Question. At the same time the British had succeeded in checking French influence in the Mediterranean, without ending France's usefulness as a continental balancing force against the eastern powers. Through most of the 1840's France drifted away from Britain in foreign policy without becoming firmly attached to Austria, Prussia, and Russia. Czar Nicholas of Russia visited London in 1844 and returned to Saint Petersburg with the delusion that when the time was ripe Russia and Great Britain would be able to agree on the partition of the Ottoman empire. This misunderstanding was to contribute to the Crimean War in the 1850's, but before that time the attention of everyone was captured by the Revolutions of 1848.

1848–1850: THE DIPLOMACY
OF REVOLUTION

In their first onrush, the revolutions of 1848 seemed to overturn irrevocably the Vienna settlement of 1815. That settlement had been the work of the sovereigns, not of the peoples. Its defense through the years had been the work of a conservative international organization of sovereigns. Now the rulers were being limited by constitutions, if not overthrown outright. The peoples were taking matters into their own hands. In place of the international organization of kings it appeared that an international fraternity of liberals and nationalists would give Europe a new organization. There even appeared on the horizon Marx and Engels, who dreamed of an international movement of the working people.

In 1848 the rulers of Austria and Prussia were thrown off balance in the first assault. Metternich and his feeble-minded master Ferdinand I passed from the scene. The unstable Frederick William IV of Prussia almost conceded the game to the Berlin liberals—"his dear Berliners." And indeed the game seemed lost for the old concert of princes over which Metternich presided. In France Louis Philippe, who was not even a full member of the conservative sovereigns' club but had tried very hard to gain admission, went down before republicans and socialists. But across the Channel, Great Britain stood almost untouched. And in the east, irritated but unscathed, was Nicholas I of Russia, who became Metternich's heir in the job of organizing the conservative forces.

The reaction, which was a miracle for the frightened upper classes and a tragedy to the liberals and nationalists, is not in retrospect very hard to explain. The early exuberance of the revolutions hid the fact that affairs in Central Europe in 1848 were in a very different state from those of France in 1789. The conservative officials, armies, and aristocracies were stronger, the coalition of middle and lower class elements weaker than their past counterparts of 1789—or their future ones of 1917. The revolution in France was indeed very radical, but in the end its radicalism turned out to be more Parisian than French. Neither the Provisional Government in Paris nor Louis Napoleon, when he became President, went beyond a cautious policy of non-intervention in the rest of Europe. Both were pledged to an overturn of the Vienna settlement, but by diplomatic means. The liberals and radicals with visions of 1793 in their eyes, who expected France to dash across the Rhine and Alps to bring succor to struggling revolutionaries, were mistaken.

French troops did move. Louis Napoleon sent troops to Rome. They went to mediate between the Pope and his subjects but stayed until 1870, supporting a conservative papal government. This tortuous Roman policy was largely for the consumption of French Catholic opinion, and in foreign affairs was chiefly designed to forestall Austrian intervention in Italy. It was certainly not intended to succor revolutionaries. Britain, under Palmerston's leadership, was sympathetic to the Italians, but Britain and France were still suspicious of each other. There was no concerted effort on the part of the western powers to recast Europe along more liberal lines during Austria's and Prussia's discomfiture.

As things turned out it was Nicholas of Russia whose armies marched, and in the interests of the "monarchical principle," as the eastern governments vaguely but impressively called their brand of conservatism. Austria disciplined the Italians and the Czechs without outside help, but could not subdue the Hungarians. Russian troops sent by Nicholas helped. Frederick William IV of Prussia undertook on behalf of the Frankfurt Assembly, the nationalist and liberal reorganizers of Germany, to fight Denmark over the provinces of Schleswig and Holstein. When the great powers frowned on this enterprise Prussia withdraw the troops and, comforted by their return, disposed of the Frankfurt Assembly. But when Frederick William IV tried to form the "Erfurt Union," a north German confederation dominated by Prussia, Nicholas of Russia supported the objections of the Austrians, who wished to restore the old German Confederation of 1815. Frederick William IV had to back down, in the "humiliation of Olmütz," in 1850.

By 1850 the work of the Congress of Vienna seemed once more to have been saved from "the Revolution," as the conservatives called the principles of 1789. In the next two decades the map was to be considerably revised, but not primarily by the liberals.

1850–1870: THE DIPLOMACY OF REALISM

After the Revolutions of 1848 the flavor of European history changes. During the Metternich era there were many radical ideas but the conduct of affairs was in the hands of aristocrats with a traditional outlook. After the dreams of 1848 were shattered, the traditionalists did not inherit the earth. The problems which had been accumulating for half a century did not go away, and the more successful statesmen, whether liberal or conservative, were men like Louis Napoleon, Cavour, and Bismarck, who were willing to work with the new conditions. The word *Realpolitik,* popularized by a German book in the 1850's, meant paying attention to realities—and the realities included armies and national ambitions and popular demands for constitutions. Louis Napoleon, Cavour, and Bismarck were not without personal beliefs, or even illusions, but in the two decades after 1850 they demonstrated enough mastery of reality to bring about substantial changes both in international frontiers and domestic institutions.

In the course of those changes the Concert of Europe and the settlement of 1815 were not obliterated altogether, but neither remained what it had once been. When a number of clever and opportunistic statesmen—not revolutionary outsiders—sought definite changes in a short space of time, the green-topped tables of the Concert were by-passed. "Blood and iron," as Bismarck put it, replaced "speeches and majority resolutions." The result was a forcible revision of the Vienna settlement to the extent of a united Italy, a new German empire, and an Austria-Hungary facing southeast among the Slavs, to mention only the most striking developments.

An important aspect of these shifts was the realignment of the great powers. In the Crimean War (1854–1856) the Eastern Question appeared again as a major fact in western politics. Russian ambition to partition the Ottoman empire provoked a British and French expedition to the Crimea, aided by Sardinia. The limited defeat of Russia in the war did more than preserve the integrity of the Ottoman empire, and provide for the respect of Christians therein, and neu-

ON THE POINT OF DROWNING by Honoré Daumier. The Russian bear is about to go under, while Prussia stands by, calmly smoking a pipe. The drawing appeared in *Charivari*, October 9, 1855. (Courtesy of Robert M. Walker, Swarthmore, Pa.)

tralize the Black Sea. The peace conference, held in Paris, was in the best tradition of a concert of the great powers, but it also marked the triumphant return of France—and of France under a Bonaparte—to a position of European eminence. Waterloo and the Congress of Vienna could be considered avenged.

But there was more. Whereas Britain and France stood together once more in *entente cordiale,* the three conservative eastern powers of the old Holy Alliance were badly split. Austria, in spite of its debt to Czar Nicholas for his suppression of Hungary in 1849, had during the Crimean War thrown its diplomatic weight on the allied side, to an extent which had compelled Russian withdrawal from the Rumanian principalities (technically Ottoman possessions, but granted autonomy at the peace conference) and had played no small part in Russia's acceptance of defeat. The Austrians had so betrayed their late rescuer because they feared the czar's propensity for staking out spheres of influence in the Balkans and encouraging Balkan nationalities to rise. This "Habsburg ingratitude" would not soon be forgotten by the Russians. Furthermore, Russia, so long a menacing giant feared by everyone since its ponderous advance into Europe on the heels of the first Napoleon, was revealed in all its backwardness by the ineptitude of its defense in the Crimea. It would be some time before Russia, faced with serious problems of reorganization at home, would again play a major part in European affairs.

Britain and France, on the other hand, played out one more scene before they again cooled to one another. In the turbulence of 1859 to 1861, Cavour's superb opportunism, coupled with Louis Napoleon's incautious calculations of risk, set afoot the unification of most of Italy. Louis Napoleon had not intended to lose the initiative or let things go so far. After the defeat of diplomatically isolated Austria, he tried to call a halt and could not. While Garibaldi's filibuster was bringing the Two Sicilies and part of central Italy into the new kingdom, the very benevolent neutrality of Britain and France protected him and so contributed to the making of Italy.

In the 1860's, however, there was no Concert to talk away Bismarck's schemes, and no firm alignment either to the east or to the west. Russia was still aloof, nursing its wounds, and Bismarck assured himself of Alexander II's friendship by applauding the brutal Russian repression of a Polish insurrection in 1863. Austria was isolated, and could be manhandled by Prussia without provoking the hostility of any friends save for the lesser German states. Louis Napoleon, it will be recalled, underestimated Prussia's ability to defeat Austria in what turned out to be the Seven Weeks War, and overestimated his own ability to secure compensation for his neutrality. Worse still, from the French point of view, Louis Napoleon had overextended his resources and alienated Britain by his imperialistic ventures, especially his Mexican enterprise. Britain was disinclined to mix in the affairs of the continent—isolated, as it were, by choice. Bismarck could scarcely have asked for a better international situation in which to fight France, and in 1870 he did not resist the temptation to do so. The Franco-Prussian War, the most important conflict in Europe between 1815 and 1914, found France without allies. The breakdown of the Vienna system had led to a situation where the determined realist, Bismarck, could singlehandedly undertake an epochal reorganization of affairs. After 1871, a new Europe existed. France, its greatest power since the defeat of the Habsburgs in 1648, was displaced. In Central Europe diversity had given way to a powerful German state.

EUROPE AND THE WORLD

From 1789 to 1870 the gap between Europe and the rest of the world widened—in military power, commercial enterprise, productive capacity, wealth, well-being, and intellectual sophistication. This period, notable for drastic economic and political change at home, is often assumed to have been accompanied by a decline in overseas activity. It is tempting to believe in such a decline because it fits well with the rise of liberal theories which played down or denied the importance of colonies. Further, the conspicuous growth of the "new imperialism" after 1870 tends to emphasize the comparative inactivity of the preceding period, and contributes to the conclusion that Europe's attention in the early nineteenth century was turned inward upon itself.

These are the familiar generalizations, but they must be qualified almost out of existence. To be sure, the theory that Europe was "busy at home" seems adequately supported by the 1789 to 1815 period. Napoleon kept the great continental powers busy, himself included.

But Britain, virtually alone in having access to the rest of the world, profited from the situation to become the unchallenged mistress of overseas empire. Napoleon's allies, however unwilling, became the prey to British sea power. In 1806 Cape Colony, the tip of South Africa, was seized from Holland by the British. Spain's involvements with France gave its American colonies a chance to revolt in the decade and a half after Napoleon's seizure of Spain in 1808. Portugal's colony of Brazil opened its ports to foreign commerce during this period, and in 1822 achieved independence. India and Australia were left to British influence, owing to the preoccupation of the French and Dutch with the European situation. Napoleon's sale of Louisiana to the United States, and the fateful slowness of Spanish, British, and Russian penetration of California were direct or indirect results of the Napoleonic wars.

Waterloo seemed to introduce a new era of factory smokestacks and Victorian businessmen and statesmen and reformers preoccupied with domestic social questions. Now indeed Europe appeared to be "busy at home." Yet there were demobilized French officers who did not return from the wars but preferred to serve in the Latin American revolutions or in Egypt. There were Englishmen working in India and Cossacks extending Russian influence in Siberia and Central Asia, and there were Americans pushing westward toward the Pacific. The continuing European and American expansion had its literature, as in earlier times, and its scientific side. There were geographical societies interested in the yet largely unknown interior of Africa; this was the period of David Livingstone's exploring and missionary activity. The polar regions were penetrated. Russians and British were seeking to find northeast and northwest passages between the Atlantic and the Pacific, and were probing Central Asia from Russia and India. Missionaries like the Frenchman Evariste-Régis Huc explored parts of China and Tibet. The nineteenth-century religious revival played its part in European expansion by sending out missionaries who took European culture and sometimes political influence with them. There was population pressure, too, as thousands of people from the British Isles, Germany, and Scandinavia sought greater opportunities in such places as America and Australia. The economic motives for European expansion in this period were still more a search for raw materials than for markets or places to invest capital. Strategic considerations played a part. The prospect of a Suez Canal gave bases in the eastern Mediterranean and Red Sea a new importance.

Technology was making the west irresistible. Europeans were still not entirely secure against African Zulus or the nomads of Turkestan who fought the Russians so stubbornly, just as the American Indians resisted the westward movement of settlers in the United States. But inventions like the breechloading rifle and the revolver, the railroad and the telegraph, were to prevail. The fire power of warships, of Commodore Perry's flagship *Powhatan* with its sixteen 9-inch guns at Tokyo Bay in 1853 and 1854, was enormous. With these floating platforms of artillery at their door, the Japanese granted trading rights to the Americans.

The opening of Japan, which had been closed to all foreigners except the Dutch since the seventeenth century, became part of an internal Japanese revolution toward modernity which was to have vast consequences for world history. In China the decaying Manchu-ruled empire had already surrendered to the British several coastal ports in 1841 and 1842. Concessions to Europeans and Americans continued, in spite of outbursts of xenophobia. The uncultured foreigners, though few and far from home, were too powerful to be resisted. In 1860 17,000 British and French troops occupied Peking, the capital, to enforce respect for their diplomats, missionaries, and trade agreements. And China was at the same time losing its somewhat shadowy authority over its extremities. The French were penetrating Annam and Cochin China, the British Burma, and the Russians Turkestan and Manchuria. In other parts of the world—in India the British, in the islands of Southeast Asia the Dutch, and the penetration of Africa from former trading centers along the coasts—the discrepancy in power and energy was coming into play which was to make possible the burst of imperialism at the end of the century.

The story of Europe's colonial empires is too long to be told here. It is enough to remember that despite the loss of their American colonies by Spain and Britain, colonial empires continued. Missionaries, traders, and administrators, both military and civilian, were at work in spite of the preoccupations at home and the indifference or hostility of opinion. The abolition of the slave trade and the decline, by stages, of slavery itself posed problems in many colonies of the plantation type, such as those in the West Indies.

There were varieties of political control too numerous to list. Where there were few natives and many inhabitants of European stock it was possible to permit institutions of self-government to develop. An outstanding example was the Dominion of Canada formed in 1867, which had its own parliamentary government under the authority of the Crown. Cape Colony, in South Africa, and most of the settlements in Australia were also developing self-rule. But where large native populations existed, the territories remained under political control of the home governments. In India, after the great rebellion of 1857–1858, the old East India Company which had ruled the subcontinent was finally suppressed. From 1861 the India Office, with a British cabinet member at its head, governed through a viceroy with provincial assistants.

In spite of its predominance, Britain was not alone in the colonial field. France, almost without the knowledge of its own population, was quietly constructing a second colonial empire. Beginning with Algeria, in North Africa, the French were adding to the remnants of their former overseas holdings large segments of West and Equatorial Africa, together with Asiatic footholds in places such as Cochin China and Cambodia. France also had religious or financial interests in Syria, Tunis, and Egypt, testifying to an expansive energy which was to play a part in the imperialist age to come. Of the older colonial empires, Spain still had important holdings in the West Indies and the Philippines. The Dutch were strong in the East Indies islands. Portugal retained some important remnants of a once widespread empire. The apogee of Europe's global influence still lay in the future. But its foundations were laid and its materials were at hand.

PART FOUR

PLEBEIAN AND IMPERIAL EUROPE

1870–1914

34

ECONOMIC POWER
AND CHANGING
ATTITUDES

THE YEARS BETWEEN 1870 and 1914 are the years when the contemporary world begins to take shape—the world of airplanes, automobiles, labor unions, and telephones. In this period, the industrial system and the accumulation of industrial wealth spread rapidly. It affected the lives of masses of people and made itself felt far from its original home in Western Europe. It affected not only ways of life, but social systems, legislative action, and notions about man and the universe. There were vastly more *things* in the world than there had been before. In Western Europe there was so much to go round that it could be shared by the average citizen.

Always before, accretions in the total amount of wealth had meant new comforts principally for the people who were already well-to-do. There now became available through taxation or charity an increase in things like schools and, later, direct aid to the ill, the elderly, and the unemployed. The feasibility of providing such services was the subject of spirited debates. Out of them emerged a characteristic function for the modern state—the paternal, or welfare function. It was not wholly new, but previously the welfare institutions had mostly been operated by other agencies, generally ecclesiastical; and in the countryside, where families and neighbors cared for their own, they had been less necessary than in the growing cities. A new segment of state apparatus—the modern bureaucracy—appeared, and a great controversy raged between those who opposed the expansion of the government's power as leading toward tyranny, and those who felt that its accomplishments were grossly insufficient.

Of necessity, the organization of the economy underwent drastic revision with each step in the development of new manufacturing processes. The most conspicuous feature of this revision was the growth of very large business units which rapidly reached such a degree of size, complexity, and influence as to constitute states within states. As technology grew more and more intricate, making possible greater production and profits through the use of more machines, more and more money was required to get a firm started and to keep it going. A moderately wealthy man might himself have financed a cotton mill in the early nineteenth century; it took hundreds of wealthy men to provide enough money to start a company to manufacture locomotives or ocean liners. The result was that joint enterprises grew up, staffed by large corps of hired experts and managers, administering huge amounts of capital and employing thousands of employees. Nothing quite like them had ever been seen before, and their relationship to the state, to their employees, to the consumer, and to the rest of the economy had to be improvised and argued as they grew.

There were all sorts of by-products of the growth of the large business unit. A class of people who worked in offices for large firms in sub-executive or super-clerical jobs appeared. They shared many of the characteristics of the older professional groups—their social position was moderately "genteel," like that of teachers, doctors, soldiers, and priests. They were "white collar" people who wore what we call street clothes and they worked by their brains and not their hands. But they lacked the personal independence of the professional man. They worked regular hours, and for a salary. They constituted a new class in society. The more complicated the machines became, the more numerous the scientific advances and the more intricate the routines of offices, the more skills were required. All over Europe, education, particularly technical education, grew more important, and countries which lagged behind found themselves outdistanced in economic development by their better trained neighbors.

But there were repercussions beyond these. The new kinds of productive techniques provided not only wealth but also power. On an absolute basis, there was now more power in Europe than ever before—power of all sorts and sizes. People could move faster; steam hammers could flatten more effectively; guns could shoot farther. But also there perpended more abstruse forms of power. Literacy brought a sort of power to the literate—intellectual power. It also brought a sort of power to the people who wrote and published. Now that large masses of the population could read, they could be influenced by crusaders and demagogues. Further, accumulations of money and control over business brought a new— or at least more conspicuous—form of power to the accumulators. The heads of a very large business had fairly direct control in many cases over the welfare and livelihood of their employees. They also had an enormous influence over the people whose manner of life became dependent on their products. Through their means and prestige, they frequently had a measure of influence over governments. On the other hand, opposition to wealth and even to property itself was organized on a vast scale in the form of labor unions and socialist parties. Since the nature of this power was mainly new, its distribution and its management could not be handled by familiar institutions. It created many of the tensions of the twentieth century.

Clearly, the state was the most powerful and effective organization in European society. It turned out to be in almost every case the ultimate beneficiary of the new sources of power. Parties and classes might fight among themselves; the state could, and must, arbitrate among them.

The effects of industrialization and the other changes which accompanied it reached into every phase of European life. Airplanes, newspapers, schools, and hospitals. Mass meetings and department stores. Automobiles and summer resorts. Suburbs and machine guns. Telephones and slums. Typewriters and street clothes. Unemployment and cheap pottery. Ideologies and sewing machines. Old-age pensions and World War I.

THE GROWTH OF ECONOMIC POWER

The Age of Coal and Cotton began to change into the Age of Steel at about the time when industry was spreading from its first homes in England, northern France, and Belgium into the other parts of Europe. Perfection of better methods of steel production took place in the 1870's. The Bessemer converter, invented in 1856, had been supplemented by the more satisfactory open-hearth methods of Siemens and Martin in the 1860's. To them were added, in the 1870's, the Thomas-Gilchrist methods for making steel out of lower-grade iron ore.

Lower-grade ores were present in the major iron deposits then known in

INDUSTRY AND ECONOMIC GROWTH IN EUROPE ABOUT 1910

Europe, the Lorraine basin, divided between France and Germany after 1871. Beginning in the late 1870's, these ores were exploited. The price of steel declined steadily. Between 1865 and 1910, the world production of steel increased from half a million tons to almost sixty million, of which well over half was in Europe, mostly in France, Britain, and Germany.

Steel was, as it still is, the most important substance of an industrial society; it is essential in the manufacture of machines of all kinds. Once it became freely available a vast expansion was possible in the number and efficiency of textile machines, bridges, trains, farm implements, and every other mechanical invention. Things like sewing machines and typewriters, which were in themselves to have a dramatic impact on the lives of people who used them, became practicable for the first time and, being practicable, were accordingly invented. The availability of cheap and versatile steel revolutionized the production of every existing commodity, from wheat to chinaware, and made possible the creation of thousands of new ones.

Behind steel, and everything else, however, lay the facts of fuel and power. Coal was still, in 1914, sovereign. Without it, steel could not be manufactured and, indeed, nothing could be manufactured very conveniently. Water-wheels still turned, and wood was still burned on domestic hearths, but neither of them was strong enough or cheap enough to furnish the needs of a considerable factory. The coal-producing areas of Europe were thus the root sources of wealth, and from them industry spread in concentric circles. The major coal deposits known in 1870 were in Britain, in northern France and Belgium, and in western Germany (conveniently near the iron ore of Lorraine). These were mined with increasing thoroughness, and other deposits came gradually into production, mainly in Russian Poland. Coal production in Britain increased three and a half times in the period; in France, fivefold; in Germany, over fifteenfold.

Alternatives to coal, which were to supplement it in the first half of the twentieth century (and, conceivably, to replace it in the second), were already coming into existence. The first of these was electricity. The principle of electricity had been roughly known since the early eighteenth century. By 1914, the dynamo and the transformer had been invented and perfected. But so far electricity was generated mostly by motors which used coal, and its use was mainly for lighting, not for industrial power. Not until the development of hydroelectric power, after World War 1, was electricity to dethrone coal. The second alternative source of power was petroleum. Since it was early discerned to be the best available source of propulsive power, it became more and more important by 1914.

Mobility was an essential form of power, and it was a requirement for marketing which was, in turn, the requirement for all large industrial growth. People had to be got to the factories to work in them, and the goods produced had to be gotten from the factory to the consumer. The period from 1870 to 1914 was still the age of the railroad. The automobile, not yet mass-produced, was still a toy. Railways spread out with incredible rapidity. By 1914, Europe was equipped with a very complete network and with exceedingly efficient rolling stock and management. England, which already had a well developed rail system by the middle of the century, increased its miles of track fourfold. With only a few hundred miles of railroads in 1860, Russia's track length had risen by the 1880's to fifteen thousand miles and continued to expand rapidly. Railways became a symbol, symptom, and prerequisite of economic growth.

But railways also involved an exceedingly high capital investment. The land through which they had to pass to reach the most useful destinations—the centers of cities—was the most expensive land to buy, and the costs of materials and operation were very high. Many of the railways failed to make money for their investors. Others yielded an extremely low return. As a consequence, tendencies which were noticeable throughout many other spheres of the European economy were especially conspicuous in railways: there was an increasing inclination on the part of the companies to eliminate competition and to pool their resources through mergers. And there was a similar inclination on the part of governments to subsidize or to take over unprofitable but useful lines. By 1914, one of the major railway companies of France was state-owned and operated, and over 90 percent of Germany's were. The Russian railways were all state-owned, and so, by 1914, were those of Belgium, Italy, and Switzerland.

These tendencies—toward merger of competing private firms, and toward state control—were the first and biggest breach in the citadel of private enterprise and free competition in the European economy after 1870. The industrial growth in almost all countries had to some extent (greatest in Britain, least in Russia) taken place under the aegis of the idea of a free economy which was intertwined with the doctrines of political liberalism, and monopoly was feared because it concentrated power in the hands of the monopolist. But railways, like many another industry afterward, posed a problem: they were essential to the public welfare and to general economic progress, but they were in some cases losing money. Competition was frequently unfeasible. For the apostles of free capitalism, a neat dilemma was posed, and in cases where it became acute it was invariably solved—in the end, even in England—by government ownership. Only the state had large enough resources to underwrite the losses which seemed to inhere in the railroad business.

A somewhat comparable set of tendencies was perceptible in the sphere of finance. Many causes led to larger and larger banking units and toward state control or direction. The right to issue banknotes had come by 1914 to be limited to the "central" bank in most countries, and while the central bank usually remained theoretically a private institution, as with the Banks of England and France, the connection with the state treasury was of necessity close.

In industry and commerce, free competition showed more vigor than in banking or railroads, and state-owned enterprise was much rarer, but there was a similar tendency to combination. The requirements for larger amounts of capital to finance the new and costly equipment of modern industry were so great that individuals could not raise them or, if they could, did not care to risk their entire property in one venture. In the 1850's in England and the 1860's in France, limited liability companies—what we call corporations—had become legal, and they spread rapidly. By 1914 new ones were being formed in France at the rate of 1,500 a year. They permitted an enormous expansion of the capital and thus of the size of companies. Great international businesses, controlling vast numbers of factories and many different sorts of manufactures—and owning, perhaps, their raw-material sources in distant colonies—became common. The small producer, at a disadvantage in marketing and in raising new capital for improving his plant, was more and more often driven out of business.

As the titans of industry came to dominate it, they also came to cooperate with one another. Agreements were frequently entered into to divide markets, to share raw-materials sources and, most of all, to stabilize prices. Such agreements became progressively more common and more formal. In Great Britain, with its strong traditions of free competition, they were unenforceable and might be illegal, but on the continent there were few such inhibitions, and indeed in Germany such arrangements were encouraged and sponsored by the government, as tending to stabilize prices and eliminate business bankruptcies.

These arrangements were known as pools, or cartels, and they were a form of monopoly. The first formal cartel was established in the German coal industry, in the 1890's; dozens of others soon followed. Less formal but scarcely less effective arrangements were made in Britain, where single firms or groups of firms early secured far-reaching control over such enterprises as the sale and manufacture of salt, of sewing thread and, in the 1900's, of part of the great British merchant marine. In addition, international cartels were established for the control and price-fixing of transatlantic shipping, rubber, and other products.

The essential features of business and finance, then, were the tendency to consolidation, the use of more and more capital, and sometimes increasing government control.

CHANGING SOCIAL AND ECONOMIC PROBLEMS

Underlying the growth of economic power and of the size of business units, was the growth of the market. A part of this expanding market was overseas. Europe's foreign trade was bounding upward—it increased about fourfold from 1870 to 1914. But much of the growth was within Europe. The population was still rising rapidly—from 266,228,000 in 1850 to 462,828,000 in 1914. The distribution of this increase was very uneven—the French population averaged an increase of only about ⅓ of 1 percent a year, while in parts of Eastern Europe the annual increase was nearer 2 percent.

The European population would have been much larger than it was had not so many of its more adventurous citizens left home. In the century after the Congress of Vienna, some fifty million emigrated to other continents. Logically, they came from the places where the population growth—and hence the pressure on employment opportunities—was greatest: Britain and Germany in the earlier period, Italy and Russia later. Overseas, they not only helped to build new societies like the United States and Argentina; they also helped expand the overseas markets for European industry.

Within Europe, the continuing concentration of the new population in cities helped to increase the market. Country people still provided for many of their own needs of shelter, food, and clothing, but city people had to buy everything they used. The towns were growing faster than ever. London in 1870 had about three and a quarter million; by 1914, it had more than doubled. During roughly this period the spread of manufacturing to new areas is indicated by these figures for population growth: Barcelona (in Spain) from 180,000 to 587,000; Milan (in Italy) from 196,000 to 600,000; Warsaw (in Russian Poland) from 180,000 to 790,000, Dusseldorf (in western Germany) from 63,000 to 358,000.

These new urban populations were becoming the "typical Europeans," replacing the peasant. They depended upon a complicated and highly specialized economy to house, nourish, and employ them. They had interests and demands different from those of the simpler societies of the past, and their concentration enabled them to discuss and organize into movements and parties. From their needs, and from those of the rural populations still existing beside them, more complicated economic and social problems ensued.

In 1914 there were still more people engaged in farming in Europe than in any other occupation, though in some countries like England and Belgium there were many fewer in farming than in all branches of industry considered together. The vast increase in urban populations meant of course that the market for farm products grew. But the position of European farmers was precarious. The greatest single crop in Europe before 1870 was wheat. Then proliferating railways and the invention of steamboats made wheat from overseas available on the European market; in North America, in Russia, and in Argentina, the fertile vastnesses could be made to grow wheat far more cheaply and in far greater abundance than on the small and highly fertilized farms of Western Europe. The European farmer was threatened with extinction.

He escaped it, if at all, by one of two methods. In the case of the Danes, the Swiss, and the Dutch, the sophisticated farming populations hurriedly shifted from grain crops to dairying and to livestock; they became suppliers for the great industrial regions which lay near them, in Germany, Belgium, northern Italy or, especially, Britain. They became the richest as well as the most forward-looking farmers on the continent. Similarly, in areas near big cities, farmers turned to truck gardening, for whose perishable products there devoloped an almost inexhaustible demand.

Secondly, the crop farmers of all countries turned to their governments for aid. What they wanted, specifically, were tariffs to bring the price of imported foods up to the level at which they could profitably produce. In most cases they got them; France and Germany both imposed taxes on imported wheat, wine, and other major farm products in the late 1870's or 1880's. Most other continental countries followed suit.

England did not. By 1880, so large a percentage of the English population was employed in industry or commerce that food purchasers far outnumbered food producers, and the former naturally opposed a duty which would raise the cost of living. Moreover, the free trade tradition, which had lately won its final great battles, was now very strong. On the continent, where laissez faire had never been so popular, the prejudice against tariffs was much smaller. The farmers were frequently supported by the businessmen of France, Germany, or Italy in the demand for tariff protection, since the manufacturers also wished to protect themselves against foreign (and especially British) competition. In every case they got their wish; by 1900, virtually every major continental country except Holland had adopted tariffs, and the tariffs tended inexorably to mount.

The opening up of the United States' and Canadian farms, occurring simultaneously with the rapid expansion of world industrial production, started a downward trend in farm prices which has never been reversed except during wars. Only by subsidies, tariffs, or other controls have governments been able to keep the farmer going. The tariffs which European countries adopted in the late nineteenth century were never sufficiently high to save the farmer from financial difficulties. In Russia, as in the United States, more and more owners lost their land to city banks. In Prussia, the aristocracy preserved enough enterprise and enough political influence to stay in business, but they did so by wangling ever higher tariffs and, after 1900, direct subsidies from a regime which regarded them as essential to its survival. The Prussian *Junkers,* in turn, found themselves more and more reluctant to lose their special influence in a government whose benevolence was indispensable to them, and a strange and ominous political problem ensued.

In the most successful farming regions—Denmark, Holland, West Germany—the dilemma of the small peasant was partly resolved by Cooperation. The cooperative movement, which had originated in Britain in the 1840's, was increasingly applied to farming. Voluntary village groups, often with government aid, banded together to buy farm machinery and fertilizers, to learn and apply the results of modern research, and to dispose of their products. The farmers' cooperatives became, throughout Northwestern Europe, the most effective and characteristic form of agricultural self-help.

The hardships of the farmer were continuous. Those of the manufacturer, worker, shopkeeper, and banker were cyclical. The opening years of the 1870's marked the culmination of a long period of prosperity. A high, and rapidly expanding, prosperity had prevailed for two decades throughout most of Europe. The period had been relatively free of social and economic tensions. In 1873, however, the age of prosperity began to end. A depression spread over the world, inaugurated by a bank panic in Vienna and a speculative boom and collapse in Germany. It lasted, in one form or another, and with intermediate ups and downs, for over twenty years.

The period was one when industry and wealth were expanding rapidly. Three things caused the period to be regarded as one of depression by contemporaries: one was the plight of agriculture; second, prices generally declined, or hovered at a point below that of the previous decade; third, there were frequent business failures, with consequent widespread if sporadic unemployment.

The decline in prices may be ascribed to several causes. The most conspicuous was the general governmental policy of balanced budgets and "sound" currencies. This policy, which corresponded with one of the basic tenets of clas-

SHIP BUILDING ON THE CLYDE 1917–18 by Muirhead Bone. British school.
(Courtesy of The Metropolitan Museum of Art, Gift of Muirhead Bone,
1919)

sical economists and indeed of most businessmen, was adopted by one after another of the major trading countries of the world. The gold standard, by which currencies were valued and measured in an almost unvarying relationship to the extremely stable price of gold, had been universally adopted by 1900, except for a few silver-standard countries like China. It had a very beneficial result for those members of the population who were not unemployed. Wages, declining on the whole much less than prices, became more valuable. As a consequence, the standard of living of many European workers rose.

The rise was, however, accompanied by insecurity, by fear of unemployment, and by an increasing sense of power and also of injustice on the part of working men. The period after 1870 was by no means so tranquil, as regards social and economic issues, as the previous era. It was accompanied by sharp industrial conflicts and, in every country, by the founding or the extension of socialist parties—and of labor unions—but there were no revolutions in Western Europe.

The growth of unions was one of the spectacular features of the age. By 1914, the numbers involved in the major countries were very large; over four million in Britain, almost three million in Germany, almost a million in Italy. In every case, membership still counted only a minority of workers, but often the unions were best organized in the most essential industries. They had connections and implications beyond the purely economic ends for which they organized and struck. Almost all European unions were associated with political movements, or at least with political ideas. In most cases these ideas were boldly reformist, in many cases revolutionary. In Germany, the largest union organization, the Free Unions, was closely associated with the Social Democratic party. In England, the unions were among the sponsors of the Labor party. In France, by 1914, unionism was strongly colored by the syndicalist movement, which openly preached that the ultimate purpose of unionization was to bring about the General Strike, which would in turn bring about the destruction of the state and of bourgeois society.

Most working people never really meant to be revolutionaries but they nevertheless became a powerful and independent political force, difficult to assimilate into the old political order. Working men in practice showed a marked reluctance to abandon the capitalism which was increasing real wages by producing cheap commodities. But very strong pressures were brought by the working class unions and parties for social reforms, and in most cases the "bourgeois" governments proved willing to make concessions. In country after country in the years before 1914, laws were passed providing for insurance (generally paid for in part by the employer, the worker, and the state) against illness, old age, and accident. Other laws regulated hours of work, safety conditions, and the employment of children. In these fields, Germany and the Scandinavian countries had advanced furthest by World War I. France and the eastern countries were the most backward, but almost all governments had passed some sort of social reform measures.

These concessions, always expensive, were possible and effective only when the wealth of the community was great and expanding. They were a symptom, a luxury as it were, of a rich society. And there was no question that

Europe in 1914 was rich and getting richer. It was able to produce far more than ever before. By selling its surplus abroad it could purchase the raw materials which were needed for its factories and could import the foodstuffs—and luxuries —which it no longer produced in adequate supply for its growing populations. Moreover, out of the profits of the past there had been built up large investments in other parts of the world, and the interest from these paid for a considerable part of the imported raw materials, food, and luxuries.

By 1914 Britain, France, Germany, Holland, and most other western countries were buying from foreign countries more than they were selling. The surplus was being paid for with the income from foreign investments. Europe, still in the full vigor of its own industrial growth, was already in the position of an heir living off inherited securities. It was an extremely fortunate situation, and while many of the social and administrative problems which had accompanied the expansion of wealth and the transformation of the economy were still unsolved, the likelihood of almost perpetual enrichment was generally agreed on.

World War I was to disrupt and, in some essentials, to destroy the foundations upon which Europe's prosperity and growth rested.

CONFLICTING IDEALS

As Europe reached a new physical maturity it was beset with conflicts about beliefs, and these in at least simplified form reached the multitudes as nothing had since the Reformation.

The traditional religions carried on, but they faced powerful competitors in nationalism, liberalism, democracy, socialism, and other secular interests. Churches were less closely associated with education and charity as states took over these functions. The growth of big cities and the shifts in population separated many people from religious practices. Intellectuals had long been attracted by the secular ideals of science, of progress through reason. Now, with spectacular technological achievements before their eyes, and with popularized versions of scientific principles in their heads, people were tempted to discern a rivalry between science and religion. A conflict for influence over the public developed between the clergy and spokesmen for science, each believing that the other threatenend fundamental values. Moreover, as states sought to assure themselves of the exclusive allegiance of their citizens, they came into conflict with churches.

Within the Roman Catholic Church, a firm stand was taken against the innovations of the age. In 1864, Pope Pius IX issued a *Syllabus of Errors* denouncing liberalism, rationalism, science, and "progress" as these ideas were being interpreted by many European intellectuals. In 1870 an ecumenical council proclaimed the dogma of papal infallibility: that the Pope speaks with supernatural authority when pronouncing *ex cathedra* on matters of faith and morals. In general, the tendency among Catholics to look to Rome for guidance—called ultramontanism—was winning out over the tendency of "national" churches, such as the French Catholic Church, to maintain a high degree of autonomy in the management of their affairs. The Catholic Church, in spite of its loss of temporal power, was able to maintain the loyalty of its adherents and indeed to strengthen its spiritual leadership.

It proved able, too, to adjust itself to new conditions of science and society. Leo XIII, who became Pope in 1878, encouraged scientific research, and in his famous encyclicals *Immortale Dei* (1885), *Libertas* (1888), and *Rerum Novarum* (1891) interpreted the problems of modern society in terms of Catholic doctrines. This movement of Social Catholicism condemned materialism—the widespread tendency to interpret human destiny in terms solely of material success and comfort in mortal life—and socialistic efforts to abolish private property. The encyclicals emphasized the opposition between Christianity and certain aspects of liberalism as well, notably those that seemed to ennoble extreme and competitive individualism. They dwelt upon the desirability of a cooperative society, of action by groups to secure social reform. They attacked the abuses of capitalism and welcomed efforts such as the formation of Catholic trade unions. Leo XIII also stated the view that Catholics were not compelled to subvert particular forms of government. For example, he urged Frenchmen to accept the Third Republic and take part in politics. But these adjustments were made without relinquishing fundamental doctrines or permitting adherents complete freedom to interpret the relationship of scientific discoveries and new social conditions to Catholic dogma.

Within Protestantism there continued to be many sects and tendencies. In the new conditions of increasing discussion of scientific discoveries and insistent social problems, some Protestants remained "fundamentalist," refusing to accept any scientific discoveries or social attitudes which did not agree with the Bible as the literally inspired word of God. Others became "modernists" who in greater or less degree were willing to reinterpret Christian truths in the light of accumulating human experience. Having no international center of authority like that of the Roman Catholics, Protestant churches entered into almost no conflicts with the national states. As in Catholicism, there were within Protestantism movements for social betterment, such as the Christian Social Union founded in Great Britain in 1889 which tried to apply Christian principles to problems of social reform.

Judaism had its "modernist" movement, especially in Western Europe. The Jews of Eastern Europe tended to remain Orthodox. Socially, the Jews of Western and Central Europe tended to become assimilated as the spread of liberal and democratic principles led to the removal of ancient discriminations. However, the frustrations experienced by many Europeans during the rapid social changes connected with industrialization and urbanization and democratization contributed to the re-emergence of anti-semitism. Nationalist extremism, which in many cases sprang from the same social dislocations, made anti-semitism worse. In Eastern Europe, especially in Poland and Russia, anti-semitism was actually encouraged at times by the Russian government and took the form of pogroms (massacres). Many Jews fled toward the west. In 1897, the first congress of the Zionist movement which sought to make Palestine into a Jewish national home was held in Switzerland. Anti-semitism, besides being encouraged by social problems and nationalism, was fostered by racist doctrines which fed on the same sources and were bolstered by pseudo-scientific generalizations from biology.

The growing prestige of science is best illustrated by the work of Charles Darwin, whose *The Origin of Species* (1859) was one of those enormously influential books comparable to Adam Smith's *Wealth of Nations* or Isaac Newton's *Principia*. Like the earlier books, Darwin's appeared to sum up a subject about which much had been said but which had until then not quite come into focus. The idea of evolutionary change was in the air in the nineteenth century, and had been demonstrated by geological findings which helped to measure huge stretches of time. The idea that living things were all related to each other had already captivated the imaginations of biologists. In agriculture much had been done with the breeding of animals and the improvement of crops. The conviction that society and institutions were influenced by environment went back at least to Montesquieu and Locke. More recently, the theories of Malthus on population had suggested the notion of a struggle for survival, and the classical economists had emphasized the beneficence of competition. Charles Darwin suggested the applicability of these notions to biology. He was not, however, a mere synthesizer of other people's ideas, but a working biologist who had spent decades in field work all over the world. His basic idea was simple enough: living things had evolved into the various known species by a process of constantly adapting themselves to the environment. This process consisted of "natural selection" in the struggle for survival; that is, of thousands of minor variations, some helped their possessors to survive. Through the generations these useful variations were accentuated in a gradual differentiation of species. It was Darwin's years of collecting evidence and arranging it according to geographical distribution and order of appearance through geological time which appeared to prove his thesis.

Darwin's theory was one of those great, illuminating explanations of cosmic significance, characteristic of the nineteenth century. It could not fail to arouse tremendous controversy, for it appeared to many people to refute the Biblical story of the creation and to deprive man of the significant role assigned him by the Christian interpretation of history. For if man had evolved from lower forms of life, whence came the soul that Christians believe to be the peculiar treasure which God has bestowed on the human species? Darwin's theory was not alone in disturbing settled beliefs, but it was the most spectacular among many findings—in anthropology, archaeology, and historical scholarship, for example—which were doing so; and it appeared just in time to reverberate widely in the broadened public opinion of the late nineteenth century.

Darwinism stood for "science," but there were immediately very unscientific efforts to bend his ideas to all sorts of uses. The idea of a struggle for survival in which the fittest survived was used to justify *Realpolitik,* armaments, imperialism, and class warfare. The "fittest" could be interpreted to apply to a nationality, a race, or a social class, which had the upper hand, or the tables could be turned and the struggle for survival used to justify a struggle against those who had the upper hand. To some, Darwinism seemed to suggest the naturalness of free competition in economics, while to others it suggested cooperation for survival. Finally, Darwinism could be used in defense of the proposition that man and his reason and his moral standards were simply products of a nature "red in tooth and claw."

Darwin's serious scientific work, and the efforts—usually called "social Darwinism"—to use it in justifying some particular group of the "fittest," are indicative of the thought of late nineteenth-century Europe. There was much careful, scientific work in complement to the visible transformation of the continent being made by industrialization. This work seemed at first to explain so much that a great impression of rapid scientific progress was given, and it seemed as if all the secrets of life and society must be explicable and would soon be explained. This optimism proved to be premature. When it came to summing up what had been learned, the disinterested and wise admitted that while a great stride forward had been taken there were still many mysteries unsolved. Finally, with the broadening of public opinion to whole nations the popularizing of scientific discoveries such as Darwin's and the deification of science contributed to demagoguery, hysteria, and nationalistic and racist prejudicies. This misuse of science, it began to appear, might possibly threaten the very ideals of individual liberty and rationalism which had always been associated with scientific inquiry. But if the shadow of this possibility fell on a few minds, for most people before World War I faith persisted in progress resting on scientific research and made visible by ocean liners and automobiles.

LIBERALS AND CONSERVATIVES

Liberals had always been optimistic about man and his prospects. The optimism, while it harmonized with liberal theories about human nature, the state, and the history of Europe, was not entirely a matter of theory. Like all social philosophies, it was based on experience, or what its adherents took to be experience. In the late nineteenth century a host of new facts confronted liberalism, challenging the liberals to account for them or change their beliefs. Rival philosophies on all sides challenged persons of liberal inclination by offering their own interpretations of what was happening to Europe and to the world.

The new facts are already familiar. Among them were: the "long depression" from the 1870's to the 1890's, with its attendant hardships; intensified economic competition among nations as industrialization spread; the rise of trusts and cartels within nations, and the intensification of imperialism overseas; increasing political and economic action of the lower classes, following the extension of the suffrage and the growth of labor unions and socialist parties; the intensification of nationalism with the growth of popular education and literacy and universal military service in the older states, and the awakening of nationalism among hitherto passive peoples, especially in Eastern Europe; and finally, decisions of policy associated with all these problems—decisions about tariffs, colonial expansion, social legislation, alliances, and armaments.

On one side, the liberals before World War I found that conservatives were in many ways better prepared than themselves to deal with these changing conditions. First, the conservatives of all shades of opinion had never taken the optimistic view that all would be well if the inequalities and special privileges of the old regime were abandoned in favor of policies of laissez faire. Disraeli in Britain and Bismarck in Germany found it easy to recommend tariffs and social legislation regulating conditions of work and wages and setting up programs of insurance against sickness and accidents. Conservatives were not in any way committed to an individualistic society. They could with consistency accept trusts and labor unions, and some of the more philosophical of them recommended a "corporate" organization of society in which both employers and employees would be grouped according to the industries or occupations in which they were engaged. Another sign of their flexibility was this: some conservatives in the period after 1870 found it possible and convenient to extend the suffrage to the great mass of the population, thereby outbidding the more rigid of the liberals, who were committed to a property qualification for voting. And, most helpful politically, many conservatives from Great Britain to Russia overcame their former aversion to nationalism, realizing that nationalistic appeals, often coupled with imperialism, touched the pride of the populace and rendered palatable military service, armaments budgets, and expansion. Nationalism could easily be made to harmonize with the conservative affinity for group organization and respect for past traditions.

From another side liberals in the late nineteenth century were faced with the powerful theoretical and practical appeal of democracy and socialism (see below).

Liberalism was split by these challenges into two principal divisions. On the one hand, many liberals continued to affirm the major tenets of earlier "classical" liberalism, regarding liberty as an end in itself, and also as a collection of practical recommendations such as free trade or opposition to welfare legislation.

On the other hand, a few liberals from the 1880's, and afterwards increasing numbers of them, revised their beliefs about *means*, while insisting that their *end* (the liberty of the individual) was unchanged. In general the revised liberalism moved toward the democratic beliefs, already described, of such pioneers as J. S. Mill in Britain and Alexis de Tocqueville in France. This led liberal factions like the French Radical or German Progressive parties to accept the idea of protective legislation for workers as tending to make them more free, even if it encroached upon the freedom of employers or taxpayers.

On a philosophical level the most important modification in the view of man and his liberty was recognition that the individual could not be thought of as independent of and prior to society. Man was still viewed optimistically, but his freedom was thought to consist of the development of his potentialities and human qualities *in society*. A man alone was a useless abstraction. It followed from this view that the state need not be a mere defender of absolute rights to specific properties or liberties. The state became an instrument whose power could be used to create a good society: one in which individuals could develop their talents. Liberalism in this guise retained its optimistic and rationalistic and utilitarian traditions, but said goodbye to *laissez faire*.

THE EUROPEAN LEFT

To the left of liberalism in the period from 1870 to 1914 lay social democracy. Europe in those decades was still overwhelmingly monarchical and aristocratic, with the large exception of republican France and the minor one of Switzerland. Monarchical and aristocratic Europe was, however, opening the gates of its city to the plebeian multitude. Much depended on how the masses of new voters would use their power. When war came in 1914, the outcome of the drift into popular participation in government was still unclear. But the revolutionary landslide so long predicted by conservatives had not taken place. Many of the new voters supported traditional parties. And there were several rival kinds of socialism.

Of the socialisms, Marxism was to play the greatest part in European and world history. It was a product of the mid-nineteenth century, and was built of much the same materials as liberalism, particularly in its assumption that men were animated primarily by materialistic motives. Marxism was one of those all-encompassing systems so characteristic of the nineteenth century's self-confident urge toward synthesis of everything. It was, however, so universal in its pretensions and so apparently scientific that, for many people who hungered after certainty, it became a secular religion. Far into the twentieth century, followers of Marx forgot that hypotheses are made to be broken, or science is nothing. On the other hand, later critics sometimes forgot, in their disgust with the idolatry shown Marx, that the system was a work of some merit, and built in good faith.

Marx himself contributed to the impression that his philosophy was a thing apart, unique and untouchable, when he called the early socialists such as Owen, Fourier, Blanc, and Proudhon "Utopians." The name has stuck. What Marx meant by it was that these men, whose works he had devoured as a young German Ph.D. studying in Paris in the 1840's, were unscientific compared to himself. They were moralists, who knew what was right but did not understand how it was to come about. Marx and his friend Friedrich Engels, another German, thought, at least as early as 1848, that they knew how socialism was to come about. They thought that they had mastered the science of social change, of history's direction. They were "scientific socialists."

Karl Marx (1818–1883) was born in the Prussian Rhineland of middle-class parents and educated in German universities until, at 23, he took his doctorate and became a radical democratic newspaper editor. When his paper was suppressed, he moved to Paris, in 1844, and began to wade through the enormous literature on social and political questions which had accumulated in France since 1789. In Friedrich Engels (1820–1895), son of a wealthy German businessman who owned shares in a factory in Manchester, England, he found a philosopher and economist able to acquaint him with the *Condition of the Working Class in England*, the title of Engels' book published in 1845.

Under French and English influences the two German philosophers, already democrats, learned to be socialists. After four years of activity with small underground revolutionary groups in France and Belgium they published, in January, 1848, the *Communist Manifesto*. It attracted small notice in a year which was soon deluged with revolutions, but it contained the outline of an imposing theory of revolutions. After futile political activities in western Germany in 1848–1849, Marx took refuge in London, where he was to spend the rest of his life in obscurity, writing in the British Museum. Engels followed in 1850, to tend his business interests while giving his main attention to socialist questions and considerable financial support to Marx.

Marx remained poor and obscure all his life—a shabby refugee. He wrote a few commentaries for Horace Greeley in the *New York Tribune* in 1851 and 1852 (*Germany: Revolution and Counter-Revolution*) and for a German language newspaper in the United States (*The Eighteenth Brumaire of Louis Bonaparte*, 1852). Most of his vast and painstaking composition remained unpublished. In 1859 two chapters of an economics book appeared in Germany as *The Critique of Political Economy*. In 1867 the first of the four volumes of his master work *Das Kapital* was printed in Hamburg. Later volumes were edited and published by the loyal Engels after Marx's death in 1883. Engels lived to enjoy some of the fame which the slow-starting but weighty reputation of Marx's work, together with his own writings, earned toward the end of the century.

Marx's activities as founder, in 1864, of the first International Workingmen's Association, and his numerous polemical writings in the socialist press, attracted little attention. Englishmen never took in large numbers to the ponderous German brand of socialism. In France, the working class tended to follow Proudhon and to distrust the state which played so large a part in Marx's philosophy. The anarchists, exemplified in the brilliant, unstable Russian conspirator Michael Bakunin (1814–1876), contested Marx's leadership in the International, which in any case broke up in the 1870's after the suppression of the insurrectionary (though not Marxian or even very socialistic) Paris Commune of 1871. In spite of these setbacks Marxism became by 1914 the dominant socialist impulse in Europe, partly owing to its comprehensiveness and scientific trappings, and partly to the prestige of German thought and of the German Social Democratic (Marxist) Party, the largest in the Second International founded in 1889.

It is often said that Marx made a synthesis of German philosophy, French revolutionary tradition, and English political economy. This statement should be more useful after a sketch of the main facets of Marxism.

Philosophy. Like most of the German university students of his generation, Marx had been influenced by the philosophy of Georg Wilhelm Friedrich Hegel (1770–1831). Hegel was one of the great nineteenth-century system-builders. He shared the desire of the men of the Enlightenment to find laws of nature, and he had the nineteenth century's appreciation of evolutionary change through history. Hegel reconciled the two by finding what he took to be the laws and meaning of history. What Edmund Burke and Joseph de Maistre had done as near-poetry, Hegel undertook in the form of systematic philosophy. He described in detail how the historical process attained its end through a kind of logic of its own called the *dialectic*. The end of history, the great idea which was the point of the whole thing, was freedom. Each historical stage had a key idea (*thesis*), which because of its imperfections generated its opposite (*antithesis*). The two after a period of conflict became fused (*synthesis*), but this new stage had its shortcomings and turned, therefore, automatically into a new *thesis*—and so the process of antithesis, synthesis, and so on, was bound to continue.

This philosophy of change had great charm for the young students of the early nineteenth century, for it tied everything together—history, philosophy, science, arts. And although conservatives liked Hegel because everything that existed was justified by its part in the drama of history, and the philosopher seemed to be saying that "whatever is, is right," the impatient youth liked him because he proved that all would pass away, including their elders and their elders' institutions.

Marx and Engels in their student days were among the impatient youth who adored the historical process but refused to look upon it (as Hegel did) as consisting of ideas. Such things as ideas, philosophies, and religions they considered to be projections of human needs in everyday life. Changing material conditions, not changing ideas, provided for them the key to history. Human minds could become aware of the historical process as it went its inevitable way— they could even be free, and want what was right. But freedom and rightness consisted only of recognizing and being in harmony with the inevitable march of economic and social realities.

Science. Marx's "science of history" was patterned after Hegel's. It described what the Enlightenment would have termed natural law. He claimed to be a scientific socialist because he had found these truths, in which lay the solution to mankind's problems. Everything that we shall describe below was considered by Marx and his followers to be "science."

Sociology. Marx's description of society's structure began with what he took to be basic: the material needs of mankind. To provide themselves with food and clothing and shelter men entered into "production relations," that is, patterns of economic activity. Since people did different kinds of work, they became different kinds of people, that is, social classes. The classes depended on the activities, which depended on the state of the techniques of production. Whatever the society, its pattern was determined by the necessities of production. Activities at the upper levels, those of, for example, lawyers, teachers, and priests, depended on the more fundamental arrangements for material survival. Systems of law, education, and religion were a superstructure which was shaped by what lay beneath. They were not "true" except as they justified the production-relations.

History. As the basic technology changed, bringing new activities and, therefore, new relations among men, the whole superstructure would have to change too. When Marx came to explain how society evolved from one stage to another, he made an imaginative leap in order to bring his materialistic description of society into line with Hegel's dialectical process of change in history. He saw in class struggle the dialectical motor of change. Every historical era was based on exploitation of the kind he saw around him in the mid-nineteenth century: ancient times, based on slavery; medieval, based on serfdom; modern, based on exploitation of the wage earners. But history solved its own problems. For example the new class of *bourgeoisie* was formed by economic changes within the society dominated by nobles. The *bourgeoisie* defeated the nobles and brought the present era of constitutional governments. This was the meaning of the French Revolution. But by building factories, the *bourgeoisie* created its own future destroyer, the proletariat.

Politics. In every historical era the "state" was the machinery of coercion used by the ruling class, the owners (along with other devices, such as religion, which was a drug to keep the people docile). Marx called the state of his own time a "committee of the *bourgeoisie*." He forced this impression into a gigantic mold which he then applied to all times and places. (For every era he assumed a coercive state manned by a ruling class. Revolutions came when an old ruling class which no longer corresponded to the economic realities was being dispossessed by its successor.)

Economics. The conditions of Marx's own times were those of the early Industrial Revolution in Western Europe, and it is not surprising that his economic theory used many of the ideas of contemporary analysts. The definitions of the classical economists in particular proved useful to him: much of Marx's economics was just classical economics seen from the other side of the barricades, just as his famous attack on religion as the opiate of the people was an angry version of what the conservatives had been saying with approval.

Without changing them very much, Marx rewrote the orthodox explanations of the value of commodities as depending on the amount of labor put into them, of capital as stored-up labor, and of wages and dividends as rewards for labor and capital. The value of commodities in Marx's view still depended on the amount of labor put into them. The workers, however, did not receive back a value equivalent to the number of hours they worked. They were paid a lesser value. The food, clothes, housing, and so on, which their wages purchased took less labor to produce than the products which they were making for their employers. The difference between the value returned in wages and the value produced by the workers was what Marx called "surplus value," which went to the factory owners. It followed that by paying workers less than they produced, the factory owners were accumulating wealth while the working class, as Ricardo's iron law of wages had said, remained at a level of subsistence.

The Future. In the long run, however, Marx expected the historical process to rescue the working class. Economically, the exploitation of the workers meant that they would be unable to buy the products they produced, with the result that in a competitive scramble of the capitalists for customers there would be depressions and wars. The stronger capitalists would devour the weaker. Socially, this meant that the number of exploiters would decrease and the number of the exploited would increase. Culturally and politically, it meant that the proletariat, growing more class-conscious as it learned from experience, would ultimately overthrow the few remaining capitalists and the state. The proletariat would for a time set up a state of its own while the remnants of capitalism were being dismantled. After private property and the wage and profit system had been removed, there would be no classes or class warfare. Then there would be no need for a state. The state would wither away and there would be a classless society. In it, each would contribute according to his ability and receive according to his needs.

And so Marx's theory ended in a Utopia, like the dreams of so many of his predecessors. To be sure, he expected no immediate results, either from persuasion or from insurrection, and did not allow himself the luxury of dwelling on the details of the future society. Results would come from the historical process. One could only learn to understand and cooperate, and leave to history the working out of the details. Marx's utopianism was sophisticated and intricate enough to obscure for many years the imaginative and essentially poetic character of its vision, which was like Hegel's in that it purported to tell history's secret *wish*— a prize not attainable through scientific investigation. On the other hand, Marx's procedure was closer to scientific method than pure guesswork. He fitted together hypotheses from practically every social science, drawing upon the boldest minds in a century of system-builders. The generalizations of the nineteenth century were as crude as they were bold, but they had some relation to reality. This relation declined as reality went on developing, but the Marxian synthesis grew in potency as a myth even while its scientific content was evaporating. The myth itself was to be a force in history.

Orthodox Marxists in the socialist parties of the Second International were obliged to struggle to keep their official doctrine pure of "revisionism," the tendency of Marxists like the German Eduard Bernstein to revise Marx's theories, making them less revolutionary in view of the same new conditions which were perplexing the liberals. Bernstein and others like him wanted to cooperate with the governments as they became more democratic and with the other political parties and to approach socialism by little steps, by whatever legislation could be achieved. They paid lip service to the ultimate revolution, but they were condemned by the orthodox party leaders for abandoning the revolution. In their hearts, however, both the orthodox and the revisionists had accepted democratic socialism which meant a peaceful and gradual revolution. When war came in 1914, the great majority of them joined their regiments. The Second International, which was only a loose federation of autonomous parties, had been unable to agree on a policy to follow in the event of war, although in principle they held that the workingmen of rival countries should not fight each other.

Democracy, economic progress, and nationalism tended to weaken class antagonisms and to quiet the revolutionary fervor recommended by Marxism. This softening was particularly noticeable in highly developed Great Britain, France, and Germany. There were few Marxian socialists in Great Britain, where the most influential socialists were the Fabians, named after the Roman general famous for delaying tactics. The Fabians were not by any means a mass movement. They were a small group of gifted intellectuals who believed that the advance of democracy and education, combined with the decline of economic individualism and the increase of social legislation, would bring about socialism gradually. They were anything but Marxist, rejected class warfare and violence, and were frankly patriotic; they even accepted the British empire, provided it could be rationally managed in the interest of the general welfare.

On the continent there were also moderate socialists of various kinds. In Germany the so-called "socialism of the chair" was not a revolutionary movement but fortified by studies of economic history the tradition of state intervention in the economy and prepared the way for paternalistic social legislation. Among Catholics in various parts of Europe a movement called "social Catholicism" deplored un-Christian policies of violence and class struggle and sought social harmony through cooperation of employers and workers. Social Catholicism combined religious idealism and humanitarianism with a liking for group organization by professions, reminiscent of the estates of the old regime.

Of quite another sort was the movement known as revolutionary syndicalism which became popular in France, Italy, and Spain. The word "syndicat" in French means labor union. Syndicalism was, in brief, an effort to remake society in a socialist image, not through state action, but through the revolutionary action of the workers themselves in their unions. Syndicalists distrusted the state, which, in France had crushed workers' revolts in the June Days of 1848 and in the Paris Commune of 1871. They distrusted socialist politicians, who tended to be intellectuals who sometimes aimed at taking office in the government. Furthermore, in France, Italy, and Spain the economy developed more slowly than in Great Britain and Germany in the late nineteenth century, with the result that many enterprises remained small and relatively poor and offered their workers less prospect for betterment than the expanding industries of Great Britain and Germany. With less sense of sharing in industrial advance, and with less money in their treasuries, unions tended to feel that they had little to lose by strikes, sabotage, and violence. In France, Italy, and Spain, moreover, workers tended to be volatile, independent-minded, and undisciplined, and to resent the stolid placidity of their none-too-enterprising employers. In France especially, the revolutionary tradition played a part in shaping the attitudes of workingmen. The great dream of syndicalists was the general strike of all workers, designed to destroy bourgeois society at one stroke, but in fact syndicalists were never in the majority in the labor force. The idea of the general strike was popularized by an engineer, Georges Sorel, who was not a rank-and-file syndicalist.

Revolutionary syndicalism was closely related to anarchism but differed from it in several respects. Anarchist leaders tended to be idealistic intellectuals, few in number, extremist devotees to liberty from both private property and from the coercion of states. In the 1880's anarchists in Western Europe adopted terrorist methods of assassination and damage to property, but toward the end of the century this tendency slackened in the west while continuing in Russia. Unlike anarchism, syndicalism was a broad and more or less spontaneous movement among workingmen, although there were anarchist workers who contributed to the flavor of syndicalism. As the year 1914 drew nearer, syndicalists in France turned away from violence. Syndicalist suspicion of the state and of politics persisted far into the twentieth century among workers in France, Italy, and Spain.

Europe between 1870 and 1914 grew enormously powerful and reached new heights of global influence. But when World War I came, Europe still had not fully succeeded in drawing its working classes into the peaceful game of constitutional politics.

35

THE WORLD REIGN
OF EUROPE

THE SPREAD OF Europe's influence through the world has been the sign and symptom of Europe's vitality. It has also been a cause of Europe's vitality. As the explorations and the dominions of Europe were extended overseas, the riches and the trade and the strange cultures which Europeans found fed the growth of European civilization. The independence of the rest of the world, its creativity and its authority, were progressively reduced. The gap between it and Europe steadily widened. Europe conquered the planet.

In 1914 there was almost no part of the world's surface which was not under the control, direct or indirect, of Europeans. All of America was dominated by their descendants. The Western Hemisphere, with a few colonial exceptions, had won political independence for European governments, but its societies were still characteristically, if not entirely, European in nature. All of Australasia was British. Almost all of Africa was divided into colonies or protectorates of European nations. Only the remote empire of Ethiopia and the little coastal republic of Liberia maintained a precarious independence. Most of Asia, the largest of the continents, rich in ancient civilizations and densely inhabited, was in one way or another controlled by Europeans. The entire northern part of the enormous land-mass was part of the Russian empire. The subcontinent of India, with its appendages, was British. France governed Indochina, and the Netherlands most of the Indonesian archipelago. The United States of America had recently annexed the Philippine Islands. There remained a number of small kingdoms, obscure or fictionally independent, like Siam, Nepal, and Afghanistan, and four large empires. Of these, Persia was being partitioned between Russia and England. Two others, China and the Ottoman empire, had lost their vitality, and

both were infiltrated by European powers. The principal reason why their governments had maintained a titular independence was that the European powers
could never agree how to go about dividing them up into colonies.

The only genuinely independent country in Asia, and the only important
non-European government in the world in 1914, was Japan. And Japan was an
instructive exception, for the Japanese had survived the expansionist ambitions
of Europeans by adapting their own economy and institutions to western models.
They had been saved, as it were, by fighting Europe with its own weapons: their
government had been rapidly modernized and their industry had in fifty years
developed to the point where they could match Europe or America. Although
most people did not realize it in 1914, the success of Japan as a great power
showed that other peoples wishing to safeguard or recover their independence
could do so by remaking themselves, politically and economically at least, in the
European image.

This extraordinary predominance of Europeans in a world in which they
were overwhelmingly outnumbered was due to peculiar skills and talents. Europeans, like Romans, knew how to run things—things like shops and post offices
and banks, corporations and armies. They knew how to mingle this skill at running things with scientific knowledge about the universe, so that they could
manufacture things as well, the very things most useful in subduing other people:
guns, battleships, brightly colored cloth and beads. And they had—what was just
as essential to their success—a nice combination of freedom and obedience to authority, of ambition and self-restraint, of competitiveness and willingness to cooperate.

This geographical expansion has been called "imperialism." The word in
our day has become a controversy: "imperialist" is an insult delivered by Mexicans
against the United States, by Algerians against France, by Indonesians against
the Netherlands, by Arabs against the western world, by the Communist world
against the non-Communist world. It is now so vaguely used and so incrusted
with emotion that it does not seem to mean anything at all precise. As the range
of Europe's political control has receded in the past generation, people who still
think of Europe as "imperialist" have sought subtler meanings of imperialism
than the existence of colonies—financial influence, military superiority, cultural
arrogance. But in this chapter we shall use "imperialism" in a strict and definite
sense to describe: the extension of political and territorial control by the European governments over places not inhabited by Europeans. This control was
usually accompanied by economic interests and influence, but such influence is
not what we mean by imperialism. By that word we mean the building of empires
and popular enthusiasm for the building of empires.

After 1914, the tide of Europe's political and territorial dominance abruptly
began to ebb. More and more parts of the world challenged their European
masters, and more and more parts of the world followed the course of Japanese
development, growing into nation-states on the European model, turning European technology and political organization to their advantage. Two non-European
powers had already by 1914 inflicted first-rate military defeats upon two European

powers: Ethiopia on Italy, in 1896, and Japan on Russia nine years later. The possibility of military defeats by non-European countries was growing at the same time as the will to inflict them. Sleeping giants were beginning to awaken. China and the Ottoman empire had both, in the decade before 1914, undergone revolutions which were *nationalist* revolutions, embodying the ideas of a new generation of thoughtful and energetic men who were intent upon asserting the independence and the greatness of their countries, ejecting European influences and competing with European power. Powerful nationalist sentiments were beginning to stir in British India.

Nationalism was a European idea and tradition. Perhaps none of Europe's exports to the world was more important than the explosive ideas of freedom and equality, for both individuals and nations, which had so high a fashion in the nineteenth century. These ideas, like European political and economic methods, were being turned against the empire-makers at the very moment when imperialism reached its height. It was the beginning of the most important movement of the twentieth century.

THE COLONIAL WORLD IN 1870

In 1870, a relatively small portion of the world map was splashed with the colors of European nations. The largest areas were Asiatic Russia—if that could be called a colony—and India and Australia. The Western Hemisphere was largely free; Canada, the principal colonial area remaining, had in 1867 been federated into a single dominion equipped with extensive rights of self-government and (what was most striking) freedom to pursue an independent commercial policy, which meant freedom to put tariffs on goods from Great Britain. It was still a "self-governing colony," but it was now organized to move toward freedom and equality with Great Britain. For the rest, there persisted on the mainland only the obscure and unwholesome colonies of French, Dutch, and British Guiana, British Honduras in Central America, and a wide selection of decaying sugar and fishing islands—the British, Spanish, French, Dutch, and Danish West Indies, British Bermuda and the Bahamas, all now sunk in poverty and neglect, and scattered others such as self-governing Newfoundland and the miniscule French islands near it, Saint Pierre and Miquelon.

Africa, in 1870, remained largely unexplored and uncolonized. At its northern end, France had conquered Algeria (formally part of the Ottoman empire, actually for years a piratical kingdom of its own) in 1830. At Africa's southern end, the stragetically important Cape Colony had been taken by the British from the Dutch in the Vienna Treaty of 1815. By 1870, many of the Dutch settlers, called Boers, had migrated northward to escape British control and had founded islands of semi-European civilization in the heart of south Africa, in their own free states called Transvaal and Orange Free State republics.

Scattered around the edges of the continent were other colonies, most of them no more than forts and trading posts and most of them dating from earlier spurts of colonization. The oldest and best established were two Portuguese holdings on either side of the southern bulge of Africa, in Angola in the west and Mozambique in the east. Around the western bulge were others, mostly French and British. These were to become the take-off points for vast expansions of territory in the next two decades. In 1870, however, except for Algeria and the Cape, they were still minor, obscure and neglected, and most of Africa was still under its native chieftains.

In Asia, aside from India and Russia, there was in 1870 still no territorial penetration of any importance by European powers. The Dutch East Indies—now the Republic of Indonesia—were being built up around the old settlement on Java, the British had installed themselves in Singapore and the Malayan peninsula north of it, and the French were beginning to take an interest in Indochina. But colonial (as distinct from commercial) activity in Asia was still very limited, and except for Hong Kong and Singapore, the most important colonies were the old seventeenth- and eighteenth-century ones. There was already, it is true, a good deal of international rivalry for favors from the celestial but distraught regime of the Chinese emperor. The empire was in the throes of dissolution. A shattering revolution of 1850, conceivably the bloodiest in any country's history, had caused the loss of something like twenty million lives. The British, in an effort to safeguard the market for their exports of India opium, had been led into a singular and shameful war in 1841 which was renewed, with French assistance, in 1857. As a result of these two wars, Hong Kong was ceded to Britain, European settlements were given what amounted to colonial status, and Chinese commercial policy passed under the control of European advisors. But the huge Chinese empire, while infiltrated, was still whole in 1870, and the European interest in it remained sporadic and commercial, not territorial.

There was also a long list of little colonies, mostly islands and mostly held for many years, in addition to the mainland territories. There were for example the British Gibraltar and Malta in the Mediterranean, and Saint Helena and Ascension in the middle of the South Atlantic. There was the Spanish Fernando Po off West Africa. There were the Portuguese Madeiras and Azores in the north Atlantic. These were often of some strategic importance but yielded little or no commercial profit.

The picture of the colonial world in 1870 was, then, spotty. The map was splashed with slowly spreading patches of color, but enthusiasm for colonial expansion was probably at the lowest ebb in four hundred years. There were a few rather cranky enthusiasts, like Edward Gibbon Wakefield in England, who saw in colonies a solution for the "overpopulation" of England, or the Saint-Simonians in France, who blended an enthusiasm for modern transport and technology with some rather peculiar religious ideas which gave them a theological concern for French influence in the Middle East. But these were or seemed to be exceptional. At the time of the triumph of liberalism in Europe, colonies played a relatively small role in European ideas and affairs.

European Colonial Empires in 1914

THE NEW IMPERIALISM, 1870–1914

After 1870, the pace of colonial expansion increased rapidly, so that by 1900 almost the entire Eastern Hemisphere had been divided amongst European governments. Attitudes toward the value of colonial empires were drastically revised. The partition of the world was much more than just a speeding up of the slow processes of accretion which had been in progress since 1815—it was also Europe's last expansive burst. So rapid was it that it occasioned tumults of a most fundamental sort. The controversies which attended this last great phase of empire-building sent down roots from which growths both noxious and beneficent still proliferate.

In the next section the course of empire-building will be briefly traced. First, it is expedient to investigate the cause and nature of late nineteenth-century imperialism.

The question of causes is vexed indeed. Whole schools of thought, then and since, have argued the matter. The most systematic of these schools, and the most influential, are those which have emphasized economic causes. The economic interpretation was first systematically set forth in 1902, by John Hobson. His analysis formed one of the bases of the Marxist theory of imperialism which was developed by N. Lenin, the great theorist and mover of the Russian Revolution, but not all of its supporters were by any means Marxists, or economic determinists. The main theme of their beliefs is the primacy of economic motives in late nineteenth-century imperialists. One version of their argument (not the Leninist version, although they have a family resemblance) runs as follows: Europe, and especially Western Europe, was faced after 1870 with a rapidly expanding industrial establishment, virtually all of it operated by private and competing businessmen. Businessmen could foresee the day when the domestic market for their goods would be saturated—the "long depression" from the 1870's to the 1890's was a warning, and so were the tariffs which began to rise almost everywhere except in Britain. Businessmen therefore urged their governments (and as the wealthiest and most influential people in each nation, they could count on the governments doing what they wanted) to assure new overseas markets by extending political control over them. The governments (the argument runs) obligingly undertook to bring their political control vast areas and populations overseas. And there were other economic motives: the European investors were looking for places to invest surplus capital; the European industrialists relied increasingly on imported raw materials. Europe was rich in coal and iron, but it lacked (or was thought to lack) many of the increasingly varied commodities essential to industry: tin, nickel, magnesium, rubber, oil, to name a few. In order that (for example) French manufacturers might have safe, *French* sources of the raw materials not available in France itself, colonies were necessary.

This analysis of the causes of imperialism has unquestionably considerable basis in fact: many colonial ventures, such as the German colonization of southwest Africa in the 1880's, were without doubt first undertaken at the behest of commercial interests. Moreover, the theory was strengthened by the fact that it was businessmen themselves who first proposed it. The most ardent imperialists in France, Germany, and Britain were people who argued quite openly that new and larger markets and sure sources of raw materials would safeguard and enrich the economy of the mother-country. Only later was the theory turned against capitalists by the Marxists and socialists, who branded as sinister and criminal motives which had been proudly advanced as justifications.

But the investigations of impartial historians in the last thirty years have qualified both Hobson's and Lenin's analyses as *exclusive* explanations of late nineteenth-century imperialism. Many facts simply do not support the theory. As will be seen later, it was not always businessmen who initiated colonial expansion, and governments were often wary of it. Moreover, although no one realized it in advance, few of the colonies acquired in the second half of the nineteenth century became vital or even important markets for the exports of the mother-country. The exports of industrial countries continued to flow, overwhelmingly, to other industrial countries, not to the poor and primitive colonial areas. Unquestionably many businessmen made enormous profits out of particular colonial ventures. They were much fewer, and their profits much smaller, than those of people concerned with trade among the large and wealthy and "mature" economies of the west, but they were naturally ardent supporters of imperialism. Most mother-countries by 1914 were spending vastly more in administering and defending and developing their colonies than they were deriving from them in the way of trade profits.

A second systematic explanation which has enjoyed great popularity is the theory of "the place in the sun," or a national itch for fame and power. The frenzied scramble for colonies reflects, by this line of thinking, not rivalry for economic advantage among France, Germany, Britain and the lesser colonial powers so much as a competition for prestige. Imperialism is seen as an extension of sentimental nationalism: the same emotion which led Italians to think that it would be more *respectable* to be citizens of an Italian state than subjects of exotic princelings, also led Italians to think it would be more *splendid* if Italy were to acquire some nice colonies, like other great powers. Imperialism then is taken to be a sort of projection of the proud identification of individuals with their nation's reputation and glory.

Just as there is a great deal of truth in the argument that imperialism was the consequence of profit-seeking by businessmen, so there can be no doubt that it was also motivated by eagerness for a place in the sun. One case will suffice to illustrate the point. The French colonial expansion after 1870, and particularly in the 1880's and 1890's, explicitly aimed at satisfying the French thirst for national adventure after the injuries and humiliations in the Franco-Prussian War. The principal architect of the modern French empire, Jules Ferry, was widely—and accurately—accused by his enemies of trying to divert French attention from Alsace-Lorraine by exciting it with vast acquisitions of territory in Africa and Asia. Prince Bismarck, the German chancellor, enthusiastically and openly supported France's imperial expansion for this very purpose. The more that French frustrations were assuaged by glories abroad, the less likely they were to menace Germany or European peace. On one occasion, when both France and Italy were plotting the seizure of Tunisia, Bismarck specifically backed the French. "The Tunisian fruit is ripe," he whispered in effect to the French representative at Berlin. "Pluck it!"

There are other aspects of the colonial scramble in the late nineteenth century which were undoubtedly part of its cause and which relate only obliquely to either the Leninist or the Place-in-the-Sun notions.

There was first of all the matter of missionaries. This was in England—and to a lesser extent elsewhere—an age of evangelical religion. By "evangelical" is meant a religious feeling marked by eagerness to expand the Faith and to convert heathens to it, and usually marked too by outward displays of religious enthusiasm. At the time the evangelical revival was going on, Europe's wealth was expanding, and so were the means of travel. Religious groups had the means as well as the will to spread missionaries throughout the world.

The missionaries were frequently at odds with governments; in some cases, in Nigeria for example, they disliked and opposed the government's interference with their work. In others, they vainly sought government protection. And sometimes the missions were used as pretexts for a policy of annexations which had already been decided on for other reasons.

In addition to missionaries, many, many European empire-builders professed more general humanitarian motives, often undoubtedly sincere. Almost everybody who annexed a "primitive" region (or any non-European region for that matter) spoke of the benefits of modern civilization which it was proposed to bestow on it. Modern civilization involved very real benefits, such as postal services, public works and communications and (less clearly) European education and medicine. It also involved more dubious benefits, such as "law and order" (most of Africa was remarkably orderly under its native chieftains) and European social and economic institutions which broke up the old culture and economy of many a native society and left it orphaned in the twentieth century. Most real of the benefits was the stoppage of the iniquitous slave trade which still, at the end of the nineteenth century, flourished in Africa. But whether the innovations were good or bad, it was easy for the self-assured Europeans and Americans of the nineties to assume the infinite preferability of their culture to that of African natives. It was easy for them, quite genuinely, to *equate* colonization with humanity. One empire-builder wrote, berating the British Treasury which hesitated to supply funds for the conquest of Central Africa, that the Treasury was "a Department without bowels of compassion or a throb of imperial feeling."

The most common of the real reasons for annexationist policies, at least in Britain, was apprehension about the annexations of some other government. The final, unanswerable justification for seizing additional territory was strategic: that unless given lands were conquered, they would fall into the hands of colonial rivals—mainly France, Germany, or, in Asia, Russia. To take one case: if the hinterlands—commercially valueless and extremely inaccessible—of the British coastal holdings in West Africa were not conquered by Britain, they would fall into French hands, and France would be able to threaten the entire British position in West Africa and perhaps even to push the British coastal holdings into the sea. Similarly, the strategic requirements of the route to India, which led by British Gibraltar and British Malta to British-controlled Suez, suggested the desirability of annexing Cyprus, in 1878, of occupying Egypt, in 1881, and then of safeguarding Egypt by extending British control southward from it through the vast areas of the Nile and its sources. Indeed, most of the gigantic British colonial holdings in Eastern Africa and in Arabia were at least partly acquired to defend the passage to India.

When these things have been said, there is still no complete explanation of the flowering of imperialism. It was far more than a set of reasonable political reactions: it was also a fad and a dream. Enormous popular enthusiasm, and a vigorous competitive spirit among the colonizing powers, flowered. People wrote odes to colonialism. Crowds applauded Indian rajahs who rode through London on elephants. Whole libraries were written to demonstrate the superiority of the white race—such writings, while they had the most lasting effects in Germany, South Africa, and the United States, were in their day equally copious and virulent in Britain, France, and elsewhere. If Germany had its Nietzsche, Britain had its Houston Chamberlain and France its Gobineau, all adherents of an entirely fallacious theory of racial supremacy. And the United States had a President—Theodore Roosevelt—who spoke of the Yellow Peril.

There were many countries concerned in colonial conquest, and many areas being conquered. For each, motives were intricate and various. For each, the conquest was a matter of details. In order to have a truer picture of the extraordinary process whereby Europe completed its world rule in the two decades before 1900, it is worthwhile to look briefly at one example, as a sort of case-study.

A CASE STUDY IN COLONIZATION: BRITISH CENTRAL AFRICA

One of the last habitable portions of the world's surface to be explored and brought under the control of Europeans was the territory of what is today the Central African federation, a part of the British Commonwealth. A summary account of its acquisition by Great Britain illustrates the many and mingled motives and methods of colonization: the role of the individual and adventurous "empire-builder"; the role of commercial interests and missionaries; the complex attitudes of home governments; the local tribal politics of the colonial areas; the competition among European powers; and the decisive role which was *always* played by the military superiority of the Europeans. It was this fact, that European technology and organization permitted a very few men with a very few arms to conquer and hold huge areas, more than any other which lured governments and empire-builders into more and more far-flung but inexpensive annexations.

Prior to the late 1880's, there was little interest in the region, which was left to its numerous chieftains, except for the presence of a few merchants and a number of missionaries, mostly Scottish Presbyterians. By the late 1880's, however, British agents in surrounding settlements—Portuguese East Africa and British South Africa—were beginning to see both possibilities and dangers in it. It was, in fact, an important area. High country, with a healthful climate and amply watered by numerous navigable lakes and rivers, it was surrounded by the expanding colonies of many powers: the Portuguese to the east and west in Angola and Lourenço Marques; the British to the south in the Cape colony and its northern projections; the independent Dutch-Boer republics to the south; German settlements in southwest Africa and to the northeast, on the coastal strip of east Africa which extended inland to Lake Tanganyika; and the International State of the Congo, controlled by the king of the Belgians (of which more later) on the west. All of these colonial powers were ambitious and indeed predatory. And some of their citizens were afflicted by dreams of empire more remarkable for their grandeur than their realism.

Two such dreams may be briefly mentioned. The Portuguese, a small but determined people, had thought of the idea of uniting their two vast colonies on the eastern and western coasts by annexing the huge territories which lay between. At the same time certain Englishmen, most notoriously the local chairman of the British South Africa Company, a man named Cecil Rhodes, dreamed of an unbroken stretch of British territory from Cape Town to the Mediterranean which would eventually become the site for the fabulous "Cape to Cairo rail-

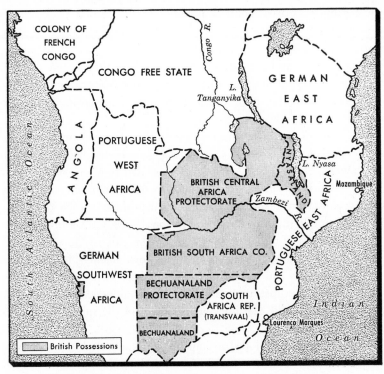

CENTRAL SOUTHEASTERN AFRICA, LATE 19TH CENTURY

way," a project which, while it never materialized and would probably have served little commercial purpose had it done so, fired the imagination of many Englishmen imbued with the idea that railways always brought enormous riches, power, and prestige. Such a railway would have covered over two thousand miles, much of it inaccessible and almost uninhabited.

The boundaries of the colonies surrounding Central Africa were extremely vague, although some of them—notably the Congo—had been defined in 1885 at the Berlin Conference (see below, p. 596). The field was wide open.

The principal operators in its conquest by Britain were two: an intrepid and quixotic British consul in Portuguese East Africa, Sir Harry Johnston, who annexed whole regions on more or less his own authority, sometimes against the explicit orders of his government; and Cecil Rhodes acting in the name of the British South Africa Company. In recognition of the latter's achievement, the two larger states of the present-day Central African federation bear his name—Northern and Southern Rhodesia.

The British South Africa Company, a chartered company in the tradition of the great seventeenth- and eighteenth-century companies, was one of many operating in Africa. There were large profits to be made through trading with local tribes, and such companies' directors, at home in London, were frequently businessmen interested primarily in such profits. But there were other aspects. In the first place, the companies were inevitably led into political dealings with the local chiefs and tribes and, by backing one favorable to their interests against others who opposed them (or tried to overcharge them by price-fixing for native wares), came to occupy a decisive political position. In the second place, the British government chose to use these companies for the purpose of extending British influence, for a very good reason: it was cheap to do so. The companies paid for the exploration, defense, and policing of the areas where they operated. In an age when balanced budgets and low taxes were a major concern of European politicians, this meant that the governments were given large colonies at no expense and therefore no political risk to themselves.

The work of conquest began in 1889, when Harry Johnston moved into the region between the lakes of Nyasa and Tanganyika and began to sign treaties with the chiefs. These treaties were simply printed forms in which the chiefs (usually in return for gifts bought at London department stores on Johnston's personal account) agreed to permit Englishmen to trade in their dominions and to make no treaties with other European nations. Some went a little further and acknowledged a sort of vague overlordship on the part of Queen Victoria, but these were discouraged by the cautious London government. The treaties did not mean much, but they did give Britain a bargaining advantage in negotiations with other powers, by constituting a prior claim to "influence." It was, in fact, by means of such documents that the rough outlines of the spheres of colonization were sketched.

Several hitches developed to impede Johnston's work. The native chiefs proved in a few cases recalcitrant, and wiped out the little expeditions which were sent to keep order. The government at London, pushed by the Treasury (which worried about expense) and the navy (which scorned all inland activities), refused to back up their aggressive agent with funds or gunboats for the lakes. And the Portuguese protested vigorously against British operations in territory which they regarded as theirs. But these difficulties were gradually overcome. Funds were made available to Johnston by the South Africa Company. The Portuguese were obliged by strong British pressure to agree to a treaty in which they abandoned their dream of a trans-African colony. The Germans, strategically located in the north, were induced to accept British installation on Lake Tanganyika by the cession to them of the island of Helgoland, in the North Sea, in 1890. The British Government thus cheaply (and not very enthusiastically) eliminated the major foreign threats to the territory, and by 1893 the control of the South Africa Company over the western part of the territory was confirmed, and a protectorate over the local rulers in the eastern part had been recognized by both the British administration and by foreign countries.

What is striking in all this is the interplay of motives. At no time did the London government deliberately plan the conquest of Central Africa. Generally, it held back, and conceded support or even permission only after long delays, and only when the threat of prior conquest by foreign powers seemed imminent. The missionary societies urged government action, but they were only one of several pressure groups operating in different directions. Nor were the directors of the South Africa Company very forward. They, too, viewed the activities of their agents on the scene as likely to involve them in risky and profitless adventures. It was in fact the two men, Johnston and Rhodes, who took the steps which made possible the establishment of British rule in the area. To them, it seemed *obvious* that it was desirable to establish British rule in Central Africa, that this was what *must* be done, and they fought local tribes, foreign governments, and their own superiors to secure their purpose. A blending of enterprise, derring-do, and patriotism prompted them; but really, the explanation was in the attraction for brave, imaginative, and not very logical-minded men of the vacuum at the heart of a continent.

PARTITION OF THE WORLD: AFRICA

The years 1870–1914 saw the partition of Africa amongst the European powers with the dramatic exception of Ethiopia and the negligible exception of Liberia. From the point of view of contemporaries, the principal interest in the partition arose from its effects upon the mother-countries and particularly upon the relationships among the European powers. For the imperialist rivalry caused deep tensions; and while all the colonial rivalries were peacefully settled, they seemed at many times to threaten a general war.

The immediate cause for the scramble was the exploration of central Africa and, specifically, the valley of the Congo, a vast watershed of about 4,500 miles of navigable waterways heretofore entirely unknown. Its exploration in the 1870's was mainly the work of a New York newspaper reporter, H.M. Stanley, who was sent out to interview the British explorer Livingstone who had preceded him and was thought to have become lost. Stanley perceived the extraordinary possibilities of a European commercial exploitation of the region and interested the king of the Belgians, the wealthy and wily Leopold II, in the project. In 1876, an International Association of the Congo was formed which was in theory a private commercial company but, like other private commercial companies operating in Africa, shortly became a sort of private government for the region. The penetration of the Congo watershed, and the extraction of its riches, proceeded apace. It was eventually to become the scene of scandalous exploitation of native labor and to give its royal proprietor an exceedingly unsavory reputation.

Simultaneously, the French, the British, and the Germans were beginning to undertake similar penetration from other parts of the west coast, signing "treaties" with native chiefs or kings. In North Africa, in the early 1880's, the French had established a protectorate over Tunisia and the British had occupied Egypt. In Eastern Africa, British influence over the sultan of Zanzibar (a Moslem island which exercised suzerainty over some of the mainland) was increasing, and the Germans were beginning to establish themselves near Tanganyika. By 1885, it was necessary to make some delimitation of spheres of activity, and Bismarck sponsored a conference of the African powers at Berlin, where the first frontiers were drawn. The "Congo Association," transformed into something called the Congo Free State, was recognized as an independent state run by the international company, but was really ruled by King Leopold. Also at Berlin, and at a later conference at Brussels in 1889, the Powers agreed to (a) efforts to eradicate the slave trade, which was widely practiced by the scattered Moslem elements among the indigenous Negroes (b) certain standards—widely disregarded— for treatment of the natives (c) free international use of some of the main waterways (d) "free trade" in all parts of Africa—which meant simply that no power, company, or tribe should be granted a monopoly of trading rights in the newly colonized areas (e) certain ground rules for further expansion, which boiled down to the principle that the powers could not despoil one another's territory but that hitherto unclaimed areas were free game.

By 1895, most of the continent had been thus peacefully divided. There remained, however, several areas of great strategic and commercial importance, over which serious and nearly fatal conflicts were to arise. These were, first, the Ethiopian empire and the areas west and north of it, which controlled the headwaters of the Nile and which bordered on the Congo Free State, on French Equatorial Africa, on some unpromising east-coast territories which the Italians had picked up, and on British Egypt and British Kenya. Secondly, the decaying sultanate of Morocco, on the Atlantic in the northeast corner of Africa, became a center of conflict.

The first region produced the first crises. Italy attempted to conquer Ethiopia and, in 1896, at the disastrous Battle of Adowa, suffered the first defeat inflicted by an African people on a European army. Ethiopia was in a different position from most of Africa. It was a Christian nation, and it had a much more organized central government which was able to put an army in the field. The defeat eliminated the Italians from the competition. Ethiopia was safe. But in the ill-defined area to the west, the remaining contenders, France and Britain, undertook a hasty effort at penetration. In a general way, the British were seeking to protect not only Egypt but the putative Cape-to-Cairo belt; the French dreamt of linking their west-coast possessions to their small holding on the east coast at Djibouti. Both sent expeditions, and in 1898, at a place called Fashoda, the generals of the two expeditions met, each with instructions not to give way.

It was a bad moment for Franco-British relations—the worst since the Treaty of Vienna. There was a two-century-old background of colonial rivalry and bitterness between the two countries. France had sulked over the British occupation of Egypt, which since the Crusades the French had regarded as their sphere of influence. And the British had sulked over French expansion behind and around their west-coastal colonies, which had left Nigeria, the Gold Coast, Sierra Leone, and Gambia as British islands in a vast French sea. It looked in 1898 as if the struggle for Africa might at last find its climax in a European war.

It did not do so. Peaceful—if not, for some years, friendly—relations survived. The French gave in, largely because of French domestic instability at the time—the Dreyfus Crisis was in course. And with the French retreat, the last great colonial issue between France and Britain was solved. Thenceforth, though no one at the time could have foreseen it, the traditional enemies were to be friends, for the next threat to France's empire came from Germany.

It came in 1905, in Morocco. In the meantime, the British and the French had signed an amicable colonial agreement, interring their disputes by mutually recognizing the supremacy of Britain in Egypt in return for the priority of France in Morocco. This agreement, initiating the cooperative understanding called the "entente cordiale," was to prove a turning point in European history and to determine the alignment and eventual outcome of World War I.

In 1905, the Germans (having changed their views about encouraging French colonial expansion) challenged the increasing French influence in Morocco, which was visibly leading toward a protectorate over that disorderly state and thus toward French predominance in the whole of North Africa from Tunis to the Congo, some two thousand miles or more around the coast. Another European crisis developed, and this time it was the Germans—faced by a united Franco-British front which they had not expected—who backed down. By 1912, after further crises and negotiations, the French protectorate was established.

Peace had been maintained in the process of getting Africa partitioned. But Italy had been humiliated, France and Britain drawn together, and both then alienated from Germany. As an incident of the scramble, Belgium (to which Leopold had willed his now notorious private property of the Congo) had become a major colonial power. Because of the rivalries of its peers, Portugal had survived as one. The frontiers which were to determine Africa's future had been laid down, and the divisions which were to determine Europe's had been built up.

But the great age of imperialism was already ending by 1914. Its end was clearly shown in the British experiences in South Africa, the high-water mark of British enthusiasm for empire-building. This apogee was reached in a war between two European peoples, the British and the Dutch-Boers, for control of South

Africa and its native wealth and population. There had been a long and bitter history of conflict between the two. The Boers, descendants of Dutch settlers, had left their homes and founded new states in the interior. These states, the Transvaal and the Orange Free State, had been more or less under British "protection" for a generation. The Boers, dour, conservative, and suspicious, began to seek to safeguard themselves and their rich gold and diamond mines by excluding British enterprise. Their suspicions were, in fact, well-founded. Cecil Rhodes and other enterprising empire-builders had their eyes on the republics, and in 1895 they organized a filibustering raid which was apparently aimed at overthrowing the Boer regime and substituting one which would at least be more favorable to the British. The "Jameson Raid," arranged without the approval of the British government, failed, but it embittered relations still further. In 1899, war finally broke out between the intractable Boers and the ambitious British. European opinion was solidly against Britain's aggression. A strong section of British opinion opposed the war and developed an anti-imperialist literature. The Boers proved extremely difficult to subdue. The war dragged on, under horrifying circumstances, for three years. By the time it was over, zest for imperial expansion had cooled noticeably. A small but determined enemy had stopped the British empire in its tracks for three years and laid it dangerously open to hostile maneuvers from its European rivals.

Even the most ardent imperialists were sobered by the dangers to which their wars had exposed them. From 1901 on, there was in Britain a decline in imperialist exuberance. Rivalries continued, and in some areas grew sharper than ever, but the old enthusiasm for colonial expansion and the old spirit of imperialist adventure was beginning to die in many quarters before World War I drowned in blood the impulses which had given rise to it.

PARTITION OF THE WORLD: ASIA

Asia was never partitioned so thoroughly as Africa. Although most of its parts were brought at least indirectly under European influence before 1914, their complicated civilization and far more advanced governments enabled Asians to preserve some semblance of self-government in Persia, China, the Ottoman empire, and Siam, a true independence in Japan, and, in areas which fell to western empires, to retain some unity and some measure of control over their destinies.

However, despite the very striking contrast between densely populated and highly civilized Asia and thinly populated, "primitive" Africa, the extension of European influence into the two bore a close likeness in effects upon the native peoples and on the relations among the European powers. The international tensions which arose in Asia were if anything more intractable and more threatening than in Africa. This was due mainly to the fact that Russia, absent from Africa but very much present in Asia, was the most feared and probably the most aggressive of the European powers. The Russian emperor and many of his people added to the normal, slightly hysterical, enthusiasm for expansion in that day a tendency toward political irresponsibility which even the Germans rarely equalled in their foreign policy adventures. But, while very grave and persistent tensions arose over Asian affairs, and while they led to a war between Japan and Russia, they never led to a war amongst European powers. In this, too, the diplomacy of Asian imperialism resembled that of African.

The most alarming of the Asiatic conflicts among great powers was, naturally, between the two which were already established there, Russia in Siberia and the Caucasus, and Great Britain in India. The two had clashed at almost every point in Asian politics for a generation before 1870; over the Straits and Constantinople; over Persia, the dilapidated empire that formed a buffer between them; over Afghanistan and the northern frontier of India; over Russia's influence in northern China. The principal reason for these ubiquitous stresses was the British fear—well-founded—that Russia was conspiring expansions which would threaten India and China and the routes to them. Russia and Britain had become, by 1900, "traditional enemies"—just as France and Britain always had been.

Russia had moved, and was still moving, southward in Central Asia. In the 1880's, however, a fairly stable frontier was established after the British fought a war to safeguard their position in Afghanistan, which thereafter survived precariously as an independent, if wholly remote, kingdom. The struggle in Persia was eventually resolved when, in 1907, the Russians and the British agreed to what amounted to a partition of that empire into spheres of influence. The conflict over the Straits and Turkey belongs to the diplomatic history of Europe (see Chapter 42). It was in China that the most bitter, intricate, and lengthy conflicts took place.

From the 1850's on (when Japan was beginning systematically to modernize itself) China was in a dismal condition of decay. Like the Ottoman empire, which it in some respects resembled, it was increasingly subject to humiliating

HARBOR SCENE AT YOKOHAMA. A printmaker records the beginnings of large-scale European trade with Japan. (Brooklyn Museum Collection)

demands and concessions to western powers, each of which made internal reform more difficult than ever. Harbor privileges, extraterritorial rights, commercial favors, were extracted one by one, and ambassadors at Peking took on the role of protectors or even bosses. Moreover, again like the Ottoman empire, its more remote provinces, inhabited mainly by non-Chinese groups, were being snatched from its control. The British annexed Burma (which adjoined India) in the middle 1880's. The French gained control over the provinces of the extreme southwest—that today form northern and southern Vietnam and the kingdoms of Laos and Cambodia—to create the French colony of Indochina. Russia was already munching contentedly on the ill-defined provinces of the extreme northwest and had, in 1860, established its principal Pacific port of Vladivostok in what had once been Chinese territory. Hong Kong had been annexed by the British in 1842. The Germans, entering the scene late, wrung special trading privileges and the port of Kiaochow from the Peking regime in 1897.

The worst treatment, however, was inflicted on China not by any western power but by its resurgent neighbor, Japan. In 1894, Japan attacked and defeated China and, in the Treaty of Shimonoseki, displayed its capacity, not only for imitating western military prowess but also for imitating western imperialism. China surrendered the outlying province of Korea (to become a theoretically independent empire, eventually annexed to Japan in 1908). The Liaotung peninsula in central China and the off-shore island of Taiwan (Formosa) were ceded to Japan.

The Sino-Japanese War of 1894–1895 was fateful in many ways. In the first place, it projected Japan deep into the tangled heart of northern China, which the Russians had long considered their private preserve. The resulting clash led to the amazing defeat of Russia by Japan in 1904–1905. In the second place, it announced to the startled west the emergence of a new great power—the first non-European great power. Japan's feats—which continued to startle the west until the atom bomb on Hiroshima in 1945 spelled the end of Japanese military greatness—attracted at first very favorable attention. Japan was seen, at the end of the nineteenth century, as an extraordinarily valuable ally, and in 1902 Great Britain signed an alliance with Japan, aimed principally against Russia, which was another milestone: for the first time, a non-European power was drawn as an ally and an equal into European diplomatic politics.

And finally, the defeat by the Japanese marked the beginning of a revolution in China. For one thing, the United States—unwilling to see China and its rich commerce fall under the control of European empires—stepped in with demands for protection of the territorial integrity of China and the "open door," equal trading privileges for all. More important, Chinese national consciousness began to assert itself. At the beginning of the century it showed itself in a blood-curdling anti-western movement called the Boxer Rebellion which required the united efforts of all the European powers to suppress. Later, and more respectably, in 1911, it took the form of a republican revolution led by the Nationalist Party, devoted to asserting the country's independence and reforming its decadent institutions. A long and arduous process of national regeneration had at last begun.

By 1914, then, the situation had begun to change in the Far East. China had at last turned away from complaisant acceptance of partition. Japan had become a modern and aggressive empire which had defeated the great Russian state. But elsewhere, Asia still slumbered beneath the weight of its elementary economy, its moribund social structure, and its European suzerains. The Ottoman empire was nearing its final, awesome disintegration. Persia was divided and misgoverned. Southeast Asia was, except for Siam (which served as a buffer state between the regions of French and British predominance) wholly under the sway of Britain, France, or the Netherlands. And from Singapore to the Suez Canal British power on land and sea commanded the southern half of the continent.

The expansion of Europe had reached its climax.

36

GREAT BRITAIN

In 1870, the Kingdom of Great Britain was emerging from a period of revolutionary change which, though peaceful, had in a century completely transformed
the life and government of its people. In every sphere, the Great Britain of 1870
was profoundly different from that of 1770. Its population had increased to over
31,000,000—an increase of more than threefold. Even this comparison tells only
part of the story, since the rapidly growing populations of Canada, Australia, the
United States, and many overseas territories were in considerable part descendants
of inhabitants of the British Isles. A farming and trading country had been converted into the world's leading manufacturing nation. The former system of government, impeccably constitutional but haphazard in its operations and almost
entirely controlled by a small group of landowners and merchants, had been transformed into a smooth-working representative government dominated by a House
of Commons elected by a large percentage of the citizens. In 1870 Great Britain
was not only the workshop of the world, as its manufacturers liked to call it. It
was also the leading nation in economic and naval power, in effective constitutional government, in colonial holdings, and, not least, in prestige.

From 1870 to 1914 progress continued in almost all fields. The colonial
empire continued to grow. So did commerce. Industry continued to expand, and
the standard of living continued to rise. The population increased. Representative
government was gradually and on the whole painlessly transformed into democracy. But the change was now less rapid—much less rapid than the changes which
took place in countries like Russia, Germany, or the United States during the
same period—and it was along lines already familiar. Britain in 1914 did not seem to
be much affected in its basic structure or direction by the developments since 1870.

The men and women who reached maturity after 1870 devoted themselves
to sorting out changes which had already taken place, to adjustment, rearrangement, and reform of systems and institutions which had already come into exist-

ence. Rights already achieved for many—like the franchise, and the control of working hours and conditions—were extended to others in the community. Material wealth almost constantly expanded. Patterns for colonial development like the extension of self-government to Canada (which had begun in the 1840's) were applied to other colonies. Foreigners tended to regard the British as smug; almost everyone regarded them as fortunate. In contrast to most parts of the world, Britain was remarkably stable. There was, however, a sort of storing up of revolutionary developments, a backlog of subsurface changes which began to make themselves felt in the years just before World War I and were to lead to radical readjustments in the thirty-five years that followed, until a new equilibrium was achieved in the decade after World War II.

Moreover, perceived by only a few, the British economy was faced with serious threats by 1914, both from the gradual slowing down of its own rate of expansion and from the vigorous competition of more dynamic regions abroad. As more and more Britons pointed out in the early years of the twentieth century, there were grounds for serious alarm about Britain's future. Furthermore, the evolution of democracy—and of material security and rights for the working classes—seemed to have reached a point where the propertied and dominant social groups would make no further concessions without being forced to do so. The social and political elasticity of Great Britain appeared to be diminishing, and in certain parts of its empire, most especially in Ireland, concessions were being demanded which no British government cared to permit. World War I postponed and concealed some of these difficulties and divergences. But in the end it aggravated most of them. After the Armistice at length was signed, it was gradually discovered that the Golden Age had come to an end and that Great Britain had lost not only its supremacy but some of the sources of its power and prosperity.

POLITICAL AND CONSTITUTIONAL DEVELOPMENT

The British constitution, arising from ancient custom and modified at intervals by parliamentary enactment, by administrative habit, and by rebellion, had tended to freeze in the eighteenth century. In the nineteenth it had thawed again, and after 1832 British institutions were very extensively reorganized. But this reorganization was in the main completed by 1870. The lines for development for the next eighty-five years were clearly laid down.

The British crown had been shorn of its political powers and was being given a new role in government. Unlike most other monarchs in Europe, the queen of Great Britain was excluded from proposing legislation, appointing her own ministers, nominating members of the administration, or carrying out policies in any sphere. Victoria (1837–1901) still fancied that she had a special influence in foreign and military affairs, but this influence was largely imaginary. On the other hand, her peculiar personality—prim, possessive, obstinate, uncreative, and

Four Generations of British Royalty. Queen Victoria, in 1894, with her daughter-in-law Alexandra (wife of the future Edward VII, reigned 1901–1910), her granddaughter-in-law Mary (wife of the future George V, reigned 1910–1936), and her great-grandson, the future Edward VIII (reigned January to December, 1936). The coziness of the family group as depicted here, domestic rather than glorious, may be contrasted with the imperial splendor in which Elizabeth I was shown in the engraving on page 103 or Maria Theresa in the painting on page 240. The comparison illuminates the durable but drastically changing role of royalty in national life. (Radio Times Hulton Picture Library)

inartistic—was in some respects extremely congenial to the majority of her sub-jects. Her extreme longevity—she was eighty-one when she died in 1901—and the period of progress and tranquility over which she presided, eventually endowed her with enormous prestige and popularity. In 1870, her personality and the monarchy itself were still controversial, but they soon ceased to be so. Moreover, her office, stripped of real authority, came to occupy a convenient (if mainly fictional) role in the mechanics and symbols of government. The theme of monarchy was interwoven with Britain's relations to its colonies and with the routine of appointing prime ministers. These functions, at once indispensable and innocuous (if rather expensive), contributed to the stability and color of the British state and provided to the populace a sort of emotional outlet. No other dynasty in Europe could boast a crown more secure in 1918.

The real center of authority in the British government was, in 1870, as it had been for a generation or more, the House of Commons. The great constitu-tional issues of the preceding age had revolved about how that House was to be selected, rather than about its well-established prime importance in the political scheme. By 1870, a midway point had been reached in the transformation of the House from an aristocratic to a democratic body. The old landed classes, both the great, sophisticated noblemen and the small, bucolic squires, were still rather overrepresented. But the electorate now included most of the manufacturers and, since the Second Reform Bill, of 1867, it also included a large number of ordin-ary householders in the growing cities. In 1884, a Third Reform Bill expanded the franchise further by including most of the country people. England was still not technically a democracy—not until 1918—since the right to vote still depended on membership in one of several classes, determined by income received, or rent or taxes paid, or place of residence. But after 1884, the great majority of adult males belonged to one of these classes. The average Englishman could vote; as yet he did not vote for members of his own class, but before the century was over, he was beginning to do so.

The House of Lords, consisting of prelates of the Church of England and the hereditary holders of noble titles in Great Britain (including some elected peers from Scotland and Ireland), was still influential. It could still veto legisla-tion passed by the Commons. It still supplied a large majority of ministers and other high officials (the last titled prime minister, Lord Salisbury, retired in 1902). But in an age when public opinion was growing more self-assertive, the peers did not care to exercise their powers unless the basic institutions of the class structure were challenged, and until 1905 they were not. Moreover, the Lords were growing less narrowly aristocratic. The prime minister (in theory, the queen) could create peers at will, and did not hesitate to do so. The House of Lords increased rapidly in size and many of the new "creations" (as they were called) were persons of present eminence but past simplicity—brewers, railway magnates, poets, or steel manufacturers.

Commons' great prerogative, control over the budget, had gradually helped to give it control over the queen's ministers. By 1870, the sovereign was obliged to appoint only prime ministers acceptable to the majority of Commons, and the prime minister filled, at will, the other high offices of state. The ministry (or more especially, its principal members, who formed the cabinet), were assured of the support of the majority of the House. It formed a smooth-working committee which could be removed from office only by persistent defeats of its measures in Commons or by an election in which its political opponents were voted into a majority in the House by the electorate.

The cabinet controlled appointment to all offices in the administration—postmasters, army sergeants, bishops, governors of colonies, ambassadors, and janitors. In the past, appointments had been given largely to friends and relatives of the ministers, and the administration had been both slovenly and aristocratic. By 1870, however, the business of government was too intricate and exacting to permit such conditions to continue. In any event, the newly powerful manufacturers and professional people were anxious to end them. By 1870, the civil service, systematic and professional, based upon merit and skill, was slowly becoming established, although it as yet extended only to a few offices of government.

This system of government, combining many of the traditions and habits of an aristocratic age with recent innovations, sponsored in some cases by the reforming liberal philosophers, operated and operates today extremely well, perhaps better than any other which men have devised. Its success depended in large part, however, upon the existence of political parties; it was through political parties that the wishes of the electorate could be translated into electoral programs and candidates and made known in Westminster, where Parliament sat. It was political parties which permitted an orderly arrangement of majorities and an orderly alternation of cabinets. Until very recently, in 1870, the parties had consisted mainly of groups of friends of individual politicians, without national organization or national programs of action. But this age was passing. The division of the House of Commons into two fairly coherent groups, each with its own characteristic outlook on life, was proceeding rapidly. In the decade after 1870 a "grassroots" structure was developed in the form of the caucus, or local meeting of party faithful in each locality, where candidates, strategy, and platform could be discussed and decided.

THE POLITICAL PARTIES

The two parties which had coalesced by 1870 were called Conservative (or Tory, after their remote ancestors) and Liberal. The Conservative party, out of power in 1870, was remarkably coherent and well-unified under the leadership of Benjamin Disraeli (1804–1881)—soon to be transformed by a grateful queen into the Earl of Beaconsfield. Some of the party strength came from the influence of the country landowners, and the party preached their faith in very gradual change, devotion to monarchy and established Church, the importance of private property in land, and old-fashioned virtues and values associated rather vaguely with the England of the past.

But Disraeli, an imaginative and flamboyant leader, had added something new. He perceived that a party of conservatives must make some rather special appeals in order to succeed in an age when so many of the simpler people in the population could vote, and he fashioned such special appeals with striking skill. In the election campaign of 1874, he succeeded in persuading the Conservatives to place special emphasis upon promised laws to protect, aid, and please the working man—public housing and health, factory safety legislation, protection of trade unions, and more beer parlors. He also sought to bait and flatter the average voter with appeals to patriotism, with romantic build-ups for the monarchy, with extravagant applause for the glories of the empire and the natural superiority of the British nation. This combination of nationalism, social conscience, and tradition came to be called Tory Democracy.

In 1870, the Liberals were at the height of their political power and prestige. They had come to office after winning the first election held under the Reform Bill of 1867. The newly enfranchised householders of the towns had shown their confidence that the Liberals were the party most friendly to the interests of the average man. Like the Conservatives, they were held together in a coherent party through the skill and force of their leader, in this case the prime minister, William Gladstone (1809–1898). But the Liberals were more diverse than the Tories. The party consisted of assorted elements thrown together by historical accident. There were, first of all, the old Whigs, remnants of the great noble landowners who had run the country in the eighteenth century and who retained their taste for power. Secondly, there were the so-called Radicals, for the most part manufacturers, professional men, and doctrinaire intellectuals, who were devoted to the ideals (or some of them) of what was called earlier Philosophic Radicalism—what we think of as "laissez-faire liberalism." The Philosophic Radicals had fashioned a cosmology out of free trade, free enterprise, inexpensive government, and civil liberties. But by now most of their demands had been met, and the Radicals were coming to represent points of view either old-fashioned or divergent. Some of them, like Charles Dilke and Joseph Chamberlain, were espousing extreme causes like republicanism and even a mild form of socialism.

The Liberal party appealed to almost all groups who had in the past been treated with intolerance or even persecution by the old, inflexible institutions and governing classes. Most notable among these were Dissenters (Protestants who were members of sects outside the Church of England, such as Methodists and Presbyterians), as well Catholics and Jews. Gladstone himself, and many of his party politicians, preached a vaguely puritanical but extremely tolerant sort of religious philosophy. Non-Anglicans, most notably the Irish, Scottish, and Welsh, supported the party which they believed had given them religious freedom, and the Liberals thus appealed particularly to the non-English population of Great Britain. Moreover, with its tradition of reform and its numerous members who preached and practiced charity toward the poor, the Liberals seemed the natural choice for industrial workers. Tory Democracy was to challenge this appeal, but the first working-class members of Parliament were all Liberals—there were two in 1870.

It was the job of Gladstone to hold these disparate elements together, and he did so with remarkable success. He blended lofty and rather rigid ideals, both religious and social, with prodigious learning, an exceptionally shrewd sense of practical politics amounting sometimes to hypocrisy, and a genuine and sometimes almost puerile warm-heartedness. Like Victoria, his personality was peculiarly congenial to his age. In 1870, he was in the course of his Great Ministry, which lasted from 1868 to 1874, whose vast record of legislation completed and consolidated the great reforms which had begun in 1832. The new laws seemed far-reaching at the time, but actually they merely swept away more of the anomalies and asymmetries of the eighteenth century.

A few examples of this legislation will indicate the nature of Gladstonian liberalism and the substantial accomplishments of the Great Ministry. The laws which prevented non-Anglicans from taking degrees at Oxford and Cambridge were abolished. The secret ballot (long opposed as un-English by land- and factory-owners who liked to check up on the party affiliations of their employees) was introduced. The ancient system of selecting army officers by selling commissions to the highest bidder was suppressed in favor of promotion through merit (over the dead and bleeding bodies of the officers corps, which needlessly feared the rise of officers who were not gentlemen). A thorough reform of the army and war office was carried out. The long overdue need for primary schools was faced— England lagged far behind the continent in elementary education. Elected boards were empowered to found schools where none existed, and subsidies were provided for schools which already existed (over the violent opposition of religious extremists of all persuasions, each of which felt that some other sect was going to benefit). The established Church of Ireland, a branch of the English Church, was disestablished—a move naturally disliked by the Church of Ireland, which lost most of its revenues, and sullenly welcomed by the overwhelmingly Roman Catholic majority, which was glad not to have to support a church it loathed, but regarded the step as a mere drop in the vast bucket of Irish grievances unredressed.

Such reforms as these were welcomed by the majority of voters. But the incorrigible virtue of the Liberals, their prim and conciliatory foreign policy, their antagonism to beer parlors, bored an electorate newly beguiled by Disraeli's rhetoric. In 1874 the Conservatives won a majority. Disraeli became prime minister, to hold office six years during which the Conservatives experimented with reforms along their own line of Tory Democracy—reforms more original and imaginative but less substantial in most cases than those of the Liberals. They set about a spirited foreign policy with a heavy accent on imperialism. Labor unions were freed from legal obstacles to striking and picketing. Rather inadequate health and housing acts were passed. Colonial wars were fought against the Zulus in Africa and the Afghans in Central Asia. To the accompaniment of much fanfare, the Disraeli government proclaimed Victoria Empress of India—a step pleasing to the queen but not of any great significance, since Britain continued to rule almost all of India as a colony. It acquired an important part of the stock, and with it extensive control, in the company which owned the Suez Canal. And it participated flamboyantly in the Berlin Congress which was called in 1878 to settle a war between Turkey and Russia and which ended up giving the island of Cyprus to England for no particular reason except that Disraeli wanted it.

The kind of policies displayed by the two parties in the years from 1870 to 1880 continued, with changes of emphasis and targets, to characterize them until 1918. It might have been supposed that the British could continue indefinitely with a tranquil alternation of governments and without basic change. But, despite the surface continuity and stability, several vital changes were slowly taking place in British life which led to minor explosions and presaged major ones. One of them was the painful evolution of the Irish Problem. A second was the shifting of class structure and class interests. A third was the long though rather mild economic depression which, beginning in the 1870's, lasted off and on for the rest of the century.

THE MAJOR ISSUES
IN THE LATE VICTORIAN AGE

It has been said of the Irish Problem, which ran like a green thread through English history from the fourteenth to the twentieth century, that whenever it was solved the Irish thought of a new problem. Some of its complexities have been noted earlier. Essentially, the difficulty arose from the fact that the island of Ireland, ruled by England for hundreds of years, contained a population which was of an entirely different nationality, religion, and temperament, and much poorer in material wealth. The land was mainly owned by Englishmen who were increasingly afraid to live on their estates, through a well-founded fear of assassination, and who typically paid little attention to their poverty-stricken tenants. The Irish were represented in Parliament, but the Irish members were of course a minority—sometimes they could influence governments because they held a balance of power between parties. Generally they were unable to get what they wanted for Ireland.

A majority of Englishmen (most of whom despised the Irish) were determined to maintain English control over the island, to prevent it from acquiring its own government and parliament and trying to solve its own problems. Some, however, believed that only a large measure of "home rule" could divest the British government of a wholly unmanageable problem. Gladstone, converted to the latter view, became almost obsessed by it. Determined that the Irish problem could be solved for England only by dropping it in the laps of the natives, he introduced a series of Home Rule bills. None of them passed; if they got through Commons, they were defeated by the Lords. Ireland remained a Problem, but Gladstone's efforts to solve it led, in 1886, to the disruption of the Liberal party. Most of the old Whig aristocrats, ardent supporters of the Act of Union which had made Ireland an integral part of the United Kingdom, left the party. So did a group of Radicals, led by the egregious Joseph Chamberlain, who were mostly progressive-minded businessmen with a rather naive enthusiasm for the empire and the glory of Great Britain. These dissident Liberals formed a new party, called the Liberal Unionists, which supported the Tories after 1886 and eventually united with them. It was in part their support which accounted for the long Conservative predominance from 1886 to 1905, broken only by a brief and unsuccessful Liberal interlude from 1892 to 1895.

The Tories sought to "kill Home Rule with kindness"—by gradually giving economic reforms and gentler administration to Ireland. The various measures they introduced were undoubtedly successful in improving the Irish economy and raising the lamentable standard of living of the Irish people. They helped to establish the farmers on their own land and provide them with opportunities for education and for government jobs. But they did not solve the Problem—or at least, the Irish invented a new one. When the Liberals returned to power in 1905, the Irish members of Commons supported them wholeheartedly and demanded as a price a Home Rule bill. At long last, Home Rule was passed in 1914 (after the House of Lords had lost its veto power). Conservatives, ostensibly alarmed for the rights of the Protestant and non-Irish majority in the northeastern Irish province of Ulster, reacted violently. There were riots and even mutinies. The outbreak of World War I prompted a suspension of the Home Rule Act; otherwise there might have been open rebellion in both Ulster and England. As it was, there was open resistance in Ireland, mounting into the Easter Rebellion of 1916. At the end of the war, with tempers running shorter than ever and the Problem as far from solution as ever, Ireland broke into a bloody and wearisome civil war.

Ireland was a headache for the Liberals, and it invested British politics again and again with a bitterness and an intractability which no other issue had provided since 1688. But the increasing articulateness and exigency of the working class did more long-run harm to the Liberal party and the institutions of 1870 than the Liberal-Unionist split. In 1870, England was largely run by and for property-owners; and working-class people, when they had the vote, voted for Liberals or Conservatives. By 1918, a large and powerful working class party, the Labor party, had come into existence to threaten the Liberals and to undermine and challenge the economic and social hierarchy.

Britain in 1870 possessed a small group of revolutionary socialists and anarchists, similar to those in other European countries, and there were occasional outbreaks of class strife, union violence, and social unrest. But generally speaking, there was a marked absence of the sort of hatred of rich by poor that characterized some continental countries. This relative complaisance has been the subject of much speculation; observers at the time and historians since have tried to explain it in various terms: the strong sense of national pride and unity, the rapid expansion of British wealth some of which spilled over into working-class homes, the religious sects which provided an emotional outlet for families whose lives were unimaginably hard, the great output of reformist and protective legislation passed by Parliament.

The quietude of British workers and paupers lasted until the 1880's. Until then, the unions which fought for and won recognition were organizations of skilled workers, well-to-do and generally conservative. The unskilled and discontented were not heard from. The depression of the 1880's changed the situation. Unemployment mounted (the word was invented in this period), and revolutionary ideas spread. By 1890, unskilled workers were organizing national unions, and extremist radicals were challenging the old-line control of the Trades Union Congress, the central organ of the unions. In the early 1890's a group called the Independent Labor party was organized, led by James Keir Hardie, a Scottish socialist. The ILP did poorly politically, but many people, even very conservative unionists and some intellectuals, had concluded that only through a separate political party could the working men secure a larger share in the political life and wealth of the British Isles. Persistent unemployment spurred the movement.

So did a court decision, in the Taff Vale case (1902), which menaced the existence of unions by holding that they were financially responsible for loss of profits to employers occasioned by strikes. It seemed clear that political action to bring about the statutory repeal of this decision was essential. In 1900, a group was set up called the Labor Representation Committee. The LRC contained representatives of the ILP, the unions, and the left-wing middle-class intellectuals called Fabians, including George Bernard Shaw and Sidney Webb, who provided doctrine and leadership. It proceeded to nominate candidates for Parliament and in 1906 it won 29 seats; the first working class MP's now sat at Westminster as a separate group not subject to the discipline of the older parties. The LRC, or Labor party as it began to be called, was able to press the Liberals into overriding the Taff Vale decision by statute, and passing other wanted measures.

The Liberals, who won their most sweeping victory of all time in the same election, now found themselves faced with a difficult situation. They were traditionally the party most friendly to labor and to the average man, and their electoral success depended upon working-class votes. But the Liberals were no less traditionally the party of the business interests and, even more so, the party of *laissez faire*. They had usually stood for the principle of "the less government the better," for free trade and free enterprise, for extreme restraint on the part of the state in interfering with private affairs. The working class was now moving away from these traditional Liberal notions—it was demanding, and receiving, legislative action for the remedy of its grievances which involved greatly increased taxes and a vast extension of government controls and activities.

THE LIBERAL GOVERNMENT OF 1905–1915

The ten years after 1906 saw increasing ructions within the Liberal party about how far to go in meeting the wishes of the mass constituency. But the party was capable both of great imagination and great flexibility. Far-reaching reforms were carried out, under the leadership of the two Liberal prime ministers, Sir Henry Campbell-Bannerman and Herbert Asquith, and the extremely able and fiery cabinet members, Winston Churchill and David Lloyd George. Working conditions, particularly in the smaller shops where previous controls had been ineffective, were greatly improved. The first British social security measure, the Old-Age Pensions act, was passed in 1909, with the unique provisions that the worker did not himself contribute, but received a pension out of a fund built up by the state. Then, in 1909, Lloyd George's dramatic budget, which imposed very heavy taxes on some kinds of unearned income, was rejected by the House of Lords.

The Budget was thought to strike at the very foundations of inherited wealth—and thus at the position of the aristocracy and the privileged classes—and it was not surprising that the Lords should have rejected it. A constitutional question arose. There was serious doubt as to whether the Lords could legally reject a money bill, and a hue and cry was raised in many circles over the improper use of the veto by an entirely unrepresentative legislative chamber. The cabinet replied with the Parliament Bill, which provided that acts of the Commons would, in time, become law even without the approval of the Lords. The bill passed the Commons and was, naturally, rejected by the Lords. An election was called, and the Liberals once again won a majority in the Commons (though greatly reduced). The bill was passed again, and this time, yielding to public opinion and to the prime minister's threats to create enough new peers to pass the bill anyway, the Lords let it go through in 1911. The sovereignty of the People—or at least of the House of Commons popularly elected—was at last achieved.

All these achievements and struggles should have endeared the Liberals to the working class, the unions, and progressive-minded people generally. But by this time the Labor party was already in existence. It could always outbid the Liberals, with their Gladstonian inhibitions and their middle-class leadership. From the point of view of the working man, anything that Liberals could do, Laborites could do better. Moreover, with a renewal of hard times, there was a new spread of revolutionary agitation in the years just before World War I. Strike violence grew more common, and unions threatened political action. There was even some wild talk, of a sort not heard for seventy-five years, of a general strike designed to overthrow the government. To this the Liberals (and indeed many of the Labor party people) reacted with horror. It was clear to the more farseeing, in 1914, that social unrest was blowing up for trouble and that the most serious trouble would come to the Liberals.

But it was not only with their constituents among the common people that the Liberals were having trouble. They had lost much of the support of the businessmen, who had been instrumental in building up the party to begin with, over the Irish issue. They lost more through their legislation from 1905 to 1910. And they lost more still through the Parliament Act, which alarmed a great many substantial people.

Liberal doctrine had originally represented the protest of both business-men and working-class leaders against the domination of Great Britain by land-owning aristocrats, and their desire for freedom from the ramshackle economic restrictions of the old oligarchic days. But now there was no longer much distinction between businessmen and aristocrats. Nut and bolt kings had moved into the House of Lords and bought country estates, and dukes had bought shares in industrial firms. Moreover, businessmen—like working men—were no longer so devoted to free enterprise and free competition as they had once been. Faced with rising industrial production in foreign countries often equipped with more modern factories, many of them favored tariff duties on imports—a program which ran directly counter to the most ancient and firmly held tenet of the Liberals. Others were seeking to protect themselves by making deals with the competitors to share the market and to set prices—practices which were anathema to *laissez faire*. In short, the businessmen, by 1914, partly abandoned their support of the Liberals, and the attempts of the government to play along with a working class movement which they feared and disliked did not encourage them to restore it. By the end of the war it was apparent that most of the business community—and indeed most people in Britain who owned property of any kind—had moved into the Conservative party. Henceforth, Britain's party structure was to reflect a new alignment of Labor against Capital.

In 1916, under the pressure of organizing the country for war, the dynamic Lloyd George replaced Asquith as Prime Minister and presided over a cabinet which included both Liberals and Conservatives. The coalition lasted until 1922, and when it finally broke up the subsequent election showed that the days of the Liberal party's power were at an end. Compared to the 377 seats they had won in 1906, they won only 117 in 1922. The old party structure, which was both a cause and an effect of nineteenth-century stability, had broken down with the shifting social structure of Great Britain. Uncertainties and alarms lay ahead.

THE CHANGING ECONOMIC POSITION OF GREAT BRITAIN

Behind all these developments was the changing economic position of Great Britain.

The traditional bases of the wealth and prestige of the British people had been a prosperous agriculture and a very well developed trade throughout the world, amply protected by the navy. By 1870, a new and far more fecund source of riches had been added: the manufacturing of goods in bulk, mainly in factories with machines. The new outflow of goods naturally enriched the traders, and the factory-owners. With extensive savings, Britain had already, by 1870, begun to pour out money into profitable investments abroad—in the colonies, Canada, and India, and to an even greater extent in the United States, and in places like Argentina and China. The borrowers in the fertile and rapidly developing regions could expect large profits and could afford to pay large rates of interest, which further enriched the British stockholder or bondholder. Britain's overseas investment rose steadily and, at certain periods, prodigiously. In 1885 it totalled about one and one-third billion pounds sterling; in 1914, about three and three-quarter billions. With this source of income, the people of the United Kingdom were able to buy very large quantities of goods from abroad, thus raising their own standard of living, which they certainly could not have afforded on the profits solely of their current labors and production. By 1914, Britain was in precisely the position of an heir to a successful self-made man; it was living partly on inherited income.

The accumulated capital and the new savings of the British were less and less devoted to the modernization of their own plants. As new methods developed and new factories were built abroad—often with British money—Britain's own industry fell behind. Moreover, as new industries developed abroad, foreign manufacturers were increasingly able to supply their own markets. Britain's share in world trade steadily declined, although in 1913 it was still enormous (17% of the total), and the volume of trade itself (as distinct from the percentage) was still increasing.

None of these difficulties would in themselves have raised critical problems, since Britain was still rich and inventive and there were indications of a trend toward the modernization of industry. Two other developments made the position precarious. The first of these was the almost complete destruction of British agriculture; the second was World War I.

Britain's farming, long the envy of the rest of the world, had grown steadily more efficient during the first three quarters of the nineteenth century. Although the huge increase of population meant that some food had to be imported, the bulk of what Britons ate in 1870 was still home-grown. However, cheap food imports from the great new agricultural areas of Canada, the United States, and Russia, speeded by modern transportation, easily undersold the products of British farmers. These imports began arriving in quantity in the late 1870's. When they did so, other Western European countries sought to save their own farms by imposing import duties on food products, and they succeeded. In Britain, however, the free-trade tradition was very deeply rooted. The average voter, who by this time was a factory worker, could be relied upon to vote against any party which wanted to make his food bill higher by imposing taxes on imports.

The consequence was that Great Britain rapidly became largely dependent upon imported food; the very existence of the population depended on being able to buy meat and grain abroad and being able to get it safely home. The money with which to buy it had to come from either income from foreign investments or profits on British exports. The safe transport involved control of the seas—a foreign country with a navy equal to Britain's could starve the country to death in a few weeks.

British foreign policy was to a very considerable extent a reflection of this elementary fact. So long as British naval supremacy was not seriously challenged, Britain could and did maintain a policy of aloofness from European politics. But after 1900 Germany (which was the principal economic rival as well) was embarking upon an ambitious program of naval building, and the British regarded with a more and more hostile eye the exuberant maritime activities of the

Germans. In the end, the British felt forced to draw closer to Germany's rivals on the continent, and when France and Russia found themselves at war, Britain had no choice but to join them.

At the end of World War I, the people of the United Kingdom found themselves with a navy no longer supreme, a floundering trade, an obsolescent factory system, a reduced foreign investment, an almost total absence of food and other raw material resources except coal, with a population accustomed to the highest standard of living in Europe, and with the mounting threat of social unrest. The only great resources which remained unscarred were an incomparable skill at governing themselves and a population of great discipline and technical ability.

37

THE THIRD FRENCH REPUBLIC

THE THIRD FRENCH REPUBLIC was born of the Franco-Prussian War of 1870. It died in 1940 (though some were to dispute the legal moment) in the second World War, having survived the first. The Third Republic may therefore be viewed as a long period of political stability—a period of seventy years, following the eighty years of political instability which began with the events of 1789.

This much said, qualifications may be added. The French social structure remained remarkably stable beneath the changes of regime, from the time of the Great Revolution to the twentieth century. Politically, there were times of crisis and uncertainty during the seven decades of the Third Republic. Nevertheless a large fact is not to be obscured: that the French with all their tribulations achieved democratic political institutions by the end of the nineteenth century and clung to them with remarkable tenacity in the twentieth.

THE SIEGE OF PARIS
AND THE COMMUNE OF 1871

In French history the months from the summer of 1870 to the summer of 1871 are known as the "terrible year." The Franco-Prussian War began in July, 1870. In August the French Marshal Bazaine and his army were trapped by the Germans in the fortress-city of Metz. Early in September, Emperor Napoleon III and the major French force were surrounded at Sedan. "The army is defeated and captured; I myself am a prisoner" read his telegram to Paris. In the capital a republic was proclaimed on September 4, and a Government of National Defense was organized. On September 19, Paris was cut off from the outside world by a German siege which lasted for four months, until the inhabitants were reduced to butchering dogs and rats and animals from the zoo. In October the sulphuric radical republican orator Gambetta, having escaped from Paris by balloon, took charge of a delegation at Tours, on the Loire, which attempted to organize the defense of the country. They made a heroic effort and armed some 600,000 men, but Marshal Bazaine's surrender of Metz late in October freed another German army and made hopeless the project of liberating Paris. In spite of a grand tour of European capitals made by Adolphe Thiers, help for France was not obtained. Paris was near starvation when King William I of Prussia visited the suburbs, and was ceremoniously proclaimed German Emperor in the palace of Versailles on January 18, 1871. Ten days later the capital was forced to surrender.

But the worst was still ahead. Bismarck wanted his peace terms signed by a responsible French government. In February, 1871, therefore, the Germans permitted the election of a National Assembly, while the war was still in progress and much of the country occupied. Meeting at Bordeaux in the southwest, away from the German troops, the Assembly chose Adolphe Theirs "Chief of the Executive Power of the French Republic" and authorized his entry into peace negotiations. The preliminaries of a peace which sacrificed Alsace and Lorraine and imposed a heavy indemnity, were accepted by the Assembly on March 1, and the Assembly then took up its residence at Versailles. On the same day, as part of the settlement, the Germans exacted a pound of flesh in the form of a triumphal entry into Paris. They were met with empty streets decorated with black flags, as they marched on the Champs Elysées.

But France's cup was still not full. The National Assembly represented the nation, but in a very special way. At the time of the election, the idea uppermost in everyone's mind was that this body was being chosen to make peace. The country realistically admitted the need for peace, and in the face of the furious patriotism of republican leaders like Gambetta, the voters chose moderates who wished to end the war. As a result the Bordeaux Assembly which moved to Versailles in March, 1871, had a majority of conservative, royalist, rural leaders. When they made Thiers their chief, they chose a man they knew to be an Orleanist, who had served as King Louis Philippe's chief minister. When they called the regime a republic, they expressly noted that they did not mean to prejudice the future form of government; in fact they did not wish to burden the restored monarchy with the unpopular mission of signing the peace with Bismarck.

Thiers and the Assembly were distrustful of the city of Paris, whose populace was still armed from the war, and they wished to put an end to the state of emergency there. Late in March, 1871, they sent some troops to take charge of certain cannons on the heights of Montmartre. A Parisian crowd gathered, and objected to turning over the weapons to the Versailles Assembly. The troops fraternized with the crowd. In the ensuing uprising two generals were shot after the briefest of drumhead trials. The cannon remained in the city, now in insurrection under the leadership of a revolutionary Central Committee.

So began the tragic springtime of the "terrible year," the year of the Paris Commune. The city of Paris, in rebellion against the National Assembly, resisted with weapons in its hands until the end of May, 1871. For a second time the city was besieged. During the last week, the army representing the Provisional Government at Versailles broke into Paris and conquered it street by street. Between ten and fifteen thousand Communards were killed on the barricades or by courts martial, and many thousands more were jailed or exiled to New Caledonia. The Communards, or *Fédérés,* responded to the firing squads of the *Versaillais* by burning the Tuileries Palace and the City Hall as they retreated across the city toward its radical, working class eastern section. They executed distinguished hostages, among them the Archbishop of Paris, while the German armies were still occupying the country. Europe watched with horror, thinking that the inevitable climax of all the French revolutions had come. Karl Marx, at his place in the reading room of the British Museum, scanned the newspapers and wondered whether he had been too cautious in forecasting the proletarian revolution.

But the Paris Commune was not *the* socialist revolution or even, wholly, *a* socialist revolution. It was the result of many circumstances, creeds, and emotions in a city tried by the hardships of war, furious at the need to swallow a bitter peace, and resentful of what it interpreted as defeatism and reaction in the Versailles Assembly and the Provisional Government of Adolphe Thiers. Paris had long been more radical than the rest of France, and the difference had been accentuated by the industrialism of the Second Empire and by the departure of many well-to-do people just before the approach of the Prussian armies. During the siege by the Prussians, many emergency measures had been taken in Paris, such as the payment of wages to National Guardsmen and a moratorium on rents. Suspension of these measures by the Provisional Government did much to alienate the Parisians and bring about the insurrection. The Central Committee which directed the Paris Commune was none too effective in the face of resolute neighborhood committees of all sorts. A minority of its members had connections with the First International, but the majority were followers of the Jacobin republicanism of 1793 and the ideal of a "social republic" of 1848. Such socialists as there were in the Commune leaned toward the ideals of Proudhon and decentralization (thus: *fédérés,* or "federated," suggesting loosely associated communities) rather than toward the statism of Karl Marx. The rank and file of the Communards was very diverse, consisting of thousands of artisans of the old French type—carpenters of the building trades, cabinet-makers, shoemakers—and was not dominated by factory workers.

The Paris Commune left its legend among the working class, however, together with a residue of hostility to the state, and to employers and propertied people generally, which lasted far into the twentieth century. Responsibility for the Commune was falsely and hysterically laid at the door of the First International, and the European-wide repression of labor and socialism which followed in the 1870's contributed to the demise of that body. On the other hand, the leaders of the International and their heirs in later socialist movements were glad to take the credit for the Commune and add to their cause the potency of its legend and the blood of its martyrs. In another—opposite—sense, the Commune contributed to the republican cause in France. After the ferocious repression, "radicalism" could scarcely be listed among the faults of the Provisional Government. When Thiers, its head, came out for a permanent republic his advice was not followed at once, but the moderates in France no longer thought that a republic would be unable to protect their interests.

THE MAKING OF THE THIRD REPUBLIC

On May 10, 1871, before the final climax of the Paris Commune, the Frankfurt Treaty with the Germans was signed. Thiers had been unable to keep Bismarck from taking Alsace and Lorraine, but he managed to have the indemnity reduced from six billion to five billion francs. He now set out to get the indemnity paid as quickly as possible so that German occupying forces would be withdrawn from French soil, and to everyone's surprise—for the sum of five billion francs, or one billion dollars, was enormous in those days—his objective was achieved by the fall of 1873. France had lost a war and undergone a frightful civil conflict, but the country was blessed by nature with a wealth which could survive greater upheavals than these. In the 1870's the loans which Thiers asked the public to make to the French government were oversubscribed. But before the fall of 1873 Thiers himself had been pushed out of the presidency.

The National Assembly with its monarchist majority had been almost as much of a surprise as the restoration of the Bourbons in 1814 after their quarter-century of exile. To the monarchists it was a miracle for which they were not prepared. The Legitimists and Orleanists, represented by the Counts of Chambord and Paris, grandsons respectively of Charles X and Louis Philippe, were alike in being socially conservative. Most of the Legitimists were by this time willing to tolerate some form of representative institutions, but compared with the Orleanists they were fiercely Catholic and socially more aristocratic, and most of them were still contemptuous of the Orleanist affinity for big business and parliamentary government. Legitimists and Orleanists knew that they would eventually have to come to some agreement, but first there was the more pressing need to deal with the Germans and with the Paris Commune. By 1873, however, republican victories in by-elections to fill vacancies in the Assembly became alarming, and even more so was the success of Thiers in demonstrating that a republic of a moderate kind could work. When Thiers made it plain that he wished the republic to continue, as the "regime which would divide us least," and that he wanted to go on being president of it, the Assembly forced his resignation. In his place was chosen Marshal MacMahon, a royalist who could be counted upon to step aside whenever the monarch was restored.

For a time in 1873 it was thought that everything was settled by a reconciliation of the two branches of the royal family and by an understanding that the Legitimist Count of Chambord, old and childless, would accept the Orleanist Count of Paris as his legitimate successor. But the old gentleman had been misunderstood. He was extremely devout and conscientious and, having resided in Austria for many decades, was out of touch with modern France. The monarchist majority of the Assembly tried to avoid a catastrophe by getting from him some preliminary guarantees that he would accept representative institutions and the tricolor flag, symbol of liberty. Chambord fussed a while and then published a blunt statement to the effect that his mission in France would be ruined if his first act was the acceptance of conditions from a popularly elected Assembly. The latter had no recourse but to vote Marshal MacMahon a seven-year term and hope that when it ended the Count of Chambord would no longer be available.

Within two years this waiting game had to be abandoned. Some of the Orleanists, most of whom were genuine constitutional monarchists, deserted the alliance with the right and followed Thiers into the camp of the conservative republicans. On the left the Radicals—republicans of the Gambetta variety inclined to favor the Jacobin tradition and the lower middle class—were growing stronger. But there was another threat which gave pause to the moderates, whether monarchist or republican. Bonapartism was reviving. Louis Napoleon had died in 1873 in England. His son, "Napoleon IV," represented a genuine political force, as district elections of Bonapartist candidates began to demonstrate. Against the combined threat of the Radicals and the Bonapartists, the moderate center of the National Assembly passed in 1875 a series of laws organizing new institutions. By a majority of one vote, they included the fateful word republic: "The President of the Republic is elected by a plurality of votes by the Senate and the Chamber of Deputies joined together in a National Assembly." The Third Republic had achieved legal existence.

The Constitution of 1875 consisted of only 34 articles, compared with 68 in the Constitution of 1852, 74 in the Charter of 1814, and 370 in the Constitution of 1795. But there was plenty of room for precedent-setting and evolution through custom, and through improvisation it was given life. The Constitution of 1875, the work of monarchists, has often been called a constitutional monarchy without a king. It was like the Charter of 1830 without Louis Philippe, adapted to the evolution of democracy. The republican tradition dating back to the Great Revolution was represented by the Chamber of Deputies, elected by universal manhood suffrage, which could force the resignation of ministries. But the tradition of constitutionalism, more or less on the British model, which had been the experience of 1814–1848, was represented by an upper house, the Senate, which was indirectly elected and was expected to be a conservative check on the impetuosity of the Chamber. The President of the Republic, chosen by the two legislative bodies sitting together, had a term of seven years and could be re-elected. He had real power, the key to which was his right to dissolve the Chamber of Deputies with the consent of the Senate. The regime of the Third Republic was expected to achieve, above all, balance. The power of the people flowed into the legislature, and could overthrow the executive which was the ministry. But high above, representing the general welfare like a king, was the president, and if the legislators proved to be irresponsible he could send them home to be judged in new elections, by the people.

THE PROBLEMS OF THE THIRD REPUBLIC

The Third French Republic which had taken shape so haphazardly after the ordeal of 1870–1871 was to prove far more durable than the previous regimes. But it was not the same France after 1870, nor the same Europe. There was nothing inevitable about the French defeat in 1870, but it was the first time that France had been overcome by anything less than a coalition, and it called attention to the changing European scene. There were now a united Germany and a united Italy in the central zone of Europe, so long divided. Germany and Italy by 1914 would more than double their populations of the year 1800. Great Britain, in the same period, would almost quadruple its population. The population of France would rise only from twenty-seven million in 1800 to about thirty-nine million in 1914, when Germany's was approaching sixty million. There is an illuminating and, from the French point of view, agonizing statistic in the number of males of military age. In 1870, these numbered about four and one half million in both France and Germany. In 1914, they were still four and a half million in France and more than seven and a half million in Germany.

The Third French Republic in its first phase, up to World War I, had to achieve national revival in a new international setting. For one thing, the international setting was no longer purely European. France was drawn along from colonial enterprises already begun, such as Algeria, toward new enterprises in adjoining Tunisia and Morocco, and temptations in Egypt and still more distant Madagascar and Indochina. Less powerful, relatively, in Europe, the French were faced with decisions about whether to continue, or to draw back, on the road to world power. Still rich, and blessed during most of the period with sound finances and a stable currency, France could afford either course of action in the quest for national recovery and continued greatness. But the choice between European power and imperial greatness became a crisis of conscience because of the recent defeat. To some, every expenditure of energy overseas seemed a betrayal of Alsace and Lorraine, the more so since Bismarck encouraged France to take that direction and to forget about the possibility of a return engagement with the Reich. And there were other distractions in the rebuilding of greatness.

In the years immediately after 1870 a religious question entered the picture. To the most extreme of French Catholics, the Pope's loss of Rome was as tragic as France's defeat by Germany, and they would have liked the Third Republic (or the monarchy, for which they continued to hope) to intervene in Italy in favor of the prisoner in the Vatican. Toward 1914 another disturbing new element in the French international position was the socialist and syndicalist hostility to the idea of war to defend a society of which they disapproved. How seriously to take this point of view, it was hard to decide. But hitherto the French left had been since the Great Revolution the most violently patriotic influence in politics, and now this foundation showed cracks. Among those who agitated for colonies, those who advocated a crusade to free the Pope, and those who opposed the state's existence, it was difficult for French statesmen to steer a policy toward resurrection and grandeur.

The year 1870 saw the pronouncement of Papal infallibility, which was one event in the drama of the Catholic Church's increasing sternness about certain aspects of the modern world. In general, as science and materialism won away the less firm of the Church's adherents, those who remained were the more strict in their faith. They were also more inclined to look to Rome than formerly, and ultra-montanism brought suspicion and trouble upon Catholics in all countries. In France the matter was vital. There the tradition of Catholic opposition to doctrines of liberalism and self-government seemed capable of indefinite renewal. Although it was not the case with all Catholics, there was a conspicuous connection between certain prominent and devout royalist families and a reactionary opposition to the republic. There were, as always, brilliant literary talents in the Catholic and conservative camp. Some combined fervent, exclusive nationalism with Catholicism and social conservatism: the brilliant writer Maurice Barrès preached the cult of ancestors, blood, soil, and nationalism; Charles Maurras, an unbeliever, nonetheless urged Catholicism as part of the French national tradition, and founded a royalist movement called *Action Française*. Barrès and Maurras were technically conservatives, for they sought to restore the society and state of the old regime. But in their linking of this purpose with intense nationalism they were innovators, and in some of their social programs and their advocacy of violence, they were fire-eating radicals. Nowhere more clearly than in their writings is there proof of the blurring and breakdown of the old categories of right and left. They were, in a certain sense, the precursors of the "revolutionary reaction" which in the twentieth century took the name of fascism.

In France there was a sincere and bitter conflict of faiths between Catholics and the very prevalent attitude known as anti-clericalism. Anti-clericalism was, superficially, hostility to the interference of the Church in politics. It took the form above all, of an effort to maintain the state's monopoly on education and to drive Catholic orders out of the teaching profession and religious teaching out of the schools. Catholics naturally opposed these campaigns, as they still do, on the grounds that the "godless school" would bring up a new generation of materialists without morals, and that a country was lacking in liberty if Catholics were not free to provide as they saw fit for the instruction of their children in schools of their own. Their opponents even maintained the right of the state to control, through licensing, teachers in private (which in France usually meant Catholic) schools. Deep within the anti-clerical point of view lay the conviction that freedom of opinion, reason, science, and progress required that education be free of clerical influence. In the last analysis the struggle, which reached its height in the 1880's and again in the decade after 1900, was a fight for the new generation, for the France of the future. It abated somewhat in the 1890's with the *ralliement*—the "rallying"—of important segments of Catholic opinion to the republic, after Pope Leo XIII announced in 1892 that there was nothing incompatible between Christianity and a republic. But some Catholics insisted that the Republic must be destroyed.

Particular waves of anti-clericalism in the decades after 1870 were associated with particular crises of politics and principles such as the Boulanger and Dreyfus affairs (see below). After the latter the Church and State were finally separated in France, in 1905, destroying the relationship established in 1801 by Napoleon's Concordat with the Papacy. Separation weakened the clergy financially by removing state support, but it deprived the state of all claims to regulate religious organizations, which were now free and private, and gained in stature in their new status. Anti-clericalism and quarrels over the "school question" did not, however, come to an end.

Another set of problems which the Republic faced arose from economic change. After 1870 the industrialization which had taken such strides during the Second Empire continued in less spectacular fashion, but by 1914 it had brought about even greater results.

It was true that France retained its traditional balance between agriculture and industry. Industrial growth took place in a society which seemed otherwise almost static. There was no such burst of urbanism and factory-building as in Britain and Germany. The small retail shops, the many small factories, remained, like the innumerable small farms, visible and characteristic. With them there remained that *petit bourgeois* ideal of stability, and that continuity of family enterprises passing from generation to generation, which was such an important part of French life. This ideal, comfortable and unimaginative, affected the population, which became almost stable. It affected politics, along with the inertia of a powerful peasantry which had got what it wanted in the Great Revolution, and like the large lower middle class, held fast to the old revolutionary principles but was suspicious of urban labor and socialism. It affected the labor movement, which was scattered in many small shops and many independent minded and financially poor unions, quick to strike but hard to mobilize on a large scale. Labor remained distrustful of politics and politicians, proud of its own skills and traditions, realistic in private affairs and sentimentally devoted to the great ideal of equality which had come down through the century. *Ouvriérisme* (roughly translatable as "workerism") became the name for its aloofness and self-sufficiency. Nowhere in Europe was there a finer, more human quality in the working class, but French labor was still like a nation within the nation, not yet fully reconciled to the community.

But despite the persistence of smallness and diversity, despite the loss of rich Alsace and Lorraine, the armature of heavy industry which was to see France through World War I was being built. New processes of refining iron ore were put to work. A chemical industry was developing. In 1913 France produced 45,000 motor cars. French engineering completed the great railway network, built the Eiffel Tower (almost as tall as the Empire State Building of a much later period) for the centennial exposition of 1889, and opened to the public in 1900 the first line of the Paris subway system. France entered the twentieth century as one of the four great industrial powers of the world.

The complexities which faced the Third Republic, then, were huge. But the nation had been raised from the ruins of the "terrible year." By 1900 France's diplomatic isolation was ended. Such were the vagaries of international politics that in July, 1891, the conservative Emperor Alexander III received a French naval squadron and arose to his feet at the playing of the *Marseillaise,* which had become the French national anthem but was illegal in Russia. In 1894, the Russian empire and the French Republic became allies. Overseas, France was still a rival of Britain as the century turned. The two were still, acre for acre, the leading colonial powers. But they were shortly to come together, like France and Russia, in awareness of the might of Germany and uncertainty about its aspirations.

France was accustomed to the role of great power. It was powerful and rich, able to lend millions to the Russian ally besides maintaining a large army and a navy and supporting a colonial administration. Nevertheless, its position after 1870 was not the same as in earlier times, and in the new Europe and the new world France needed internal harmony if it was to meet the challenges of the twentieth century.

THE DEFENSE OF THE REPUBLIC

French politics between 1875 and 1914 settled certain great questions, and established habits which were to have an immense staying power in the twentieth century. The most urgent task was, or appeared to be, preservation of the Republic. All of the country's major problems—foreign policy, the Church, colonies, industry, and labor—swirled in the political arena around the greatest problem of all, the century-old drama of self-government. The first five years, from 1875 to 1880, saw republicans gradually winning the most conspicuous offices of the state—the legislature, the ministry, and finally the presidency. In the less conspicuous but extremely important offices of the foreign and colonial administrations, in the officer corps of the army, and in the hierarchy of the Church, the triumph of the republicans was not so easily achieved. These positions were not elective but were manned by highly trained and carefully selected persons who, in the nature of things, tended to come from the upper ranks of society—from the great bourgeois and noble families with a tradition of service to the state, whose sons attended the great training schools—the Ecole Polytechnique, the Ecole Normale or the military academy of Saint-Cyr—or who entered the Church. In the political crises of the 1880's and 1890's the loyalties of these people were at issue. So too were mass emotions of the ordinary people. Both deepened and sometimes caused a series of "affairs" which seemed to endanger the regime.

In the 1870's the most famous and important political event after the establishment of the republic was the Affair of the Sixteenth of May. The year was 1877. The man was President MacMahon, the honorable royalist soldier who had been holding the fort since 1873. The occasion was the President's dismissal of a ministry which the republican majority in the Chamber of Deputies supported. "We can no longer march together," he told the departing prime minister, Jules Simon, and then, to settle the question, President MacMahon availed himself of his constitutional right to dismiss the Chamber of Deputies with the consent of the Senate. Back of these political maneuvers lay the differences between socially conservative and Catholic opinion and the anti-clerical views of the republican majority in the Chamber, which included the Radicals led by Gambetta. Gambetta had said, "Clericalism, that is the enemy," and it became a famous phrase. But it was the constitutional issue which was longest remembered and had the most lasting results in French political life.

The significance of the *seize mai* affair was that it altered the balance of powers in the constitution. President MacMahon's apparent wish to ignore the principle of ministerial responsibility was defeated, for in the great electoral campaign which followed his dismissal of the Chamber the republican forces triumphed, securing a popular mandate for the Republic and for the Chamber's control of the ministry. But there was another principle involved: the right of the president of the Republic to dissolve the Chamber. Because a royalist had made use of this right in an apparent effort to strike a blow against the constitution, the right henceforth fell into disuse. Later presidents did not wish to seem like MacMahon, and when this self-denial became a constitutional tradition, the powers of the presidency were reduced and its leadership was compromised. Therefore, since the president could not send the deputies home before the end of their four-year terms, they were free to be as partisan and obstructive as they wished, to make and remake parliamentary groupings according to their tastes, and to overthrow ministries without assuming the responsibility for replacing them with others having alternative programs.

This condition was aggravated by the multiplication of parties and by the lack of discipline of party leaders over the deputies. The outcome of the Affair of the Sixteenth of May was that the ministry escaped from the president but lost its leadership in the Chamber (for the ministry did not inherit the president's power of dissolution). And so the French political system lost the balance intended by the men of 1875 and moved toward a legislative supremacy reminiscent of the Great Revolution.

For the moment what was most noticed was the defeat of the royalist Mac-Mahon and the strengthening of the Republic. In the elections of 1878 the republicans gained control of the Senate, and in 1879 President MacMahon resigned rather than agree to the removal of several army generals thought to be hostile to the republic. His successor, Jules Grévy, was elderly, cautious, and republican. As the 1880's began, the revolutionary tradition was honored as the *Marseillaise* became the national anthem and the Fourteenth of July became a national holiday. Labor and socialism, after a decade of repression following the Commune, began to revive.

Beginning in the middle of the 1880's, however, there blew up another storm to threaten the republic from the right. Anti-clerical legislation, disagreements over colonial ventures, patriotic desire for a strong line against Germany, scandals about leading politicians, and above all the seeming pettiness and lack of inspiration of the middle-of-the-road regime, were all building up irritations which might be used to upset the unwary republic if the right kind of demagogue came along. General Boulanger was a demagogue, and he had his moment, in 1889, as the year opened. But he proved not to be the right kind of demagogue, and this was fortunate, for the moment of intoxication which Boulangism represented was serious.

General Georges Boulanger (1837–1891) was a Minister of War with a talent for public relations. His army reforms were of value, but because of Franco-German tension and in the absence of any other inspiration his soldierly figure attracted far more adulation than the man himself deserved or, in the last analysis, wanted. He became a dreamlike image larger than life to the multitudes who did not know him personally, and around this image gathered all kinds of dissatisfied groups having nothing more in common than distaste for the staid bourgeois regime. Bonapartists and royalists rubbed elbows with simple patriots, nationalist authoritarians, and even some Radicals and socialists. An extraordinary hero-worship evolved. Transfer of General Boulanger to a provincial command (where it was hoped he would sink into oblivion), caused women to throw themselves on the tracks in front of his train. In 1889 he was overwhelmingly elected a deputy for Paris on a dangerously vague platform of revision of the constitution —which for many of the Boulangists meant an attack on parliamentary institutions. But General Boulanger lacked the nerve or the ambition to attempt a *coup d'état* like Louis Napoleon's, and he let the moment of exhilaration pass. Later, fearing legal action as the government of aroused republicans took measures for the safety of the state, General Boulanger timidly took a train for Brussels. Suddenly France laughed, and the air was cleared. At the centennial exposition of 1889 the republic seemed healthy and safe. It had passed that fatal age of eighteen beyond which no regime since 1789 had been able to endure.

In the early 1890's the moderate republicans played down the issue of anti-clericalism, and many Catholics "rallied" to the regime. The royalists were discredited by the Boulanger affair, and the Radicals, also somewhat chastened by the attraction which the general had had for some of their number, moderated their demands for revision of the constitution. Henceforth the Radicals became what they were to remain for many decades: a democratic party in the tradition of Jacobinism, with a tendency to be anti-clerical and to work for social reforms, but with no desire to overthrow the constitutional settlement of 1875 or the social system. Radicalism henceforth had its greatest strength in the provinces and among the lower middle class. In the 1890's it was no longer the French left, for there now began to form a socialist party led by the Marxian intellectuals Jules Guesde and Jean Jaurès. In the elections of 1893 some fifty socialists were sent to the Chamber of Deputies, along with 140 Radicals and over 300 moderate republicans. There were only a few dozen royalists.

In the 1890's, with greater internal stability and its international position improved by the Russian alliance, France enjoyed several years of deceptive tranquility. Forecasting the problems of a later period, the question of doing something for the working class thrust itself forward, but the moderate republicans with the support of "rallied" Catholics of moderate views were able to maintain control of the situation, pass a high tariff, and defeat a proposal to establish an income tax. France was still run by substantial bourgeois. But near the end of the century a terrible shock threw French politics to the left.

This was the Dreyfus case. It had begun almost unnoticed in 1894, and had been prefaced in the previous year by a resounding scandal. This revolved about a long-standing conspiracy of silence on the part of certain newspapers and certain deputies concerning the fiscal difficulties of the Panama Canal Company. Eminent journalists and politicians, including a few Jews, were found to be financially involved. The explosion failed to rock the republic, but it compromised a good many politicians who had either participated or been brushed too closely by the guilty parties. Among the damaged was the Radical, Georges Clemenceau, whose career was temporarily becalmed. The rightist and anti-Semitic press, both of them small and strident, were in ecstasies. Little need be said of the frustrations of the decayed aristocrats and mean-spirited lower middle class sensation-mongers whose morale was lifted by anti-Semitism, except that they were to be in full voice when they were able to transfer their attention to the Dreyfus case.

Captain Alfred Dreyfus, an officer on the General Staff, who was a Jew, was compromised by some papers found in the wastepaper basket of the German military attaché. Dreyfus was convicted of selling military secrets to the Germans and was imprisoned on Devil's Island. The papers had in fact been written by a certain Major Esterhazy, but after several years, when the accusation of the Dreyfus family and certain independent investigations within the army began to point in Esterhazy's direction, the officers involved in Dreyfus's conviction tried to cover their blunder by falsifying evidence. A panicky colonel feared the impending scandal so much that he forged documents confirming Dreyfus's guilt. Esterhazy was court-martialed and found innocent. The novelist Emile Zola, who publicly denounced this procedure, was prosecuted and condemned, but his trial brought out many of the essential facts.

There developed two schools of thought, Dreyfusard and anti-Dreyfusard, and the case became so celebrated that families and lifetime friendships were split by it. The right and the anti-Semites, and many nationalist organizations and ordinary patriots, felt that a principle was at stake: the integrity of the army, and back of the army, everything traditional and sacred upon which social order and the safety of the national community depended. To the other side rallied other millions for whom the principles of the Enlightenment and of reason and science and justice for the individual based on the facts of the case amounted to a secular faith, so deep was their emotional commitment. On one side was the abstraction "France"; on the other, the abstraction "Justice." Although historians have since doubted that the Republic was in danger, many of the moderate republicans rallied together with the Radicals and the Socialists in 1899, when the affair reached its height, to form a republican bloc. As in the affairs of May 16, 1877, and of Boulanger, in 1889, they took the attitude that they were saving the Republic.

In the end the Dreyfus affair came to a slow, inglorious conclusion. So deeply involved was everyone connected with the case that the man himself was almost lost sight of. At the insistence of France's highest court of appeals, Dreyfus was given another court-martial. In September, 1899, the bizarre conclusion was reached that he was guilty with extenuating circumstances. He was condemned to ten years imprisonment, but was pardoned by the president of the Republic. When tempers had partly subsided, Dreyfus, in 1906, was declared innocent by

By the Seashore by Pierre Auguste Renoir (1841–1919). An excellent example of French impressionism. (Courtesy of the Metropolitan Museum of Art)

the court of appeals. He was then decorated, and promoted to the rank of major.

The Dreyfus case shook France to its moral marrow and provoked a crisis of creeds which had its roots in 1789 and earlier. It widened the abyss between the Revolution, with its secular values and egalitarianism, and the counter-Revolution, with its traditionalist, hierarchical, and clerical emphasis. The Dreyfus case had striking political effects. It revived anti-clericalism, split the moderate republicans, and brought triumphantly to power the Radicals supported by some moderates and Socialists. This coalition of the center and left remained in office, although with many changes of ministers, until World War I. Emboldened by the crisis, it purged the army of some of the anti-republican elements which had dominated it. Anti-clerical legislation leading to the separation of Church and state in 1905 was passed. The last great strongholds of the royalists were thereby attacked.

The advent of the Radicals, representative of what Gambetta once called "new social strata," was hastened by the Dreyfus case, but should not be attributed to it alone. As the most purely republican of parties, they had moved toward power with the widening acceptance of a republic. In the years before the war the Radicals assumed the posture which they were to hold through the rest of the life of the Third Republic. The Radicals were being challenged now by a new sort of left, the Marxian Socialists led by Jaurès and Guesde. In times of crisis for the Republic they behaved as if they believed in the old cry "no enemies on the left," and during the Dreyfus case had cooperated closely with Jaurès. But in fact the Radicals (together with their progressive wing, which was misleadingly called "Socialist Radical") were always to be inclined in peaceful times to follow a moderate course, lest they lose their following to the more moderate republicans. This was to be their role, one of balance between the Socialists and the moderates, until the end of the Third Republic.

ON THE EVE OF A NEW WAR,
AND A NEW PEACE

For all its stresses and anomalies, France in the decade before World War I was the finest product of the Europe that was approaching its nemesis. The country was, on the whole, prosperous. Although in those days of stable currency wages remained low, the general standard of living was slowly rising. French workingmen remained aloof but were not irretrievably alienated from the society dominated by businessmen and farmers. Workers were loosely organized in the General Confederation of Labor, and had hopes for the future. The Republic was safe. The nation was internationally renowned for its art and its intellectual life as well as for its fine craftsmanship and its luxury goods—silks, perfumes, gloves, dresses, wines. Second to none were its scientists—Pasteur in biology, the Curies in physics; its novelists and philosophers—Proust, Bergson; its musicians—Ravel, Debussy; and its painters—Renoir, Monet, Pissaro, Cézanne, Matisse.

Paris was the queen and capital of civilization. Visitors came from the world over to admire the city, to study in its universities, to taste the best in culture and in gaiety which the earth could offer. Paris became, like Venice in an earlier century, "the revel of the world." They were not the hurried tourist hordes of a later era; they had time in that twilight of the old world to appreciate the French atmosphere of freedom and love of beauty and excellence. Some discoverers of France like the American, Henry Adams, might see the challenges which the twentieth century would make, through technology and social conflicts, to the mature French culture. But for most people these discoveries were hidden beyond the year 1914.

World War I fell more heavily on France than on any other power. After the first weeks, a three-hundred-mile front was established across northern France from Switzerland to the Channel. A three-hundred-mile hemorrhage—the expression is rude but exact. One million and a quarter Frenchmen fell. After four years, the Third Republic still stood, while the German, the Austrian, and the Russian empires were destroyed. But the war was unexpectedly "total." Victory now was almost as costly as defeat. War mobilized whole populations and posed more problems in the rear than at the front—production, inflation, family allotments, draft exemptions. It was a revolution in disguise, whose effects persisted for decades afterward. Tensions were more serious, the society deformed. And while the French in 1918 won a great victory, they knew that they had not done it alone—without the French empire, the British, the Russians, and the Americans, they could not have held out. The victory hid a new and terrible disparity between France's power and its responsibilities. After 1918 the diminished French resources and the free political institutions survived under an appalling strain.

38

THE GERMAN EMPIRE

THE UNIFICATION OF GERMANY created, in the center of Europe, a new and powerful state whose presence entirely altered the European scheme of things. The very existence of a united Germany, in place of the former welter of conflicting small powers, required a revolution in Europeans' thinking. Frenchmen had to adjust to the end of a supremacy which had lasted since 1648; Englishmen had to adjust to an entirely new arrangement of the balance of power; Austrians had to adjust to the fact that, after seven hundred years, their dynasty was excluded from German affairs and ruled a largely Slavic and Magyar dominion; and Germans had to adjust to the fact that their new position imposed upon them a special responsibility for the peace and welfare of Europe. These adjustments were made painfully; some of them were never made at all.

In domestic affairs, the contrasts between divided and imperial Germany were as remarkable as on the international scene. The German Confederation founded in 1815 had been a sort of museum for European political history. Inheriting the diversity of the Holy Roman Empire, its displays included Hanseatic free cities, absolutist principalities, liberal kingdoms, governments in every conceivable state of repair and constitutional development. After 1871 these museum pieces were roofed over by a single government which constituted, in effect, a national state substantially similar, in its emotional underpinnings, to France or Britain.

In the course of a generation the German people showed a capacity for economic and administrative development unequalled even by the British and unsurpassed even by the Americans. By 1914, Germany was an entirely different place from what it had been in 1870. It had almost 50 percent more people (France's population increased only about 15 percent); what had been a predominantly agricultural population, regarded by foreigners as dreamy, poetical, and incurably romantic, became Europe's leading producers of steel and chemicals. As striking as the transformation of the German economy was the demonstration of an unparalleled talent for organization and administration. Of the major countries in the world in 1914, Germany was the best-run. Its civil service and its army and its educational system were the envy and the despair of every other people. It was an industrial country relatively untouched by the blights of urban slums and poverty. In 1913, a former German chancellor was able to write, with perfect accuracy, "Germany is like one great garden." It had managed many of its problems with superb skill.

It had managed them, however, under a system of government and in a spirit which was markedly and, to many people, ominously different from the more slipshod democracies of Europe or North America. The regime under which Germany prospered, expanded, and solved its problems was not the product of a long struggle by individuals for freedom, as was the parliamentary monarchy of Britain or the French Republic. It was planned and directed from above, by persons in authority, working in the service of their sovereign, and with the assistance of a great army and a strong militaristic tradition. There were many fighters for freedom in Germany, but they had won no victories; such freedoms as Germans enjoyed were the handouts of a discreet government.

Its dramatic success as a nation-state would have been difficult to prophesy in 1871. The Germany which came into existence in that year was the third largest state (after Russia and Austria) in Europe, to be sure, but it did not seem a very united one. It contained an extraordinary variety of landscape, traditions, and people. From the Dutch border on the North Sea to the Russian border on the Baltic, it extended some seven hundred and fifty miles. From the Danish border in the north to the Austrian in the south, some five hundred. The northern half or more was part of the great northern plain of Europe, flat and marshy at the coast-line, rising gradually to rolling country inland, fertile and well-wooded on its southern and western edges, sandy and unwelcoming on the north and east. In the south, and along the western borders, there were mountains and hilly, forested country, most of it rich for farming.

Moreover, Germany was varied and divided by history as by geography. Dialects differed—a peasant from Bavaria in the south was incomprehensible to a peasant from East Prussia. But more serious than language barriers—a standard German was the language of educated people everywhere—were divisions arising from three sources: the extremely various forms of government under which different Germans had lived; the great religious gulf between the Roman Catholics—a third of the total population—and the Lutherans; and the cultural affiliations which had caused East Prussians, from the earliest times, to regard themselves as a frontier-guard against the Slavic hordes, the Bavarians to think of themselves almost as a part of the Latin world; and the Rhinelanders to associate themselves with the France which their greatest recent poet, Heine, had so vastly admired.

Nor was it merely the variety of the German people which might have suggested disunities within the new empire. There were, within its boundaries, very considerable numbers of non-Germans, who resented their forced allegiance to the new state. Something over a million Alsatians and Lorrainers, who ranged from purely French to purely Teutonic in their language, regarded their annexation with a very doubtful eye. Something under a hundred thousand Danes in Schleswig preferred the homeland from which they had been severed in 1864. In the east, the kingdom of Prussia retained, as a monument to the century-old partitions of Poland, a population of several million Poles, who were detached from their German fellow subjects by language, race, religion, and intense national sentiment. The birth-rate of these Poles was so much greater than that of their German neighbors that it threatened the submergence of eastern Prussia in a Slavic sea.

The empire retained, moreover, the dynasties and governments which had existed before its creation. There were, in 1918 as there had been in 1869, kings of Bavaria, Württemberg, Saxony and Prussia, free cities of Hamburg and Lübeck and Bremen, grand dukes of Baden, Oldenburg and many others, and an assortment of dukes and princes to the number of twenty-six. Each of them continued to preside over his own government or court. They were, as they had been before, of highly various quality, ranging from the merchant oligarchy of Hamburg through the impeccably constitutional government of Württemberg to the medieval diet of Mecklenburg and the almost absolute despotism of a tiny principality known by the name of its dynasty as Reuss, Elder Line.

It might have been supposed, then, that the empire would suffer from these divisive forces as well as from economic backwardness. The reverse was the case; except for the Poles (and to a lesser extent the Alsatians) there was never any serious attempt on the part of anybody to get out of the empire once they were in. Local differences and traditions were obscured by a rising enthusiasm for national unity. Only the conflict between religions ever showed signs of becoming serious, and within a decade it had been appeased, or ceased to threaten disruption of national unity. And in the network of rivers, canals, coal mines and iron-ore deposits on the western border there rapidly developed an industrial system which made Germany a most modern and powerful industrial nation. By 1914, the 12,000 miles of railroad of 1870 were extended to more than 38,000 miles. The negligible steel production grew to 13,000,000 metric tons in 1910.

THE IMPERIAL CONSTITUTION

The constitution of the Empire, under which this remarkable unity in diversity was achieved, was ingenious and in some respects unique, although in its major outlines it showed a strong similarity on paper to the two experiments in federal union which had preceded it: the United States and Switzerland. It had been invented by Bismarck in 1867 as the constitution of the North German Confederation and later extended and amended to include the middle-sized southern German states who joined the Confederation in 1871. Then its name was changed to German Empire, and the king of Prussia exchanged the title of President of the Confederation for that of German Emperor.

The powers of the federal government were in theory very limited, more

IMPERIAL ARMS OF GERMANY. The arms of the German empire from 1871 to 1918 consisted of an eagle, symbol of empire, bearing on its breast a shield showing another eagle, which was the badge of Prussia, and on *its* breast a shield quartered in silver and black, the arms of the Prussian house of Hohenzollern which assumed the dignity of German emperor in 1871. The crown is that of Charlemagne and his successors.

limited than in the United States. It controlled the army (although Bavaria insisted on maintaining its own army as well), foreign affairs, the new currency and postal system. It could legislate within very narrow limits on fiscal, banking, and commercial affairs. But it was rigorously excluded from the "domestic" affairs of the member states, and it was not empowered to raise direct taxes—such as income, sales, or inheritance taxes. Its revenues came in part from customs duties and other standing imposts, but mostly depended upon voluntary grants from the state governments. The power of the central administration expanded rapidly, however, especially in financial and economic affairs. It brought almost all the German railroads (94 percent in 1910) under its direct ownership and control. Banking also grew more centralized and while remaining in theory private, came to be more and more directed from Berlin. The social security system and the varied industrial legislation were functions of the empire. In the rapidly expanding fields of trade and shipping, as well as in commercial and monetary policy, the national administration extended its responsibility.

By the time the empire was abolished, in 1918, the federal government had grown to a position of dominance and the state governments, despite their theoretical sovereignty, had become vestigial. Germany was moving rapidly toward a higher centralized and expansive government, as if propelled by an irresistible force. This movement, and the curious manner in which it flourished, uninterrupted by the revolution of 1918, was in some respects the most significant development of twentieth century Europe. It was destined to end in the final, pugnacious surge of centralization under Adolf Hitler. It involved the fighting of two wars by the rest of the world to control it, and indirectly led to the destruction of the German state.

The increasing power of the central government was manifested in its increasing inclination and ability to apply its weight in world affairs; it was in part the result of technological change as well as of the patriotism, pride, and skill of the German people. But the nature of German organization, and the circumstances of the Empire's birth, caused the affluence of power to be disposed in peculiar and alarming ways. The most important element in this situation was the extraordinary position of the kingdom of Prussia in the empire and the federal government.

Prussia contained about two thirds of the area and population of Germany, including the major industrial areas (when they developed) and incidentally the troublesome minorities.[1] Its king was *also* German emperor, and its prime minister was also usually (though this was a matter of convenience and not strictly of law) the Imperial Chancellor—that is, executive head of the federal government. In the upper house of the imperial parliament, the Council of Princes (*Bundesrat*, or Federal Council), which had veto powers over legislation, the Prussian government appointed seventeen of the fifty-eight members and controlled enough others (appointed by minor north German states under Prussian influence) to manage a majority.

[1] The French minority of Alsace-Lorraine was not in Prussia, but the provinces were administered by the federal government which was controlled by Prussia in this concern.

Prussian influence was thus very strong in the federal government, and Prussia was itself a strangely managed state. Its constitution, dating from the reaction after the revolution of 1848, confided an overwhelming influence to persons of wealth and particularly to the large landowners of eastern Prussia.

These landowners, including the country squires known as *Junkers,* were rather odd people. They were often isolated from the major currents of their day, accustomed to thinking of themselves as divinely appointed to defend Europe against the Slavs. They were often sternly Lutheran and intensely parochial. They sought mainly to be left alone and to be assured of high prices for agricultural products. They were heavily overrepresented in the Prussian parliament, administration and army. Through their reliability and loyalty, and through ancient tradition, they were influential at the Prussian court. So they were, from time to time at least, able to force their views and policies upon the Prussian ministry, and through it, the government of the German empire. This situation remained unaltered during the transformation of Germany from a sleepy collection of principalities into a vast urban and industrial power, the greatest military and diplomatic force in Europe. By 1914, the world was treated to the prospect of a splendid modern empire of sixty-five million people whose traditions had been shaped, and whose policies could still sometimes be influenced, by a few hundred thousand hayseed gentleman-farmers in eastern Prussia.

Nor was this the only oddity in imperial Germany; it contributed to and compounded many others. The empire also possessed a lower house of parliament which was elected on the basis of universal manhood suffrage—designed by Bismarck in 1867 as an expedient to purchase popular support for unity. This House of Commons, or *Reichstag,* bore superficially a close resemblance to its analogues in Britain or France. It was organized into parties, it was elected to the accompaniment of lively political campaigns, and it exercised generous powers, notably over the budget. The federal executive, headed by the chancellor, was not officially "responsible" to it—not required to resign, as in France or England, when it voted against his measures. On the other hand, a consistently hostile majority in the *Reichstag* might hold up funds and legislation needed by the chancellor, to the point where Germany would become ungovernable. On occasions, there were serious difficulties in getting the budget approved. It was therefore necessary for the chancellor to assure himself of the support of a majority of its members.

It will be seen, then, that the German federal government and the chancellor who ran it were in a precarious and sometimes nerve-wracking position. They were, first, primarily amenable to the emperor, who appointed the chancellor and could dismiss him at will. But it was, second, necessary to cooperate with and win the support of the *Junkers* and landowners who were influential in the Prussian government, with its decisive influence, and *also,* third, with the majority of the democratically elected *Reichstag.* Since these three quite often had opposing views and interests, the position of the chancellor was at times almost impossible. The German constitutional system was one of checks and balances intended in theory to balance interests—democracy, monarchy, aristocracy. But the checks threatened to lead to checkmate.

This entirely unsatisfactory situation came about because Bismarck, the first imperial chancellor, in order to secure acquiescence for a unified Germany, had to make extensive and incompatible concessions to the forces of Prussian oligarchy, to German liberal opinion, and to the king of Prussia. The resultant stresses, combined with the other conflicts which inhered in the highly various empire, might have proved fatal much earlier than they did had it not been for the extremely efficient corps of civil servants who did the real work of government, and for the skill of Bismarck himself.

BISMARCK'S MANAGEMENT OF POLITICS

Otto von Bismarck (1815–1898) does not fall into any of the standard political classifications of the nineteenth century. He was not merely a conservative, for a mark of conservatives was that they cherished the old regime and upheld Metternich's revised version of it after 1815. Bismarck destroyed the Germany of 1815 with his humiliation and eviction of Austria, his nationalistic creation of a German empire, and his project of a democratic franchise for electing its legislature. Nor was he a liberal. He loathed the notion of a responsible government and disdained the trafficking of politicians in the legislature. He was devoted to the monarchy and to the army and its interests—so flouting the fondest shibboleth of liberalism. Nor was he a socialist. He liked and trusted aristocrats and kings, and he abhorred the atheist, the materialist, the egalitarian and revolutionary qualities of socialism. At intervals, he cooperated with all three and appropriated parts of their programs. He had many of the qualities of a *Junker,* and he shared some of the predilections of the conservative Prussian landowners. He was a friend of the founder of German socialism, Ferdinand Lassalle, and agreed with him on many points. To meet the wishes of the liberals, he undertook a campaign against the Roman Catholic Church. He belonged to none of the usual groupings.

Nor will it suffice (though it may enlighten) to call him a realist. He belonged, it is true, to that generation of statesmen who are called realistic; men like Napoleon III, and Cavour, who were breaking down the mold in which Metternich's Europe was cast. With them he practiced *Realpolitik*—policy formed by considering the possible instead of the ideal, and buttressed by toughness and cynicism and self-interest. But Bismarck, like the others, had his dreams and his illusions. He was supremely ambitious for himself. He was also sentimentally attached to his king and to the traditions of the Prussian court. He was a believer in nationalism. His principal achievement and perhaps his principal purpose, like the other realists, was to safeguard the structure of the old society with its aristocrats and capitalists while engineering the political and economic changes necessary to make it palatable to others. He was the product of an age when anomalies and stresses, portending change, permitted the fulfillment of great personalities.

He was the towering monument to an era when individual statesmen might arrange and dominate the course of history.

So long as Bismarck remained in power the anomalies of the German constitution were largely concealed. He was already a national hero, almost above reproach or criticism, when he assumed the highest office in unified Germany. Moreover, he had a clear understanding of the constitution (having invented it) and rapidly perfected a technique for overcoming its awkwardness. Basically, his policy was three-fold: to manipulate the king-emperor by alternate placation and threats to resign; to secure the support of the Prussian ruling class by bribery alternating with threats of socialism and democracy if he were removed; and to maneuver majorities in the *Reichstag* by playing with party politics and with public opinion.

In the first decade of the empire, the National Liberal party controlled the largest number of seats in the *Reichstag*. The National Liberals, the rather mellowed heirs of the Prussian revolution of 1848, preached balanced budgets, cheap government, civil liberties, the defense of private property, constitutional government, and the self-determination for the German nation—this last point in their program, which had led them to back Bismarck's successful efforts to unify Germany, had originally brought about the alliance between the chancellor and the party. But the Liberals opposed, strongly and consistently, various policies and institutions which Bismarck personally liked or whose political potency he respected. They distrusted monarchies and particularly land-owning aristocracies. They disliked the Church of Rome. They disliked the expensive army, so influential at the Prussian court and so instrumental in the success of Bismarck's policies.

Despite these differences, Bismarck had little choice but to cooperate with the party, and for nine years he did so. In order to make this policy work, he had to bludgeon and tyrannize the Prussian government, and he earned the antagonism of the land-owners, who were organizing themselves into the Conservative party. He had also to handle the aged, mulish emperor, William I, and he had to initiate policies, many of which he cared nothing for, and others which he actually disliked—virtual free trade; a systematic campaign of restricting the freedom and harassing the clergy of the Roman Church (known as the *Kulturkampf*) which irritated the third of the nation which was Catholic; toleration for the nascent radical and socialist parties which the Liberals, in the name of political freedom, sought to protect. It was a most unsatisfactory basis on which to run a country, but Bismarck did succeed in sustaining the authority of the executive and most important of all, in sustaining the independence (and revenues) of the imperial army. The Liberals succeeded in imposing some of their policies upon Germany, but they never came near to storming the essential strongholds of government—the army, the independent executive, or the state government of Prussia.

By the end of the decade, Liberal influence was waning, and Bismarck determined to end his dependence on the Liberals by forming understandings with other parties, seeking to neutralize democracy and to secure a workable majority. To the Conservatives he offered a peace of forgive-and-forget enriched by the prospect of high duties on agricultural goods to maintain their incomes and their status in society. To Catholics he offered an end of the *Kulturkampf,* an agreement with the Papacy, and a share of government responsibility. To the rising manufacturing class (most of whom had hitherto supported the National Liberals) he offered tariffs on manufactured goods and laws against the socialists. Immediately after the elections in which the Liberals were defeated, in October, 1878, Bismarck caused the *Reichstag* to pass, over their protests, a measure designed to drive the Social Democratic party underground by banning its publications, meetings, and fund-raising activities. The law was strictly enforced, and German socialism remained for the next twelve years quiescent, at least on the surface.

This measure was supplemented with others, equally repugnant to many Liberals, which aimed at securing the loyalty and the contentment of the working class. Imaginative and, at the time, novel arrangements were approved by the *Reichstag* in the 1880's for insuring workers against loss of wages resulting from sickness, accidents, and old age.

By these steps, Bismarck hoped to build up in the nation and the parliament a majority of parties which would support him, replacing his old Liberal supporters. He was moderately successful. The Liberals were weakened and split, and he secured a workable majority. But the Catholics, organized into their own Center party, remained cautious and lukewarm. Once more, the army appropriations went through, and the laws suppressing the Social Democratic party were voted, but by narrow and uncertain majorities. On the other hand, the new, anti-liberal Bismarck now had the solid support of the Prussian ruling class and the monarchy.

It was not enough. Once more the *Reichstag* showed signs of recalcitrance and the chancellor adopted, in the middle 1880's, a tried-and-true formula for influencing voters to elect candidates congenial to him. He cried that the Fatherland was in danger (as a result of an international crisis and the threatening attitude of defeated and vengeful France). Parties who opposed his policies (and the army appropriations) were presented as menacing and even traitorous. The maneuver worked. Once more, temporarily, the divided forces behind the government were united.

Bismarck's downfall did not come from failure to secure the cooperation of the Prussian ruling group or of the democratic Reichstag. It was the third party to the government of the empire, the emperor, with whom he finally broke. In 1888, the aged William I died. His heir, Frederick III, succeeded to the throne already a dying man, and his reign lasted only three months. *His* son, still in his twenties, succeeded as William II. So great was Bismarck's prestige and his complacency that he never considered the possibility that the youthful emperor would dare to dismiss him, but he miscalculated seriously. William II was a complex and difficult character; sensitive, arrogant, and capricious, though withal intelligent and generally well-intentioned. He was seriously offended by the chancellor's disregard of what he regarded as the sovereign's prerogatives. Moreover, Bismarck was growing more conservative, more out-of-touch with public opinion, more inclined to disregard the interests and views of progressive politicians and of the

German people. William, on the other hand, fancied himself the "emperor of the common man."

Since the constitution was so vague on the delimitation of spheres of authority, an insoluble problem arose which ended in Bismarck's dismissal in 1890. The old gentleman retired to his country estate in the worst possible humor and spent his remaining years insulting the emperor and seeking to sabotage his successors. He thus contributed to the deepening muddle of imperial affairs.

The emperor was now more determined than ever to assert himself. The Prussian conservatives were as obstinate as ever. And some of the political parties were to become restive with the odd arrangements which deprived them of real power. It is now appropriate to examine the party structure in the reign of William II.

GERMAN POLITICAL PARTIES

German parties under the empire were already highly organized, even though their role in determining policy was limited. They were also very numerous and rather fluid. Parties tended to divide and reunite in different combinations. The contours of the larger parties, however, remained fairly stable, despite the loss or accretion of factions. By disregarding the "splinter groups" (factions which had split off from the major parties) and some of the small parties, and by overlooking the changes which took place in some of the larger ones over the years, it is possible to present a simplified picture of the German party structure.

The following were, in the years from about 1890 on, the principal political parties in Germany. The numbers in parenthesis indicate party strength in the *Reichstag* after the 1893 and 1912 elections.

The Conservatives (72; 43). The Conservatives were divided into several groups. They had originally represented the interests and ideals of Prussian landowners, and had stood for most of the characteristic planks of early nineteenth-century conservatism. As the empire grew older, their character altered. The *Junkers* were still among their supporters, but by 1914 they had been joined by many businessmen, particularly the Catholic businessmen of Silesia and the Rhineland, and by some extremist nationalist and anti-Semitic elements. For Conservatism increasingly took on the coloration of nationalism. That is, Conservatives appealed to voters on the grounds of national glory, a strong army and navy, and preservation of the national traditions (which included the *Junkers*). The Conservative parties had lost strength by 1914, but they were still influential, and they embodied a curious amalgam: vested interests of large landowners, highly colored patriotic appeals, dislike of foreigners and socialists, anti-Semitism, militarism, monarchism, private property, support of the Lutheran *and* Catholic churches; and a dislike of liberal ideas of economic freedom. They were enthusiastically in favor of protective tariffs, liked monopolies and price-fixing, and did not much object to social security legislation, providing it did not cost too much.

The Liberals (53; 45). The National Liberals gradually but consistently lost strength from 1878 on. Heirs of the Prussian liberal revolutionaries of 1848, they to some extent kept their character as a middle-class party, dedicated to representative government, anti-clericalism, civil rights, and economic freedom. But in 1867 they had accepted Bismarck, and in 1871 they accepted his imperial constitution. Later, some of them accepted protective tariffs and even cartels, and most of them accepted the monarchy, the independent executive, a strong army and navy, and in general, the existing order of society. The struggling middle-class capitalists who had supported the party in 1848 had turned, by the 1880's and 1890's, into successful princes of industry, and the National Liberals were increasingly inclined to favor whatever was good for big business. Much of their support always came from the great industrialists, but a large part of their leadership and voting power came from professional people, particularly civil servants. A remarkably high proportion of their *Reichstag* membership consisted of officials of municipal, provincial, or state governments.

The Progressives (48; 42). The Progressives were born of an earlier division among the Liberals. They inherited most of the more radical doctrines of liberalism from the parent party, and corresponded closely to the Radical Party in France and elsewhere. They were, in 1914, the most purely democratic party in Germany, standing for civil rights, a democratic franchise in Prussia (where the three-class system of elections still operated), a fully responsible ministry. They remained devoted, on the whole, to laissez-faire ideas—free trade and free competition—even after most businessmen had abandoned them in Germany, but they were not averse to moderate social security legislation. They were connected with an anti-socialist set of labor unions, and drew their voters (not very numerous) mainly from the middle class, working class, and intellectuals.

These were the older major parties. They were joined in the last decades of the nineteenth century by two new ones, which soon became the largest German parties—the Social Democrats and the Center Party. The success of these two mass parties was precisely analogous to their similar successes in Austria and, with variations, in Belgium and later in France and the Netherlands.

The Center (96; 91). The Center party was born in Germany as a Catholic response to Bismarck's anti-clerical legislation of the 1870's—the *Kulturkampf*. It reflected, also, a new generation of Roman Catholic thinkers about social questions. Of this new generation, Pope Leo XIII was the exemplar, with his important encyclicals on social questions, such as *De Rerum Novarum* (1891). In Germany, the theorist of Catholic social thought and inspiration of the Center was Bishop von Ketteler of Mainz. The Center was hard to fit in to the traditional left-to-right line-up of parties. It appealed to, and was staffed by, men of all classes—in harmony with Catholic social doctrine which abhorred class war and sought to reconcile the interests of all classes. It was generally opposed to laissez-faire ideas and advocated welfare legislation and state intervention to assure working class people respectable living conditions. It sponsored a Catholic trade union movement. On doctrinal grounds, it rejected the metaphysics of individualism but at the same time sought to protect individual rights (particularly religious freedom) against encroachments by the state.

The Center party was a party of Catholics, but it always denied that it was a "confessional" party and insisted that its interests were national and that they transcended sectarian lines. But it was and remained singularly vague on many points of national policy. It did not really have a "program," in the way that other parties did.

The Social Democrats (44; 110). Starting from almost nothing in 1870, the Social Democratic party had become, by 1914, the largest in the *Reichstag*. It was, on paper at least, an orthodox Marxist party, insisting that no good could come from collaboration with the "bourgeois state" and that the interests of workers and *bourgeoisie* were wholly incompatible. These extremist views, scenting of future violence, were incorporated in the party's Erfurt Program of 1891, and remained its official doctrine. Its constituency was mainly the industrial workers, although it secured widespread support in other quarters as well because it seemed to offer the best promise for the democratization of Germany by reform of the Prussian state electoral system, installation of a ministry responsible to the *Reichstag*, and curbing of the influence of the army and navy—all of which it enthusiastically sought. It had close connections with the largest trade union movement in Germany. It was very highly organized, with grass-roots reading clubs, hiking groups, boy scout movements and the like, and with a large bureaucracy of paid party workers.

Its official advocacy of revolution, and its hostility to cooperating with the existing state or social order, were partly a mere formality by 1914. Some of its leaders—most notably Eduard Bernstein—were "Revisionists," who challenged the theoretical accuracy of Marxism and thought that working class ends might best be achieved not by revolution but by squeezing gradual concessions from the state and the capitalists. Although it still usually opposed the chancellor, Social Democracy looked as if it might be turning into a party like other parties, seeking democratic reforms and rather mild economic legislation. But it remained, despite the trend to moderation, a nightmare to the court and government, and to most propertied people, up to World War I.

There were many other parties, to the total number of sixteen in the 1893 Reichstag. Most of them were small and represented minority or regional interests, such as the South German Peoples party, the Danish party, or the Guelph party, which objected to the Prussian annexation of Hanover in 1866. Their presence enabled the chancellor to fortify his majority by striking bargains and distributing favors.

POLITICS IN THE REIGN OF WILLIAM II

In the twenty-five years after the dismissal of Bismarck, the German political situation grew more and more involved and unsatisfactory. William II had lofty and romantic views of his own role in Germany, and the various chancellors whom he appointed found it more and more difficult to adjust themselves to the wishes of their pretentious master on one side, the increasingly clamorous demands of the *Reichstag* on a second side, and the intransigent conservatism of the Prussian landowners on a third.

At first, under Chancellor Count Leo von Caprivi an effort was made to base the government of Germany on a collaboration of monarchy with progressive popular opinion. The anti-socialist laws were repealed, liberal trade agreements were reached with foreign countries, and a policy of colonial expansion was actively pushed. Each of these policies was designed to placate an important group of public opinion, but each succeeded in arousing fears and opposition. The result of the ending of the anti-socialist laws was that the Social Democratic party, emerging from an underground existence, did handsomely in the next *Reichstag* elections and won forty-four seats. This was sufficient to alarm the emperor, the propertied classes and the army, and the government's flirtation with political liberalism came to an abrupt end. Moreover, Caprivi's trade agreements reduced duties on grain, and the Prussian landowners (already heavily mortgaged and threatened by the persistent agricultural depression which had settled on farmers everywhere) exerted their influence in Prussia to dispose of him. Their weight was enormous. Caprivi was dismissed and the trade agreements abandoned.

After 1894, when Caprivi retired, the chancellors sought to appease the landowners—with subsidies and high protective tariffs on farm products and with efforts to curb the growing influence and discontent of the Polish population in the east, which constituted the labor supply and market for many of the *Junkers*. They also sought to appease the army, the most solid support of the empire. But they had still to reckon with parliament, where in succeeding elections the Social Democrats generally increased their representation. Since the Social Democrats were always in the opposition, it became harder to find a parliamentary majority. The Catholic Center party was wooed—and won—for the government. Every effort was made to strengthen and cajole the Conservatives and the National Liberals. But German opinion showed itself increasingly eager for constitutional reform, and increasingly the government was forced to fall back on its own electoral program to achieve the defeat of the "anti-national" parties. Like Bismarck, it called out at each election that the Fatherland was in danger, and urged the election of deputies who would support the sovereign, the army, the colonial empire, and the spirited policy of an expanding world power.

It was natural that Germans should be receptive to the appeals to support a strenuous, militaristic, and even aggressive foreign policy. With the centuries-old frustration of their national spirit behind them and the material evidence of Germany's skill and success around them, they were naturally eager to assert their nationhood and to equip themselves with the standard appurtenances of greatness—colonies, a navy, overseas trade, and the right to be consulted in any international question in any part of the globe. Moreover, the end of the nineteenth century was an era of rather weird but very popular theories which gave support to Germans' sense of their own manifest destiny. A Germanized Englishman named Houston Chamberlain wrote about the "natural" supremacy of the Teutonic and Anglo-Saxon races and the "natural' inferiority of the Latin, Slavic,

Yellow, and Black races. The philosopher Nietzsche was writing obscure but effective works about the vital role in history of "the Superman." The historian Treitschke, glorifying violence, attributed past German weakness to the gentleness of the Germans, and demanded that they become hard. Everywhere, people were theorizing from Darwin about the "survival of the fittest"—and the Germans were palpably very fit indeed.

All this intellectual ferment affected the German authorities. It also gave them grounds to urge the electorate to vote for parliamentary parties which would support the army, the colonies, the monarchy, and the strong foreign policy. The socialists, with their ideas of peace and equality, were excoriated. The most important symbol of this struggle, at once metaphysical and constitutional, was the German navy, which had begun to come into existence in the 1890's. The navy was expensive, and it led to quarrels with Great Britain. But the navy was popular, its leaders were influential with the emperor and the court, and it was a good talking point for the government. In the crucial election of 1907, which was fought largely on the indicative issues of colonial policy and, indirectly, of naval expansion, the supporters of the government won handily and the Social Democrats suffered their only set-back. It was not surprising that the way out of the constitutional dilemma should have appeared to be an ever increasing emphasis on national greatness and a foreign policy best described as insolent.

GERMANY IN 1914

By 1914, the lines were more clearly drawn than ever. The monarchy was in trouble. William II's tendency to impulsive action, and his inclination to make violent speeches without consulting the chancellor, had led in 1909 to the resignation of his most loyal friend, Prince Bernhard von Bülow. Bülow was embarrassed in parliament by an interview which the emperor had granted to the London *Daily Telegraph,* in which he imprudently insulted England and embroiled Germany in an international crisis. Moreover, the sovereign became indirectly involved in several court scandals. With a new chancellor whom he disliked, and with public opinion against him, the emperor was forced to withdraw largely from public view.

By 1914, too, the Prussian landowners, fighting a last ditch battle against declining agricultural prices and against a society in which they were increasingly outnumbered, were also in trouble. In parliament, the Social Democrats had won a plurality. Demands for far-reaching constitutional change were becoming more and more difficult to restrain.

Germany appeared to be on the verge of serious political crises when the First World War broke out. There seemed no way in which a peaceful and legal adjustment could be made. If the monarchy were subtracted, there was no one to control and appoint the chancellor. The Prussian landowners refused obstinately to surrender their dominant influence in the Prussian government, through which they could preserve their own existence and prosperity. Control of the *Reichstag* by the Social Democrats was a possibility in the future. Yet it would mean a drastic reorganization of the constitution, with the violent hostility of the army, monarchy and aristocracy amounting virtually to a revolution. The only force in Germany which still had complete self-confidence, enormous prestige, and the power to take over the management of the foundering federation, was the army. Once war broke out, it lost little time in establishing an effective military dictatorship.

These grave cracks in the foundations of the empire were to some extent still concealed from contemporary view, however. They were plastered over with mortar compounded of various elements. For one thing, the country was mainly administered by the civil services—the federal service, those of the several states, and the agencies of the municipal governments. These were large, honest, energetic, and effective, and the day-to-day business of government was carried out with impressive vigor and imagination. Government expenditures on public services increased almost sevenfold under the emperor. Housing developments, railroads, post offices, schools, highways, all spread, providing Germans and visitors alike with a gratifying sense of achievement. The schools were not only numerous; they were also excellent. Prussia had established free, compulsory, and universal education before any other country, and the other German states followed suit. German scholarship in the nineteenth century dazzled and beguiled the world with its thoroughness and its "scientific" method, so suitable to the up-to-date view on which the nineteenth century prided itself. The educational system provided an increasing supply of trained scholars and technicians and government officials who staffed industry and army and civil service. German music was brilliant. And German technology was unequalled. To be sure, the gentler achievements of the humanities were on the whole, from the point of view of modern taste, weak. Most nineteenth-century German literature was colorless, and architecture inclined, for example, to massive, heavy edifices allegedly inspired by early medieval Teutonic castles, largely built of red sandstone and aptly termed Colossal.

It was in the field of material wealth that the achievement was most amazing. Coming late to the Industrial Revolution, German factories profited from the technical advances and capital accumulations of other countries, particularly France, whose savings flowed to Germany in the form of war indemnities after 1871. By 1914, German national income had about doubled since 1896. Its exports had quadrupled since 1870. Its productive capacity was the greatest in Europe. Nor were the profits of these enterprises limited to the great and haughty industrialists of the Rhineland and Silesia; they spread throughout the population. And the usual insecurity of the worker—the price of the early stages of industrialism so painfully paid by the working classes of France, Britain, and America—was largely avoided in Germany. Bismarck's most imaginative contribution had been a system of insurance, begun in the 1880's, to which both worker and employer contributed, against illness, accidents, and old age. The Bismarckian system was very incomplete and in some ways unfair, but it was a dramatic innovation in its day. It served as a model for working class demands elsewhere which led gradually to the more or less complete "welfare state" systems which exist in every industrial country today. On the other hand, it never succeeded in doing what Bismarck intended it to do, slowing down the growth of the labor unions or the Social Democratic party. Indeed, it seemed at times as if the insurance schemes merely whetted the workers' appetites for more security and further benefits. But looking back, it is clear that it made individuals, and many union and party leaders, reluctant to destroy—or even fundamentally alter—a state which proved itself capable of supplying benefits of this sort. While the industrial workers in the main were still eager to capture and control the government, they were led to accept the pattern and possibility of state action. It certainly contributed to the growth of the moderate Revisionists among the Social Democrats who, weaned from Marxism by the prospect of further profits from a bourgeois society, hesitated to assassinate the goose that laid so large a golden egg.

The widespread scope of government action in Germany—the many excellent public services, the housing projects, the social insurance—met with only mild opposition from the businessmen and bankers and almost none from other segments of society. Germans were accustomed to strong and extensive government planning. The theoretical objections to it, so deep-rooted in Britain and France, had never been seriously adopted by most Germans. Laissez-faire liberalism, and the Jeffersonian notion that the government is best when it governs least, were unfamiliar in a country which had passed so rapidly from the age of enlightened despotism to that of the Industrial Revolution.

Throughout the whole of German society the ideas of paternalism, of strong government, of discipline, order, system, thoroughness, were deeply implanted. It was clear to the most casual reader of history that the national success of Prussia—prelude to the national success of the German empire—was attributable to discipline, order, and sound administration by the government, and to loyalty, obedience, and organization among the subjects. In the twentieth century, these traditions were as lively as ever. Even among the people who opposed the regime with its militarism and authoritarianism, they were evident. Even among the Social Democrats, with their elaborate party organization, their discipline and obedience, their paid vacations for party members, their training courses and kindergartens, the importance of authority and system was universally recognized.

To these traditions was attributable the magnificence of the German achievements. To them too was attributable the weakness—almost universally unperceived—of the German imperial structure.

39

THE FAILURE OF
THE HABSBURG
MULTINATIONAL
STATE

The austro-hungarian monarchy was the most peculiar country in Europe. Its population consisted of an almost endless variety of peoples of different language, culture, and racial stock. Its government was so unusual as to be unique in the annals of political science—a union of two independent states, based upon a sort of treaty-agreement and providing for the joint operation of certain government agencies. Its dynasty, the oldest and most distinguished in Europe, had a position different from that of any other reigning family—indeed, the name most commonly given to this non-nation is that of its rulers—the Habsburg monarchy. It was also known as Austria-Hungary, or the Dual Monarchy. It was, indeed, difficult to know exactly what to call it.

It was still, in the period from 1870 to 1914, a great power. Its area was greater than that of any other European country except Russia. In 1871 its population was greater than that of any except Russia, France, and Germany; by 1914 it had overtaken France. In 1870, there were about 35,000,000 people living in the Monarchy; in 1914 there were over 50,000,000. It developed during these years a vigorous industrial growth. It possessed abundant capital and was the main banking center of Eastern Europe. It was enormously rich agriculturally. It had one of the largest armies in the world. It had a large and on the whole effective administration. Nonetheless, its doom was frequently prophesied. Even among people friendly to it, it was frequently referred to as "ramshackle," and it was often regarded as having replaced Turkey as "The Sick Man of Europe." Its condition, especially after 1900, excited great curiosity of a rather morbid kind in all quarters.

The reason for this gloomy prognosis was mainly the existence within its borders of so large a number of national groups, most of them indifferently disposed toward one another and several of them seriously dissatisfied with the way things were going in the Monarchy. There were relatively few in 1870 who overtly urged the division of Austria-Hungary into its component parts, but almost everybody in the country felt that some drastic changes were in order.

Such changes had been experimented with in the previous twenty-five years. The utter disagreement as to their proper nature and direction had made the Monarchy, at various times and in several of its parts, ungovernable. After 1870, whenever further changes were proposed, they always met with strong opposition in some influential quarter. This situation forced the government to rely more and more on strong-arm methods and tended to freeze government policy into a despairing inaction—and inaction was just as unacceptable to many groups as the proposals for reform were to others. Moreover, the national diversity gradually had become mingled and confused with social tensions and troubles. These arose out of the popular desire for economic and social equality, and out of the development of an industrial, urban working class.

AUSTRIA

The Austrian Empire after 1867 formed a sort of crescent, with one point touching the Adriatic and the other, in the east, pointing toward the Black Sea. The length from end to end was roughly 800 miles; the area was over 300,000 square kilometers (somewhat larger than Nevada). The terrain was extensively mountainous. In the west, adjoining Switzerland, lay the high Alps, reaching in branches to the sea and the Danube. In the top of the crescent were the Bohemian mountains, lower but rugged; and in the east, the wild and remote Carpathians. At intervals, however, were extensive valleys and plains, most of them—especially toward the west—fertile and attractive, supporting a well-to-do peasantry and aristocracy. In agriculture, forestry, cattle-raising, and minerals, Austria was singularly well-endowed.

But the economic and social development of the empire was very uneven and tended to become more so as the nineteenth century drew to a close. The peasants of the eastern provinces were poorer and less well-educated, although they had long been legally free and had in some cases controlled their own lands since 1848. The few towns were mainly marketing centers. In the west, however, large and ancient cities were numerous; two of them, Vienna and the Bohemian capital, Prague, were great metropoles, of about a million and a half and a quarter million respectively. They were, moreover, middle-class cities, with large professional and shopkeeping groups, and wealthy bankers and business-men. To these were in time added factory-owners. Industry, when it appeared in the last decades of the nineteenth century, was mainly located around Vienna and Prague.

The social and economic diversity of the Empire was nothing compared to its linguistic and national variety. No language group was in a majority, al-though there were more Germans than anything else. In order to grasp this picture in its unnerving complexity, it is essential to study the maps here and on p. 486. Some of these groups were widely scattered through the empire, particularly the Germans who constituted the commercial and governing class in a number of provinces; those who lived in Transylvania had a special name—Saxons—and a separate tradition. But most of the people were centered in particular geographi-cal areas which in some (but by no means all) cases corresponded roughly with the lines of the provinces into which the empire was divided. There were seven purely German provinces, all in the west and approximating the present-day fed-eral states of the Austrian Republic. There was one mainly Italian province, on the Adriatic, Istria. (It contained the city of Trieste, the third largest in Austria, and also a large number of Slovenes and Croats.) The Adriatic littoral, the prov-ince of Dalmatia, was mainly Croat, with a sprinkling of Italians on the coast. In one province, Carniola, just northeast of Istria, Slovenes predominated, with a considerable minority of Germans. Three others, Bohemia, Moravia, and Silesia, in the north-central area, were about three parts Czech (predominantly country

AUSTRIA-HUNGARY IN 1914

people, although there was a Czech middle class in Prague) to one part German (mostly noblemen, city people, and civil servants, except along the edges of Bohemia, which were solidly German). The big province of Galicia (Austria's share of Poland) contained the empire's fourth city, Lemberg (Lvóv in Polish) and was divided into two sections—one purely Polish, the other, to the east, inhabited by Ruthene peasants but its land owned and governed by Polish noblemen. The remaining province, Bukovina, in the extreme east between Russia and Rumania, was a sort of ethnic nightmare: it contained Rumanians, Ruthenes, Magyars, Poles, Russians, Germans, and a very large population of Jews of various national affiliations.

The Austrian constitution provided for a fair amount of provincial self-government. Each province had a legislature (or diet) and was responsible for its own local affairs. While official business was, for purposes of convenience, usually conducted in German, and while everyone who went to school was expected to learn German, no one interfered with people speaking their native language. A fairly wide degree of toleration prevailed.

The parliament had been set up under a constitution of 1861, much amended in following years. It provided for a bicameral legislature, consisting of a House of Lords (mainly nominated by the Emperor) and a Chamber of Deputies (Reichsrat) elected, by province, by electors. The electors were chosen under an odd franchise, which was a transition stage between medieval "estates" or "diets" and democratic representation. The populace was divided into four classes, or curias—one class was great landowners, another townspeople, another chambers of commerce, another small landholders and other royal taxpayers. In 1896, a fifth class, including the whole male population was added. Each class chose an equal number of electors; the well-to-do, and particularly the nobility were thus greatly overrepresented.

The ministers were appointed by the emperor, and it was never wholly clear whether they were to be his personal assistants or rather the agents of the Chamber. The problem was that the Chamber was not organized into parties in the usual way—there were parties, but they were so divided by national rather than doctrinal disputes that no coherent majority ever emerged. The ministry was thus rarely assured of parliamentary support for its measures. It was often obliged to govern by decree, and as time went on the Reichsrat exercised less and less control over the executive authorities. This was, of course, the Reichsrat's own fault.

The failure of the Reichsrat to control the ministry meant that the emperor, who appointed it, played a decisive role in the government. Francis Joseph I (1848–1916) was a well-intentioned man with a strong sense of duty, but he was timid, rigid, and not particularly intelligent. His impulse was to conserve, not to invent. And he was enclosed in a court which was narrowly aristocratic and rather bigoted. Its ideas tended to be old-fashioned. Much emphasis was placed on court etiquette and pedigree. In line with Habsburg traditions, it regarded the army and the Church as the chief instruments for holding the empire together, and the police as its principal mainstay. Neither the politicians of the Reichsrat nor the unimaginative emperor was able to initiate strong policies. Therefore, its enemies claimed with some justice that Austria was ruled by "a standing army, a kneeling clergy, a sitting bureaucracy, and a crawling police force."

HUNGARY

The Kingdom of Hungary, as re-established in 1867, was a Magyar state. It was ruled and dominated by the Magyar people, whose language was the official language and who monopolized state office. Its boundaries included, however, a great many people in addition to the dominant Magyars. Of a population of about twenty million in 1910, approximately fifty percent, or ten million, were Magyars, concentrated in the center of the country, in the great Hungarian plain on either side of the Danube. Around the edges were some two million Slovaks—Slavs, closely related to the Czechs; almost three million Rumanians; almost two million German-speaking people; and two and a half million Serbs and Croats.

The percentage of Magyars was not much greater in Hungary than the percentage of Germans in Austria. But while Austria, governed with considerable decentralization, was regarded as frankly a polyglot state and not a German one (although the Germans might enjoy a priviliged position in it), the Magyars regarded Hungary as a national state. The administration was highly centralized, and it was entirely in the hands of Magyars. This had not always been the case. Some of the outlying provinces, such as Transylvania, where the bulk of the Rumanian population lived, had traditionally enjoyed a separate administration. The kingdom of Croatia-Slavonia, in the south, had once (in the eleventh century) been independent, and under the terms of the *Ausgleich,* the Dual Monarchy arrangement, it was guaranteed a parliamentary assembly of its own, the right to conduct schools and public business in its own tongue, and control over religious affairs, education, the courts, local government and police. Croatia was also separately represented in the House of Lords and the Chamber of Deputies of the Hungarian Kingdom, in Budapest.

The tendency of the Magyars, once they recovered their independence in 1867, however, was highly nationalistic. They disliked the division of their country, they disliked its linguistic diversity, and they regarded the Rumanian and Slavic populations as troublesome and, it is not too much to say, inferior. The rights of Transylvania were early suppressed. Those of Croatia, protected by treaty and law, were constantly encroached upon. The Croatian diet was packed and manipulated, and the Croatian leaders were harassed. This was in part due to the collusion of the native Croat aristocracy, which feared social unrest in their own country, and feared especially movements aiming at separation from the Habsburgs and union with Serbia, more than they feared the Magyars. By 1914 Croatia-Slavonia had lost most of its self-government. Moreover, beginning in the 1880's, a strenuous effort was made to "Magyarize" all other groups in

Hungary—to impose the Magyar language, to eliminate so far as possible all traces of national diversity.

The Magyars were flamingly nationalistic—perhaps more spectacularly so than any other people except the Poles in Europe during the period. But these sentiments, while they may have been shared by the mass of the Magyar population, were articulated mainly by its government; and the government of Hungary was entirely in the hands of a small class of landowners.

The landholding system of Hungary was very retrograde—more medieval than any in Europe outside of Russia, parts of Prussia, and perhaps Rumania. The legal and economic position of the peasants was decidedly inferior. Their political position was non-existent; the franchise was extremely limited and the parliament was almost entirely controlled by representatives of the aristocracy. Moreover, county government—very important in an entirely agricultural country—was wholly run by the landowners.

The party which was in power during almost the entire period from 1867 to 1918 was the Liberal party, which had been born out of the events of 1848. The Liberal party shared the ideals of the mid-century liberals throughout Europe in two respects. It was fiercely nationalistic, loathing domination from German Vienna. And it was ardently in favor of representative government, and opposed to autocratic, but willing to accept constitutional, monarchy. And representative government meant representation of the landowners.

Hungary was stable—not to say static—during the years from 1870–1914. The population increased but the economy of the country was little changed. The social structure was static. The principal show of dynamism was in the rambunctious display of national spirit on the part of the Magyars—the increasingly tight rein with which they curbed localism or nationalism or even ordinary civil liberties among the Slavic and Rumanian people in Hungary. Their growing independence was shown, too, in the increasingly hard bargains which they tried to impose on their partner, Austria, in the periodic renegotiation of the commercial treaty. They also tried to influence the foreign policy of the Monarchy in the direction of strictly Hungarian interests. But little other development or change was visible in Hungary.

THE HABSBURG MISSION
AND ITS FAILURE

Austria-Hungary, in view of its composition, could not depend upon the national patriotism of its subjects to provide obedience to the state and a sense of community among its citizens. In this it was at a unique disadvantage among European states. There was, however, a substitute for patriotism, and this was loyalty to the House of Habsburg. The dynasty was very ancient and very proud, and it undoubtedly commanded the awe and attachment of its subjects in a way which Americans can scarcely understand. Moreover, Francis Joseph I was a popular figure. Toward the end of the century he was already so familiar—and so old (he was born in 1830)—as to command a sort of automatic affection. His personal life had been unhappy; at intervals, he lost his son and heir, his brother, his wife, and his nephew through violence. These sorrows provoked a sentimental sympathy among many subjects.

But more than Francis Joseph was supposed to commend the dynasty and the Monarchy to its subjects. The Habsburgs had a Mission, about which quite a lot was said by their supporters. This Mission was supposed to involve the bringing of peace, order, prosperity, Catholicism, and western culture, to Central Europe. In pursuit of it, the Habsburgs had annealed their disparate holdings. They had turned back the Turks and driven them from the Danube valley. Now, in an age of rising nationalism, they were supposed to protect the nationalities of their realm from one another and to provide unity and concord among them, safeguarding the rights of each and protecting the welfare of all.

This Mission was plausible enough. The national minorities were so numerous and many of them so small that it was not imagined by anybody that they could be sorted out into national states of their own—Central Europe thus sorted out would have constituted a series of Luxemburgs and Liechtensteins, politically and economically chaotic. More than that, the nationalities were not only numerous but snarled up. In village after village, one street would be (say) Rumanian-speaking and the next street Magyar with Germans in the suburbs. A large-scale ethnic map of Transylvania, Bukovina, or Istria looked like an Oriental rug. In almost every province there was at least one area with national tangles that could not be sorted out.

Furthermore, the Monarchy formed an economic unit of a sort. It was the largest customs union in Europe outside of the primitive Russia, and it formed a rough economic region of its own. With the rise of industry in Vienna and Bohemia, it was well-balanced, providing many of its own raw materials and, particularly from Hungary, its own food supply. This economic unity in some respects grew with the growth of modern business methods; trade channels followed political frontiers, and so did banking. The expansion of commerce and production, and the growth of Vienna as a banking center, strengthened the unity of the Monarchy. There were, to be sure, some disruptive economic factors as well. The dependence of the Austrian half on the Hungarian for its wheat gave the latter an all too powerful bargaining position which, during World War I, it was to use with unconscionable effectiveness. There were serious competitions between different provinces, and some of them found their natural markets and sources of supply outside the empire shut off from them by tariff walls. But on the whole the extreme inconvenience which would have followed disruption of the Monarchy's economic unity was one of the forces which strengthened loyalty to it.

The Habsburgs' political Mission, however, was a failure. The most serious failure was in Hungary. The Habsburgs failed to protect the Slavic and Rumanian peoples of Hungary against the Magyars. From the point of view of the Croats, for example (and they were among the most devoted adherents of the Crown), the Crown failed them when it failed to prevent the dominant Magyars from persecuting them. So, the Croats gradually lost their enthusiasm for the

Habsburgs and began to think of alternative ways of protecting their national rights and freedoms. The creation of the Dual Monarchy out of the Austrian Empire spelled the abandonment of the Habsburg Mission in Hungary.

In the Austrian half as well, the fact (or myth) of the Mission began to break down. The government, fearing that the Poles might become as troublesome and dissatisfied as the Polish populations of Germany and Russia were, did everything in its power to gratify them. It succeeded. Not only were the Poles in Austria far more contented and less eager for the revival of a Polish state than in the other two empires; they were among the most loyal of the Habsburg subjects. Giving the Poles what they wanted, however, meant giving them the power to persecute the Ruthenes, who constituted the rural working population in part of the Polish province of Galicia. The Habsburg Mission showed another anomaly: to keep one nationality happy it seemed to be necessary to sacrific another.

This process of compounding national conflicts spread. By 1914, it was extending to the Czechs. The chief antagonists of the Czechs were the Germans, who constituted a strong minority of the population in the "Lands of the Crown of Saint Wenceslas"—that is to say, the ancient Bohemian Kingdom. It had been (rather vaguely) suggested that after 1867 the Vienna government would do for the Lands of the Crown of Saint Wenceslas what had just been done for the Lands of the Crown of Saint Stephen (Hungary). A Triune Monarchy would replace the Dual Monarchy, with Bohemia as the third independent state under the dynasty. The suggestion was never carried out. The Germans in Bohemia were bitterly opposed to the creation of a separate government in which they, the more wealthy and influential part of the population, would constitute a numerical minority. They were (not entirely without reason) convinced that a Kingdom of Bohemia would be a Czech kingdom, and that they would suffer the fate that the Croats and Rumanians were suffering in the Kingdom of Hungary. The Germans of Bohemia, including a large portion of the imperial aristocracy, were in a position to stop the granting of autonomous rights to Bohemia, and they did.

The result was that the Czechs, or some of them, became more and more dissatisfied. Several Czech nationalist parties appeared (aiming not at separation from the Monarchy but at restoring a self-governing Bohemia within it). They boycotted the *Reichsrat* and encouraged sedition. The Czechs thus came to constitute a danger to the peace of the Monarchy, even though none of their leaders advocated its destruction. The government was forced more and more to rely upon the loyal Germans, which meant moving further and further away from Czech wishes.

Entirely different problems were presented by the Italians and Rumanians and Serbs. These people all were able to look across the borders at national states of their own nationality, unlike the Poles or Czechs. The Italians were the smallest group but in some ways the most intractable. Opinions might differ as to the wisdom of leaving the Dual Monarchy to become subjects of backward, poor, and unstable countries like Rumania or Serbia, but Italy was a modern, constitutional state with a standard of living and administrative efficiency almost as high as Austria-Hungary's. Italian discontent was, however, held within bounds by diplomacy. Italy was an ally of Austria-Hungary, and its government (most of the time at least) sought to discourage inflammatory propaganda aimed at fanning the nationalistic fires of the Austro-Italians. The Rumanians and Serbs were also at the beginning of the period allies, but they were harder to control. By 1914, all three alliances had become a dead letter; that with Serbia had been openly denounced by the Serbs.

Complaints and threats from the Kingdom of Serbia, on the southern border of Austria-Hungary, were the most serious of all. The Serbs in the Dual Monarchy were part of the same nationality as those in the Serbian Kingdom, and they were probably worse treated than the Italians or Rumanians. Moreover, they were close cousins of the Croats, and both Vienna and Budapest were haunted by the nightmares of united Serb-Croat action to remake or destroy the Empire. For increasingly the Croats showed themselves open to the suggestion of united South Slav (or in their own tongue Yugoslav) action. Furthermore, after 1878, the Monarchy administered the Turkish provinces of Bosnia and Herzegovina which lay on its southern border and adjoined Serbia. The provinces were mainly Serb, and their administration was on the whole backward. The Monarchy (Austria and Hungary were jointly responsible for the provincial government) deliberately discouraged education, on the grounds that literate Bosnians would be able to read Serb nationalist propaganda. In 1908, the two provinces were seized outright from Turkey, and the Serbs were infuriated by this frustration of their dreams of liberating them. Serb secret societies operated widely, not only in the two provinces but in the other Serb and Croat territories of the Monarchy.

There were frequent suggestions made in Vienna of ways to assuage Serb and Croat nationalism. The most common was the creation of a Yugoslav state on the same footing as Hungary (if Bohemia had ever received equal treatment with Hungary, this would have meant a Four-Part Monarchy). Since almost all the regions included in such a country would have come from Hungary, the Magyars naturally fought it tooth and nail—in any case, they did not wish to have any more equals under the Habsburg roof.

Instances of national dissatisfaction of this sort could be enumerated for dozens of pages. They illustrate the difficulties which lay in the path of any proposal for reform of the structure of the Monarchy—and in the path, too, of managing its day-to-day affairs. It is scarcely surprising that more and more responsible subjects of Francis Joseph should have been driven to one of two conclusions—either to go on, making do as well as possible and shutting the door on change and talk of change; or else to blow the House of Habsburg sky-high and see where the pieces fell.

Neither viewpoint was very helpful, but the destinies of the multinational state eventually fell into a sort of prize-fighting ring in which the two philosophies contended. In the last years, these two points of view were joined by two others, the Socialists and the Christian Democrats, products of twentieth-century social and economic developments, who converted the prize-fight into a free-for-all which the aging emperor sadly watched.

AUSTRIAN POLITICS, 1870–1907

The Austrian Empire in 1870 was being governed, like most European countries, by a Liberal party. The Liberals had gained control of the ministry after 1867. They shared the secular ideals of most liberals—they believed in efficient, lay administration, civil liberties, and freedom of business enterprise from government regulation. Under the prime ministerships of Count Beust and, after 1871, of Prince Auersperg, the government was operated like other representative governments, with the ministry responsible to the parliamentary majority (elected it will be remembered with a very limited franchise). The Liberals passed a number of measures aimed at modernizing the Austrian legal and social structure, which was in some ways very old-fashioned. Full legal rights were extended to Jews and Protestants, civil marriage was recognized, old economic restrictions were lifted, civil liberties (guaranteed by the constitution) were strengthened.

The Liberal party, however much it might act like other liberal parties, was necessarily different in multinational Austria. Its peculiar problem was that it was overwhelmingly a German party. Its largest support came from the German middle classes of Vienna and other cities, and its program was designed mainly to satisfy German ideals and German business interests. It was strongly opposed by the other Austrian nationalities, two of which were sufficiently numerous to have strong parties of their own: the so-called Polish Club, and the Czech Nationalists (who made things easier for the Liberals by refusing to attend the parliament). For the rest, the *Reichsrat* consisted of a multitude of minor parties and a large unorganized group of conservatives, whose principal concerns were the defense of the dynasty and the Church and the protection of the rights of landowners.

Elections were held in 1879, and the Liberals lost their majority. There had been an economic crisis in 1873 which had shaken the faith of business interests in the Liberals and had disillusioned and frightened the country generally. The government's foreign policy had been unpopular in many quarters, and its mildly anti-clerical measures had outraged many of the devout. The non-Germans, especially the Czechs, naturally voted against a party which was mainly German. In the new parliament, where the conservative and Czech groups were strengthened, no party had a majority. The new prime minister appointed by the emperor was a member of no party himself; he sought to reconcile all the groups.

The appointment of Count von Taaffe really represented the end of Austria's brief experience with representative government. Although the *Reichsrat* continued to meet, and to pass laws, the Ministry was henceforth independent of it. Eduard von Taaffe (1833–1895), who was perhaps the ablest Austrian statesman in the period, recognized that a ministry could not be responsible to a parliament in which nothing except conflicting national interests were represented. He was determined to "stand above nationalities," and to strengthen the one real unifying force in the empire, the crown. He described himself as the "Emperor's Prime Minister" and, supported by the crown, tended to govern secretively and rather autocratically.

He had considerable success. The Czech Nationalists were lured into abandoning their boycott of the *Reichsrat* by making Czech an official language for government offices. From 1879 until 1895 a very considerable measure of internal tranquility was maintained. The nationalist parties felt themselves more fairly treated and held their more extreme demands in abeyance. Prosperity had returned, and with it came development of a considerable industrial establishment. The ministry was skillful at dispensing favors, which took people's minds off large issues of principle. Public works were greatly expanded and, more especially, the administrative staff grew rapidly. Indeed, political patronage became a technique of government—as it has been many times and in many places. Politicians who showed signs of dissatisfaction were given government jobs. By this means, nascent nationalist movements were deprived of their potential leaders, and a vast, expensive, but generally able government service burgeoned.

There were certain disadvantages to this highly opportunistic system of government: it rested, for one thing, upon monarchical initiative in a day when more and more people felt that monarchs should be seen and not heard, it constituted a sort of freezing of the national problem, with no structural changes proposed or desired. And it irritated the Liberals. During the Taaffe ministry, the Liberals grew more and more explicitly German, while at the same time growing more radical in their political programs. Some of them began to advocate a very limited monarchy and universal manhood suffrage. At a party conference at Linz, in 1882, they drew up a program which in practice would have meant a highly centralized Austrian government dominated by the Germans.

The groups in the *Reichsrat* on whom Taaffe increasingly counted to vote his budgets and his laws were socially conservative—landowners, clericals, arch-monarchists. Among the unenfranchised working classes and peasants, and among progressive spirits everywhere, his rule was thought reactionary. In the *Reichsrat*, a stronger and stronger opposition showed itself. In an effort to overcome it, Taaffe sought to appeal to the average citizen by what seemed a startling reversal of his policy: he announced to the *Reichsrat* that he favored something like universal suffrage. Almost none of the parties was prepared for this, least of all his own conservative supporters. The emperor disliked the suggestion. In 1893, Taaffe was forced to resign.

If his appointment had meant the end of conventional parliamentary government, his resignation meant the temporary end of parliament. The three years that followed were of such political confusion and such violence in the *Reichsrat* that they paved the way for government by decree. The issue which bulked largest during these years and which brought down the shaky coalition government of Prince Windischgrätz was significant and baleful. It concerned a school in a town called Cilli (or Celji, in the language of the Slovenes). Cilli was in the province of Styria, which was mainly German but which contained a large number of Slovenes in its southern parts. The Slovenes, South Slavs like the Croats and Serbs, were rural, devout, and not very numerous; they were among the most obscure and loyal of the Slavic nationalities. Taaffe, in his effort to head off trouble, had set up several schools in Styria where instruction was in the Slovene tongue. The Slovenes of Cilli, a mixed town, were promised a similar school. The issue was carried to the parliament, where Slavs and Germans lined up on it and came to blows. The government stuck to its promise of a Slovene school, and the German deputies voted against it. The ministers resigned. The crisis indicated the ways in which the national issues made parliamentary government unmanageable. It was inconceivable in any other country that the curriculum of a single village school could cause the resignation of the national government. Parliament had become a shambles, and debates were characterized chiefly by the tossing of inkwells. Five ministries followed one another in rapid succession.

Fortunately for the Empire, the constitution contained a clause which permitted the emperor to legislate by decree when parliament was not in session. The parliament could later void such decrees, when it reassembled. For the next six years, the *Reichsrat* met regularly, received bills from the government and invariably failed to approve them. When it adjourned, the bills were made law by imperial decree. When parliament met again, motions were invariably introduced to void the decrees—and invariably the *Reichsrat* again failed to agree. The *Reichsrat* thus made itself ridiculous, and the Austrian Empire was transformed perforce into a rather comical despotism.

The major development of these years was the growth of the two great new parties. The Social Democrats were similar to Marxist socialist parties in other countries. They were in theory orthodox Marxists striving for the overturn of capitalist society and the creation of a working-class state. In point of fact (like most socialist parties) the Austrian group contained a high percentage of very moderate reformers who were more interested in political democracy and mild welfare legislation than in social revolution. The leadership was mainly in the hands of middle-class intellectuals.

The Social Democrats were differentiated from the older parliamentary groups by more than their demands for drastic social reforms. They were also, strangely enough, supporters of the unity of the empire and even, in practice if not in theory, of the Habsburg dynasty. As Marxists, they were unenthusiastic about nationalism and national states, which they regarded as bourgeois inventions calculated to lead to wars and to facilitate the exploitation of the working class. In the classless Utopia to which they looked forward, there would be no national states and no national oppression. Their immediate concern was with class war, not with national rivalry. Moreover, they were for good economic reasons averse to the break-up of the state whose capital they inhabited and on whose existence the prosperity of the city depended.

The Social Democrats were, among all political groups, theoretically the most tolerant, the most internationalist, and the most sympathetic to the grievances of the minorities. Ironically, the fact that they were mainly a German party and that they supported the unity of the Empire led most of the working classes of other national groups to eye them coldly. They had some supporters in Bohemia among the Czechs, but elsewhere outside the German provinces they were weak. Ironically, too, the court and the aristocracy came to look upon the socialists as their saviors from the separatist national groups.

The second of the great parties which grew during these years was the Christian Socialist party. Like the Social Democrats, its main strength was in Vienna and the German areas. Also like the Social Democrats, the Christian Democrats stood for extensive social reforms and for the unity of the Empire. Here, however, the resemblance ended. The Christian Socialists were devout Catholics, while the Socialists were explicitly anti-clerical. The Christian Socialists were mainly middle class in origin, and their main social and economic demands were for the protection of the *kleinbürgertum*, the little bourgeois people, against harassment by the forces of wealth and conservatism. They reflected the prejudices and narrownesses of the lower middle classes; many of the Christian Socialist leaders were anti-Semitic (Jews were associated with the great banking and business interests, and were popularly regarded as hostile to the "little man," especially the shopkeepers). The party was also enormously successful politically, and some of its leaders were very able. Karl Lüger, who became mayor of Vienna in 1897, was the leader of the party. He was also the most imaginative and energetic mayor Vienna had ever had, and he became the idol of the Viennese.

Both Social Democrats and Christian Socialists urgently demanded manhood suffrage. After lengthy delays and much reluctance, the emperor and the ministers finally concluded that the system of government by decree could not continue and that the only way to break it was to yield to this demand. A bill for a democratic franchise was introduced and eventually, in 1907, it passed. Austria had become a democracy.

It did not remain one long. The franchise reforms of 1907 led to chaos. In the first democratic election the Christian Democrats received 96 seats and the Social Democrats 87. There were no fewer than twenty-three other parties, every one of which represented a nationality interest. The two major parties could not agree on a program, and all the other groups were so intent on local interests that they could not form a coalition with either of the two. A deadlock even more complete than that which had existed in 1897 now ensued. Again there was rule by decree.

DISINTEGRATION, 1907–1918

By 1908, almost all the national political groups were growing more extreme, and their leadership was passing to more and more demagogic leaders. The most immediate problem was that of the Serbs, who were daily lured, blandished, and agitated by the propaganda from Belgrade, the capital of the Serb kingdom. Many people thought that unless something were done to suppress Serb nationalist agitation, the Serbs and all the South Slavs in the Monarchy would violently secede from it and bring the whole Habsburg structure crashing down.

It was therefore natural that people close to the dynasty should begin to think in terms of forceful measures to preserve it. They found themselves more and more prepared to listen to the army generals, who preached strenuous action to restore the prestige of Austria-Hungary. In the end, they preached war against Serbia, which immediately widened into World War I.

The story of the outbreak and course of the war is told elsewhere. Here it is necessary only to note the epilogue of the Monarchy. The *Reichsrat* was adjourned for the duration, and what amounted to a military dictatorship was instituted. Very strict mobilization measures were promulgated; Austria-Hungary, to a greater extent than any other power, had previously prepared plans for its economic mobilization. Financial measures, rationing, and industrial controls were instituted. Very extensive political controls were set up. These were natural and perhaps necessary. The minorities were so exceedingly unreliable, and the government so convinced that they would take advantage of the war crisis to press their own demands, that no belligerent government could have permitted much civil freedom to remain. In fact, Austria-Hungary was converted into a police state; there were massive arrests and repressions.

These wartime measures defeated their own purpose, however, owing to the course of the war. The imperial armies, badly officered and badly equipped, fought badly. Soldiers of the minority nationalities deserted to the enemy in increasing numbers. Informed of the arrest or oppression of their co-nationals at home, they naturally saw little point in fighting to defend the government which was persecuting them.

The economic situation also rapidly deteriorated. Despite the efficient war administration and despite Austria-Hungary's own great resources, the Allied blockade of the Central Powers soon began to have disastrous effects. By 1916, Vienna and the other major cities were on the verge of starvation.

The government was faced with a complete breakdown of the war effort, if not with revolution. At this crucial juncture, Francis Joseph finally died. He was succeeded, in December of 1916, by his great-nephew, the King-Emperor Charles I. Charles was clear-headed and well-intentioned. He saw that if the Monarchy and his own thrones were to be saved, urgent measures were necessary. The most important things to be done were to end the policy of repression, to restore some measure of popular government and, most of all, to end the war as soon as possible. In quick succession, he issued an amnesty, pardoning and liberating all political prisoners; he recalled the parliament; and he entered into secret negotiations with the Allies in which he offered to abandon Germany and make a separate peace.

These measures came too late, and they had a most unfortunate effect. The amnesty, instead of mollifying its beneficiaries, merely permitted them to recommence their seditious operations. Many of them left the country to propagandize for the dismemberment of the Monarchy in Allied capitals. The re-calling of parliament merely gave the deputies an opportunity to vociferate their many complaints. And the peace negotiations, which were disdainfully rejected and published by the Allies, frightened and infuriated the Germans.

The consequence was that German influence, which had been growing in proportion to Austria's military and economic difficulties, now became supreme. The Germans practically took over the command of the Austrian army (and led it to its most spectacular victory, over the Italians at Caporetto in 1917). They moved into Viennese government offices and dictated policy. By the spring of 1918, the Austrian Empire (and to a very much smaller extent, Hungary) had become a prisoner and indeed a protectorate of Germany.

The end of the Habsburgs was now at hand. The Allies (experiencing their own military difficulties) adopted a policy aimed at encouragement of the nationalities to revolt. The principle "self-determination"—which suggested small, independent national states—was sponsored, and governments-in-exile were formed for some of the minority groups. A Czech state came into existence, outside of the Empire, and was recognized by the Allies. The Russian Revolution inspired and encouraged extremist socialists, and its ideas (and apostles) spread rapidly in the hungry cities. By the spring of 1918 Austria, barely holding its own with German support on the fronts, was seething internally with rebellion.

The German defeats in France in the summer of 1918, brought the end of the war and they also brought the end of the Monarchy. An Allied army, advancing rapidly through the Balkans, threatened from the south, and the Italians won a great victory at Vittorio Veneto and started across the Alps. The exiled nationalist leaders re-entered the country. In October, Emperor Charles proclaimed that the empire was to be federalized. It was far too late; national governments were already being set up in Prague, in Lemberg, in the Croat capital at Zagreb. On November 3, an armistice with the Italians was signed, and during the next week the Socialists seized control of Vienna. They proclaimed a republic. The Hungarians did so a few days later. Charles I (and last) renounced his two crowns and withdrew to Switzerland.

The imperial Habsburg dynasty had long worn the crown of the Holy Roman Empire, and it traced its constitutional descent, and a certain kinship of spirit, from the Roman empire of Augustus, Constantine, and Charlemagne. The Emperor Charles was the last of the Caesars. The tradition of almost twenty centuries now came to an end. With Charles's exile also came an end to the only attempt in modern times to build a great European state on any basis save nationality. The multinational empire had ceased to exist.

40

THE TRIALS OF
ITALY

THE KINGDOM OF ITALY was newly completed in 1870. But unification brought no tranquility. In contrast to the almost miraculous stability and growth of Germany, Italy remained a country of armed conspiracies and uprisings, parliamentary turbulence and unstable governments, and, in some regions, of primitive economic life and grinding poverty.

And yet, there had been progress by 1914. The country was changing, and in important ways advances were being made. The most striking of the advances were, it is true, in the field of public works, more impressive to the banker and the tourist than to the native. A network of railroads traversed the tortuous terrain. Industry, that fashionable barometer of twentieth-century economic health, began to establish itself on a large scale in the 'nineties, and by 1914 Italy was an important exporter of textiles. Shipping had increased, and Genoa had nosed out Marseille as the first port of the Mediterranean. The government revenues had doubled and tripled. Colonies (the fashionable barometer of nineteenth-century national greatness) had been acquired on a modest scale. A degree of national loyalty and enthusiasm seemed to have replaced the ancient attachments of divided Italy. A peculiar but not entirely unworkable method had been evolved for dealing with the intractable factionalism of the Chamber of Deputies. Virtual democracy had been at last achieved, with the extension of the suffrage in 1912, in contrast to the extremely narrow electorate of 1870.

In short, Italy from 1870 to 1915, while capricious and backward, seemed to be moving in the same general direction (almost universally regarded as commendable) as the rest of Western Europe.

ITALY IN 1870

The new Italy was a nation of over 117,000 square miles (compared to France's 212,000 and New York State's 48,000). In 1871, it had a population of 26 million people (compared to France's 36 million and New York State's 4½ million). It thus ranked as one of the largest and most populous countries in Europe. But it had a trying geography.

Of all Italy's surface, perhaps one tenth is fertile and arable in the way that all of northern Europe is. The high mountains cannot be tilled, and many of the plateaux and valleys suffer from floods or drought, and from the effects of bad farming and deforestation. Nor is the unpromising peninsula equipped with compensating wealth in raw materials—it was not known until the middle of the twentieth century that Italy was rich in oil. More than any comparable area in Europe, Italy turned out to be poor in raw materials when the industrial age at last arrived and such matters were investigated. There is almost no coal and no iron, which were the essentials of nineteenth-century progress and prosperity. There were in 1870 no known supplies of any other mineral except sulphur, which was abundant in Sardinia but was, symbolically, to be driven out of the world market by cheaper American sulphur. The national income per person was calculated at $40 a year; that of Great Britain was over $150.

Italy's main economic assets were its ports, several of which were first-rate and many of which were useful, and its gifted population. Even the latter, through a tendency to expand with breathtaking rapidity, showed signs of becoming a liability. In this country bare of natural wealth, the population had increased to thirty-four million by 1914. The liability would have been a catastrophe, for the actual number of Italians in the world was vastly greater than this, had it not been for the emigration of an average of more than half a million each year to other parts of the world.

The old division of Italy officially ended in 1870. The Kingdom of Italy, as then constituted, was made up of what had been seven pieces: the kingdom of Piedmont-Sardinia, the Austrian Provinces (Lombardy and Venetia), the small independent duchies of Parma and Modena, the grand duchy of Tuscany, the States of the Church, and the Kingdom of the Two Sicilies. (There were several pieces still left over: the Austrian provinces of the South Tyrol, in the Alps, and of Istria, on the Adriatic, which were to be conquered in 1918; the Swiss canton of the Ticino, also in the Alps, which is still Swiss; and, significantly, the smallest and the most mountainous of all the Italian states, the Republic of San Marino, which is still independent. It was so small and so mountainous that the Italians never even tried to annex it.) All these countries had had entirely different forms of government and institutions, cultural and economic systems and affiliations, and social structures, since the days of the Roman empire.

What was to prove significant, however, was not memories of the old independent states, which most of the population regarded as obsolescent. The crucial fact was that each state was itself diverse. Piedmont, the mother of Italy, is a case in point. Its home province was the upper end of the Po Valley, hedged on three sides by Alps, with a prosperous and progressive agricultural people strongly Alpine in appearance and tradition, regarded by other Italians as dour and penny-pinching. The Piedmontese language was Italian strongly influenced by French, and its wealthier citizens spoke Parisian French natively and sometimes exclusively. The inhabitant of Rome would find few people in the Piedmontese capital of Turin to understand his language.

Piedmont also included, however, the former Republic of Genoa, on the coast beyond the mountains, which it had picked up in 1815. Genoa was a fishing and commercial province with a proud bourgeois past similar to that of Venice and with dying but well-remembered commercial and cultural associations with the east and with America, which had been discovered by its most famous son, Columbus. A thousand years of history, as well as the mountains and mutually incomprehensible dialects, separated it from Turin. And Piedmont included as well the island of Sardinia, malaria-ridden, primitive, sparsely inhabited, with a ferocious native population as different from the haughty Genoese or the bustling Turinese as a Tibetan peasant from an English lord.

Nor were these provincial differences lessened as one moved south to other Italian states. The Papal provinces, astride central Italy, exhibited comparable variations. In the primitive south, the poorest part of the mainland, they were accentuated. Moreover, underlying them, were larger contrasts between southerners and northerners in general. Milan and Turin might show the differing effects of Austrian and French influence; both were, however, essentially northern cities, inhabited by a population mainly blond in complexion and commercial in outlook. Both were accustomed to, and had profited from, an extensive trade and manufacture and, in their different ways, an excellent administration. Both were wealthy, efficient, and forward-looking, surrounded by a rich agriculture and a relatively prosperous peasantry. But in Palermo, the Sicilian capital, or in Naples, entirely different conditions prevailed. Here there had been centuries of misrule, banditry, poverty. Here was a population predominantly short and very dark, showing marked indications of the Greek and African emigrations of earlier days. Here was squalor, corruption, and poverty without parallel in Europe. Here too was a system of aristocratic control, based upon landed estates and life-and-death power over the peasantry.

There was, in 1870, an Italy. But Italy consisted of a political system, a gleam in the eyes of a few million militant nationalists, and a language which was spoken by the wealthy and cultivated.

To these diversities was added a constitutional question, which rapidly turned into a political and social one.

THE INSTITUTIONS OF UNITED ITALY

The institutions of Italy after 1860 were those of Piedmont. The Kingdom had been unified, hastily and high-handedly, by Count Cavour and his

Piedmontese Liberal followers, and their own constitution—the *Statuto* of 1848—had been applied without change to the new state.

The monarchy was Piedmontese. The throne was occupied by King Victor Emmanuel II (until his death in 1878; then by his son, Humbert II) of the House of Savoy. The monarchy, a native dynasty in contrast to the imported rulers of the previous states, was generally popular. It was also innocuous; the constitution bestowed upon the king extensive executive powers, but Victor Emmanuel II never sought to exercise them and his successors did so only when the government seemed to be breaking down. The crown was mainly ornamental and served the useful function of providing a permanent, symbolic head to a government which was otherwise often rather chaotic.

If the crown was harmless, other features of Piedmontese rule were more controversial. The suffrage was extremely narrow. Only those with rather elaborate property and educational qualifications had the right to vote. Less than half a million did so, and they were concentrated in the prosperous north. In the Chamber, the old Piedmontese factions continued to dominate the scene. Other groups could get no foothold. Republicans, socialists, and anarchists were barred by their seditious principles and by the franchise restrictions. All who opposed the Pope's loss of his territorial power—called Papalists—and all who favored a restoration of the old, local dynasties—called Legitimists—were also regarded as seditious, and they abstained from elections on orders from the Pope, and so were excluded from roles in the new Italy. There remained, in 1870, two ill-defined political groups, both of which had been formed out of issues attending the unification. In power at the beginning of the period was the right—the old Cavourian liberals whose main principles were devotion to the existing constitution and the House of Savoy and (now that Italy was unified) to the existing state of things generally. The other group, the left, were the erstwhile followers of Garibaldi and Mazzini. They had favored violent methods for unification and now were flamboyant in their demands for strong measures to secure the "unredeemed" Italian provinces of Austria. They were, they said, in favor of a broader franchise, and they were thought to be friendly to the interests of the simple people.

But neither of them was a party. Both were groups of politicians, orators, and theorists without much organization and certainly without any serious programs or actual policies. Both were, in their effective leadership at any rate, strongly inclined to the liberal doctrines of the day about social and economic matters. They believed in keeping the government out of the economic system, in sound currency, and in balanced budgets. Since the costs of unification had been extremely high, and since Italy was a poor coutry, this last requirement involved extremely high taxes. The left claimed that it wished to ease taxation burdens on the masses. In point of fact it never did so, for its well-to-do constituents and its economic theory both demanded balanced budgets.

The tax structure of united Italy was an illustration of the handicaps involved in applying Piedmontese institutions to the entire kingdom. In the prosperous north, the Piedmontese taxes fell fairly lightly. But the major sources of revenue were purchase taxes and wheat taxes. The rates which were bearable in the north were intolerable in the south, and they bore with especial weight upon

ROYAL ARMS OF ITALY. The Italian kingdom acquired, as its coat-of-arms, the shield of the Savoyard duchy, a silver cross on a red field, surrounded by the ribbon of the knightly Order of the Annunciation and surmounted by a royal crown. The use of the coat-of-arms of the Piedmontese rulers was a symbol of the imposition of the constitution as well as the dynasty of Piedmont upon the entire peninsula.

Savoy was an Alpine country, and the colors red and silver, or red and white, are associated with almost all the regions of the Alps, including the modern republics of Switzerland and Austria. The Swiss coat-of-arms is the same as that of Savoy. When an international relief and service organization was founded, with its headquarters in peaceable, neutral Switzerland, it took as its badge the Swiss shield with the colors reversed— a red cross on a white field. Hence, the familiar name of the Red Cross.

the very poor, who thus became poorer. The ironic effect of extending Piedmont's liberal fiscal system to the primitive Naples and Sicily was to impoverish the latter and to increase the gulf between rich and poor. In this respect, the southerners were worse off after unification than before, and they showed their dissatisfaction by a continuance of the methods of protest at which they had become adept during the period of Bourbon tyranny— tax evasion, banditry, gang wars, larceny, assassination, and frequent riots. Most of the political disorders which took place in the thirty years after 1870—and they were incessant—were in the southern provinces of the mainland, or in Sicily.

The evils were compounded by the administrative system imported from Turin. It was highly centralized. The prefects and subprefects, appointed from Rome by the Minister of the Interior, in effect governed the provinces, which had replaced the old state boundaries. The administration was, moreover, top-heavily northern and Piedmontese. It was natural that the inexperienced south should have a smaller share in cabinet posts, civil-service jobs, and judgeships. But the country south of the Po was governed almost like a colony. Both high policy and administrative practice favored the economy and development of the Po provinces.

Moreover, the poverty and inexperience of the southerners was largely untempered by educational advances. Italy, mainly for budgetary reasons, remained among the most backward of western powers in its establishment of schools. In 1879, for example, illiterate Italy spent twenty-eight million lire on education, while literate France spent the equivalent of fifty-five million. In the north, schools were privately or locally maintained, while in the south there were no resources for them.

The difficulties of government were further complicated by the question of the Church. The government and dynasty already had a long history of anti-clericalism behind them in Piedmont. When Rome was successfully invaded and annexed to the Kingdom in 1870 Pope Pius IX protested vigorously, condemned the government in strong terms, excommunicated its leaders, turned his throne to the wall and proclaimed himself a prisoner of the state. The Italian government, exceedingly sensitive on religious questions, sought to behave with generosity, while refusing to yield its new capital. The parliament passed the Law of Guarantees, which provided for the sovereignty and independence of the Pope in the Vatican and for a suitable payment to the Church to replace the revenues lost with the Church States. While the payments were in fact made, the Vatican did not recognize the Law of Guarantees. Catholics continued to be ordered to exclude themselves from Italian politics, and the Pope continued to proclaim himself a prisoner.

This strange situation, heart-rending for the devout, had repercussions in every area of Italian life. The Church was intertwined with education, with charity and social services, with the daily routine of villagers and noblemen. The cleavage between government and Faith led many political thinkers, bred in the secular and anti-clerical tradition of the liberalism which Pius IX so vigorously denounced, to seek the extirpation of the clergy from Italian life. The devout reacted accordingly. Opposing extremist groups stirred political difficulties and profoundly affected foreign policy: the anti-clericals drew their inspiration from Republican

France, the clericalists from Apostolic Austria. Pro-clericals thus favored an abandonment of the territorial claims against Austria and a policy of amity with it,
while anti-clericals sought to enflame nationalist antagonism to the Habsburg
empire.

ITALIAN POLITICS, 1870–1896:
THE BIRTH OF TRASFORMISMO

Under the circumstances, it was perhaps surprising that Italy was as well
run as it was, and that disaster engulfed neither the economy nor the constitution.
The relative ease with which successive cabinets rode the storms of hardship and
periodic revolt was due partly to the tranquility of Europe as a whole and to the
general economic advances which the world was making. More specifically, in
the early years, the absence of national upsets was due to the impetus of unification: the right, heirs of Cavour and the great tradition, governed cautiously and
prudently, if with little positive accomplishment. Their leaders, men of personal
distinction and integrity, were not first-rate statesmen, but they succeeded in
putting the administrative system into working order, in modestly expanding communications and transport services, and in balancing the budget.

In 1876, the right was defeated in the national elections. It was divided
and without a program, and it had little left to offer the country. The left, the
heirs of Garibaldi and Mazzini, gained the majority in the Chamber. For two
years, the country floundered under several cabinets, the last dominated by
Zanardelli, a fire-eating radical who unleashed the anti-Austrian nationalists and
talked of drastic reforms. His leftism was sufficiently violent to frighten his moderate colleagues, although it was highly theoretical and largely bombast. Several
ministers resigned, and the prime minister was forced to follow. The left was
divided between those who demanded basic changes—lower and fairer taxes, a
wider franchise, and an anti-clerical policy—and those who sought in the main to
continue the old liberal tradition. It was to the second (and smaller) group that
the king turned for the next prime minister, Agostino Depretis.

The Depretis ministry coincided, within a few months, with the death of
the king, Victor Emmanuel II, and of the Pope, Pius IX. The new king, Humbert I (1878–1900), and the new Pope, Leo XIII (reigned 1878–1903), were
less involved in the old problems than their predecessors, and the old political
issues were dying. A new era began, marked by hopes for a general conciliation
and an easing of political tensions.

Although no real changes took place in the structure of the country and
no real advance was made toward solving its problems, a degree of tranquility did
ensue. The decay of the old political groups gave Depretis an opportunity to
practice a new technique of government which evaded factional disputes and
basic issues alike. The technique consisted simply of seeking parliamentary support wherever it could be found. Chosen as a moderate leftist in a parliament
dominated by the left, Depretis realized that he could not govern without the

support of the right. Rightists were brought into his cabinet, and the policies which were adopted were compromises between opposing principles. This method of cabinets selected entirely on the basis of political expediency, without regard for the beliefs of the men and groups who supported them, was known as *trasformismo* and was the basis of Italian ministerial government from 1876 to 1922.

A deputy was induced to abandon his principles by the emoluments of supporting the party in power—a cabinet post for himself, government jobs for his friends. The voters were induced to vote for his re-election by political machines which developed rapidly: bosses, fed on government jobs and bribes, controlled the voters. This involved, among other things, an increase in government jobs. Italy began to bristle with party officials, which in turn increased the tax burden. *Trasformismo* meant that no systematic policy, principle, or program could ever be adopted. This meant, in turn, that government was a purely makeshift and practical affair, devoid of the idealism which figured so consistently and colorfully in all political utterances of all Italians. It also meant that the deputies who supported the government were likely to be in trouble with their electors—leftists elected on a platform of repealing the hated tax on flour-milling in 1876 found themselves supporting its continuation, since the government (dependent on rightist votes) was forced to do so.

Politicians involved in *trasformismo* could not, of course, admit publicly that the system which they supported was crassly and squalidly practical. They continued to speak in highly colored terms about ideals, and to blacken their opponents' reputations with dark accusations. As a result, Italian political life degenerated into a mixture of rhetoric and name-calling, wholly without relation to the realities, which were dealt with quietly in the deputies' palace of Montecitorio in Rome or in the village bar where the local bosses met.

Trasformismo meant that parliamentary government was replaced by the dictatorship of a prime minister who maintained his position through corruption. Each succeeding practitioner of the technique perfected it further. Idealistic but impotent opposition naturally also increased. The "parliamentary dictatorships" thus installed were on the whole feeble and precarious, and they dared only sporadically to interfere very seriously with the civil liberties which the liberal constitution guaranteed. The press, while venal, continued to be more or less free. Elections, manipulated and corrupt, continued to be held. Concessions were from time to time made to the rising demands for democratic suffrage. But a pattern had been established: strong-man government based on sordid political deals and opposed by an increasingly impractical and rather demagogic, although frequently sincere, idealism. It was a pattern complemented by the national facts of disunity combined with rather pyrotechnical jingoism. Taken together with backwardness and hardship they were to prove in the end catastrophic.

By the time he died in 1887, the inventor of this peculiar mode of government had chalked up a few solid accomplishments. The milling tax had been gradually reduced (although the total volume of taxation increased). Some advance was made in the building of schools. The work of extending telegraphs, roads, and railroads (whose construction was a minor miracle of engineering, given the Italian terrain) progressed. The franchise was widened, to include two million instead of half a million voters. A colony of a sort had been acquired on the shores of the Red Sea—named Eritrea and equipped with the worst climate in the world. Italy had joined the Austro-German Alliance, drowning its dislike of the Habsburg empire in its need for diplomatic security and in the intense annoyance with France. Anti-French feeling arose after the French annexation of Tunisia, which the Italians had regarded as their proper sphere of expansion. The French seizure of it threw them into an attitude of hostility toward France which was to color Italian actions for decades to come.

In the last years of the Depretis government, however, ominous developments took place. The acquisition of Eritrea was accompanied by a military setback, which turned into a disaster, at the hands of the tribesmen. And the tension with France was accompanied by a financial crisis in which, to raise urgently needed revenues, import duties were raised. The French retaliated with new duties on Italian goods. A first-rate tariff war ensued, and trade between the two countries came virtually to a standstill. France was not only Italy's most important market, it was overwhelmingly its major source of supply for many manufactured goods and most raw materials. The consequence of the tariff war was the collapse of Italian commerce, impoverishment of the peasants, and unemployment of the workers. This led, not unnaturally, to protests and riots, one of which amounted virtually to a Sicilian revolution. It was a difficult legacy which Depretis left, upon dying, to his successor.

That successor, Francesco Crispi, (1819–1901), was the most colorful and the strongest of the strong-men. A Sicilian and a former extreme leftist, he had gradually espoused most of the causes he had once detested—the monarchy, the extremely hierarchical class structure, colonialism, the Triple Alliance, and extreme jingoism. He had thus earned the hatred of the left. Moreover, his regime was marked by frequent failures, culminating in an unexampled military disaster in Africa. In spite of these liabilities, however, his force of personality, and the efficacy of *trasformismo*, permitted him to remain in power during two ministries —1887–1891 and 1893–1896—amounting to seven years.

He was sufficiently strong to carry out several controversial but useful measures—a Health Act, and a measure extending local government powers. He rescued the currency from its perpetual precarious state. But, more than any other of the prime ministers, he attacked civil liberties: first, through a bill practically prohibiting political parades, and second, through his bloodthirsty suppression of the riots of 1893, when workers in Sicily and other parts of Italy rose against what amounted to famine conditions. Moreover, he pursued a policy of irresponsible adventure in foreign policy, characterized by a reckless antagonism to France (it was rumored that he hoped to use the Triple Alliance to back an attack on France), and by the attempt to annex the African empire of Ethiopia. This venture led to war, and to the defeat in 1896 of an Italian army at Adowa, by untrained and unequipped Ethiopian tribesmen. It was the first time that a non-European army had decisively defeated a European one, and Europe as well as Italy was shocked by the disaster. It seemed clear that an almost criminal incompetence had marked the preparations for war, and in 1896 Crispi resigned.

His successor, Rudini, faced further unrest. Defeat and continued famine gave grounds for further riots, sparked now by socialist organizers. The riots began in the south and extended into the north, climaxing in the industrial city of Milan, where serious risings lasted for three days and over a hundred citizens were shot by the troops. Order was at last reimposed, to the accompaniment of censorship and mass arrests. National dissatisfaction prevailed, and there were cries of outrage. In 1898, Rudini resigned. A frightened Chamber selected the extreme conservative, General Pelloux, as prime minister. There were further troubles, and further repressions. Efforts were made to govern by decree, without parliamentary approval, and even to suppress parliamentary institutions. Civil liberties were further abridged and police control extended. But the deputies clung to their prerogatives; conservative, disheartened by defeat and terrified by social unrest, they nevertheless distrusted the authoritarian methods of Pelloux. He was forced to resign. After several years of almost total ministerial confusion, and unavailing efforts at far-reaching social reform by a weak left government, the third and last of the parliamentary dictators and masters of *trasformismo* was called to power. Giovanni Giolitti (1842–1928) became prime minister in 1903.

THE RISE OF INDUSTRY AND SOCIALISM

The repressions and experiments of the period from 1896 to 1903 resulted in part from the alarm which propertied and conservative people felt at the rise of the Socialist party. It was the specter of a drastic revolution against the social order which caused the government and the governing classes to lose their poise so seriously. And indeed, while it did not in the event lead to any serious readjustments of the social order, the mushroom development of Italian socialism was a symptom of revolutionary changes in Italian life. The generation of the unification had now disappeared, and with it the easy avoidance of basic issues. Gone, too, were the old problems and disputes, and the old intellectual lethargy which had made the period around 1870 the least creative, in art and literature, of any Italian age since the fall of Rome. A sort of renaissance had begun in the 1890's.

The most tangible and earliest indication of the new shape of the Italian nation was the growth of industry. There had always been, in the north, small manufactures, mostly for the local market. By 1914, Italy was exporting considerable quantities of manufactured goods as well as producing for an expanding domestic market. There were several consequences: an increased dependence on imports of the raw materials which were wholly lacking in the homeland; a further spread in the economic gap between south and north, where the industry was almost wholly located; the rise of an organized urban industrial working class, largely literate and intensely articulate; and the corresponding spread of unease and alarm among the well-to-do.

The industrial development started (as it usually did) in the textile field. By World War I, Italy was exporting $120,000,000 worth of silk and silk cloth and a quarter of that value of cotton goods (total textile exports thiry-five years earlier had been under $5,000,000). The old exports—fruits, olive oil, vegetables, and wood products—were still considerable, but none of them was worth as much in foreign trade as the entirely new item of chemical products. For both domestic use and foreign trade, Italy was also building boats, automobiles, and electrical goods. In the two latter fields the Italians were pioneers.

Much of this industry was concentrated in Milan and Turin, the old commercial cities. Here, where adequate capital and skilled labor were available, there was a rapid growth of labor organization. Unions developed quickly. As in most continental countries, they were from the beginning affiliated with socialist parties and politics, and, as in all Latin countries, they early displayed a proclivity for strikes and violence. By 1903, when Giolitti began his long reign, the Socialist party possessed several newspapers—one of them, the *Avanti* of Milan, of national importance—and thirty-three members of the Chamber of Deputies. The language of the Socialists was frequently intemperate, their avowed doctrines were Marxist, and their methods, on occasion of strikes or agitations, forceful. It was scarcely surprising that the people long accustomed to an unchallenged enjoyment of influence and property in Italy should have been deeply alarmed.

The Socialists were, however, deeply divided among themselves. The divisions (publicly concealed, for the most part, and not generally perceptible in all their depth until the Libyan War crisis in 1911–1912) reflected the highly individualistic and factional political tendencies of Italy—and of Latinity generally. They also corresponded to similar divisions among socialists everywhere. There were, in the first place, orthodox revolutionaries—pure Marxists who saw no possible good in the existing "bourgeois" order and operated on the assumption that it must be overthrown. These were opposed by moderates (who corresponded roughly to the British Laborites or to the German Revisionists) who sought to work within the existing constitution and social order to achieve immediate amelioration of working class hardships and grievances. Thirdly, there were strong syndicalist elements—stronger than in any other country except France. The syndicalists, followers of Sorel, were primarily industrial organizers and practitioners, on principle, of civil and industrial violence. They anticipated the early crumbling of the state, and their violence (particularly in regard to the Church) was greater, their language more inflammatory, than those of other groups. The endless polemics and conflicts among the socialist theorists and writers struck sparks of a rather high literary—or at least journalistic—quality. Quick and shrewd minds were stimulated. But they naturally led to animosities and divisions which reflected the entirely different philosophies of life which the various leaders held.

The Socialist party was highly organized and at times reasonably well-disciplined—much more so than any other in Italy. Indeed, it was the first Italian political party in the modern sense (as distinct from a vague faction or "grouping"). It was, however, exceedingly fragile. Giolitti knew and played upon its weaknesses, and brought about its cleavage.

It was not only on the left, however, that the ebullition of the turn of the century was throwing up new ideas and new movements. A new nationalism was also being born. In the old days, the extreme nationalists had been men like Mazzini who thought in terms of Italian unity as part of a confederacy of free nations. Now, in Italy as elsewhere, nationalism was acquiring a new meaning. It was more a case of Italy against the world. A group of intellectuals was evolving an elaborate philosophy suggesting that "all history" indicated that true creativity and progress were possible only in a highly united and expansive national state. Most leaders of the movement were almost purely theoretical and did not advocate aggression or war, but their writings were used by those who did.

The most famous of them, Gabriele D'Annunzio, was Italy's best-known poet. He was erratic, passionate, irresponsible, and influential, and he came in time to epitomize the most extreme and quixotic of Italy's national aspirations— and, before long, to advocate war and violence as a means to national "fulfillment."

Less bellicose and far more respectable were the two principal philosophers of early twentieth-century Italy, Benedetto Croce and Giovanni Gentile. Both of them were serious students of Marxism, with which they sympathized. Both of them, however, moved *via* syndicalism toward a new doctrine which they called Futurism, and both of them were enormously influential. In Italy, perhaps more than anywhere else, the professional intellectual and thinker is attended to by the rest of society. And while Croce never espoused the more violent forms of nationalism, and Gentile did not do so until after the war, their acceptance of violence and their eagerness for national "regeneration" sometimes blended with the views of the more inflammatory and rigid expansionists. Their arguments, so interpreted and widely read, affected a whole generation, even though they were couched in the most abstruse metaphysical terms.

In still other spheres, a new and vital effusion of ideas was in course. Under the pontificate of Leo XIII, the Church had sought to interpret the possibility of social justice and social progress in terms of Catholic doctrine. The result had been a series of encyclicals designed to encourage Catholic workingmen to seek their material salvation within the limits of orthodoxy. This had led throughout the world to the evolution of Catholic social theories and to progressive Catholic Action groups. Moreover, circumstances had dictated a working compromise between Church and Italian state which led to increasing mutual toleration. With the ascension of the Papal Throne by the saintly Pius X in 1903, a formal relaxation of tension began. Catholics were first permitted, and then encouraged, to participate in politics. While the Pope continued to be, officially, a prisoner in the Vatican, aspiring Catholic politicians were now no longer prisoners of their consciences.

The result of these two facts was the development of religious-political movements. Some of them (espousing the heresy of "Modernism") erred theologically and had to be denounced and banned by the Church. But some, under the intelligent and energetic leader Father Don Luigi Sturzo, remained perfectly orthodox and gathered able men and numerous followers who attacked the corruption, the landlord-dominated society, the oppression of the poor. They were shortly to coalesce into the second of Italy's major political parties, the Popular party—and were, many years later after the interlude of Fascism, to be transformed into the governing majority of the Italian Republic.

These movements, and others, indicated that the younger generation of

Italians was eager for change, was capable of original and forceful thought, and suggested that the old forms and malpractices could not long endure. They continued to do so, however, thanks to the extraordinary skill of Giolitti.

The prime minister adjusted *trasformismo* to the dynamic circumstances of twentieth-century Italy. It was clear that parliamentary majorities must be obtained through the acquisition of support among the new forces, and he set about his task with vigor and effectiveness. To each of them he offered something new and important. The consequence was that the new forces were divided among themselves. Most of them were inclined to do business with Giolitti—but their more intractable and ferocious members were left outside the parliamentary majorities as agitators and revolutionists.

To the Socialists, with whom he made repeated deals and bargains, and whose teeth he eventually drew, Giolitti offered democracy. The manhood suffrage bill, explicitly designed to meet Socialist exigencies, was passed in 1912. Later, Socialists were taken into the cabinet. Social reforms, long demanded, were granted.

By 1912, the majority of socialist deputies were prepared to support Giolitti. The syndicalist minority split off, over the issue of the Libyan War of 1911 against Turkey, which was undertaken to acquire the Turkish provinces of Tripoli and Cyrenaica for Italy. It was a case of pure and sordid aggression, indefensible on any abstract grounds but on the whole popular in Italy. The inflexible Socialists who resisted it captured control of *Avanti;* the new, anti-war editor chosen was a rising young fiery republican and anti-clerical syndicalist by the name of Benito Mussolini.

It was characteristic of Giolitti's skill that he avoided taking the responsibility for measures which might irritate his highly diverse supporters. In 1913, after the first elections held under the widened franchise law, he turned the power over to a nominee, Antonio Salandra. Salandra was faced (as Giolitti knew he would be) with a recurrence of social unrest, sponsored mainly by the extreme Socialists under Mussolini. These commotions, involving strikes and assassinations and riots, centered in Mussolini's home territory of Emilia. But while they had nothing to do with provoking them, the rest of the Socialists could hardly abstain from criticism when the police and army used the accustomed strong-arm methods to quell the populace. The blame for the spilt blood fell on Salandra, not on Giolitti—although the prime minister was his appointee and his puppet.

In similar ways, Giolitti wooed and won considerable portions of nationalist and conservative, and also Catholic, parliamentary supporters. To each group he promised (and provided) congenial measures. He reached an understanding with the pro-clericals for electoral support (aimed from the Catholic viewpoint at stemming the growth of atheistic Red Socialism), although he also backed open anti-clericals when they agreed to vote for him. To the nationalists, eager for the annexation of Austria's Italian provinces, he offered support for the French in foreign affairs, slackening the ties of the Triple Alliance—which remained in formal existence, however, to appease conservative pro-clericals, who were friendly to Catholic Austria. To all, he offered law and order, a continuation of the rapid expansion of industry and national income, and minor reforms affecting the now prosperous Treasury, charitable institutions, and the civil service.

All in all, Italy was probably as efficiently governed under Giolitti as at any time during its modern history, but it was governed by corruption and by compromise. Voters were bribed and suborned. And the parliamentarians who were led into supporting the prime minister lost their reputations and their standards of values. *Trasformismo* had achieved its greatest triumph and its greatest squalor.

THE COMING OF WAR

The effect of the Giolitti regime was to leave the leadership of those groups not prepared to engage in political deals in the hands of extremists, both socialist and nationalist. A serious citizen who was disgusted by the government found no alternatives except such inflammatory and highly anticonstitutional groups. The majority of Italians were not prepared to turn against the regime in 1914. Nor were the revolutionary dissenters as yet able to unite with one another. It was adversity, and World War I, which dissolved the remaining confidence in the parliamentary regime.

Italy, long if reluctantly united to the Triple Alliance, had in the decade prior to the outbreak of war, been re-establishing its friendship with France, so rudely shaken by Depretis and Crispi. The fact was that Austria and Germany now had little to offer Italy, while the opposing camp, France and Russia, had no special interest in blocking Italy's aspirations. Loudly voiced by nationalists, these lay mainly in two areas—North Africa and the Adriatic. The former involved the acquisition of Turkish provinces, the latter of Austrian. Italy won French and Russian consent to the attack on Turkey in 1911, which led to the annexation of the Libyan desert. It was clear that only through the defeat of Austria could the Adriatic provinces be acquired. Italians were therefore extremly loath to enter the war on the side of their allies, Austria and Germany, and they found adequate legal grounds for not doing so. Italy, in August of 1914, proclaimed itself neutral.

The Salandra ministry, under the guidance of Giolitti, now pursued the Giolittian tradition in fine style: Italian participation in the war was, in effect, offered to the highest bidder. The Allies bid higher. They offered to Italy, in case of victory, very extensive tracts of Austrian real estate, including not only the strictly Italian regions of Trent and Trieste but the Bolzano district of the Tyrol, purely German, and much of the Dalmatian coast (across the Adriatic from Italy) which was mainly Slavic. They also were generous with the territory of Turkey, and agreed that Italy should have about a quarter of Asia Minor once the Turkish proprietors were disposed of. These inducements fortified Italy's natural proclivities toward the democratic west and the traditional friendship with Britain. In 1915, in May, Italy declared war on Austria-Hungary.

The bargaining, only thinly concealed behind diplomatic secrecy, was outrageous. But the war was at first supported by the people who were most critical of the government's methods. Nationalists were eager for the new territory. Sincere liberals, democrats and idealists, enthusiastically supported the war of democracy against the supposedly autocratic Central Powers. For once, Italy was united. But military events dispelled the unity. Stalemate on the exceedingly difficult Austrian front was followed by catastrophe. In the fall of 1917, the Italians were routed, and it looked for a time as if they might have to withdraw from the war. Only able administration and abundant support from France saved the situation after Caporetto.

Recriminations naturally followed. The government said that national and especially army morale had been undermined by socialist propaganda. Socialists said that nobody could be expected to support with zest a war so sordidly begun and so badly administered, and that in any case the nation was half-starved from shortages and economic disorganization. The nationalists, saying that the government's lack of idealism had deformed and dispirited the war effort, called in ringing tones for a National Rebirth. General dissatisfaction prevailed, and the economic situation deteriorated dangerously.

The end of the war found Italy faced with a breakdown not only of its economy but, it seemed, of the very fabric of its society, ready for desperate measures to find a substitute for the dusty and venal expediency of the parliamentary monarchy. None of the great problems had been solved—regional division and inequality, a stratified and oppressive class structure, and abysmal poverty, persisted as always. Over them had been plastered the new industrial wealth, in much the same way that a generation earlier the constitution of Piedmont had been plastered over the disunited peninsula. Extremist criticism was louder than ever. The destinies of Cavour's kingdom were about to fall into bizarre hands.

41

RUSSIA'S FIRST
INDUSTRIAL AND
POLITICAL
REVOLUTIONS

Russia like other European states from 1870 to 1914 played its part in the European state-system, which was becoming a world state-system. Russian expansion in Asia, and the Russo-Japanese War of 1904–1905, evidence its participation in imperialist enterprises. Russia also shared in the other great movements of those years—industrialization, urban growth, the formation of cartels and labor unions, the spread of socialism, and the dangerous and inspiring prospect that the lower classes would enter politics. Superficially, as at the end of the eighteenth century, Russia looked like a European country with typical European interests. The serfs were long since free. There were industries, big businessmen, bankers, labor unions, and after 1905 even political parties and a parliament.

As in the time of Catherine the Great, however, the European façade hid a rough kind of reality. Russia was indeed having an industrial revolution by the turn of the century, but it was taking place in the midst of land-hungry peasants, and to a high degree at their expense. Almost simultaneously, the Russians were undertaking, in the revolution of 1905, to shift from absolute monarchy to representative government. In making these changes, Russia had available Europe's most advanced ideas, but in its rude environment these ideas took on an explosive quality which they had lost in the west. It was as if Russia were trying to solve

677

IMPERIAL ARMS OF RUSSIA. Like the Habsburgs, the Romanovs of Russia used the double-headed eagle as the emblem of their empire. In the Russian case, the eagle indicated the tradition that Moscow was the Third Rome—the legal and religious heir of the Byzantine empire after the latter's suppression by the Moslem Turks in 1453. The shield on the eagle's breast carries the arms of the principality of Moscow, the cradle of modern Russia, with the equestrian figure of Saint George, the Muscovite patron. On the wings are scattered the shields of the provinces which composed the empire.

all at once the problems which Western Europe had taken in turn: the problem of land and peasants; the problem of absolutism and representative government; the problem of working conditions in the early stages of industrialization. The strain was very great, especially since there was no respite from international politics.

THE STATE, TO 1905

When Alexander II was assassinated in 1881, he was succeeded by his son Alexander III, a powerful, hard-working man with a strong will and little imagination. His reign, from 1881 to his death in 1894, is sometimes referred to as an "enlightened despotism," and it is true that Alexander made some good appointments, consulted with experts, and brought about reforms in the interest of the peasants. Redemption dues were reduced, the poll tax was abolished, and a Peasant Bank was founded. But Alexander's distrust of political change was not unnaturally strengthened by the murder of his father, and the keynote of the reign was internal order.

One of his first acts was to drop the Loris-Melikov plan for consultation with representatives of the zemstvos and towns. The conspirators involved in the assassination of Alexander II were rounded up, their leaders executed, and their revolutionary organizations virtually destroyed. Something resembling martial law was inaugurated and continued until the Revolution of 1905.

Alexander's son, Nicholas II (1894–1917), last of the Russian emperors, was a weak-willed, charming man, devoted to his family and extremely considerate of those with whom he dealt personally. Like Louis XVI, he was usually under the influence either of his wife or of the last person with whom he had talked. He meant to carry on unchanged his father's autocratic regime; yet he was so reluctant to face unpleasantness that when he dismissed a minister he usually did so by mail. Strong-minded people who had access to Nicholas could persuade him to follow a personal policy which contradicted that of a ministry. Such a monarch could lead a blameless private life and win the sympathy of those who knew him well, yet at the same time do nothing to soften the injustices beyond his immediate entourage or check his country's course toward war and revolution.

The key problem in Russia's political life between 1881 and 1905 was the one inherited from the reign of Alexander II, the liberator of the serfs. The reforms of Alexander II had been made in self-defense by the autocratic regime, without checking the autocracy except at the local level. In the peasant villages and groups of villages (cantons, volosts) a measure of self-government had been permitted. Above this basic peasant government were the district and provincial assemblies, or zemstvos, with limited functions, and in addition, the elected city governments. At the national level, however, and reaching down into country and town for police and other affairs, the czar's bureaucracy continued to rule. There were thus, side by side, two systems, the one autocratic, the other representative.

Each of these two systems tended to encroach upon the other. Alexander III and Nicholas II were determined to check any further advance of representative institutions. Alexander III let the bureaucracy begin to overwhelm the local representative bodies. Nicholas warned at the start of his reign that the extension of zemstvo practices to the national level was a "senseless dream." Yet in spite of their restrictions the zemstvos continued to do much good work and to develop men experienced in looking out for community interests without the direction of the centralized bureaucracy. The zemstvos were seedbeds of political liberalism. When the autocracy failed to keep up with the times —and the pressure of the times was great—the zemstvo men and their sympathizers were bound to push for a system of national representation.

To anyone familiar with Western European and American history the most insistent question is why Russia was so slow in bringing the issue of representative government to a head. In the nineteenth century, when Western Europe was moving away from absolute monarchy, Russia's bureaucratic machine, the tool of autocracy, was being perfected without opposition from the rank and file of the nobility. The latter were contented with the absolutist system so long as their privileged social position was maintained. When the Crimean War dramatized weaknesses which had long been a matter of concern, the czar and his bureaucracy made reforms which left the nobles substantial advantages. In the decades after 1861 the autocratic regime continued to be based on the support of this declining section of society. The fears and prejudices of the nobles were only reinforced by the growing contrast between Russia and Western Europe, and by the bloody violence of 1881.

Even as late as the end of the nineteenth century the Russian nobles lacked the incentive of competition with a strong middle class. In the absence of rivals and critics who commanded attention, the nobility was slow to realize the inadequacy of the czar and the autocracy as guarantors of public order. When social unrest was becoming serious at the end of the century, the danger appeared so great that moderate reformers tended to be regarded as subversive. This condition handicapped what liberals there were and kept the upper classes from standing together for a program of change. The process of limiting the autocracy, like the emancipation of the serfs, was postponed until defeat in war and the danger of domestic explosion made it appear unavoidable.

If the Orthodox Church had not been (since Peter the Great) kept in a position of subservience to the state, its high officials probably would have enjoyed greater respect, popularity, and public influence and been able to temper the autocracy.

There were men, like the railroad builder and industrializer Sergei Witte, Minister of Finance from 1892 to 1903, who tried to modernize the society without touching the autocracy. This kind of program was theoretically possible but in practice a failure owing to the very nature of autocracy—when there was a weak ruler, there was a kind of anarchy at the top of the state. Russia's experience with Far Eastern imperialism and the war with Japan will illustrate this point.

As related elsewhere, the three conservative eastern powers, Russia, Prussia, and Austria—the partitioners of Poland—had stood together during much of the nineteenth century. The Romanov, Hohenzollern, and Habsburg dynasties were drawn together by their common interest in social conservatism and maintenance of the partition of Poland, but were increasingly driven apart by Russian-Austrian rivalry in the Balkans. Eventually the rift between Russia and Austria-Hungary became permanent and Germany aligned itself with Austria-Hungary. The extremely conservative Emperor Alexander III of Russia found himself, in 1894, allied with the Third French Republic. French loans poured into Russia, and Franco-Russian cooperation in the Far East ensued, contributing to the Russo-Japanese War of 1904–1905.

Russia had continuously expanded toward the east, and in the intervals when its Balkan ambitions were rebuffed by the European powers, had accelerated this expansion. Such was the case in the late 1880's and 1890's. In the 1890's Witte hoped that the Trans-Siberian railway would win for Russia an advantage in trade with China and would strengthen the Pacific fleet to a point where in an emergency it could control the western Pacific. Witte was an imperialist, but he was opposed to dangerous military adventures. He was not, however, able to keep the impressionable emperor from being won over to an extremely reckless Far Eastern policy advocated by the Minister of the Interior, Plehve, and by certain financial speculators and adventurers.

When Japan defeated China in 1894–1895, Russian diplomacy helped to limit Japan's gains, and Russian loans to China opened the door to Russian penetration of Manchuria by way of railway concessions and the building of a naval base at Port Authur. After the Chinese Boxer Rebellion against the western powers in 1900, Russian troops remained in Manchuria. Moreover, Russian soldiers in the guise of lumberjacks began to penetrate North Korea. The Japanese regarded Korea, which they had detached from China in 1895, as theirs, and they considered Russian penetration there a strategic threat to their home islands. They secured in 1898 a Russo-Japanese agreement to respect one another's interests in Manchuria and Korea. Russia also responded to pressure from Britain, Japan, and the United States by promising in 1903 that Russian troops would be withdrawn from Manchuria.

But friends of the Emperor Nicholas persuaded him to dismiss the cautious Witte in 1903 and to continue an aggressive policy in both Manchuria and Korea. The Minister of the Interior, Plehve, who was a reactionary more concerned with keeping order than with economic development, urged Nicholas to consider the possibility that a war would build up the prestige of the monarchy. Japanese requests for another agreement were ignored, and the Japanese prepared for war.

Japanese warships in February, 1904, struck at Port Arthur, and in April attacked Vladivostok. Landings above Port Arthur cut it off from the sea and forced it, finally, to surrender in January, 1905. Land battles near Mukden were victories for the Japanese armies. Russia sent its Baltic fleet around the world between October 1904 and May 1905, only to have it sunk at Tsushima Straits. Russia was not in condition for a long war. Few Russians had any interest in the Far East. Russia's investments there were a drain on the treasury, and trade with China was negligible. At home revolution was brewing. In July, 1904, Plehve had been murdered by a Socialist Revolutionary. In January, 1905, occurred "Bloody Sunday," the irresponsible firing of soldiery into an unarmed petitioning crowd. With the mediation of Theodore Roosevelt the war came to an end in the Treaty of Portsmouth, New Hampshire (September, 1905), by which Russia gave up its interests in Korea, its rights in the Liaotung Peninsula, and the southern half of Sakhalin Island. Prominent in the Russian delegation which broke its instructions to make these concessions and win peace was Sergei Witte, who was to play an important role in the Revolution of 1905.

THE SOCIETY

Russia had felt the challenge of Western European society since before Peter the Great. Since the 1830's westernizers and Slavophiles had quarreled over what to imitate and what to spurn. After the emancipation of the serfs in 1861, Russian society seemed to be a compromise between Europe's old regime and its nineteenth century.

Emancipation was a step toward equal citizenship for all, but there still remained differences of legal status. The peasants were a group apart, with their own local government, courts, and collective responsibility for taxes and redemption payments, while nobles were still privileged, and townsmen still remained in various classifications peculiar to their situations. Not all property was free—subject to purchase and sale—for peasant allotments were held collectively. Although peasants as individuals could buy or rent additional land, those who were shareholders in village communities could not forsake their responsibilities or leave without permission. The nobles, moreover, still had their own corporate organizations. These conditions were to give a peculiar shape to the development of agriculture and industry.

Russia's population growth is indicated by the following table.

Date	Population	% rural	% urban
1859	74,000,000	94.3	5.7
1897	129,000,000	87.4	12.6
1914	170,000,000	80	20

The rapid growth of total population contributed to the straitened condition of the peasantry and to the intensity of their desire for more land, which played so important a part in the twentieth-century revolutions. The growth of towns, although small by Western European standards, was rapid. More important, town growth was mostly concentrated in a few big cities, particularly St. Petersburg and Moscow, and made them politically vulnerable to the new labor movements.

Russia remained primarily rural and agricultural, however. The key fact about Russian agriculture was its backwardness and low output. It is true that grain production increased faster than the population. Yet in spite of this improvement—which is measured against previous low levels of accomplishment—Russian methods lagged far behind those of more advanced countries. The Russian wheat harvest in 1900 amounted to about 406 pounds per acre, in comparison with 868 in the United States and 1,109 in Germany.

Russian agriculture was held back by the tools and methods of the peasants, who for the most part went on farming as their fathers and grandfathers had done. Emancipation had, after 1861, placed land (usually less than they had had before) in the possession of peasant villages, the *mirs,* and arranged for them to pay for it as if paying off a mortgage (except that they owned and paid collectively). There was nothing in this arrangement likely to improve agricultural methods. The need to make redemption payments to the state, combined with less land with which to earn them, meant that in one way or another the peasants had to go back to work for their former masters. Activities outside of the collective village economy—work for wages, share-cropping, sometimes renting of land and hiring of labor—differentiated the able and energetic from the dull and lazy and unlucky. Side by side with the community enterprise private enterprise grew up. In spite of the *mir,* the peasantry was being sifted into owners and wage laborers, and this process was encouraged by the increased need for money in daily life—not only for redemption payments but also for household articles which had once been produced at home.

The sum of all these circumstances was that a minority of enterprising farmers prospered outside the restraints of the village economy, and thereby improved output, while the great majority of the peasantry used the old methods on less land and spent the rest of their time working for someone else, usually with the same old tools and methods. Population growth simply made matters worse by reducing the amount of land per person.

This situation might not have been so serious if the Russian nobles had taken the leadership in improving agricultural output. But they lacked both capital and enterprise. Because so many of them had mortgaged their lands and serfs before 1861, the emancipation did not provide sufficient capital for modernization, and in any case the majority of Russian landowners were no more businesslike after emancipation than they had been before. The great majority went on borrowing money, selling parcels of land when they had to, and farming the rest through various share-cropping or other arrangements, all of which resulted in the same old scraping of the earth with the same meager results. Although financial necessity instead of legal serfdom now bound the peasantry to their former masters, the daily routine of the countryside was not much changed. Gradually the nobles lost possession of their land, and the more enterprising peasants and townsmen acquired much of it. Russian nobles in 1914 owned less than half as much land as they had owned in 1861.

On the other hand, it would be misleading to overlook the fact that among the nobles, as among the peasants, the abler and more enterprising were amassing properties. In the thirty years after 1861, nobles purchased about 40 percent of the land which was sold. Privately owned land (as distinguished from the collectively owned land of the villages) was, moreover, being concentrated in the hands of a minority. Most such land was in the form of huge estates of thousands of acres, while the private holdings acquired by the peasants were numerous but small in total acreage.

Concentration of land ownership in the hands of an efficient minority helped Russia to raise its total agricultural output in spite of the inefficiency of the majority of farmers. Although population was rising, there was grain left over to feed the towns and to export. Russia could begin to pay for its industrial revolution. But this is not the whole story. Much of the grain sent abroad or to the cities would not have been "left over" if the majority of the peasants had had their way. To understand the peasants' complaints one must see how Russia's entry into world trade and industrialization was adding new strains.

The following table will give some idea of Russia's industrial growth.

Year	No. Factories	Workmen (thousands)	Annual Output (millions of Rubles)
1870	26,300	435	500
1890	32,200	1,400	1,500
1912	29,900	2,900	5,700

The slow increase, followed by a drop, in number of factories reflects the important fact that Russian industry, coming late, and mainly in a few great centers, was nevertheless built on a large scale from the first. There were not many factories, but they were big ones. This fact has a bearing on Russia's vulnerability to European and other revolutionary ideas. Russia's increased output is borne out by the following:

RUSSIAN PRODUCTION IN MILLIONS OF TONS

	1860	1900	1913
Coal	.28	16.	36.
Steel	.0016	2.5	4.0

But a comparison with other countries shows Russia's relative position:

PRODUCTION IN MILLIONS OF TONS IN 1913

	U.S.	United Kingdom	Germany	France	Russia
Coal	509	287	190	40.8	36
Steel	31.3	7.7	18.3	4.7	4.

Russia was the least of the great powers industrially, but it is clear that by World War I it had developed a certain amount of industry. This fact helps account for Russia's important role in the war, even though the effort contributed to exhaustion and to revolution in 1917.

Russia's industrial development became rapid and conspicuous in the 1890's. Before that, it had been getting gradually under way, aided by a number of factors. The building of a railroad network on a large scale from the 1870's helped commerce and the metallurgical industry. The government had begun to sponsor industry. There were huge government contracts, high protective tariffs, close links between government officials and industrialists. Foreign investment was encouraged. To win the confidence of foreign investors in Russian government bonds, banks, and corporations, there had to be a sound currency, a favorable balance of trade, and a gold reserve. There also had to be taxes heavy enough to ensure that the government would be able to balance its budget. These things—especially railroad building (from the 1890's on, the state owned most of the railroads) and the gold standard (1897)—are associated with Sergei Witte's service as Minister of Finance from 1892 to 1903.

In terms of everyday life the Witte policies meant that the consumer had to pay high prices because of protective tariffs and heavy indirect taxes. Tax policies favored nobles' estates and inheritances and bore heavily on peasants. Because of his heavy taxes the peasant had to sell his grain and restrict his own consumption. If he worked full or part time for a well-to-do neighbor, or for one of the great landowners, he had to content himself with low wages, for the growing population provided plenty of competition for jobs. If he rented or bought land, he had to pay dearly, for the demand was great. Peasant land-hunger was part of the price Russia was paying for the great estates which were its best producers of a grain surplus. With tariffs, high prices, taxes, the rising population, and concentration of land ownership, it is fair to say that peasant sacrifices were to a large extent paying for Russia's industrial revolution. If there had been no wars and revolutions these policies might have helped the peasant eventually by building up industries and providing goods at low prices, but events took another course.

By 1897 there were more than two million factory workers. Many of them still had ties with their villages, but an industrial proletariat was forming. There were important strikes in St. Petersburg and Moscow in 1878, 1885, and 1896–1897. During the depression of 1899–1903 revolutionists organized political demonstrations, and there were some strikes of a political character. Labor unions were illegal before the Revolution of 1905 except for the short-lived experiment of the police official Zubatov who in 1902 set up a society of workers under police direction, only to see it get out of hand.

In addition to a new proletariat, there were also new groups in the middle class: westernized bankers, industrialists, promoters, and engineers, the kind of men championed by Witte. Some were given official ranks. Some of the middle class were old-style Russian merchants who had prospered in wholesale business, grain brokerage, or textile manufactures, men with little interest in culture or politics but often daring entrepreneurs. Few in number, both middle class types were for the most part politically conservative. In this they were like the Russian nobles who, largely created by the state and allied with it against the lower classes, had failed throughout the nineteenth century to limit autocracy.

1878–1883 by Olga Sakhnovskaya (Russian, 1902–   ). This wood engraving appeared in 1932 as part of a series on women's role in the revolutionary movement. (Philadelphia Museum of Art, Prints Division)

CONFLICTING SOCIAL THEORIES, 1870-1905

In the last decade of the life of the "Czar Liberator,"Alexander II, and contributing to his assassination in 1881, there occurred a new chapter in the history of the revolutionary movement in Russia. In the 1870's, reinforced by hordes of students recalled by the conservative government from study abroad, the Populists made an all-out effort to realize their dream of "going to the people." Their crusade was rebuffed in a manner at once ludicrous and tragic, as the peasants shrugged them off without comprehending their aim, and the police treated them as subversives. After 1876 a society, "Land and Freedom," turned to efforts to bring about a change of heart in the government. Some populists, after 1879, became the "Black Partition" party, dedicated to agrarian socialism. Others, yielding to the temptation to respond with violence to the police repression, determined to frighten the government and its officials into awareness of the need for reforms. A group known as the "People's Will" was formed, an through its "Executive Committee" made horrible the last years of Alexander II's reign with a series of atrocities, eventually setting their sights upon the Emperor himself, whom they killed with a bomb in 1881. But this success was a failure, for in the repression which followed the terrorist movement lost its most daring practitioners. Violence and counter-violence only hardened the autocracy.

In the period between 1881 and 1905 the contest between radicalism and reaction continued, with moderate liberalism gaining some ground. In general the 1880's were a period of repression. In the 1890's, however, unmistakable evidence of mass dissatisfaction with the agricultural settlement dating from emancipation, and with the conditions of Russia's new industrial revolution, put the regime on the defensive. Like the French Revolution of 1789 in Western Europe, the Emancipation of 1861 had stimulated thought about the structure of society. Like the Industrial Revolution in the west, the Russian economic changes at the end of the century suggested new possibilities of social organization. As always, Russia had the example of European practices and ideas and the urge to avoid Europe's mistakes.

The official philosophy of the government in the period from 1881 to 1905 was the "power and truth of the autocracy," which in his first imperial manifesto Alexander III promised to defend. The growth of nationalism in Europe, and its conspicuous progress in Germany and Italy, stimulated the self-consciousness of the many nationalities within the Russian Empire and brought forth from the Great Russians a heightened nationalism of their own. The government's policies of Russification of subject nationalities and enforcement of Orthodoxy in religion reflect this fact. Anti-semitism was an official policy of the government. The *Protocols of the Elders of Zion*, published in 1903 as proof of a Zionist conspiracy to rule the world, were fabricated by the political police. Pogroms against Jews, in which ignorant mobs gave vent to nationalist feelings and the urge to find scapegoats for their economic and social dissatisfactions, were not checked by the government. The old, reforming Slavophilism of the 1840's to 1860's had been replaced by a more chauvinistic variety much more prone to promote autocracy and imperialism. Since the defeat in the Crimean War of the 1850's and the checks to Russian ambitions in the Balkans there had also grown up a new Pan-Slavism. Unlike the more democratic aspirations of the Pan-Slav Congress at Prague in 1848, the Pan-Slav doctrine of the late nineteenth and early twentieth centuries emphasized the Russian mission to liberate and unite the Slavs and lead the struggle against Western (especially German and Magyar) Europe. Pan-Slavism was not official Russian policy, but many Russian officials were Pan-Slavists.

The outstanding example of Russian reactionary social philosophy in the late nineteenth century is provided by Konstantin Pobedonostsev (1827–1907), who besides being a distinguished jurist was tutor to both Alexander III and Nicholas II and also held office as Chief Procurator of the Holy Synod from 1880 to 1905. During much of this period he was probably the most influential man in Russia. He was widely traveled and well-educated, an accomplished linguist, a writer and translator who appreciated much that the west had to offer and had no objection to the spread of knowledge among a small elite of persons like himself. He was aware that different parts of the world had differences of culture and institutions, and was even willing to admit that representative government was probably appropriate in England and the United States. His ideal for Russia, however, was an absolute monarchy ruled by divine right by a shepherd czar whose duty was to care for the great multitude of essentially childish and irresponsible people. The latter should be managed through their sentiments, prejudices, habits, and faith rather than through attempts to educate their reason.

It was typical of late nineteenth-century Russia—and indeed of less highly developed societies generally when they came into contact with more highly developed ones—that such conservatism as Pobedonostsev's should exist side by side with the most radical social theories. Western Europe was spared this kind of sharp contrast, for in the days when an English or French variant of Pobedonostsev could occupy an important public office there were as yet no revolutionary movements to compare in size or appeal with, for example, Russian Marxism of the 1880's and after.

The first important Marxist in Russia was Georgi Plekhanov (1857–1918). He was a former Narodnik who like many others was discouraged by the movement's failure to reach the peasantry but could not approve of terrorism. Plekhanov absorbed European Social Democratic ideas in Switzerland in the 1880's and began to hope that the industrialization of Russia would create a proletariat capable of making the socialist revolution. He founded abroad in 1883 an "Emancipation of Labor" group. In 1898, after several failures, the Russian Social Democratic Labor party was founded.

Marxism had a doubly powerful appeal to the Russian revolutionary intelligentsia. Never before had they had on their side such a heavy armament. With its claim to scientific insight into the structure of society and the laws of historic change, Marxism convinced such men as Plekhanov that terrorism and the cooperativeness of the Russian village were equally childish. The best teachers were great historic forces, industrialization and the building of cities with their factories and slums. People would learn from their condition. When life became socialized, the people would. On the other hand, Marxism had an appeal similar to the old familiar themes of Orthodoxy: it was a universal, the true faith demanding recognition. The Russian intelligentsia with their longing for total justice and a total explanation of life and society were as thrilled with the mission of the proletariat as they had been with that of the peasantry.

Plekhanov emphasized the scientific, inevitable, gradual side of Marxism. A similar attitude was taken by the "Legal Marxists," so-called because the government saw no need to forbid their learned articles on the coming of industrialism to Russia. The "Legal Marxists" were revolutionary in their long-term plans, but for the moment most of their attention was given to industry as to a new toy. Another group, the so-called "Economists," were Marxists who wanted to encourage the labor movement to better its condition through organization and collective bargaining.

These tendencies were opposed by the more radical Marxists, who wished to get on with the revolution as soon as possible. To a willful revolutionary like Lenin the evolutionary, scientific, gradualist side of Marxism did not appeal as much as the ethical, messianic, inspirational side.

The formula

$$\text{CAPITALISM} \rightarrow \text{INDUSTRIALISM} \rightarrow \text{LIBERALISM} \rightarrow \text{DEMOCRACY} \rightarrow \text{SOCIALISM}$$

had disadvantages which Marx had not had to face when he was thinking of Western Europe. In an undeveloped area where constitutional and industrial revolutions had not yet occurred, a Marxist was forced to wish for the coming of the people's capitalistic oppressors, for concentration of wealth, for increasing misery, and for all the unpleasant stages which in Western Europe had already taken place. This difficulty of having to welcome capitalism and wait while it exploited the Russian people was eventually to be avoided by Lenin. He was to emphasize the weakness and cowardliness of the Russian *bourgeoisie,* the common interest of workers and peasants in overthrowing the old regime, and the things which could be accomplished by an exclusive and tightly organized revolutionary party working under leaders who understood better than the masses the direction history had to take. This was not exactly the Marxism which Plekhanov had imported from Europe. It was like a Marxism Russified, taken back toward Populism. This was to be Bolshevism, so-called because Lenin's following at the Social Democratic party congress of 1903 claimed to have a majority (*bolshinstvo*) and their opponents a minority (*menshinstvo*—thus Mensheviks).

Meanwhile the remnants of the Populists, bearing the Narodnik tradition and still hoping that Russia might skip the mistakes of nineteenth-century European individualism and industrialism, continued to meet in the 1890's in scattered groups. Starting in 1897, there was talk of uniting, and in 1901 the union of some forty-nine groups came about and the Socialist Revolutionary Party was born. It still looked to the peasants for the reform of Russia. Its program was the calling of a constituent assembly which, it was hoped, would turn Russia into a democratic republic with socialist ownership of the means of production. The land would be distributed to the peasant villages to be farmed collectively. Industry would be adjusted to the needs of the villages which, through their prosperity, would form a big internal market. The Socialist Revolutionaries were led by members of the intelligentsia, but, unlike their Narodnik predecessors, did succeed in winning some peasant support. The tradition of terrorism stemming from the People's Will was continued in the left wing of the Socialist Revolutionaries, and a good many public officials were assassinated by their "Fighting Organization."

At the opening of the twentieth century Russia had an unsolved peasant problem and a Socialist Revolutionary party appealing to the peasants. It had also an industrial revolution in an early stage, with a Marxian Social Democratic party hoping to organize and control the labor movement.

Between the reaction and the revolution there were liberals in Russia, and they were slowly growing in numbers. Because the reactionary nobles tended to ignore the zemstvo assemblies of district and province, these bodies were mainly controlled by the minority of liberal nobles. They and their professional employees—teachers, doctors, agronomists—tended to be liberal in varying degrees. The notion of capping the zemstvo system of local representation with a national representation was irresistible to Russian liberals. It was people like these, meeting more and more frequently in the first years of the new century in national professional congresses, who formed the Constitutional Democratic (Cadet) party in 1905.

THE REVOLUTION OF 1905 AND AFTER

The Russian revolution of 1905 is often called "the rehearsal," because of the greater revolution which was to follow in 1917. The two revolutions are in some ways similar, for both grew out of the same long-term conditions. In 1904 and 1905 the war with Japan called attention to the defects of the autocracy, and set up economic and social irritations which would not have been so dangerous if there had not been in the background explosive accumulations of peasant and worker discontent. The draft, war casualties, and economic tie-ups were especially dangerous in Russia in the aftermath of the 1861 land settlement and in the conditions of early industrial revolution.

In the case of liberals like the zemstvo nobles and professional workers, action, when it came with the war, took the form of congresses and resolutions. In November, 1904, for example, a convention of delegates from all the Russian zemstvos demanded a representative assembly. Similar demands came from national associations of professional people. The Constitutional Democratic party (Cadet) led by such men as the historian Miliukov took shape.

To workers and peasants, action meant strikes and attacks on the manor houses of landlords. "Bloody Sunday" in January, 1905, was more than any other single event the signal for strikes and political assassinations. On that day unarmed demonstrators of the labor organization built with government permission by the priest, Father Gapon, were fired on by troops as they approached the Winter Palace to petition the czar. About 150 people were killed and 200 wounded. In the face of the wave of strikes and disorders which followed, the government continued to rely, unimaginatively, on force. Attempts to coerce the railroad workers led to a big railroad strike which tied up the economy and stopped food shipments to the capital.

By the fall of 1905 there was a general strike, and representatives of working people had formed a *soviet* (council) in St. Petersburg. Through the countryside, peasants, once the crops were in, met together to announce their grievances and in many cases to organize local "republics" and chase the manor lords from their districts. The peasants were not much concerned with politics, but Socialist Revolutionary leaders tried to interest them in the nationalizing of the land and the calling of a constituent assembly.

In the spring of 1905, Nicholas II was faced with an unfinished war with Japan and with worsening disorders at home. At first he tried to stand firm, declaring that autocracy could not be touched and that no territorial concessions to the Japanese could be made. Later he promised a consultative assembly, but this concession satisfied no one. In September Witte's concessions at Portsmouth made peace with Japan possible, and in October he convinced the czar that his only alternative to military dictatorship was the granting of a national duma, or representative assembly, with power to accept or reject the laws. The czar in his alarm issued the October Manifesto, which made this concession and guaranteed the Russian people civil rights.

Witte, who had become a sort of prime minister, reduced the redemption payments of the peasants for 1906 and abolished them thereafter. The revolution began to subside. Peace with Japan made possible the return of troops from the Far East. The Liberals were split by the October Manifesto, some of them, the "Octobrists," arguing that its concessions were sufficient for the moment, while others, the Cadets, wanted more. For a time in late 1905 people speculated as to whether Witte would be able to disband the St. Petersburg soviet or would be arrested by it. In December Witte had the soviet leaders arrested, including Leon Trotsky, who used his trial as an occasion for Social Democratic propaganda. There was no serious opposition in the capital, and only a ten-day uprising in Moscow. Witte in the spring of 1906 fortified the government by borrowing 2.5 billion francs from France, and prepared to meet the First Duma.

In the spring and summer of 1906 the backswing from the revolution was fully apparent. The First Duma was dominated by the liberal Cadets, but they could get nowhere against the government. Although their consent was necessary to new legislation, they could do nothing by themselves, for the October Manifesto had not granted ministerial responsibility in the English sense. The Emperor's Council of State had been altered to make it into a kind of House of Lords. The Duma could refuse to approve of the budget, but in this case last year's budget remained in effect. Article 87 of the fundamental laws permitted emergency legislation in the absence of the Duma, provided it was ratified later. The First Duma, faced with these obstacles, lasted only until July, 1906, when it was dissolved. In May, its creator and the limiter of its powers, Witte, had been forced to resign. Czar Nicholas hated to admit even to himself that Witte had saved the situation and that it had been necessary to abandon absolute monarchy.

Witte's successor was Peter Arkadyevich Stolypin (1862–1911), who for five years—until his assassination in 1911—made a bold, imaginative effort to prevent further revolution. He did not object to a duma, provided it was docile enough and could be swayed by his nationalistic appeals. The Second Duma, which met from February to June, 1907, was not to his taste, for it was dominated by Cadets and representatives of labor. Stolypin managed the dissolution of the Second Duma on the pretext of socialistic disloyalty and conspiracy. Then, having changed the electoral law unconstitutionally to make it count against the towns, the poor, and the peasants, he secured a Third Duma with a majority of Nationalists (conservative country gentlemen like himself) and Octobrists (somewhat more liberal country gentry and big businessmen) to offset the reactionaries and socialists. It ran its full course of five years (1907–1912), and was followed by a Fourth (and last) Duma of similar composition. Meanwhile Stolypin cracked down on the remains of unrest in the countryside, using military courts martial, and put into operation his land legislation designed to make peasant revolution unlikely in the future.

For some time there had been a growing opinion that the Russian peasant would be more efficient as a farmer and more conservative politically if he were freed from his ties to the village community and made the outright owner of a farm. The poor and lazy, to be sure, would suffer from competition and would probably lose their land. In so doing they would form a labor supply, and the land would be in better hands. The adherents of this point of view were reinforced by the Revolution of 1905, which disillusioned many Russians with the *mir* as a conservative institution. Stolypin's "wager on the strong," begun in 1906, was political as well as economic. In a series of steps the land allotments dating from the 1861 emancipation were to be (1) turned into hereditary tenures, and (2) consolidated so that each peasant would own a farm instead of scattered strips. Land would no longer be collectively owned or periodically realloted, unless the peasants themselves made no move to take advantage of Stolypin's laws. Theoretically the majority in each village decided, although in practice government pressure favored the change.

Stolypin's land legislation cannot be fairly judged, for World War I intervened and the changes of tenure came to a virtual halt after 1915. By the end of 1915 about half the peasant households formerly immersed in their village communes had switched to hereditary tenure, but of these less than half had consolidated their strips of land, even in part, and only a small minority had managed to round out fully consolidated farms. Quite apart from the Stolypin land laws, the peasants between 1906 and World War I continued to buy land, perhaps more than they could afford. The population was still rising rapidly, and such measures as emigration, migration to Siberia, and the shift to still growing urban industry provided an insufficient outlet. The living standards of the peasantry remained very low. The Stolypin laws did not attack directly the problem of insufficient land in the hands of the peasantry. These laws pointed, in the long run, toward both political stability and a more efficient agriculture, at least on the farms of the more successful peasants, but there was to be no "long run."

Russia's experience in the Revolution of 1905 differed in several important respects from the ordeal of 1917. In 1905 peace was made before the worst peasant and proletarian disorders. The army, though it consisted of peasants in uniform, remained for the most part under discipline. Along with the police and the whole bureaucratic network of the regime, the army retained its effectiveness in restoring law and order. In 1905 despite the Emperor's weakness and inconstancy it was still possible for able men like Witte and Stolypin to remain in office long enough to serve the country according to their lights. The peasants in 1905 were unruly but were less determined than in 1917 to seize the Russian land for themselves. The urban workingmen gave temporary force to the revolution of 1905, and at the outset their unruliness, which exacted concessions from the state, had the favor of liberal employers, but the latter soon became frightened of revolution. Revolutionary leaders such as the Bolsheviks and Mensheviks were negligible in number and unprepared. The institution of the soviets, which was to mean so much in 1917, took them by surprise. In many respects the Russian Revolution of 1905 was more like the Central European revolutions of 1848 than like the Revolution of 1917. The deeper political and social discontents of 1905 and 1917 were, however, essentially the same.

After the Revolution of 1905 Russian big business was once more reluctant to meddle with opposition to the state, although the employers' associations deplored government concessions to the now legal labor movement. The lower middle class tended to divide between reaction and liberalism. The landowners were split three ways, among the reactionary Black Hundreds, the Octobrists, and the Cadets. As indicated by the Stolypin land legislation, there was loss of faith in the peasant commune as a conservative institution. Among the revolutionists, the Socialist Revolutionaries still pinned their hopes on the commune. It is virtually impossible to say how the mass of the peasantry felt about this institution.

Between 1905 and 1917 the Bolsheviks and Mensheviks, whose final split came in 1912, argued bitterly about the lessons to be gleaned from Russia's recent experience with revolution. They agreed that the *bourgeoisie* had neither made nor defended the gains of the revolution, and that the urban workers had shown unexpected power. The potential of the peasantry was less certain. According to the Mensheviks, 1905 simply proved that there could be no socialist revolution without a much larger and stronger proletariat, no larger proletariat without the further development of capitalism, no flowering of capitalism without the victory of a bourgeois revolution along western lines. The role of the proletariat was to help the *bourgeoisie* make their revolution. The peasantry could not be relied on. The Social Democratic party should remain large and open, since there was no hurrying history and no need for excessive discipline in anticipation of a socialist coup. Even if Europe went socialist, Russia would have to wait its turn.

Leon Trotsky (Lev Bronstein, 1879–1940) had played an outstanding role in the St. Petersburg Soviet in 1905—and was to be even more important in

1917. In these years, he continued to defend the Menshevik conception of the party and to urge reconciliation of the Bolsheviks and Mensheviks. In other respects, however, he took a position which was in extreme opposition to the Menshevik philosophy. After 1905, he argued for what he called "permanent revolution," which meant that the coming bourgeois-democratic revolution would be forced by circumstances to keep going until Russia was socialized. He even conceived of the possibility that more advanced Europe, catching fire from the Russian revolution, might enable the socialist revolution in Russia to remain alight. Trotsky argued that Russia's late, concentrated, and state-sponsored industrialization had created a powerful proletariat while the *bourgeoisie* was still weak and dependent. When the autocracy fell, as it was bound to do, the *bourgeoisie* would be afraid to make a genuine constitutional democracy. Their procrastination, accompanied by refusal of even modest concessions to the factory workers, would force the proletariat to choose between reaction and socialization. Incapable of choosing reaction, the proletariat would be forced to socialize the revolution in order to keep it alive. In a similar manner, the proletariat would be forced, ready or not, to socialize agriculture in order to keep the peasantry from defeating the revolution. This sequence of events in Russia could not succeed unless the chain reaction spread to Europe and ultimately the world. While Trotsky objected to the undemocratic character of the Bolshevik conception of the party, he predicted that the proletarian minority in Russia would be obliged to force the rest of the country along the road history was taking.

Nikolai Lenin (Vladimir Ilich Ulyanov, 1870–1924), was the leader and disciplinarian of the Bolsheviks. He fought savagely against Trotsky's Menshevik conception of what a socialist party should be, and insisted that the party should remain small, single-minded, and maneuverable. He protested against Trotsky's undemocratic casting of the Russian proletarian minority in the role of leader of the permanent revolution. Actually Lenin was very close to Trotsky on everything except the organization of the party. He would not commit himself on how much time would have to pass before the first, or democratic, revolution would turn into the second, or socialist, one. Lenin saved democratic appearances by saying that when the weak Russian *bourgeoisie* failed to make the democratic revolution the proletariat and peasants would make it together. Although the peasants were not socialistic, he saw that their desire for land was making them revolutionary, and could be enlisted in the overthrow of autocracy. Thereafter (though Lenin would not say how long thereafter) the poorer peasants might be induced to join the proletariat against the richer peasants and the *bourgeoisie,* and if Europe led the way to socialism Russia could follow. Trotsky and Lenin were pioneers in revising the Marxism of mid-ninteenth-century Western Europe in a direction better suited to their determination to revolutionize Russia. World War I was to give them their chance, and in 1917 they were to work together, Trotsky abandoning his scruples about the party and Lenin his reluctance to assign a leading role to the proletarian minority.

42

THE INTERNATIONAL STATE SYSTEM AND ITS UNDOING

FROM 1871, when the Franco-Prussian War ended, until 1914, when World War I began, no big battles were fought in Europe. There were conflicts overseas, some of them important and gory: the Spanish-American War (1898); the Boer War (1899–1902); and the Russo-Japanese War (1904–1905). There were also endemic campaigns in places like Afghanistan and the Sudan. But practically the only fighting on European soil consisted of militarily insignificant campaigns in the Balkans. This was a period of peace without parallel in modern history.

The very uniqueness of this tranquility was important. Men born in 1870 were forty-four years old in 1914. A generation had grown up without knowing what a war at home was like. The great struggles of the middle of the century— the American Civil War, the Crimean War, the Seven Weeks War, the French wars against Austria and Prussia, were distant and dream-like to middle-aged people in 1914. When they became conscious after 1900 that a new European conflict might be in the making, few of them had any realistic idea of what to expect or what sort of military effort to prepare for. Many of them, from chiefs-of-staff down, thought in terms of the quick, decisive battles of the middle of the past century. Almost no one realized that twentieth-century war might, like a high persistent fever, exhaust and alter beyond recognition the nations and their social and economic structures.

THE NATURE OF THE EUROPEAN
STATE SYSTEM

While peace reigned, men prepared for war and so made it more likely. The European state system made this paradox possible, and perhaps inevitable. Europe consisted of a series of separate states which possessed, in this period, remarkably stable frontiers and institutions. Their separateness was the essential characteristic of the system. The basic law of the world order was the notion of "sovereignty," which meant that every government had final and complete authority to do whatever it wished, and that no other government, and no individual from another country, had any power over it whatever. The idea of sovereignty meant that governments had a constitutional and legal obligation to defend it. This involved defense against possible attack, which meant the maintenance of a suitable defense establishment, and the protection of the "national interest"—the security of an ally for example.

In both theory and practice, there were things which could limit this authority. The practical limitations were the more striking. Clearly a country like Denmark was bound to be influenced by its almost total military impotence and the presence of powerful neighbors. Every government was inhibited, too, by the moral scruples of its statesmen and its public, and by regard for public opinion in the world at large.

The relations among the sovereign states were in practice governed by numerous conditions, habits and customs which taken together added up to the profession of diplomacy and to the public law of Europe. The following points may be cited as its fundamental aspects.

1. In every country, foreign policy and foreign ministries in the nineteenth century resisted the general movement toward popular control. The destinies of the nation were too deeply involved to be entrusted to party politicians. International negotiations were too delicate to be subjected to public discussion. This meant that foreign relations were largely carried on behind closed doors, and that the personnel of diplomatic services remained highly professional and, for the most part, aristocratic.

There were degrees and qualifications to this detachment of foreign policy from popular politics. In Great Britain, and to some extent in all countries with cabinet governments, foreign policy was subject to change with changes of party control. But even in the countries where public opinion and parliaments exercised the fullest control over government operations there persisted a high degree of secrecy in actual diplomatic negotiation. Despite changes of ministry and party control, the constitutional governments in fact displayed a great degree of continuity in their foreign policies.

2. Diplomacy in this period was a game played by elaborate and rigid rules. There were certain things which no one was supposed to do, such as invading a European neighbor (it was all right to invade overseas countries if you

thought you could get away with it), or seating the Costa Rican minister nearer to the host than the Papal Nuncio at a dinner party. These rules were all based upon a few principles which were regarded as having the force of law. The most important of them was that all treaties were inviolable. A contract between governments, once made, could not be broken. Another was that nobody could change the existing international arrangements without consulting the interested parties. If for example (and this was always the case) the Russians wanted to force the Turks to permit Russian warships to go in and out of the Straits at will (which had been forbidden in various earlier treaties), it would not do simply to persuade the Turks to let them do it. For this was a "European Question," involving basic changes in the power situation in the Mediterranean, and the approval was needed of all the great powers, which, acting jointly, were supposed to constitute a sort of executive authority—called the Concert of Europe.

Throughout most of the period from 1870 to about 1908, the rules were generally obeyed. Ambitions and fears were submitted to the powers for adjustment. Single-handed revisions of international arrangements were rarely attempted and, when they were, often re-revised later by the Concert of Europe.

The system of legal and traditional restraints was strengthened by some very important realities. If anybody tried to rearrange the map of Europe, he was likely to tread on so many toes that he would find an overpowering force aligned against him. When, in 1875, Bismarck was rumored to be considering fighting a new war against France (allegedly to prevent the French from regaining enough strength after 1871 to permit them to contemplate an attack on Germany), the British and Russians told Bismarck that they would not allow France to be further weakened. Any one country which became too powerful would pose a constant threat to all others. There was, thus, still in operation the automatic regulatory device familiar in earlier eras—the balance of power. The phrase has meant different things at different times and in different places, but it is this situation to which it is properly applied in the nineteenth century.

3. At the root of sovereignty was the institution of the national state buttressed by the loyalty and affection of its citizens, and the national state had defects which impaired the workings of the international system.

For several hundred years, and with increasing rapidity as the nineteenth century wore on, people living in each nation-state had been becoming more like one another and less like people across the borders. In 1500, a Frenchman in Burgundy was much more like a Swiss across the border than like a Frenchman in Provence. By 1900, frontiers had grown much sharper. This was partly due to the increasing uniformity of national administrations, especially since the French Revolution. People throughout one country mostly lived under a system of common laws and institutions. It was also due to the spread of universal education, which standardized language. Statesmen now knew that they could generally rely upon the people of their own nationality to back them up in moments of national emergency. The *independence* of nations, and thus the freedom of action of diplomats, was very deeply and strongly rooted.

But the national states all contained some citizens who were not part of the majority nationality. It was natural that people who lived within a country against their will, and were thus disloyal to it, should be the most troublesome and nerve-wracking concern of national policy. And it was, moreover, natural that a government should regard with an especially eager and solicitous eye people of their own nationality who happened to be in other people's countries. For example, the presence of more than a million Frenchmen in the provinces of Alsace and Lorraine, annexed by Germany in 1871, was a first-rate international issue. The Germans were aware that France wanted the provinces back more than anything else in the world, and the German nation developed a mass feeling that it was being followed by forty million vengeful French citizens.

The most unpleasant situation of all existed in Austria-Hungary, for it consisted of very diverse peoples, none of them moved by the same *kind* of solid loyalty as animated the great bulk of Russians, Dutch, or Italians. Austria was the only major European state in this position. Even those like Russia which had very large minorities also had a core of citizens devoted to Russia simply because they were Russians. Austria was faced on all sides with the kind of problem which faced the Germans in Alsace and Lorraine. The Italians were licking their chops for Trieste, the principal seaport of Austria; the Serbs yearned for about a quarter of the empire; the Rumanians coveted Transylvania—all territories inhabited by their co-nationals.

The Austrian problem was acute and, in terms of the existing European order, insoluble. It was not surprising that Austria should have been the scene of the explosion which finally blew up the system.

EUROPE IN 1914

THE AGE OF BISMARCK, 1870–1890

There had never before been a Germany. In 1871, Germany was made; it possessed the largest and most efficient army in Europe and it also possessed the ablest diplomat. The balance of power, and with it the workings of the European system, were revolutionized, and the shape of the new situation was largely determined by the German chancellor.

Even now, more than half a century after his death, it is impossible to secure any general agreement upon Bismarck's stature as a diplomat. To some historians he was an infallible genius, well-intentioned and Olympian. To others he was sinister and bungling and upon his resignation, left an international mess which could never be cleared up. But everyone agrees that he dominated European diplomacy with almost the same degree of authority as he dominated German domestic politics.

The basic aim of this titan was undoubtedly to maintain the peace of the Europe which he had so drastically reorganized. Germany, he proclaimed with evident sincerity, was "sated;" it had nothing to gain and much to lose from war. The history of international relations during the two decades of his chancellorship is in large part the history of Bismarck's efforts to untangle dangerous snarls and make sure that there were no potential enemies on Germany's borders.

To the north there was no menace, only forlorn little Denmark, bludgeoned into almost total dependency on Germany in 1864. But to the west was France, so seriously alienated by the loss of its European supremacy and its border provinces as to be irreconcilably hostile and dangerous. Bismarck consistently strove to minimize the western danger by a variety of means. He dabbled, directly and indirectly, in French politics in order to further the cause of the moderate republican group, which was the least bellicose of French parties. He tried to assuage French pride by feeding it on other people's territories, especially in Africa where, under his urging in 1881, the French snapped up Tunisia, a country which the Italians wanted and whose loss made them conveniently anti-French. And he tried to prevent the French from winning friends among other countries lest he be faced with a French-led coalition against Germany. To this latter end, he welcomed and perhaps furthered the tensions which mounted between France and both Italy and Britain over African affairs. If the Italians were put out by the seizure of Tunisia, the French were even more put out by the British occupation of Egypt a year later, for the French had long nourished their own ambitions in the eastern Mediterranean.

The main threat was of French understanding with Russia or Austria, the powers on Germany's eastern and southern frontiers. Bismarck strove to avoid this threat by maintaining close relations with both of them. Emphasizing the gulf which separated the three empires from democratic France, he talked of "monarchical solidarity" and secured in 1873 a rather vague understanding called the Three Emperors' League.

The course of monarchical solidarity did not, however, run smoothly. The

Austrians, ejected from German affairs in 1866, found that their empire was now a Southeastern European one, polyglot and precarious. They were extremely sensitive to nationalist movements among the Balkan peoples and the subjects of the shaky Turkish empire, since outbursts of nationalism in that part of the world would undoubtedly compound the difficulties of governing a huge country consisting entirely of minorities. The Russians, on the other hand, showed an obsessive, if intermittent, desire to meddle in the Balkans, usually in the way of protecting or expanding the rights and welfare of the Orthodox and Slavic Balkan nations. The interests of Germany's two sister empires were almost constantly in conflict.

The conflict burst forth in 1877, and led to the disruption of the Three Emperors' League. The Christian and Slavic inhabitants of Bosnia and Bulgaria, backward and sparsely inhabited Turkish Balkan provinces, revolted. The revolts were suppressed with energy and brutality. Europe shuddered over sensational reports of the "Bulgarian Atrocities." Russia rushed to the defense of the oppressed Christians. Austria rushed to the support of Moslem Turkey. Russia went so far as to declare war and, with some difficulty, reached the gates of Istanbul. A peace treaty was hastily negotiated at San Stephano, setting up an independent and very large Bulgaria, which included many people besides Bulgars and was intended to be a Russian client. Austria and Britain objected, and Bismarck called a European Congress at Berlin. Bulgaria was cut down to size, and Austria was appeased by the right to occupy and administer the troublesome province of Bosnia. But the Russians were infuriated at the loss of the fruits of victory, and the inter-imperial cordiality was abruptly broken off.

In this situation, Bismarck strengthened his connection with the remaining partner and in 1879 signed a treaty of alliance with Austria. It was a natural step. Austria was governed by a German dynasty, and there were strong sentimental and economic links. The Austrian alliance created a large, defensible territorial unit in the heart of Europe. Any other power would hesitate to attack so formidable a combination. The alliance was regularly renewed; it remained the principal bulwark of the foreign policies of both countries until 1918 when the defeat of one and the disintegration of the other put an end to it.

The alliance was in its essentials a simple defensive agreement: if one country were attacked, the other would come to its assistance. These simple terms concealed many intricacies, however. For one thing, this was almost the first time in modern history that a permanent, peacetime alliance had been signed between great powers, aimed not to meet a wartime situation or the threat of a war but as a permanent and regular means of securing the peace. The invention of the peacetime alliance led to its spread—other nations gradually adopted the idea, and in a few years every major country of Europe was allied, or aligned, with some others. As will be seen shortly, this welter of alignments gradually sorted itself out into two grand systems of allies; Europe was, in the cliché, to be divided into two armed camps.

But in addition to a future development of this sort the Austrian Alliance portended other things. By uniting itself so closely to the Habsburg monarchy, Germany became in a sense dependent upon it; and Austria was increasingly a poor country to depend upon, owing to its developing problems of national dis-unity. In the end, long after Bismarck's death, the Germans found themselves compelled to shore up their ally, to support its ill-judged ventures in diplomacy, finally to defend it with their own armies.

After 1880, the Germans sought to mend their Russian fences again, and they succeeded admirably. The Three Emperors' League, shadowy at best, was revived and converted into an alliance. The Russians had recovered from their irritation of 1878, and the influences in the court of Petersburg which had been most active in the Balkan adventures had subsided.

Germany's security system was extended in other directions, too. After the Tunisian episode, the Italians were brought into the Austro-German Alliance (which remained separate from the Three Emperors' Alliance). While the Italians mostly regarded Austria as their public enemy No. 1, owing to the fact that so many Italian-speaking provinces were still part of Austria, they were at the moment so annoyed with the French as to swallow their Austrophobia. The Dual Alliance thus became the Triple Alliance and, by a series of intricate bar-gains, the minor kingdom of Rumania was lured into adhering to it. Austria also bought off the king of Serbia and converted his country into a sort of informal protectorate, so that its southern frontiers were secured. For the moment, in the middle 1880's, the Austro-German combine was prospering mightily.

Difficulties, however, lay ahead. These arose again from Bulgaria, which showed an extreme reluctance to remain as small as the powers had made it in 1878. A long and incredibly intricate series of events developed from the deter-mination of the Bulgars to annex some neighboring provinces, from their reluc-tance to do what their Russian protectors told them, and from their eagerness to beat up their neighbors the Serbs. All this, accompanied by an enormous amount of negotiation among the great powers, led to such peculiarly Balkan develop-ments as the kidnapping (by Russian agents) of the Bulgarian sovereign, and a brief war with Serbia in which the latter country had to be rescued by the Austrians. This muddle led to a renewal of violent animosity and conflicting interests between Russia and Austria, which was always near the surface of Euro-pean diplomacy. The Three Emperors' Alliance became unmanageable and was allowed to lapse. But Bismarck, determined to retain the friendship of Russia as well as the alliance with Austria, signed in 1887 a "Reinsurance Treaty," which was a promise that Russia and Germany would remain neutral if either were at war with a third power—unless one of the two attacked France or Austria, in which case the other might go to the assistance of the victim. This latter provision was intended by the Russians to protect France and by the Germans to harmonize the Reinsurance Treaty with their obligations to defend Austria under the 1879 alliance. Austro-Russian relations remained ice-cold, and Russian propagandists were writing books that blueprinted the dissection of Austria-Hungary into small, Slavic bits which would be partners of the Slavic Big Brother Russia. But Germany's relationship with each remained sufficiently cordial to eliminate the danger of attack.

The position of Britain throughout this period was also satisfactory to the Germans. British statesmen traditionally eschewed commitments and involvements in continental affairs. For a number of reasons, the British after 1870 were less concerned in continental affairs than ever.

Their major interests lay on the high seas, in colonial affairs, and in trade. These interests suggested the need for peace and the avoidance of continental quarrels, especially since Britain's naval and commercial superiority made allies unnecessary. The only occasions when the British offered more than advice to continental powers were those involving the position of Turkey and the eastern Mediterranean. The maintenance of Turkish control (harmless from the British viewpoint) over the Straits and the Near East was a basic British concern, for the sea routes to India—the "life line of Empire"—were involved. The great danger was an extension of Russian power, for Russia was aggressive and was traditionally regarded by Englishmen as The Enemy. After 1881, by which time the Suez Canal had passed under British control and Egypt had been occupied, the sensitivity of Britain to Near Eastern problems was greater than ever. This concern had led to the one important British participation in a European negotiation, the Congress of Berlin. Afterward, the British found themselves dependent, in a degree, upon German friendship to counteract the fear of Russia in the Straits and of France in Egypt and in other parts of Africa. An alignment with the Triple Alliance gradually developed. Neither party was disposed to convert it into a military or formal alliance, but relations were close and cordial.

This was Germany's situation when Bismarck was dismissed by the young Emperor William II. Throughout the chancellor's stay in office, the peace of Europe had been maintained, France had been restrained and to some extent diverted, alliances with Austria, Russia and Italy had been won and strengthened. Friendship with Britain seemed assured. And the acute Balkan and colonial conflicts, in none of which Germany had any great interest, had been prevented from embroiling Europe in hostilities.

This situation began to alter rapidly after Bismarck's dismissal.

THE BREAKDOWN OF THE GERMAN SECURITY SYSTEM

The most ominous of European realities after 1890 were the Balkan tangle and the resultant antagonism of Russia and Austria, and the changing attitude of Great Britain.

Bismarck's Reinsurance Treaty with Russia was not renewed after his dismissal. William II and the new chancellor believed that renewal was impossible. The Austrians, at swordspoint with Russia in Balkan affairs, objected to their ally being allied with their enemy, and so did the Russians. The treaties were all secret, but their general outlines were known, and the Reinsurance Treaty appeared inconsistent in spirit, though not in its actual text, with the Triple Alliance. After 1890, while the courts of Berlin and St. Petersburg remained cordial, there was no written commitment between them.

The Russians felt that Germany had already made its choice as to which side it would back in case of an eventual conflict between Russia and Austria, and they felt themselves isolated and vulnerable. Moreover, they were now beginning an active phase of industrial development, of railroad building, of conversion of the vast, primitive Russian economy into a modern society. This required money. There was in Europe a great power which, also diplomatically isolated and also acutely vulnerable to Germany, possessed a great abundance of capital ready for lending abroad. This was France, and while the Russians had long feared and disliked French democracy, their need was urgent. Negotiations for closer relations led first, in 1892, to an agreement for the export of French credits to Russia and to a rather informal military agreement to cooperate in case both countries found themselves at war with Germany. In 1894, a secret military alliance was signed.

The Franco-Russian Alliance marked the end of Bismarck's system. The balance of power had reasserted itself in the new form of two opposing systems of allies. Their existence tended of itself to strengthen the bonds of alliance. In the next twenty years, heavy strains were placed on Franco-Russian friendship, but it survived because neither France nor Russia dared to face, alone, the possibility of a new war.

The second ominous reality of the 1890's was Great Britain's changing position. The overwhelming preponderance of British economic and colonial power was visibly dwindling as other nations industrialized and extended their empires, and its diplomatic detachment meant that Britain could not count on any friends when it found itself involved in the innumerable overseas disputes which flecked its horizon. In Venezuela, in 1895, it found itself at serious odds with the United States; in the Sudan, in 1898, with France; in the Far East and the Near East, with Russia; in South Africa, in 1896, it found Germany giving comfort to its small enemy, the Transvaal Republic. Everywhere in the globe, Britain was heavily involved, and everywhere it found antagonists among the other world powers. With no army to speak of and no allies at all, the British became alarmed at their position.

A withdrawal from exposed positions, and appeasement of some antagonists, was clearly indicated, and this was systematically undertaken. The most important emendation was in connection with the United States. Disputes in the Caribbean, where Britain had long been the principal naval power, were liquidated, and the American sea was gradually and tacitly confided to United States dominance. In the Far East, British and Americans established a close understanding and parallel policies. In a remarkably short time, Britain had transformed bitter controversy into cordiality. There was never any serious question of an alliance (although some British statesmen suggested it), but a nascent English-speaking bloc appeared. It was to develop into the most important single fact in the diplomatic history of the twentieth century.

The hostility of the other powers persisted. The British began to draw in their horns in various other regions, blunting some of the sharp disputes in the Near East, the Pacific, and the Orient. Affairs in South Africa brought things to a head. In 1899 the government at London drifted, or was pushed, into a difficult

and (it appeared) wicked war against the small semi-independent republics maintained by Dutch (Boer) settlers north of the British colony of the Cape of Good
Hope. The Boers put up a much stronger defense than anyone had supposed
possible. A large part of the British army and navy was tied up for two years, and
the depressed and bewildered populace of Great Britain found itself with weak
defenses and no allies looking across twenty miles of channel at an unfriendly
continent.

The glee and malice with which the British predicament was welcomed
in Europe was unanimous, and it was an eye-opener. French newspapers took the
opportunity to cast aspersions on Queen Victoria's personal morals, and the
Russian czar dallied with the thought of attacking India. There were serious
suggestions of a continental coalition against the British empire, ostensibly for the
purpose of avenging the poor Boers of South Africa. It seemed barely possible
that the rivalries of continental nations might be immersed in an anti-British
crusade. The Germans were the most serious sponsors of such a program, and it
was their hostility which came as the greatest shock to British diplomats, and
foreshadowed the dramatic events shortly to take place.

Britain quite clearly had to take some active measures to prevent itself
from being ganged up on in the future. There were two sets of allies; more friendly
relations had to be established with one of them. The British chose the Franco-
Russian side and so determined the line-up, and the outcome, of two world wars.

There were many and complex reasons for the British choice. For one
thing, the retirement of the prime minister, Lord Salisbury, in 1902, brought into
prominence and power a group of francophiles, who, through fear of Germany or
confidence in France, urged an understanding with the latter. Salisbury had been
the architect and author of "splendid isolation" and so long as he remained no real
change was possible. But in 1902 the change began to be made by men who, like
the new Prime Minister Arthur Balfour and Foreign Secretary Lord Lansdowne,
were sentimentally attached to France, as was the new king Edward VII
(1901–1910).

Far more than personal feelings dictated the choice. There were also
people like Joseph Chamberlain in the cabinet who would have preferred an
alliance with Germany. But the Germans, when approached very informally, had
their own doubts. They distrusted what they thought of as the instability of the
British cabinet system, and they were particularly unwilling to be involved in
Britain's constant affrays with the Russians, especially in the Orient. Moreover,
it never occurred to them that the ancient hostilities between Britain and the
Franco-Russian allies could be overcome. The emperor, Chancellor von Bulow,
and the influential chief of the foreign office, Friedrich von Holstein, thought
that Britain was so bound to come in conflict with the French and Russians that
they could make their own terms for a German-British understanding.

They were mistaken, for their own conduct was such as to frighten the
British into allowing the French to make *their* own terms. Whether the Germans
really seriously intended to undertake a long-run assault against the British empire
is very doubtful, but they acted as if they did. Their hostility in connection with
South African affairs was matched by a flavor of highhandedness in other deal-

ings with London. They were increasingly engaged in expanding their influence in Turkey, where they were shortly to make plans for constructing a Berlin-Baghdad railway connection which would have brought them to the borders of India. They were now busily engaged in developing and expanding their own colonial empire, in Africa and the Pacific, often in territories which the British would have liked to have. Their businessmen were aggressively competing with (and underselling) the British in world markets. And, most of all, they had begun in 1898 to build a navy. In 1902 it was still a very small navy, but its presence alarmed the British, who asked themselves what purpose a German navy could have except ultimately to challenge the British on their home waters.

Even after the first understandings had been reached with France, Anglo-German relations need not have deteriorated further had it not been for the way the Germans talked and acted—about their colonies, their trade, their navy, their "world role." The Germans were forever flexing their muscles in public. It may have been no more than the posturing of a neurotic emperor and his inept advisors, combined with the wild oats of a young and fabulously successful nation, but it frightened the British. By strengthening the hands of the anti-German groups in the London government, it converted apprehension into hostility.

The British conversations with France were, in their beginnings, simply an attempt to eliminate sources of friction. Talks were opened on conflicts of interest in North Africa, and a simple formula was found to eliminate a long and tangled cause for mutual suspicion. Britain's occupation of Egypt had long been opposed by France; France's growing influence in Morocco had long been opposed by Britain. The two countries simply promised not to interfere with one another in the two areas. Less important areas of overlapping interests in other parts of the world were similarly dealt with, and the centuries old rivalry of the two western powers came abruptly and permanently to an end. In the presence of a new and menacing colossus in Central Europe the old enemies found that they needed one another's friendship.

The friendship was soon put to the test, in North Africa. France was rapidly extending its influence in Morocco and converting that senescent sultanate into a sort of semi-colony. To this the Germans objected, saying that their great interests in this part of the world (no one could find out just what they were) required their assent to any new arrangements there. Sharp words, and a sharp crisis, ensued in 1905, and a conference of all interested powers was called at Algeciras, in Spain. To their intense embarrassment, the Germans found themselves entirely unsupported in their efforts to preserve the independence of Morocco. Only the Austrians voted with them, and the British were notably firm in their backing of the French. The creation of a French protectorate was allowed to proceed.

The French now found themselves in a stronger position than at any time since 1870, and they sought ardently to fortify themselves still further. Two measures were indicated: first to convert the *entente cordiale* (or, in English, friendly understanding) with Britain into some more binding engagement of aid in case of war, and secondly to engineer some similar *entente* between Britain and Russia.

The first aim was only partially achieved—indeed nobody was sure, even in 1914, that Britain would join its French friends in the European war. British opinion remained stoutly opposed to continental commitments and entanglements, but increasingly close relations were achieved, and beginning in 1906 there were quiet conversations (even the Prime Minister of Great Britain did not fully apprehend their scope, although the foreign minister, Sir Edward Grey, supported them) between the military and naval authorities of the two countries. These conversations led to joint plans for defense in case of a German war. While there was no legal alliance, the fact that each country was in some measure depending on the other's execution of the defense plan meant that there was almost a practical alliance.

The second French aim, of promoting Russian-British cooperation, seemed more difficult. Russia's endemic expansionism had been aimed in several directions. In the Balkans and Turkey it had for a hundred years met the cast-iron British determination to prevent the entrance of a rival great power into the eastern Mediterranean and the Middle East. Russia had once threatened India, and now threatened Persia, which lay along the route to India. In the Far East, the Russians showed signs of intending to consume most of northern China, where Britain had vast commercial and strategic interests. Russia was concentrating on securing control over Manchuria in the late 1890's. This effort had brought the Russians into head-on collision with the Japanese, who themselves were eyeing the same region. The British naturally backed the Japanese and, in 1902, had signed an alliance with them—Britain's first peacetime alliance, and the first abandonment of isolation. The Japanese, emboldened, took an even firmer stand, and in 1904 Russia and Japan found themselves at war, with Britain benevolently neutral toward Japan. It appeared that the cause of British-Russian understanding was quite hopeless.

But the situation now altered drastically, owing to the disastrous defeat of the czar's forces. The Russian fleet was unexpectedly sunk by the Japanese, and the Russians' position in Manchuria became untenable. They were forced to accept a humiliating peace—and, at the same time, to face domestic revolution provoked by the defeat. So the Russians were in no condition to engage in foreign adventures, certainly not in the Orient, and they were a great deal more amenable to settlement of outstanding issues with Britain. Discussions began in 1905, and followed the same pattern as with the French. The main area concerned (since the Russians were now effectively removed from China) was Persia. It was agreed to carve that country into spheres of influence, reserving the southern part for Britain and the northern for Russia. Similar arrangements were made in Tibet and Mongolia; and suddenly another ancient enmity was interred. To be sure, neither party was comfortable with its new friend. The British remained suspicious of Russian motives, and the Russians were convinced that the British were insufficiently generous with their new friend. But no open breaks occurred. The French at last had their dearest wish, and Bismarck's nightmare had materialized: a moderately firm understanding united Russia, France, and Britain. Germany and Austria were surrounded.

THE TWO SETS OF ALLIES DRIFT TOWARD WAR

The lines were drawn, and they were progressively tautened in the next seven years, as mutual suspicions and mutual defenses rose. The German diplomatic position was growing difficult. In the fifteen years since Bismarck's death, a ring had closed around the German empire. Naturally apprehensive, the Germans determined to secure their position by expanding their navy—thus in the end ensuring British enmity. Austria alone remained a reliable friend. The third member of the Triple Alliance, Italy, at length reconciled to the French acquisition of Tunisia, was turning its eyes on neighboring Libya. And here the Italians found themselves encouraged by the French and opposed by the Austrians and Germans. Libya was more or less part of Turkey, and Italy's allies were hoping to convert the Turkish empire into an ally. At the conference on Moroccan affairs in 1906 at Algeciras, Italy voted against its allies. The Triple Alliance, still standing on paper, was extremely weak in its southern link.

At this juncture the old problem of Russian-Austrian relations in the Balkans again arose. Russia, ejected from the Far East by Japan and curbed in the Middle East by Britain, turned its attention anew to the Near East and the Balkan peninsula. The situation was vastly different now from the days of comic-opera politics in the 1880's. Austria's internal situation was growing more difficult as the various nationalities grew more eager for greater rights within the monarchy—or separation from it. Serbia, after a violent revolution in 1903, had abruptly ceased to be a pawn of Austrian policy and become ardently nationalist. Its government was believed (with some reason) to be disseminating nationalist propaganda and encouraging terrorist activities among the southern Austrian provinces where persons of Serb nationality were in a majority. It was thought that Russia was conniving in this agitation. The Vienna government, beset with anxieties, was alarmed, even terrified. There seemed to be no solution to the Balkan problem except a forceful suppression of the Serb state by Austrian arms and this "solution" gradually came to be accepted in Vienna as inevitable. The stiff-necked military, led by ferocious Conrad von Hötzendorff, the chief of staff, backed it. The old emperor and the foreign minister, Count von Berchtold, were won over.

The Serbs now sought, and found, solace and support in Russia. They were Slavs and Orthodox Christians, suitable objects for Russia's solicitous concern.

The most immediate aim of Serb nationalists was the province of Bosnia, which was still more or less part of Turkey, although it had been occupied and administered by Austria since 1878. So long as it was legally Turkish, there was some hope in Belgrade, the Serbian capital, that it might eventually be acquired by the Serb kingdom. Since they were mainly Serb-speaking, the Bosnians were sympathetic to this aspiration. The Austrians were determined to prevent any such development, and in 1908 they announced that they were going to annex the province outright.

The Russians (who had been consulted, but vaguely and rather deceptively) were furious. In London and Paris, there was enormous irritation at the singlehanded (and therefore illegal) Austrian action. There was talk of war. But the Germans stood staunchly behind their ally, and frightened off the opposition. The Russians, still shaken from their mauling of 1905, were in no position to engage in a major war. The crisis passed over.

Four uneasy years ensued, marked by frequent if rather minor diplomatic clashes, mostly between France and Germany, and by mounting alarm and mounting armaments. Then, in 1911, the Italians went to war against Turkey to secure Libya which they had long coveted for an Italian colony. While the Turks were thus engaged, the Balkan countries abandoned their incessant mutual bickering to join hands. They attacked Turkey and forced the Turks to abandon most of what was left of their once vast European holdings. Only the capital, Istanbul, and the shore of the Straits was saved. No sooner had the Turks admitted defeat, however, than the victorious Balkan allies fell to quarrelling among themselves. Greece and Serbia felt that their partner Bulgaria was getting too large a share of the booty, and war broke out among them. The Turks joined in, recovering some territory which they had lost the year before.

The Balkan Wars ended late in 1913 after the energetic and more or less harmonious intervention of the great powers to secure peace. But the settlement was entirely unsatisfactory to two of the participants. The Bulgars, with their voracious appetites whetted but unappeased, sulked over territories they had almost won. Even angrier were the Serbs. They had won in both wars, and they had doubled their territory. But they had been prevented from securing their dearest ambition, which was access to the sea. They thought that an outlet to the Adriatic would give them economic independence—as it was, all their trade had to pass through Austria or on Austrian-controlled railroads, which gave Vienna something of a stranglehold over the livelihood of the Serbs. Precisely for this reason the frightened Austrians talked the other powers into frustrating the Serb hopes. The available seacoast was taken from them (under threats of war) and converted into something called Albania, which was duly provided with a German prince for a ruler.

The Serbs were now thoroughly enraged. They had been done out of their seacoast, and they had lost Bosnia, and their "brothers" were (they claimed) languishing by the million under an oppressive Habsburg rule. A good many Serbs were convinced that they could never have their way until the entire Austrian empire was destroyed. At Vienna, understandably, a "solution" to the Serb problem was regarded as most urgent.

In order to appreciate what happened next, it is necessary to see the two opposite viewpoints toward this Serb-Austrian dispute. First, the Austrian viewpoint, which was also shared by the Germans. The Habsburg dynasty was the oldest and proudest in Europe; it had liberated Central Europe from the Turks; it had presided for more than seven hundred years over most of Germany and Italy. Austria-Hungary was the second largest state in Europe. It was rich, and in its western parts at least, modern and progressive. Its cultural achievements were second to those of no other state in modern times save France. Its capitals, Vienna and Budapest, were among the finest, largest, richest, and most civilized in the world. It had a population of fifty million people, well-governed and relatively well-educated. It was one of the great powers of Europe. And the *very existence* of this great empire was, incredibly, being threatened by a nation of three million, mostly pig-herds, almost entirely illiterate, primitive, impoverished, given to barbaric and frequent revolutions, whose capital was a town with unpaved streets and a population of nine thousand. From the point of view of the exquisitely cultivated Viennese, the situation was unthinkable.

There was, however, another point of view, mysterious to the Viennese but widely (though not unanimously) held in France, Britain, and Russia. From this point of view, Austria-Hungary was a ramshackle empire, ridden with a corrupt and top-heavy civil service and a medieval social structure, with no national tradition and no nationality of its own. It appeared that it was bound, in time, to disintegrate, and, in the meantime, was engaged in a campaign of merciless exploitation and oppression of its minorities such as the Serbs in its southern provinces. On the other hand, the Serb nation was young and brave (if somewhat elemental), understandably maddened by frustration. The Serbs had the cause of freedom on their side. They were a democratic people, with vigorous (if somewhat unstable) representative institutions, and they had been repeatedly bullied by the proud and aristocratic Habsburgs. They were the underdogs. They represented national rights. And, in the end, they were deliberately attacked by the Austrians, who made no secret of the fact that they intended to weaken and perhaps destroy the independence of the kingdom of Serbia.

The two points of view, each exaggerated, were both basically correct. They were also mutually incompatible.

On June 28, 1914, the heir to the Austrian throne was assassinated by a Serb nationalist during a state visit to Sarajevo, the capital of Bosnia. The murder of the Archduke Francis Ferdinand, and his wife, was for Austrians the final blow and insult. It was believed (or at least alleged) that the murder was planned in Belgrade with the knowledge of Serbian officials, as a first step in the "liberation" of the South Slav areas of the empire. The murder was generally regarded with outrage throughout the world. In Vienna it was quite frankly viewed as a pretext for a final "solution" of the Serb problem. For a month the Austrians deliberated on what to do. They consulted the Germans, who appear (it is not perfectly clear what happened, since the consultations were largely verbal) to have told them to go ahead with any steps they thought necessary. In the end, on July 23, they presented the Serbs with a long series of demands which involved such things as the right of Austrian judges to sit in Serbian courts. The demands were meant to be unacceptable, and they were. The Serbs rejected them; and on July 28 the Austrians declared war and began shelling Belgrade. World War I had begun. Though nobody knew it, the destruction of Europe was under way.

Between the time when the Austrian ultimatum was presented and August 4 when Great Britain declared war on Germany, the European powers fell into hostilities like a line of dominoes, although strenuous efforts were made to prevent a European war. The diplomats at the foreign offices stayed up all night for two weeks, and code clerks collapsed from exhaustion in the effort to find a peaceful solution or at least to prevent the war from spreading. But the efforts were to no avail, for the governments feared the loss of their allies more than they feared war itself.

The story of those two weeks has been repeatedly told, in infinite detail and from every conceivable viewpoint. At few points in history do historians find so complete a documentary record of events, and in no other fortnight were the issues so vast and so palpable. The story is intricate, and at any point in it different policy, or a more skillful diplomacy, might have saved the peace. Viewed in large and from a distance, however, the course of events looks very simple, and so logical as to seem inevitable.

The first of the dominoes to go down was Russia. The Russians were particularly trigger-happy for many reasons. The French alliance was, at the moment, in an unusually healthy state. The French president and foreign minister were actually in Petersburg for a very successful state visit when the crisis broke, and the Russians knew in advance they could count on their ally. Their army, reorganized and rebuilt after the humiliations of 1905, was in better condition than it had been for years. They were anxious to re-assert themselves in foreign affairs. They believed (correctly, it turned out) that a foreign war would bring an outburst of enthusiasm and national solidarity which would divert attention from a troublesome domestic situation. They had for some years cherished a growing dislike of Germans and contempt for Austria. They were in no mood to permit a small and helpless friend like Serbia to be battered to death by Austria. Vienna was duly warned, and Vienna continued its private war. The Russian ministers, after some argument among themselves and with the peaceable czar, decided to mobilize their armies.

Mobilization did not necessarily mean war, but it was the next thing to it. One nation faced with a fully mobilized army across its frontier must of necessity also resort to mobilization or else be taken unprepared by invasion. And the Russians were in a curious position—their mobilization plans, drawn up on the assumption that they would be fighting Austria and Germany simultaneously in any war, provided for the manning of defenses and the calling up of reserves along the whole western frontier. The plans had taken years to develop and could not be changed; and so a measure which was in its origins designed to frighten the Austrians out of Serbia also constituted a life-and-death threat to Germany. The Germans, prepared in any event to back their Austrian ally, demanded that the Russians cease their military measures. When they declined to do so, Germany declared war. This was on August 1.

There was never any question about France. The French were in something of the same position in regard to Russia as Germany was to Austria. No matter what the cost, they dared not abandon to humiliation and possible defeat an ally whose power and loyalty was their main safeguard in Europe. When the Germans inquired of France's intentions, the French mobilized. Germany also declared war on them.

The two systems of allies were now fully engaged in hostilities, save for Italy, which refused to join its allies on the Austro-German side and declared its neutrality. The position of Britain remained unclear, for Britain insisted (correctly, so far as the letter of the law went) that it was under no commitment to either side. There was strong anti-war sentiment in London, in the cabinet itself, and Britain was moreover faced with an extremely serious crisis in Ireland. But the Foreign Minister, Sir Edward Grey, and the other leading apostles of the *entente cordiale,* emphasized the moral commitment to France and the threatening and aggressive character of German actions. The long backlog of German-English hostility, and the allied interpretation of the Austro-Serbian dispute, now came into play. And on August 4, in pursuance of long prearranged German military plans, the German army invaded the kingdom of Belgium on the way to its objective, Paris.

Belgium had several claims on British attention and sympathy. It occupied a piece of shore-line, across the channel from the British Isles, which Englishmen had sought for many centuries to keep under the control of a friendly power. It was, moreover, legally "neutral" under the terms of a treaty of 1839; the great powers had agreed to respect its territory and its sovereignty, in return for which Belgium agreed to abstain from any alliance, alignment, or hostile action. The Belgians had found it convenient to observe their own obligations. The Germans now spectacularly violated theirs, and the German chancellor was so exceedingly unwise as to refer to the treaty of guarantee as "scrap of paper"—suggesting that the interests of great powers must always take precedence over legal obligations.

The invasion of Belgium turned the trick. Britain might have been forced into war against Germany sooner or later, but the "rape" of the almost defenseless but undoubtedly courageous little kingdom unified British sentiment and brought the whole weight of British opinion against Germany quickly and solidly. The British government, more concerned with strategic considerations than with the sanctity of treaties, was enabled to act. On August 4, Great Britain declared war upon the German empire.

There remained only the persuading, the bullying, and the bribing of neutrals until every major power and most of the minor ones in the entire world should be engaged in hostilities.

In the years that followed, the peoples and prophets on both sides became convinced that they had been deliberately and gratuitously attacked, and a vast mountain of documents was adduced to prove their case. The Austrians blamed the Serbs for intolerable provocation. The Russians blamed the Austrians for a bullying attack upon a small neighbor. The Germans blamed the Russians for unprovoked aggression, and the British for a duplicitous concealment of their engagements to France. The French blamed the Germans for general over-all wickedness, and the British blamed them for raping Belgium. It rapidly became a conviction, deeply held on each side, that the other had been plotting for years. As early as the fall of 1914, the British were busily telling one another, and everybody else, that the Germans had planned the war to the day and hour many years earlier. The German emperor—the kaiser—was presented in allied countries as a blood-thirsty autocrat who had designedly plunged the world into war, and a whole generation of children in the western world grew to maturity steeped in this myth.

In point of fact, the Germans had least to gain from a war. Germany contained, to be sure, more than its share of chauvinists, people who planned and believed in a world, or at least a Europe, dominated by German power. Some of these people were highly placed, and all of them were vociferous. But there is no real evidence that they had any decisive influence on policy in the crucial stages of the crisis. The real, and sustainable, charge against Germany is that its statesmen failed to try to curb Austria until it was too late—and this was a charge which could be levelled with equal justice against France in its relations with its bellicose Russian ally. The Germans were not alone in their guilt. They knew that they were playing with fire, but they were so solicitous of Austrian interests and so indifferent to the possibilities of war as to make little effort to quench it. They were guilty, in the last weeks, of two illusions: they believed that the war to come would be quick, decisive, and relatively painless, like wars in the recent past; they also believed they could win it.

But every other nation thought it could win, too.

PART FIVE

THE FORFEITURE OF WORLD POWER

1914–1939

43

CATASTROPHE, 1914-1918

In 1914, Europe was at the height of its grandeur. Its citizens were far better fed, better educated, better housed, freer and longer-lived than any Europeans had ever been before. It occupied a position never before approached in human history. By 1918, both the outward signs and the deep foundations of this wealth and power had been damaged. Europe's world dominance was lost, its society shaken, its political institutions undermined or destroyed.

The real causes of the catastrophe of World War I, and the real reasons why it proved to be difficult to recover from it, were hard to discern and harder to cure in the years after 1918. Europe had consisted of a balance between unity and diversity—unity in the underlying similarity of its social institutions, its moral and religious composition, its traditions and its economy and its political ideas; and diversity in the different nations and nationalities which, rubbing shoulders with one another, had organized themselves into competing states. Each part of the whole had for centuries stimulated and challenged the others, and despite the wars and conflicts there had always survived enough of a balance between the unity and the diversity of Europe to prevent mutual murder and to permit recovery. In 1914, diversity at length overbalanced unity and in the war that followed, the remnants of the unity were largely lost and the divisions were deepened.

THE STALEMATE

Most people supposed that the war which broke out in 1914 would be a short one. It was argued, for one thing, that modern weapons and means of communication, particularly artillery and railways, would permit a rapid concentration of power to assure a decisive engagement early in the campaign. Secondly, it was widely supposed that modern war had become so costly that no government could afford to engage in a long war. It was imagined, therefore, that the war would be fought with the forces in existence, the standing armies, trained reserves and munitions with which the powers had already equipped themselves. Before these were exhausted, it was thought, a decision would have taken place, possibly within a few weeks, certainly within a few months. Some did fear that the hostilities might bring the end of the old Europe: Foreign Minister Sir Edward Grey, looking out from his window as the summer dusk fell on London the night before Britain's entry into war, made a famous remark as he watched the lamplighters turn up the gas street lamps: "The lamps are going out all over Europe; we shall not see them lit again in our life-time." But his observation was more prescient than representative. Almost everyone expected the conflict to follow the brief course of the nineteenth-century wars.

It very nearly did so. The German General Staff had worked out a masterly plan of campaign. A quick, decisive blow would be struck against France, with the German army advancing through Belgium. Paris would be occupied, and France put out of the war, as had happened in 1870 and was to happen again in 1940. Thereafter, Germany could devote its entire attention to Russia, whose conquest would then be-certain, while Austria finished off Serbia. Germany prepared thus for a holding operation in the east and a decisive thrust in the west, involving a quick occupation of Belgium and Luxembourg.

Had this plan worked, Germany might have emerged victorious. The German empire would have dominated European affairs, but neither the economy nor the social and political structure of European countries would have undergone the shocks which they did.

Several things upset the German plan. The advance was costly and it was confused by tactical errors. It halted abruptly after a crucial battle, the First Battle of the Marne, which began on September 6, 1914, on the eastern approaches to Paris. The French held their positions along the river Marne; an army was rushed to the front from Paris in taxicabs, and the road to Paris was barred, the front was stabilized, the French government and armies survived, and the German plans broke down.

Other facts contributed to the German failure and the stabilization of the western front. One was the unexpected rapidity of the Russian mobilization, which enabled the Russians to launch an eastern offensive, against East Prussia, before anyone expected that they could. They were defeated at the great battle of Tannenberg on August 27–30, by German armies under the leadership of General von Hindenburg, but not before they had forced a diversion of important—conceivably decisive—German forces from the west to counter their advance. Another important fact was the entrance of Britain into the war, partly as a result of the engagements with the French in the past ten years, partly because of a rapidly mounting distrust of Germany, and partly because of the German invasion of Belgium. Both the speed of Russian mobilization and the entry of Great Britain meant that Germany's plans were seriously compromised, and

The Road to Arras by Christopher R. W. Nevinson (British, 1889–   ).
Lithograph. (Courtesy Museum of Fine Arts, Boston)

might have broken down even if Paris had been captured. The position of France, even after a decisive defeat, would not have been hopeless, as it was in 1870, and a long, defensive war might have ensued in any case.

The frustration of the German advance did not, however, mean that the initiative had passed to the Allies. German power, while halted, was not weakened. The Allies had not the means to undertake a successful offensive themselves. The Germans, instead of retreating, entrenched themselves in almost impregnable positions in northern France. For the next four years, every effort on either side to grasp the initiative and to break the opponent's lines failed. New weapons such as machine guns, and new techniques, such as the use of barbed wire and trenches, made defensive operations vastly more effective at this stage of the history of warfare. Huge battles were fought at regular intervals, but none was successful in securing advances of more than a few miles. The major defensive positions were constantly strengthened, so that they were ready to meet the attack of ever larger forces and ever stronger weapons. The two lines, which were extended after the short period of movement before the Marne until they reached from the English Channel to Switzerland, remained intact until the Armistice of 1918. On the western front, the situation which developed was the very reverse of that which had been envisioned.

The two biggest German efforts to reach a decision after 1914 were made in the spring and summer of 1916 and 1918 (winter weather was not suitable for large offensive operations). On the first occasion, a direct assault was launched upon the French fortress of Verdun, which dominated a large portion of the line and made German advances around it dangerous or impossible. The battle raged for months, and about 350,000 casualties were suffered by each side. In the end, the fortress stood, to provide the superb French defense with a slogan that became one of the famous phrases of the war: *Ils ne passeront pas.* In 1918, the German Command undertook a great "Peace Offensive," designed to break the Allied line and end the war. In the meantime the Russians had been defeated and had made peace, so that the Germans were at last able to concentrate their full strength on one front. Considerable progress was made, and the Allies were on several occasions in serious danger of suffering a breakthrough. The Second Battle of the Marne ended, however, as had the first; the Germans were held on the edge of Paris. Subsequent major German efforts nearly cracked the British lines, but by July the offensive had to be abandoned without any major changes in the western front, and since German resources and staying-power were beginning to fail, no further offensive operations could be envisaged. It was after the failure of the July, 1918, offensive that the German command and government began to consider negotiating an armistice.

The Allies made several comparable offensive attempts. The French launched an entirely unsuccessful offensive on the center of the front in the summer of 1915, with losses so high that they nearly led to the mutiny of the French armies. The next summer, it was the British turn, in their sector to the north, on the Somme river. Gains were minor, and over half a million men were casualties. There were other large but unsuccessful efforts in 1917. Not until 1918, after the dwindling of the great German effort of that summer and after the arrival of American troops, did a successful offensive take place. The Germans, though their lines never broke, were pushed back from important positions. And these losses, coupled with their own failing resources, with internal perturbations, and with the advance of Allied armies in Italy and in the Balkans, determined the German decision to abandon the war.

This situation of equally matched strength, the great stalemate of World War I, was in no way paralleled on the other major front, in the east. Here, by contrast, armies surged back and forth through thousands of square miles. There was a vast seesaw, in which the offensive efforts of the Russians (meant to complement offensives in the west) usually were successful against the Austrians on their southern flank and unsuccessful against the Germans to the north. As a consequence, after each victory over Austria, the Russian strategic position became difficult and the Germans were able in their turn to take advantage of it with attacks which invariably forced Russia back deep into its own territory. The last of these gigantic seesaw operations took place in the summer of 1917, when a final Russian offensive was undertaken. It failed completely, and (Russia having begun to collapse internally) the Russia army went to pieces and the Russian government entered into peace negotiations which ended in March of 1918.

There was also a southern front after 1915, when the Italians entered the war against the Austrians and, later, when an Allied army succeeded in landing in the Balkans and eventually forced its way northward toward the Austrian border. The Italians suffered one major disaster (after German troops had arrived to strengthen the Austrian army) in the autumn of 1917, at Caporetto, but French forces, hastily imported, succeeded in stabilizing the lines. It was not until Austria—following Russia—began to weaken internally in the summer of 1918 that the Italians and the Allied Balkan army were able to advance.

The important thing to notice about each of these fronts is the universal difficulty of securing any kind of decision. Even in Russia, after the peace was signed, the Germans experienced such difficulty in occupying and controlling the territory which they had won that they were not able fully to exploit their victory. From almost the first month of the war until the day of the Armistice, November 11, 1918, the prospects of securing a quick victory were for either side hopeless. And the Armistice, when it was signed, although clearly an Allied triumph, was in the *form* of a negotiation between two undefeated armies. The Germans, at least, expected the Armistice to be followed by a negotiated peace between equals.

There was, in other words, a military stalemate in the years 1914 to 1918. This gave rise in both camps to a difference of strategic opinion, among those who wished to concentrate every resource on breaking the stalemate on an established front, and those who sought new weapons and new techniques and new theaters with which to win the war quickly. In neither camp was either point of view entirely victorious; on both sides the policies adopted were compromises between the two schools, or oscillations between them. As each contrivance failed, its backers would be discredited and the opposition would temporarily prevail in this secret, internal strategic conflict.

A most spectacular struggle of this sort took place in Great Britain. In

1915, the leader of the school which sought to divert British strength from the western front to more exotic campaigns, Winston Churchill, the First Lord of the Admiralty, succeeded in getting one of his pet projects undertaken. This was the forcing of the Dardanelles. Since Turkey had entered the war on the German side in October, 1914, the Straits had of course been closed to Allied traffic and Russia had been deprived of any ice-free sea connection with its Allies. Some strategists like Churchill, with a sure sense of historical values, understood the importance of this situation. If the enemy control of the Straits was preserved and Russia kept cut off from western supplies, then the enfeebled and primitive Russian economy would certainly collapse under the strain, Germany would conquer in the east, and the position of the western Allies would become desperate. In 1915 British and French naval squadrons were therefore sent to the east. They narrowly failed to force a passage through to Constantinople. An assault on land was then launched upon the Turkish positions on the Dardanelles, in the Gallipoli peninsula which controlled the entrance to the narrow waterways. A lengthy and painful campaign ensued, in which the British forces were several times within sight of success. But the project was not wholeheartedly backed in London, where adherents of the "western" camp withheld supplies and men which they feared to divert from France, and the British forces eventually withdrew after suffering terrible losses. The Straits remained closed; the fate of Russia was, as Winston Churchill had anticipated, sealed.

This was an important example of the difficulty of weighing the relative demands of the main fronts and of side actions. Another, and equally crucial example, was in the decision which the Germans made to try to break the stalemate by the unrestricted use of submarines against shipping. Here the two opposing camps were, approximately, the navy on one side and the diplomats (who feared political repercussions among neutrals) on the other. Germany was blockaded by the British, and in the inconclusive naval battle of Jutland, in the spring of 1916, failed to break the blockade. Its economy was suffering grievously. But the German navy argued, with some justification, that by a proper use of submarines—then a very new form of weapon—Britain itself could be blockaded and all merchant vessels carrying the vital supplies from America could be sunk. Great Britain was, in fact, extremely vulnerable to such a campaign, since it was almost entirely dependent for both food and munitions upon its sea traffic. The trouble (from the German standpoint) with this program was that it was "illegal"—that is to say, it involved sinking merchant vessels, imperilling lives, including those of citizens of neutral powers, without warning, which was contrary to rules of war universally subscribed to and theretofore generally observed. The Germans, at once desperate and optimistic, nevertheless embarked on their program of unrestricted submarine warfare. It was nearly successful: in the summer of 1917, after six months of it, the British were near starvation. But it failed because it was met, as so many of the military inventions of the war were met, by adequate defensive inventions, in this case the convoy. From the summer of 1917 on, transatlantic transport was grouped into fleets and protected by destroyers, which frustrated submarine attacks. The threat to Britain's food supplies was immediately lessened. Moreover, as one of the incidents of Germany's illegal operations, the United

States entered the war. Just as the outcome of the Gallipoli campaign doomed Russia, so did the outcome of the submarine warfare doom Germany by bringing into the conflict a great power, fresh and rich, whose resources threatened at last to bring the long-sought decision.

Another way in which the belligerents sought to break the stalemate was by bringing more and more allies into the war. The Germans succeeded in luring the Turks and Bulgarians into entering on their side. The Allies, over the years, induced the Italians, the Rumanians, the Greeks, the Portuguese, the Chinese, the Japanese, the Brazilians, and some other countries, to take part. Most of these additions to the original list of belligerents were secured by extensive (and secret) bribes and promises. The Italians, for example, in the Treaty of London of May, 1915, under which they entered the war, were promised the Austrian provinces of South Tyrol, Istria, and part of Dalmatia, and spheres of influence in the Balkans. Later they were promised parts of Turkey. Similar lures, more or less definite, were held out to the Greeks and Rumanians, while promises of "compensation" were made to encourage the harassed Allies, Belgium, Serbia, and Russia. The latter, for example, was promised Constantinople. All of these aggrandizements were to be at the expense of Austria, Germany, Turkey, or Bulgaria. When the peace treaties eventually came to be discussed, these pledges hampered efforts to draw just and sensible new frontiers.

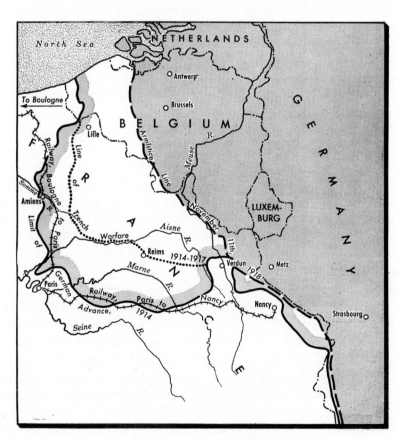

THE WESTERN FRONT, 1914–1918

The proliferation of belligerents did not much affect the course of the war and certainly did not help to break the deadlock until the entrance of the United States in April, 1917. But the progressive engulfing in the war of more and more remote regions—involving hostilities such as the Japanese seizure of the German colonies in the Pacific and the British occupation of the Ottoman provinces in Palestine and Arabia—shows how the stalemate contributed not only to the war's prolongation but to its spread, until it became quite literally a "world war," to be decided by the intervention of a non-European power, the United States. It might have been said in 1917, as Canning had said almost a century earlier, that a new world had been called into existence to redress the balance of the old. And this time the old world was so weakened that it never again became mistress of its own fate.

THE DOMESTIC RESPONSE
TO THE STALEMATE

It may well be asked why, in view of the mounting costs of operations and the apparent hopelessness of victory, the war was not called off sooner than it was. The answer is threefold. In the first place, the cost which was being paid was only gradually revealed, and by the time its dimensions had become evident, the warring peoples were too deeply committed to withdraw without catastrophe. Victory had become a sacred cause; talk of peace became a form of treason.

Secondly, very real hopes, ambitions, and aims which had nothing to do with the *causes* of the war soon became attached to the national effort. To take the simplest illustration: the French provinces of Alsace and Lorraine, lost to Germany in 1871, were irrelevant to the outbreak of a war which France entered because it was bound by alliance to come to the aid of Russia. But once the war began, no French government would have dared to make a peace which did not provide for the recovery of the provinces. Nor could any German government make a peace which provided for their cession, until disaster faced Germany. Public opinion and government commitments, once a war had broken out, soon came to include many national ambitions, like the Italian desire to control the whole Adriatic Sea. In a sense all old tensions and disputes suddenly came to the surface, and peoples were determined to fight until they were settled. The most grandiose example is the national ambition of the peoples of Austria-Hungary for independence. Their urge to independence was in some cases ancient, but in very few was it urgent in 1914. By 1918, it had become so, and the Allies—to weaken and divide their Habsburg enemy—had lured the nationalities by promising "self-determination," which meant national independence.

Which leads to the third point: with each month that passed, the horrors of defeat grew greater in the minds of the belligerents. If Austria-Hungary had lost its war in the first few months of the fighting, its eventual disintegration might have been brought nearer but would not have become imminent.

By 1918 defeat had come to mean for Austria-Hungary total destruction. In the same way, if the war had ended in 1914, Belgium would presumably have been evacuated and restored to freedom. By 1918, the experience of the German high command had convinced its members that the future security of Germany demanded the annexation or control of Belgium. A question which had been for the Belgians a matter of honor and safety had become one of national survival: if Germany won, Belgium would cease to exist.

In short, the effect of the war was to make its issues more urgent and vital and complex as the four dreadful years progressed. It was harder to make peace in 1917 than it had been the week the war began.

But the basic reason for the prolongation of a war in which military stalemate seemed to have been achieved was the extraordinary capacity of nations for waging it. The modern nation-state, with its unprecedented power for organizing its resources and evoking the loyalty of its subjects, was fully tested for the first time in history; and in the west, at least, where it was most highly developed, it was found to possess incredible resiliency. Complex societies withstood the shocks and amputations and disillusionments which the stalemate involved.

Even in the less developed and less solid states of the east there was remarkable resiliency. In Russia, the most archaic and the worst governed and least developed of the great European powers, collapse was postponed for three years. The areas in which the state and society failed to hold together through the strain will be examined in separate chapters. It must, however, be borne in mind that the Russian Revolution was undoubtedly the most important single development to come out of the war, and its effect upon the course of events in the west was instantaneous and profound. Nevertheless, the Russian experience was so large and special as to require separate treatment.

In the western countries—Great Britain, France, and Germany being the ones which deserve closest attention—the methods by which the governments mobilized their resources and carried their societies through the struggle were very similar. They may, for the purposes of brevity and clarity, be considered together.

All three countries, and all other belligerents, experienced a moment of exuberance when hostilities began which drowned opposition to the war and assured national unity at the outset. Each was convinced that it had been attacked by somebody else—Britain and France by Germany, Germany by Russia, Austria by the Serbs, Russia by Austria. As a result, even the doctrinaire anti-war groups, mainly the several Social Democratic parties, abandoned their pacifism to fight a war of self-defense. In each country, parliamentary coalitions of Sacred Union (as the French called it) were formed. By the time this exuberance had subsided, the governments had come to find ways to impose patriotism.

They did so by censoring the press—totally and ruthlessly in Germany, moderately and with consent in Britain, capriciously and against protest in France. They also did so by what later came to be called "positive thought control" —that is, propaganda. Each nation was treated to frequent, emphatic, and flattering explanations of its own innocence and the enemy's culpability. Domestic opposition was systematically disarmed, usually with the enthusiastic connivance of the majority of the people. Anyone who opposed the war was regarded as so dangerous as to justify imprisoning if not executing him. The effect of this was to deform ordinary political processes. On the most important issue of the day, there *could* be no respectable difference of opinion.

As a result of this imposed uniformity, two things happened. First of all, each country was led more and more in the direction of dictatorship. Quick and authoritative power of decision necessary for wartime policy-making, and the threat of internal subversion, demanded the suspension of the ordinary guarantees of civil liberty. It was—oddly enough—in Britain that this suspension came first and most quickly and thoroughly, with the Defense of the Realm Act. This comprehensive statute in effect gave power to the government to do anything it wanted, notably by suspending habeas corpus. Thus, ordinary individuals could be and were arrested, and imprisoned, without trial or explanation. The British government remained impeccably parliamentary, but while subject to the control of the House of Commons it was nonetheless empowered to act with an absolutism that James I might well have regarded as excessive. A similar parliamentary dictatorship evolved, more slowly, in France, which ended the war under the one-man rule of Georges Clemenceau. In Germany, the trend of events was to convert the civilian government into a paper facade for a hidden dictatorship by the high command. Chancellor, *Reichstag,* and Kaiser all became puppets of the general staff.

The second result of coercing opinion was that an opposition *did* arise, an illegal opposition. This was at first small and uninfluential, but toward the end of the war, and especially after the Russian Revolution had shown that a country *could* make peace, it grew to rather alarming dimensions. It was most important in Germany, where a growing number of Social Democrats (called Independents) refused to support the war effort. Smaller groups of Social Democrats in other countries—together with some conscientious pacifists and some anarchists—joined in an attempt to stop the war, which automatically made them traitors and revolutionaries. Most of these were followers, or sympathizers, of Lenin and the Bolsheviks. They were feared and harassed and persecuted in almost every warring country. But their existence foreshadowed the future growth of revolutionary Communism and it marked, significantly, the end of the late nineteenth-century era of good-feeling, when almost all political parties in Western Europe had consented to operate within the framework of parliaments and of constitutional rules.

All governments found it necessary to undertake, sooner or later, a thorough regimentation of the economic life of their countries to provide the necessaries of the war effort and to maintain some kind of order in the surviving civilian economy. The first and most important form which this mobilization of the economy took was military conscription. Conscription of labor and of women, formally instituted only in Germany, was nonetheless approached by various restrictions and exhortations in both France and Britain.

Industrial and economic mobilization came more gradually. When the original military supplies which had been available at the outbreak of war were used up, it became necessary to organize the economy very strictly to replace them. In the first months of the war the British government's slogan had been "business as usual." By the spring of 1915, however, a munitions crisis actually led to some shortage of ammunition among men in the front lines. The slogan of "business as usual" had to be reversed; both labor and capital had to be cajoled or forced into arranging their available resources so as to increase to the fullest the output of war goods and reduce to a minimum the output of civilian goods. Raw materials, particularly imports, had to be controlled, to make sure that there was no wastage, that the necessary minimum (but only the necessary minimum) indispensable to the civilian economy was maintained. Consumption had to be regulated by rationing, to assure a just distribution of available supplies and to prevent price inflation. All this involved a progressive suspension of a normal market economy and of the freedom and mobility of labor and capital. Working conditions were regulated, strikes suspended (by mutual agreement bolstered by government threats), the direction of investment planned, all trade controlled, consumer goods brought largely under government restrictions. This involved a degree of what has since been called "planning" which spelled the virtual end of the free economy and the total dominance of the government. So large a revolution in laissez-faire Britain did this entail that, even in war-time, it meant a change in government. The replacement of the laissez-faire Asquith by the all-out war leadership of Lloyd George was, at least symbolically, a sign of the revolutionary change in Britain's economic system which was required and achieved.

In France, similar steps were taken. France was better able to supply itself with food than Britain but, owing to the fact that most of its important industrial areas were occupied by the enemy, it was harder pressed for manufactured goods. In Germany, the situation was worse than elsewhere, for Germany was cut off by the British blockade from most of its sources of raw materials. Controls more far-reaching than in Britain and France were early adopted, although they operated in some cases very badly indeed. In one field, however, the German war government was superlatively efficient. In the planning of the use of available raw materials, a remarkably successful effort was made, under leadership of a businessman who became one of the most eminent figures of wartime and post-war Germany, Walter von Rathenau. Installed as an economic dictator, Rathenau not only rigidly and efficiently distributed raw materials but helped develop substitutes for those which were not available. Here the great German chemical industry came to his aid with synthetics, on a scale hitherto undreamt of—the famous *ersatz*. For example nitrates, essential to the manufacture of explosives and hitherto available only from natural deposits in Chile, were manufactured by fixing nitrogen from the air. Extraordinary things were done to convert coal, potatoes, and seaweed, which were practically the only resources which Germany possessed in abundance, into foodstuffs or munitions. The effect of these efforts was not only to maintain Germany's warmaking capacity but also to create an industry and a branch of technology which—in the form of contemporary plastics —has become one of the most significant of the twentieth century.

In all three countries, then, a program of national mobilization necessarily turned into a program of national regimentation and government planning. The forms differed profoundly among the nations affected, and each was informed by the traditions and temper of its people. In Britain and France, the concentration of power in the government, and its planning of the economy, was the subject of constant public debate. In Germany, an exceedingly stiff and oppressive control of individual liberty developed from the moment war broke out, and the regime was operated in many spheres directly by the military. In Britain and France, on the contrary, the civilian governments never lost control of the military leaders, and indeed in France the war effort was in the end directed by the man who said "war is too important a matter to be left to generals," a sentiment which would have been treasonous if expressed in Germany.

One striking fact, however, was common to all three countries: the governments were able to extract from the nations energies and production on a scale previously unimagined. Two things were clearly shown. The national state was the most powerful and efficient way of organizing human beings that had ever been known. *By government action* apparently limitless effects in the production and utilization of manpower and goods and ideas could be achieved. This was the lesson taught by the successful war efforts of the belligerents, and it dealt a grave blow to the notion, which had been the root of nineteenth-century liberalism, that it was almost always better to let individuals work out their destiny and solve their own problems without recourse to government action.

THE WAR TO MAKE THE WORLD
SAFE FOR DEMOCRACY

The nations of Europe went to war either to protect their vital national interests or to fulfill their obligations to their allies. An impartial appraisal may distribute blame for the outbreak among the governments, but it cannot allocate justice, liberty, and high-mindedness to either side.

It became, however, necessary to present moral motives. Once the patriotism which everywhere exploded in 1914 had subsided, citizens demanded a formulation of moral purposes, and moral purposes were also desirable to impress neutral world opinion. Such formulations came to be known as "war aims," and they played an important part in the propaganda of both sides. The Allied powers had an enormous advantage. They were able, in the beginning, to exploit the fact that Germany had undoubtedly committed one monstrously illegal action—the invasion of Belgium—and was presently to commit others, varying from submarine warfare to the shelling of Reims Cathedral, the superb medieval church which was also a French national shrine. The French and the British could present themselves as fighting for the sanctity of international agreements and against "barbaric" and "anticultural" Germany. They could also present themselves as defending humanity against an aggressively militaristic Germany, for it was widely believed, on very doubtful and partly fraudulent grounds, that the German War Lords had been plotting an aggressive war for many years. Especially after the Russian Revolution had relieved the Allies of the embarrassment of an autocratic ally, they could present themselves as fighting for the defense of liberty and democracy against what was, quite wrongly, labelled "the Kaiser's absolute rule."

Moreover, both Germany and polyglot Austria had a bad reputation for their treatment of minorities. Rather cautiously (for they had their own discontented minorities, such as the Irish in the United Kingdom) the Allies embarked upon a program of promising freedom for oppressed nationalities and presenting themselves in the guise of liberators. When the United States, with its reputation for freedom and idealism, and with its President and public sincerely devoted to the expressed aims of the Allies, entered the war, these formulations of moral motives acquired more force and reality. By 1918, a great many people all over the world, including many in Germany and Austria-Hungary, had become convinced that the Allies really stood for freedom, democracy, peace, and a scrupulous respect for human rights and international law. In January of that year, Woodrow Wilson enunciated his Fourteen Points, which summed up the morality of the Allies and outlined the basis for the kind of peace which they were seeking. These fourteen points became a text for the Allies, and it was on the basis of them that the German government finally negotiated an armistice.

The Germans were in a much less favorable position for formulating attractive war aims. They tried, with some success, to use the appeals of the Allies. In dealing with Russia, they turned the Allied slogan of "self-determination of nations" against its authors, for Germany appeared in the guise of a liberator of the oppressed Poles, Lithuanians, Estonians, Latvians, Finns, Ukrainians, and others who labored under the very heavy yoke of imperial Russia. They could promise justice for Ireland with sufficient persuasiveness to contribute to a revolution against English rule in that island. They could promise their own people to convert the German empire into a responsible parliamentary democracy after the war. But there were limitations: they could do nothing about promising liberty to the Alsatians or the Poles in Prussia and Austria, nor about the rest of the nationalities of the Habsburg monarchy.

And they were genuinely stifled by internal German differences about the true purpose of the war. The German political parties had agreed to vote war credits on the guarantee that the war was one of defense, not of conquest, and the Center and Social Democratic parties, which controlled the Reichstag, were insistent that this promise be honored. But in point of fact, the German government and general staff had very different ideas. They came more and more to envision very large annexations indeed, and a total reorganization of Europe under German domination. It was never possible for the Germans to give an authoritative statement of their war aims which was more than a negative evasion. The perfectly reasonable statement that they were fighting to save themselves from foreign depredations (notably Alsace and Lorraine) was not very appealing or exciting to anybody outside Germany. Power passed more and more openly to the military, and the military more and more openly revealed its true and horrendous war aims. The most spectacular demonstration of their true character was in the harsh peace treaties which were imposed upon defeated Rumania, in May, 1918, and upon Russia, in the Treaty of Brest-Litovsk in March, 1918.

The latter was particularly "carthaginian"—the treatment of the vanquished was so severe as to imply a desire to wreck it for all time and to seize for the victors economic and territorial advantages of a most extensive and imperial sort. The treaty, ineffectually protested by civilian party leaders within Germany and Austria, helped to convince the world of the selfish and brutal motives of the Germans and, by contrast, of the moral and disinterested motives of the Allies.

The west thus emerged from the war committed to a series of appealing slogans and ideas as a basis for peace. They had fought a "war to make the world safe for democracy"; they had fought "a war to end wars"; they had fought a war to secure "self-determination for all peoples, great and small"; they had fought a war to secure "the sanctity of treaties" and to destroy "militarism and autocracy" as embodied in the German "ruling classes." They had fought, lastly, so that an international organization might be set up to regulate disputes, ensure freedom, prevent future wars, and promote international cooperation and prosperity. So appealing were these ideas that much of a war-weary world was infected with feverish enthusiasms and hopes for an imminent Utopia.

But among the Allied governments, even in America, there was no inclination to abandon important national safeguards or aspirations. Italy, for example, could not be persuaded to give up in the name of slogans the provinces for whose acquisition it had entered the war. France could not be convinced that a future free Germany would really be so peacefully intentioned as to make it safe to allow the Germans to control the Rhineland. Britain could not be expected to abandon the navy which, it had been shown, was its one sure bulwark against starvation, in the interests of a hopeful notion called disarmament which was provided for in the Fourteen Points. The United States could not possibly have persuaded its businessmen to abandon tariffs and protectionism simply because another of the Fourteen Points called for a reduction of obstacles to international trade.

So there was a good deal of unreality about the Allied war aims from the moment they were enunciated. But the principal unreality lay in the empty hopes for a better world and a better, richer, and freer Europe on the morrow of a war which had generated unprecedented hatreds and fears and ambitions, which had devastated the populations and the economy of the continent, and which had shattered the poise and the wealth and the institutions upon which the whole structure of European civilization depended. The consequent disappointment and disillusionment were themselves potent elements in the chaos of the quarter century which followed.

THE WRECKAGE

In four years of war, Europe lost over seven million of its population. This was an appalling proportion of the total, but as a proportion of the *economically* important part of the continent it was more appalling still. For the great majority of the people killed in the war were young men—the people who, had they lived, would have been the workers and leaders and thinkers of the next twenty years of European history. The blood-letting, tragic and depressing in human terms, was disastrous to industry and government in the years to come, and it was serious for cultural growth and for the renewal of the population.

The loss of life was undoubtedly the most serious of the crippling shocks which World War I delivered to the intricate organism of European greatness. But there were others which proved scarcely less lasting than this horrible amputation. The entire economic mechanism of the continent was disarranged.

European industries suffered in three ways from the war. First, there was actual physical devastation, most important in France and Belgium whose principal factory regions were battlefields. Second, there was obsolescence: machinery was used, often for purposes which had not been intended, until it almost literally fell apart. This was most serious in Great Britain and Germany. Finally—and this burden, the heaviest of all, fell equally upon all of the European belligerents —there was the negative damage which resulted from lack of growth. That is to say, the new investments, new factories, new methods, and new markets which should have been growing up for four years simply did not exist. The 1913 level of industrial production was not reached again until 1928. In those fifteen years of destruction and rebuilding, grave discontents had grown up and dangerous remedies had been proposed, and the rest of the world had moved on.

Europe's export trade, for instance, was gravely affected. During the war, it had proved impossible to supply the hungry markets overseas with the finished products which Europe had normally provided. The markets could be recovered, and to some extent were, but the competition was stiffer and the things which were in demand were different. A drastic change in Europe's commercial and manufacturing habits was needed, and it was difficult in times of stress and insecurity to achieve it. In any case, the old predominance of Europe was gone forever, and the old patterns of commerce were shattered. A major source of Europe's income, which had provided part of the costs of its indispensable imports, was lost or compromised.

This would have been less grave had the loss of markets not been accentuated by the loss of merchant marines and foreign investments. The great creditor nations of Europe in 1914—Britain, France, Germany, Belgium, Italy, and Austria-Hungary—had imported much more than they had exported. The loss of markets meant that the portion of vital imports which had been paid for by exports was endangered. But the pre-1914 import *surplus* had been paid for mainly by two means—the hiring out of Europe's merchant vessels for carrying foreign goods; and the income from investments abroad. Both of these sources of income suffered even more drastically than did the foreign markets.

In 1918, in place of the precious overseas investments, the major European trading countries had huge debts. Germany was charged with enormous reparation bills. Britain, France, Italy, and most other countries had been obliged to borrow enormous sums from the United States either during or immediately after the war. Instead of having large surplus incomes of foreign money, they had large debits of foreign money owing.

The war's economic whirlwind had far-reaching social effects, partly caused by the disruption of the value of money. The most spectacular of European inflations, in France, Italy, Austria, and Germany, did not occur until several years after the war, but in every case inflation began before 1918, and the impossibility of curbing it later was due to the disorganization of the war itself. Most currencies had depreciated by something like 40 percent of their value by 1918; this was due in part to the rise of prices as consumer goods became scarcer and scarcer (five marks might buy a sweater in 1914; it took eleven to buy one in 1918) and also to the increase in the volume of money. Every government paid its enormous wage bills (to the soldiery, most importantly) and its bills for war supplies (to the munitions makers) by simply printing more money. The gold standard of 1914, the most important basis for international monetary stability, was abandoned by everyone as soon as the war began. More money, fewer goods, and higher prices add up to inflation, and inflation invariably means that people living on fixed incomes and on the income from savings are hard hit. The most frugal, law-abiding, hard-working, stable elements of Europe, the ones who had staffed middle class liberalism and who had produced much of the capital which paid for industrial progress, were shaken to their roots. The people who lived on savings and fixed incomes were never to recover their prosperity or their confidence in the future.

There were political effects too, hardly less painful or ominous. The concentration of power in government hands, the willingness on the part of the citizenry to abandon its own liberty and power over its own destiny, had permanent effects: people were, after 1918, far more willing to look to the state for the solution of their problems than they had been before. In every country, the political parties which were strengthened by the war were those—on either left or right of the traditional political gamut—which favored *government* action for improving conditions and protecting individuals and values. In every country, the political parties which were weakened or destroyed were those which sought to reduce the sphere of government action.

Scarcely less important than this effect of the war were the divisions in European society which were created or revealed by it. Several things were involved. Most disturbing was the Russian Revolution, which appalled respectable people, so that socialism appeared more alarming than before. A real, live, blood-curdling social revolution now existed as a warning to them, and they reacted fiercely, with fear, hatred, and sometimes repressions of their fellow-citizens whom they suspected of sympathy with it. Many people and trade unions who were wholly innocent of revolutionary aims were tarred with the Communist brush. European labor had on the whole improved its position during the war, as a result of the unions' willingness to undertake the necessary jobs of organization and economic mobilization. Now as the war reached its end, conservative people were all too eager to try to put the unions and their political parties back in their place. The result was social bitterness, social fear, and social unrest on both sides.

A comparable deepening of divisions between nations was even more conspicuous and baleful. Hatreds and suspicions were exacerbated. For four years, the Germans listened to the incessant and often venomous propaganda of their government and fellow-citizens portraying England as a nation of subnormal murderers whose particular pleasure was the starving of German babies. The French and Belgians—and other Allied peoples—were constantly informed that the Germans were autocratic, militaristic, law-breaking brutes whose special pleasure was the mutilation of Belgian and French babies. The tenuous but subsisting structure of mutual acceptance and mutual confidence among European nations had been destroyed. Almost everybody had learned to regard some of his neighbors as subhuman monsters.

This popular (and fortunately not very long-lived) virulence of opinion was matched by an *institutional* breakdown of Europe's international links during the war. All commerce stopped between belligerents, and that among Allies and neutrals was diminished and deformed. The gold standard, the basis of European commerce, was suspended and more or less permanently abandoned. Free circulation of ideas practically ceased, since ideas were subject to rigid controls. Free circulation of peoples also ceased. In 1914, it had been possible to travel freely among almost all European countries except Russia without passports or official papers of any kind. During the war travel by private persons almost stopped, even among neutral countries, and it was never resumed again on the old basis. Further: it had been, in the old days, the aristocrats and the upper middle classes who had formed a community of European culture. They had intermarried, they traveled freely, they usually spoke several languages, they often had large interests in land, business, or banking in several countries. By 1918, after a war fought victoriously in the name of democracy, the upper classes were often discredited and even more often impoverished. The Common Man was in vogue. Even where, as in Spain, Hungary, or Italy, the old ruling classes persisted in their power, they dared not openly appear cosmopolitan. They espoused nationalism in deference to the wishes of the electorate. By 1918, the community of Europe, if not dead, was gravely injured.

The old frontiers and stabilities were gone. The Russian Empire was in the throes of disintegration and civil war, with a chilling experiment in communism taking shape at its core. Austria-Hungary was gone, replaced by a series of small states with ill-assorted economies. Germany, battered and bitter, had undergone a revolution which few of its citizens wanted and a defeat which none of them accepted. Italy had suffered heavy losses to its self-respect as well as to its economy. France, with a declining birth rate, had lost a million and a quarter men and the financial foundations on which its stability was built. Great Britain had lost forever its primacy in the world economy.

All of these economic and social developments were in the making before 1914. Europe was already growing more nationalistic and more democratic. Europe's social cleavages were already growing noticeably deeper. Its economic primacy and security were already beginning to decline. But the tendencies most unsettling in the Europe of 1913 were enormously speeded and aggravated by World War I. The very violence and rapidity with which they were accomplished gave them a disintegrative character which they might have lacked if carried out slowly and gradually. There was no time for adjustment nor for comprehension.

And they were accompanied by human tragedy and by shock on so vast a scale that the peoples of Europe were not able quickly to recover from them. A new generation was to be required before the old sources of vitality, imagination, and poise could be restored.

44

THE PEACE
SETTLEMENT

AT THE PEACE CONFERENCE which was held in 1919 in Paris, the world's statesmen failed to make a lasting peace settlement. Tensions and instabilities persisted
throughout the next decade. After 1929, Europe was shaken by depression,
civil strife, and exotic dictatorships that practiced barbaric policies and produced
World War II.

The largest of the many difficulties which beset the statesmen was their
inability, and the inability of their peoples, to welcome or even imagine the kind
of changes needed to adjust the world's institutions to the vast alteration which
the war had wrought. Nations were not prepared to give up their cherished
traditions. The ideal of many people after the war was summed up in the plain-
tive and ungrammatical plea of the American President, Mr. Harding, for a
"return to normalcy." The fact was, there was no longer any normalcy to return
to. Profound readjustments in such things as national defense establishments,
tariff and currency policies and wage scales were required to establish a new
normalcy, and nobody was willing to make them.

The hardest adjustment was to realize that Europe no longer was supreme
in the world, and that the decisions of the great European nations were no longer
the only decisions that mattered. In the peace negotiations, Russia was treated
as if it did not exist. Afterward, the United States chose to behave as if Americans
could withdraw again from world affairs and leave everything to Europe. Since
Germany was ostracized and Austria-Hungary had ceased to exist, this meant
that the world leadership and responsibility for reconstructing a stable world
order devolved largely upon the French and the British, who for twenty years
struggled to keep control of their own destinies and of world diplomacy. Neither

the stature of their statesmen nor the power of their nations was sufficient to so vast a responsibility.

The major novelties of postwar international relations were the "new diplomacy" and the League of Nations. These were both outgrowths of the Allied war aims and Wilson's Fourteen Points, which formed the basis on which the Armistice had been negotiated and on which the treaties were supposed to be constructed. The New Diplomacy was intended to be democratic. "Open covenants openly arrived at" were contrasted to the secret negotiations and alliances of prewar years in which governments could commit whole nations to policy and even to war without their knowledge. It was Wilson's belief that "the common man" would be peaceably inclined, and that if consulted about foreign policy he would influence it in a wholesome direction. There was a tendency to negotiate international arrangements in public and to introduce popular discussion of foreign policy. "Diplomacy by conference," freely covered by the press, became a characteristic of international affairs after 1918. But it is arguable that the effects were not what Wilson intended. Discussion tended to be uninformed, and foreign policy tended to become a subject of slogans for propagandists and politicians rather than an art for professionals.

The League of Nations, which was also, in the main, Woodrow Wilson's brain child, represented a serious and even noble effort to provide an international organization which could prevent wars by adjusting disputes. It too represented a belief in democratic processes and public discussion. But several handicaps prevented the League from operating successfully. For one thing, its organs could not coerce the member nations into obeying its decisions. Second, the mightiest of its supporters, the United States, never joined it. Third, the whole idea of the League was that it was a free association of free governments of free men. It could not operate successfully if some of its members were tyrannies, for its whole structure was attuned to the idea of world democracy.

The basic trouble with the League, perhaps, and with other aspects of the peace settlement, was that they were born into a world of economic dislocations. The League's machinery was almost all designed to deal with political disputes—designed, as has been said, to solve the problems of the prewar world. The most useful thing that statesmen and citizens could have done after 1918 was to think how to go about providing capital for European reconstruction, solving the problems of Europe's new status as a debtor, freeing world trade, stabilizing currencies, and preventing unemployment. Almost no effort was made to deal with these problems on an international scale. Instead, governments resorted to traditional economic policies while well-intentioned orators wrangled about borders and minorities.

THE SETTLEMENT WITH GERMANY

The worst weaknesses of the peace settlement arose from these errors of omission. But its positive decisions also led to trouble. Some of these were on matters which could not possibly have been settled to the satisfaction of everybody. It is profoundly true that after a great and bitter war, justice is especially hard to achieve, for peoples' ideas of justice are then more divergent than at any other time. In the all-important treaty with Germany, the Treay of Versailles, this maxim was clearly illustrated.

The basic obstacle to a lasting peace with Germany was a difference as to who had won the war. The Allies thought of themselves as victors and of Germany as defeated, whereas the Germans understood that they were to negotiate peace, and they clung to the fact that their army was never defeated in the field. The Treaty of Versailles which was drawn up and presented as an ultimatum to the young German republic in May, 1919, was perfectly reasonable as a treaty imposed by victors on the vanquished; as a settlement between two stalemated opponents it was outrageous, and was so regarded by the Germans. Rather than sign it, they even contemplated renewing the war in the spring of 1919, and they never got over the sense of betrayal until, twenty-five years later, they were decisively defeated in a second war.

Outrageous though it seemed to the Germans, the treaty would have been still more harsh if the French had had their way. There were many people in France who favored undoing Bismarck's unification and dividing Germany again into small independent states. There were still more (and they included the French ministers) who hoped at least to detach the Rhineland provinces from Germany in order to form a buffer between the two countries.

The American and British viewpoints were quite different. They held

GERMANY'S LOSSES AFTER WORLD WAR I, 1918

that if Germans were justly treated, and led into paths of democracy, they would reform their ways. A "punitive" peace was entirely out of keeping with Wilson's noble vision of the brotherhood of man. As for the separation of the Rhineland, he saw in it merely the seed of future conflict—"we want," he said, "no more Alsace-Lorraines." There were thus two points of view sharply opposed, and the resulting treaty was a compromise between them. It was, perhaps, the worst possible outcome, for enough damage was done to the Germans to enrage them without its being enough to weaken them permanently. A peace which was at least half punitive was irritatingly enmeshed in high-flown language about democracy and justice, which salted the Germans' wounds.

What *was* done to the Germans was sufficiently drastic. First, let us consider the territorial changes. Germany lost about 13 percent of its territory. These losses included Alsace and Lorraine, which the Germans were willing to accept, and a negligible and foolish frontier "rectification" in Belgium's favor. The land west of the Rhine was to be permanently demilitarized and occupied for fifteen years by the Allies. The small (and completely German) Saar territory, which contained most important coal mines, was to be put under a League of Nations administration, with France receiving the coal, for fifteen years; then a plebiscite would be held to determine its fate. The province of Schleswig, taken from Denmark in 1864, was to be disposed of by another plebiscite, and in the end the northern half of it was returned to the Danes. These were minor, temporary, or acceptable losses. It was on the eastern frontier that there were the largest, most galling, and most intractable frontier problems. There, the Allies were faced with the need to delimit the resurrected state of Poland, now emerging from the shattered empires of Habsburg, Hohenzollern, and Romanov, which had divided it a hundred and twenty-five years earlier.

The Poles (strongly backed by the French, who reverted to their traditional alliance with Poland as soon as there was a Poland to ally with) demanded and got the Prussian provinces of Posen, West Prussia and Upper Silesia. On the face of it, this seemed fair enough. In most of these lands there was a Polish majority, and that majority had been notoriously badly treated by the Prussians for a century and a quarter. But there were problems. All the lands now contained a large German minority, which composed the wealthiest and best educated class. The cession of West Prussia (which was required in order to give Poland access to the sea and control of its main waterway, the Vistula river) cut Germany in two—East Prussia, still German, was entirely separated from the rest of the country. Moreover, the major port of Danzig, which was purely German, was also detached from Germany and made into a free city under League control, in order that the Poles might not have to depend on Germany for a harbor (they later built a new port of their own, wrecking the economy of Danzig). The problem of Upper Silesia was the most acute of all. It was one of the most important industrial areas of Germany. The population was in part Polish, but it had been under Germanic rule for some thousand years and was well assimilated. Moreover, the factory towns were German in population. When the cession of Upper Silesia was discussed, the Germans objected strenuously. The settlement was deferred. In the end, a plebiscite (unconscionably rigged by the French and Poles) was held, and the richer half went to Poland.

These arrangements caused Germans more pain than any other part of the peace settlement. The frontier was in fact extremely unsatisfactory, cutting through the middle of towns, across railroad lines, separating farms and factories from their markets. But any frontier was going to be unsatisfactory. If there was to be a Poland at all it must have some of the territory, and any substantial loss of German territory to Poland was bound to be unsatisfactory to the Germans, for most of them were accustomed to viewing themselves as "Europe's historic bulwark against the Slavic sea" and to regarding the Poles as inferior and undesirable people. Here clearly was an insoluble problem, a real clash of national interests and demands; here was the greatest single point of irritation in the interwar years; and here, indeed, was the scene and cause of the outbreak of World War II.

The territorial losses were by no means the only ones Germany suffered. It would be tedious and depressing to list all the others, but they were innumerable, and the very multiplicity of losses was one of the things which shocked German (and, when there was time to think about it rationally, Allied) opinion. Germany lost its overseas investments. Germany lost its merchant marine. Germany lost its colonies. Germany lost its air force and navy. German rivers were subject to international control. German commercial policy was controlled (to assure a market for Allied goods) for five years. Germany's wartime leaders were to be tried for "war crimes" by an international court. Germany was to be permitted an army of only a hundred thousand men. And, most serious of all, Germany was forced, in the so-called "guilt clause," to admit starting the war and, in expiation, to pay reparations. The figure for reparations which the Allies had in mind was so monstrous that they did not dare put it down in the treaty— the Germans had to agree, in effect, to pay whatever might be demanded. When the bill was first computed in 1921, it came to thirty-three billion gold dollars.

The disarmament of Germany was described in the treaty as a first step in world disarmament, but no one except the Germans ever did disarm. The result was that Germany was, in its own view, left humiliated and defenseless. The Germans systematically and successfully violated the disarmament clauses of the treaty, so their plight was not as grave as they claimed, but it was bad enough to instill conflict and bitterness. The persistent secret violations were an indication that the Germans not only felt they had no obligation to respect the treaty but rather had a patriotic duty to evade it.

Reparations constituted an even more serious problem for postwar diplomats. The Germans believed, with some reason, that the reparations were so large as to be unpayable and that they were intended not to cover war damage, as advertised, but to break Germany economically. For a country already profoundly shaken and impoverished, with its exports largely strangled, the problem of regular transfers of large sums of money abroad was serious if not insoluble. Since payments were to extend to 1971, the future seemed mortgaged. And the German cries of anguish were echoed abroad. In 1919, even before the arrangements were finally made by the victors, an English economist, John Maynard Keynes, wrote a book called *The Economic Consequences of the Peace,* as influential in shaping the course of events as any book of this period. Keynes argued that the prosperity and stability of Germany were essential to the world economy, and that by destroying them through reparations and confiscations the Allies were really damaging themselves and undermining all hope for future economic recovery. It has since been doubted whether Keynes' reasoning was accurate, but its impact on American and British opinion was enormous. Even before the reparations question became critical, as it did in the early 1920's, a large body of opinion in the United States and Britain had become sympathetic to the German view. This made it possible to arrange more manageable systems of reparations payments in 1924 and 1929, but it also opened a rift between British and French policy, for the French remained adamant on the question.

The divergences between Britain and France became one of the major obstacles to maintaining the peace settlement and to international cooperation. At the root of them was "the security problem." In essence it was simply the problem of French security from a possible German effort at vengeance. The treaty was hard on Germany, but in one way it was hard on France as well. The French were deeply concerned about Germany's probable desire to reverse the peace settlements by force as soon as possible. They were convinced that the Germans were inveterate aggressors. They also knew that the German population and economy were growing fast, whereas those of France were nearly stable, so that Germany's resources were bound greatly to exceed those of France—its population, five millions greater in 1870, was in 1920, twenty millions greater. The French first demanded the cession of the Rhineland, and were turned down. Next they asked for an international army which would enforce the peace treaties and resist aggression, and were turned down. Next they turned toward a tight defensive alliance, known as the Pact of Guarantees, whereby Britain and the United States would automatically come to the aid of France in case of attack. When the United States refused to ratify the Versailles treaty, the Pact died, for Britain also declined to approve it. The French were left with few comforts save German disarmament and the temporary occupation of the Rhineland.

In the years that followed, the security problem dominated all European diplomatic developments. It led the French into a ferocious attitude toward Germany and a resentful one toward Britain. The history of the 1920's was to a large degree shaped by efforts to solve this problem.

THE SETTLEMENT IN THE
REST OF EUROPE

Germany presented by no means the only problem which had to be settled before peace was made. There were the other enemy states—Austria-Hungary, Bulgaria, and Turkey. There was chaotic and ostracized Russia. There was the

League of Nations to be built. And there was the general feeling, insistently propounded by Wilson, that the Allies were not only adjusting disputes but building a new world order, which meant that everything under the sun came within their purview. The arrangements made in a wide variety of spheres were in many cases just as pregnant with future conflict as the treaty with Germany.

Throughout Eastern and Southern Europe, and in the Near East where the territories of the ruined Ottoman empire had to be dealt with, frontiers were very liquid. In no place did they correspond to nationality lines. National groups, each with its own strident pride and plans, overlapped and rubbed shoulders in baffling confusion from the Alps and the German border to the Gulf of Persia. It was, perhaps, folly to try to sort out Southeastern Europe and the Levant into national states. Most of the nations were underdeveloped, ill-defined, or too small to maintain states like the western ones. But the effort had to be made—partly because the nationalities demanded it, partly because the Allies' war aims had promised it, partly because nobody could invent any other kind of organization except the national states which had been so successful in the west.

One special difficulty was the fact that the great powers had no real military forces in most of the area. This meant that even if the counsels of Britain, America, and France had been wise, they could not have been enforced, and the final decision was really in the hands of the armed bands which operated under the guise of armies of "liberated peoples." The clearest example of this problem was in Hungary. There, despite the pleadings and orders of the Allies in Paris, the Rumanian army invaded defeated Hungary in 1919 and plundered the country. There was no force to oppose it.

Secondly, a good many far-reaching decisions about boundaries had already been taken in secret treaties signed among Allies during the war. France and Britain were bound by these treaties, the honoring of which would have made hash of Wilson's demands for frontiers drawn along clearly determined lines of nationality. Fortunately, the most egregious one, the Treaty of London with Russia (which had promised the Russians Constantinople), had already been renounced by the Soviets. Of those that remained, the agreements of France and Britain with Italy were the most troublesome. Despite (or perhaps because of) Italy's far from brilliant war record, the Italians were in a most nationalistic and grasping mood. They demanded all that they had been promised, and more: German-inhabited south Tyrol, Slovenian-inhabited Istria, Croat-inhabited Dalmatia, Albanian-inhabited Albania, enormous chunks of Asia Minor.

The collision between Wilson's principles and the Italian claims, some of which were based on the secret treaties and others on vague grounds such as "a defensible frontier" and "historic right," was one of the most illuminating of the peace conference. It was obvious that if the Italian claims were granted all pretense that the conference was acting on principles of justice would have to be abandoned. Wilson, convinced that the Common Man was more moral than the politicians, made a speech to the Italian people begging them to renounce the demands which their Prime Minister and Foreign Minister, Signori Orlando and Sonnino, were pushing at Paris. The consequence was an explosion. Instead of backing Wilson against its own leaders, Italian public opinion regarded the

American President as guilty of intolerable meddling in Italian domestic affairs. The Italian delegates withdrew from the conference, and total rupture was avoided only by conceding some of the more important Italian demands. Nowhere was the clash between abstract principles and national ambitions more clearly illustrated.

Many of the other territorial arrangements followed similar deplorable patterns. Tepidly backed by Lloyd George and the British, Wilson and the American delegates wearily protested the bartering of populations. The French, wise in the ways of European politics and eager to form friends and allies among the new states, generally backed the ambitions of any government which was demonstrably anti-German. In the end, the picture which emerged in Southeastern Europe looked like this: Poland, Czechoslovakia, Rumania, Yugoslavia, and Greece (all friendly to the Allies) were gorged with enemy territory. Poland was carved out of the three defunct eastern empires. Czechoslovakia was made of the old provinces of the Habsburg kingdom of Bohemia, plus some provinces from Hungary. Rumania, more than doubled in size, was given Transylvania and some Austrian provinces, plus Bessarabia, which had been Russian. Serbia—expanded by the annexation of Montenegro, the Hungarian province of Croatia, and the Austrian province of Carniola—changed its name to the Kingdom of the Serbs, Croats, and Slovenes, later called Yugoslavia. Greece was awarded southern Albania, and eastern Thrace, which had been Bulgarian.

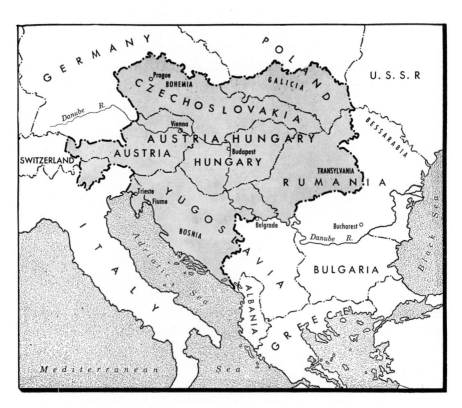

THE DISINTEGRATION OF THE HABSBURG MONARCHY, 1918

The Habsburg Monarchy ceased to exist. The Habsburg dynasty had been overthrown in November, 1918. The purely German and Magyar areas which had formed the core of the empire of Austria and kingdom of Hungary became independent states, with which the Allies signed the separate treaties of St. Germain and Trianon. The developments which so suddenly disintegrated vast and ancient Austria-Hungary were not the result of decisions taken at Paris. The polyglot monarchy fell under its own weight. No decision at Paris could have revived it. Nor could any decision at Paris have prevented the bloating of the "succession states" at the expense of the vestiges which became the Republic of Austria and the Kingdom of Hungary. The main concern of the Allies was to prevent total chaos and the spread of Communism into Eastern Europe. They succeeded in the end, although Hungary went through a few months of being a Soviet republic in 1919.

Whatever its sources, the settlement which was reached was most unsatisfactory. Austria, forbidden by the treaties from union with Germany, was left impoverished, an Alpine hinterland around the vast and orphaned imperial capital. Hungary, the proudest of nations, stripped of two thirds of its lands and all its glory but not of its oppressive aristocracy, was reactionary, sullen, and vindictive. Nor did the division of the Habsburg monarchy eradicate the problem of minorities. Yugoslavia, Rumania, Czechoslovakia, and Poland were all amalgams of varied nationalities.

Minorities were no less serious than they had been in 1914—before the war and peace which were supposed to result in frontiers drawn along clearly defined lines of nationality. Their situation was never satisfactory and was sometimes genuinely deplorable.

Nor was adequate provision made for financing the economic stability of the new countries or of the shrunken old ones. In every case, the frontiers cut economic lines—railroads, roads, and natural markets. New tariffs and new currencies replaced old ones. Banking systems were disrupted. The new governments possessed neither the revenues nor the wisdom to undertake the kind of capital investment which was necessary to make them going concerns. Capital was short throughout most of the world, and little was available for large-scale international development. The League did make loans to bail Austria and Hungary out of bankruptcy, and the French made extensive investments, but they were not designed to construct a new Eastern European economy.

The expectation that facsimiles of western national states and western democracy could survive and flourish in Eastern Europe was to be disappointed. National rivalries, artificial boundaries, national poverty, all led to international conflict and in the end to dictatorship, and invited conquest by the Germans and later by the Soviets. It was one of the failures of the peace settlement that these difficulties were not foreseen. But the eventual tragedy in the east stemmed less from the peace than from a lack of vision and statesmanship in the years which followed.

We cannot here investigate the domestic developments of strife-torn Russia, but a word must be said about the policy of the western Allies. By the time of the Armistice, in November, 1918, the Soviet regime had already been installed for a year in Russia. Lenin and Trotsky were in power, the Communist party was establishing its dictatorship, and the Red Army had been organized. One of the terms of the Armistice in the west was the evacuation by the Germans of Russian territory, and one of the Fourteen Points was the "restitution of Russia."

Restitution meant, to the western Allies, the destruction of Communism as well as the evacuation of the German-occupied regions. The Americans, British, and French were all extremely bitter about the Soviet regime, partly because it had made peace with Germany and so betrayed them, partly because of its confiscation of Allied property and investments (an especially heavy blow to France), and partly because of the brutal and repressive nature of the regime as it was presented to them by their diplomats and journalists. There were efforts to make some contact with the Soviet regime, but they were fruitless—neither side had anything to offer the other, since Lenin would not restore the foreign investments and the west would not deal with him until he did. Moreover, the civil war between the Reds and the Whites was beginning in Russia and it was thought that the Communists were doomed. There were British, French, American, and Japanese forces in Russia, fighting alongside the Whites. Nobody at Paris could think of anything to do except to attack the Bolsheviks halfheartedly on their own soil and give all possible aid and comfort to the reactionary White armies, which had little chance of success.

In the long run, the worst outcome of the peace was the survival of a violently hostile, vengeful Soviet regime in the largest country in the world. The attempt to build peace without including Russia was doomed to confusion and failure—the country was too big a part of the world which the peacemakers were trying to pacify and rebuild. On the other hand, it is difficult to see what could have been done. War-weary publics simply would not support a full-scale war against the Bolsheviks—the intervention which did take place was enough to cost Lloyd George significant support in England. And it was unlikely that, had a conciliatory policy been pursued, the Soviets would have become less relentlessly hostile to the capitalist countries.

In the rest of Europe, then, the settlement was as inadequate as it was with Germany. Rarely were the important problems solved by anything but makeshifts. Rarely were new frontiers satisfactory to the parties on both sides. Nowhere was adequate account taken of economic needs and conflicts. Russia was perforce left antipathetic, outside the "Versailles system." But at no point is it easy to see how the peacemakers—Wilson, Clemenceau, and Lloyd George— and the delegates of the smaller powers could have done much better. The problems were too big, and they had developed too suddenly, in an atmosphere of too much hatred and ambition, to have permitted a just and lasting peace.

Outside of Europe, the problems of peacemaking were scarcely less vexatious, and they revealed the same sorts of conflicts. The enormous demands of Japan, an ally, collided with the security of China and the wishes of Australia. The distribution of the German colonies and the outlying provinces of the Ottoman Empire raised rivalries and arguments. The Allies' effort to partition Asia Minor among themselves failed, owing to the resistance of the Turks, who organized and defended a new Turkish state in the heartland of the old Ottoman Empire.

THE YEARS OF STRESS:
VERSAILLES TO LOCARNO

The seven years which followed the Armistice, from 1918 to 1925, were a period of recurrent disorder, economic troubles, and despondency. With the end of the great incentive to sacrifice and national unity which the war had provided, nations became deeply divided. Social conflict, partly a product of the Russian Revolution and partly of economic distress, appeared and spread. The international situation grew less settled each year.

The major features on the international scene in these years were: the postwar depression, beginning in 1920, and its attendant problems of reconstruction; the organization of the League of Nations; the series of conferences which sought to liquidate the formidable postwar problems; the French invasion of the German Ruhr industrial area in 1923; and finally, the beginnings of some sort of economic and political stability with the return of prosperity, the completion of reconstruction, the Dawes Plan for reparations, and the Locarno Pact. By the end of 1925, a very much brighter era was dawning. But it was to be short-lived, and by 1930 it was becoming clear that few of the basic problems had been solved.

The depression which followed the Great War was similar to those which had followed most modern wars in the past. Its consequence was to make societies more unsteady and governments, therefore, less conciliatory to one another. In the case of Britain, the depression emphasized the importance of the lost German market for British exports and led to a desire to rebuild Germany as rapidly as possible. French troubles expressed themselves in foreign policy through a strenuous determination to collect every cent of German reparations, by force if necessary. In Italy, the economic crisis was in part responsible for bringing to power an intensely nationalistic dictatorship.

The League of Nations, set up by the Treaty of Versailles, was intended to settle the tensions which might arise after the war. It consisted of: an Assembly, wherein each of its members had one vote; a Council composed of permanent members, the delegates of the great powers, and semipermanent members who usually represented different regions; and a Secretariat consisting of salaried administrators who formed something like an international civil service. The function of the Assembly was to discuss and advise on matters affecting peace. The function of the Council was to propose solutions for international disputes and to seek to enforce them—if necessary by what were called "sanctions," which meant embargoes or even military action against aggressors and treaty-breakers. The function of the Secretariat was to collect information and make recommendations on the numerous international matters which came within the League's purview. In addition, there were two related organizations: the World Court, which was to adjudicate disputes on the basis of international law; and the International Labor Organization, which was to discuss labor problems and to make recommendations for improvement of working conditions and related matters.

STAMPS. Postage stamps came into general use in the 1840's, as other governments followed the example of the British, who first introduced the idea of a standard prepaid postal rate. Until 1840, postage had always been paid by the recipient of the letter upon delivery. Many postal services had until fairly recently been privately operated, on a rather hit-or-miss basis. The postage stamp is thus a symbol of the development of modern government services, and also of improved transportation and the growth of a more complicated society which required cheap, fast, reliable postal service. Stamps came gradually to be more than merely useful indications of a fee paid. Governments learned to use them for propaganda purposes, to commemorate great national occasions, to popularize national figures, to emphasize cultural accomplishments.

1   2   3   4   5

Stamp 1 above was issued by the government of Austria-Hungary for use in the province of Bosnia, to commemorate the death of the heir to the Habsburg throne, whose assassination in the Bosnian capital of Sarajevo was the cause of the war crisis of 1914. The stamp shows the murdered prince, the Archduke Francis Ferdinand, and his wife, who was killed with him.

Stamp 2 records the disintegration of Austria-Hungary which took place as a consequence of the war that started in 1914. It was issued by local authorities in the Austrian province of Carniola after the revolution against the Habsburgs and the decision of the Carniolans to attach themselves to the newly formed South Slav kingdom of the Serbs, Croats, and Slovenes. The picture depicts Carniola breaking free from the fetters of Habsburg rule.

Stamps 3 and 4 record the Russian Revolutions of 1917. The first is one of the last series of stamps issued by the Czarist government, showing the last Emperor Nicholas II. The second, the first stamp issued by the Soviet government, is another portrayal of the idea of liberation, represented by the breaking of chains.

Stamp 5 is a grim reminder of another effect of World War I, the inflation of currencies. This German stamp, used for ordinary postage, had a value of twenty milliard marks—that is, twenty billion. Before 1914, the mark had been worth about twenty American cents.

The League, whose headquarters was in the Swiss city of Geneva, was intended to be a world organization, but it was in practice very European. Though most nations, excluding the United States, Russia, and Germany, were members of it, and although Japan had a permanent seat on the Council until it resigned in 1933, most of the problems and most of the leaders of the League were European.

Its record was rather encouraging up to 1925. The Secretariat was proving itself efficient in dealing with such technical matters as international narcotics control. The League was, moreover, moderately successful in supervising the "mandates"—that is, the former German colonies and Ottoman provinces which by the peace treaties were confided to the Allies—Japan, Britain, France, or Belgium—for administration under League supervision, while they were theoretically being prepared for nationhood. The Council, the most important part of the League, also could point to several successes—and near successes. Most of them were cases arising out of the war and the redrawing of boundaries. All of them were between fairly small countries, in which none of the great powers had vital interests. The Council, for example, settled a dispute over the Aland Islands between Sweden and Finland. The Upper Silesian boundary was settled, though not very satisfactorily. In the Balkans, the League arranged settlements of disputes between Turkey and Greece and Bulgaria and Greece, and carried out exchanges of populations.

But all these matters were easy because the parties to them could be overawed by the League and the major powers behind it. The one case involving a great power in these years was between Greece and Italy, when Italian battleships—with little justification—bombarded and wrecked the Greek island of Corfu. Here it was not the malefactor Italy which backed down: it was injured Greece, and the League. The incident was extremely significant, for it showed that open aggression by a great power could not be controlled.

The most important questions of the day, however, the relations between the defeated nations and the Allies, did not appear on the League agenda. These were dealt with—or at least discussed—by a Council of Ambassadors, or by conferences of experts. There were endless meetings, on reparations, on the Near Eastern question, (peace was not finally made with Turkey until 1923 after a series of minor wars and crises), on such eastern problems as the war between Poland and the Soviet Republic which broke out in 1920, and which ended with vast accessions of territory to Poland on its eastern border. Some of these problems were settled, but many were not.

The most important of the continuing problems was reparations, and it was this which gave rise, in 1923, to the most portentous and distressing international event of these years, the French invasion of the Ruhr. This was precipitated by a failure of Germany to keep up its reparation payments, but its real causes were different. The government in France was that of Prime Minister Raymond Poincaré, the war-time president, a Lorrainer, a conservative nationalist, and a Teutonophobe. He represented a widely held French belief that France had been done out of its right to "security" at the peace conference. The French had already sought new paths to security—mainly by signing treaties of alliance with Germany's smaller neighbors, all of which had profited at the expense of the Central Powers: first with Belgium, and later with Poland and with the "Little Entente"—Yugoslavia, Rumania, and Czechoslovakia, which shared a vital interest in maintaining the peace settlements. Now, the French embarked upon what looked like a direct attack on the distraught former enemy. Together with those of Belgium, its armies invaded and occupied the Ruhr valley, the most important industrial area in Germany. Most people—especially the British, to whom the action seemed irritating, illegal, and arrogant—suspected a desire to crush Germany. At the same time, the French began to arrange conspiracies in the adjacent Rhineland (which they already occupied under the treaty), which led to the proclamation of a separate Rhineland Republic by French-sponsored intriguers. Nothing came of it, but it suggested to the world that the motives of France were more political than economic.

In the autumn of 1923 Germany gave in, and promised to resume full reparations payments. The French forces withdrew. An international commission set about studying the rescheduling of reparations, and shortly thereafter (1924) general elections in France brought to power a leftist majority under the conciliatory Edouard Herriot. The German mark, after an incredible inflation rocketed to new heights by the Ruhr invasion, was stabilized. And at about the same time, world economic recovery was bringing prosperity again to most countries. France had completed most of its reconstruction and was no longer so dependent upon large payments from Germany for its own financial stability.

These developments all contributed to a better climate of opinion. So did the almost simultaneous coming to office in Britain, Germany, and France of three talented, tactful, and strong foreign ministers: Austen Chamberlain in Britain; Aristide Briand in France; and Gustav Stresemann in Germany. All three sought peaceful relations: Chamberlain because Britain wanted a peaceful Europe in order that its own commitments might be reduced; Briand because he thought weakened France could not live except in a peaceful and united Europe; and Stresemann because he thought that cooperation with the western powers was necessary to permit Germany to recover its strength and to work for the undoing of the Versailles Treaty.

It was generally recognized that the French sense of "insecurity" was the root cause of much of the instability, and some satisfactory formula for remedying this situation had been sought unsuccessfully for years. Now the three foreign ministers found a formula. France and Belgium on the one hand, and Germany on the other, were to promise never to attack one another and never to cross their common frontiers. Germany also undertook never to permit troops to enter the Rhenish areas of its own territories which were demilitarized by Versailles. This agreement was to be "guaranteed" by the remaining two great western powers, Britain and Italy, which agreed to come to the aid of the victims if either side violated its undertaking. The treaties embodying these arrangements, including an understanding that Germany should enter the League of Nations and be restored to respectable membership in the family of nations, were signed at the Italian resort town of Locarno in October, 1925.

Locarno was widely heralded as "the real end of the war" and, by Chamberlain, as assuring "peace in our time." So exhilarating was the belief that French security was now achieved, and that good will would prevail, that most of the other issues of European politics seemed to dwindle into insignificance. The fact that Locarno followed soon on the Dawes Plan, which had made a workable arrangement for reparations, and upon the beginning of a world economic boom, consolidated the impression. An era of good feeling was inaugurated. It lasted a mere five years.

THE ERA OF GOOD FEELING: LOCARNO TO THE DEPRESSION

So long as prosperity lasted and the three great foreign ministers remained in power, it seemed as if nothing but improvement could be looked for in the "European situation," as it was called. Disarmament talks, so long projected, at last commenced. The Allies evacuated the occupied German Rhineland, five years ahead of schedule, in 1929. A new more liberal arrangement for reparations payments was achieved. The League continued to develop, strengthened by the presence of Germany after 1926. Even sinister Russia, apparently losing confidence in the imminence of world revolution, began to enter into more or less amicable relations with its neighbors and even with western countries.

All this was very encouraging. But the hopes were shortly to be drowned in the whirlwind of the Great Depression, which wrecked the world's economy, bred extremist policies and bellicose dictatorships, and deranged even the reasonable men of Europe to the point of folly and war. By 1932, Stresemann and Briand were dead and Chamberlain out of office. The German republic was staggering to perdition. All of the careful and painfully worked out arrangements of the 1920's were about to be destroyed.

But indeed the atmosphere of peace itself rested upon illusions, even before the Depression swept them away. Let us take, as a sample, the disarmament problem. It was generally believed that disarmament was the most important element, next to "security," of a lasting peace (a belief open to question in the first place, since no matter how low the general level of armaments, a determined aggressor might still aggress). Disarmament had been projected in the treaties, and in the early 1920's its easiest aspect, naval disarmament, had been tackled. The outcome was the Washington Naval Treaty, signed by the major naval powers in 1922, Britain, France, Japan, and the United States. Even this agreement dealt with only one class of naval vessels—battleships—and even it had been subject to acrimony and discontent. Efforts to extend the agreement to other kinds of ships in 1927 failed; and in 1930, at the London Naval Conference, it was found impossible to agree to any other reductions.

Naval disarmament was difficult; land disarmament proved impossible. A preparatory conference met at Geneva in 1927, nine years after the principle had been agreed on, but it became hopelessly snarled. The French insisted that agreements meant nothing unless accompanied by international inspection to make sure they were being observed, and all other states objected to this as an intolerable infringement of their independence—an issue remarkably similar to that between the United States and the Soviet Union in the disarmament talks of the 1950's. Countries which had conscription objected to counting former conscripts—trained reserves—in the totals, while those which did not have conscription—mainly Britain and Germany—insisted on it. Hundreds of other differences, general and particular, appeared. It took three years to draw up an agenda for a General Disarmament Conference, which did not meet until 1932, after the international situation had gone to pieces.

The evacuation of the Rhineland by the Allied occupying forces was achieved by Stresemann, who had come to inspire such confidence abroad as a man of peace and cooperation that his proposals were very favorably received. It was thought that this measure would contribute to "appeasement," a word which ten years later acquired a very sinister meaning. The evacuation was commenced in 1929, on the eve of Stresemann's death and the crumbling of the German republic. But even had subsequent events been less unfavorable, it is doubtful that the evacuation would have contributed much to appeasing Germany. The Germans were determined to rearm, and many of them, even the pacific Social Democrats, were sympathetic to the idea that in the foreseeable future they might become strong enough to be able to force the liquidation of the Versailles Treaty and, perhaps, recover the territories lost to Poland. Stresemann was aware of, and enthusiastic about, the persistent violations of the disarmament clause. As a result of secret agreements with the Soviet Union, German troops were being trained in Russia, and German firms there were manufacturing guns, grenades, and even poison gas for shipment to the Fatherland. The evacuation of the Rhineland, or indeed anything in the way of concessions, was unlikely to alter the attitude of the German army or much of the German public toward the Versailles Treaty and Germany's subordinate position in Europe. For similar reasons, the new reparations arrangements, the Young Plan of 1929, contributed very little to a permanent peace.

Another gaping weakness of the era of good feeling was in the failure to achieve any guarantees of security in Eastern Europe. While Locarno gave at least an impression of stability in the west, the new states in the east had no comparable safeguards. It was, for example, Poland which was most exposed to a new German attack, and the Germans showed no inclination to give assurances of accepting their losses to Poland. Indeed, their conciliatory attitude in the west was intended to free their hands for a revision of the peace settlement in the east.

Nor was the League in any better position to solve basic problems or prevent wars. The United States continued to be absent from it. But American absence from Geneva did not preclude an active role in world affairs. The Secretary of State, Frank Kellogg, proposed in 1928 that all the nations of the world agree to "renounce war as an instrument of national policy." When publicly requested to renounce sin, it is embarrassing for anyone to decline; the nations rushed to sign the Pact of Paris. Several of them added reservations, which Kellogg tacitly accepted. In this way, wars of self-defense were excluded, but nonetheless by this extraordinary document aggressive war became formally illegal. The pact was signed by forty-five states, including Japan and the Soviet Union. Its long-run effect was, of course, *nil*. Its immediate consequence was that the first few aggressive wars which took place after its signing were not preceded by formal declarations of war and were referred to as "incidents" by their authors.

Soviet foreign relations in this period reflected great changes which were taking place in the internal affairs of Russia and which brought to supreme power the tough and realistic Joseph Stalin. Stalin, compared to his predecessors, was both less interested in immediate world revolution and more prepared to lie about his aims. Relations had already been resumed with France and, for a few months, with Britain—they were broken off when it appeared that the Soviet diplomats were seeking to meddle in British politics. Relations with Germany had been fairly good since 1922, when an economic and secret military agreement had drawn the two outlaw nations together. In 1927 and 1928, efforts were made by the Soviets to eliminate some of the tensions with their neighbors in Europe and the Near East, all of which without exception had been suspicious and hostile. Non-aggression pacts were signed with Iran, Turkey, Rumania, Yugoslavia, Poland, and the little Baltic states. There were some grounds for believing that the Soviet regime under its new leader was moving toward a respectable foreign policy. But in point of fact there was little hope that the regime could be welcomed into the family of nations as a national state like the others.

There were other problems which persisted. One of the most ominous features of Europe in the late 1920's was the inability of the Central and Eastern European states to develop internal stability or international harmony. The high hopes for democracy were being destroyed. Poland had already drifted under an undemocratic regime, and so had Hungary and little Albania. Yugoslavia, ridden by rivalries among its national groups, was about to do so. And in the countries where representative government still survived in 1930, it was growing increasingly corrupt, inefficient, and violent.

Despite the breathing space of the period 1925 to 1930, then, the basic problems had not been solved. A makeshift structure had been constructed out of the war ruins, but the deep maladjustments remained. The breathing spell was important for Europe, for it permitted recovery from the material devastation of the war. By 1930, Europe's trade and industrial output, its standard of living and its finances, were back to where they had been in 1913. But the stage was already set for the black disasters which began the next year.

45

THE ECONOMIC
AND POLITICAL
CRISIS IN EUROPE

IN THE PERIOD BETWEEN THE WARS, Europe tried to adjust its economy and its political arrangements and ideas to its altered position in the world and to its own shaken societies. These efforts gave rise to debates and emotions of the most violent sort. Europeans had been bred, before 1914, on the expectation of constant progress and improvement. After the war, their condition was disorganized and disappointing, and threatened to grow worse.

The disappointment was particularly exasperating because it was clear that the possibility of economic expansion still existed after 1918. Its physical signs—increased technical knowledge, expanding factories, methods of mass production—were visible on every hand. But in the midst of plenty there was crisis, insecurity, and unemployment. Business depression on a scale unknown in living memory spread suffering and alarm in the 1930's. Many people felt that somebody must be to blame, and it seemed to some that there must be a formula which would remedy the situation. Doctrines of the most diverse sort were expounded, and some of them adopted. Where they captured the government, as in Soviet Russia or Italy, such doctrines led to bizarre and brutal experiments. Where, as in France and Britain, no one doctrine secured acceptance, frustrating debate ensued against a background of inaction.

In the west, nineteenth-century liberal traditions were still fairly strong in 1918. There had been emendations, particularly in the practice of laissez faire, and even liberal parties had accepted social legislation to protect the rights of workers and restrict the powers of employers. But the basic assumptions of both political and economic liberalism were still unchallenged by any respectable body of theory except Marxism. In the 'twenties, a new form of political organization called fascism appeared. There seemed to be no alternative to a free society, with a minimum of government action and a maximum of bruising booms and busts, except a regimented tyranny like the Communist or fascist.

By the time the Great Depression reached its depths this situation had begun to change. In the countries which rejected the more drastic panaceas, a new economic theory began to emerge which proposed ways of eliminating the shocks of a wholly free economy while preserving the merits of political freedom. This hopeful vision did not, however, materialize until it was too late to prevent a world economic breakdown and its resultant social conflict, or to save Europe from the triumph of German Nazism, the internal division of the surviving democracies, and the advent of World War II.

THE WORLD ECONOMIC BREAKDOWN

World War I had left the European economies exhausted, and drastically affected Europe's position in the world. The most sensational of these changes was the conversion of the old, mature economies of Western Europe from creditor into debtor nations. Instead of regularly receiving from abroad large sums in foreign currency, used to pay for the imports which made them prosperous, Europeans were now obliged to send money overseas. This change was a symptom of a larger one, the growth of non-European countries, particularly the United States. The displacement of the old center of the world economy showed itself in many ways, most especially in dependence on the United States for aid and capital. It is most easily demonstrated in two sets of figures.

First, the production of farm and industrial products in Belgium, France, Germany and Great Britain in 1920 stood at 60 to 90 percent of the 1913 figure, while that of the United States stood at about 113 percent.

Second, Europe's share in world trade fell from 54.5 percent in 1913 to a low of 46.9 percent in 1926.

These two sets of figures indicate the *comparative* decline of Europe after 1913. They do not necessarily indicate that Europe had stopped growing, but rather that other places were growing faster.

The first task after 1918 was reconstruction, which meant both repairing war damage and overcoming the appalling dislocations left by the catastrophe. Europe lacked the necessary capital, and this meant that Europe's destinies were no longer under its own control. Europe's need for capital, which only America could supply, increased dependence upon the United States, whose policy was the decisive force in world economic affairs.

The United States had been accustomed throughout its previous history to a debtor position—that is, it owed money abroad. This meant that its own commercial and economic policies had little effect upon the history of foreign countries until 1918. By then, however, the situation was reversed. But American politics and opinion were not correspondingly altered. American imagination failed to keep up with events. The failure was reflected, in politics, in a determined effort to return to "isolation," which meant withdrawing from commitments outside the Western Hemisphere and refusing to join the League of Nations. In economics, it was reflected in insistence upon repayment of the war debts owed by the Allies. By the end of 1919, some $9.5 billion were owing to the United States, the bulk of it by Great Britain, France, and Italy. The loans had been made as business transactions, although they had been designed to assist the common war effort and Europeans argued that they had not expected to have to repay them.

There was, perhaps, no moral reason why the money should not have been repaid, but there was an economic one. Europe was now in debt; the problem of earning enough dollars to pay even the interest of the loans was difficult, and efforts to do so put severe strains on the war-racked Allied countries. It led, among other thing, to the Allies' continuing demand that the defeated Germans provide them with means of payment in the form of reparations, and this caused bitterness and economic calamity in Germany. The only wholesome means of payment open to France, Britain, and Italy was an increase in their exports to America. Such substantially increased purchases by American consumers would have meant competition for American manufacturers. Congress and much of the public were strongly averse to permitting foreigners to sell freely in the American market, and in 1924 the United States tariff was actually raised to deter them.

Economic logic, however, forced an informal solution to the debt problem in the late 1920's. Instead of cancelling debts all around, they were indirectly financed by American surplus capital. Starting in the middle 'twenties, large private American loans were made to Europe, especially Germany. These were used in part to pay German reparations to the former Allies, who in turn sent the money back to America in the form of interest on war debts.

After 1924 or 1925, the confusion and disorganization of the postwar period began to clear, thanks partly to this munificence of American lenders. The costly job of physical reconstruction was complete. The postwar depression had ended, and both production and trade were reviving. By 1927 or 1928 virtually all parts of Europe except, perhaps, Great Britain had attained the prewar level of commerce and industry.

The new prosperity was, however, uneven and peculiar, and based on sagging foundations. Certain groups, such as British coal miners and American wheat farmers, were not sharing in it. Some prices, especially securities, were rising, while others, especially farm products, were declining, and this meant that many people found it hard to buy necessities. The entire structure was based upon an unhindered flow of American capital, which greased the wheels and permitted the expansion of European economies. In 1929, the precarious boom turned into depression.

The Great Depression of the 1930's was the most important episode of the period between the wars. Had it not happened, there might well have been no second war, for the economic and political events which it set in train would not have occurred: there might have been no Nazi dictatorship, no fatal aggressions against the nations of Europe. The depression sharpened disputes and social conflicts. It hastened a whole array of little revolutions, some of which changed regimes and all of which changed policies and attitudes.

The causes of the depression are as complex as its effects, and they are less clearly understood. It is, perhaps, safest to begin with the event which was most concrete, the collapse of the American stock market, and proceed thence to mention of larger causes.

The American stock market had reached, in September, 1929, a level of unprecedented prices and volume of sales. The rise had continued—not without interruptions, since 1924. From the beginning of the summer of 1929, the price of stocks had increased by about one quarter. After the middle of September it remained steady for a month, and then selling began in a panic. From October 24, 1929, to November 15, prices fell by half. The financial slaughter was very great.

The dependence of the world economy on the United States was now graphically demonstrated. In America, loss of savings and of confidence led to a

ANXIETY by Edvard Munch (1863–1944). Color lithograph, 1896. (Museum of Modern Art)

sudden contraction of consumption and investment. By 1930, business had followed finance into a decline. The falling demand for foreign goods led in turn to a contraction of world trade, which hit Western European business. But the stock market crash had more immediate and disastrous effects: it cut off the supply of American capital to Europe, the capital which had paid for Europe's economic recovery and made possible the honoring of its numerous and heavy debts.

There was certainly more to the causes of the depression than the Wall Street crash. Some economists have argued that a business recession was already in course. There had, indeed, been a fairly steady decline in commodity prices—that is, prices of unfinished primary materials—since 1926. Most farm products had been produced in greatly expanded volume during World War I. After it, productive capacity remained but demand fell. Commodity prices had generally been low everywhere since 1918, and had gone further down after 1926. This meant that half the world's economy was already in trouble by 1929. The other half, the industrial half, was bound for trouble too, crash or no crash. Decline of income for farmers meant a declining market for manufacturers. Overconfidence and cheap money in America had led to an excessive flow abroad of capital, which had led to industrial over-expansion in many parts of the world. Manufacturers were producing more than they could profitably sell.

Whatever its deep causes, the effects of the Great Depression were prompt, concrete, and harrowing. World prices had fallen in 1930 by 10 percent, and, two years later, by 30 or 40 percent. Many firms simply could not make a profit and went out of business or restricted operations. Unemployment spread, rising in Germany from one and a third million in 1928 to five and a half million in 1932. In Italy, despite its rigidly controlled economy, unemployment rose by 200 percent in about the same period, and in Great Britain by about 250 percent. The situation was similar everywhere, except in the Soviet Union, which was almost entirely isolated from world economic movements.

As unemployment rose, purchasing power declined and government revenues fell. Perhaps the most drastic effects of the depression are seen in the figures on world trade, whose total volume fell by more than two thirds from the 1929 high to the 1934 low.

It would be difficult to exaggerate the effects of the Great Depression in almost every aspect of life throughout the world. Except for the Soviet Union, and a few countries like Sweden where strenuous measures kept the effects within endurable bounds, the crisis spread hardship and engendered bitterness everywhere, and provoked extremist policies and demands of the most unsettling sort.

THE WORLD IN DEPRESSION

Each European country adopted its own measures for dealing with the depression. There were few efforts at international programs, and those few abortive. But in the end, the recovery policies of the major western countries, and of the United States as well, developed in not entirely dissimilar ways.

All were nationalistic. Each government used its authority to secure recovery at home without much regard for effects abroad, and to insulate and cushion the domestic economy against foreign uncertainties. The most conspicuous casualty of the depression was the gold standard—that is, the international standard for measuring the value of national currencies—which had been almost universally accepted in 1914 and largely restored to that status by 1929. Another important casualty was what economists call "multilateral trade"—that is, the buying by country "A" of goods from country "B," which in turn buys from country "C," while country "C" in its turn buys from country "A." Such multilateral trade permits countries' international accounts to even out in the long run, and it also permits them to buy in the cheapest and sell in the dearest market. In the depression, nations were frequently obliged to make "clearing agreements" with one another, so that their mutual sales and purchases would come out even. This process, known as "bilateralization," broke up the natural pattern of buying in the cheapest market. In order to make accounts balance, two countries might have to buy from one another goods which they could have found more cheaply elsewhere. The consequence, like that of most of the expedients of the 'thirties, was to help solve immediate problems of unbalanced international accounts, while at the same time making for inefficiency and restriction of the total volume of trade.

Secondly, governments extended their sphere of action greatly, sometimes to the point of planning what and how much should be produced, what the price should be, and who should buy it. This sort of "intervention," as liberal economists in the nineteenth century would have called it, was at least partly inspired by the experiences of World War I. Mobilization had shown that governments could ration limited resources and allocate supplies to achieve really remarkable results. As one historian observed, the war experiences of the nations did more to further the cause of socialism than the efforts of all the socialist parties in history. If by socialism one means government planning and regulation, then this statement is plausible, and the depression added what the war had left unfinished.

Third, almost every government engaged in currency manipulation, which enabled it to control prices, to encourage exports (by reducing domestic prices in terms of foreign money), and to discourage imports (by raising foreign prices in terms of domestic money). It also enabled governments to meet the huge demands upon them, such as relief for the unemployed and for foundering businesses. Virtually every government expanded its budget to succor some portion of its citizenry. French public expenditures rose by a half in the decade after the crash, and so did the British. The discovery of the potent effects which the manipulation of credit and currency could have, placed a gigantic weapon in the hands of the state, as powerful as the weapon of taxation, for ordering the economy and rearranging the social structure.

The experience of three countries will illustrate the policies which many adopted.

Great Britain suffered earliest in Europe, and the British were the first to evolve drastic measures. Unemployment spread rapidly in 1930–1931, and the expensive pound sterling, painfully revalued in 1925, produced a grave decline in exports. Combined with great deficits which were produced by unemployment relief payments, the effect was to raise the spectre of national bankruptcy. After 1931, the following measures were adopted: the pound was detached from gold and reduced in value, henceforth subject to regulation by government fiat; free trade was abandoned and tariffs of 10 percent (later raised) were imposed; arrangements were made with other countries of the British Commonwealth for reciprocal preferential trade treatment—that is, Canadian or Australian goods entered Britain subject to a lower duty than goods from, say, the United States, and British goods enjoyed a similar preference in Canada or Australia; finally, efforts were made to prevent cheap money and dearer imports from leading to an uncontrolled price rise, mainly through strict government economy including reductions in unemployment relief. These measures stimulated purchasing power through various means, notably because they led to the founding of firms to manufacture and sell, behind the new tariffs, goods formerly bought abroad, and these helped soak up unemployment. But the consumer paid higher prices, and foreign countries which lost their markets in Great Britain felt considerable distress.

The country most adversely affected by the depression was Germany. There, unemployment reached even more shocking levels than in Britain. By 1932, the German situation was critical and revolution was widely apprehended. After the devaluation of the pound, the obvious course for Germany was a corresponding devaluation of the mark, which would have eased the budgetary, banking, and foreign trade crises. But this would have been inflationary, and memories of the inflation of 1923 were so vivid and distressing as to preclude a policy aimed in that direction. Little was done until the advent of the Nazi dictatorship.

Nazi economic policies were intricate and diverse, but a few highlights may be mentioned. Enormous public works were undertaken to put the unemployed to work. Wages, however, were strictly controlled, so that demand did not immediately rise, and prices were also controlled, preventing inflation. Foreign trade was closely regulated. Importers were told what they could import, preference being given to basic raw materials. Exports were stimulated by permitting foreign purchasers to buy marks at a reduced rate. Trade agreements with many countries provided for the balancing of purchases and thus of currency transfers. These steps involved the extension of government control to all sectors of the economy. Farmers and industrialists and shopkeepers alike had their production, prices, and wages planned for them. The results were in some degree gratifying. Unemployment, Hitler boasted, was reduced from six to one million in three years, and industrial production rose 75 percent. Prices were held fairly steady, and the mark remained at its nominal gold value. The price paid was also high, however. The recovery was carried out only by a brutal and total destruction of liberty, and the rigid economic structure remained in some ways precarious.

In France the depression came late, and little was done to develop a consistent program until 1936. Before that, a conservative policy of rigid economy and adherence to the gold standard was accompanied by measures to restrict imports and salvage tottering businesses. Import quotas were adopted, disrupting the normal flow of trade, and subsidies were extended to various interests. In 1936, however, a predominantly Socialist ministry took office and undertook far-reaching reforms. They were designed, among other aims, to increase the purchasing power of the ordinary man, so creating new demand. Minimum wage laws were passed, shorter working hours decreed, paid vacations provided, and the franc was devalued. Recovery remained slow, however, and the most visible consequence of these measures was the fury of conservative opinion.

But by 1939 a measure of revival had taken place everywhere. Rearmament was a most important economic stimulant, diverting large government funds into industry, augmenting employment and purchasing power. It represented a form of public works and government enterprise on the largest possible scale.

While the depression persisted, some patterns and tendencies dating from an earlier time continued and added to its revolutionary effects on society. The most important of these was the distress of agriculture, which accounted for more than half the jobs in Europe during these years.

The condition of agriculture was endemically unfavorable. It had been so since the 1870's, when railroads and steamships first opened up European markets to the cheap produce of Russia and America, precipitating a general decline of farm prices. The consequence was an increasing imbalance, which worsened in the 1920's and 1930's, between the standards of living of people concerned with manufacturing and those concerned with farming. This widening spread was given, by Lenin, the name of the "scissors." In revolutionary Russia it appeared in a peculiarly acute form, but it was widespread in most agricultural areas. The varied medicines with which governments dosed their farms had little effect. Great Britain subsidized beet sugar. The French government bought large surpluses of wine, and the Brazilian of coffee. In Germany, foreclosure on mortgages was forbidden outright, and minimum prices were set for farmland. Such remedies availed little.

The fault was the relative inefficiency of agriculture. This was most noticeable in places like Rumania, where methods were backward, machines few, and output per man small. It was also true in the United States, where output was very high. Even highly mechanized farmers could still not produce as much value with a day's work as could a man in a factory.

Various solutions were tried. In the United States, prices of farm products were simply pushed upward by act of Congress. In less advanced countries, efforts were made to increase efficiency by supplying more tools and scientific methods, and by improving marketing. But there were difficulties. In underdeveloped countries like Rumania, more output per acre would mean that fewer farm workers were needed, and there was no place for the surplus labor to go. Moreover, the principal urge of eastern peasants was to own their own land. This meant dividing farmlands into small holdings, as had been done in France during the Great Revolution. But the French example showed that small farms, while they might contribute to social stability, were not very efficient, for the individual farmers could not pay for the necessary equipment.

The most original approach toward a solution of these problems on a large scale was in Russia. There, collective farms offered an alternative to both the small-scale peasant farming of France and the great landed estates of Poland and eastern Germany. The Soviet experiment was not very satisfactory as a guide for the west, however, for its inauguration required an iron dictatorship and much suffering. Nor was it, by 1939, demonstrable that eight years of collective farming had done very much to increase output or improve conditions on the land.

As World War II approached, European agriculture was in a serious plight, whose effects were felt in every sphere. In the east, it was distressed farmers who contributed most to political discontent and whose demands helped to make the sordid dictatorships of the 1930's. In Germany, small farmers (among others) voted solidly for the Nazis, and it was the frightened Prussian landlords in the east who sought most vigorously to undermine democracy and the republic.

It was natural under these circumstances that rural regions like Rumania should seek to build up their industries through government planning and investment. "Planning" was very much in fashion, especially after the widely advertised success of the First Five-Year Plan in Soviet Russia (1928–1932). It represented the fruit of an understanding, born in World War I, that it is possible to secure dramatic effects through government decision and investment, and it was taken up as a means not only of developing industry but also, as in Britain, of alleviating depression or, as in Germany, of nurturing self-sufficiency.

The motives of the various plans proposed or adopted were as various as their methods, but the most complete ones, in Russia and Germany, were in some respects very successful. Germany was prepared for a grandiose war effort. Soviet industrial output is said to have quadrupled under the first two Five-Year Plans (1928–1938), a rate of progress much greater than that of any other country.

In Great Britain, despite much discussion, no systematic plan was ever worked out, but the Conservative governments were inaugurating policies which resembled piecemeal planning, designed to eliminate the damaging effects of competition and, to some extent, dependence on imports. In many fields—shipping, steel, chemicals, air transport, radio and electricity—the government sponsored or subsidized group investment, group price regulation, and sometimes outright monopoly.

In every country, the most grievously injured victim of the depression was the liberal ideal of a world of free economies with stable currencies, low tariffs, and a minimum of government intervention in the economy. The liberal prescription for depressions—smaller budgets, unhampered price and wage declines, unrelieved unemployment—had proved unworkable, even in those countries where the tradition was strongest, like the United States.

Nor were the solutions adopted in the democracies or the fascist dictatorships "socialist" in any traditional sense. Socialist parties were, and remained, devoted to the central idea of nationalization of industry, banking, and commerce. Except for a few cases, such as the Bank of France and the perpetually insolvent French railroads, few enterprises outside of Russia were actually taken over or operated by the state, although there was a considerable extension of state enterprise in Nazi Germany.

Most of the measures were regulatory, like those of the New Deal in America, not confiscatory. Most of them were intended either to salvage threatened businesses or to stimulate purchasing power—aims which precisely controverted the basic precepts of *both* old-fashioned capitalism and old-fashioned socialism. They were achieved mainly through government action, whether it was called Planning or not—manipulation of money, credit, wages, and prices, and aid to agriculture. The important feature of recovery, wherever it took place, was that money was being put into the hands of consumers and investors. This was the real revolution which emerged from the depression, outside the Soviet Union. It was accompanied by a revolution in economic thought which shortly led many economists and businessmen to abandon their previous assumptions about how economies worked.

THE REVOLUTION IN ECONOMIC THOUGHT

John Maynard Keynes (1883–1946) was the father of this revolution. Son of a distinguished Cambridge mathematician and philosopher, he was himself a brilliant economist. He was a member of influential intellectual circles in Britain, and a member of Lloyd George's staff at the Paris peace conference. Here he collected the materials and the anger which inspired *The Economic Consequences of the Peace*, a polemical book which brought him world fame.

In 1919, when he wrote it, his assumptions and theory were still basically those of the nineteenth-century economists, but his ideas shortly began to change along original lines. In the *Tract on Monetary Reform*, in 1923, he came out squarely against the orthodox deflationary policy, and the effort to return the pound to the gold standard, then being pursued in Great Britain. Such a policy, he said, reduced prices, constricted consumer spending, and slowed down economic growth. Many of his later conclusions were contained in the *Tract*, but the elaboration of their theoretical foundation awaited his two great works, the *Treatise on Money* and *The General Theory of Employment, Interest and Money*, which were published in 1930 and 1936. The following elementary summary of some of his principal contributions will help to make clear the nature and scope of the intellectual revolution which they evoked.

Earlier economists had argued that the basic forces in economic change are supply and demand. They had said, to put it simply, that prices were determined by the interaction of supply and demand—for example, whenever supply increased and demand remained the same, prices would fall. A doubling of supply (that is, production) would reduce prices, but there would always be a market for almost anything if the price were low enough. The suitable policy for a government to follow in a depression, the older economists thought, was inaction: there was nothing to do but wait for prices to fall so low that businessmen would stop manufacturing goods. Supply would then diminish, and prices would automatically start to rise again.

To these notions Keynes added an entirely new element, which was the role of *spending,* or, more precisely, the way in which the willingness to expend savings bore upon the operation of economic laws. Spending, in modern economies, takes two forms: buying consumer goods, or investing in new plants and equipment by businessmen. Businessmen who wish to get money to build, say, a new plant, get it in the form of loans from banks or from securities—stocks and bonds—sold to private investors. The average citizen who has some money has three choices of what to do with it—to buy goods, to invest it, or to keep it in cash. Keynes pointed out, for the first time, the decisive importance of the way in which this choice is made.

Let us suppose a time of recession. Businessmen will hesitate to expand their plants or start new ones, fearing a falling off in demand for their product. People with money will hesitate to buy refrigerators, cars, or anything else, thinking that prices may go down. As a result, the total level of spending declines. This means that prices decline, business finds itself in trouble and lays off labor— or perhaps lowers wages. The effects spread out at a geometric rate of progression. Keynes demonstrated that for every dollar decline in investment there would be a three or four dollar drop in the amount of money available for spending, for each dollar invested is multiplied by being passed along among workers, consumers, shopkeepers, and so on. Small changes in investment therefore show up as large changes in the economy, a phenomenon known as "the multiplier effect."

The opposite danger to depression is inflation. This occurs when investment grows more rapidly than savings—when businessmen are so confident that they invest in new plants on the largest scale, and there is increasing competition for savings, for labor, and for equipment. Prices are driven up. The multiplier effect is present here as well. For every new dollar invested, total spending rises several dollars. Demand for consumer goods expands accordingly, encouraging businessmen still further and pushing prices higher. An upward spiral as perilous and, for some groups, as painful as depression, ensues.

Keynes introduced a new element to economic theory: the relationship between saving and spending. This relationship he saw as decisive in determining the course of economic change. The effects of his theories on practical affairs were very great. What was needed to prevent depression and curb inflation, according to Keynes, was government action. When businessmen were hesitating to invest and consumers hesitating to consume, the government could forestall depression by government spending and by measures to ease credit. For example, the government could undertake public works. By going into debt itself, it could inject money into the economy which, with the multiplier effect, would spread through it, causing an increase in savings, in purchasing power, and in investment, and reversing the downward tendency. Or it could reduce interest rates by appropriate changes in the policy of the central bank, which would encourage borrowing and new investment. Or it could, perhaps, devalue the currency, so raising prices and stimulating spending. Any or all of these would have the effect required: the increase of purchasing power and willingness to spend. Conversely, in time of inflation, the government could rein its own spending and reduce investment by raising interest rates, so decreasing the volume of credit and hindering price rises. It is important to remark that *only* the government can operate in this way to stabilize the economy: businessmen cannot be forced to invest when they feel it unwise to do so, nor can consumers be forced to buy goods if they do not want to. Governments, however, have practically unlimited credit and unlimited power to decide when they will inject money into or drain money out of the economy.

Keynesian economics showed how government might act to stabilize economies. The old objections to government intervention were discredited. But the action for which Keynesians called stopped far short of socialism, or of wholesale planning. There was to be no direct interference with economic freedom or private enterprise. Capitalism was to be saved, not sacrificed, by government action.

The new theory liberated its followers from the antagonism between humanity and economic laws which had characterized nineteenth-century theories and had caused people to call economics the "dismal science." Ricardo had seemed to say that it was economically wholesome for people to suffer and starve. Keynes now said that it was economically disastrous for them to do so. The "Keynesian revolution" thus provided the philosophies of freedom and political democracy with a kindly and hopeful creed and counterpart.

THE REVOLT AGAINST POLITICAL FREEDOM

As war and depression provoked a systematic attack on liberal economics, so did they generate a crusade against liberal political ideas and their democratic legacy. In both assaults, older critical theories were drawn upon, blended with new and more radical ideas, and recast. Against the notion of the free economy were arrayed such varied rebels as Communists, socialists, and Keynesians. Against political freedom and representative government were arrayed Communists and fascists—for most socialists and all Keynesians remained devoted to political freedom and democracy.

Fascism is not a very good word. Strictly speaking, it means the political party and ideas which dominated Italy in the years from 1922 to 1943. Loosely used, it is sometimes made synonymous with "dictatorial," or even with "conservative," which is certainly improper. Like so many other terms in the lexicon of the twentieth century, it was early taken over by Marxists and given a meaning harmonious with their own uses. Fascism for the Marxist means "the final stage of monopoly capitalism, in which capitalists, frightened by the threat of social revolution, impose their own dictatorship." In each country where it flourished, furthermore, there was a native word for the fascist movement—National Socialism (or, more commonly, its nickname, Nazism) in Germany; Rexism in Belgium; Falangism in Spain; Integralism in Brazil. But despite its lack of precision there is no other single word satisfactory to describe the political movements which came to power in Italy and Germany between the wars.

There is another difficulty in defining or analysing fascism. Its leaders emphatically and repeatedly explained that their principal purpose was to destroy "the myth of reason." Since reason is the only tool most people have for explaining and classifying things, the explicit rejection of it made it easy for fascists to say anything they wanted without need for consistency. The German leader Adolf Hitler might in one speech adulate the glories of war and in another the beauties of peace, to both of which he professed himself greatly attached. Charged with inconsistency, he would have replied that consistency was a criterion of reason and that he disdained it, knowing a more reliable path to truth. Precisely what this path was he never made entirely clear, but it seemed to consist mainly of his own intuition and his mystical communion with the Folk Soul of his people.

Perhaps the best way to understand fascism is to list the things which its proponents disliked. Very simply, they were these.

1. The notion that each individual is equally valuable. For fascists, some individuals were not only less valuable but positively undesirable and ought to be exterminated. All western societies have at some time practiced a version of this belief—in the death penalty for treason or murder, most often—but few in modern times have ever proposed the extermination of large groups.

2. The notion that the individual is the best judge of his own welfare. This was replaced by fascists with the idea that most individuals have no sensible basis for making decisions, which ought to be made by someone "superior" and better informed.

3. The notion that if all individuals express their choice about how they should be governed, the greatest good for the greatest number will result. Fascists believed that government by individual choice merely led to control by cheap politicians who knew how to pander to vulgar tastes and to manipulate voters.

4. The notion that individuals, if accorded the greatest possible freedom consistent with public order, will make the greatest possible contribution to humanity. The fascists held that it is society—the group—which by joint achievement confers culture on individuals. The measure of an individual's worth was his capacity to contribute to the group, and the standard of all morality was the welfare of the group.

5. Political parties, which sacrificed the interest of the nation to a faction.

6. Freedom of expression, which allowed enemies of society to mislead the public.

7. Capitalism, which encouraged individuals to profit at the expense of the public.

8. Representative government, which led to confusion and factionalism and to distortion of the "national will," in contrast to rule by a dictator who could embody it.

9. Minorities and non-national groups, which were thought incapable of behaving in harmony with the nation.

Finally, fascists were (though not consistently) opposed to the gentle virtues of tolerance, patience, and forgiveness. They lauded the more vigorous virtues of strength, courage, sacrifice, and honor. Against the enemies of the state they advocated violence; indeed, they often advocated it simply as a form of self-expression.

The reverse of these aversions constituted the positive program of the fascists. They were in favor of: an "elite"—people peculiarly equipped to protect and enrich the group, who would have special privileges and power; a "leader," who would substitute his own decision for the processes of representative government; the nation, which all fascists saw as the ultimate "group." Fascists differed as to just what a nation was. The German Nazis thought in racial terms. Their nation was conceived as a tribe whose members were determined by heredity. Italians, however, defined their nation in terms cultural rather than genetic. Finally, fascists were in favor of the State, which meant the sum of the preceding things welded into a powerful body which supervised every aspect of life and constituted (as Mussolini grandly put it) "the recapitulating unity of countless generations."

In actual practice, these rather spongy absolutes were taken to involve dictatorship, large armies, spirited foreign policies, repression of subversive opinions, and elimination of groups like labor unions and socialist parties. There was a tendency to deify state and dictator, which led in Germany to altercations with the churches. On religious matters, fascists were divided, for in Catholic countries they tended to be at least formally Catholic, while in Germany they were hostile to all religions.

The philosophical origins of fascism have been much discussed. It is easy now to see that fascists borrowed any idea from the past which suited them, and they remained relentlessly opportunistic. But the systems which they installed undoubtedly owed something to the thought of various predecessors.

The most important of these, in the case of Italy, were the syndicalists, and their popularizer, the Frenchman Georges Sorel. Mussolini had grown up as a syndicalist agitator, and he carried some of its ideas through his transition to Fascism. Two ideas, in the main, were borrowed from the earlier movement: first, a belief in the social utility of violence; second, the idea of organizing society into "functional groups," which Mussolini called corporations. Since work was the most important part of anyone's life, primary allegiance and association ought to be through a professional group. It was hoped that this banding together of everyone concerned in (say) the steel industry would give all members a common and constructive goal. As used by fascists and sometimes by non-fascists as well, "corporatism" was meant to be an antidote to Marxian class warfare. The corporation grouped together the employer and the employees as a family. Theoretically it functioned for the welfare of all, but in Fascist hands corporate organizations became the means of destroying an independent labor movement and giving Fascist party bosses a voice in the business community at a substantial but by no means intolerable cost to the latter.

Another source of fascism, particularly of German Nazism, was the philosophy of Friedrich Nietzsche (1844–1900), an eminent German philosopher and misanthrope. A good deal of Nietzsche had to be carefully edited before his works were acceptable to the Nazis (he had, for one thing, regarded Germany as the most decadent and contemptible of nations), but nonetheless his works became an official gospel of the regime. He had inveighed against ideas of liberty and equality, and denounced the soft, middle class qualities of materialism and individualism. He urged instead the confiding of society's destiny to a new race of Supermen—bellicose and muscular idealists who would guide civilization back to more heroic values.

An important source of Nazi doctrine was the racism of nineteenth-century writers. Such men as Sir Henry Maine in Britain or Count Gobineau in France had suggested the inherent superiority of some races over others, and the superiority of "pure" (as opposed to hybrid) races. In the sense in which these writers used the words, no European "race" was "pure," or anything like it. But the wholly unprovable idea of the superiority of—say—the Teutonic peoples, and the desirability of their remaining pure, was converted by the Nazis from a naive theory to a mystical theology, and it was used to explain history and to justify extermination of Jews, war against Slavs, and the hegemony of Germans.

In addition to these, there were many other ancestors of fascist doctrine, some of them very unlikely. The gentle Idealists, mostly Liberal Oxford professors of the late 1800's, provided some of their ideas. The Idealists had set forth the fact (which earlier Liberals had disregarded) that the "group" is at least as important to the individuals as the individual is to the group. It is from the family, the school, the church, the nation, the state, that children learn ideas of right and wrong, the great thoughts of the past, language iself. Roman Catholic writers had emphasized the importance of "associations"—family, parish, trade union—in inculcating culture and morality. From these and many other sources the fascists drew, to produce their transmogrified version which deified the state and made all signs of individuality into crimes against society.

Fascism was not alone in winning large numbers of people away from a faith in freedom and democracy. Marxian socialism, with its almost mystical faith in the working class and its claims to scientific understanding of history, continued to appeal to workers and intellectuals. Its popularity grew as a result of the Great Depression and of a general lack of precise knowledge about the Soviet Union. To many, the "socialist homeland" appeared from afar to be the only hope for a rational and peaceful society in a world dominated by Hitler and Mussolini. Marxism became a kind of "opium of intellectuals," as one French observer put it.

Since the split between Socialists and Communists at the end of World War I, the latter, associated with the Third International at Moscow, had increasingly become the agencies (unwitting on the part of the rank and file) of the Soviet government and Soviet foreign policy. Communist intellectuals and party leaders in Central and Western Europe clung to their faith that in Russia a model society—"a new civilization," as the British socialist Sidney Webb called it—was being constructed. Fascism, the depression, and the approach of World War II helped to obscure from view the Stalinist purges of the 1930's and other evidence that Russian Communism was far more savage than most western intellectuals imagined. In Western Europe, the split between Socialists and Communists, and their application of more energy to mutual vilification than to combatting the depression and fascism, was a crippling handicap to both the labor movement and to democracy.

The split between Socialists and Communists was part of a larger division in Europe's political life. During the 1930's, two camps (each gravely divided within itself) were arrayed against one another. On one side were the old conservatives and liberals, the socialists and radicals and democrats, all believers in the traditions of self-government. On the other were Communists and fascists, both supporters of a notion of the state which came to be called totalitarian. Totalitarianism meant the insertion of the state's power into every aspect of life; totalitarians discerned political significance in everything. The totalitarian state left its citizens no privacy; no occupation was untouched by political control. This total organization of human affairs by governments in the name of some dogma—whether class or nation—was perhaps a response to the uncertainties of a generation familiar with war and depression. It undoubtedly reflected the growing number of instruments, scientific and political, which were at the disposal of the state for controlling its citizens. Whether many people were genuinely tempted to "escape from freedom," or whether they were simply confused by the appeals of fascism and Communism, totalitarianism posed the greatest menace to human freedom which the world had known.

46

THE RUSSIAN
REVOLUTIONS OF
LENIN AND STALIN

THERE ARE MANY WAYS of looking at Russian history from 1917 to 1939. It may be viewed as the story of the great power which is the Union of Soviet Socialist Republics today. A social revolution took place, the most striking since 1789. It produced the strongest of the twentieth-century dictatorships. Its ideology worried and confused intellectuals in the west. In the less fortunate parts of the world peasant and nationalist leaders watched with interest while Russia raced to catch up with western Europe and America.

The Russian revolutions—first the liberal one of March, 1917, then the Bolshevik one in November, then Stalin's revolution "from above" in the Five-Year Plan—were at once inspiring and repulsive. They were a drama of social science, of man using his will and knowledge to make over his environment. Yet they demonstrated man's weakness and cruelty.

For a time Russian history was a story of the failure of czar, generals, and police officers to cope with the strains of World War I. Then it became a story of the failure of liberals and moderate socialists to master those same problems. Then it turned upon Bolshevik maneuvers from one policy to another as they tried to stay in power. The old Russia of brutality and orthodoxy and one-man rule kept showing through as the Communists tried to cover it with acceptable democratic garments. Even such a crafty player as Joseph Stalin had to leap clownishly from one policy to another to keep himself and his party from being crushed by giant economic and social forces.

But there is another side to the story. The Communists in Russia did not simply scramble to stay in power. They exerted their will, and cut, ever so clumsily, the pattern of a new society.

WORLD WAR AND LIBERAL REVOLUTION[1]

World War I provided the setting but not the fundamental causes of the Russian Revolution. Russia since the start of the century had been carrying a whole set of weights which the other European countries had lifted one or two at a time. Politically the transition from autocracy to representative government was not far enough advanced to insure its success. Socially a peasant problem more serious than that of France in 1789 existed side by side with urban conditions which resembled those of England during the early Industrial Revolution. Intellectually and psychologically, Russia's condition was aggravated by the fact that the old government and society had lost the allegiance of most educated people, including many of those in positions of responsibility and privilege. A backlog of untried political and social theories had piled up.

Russia's participation in World War I aggravated the irritations caused by unsolved problems; it turned the long-term causes of upheaval into immediate causes and brought the shift of power and property and official philosophy which was the revolution.

When war came in 1914 most Russians supported it patriotically, the exceptions being on the far right and the far left. Some reactionaries at court wanted peace with Germany on the ground that the Hohenzollerns cared more for social order than did England and France. The Empress Alexandra Fedorovna was of German origin as well as being devoted to autocracy, but there is no evidence that she had German sympathies. The royal family was deeply influenced by the uncouth but powerful holy man Rasputin, who was able to ease the pain of their hemophilic son. Rasputin was devoted to autocracy, which had enabled him to reach a point where his scribbled notes wrecked ministries, and great aristocrats paid him court. Rasputin was true enough to his peasant background to be against the war, but he worked with no party.

The more liberal cabinet members and the educated public favored the war, distrusted German political and business influence, and were glad when the name St. Petersburg was changed to Petrograd to make it sound less German, more Slavic. In general, educated people thought that the war would force the autocracy to consult them and permit their participation in the management of the country. In this way, they expected, Russia would become a constitutional state like its allies Britain and France.

[1]Russia retained until February, 1918, the old Julian calendar, according to which the first, or liberal revolution of 1917 took place on February 23 and the second (Bolshevik) revolution on October 25. In this book all the dates for Russian history are given according to the Gregorian calendar used by western countries, and by Russia since February, 1918. Thus what the Russians call the February and October revolutions of 1917 are to us the March and November revolutions.

Even most of the socialists in the Duma were patriotic. At first both Bolsheviks and Mensheviks opposed the war, but the Mensheviks, in keeping with their more moderate views, for the most part repented. The Bolshevik leader Lenin, living in Switzerland, said that the workers should spread defeatism and try to turn the war into a revolution. In his book *Imperialism* Lenin argued that workers and the moderate socialists who were now making war on each other in the uniforms of their respective countries had been seduced by their small share in the spoils of Europe's imperialistic exploitation of the rest of the world.

Russia's huge if clumsy contribution to the Allied cause has been described elsewhere. With Lenin in Switzerland, Trotsky in New York, and Stalin exiled to Siberia, the Russian Revolution cannot be said to have come from the actions of its ultimate beneficiaries. The extraordinary wartime strain on production and the unforeseen need for planning were disastrous to the old quasi-absolutism, only slightly altered by the Revolution of 1905. Cumbersome at all times, the machinery of autocracy reached a new low during the wartime crisis owing to the isolation of the royal family and the resulting virtual anarchy at the summit of the state. Rasputin's sickly ascendancy over the empress, and her strong-willed but ignorant influence on her husband, Nicholas II, sealed them off from the advice of even their nearest relatives. Especially after Nicholas went to the front in early 1915, leaving the empress as virtual regent, Rasputin's erratic behavior served to guarantee the absence of able, independent men from high public office. After Rasputin was murdered at the end of 1916 there was no improvement in the leadership provided by the sorrowful empress and her apathetic husband.

Meanwhile another tendency, existing in embryo since Alexander II's zemstvo reform, and somewhat enlarged by the Revolution of 1905, worked to save the situation. The zemstvos and the Duma lacked deep roots in the Russian people, but they did what they could to provide medical supplies, food, transport, and production. To Russia's misfortune the contest between the autocracy and an all too feeble upper class liberalism continued to the March revolution of 1917. As they had in France in 1789, the conservatives and moderate liberals failed to form a coalition ready to make the absolutely necessary concessions. The complete absense of effective leadership on the part of the autocracy, and its refusal to let the liberals try to dominate the situation, proved disastrous.

Confusion in the government was accompanied by deterioration in the country. The mobilization of some fifteen million men by 1917 hurt industry by taking irreplaceable skilled workers. Agriculture suffered too, particularly the large estates that customarily produced the surplus which fed the towns. Enemy invasion cut down the amount of land. Casualties—in all some seven million, of which about 650,000 were deaths—impaired morale. The price of food rose about 300 percent between 1914 and 1917. Real wages declined. Town producion simply could not meet the needs of the war, much less the wants of the peasants. Inadequate equipment and heavy casualties discouraged the troops. Desertions were monumental. Rumors about a coming redistribution of the land disturbed the army. By 1917 the whole front threatened to disintegrate.

In March, 1917, the venerable imperfections in Russian politics and society were finally translated into revolutionary action. Russia slid into revolution. There was no explosion of wrath, just a gradual withering of the government's authority until, one day, it was gone and could not be revived.

On March 8, 9, and 10, 1917, crowds increased in the streets of Petrograd, demonstrating against food shortages, in favor of socialist Woman's Day celebration, and in sympathy with the locked-out strikers of a large factory. On March 11 the government decided that the Duma should be dissolved. But on the night of March 11 the soldiers in their barracks decided not to fire on the people, and so on March 12 the troops disobeyed orders and joined the popular demonstration, which turned to hunting down the police and seizing arms from the arsenals. The dismissal of the Duma on that same day does not seem to have played a major part in revolutionary events. The members of the Duma obeyed orders and closed their session. The only suggestion of irregularity on the part of the Duma was that upon hearing of the disintegration of military authority in the city, they formed a Temporary Committee which continued to meet, unofficially, to follow events and if possible to help in the restoration of order.

But if the public in those tumultuous days supported any representative body, it was not the remains of the Duma, but rather the Soviet (Council) of Workers' and Soldiers' Deputies which also held its first meetings on March 12. The Soviet appeared almost spontaneously, nobody knows quite how.

Nicholas II was not in Petrograd but at army headquarters. On March 12 he sent a force to restore order in the capital, but when it reached the suburbs it melted away into the revolution. When Nicholas learned that his generals as well as the members of the Duma thought his abdication to be necessary, he retired in favor of his brother, Grand Duke Michael. Public hostility to a monarchy was so strong, however, that Michael did not dare accept the crown except from the hands of a constituent assembly, and so Russia became in fact a republic, although technically it was still a monarchy without a monarch.

In other parts of Russia the revolution had been paralleling the events of Petrograd. Committees of revolutionaries took over the authority in most Russian cities. There was on the whole little bloodshed, for scarcely anyone wished to defend the czar. At the front the armies neither disintegrated at the news of the revolution nor showed any displeasure with it.

Almost simultaneously with the czar's abdication a Provisional Government was formed in Petrograd (March 16). It was headed by Prince George Lvov, a liberal idealist who had been prominent in the work of the zemstvos. The Provisional Government was pledged to establish civil liberty, abolish legal restrictions based on class, nationality, and religion, and call a constituent assembly to decide on Russia's future government. The Provisional Government was in reality dependent for its existence on the benevolence of the Petrograd Soviet, the only body which had the respect of the armed workers and of the city's garrison, which had thrown off discipline.

Everywhere the old state machinery had withdrawn its tentacles as officials fled or gave up their functions. The Provisional Government, product of the old regime's Duma, hung, as it were, in mid-air.

The Soviet, on the other hand, was a huge, unwieldy meeting of some 2,500 deputies, whose membership was in constant flux. Most of those in attendance were moderate socialists of one kind or another. They did not wish to take the responsibility of governing Russia themselves, for they felt unprepared and believed that this duty should fall to the non-socialist parties. But they had no hesitation about safeguarding the revolution. One of their first acts was to issue the famous "Order Number One" to the troops, directing them to elect their own representatives in all units in order that there might be someone to keep an eye on the officers. Order Number One contributed to the crumbling of army discipline. Another of the Soviet's actions was to compel the Provisional Government to arrest the Czar and his family.

In effect, there was in Russia at this time a "dual power," the Provisional Government having nominal authority but only moral influence, and the Soviet having very real power but little or no formal authority. The liaison between the two was provided by Alexander Kerensky, a brilliant and self-confident young right-wing Socialist Revolutionary who had been leader of a labor group in the Duma. Kerensky was to be the incarnation of the liberal revolution.

Looking back at the Provisional Government and the high hopes of the March Revolution, anybody today must wonder at the contrast between the excellence of its intentions and the brevity of its career. For a few months Russia was for the first time really free. Civil liberties had been won, there was an eight-hour day and freedom of labor to organize, nationalities were to be emancipated, the peasants were promised the redressment of their grievances, and the whole was to be crowned by the work of a constituent assembly which would presumably make a democratic republic. For the moment, at least, the army in spite of its hatred of its officers and of the war was not ready to cease defending the country. The peasants, in spite of their dislike of the war and their desire for more land, were not as yet in a state of insurrection. The labor movement in the cities was still led by moderate socialists. Yet the abyss lay ahead; and one cannot help asking whether the March regime had any real chance of success.

There were forces at work in Russia which had to be coped with if disaster was to be avoided. Russia's allies, Britain and France, deep in their own struggle, were pressing for a continuation of the war. And indeed the alternative was bleak if peace meant that Germany would be enabled to win in the west and then turn east with all its force. Russia's traditional aims, expansion in the Balkans and seizure of the Straits from Turkey, were still temptations. Yet continuing the war threatened to disintegrate the armies and, muliplying desertions, bring active elements in the peasantry home to arouse the others.

Every week which passed increased the unrest in the countryside as the peasants learned of losses of life at the front and grew more impatient and nervous waiting for some kind of land settlement. As shortages and disorganization cut down deliveries of manufactured products to the countryside, the peasants' willingness to deliver grain to market decreased. In the towns rising prices and food shortages were complicated by strikes, lockouts, and factory shutdowns.

In brief, unless the Provisional Government could find a way to rally the army at the front and the public at home, it would find the army refusing to fight any more, and the people at home seizing the land and the factories. The situation might have been saved if the Constituent Assembly had been called at once and if it had at once made the right decisions about the war, the land, and the labor movement. But could the Constituent Assembly be called without first stopping the war? Was the stopping of the war one of the "right decisions," and what were the others?

No one can know what other turns Russian history might have taken. Neither the Provisional Government nor the Soviet, in the summer of 1917, found a way to counter the worsening military, social, and economic situation which had brought the March Revolution and was to make possible that of November.

The Provisional Government first lost face on the question of war aims. Miliukov, the Cadet foreign minister, represented the point of view held by many liberals: that Russia should stand by its allies and share in the coming victory by taking Constantinople and the Dardanelles. The moderate socialists of the Soviet wanted a peace without annexations or indemnities. Miliukov tried to continue his policies, but public indignation threatened the Provisional Government, and Miliukov resigned. A new period began in which members of the Soviet consented to take part in the Provisional Government.

In the middle of this first stage of the revolution Lenin arrived in Petrograd (April 16) from Switzerland. He had taken advantage of the German government's willingness to transport agitators like himself back to Russia. Others were already on the scene, notably Stalin, who had returned from Siberia and was playing a rather obscure role while awaiting firm direction. Trotsky was on his way from New York.

Lenin's "April Theses" at first struck such a bold and jarring note that he was at once voted down by the Bolshevik leadership. With his fanatical single-mindedness, determined to have a socialist revolution in Russia, he wrung the last ounce of reinterpretation out of Marxian theory. The only way to have peace was to overthrow capitalism and capitalist governments. This could be done in Russia by the proletariat in alliance with the poorer peasants. The revolution had to move to a second stage in which power would pass from the Provisional Government to the Soviets, the only true representation of the workers and peasants. Lenin was not entirely clear about who would direct the Soviets when they took power, or how the peasants would share the nationalized lands, or how "social production and distribution of goods" would work. But he was a confident improviser, sure of his ability to ride the tide of events. And his program, translated into slogans, had a powerful appeal to people who saw a vision of soldiers coming home to share the land, workers managing their own industries, and government in the hands of ordinary people living at the level of their fellow workers. His tireless repetition of this program had such an effect on the public that by May the Bolsheviks were won over. Lenin showed them how they could draw strength from the hurricane which was tearing away the authority of the Provisional Government.

By midsummer, 1917, Lenin's tactics began to bear fruit. In early July Kerensky's military offensive against the Germans and Austrians turned into a disaster. A great popular insurrection on July 16–17, carrying Bolshevik banners and slogans, besieged the meeting of the Petrograd Soviet, demanding that it take over the direction of the government. The Soviet leaders, mostly Mensheviks annd Socialist Revolutionaries, refused to do so. In the next few days order was restored in the city in spite of the disquieting news from the front. The government claimed to have documentary proof that Lenin was a German agent, and there was a crackdown against the Bolsheviks, some of whom were arrested, while others, including Lenin, went into hiding. At the front discipline was restored by machine-gunning deserters.

In this "July crisis" the Bolsheviks tried to lead and channel the popular energies, but they did not dare to attempt the seizure of power. Had they done so, they might have taken Petrograd only to find themselves repudiated and destroyed by the rest of the country. In the next few months they were able to profit from the further deterioration of Russia's economic and social condition.

After the July crisis two leaders attracted men's eyes and hopes in Russia. In Petrograd Alexander Kerensky emerged at the head of a new coalition government. At the front General L. G. Kornilov at the end of July became commander-in-chief. He was a forceful officer of plebeian background who had reconsolidated the front following the July offensive's failure. Kerensky appointed him in the hope of reinvigorating the army, but Kornilov, who was rather naïve about politics, was known to be contemptuous of the premier, of socialists in general, and of the Soviet. He soon became a rallying point for conservative enemies of the regime.

Kornilov and his backers did not consider themselves to be counter-revolutionaries, but planned a reorganization of the government, by force if necessary. Kerensky, hearing of the plan, dismissed the general and sought support from the workers and soldiers in Petrograd. The Kornilov rising was attempted early in September, 1917, but the troops would not follow the general and the railroads would not transport the conservative forces. The Petrograd Soviet and workers were in armed readiness for a threat which never materialized. The upshot of the affair was that Kerensky found himself more or less at the mercy of these armed saviors, many of whom were Bolsheviks.

From mid-September to early November Kerensky's Provisional government was being left behind by events. It reserved land reform for the Constituent Assembly representative of the whole people, but postponed the Constituent Assembly. It would not take steps to stop the war against the wishes of Russia's allies. Although there were great difficulties in the calling of a representative Constituent Assembly in wartime, it is probable that Kerensky's Provisional Government, in not doing so more promptly, was losing its last chance to keep power out of the hands of the Bolsheviks.

Kerensky's party, the Socialist Revolutionaries, was split between his own right wing and the much more radical Left Socialist Revolutionaries, whose demands for peace and land reform were closer to the people's wishes than the program of the Provisional Government. In the cities the Mensheviks were losing ground as the workers reacted more and more savagely in the face of inflation, food shortages, wage disputes, and work stoppages from lack of raw materials. By September 12 the Petrograd Soviet had a Bolshevik majority, and on the 18th the Moscow Soviet followed suit.

BOLSHEVIK REVOLUTION AND CIVIL WAR

So it came about that by early November all the real military force in the capital was in the hands of the Soviet, which was in the hands of the Bolsheviks. It was an easy matter for the Bolsheviks to seize the city, and with the support of the Left Socialist Revolutionaries their chances of controlling the country were good. Lenin returned from hiding in Finland in October and convinced the majority of the Bolshevik Central Committee that a Bolshevik revolution in Russia stood a good chance of being followed by a revolution in Germany. Leon Trotsky, who had joined forces with the Bolsheviks and with Lenin, supported this view, and was a tireless agitator in the Soviet and in the shops and garrisons of the capital. Joseph Stalin, less known, but a seasoned Bolshevik party worker and a member of the Central Committee since 1912, also supported the coup, although he did not play a leading role.

The challenge to the Provisional Government took place, after careful preparations, on November 7, employing troops and armed workers under the command of a committee of the Petrograd Soviet. Kerensky was able to offer little resistance, and escaped with the help of an automobile flying the flag of the American embassy. Power slipped from his hands into those of an All Russian Congress of Soviets, dominated by the Bolsheviks with the help of the Left Socialist Revolutionaries. At the departing backs of the minority of Mensheviks and Right Socialist Revolutionaries, as they walked out in protest, Trotsky shouted with vanity and derision that they were passing "into the garbage can of history." In the huge expanse of Russia outside the capital there proved to be little organized resistance to the Bolshevik coup. In Moscow the fighting was severe for a time, and there was nationalist opposition in some areas of Russia, but the Bolsheviks were able to take over the command of what remained of the armies at the front.

There was still the prospect of the much heralded Constituent Assembly. The Bolsheviks did not wait for it. They made an armistice with the Germans, abolished private property in land, and turned over to peasant soviets the problem of distributing it to families for their use. Far from being the kind of socialism in which the Bolsheviks believed, the distribution was a concession to the Socialist Revolutionary point of view. Lenin's revolution depended on keeping the support of the peasants.

The Constituent Assembly, which met on January 18, 1918, was elected without substantial interference from the Bolsheviks and may be considered a roughly accurate survey of opinion, although people were influenced by the turbulent times. The Cadet party had been discredited by its sympathy for Kornilov, and many of its leaders were in prison or in hiding. Of the 703 delegates to the Constituent Assembly 168 were Bolsheviks, 380 were Right Socialist Revolutionaries, 39 Left Socialist Revolutionaries, 18 Mensheviks, 17 Cadets and representatives of other "bourgeois" groups, and 81 representatives of national groups, most of them anti-Bolshevik. The Bolsheviks and the Left Socialist Revolutionaries together had only 207 of the 703 delegates. Lenin revealed his intentions by stating in advance that such a form of representation was old-fashioned and "bourgeois" and that representation through soviets was a higher form. What he was saying was the dubious thesis that representation of a class (or, strictly speaking, of two classes, workers and peasants) was superior to representation of a society of individuals. The Constituent Assembly was allowed to meet for only one day. Then another Congress of Soviets under Bolshevik control assumed the state power.

A Congress of Soviets representing the great mass of Russian peasants and workers could have been a fairly democratic instrument. This was not to be its purpose, however. As events developed through the period of civil war and foreign intervention, the device of Soviet meetings became a screen for Bolshevik rule. The "dictatorship of the proletariat" tended to become a dictatorship *over* the proletariat.

From 1918 to 1921 Russia passed through a period of civil war and foreign intervention which, along with the terrible economic disintegration, made a frightful ordeal of those years. The Bolsheviks rode out the storm and managed to stay in power, and in so doing hardened their dictatorship. Outside forces failed to unseat the Bolsheviks, and the Bolsheviks failed to realize their hopes of a European revolution which would come to the aid of the Russian.

The period opened with the Treaty of Brest-Litovsk, in March, 1918, with the Central Powers, which the Bolsheviks signed with extreme reluctance under the prodding of Lenin. Russia lost Poland, the Baltic shoreline, and parts of the Ukraine—roughly Russia's territorial gains in the west since Peter the Great. The Allies, against whom Germany could now transfer troops from the east, were injured. By encouraging the German empire, the treaty hurt the chances of German socialism. For this reason and because of the enormous loss to Russia, most of the other socialist parties condemned the Treaty of Brest-Litovsk. Russia was on its way to becoming a one-party state, and many of the moderate socialists were on their way to joining the counter-revolution. Terrorist acts—for example by Left Socialist Revolutionaries—accentuated the growing Bolshevik reign of terror. The Treaty of Brest-Litovsk also spurred the Allied intervention in Russia, which began with the idea of keeping supplies which they had sent to Russia from falling into the hands of the Germans.

All of these results give the measure of Lenin's determination and Machiavellianism. He argued and threatened his party into acceptance of this bitter tactic because without some kind of peace the Bolsheviks would have been overthrown. The Russian armies would no longer fight for the Bolsheviks any more than they had for Kerensky. They were deserting in crowds. If the new Communist government—the party took that name in 1918—was to stay in power and the flame of this particular revolution was to be kept alight, there had to be a breathing spell for the building of a Red Army. In the end Lenin was vindicated. The Allies defeated Germany later in the year, and Russia regained much of what it had lost. But it was not the hoped-for socialist revolution in the west which saved Russia from the Germans.

Meanwhile civil war, complicated by foreign intervention, began to rage in 1918, and reached its worst in 1919 and 1920. Moderate socialists and liberals, attempting to overthrow the Bolsheviks, joined the "White" forces recruited by czarist officers, and tended to fall under their sway. The Allies—Britain, France, the United States, Italy, and Japan—invaded Russia with small forces from the north, south, and east. Their original motive of restoring the Eastern Front gave way to a rather irresolute wish to overturn the regime if this end could be achieved without too great an expenditure. The Bolsheviks had had just enough of a breathing space after Brest-Litovsk to organize a Red Army, under Trotsky as People's Commissar for War. In March, 1919, they also founded a Communist International—the "Third International." To complicate matters further, the new Polish state was at war with Russia from April, 1920, to the Treaty of Riga between Poland and Russia in March, 1921, and the Russians on their side tried unsuccessfully to support Soviet regimes among the nationalities such as the

LENIN. Here the Bolshevik leader is addressing troops leaving for the front in 1920 during the civil war. (Sovfoto)

Estonians and Latvians in the western borderlands of the former Russian empire.

The period of civil war and foreign intervention was desperate. At times, Russia was reduced to the size of the original Muscovite state. There were atrocities by both the Reds and the Whites. In the end it became clear that neither the Communist hopes of world revolution nor the western abhorrence of Lenin's regime could be satisfied. The size and isolation of Russia saved the Communist regime at its start, while Communist attempts farther west—notably in Hungary and the new Germany—failed. In Russia the desperate leadership of Lenin and Trotsky and their aides, together with the reluctance of the peasants to choose the known failings of the Whites over the as yet largely unknown intentions of the Reds, made the difference.

Through these years the economic situation in Russia was a vicious circle in which the cities and the country supplied each other less and less. Peasants seized the land and divided it up, so that each peasant family had perhaps 20 percent more land than before. But since the great estates had been the best producers of a surplus, there was now less food for the towns. The Bolsheviks, if they did not provide for the towns, would be overthrown by the very workers who had placed them in power. Yet there was famine in large parts of the country. The big cities, short of food and employment, shrank to a gray fraction of their former selves, and production sank to about 18 percent of its prewar level. The Bolsheviks had encouraged "workers' control," that is, factory committees as watchdogs to safeguard industry while owners, managers, and laborers worked together. But the workers began to take over the shops for themselves. The Communist government was forced to try out socialism sooner than it wished and to assume responsibilities for which it was not prepared. This phase came to be known as "war communism."

When the Bolshevik Revolution first seemed to promise a new life for everyone, all sorts of guarantees of unemployment and sickness benefits were made to labor. But with the war crisis and the necessity of maintaining some kind of production, the Bolsheviks turned to compulsory labor, rationing, and one-man management in industry. From "workers' control" the Bolsheviks turned to getting control *over* the workers, and did so by merging the factory committees with the labor unions and controlling the labor unions through party cells.

The Bolsheviks survived in the towns because they used force to take the peasants' grain at fixed prices, and encouraged the poorer peasants against the richer. They managed to keep enough industry going to provide for the Red Army, but they were unable to satisfy the peasants with manufactured goods. Their methods in industry came dangerously close to alienating the working class as much as their grain requisitions alienated the peasantry. When the civil war crisis eased in 1921 they were almost isolated in a population sullen or in opposition. Their revolution was in danger.

Politically the period from 1917 to 1921 saw the gradual formation of a one-party dictatorship in the Russian state. Parallel to this development, but moving more slowly, there was a tendency for the party itself to be controlled by an elite of its own members.

In July, 1918, the Soviets accepted a constitution proposed by the Communist party. This set of fundamental laws of the Russian Socialist Federated Soviet Republic was something less than descriptive of the actual government of Russia in the years to come. The makers did not regard it with any great veneration, but considered it a working program and a document of some propaganda value. One of the elements expected to be attractive was the "federal" idea in the name of the new republic. It was maintained that nationalities had the right to break away from the new Russian republic if they wished. It was in fact hoped that soviets under Bolshevik control would keep the former czarist territories together. In practice, the constitution did not create a federal system, but merely one with a certain amount of lip service to the autonomy or independence of minorities. The same Communist leadership controlled all of them; but it is true that they were encouraged in the development of their own languages and cultures.

In form the soviet system of government was like a child's pyramid of building blocks. At the base were the village soviets, which sent deputies to rural district (volost) soviets, which sent deputies to county (uezd) soviets, and so on, up to the All Russian Congress of Soviets. The big cities were favored over the rural areas, for the Communists trusted the city workers more than they did the peasants. This plan was based largely on what was already there: the soviets which had formed during the revolution. If it had worked the way it looked, Russia would have been democratic, even though the elections to the All Russian Congress were indirect. By dominating the soviet system from the top down, the Communist intelligentsia managed to use the gigantic representative machinery as a facade for their rule.

Above the All Russian Congress of Soviets the pyramid continued to its summit. The Central Executive Committee of about 200 members was the next level. From it came the smaller Council of People's Commissars (Sovnarkom), which came to be the directing body. The vast network of soviets was in theory the channel through which the people's will flowed upward with the chosen delegates. In practice the soviet network helped impose decisions from above.

The Communist party's control over the Soviets was solidified in the period of the civil war, first at the summit, then gradually down to the grass roots. By 1921 the Bolsheviks ceased to pretend that there could be other socialist parties. Moreover, during the civil war period and in the first years after its close, there came into being a dictatorship within the Communist party itself. In theory the party was democratically organized, even though the members were expected to be true to the tenets of scientific socialism. After free discussion of a given situation—so ran the theory—members were expected to conform absolutely to the decision reached. In practice the Politburo, consisting of the leading party members, came to direct the thinking of the whole party. The Politburo could reward or coerce the members of the party. The party could reward or coerce the members of the Soviets. It was like a revolution turned upside down.

By 1921 Lenin and his colleagues had to prepare to make economic concessions to the Russian people so that the Communists would not be overthrown. But at the same time they made sure that there would be no political concessions, no loss of control by the little band of revolutionary intelligentsia who had captured Russia.

THE NEW ECONOMIC POLICY

Lenin's "New Economic Policy" of 1921 was a tactical retreat. Unlike the czar, he made concessions to the public before it was too late. Economically this meant concessions to private enterprise in order that the pulse of exchange between town and country might regain its strength. Socialism was not abandoned—the "commanding heights" of the economy remained socialized—but a large private sector was allowed to flourish alongside the socialist sector. The two were to compete, and Lenin expected that the socialist part would gradually eliminate the private.

In commerce there was a considerable return to private trading for profit, but the state kept its foreign trade monopoly. Some concessions were made to foreign capital invested in Russia. The money economy was revived after the inflation and near-barter of the civil war years. In industry the large enterprises were still government-owned. Small industry was permitted to return to private hands. If industrial output for 1913 is marked with the index number 100, it will be found to have fallen to 20 by the year 1920, so great was the disruption of World War I and the civil war which followed. By 1928 it had climbed to 132.

Neither the 1917 revolution nor the later period of "war communism" socialized rural life. There were a few state farms on which peasants worked as wage laborers, but the great majority of Russian farms remained as they had been when the peasants seized the land during the revolution. The large estates which had formerly produced most of Russia's surplus were gone. The N.E.P. tried to cajole the peasants into marketing a surplus by limiting the state's share of the harvest and letting the farmers dispose of the rest. Although in theory the land all belonged to the state, the peasants were reassured concerning their rights to the lands which they held. After a terrible famine in 1921, in which millions died, there was difficulty in relating farm prices to the prices of manufactured goods. But by the late 1920's agriculture was reaching something like its prewar output.

In the 1920's Russia was given another constitution, that of the Union of Soviet Socialist Republics (1924). It was a linking in law of the Russian Socialist Federated Soviet Republic with other socialist soviet republics such as the White Russian and Ukrainian. The new U.S.S.R. was in form a federation but in reality a "union" as expressed in its name. It had the same structure of soviets as the R.S.F.S.R., culminating in an All Union Congress of Soviets, out of which rose an All Union Central Executive Committee with two chambers, one for nationalities, and one for the constituent republics in proportion to their populations. At the top of the pyramid was a Council of Commissars (Sovnarkom).

In the 1920's Lenin, who had been the genius of the revolution, passed from the scene. The little band of dominant leaders then broke into factions and quarreled among themselves until Joseph Stalin emerged as dictator. It was natural, once other parties were forbidden, that the various points of view should be debated *within* the Communist party. But in a country where only one party was allowed, the same machinery which was used against outsiders could be used by the insiders against each other.

Lenin suffered a stroke in 1922; from the spring of 1923 to his death in January, 1924, he was effectively out of politics. In the struggle over the succession Joseph Stalin produced his slogan, "socialism in one country," which was an effort to discredit Leon Trotsky's hopeful theory (known as Permanent Revolution) that Russian socialism would be reinforced by socialist revolutions which it would stimulate elsewhere. Stalin said in 1924 that Russia could go ahead and build socialism no matter what happened in Europe. Stalin's view did not renounce world revolution, but it made Russia the center, not the periphery, of that revolution. It appealed to national pride and came as a relief to many Russian Communists who knew little of Europe and were tired of feeling dependent on events outside of Russia.

Stalin's success hinged mainly on canny maneuvering while his potential enemies destroyed each other. There was a big argument in the 1920's between those who stressed the need to industralize rapidly, lest Russia be overwhelmed from outside, and those who held that Russia was in no immediate danger. The former wanted to tax the richer peasants severely in order to get capital for industrialization. They wanted to base their power on the town workers and on the poorer peasants. The latter wanted to continue the New Economic Policy, encouraging rather than discouraging the more productive peasants, and develping industry gradually. They stressed endurance rather than urgency and said that European capitalism, with American help, would last for some time.

In this truly dramatic debate over Russia's future, Stalin cleverly assumed the role of practical man mediating between extremists. Actually he swung the balance toward moderation. Trotsky's intellectual brilliance and repeated calls for greater freedom of discussion within the party were of no avail against Stalin's control of the party machine. Trotsky fell victim to the system which he and Lenin had built when they accepted the convenience of a one-party state. In 1927 Trotsky was expelled from the party, and in 1929 he was exiled from Russia. He was murdered by a Communist agent in Mexico in 1940.

By the end of the year 1929 Stalin had discredited all his rivals. He was able to celebrate his fiftieth birthday in the midst of the adulation of a large following.

THE FIVE-YEAR PLANS

The start of the First Five-Year Plan in 1928 coincided with the last phase of Stalin's drive to personal power. The Plan was a large part of Stalin's attack on his rivals, together with much talk of the need for factories and for resolute blows at the kulaks (well-to-do peasants).

Stalin used the conditions of 1928 to his personal advantage, but those conditions were real. In international affairs Russia was more than ever isolated.

The friendship with Germany which had begun in the early 1920's when the two nations were outcasts was fading now that Germany had borrowed a lot of American money and joined the League of Nations. The Comintern—the international organization of Communist parties, increasingly a tool of Russian foreign policy—was meeting with rebuffs in western countries. The U.S.S.R. in the 1920's had hoped to win support in the nations from Turkey to China by playing upon themes of national self-determination and anti-colonialism. This policy was not bearing fruit, and—crowning blow—the Chinese nationalist party which Russia had supported, the Kuomintang of Chiang Kai-shek, had broken with the Communists in 1927. Stalin was able to make use of a sense of urgency as he seized the leadership of the party and set afoot the Five-Year Plan for strengthening Russia.

There were domestic reasons for ending the New Economic Policy before it was too late. With every passing year the peasant farms became more like private property. There was danger that these peasant proprietors might become an invincible political force. Ominously, on the eve of the First Five-Year Plan the grain surplus essential to the feeding of the towns fell off. The peasants were evidently eating more of their grain themselves or turning their fields to more profitable uses. If this change were not arrested the Communist party would be faced with unrest and possibly rebellion by townspeople. Students of rebellion, the Communist leaders (as in 1921) did not mean to let it happen to them. But even if this threat never materialized, and a prosperous peasantry began selling foodstuffs in order to buy factory-made goods, the future would not please the Communist party. In that case Russia would have more factories. But not steel and heavy machinery, the musculature of a powerful state, but furniture and phonographs and other consumer goods would be the products of the Russian industrial revolution.

And so began the Five-Year Plan, first of the series which was to industrialize Russia and become a continuing part of Russian life. These plans were to make enormous changes in the physical appearance of the country, in the lives of its inhabitants, in the power of its armed forces, and in the place of Russia in international affairs. They were to be accompanied by a great assault on the Russian peasantry, pitting the poorest peasants, backed by all the force of the state, against the rich and indeed against the rank and file. This assault took the form of a gigantic reshuffle, the collectivization of agriculture, calculated to remove the power of the peasantry to resist the new masters of Russian destiny. After all the tumult, the injustice, the suffering, the waste, and the enthusiasm of many Russians, particularly the educated young with careers to make and a hatred of past darkness and ignorance and national disgrace—after all this, Russia assumed an aspect of modernity and a continuing momentum. The old stagnant society, at an enormous cost, was stirred into historic motion. The Plan and its successors gave Russia heavy industry. They prepared it for World War II. They clothed it with an allure which was to fascinate impatient intellectuals in the economically backward parts of the world.

Space does not permit an account of all the projects contained in the half dozen volumes assembled by the State Planning Commission for the First Five-

Year Plan. In brief, Russia, by consuming less and investing the difference in modernization, would build a socialized industry without becoming dependent on foreign loans to any great degree.

What actually happened between 1928 and 1932, when the Plan was declared completed after four years, is usually referred to with some justice as a "second revolution." Like all revolutions, it contained much that was unexpected. There was peace, as expected, but Hitler came to power in Germany. The Great Depression reduced the Russian income from exports. Poor harvests and a frightful disorganization of rural life led to famine. Once started, collectivization of agriculture ran wild in 1929 and 1930 until Stalin called a halt to the strong-arm methods of the party and tried to put a good face on the matter in a pamphlet called "Dizzy with Success." Violence and near civil war led to the extermination of people and livestock. Food was rationed. Incentives for workers took the form of piecework rates and much brutal coercion. Writers, artists, musicians, education, and the press were mobilized and directed. The Communist party was purged and welded together into a more powerful instrument. A drive on religion was intensified, and Stalin drew upon nationalist inspiration by picturing Russia as an underprivileged nation beaten like a slave in the past and now fighting its way toward equality.

A Second Five-Year Plan followed the First, and a Third, intended for the years 1938 to 1942, was greatly modified with the approach of war and then during the war. None of these plans turned out as expected, but each served its purpose of achieving a few major additions to the productive machine even though the cost was great and other parts of the economy were disrupted. With all their

HARVEST by Fedor Konstantinov. A wood engraving, 1938, inspired by the idea of collectivized agriculture. (Philadelphia Museum of Art, Prints Division)

faults the plans—and the efforts which they exacted—strengthened Russian industry and set the nation on the road to modernity. Making allowance for the pitfalls in Soviet statistics, objective foreign observers recognized that Soviet industrial output by 1940 was perhaps four and a half times what it had been in 1913, with most of the increase coming after 1928. The rate of increase through the 1930's was greater than that of the 1890's (perhaps 12 percent per year, as compared to 8 percent—the average annual rate of increase in the industrial production of the United States from 1900 to 1950 was 4.1 percent). Perhaps Russia would have done as well or better under capitalism, but the Revolution of 1917 was a fact. The Soviets did not let the consumer decide what should be produced with the capital which was being withheld from his standard of living; the state decided what these sacrifices should pay for and decided in favor of producer goods and arms. But the multiplication of factories and factory workers was no less real.

Above all it was the farmer who paid. The amount of agriculture which remained outside of the collective farms was negligible. The Russian peasant now worked as part of a group which had thrown its lands and fortunes together, but he was allowed to keep his house and garden plot—a "private sector" which tended to compete with the socialized part of his life. The tractors and combines which were supposed to transform agriculture came more slowly than had been pictured, and the machine tractor stations which lent them to collective farms proved to be devices for political control as well. Agricultural output increased scarcely at all under collectivization, and the standard of living in the villages remained low. But the wealth and the young men taken by the state from the villages built the industrial revolution. Collectivization enabled the party to control the countryside while this forcible transformation was taking place.

STALINISM

The Five-Year Plans were more than an economic change. By the early 1930's a new society began taking shape, with more cities, more education, and more trades and professions. The demands of production were victorious over the egalitarianism of the old revolutionaries. Piece rates and hourly rates for workers and high salaries for executives were accompanied by incentives such as housing, bonuses, and publicity. The Stakhanovite movement propagandized the need for improvements in efficiency. Stalin by 1934 was saying that egalitarianism was infantile. He appealed more and more to the younger generation—not to the radical idealists, but to the shrewd, apolitical, ambitious new intelligentsia of experts. The party became less proletarian as these new men were brought into it. In the great social shake-up which accompanied industrialization the drive for personal advancement gave the regime a power comparable to that of France under Napoleon.

The scope of the social change may be seen in the estimate that by 1939 the peasantry and remaining craft workers were only about half of the population, the rest consisting of office and factory workers. Labor unions became agencies, not for the formation of policy, but for the carrying out of government (party) policies. Their chief goal was to stimulate production and help state officials to administer social insurance, housing regulations, and safety rules. In theory there was supposed to be no conflict of interest between the worker and the workers' state. Education became more formal, more disciplined, and more vocational. The importance of the family was reemphasized when it was found that the old revolutionary attitudes of tolerance toward individual freedom—for example in obtaining divorces—interfered with regular habits and work discipline. Literature and the arts, which had been relatively free in the 1920's, were mobilized for propaganda purposes. The official style, "socialist realism," was designed to reach the masses. Religious practices were tolerated without being officially approved when it was found that persecution interfered with work and production. A phrase, "the new respectability," sums up all these tendencies of the 1930's.

In 1936 Stalin sponsored a new constitution. It did not substantially change the rule of Russia, although the system of soviet representation was altered to permit direct elections in place of the former pyramid, and a secret ballot was added. There was still only one party, and the elections were still in fact a kind of cooptation from above of representatives committed to the regime. Indeed, the same cooptation took place within the Communist party, which held the key positions in the army, bureaucracy, and secret police as well as in the soviets. The little oligarchy of Communist leaders controlled the Russian state by controlling the party. Stalin maintained personal ascendancy over the oligarchy of Communist leaders by keeping them individually in fear of him and his informers and by playing upon their rivalry for his favor. These measures kept them from combining against him. The constitution of 1936 was prepared at a time when Russia wished to impress upon the rest of the world its democractic progress. After the rise of Hitler in Germany, Russia joined the League of Nations (1934) and became an outstanding exponent of collective security. On the other hand the Constitution of 1936 did reflect a certain easing of tension within Russia following the First Five-Year plan. The elaborate structure of soviets and the ritual of elections helped solidify the power of the party. The elections were a kind of plebiscite, and gave the party chances both for propaganda and for pulse-taking. The Communists did not mean to repeat the mistake of the czar's government by failing to maintain contact with the mass of the people.

Stalin said at the time of the 1936 constitution that the regime was still a dictatorship of the working class. He admitted the continuing existence of the two "strata," workers and peasants, but said that their interests were identical. Since there was no more class struggle, there was supposed to be no need for more than one party. Stalin and the Communists maintained that their dictatorship was democratic because the party spoke for the proletariat, which spoke for humanity. In other terms, the Communists claimed to have mastered the science of social change, to know what history had in store for mankind, and to be acting in mankind's interests. They did not claim that communism had been achieved—obviously there were still not enough goods to meet everyone's needs, and the state had not withered away—but they claimed to have achieved socialism, and this is what they meant when they said that their state acted in the interest of the proletariat.

The party not only dominated the people through the state but also dominated society directly through its control of labor unions, collective farms, industry, the professions, the arts, and indeed almost all group activities. This was the totalitarian side of Soviet Communism, and what it meant in practice was that a little band of revolutionary intellectuals had built up an autocracy more effective than that of the czars.

In the mid-1930's there began, secretly at first, the imprisonment and execution of young radicals accused of plotting the overthrow of the regime. This "purge" gained in momentum from 1936 to 1938. Thousands upon thousands of persons were arrested for complicity with the exiled Leon Trotsky and with the Germans in a conspiracy against Soviet Russia. Great public trials were held, in the course of which some of the most famous "Old Bolsheviks" of the original 1917 revolution were forced to confess publicly to charges of conspiracy. Prominent army generals were executed. By 1939, when the worst of the purging ended, nearly everyone in Russia had a relative or knew someone personally who had been arrested. In many cases the arrested persons had disappeared into concentration camps devoted to forced labor, or had been killed.

The great purges eliminated the Old Bolsheviks and their followings and made over the chains of command in the army, party, and bureaucracy. A new generation of tough careerists stepped into the vacated places, and the dictatorship carried on. The great powers thought Russia seriously weakened. The purges caused much bitterness and opposition to the terrible injustices committed by the regime, but they also spread fear: they were a reign of terror. Stalin later claimed that they cleansed the state so that it could be strong in World War II. It may well be that Stalin, seeing the war coming, wished to eliminate those critics who might replace him if things went badly. It is probable, also, that the purges were the outcome of the dictator's wish to get rid of entrenched officials who might have removed him or limited his power in order to protect their positions. In any case, the purges opened the way to new men eager for Stalin's favor and willing to glorify him and go to almost any lengths to keep the regime going.

A composite picture of the events of the 1930's in Russia best expresses what later came to be known as "Stalinism." The personal dictatorship, the cultivation of legends about Stalin's greatness, the terror and the purges, the seeming abandonment of the egalitarian ideals of socialism, the growth of bureaucracy, the silencing of discussion, the regimentation of thought and of the arts, the nationalistic appeals, the betrayal (described elsewhere) of Communist parties and working class movements in other countries in the interest of Russian foreign policy—these eventually came to be associated with Stalin's name, along with the material and social revolution which set Russia upon an irreversible process of growth. What Russia had been and was becoming was long obscured by propaganda, by the more showy exploits of Adolf Hitler, and by the exigencies of a wartime alliance. At the close of World War II, Russia was to loom suddenly large on the horizon—so large, indeed, that Europe's independent existence seemed in doubt.

47

DICTATORSHIPS IN ITALY AND SPAIN

In october, 1922, Benito Mussolini was appointed prime minister of Italy by King Victor Emmanuel III. His party, the *fascisti*, did not control a majority in parliament, and it certainly did not command a majority opinion in the nation. Nevertheless, over a period of about five years Mussolini was able to suppress the other political parties, destroy the civil liberties guaranteed to Italians by Charles Albert's *statuto,* and establish for himself and his party virtually absolute power over the Italian state, economy, and society. Nor was this one-man rule an improvised and temporary dictatorship, like the contemporary regime of Primo de Rivera in Spain, nor a despotism politely concealed in parliamentary forms, like that of Mussolini's predecessor, Giolitti. Fascism was an open and systematic attack on freedom and democracy and parliamentary government. It proclaimed itself perpetual, and it set out to remake every aspect of Italian life according to its ideals. The dictator—*Duce,* or leader, he called himself—announced repeatedly that he was the leader of a violent and total revolution.

This immense dislocation caused by Fascism was to some extent the result of serious efforts on the part of sincere but desperate men to meet the real and terrible needs of an age in which the rise of industry, the expansion of the population, and the disaster of World War I had bred dilemmas of a size previously unknown. It was to some extent merely the triumph of political gangsterism, whose leaders were to a really remarkable degree moved by vulgar and sordid considerations. But societies do not normally allow themselves to be governed by criminals, and the willingness to accept them was in itself an indication of the disorders of Europe between the wars. The nature of fascism as a theory has been dealt with elsewhere. The story of its triumphs in Italy, and of its echoes in Spain, forms the subject of this chapter.

FASCISM

The essence of fascism was a systematic attack on ideas of liberalism and democracy—of the value of the individual. Its core was nationalism. To justify itself, fascism elaborated an intricate political theory. The fascist party leaders and organizers were politicians, however, not theorists, and we know now from the information about them which has become available since their dethronement that they were ruthlessly practical—eager to achieve power and skillful at doing so, and not greatly concerned with what would happen once they were in office. Their stock-in-trade, both while they were on the make and once they were in power, was quite frankly the stirring up of animosities against their enemies. Fascism was rule by scapegoat. In both Italy and Germany it achieved success mainly through the manipulation of grievances. It is therefore to real conditions, not to philosophical ideals, that we must look for the explanation of its sudden triumph.

Neither in Italy nor Germany nor anywhere else did a majority of voters ever freely vote for a fascist party. The fascist successes were only partly electoral. Once in the government, fascists gained control by manipulation, intimidation, and illegal repression. But in Italy, as in Germany, the parties relied on the *acquiescence* of the majority of the population. In order to achieve even this much public support, they had to have a very broad and definite appeal. There had to be, and was, something in the temper of Italy in the 1920's and Germany in the 1930's which inclined their peoples to acceptance of such extremist regimes. And there must have been something in the temper of the world which converted what was in essence a program of frenetic nationalism into an international movement.

The most important of the conditions which permitted fascism to flourish was undoubtedly the disequilibrium into which World War I had thrown all Europe. The war destroyed old values and old inhibitions. It forced entire populations to applaud the notion that violence, if directed against undesirables, was praiseworthy. And it disillusioned large parts of the populations, particularly war-veterans who had fought for ideals which, in the after-war period, seemed preposterous. The war also demonstrated the power of governments, if they were untrammeled by party politics and public opinion, to accomplish miracles of organization and production. The incredible versatility and flexibility of the national state had been proved. Once the national emotion was invoked to secure governments' freedom of action, they had multiplied their industrial production, equipped vast armies, survived shocking crises, provided full employment. Moreover, the war had left in its trail economic disruption whose principal manifestations were recurrent unemployment, housing shortages, inflation, insecurity, and social conflict. It was natural that periods of extreme economic stress, such as that in Italy in 1922, should lead people to demand strenuous government action to solve the problems.

Secondly, parliamentary democracy was, bluntly, a failure in Italy in the years before the fascists came to power, and in other countries where they flourished—the Balkans, Spain, France, Brazil—it was either unsatisfactory or a mere mockery. When strenuous, authoritative action was required, the German republic or the Italian kingdom could produce only party squabbles over what action to take. A great many people turned against democracy and all of its associated moral and political ideas as a consequence of its poor record. This could not have happened in the nineteenth century, when misfortune could still be blamed on the *absence* of democracy.

Thirdly, the insecurities of the interwar years produced an almost neurotic anxiety among well-to-do and propertied people. They were, understandably, frightened of socialism and Communism, both of which in one way or another seemed to threaten not only their material existence but their whole world. The drift of parliamentary governments, accompanied in years of depression by the rapid growth of socialist and Communist parties, plus the hideous example of Soviet Russia always before their eyes, inclined them to support whatever was the most anti-Communist party that they could find. In the years when they were on the make, Nazis and Fascists distinguished themselves by violent action against Communists. Squads of party members beat up Communists—and often liberals and socialists—in the street. In Italy they seized factories occupied by socialist sit-down strikes. Their leaders excoriated Bolshevism as the number one enemy.

In return for the support of the wealthy, Mussolini agreed to play down the socialist and radical content of his program. Fascism was in its origins partly a working class movement. It presented extensive demands for social reform which read almost like Marxist proclamations with the addition of strong nationalist and mystical infusions. Like the socialists, Fascists recommended state ownership and control of much of the economy. In the event, very little that resembled socialism, or even social reform, ever emerged in Fascist Italy: it remained a "bourgeois" society. Some—although not very many—working class people supported fascism in its early years. The appeal to the proletariat was less successful than the appeal to the propertied, but it was real.

Fascism offered something for everybody. But what it offered most flamboyantly and most persuasively was nationalism. In modern times one of the most effective justifications a government can make for imposing regulations on its citizens is "national need." The modern state has presented itself more and more in the guise of a guardian of the national welfare. The sentiment of nationalism has been more and more often evoked and flattered, until it has come to take on, in many eyes, the status of a moral value and even a religious ideal. Of this tendency, fascism was the most extreme example the world has seen, for fascism defined morality almost exclusively in terms of national welfare: what was good for Italy or Germany was good; what was bad for them was bad.

In Germany and Italy large numbers of people were aggrieved and disappointed as a consequence of World War I. In both countries, huge sacrifices had been asked and made in the name of the nation, and in both the sacrifices had proved vain. Italy had fought for (and had been promised) very large accretions to its national territory, power, and prestige. Large territories—the south Tyrol and Trieste and Istria—had been won. Others—Dalmatia, parts of Asia

Minor, Albania—had not. Moreover, the Italians had been treated by their Allies at the Peace Conference rather like greedy children. This treatment, combined with the stinging memory of a rather indifferent war performance, made Italians extremely sensitive, and extremely receptive to a leader who promised national glory, national renascence, national revenge.

It was, conceivably, no accident that fascist nationalism triumphed in the two great powers of Europe whose unification had taken place only within living memory. Tardily, the forces of their nationalism had matured, armed, and won nationhood. Unification had required an energy and a forward motion which could not be and were not dispelled when unity was at length achieved. Nationalism overshot its mark, so to speak. A lingering dissatisfaction and a lively national consciousness persisted after 1870 in both countries, and, persisting, was then subjected to the shocks and distresses of World War I.

There was, then, a coincidence of circumstances which favored the growth of fascism: the shocking economic and social state of the two countries; the inadequacy, in each of them, of democracy and parliamentary government; and a peculiar receptivity to doctrines of extreme nationalism (which is perhaps another way of saying that nationalism was not attached to any particular political traditions). And to these must be added the division and inefficacy of their opponents at home and abroad, and the ruthless skill of fascists themselves at exploiting situations.

We must now turn to a factual consideration of the rise and regime of Fascism in Italy.

MUSSOLINI'S MARCH ON ROME

Italy had, since its unification, lived with an unedifying series of "parliamentary dictators" who brought some sort of order out of the corruption and confusion of party politics. Italy had prospered. Democracy, at least in the form of universal manhood suffrage, had been won in 1912. But Italy's government remained uninspiring, its social conflicts were sharpening with the rise of militant socialism, and in international affairs it had suffered humiliations and defeats.

After World War I, Italy's difficulties were greatly aggravated. Two young political parties emerged. Catholics, reentering politics after the relaxation of the Papal ban, flocked to the progressive Catholic *Popolari* and its leader Don Luigi Sturzo. Socialism burgeoned; the party became the largest in Italy. Both of these were entirely different from the traditional right and left groupings of the parliament. Products of democracy, they were "mass parties" with strong grass-roots organizations, led by devoted doctrinaires instead of polite groupings of flexible gentlemen. Both of them stood for drastic changes in the established order of society. The Socialists, although divided between those who supported and those who opposed the Russian Revolution and the Communist International, did not split openly, and it was thus feared that a Socialist government in Italy would bring Communism to power in the west.

There were other difficulties. Many Italians, feeling themselves betrayed by their allies, developed a frenzied zeal for the acquisition of the territories which were withheld from them—most notably the port-city of Fiume (largely Slavic in population), which was claimed by Yugoslavia and whose status was still under negotiation in 1919. A good many people, particularly veterans, were at once outraged and energetic, and in 1919 Italy's most eminent poet, Gabriele D'Annunzio, led a filibustering expedition to Fiume, set up a weird Free City government whose officials wore medieval robes designed by D'Annunzio himself, and defied the world. D'Annunzio was in 1920 finally ejected from Fiume by the Italian government, an act which discredited it in the view of super-patriots.

Still more serious was the economic crisis. The Italian lira, like most European currencies, fell during the war to half its former value. Thereafter it continued to sink. This inflation meant rising prices, declining real wages, impoverishment for people on fixed incomes, mulcting of creditors, and insecurity for everyone. And, like the rest of the world, Italy was hard hit by the postwar depression of 1920–1922. Factories closed; unemployment spread. Worst of all, social strife spread with it. In 1921, a development which terrified respectable people took place: workmen began to seize factories, turning out the owners. It seemed as if Red Revolution had indeed begun.

In the face of this, the government showed itself increasingly unstable and limp. Premier followed premier; majority after majority dissolved. It seemed—and perhaps was—certain that the ordinary processes of constitutional government could not provide Italy with the stable and determined government which was clearly needed. Even the old master at bringing order out of political confusion, Giolitti, failed in his brief postwar tenure of the premiership, in 1921. He found himself quite unable to build a majority around a program for dealing with the economic crisis, the strikes, and the factory-seizures. In the course of the next year, the economic situation eased, but the political crisis did not. In October, 1922, the last of the constitutional prime ministers, Luigi Facta, requested permission of King Victor Emmanuel to use the army to dissolve the most troublesome of the political action groups which were threatening disorder. The king refused, and instead he accepted Facta's resignation and called as prime minister the very man whom Facta had hoped to jail, Benito Mussolini, leader of the *fascisti*.

The young party which now found itself in control of the ministry had already had a peculiar history. Its founder and leader had spent his youth as a socialist-syndicalist agitator, rising, before 1914, to be head of the Socialist party and editor of its newspaper, the *Avanti*. Although most Italian Socialists opposed Italy's participation in the World War, some became ardent backers of intervention on the Allied side, ostensibly to save the world from the "militaristic autocracy" of the Central Powers or to aggrandize Italy at the expense of Austria-Hungary. In the case of Mussolini the change of heart from pacifism to bellicosity proved permanent and revolutionary. In the Italian army, Mussolini's views evolved further. He remained a revolutionary socialist, but he abandoned all of the internationalism of the ordinary Marxists and blended socialism with extreme nationalism. The "nation" replaced the "class" as the ultimate unit in his thinking. He found, or converted, a number of like-minded men, and they began to organize. When the war ended, a Fascist party was founded with *squadristi*—strong-arm groups—as its militant branch. Its first program was extremely leftist: it demanded an end to the monarchy, the nobility, and the House of Lords; it attacked private property and the Church, while extolling the glories of Italy.

In the year or so that followed, a very drastic change overtook Fascism. The party ceased to be anti-monarchist or anti-clerical or anti-noble or even very conspicuously anti-private property. It became instead principally anti-Communist and anti-socialist. While most of the substance of the left-wing programs thus disappeared, much left-wing window dressing remained, blended with right-wing ideas. The resulting mixture was of a sort wholly unclassifiable by the usual left or right criteria, and its emergence marked the end of any real meaning to the words which had grown up to describe the relationships among parliamentary parties. Fascism was neither rightist nor leftist. In fact, it was very hard for anyone to say what it was.

Once it became anti-Communist, however, and its *squadristi* devoted themselves to beating up socialists and labor unionists, it received considerable support from frightened and wealthy Italians. Emboldened by the government's failure to stop his strong arm methods (and perhaps also alarmed, for the economic situation had begun to improve, foreshadowing an end to extremism in Italy), Mussolini decided to stage a "March on Rome." It was this action which led Prime Minister Facta to seek military action against the Fascists. Actually, the March on Rome was carried out mainly by party members traveling on suburban railroad trains and was neither military nor particularly dramatic. By now, the Fascists had enough followers to command respect and fear, and enough parliamentary support to provide a nucleus for a ministry. In October, 1922, the king invited Mussolini to form a government. In November, King and parliament granted him dictatorial powers for a year, to restore order and produce reforms. Mussolini began a gradual but systematic destruction of constitutional government.

This change was not completed for five years or more. Indeed, in one sense it never was completed, for numerous relics of the pre-Fascist era survived as ornaments of the Fascist landscape, including the monarchy itself. Victor Emmanuel III retained his throne, and the House of Savoy continued to reign, although its prestige diminished and its powers disappeared. The aristocracy also survived, although not the House of Lords, and so did a shadowy Chamber of Deputies, eventually consisting entirely of Fascists. In theory, the *Statuto*, Italy's constitution, was still in existence, although entirely transformed.

The steps by which Mussolini made himself a dictator and Italy a totalitarian state are instructive. In the last analysis, they depended upon the backing of his party as a militant arm of his power, and upon his control of the police. Once these were available, the transformation of an ordinary prime minister into a dictator was possible. The first action was the forcing of a law through parliament which provided that any party winning a plurality of the popular vote should have a majority of seats in the Chamber. This, together with pressures and corruptions at the ensuing election, provided the government with control of parliament—the first time a single party had ever had a majority in the Italian Chamber. Restrictions—both by law and by decree—on personal freedom and freedom of expression followed, and the prime minister was given emergency powers by special law. The local governments, many of which had already been seized (or legally won) by Fascists, were now placed entirely in their hands. The respected leader of the Socialist party, Giacomo Matteotti, was murdered by Fascists in 1924. The non-Fascist parties in the Chamber, finding their position impossible, attempted to rouse the country by withdrawing from parliament and demanding an end to illegal action and dictatorship. This movement, called the "Aventine Opposition" led to dissolution of these parties in 1926; and in 1928 a new electoral law restricted future membership in the Chamber to members of the Fascist party. At the same time something was set up called the Grand Council of Fascism, in which the high organs of the party acquired a function in the state as a sort of executive debating society. In 1929 the long hostility between the Italian State and the Church of Rome was ended. The Lateran Treaty established the tiny sovereign state of the Vatican within Rome, restored the temporal power of the Pope, and recognized the right of the Church to operate schools and other institutions in Italy. This dramatic change in the relations of Italy with the Church was barely less revolutionary than Mussolini's constitutional changes.

By 1930, Italy was a Fascist state, dominated by the *Duce*.

THE FASCIST STATE

It will be observed that, compared to what happened a few years later in Germany, this revolution was very gradual, and compared to German experience it was, too, rather genial. Aside from the banning and persecution of Communists and Socialists, violence and terrorism by the government were limited, though shocking. Moreover, the policies adopted by the government were conventional enough. No drastic overhauling of Italian society accompanied the destruction of Italian freedom.

Enormous plans were made and broadcast, it is true, for the establishment of a "corporate state." This meant the organization of everyone into "corporations" according to his occupation—industry, commerce, the arts, and so forth. The corporations consisted of employers, employees, and Fascist civil servants, and they were to regulate their own spheres of activities and to form the basis for political representation—a Chamber of Corporations was set up in 1938 to replace the Chamber of Deputies. The Corporate State was, superficially, in the tradition of syndicalist theory, which urged the organization of society along "functional" lines. Something like it had been advocated, too, by Catholic and conservative opponents of liberalism in the nineteenth century. The Corporate State, aimed at eliminating class conflict and providing each individual with a legal niche in society, was advertised as the most daring and salutary of Fascist innovations. But the Italian corporations never got off the ground. Their organization was not fully developed until 1934, and when they came into operation they turned out to be little more than a convenient method for employers and bureaucrats to control employees. They were the most grandiose example of the fact that in practice Fascism was a rhetorical cloak to conceal the old order.

Indeed, one of the most serious criticisms of Mussolini was that he altered very little except to install a rather ruthless tyranny and to set his government about with a vulgar panoply of Black Shirts, meaningless verbiage about the Italian Soul, and souvenirs of Imperial Rome.

He had, however, achieved two things of great importance: he had created and popularized a revolutionary "ideology," suitable for export; and he had reorganized the economic policy of Italy so that, by 1930, the economy was fairly stable.

The first was largely a matter of public display and propaganda. Mussolini's own speeches and writings, while often vague, were nevertheless inflammatory and contagious. There was much talk about youth—*Giovinezza* became an official hymn of the New Italy—and about sweeping away the musty debris of nineteenth-century liberalism. There was also much talk about the revival of the glories of Rome. There was the indubitable fact that a small, highly organized, fanatical "action group" had seized and held the government of a great country. These were enough to make many people think that here was, indeed, a new, vigorous, and revolutionary force in the world.

His domestic achievements gave substance to some of his claims. Italy, like many European democracies, had been troubled by the absence of any authority that dared to give orders and to have them enforced. The result was an oppressive air of inefficiency about the government and the economy. Mussolini did give orders, and achieved superficial but electrifying changes. Employment reached high levels. The money, and with it prices, was stabilized. Large public works were undertaken. Exhilarating plans were set forth for the expansion of Italian industry. Efficiency-by-decree was attempted, notably in the state-owned railways, which had been notoriously unpunctual. A sort of slogan of the regime emerged from this minor improvement in timetables: it was said, with breathless admiration, that "Mussolini made the trains run on time," a reform regarded as symbolic.

In point of fact, the economics of fascism were elementary and costly. The Italian labor unions were dissolved, and this made possible a policy of deflation—of forcing down wages and prices. Taxes were raised, largely at the expense of the poorer classes. Unemployment was soaked up through grandiose public works which made a favorable impression on visitors and actually did contribute to the capital improvement of Italy: new railroad stations, the draining of the Pontine Marshes, housing and highways. More doubtfully, a hopeless but elaborate program was set in train to make Italy self-sufficient. "Autarchy," which means that there need be no reliance upon imports, was a goal of Fascism. Autarchy was preposterous in Italy, a country possessed of poor soil and few abundant raw materials except sulphur and mercury (oil had not yet been discovered). Nonetheless, steel works (in the absence of iron or coal, which had to be imported at

THE ETERNAL CITY by Peter Blume. An American's impression, 1934–1937, of Fascist Italy. (Museum of Modern Art, New York)

huge expense) were established. Shipyards were expanded and a magnificent merchant fleet provided. "The Battle of the Wheat" was launched, to improve agricultural output and bring new land under cultivation. And all of these projects, showily advertised, produced results.

The results were hardly worth the cost, which was never mentioned. All the large ventures were expensive, and most of them led to the production of commodities for which Italy was poorly equipped. And they were, in the last analysis, paid for by a reduction of wages and a diversion of capital from more useful investment. In the twenty years of Fascism, the productive capacity of Italy rose very little, and the purchasing power of the population declined considerably. This record is to be compared with the expansion of both production and purchasing power in the years before 1914 and, especially, under the democratic regime since 1945. By 1956, despite the loss of one fifth of its factories in the war, industrial production in republican Italy had risen by 90 percent over the 1938 level. This was a vastly greater increase than that achieved under Fascism.

In the years before 1932, the diplomatic record of Fascism precisely corresponded to its social and economic record. That is to say, the appearance was dramatic, even flamboyant, but the substance was on the whole trivial and conservative. Mussolini threw his arms, and his weight, around in international conferences. He baited Italy's wartime allies, particularly France, and spoke in large terms of "Mare Nostrum" and a revival of the Roman Empire. He openly competed with Yugoslavia for control of the Adriatic, and to that end conspired to create what amounted to a protectorate over Albania. He sought to expand Italian influence in Central Europe and the Balkans by encouraging intimate relations with the defeated and therefore discontented states—Bulgaria, Austria, and Hungary. And on one occasion he committed a violent and outrageous act, by shelling the Greek island of Corfu, as reprisal for the murder of an Italian member of an international commission at work there. This action, an open violation of Italy's obligations under the Covenant of the League of Nations, was the first blatant act of armed aggression which had occurred since the war.

Despite these alarming indications of bellicosity, bombastic or real, Italian international conduct during the first ten years was on the whole respectable, if not very brilliant. Italy continued to act as a member of the Council of the League and of many other international organisms. Italy was a sponsor of the Locarno agreements. Italian foreign policy showed few hints of a desire for war. With the partial exception of Albania, no further territory was added or even demanded. An observer in 1930 might have supposed that the references to Imperial Rome, to control of the Mediterranean, and to the virtues of war, were mainly for internal consumption.

In the 1930's, however, the situation began to change. The change may be attributed to two things: the Great Depression, which brought serious problems to Italy and its dictator; and the rise of Adolf Hitler, who provided support and encouragement for some of the Fascists' more ambitious international projects. The world collapse of prices and markets placed a heavy strain on the rigid and artificial economy of the country. Revenues to support the stable lira and pay for the vast public works projects declined. Supplies of foreign exchange with which to purchase raw materials declined. Italian purchasing power declined. Wages were lowered, and lowered again, by decree, but cheaper labor did not lead employers to hire more of it. Unemployment reappeared, and by 1932 it is estimated that almost half the labor force was out of work, at least part of the time. The assurances of the Fascists that they could guarantee stability were imperiled. It was mainly to solve this situation, by distracting public opinion and by expanding the army and navy, that Mussolini was led into a large international experiment, a war against the African empire of Ethiopia, which was undertaken in 1935.

The purpose of this venture was frankly to add to the territory, power, and glory of the Italian empire, and it was quickly successful. The Ethiopians were rapidly defeated and their land annexed. King Victor Emmanuel III assumed the exotic emperorship. It was the kind of war which might have passed almost unnoticed in the later nineteenth century. In the twentieth, however, it led to formidable complications. Mussolini found himself opposed by the League of Nations and (rather half-heartedly) by its principal members, France and Britain. Threatened with diplomatic isolation, he turned to the state which had stood by him in the crisis, and in 1936 and 1937 cemented his relations with Nazi Germany into an "Axis," which meant a diplomatic alignment and an international treaty ostensibly aimed at protecting the world from Communism.

The relationship with Hitler, who frequently proclaimed himself "the pupil of Mussolini," had begun with the former's accession to power in 1933. The two dictators had met in 1934, amid a flurry of flags and propaganda, and had given the world an impression of two kindred fanatics determined to revolutionize Europe. The impression was strengthened after the Ethiopian crisis had forced Italy into Germany's arms. It was exceedingly embarrassing to Mussolini, and it was to lead to his downfall.

Neither Mussolini nor his principal advisors were eager to follow Hitler in the war-policy to which the Germans were devoted. The Italians, with few illusions about their military or economic strength, and with little liking for the Germans and their Führer, were cautious. But they were imprisoned by two things: their incessant utterances about the glories of war and the need for winning Italian greatness on the battlefield (which Mussolini himself sometimes took seriously); and the diplomatic isolation after Ethiopia which made them dependent upon Germany. In May, 1939, they rather reluctantly entered into something called the Pact of Steel with Germany, which promised eventual support in a possible war. When war came, Mussolini held back, but when the Germans seemed to have won it in the spring of 1940, he hastily entered it himself.

German Nazism had other bad effects on Italy. As it drifted more and more under the influence of its German pupils, and as the stringencies of both the international and the domestic economic situation tightened, the Italian government found itself obliged to resort to more and more forceful imitation of the shibboleths of international fascist "ideals." Domestic repression became more brutal and pervasive and, as it generated greater opposition, more brutal still. In the end, the Italians were obliged by Hitler to introduce anti-Semitic measures which, considering the rarity of Jews in Italy and the total lack of anti-Semitism in Italian history, were as bizarre as they were horrifying.

The ironic fact was that Mussolini, like Frankenstein, had helped to create a monster which came to dominate him, and which forced him to try to live up to his demands, blusterings, and threats which had been mostly mere verbiage. A repressive and old-fashioned dictatorship clad in revolutionary garb turned into a real revolution. As a consequence Italy fought and lost a painful war, and with it its colonies and its reputation as a great power.

TWENTIETH-CENTURY SPAIN

The history of Spain between the wars was as bloody and as tragic as that of any European country, and this was true because the great ideas and issues of the twentieth century there encountered one another in a background that was extremely old-fashioned.

Spain was poor, its economy and institutions backward. Most of its population and many of its institutions were little changed in their habits from the eighteenth century. But this extreme conservatism—or stagnation—had dramatic exceptions. The ideas and economic innovations of the rest of Europe had secured sporadic footholds here and there. By 1920, Spain had important industrial centers—mainly in Madrid and Barcelona—where highly protected manufactures, often foreign-owned, had produced isolated communities of capitalists and laborers. There were middle classes and a proletariat, and there were middle-class and proletarian ideas, in wild variety. Liberalism flourished, in many forms. So did Marxism, both Trotskyite and Stalinist. So did anarchism—which survived as a serious political force only in Spain in this century—and so did syndicalism.

But these centers of modernity subsisted in a sea of ancient habits. In 1920, wine and fruit exports were still three times as great as those of cotton textiles, the largest manufactured item. Spain was still overwhelmingly agricultural. An antique landowning class, a powerful clergy, old-fashioned political bosses, and an even more old-fashioned army dominated the scene. The consequence of this mixture was a scene of vast confusion in which each baffled element was led, or forced, to extremist positions and to the practice of violence.

In 1936, there broke out in Spain a passionate and costly civil war which lasted for three years, devastated the country and led to the installation of a military dictator whose regime at times manifested some of the symptoms of international fascism. The winning side of the civil war, called "rebel" or "fascist" by its enemies and "nationalist" by its proponents, was ardently and openly backed, and with very large military aid, by Mussolini. It was also backed, though with less enthusiasm, by Nazi Germany. The losing side, called "loyalist" or "the government" by its friends and "Communist" or worse by its enemies, was supported at home and abroad by progressive and democratic political groups of all sorts and, as the war progressed, by the Soviet Union.

As a consequence of these two sets of friends, the war in Spain appeared to contemporary opinion as a testing ground for two great forces, Fascism and Communism, and as a crucible for twentieth-century ideas. To others, aware that the Nationalist cause was not by any means exclusively fascist and that the Loyalist side contained, in fact, very few Communists, the issue seemed to be an old fashioned dictatorship *versus* democracy. The Spanish Civil War was all of these things and more: it was fundamentally the haphazard and intricate eruption of a society which had progressed with notable unevenness.

Nonetheless, the regime which emerged victorious in 1939 was ostensibly fascist, and it was supported by (although not composed of) a party which in its organization and aims was undeniably fascist. It is therefore appropriate to consider Spain in connection with Italy.

There were many resemblances among the problems of the two countries. Conflicts between regions in Spain were even worse than in Italy. Several portions of Spain, notably the rich northern provinces of Catalonia and Vizcaya, were inhabited by people (in these cases, Catalans and Basques) who did not speak Spanish natively. Among the purely Spanish areas, moreover, there were differences of economic and political development which made them almost like different countries. Spain, like Italy, was troubled with a mountainous and frequently arid terrain and, like Italy's, its limited agricultural opportunities were further reduced by centuries of deforestation and bad farming. Like Italy, too, Spain's people and resources were very poor indeed. There were comparable problems of land-holding, for in much of Spain the peasantry was landless and worked as tenants or hired labor on the estates of the nobility. Spain's constitutional monarchy, in theory liberal and democratic, but in fact corrupt and confused, was a façade for politicians and for the real powers of Chuch and nobility and army. Italy suffered from a comparable, though much less serious, problem. Like Italy, too, Spain had undergone a marked cultural and political renascence in the first decade of the twentieth century, with new ideas, new writers, new political demands, and new parties developing in an atmosphere which was always ebullient and sometimes violent.

In the 1920's the two countries seemed to be undergoing comparable developments. To match Mussolini, Spain developed a rather similar dictator, in the form of an army officer named Primo de Rivera, who ruled from 1923 to 1930. The facade of liberal, constitutional government was abandoned. The dictatorship oscillated between extensive social reforms and strict military rule. Primo, however, did not, like Mussolini, base his power upon the unquestioned obedience of a highly organized and militant party. In 1930, having lost the support of the king and the army, Primo de Rivera resigned, and the constitution was declared again in force.

The end of the dictatorship came at a difficult moment. Pressure for really drastic reform of the antiquated structure had been building up and, suddenly liberated, proved impossible to control. Moreover, the return to a relatively free atmosphere coincided with the world economic crisis and with spreading hardship and discontent. The republicans, liberals, and socialists girded for action. They were met with arrests and imprisonment and then, in April, 1931, by the capricious decision of King Alfonso XIII to hold local government elections, preparatory to elections for the national parliament. The revolutionaries—mainly the middle class liberal republicans—swept the field. The king, alarmed and hopeless, unexpectedly left Spain, and a republic was proclaimed.

Liberals now found themselves in power, supported by extremist proletarian elements and by strong separatist movements in Catalonia and Vizcaya. These ill-assorted groups—the liberals striving to jerk Spain from its antique torpor at least into the nineteenth century, and the working class movement aiming at the twenty-first century—composed for their republic a constitution. Their efforts led to their downfall, for the constitution was openly and squarely aimed at a drastic revolution of Spanish society, which meant the dispossession of Church, nobility, and army from their wealth, position, and power. The separation of Church and state, the dissolution of the religious orders which had dominated education and social service, the expropriation of the landed estates, and the elimination of the army from its proud position as arbiter of Spanish policy, were all of them analogues of steps which had been inaugurated in the Great Revolution in France and painfully consolidated there in the course of the next century, to the accompaniment of violent dissension. In Spain, the reforms proposed were explosive; the mounting troubles of the next years represented a twentieth-century version of the French Revolution complicated by Marxist, syndicalist, and Trotskyite diversions.

A good many of the none too numerous middle class supporters of the republic were alarmed by the drastic changes written into the constitution of 1931. The rightists were even more opposed. In 1933, a coalition of conservatives won the majority in the parliament, and engaged to undo the changes which had so far been carried out. The left, supported by a huge and flaming resentment among the common people, responded by uniting into a Popular Front, and three years later won an overwhelming majority in the national elections. A new government, largely influenced now by socialists under the determined leadership of the extreme revolutionary leader Largo Caballero, took office at the beginning of 1936. Riots, repressions, and murders were undertaken by extremists on both sides. The government, unable to count on the army, found itself powerless to enforce its decisions and, in some areas, to maintain order. A situation approaching anarchy threatened, and the diverse factions of the Popular Front found themselves in mounting disagreement. In July of 1936, the army rose in rebellion. The Civil War had begun.

THE SPANISH CIVIL WAR

Fighting was to last for almost three years, and was fought with great bitterness both on the battlefields and in men's minds. The military division between the two Spains was geographical. Those areas in the western half of Spain which the rebels captured in the first days remained in their hands throughout the war. The areas, mainly the eastern and the northeastern part of the country, the province of Vizcaya, and the capital, which the Government held, continued —with steady attrition—in Government hands until finally the Loyalists were shut up in the northeastern corner of Spain. On the rebel side was almost all the army and the nobility, the parliamentary conservatives, the upper clergy, and most people of position and wealth. On the Loyalist side were the liberals, re-publicans, socialists, Trotskyites, anarchists, syndicalists, and Communists, along with many intellectuals, much of the population of Vizcaya and Catalonia (which had been given self-government by the republic), a part of the lower clergy, most industrial workers, and some peasants. The Nationalist rebels saw the war as a defense of religion, of private property, of government by responsible leaders, and of traditional Spanish values. The Loyalists saw it as a defense of democracy, prog-ress, and the common man against obscurantism, privilege, and dictatorship.

The initial advantage of the rebels, resulting from the fact that they con-trolled the army, was surprisingly and quickly offset by the republic's arming of the populace. Hastily summoned levies fought with great passion and skill. Madrid was saved for the republic after long and close battles, and armies were soon trained and equipped. What turned the balance and assured the eventual victory of the Nationalists was the foreign assistance which they received. Britain, France, and United States imposed an embargo on arms to either party, partly in the hope of preventing the war from spreading and partly as a result of strong pressure from opinion at home, which deprecated assistance to the anti-clerical, socialist-dominated legal government. Italy ostensibly joined the embargo agree-ments, but it consistently violated them, and the rebels were soon enjoying very substantial shipments of Italian arms, planes, officers, technicians, and, indeed, whole fighting units. On the republican side, no foreign aid was forthcoming at the beginning. Later, some was sent by the Soviet Union. It arrived too late and in too small quantities to affect very much the outcome of the war. Its principal consequence was to convince the world that the republic was, indeed, Communist, and to enhance the influence of the few Communists who were present in Spain.

The military history of the war was a slow and painful progress for the Nationalists, who first subdued Vizcaya (and in the process gave the world its first horrifying taste of indiscriminate aerial bombardment of civilians by wiping out the city of Guernica), and then advanced slowly in central-eastern Spain, ultimately reaching the sea and cutting the republican territory in two. The military operations were accompanied by atrocities and brutalities on both sides.

The outcome was also influenced by the differing internal arrangements of the two parties. The republic was beset by faction and cleavage; the major conflicts were between those who wished to push social revolution while the war was being fought—mainly socialists and anarchists—and those who wished to delay it—mainly liberals and Communists. These disputes grew more serious as the war progressed. It was ultimately the Communist view—of maintaining the existing order and avoiding all reform measures—which prevailed and which undoubtedly weakened the enthusiasm of the republic's supporters among the peasantry and the populace at large. This Communist policy resulted from de-cisions in Moscow. On the rebel side, the government which was organized at

Burgos and soon recognized as legal by Italy and Germany, was frankly a military dictatorship. The leaders were, at the outset, four army generals. But Emilio Mola, the most prominent, was killed in an airplane accident, and two others fell into obscurity, leaving General Francisco Franco as leader and dictator. Control was much tighter than on the republican side, and the rebels were much more efficiently organized for war.

There were, however, abiding cleavages among the Franco supporters. The two most important groups may be delineated roughly as "traditionalists" and "fascists." The traditionalists—monarchists, churchmen, landowners, and army leaders—were fighting mainly to preserve the ancient institutions and privileges threatened by the reforming and virulently anti-clerical republic, and sometimes to turn back the clock to the early nineteenth century, before Spain had acquired its troublesome veneer of democracy. The fascists, however, saw the civil war as a crusade for "revolution" along Italian and German lines. They were almost as impatient of traditionalism as they were of socialism. They sought a one-party state, a renovation of Spanish culture, modern economic development, social legislation, and an elite based upon virtue and not upon birth or wealth. There were, at the outset, many and various fascist groups. As the war progressed, they coalesced into a single party, the Falange, which became the only legal party in Franco's Spain. The Falange did not, however, control government or policy as it did in Italy. Its symbol—yoke and arrows—decorated walls and public buildings as did the *fasci* in Italy or the swastika in Germany. Its uniform and its leaders were ubiquitous. Its programs and its ideals were widely publicized. But Spain never became quite a Falangist state. General Franco was able to balance the two groups of his supporters, and they were in turn able to agree upon his dictatorship, the aggrandizement of the army, the restoration of the Church, and a policy of extreme nationalism for Spain—whose first victims were the self-governing provinces of Catalonia and Vizcaya.

The regime which emerged from the Civil War to preside over an exhausted and ruined Spain was thus a combination of old-fashioned jobbery, military dictatorship, and monarchist influences, set about with the decorations of fascism. Fascism—like socialism—was a twentieth-century movement which was too weakly based to prevail in antique Spain.

48

GERMANY, THE NEMESIS OF EUROPE

In 1914, Germany was the most powerful nation in Europe. Its people were efficient, intelligent, and well-educated, its industries productive and numerous, its army splendid. The Germans were rightly proud of their achievements since the German empire was established in 1871. They were confident that the future would bring them greater riches and glories.

This empire of sixty million people in the following four years fought and lost World War I. Its people later installed the most barbaric regime that Western Europe had seen in a thousand years, and this regime in 1939 undertook a renewal of the world war of 1914.

The story of Germany from 1918 to 1933 is the story of a gifted people struggling to find unity and greatness in the face of appalling odds. The odds were produced partly by external circumstances—defeat in war, world economic disorganization, hostile and imprudent neighbors. They were partly a product of Germany's own traditions and experiences, of past and present struggles between liberals and conservatives, between Communists and the established order, between the army and civilians, between monarchists and republicans, between chauvinists and internationalists. In the end, unity and greatness were sought through the National Socialist dictatorship and its leader, Adolf Hitler.

Like the Italian regime of Mussolini, that of the Nazis from 1933 to 1945 seemed at the time to be a serious response to the problems and complexities of the twentieth century. Fascism—which is a word used to describe both the Italian and German dictatorships—presented itself as a system for unifying societies riven by political and class disputes. But we know now that for many of its adherents Hitler's doctrine was a vulgar racket and its true nature was an effort by its creator to conquer Europe. For all the Nazis' flashy and intricate "philosophy" of the nature of man, the state, and society, in essence it was the latest effort by the most vigorous of European states to secure the unity of Europe by military means. Hitler was the squalid and perhaps insane successor of Charlemagne and Napoleon.

When Hitlerism is so viewed, it is less difficult to answer the question as to why Germany should have fallen prey to gangsters. The gangsterism was perhaps a continuation of a drive to power and prestige which had begun under Bismarck and which the progressive decay of the old Europe made easier and more inviting. Seen from another standpoint, the National Socialist phase was the re-action of a people tempered by traditions of strong government and military glory to a period of humiliation, weak government, and economic distress. In the minds of many, the public visage of Nazism was a vigorous and practical answer to the problems of Germany in the postwar period. The extremism of the Nazi methods was invited by the disarray of Germany itself after 1918. Strong-arm methods were encouraged by the ineffectiveness of the Weimar Republic.

The beginnings of Germany's collective madness are to be found in its history after 1914. These beginnings were in turn the product of circumstances before 1914, but until that date there was no connected history of movement toward disaster. After it, German history takes on the symmetrical outlines of a stage tragedy.

WORLD WAR I AND THE 1918 REVOLUTION

Germany, to a greater extent than France or Britain, experienced pro-found shocks to its constitutional and psychological system. When Germany lost the war, blame and shame were passionately allocated by each leader and group to others. The army command, which had exerted a military dictatorship over people and politicians, had concealed from everyone the precariousness of the military situation. When defeat became imminent, the army command merely washed its hands of responsibility and turned over the tasks of securing peace and reorganizing the nation to politicians whom it then attacked as traitors.

In 1914, the outbreak of hostilities brought a sudden and nearly complete consensus of patriotism in Germany, as in every warring country. There were deep differences among the parties, involving such basic matters as the position of the monarchy, the ruling class, the army, and private property. But these dif-ferences were forgotten in the need for "defending the Fatherland against its attackers." Even quite extreme socialists tended to be rather sentimentally nation-alistic when the test came, and almost none of them could regard with equanimity a victory by the Slavic hordes of autocratic Russia. In any case, the Social Demo-cratic party would not have dared to take a position against the war: it would have lost all its electoral support if it had done so.

This patriotic zest showed itself in the *Burgfrieden*, a pact to abstain from interparty rivalries while the nation was in danger. The parliamentarians hastened to vote the funds required to prosecute the war.

A good many deputies, and much of public opinion, supported the war in the belief that Germany had been deliberately attacked. Three of the parties insisted upon the defensive nature of Germany's war aims—the Center, the Progressives, and the Social Democrats—and, supposing that their view was shared by the great authorities of the state, continued for several years to accord them enthusiastic support.

Behind the wartime censorship, great changes were taking place in the structure of the German empire. Emperor William II, long regarded as irresponsible by almost everybody, was eased by his officials into a position of ornamental impotence. The chancellor, head of the imperial civil government, was the helpless Bethmann-Hollweg, who was obliged to take orders from the army chiefs, who could argue that in wartime military considerations must govern everything. In 1917, the army forced Bethmann-Hollweg out of office and replaced him with its own appointees. There was left no force in the German state capable of challenging the army leaders, of whom the most influential were General Ludendorff, the First Quartermaster General, and the Chief of General Staff, Paul von Hindenburg. The political parties were imprisoned by their own early acceptance of the war and of the army's usurpation of civil power. So long as Germany appeared to be winning (which, because of censorship and the army's distorted communiqués, was much longer than the military facts warranted) the politicians neither wished nor dared to try to seize power which they had never held and did not want to hold.

The only open opposition to the war policy and the high command came from an avowedly revolutionary group which developed around the person of Karl Liebknecht, a Social Democratic deputy who had voted against war credits in 1914. He had by 1918 won the support of more than a score of Reichstag members, and he had a considerable following among workers, soldiers and sailors. The group was split within itself between those who wished to seize the opportunity to effect a social revolution and those who merely wanted to stop the war. The former, led by Liebknecht and a remarkable and ferocious lady named Rosa Luxemburg, were in close touch with the Bolshevik leaders after the Russian revolution. They called themselves "Spartacists" and their followers later became the core of the German Communist party. The others, far more moderate, organized the Independent Social Democratic party. These factions, divided by much bitterness from the Majority Social Democrats, were the only people in Germany who wholeheartedly opposed the war and sought drastic changes in the institutions of Germany. This was to be a fatal element in the future of German freedom, for the Spartacists, in attempting to seize control after the war, forced the Majority Socialists into dependent cooperation with the army and the conservatives.

In August, 1918, the army command became convinced that the war could not be won, and in September it requested—or ordered the government to request—an armistice from the Allies. Moreover, it indicated its belief that changes in the German constitution of a democratic sort might make it easier to secure favorable terms from the enemy. The results of this change of policy by the army were dramatic. A new and liberal-minded chancellor, Prince Max of Baden, was appointed. Requests for an armistice were forwarded to the Allies. And in October a drastic overhauling of the regime took place, with extensive democratic rights written into the constitution and a ministry responsible to the parliament established. In a few weeks the old Bismarckian order was completely destroyed. Further, Prince Max and the army both became convinced that the emperor, who had become a symbol and target of Allied antipathies, must abdicate. On November 9, Prince Max announced the abdication (before it had taken place) and turned his office over to the moderate Socialist leader, Ebert. A republic was proclaimed.

The Socialists who took power were moderate men who were still awed by the might of the army and the splendors of the old tradition. They were also frightened of Bolshevism, and one of the first acts of Ebert was to secure the promise of support and cooperation from General Groener, Ludendorff's successor.

A German revolution had taken place, but it was a strange one. The revolutionaries were reluctant and unhappy and they were in league with those they had displaced, the military leaders. There was no enthusiasm in their ranks, or indeed in any ranks, for the birth of the republic. The government was saddled with the terrible responsibility of ending the war and of fighting off the threat of the extremists—the Workers' Councils, and the Spartacists whose agitation had begun to spread rapidly in November, 1918. These truly revolutionary groups, convinced that the moment of triumph was at hand, attempted a rising in January, 1919. It was put down with the greatest violence by the army and by groups of veterans called *Freikorps,* organized and armed by the government. Both Luxemburg and Liebknecht were killed. The government had been forced further into the debt of the army and the conservatives. The German republic was born under an ominous sign.

An even more ominous element was soon to enter the situation. The Armistice had been signed in November. In the winter German elections were held for a constituent assembly. They resulted in a large majority for the combined forces of the liberal groups—the Center, the Majority Social Democrats, and the Progressives (now renamed the Democrats). A new government, representing these parties, was formed, and it was this ministry which received the Allied peace proposals in May with orders to accept them unchanged or face invasion. When the terms became known, shock and outrage swept Germany. The nation (or an important part of it) felt it had been betrayed and persecuted, and serious consideration was given to rejecting the terms. There was, however, no possibility of military resistance to an allied attack, and eventually on June 28, 1919, the Treaty of Versailles was signed. The extreme violence of the German reaction against it colored all subsequent German history and helped to disgrace the regime and the parties which signed it.

The extent to which the odium of signing the Treaty of Versailles discredited the moderate republican parties is shown in election figures. In the elections for the constituent assembly, Rightists won 64 seats, Centrists, 89, Democrats, 74, Social Democrats, 165. In those of June, 1920, for the first *Reichstag* of the new republic, Rightists, 128, Centrists (including its Bavarian wing) 89; Democrats, 45, Social Democrats, 113.

The treaty seemed so monstrous to the German people because they did not realize the completeness of their military defeat. The army high command, to protect its skin and its reputation, had always concealed from the nation the hopelessness of the military situation. The Armistice had been explained in terms of a negotiated end to a stalemate. The German armies, until the end, had stood firm on all the fronts. They had completely crushed their largest enemy, Russia. Not one foot of German territory had been occupied. Germany imagined that the peace would be a compromise negotiated among equals. Instead, it was presented as what Germans called a *Diktat*—a word implying imposed terms.

An explanation of this situation was demanded and provided—by the army itself. The army adopted the position that it had been "stabbed in the back" by traitors at home. Republicans, Socialists, Communists, labor unions, Jews, and all sorts of other people were charged with having created the internal disorders of the fall and winter of 1918–1919 which forced the army to retreat and to become so weakened that it could not continue to fight. This theory was the reverse of the truth, of course. In fact, it was the high command that had originally told the astonished civilians that they must negotiate an armistice. But the theory was appealing and clinging, it convinced many people, and it gave them a scapegoat for their woes. A great many Germans—otherwise sensible and certainly patriotic—were henceforth to devote their lives to destroying the "internal enemy" and its creature, the new republic.

THE WEIMAR REPUBLIC

The constitution of the German Republic was drawn up by the constituent assembly which met in the winter and spring of 1919 in the town of Weimar, and the regime which it inaugurated was known as the Weimar Republic. In form, it represented a blending of German traditions and socialist ideas with United States, French, and British models. Germany remained a federal state, and Prussia remained as it always had been, overwhelmingly the dominant member of the federation. But now the states were to be democratic republics, and, deprived of their princes, they were to be more subordinate to the much stronger central government. The emperor was replaced by a president shorn of most of the old monarchical powers except for an emergency authority to govern by decree if necessary—Article 48, which eventually became notorious. Appointed by him was a chancellor, but now the chancellor was the head of a ministry responsible to the *Reichstag*. The *Reichstag*, elected as it always had been, on the basis of universal suffrage, exercised much more extensive power than had the imperial parliament. There was a second house, the *Reichsrat*, representing the states, with less extensive powers than the old federal council. In addition, there were guarantees of civil rights and of rather vaguely defined economic rights, which looked toward eventual control of the workers over industry and embodied the ideals of a welfare state.

Considering the dimensions of the events which had taken place, remarkably little was really changed. The economic charter of the constitution remained largely unimplemented. The regime tended to fall into the patterns of conduct familiar under the monarchy. There was no systematic effort by the Republic to alter the social structure of Germany—that is, no attempt was made to alter the distribution of private property, nor to dispossess the old ruling classes, the nobility and the great industrialists. Even the former ruling families, including the Hohenzollerns, retained their estates and their bank accounts.

The major branches of the state remained largely unaffected. The civil service, which had been the pride of imperial Germany and the best in the world, continued little changed. Little was done to alter the educational system, apart from founding new universities and schools. German education remained in some of its aspects rigid, conservative, and militaristic; school teachers continued to inculcate in the young the glories of the Prussian tradition and the German army. Nor was the court system revised. The judiciary remained a stronghold of conservative jurists who were quick to convict "revolutionaries" but very slow to condemn participants in rightist or army plots against the regime. Most important of all, the army officers were left unmolested. Although the army was limited by the treaty to a meager 100,000, ways were found to retain the traditions and most of the personnel of the old officers corps—the 100,000 consisted to a remarkable extent of officers. The General Staff, although outlawed, was reorganized under different names. The police forces became a haven for former army men, and the outlawed air force took new form under the guise of civilian airplane "clubs." There were persistent and fairly sizable violations of the treaty. But it was not so much the violations of the treaty regarding the size and equipment of the army which were important as the preservation of its essential organization, spirit, and prestige. When large-scale rearmament became possible, it could be carried out quickly and under highly professional leadership. The Prussian military tradition survived, and its commander in chief in the 1920's, General von Seeckt, frankly observed to the foreign minister, "We must regain our power, and when we do, we naturally will take back everything we lost."

The Weimar Republic was to some extent, then, merely a façade behind which the old and now vengeful institutions of the empire survived. The men who rose to prominence in the Weimar Republic reflected the continuity with imperial days. Friedrich Ebert, Philipp Scheidemann, and Hermann Müller were among the most notable of the Social Democrats. The greatest statesman of the period, Gustav Stresemann, who was foreign minister from 1923 to 1929, was a member of the rightist People's Party, which was composed mainly of former National Liberals. Heinrich Brüning, the last republican chancellor, was a Centrist. All of them were professional politicians, with experience under the empire. All of them were, in the broad sense, patriots, who regarded the defeat as a great calamity. All of them were eager to avert "social revolution" and were prepared to support the army with varying degrees of enthusiasm. Brüning and Stresemann, and even the Socialist President Ebert, were sympathetic to the defunct monarchy. Stresemann, although he made his reputation as an exponent of a peaceful foreign policy, was eager to strengthen the army and ultimately to recover the lost provinces in the east, and none of the others was prepared to accept as more than a necessary and provisional evil the Versailles settlement. None of them showed any inclination to tamper with the German social structure or with the

Der Gefangene (The Captive) by George Grosz (1893–   ). Grosz, who emigrated from Germany to the United States in 1932, made this biting attack on German authoritarianism even before the advent of Hitler. (Courtesy of the Metropolitan Museum of Art, Dick Fund, 1926)

old centers of power and influence. None of them was in any degree inclined to reverse the old and well-established tendency of the German economy to become more and more concentrated and controlled in the hands of the state, the banks, and a few large monopolies. None of them even considered any dramatic or imaginative policies for the construction of a new sort of Germany.

The President of the Republic after 1925 was the ancient and hallowed soldier von Hindenburg (1837–1934), the purest sort of *Junker* and army officer, a devout monarchist, a believer in the traditional creeds of his class and calling. Hindenburg was already approaching senility when he was elected, and he had never been a serious thinker along political lines. While his presence lent a certain respectability to the Republic in the eyes of its detractors, it also symbolized the thinness of the democratic veneer.

These built-in weaknesses were not the most serious in the Weimar Republic. There were others which were even more lethal. Two sorts, political and economic, may be discerned.

The party structure of the Republic was unfortunate, if not fatal. All the parties of the imperial *Reichstag* survived, in slightly altered form. The Conservatives and Free Conservatives, chauvinist, reactionary, and royalist, were now united under the name "Nationalist." The old National Liberals, called now the People's Party, continued, small but influential. The old Progressives, the most genuinely liberal and democratic of the parties, survived weakly as the Democrats. The two largest parties of the empire continued as the two largest parties of the republic, the Catholic Center (which had no clearly defined program except to be constitutional, Catholic, and centrist) and the Social Democrats, whose socialism became more and more watery and whose democracy did not in practice include systematic opposition to the old ruling class.

In addition, there were other groups which had not existed under the empire. One was the fast growing Communist party, which was dedicated to the violent overthrow of the existing order, which refused ever to cooperate with the Social Democrats or any other group, and which indeed preferred to see the growth of the reactionary right rather than the stabilization of a democratic society which might wean away its share of the working class electorate.

There was also a congeries of small, violent, rightist parties, dedicated to overthrow of the Republic in the interests of fanatical nationalist aims. These groups were small throughout the 1920's, but they had some influence, and they enjoyed the friendly support of various army officers, noblemen, and businessmen, and the friendly tolerance of some of the state governments, especially in Bavaria. They were anti-democratic, flamingly militarist and nationalist, and anti-Semitic. They sometimes spoke in terms of a "popular" revolution and paraded as friends of the workers and exponents of an altogether new order, but they were mostly deeply reactionary. The most important of them was a clique of army veterans and newspapermen, led by an inspired propagandist named Hitler, and called the National Socialist German Workers Party, which tried to seize the government of Bavaria by a *putsch*—a quick insurrection—in 1923, and failed ludicrously in the effort. Many of these groups maintained semimilitary organizations of their own, halfway between Boy Scouts and armies. Their avowed purpose was to "maintain order," which meant preventing social revolution. But their real purpose was to inspire awe among the populace, to beat up political opponents, and to attract fun-loving veterans and juvenile delinquents with promises of unlimited opportunities for brawling. It was thought impossible, in view of the army's favorable attitude, to outlaw them, so their opponents responded by organizing para-military outfits of their own, which only compounded the difficulties.

A fundamental weakness resulted from this party structure. In order to govern, the ministry had to have the support of a majority of the parliament. This meant that a majority had to be formed by agreement among several parties, since none ever controlled a majority of seats by itself. And this, in turn, meant weakness and constant changes of government. The separate parties could rarely agree on basic problems, and each of them was naturally inclined to save its own voting strength whenever any unpopular measure was proposed by withdrawing from the coalition. In the Weimar Republic, from 1919 to 1933, there were no fewer than twenty-one ministries, *none* of which ever enjoyed a stable enough majority to undertake a coherent program of legislation.

Instability made more and more people dissatisfied with the Republic. A vicious circle existed. The more people became dissatisfied, the more they tended to vote for the extremist parties which looked to the overthrow of the regime. And the larger the extremist parties grew, the more difficult it was to achieve stability. In the end, it was necessary to govern by decree—parliamentary approval could not be secured for *any* ministry at all. By the end of 1932, senile and reactionary President von Hindenburg was exercising more nearly autocratic powers than had the emperors before 1918.

Economically, Weimar Germany began its career with three handicaps. The first of these was the loss of some of its richest territories (inclining 26 percent of its coal and nearly 75 percent of its iron), its merchant marine, and its overseas investments, by the treaty. The second was the inflation which started during the war and had already in 1918 reduced the mark to half its 1914 gold value. The third was the "reparations" which the Allies demanded.

The Allies had agreed, rather casually, that Germany should pay for "the cost of the war." There were several obstacles in the way of the vast payments demanded. For one thing, the German economy was battered and depressed. For a second, there was the "transfer problem"—even if the Germans could collect enough German marks for the payments, they had somehow to turn them into francs and pounds, which meant buying those currencies abroad. Since few people wanted marks and everybody was buying francs and pounds, demand drove up the price of the latter and drove down the price of German currency. In the third place, nobody in Germany really *wanted* to pay the reparations. The Germans naturally wanted it to appear impossible for them to pay, and were even more naturally reluctant to work harder and harder to earn money which was going to do them no good at all.

The reparations question led to two disasters: in an effort to make money, quite literally, the government took to printing marks, which led to a fabulous and calamitous inflation in 1923. And Germany's extreme aversion—or inability—to keeping up the payments encouraged the French to invade the German industrial area of the Ruhr valley in 1923 to try to extract payments themselves.

The Ruhr invasion, coinciding with the horrible inflation, had drastic effects. It solidified the hatred of many Germans for the Republic, which had been unable to defend them. It encouraged extremists—it was no coincidence that the National Socialists' first effort to win power came at the time of the Ruhr episode.

The most dramatic and permanent effect of the inflation was to scare the wits out of the German middle classes. The mark had been worth about twenty American cents in 1914. By the end of 1923 it was worth something like one trillionth of its old value. Prices rose accordingly, and it required a bushel basket full of paper money to buy a loaf of bread. The result was to wreck the finances of anybody who was owed money and to make the fortune of many speculators. The government (which owed money in the form of loans, bonds, and pensions to its citizens) profited. So did businessmen, who could pay off all their corporate indebtedness. Wage earners suffered hardships because their wages did not keep pace with prices, but these were temporary handicaps, and when the inflation was over, the workers were not much worse off than they had been before. But everyone whose income was more or less fixed—people who lived on rents, dividends, pensions, and savings, all of which made up a large part of middle class incomes—was ruined. Such people not only lost their income but their capital, and with it their status and way of life. They were frightened and embittered and, like most other people in Germany, determined that, cost what it might, nothing like the inflation should ever be permitted to happen again.

The economic stability of Germany was rapidly restored in the years that followed. The Ruhr was evacuated. An altogether new currency was issued. The capital-rich investors of the United States poured loans into Germany at a great rate, which enabled it to pay its reparations bills and to have a great deal left over for public works and industrial expansion. By 1928, Germany had reached or overtaken the levels of industrial production for 1913. The merchant marine, lost in 1918, was built anew, more modern and larger than ever. New "cartels" in the steel and chemical industries permitted larger investments, more efficient methods, and more orderly marketing, which enabled German firms to recapture their preeminence in world markets. The huge steel trusts of Thyssen, Stinnes and Phoenix, the Farben Chemical Trust, and many others, became mammoths of world industry. The standard of living of the average industrious German citizen rose higher than it had ever been.

This fortunate period of five years, from 1924 to 1929, was only a happy interlude between disasters. In 1929, the great world depression began, and its first effect was a collapse of world prices and of world markets. Banks failed. Factories closed. Foreign trade declined. Unemployment mounted. By 1932 there were over six million jobless in Germany. Desperation engulfed the country. Elsewhere, easing of the depression was achieved by inflationary measures—pump-priming as it was called in America. But in Germany the memories of 1923 were too fresh to permit any policy except the reverse, of forcing prices down, maintaining the value of the mark and reducing government expenditures. The consequence was to deepen and prolong the economic crisis and to make the Germans more anxious than ever to find a strong and determined government to replace the floundering Weimar Republic.

THE NATIONAL SOCIALISTS COME TO POWER

The story of the coming to power of the Nazi dictatorship is a story of skillful maneuvering by Hitler and his followers and of mistakes and miscalculations by almost everyone else.

The most conspicuous figures in the drama were: the decrepit president-hero, Paul von Hindenburg; Franz von Papen, a Rhenish nobleman who was theoretically a member of the Center party; General von Schleicher, an ambitious and unscrupulous old-line army officer; and a group of industrialists who at the crucial moment provided the Nazis with much-needed funds and support.

In 1930, Heinrich Brüning, a conservative but very respectable Centrist, and a protégé of Hindenburg, became chancellor. Ruling by presidential decree and pursuing a relentless policy of economy throughout the worst of the depression, he stayed in power through presidential grace for two years and in March, 1932 engineered Hindenburg's reelection, which was won against the rival candidacies of Hitler and a Communist. But he lost the president's confidence, partly as a consequence of intrigues by his successors, Papen and Schleicher. Brüning was dismissed in 1932, at the very lowest point in the depression. Papen, another and less worthy protégé of Hindenburg, was appointed in his stead. He too ruled by decree; in two successive elections which he called, he failed to secure any popular support at all.

Papen and his extremely baronial cabinet established something like a dictatorship. He disbanded by force the Social Democratic state government of Prussia. He clearly aimed at destroying the constitution, and he tried to bring the Nazis into his cabinet to support his efforts. But he worked in vain, and in November he was forced to resign, largely by the intrigues of General von Schleicher, who was appointed by Hindenburg to replace him. But he too, however conservative, was unable to govern without the support of either the democratic parties or the Nazis, he displayed no abilities at all in handling the economic crisis, and he lost the confidence of the president. In January, 1933, he resigned. There was now little choice left to the president and his advisors but to call Adolf Hitler to the chancellorship. The Nazis refused to accept office on any other terms than complete control of the ministry, and since the Social Democrats and Communists refused to support any conservative government, or to cooperate with one another, no parliamentary combination was possible unless it included the Nazis, who had won the largest number of seats in the *Reichstag*. It was believed by the President and by Papen, who engineered Hitler's appointment and who became vice-chancellor in his cabinet, that the Nazis once in power could be tamed and controlled. Accordingly, on January 30, 1933, Hitler took office.

It was the eleventh hour for the Nazis, despite their great electoral strength. In the last of the two elections which had been held in 1932, their *Reichstag* seats had fallen from 230 to 196. Their party funds had been exhausted, and popular opinion was apparently turning against them, owing partly to their extreme irresponsibility and perhaps to a marked improvement in the economic situation which had begun in the summer of 1932. But from their difficulties they had been rescued by money offered by a group of Rhenish industrialists. It was, therefore, as a consequence of the efforts of the *Junker* Hindenburg, the aristocrat Papen, the general Schleicher, and the Rhenish business leaders, that Hitler was installed.

The strange alliance of Nazis and desperate conservatives was a symptom of a malady of the age. The landowners, industrialists, army officers, civil servants, aristocrats, and monarchists, who feared democracy and had long sought to replace the Republic with a more authoritarian regime, tried to accomplish their purpose by *using* the National Socialists. They disliked the Nazis, whom they regarded as irresponsible, vulgar, and crazy. But they found the Nazi hatred of democracy congenial, and they especially liked the Nazis' virulent antipathy to the Communists, and the army liked Hitler's extreme nationalism and promise of rearmament. They thought that by bringing them to power they could control and exploit the Nazis' enormous popular following, a following which the old-fashioned conservatives had never been able to achieve. They saw in Hitler, with his enormous electoral appeal, a sort of catspaw with which their own goals could be achieved. Seldom has any group of experienced and mature men been more wrong in their calculations than were the German conservatives who permitted the appointment of Adolf Hitler as chancellor.

In the six months that followed, Hitler and his lieutenants succeeded in destroying the institutions of the Republic and of freedom in Germany, and in gaining so complete an ascendancy over the German state and nation that they were eventually able to bring to heel the very elements, army, industrialists, and conservatives, who had brought them to power. The first step was the suspension of civil liberties, followed by a new election, held on March 5, 1933. As a result of intimidation, corruption, and strenuous propaganda (including burning down the *Reichstag* building and blaming the Communists for it) the Nazis succeeded in achieving 288 seats in the *Reichstag*—still far short of a majority. They then sponsored and passed an Enabling Act, which permitted them to legislate as they pleased. The Gestapo, the secret political police, began to root out opposition. One by one, the bulwarks of representative government were destroyed during the summer of 1933. The other political parties, first the Social Democrats and later the Centrists and Nationalists were dissolved, so that only one party remained legal. The labor unions were dissolved. The state governments were all replaced by Nazi agents. Freedom of the press and of speech were abruptly ended. In all these ventures, the Nazis enjoyed the encouragement of the great strongholds of conservatism—the president, the army, the aristocracy, the industrialists, the foreign office. These groups and institutions remained for a time immune, but their turn was coming too. The Nazi regime was a government by terror, and to its sway no group or individual was invulnerable.

By the end of their first year in power, the Nazis had established a complete dictatorship. Reparations payments, suspended by Brüning, were declared ended. Rearmament began in earnest. Germany withdrew from the disarmament conference and from the League of Nations.

The man and the party which carried out these remarkable changes represented a peculiar combination of motives and forces. In the 1920's, when the party was founded, it contained many genuinely socialist elements, friendly to the aspirations of the working man and contemptuous of the old conservatives. The para-military arm of the party, the Storm Troopers (*Sturm Abteilung*, called the SA) was decidedly plebeian, and its commander, the unwholesome Ernst Roehm, hoped that his organization might one day absorb or replace the regular army. The majority of the party leaders, at least below the top level, were middle class and lower middle class people, many of them war veterans or bureaucrats who had been stunned by 1918 or bankrupted by 1923, and who worked off their hostilities by becoming the posturing bully-boys of a "new order," responsible for many killings both before and after 1933. As in Italy, it seems to have been fear of Communism, disgust with the flaccidity of the regime, and economic desperation which led most people to join, or vote for, the Nazis. In general, their greatest appeal was in rural areas, where frightened and conservative peasants saw safety in them, in Munich, which was the center for all the most reactionary thought in Germany, and among the desperate and dispossessed lower middle class. In industrial cities, and particularly in Berlin, they were less successful than in rural areas and small towns.

The Nazis boasted a weighty system of political theory, upon which they theoretically united. Elaborated by the party's propagandist Joseph Goebbels and its theorists Alfred Rosenberg and Julius Streicher, and inspirited by the lengthy and hysterical memoirs of Hitler himself, *Mein Kampf*, the Nazi program boiled down to drastic anti-Semitism and anti-Communism, set about with extreme chauvinism, hatred of democracy and vague denunciations of "interest slavery," which was taken to mean opposition to bankers and capitalists. There were elaborate genetic trappings, too, purporting to demonstrate the superiority of the German race and the dangers of hybridization. But in point of fact, Nazi dogma (like Fascist dogma in Italy) never meant much. The "revolutionary" wing of the party, embodied in the person of the young socialist leader Gregor Strasser, was sloughed off in 1932, and most of the avowed "revolutionary" aims were tacitly abandoned later that year, when Hitler sought and secured the support of the Rhineland industrialists. So far as political theory went, Nazism was contradictory and meaningless. In fact, the only thing which the party stood for was what Hitler said it ought to stand for. His weird but compelling personality, his whims and prejudices, his capricious and sometimes paranoid views on all subjects—these were the true program of National Socialism.

Adolf Hitler (1889–1945) was a great orator and a man of intermittent charm and brutality. Born the son of a minor official in Austria, an unsuccessful draftsman in his youth, he unquestionably believed that destiny intended him for greatness and that he was relieved of all conventional moral obligations and restraints. He never hesitated to lie, even to his own followers, whenever it suited his purpose. He—like his aides—was a master of rationalization. Total reversals of opinion were hastily explained away with double-talk which sometimes convinced even his enemies. He was equally at home receiving bouquets from fresh-faced "Aryan" children and declaiming about the glories of total war. He embodied, and infected the world with, the thing which was the very essence of fascism: a rejection of reason and logic and consistency and, indeed, of human thought as a guide to truth and wisdom. And he embodied as well a pathological hatred—of Jews, of Slavs, of democracy, of all who thwarted him—which he converted into a system of government.

Hitler had, nevertheless, an almost magical sense of the crowd, of what would appeal to masses of hard-pressed, half-educated citizens. It was this talent which enabled him to control the party and lead it to supremacy in Germany. His program was nonsense, and his party was corrupt and cloven with concealed rifts. Nowhere is this more clearly evident than in the terrible blood purge of June, 1934. On this occasion as many as a thousand people were killed, including former Chancellor von Schleicher. Most of the victims were Nazis, who were executed either because Hitler feared or disliked them or because the SA, the principal sufferer, was regarded with distaste by the army whose support he still needed. After that, he was supreme in the party and secure within the state as all public offices, including the police, came to be more and more thoroughly infiltrated by Nazis. In August, 1934, Hindenburg died, and Hitler succeeded him, holding the offices of both president and chancellor. He called himself "*führer*" or leader.

THE NAZI STATE

In the years that followed, the conservative strongholds were reduced. In 1938, after trumped-up "scandals" in the army. Hitler replaced the old High Command by nazified army officers. In the same year, the conservative foreign minister, Neurath, was replaced by a pure-blooded Nazi, Ribbentrop, and the purge of the diplomatic service began. Several of the great industrialists, including the steel magnate Hans Thyssen, were imprisoned or forced to flee. The former reigning families and the aristocracy were mostly treated with contempt and disdain.

While he was disposing of his earlier allies, Hitler was persecuting and destroying his earlier enemies. The Jews were the most afflicted of these groups. Beginning in April, 1933, boycotts of Jewish shops were encouraged, and Jews dismissed from government positions. In 1935, the "Nuremberg Laws" were decreed, which closed professions to Jews, stripped them of all civil and legal rights, forbade intermarriage with non-Jews, and imposed other humiliations upon them. There was considerable emigration, and the number of German Jews remaining was reduced by arrests and murders. The worst blow for those who remained came in 1938, following the murder of a German diplomat in Paris by a Jew. Upon this pretext, armed bands of SA men and others, officially encouraged, ran wild in German streets, looted shops, arresting all Jews they came upon and murdering many. Almost two hundred synagogues were set afire. By 1939, only about 285,000 (out of 790,000) were left in the German and Austrian Jewish communities. Most of them were murdered in the course of World War II. Throughout the whole of Europe, almost five million Jews were killed by the Nazis between 1933 and 1945.

These outrages were carried out in the name of "racial purity" and "freeing Germany from the international Jewish conspiracy." The anti-Semitism of the Nazi regime was compounded of several causes—the pathological anti-Semitism of the Führer himself; the convenience of using Jews as scapegoats; greed for the property of wealthy Jews, most of which passed into the hands of Nazi party leaders. Never in the history of Europe in the past several centuries has any large group of people wholly innocent of any wrong-doing suffered so dreadful a fate.

The core of Nazi Germany was bloodthirsty violence, highly organized into a police state with its secret police, its Storm Troopers and its elite guard, the "Aryan" SS. The terror was bolstered by an equally elaborate system of propaganda. Not only were the press and all private discussion rigidly controlled, but a positive ocean of publicity was unloosed on Germany and the world, under the direction of the Ministry of Culture and Enlightenment presided over by Dr. Joseph Goebbels. Nazi propaganda was highly flexible. To foreigners it stressed the Nazis as a bulwark against Communism, as friends of peace or (alternatively) irresistible conquerors, as "Good Europeans" protecting Europe from such mixed menaces as capitalism, Communism, American materialism, Jews, socialists, the British empire, racial impurity, the yellow menace. To Germans, it presented a flood of ideas woven around the superiority of Germans and their culture, the restoration of the economy, the natural right of Germany to world power, and the lovable personality of the Führer. Whatever its tenor, Nazi propaganda was within certain limits effective. At the least, it deadened the minds and consciences of many, many people who were prepared to take the easy course of non-resistance and who were aware of the real improvements which the Nazis had brought.

The most important improvements were Hitler's international triumphs, dealt with elsewhere, and the very marked improvement in the economic situation. By 1939, the most shocking symptom of the depression, unemployment, had largely been overcome. German factories were once again producing to capacity. German exports were again being sought on world markets, and the German currency was far solider than it had been in 1933.

This remarkable change was due to three factors. First, there was general improvement in the world economy, which began at the time when the Nazis came to power and from which they automatically profited through rising prices and expanding trade. Second, there was rearmament, carried out furtively before

1935, openly and on the largest scale thereafter. The expansion of the army, the building of new naval vessels, airplanes and fortifications and munitions, soaked up unemployment, multiplied purchasing power, and started the wheels of industry and commerce turning. It was complemented by very extensive public works of a less war-like sort, including the building of the famous superhighways, the autobahns. Third, the economic revival was made possible by very tight controls which a democracy could not have instituted. Imports, raw materials, and labor were strictly regulated and allocated where they would do the most good. Price levels were set and rigidly enforced. Foreign transactions and government expenditures were manipulated. The result was, not abundance, for consumer goods remained in short supply, but full employment, industrial expansion, and economic stability. There were serious shortcomings. The burden placed upon Germany's limited gold supply was grave, and was relieved at the last minute only by the annexation of Austria with its large gold reserves in 1938. The standard of living among those employed actually declined; that is to say, an employed worker in 1939 could buy less than in 1933. But this was a small price to pay—most people thought—for the ending of disorder and of unemployment and the restoration of national self-esteem.

Like the economy of Italian Fascism, that of Nazi Germany contributed very little to the enrichment of the nation. It was aimed at stability, at keeping down wages, at maintaining financial solvency, and most of all at preparing for war and reducing Germany's dependence upon imported goods. In these purposes it was remarkably successful, but from the point of view of increasing the real wealth of the nation, the Nazi era was markedly less successful than that which preceded or followed it.

Nor were the innovations in governmental and social institutions which the Nazis introduced in the years before the second war of particular interest. One of the most advertised was the Labor Front, which replaced the dissolved unions. The Labor Front organizations had no right to strike, or to bargain for better wages or working conditions. But they did provide their members with paid vacations and holiday outings which were one of the main showpieces of the Nazi regime. The supporters could also point with pride to the various pervasive youth organizations, which substituted wholesome entertainment and work camps for the more relaxing pastimes of democracy. The Nazi farm program was also vaunted as a means of relieving the hard-pressed farmers, mainly by fixing farm prices and forbidding mortgage foreclosures. It was also intended to encourage the traditional virtues of the German peasantry by tying landowners to the soil through legal barriers to land sales and through elaborate regimentation of production. Farm prices rose somewhat, and the heavily mortgaged farmers were enabled to survive. On the other hand, some of the restrictions on the sale of property and the efforts to prevent the departure of peasants for the cities bore a peculiar resemblance to serfdom.

The atmosphere of Germany in the six years between the accession of the Nazis to power and the outbreak of war was a peculiar combination of exhilaration and nightmare. There were the triumphs of foreign policy, which brought the Rhineland, the Saar, Austria, and the German portions of Czechoslovakia into the Fatherland. There was the prideful rebuilding of the army and of Germany's international prestige. There were the economic recovery and the paid vacations. There were the incessant pageants of the Nazi party. There were enormous displays of youthful athleticism, there were party meetings, there were exciting new building programs. But on the other hand, there was the appalling persecution of dissenters, the disappearance of any belief in reason, logic, moderation, or truth. There was the oppressive omnipresence of the secret police, and the total regimentation and regulation of every aspect of human life and activity. The individaul, as he was constantly told, existed for the glorification of the nation and the Führer, and the enrichment of the race. There was the quiet but systematic harassment of the Protestant churches, and more open defiance of the Church of Rome (which denounced Nazism and all its works in 1939) and the total extinction of Judaism. There was the encouragement of an idiotic "German" cult, on whose altars were placed a sword, a swastika, and a copy of *Mein Kampf*.

It was all very different from the free and easy days of Weimar. It was all very different from what the stiff conservatives of the army and the civil service had expected. For perhaps a majority of Germans it was inspiriting. For a great many it meant torture and death. For the world it meant the approach of a second world war.

49

THE TRAGEDY OF
EAST CENTRAL
EUROPE

BETWEEN THE First and Second World Wars there were two decades of freedom for the peoples of East Central Europe. By a kind of explosion at the end of the first war, there shot forth from the wreckage of the Hohenzollern, Habsburg, Romanov, and Ottoman empires thirteen nations. Of these, most were making a fresh start or were so thoroughly reorganized as to be almost unrecognizable. The area from the Baltic to the Adriatic and Aegean was filled with new constitutions, like the rockets of a great Fourth of July. This act of self-determination was one of the most inspiring of the events which took place at the close of World War I. One of the greatest illusions of the era was the assumption, widely held in Western Europe and America, that the drama was over, and that this freedom was permanently enshrined as a part of European progress.

The peoples of East Central Europe were many and ancient, but they had almost disappeared from view by the nineteenth century. With the second and third partitions of Poland in the 1790's the last of the nations between the Russians and Turks, on the one side, and the Germans, on the other, was overrun. "Overrun" is a military and political expression, and "disappeared from view" is even less precise. From the Finns to the Greeks, these nationalities lost neither their sight nor their hearing, and as the nineteenth century advanced, so did their self-awareness. But while the overpowering empires remained, the peoples of East Central Europe were unable to follow the Italians and Germans to statehood.

Such liberations as there were in the nineteenth century arose from clashes among the great empires. Greek independence in the war of 1821–1831, and the independence of Serbia, Rumania, and Montenegro in 1878, followed Russian wars against the Turks. Bulgaria, made autonomous in 1878, declared its independence in 1908 on the occasion of a sharp disagreement between Austria and Russia. Albania secured independence in a similar situation in 1912. But in the north the partitions of Poland held firm, and so great was Russian power that the prospects of the Finns, Estonians, Latvians, and Lithuanians for independence seemed dim indeed. It was not until the Revolution of 1905 set up tremors of self-government in the Russian Empire that a new stage was reached. Thereafter the unceasing efforts of the Poles, and the nationalist movements of their northern neighbors, began to appear to have some chance of success.

In the last years before World War I the Habsburg international state of Austria-Hungary, and also the German empire in its Polish regions and the Russian empire inside its western borders, experienced nationalistic opposition. Many of the subject nationalities, unable to prevail against the enormous weight of the three empires, not unnaturally hoped that disagreements, or even a clash between Russia and the dual alliance of Germany and Austria-Hungary, would open an avenue of escape.

THE EXPLOSION

The World War opened this avenue, but at a cost and with consequences which no one had foreseen. The great empires fought each other and so enabled their subject peoples to escape from them. The peoples of East Central Europe were, however, caught on the battlefields of the eastern front. It was their lands which bore the brunt of the campaigns. And until the very end, liberation from one side in the conflict bore the appearance of conquest by the other.

In Eastern Europe the war was, in a strict sense of the word, "imperialist." The Austrian, Russian, and German empires were all striving to maintain themselves and to consolidate their imperial positions. Within the Austrian empire, to be sure, there had been in recent decades signs of a possible evolution toward autonomy for the subject peoples. The possibility of "trialism"—autonomy for the South Slavs of the Adriatic coast as well as for the Germans and Hungarians—was being discussed on the eve of the murder of the Archduke Francis Ferdinand in June, 1914. This kind of evolution, promising in principle, aroused the suspicions of the Hungarian Magyars and made the Czechs of Bohemia demand the equivalent. In the event, the men in power chose a military solution to the immediate problems of the Habsburg empire. In the case of the Russian empire, the most pressing problems were somewhat different, but Russia's rulers also elected a military solution, and like the Austrians and Hungarians, entered upon a disastrous course. Whatever one may think of German motives at the outbreak of the war, the German empire, even more than the Austrian and Russian,

was soon fighting for imperial interests. For in Germany the idea of *Mitteleuropa*
—organization of all of East Central Europe into some form of German-led unity
—grew in strength as the war progressed. What the Germans would have made
of victory is suggested by the immense concessions which they exacted from
Russia in the Treaty of Brest-Litovsk in 1918.

The difficult position in which the subject peoples of East Central Europe
found themselves during the war is illustrated by the diversity of their programs.
Some of the Poles, regarding Russia as the chief obstacle to their liberation,
fought on the German side. Others served with the Russians. There were also
Czechs on both sides—the Czech statesmen Thomas G. Masaryk and Edward
Beneš were in exile in the west and were working for an independent Czech
nation. In the Balkans, the Serbs and Bulgarians, bitter after their recent quarrels,
were on opposite sides. In 1917 the Russian Revolution and the entrance of the
United States into the war further complicated matters. In the United States
were many immigrants from East Central Europe who had hopes and plans for
the future of their former homelands. In Russia the change of regimes seemed
to remove its imperialist menace from East Central Europe, but the Bolshevik
Revolution of November, 1917, confused the issue by mixing revolutionary
propaganda with promises of self-determination for all peoples.

EAST CENTRAL EUROPE

1914   1920–1938

In the end something like a miracle happened for the hard-pressed nationalities of East Central Europe. They had been caught in the middle of a great war between ruling empires, and then *both sides lost*. First the Russians collapsed in 1917, and the prospect of German domination spread across the whole area. But then, in November, 1918, Germany lost the war, and the whole situation in East Central Europe became fluid. Or, more accurately, it was already fluid. The Habsburg monarchy was in a state of collapse. Austria had tried to make a separate peace, and then to proclaim a federal empire of autonomous peoples. It was too late. The center no longer controlled the extremities. The emperor's last appeals had no effect on the independence movements of the Czechs and Slovaks to the north or of the Serbs, Croats, and Slovenes to the South. Out of the former came Czechoslovakia. Out of the latter, when the other South Slavs (including the Montenegrins) joined with Serbia, came the Kingdom of the Serbs, Croats, and Slovenes—later to be named Yugoslavia. There was nothing left of the Habsburg monarchy but the prospect of disorders unless something were done quickly in Vienna and Budapest. After concluding an armistice on November 3, 1918, the Habsburg Emperor Charles I withdrew to exile. Republics were proclaimed in Austria and Hungary. Uneasy peace reigned over the wreckage of the Habsburg empire.

In the fall of 1918 an Allied offensive northward from Greece knocked Bulgaria out of the war by the end of September. Rumania, which had been defeated and forced to make peace by the Central Powers, reentered the war. Rumania was to profit greatly from the fact that both Bulgaria and Hungary, as well as its former ally Russia, were in no condition to resist the expansion of its borders.

To the north of Rumania, in a broad band of territories stretching all the way through Finland, the German defeat of Russia, followed by the defeat of Germany at the hands of the Allies in the west, opened the way for the subject peoples.

A year earlier, by the time of the Bolshevik Revolution in November, 1917, much of this western frontier region was already out of Russian hands. The Bolshevik program, which offered self-determination for all nationalities even if it meant separation from Russia, was taken at its face value by the Finns, Estonians, Latvians, and Lithuanians. The Poles had already determined to have independence. The White Russians (Byelorussians) showed some tendencies in this direction. The Ukrainians, with a more fully developed sense of nationality, tried under German sponsorship to set up an independent republic.

The Soviet regime in Moscow hoped that all of these peoples would form Communist republics and associate themselves with Russia. The Russians were, however, unable to resist the German advance, and were forced in the Treaty of Brest-Litovsk, in March, 1918, to relinquish all of these territories. It then became apparent that the formerly subject peoples of these borderlands were all in danger of German domination. In November, 1918, when Germany was defeated, the danger seemed to disappear.

There followed, however, two years of confusion. Russia immediately denounced the Treaty of Brest-Litovsk. As civil war raged in Russia, German irregulars fought to prevent loss of German control over the Baltic shores. Red armies attempted to support soviet regimes in as many as possible of the former Russian territories. In the spring of 1920, Polish forces pushed as far as Kiev, in the Ukraine, but in the following summer the Red armies threw them back and advanced toward Warsaw, only to be checked in their turn. In the end it was force which determined the frontiers. Finland, Estonia, Latvia, Lithuania, and Poland emerged as independent states, but the Russians were able to maintain Soviet regimes in most of the Ukraine and White Russia. Treaties were finally signed with the Baltic nations in 1920, and with Poland in 1921.

It would be a mistake to overestimate the ability of the treaty-makers at Paris in 1919 to influence the shape of postwar East Central Europe. To be sure, the peacemakers, and later the League of Nations, had some influence on the settlement of boundary disputes. The great powers at Paris made crucial decisions like the creation of the so-called Polish Corridor between Germany and East Prussia, the refusal to allow *Anschluss* (union) between Austria and Germany, the inclusion of the Sudeten Germans in the western edges of Czechoslovakia, and the recognition of an independent Albania. Peace terms were much harsher for the losers such as Austria and Hungary and Bulgaria, than for the countries which, like Czechoslovakia and Rumania, were recognized as allies. On the whole, however, the new regimes in East Central Europe were the work of the peoples themselves, taking advantage of unusual circumstances. In the coming decades much was to be said in Europe and America about the insufficiencies of nationalism and of the principle of national-self-determination as guides to peace. To the peoples of East Central Europe, who were usually the targets of remarks about the "Balkanization of Europe," self-determination was more than a topic for academic discussion. It was the fundamental fact of their existence.

THE PROSPECTS

The countries of East Central Europe all set forth into the postwar world armed with national pride and with democratic constitutions. One hope for the future which most of them shared was the "green revolution," so-called because it contrasted to the "red revolution" in Russia, and because it concerned the peasants and the land. From Finland to Greece programs of land distribution were undertaken in an effort to achieve social justice and guarantee the loyalty of the rural districts against the possibility of Communism. Another common characteristic of the states of East Central Europe was their location in the relatively less commercial and industrial part of Europe east of the Elbe-Adriatic line. A fourth was the great extent to which their future—like their past—depended on outside forces, particularly those forces which determined the fate of Germany and Russia.

In most respects the countries of East Central Europe differed from each other so greatly that space does not permit more than the most conspicuous illustrations. Politically, all had to organize or reorganize their institutions, but the specific obstacles to success varied widely. Poland, in spite of its independent existence in earlier times, now had to unify districts which had grown accustomed to German, Austrian, and Russian administrations and ways of life. There were minorities of Germans, Ukrainians, White Russians, and Jews. Poland was deeply influenced by the war with the Bolsheviks and by the continuing presence of Communist Russia on the other side of its long eastern frontier.

Hungary had a similar experience, for in 1919, just as the new state was getting its start under a liberal government, a Communist regime was formed under the leadership of Bela Kun, a Russian-trained Hungarian Bolshevik. At that time, in the midst of disastrous defeat and dismemberment, it was difficult for any regime to stand. Bela Kun and the Communists got their chance when the democratic regime headed by Count Karolyi was discredited by the huge territorial losses being imposed on Hungary by the Allies, and embarrassed by the return of Hungarian leftists who had been in Russia—among them the journalist Bela Kun. The disturbed conditions were a little like Russia's in 1917: defeat, a constituent assembly, a radical capital and a countryside of big estates, and a great majority of peasants with little or no property. But Hungary was not as isolated as Russia had been, and the aristocracy was by no means as ineffective as Russia's. The soviet regime led by Bela Kun was forced by public opinion to resist the Allied peace terms. Budapest was occupied by the Rumanian army in the summer of 1919, and Kun escaped to Russia. When the Rumanians withdrew in the autumn, "White" forces led by Admiral Horthy took control in Hungary. This experience with Communism was to leave Hungary politically and socially conservative. The Horthy forces remained in control, and truncated Hungary became what it had been before 1914, a kingdom dominated by its landowners.

The prospects of the Kingdom of the Serbs, Croats, and Slovenes (later Yugoslavia) were greatly influenced by the fact that the energetic Serbs had already had a country of their own and tended to dominate the new one. The Croats, accustomed to struggling for autonomy within the Habsburg empire, were determined to maintain their rights within a federal system. The Slovenes were a cultivated but not very numerous people, and did not play a very large part in the struggle between their South Slav brothers. There was a similar, but much less serious, problem of federalism in the new state of Czechoslovakia, which contained the Czechs of Bohemia (from the Austrian half of Austria-Hungary), the Slovaks (from the Hungarian half) and some Ruthenians (also from the Hungarian half; they lived at the extreme eastern tip of Czechoslovakia) as well as a large German minority. The Slovaks complained of too much centralization and of domination of the government by the Czechs, but as a Slovak intelligentsia developed, more of them took part in the direction of the country. The Ruthenes were supposed to have autonomy, but had few educated leaders of their own.

In most of East Central Europe the great mass of the people were peasants whose experience and outlook were based on village traditions and whose lives, materially meager, were paced by the seasons and the weather. These people, like a great ocean, had among them islands of urban life in which another kind of being lived: the shopkeeper, the banker, the ubiquitous lawyer, the government official. There was some connection between factory workers in the big towns and the peasantry from which they had sprung, but in general there was not much industry. Transportation was so poor that the peasantry lived a life apart. Conditions which had shaped old-regime Russia were also decisive in this region: population growth; inefficient agricultural methods; overpopulation in the rural areas, but insufficient industry to attract people to the towns.

The map of East Central Europe illuminates the extent of these agrarian conditions, which existed in Bulgaria, Yugoslavia, Rumania, Hungary, Poland, and parts of Czechoslovakia and Greece. The responsibility of the leaders of these countries was to provide conditions which would contribute to the improvement of the peasantry, of which the countries so largely consisted. The area might continue to be, in comparison with Western Europe, a vast rural slum, in which only a few townsmen and important landholders lived well and had some understanding of national and world problems. For any other destiny, there would have to be leadership of the masses: to conduct them toward citizenship; to provide schools and research; to build industries for employment and for the production of tools and household goods; and to find the capital with which to increase the nation's output, so that it could afford all these improvements. This was the main problem which faced the leadership in East Central Europe. These countries were in a condition similar to that of many "underdeveloped" areas in Asia and Africa today. The virulence of their nationalisms tended to obscure from outsiders and indeed to hide from the peoples themselves the enormous economic and social challenge. Yet this backwardness was itself one of the causes of the intense nationalism of some of the leaders, as it is today in the case of some of the non-European peoples most fiercely determined to be respected. These nationalisms, and the problems of minorities, and the bitter quarrels over bits of territory in which every nation engaged, attracted the most attention in the postwar period and hid the real challenge to Europe's continued progress which this East Central European area represented.

Apart from its other problems, the area had difficulty in recovering from the surgery which its boundaries had undergone. The most striking example of this problem was that of the republic of Austria, where the metropolis of Vienna with its banks, commercial establishments, and factories accustomed to meeting the needs of a great empire sat like a spider at the center of a web of railroads which now led outward through a few miles of countryside to insignificant borders. Its former markets were now separated by tariffs and customs officials. If Austria had too much industry, most of the other countries had too little. Only Czechoslovakia had the prospect of a balanced economy without truly massive injections of capital and technical education. If the capital came from abroad, the nation's economy might fall under foreign control, and the investments might not be in the best interests of the country. If the capital came from within the country, it posed problems of taxation and favors to industry or to agriculture—problems comparable to those which the Russians were facing in the same period. No doubt, divided East Central Europe would have been better off with economic cooperation among the parts, but in view of rivalries and nationalisms this ideal would be hard to attain.

All decisions about economic matters had to be made in the political arenas of the new states. Economic programs depended upon the form of political institutions and the distribution of political power. In most countries the crucial political issue was whether cynical "management" of the mass of rural voters would permit the domination of the country by a minority governing class and if so, what the nature and interests of the ruling group would be, and how it would use its power. In view of the nearness of Russia, Communism was bound to be an issue. In the more advanced industrial regions such as Austria and parts of Czechoslovakia and Poland, socialism was already well-established and would play an important political role, as it did in Western Europe. Nationalist and foreign-policy issues were bound to arise within the many new and rather arbitrary boundaries. But none of these problems seemed insoluble. Given time, the East Central European countries might develop habits of government and the confidence of the peoples in their political institutions.

POLITICS

As things turned out, time was short. From Finland to Greece, the disorders following World War I did not end until 1920 or later. In 1922 the Greeks were still fighting battles to determine the settlement of postwar boundaries. The early 1930's brought the depression and the rise of Hitler, both of which made politics very difficult in the small Eastern European countries. Lacking other markets, the agrarian countries tended to become economically dependent on Nazi Germany in the 1930's. By the autumn of 1938, with the disappearance of Austria and the partition of Czechoslovakia, the breathing space "between the wars" was over for East Central Europe.

During this all too brief independence, democracy was not achieved in these countries, with the exception of Czechoslovakia and with qualifications concerning Finland and the Baltic states. Czechoslovakia, under its renowned philosopher-president, Thomas G. Masaryk, had a democratic constitution influenced by the French and American models, a land reform which divided the great estates (many of them the estates of Austrian Germans) among the peasantry, and a healthy balance between industry and agriculture. There were many problems, one of which, the minority of Sudeten Germans, was to lead directly to conquest by Hitler's Germany when the country was abandoned by its allies. Czechoslovakia was well-governed, however, and proved itself capable, barring overwhelming outside forces, of solving its problems.

Austria was even more advanced culturally than Czechoslovakia and, having lost the war, did not have serious minorities problems. Austria did, however, have grave economic problems which stemmed from its sudden drop from a country of 28,000,000 to one of 6,500,000 persons, of whom 1,500,000 lived in Vienna. Austria was saddled by the victors with the entire debt of the former empire. The little country was, moreover, so advanced socially and economically that it suffered from the strains characteristic of the most highly developed societies. Its very democratic government was handicapped from the outset by division between Social Democrats, a Marxian but gradualist party which dominated Vienna and some mining and manufacturing districts, and the Christian Socialist party, which had a lower middle class following in Vienna but drew its chief strength from conservative peasants and landowners in the rural districts. Both of these parties, so sharp was the cleavage between them, soon developed private military forces. A conservative German Nationalist Party cooperated with the Christian Socialists in the 1920's, giving them the advantage, but abandoned them in the 1930's, making it virtually impossible for any group to get a majority.

Austria, an advanced, Catholic country with its peculiar new geography and its deep urban-rural, religious, and class antagonisms, also suffered from anti-Semitism and differences concerning *Anschluss* with Germany, particularly after Hitler's rise to power. The outcome in the 1930's was a peculiarly Austrian brand of Catholic dictatorship on the part of the Christian Socialists, led by Engelbert Dollfuss. This regime resisted the Nazis, with Mussolini's help, but crushed the Social Democrats in a civil war in Vienna in 1934. A Fatherland Front of rightwing groups (except the Nazis) was established, and transformed Austria into something resembling a fascist, single-party state. Dollfuss was murdered by the Nazis in a *coup* which failed in 1934, but his successor Schuschnigg was unable to resist Hitler's pressure in 1938, and Austria was taken by Nazi Germany. The Austrian case, however, was special; it illustrates nothing typical of East Central Europe.

Hungary, on the other hand, had many economic and social problems which may be called characteristic of East Central Europe. After the failure of Bela Kun's attempt to found a Communist republic, Hungary was returned to the management of aristocratic Magyar gentlemen. Admiral Horthy became Regent of the Kingdom which, however, had no king. It was impossible to allow the Habsburgs to return, since their presence was strenuously opposed by the neighboring states which had succeeded to their territories. Throughout the 1920's the aristocratic Count Bethlen was prime minister. The election law, originally democratic, was changed to a complicated system with residence and education requirements and an open ballot in the rural districts. In practice, therefore, the suffrage was severely limited. And although there continued to be numerous parties, including Social Democrats as industries grew up in Budapest and elsewhere, and Small Landholders representing the peasantry, the aristocratic conservatives who had always ruled Hungary continued to do so. Under these conditions there was no substantial land reform in Hungary, and the country continued to be characterized by huge estates and a numerous peasantry with tiny holdings or with no land at all. On the other hand, there continued to be a kind of aristocratic liberalism in Hungary which permitted free discussion among intellectuals, although political movements of peasants and workers were carefully watched. Anti-Semitism grew as Hungarians entering commerce and manufacturing encountered the competition of Jews who had traditionally managed such enterprises, but it was characteristic of the regime that anti-Semitism was discouraged by the government. In the 1930's, after the retirement of Bethlen, prime ministers such as General Gömbös and the economist Imrédy gave Hungary the appearance of a fascist state. They were admirers of Mussolini and Hitler, and a fascist Arrow Cross movement grew up. But the government did not change in its essentials. Hungary's traditional ruling groups retained power in spite of the fascist threat, and this, as we shall see, was characteristic of some of the other countries of East Central Europe.

Poland with 27,000,000 people was the largest state in the area. Reborn in a fierce struggle against both Germans and Russians, it fought determinedly for its ancient borders, contending with the Czechs to the south, the Lithuanians to the north and the Soviets to the east. The new republic emerged in the 1920's with minorities of 5,000,000 Ukrainians and more than 1,000,000 White Russians. There were also some 800,000 Germans and more than 3,000,000 Jews, the latter in many cases Polish-speaking. Poland was still mainly agricultural, traditionally a country of vast estates surrounded by innumerable small holdings, and with a large landless peasantry. There were rich resources, many of them undeveloped, and Poland made remarkable though clumsy economic progress between the wars. The country was also rich in political movements and points of view. Indeed, it was this diversity which weighed heavily upon the new political machinery of the early 1920's with its universal suffrage, bicameral legislature, president elected by the two houses of the legislature, and cabinet responsible to the parliament.

The green revolution came to Poland in the form of a great land redistribution program. By the mid-1920's, however, its application was slowed by the influence of the great landowners. They were the national leaders, respected by bankers and big businessmen in much the same way that the middle class in Germany and Russia before World War I looked to the state for favors and to the landed aristocrats for political guidance. In the towns there grew up an active proletariat and many lower middle class people, shopkeepers and petty civil servants, a seedbed for anti-Semitism and political conservatism. The Communists in Poland were not very strong, although the presence of Russia across the eastern border made them a threat. Socialism flourished in the trade unions. There were many peasant parties, which finally joined together in the 1930's. The army, which had so recently defended, and indeed helped to make, the nation, was a powerful force.

The national leader, Marshal Pilsudski, had been a heroic organizer of resistance to both the Russians and the Germans. An aristocrat and a nationalist, he had been a Marxian socialist who had been sent to Siberia for five years by the Russians. He had organized socialist resistance to the Russians, been jailed, escaped, and during the war had organized a Polish Legion to work for independence. He had a great personal following among all classes, and had learned to organize diverse social groups in the cause of nationalism. After the war he tried to rise above politics. He refused the presidency but, believing in a strong executive and insisting on retaining control of the ministry of war, in 1926 he overthrew the government and became, in effect, dictator. In the late 1920's he tried to work with the parliament, but he was unable to obtain a majority when many of the left deserted him because of his association with the conservatives. He built up a party of his own, a so-called Non-Partisan Bloc, and by intimidating or nullifying opposition groups controlled the parliament. In 1935, the year of his death, a new constitution changed the electoral laws and increased the powers of the executive.

Pilsudski's rule was efficient, and the country attracted foreign loans. He was more of an old-fashioned authoritarian than a fascist, although there were fascist movements in Poland. Indeed, in Poland all kinds of political and social movements persisted in the gifted, energetic population, and opposition to the authoritarian regime grew under Pilsudski's successors as World War II drew nearer.

In the Kingdom of the Serbs, Croats, and Slovenes, representative political institutions capsized on the rock of antagonism between the Serbs and Croats. Perhaps if there had been abler leadership or a more experienced electorate this outcome might have been avoided. The new kingdom was governed from the start by the Serbs, who made a strongly centralized constitution in 1920, when the Croats boycotted the Constituent Assembly. The Croats and Slovenes were accustomed to the more efficient administration of the Habsburg monarchy, and to its more sophisticated culture and economy, but they were outnumbered six to four by the Serbs in the population of roughly ten million South Slavs. The Croats in particular held out for autonomy and most of the time refused to cooperate with the government. Although the green revolution was undertaken in the largely agricultural country, as elsewhere in East Central Europe it performed no miracle for the impoverished economy. Landholding systems had been varied and intricate, and efforts to distribute holdings often raised more problems and complaints than they settled. Small peasant holdings were satisfying to the owners, but inefficient. The unresolved political stalemate postponed constructive planning to solve the country's problems.

The drama of South Slav self-government reached a tragic climax in 1928 when the Croat Peasant Party leader Stepan Radich, a great orator revered by his people but seemingly incapable of producing a coherent program, was murdered by a Serb deputy during a session of the parliament. In 1929 King Alexander inaugurated a dictatorship, renamed the country Yugoslavia, and tried to wipe out all vestiges of national antagonism, including the political parties. During a visit to France in 1934 Alexander was himself murdered by an assassin associated with Croat extremists whose party was subsidized by Mussolini. The Yugoslav dictatorship continued under the regency of Prince Paul, the late king's cousin. Again it was a case, not of fascism, but of old-fashioned authoritarianism which in Yugoslavia did not furnish good government but simply administered while holding the lid down on a difficult situation.

With local variations which it is impossible to recount in a brief survey, Rumania and Bulgaria exhibited some of the same tendencies as Yugoslavia. Both experienced the green revolution, yet failed to overcome the social gulf between the peasantry and the towns. In the politics of both countries there was a high degree of personal ascendancy by individual political leaders over their followings, coupled with a tendency to "manage" elections on the part of whichever party was in power. In both there was frequent violence and an "all or nothing" mentality partly inherited from generations of opposition to oppressive foreign rule. Both had peasant parties which proved ineffective, although in the Bulgarian case a remarkable peasant leader, Alexander Stamboliski, gave the country a regime so firmly dedicated to the peasantry that he was murdered by his opponents in 1923. Both ended in royal dictatorships after the failure of party politics. King Boris III in 1936 became dictator in Bulgaria. In Rumania King Carol became dictator in 1938 after defeating an attempted *coup* by a fascist and anti-Semitic group called the Iron Guard.

In East Central Europe after World War I there were great hopes for the peasant parties of men like Radich and Stamboliski. They seemed to combine social justice and democracy with overwhelming political power. Some observers thought that the "Green International" of peasant parties in which Stamboliski and others were interested would not only check the "Red International" of Communism and the "White International" of reactionary kings and landlords, but would also overcome nationalistic rivalries and reduce the possibility of war.

But the peasant parties, like the economics of small peasant farms, proved to be disappointing. In spite of their numbers, the peasants were not a decisive political force or even a very cohesive social group. Most of them were ignorant, and the political leaders who represented them tended to be lawyers or urban intellectuals or, if they came from peasant villages, tended to become engrossed in the life of the towns and to forget about peasant interests. Moreover the great depression hurt a peasant economy which was weak to begin with and doomed hopes for cultural advance based on economic progress.

Greece, the southernment outpost of East Central Europe, was in some ways not typical of the region. Like Finland and the Baltic states of Estonia, Latvia, and Lithuania, it had to some extent mediated between east and west. Greece was a poor country but profited from the sea by means of its shipping. For almost a century it had been independent, but like the Balkan kingdoms which had escaped from Ottoman domination in the nineteenth century Greece was for a long time ruled by an oligarchy separated by a wide gulf from the mass of the population.

After World War I Greek political life was embroiled by struggles between, on the one hand, the king and the conservative groups who had been accustomed to running the country, and, on the other, new liberal and republican factions. On both sides the level of political behavior was low, characterized by managed elections and frequent shifts back and forth between the monarchy and a republic. Nationalistic aspirations complicated the situation by leading to an ill-starred war from 1920–1922 against the equally nationalistic Turkey of Mustapha Kemal Pasha. The Greeks were thrown back from Asia Minor and eventually forced to find homes for more than a million of their nationals—a problem which worsened the economic and political situation in the small homeland. Like Yugoslavia, Rumania, and Bulgaria, Greece finally took refuge in a royal dictatorship in 1935, which was shortly followed by the military dictatorship of General John Metaxas.

FASCISM AND ROYAL DICTATORSHIPS

In East Central Europe fascist organizations drew their followings from frustrated lower middle class people and, occasionally, peasants, who could not understand the complications of economic phenomena, in particular the depression of the 1930's and the social dislocations resulting from changes in the value of money. These people found solace in garbled doctrines of nationalism, anti-Communism, and economic reform.

The leadership of these and other political movements was over-supplied from reservoirs of "intellectuals" who had managed to secure a measure of education which placed them above the peasant masses. Such persons, unable to find employment in the still relatively undeveloped economic enterprises of the region, turned to politics as a suitable profession. They were motivated by confused nationalistic aspirations and by a desire to get jobs in the proliferating bureaucracies of the new states, which gave their members power and status. The bureaucracies of East Central Europe weighed heavily upon the uneducated peasant communities by their costliness and an arbitrariness tempered only by corruption.

The success of royal dictatorships against fascist movements in East Central Europe is explained by the persisting strength of old-fashioned ruling groups in an underdeveloped society. The weakness of fascism is explained by the absence of those mass followings of confused and unhappy people which were made possible by economic and social dislocations in the industrial and urban societies of western countries where a little education became a dangerous thing.

In a manner of speaking, the countries of East Central Europe were—most of them—unprepared for fascism, which was a sickness of the more highly developed societies. This was one of the few benefits of their still largely rural condition. But the royal dictatorships were scarcely less oppressive than the fascists. In retrospect the real tragedy of the region was that the great powers which hemmed it in allowed it so little time to find its way and provided so little help. The fate of East Central Europe was a measure of Europe's failure in the years between the wars.

50

THE DEFAULT OF
THE VICTORS:
BRITAIN AND
FRANCE AFTER
VERSAILLES

GREAT BRITAIN AND FRANCE had fought a war for the mastery of Europe, and they had won. Their people had borne without flinching almost unbearable strains. Their ideals as well as their armies had been victorious; freedom and democracy were in 1918 triumphant throughout most of Europe. The great gift of the west, the gift of humane liberty, could now be offered to the world.

In the event, the years after 1918 were years of disillusion and hardship. The problems which the war produced were more intractable than those which it solved. The British found themselves with a faltering economy. Their leadership was in the hands of men who were at best uninspired and at worst incompetent. Their international position was being quietly eroded. The French, faced with nearly total destruction of some of their richest provinces, rebuilt them with remarkable speed but at the cost of the solidity of their currency and the savings of their most industrious citizens. Then the economic whirlwind of the Great Depression struck the French economy, laying waste its tidy, hard-earned solvencies, spreading unemployment, revealing class bitterness and social conflict. The French Republic was torn by party disputes and led by men who were without the stature of the prewar statesmen and were, at worst, scoundrels. The society, bleeding from its wartime amputations and shaken by the loss of its savings, was sullen or embattled. In the end both countries were brought to another war which they could have prevented.

These problems arose from World War I which, like the French Revolution, had the effect of shaking up people and institutions so thoroughly as to leave a legacy of confusion and extremism. Physically exhausted by the efforts of the war, some citizens reacted with a determination to mind their own concerns and seek their own pleasures, being convinced of the worthlessness of governments and the transience of all things. At the same time, other citizens were accustomed to the violence of wartime and infected with ruthlessness in fighting for their aims. In the war, moreover, a generation had been, almost literally, killed off. Almost all the top leaders of the interwar years were men who had made their reputations before 1914, and who were essentially prewar in their outlook. Among the outstanding members of the British cabinet, only one, Anthony Eden, was of the generation who had fought in the front lines in 1914–1918.

Despite the weary story which must now be told, it must not be supposed that there were no successes or achievements in France and Britain. Out of the postwar sense of dispossession arose a vigorous artistic striving and an experimentation with new ideas and media. The standard of living and of civilization was perceptibly rising. In 1939, Frenchmen and Englishmen lived more decent lives, in greater comfort and with more material goods, than ever before. The interwar years saw a gradual extension of the notion that society must protect its members against some of the losses and suffering occasioned by old age, sickness, unemployment, destitution, ignorance, and disease. Democracy was adjusting in some ways, though not in all, to the demands of a new age of equality and the opportunities of the new age of technology.

GREAT BRITAIN IN THE 1920's

A general election was held in Great Britain a month after the Armistice of November 11, 1918. In the slightly hysterical atmosphere of the day, the wartime coalition of David Lloyd George backed by the Conservatives and some Liberals was returned to power on a slightly hysterical platform of "Hang the Kaiser," "Make Germany Pay," and "We Promise a Home Fit for Heroes." The combined opposition numbered 33 Liberals and 63 Laborites. The coalition majority in the House of Commons controlled 526 seats.

Lloyd George and his coalition remained in power for four years, but the wartime hero saw his popularity disintegrate and his ridiculous electoral program come to nothing. The Kaiser (safely ensconced in neutral Holland) was not hanged. Germany was found to be too poor to pay. "A home fit for heroes" turned out to be a land battered by strikes and civil war.

The most conspicuous and painful development of the period was the postwar depression. After a brief period of prosperity, lasting through 1919, a heavy economic pall descended on Great Britain as on most of the rest of the world. Throughout 1920 and 1921 it deepened. Unemployment spread, rising from practically nothing to over two million—almost 18 percent of the working force.

There were violent labor disputes. These reflected to some extent the growth of unions during the war and the accumulation of unsettled claims during the four years of patriotic forbearance. But they also reflected other, more ominous, conditions: workers were now determined to force their fellow citizens to make good on the promises of a better world after the war, for appetites and ambitions were never so great as at the moment when the economy was least capable of satisfying them. They reflected a growing impatience in the labor unions with peaceful and gradual methods. There were more strikes in June of 1919 than in any previous month on record. In April, 1921, the miners went out. Their strike was directed not only toward demands for higher wages (which were almost unthinkable in view of the crisis of the coal industries) but toward a "root solution," nationalization of the entire coal industry. Behind the strikes there seemed to many respectable folk to be a specter of something worse, of social revolution. A British Communist party had been organized and was infiltrating some of the unions. The Labor party had voted against having any connection with it, but nobody could tell whether it might not attract the constituents of Labor and become a serious threat.

Prosperity began to return, in some measure, in 1922, and the social conflicts subsided, but in the meanwhile the Lloyd George government was forced to face an even more disturbing situation. The United Kingdom was in the throes of a civil war which was shortly to lead to its partition. This distressing state was the climax of the long history of difficulties with Ireland, which had been governed as a part of the United Kingdom of Great Britain and Ireland since 1800. During the war, Sinn Fein, a movement demanding absolute independence, had gained in strength, and at its end resorted to arms in an attempt to eliminate all connection with Great Britain.

The most pressing issues in Ireland in the early 1920's were: what was to be the degree and nature of the link between Ireland and the British crown; and what was to become of the northeastern province of Ulster, which the Irish claimed but which was in large part Protestant, Scottish, and ardently loyal to the crown. A Home Rule bill of 1914, postponed by the war, had provided a separate government and parliament under the crown for Ulster—Northern Ireland, as it was called. In 1921 this regime was duly inaugurated. In the meanwhile, Sinn Fein had set up a rebel "Irish Republic" in the South. The British, after bitter fighting, sought to negotiate with Sinn Fein and succeeded in reaching agreement with its leader, Eamon de Valera. The agreement provided for a free but partitioned Ireland, enjoying the same status in the Commonwealth of Nations as Canada. But the prestige of the Lloyd George government was severely shaken.

As serious as the social conflict and the Irish war was the deep economic maladjustment, of which the strikes and depression were partly a symptom. The British Isles were dependent on imported food and raw materials to feed their people and their factories. Now, sources of foreign currencies to pay for these imports were compromised. Foreign investments had been in many cases liquidated to pay for war materials. The export trade lost its former dominance. Many industries were growing inefficient, especially those upon which the world supremacy of British commerce in the nineteenth century had been constructed:

coal, shipbuilding, and textiles. They were simply unable to compete with new methods used abroad, and they had no attraction to investors which might have permitted them to raise new funds for re-equipment.

This problem of lack of new investment underlay most of Britain's subsequent economic difficulties, but none of the governments made any real attempt to deal with it. The Lloyd George government and its successors in the 1920's applied the economic policies which were judged most fit to meet the situation according to the lights of orthodox economists. This involved reducing costs, to reduce the prices of export products and make them more competitive in foreign markets. This rather grim policy had several serious weaknesses, for reducing prices involved reducing wages, since wages were often the most important part of a manufacturer's costs. This in turn meant more work and a lower standard of life for workers, and workers in the 1920's were simply not willing to put up with it. This was the root cause of the strikes of 1919–1921, and later of the General Strike of 1926. In the end, it proved impossible to reduce wages very substantially, so costs remained high and so did export prices, and the deflationary policy was only modestly successful.

The economic policy did have some good points. Britain was spared the terrible shock of inflation which shook the middle classes in most of the continental countries. By 1925 the pound had been revalued at its 1914 gold value and was—briefly—again the strongest currency in the world. This served the important interests of British banking, which financed a huge proportion of the world's trade. Moreover, the continued adherence to the idea of free trade helped to assure low prices for the consumer. Nevertheless, the policies inaugurated by the Lloyd George administration did not do the necessary thing, which was to build more modern factories. That had to wait for its beginnings until after the economic revolution of 1931.

The most conspicuous problems of the period 1918 to 1922 were in foreign affairs, where the aftermath of the war and all its complications had to be dealt with. Here, the record of the Lloyd George government and particularly of its distinguished foreign minister, the Marquis of Curzon, was on the whole better. The treaty was written and signed; and settlements of most of the thorny problems were achieved. But there were three areas where Lloyd George failed, or where success was long delayed, and these contributed to the undermining of his government. One was Russia—which Britain treated like an international criminal, to the indignation of a certain portion of the public which saw in the new Communist regime the hope of the world. The second was France, which Britain had declined to guarantee against possible future aggression from Germany and which drifted in bitterness away from its ally. The third was the Near East, where a most intricate and intractable situation led to recurring wars and crises which gave weapons to the prime minister's opponents.

By the end of 1922, Lloyd George's unpopularity was becoming so noticeable that the Conservatives decided to detach themselves from him. The prime minister resigned, and the Conservative leader Andrew Bonar Law took his place, to be succeeded after a few months by Stanley Baldwin.

Stanley Baldwin was a lazy, unimaginative man, a successful manufacturer who embodied the new, businessmen's Conservative party which gradually had replaced the old landowners' and aristocrats'. He had no attachment to the nineteenth-century liberal ideal that the government should refrain from meddling with the economy. He was, on the contrary, as much in favor of meddling as was his opposition, the Labor party, only he believed that the state action should be in aid of businessmen. In his administrations, he encouraged the very thing which had been anathema to nineteenth-century thought: state-sponsored and state-subsidized monopolies. In shipping, air transport, radio broadcasting, the electrical industries, and several others, the Conservatives sponsored combinations of private industries, sometimes (as in radio broadcasting) going so far as to give a semipublic corporation, in this case the British Broadcasting Company, an exclusive charter and control over specified sources of revenue, a status rather like that of a turnpike commission in an American state. This was neo-mercantilism with a vengeance, developed out of a belief that competition weakened rather than strengthened business.

The Conservatives were defeated in the election which Baldwin called in 1923, and lost their majority in the Commons, although the popular vote showed relatively little change. No party had a majority, so the only possibility was a Labor government supported by Liberal votes. The Labor leader, Mr. Ramsay MacDonald, accordingly became the first socialist prime minister to take office in Britain, or indeed in Western Europe.

MacDonald was a working class man. He had fought his way up the trade union ladder, and he was one of the great orators of the twentieth century—he had, as one observer said, power to win audiences by his voice even when his words meant nothing, which occurred frequently. Like the party which he led, he was by program radical and by temperament conservative. Although Laborites talked socialism and class war, they were gentle in practice; they bore the stamp of the Fabians' "gradualism," and of the trade union tradition of seeking immediate advantage for the working man rather than revolution.

The first Labor Government was in office for less than a year, and it was imprisoned by its dependence on Liberal votes in the Commons. Its record was therefore not very significant, but it showed itself "respectable," and moderate in all ways. A few rather wholesome housing and tax measures were passed, and in foreign affairs a policy of greater affability to France and greater support for the League was initiated. There was no talk of nationalization. The only thing that was done that betrayed any "leftist" inclination was the recognition of the Soviet Union.

The government was weak, and the defection of the Liberals over a minor issue brought it down. A new election was held in 1924. Labor increased its popular vote by a million. But it lost some forty seats in the Commons, and the Liberals lost over a hundred. The Conservatives once again had a majority, and Baldwin returned to office.

His return coincided with the beginnings of the prosperity of the late 1920's, which concealed the maladjustments of the British economy. It also coincided with the general improvement in the European situation which attended the signing of the Locarno Treaties and other soothing events. These two developments permitted the second Baldwin government to live out its five years with many fewer problems and responsibilities than its predecessors. Some of the war-time injuries were restored, the pound remained strong and stable, new British industries developed and began to capture new foreign markets—particularly the automobile and electrical appliance industries—and something was accomplished toward rebuilding the foreign investments. For the most part, however, the second half of the decade saw no dramatic legislation and few dramatic events.

To this generalization there is one outstanding exception. The year 1926 saw the General Strike, the first and last in British history and one of the most alarming developments of its day. The strike grew out of the perennial problems of the coal miners. In 1925 the new Chancellor of the Exchequer, Winston Churchill, had completed the job of revaluing the pound, returning it to the gold standard at the 1914 rate. This meant that pounds were costlier for foreigners, and British exports, notably coal, suffered. Coal mine owners sought to counter slipping sales by reducing prices, which to the owners seemed to demand reducing costs, which meant reducing wages. The coal miners, already badly paid and forced to work under the worst conditions in any industry, struck. Since their demands went unsatisfied, they were joined by other unions. In May, 1926, the wheels of British society stopped turning.

The General Strike failed. The government, backed by the thoroughly distraught upper and middle classes, brought every resource to bear to break the strike. It was denounced as unconstitutional, and even working class people were so greatly inconvenienced that many of them opposed it. After a melodramatic week of no trains, no papers, no deliveries and no production, the unions called off the strike. But it was important; it convinced the unions that such drastic action was impracticable, and it shook the workers' confidence in their union leadership. Union membership, which had been growing, began to decline, and continued to do so for many years, a process speeded by restrictive legislation which the government shortly enacted. It showed everyone that "bourgeois" society was not so easily upset as naive revolutionaries had once imagined.

The statutory life of the 1924 Parliament ran its course peacefully after the General Strike. Most parts of Britain were relatively prosperous now, and relatively content. The Conservatives fought their next election with the slogan, "Safety First," and confidently expected to be elected. But the electorate, if not exactly discontented, was bored, and among working class people the memory of the broken strike still rankled. In the election of 1929, the Conservatives lost over a hundred seats, and the Laborites won over a hundred. MacDonald again became prime minister with Liberal support.

FRANCE IN THE 1920's

In many respects, the problems of France resembled those of Britain—war-weariness and disillusionment; social unrest and a shaken economy; a lack of inspiration in political leadership. But France lacked the great economic problem which faced the British and which the British, in 1929, were still refusing to face; the French economy was basically healthy. On the other hand, France had problems which the British did not, problems which, some of them, went back as far as the French Revolution: the relation of church and state; the singular bitterness of class conflict; the extreme instability of French ministries, arising out of the many factions which passed for parties in the French parliament.

The French did not need to import food. Moreover, unlike the old, basic British industries, the French industrial structure was in 1929 far from obsolete. The main industrial areas, in the extreme northeast, had been fought over in the war, and most of the factories wrecked. This was a blessing in disguise, for capital which might not have been volunteered merely for re-equipment *had* to be found for reconstruction, and was provided by the state.

If the necessity for rebuilding the devastated areas was in some ways a blessing, in others it was a curse. The state had to pay out, suddenly, huge sums for what amounted to capital investment. The capital for reconstruction had to be provided by the French taxpayer, or by printing money, which in turn meant that the entire population paid in the form of higher prices. During the early 1920's the franc fell by three quarters of its prewar value in terms of gold.

There were, in the twelve years which followed the Armistice, three elections for new parliaments in France: in 1919, in 1924, and in 1928. The first resulted (in contrast to the Khaki Election of 1918 in Britain) in throwing out the wartime leader, Georges Clemenceau. Clemenceau was an old-line Radical; the new Chamber was conservative and Catholic. It was indeed the first Chamber with an openly conservative majority elected since the Third Republic was founded. There was little to hold together the loose groupings which formed the majority. Ministries rose and fell at the usual rhythm until 1922, when the ardent nationalist Raymond Poincaré, the wartime president, came to office and remained there for two years carrying out the ill-fated Ruhr policy.

The Ruhr invasion (as is explained elsewhere), was an effort not only to collect German reparations but also to weaken Germany financially and politically, in the hope of postponing the time when German recovery would permit the Germans to entertain thoughts of revenge against their conquerors. It involved the occupation of the main center of German industry and an effort to operate the factories to French profit. In almost every way it was a failure. German passive resistance, while it wrecked the German economy, prevented the French from realizing much profit. The French voters, or a majority of them, were prepared to vote for parties which promised a more conciliatory and less expensive policy toward Germany.

The Chamber elected in 1924 contained a large majority for the parties which had opposed the Poincaré government, the most leftist majority yet known to the Third Republic. It was composed mainly of two parties: first, the Radicals, led by Edouard Herriot, the party which had dominated the Republic after 1900 and was radical by very old-fashioned standards—it stood for sound money, low taxes, civil rights, and anti-clericalism; secondly, the Socialists, who agreed to a Radical ministry but declined to participate in it. The Socialists, led by an extremely wealthy and brilliant lawyer named Léon Blum, were (like the Radicals or the British Laborites) more moderate than they sounded. They preached Marxism and class warfare and nationalization of the means of production, but their backbone consisted of intellectuals, civil servants, and trade union members who were eager for immediate advantages rather than for social revolution. Moreover, the Socialist party had been purged of its extremists in 1920 when, at the party congress at Tours, those of its members who wished to affiliate with the Communist International at Moscow had broken off to form the French Communist party. At Tours, the pro-Communist delegates had been in a majority, and they had thus acquired the party property, the newspaper, *l'Humanité*, legal continuity with the prewar Socialist party, and some of its traditions and leaders. But the elections of 1924 had shown that the voters preferred the Socialists with their Radical alliance, their moderation, and their freedom from links with Russia. While the Radical and Socialist alliance elected 266 deputies, more than ever before, the new Communist party won only 26 seats.

The *Cartel des Gauches* (Combination of the Left), as the coalition of Radicals, Socialists, and other moderate leftists was called, at once set about rectifying what it regarded as the mistakes of the right. The German policy was reversed. The Dawes Plan, a moderate arrangement for reparations payments, was approved. The peaceable Locarno Treaty was signed and Germany was welcomed into the League of Nations. Relations with the Vatican (restored by the preceding government) were broken off, and the old, prewar laws against religious orders were invoked with strictness—a policy which got the Herriot government into trouble in the restored province of Alsace, whose devout Catholics regarded this as intolerable meddling by their French rulers.

Alsace and Lorraine were problems in several ways, for their populations were accustomed (whatever their complaints) to fifty years of German rule, during which they had shared in the rapid economic growth of Germany, and they found that reintegration into highly centralized France had forced sudden changes in their way of life. An Alsatian Self-Government Movement developed, and proved a serious embarrassment to the *Cartel des Gauches*. But it was nothing to the embarrassment provided by the financial situation, which now became impossible. The franc fell disastrously. The Radicals and Socialists, united on foreign policy and religious questions, were deeply divided on financial matters—the Socialists favored a capital levy, repulsive to the Radicals, who were connected with business interests. The credit of the state was endangered, and government loans were poorly subscribed. The ministry hesitated either to raise taxes or to cancel public indebtedness—and was forced to resign. Its place was taken, after several other short-lived leftist cabinets, by one containing many of the same ministers but presided over by the arch-conservative Poincaré—such was the eccentricity of republican politics—supported by a majority made up of the Radicals and the center parties without the Socialists.

Poincaré worked what at the time was called a miracle. Parliament voted him emergency financial powers; the franc was devalued; rigid government economies were inaugurated; taxes were raised—and in a few weeks the state's credit was sound again. The franc, shortly re-attached to the gold standard, became one of the world's most stable currencies, and so it remained for the better part of a decade. French foreign trade expanded quickly, and French production rose. For the next few years, France enjoyed the greatest prosperity of its history. By 1929, the index of production had passed 1913. Unemployment, in 1928, was negligible.

These benign developments were in fact due as much to external circumstances as to Poincaré's policies. World prosperity was running high, and France shared in it. But the outside causes received less publicity than the policies of the prime minister, and this fact gave rise to a curious and significant political rift. The right, whose man Poincaré was, took credit for his success, arguing that only conservatives knew how to manage finances. The left, on the other hand, noting that Herriot's troubles had resulted from the bankers' refusal to lend the state money, and Poincaré's success from their willingness, drew other conclusions. They insisted that the bankers and the groups who controlled the wealth of France had erected what they called "a wall of money" around the government; by withholding credits, they were in a position to overthrow any progressive or leftist government.

The Wall of Money became a battle cry for the French left, and the widespread credence given to the notion of a "capitalist conspiracy" led to far-reaching bitterness and to political extremism.

But this fruit did not ripen until after the depression struck. Prosperity in France survived the flood of 1929 longer than in most countries, and there was no great need for strenuous measures. By 1931, however, the depression had begun, and there was nothing to meet it except the politicians of the center with their lack of ideas and their insecure parliamentary majority.

The French story in the 1920's seems, in many ways, brighter than the British. For all that it had suffered heavy losses in the war and the terrible shock of inflation, which wiped out earnings and impoverished many middle class people, French society held together. But in this stability were the seeds of the real problem of France, for the economy verged on stagnation. The population was actually declining—the first time such a thing had happened in a major country in centuries. While plant equipment was new, management practices were old. French businessmen, surrounded by tariffs and comfortable price-fixing arrangements, were content to keep things as they were. The French farmer was content to cultivate his small and uneconomic holding with old-fashioned methods. There was an almost conscious attempt on the part of the peasants, the businessmen, and the huge class of small shopkeepers to freeze the economic structure.

Moreover, the old problems were still unsolved. There was still a portion of the populace which distrusted the Republic and democracy. The relations of the state to Roman Catholicism were still unsettled. The amorphous party structure, whose diversity led to recurrent ministerial crises, was still an historical museum, reflecting every political interest which had ever been proposed, from old-regime royalism to anarcho-syndicalism.

For all its wealth and stability, France was ill-equipped to confront the nightmares of the 1930's—the Great Depression and the rise of Hitlerism.

GREAT BRITAIN IN THE 1930's

In both of the great western democracies, the decade of the 1930's was largely occupied by attempts to cope with the shocking economic situation and the mounting threat of war. The stories of these two crises are told elsewhere. What concerns us here is the political narrative, the Iliad of division and weakness within each country, as the dreary years ground on toward the catastrophe.

There are sharp contrasts between Britain and France in the 1930's. The British remedies for depression and for international tension were, whatever their shortcomings, consistent and systematic. Politically, the United Kingdom was stable to the point of atrophy. In France. drastically opposing policies were urgently proposed until at the end something not altogether removed from civil war shook the nation. The last years of the Third Republic—which dissolved in 1940—saw its capacity to produce decisions further enfeebled. It resembled an elderly paralytic observing, with considerable courage but not much hope, the preparations of his murderers.

The era of misfortunes began for Britain as Ramsay MacDonald returned to office in the second Labor government, again supported by the Liberals in the House. Before it had been in power a year, the depression struck Great Britain. Prices and exports fell, trade stagnated, and unemployment rapidly spread. A business depression turned rapidly into a human tragedy and a national crisis.

In the face of this situation, the MacDonald government did almost nothing, and there was in fact little it could do. Opposing voices were advocating, in some cases, an inflationary policy, in others resort to tariff protection, in others strict government economy and paring of unemployment relief. None of these was possible for the Labor government. It was sworn to protect the pound and to preserve free trade, and no government which owed its existence to working class votes could in honor reduce the payments to the rapidly growing unemployed.

Yet these payments had by the middle of 1931 brought the British Treasury within sight of depletion. The situation was compounded by a flight from the pound—that is, owners of British currency were so alarmed as to use it to buy francs or marks or dollars, which caused a drain on the gold supply and forced down the price of pounds. By August of 1931, bankruptcy was nearer than it had ever been in British history.

Unable to secure the agreement of his party to government economies, MacDonald resigned. He was, however, immediately reappointed, this time as head of a ministry which included Conservatives and Liberals. It was called a National Government and was, in theory, a coalition. But both the Labor party and the Liberals were split, and the majority of their members went into opposition. In the new government, the aging MacDonald became more and more of a figurehead, and the real power lay with the Conservative majority and the Conservative leader, Stanley Baldwin.

The National Government was a constitutional anomaly, based on an "agreement to disagree" among its members. In October, a general election was called, and the coalition fought it on the vague and silly slogans of "a doctor's mandate," and "a vote against the National Government is a vote against the king." (The monarch, King George V, was supposed to have taken the initiative in its formation, although the extent of his activities was never clear.)

Despite the disagreements of its varied membership, the National Government won the election, and did adopt a drastic and coherent policy. The pound was devalued. Tariffs were hastily imposed, ending the seventy years of free trade, to protect the domestic market for British manufacturers. Unemployment relief was reduced, a measure which occasioned the greatest bitterness. Preferential trade arrangements were worked out with the self-governing dominions, Canada, Australia, New Zealand, South Africa, and Ireland. The tightening of economic bonds of empire coincided with their political loosening. In 1931 there was passed the Statute of Westminster which wrote into law what was already customary: that no act of the British Parliament could bind any of the five dominions against its will. Henceforth, few constitutional links except the titular monarchy subsisted to unite the free members of the British Commonwealth. They had been replaced by ties of economics and sentiment, to form an association of countries unique in history.

The program of the National Government helped to stem the hemorrhage of public money and contributed to a modest recuperation. Although unemployment remained high through the 1930's, and began to disappear only with the advent of rearmament, a business recovery in Britain was afoot by 1933 and a modest and uneven prosperity was achieved by the late years of the decade.

It was achieved in a greatly changed economic structure. Behind the new tariffs grew up a whole constellation of energetic new firms—light consumer-goods industries, for the most part, supplying goods which had formerly been imported. The centers of these new industries were in Birmingham, Coventry, and the octopus of London, which now contained something like eight million people. The old manufacturing centers in Lancashire and Yorkshire languished; their heavy industries, dependent upon exports, did not share in the hustle of recovery and expansion.

By 1939, the free economy of Britain, heritage of liberal enthusiasms in the middle of the nineteenth century, was thoroughly eroded. A very extensive (though very incomplete) social security system existed. Combination of industries and cooperative price-fixing were encouraged. Subsidies were extensively used. Tariffs had been adopted. The path was cleared for the planned economy which the Labor party advocated, and it made little practical difference that these preliminary steps toward it had been taken by Conservatives acting to shield businessmen from the shocks and pains of free competition.

The second General Election of the decade—and the last held before World War II—took place in 1935. By then MacDonald had retired and Baldwin had replaced him, and the National Government was almost purely composed of Conservatives. By then, too, the international situation had become more grave and its issues obscured domestic questions. The Labor Party went into the election with divided counsels and emerged from it without a majority, although it recovered from the splits of 1931. The National Government lost half its majority, but it still had 387 Commons seats to 158 for Labor. The election confirmed, too, the disappearance of the Liberals as a major party; their representation fell to seventeen seats. The mechanism of a two-party system was at last restored.

Baldwin retired in 1937. His place was taken by Neville Chamberlain. Chamberlain had been an excellent minister for local government in the 1920's and a very good Chancellor of the Exchequer in the early 1930's. Now, however, he was to devote almost his entire energies to foreign policy, a field in which his training and his gifts did not lie. After 1935, indeed, there was little of note in the field of domestic legislation or politics. The international situation dominated the scene.

The last half of the decade did contain one strange event. This was a storybook royal romance which led to the forced abdication in December, 1936, of Edward VIII, who had succeeded his father on the throne a few months before. Edward was forty-two, a man of the war generation, unmarried, and with more fresh ideas than was safe for a British sovereign. He announced that he wished to marry an American woman of fashion, the twice-divorced Mrs. Wallis Simpson. The national Church, of which the King was the head, refused to recognize divorce, and Edward refused to abandon the lady. Despite much sympathy and divided opinions about his rights, the King bowed to the insistence of the episcopacy, the dominions, and the prime minister, and abdicated in favor of his younger brother, who became King George VI (1936–1952).

HOUSING ESTATE, ENGLAND. In the years between the two world wars, Great Britain suffered from deep economic dislocations. It was also undergoing extensive social changes which involved the growth of a huge "middle-middle class," replacing the old hierarchy of aristocrats, factory-owners, industrial workers, and peasants. The typical Englishman of those days was more and more a clerical worker, semiprofessional, who lived in comfortable but drearily uniform "housing estates" like this one, which is shown symbolically engulfing the farmland and the old villages in the country around London in 1935. (Radio Times Hulton Picture Library)

The Crisis of the Throne inspired the sob-sisters of the world to an unparalleled output of sentimental twaddle, and it helped the sales of newspapers and magazines. Beyond its publicity value, it had a certain importance in illuminating the position of the monarchy, which had appeared to be purely decorative. For the crisis showed that the throne was more than decorative. In Great Britain, it was cherished as the link, symbolic but significant, between the almost completely independent countries which had once been colonies and were now dominions of the British Commonwealth. The unpopularity of the king's proposed marriage had been greatest in the dominions, and it was thence that decisive pressures had come.

If there were disturbances at the top of the social structure, there were remarkably few at the bottom. Economic recovery eased social discontent, and international crisis distracted it. In the depression years, as in the early 1920's, there had been fear of extremism and Communism. But the Communist party failed to grow substantially. The bad years saw few riots and little violence. Even strikes were less numerous than they had been. But, nonetheless, there was a latent social conflict. The conservative policies of the decade helped to confirm many working class and some middle class people in the belief that they were the subjects, if not the victims, of an oligarchy of wealth. The sense of class conflict was moderate, but it was definite. The seeds of a dramatic, if serene, reconstruction of Great Britain had been planted and were growing. After World War II they were to bear a copious harvest.

Great Britain drifted into war under inept leadership and despite the hopes and wishes of almost the entire nation. The country was unprepared, militarily and psychologically. And in 1940, military defeat threatened. Then, under inspiring leadership at last in the person of Winston Churchill, the kingdom fought with determination and skill, and closed its ranks with vigor and heroism. The interwar period with its mediocrities and its apathy were revealed in the nature of a long and feverish sleep. The vitality of Great Britain had survived.

FRANCE IN THE 1930's

The depression struck France late. When it came, it was worse and more intractable than in many other countries. By 1935, French exports stood at less than a third of the 1928 figure. The French export trade was not as important a part of the economy as the British, but it was important enough to affect business, and sinking prices and slow trade spread throughout the nation. The French government by reason of its multi-party character and its precarious parliamentary tenure was never able to agree to the sort of consistent and firm program which brought about a measure of recovery in the United States, Germany, and Great Britain. Not until 1936, when the Socialist-dominated Popular Front came to power, were drastic and consistent reforms inaugurated, and these were better calculated to achieve social justice in a prosperous country than to rescue a drowning economy. Prices had recovered their 1929 level by 1938, as a result of cutting the value of the franc. But industrial production did not fully recover, and unemployment was higher in 1938 than it had been in 1932—a baleful situation paralleled in no other industrial society. French unemployment never reached anything like the dreadful figures in Germany or Great Britain—the highest was under half a million in 1936—but it seemed to be irremediable. Taken together with other hardships, it formed the background for many political troubles.

The governments which presided over these developments were numerous and unstable. The parliament which had been elected in 1928 was predominantly middle-of-the-road and conservative, and the ministries which its majority supported reflected conservative views on economic policy. This meant deflation and retrenchment, a policy espoused by the successive governments of Chautemps, Laval, Briand, and Tardieu. In the election of 1932, a new *Cartel des Gauches,* led by the Radical party again, displaced the centrist and conservative majority. It was the product of economic distress, but it was unable to follow any strong economic policies. By the end of 1932, the deficit was four hundred million dollars and was continuing to mount. It could be stopped only by rigid government economies, and this the Radical and leftist deputies could not yet accept, since it meant hardship for government employees (very numerous and influential in progressive circles) and for the workers. The situation was remarkably similar to that in Britain eighteen months earlier.

The climax did not come until February, 1934, but it came with an explosion. By then the country was in deep depression and the futility of the government was evident. Something like despair, mingled with disgust at the maneuvering of politicians, was widespread. It took two forms: on the one hand, it sharpened the appetite of the leftists for social revolution; on the other, it increased the followings and boldness of those who insisted that republicanism was corrupt and moribund and who demanded some sort of nationalist dictatorship. Prominent among the latter, picturesquely enough, was a monarchist group which wanted a stream-lined version of the old regime that had ended in 1789. There was even a party called the Franquists who claimed that they wanted to restore the culture and virtue of France as it had existed under the ancient Franks, in the seventh century. The rapid proliferation of these extreme rightist action groups represented something much more up-to-date than an admiration for the regime of Louis XIV or the glories of the Merovingians. It represented the reaction of conservative but desperate people to a situation of decay, to the spread of socialist and Communist influence, and to the stimulating examples of Mussolini across the Alps and of Hitler across the Rhine. The depression and the international situation highlighted the shortcomings of the Republic and made people feel that some drastic changes were indispensable.

Such drastic changes were sought, and nearly achieved, in the Paris insurrections of February, 1934. These riotous events were precipitated by a scandal in high places, a symptom of what its opponents took to be typically republican corruption. An undesirable pawn-broker named Stavisky committed suicide. On investigation he was found to have been engaged in many shady deals, and (it seemed) to have been protected from police action by the intervention of numerous republican politicians who presumably received benefits. In the face of a flood of sensational revelations, the ministry resigned. A new ministry under Daladier, remarkably similar to the old, took office.

The "action groups" of the right, apparently believing that the moment was ripe to overthrow the Republic, staged a monster demonstration in central Paris on February 6. The crowd broke through the police lines and almost succeeded in seizing the Chamber of Deputies. Order was restored, with difficulty, and with eleven dead and several hundred injured. It was the first time since the Commune of 1871 that blood had been spilled in a revolutionary disturbance in Paris.

The Republic survived, but its existence was threatened, and the Leagues (as the semifascist action groups were called) continued open preparations for new disorders, which again broke out on February 12. Now, however, new and unexpected support came for the Republic. The Socialists and Communists (who had cooperated with the Leagues in the troubles a week before, to express their hostility toward the "bourgeois republic") now reversed their position. They had remembered the old Jacobin devotion to republican institutions, and they had understood that a republic, no matter how bourgeois, at least allowed them freedom to operate, which would be lost under a rightist dictatorship. Accordingly, they not only fought on the side of the police on February 12, but threatened a general strike against the rebels. The Daladier ministry resigned, but once again French democracy was saved.

The new premier was the most eminent politician in France, former president Gaston Doumergue. He was a man of the right (installed, like Poincaré, by a leftist Chamber) but he enjoyed wide prestige. Strenuous financial measures averted the endemic crisis. Confidence and calm were immediately restored.

Conservative opinion, temporarily mollified, continued to grow in numbers and in willingness to use violent means. But if the extreme right was growing, so was the extreme left. By 1936, the Communist International had begun its policy of encouraging co-operation between Communist parties and democratic parties to stop the growth of fascism. In preparation for the elections of 1936, an entirely new alignment took shape in French politics: an electoral alliance (the Popular Front) was arranged among the Radicals, Socialists, and Communists. For the first time since 1920, the left was united, the Communists were talking like good Frenchmen and good democrats, and the electorate was sufficiently aroused by the threat of fascism and the need for far-reaching change to promise electoral success.

Electoral success was indeed won. The elections, in May, gave the Popular Front parties 64 percent of the seats in the Chamber. The extent of social unrest was shown by the fact that the Communist representation jumped from 12 deputies to 72. The Communist party was, for the first time, a major force in French politics. The Socialist Léon Blum took office as prime minister, with a cabinet of Radicals and Socialists (the Communists, while supporting the government, declined to participate in it), and well-to-do Frenchmen awaited revolution.

No revolution took place, however. What was done was to jerk France suddenly up to the level of social progress long since reached by Britain, Germany,

Scandinavia, and, very recently, by the United States. Following a great wave of sit-down strikes, labor unions were given rights of collective bargaining. A forty-hour work week was decreed. Paid vacations were instituted. The rather modest social security legislation of 1928 was expanded. The airplane and munitions industries, and the Bank of France, were nationalized.

Léon Blum's downfall was brought about, like that of so many other premiers, by budgetary troubles. Faced with mounting shortages of funds, he asked for emergency powers and was refused them. He resigned; and for the next two years France reverted to its dreary round of ministries run by famous, or infamous, Radical party politicians. The Popular Front was still formally in existence, but as had so often happened in the past the government moved further and further to the right. By the end of 1938 it was faced with the open hostility of the Communists and the disaffection of most of the Socialists. There was one change from the period before 1936, however: the Blum administration had cracked down hard on the armed fascist action groups. There were no longer any disturbances from the extremists on the right.

The last years were largely occupied by the mounting international crisis, which also opened deep sores in the body politic. The Communists and most Socialists demanded a strong and determined anti-Hitler policy. Some of the fascists demanded cooperation with Germany. Conservatives, Radicals, and centrists divided, some believing that resistance was hopeless and aiming at appeasing Hitler by negotiation, others believing that only a spirited foreign policy could prevent disaster. The international question became entangled with domestic issues; leftists charged the right with betraying the country to Hitler in order to prevent social progress and safeguard their position. Ultra-rightists charged that attempts to stop Hitler were a Communist plot.

By the time war came, the French political situation was thoroughly confused and the nation deeply split.

These difficulties portended grave problems after the war was over. The French Republic had been successful in the nineteenth century at least partly because it was unable to adopt strong and positive policies. For an era when economic progress and political tranquility had demanded government inaction the French political system was ideally constructed. In the twentieth century, however, with the huge problems of social adjustment and international crisis and depression, the Republic's inability to act was serious and in the end fatal. But it would be a mistake to suppose that the disaster which overtook the nation and the Republic in June of 1940 was the inevitable product of these divisions and weaknesses. Most Frenchmen rallied to the war effort, in the months from September, 1939, to May, 1940, with grim solidarity. The Republic fell, in the end, as a consequence of a successful invasion, which the British never had to face. The fortunes of the Third Republic, and the fortune of the country, were decided on the field of battle, and it is likely that even the healthiest nation would have fallen before the onrush of the German armies in 1940.

51

THE FAILURE
OF DIPLOMACY

In 1930, twelve years after the Armistice that ended World War I, Europe and the world had worked out a makeshift way of living at peace. The devastations of the war had been made good. European standards of living and production had reached and in some countries had passed the 1913 level. Some new and promising ways of dealing with diplomatic problems had been worked out. To be sure, the most important changes in the old nineteenth-century order had yet to be faced. The United States, now the greatest power in the world, was still aloof. The Soviet Union was sulkily outlawed. Europe itself was as deeply divided as ever by emotions and by the tangible barriers of frontiers. Nevertheless, a way of living with the deep dislocations had been found, and as the decade of the 1930's opened, most men were convinced that it would survive and perhaps grow into a peaceful and practical system.

Ten years later, Europe was again at war. All of the adjustments of the 1920's had been swept away. Soon to join them in the rubbish pile of history were many of the most ancient of European institutions and splendors and illusions. The national state system itself, the most deep-rooted and characteristic feature of modern Europe, was now under attack. Small but venerable nations like Holland and Denmark, and great ones like France and Italy, were shortly to fall. Adolf Hitler was making his play for the mastery of Europe and by 1939 his game had proceeded far enough to permit a frontal assault on the opponents whom he had already undermined by guile and gambit.

The story of the 1930's is the story of Hitler's advent to power and of his systematic attack on the European system which had been put together in the years since 1918. It is also the story of the retreat of Britain and France from the dominion which they had loosely exercised over most of Europe west of Russia, and of the withdrawal of their power and influence to the confines of their own frontiers, where they eventually found themselves vulnerable to the military edifice which they permitted to be erected in Germany.

The *causes* of the skillful and determined German policy, and of the weary and inept responses of the British and the French, can be dealt with only summarily. They arose in main part from the internal histories of the three countries, described in other chapters, and from the shocks which they had suffered between 1914 and 1918, which affected Germans with a determination for revenge and Frenchmen and Britons with a dread of war. They were the reflection, too, of the difficulties which free societies face in dealing with dictatorships, where the former are slowed and harassed by debate and opposition and publicity and the latter can act suddenly, secretly, and without internal divisions. But the most immediate and important cause for the sudden disintegration of the European situation after 1930 was the world depression. This calamity wrecked the German republic and brought Hitler to power. It paralyzed the governments of Britain and France and their allies. Every government was facing a domestic economic crisis which at least distracted its energies from foreign policy and at most threatened to destroy it by social revolution. Since every government resorted to nationalistic experiments and programs for solving the economic crisis, collaboration among them was made difficult and sometimes impossible.

By the time the crisis began to ease, Hitler was in power and the democracies had already begun the series of retreats before him which was to persist without interruption until the war began.

THE COLLAPSE OF WORLD ORDER:
1930–1934

The makeshift peace of the 1920's depended fundamentally on four things: the effectiveness—however limited—of the League of Nations to prevent aggression and maintain the rule of law; the economic stability of Europe, which depended in turn upon expanding world markets and upon a continued flow of credit from America to Germany; the willingness of Germany to accept—or of others to enforce—German disarmament and peaceable policy; and the security of France from danger of attack. The latter meant German disarmament, plus the French system of defensive alliances with the small powers of Eastern Europe, plus the Locarno Treaty of 1925, under which Britain and Italy had guaranteed to prevent violations of the Franco-German and German-Belgian frontiers and of the demilitarized zone of western Germany. In Eastern Europe, peace depended upon the willingness and power of France to defend its Polish, Czech, Rumanian and Yugoslav allies.

By 1934, the first two of these fundaments had disappeared completely. The third was almost gone. The peace of Europe hung then on the slender thread of the French security system, which was to crumble in 1936. In the years after 1934, while the French conceived and began to execute a substitute system to save the peace, their British allies were pursuing contradictory policies which wrecked it. The period from 1934 to 1938 was one of Franco-British friction, which prevented the steps which might have prevented the war. By the time cooperation between the two was restored, the last bulwarks were gone.

The first condition of peace to disappear was economic stability. As elsewhere related, the effect in Europe of the American crash was to shut off the flow of short-term loans from America to Germany. The circuit flow of capital was interrupted and the delicate mechanism of world finance broken.

In 1931 it became obvious that the staggering European economies could not fulfill their international obligations. President Hoover then suggested a "moratorium"—a postponement—for one year of all interest payments due the United States on its war debts. A year later, in July, 1932, a "gentleman's agreement" was reached at Lausanne which involved the virtual cancellation of reparations. The United States attempted to collect the war debt payments due it after the expiration of the moratorium, but the European nations were unable and unwilling to pay, and went into default. This default of international obligations had the effect of exasperating American opinion and causing the United States to withdraw further from participation in European affairs—a withdrawal embodied in the American neutrality legislation of 1935–1937. These acts provided that no arms should be sold nor loans made to belligerents, and that other purchases should be carried away in the belligerents' own ships. It was a symbol of the breakdown of community, confidence, and joint responsibility among nations.

The first political explosion which followed the onset of the depression came in the Far East. It is not possible here to examine its causes or character in detail; it is sufficient to say that a strongly expansionist military faction had gained influence, if not control, over the Japanese government. Spurred by desperation which resulted from the loss of Japanese markets abroad, this faction embarked in 1931 upon a program of aggression designed to provide Japan with a great mainland empire in Asia. Japanese troops attacked and shortly annexed Manchuria, the huge northern province of the Chinese Republic.

This remote event had the greatest importance for the progress of European affairs because of the reply which it evoked from France and Britain and the League, whose function it was to protect its members from precisely such attack. The reply of France, Britain, and the League was feeble in the extreme. An unprovoked military assault, openly a violation of the League Covenant (and, for what it was worth, of the Peace Pact of 1928 in which everybody including Japan had renounced war as an instrument of policy), was met with an investigative commission sent out by the League and by a fruitless debate of its report. The most was done by the United States (where public opinion was strenuously anti-Japanese), whose Secretary of State, Mr. Stimson, announced a spirited but futile policy of refusing to "recognize" changes brought about illegally by armed force. The only consequence of these moves was that Japan resigned from the League.

The causes for the feeble attitude of Britain and France are clear enough. China was a long way off, and neither cared to become involved in a remote dispute fraught with possibilities of war. Both countries were deeply involved in

European politics and, especially, in their efforts to solve their economic problems. Public opinion was cold to spending time, money, and perhaps men in curbing Japan. The effects were equally clear: after 1931, it was obvious that no country could rely upon the League and its principal directors, the French and the British, to protect them. The fragile structure designed to inhibit war had been tested and found wanting.

The lessons which the Japanese had taught the world were very shortly applied in Europe itself. Adolf Hitler came to power in Germany, in January, 1933.

There were some observers who discerned at once the fundamental qualities of the Hitler regime: that its leader was determined to make war and to reverse the verdict of 1918; that he was determined to conquer Europe, if not the world; and that his whole policy and government were to be directed toward these ends so completely that he would shortly be unable to draw back from them even if he wished. Among the observers who grasped these truths were many in high places, including the Permanent Undersecretary for Foreign Affairs in London, Sir Robert Vansittart; the former Chancellor of the Exchequer, Mr. Winston Churchill; the French Socialist leader, Léon Blum. But there were others throughout Europe whose attitude ranged from adulation of the new regime to a belief that the German Nazis could be mollified by concessions. Ordinary people could not be sure which group was right, and merely hoped for the best.

The first eleven months of Hitler's conduct of foreign policy were unclear in their implications. At times, he conducted himself in a most pacific and affable manner with other nations, presenting himself as the guarantor of the west against Bolshevism and cheerfully signing, in the spring of 1933, a four-power pact with Italy, France, and Britain whose vague provisions affirmed perpetual friendship. Then, in October, just as the disarmament negotiations which had aroused such hopes and had for so long been regarded as a cornerstone of Europe's future tranquility were at last nearing completion and agreement, Hitler announced German withdrawal from the Disarmament Conference—and also from the League of Nations. This decision was presented to the German electorate and ratified by virtually unanimous (if highly rigged) approval. But it was followed by more talk about German willingness to begin disarmament negotiations all over and form a new peace organization, once the old ones—symbols of German degradation arising from the Versailles Treaty—were abandoned. From then on, whenever he did something particularly outrageous, Hitler always promised that he was now ready to enter into negotiations for a new European order which would assure peace. Some people believed him.

The makers of French policy were not among them. There was some feeling in France that Hitler was too powerful to resist and must, therefore, be appeased, but there was almost no tendency to believe what he said or have confidence in his good intentions. By the spring of 1934, the French government had set out on a policy of trying to stop Hitler. To this end, they tried to fashion a large continental coalition against Germany, a sort of universal dike. This involved three separate actions. First, the alliances with the small powers in Eastern Europe must be shored up. This presented difficulties, because the most important of the eastern allies, Poland, was in the hands of an extremely conservative military faction and already showed signs of marked cordiality to Berlin. Second, the Soviet Union must be brought into the European system as a defender against Germany. Third, Italy must be wooed and won to an anti-German policy. At the same time, a measure of harmony with Britain (whose support in case of war was basic) must be maintained.

The French foreign minister, Louis Barthou, set about the execution of this policy with vigor. The obstacles were enormous. The British disliked anything which seemed to increase Soviet influence or draw it westward. The eastern allies, particularly the Poles, were even more suspicious of the Soviet. Italy, led by Mussolini who regarded Hitler with some respect and friendship as a pupil of his own methods and ideas, was clearly an unpromising target. Nevertheless, Barthou went to work, with visits to the allied capitals and with invitations to the allied leaders. One of them, King Alexander of Yugoslavia, came to France in October, 1934, and was met by Barthou in Marseilles, where both of them were assassinated.

The death of Barthou did not mean the immediate end of his policy, for it was carried on by his successor, Pierre Laval, who in the next year was to work out an alliance with the Soviet Union and a deal with Mussolini. But after the assassination the policy began to misfire. From then on, owing to the deal with Italy and to the growing boldness of Hitler, French initiative was lost and the leadership of the free countries passed to London, where there was little disposition to try to stop the German advance.

1935 OR THEREABOUTS—ANOTHER VISIT UNLESS THE JOB IS FINISHED Now by William H. Walker. This prophetic drawing appeared in *Life* on July 4, 1918. The specter it predicts materialized almost on schedule. (Courtesy of Robert M. Walker, Swarthmore, Pa.)

THE BRITISH EFFORTS AT APPEASEMENT: 1934–1938

By the end of 1934, German rearmament was proceeding openly. Nazi methods had received some striking illustrations—domestically, in the shocking Blood Purge of June, which wiped out several thousand Nazi party members, and internationally in the assassination of the Austrian Chancellor Dollfuss in July in the course of what was clearly a Nazi effort to wreck the Austrian Republic and unite it to the Nazi Reich. None of these events, however, had done more than confirm the apparent conviction of the British cabinet that the only way to preserve peace was to find out what Hitler's terms were and then to satisfy them.

British policy in these years was conditioned by personalities. The foreign minister from 1931 through the spring of 1935 was Sir John Simon, an eminent Liberal lawyer who knew relatively little of foreign affairs. He was succeeded by Sir Samuel Hoare, a diplomat better trained at negotiation than at perceiving unpleasant truths. These leaders were aware of the extreme aversion to war of the British people, and of the extreme costliness of rearmament at a moment when the government was devoted to economy. Aware, too, of the fact that Germany had been badly treated at Versailles and in the 1920's they were inclined to think that Hitler was merely trying to undo past injustices. Nor was the Laborite opposition such as to insist on a stronger policy against the Nazis, for Labor's leadership was in the hands of men like George Lansbury who were deeply pacifist, convinced that wars benefited no one except capitalists, and that rearmament was a costly plot against the workers. The Tories had more far-seeing critics in their midst, like Winston Churchill, and so had the Laborites in men like Ernest Bevin, who was years later to be a brilliant foreign minister, and Clement Attlee, who was to become premier. But the leaders paid little attention to Churchill or Bevin or Attlee when the latter inveighed against the dangers of trying to accommodate Adolf Hitler.

British policy was based then upon several convictions and purposes. First, war must be avoided at almost any cost (except, perhaps, the cession of British territory). Second, Hitler could and must be negotiated with as a reasonable man. Third, the rearmament of almost unarmed Britain was expensive, unpopular, and unnecessary, and must be avoided or delayed. Fourth, the great goal to be sought was "a general settlement," which meant in practice giving Hitler as much as was necessary to keep him happy.

French policy was, as we have seen, very different. But in the year or two that followed Barthou's assassination, the French position crumbled and the British prevailed. The process weakened both parties, for it caused divisions between them at a time when close cooperation was needed. And in the end it led, in France, to the emergence of men as fatally conciliatory as the British leaders.

Two great and terrible events in 1935 illustrated and confirmed this process. The first took place in March, when Hitler denounced the disarmament clause of the Treaty of Versailles and announced, in effect, that Germany no longer regarded itself as bound by it. This meant that the balance of military power in Europe was going to shift rapidly against the western powers. An effort was made to counter this development by a meeting of the three principal signitories of Versailles, Britain and France and Italy, at Stresa, in the spring. The "Stresa Front" warned Germany against further violations and indicated forcible resistance to any that might take place. For a moment it looked as if a stand had at last been taken.

But it was a paper front, and its members defected almost at once. First, the British announced in June that they had signed a naval treaty with the Germans, which—for them at least—legally terminated the Versailles treaty. This indicated publicly the British feeling that the way to prevent war was to negotiate with Hitler, not to frustrate him, and had the practical effect of giving British consent to the construction of a new German navy, which had previously been entirely outlawed. The French were appalled.

Still more serious events took place in the summer, when it became clear that Mussolini was preparing to attack the African empire of Ethiopia, which the Italians had long hankered after. Here the attitudes of the British and French were very different. The British would accept from the dictators anything short of armed aggression. The French were prepared to resist any of Hitler's provocations, whether armed or not, but were willing to concede Mussolini whatever he wanted. Indeed, there is strong suspicion that the French had secretly agreed in advance to letting Mussolini annex Ethiopia as a price for his collaboration in an anti-German coalition. The French believed that the only real menace came from Germany, while the British believed that a menace to peace came from "overt"—which meant armed—action on anybody's part.

When Mussolini began his African march, Ethiopia appealed to the League of Nations and the British government, strongly backed by public opinion, felt constrained to support its request for assistance. The French demurred, but they could not risk a public split with Britain, nor dared they openly encourage what was clearly an illegal and immoral act of aggression. Accordingly, the League took action of a sort, after failure of undercover efforts to make a deal with the Italians by ceding them part of Ethiopia. What the League did was to vote that its members should refuse to ship arms to Italy. "Sanctions"—which meant an embargo—were imposed for the first and only time.

But sanctions failed to deter Italy, mainly because oil was not included in the list of prohibited items, and oil was the one import really indispensable to the Italians. It was deliberately excluded mainly because Mussolini had let it be known that any attempt to embargo it would lead to his making war on Great Britain. The British were prepared to support the League, but not to the point of risking war. In other words, they were willing to support the League, but not to the point where it might prove effective. Italy continued its war. By the spring of 1936, Ethiopia had been overrun. The chief result of sanctions was that the link between Italy and the democracies had been broken. The Italians had turned for economic aid and diplomatic support to Germany. They had left the League and were presently to form an "Axis," which meant a diplomatic alignment, with the Nazis. The hope of a united front against Hitler was gone.

Before the Ethiopian war had run its course, however, two other events of great importance had taken place. For one, the British and French (seeing that Mussolini could not be stopped without war) had secretly tried to make another deal with Italy in December, 1935. This entirely futile endeavor, known as the Hoare-Laval Pact, was prematurely publicized at a moment when the two countries were still officially trying to frustrate the Italian government. It suggested a lack of good faith in the League, a high degree of cynicism, and a conviction that aggressive dictators could and must be bargained with, at the expense of defense-less nations like Ethiopia. In both France and England there was a public outcry which led to the fall of the ministry in France and the dismissal of Hoare in Britain. It did not serve to alter appreciably the policies of either government, but it did weaken their authority when the next test came, in March of 1936.

In that month, the French parliament ratified a treaty of alliance, which had been signed the previous May, with the Soviet Union. This treaty was the fruit of Barthou's and Laval's policy of reintroducing Russia into European affairs as a counterweight and bulwark against Germany, and it had been accompanied by the Soviet's entrance into the League of Nations. It was the consequence not only of French efforts but also of a shift of Soviet policy. Since 1934, the Russian government, alarmed by the growth of fascism, had been eager to form friend-ships and alliances with the bourgeois democracies, to cooperate with the League which it joined in 1934, and to form a united front against fascism and aggression. This policy was associated with the foreign ministry of Maxim Litvinov and the encouragement of "popular front" coalitions of Communists and democratic parties throughout the world.

In response to the French ratification of the treaty, Hitler now proceeded with his next and most dramatic step thus far, the remilitarization of the Rhine-land. His action was an open violation of the Locarno Pact, and he justified it by saying that the pact had been previously violated and negated by the Franco-Russian Treaty—an assertion of doubtful accuracy and total irrelevancy, since the Rhineland "invasion" had been planned earlier.

The Rhineland operation was exceedingly serious. The German areas west of the river had been demilitarized—that is, closed to German troops and fortifications—by the Treaty of Versailles, in order to provide a military neutral zone between the French border and the German army and to leave Germany's industrial heartland east of the Rhine unprotected. It was of very great strategic importance to France, for the demilitarized zone provided an area which the French could hastily occupy in case of trouble, as well as withholding it from Germany as a jumping-off place for an attack similar to the one of 1914.

It was expected that Hitler's action would produce violent reaction in France. Indeed, it was so expected by the German army. The general staff knew (as the French did not) that the force which occupied the territory on the day of Hitler's bombastic announcement was small and badly armed, and the generals had advised strongly against a step which they thought would lead to a French invasion of Germany and bring to nought all Hitler's previous work of restoring German power and prestige. Indeed, the German generals were so apprehensive that they even planned to revolt against Hitler in case the action failed; to remove him from office and exculpate themselves of responsibility for the violations of the treaties. Hitler disregarded their advice and proceeded on his perilous course, although he prudently gave orders for withdrawal in case the French moved.

Hitler was right, and the generals were wrong. The French did not react with armed resistance. Their failure to do so meant that the last chance to stop Hitler without a major war was gone. The reasons for French flaccidity are complicated and even today unclear, but they are of two kinds. In the first place, the government relied very heavily upon the advice of the service chiefs, and the French generals (as cautious as the Germans) greatly overrated the strength of the Greman forces involved. As a result, the cabinet agreed that they could not act unless they were assured in advance of the support of the British. The dangers of fighting a war single-handed against Germany were too great in their view. The next step was, therefore, to consult the British—and here the second and more complicated set of causes came into operation. For the British were exceedingly reluctant. They were convinced, it seems, of two things: first, that a major war would surely result from such an action; and, secondly and less understandably, they felt that there was much to be said in Hitler's behalf. The Germans were, after all, merely occupying their own territory. And anyway, Hitler—in the same breath that he announced the Rhineland action—also had announced that he was eager to begin negotiations for "a general settlement."

So, in the end, the French had to be content with protests to Berlin, which of course had no effect. And Europe sat back to await the next crisis. It was not long in coming; the civil war in Spain began in July of 1936.

It was clear from the beginning that the rebel regime of General Franco was dictatorial and that it was supported by Mussolini and Hitler; the republic which was defending itself against General Franco was legally and democratically elected, and its cause was espoused by many believers in freedom and democracy and by the Soviet Union, then at the apex of its posture as the champion of democracy against tyranny. Anxious democrats and liberals throughout the world thought they saw, more and more clearly, a microcosm of the world struggle between rival ideologies.

The facts were different and more complicated. Mussolini's interest was as much strategic as ideological, and as much quixotic as strategic. On the other side, there were important people who were deeply antifascist who preferred Franco's cause to the republic's. This group included most Catholics and many honest conservatives like Winston Churchill who saw in the republic a Communist threat at least as great as the fascist threat in the opposing camp.

The policy of the French and British governments—and of the American— was one of non-intervention, which meant giving arms and financial assistance to neither side, even though they continued to recognize the republic as the legal government of Spain. Efforts were made to set up an international embargo on arms to the two belligerent factions; agreement was reached on paper, but was openly disregarded by the Italians, Germans, and Russians. The French and British merely deplored the violations.

This terrible episode of Spanish history was to cause deep divisions in opinion in the democratic countries. Their governments were accused by progressive opinion of being excessively soft on the fascists, and even of colluding with them. Sparked by Communist attitudes and propaganda, the policy of France and Britain toward the fascists and their now rather numerous aggressions was widely charged to their desire to preserve and encourage fascism as a bulwark against Communism and liberalism. In return, those who supported the British and French policies accused their critics of being Communists.

THE CLIMAX OF APPEASEMENT: JANUARY, 1938, TO APRIL, 1939

By the end of 1937, British policy was in the hands of the new prime minister, Neville Chamberlain, a successful manufacturer of bolts from Birmingham. He was elderly and stubborn, very fearful of war, and very conscious of his responsibility to secure peace. Surrounded by people who were convinced of the dangers of trying to thwart Hitler, Chamberlain undertook to pursue as a systematic policy the attitude which the British had previously taken as a result of fear and confusion. This policy involved putting trust in Hitler's word as a gentleman and trying to satisfy his demands through negotiation. It was based upon the assumption that the Führer's aims were finite and that they could be negotiated about and perhaps limited. This assumption was false.

From the very beginning of his career, Hitler had aims which could not possibly be achieved without war. By the end of 1937, a more or less precise timetable for the achievement of his preliminary territorial aims had been developed. The German strategy, since revealed in captured German documents, was this: to break the circle of French alliances around Germany and to consume the Slavic states—Poland and Czechoslovakia—on his borders. Then, he would be prepared for the next step, the destruction of the Soviet Union. He hoped that this might be done without provoking war with France and Britain, but he did not really expect so, and therefore made plans for military conflict with them. The first need was to destroy Czechoslavakia, which had a powerful defense system and a large, French-trained army, and which was bound by treaties of alliance with France and the Soviet Union. So long as Czechoslovakia and its army remained intact, Germany was threatened with the possibility of a three-front war. The elimination of the Czech bastion on his flank had in turn to be prepared by the annexation of Austria. The map will show why this is true: Austria had a long common frontier with Czechoslovakia, not equipped on the Czech side with defenses such as those which bristled along the Czech-German frontier. If Austria were in German hands, the Czech state would be surrounded on three sides, one of which was undefended and perhaps indefensible. The prospect of a successful defense against German attack would then become almost impossible for the Czechs and the possibility that French and Soviet aid might in the end prevail against Germany would not much compensate for the prospect of immediate occupation and subjection to the machine of Nazi terror. It was, therefore, to Austria that Hitler first turned his attentions.

The Austrian Republic at the beginning of 1938 was in a lamentable state. Its economy, never strong, was badly battered by the depression. Its government was in the hands of a rather old-fashioned and conservative faction of the so-called Christian Socialist party, predominantly a middle class, peasant, and aristocratic group which was governing through a dictatorship of the chancellor, Kurt Schuschnigg and against the determined wishes of the suppressed Social Democrats. The country possessed a large National Socialist party, bent on union with Hitler's Germany, and there were no military defenses to speak of. Moreover, a very large proportion of the population was at least acquiescent toward "*Anschluss*," as union with Germany was called, although it was naturally opposed by all Jews and Social Democrats. Italian policy, the only real support of Austrian independence, had strenuously opposed the presence of the German great power on the northern frontier of Italy. But since 1935, Italian resistance to *Anschluss* had diminished, for the Ethiopian adventure had alienated Italy from France and Britain and made it dependent upon Germany and upon the "Axis" alignment. The Italians no longer had enough freedom of action to try to save Austria.

On March 12, 1938, Hitler gave orders for his army to cross the frontier and to march on Vienna. In the Austrian capital, Nazis simultaneously seized

HITLER'S ACQUISITIONS ON THE EVE OF WORLD WAR II, AUGUST, 1939

the government and imprisoned the chancellor, and a few days later Hitler announced the incorporation of the republic into "Greater Germany." The dream of the unionists of 1848 was at last achieved, under weird auspices and, as it turned out, temporarily.

The reactions in France and Britain were anxious but in the end negative. It was argued that, after all, Austria *was* German—and that in any case nothing could have been done to prevent the *Anschluss* without a war.

Next came the turn of Czechoslovakia, the best-armed state of Central Europe. Its position was now gravely compromised. It faced the German army on three sides. Its ally, France, was by now entirely under the influence of British policy, and the British prime minister observed in March that "we must not delude" small European countries into supposing that Britain would come to their assistance if attacked by Germany. Most serious of all, the Czechs faced almost one third of their fellow citizens who were German-speaking, who had many grievances, and who proved extremely receptive to the German Nazi party.

Starting almost immediately after the annexation of Austria, German policy and publicity showed a single-minded and unnerving preoccupation with the "plight" of the Germans in Czechoslovakia—the "Sudeten" Germans they were called, since the majority of them lived in the Sudeten mountains near the German border. German press and radio reiterated constantly the hideous (and mainly imaginary) persecutions to which the Sudeten Germans were subjected by the Czech state, and Hitler announced his intention to relieve their sufferings.

The Germans during the spring and summer were completing their plans for a military attack on Czechoslovakia, which was to take place at the end of September. This was, however, not known publicly and not suspected by Neville Chamberlain and the British cabinet. As usual, the British saw much justice in Hitler's claims—it was only natural that he should wish to unite all Germans in the German state—and much danger in resisting them to the point where armed force might be used. The Chamberlain syllogism was simplicity itself: war comes when armed force is used; if negotiations are carried on, granting peacefully what is sought by armed force, no war will result. As a consequence it was decided to bring pressure to bear on the Czechs to take a "reasonable" attitude toward the demands of the Sudeten Nazi leader, Konrad Henlein. The Czechs consented to hold conversations with Henlein and, in September, even consented to grant all his demands for special privileges and self-governing rights for the German minority. But Henlein did not accept the government offers. The Sudeten Nazis, and Hitler behind them, did not wish their public demands to be met; what they wished was a pretext for military attack.

Once the Czech offers were rejected, and Hitler had announced in September at the Nazi Party Congress his intention of "solving the Czech problem," the crisis was on. It was not exactly clear what the German demands were—they kept changing, from guarantees of civil rights, to autonomy, to "liberation," which meant cession of German-speaking regions and the partition of the Czech state. Nor was it entirely clear what the French and British position was: the French insisted they were going to honor their alliance, but it was fairly clear that they would not or could not do so without British support, and the

British still argued that if the Czechs were "reasonable" and would "negotiate" with the Germans and give them what they wanted, there would be no military action and no need to invoke the French alliance.

In the end the British view prevailed, but not before a crisis which shook Europe to its roots. The real reason for the crisis was that Hitler *wanted* to invade Czechoslovakia (apparently for practice) and therefore resisted formulating his demands so that they could be granted without war. Chamberlain flew twice to Germany to confer with the Führer. Both times he received a somewhat muddled list of demands, including cession of some Czech border regions. Both times, Chamberlain got the British cabinet and the French and, through them, the Czechs, to agree to the list. Then Hitler said that the cessions were insufficient and asked for more. Toward the end of September, it looked as if there was no pleasing him, and with the greatest possible reluctance the British government began to face the prospect of going to war to support the ally of an ally, about which, as Chamberlain wistfully put it, "we know little."

At this grave juncture, Hitler's friend Mussolini (who dreaded the thought of a war for which he knew Italy was ill-prepared in every way) intervened. He urged a four-power conference, and it was duly held, in the last days of September, 1938, in Munich. Hitler was annoyed to discover that the British and French were willing to grant his most extreme demands for the cession of Czech territory. Areas with a German majority were to be ceded outright. Others, where the wishes of the populace were in doubt, were to hold plebiscites under German auspices. The Czech government was to be replaced in the remaining territories by one friendly to Germany. The rump state remaining was to be guaranteed by all four powers—a guarantee which was never mentioned later. The statesmen agreed on this solution. Hitler announced, "I have no more territorial demands in Europe" (which was a lie); and Chamberlain returned to a relieved and cheering London to say (plagiarizing his half-brother Austen's observation about the Locarno treaties thirteen years earlier) that he had assured "peace in our time," which was also a lie but not a conscious one.

The Munich crisis had momentous effects. It destroyed the Czech bastion of Germany's southern border. It insulted and infuriated the Soviet Union, which had hitherto shown willingness to cooperate with the western powers in an anti-fascist policy and which had repeatedly asserted its willingness to come to the support of Czechoslovakia if they did. In the final settlement, the Russians were pointedly disregarded, and it looked almost as if the four powers were prepared to cooperate among themselves against the Soviet Union and its interests. It lowered French and British prestige throughout Europe and the world. Finally, it further sharpened the domestic divisions in France and Britain.

It is conceivable, though unlikely, that Chamberlain really intended what his critics accused him of: to distract German attention from the west by concessions in the east until Germany was brought into conflict with the Soviet Union and the two eastern colossi were left to fight it out while the west husbanded its resources and watched in peace while the equally detestable foes, Communism and Nazism, destroyed each other. This policy, if it existed, would have been at least a rational one. It seems more likely that Chamberlain and his cabinet actually believed what Hitler said, and thought that he now had no more demands to make and that a "general settlement" was possible. But whatever the motive, it proved incapable of realization after Munich. For both French and British public and even official opinion was now outraged by the thought of further concessions to Hitler, and a government which acceded to them would have found itself in grave political danger. This aversion to Nazi Germany was, moreover, greatly strengthened by events in Germany in the fall of 1938; a pogrom against the remaining Jews, of hideous scope and violence, was then undertaken. World opinion was appalled, and it became more and more difficult for the British government to do business with Hitler.

The turning point came in March, 1939. Hitler summoned the president of the rump Czech state to his presence, issued an ultimatum, and sent the unhappy statesman home. There were risings engineered simultaneously in the Slovak province, and German armies crossed the Czech frontier and occupied Prague on March 15. The elaborate details of the Munich Agreement were negated. Czechoslovakia divided in two was incorporated into Germany as the Bohemia-Moravia Protectorate and the Protected State of Slovakia. Hitler's promise about the last territorial demand in Europe was belied.

The Prague Crisis, as this one was called, brought the end of appeasement and the beginnings of the Franco-British stand which finally led to war. Public opinion was outraged, and so was Neville Chamberlain. It was clear that all the assumptions on which he seems to have based his policy were falsified and, not without some tergiversation, he eventually denounced Hitler's seizure in the most categorical terms. Moreover, the British rather impulsively announced that they would fight if similar aggressions were committed against any of the threatened Eastern European countries—including Poland, Rumania, and Greece. This tardy, hasty reversal of the appeasement policy meant that the British and the French, if they had to fight, would fight under very unfavorable circumstances. The Czech bastion was gone. The Rhineland was remilitarized. German armament was far advanced. Austria was lost, and so was Italy. The Soviet Union was disaffected and distrustful. But there was no longer any alternative. The British and the French set about the weary task of trying to rebuild a diplomatic and military fence around the fascist powers in the hope that threats and defenses might prevent what conciliation and concession had failed to prevent—armed aggression. It was too late, much too late, to achieve their purpose.

THE FINAL CRISIS: APRIL TO SEPTEMBER, 1939

The hastily offered guarantees to the smaller Eastern European states had extended and rigidified Franco-British commitments without increasing their power. An effective "stop Hitler" program demanded that the Nazis be confronted with overpowering force, and this could be provided only by bringing the Soviet Union into line again. The obstacles were very great: the Russians now took the proposals of France and Britain to mean that they wanted the Soviets to pull their chestnuts out of the fire. Each side in the negotiations for alliance which took place that spring and summer of 1939 was deeply suspicious of the other, and each regarded the other as a menace only less serious than the one which they were supposed to be defending themselves against. The Russian reception was chilly, and it was not made more friendly by the dismissal, in May, of Foreign Commissar Litvinov, who was the living symbol of the mid-1930's policy of cooperation with the democracies. His replacement was the grim and uncooperative Molotov.

The negotiations for an anti-Nazi alliance never overcame one basic obstacle—the position of the states which lay between Russia and Germany: Poland, Latvia, Estonia, and Lithuania. The Russians demanded that they be empowered to operate in the territories of these states, which lay like a protective zone along their own frontier, in case of German attack or threat of attack. The Russians, understandably, were unwilling to see Nazi puppet regimes established in the border states while they stood helplessly by, waiting for invading armies to reach their own soil. The border states, especially Poland, were naturally strongly opposed to allowing any kind of Soviet operation in their territory, and the British took the position that since they were seeking to defend the independence of small powers they could hardly begin by agreeing to give the Russians permission to occupy four of them.

Even before this deadlock had been reached, however, the Soviet government had begun making advances to the German government, the first steps in a stunning "diplomatic revolution." The Soviet position seems to have been this: both the western powers and the Nazis are potential enemies. We cannot fight both and prefer to fight neither; therefore, let us put our policy up for sale and see who will pay the higher price.

The British and French were not in a position to pay any price at all, and the Germans could offer a very high one. They asked, not armed participation in war, but only neutrality from the Russians. In return they offered substantial commercial enticements and vast territories: the three Baltic states as a Soviet sphere, and almost half of Poland. Since the Germans were intending to make war, not prevent it, it was easy for them to proffer a share in the loot.

On August 23, while lackluster negotiations with the French and British were still proceeding, the world was astounded by the announcement of the Soviet-Nazi Pact of friendship, neutrality, and commerce (the territorial arrangements were naturally not published). This represented a basic and complete reversal of policy on both sides. The two parties had always regarded one another as enemies and had for years emitted poisonous floods of propaganda against one another. Now, at a single signature, all this was changed. The German press became cautiously but definitely friendly to the Soviet Union; and Communists throughout the world suddenly espoused the position that Nazi Germany was no more wicked than the democratic governments and that what mattered was the defense of the Socialist Fatherland. Hitler need no longer apprehend hostile major powers on both frontiers.

For months the propaganda war against Poland had been in progress, as it had against Czechoslovakia a year before. The Poles were accused of endless atrocities against their considerable German minority. Vague but shrill demands for a new Polish attitude and for special privileges in Polish territory (mainly the Polish corridor between East Prussia and the rest of Germany) were broadcast. In contrast to the position of the Czechs a year earlier, the Poles were advised now by the French and British not to yield or to negotiate. There were tense and painful pleas and consultations. The appeasing British ambassador to Berlin, Sir Nevile Henderson, begged for a postponement of Hitler's "revenge" on Poland. But there was never the slightest hope of a postponement. This time Hitler was going to have his military invasion. On September 1, his army crossed the Polish frontier and his airplanes bombed Warsaw. Two days later, honoring at last their obligation to defend an ally against attack, Great Britain and France declared war on Nazi Germany. The long armistice was over. The last chapter of the war that had commenced in 1914 was begun.

PART SIX

DIVIDED EUROPE: SINCE 1939

52

WORLD WAR II

THE SECOND WORLD WAR, which lasted from 1939 to 1945, has often been called a concluding chapter of the First, and the years between them are sometimes known as "the long armistice." In many ways this is a fitting description. World War II was a climax of the same struggle for German supremacy which had begun during the first. It completed the reduction to impotence of the competing titans who had, before 1914, controlled the world. The arbiters of European affairs, by the middle of the Second World War, were semi-European nations, the United States and the Soviet Union, and the most important feature of the war was that it ended with Russian and American troops occupying and controlling almost the entire continent of Europe.

The Second World War enfeebled the competitive spirit as well as the power of the Western European nations. The events of 1914 to 1918 had heightened animosities among European peoples and left the European economy in disorder, and in so doing had contorted the history of the interwar years. So large were the losses of Europe after 1939—especially the loss of its power to determine its own destiny—that the old rivalries had become by 1945 largely irrelevant. The great continental countries—France, Germany, Italy—no longer had the will, the means, or the temptation to indulge in the dreams of grandeur or the lethal competitions of earlier days. In the western countries a new reasonableness and a new cooperation were born out of the disaster. In the two spheres of defeated Europe, one under the iron control of the Soviets in the east, the other under the relatively genial influence of America, there was greater cohesion than had been known before. The governments of each region, under the leadership of its gigantic sponsor, armed for defense and were led to a high measure of cooperation with one another. The many little rivalries were submerged into one great one.

All these developments were the consequence of German aggression in 1939. The Germans were making the latest in the old series of efforts to unify

Europe under the domination of one of its regions, and the effort came very near to success: the ancient fortresses of European diversity—Paris, Vienna, Prague, Rome, Warsaw, and a dozen others—were overrun by the German army. In the end the great German empire was wrecked by outside forces, and the submerged nations found themselves under the control of their liberators.

The course of the war was intricate. It may be divided into two parts, a preliminary European phase in which the original contestants, France, Great Britain, and Germany, fought it out among themselves, and a world phase, beginning when the Soviet Union, Japan, and the United States entered the scene and the issues and the combats spread across the face of the earth.

THE EUROPEAN PHASE: SEPTEMBER, 1939, TO JUNE, 1941

The war began with a German attack on Poland, on September 1, 1939, preceded by many stirring events and crises. In March the British and French had guaranteed that they would come to Poland's aid if Hitler attacked it. The Russians and Germans had startled the world by reversing their previous policies and entering into a pact of friendship which contained secret annexes promising the Soviets' benevolence toward a German seizure of western Poland, in return for Soviet rights to acquire eastern Poland and a predominant influence in Finland and in the Baltic states of Lithuania, Latvia, and Estonia.

Poland was no match for Nazi Germany, and its allies, Britain and France, were incapable of helping it. The Germans used tanks and airplanes against the poorly equipped Polish forces with crushing effect. By October 1 Warsaw had fallen, the Polish armed forces had disintegrated, and the triumphant Germans met the Russians, who had begun on September 17 to advance to the line of demarcation which they had earlier agreed upon. The old Prussian provinces along the western and northern borders were restored to Germany. The Russians occupied and annexed the eastern provinces. In between was left the capital and its hinterland, organized under German control into the "Government General" of Warsaw. The Fourth Partition was complete.

It was generally but erroneously believed that the speed of the victory had owed much to "The Fifth Column." A Fifth Column was an organized band of traitors who were supposed to prepare the way for enemy advances by espionage, by seizing control of strategic points, by spreading consternation and despair. The Nazis were imagined to have developed such Fifth Column networks throughout the world. The notion was only about 10 percent based on fact; the rest was a combination of panic and of German propaganda—which *did* become weapons in the German conquest of Europe. In fact, the idea of a Fifth Column was one of many explanations of the stunning blows which were in reality the product of careful and imaginative planning.

The German success in Poland, and later in Scandinavia, Holland, Belgium, France, and the Balkans, was in fact due mainly to military superiority whose essential feature was superior air power. Close cooperation of fast-moving tanks and motorized units with tactical air units made possible the most characteristic military feature of the 1939–1945 war in Europe—the break-through. In World War I it had been regarded as dangerous for forces on one part of a battle-line to advance to the rear of the enemy, where they could be attacked on all sides, surrounded, and cut off. Now, with air power to harass the enemy and speedy motorized units, what had been regarded as danger to be avoided became an opportunity to be sought. A hole could be pierced in the enemy lines and fast-moving units sent through it, to spread out behind the enemy, cutting his supply lines and communications and hastily occupying large areas of his territory.

Once Poland was defeated by such methods, the war passed into a peculiar phase of inaction for five months. There were no considerable battles from October of 1939 to March of 1940. The only campaign fought during the period was separate from the main war: a small struggle between the Soviet Union and Finland. To make good its domination over Finland, which the Germans had agreed to in the pact of August, 1939, the Russians determined to annex some strategic portions of Finnish territory and to subject the Finnish state to Russian control. Unexpectedly, the Finns fought back with great effectiveness when they were attacked in November, 1939. By March, 1940, Finnish resistance had finally cracked, and the Russians were able to secure a treaty extracting the desired Finnish territories.

On April 9, 1940, the Germans occupied Denmark (which offered no resistance) and attacked Norway, whose capital, Oslo, fell on the first day of the new campaign. This operation was evidently intended mainly to provide naval and air bases for attacks on British shipping, and to discommode the British blockade of Germany. It presented a difficult problem for the British and French. Their position in the west was not strong enough to permit the diversion of large forces to assist the Norwegians. On the other hand, committed as they were to defending the freedom of small nations, it would have been a serious political embarrassment to them if they made no sign at all of coming to the aid of a fellow-victim of German aggression. In the end, aid was sent. It was not substantial enough to do the Norwegians any good, although it did prolong the campaign of conquest, and may have helped the British by delaying the German attack in the west and seriously weakening the German navy. The British units in Norway were either defeated or ejected. By the middle of May the Germans were in control of most of the country. King Haakon and his government were in exile in London, and a Nazi puppet regime was installed.

One effect of the northern campaign was a change of government in London. Neville Chamberlain had been prime minister since 1937, and his name was closely associated with the policies of appeasing Hitler in the last years of peace. The Norwegian failures brought to the point of explosion a widespread conviction that the war measures were being executed with a sluggishness approaching languor. On May 10, 1940, after the expression of much antipathy in the House of Commons, Chamberlain resigned, and Winston Churchill was appointed prime minister. He was the first man of first-rate talents to lead Great

Britain since 1922, and he was, it turned out, one of the few clearly great men of his century. His gifts were badly needed.

While the Churchill government—a national coalition including Labor party leaders—was being formed, the Germans had launched their great western offensive with simultaneous attacks on Belgium, Holland, and Luxemburg, on May 10, 1940. The outlines of the German attack were superficially similar to that which had been attempted in 1914—a march through Belgium and across northern France—but this time the major objective was not to sweep the Allies back toward Paris but to cut through their lines to the Channel, separating their armies in the north from the main French forces farther south; in 1940, too, the program included the occupation of the Netherlands. It was carried out with masterly use of parachutists, armored and motorized units, and tactical air power. The result was a staggering success which surprised even Hitler by its thoroughness and rapidity.

The Netherlands collapsed after five days fighting. Queen Wilhelmina and her ministers, barely escaping capture, withdrew to exile in London, there joining the Polish and Norwegian governments. The Belgian defenses also crumbled. Within a week, Brussels had been occupied and the advancing Germans had reached the French border.

There now took place the most dramatic and momentous of the many break-throughs of the war. Charging at the Meuse river near the Belgian border, German units breached the French lines and rushed to the sea. The success of the break-through was due to a number of conditions. The Allies were unprepared for the overwhelming weight and speed of the attack and for its location—they expected the main assault farther north, where it had fallen in 1914. They were unable to summon sufficient strength in fighter planes to break up the air cover for the German advance. The French defenses along the Belgian frontier were much weaker than in the south, and this weakness was compounded by an advance to assist the Belgians after the German attack began. The lightning German penetration took place at the hinge between the French lines on their own border and those advancing into Belgium.

The king of the Belgians surrendered his armies to the enemy. The situation of the British and French armies cut off in Flanders was desperate. A tremendous effort was made to form new lines and hold off the attack while evacuation could take place through the only usable port, Dunkirk. Against overpowering odds the evacuation was completed, on June 2. Over a third of a million troops, including a number of French units, were withdrawn to England; the losses were only 30,000. The "miracle of Dunkirk" was made possible by temporary control of the air, and control of the sea, which permitted the Royal Navy to protect and assist the six hundred private vessels, including yachts and rowboats, which ferried the army across. The British army had lost 10 percent of its numbers and all its equipment, but it was still in existence, ready to defend the island against attack by the Germans.

After Dunkirk the Battle of France proceeded swiftly, a military catastrophe on the largest scale. The French position was already almost hopeless. Ger-

THE WITHDRAWAL FROM DUNKIRK by Charles Cundall (detail). Between
May 28 and June 5, 1940, in the course of France's defeat by the German blitzkrieg, many Englishmen crossed the Channel in every sort of
military, fishing, or pleasure craft (including 203 private motor boats, 27
yachts, and 19 lifeboats) and brought home 338,000 of their troops, and
some French, from the continent. This feat, a moral victory in the midst
of disaster but also a substantial physical operation, was made possible by
British sea power, which maintained command of the surface of the
Channel, and by British air power, which protected the ships and fought
off the German Luftwaffe—though not without substantial losses in the air
and on the sea. German hesitation to commit ground forces, particularly
tanks, on the marshy terrain of Dunkirk before the rest of France was
defeated helped make possible the "miracle" which was to inspire the
British as Churchill called for continued resistance. This episode was a
prelude to the "Battle of Britain" in the autumn, in which Hitler, unprepared with landing craft and much less adequately armed at sea than
Germany had been in World War I, tried unsuccessfully to defeat Britain
from the air. (British Information Services. The painting hangs in the
Imperial War Museum, London)

mans poured through Belgium and occupied most of northern France, where there were no French forces to resist them. With the loss of the British and Belgians, the French were outnumbered two to one. A large proportion of the troops available were caught in the Maginot Line with their backs to the Germans, and others were defending the Spanish and Italian borders. The latter saw a few days of fighting after Mussolini hurriedly entered the war on June 10.

The choice which confronted the French cabinet, hastily transferred to Bordeaux, was whether to abandon the war altogether or to evacuate continental France and attempt to continue fighting from North Africa and other overseas parts of the French empire. The British and an important part of the French cabinet favored the second course; the cabinet majority and others of the French politicians who had gathered in Bordeaux favored the first. Majority opinion viewed the war as already lost, and the cause of continued resistance was outvoted. A new premier, the elderly and very conservative hero of World War I, Marshal Pétain, was appointed, and requested an armistice, which was granted by Hitler on June 22, 1940. By its terms more than half of France, including Paris, was to be occupied, and all French forces on the continent were to surrender. But the Germans were not to occupy the colonies or to gain control of the French navy, and a French national government under Pétain was to continue in existence. It chose as its capital the resort town of Vichy, in central France.

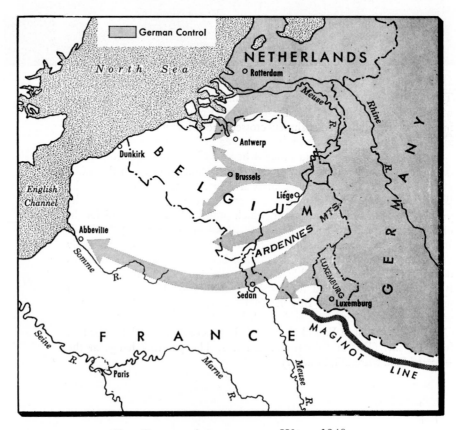

THE GERMAN ATTACK IN THE WEST, 1940

Hitler now turned his attention to the destruction of Great Britain. During the summer of 1940 a deeply anxious but solidly united British nation awaited momentarily the invasion of the island. The British were, however, safer than they realized. The best invasion weather was squandered by the Germans while they tried to agree on a plan of attack. The Germans were handicapped by their lack of naval and landing craft and by their inexperience in maritime warfare, but a plan was eventually made for September landings, which were to be prepared by all-out air attacks intended to break the British resistance in advance. Air attacks commenced in August, and were almost successful in wrecking the crucial Royal Air Force fighter bases in southern England. But the RAF succeeded in beating back the German Luftwaffe. London and other British cities were subjected to heavy raids, but German air control over Great Britain was not established, and Hitler abandoned—or postponed—the plan for landings. As Churchill said, appraising the contribution of the understaffed RAF fighter command, "seldom in human history have so many owed so much to so few."

The Battle of Britain was the first setback for the Rome-Berlin Axis. Other small but significant setbacks followed in the autumn. In October, Mussolini —acutely jealous of the brilliant achievements of his ally—undertook two offensives. He attacked the kingdom of Greece. The Greeks, like the Finns a year earlier, astonished the world by the vigor of their resistance, and turned back the attack. And a much more serious defeat was taking place simultaneously in North Africa. As part of a gigantic plan to seize the Suez canal, cut British communications from India and the east, and gain control of the Mediterranean, Mussolini attempted an attack on Egypt from the adjoining Italian colony of Libya. The British frustrated the attack and advanced deep into Libyan territory. By the end of the year the Italians had suffered humiliation on both their Balkan and African fronts. As Germany prepared to come to the rescue, Italian military and diplomatic policy drifted under German control. A second European great power was reduced to impotence.

The next campaign of the war, and the last of its purely European phase, came in the spring of 1941, in the form of a German offensive in the Balkans. The motives for this campaign were mixed. It was a way to rescue the Italians from their dreary failure in Greece. It was part of the enormous plan which looked toward the driving of the British from the eastern Mediterranean. And it was designed to bring Yugoslavia under German control as part of the program which was now being developed for an attack upon the Soviet Union, a preliminary designed to safeguard the German flank. The Yugoslavs unexpectedly resisted, but in April, 1941, the Germans attacked their country; by May 1, the whole of Yugoslavia and of continental Greece was in German hands. Greek forces, strongly supported by the British navy and army, were still installed in Crete, however.

The Cretan battle ended in German conquest of the island, but though nobody knew it, it marked the high tide of the Axis victories in the Mediterranean region. The British and Greeks fought heroically. The Germans, using parachutists for the first time on a large scale to accomplish an invasion across water, suffered huge losses of their best units. This costly victory was one of the reasons why the Germans now abandoned their effort to close the eastern end of the Suez pincers.

By June of 1941 the British position was a great deal more promising in several respects than it had been a year earlier, for their island was safe and their Mediterranean position was holding firm. Although no one knew it, the German situation was less favorable than it appeared. German industrial mobilization was inefficient and quite insufficient to provide for a long war. German military planning was hampered by the strategic views of Hitler, which were sometimes inspired but more often puerile.

Across the Atlantic, moreover, great and hopeful developments had taken place. The policy of the United States was changing. In the beginning of the war, strict neutrality legislation had prevented any aid to the Allies. But the Neutrality Law had been revised, in view of the widespread American conviction that Hitler was a repellent outlaw and that his victory would endanger American security. The revision permitted the sale of munitions to the Allies, but after the fall of France it was clear that this was not enough. Two things were needed: credits, to permit the British to purchase in America the enormous quantities of supplies needed; and assistance in transporting them across the submarine-infested North Atlantic. The first was provided by the Lend-Lease Law, which passed Congress on March 11, 1941. It allowed the United States to lend or rent to the British and their allies any war materials and services which could be spared, including such items as the repair of British naval vessels in American shipyards. Repayment would be made by returning the materials and services, or their equivalent, or by providing American forces with facilities which they might require. This time there were to be no war debts to complicate the postwar world; no credit was extended by the United States. The second requirement, transport assistance, was provided by armed American escorts across at least the western Atlantic.

These steps marked a revolution in American foreign policy, and one which was to be permanent. Isolationism, the determination to avoid taking part in another of Europe's wars, had dominated the making of American policy since 1918. By June of 1941 Great Britain was no longer alone. The United States was moving toward a program of "all aid short of war," which meant in fact "we shall fight if we have to."

And on June 22, 1941, Germany attacked the Soviet Union.

THE PERIOD OF CONTAINMENT: JUNE, 1941, TO NOVEMBER, 1942

The pact of August, 1939, between Hitler and Stalin had been a work of pure opportunism. The two parties remained, covertly, one another's bitterest enemies, and Russian-German relations were far from smooth. The biggest causes of mutual complaint were territorial: Stalin had been promised merely a sphere of influence in the Baltic states, but he had annexed Lithuania, Latvia, and Estonia outright in 1940, and had attacked Finland. In the south where the agreement had promised to safeguard Soviet interests in Rumania, the Germans had moved in with occupying forces and were enjoying the smiles of a pro-Nazi satellite regime under General Antonescu. Nor could the Russians approve of the German conquest of Yugoslavia (April, 1941) and the reduction of Bulgaria to satellite status the month before. Despite these tensions, however, the Russians were apparently unaware of the plans which Hitler had been mulling over for months.

The first stages of the invasion were most satisfactory from the German standpoint. Three major thrusts, toward Leningrad in the north, toward Moscow in the center, and toward Kiev and the rich Ukraine in the south, aimed at conquering the major centers of European Russia and also at surrounding and destroying the Red army. By the end of the summer these objectives seemed in sight. The German armies were deep in the Ukraine and within a few dozen miles of both Leningrad and Moscow. By the time winter set in with unexpected suddenness and punishing cold in early December, the Germans had been stopped in the suburbs of Leningrad and Moscow, and despite enormous losses Russian armies were still in being. The Germans' failure was due to their poor tactics, to the immense distances involved which placed an unexpectedly heavy strain on mechanized equipment and supply lines, and to the vigor and skill of the Russian defense. The Germans, moreover, stiffened resistance in occupied areas by their brutal treatment of the population. By December the Russians had succeeded in mounting local counterattacks to relieve the pressure on Moscow.

The following summer saw a new German effort to reach a decision. The pattern of 1941 repeated itself. The Germans approached to within one hundred miles of the Caspian Sea, threatening to cut Soviet communications with what remained of the agricultural and industrial southeast and to cut off the Russian oil supply in the Caucasus. By August, 1942, they had reached Stalingrad on the Volga and had it under siege. Its fall would have been critical, and very damaging to Russian morale, but Hitler set too much store by this propaganda opportunity and stubbornly persisted at Stalingrad when he might have done more damage by taking a larger area in southeast Russia. Stalingrad did not fall. The battle was fought for days, weeks, months. The defense held. And in October, the Russians launched a counteroffensive which inaugurated the long but steady series of advances which forced the Germans back to Berlin and defeat in the course of the next two and a half years.

Equally decisive developments had meanwhile taken place in the west. The United States had been moving nearer to war throughout the autumn of 1941, and in December the Japanese attacked Pearl Harbor. The Germans and Italians, by previous agreement, came to the aid of their partner, and the United States was at war with all three of the Axis countries.

It had already been decided by the American strategic leaders that in case of war the major energies of the United States must first be concentrated upon defeating Hitler while holding off the Japanese in the Pacific. In the first months of the war, the Japanese overran the Philippines, Malaya and the great British base at Singapore, and the Dutch East Indies, threatening Australia. Under the shock of these defeats there was a strong temptation to alter the strategy, but it was persisted in, and preparations for the war in Europe were given priority.

The most obvious target for Britain and America was an assault upon the western part of Europe, but this was bound to be a venture of great risk and cost which must be carefully prepared. It was thought essential nonetheless to take some steps at once, to reassure Russia, to stimulate British and American opinion, and to encourage the conquered peoples of the continent. A landing in French North Africa—which had been more or less in the position of neutral territory since the 1940 armistice—was therefore planned to coordinate with a strong offensive from Egypt, against the Libyan forces which had been strengthened by German units and a brilliant German commander, Erwin Rommel. The Germans and the Italians might then be squeezed from both ends of the Mediterranean, and ejected from Africa altogether. The Mediterranean sea routes would be safe and Italy and Southern Europe made vulnerable to assault. Accordingly, in October, 1942, the British General Montgomery struck from his base in Egypt with overpowering force against the German-Italian army in Libya and commenced an advance which was to lead him across the entire length of that colony and into French Tunisia on its western border. On November 8, 1942, British and American forces under General Dwight Eisenhower landed in Morocco and Algeria. The importance of air and sea power was illustrated again. Allied naval and air forces dominated the Mediterranean and prevented the reinforcement of the Axis. By the end of the month, the Allies were preparing for an attack on Tunis, the only Axis-held area left in Africa.

October and November, 1942, mark the high water mark of Hitler's success and empire. From then on, German and Italian defeats multiplied, and the territory under their control began to shrink. By the time this turning point was reached, relationships among the Allied powers had already begun to take the forms which were to persist throughout the rest of the war.

Between Great Britain and the United States relations were close and friendly. Even before the United States became a belligerent, agreement had been reached between Churchill and Roosevelt concerning the aims and purposes of the two democracies. They had met on a warship off Newfoundland in August, 1941. Here they had worked out the Atlantic Charter, which formed thereafter their basic statement of principles. They pronounced themselves opposed to aggression, announced that their countries sought no territorial aggrandizement and that after the destruction of the Nazi tyranny they would strive for universal peace, through some sort of international security system, and for greater freedom —from fear and from want, as well as from oppression. Relationships were later expanded to include joint strategic planning. The British and the American aims were in many cases alike. Their leaders, Churchill and Roosevelt, understood and liked each other. Despite many differences, cooperation between Britain and America was never in doubt.

With Russia the case was different. The Soviet leaders had been ostracized, treated by both British and Americans for years with distrust, fear, and

sometimes hatred and contempt. The Soviet Union embodied an idea of government and social revolution which most British and Americans loathed and feared,
and they had rarely attempted to conceal their attitude. The Russians were deeply
convinced that all capitalists sought the destruction of their state; further, they
probably hoped the war would provide an opportunity to extend Communism.
Misunderstandings between these ill-assorted allies were inevitable, and the wonder was that they managed to cooperate as well as they did.

When Russia was attacked, Churchill at once announced that he regarded
the Soviets as a full ally in the war against Hitler and promised to send them as
much aid as possible, and the government at Washington followed the same line
before and after Pearl Harbor, despite considerable domestic opposition. Efforts
at cordial relationships were strenuous. Missions were sent. Stalin was induced to
sign the United Nations Declaration, which embodied the points of the Atlantic
Charter, and the British agreed to enter into a treaty of alliance with Russia.
But difficulties persisted, and they arose basically from the western allies' inability
to meet the principal demands of the Russians.

The Russians were concerned with two things above all others: first, the
opening of a new front in Western Europe, the "second front," which would
divert some part of the German forces from war in Russia; and second, British
and American recognition of the Russian frontiers of 1941. Both these demands
were unacceptable.

The British and Americans agreed that a second front must ultimately be
established, but felt that they were unable to undertake it in 1942 or, they later
decided, in 1943 either. The Russians were left for a time to bear the brunt of
German power. There was a suspicion in Moscow that the west was not unwilling
to see the Russians exhausted or even defeated, and whether this suspicion was
justified or not, it did nothing to improve relations.

The matter of Soviet frontiers was even more complicated. Before the
Soviet involvement in the war, the three Baltic states, large areas of Finland, a
third of Poland, and a Rumanian province had been incorporated into Russia,
whose western frontiers were thus returned almost to the line of the czarist empire
of 1914. The Russians were urgently desirous that the British and Americans
recognize these gains immediately. But the western allies were in theory fighting
the war to protect the rights of small nations. They had repeatedly insisted upon
the right of self-determination for all peoples. They were bound by agreements
with Poland, in whose defense Britain had entered the war in the first place. And
they were profoundly distressed by evidence of a predatory spirit in Moscow. They
insisted that no territorial settlements could be made until after the war.

The refusal by the westerners to meet the most basic demands of the
Soviet Union was not understood in Moscow, and a sinister interpretation was
put upon it. To Stalin and his colleagues it seemed self-evident that Russia
must have the territories which it was already ruling, as a matter of defense against
future aggression if for no other reason. They were perfectly willing to allow the
British and Americans to make corresponding acquisitions elsewhere, and attributed their refusal to consider the Soviet demands to a wish to cheat and perhaps
undermine their ally. By the middle of 1942 a very considerable flow of war

materials was entering Russia from the west—enough, perhaps, to have made the difference between survival and defeat—but not nearly enough to banish Soviet fears and ambitions or to compensate for the lack of a second front.

On the other side, in German-occupied Europe, the rifts between the Axis powers were even deeper, although they were more easily controlled, since the Germans were in a position to issue orders to their allies. By the end of 1942 Hitler exercised a virtual dictatorship over most of continental Europe, excluding Sweden, Switzerland, and Portugal and, rather unexpectedly, Spain, where General Franco had vigorously rebuffed Hitler's efforts to get him into the war. Elsewhere, however, Germany was in total control.

After the North African landings of November, 1942, the Germans occupied the whole of continental France, and Marshal Pétain's Vichy regime lost even the limited freedom of action it had had since 1940. During those two years it had represented a force capable on occasion of independent policy, backed by French conservatives, and seeking to bring about in France a Catholic, authoritarian, and very old-fashioned sort of "revolution." After 1942, however, few sensible patriots could fool themselves into thinking that Pétain was anything but a German puppet. French public opinion turned strongly against the government, and German occupying authorities were obliged to take more and more control.

In Italy a rather similar situation existed. More and more, Italy and its war effort were being controlled by German "advisers," and in 1943 it was reduced to a status of subordination at least as low as that of France.

Administration in the other German-occupied areas varied, but everywhere the German policies were the same: persecution and extermination of Jews;

AXIS EUROPE, 1942

terrorism of all political opponents; heavy economic exactions; conscription of labor to work in German factories. The most fortunate regions were those for whose "culture" the Germans had some respect and where army rather than Nazi party officials were in charge—Belgium, Denmark, France. The least fortunate were those whose populations were Slavs, whom the Nazis regarded as an inferior race—Poland and occupied Russia—and where the party controlled the occupation.

The Germans presented themselves as fighting in the interests of European culture. After the war with Russia began, the British and the Americans were presented as dupes of Stalin, and the major propaganda effort was directed against Slavic Bolshevism. There was much talk about the New Order which Hitler was building for a happy future of the European peoples. But remarkably little was said about what Germany's postwar plans for Europe—and presumably the world—really were. Not even so vague a prescription as the Atlantic Charter was forthcoming from Berlin. Such plans as existed envisaged the enslavement of Europe and could not be publicly proclaimed. And indeed, as we now know, Hitler himself had not worked out any form for a postwar world. His thoughts seem to have been extraordinarily vague and trivial, and the only precise program which he had in mind was the decimation and enslavement of the Russian people.

From the end of 1942 on, there was little need or time to consider programs for a future world dominated by Germany. The Nazi dictatorship was at last on the defensive, and its armies were retreating. The end of the war was already in sight and its outcome was certain.

THE DESTRUCTION OF THE AXIS: DECEMBER, 1942, TO MAY, 1945

The task which remained to the United Nations once they had grasped the initiative was lengthy and costly. The German army and air force were still intact, although their resources were greatly strained by the enormous areas which they covered. It was generally recognized that before victory could be won, a Channel crossing and an invasion of France must be undertaken, a venture without parallel in modern war.

The course of military events which led up to the surrender of the German forces in May, 1945, may be quickly summarized. In the east, the two and half years after Stalingrad saw a fairly steady Russian advance. By February, 1945, the Red Army had entered the territory of Poland, and occupied most of Rumania and Bulgaria and part of Hungary and Czechoslovakia. Most of the Danubian valley and of the Balkans except Greece and Yugoslavia (which had been liberated by the efforts of its own resistance fighters), almost all of Poland, and a part of prewar Germany were under Russian control, and the losses to the German army in men and arms were staggering. The western advance of the Red Army was inexorable and the western Allies could have done little to prevent it. The Communist control of Eastern Europe after the war was made possible by the Soviet successes.

The western efforts were devoted, throughout 1943, to the Mediterranean theater and to the mounting air attack on Germany. There were heavier and more frequent raids on German cities, almost all of which suffered unimaginable damage, including almost a quarter of a million casualties in Hamburg alone. German morale was shaken, and industrial production was markedly affected by these terrible depredations.

In the summer of 1943 the British and Americans attacked Sicily and, later, the Italian mainland. In July, 1943, Mussolini was dismissed from office by the king of Italy, Victor Emmanuel III and his new prime minister, Marshal Badoglio, secretly negotiated a surrender to the Allies which became effective on September 3, the day when the British Eighth Army crossed from Sicily to the Italian mainland. The new government took refuge in Allied-occupied territory, and thus temporarily saved itself and the House of Savoy from the wreck of fascism. But Germany quickly occupied and took over the northern half of the country. A new fascist regime, called the Italian Social Republic, entirely subservient to the Germans, was installed in the north. The Allied advance stalled before Monte Cassino, north of ruined Naples.

In the meantime, preparations were being made for the long-awaited invasion of France. A brilliantly planned cross-Channel attack on the beaches of Normandy was launched on June 6, 1944, and despite many fears and misgivings it was a success. The German defense was harassed by the now demented strategic ideas of Hitler, who imprudently forbade his armies to retreat, so permitting the Allies to destroy them piecemeal. In a few days the coastal areas were safely in British and American hands, and within the narrow bridgehead the build-up proceeded for an offensive. It began at the end of July, 1944. The German lines were pierced at Avranches, and the German tactical invention, the break-through, was now turned against them. The Americans (who now composed the majority of the invading force) surged south and west behind the Germans under the audacious command of General George Patton. By September the Allies had crossed the Seine and were driving toward Belgium, and Paris had been liberated.

During the autumn, however, the advance slowed down and finally stopped in the difficult country on the Rhine and at the German border. The Germans had organized an effective defense of their own lands, and were even able to undertake an ambitious but unsuccessful counterattack in December, 1944. During the rest of the winter, the line held along the Rhine. In March, 1945, however, as the Russians were approaching Berlin from the east, the western Allies began the final offensive. The Rhine was crossed late in the month, and the British and Americans, now joined by French and Belgian units, spread out through western Germany. Simultaneously, the German lines in Italy began to give way, and a long retreat to the north began.

Throughout the month of April, 1945, the German army began to disintegrate. Hitler committed suicide in his Berlin air raid shelter just as the Russians occupied Berlin. The Russians and Americans met on the Elbe, to the west of the city. Admiral Doenitz, whom Hitler had appointed his heir, surrendered the remnants of the German army. On May 7, 1945, the war in Europe ended. The German state ceased to exist. What was left of it was an impoverished and terrified population and a mass of ruins unprecedented in human history, governed by the military commanders of Great Britain, the United States, France, and the Soviet Union.

The war in Europe was over, but the Far Eastern struggle between Japan and the United States and Britain continued. In the Pacific, too, battles were being won by the Allies. After the first disasters, in the winter of 1941–1942 when the Japanese had damaged the Allied navies and won the Philippines, Malaya, and Indonesia, American sea and air power were gradually rebuilt. By painful stages, the islands of the western Pacific were recovered; China, India, and Burma were successfully defended. After Japan's great naval defeat at Leyte Gulf in October, 1944, the Philippines were reconquered, and American forces then proceeded to the seizure of Okinawa, near the main Japanese islands, which fell at the moment when the European war was ending. Japan's naval and air forces were badly battered, and the difficulties of supplying its vast conquests were made almost insuperable. But on V-E Day the very formidable task of invading Japan itself still had to be faced. No one yet knew, in May, that the atomic bomb would shortly bring Japan to surrender without invasion, and the Americans believed that a long and bloody war lay ahead. No one yet knew that an era of history was about to end with the harnessing of atomic power, that a new age of technological progress and hazard was opening, or that the defeat of Germany was the last, dramatic event in the long reign of gun powder.

ALLIED DIPLOMACY, 1943–1945

Military activities were not the only important events of the years 1943 to 1945, painful and stirring though they were. Equally weighty were the relations among the major Allies who were to be responsible for the rebuilding of the ruined continent. In certain ways, the Big Three of the United Nations (United States, Great Britain, and Russia) were able to cooperate fairly effectively. After the opening of the "Second front" in France, they had established a moderately amicable and workable arrangement for some sort of military cooperation. Public opinion in the three countries had developed a fair degree of cordiality. The personal relations among Churchill, Roosevelt, and Stalin were quite genial, at least until the last two months of the war.

In order to understand western policy during and after the war, it is important to realize two things. First, Stalin's conduct, and the evidence of their own observers, gave the British and American governments some grounds for supposing that the era when the Soviet was aiming at international Communist revolution was over. The Third International had been abolished in 1943. Communist parties abroad enthusiastically supported their national governments and made a great display of patriotism. There were many other developments, such as the restoration of the Moscow Patriarchate and the growth of freedom for religion in Russia, which led the westerners to hope that the Soviet Union would henceforth behave not as a center of world revolution but merely like another national state, defending its own interests but cooperating for the maintenance of peace. Second, the prospect of *another* war, against the Soviet Union, was quite unthinkable; the only alternative was to try to get along as well as possible with the gigantic partner which Hitler and history had forced upon the west.

Soviet cooperativeness was reasonably evident through the years 1943 and 1944. In November, 1943, the three leaders and their advisors met at Tehran. Their conference was an almost complete success. Stalin agreed to various commitments which the western powers wanted, including promises for the postwar evacuation of Iran—occupied by both British and Russian troops—and the restoration of its independence. The next year, in October, Churchill visited Moscow and found the Russians still willing to bargain and negotiate. At that meeting, for example, a disposition of the Balkans was agreed upon by Churchill and Stalin: Greece was to be a British sphere of influence, Bulgaria and Rumania Russian spheres, and there was to be an equal partnership in overseeing the affairs of Yugoslavia.

Moreover, planning for the postwar period was shaping up. At Dumbarton Oaks, in Washington, a conference on international organization in October, 1944, made a blueprint for the new international security organization, promised at the Tehran meeting. The charter for the United Nations Organization drafted there was provisionally agreed to by the Russians. There were other meetings —dealing with a whole array of technical matters—in which the Russians proved cooperative.

The major problem which remained was that of the Soviet frontiers, and this difficulty focused on Poland. Relations between the legal Polish government in London and the Soviet Union were venomous. The Poles were reluctant to yield any of the lands which they had governed before 1939, including regions populated by Russians and Ukrainians, and the Soviets insisted on a line well to the west of the old frontier. The matter remained undecided at the end of 1944, when the Russians had already occupied part of Poland and set up a Communist committee, which they treated as a provisional government, in the liberated city of Lublin. There were other problems which gave rise to concern as the end of the war approached. When the British landed in Athens, in the fall of 1944, they tried to restore the old Greek government which had fled in 1941, and found themselves opposed by resistance movements which were partly Communist led. In Yugoslavia, a Communist resistance leader Marshal Tito had seized power (with British and American support) and was systematically eliminating domestic opposition and refusing to permit the return of the exiled King Peter II.

In February, 1945, at the Russian resort town of Yalta on the Black Sea, the Big Three met for the second time. There were long agenda, and already great concern among the British and Americans about the Soviet Union's behavior. The conference was reasonably cordial, but agreement was very hard to reach on a number of points.

The Americans were particularly interested in two things—securing Soviet approval of the draft charter for the United Nations organization, and securing Soviet participation in the war against Japan, which looked as if it might be long and bitter. These concerns gave the Soviets a strong bargaining position. Stalin had already agreed in principle to enter the Far Eastern War, and now he stated his conditions. They included cession of the islands north of Japan (the Kuriles) and half of Sakhalin; a Soviet naval base at Port Arthur; and control over the Manchurian railways. The Americans, believing that Russian aid would be necessary to defeat Japan, agreed to these demands. But the principal issue was Poland, and in particular two aspects of the Polish situation. One was territorial, and the British and Americans now agreed to what they had refused in earlier years—the extension of the Russian frontier several hundred miles to the west, with compensation for Poland in the solidly German territories of Silesia, Pomerania, and eastern Prussia. The other was political: how to form some kind of government which both the Russians (ardent champions of the Lublin Communist regime) and the British and Americans (bound to support the legal Polish Republic in London) could accept. A dubious formula was finally agreed on: a Provisional Government of National Unity was to be worked out in Moscow, consisting of elements from both Lublin and London.

Neither of these arrangements was liked by the westerners, and like everything else about the Yalta conference they have been much criticized. But the Russians were physically in control of Poland, and of the Balkan countries as well. The agreements which were reached are usually viewed as concessions by Roosevelt and Churchill; under the circumstances, it would be more correct to view them as concessions by Stalin. He had been argued into making some gesture, at least, toward the western demands. In a "Declaration on Liberated Europe" the Big Three quoted the Atlantic Charter and agreed that where necessary they would jointly assist peoples to form governments representative of "all democratic elements" and to hold free elections. Negotiations were to continue, and there was still the hope that a chance for freedom and democracy in Eastern Europe might be preserved. If an open break had taken place, there would have been no hope at all.

In the event, the concessions Stalin had made proved empty. The new Polish government was entirely dominated by the Communists. The freedom of western advisors and observers in Poland and the other Russian-occupied countries was so restricted that they proved powerless. There was a steady tightening of Russian influence in the Balkan countries, exemplified by the seizure of power by the Rumanian Communists over the laments of the western representatives and the protests of the Rumanian king, Michael. In the months between the Yalta Conference and the end of the war, Russian conduct proved more and more recalcitrant. Stalin's notes to Britain and America contained a larger and larger percentage of threats and insults.

It was, then, an unpromising prospect which faced the world as World War II ended. There was still no open break, and there were still public professions of eagerness to cooperate in the reconstruction and the building of a new peace. But the refusal of the Russians to permit what the west regarded as freedom and self-government in the territories which they occupied boded ill for the future.

The last great conference before the surrender of Germany took place at San Francisco in April, 1945, to approve the draft of the United Nations Charter which had been worked out in Washington the previous autumn and approved by the Big Three at Yalta. Attended by all of the 50 nations at war with the Axis (including Byelorussia and the Ukraine, two of the constituent republics of the Soviet Union) it approved the creation of an international organization similar to the old League of Nations. There was to be a Security Council of eleven governments, including five permanent members—the United States, Great Britain, France, the Soviet Union, and China—whose main function was to scrutinize and make recommendations about any situation which threatened peace—subject to a veto on consideration of any subject by any of its members— and a General Assembly of all the member states which could, in effect, consider and make recommendations concerning any problem of international affairs. Organs dealing with economic and social affairs and with trusteeships—the administration of former German, Italian, and Japanese colonies—were established.

The San Francisco Conference completed its labors in June, 1945, and achieved agreement on the Charter. There had been, however, serious difficulties between the Russians and the western allies, revolving around the admission of Argentina (strongly backed for membership by the United States) and other matters. It had even been doubtful if the Soviet foreign minister, Molotov, would consent to attend the conference, and his conduct throughout the meetings fortified the spreading conviction that the Soviet Union was rapidly abandoning its policy of cooperation with the west. The United Nations had been born, but under a sinister sign.

The Second World War was longer than the First, and vastly more costly. Among Germans alone, over five million people had been killed, and the Russian losses were astronomical. A very high percentage of all the Jews in Europe had been murdered. The victims of Nazism, Jews and others, are estimated as high as ten millions, entirely excluding deaths on the battlefield. Air bombardment had brought suffering to civilians and destruction to the economies in a way never before imagined. Almost all the German cities were reduced to rubble. Very heavy damage was inflicted on London, Vienna, Moscow, Budapest, and Naples. Great ports like Rotterdam, Antwerp, and Le Havre were wrecked. From Normandy to the Volga, from Norway to Sicily, trails of destruction crisscrossed Europe. Huge numbers of people were threatened with starvation, and millions had been chased, or had fled, from their homes. Railway and road transport was practically at a standstill in many regions. Banking and manufacturing had ceased altogether in some. The whole structure of society seemed to be fatally weakened.

And yet nowhere, not even in Germany, did the structure break down altogether. Both politically and economically, Europeans showed themselves and their traditions to be remarkably durable. The most dramatic and lasting effects came not from the horrifying loss of life and destruction of property. They were in the rarefied realm of power and sovereignty. Here, permanent changes of the most portentous sort had taken place. None of the continental nations outside of

Russia was able to count itself a major power in 1945. Even victorious Britain was gravely weakened by its struggle and eclipsed in power by its mighty American partner, already equipped with the atomic bomb. No European country could challenge or resist the will of the titans, the United States and the Soviet Union. The future of Europe lay in their hands. This was the true meaning of the long diplomatic contest with Stalin and of the Yalta Conference: where the Russian army was in control, there would develop a Communist state and society; to the west of the limit of the Russian advance, where the Americans were in control, there would be reborn states based on traditional western ideas of democracy, with societies not greatly changed from their prewar character.

Europe had been rescued from its tyrant and was now in the hands of its rescuers. The age of European supremacy in the world was finally ended.

53

THE BEGINNING OF
THE COLD WAR

THE MAKING OF PEACE after World War II was a very different kind of procedure from the settlements after the Napoleonic Wars and World War I. In those earlier times comprehensive peace treaties were signed soon after the end of hostilities and interpreted and enforced by representatives of the victorious parties for five or six years thereafter. A similar proceeding had been expected after the defeat of Germany, Italy, and Japan, and a beginning was indeed made along the traditional path of peacemaking. Treaties were, after some delay, arranged with Italy and with the smaller European enemies, Bulgaria, Rumania, Hungary, and Finland. But with the other foes, divisions among the victors made the signing of treaties impossible. Not until 1950 was there a treaty to end the war between Japan and the United States, and it did not include the Soviet Union. No general treaty was ever signed to make a German settlement; peace was restored slowly and incompletely. Hitler's Germany was divided, after stripping it of borderlands, into three parts. With one of them, the Austrian Republic, a peace treaty was finally arranged ten years after the end of the war. With the other two, which evolved into the German Federal Republic and the German Democratic Republic, no general settlement was made, and their international status continued to depend on working agreements and tacit acquiescence by other powers.

The piecemeal, partial, and peculiar way of constructing the foundations of postwar Europe was evident in small matters too. Not, for example, until 1955 was the vexed question of the Yugoslav-Italian frontier settled, after remaining for ten years explosively provisional. The existing frontiers of Poland and of the Soviet Union have never been legally accepted by the western powers. Until 1956 the status of the German-speaking, coal-mining province of the Saar was undetermined. This kind of delay was evident throughout the world. In some places outside of Europe wars were fought before any kind of generally accepted settlement was reached—in Korea, in Indochina, in China itself. Further, in the broader and more abstract questions, of reparations, of disarmament, of protection of individual rights, there were either solutions by circumstance without legal sanction, or none at all.

The slow and painful process of making a new world by hit-or-miss methods was not the consequence of anyone's wanting it done that way. For some years after the war it was difficult to apprehend or accept the only settlement which was possible in a world divided in two between the "Communist camp" and the "free world." But it is possible to perceive in retrospect that this was the real meaning of the intricate happenings of the period after 1945.

The division of the world was both difficult and unpleasant to contemplate in its European sector, but there it was achieved soonest and without bloodshed. There were crises and uncertainties, but by the end of 1948 the line between the Soviet sphere and the western sphere was drawn, with a few persisting ambiguities. It ran from the Baltic, just east of the German city of Lübeck, through central Germany, along the western edge of Czechoslovakia and the middle of Austria, down the eastern border of Yugoslavia and the southern border of Bulgaria. The westerners held an outpost within the Soviet region, in Berlin. The Soviets held an outpost in the western segment, Communist Albania on the Adriatic. Yugoslavia, Communist but anti-Soviet, occupied a unique position on the border in the south and so, in the north, did democratic Finland, which was dominated by Moscow. The only change in this frontier which took place in the ten years that followed was in Austria, where the Russians eventually withdrew from their zone of occupation. On either side of the line there developed different and opposing societies.

The story of how this division materialized is the subject of this chapter.

THE SETTLEMENT IN GERMANY: POTSDAM AND AFTER

When the war in Europe ended, in May, 1945, ominous problems were already apparent. The most important was the rapidly deteriorating state of confidence and cooperation among the three major victors, the United States, Great Britain, and the Soviet Union. Although most of the disagreements had so far been kept private, they were profound and alarming. Their focus was the conduct of the Soviet Union in the areas occupied by its armies. To many western officials it seemed quite clear that the Soviet Union was intending to control and communize as much of Europe as it could, and was well on the way to succeeding in

Poland. This disturbing impression, heightened by Russian recalcitrance and insults in other phases of interallied negotiations, was most deeply felt in Great Britain, and there by Winston Churchill, the prime minister. Churchill was urging the Americans to take a forceful stand against the Russians—only the Americans had sufficient power to do so. He urged that American troops remain at the point of their farthest advance, instead of retreating to the spheres of occupation in Germany and Czechoslovakia which had previously been agreed on. He wished in this way to force the Russians into concessions on Polish and other problems. The Americans demurred, partly at the instance of General Eisenhower, the commander in Europe. Eisenhower argued that flouting of previous agreements with the Russians would make them more intractable than ever and probably incline them to withdraw concessions which they had already accepted, especially the admission of Allied forces and officials into Berlin and Vienna, both of which lay well behind the Russian lines. As a consequence of the Americans' insistence, the previous agreements on occupation zones were punctiliously adhered to, and the western troops withdrew several hundred miles in central Germany.

Since the Russians were not to be bargained with, it was agreed that they had better be conversed with, and another "Big Three" meeting was arranged. It took place in July, 1945, in the Berlin suburb of Potsdam. The personnel was changed from the last meeting at Yalta four months before. Franklin Roosevelt was dead, and Harry Truman represented the United States. Midway through the conference, the results of Great Britain's postwar election forced the resignation of Churchill and his replacement by Clement Attlee, the new prime minister and leader of the triumphant Labor party.

The Potsdam meeting was moderately cordial, and agreement was reached on at least the most urgent problems of Germany. The ruined enemy was already divided into four zones of occupation: the largest, the Russian, in the eastern and middle sections; the British in the northwest; the American in the southeast; and a small French zone in the southwest. Each zone was thenceforth to be administered separately, but over-all planning, including the establishment of central administrative agencies, was to be arranged by a four-power control commission of the four commanders-in-chief. Berlin, also divided into four occupation sectors, was to be governed by the four local commanders. The Big Three recognized— provisionally, the western powers later said; permanently and definitely, the Russians said—the rights of the Poles to "administer" that part of Germany east of the Oder and Neisse rivers, including the purely German regions of Silesia and Pomerania, and the Soviet right to annex part of East Prussia. This amputation had already in fact been accomplished, and the expulsion of Germans from the Baltic states (where the process had begun after their annexation by the Soviets in 1940), from Poland, and from Czechoslovakia, was already in course. The problem of minorities, so painful in the interwar years, was now to be solved by wholesale transfers of population. It was also agreed that a four-power tribunal, sitting at Nuremberg, should prosecute and judge the Nazi war criminals.

Two facts governed the decisions of the Potsdam Conference. First, the war was not yet over. Japan was still fighting, and the Americans were still anxious for the Soviet Union to enter the war and help in bringing the Pacific victory. Although the Americans had just learned that they possessed a workable atomic bomb, they did not yet know that it would knock Japan out of the war a month later, making Russian assistance unnecessary. They were, therefore, extremely reluctant to court an open break with the Soviet Union by stiff resistance to Soviet wishes at Potsdam. Secondly, and even more important, everyone supposed that the Potsdam decisions were temporary and would be superseded by the work of a peace conference later.

The peace conference did not take place. The Potsdam agreements evolved into a substitute for a treaty. They evolved in curious ways, each of which profoundly influenced the fate of Europe and the world. In the first place, the boundaries (which the western powers so scrupulously insisted were merely temporary) became permanent. Nobody west of the Soviet occupation zone in Germany has ever admitted the legality or permanence of Poland's—or the Soviet Union's—western frontier. But over a period of years, in the absence of any peace conference, they became accepted in fact. On maps, western as well as eastern, Poland was shown with its Oder-Neisse line and the three Baltic states as part of the Soviet Union. The expulsion of the German population and the repeopling of the regions by Poles consolidated the new shape of Poland, but uncertainty persisted. There was still room for a wistful German ambition and for nightmarish Polish fears. The new frontier was an element in determining Poland's dependence on the Soviet Union, which accepted the new frontier, and its suspicion of the west, which did not.

Another important evolution was in the situation of Berlin. Here, the four-power occupation was supposed to be supervised and made uniform by the council of the commanders, eventually to be supplemented by a presumptive government of natives. This was what happened in the end in Vienna, where a similar arrangement was installed and worked successfully for ten years. But in Berlin four-power government shortly became unworkable. The three western sectors sponsored a single democratic government by Germans; the eastern sector developed a Communist German regime. The frontier between the two, cutting across the heart of the city, remained a frontier, subject on occasion to being barred. But Berlin was not only divided in two—the western part of the city was surrounded by the Russian occupation zone. West Berlin was almost entirely dependent for its food and its economic life on contacts with allied-occupied West Germany, several hundred miles away. As the Soviet zone became more separate and highly insulated, the Soviets and the German Communists whom they were sponsoring became more and more inclined to try to eject the western powers from the enislanded stronghold. In the spring of 1948, on the pretext of a reform of the currency in the western zones and in West Berlin, land communications were cut off by the Russians.

The Berlin blockade was one of the decisive episodes of postwar history, and one of the most important in determining the location and permanence of the boundary between east and west. The western powers, particularly the United States, reacted quickly and with quite unforeseen effect to the challenge. The great Berlin air-lift was organized. Incredibly large, if barely adequate, supplies were flown in; on the average, four thousand tons of food and fuel were supplied daily. The air-lift continued for a year, and then the Soviets abandoned the blockade. The west had won its most spectacular victory over the Soviet Union. Free Berlin survived.

The Berlin blockade had generated a sense of kinship, almost of alliance, between the Germans and their late enemies in the west, and this made possible the development of a free and friendly German state out of the three western occupation zones. This strange consequence of the war was also an outgrowth of the provisional arrangements at Potsdam. The idea of dismembering Germany had been considered by the Big Three during the war. Potsdam specifically provided for the creation of central German administrative agencies run by the four powers as soon as possible. None of the Big Three wanted Germany divided into separate zones. Each of them saw some possible advantage to itself in introducing a measure of unified rule, which would give each power a chance to get its agents into the zones of the others, and would ease the economic burdens of the occupiers.

It was the fourth power, France, which threw a monkey-wrench into the work of creating administrative agencies and a sort of prenatal government for Germany as a whole. An extremely nationalistic posture was adopted by General de Gaulle, political leader of the provisional government of liberated France. His policies were based on the conviction, still unshaken in 1945, that France would never be secure from German attack until the western provinces of Germany had been separated from the rest and provided with an independent government under Allied tutelage. De Gaulle, moreover, had been annoyed by his exclusion from the Yalta and Potsdam meetings. The French were not in a mood to submit meekly to the insistence of the Big Three that a central administration be set up in Germany.

They demanded that before a German "government" (even one headed by the victors) be created, the Rhineland and Ruhr areas, the heart of German industrial power, be given a separate status. This the Big Three, who had definitely foresworn dismemberment, declined to consider. The French on the control council thereupon vetoed any action to create the all-German administrative agencies, and the four zones continued to be administered separately and independently, with differing policies and no contact or even trade among them.

In time the French attitude altered. De Gaulle went out of power in January, 1946, and the demand for a Ruhr-Rhineland state was softened by France's increasing dependence on Britain and America. The French were led gradually to agree to fusing the *three western zones* into an economic unit and to erecting a central government for them, staffed by Germans but initially controlled by the three powers. So was born, out of agreements reached in 1948, a west German government, which took shape in the next few years and became, by stages, the independent German Federal Republic—matched in the Soviet zone by the formation of another and completely separate German state called the German Democratic Republic.

The French veto, in 1945, of the plans for central German administrative agencies was one of the most important events in the history of postwar Europe. It meant that a single German state could not be created. It meant that the Russians could not mix in the affairs of western Germany, nor the westerners in the affairs of the Soviet zone and eastern Germany. Within a short time after the French made their position clear, the British and Americans were grateful that things had worked out as they did, for increasingly bad relations with the Soviet Union would have made the presence of Soviet influence in the west intolerable. The consequence of these events was a divided Germany, which none of the Big Three at first wanted, and a Germany divided so that the bulk of the territory, population, and industrial wealth lay in the western sphere. The accidental location of the border was immensely advantageous to the western cause.

The Potsdam decisions, boiled down and contorted in the crucible of worsening western-Soviet relations, had inadvertently laid the foundations for a new, divided Europe, and for the new Germanies which were to arise.

THE SETTLEMENT IN THE REST OF EUROPE

Germany was the largest problem of European affairs, but other boundaries and problems in 1945 required immediate attention. In these, as in Germany, settlements were haphazard and sometimes arrived at through stalemate. Some were quickly reached, and others took many years. All of them contributed to the division of Europe into two spheres.

The efforts to deal with the postwar settlement outside of Germany began in September, 1945, at a foreign ministers' meeting in London. By then the war in the Pacific was over. Japan had surrendered, and the Americans were prepared to take a considerably tougher line with the Soviet Union. Two major Soviet demands, that France be excluded from negotiations for peace treaties with Hitler's smaller European allies, and that the Soviet Union be given a sphere of influence in Libya, were unanimously rejected by the west. The meeting broke up without result, but later an agreement to call a peace conference to settle the terms of the Italian and Balkan treaties was reached. The Peace Conference met at Paris in the summer of 1946. Here, most of the remaining boundaries questions were clarified after painful negotiations lasting for five months. Treaties were eventually agreed upon to end the state of war with Finland, Bulgaria, Rumania, Hungary, and Italy. In general, the frontier lines of 1939 were restored in the Balkans, with several minor exceptions and one major one: Rumania confirmed its cession of two provinces on its eastern border, Bessarabia and Bukovina, to the Soviet Union. Other boundary adjustments were small, but the three southeastern ex-enemies were all obliged to pay heavy reparations to the Russians. So was Finland, which, in addition, lost Petsamo, its northern outlet to the sea, and several important provinces in the southeast including Vipurii, the second city of Finland, to the Soviet Union.

These countries had all fought mainly against Russia, been conquered by Russian forces, and were now occupied by them. The peace treaties concerned mainly the Soviet Union, although the western powers made futile efforts to protect the freedom of the vanquished. In the case of Italy, however, a very different situation prevailed. Italy had been defeated and occupied by the British and Americans, and in the main it was western views which determined the treaty with it—the Russians even agreed to limit their reparations demands on Italy to a hundred million dollars, a third of what miniscule Finland was expected to pay. Italy was treated fairly leniently. The westerners were willing to compensate for Italian surrender and later aid against the Germans. Aside from the loss of all its overseas territories, which were to be administered as trustee territories under the UN, and very minor cessions to France in the Alps, the western powers claimed no great sacrifices. But one matter proved troublesome. Yugoslav claims, ardently backed by the Soviets, extended over most of the Istrian peninsula (which was, in fact, largely Slavic in population, though it had been Italian since 1918) and its great port of Trieste, which was mainly Italian. On behalf of their Italian protégés, the British and Americans refused the Yugoslav demands. On behalf of their Yugoslav clients, the Russians were immobile. The solution, proposed by France, was to make Istria and its port an international territory, with Trieste administered by the British and Americans and most of the hinterland by the Yugoslavs. The boundary was in general simply that of the farthest British-American advance at the end of the war, and this boundary eventually became permanent, the eastern frontier of Italy, to which Trieste city was at last ceded in 1955.

Besides making treaties with erstwhile enemies, there were other problems which had to be settled before anything like a working peace could be achieved. Austria, although it had been part of Germany throughout the war, was treated as an entirely separate and "liberated" (instead of "enemy") country. The Big Three had agreed to handle it as Germany was to be handled. Its diminutive territory was divided into four occupation zones, and the city of Vienna, jointly occupied, was subdivided into four sectors. Both the city and country had their four-power control councils. But the situation in Austria evolved quite differently, and much more happily, than that in Germany. For one thing, Austria had been provided with a government of its own for the whole republic before the Soviets even permitted the other allies to enter Vienna. This government (under the leadership of Karl Renner, who had built the old Social Democratic party to greatness in Habsburg days, before 1914) turned out to be scrupulously democratic and, despite Russian efforts, untainted by Communist influence. Furthermore, four-power control did not break down. The occupation powers remained on working terms, even fairly cordial terms, much longer than in Germany. Ten years after the war, there was still effective cooperation between Russia and the west in Vienna, a sort of island vestige of the hopes which had been held for the wartime coalition. The Austrians were fortunate indeed in the outcome of events, but they were still burdened with an irritating division of their republic and with the weight of occupying armies. The Russians refused obstinately to agree to a treaty which would end the occupation, despite dreary years of negotiation. Not until the brief softening of Soviet policy which followed Stalin's death in 1953, was a state treaty finally signed, in 1955. Here, then, with the assurance that Austria would be demilitarized and neutralized, the boundary between east and west was finally pushed back from central Austria to the Hungarian border ten years after the end of the war.

In Greece, the settlement was also long delayed, and it was more painful than in Austria, but it was also in the end made to western satisfaction. Stalin and Churchill had agreed during the war that Greece should be a part of the British sphere, and indeed its control by friendly forces was essential to the British position in the Mediterranean. But Stalin's engagement did not prevent Greek Communists from initiating a civil war as soon as the Germans were out of the way, and this struggle continued for four years, expensive for Great Britain, and harrowing for the Greeks. In the winter of 1947, when Britain was faced with a critical financial crisis, the Greek problem was dumped by the British into the laps of the Americans, who were told that if anybody were to bail out Greece, it must be they.

This event was of great importance, for it marked a turning point in American policy. New policy-makers were coming into power in the U.S. State Department, led by George Marshall and Dean Acheson, and they were determined to adopt a more spirited opposition to the spread of Communism and a more constructive program for aiding in the reconstruction of Europe. The acceptance of responsibility for salvaging freedom in Greece and for rebuilding its wrecked society was accompanied by a general statement of American policy, called the Truman Doctrine, enunciated in March of 1947. The Truman Doctrine promised American aid to any country whose independence and freedom were threatened by Communism. Congress obligingly voted four hundred million dollars to pay for executing the doctrine. Most of it went to Greece (some to Turkey), to equip its army for the fight against the Communist rebels and to rebuild the economy. A horde of American officers, economists, and technicians arrived in Athens. The civil war continued for two years. But with American help, and with the withdrawal of Yugoslav aid to the Greek Communists in 1948 after Marshal Tito quarreled with Stalin, the government was finally able to put down the long revolt. The infusion of dollars into roads, dams, schools, and factories began to do its work. In the 1950's, Greece entered upon an era of tranquility, freedom, and progress.

The Yugoslav story was still more intricate and dramatic than the Greek. Marshal Tito, an orthodox Communist entirely devoted to Soviet doctrine and leadership, had during the war led his guerrilla resistance forces to triumph not only over the German occupiers but over rival, conservative, resistance movements. The Yugoslavs were the only people in Communist Europe after the war who had freed themselves without much aid from the Soviet army. Yugoslavia, moreover, lay on the western edge of the Soviet-dominated sphere. It had been agreed between Churchill and Stalin that they should have equal influence there, and Tito, who had been substantially aided by Britain during the war, was indebted to the west. Despite this, Yugoslavia was in the first years after the war the most purely Communist, and the most rigidly so, of all the Soviet congeries in Europe. Then, in 1948, to the astonishment of the world, came a break between Tito and Stalin. The latter caused the former to be publicly denounced for heresy by the other Communist governments, and the Yugoslav people were urged to eject him. Tito and his nation held their ground. David challenged Goliath, and the Russians, afraid to venture open war, had no course but to accept his defiance. Tito thus became an *independent* Communist, and sought aid from the west, which was cautiously granted. Henceforth, he was to occupy a position of isolation and neutrality, veering from one side to the other but never committing himself to either except, much later, in the form of an alliance with Greece and Turkey. A startling and portentous rift had opened in the Communist world.

A different outcome marked the evolution of Czechoslovakia. Liberated from German rule partly by the Americans and partly by the Russians, this, the most successful and sophisticated of the Central European democracies in the interwar years, embarked after 1945 upon a precarious policy of attempting to balance eastern and western influences while retaining its own parliamentary system and a more or less capitalist society. But caution and political skill were not enough to save the Czechs. In February, 1948, an armed insurrection on the part of the Communists resulted in dispossession of the non-Communist ministers and parties, and Czechoslovakia was thrust, suddenly and completely, into the Soviet system. Just as Yugoslavia's defection was the greatest loss to the Communist sphere in the postwar years in Europe, so was Czechoslovakia's capture its greatest gain.

With the exception of Austria, the border between western democracy and

THE IRON CURTAIN, 1945–1955

Communist domination was established in Europe by the end of 1948. The division was fairly stable, and indeed the line of demarcation was not without historical antecedents. As it has been frequently remarked, the line of the Iron Curtain today follows approximately the line of the eastern frontier of Charlemagne's empire. And it follows, too, the line which in early modern times divided the development of the west into a society of small, more or less independent peasant proprietors and of the east into a region of great estates. When the Iron Curtain descended in the late 1940's, therefore, it descended along what was approximately the traditional dividing line between eastern and western Europe.

We must now turn to the nature of the Iron Curtain, and to the steps by which the deteriorating relations between the west, led by the United States and Britain, and the east, led by the Soviet Union, converted the territorial division of Europe into two opposing, hostile, and tightly insulated systems.

THE DEEPENING DIVISION BETWEEN EAST AND WEST

At the end of the war there was deep distress in high places in London and Washington at the direction being taken by Soviet policy. This distress was not, however, known to or shared by most of the public, and there was no sign of a watertight division between east and west. In most of the newly freed Western European governments—those of France and Italy included—there were Communists in the governing coalitions and in the ministries. In Eastern Europe, except for Soviet Russia itself, there were coalitions which included non-Communists, although their role was in some cases, such as Yugoslavia, very restricted. International agencies representing the whole of Europe were being set up under agreements among the Big Three—the European Advisory Commission, and the European Economic Commission—which were intended to assure cooperation on political and economic affairs.

The descent of the "Iron Curtain," as Churchill later called it, which brought about so sharp a differentiation of the two Europes, was gradual and for some time unperceived. One manifestation of it, which will be discussed in detail in later chapters, was the "purification" of governments on each side of the line of division—that is, the ejection of those groups which represented the ideals of the other sphere. By the end of 1947 there were no more Communists in governments in the west. Nor were there any groups in power in the east which were not Communist-controlled, although most of the eastern countries continued to be governed by paper coalitions called by such names as "Democratic front" which included Communist-controlled socialists and others.

It was the constriction of non-Communist elements in Soviet-occupied countries, especially Rumania and Poland, which first gave rise to concern in London and Washington. By the time the war ended it was clear that Stalin's notion of democracy and free elections was very different from Roosevelt's or Churchill's. As the next year passed, this concern hardened into certainty that the Soviet Union was intending to establish a tight control, via Communist parties, over all Eastern Europe. Each event made this intention clearer: the forcing out of the "London Poles" from the Warsaw government; illegal seizures of power in Hungary, where the majority party, the Small Holders party, was turned out of office by the Communists; in Rumania, where the appointment of a small Communist party to all high offices was forced on the king by the Russian occupiers; the taking of power by Communists in Bulgaria; the refusal of Tito to permit the king or the constitutional government to return to Yugoslavia from London. The principal, almost pathetic, demand of the western powers was for free elections in the eastern countries. On this they had insisted throughout the war, as a condition for the recognition of governments. On this they continued to insist throughout 1945 and 1946. But there was no way of making their demand effective. Elections were held. But either their results were nullified by illegal action, as in Hungary and Czechoslovakia, or else they were palpably fraudulent at the outset. In Bulgaria, in the summer of 1946, the results of the election were inadvertently announced by the Communist government the day before it took place. At the same time, police controls and restrictions on the right to move about grew more and more strict in all the Russian-controlled areas. Allied officials in the east found themselves held in futile isolation. By the end of 1948, party dictatorships were well-established and were beginning to undertake Communist social and economic programs, such as five-year plans for industry and the collectivization of agriculture.

This growing tyranny in the east was logically matched by a growing hostility between east and west, and most particularly between the Soviet Union and the United States. By the end of 1945, American public opinion was becoming anti-Soviet. The Soviet press was correspondingly anti-American; the Americans were accused of being warmongers, imperialists, reactionaries, and the enslavers of small peoples.

The milestones on this road to venomous antagonism between the world's two greatest powers, along which each was followed by its retinue of less mighty allies, had begun to appear even before the war was over. Some of them may be briefly listed.

In April, 1945, at the San Francisco Conference to prepare the charter of the United Nations organization, alarming controversies and deadlocks appeared. There were bitter disputes over the admission of Poland (backed by the Soviets) and Argentina (backed by the United States). There were many other signs of ill-will and obstruction by the Soviet Union.

At the end of the war the United States summarily ended the Lend-Lease program, which had been counted on by the Russians—and other allies—to see them through the difficult days of reconstruction. At the same time the Americans declined to consider a reconstruction loan to the Soviet Union, although it shortly granted one of almost four billion dollars to Great Britain. The disenchanted Americans were not prepared to contribute to the economic development of a hostile rival; and the Russians took their unwillingness as evidence of enmity.

In September, 1945, at the London Conference called to prepare for the peace treaties with the lesser enemy countries, the Soviet Union harshly rejected the western demand that France participate in negotiating the treaties, and itself demanded control of Libya, the former Italian colony on the Mediterranean.

When the United Nations Organization eventually met, in London, in January, 1946, there were very ominous conflicts indeed. The most important of them concerned Iran, which had been partly occupied by both Soviet and British-American forces during the war but which the Big Three had promised at Tehran, in 1943, to evacuate. The Russians now seemed determined to maintain their control over the province of Azerbaijan, which adjoined Soviet territory. Under strong pressure the Russians eventually withdrew. But the darkest suspicions of both sides were deepened.

Soviet conduct in the Far East also gave rise to alarm. The Russians had entered the war against Japan at the last moment, too late to affect its outcome, but they had demanded the full compensation promised them earlier at Yalta— and moreover, they were using the presence of their troops in Manchuria to strip that Chinese province of much of its wealth and to establish a tight political control.

The Russians made upsetting demands on Turkey (which had joined the United Nations alliance at the very end of the war), including cessions of territory and revision of the international treaty regulating the use of the Dardanelles in a manner favorable to the Soviet Union. The demands were successfully rejected, but they appalled both the Turks and the western powers.

After the explosion of the United States atom bombs over Japan, the Russians asked for—and of course did not receive—an international sharing of atomic secrets and arms. They then professed the conviction that the United States intended to use its new weapon for imperialist purposes, including, perhaps, war against Russia. In the west, on the contrary, it was widely believed that the American atomic monopoly was the only guarantee against Soviet aggression.

With each month that passed, the international conferences among the wartime allies became more and more bitter and futile. More and more, the Russians opposed everything suggested by the west, and vice versa, and each side formed a more and more sinister impression of the aims of the other. Mr. Molotov and the American Secretary of State Mr. Byrnes, the principal protagonists, argued endlessly and ever more bitterly in the long and dreary series of Foreign Ministers' Councils which met to try to reach agreement on a treaty for Germany and Austria. By the end of 1947, stalemate was complete. Further negotiations were fruitless, although a few more efforts were made. No more Russian-American agreements were to be reached, and only the most formal and chilly relations continued between the two countries and their two sets of friends. The Iron Curtain had descended shutting off the two worlds from communication with one another; what the American journalist, Walter Lippmann, dubbed "the Cold War" had begun. Henceforth, the policies of the United States and of the Soviet Union in Europe were to be directed principally at the organization and strengthening of the two regions which each could control or influence.

The breakdown of the efforts at cooperation between the two giants of the planet, and between the free world of the west and the "Communist camp" of the east, is too recent for a thorough or detached analysis of its causes. Documentary materials are still unavailable, and passions still run high. But several elements in the situation can be discerned. The existence of two such peerless powers, each with its own interests and concerns, tended *in itself*—quite aside from their ideals and forms of government—to lead to competition. The old balance of power, its mechanism and its logic, was at work. It was perhaps inevitable that each of the two should secure for itself safeguards and advantages which would lead the other to demand compensating safeguards and advantages. Seen from this viewpoint, the Cold War was merely the current version of the diplomatic struggles which were as old as the European state system, in which each government forever sought strongpoints against possible aggression by another. But added to this conflict of power was a poisonous conflict of doctrine. To judge each philosophy as it sought to be judged, one may state it thus: the Americans and their friends sought a free world in which ideas and interests of all groups and individuals might fight out a peaceful battle for markets and profits, for political control, for the discovery of philosophic truth; the Russians, being convinced that they had already discovered truth, sought a world which was safe for the construction of what they called socialism—which involved the strict control of all who opposed it, and enforced sacrifices in its behalf.

It has been noted earlier in this book that the Napoleonic era represented not only an era of battles between armies for the control of land and power, but a battle between doctrines for the control of minds. The same observation applies equally to the epoch after 1945.

THE ORGANIZATION OF THE
TWO EUROPES

The five years that followed 1948 saw the growth, on both sides of the Iron Curtain, of efforts at organization and economic development of the two groups of European countries. On the part of their leaders and sponsors, the United States and the Soviet Union, there was a mounting belief that safety demanded common measures for military and economic security. Among the governments of the countries concerned, there was a mounting disposition to accept aid and counsel from the two great powers, and to submerge old rivalries in the new need to protect themselves against enemies, internal and external. The more intense the antagonism of the two Europes grew, the greater became the interdependence among the several regions of each.

The west took major steps first. The earliest and most dramatic proposals came from the United States. Making a program for western revival and defense was associated with the coming to office of Secretary of State George Marshall, in January, 1947, who determined upon a more spirited policy. It included rebuilding American military power—which had been greatly reduced by demobilization since the end of the war a year and a half earlier—and a policy of "containing" Soviet power. The Truman Doctrine, and the Greek-Turkish Aid program of March, 1947, already referred to, were preliminaries. In June came the most important step, the Marshall Plan.

The Marshall Plan was in its simplest form a program for granting huge American credits to European countries whose economies had been weakened by the war. It was provoked by the sad state of Europe in the spring of 1947. The aftermath of the war had produced a severe economic crisis, and this had been aggravated by three other conditions—the worst winter in European history, which placed an intolerable strain on fuel supplies; the threat of inflation; and the acute shortage of dollars. The last was an intensified form of a malady which had afflicted much of the world since 1918. Since then, few European countries had been able to export enough to the United States to earn sufficient dollars to pay for the goods which they needed to buy there. The war had vastly accentuated this problem. Europe's capacity to export was curtailed. Other sources of dollar earnings, income from investments and shipping, were reduced. The materials needed to feed the war-torn populations, repair the war damage, re-equip obsolescent factories, furnish them with raw materials, and pay for the modernization and expansion of the economies, were so extensive as to require much increased supplies of dollars. The condition of consumers had become almost desperate. Rationing in many places, especially Great Britain, was more severe than it had been during the war. There were bread shortages in both France and Italy, and the west German economy had reached the point of nearly total destitution. Clearly trouble was in sight unless immediate action was taken.

What Secretary Marshall urged was that each European nation should prepare a schedule of its dollar needs, join with the others to prepare a master plan of recovery, and submit it to the United States which would (Congress willing) foot the bill. The invitation was extended to all European countries, including the Soviet Union and its satellites. The Soviet reaction was to perceive a capitalist plot: the Russians insisted that the United States was trying to buy its way into political control of the continent, and Eastern Europe declined the invitation, except for Czechoslovakia which first eagerly accepted it and then, under Soviet duress, withdrew the acceptance.

With great good will, however, the western powers worked out a program along lines indicated by Marshall. It was accepted by the United States administration, and by Congress, which appropriated the necessary money. Even before it went into effect, the United States made available emergency credits, called Interim Aid. By 1948, an imposing structure of European economic collaboration had been inaugurated, and American capital was flowing into Europe to alleviate the dollar shortage, curb inflation, and revive the economies. The restoration of Europe had begun, complemented in western Germany by strenuous measures to restore the ruined currency and get the wheels of industry turning.

The economic revival of Western Europe, discussed in detail elsewhere, was shortly supplemented by a political and military program, the North Atlantic Treaty Organization.

This momentous implement of western unity also originated in 1947, at the instance of the great British foreign secretary of the postwar era, Ernest Bevin. Its invention was a response to the final breakdown of the Foreign Ministers' Council, which marked the conclusion of all efforts at east-west collaboration. In the months that followed, the plan thought out by Marshall and Bevin took shape as the North Atlantic Treaty. In April, 1949, the document was completed and signed. There were twelve original members: the United States; France; Britain; Belgium, the Netherlands, and Luxemburg—which had joined in an economic union called Benelux—Norway; Denmark; Portugal; Iceland; Italy; and Canada. Later, Greece, Turkey, and West Germany were added. The treaty provided that each nation should regard an attack upon any of the others as an attack upon itself, and promised full assistance. It also provided for the establishment of a permanent North Atlantic Treaty Organization, sitting at Paris, to secure harmonious defense policies and to provide a supreme command for the forces of the allies. It led to the permanent installation of American forces in Europe, and to the provision of large quantities of military aid to the other members by the United States. The immediate and abiding purpose of NATO was to strengthen Europe's defenses against possible Communist attack, but in a deeper sense it created something like a confederation of its members for military purposes, armed with a cosmopolitan high command.

NATO and the Marshall Plan were striking evidence of the revolution which the ominous misconduct of the Soviet Union had brought about in the west. The sovereignties of Western Europe were partly submerged in the common effort, and with them their lethal rivalries. Even more striking was the quiet end of American isolation. Now at last Americans were interring George Washington's sanctified warning against entangling alliances.

In the east developments of a rather similar sort were taking place, as responses to western moves. Throughout 1947 the control of Communist parties in the satellite countries was being tightened. There were purges and ministerial shifts. In September—just as the Marshall Plan was taking shape—the Cominform was organized. This was in theory merely a central information agency for Communist parties. Actually, it seemed to be a revival in more discreet form of the old Comintern, abolished in 1943, which had been the agency of Russian control over Communist parties abroad. Its function appeared to be the formulation of rules of orthodoxy for the governments of Eastern Europe. It was a central agency of Soviet control over the eight Peoples' Republics which constituted the Soviet bloc. In response to NATO, the Soviets formed the Warsaw Alliance, which was a military and political confederation superficially similar to NATO.

Another step in the solidification of this bloc came later, in response to the western formation of the German Federal Republic. In the Soviet zone of Germany, a corresponding eastern republic evolved step by step. By 1950, when western Germany was approaching independence and partnership in the western alliance, the German Democratic Republic, Communist-controlled, was taking form behind the Iron Curtain, ready to assume its place in the Soviet camp. The division of Germany was in some ways the image of the division of Europe. However painful to its inhabitants, it proved a workable way of delimiting the two universes. And in one respect it contributed positively to stability, by diminishing the fears of France and other countries of a revival of German aggression.

The organization of the eastern bloc was entirely different from the western. The United States and its partners were scrupulously—almost excessively—concerned for the independence of all members, and their collaboration

THE SETTLEMENT IN EASTERN EUROPE AFTER 1946

was impeded by diverse patriotic and party demands within each country. The east spoke with a single voice. Dissent was ruthlessly suppressed. There were never any open debates among the governments of Eastern Europe. But while the western bloc was much looser and therefore freer, the two camps were similar in motives and outlook: each faced the other with suspicion and sometimes loathing, and each was organizing itself primarily as a defense against the other.

By 1950 the lines were drawn taut. Western Europe had been rescued from the bankruptcy of the postwar years and from the national divisions of centuries, and forged with American aid into something resembling a unit. In the east a different kind of unity was enforced by the brooding might of the Soviet Union. Almost all the outstanding disputes bequeathed to Europe by the war were now settled. The few that were left—the quarrel over Trieste, the evacuation of Austria, the disposition of the French-controlled coal region of the Saar, were settled in the next few years. The little conflicts were all resolved and focused into the abiding great one, the struggle between east and west. Acutely aware of this struggle and its hazards, of the deadly possibilities of nuclear warfare, and aware, too, of the pains and costs of the division of Europe, the world attended the course of events with alarm amounting to hysteria.

But there was in this unpleasant situation a sort of stability which few at first discerned. The rival giants, the United States and the Soviet Union, were so evenly matched that neither dared risk open war with the other. The unedifying series of insults which passed for Soviet-American relations in the late 1940's and 1950's was really a symptom of stability; the insults were substitutes for military adventures which no one dared to risk. The United States, in possession of the terrible secret of the atomic bomb, was able for a time to frighten the Soviet Union out of attempting adventures of conquest. After 1949, when the Russians developed a bomb of their own, a fearful balance was restored which was scarcely less effective in curbing open aggression. The effects of this stability on Europe were unnerving, but in some ways, especially in the west, they were very salutary. The United States was forced to underwrite European reconstruction and expansion, and to sponsor much-needed steps toward European unity. As Western Europe, growing each day more essential to the United States, recovered its prosperity, it also began to recover its independence. In the rest of the world, where empires were disintegrating and where ambitions clashed, the lines could not be tightly drawn between the two spheres, and it was in Asia that the most alarming international crises of the 1950's were to take place. In Europe, with the Iron Curtain defined and grudgingly accepted, stability was achieved. It was not to be seriously shaken until the Berlin question again became critical ten years later.

54

THE NEW ECONOMY OF WESTERN EUROPE

IT HAS BEEN A THEME of this book that Europe's peculiar genius has been the product of a great variety of peoples within a single civilization with many common characteristics. In World War I, national states reached the point of efficiency and power where they could undertake the destruction of unifying forces in Europe. The disintegrative process continued between the wars, reached its climax in fascism, and led to World War II. In the years afterward the continent bore the aspect of a bloody battlefield occupied by foreign victors.

In the west, however, a revival began before long to take place. Within a decade after the end of the war, this revival had taken on the shape of a revolution. Some indication of the speed and scope of the change is shown by the figures for the gross national product—the total output of goods and services for Western Europe for 1938, 1947 and 1955. (The figures for 1953 are taken as "100"): 1938, 77; 1947, 71; 1955, 111. It is clear that Western Europe accomplished more than recovery from war damage after 1945. It began to move ahead toward rapid new economic development.

That the story of Europe after 1945 was so dramatically different from that after 1918 is attributable to many causes. For one thing during the period after 1918, the United States had reverted to an attitude of chilly isolation, had insisted upon the payment of war debts owed to it, and had engaged upon a policy of increasing its tariffs, thus harassing the European export trade, although, until 1929, the United States had provided its own corrective with private lending.

After 1945, the policy of the United States was more realistic. There were no war debts to be repaid, thanks to the Lend-Lease principle. On the contrary very large grants of money were made available to European countries by the Marshall Plan and other arrangements, which served to provide both capital for investment and to pay for imports of goods necessary to rebuild the economies. Moreover, the United States had already embarked upon a program of tariff reduction which enabled the Europeans and others to find a profitable market for their exports in America. The motives for this generous and prudent policy in the United States were mixed. Most obviously, the strategic fear that an impoverished Europe would slip under Soviet control nearly forced Americans to try by massive aid to salvage for the free world those parts of Europe which had escaped Soviet domination.

Second, a number of purely technical factors contributed to European revival. One was the revision of economic thinking as a result of the writings of John Maynard Keynes. There was, too, great awareness among governments of the importance of expert economic advice. The age of purely political government was over. With the new economic information and techniques, governments could know much more clearly where their economies stood and what they required. There was greater agreement, in the western world, on what measures were necessary to assure prosperity and economic growth than there had been for many years. The maturing of the science of statistics and new studies of the economics of development through the encouragement of capital investment bore fruit in the postwar years.

Third, the European revival may be attributed to a sudden redressing, in Western Europe, of the balance between unity and diversity. In this, the very completeness of Europe's disaster proved advantageous. Dreams of empire had all turned to nightmares. One of the many motives of the steps taken toward European cooperation was fear of the predatory or imperial ambitions of Russia and America. To be free, Europe must be united. Just as fear of Russia led Americans lavishly to endow the Western European economies in the 1940's and early 1950's, so fear of Russia *and* America led the Europeans to put that endowment to wise and disciplined use.

Another source of strength lay in the domestic structure of the western countries. As a result of the war, all Western Europe (except Spain and Portugal) found itself equipped in 1946 with democratic, constitutional governments which provided for the first time since the early nineteenth century an ideological community among the nations. Moreover, there was a striking similarity in the postwar history of political parties in most parts of Western Europe. Two parties, in particular, emerged almost everywhere powerful and in many places dominant, the Catholic parties and the Socialist parties. For much of the postwar decade, Catholic parties were in control of the foreign ministries of France, Germany, Italy, Austria, and Belgium, and were influential in other countries. In most of these countries, the Socialists were the principal parliamentary opposition. In Britain, Norway, Sweden, and Denmark, they controlled the governments during much of the decade. While the Catholics and Socialists differed on many points, they had many ideas in common: they were dedicated to democracy, parliamentary government, and political freedom; they united in supporting far-reaching measures of social security and some degree of government direction of the economy, while opposing a totally regimented or planned society; and they were all, by long tradition, essentially internationalist in their outlook. Both Catholics and Socialists had as the essential core of their doctrine a cosmopolitan philosophy. Both regarded extreme nationalism as not only imprudent but wicked. But both also cherished their national traditions, independence and symbols. No Catholic, and few Socialists, had declined in the last hundred years to fight for their countries. They were thus in the main stream of history, not shut off from it by a total rejection of the nation.

Creed and science, necessity and inclination, were thus on the side of reconstructing a balance between the unity and the diversity of Western Europe.

THE MARSHALL PLAN AND
EUROPEAN COOPERATION

A former prime minister of Belgium, Paul van Zeeland, observed in 1956, "Europe will be." After World War II, the idea of "integration"—which meant anything from a customs union to a supernation—was taken up by economists, businessmen, and politicians. The most important of its architects was perhaps Jean Monnet, a French economist and industrialist, who had long envisaged the revival of his own country and of Europe as dependent upon a new technological revolution, and this, in turn, dependent upon the creation in Europe of a larger, more freely competitive market. Monnet was behind many of the ideas and led several of the organizations which gradually took form.

The first organization of Europe for economic purposes took place in 1947. It resulted from an invitation of the United States at a time when Europe's economic disarray was at its worst. Secretary of State Marshall asked Europeans to join together and present a schedule of the most urgent of their financial needs. The western countries accepted eagerly and created the Organization for European Economic Cooperation to formulate proposals. The United States accepted the program and appropriated the necessary funds—about $12 billion in four years—to finance it.

The Marshall Plan had two principal aspects. The first was provision to cover the "dollar gap," that is, the shortage of dollar exchange which prevented the Europeans from purchasing in the United States or other dollar currency countries such as Canada. The dislocation and destruction of industry, and its obsolescence, had made the problem acute. The only permanent solution was to increase European efficiency and productivity, to enable it to provide itself the things which it now must import from America, and to enable it, too, to sell goods abroad to pay for those which could not be produced in Europe. To the successful achievement of this goal was devoted the bulk of the twelve billion dollars made available by the United States between 1948 and 1952.

The second purpose of the Marshall Plan was to induce European governments to adopt the sort of financial and commercial policies which would assure the best use of the funds. This meant, in effect, avoiding inflation, undertaking basic capital improvements, and accepting a measure of intra-European cooperation.

The danger of inflation was very great. Prices were already rising rapidly; in some countries, especially Greece, the inflation had reached disastrous levels comparable to those in Germany in 1923. Stability required both discipline on the part of the governments and control of the use made of Marshall Plan funds. The former was achieved by moral suasion, the latter by the device of counterpart funds. For every dollar paid to a European government by the United States, a corresponding sum of the local currency had to be set aside in a special fund which could not be used without the permission of the Economic Cooperation Agency, the U.S. agency set up to administer the act. Thus, the need for *foreign* money was met without adding dangerously to the total amount of money available. The result of these and other measures was remarkable. By 1949, most European budgets were in balance, most prices were stable, and most currencies had stopped depreciating. Inflation, while not entirely arrested, had been brought within manageable limits, and the most disastrous of the possible consequences of war had been avoided.

The Organization for European Economic Cooperation eventually included seventeen countries: Iceland, Norway, Sweden, Ireland, Great Britain, the Netherlands, Belgium, Luxemburg, West Germany, Switzerland, Austria, Portugal, Italy, Greece, Denmark, France, and Turkey. It came into being on April 16, 1948. Its original tasks were studying and approving plans for economic reconstruction—for the best use of the Marshall Plan funds—and the allocation of those funds among its members. But once the emergency had passed, the OEEC expanded its scope to include other projects. Those which proved most important were the efforts to free trade, and the European Payments Union.

It was early realized that trade among the European countries could be expanded to their common enrichment and to reduce dependence upon overseas imports. A program for removing obstacles to trade among the OEEC members was drawn up in 1950. Its principal requirement was the abolition of "quantitative restrictions," fixed quotas on the number of, say, automobiles which might be imported into a country. By mutual agreement, it was possible to eliminate about 90 percent of the quotas in the next few years, and in other matters comparable progress was made. For the first time since the 1870's the persistent tendency of European countries to increase obstacles to trade with one another was reversed.

The most important single obstacle to trade, however, was lack of money on the part of would-be purchasers. An Italian wanting to purchase British goods might have enough lire to pay for them, but it might be difficult to find pounds sterling. For a generation, and particularly in wartime, governments had sought to protect their currencies against "flights"—impulses by their citizens to buy foreign money and thus reduce the price of their own by making it less desirable. Measures to these ends, called exchange regulation, had made it harder and harder for Europeans to secure any foreign currencies at all, thus greatly inhibiting commerce. In 1950 the European Payments Union was set up under OEEC auspices. The EPU operated, basically, by extending credit to countries whose demands for foreign exchange exceeded the demand of others for their money. Thus, governments might allow their citizens to buy foreign goods fairly freely without worrying whether the national credit would be endangered.

Many other steps were taken to reduce the economic and administrative separateness of the Western European states in the years after 1948. As an example, one may mention "Eurofina," a European railway authority set up in 1953 by the ministers of transport of fifteen nations. The utilization of energy, the production and purchasing of rolling stock, and the planning of investment through all of Western Europe was placed in its charge, and it undertook the planning of new services.

TOWARD A UNITED EUROPE

The many programs of cooperation under the auspices of OEEC, taken together, represented a very dramatic break with the past. But they shared one feature which was regarded by many as a glaring fault: they represented policies adopted by national governments which still retained the final authority in matters of policy-making. Cooperation did not mean any organic change in the structure of Europe.

From the beginning of the postwar period, there were voices loudly raised in demands for "organic integration" of Europe, which meant the creation of authorities able to issue their own orders and have them carried out by their own agents. Enough of such "supra-national" bodies would have meant the final destruction of the notion of "sovereignty" in Europe. Two schools of thought in Western Europe gradually became distinguishable. The "superstate" school advocated the creation of a federation like the United States or imperial Germany. This school held that *political* integration must precede economic integration, that a body with the political power to give orders to the member states had to be created before any substantial measure of economic unity could be achieved.

The achievements of this school of thought were not very impressive. The most important of them was the Council of Europe, set up in 1949, sitting at Strasbourg and consisting of representatives of the parliaments of the member countries. It was provided with a Secretariat, which did useful research in social and economic matters, and it served as a forum for many of the ablest and most persuasive protagonists of Western European unity. But the Council of Europe did not turn into a European parliament. Whatever its merits, it remained primarily a debating society, and its activities have attracted less and less public or official interest. The Council had no real powers and no defined functions. It passed resolutions on anything it chose but those resolutions were of no effect unless approved by the Council of Ministers, an "executive" branch of the Council of Europe composed of the foreign ministers of member states. If they approved a resolution of the Assembly, the ministers then transmitted it to their own governments for further action. But they rarely did so. In the view of its critics, the impotence of the Council had its origins in deliberate deceit: its principal sponsors, the British, and particularly Winston Churchill, were frequently accused of having developed the innocuous Council in its ineffective form in order to prevent more serious moves toward integration—an integration which Britain, with its strongly insular tradition and its imperial obligations had consistently feared and resisted.

If the Council of Europe proved ineffective, another ambitious program for integration proved abortive. This was the European Defense Community, which was an effort to create a single European army and defense establishment to replace national armies. The EDC also provided for a parliament to which the army would be responsible and which would have the power to impose taxes for its support. But difficulties attended this step. It gave rise to serious alarm, especially in France, about the relations of Germany to the rest of Europe. Great Britain, opposed as always to any organic connection with continental countries, was not to be a member. This meant that within the unified army Germans were likely ultimately to be the most powerful group. The history of German aggressions in the past two generations not forgotten, and it was feared that the "European" army might become a German army, to be used to impose German domination. There was also a basic problem in logic about the EDC. It was an army which, in the last analysis, was not at the service of, or under the orders of, any recognizable authority. It was to be controlled, in the last analysis, by six still sovereign governments. Suppose the sovereign governments disagreed— to what authority would this, the only military force in Western Europe, be subject? To create the means of enforcing a supernation's orders before creating the supernation was a logically impossible undertaking. The pact was wearily ratified by four parliaments, but in the autumn of 1954 the French Assembly rejected it.

By 1955, then, the "federative," or "supranational," approach to a united Europe had been frustrated, for the national states, and national loyalties and national rivalries, were still much stronger than any enthusiasm for a political "Europe." It was left to the second school of integration, the "functionalists," to move ahead.

The basic conviction of the functionalists was that "sovereignty" was a meaningless fiction, and that by creating more and more areas of cooperation, mainly technical and administrative, a network of international agencies which might eventually coalesce into a "Europe" would develop. One example of this approach was the Benelux union, based on substantial free trade and common economic policies, arranged by Belgium, the Netherlands and Luxemburg immediately after the war. By 1955 the functionalists had brought into existence a more impressive show-piece, a concrete and remarkably successful example of how imaginative planning for international cooperation could create a revolution in political theory and action. This was the European Coal and Steel Community.

The Community had been born in 1951. Like many of the ideas for integration, it originated in France. It was first proposed by the French foreign minister, Robert Schumann, after having been originally conceived by Jean Monnet who eventually became its head. Schumann suggested that six powers—Netherlands, Belgium, Luxemburg, West Germany, Italy, and France—establish free trade in coal and steel, and set up an organization to supervise this free trade, and to plan and regulate the industries. The coal mines and steel mills of Europe (continuing to function as private property owned by the stockholders) would be removed from the control of the national governments in whose territories they happened to lie and be made subject to a new government of their own. This new government would be, in some respects, like a national government: it would have its own agencies and laws, its own powers to enforce and to finance and to plan. Unlike any other government in modern times, it would have no territory and no citizens. It would operate *among* and *within* the spheres of national governments, not by tolerance but by right, and would have over its own subjects the same sort of final and coercive power which governments have over their citizens.

The purpose of the Community was not, however, to adumbrate a revolution in the theory of government but to increase the efficiency and output of the industries to which it applied. In the first two years of its operation, from 1953 to 1955, production of steel and coal in the six countries rose by the dramatic figure of 93 percent. This was a rise considerably more than 50 percent greater than in all other industries.

The success of the ECSC, and the relative painlessness of its birth, emboldened the functionalists to proceed to other schemes. In 1955 negotiations among the Six began on two comparable but much larger projects: the Common Market, and Euratom. The treaties embodying them went into effect in 1958. The Common Market was to eliminate, over a twenty-year period, virtually all tariffs and related obstacles to trade among the six nations of the Community and their overseas colonies. Euratom was to provide for international regulation and development of atomic energy in the Six. Each was to be managed by an administrative and political structure similar to that of ECSC, and they were to share the same Assembly and Council of Ministers. There was thus coming into existence a European government for certain functions and purposes. Europe was being made, but in a fashion so novel that no one had ever foreseen its outlines.

There were, however, and are, serious obstacles to the making of an "economic Europe" along lines of the ECSC, the Common Market, and Euratom. The first of these concerned its extent. Not all of the free countries of the continent were involved. The Scandinavian and Iberian countries, Switzerland, Austria, and Greece remained outside of these arrangements, and so did Great Britain. This aloofness, in the case of continental countries, sprang from several sources. Denmark, for instance, had Great Britain as its major market and an important source of manufactured goods. The Danes, if included in a common customs union with the Six, would have had to pay higher duties on goods from Britain and might well have experienced difficulty in selling to them. Switzerland, with its extremely strong export position and its rock-like currency, hesitated to become enclosed in a union of countries with weaker economies, which might lead to the loss of dollar markets. Great Britain was the most important holdout. The British had never regarded themselves as part of Europe, and they had, in the last half-century, concentrated their major efforts on developing closer bonds with the empire and commonwealth countries. To enter into a European Union of any sort would involve the sacrifice of at least some of these bonds. On the other hand, a close European union formed without British participation might lead to the exclusion of British goods from the continental market. The United Kingdom exported more to distant New Zealand than to neighboring France, but the French share of its trade was very important, and if France were to admit German goods free but impose European duties on British goods, the British economy would suffer severely. British policy therefore tended to discourage European integration.

The most important obstacles within the six nations which took shape as the European Community were the vested interests of particular groups. One of the most difficult problems to adjust in the negotiations for the Common Market was the fact that the different nations, with their different levels of wealth, had provided different degrees of social benefits—old age and sickness insurance, unemployment compensation, and the like—and different levels of wages. The French (who enjoyed much the higher level of wages and social benefits) were afraid that free competition with Germany would be on terms very unfavorable to France, since French costs were higher. They therefore demanded that equalization of wages and social security arrangements precede—or accompany—the elimination of tariff barriers. Similarly, French businessmen, accustomed to sell to a market protected by the highest tariffs in Europe and thus enabled to charge higher prices and pay higher wages, were alarmed lest they be driven out of business altogether. Comparable, if varied, considerations agitated other groups.

Overriding all other considerations, however, was the realization that all the European economies had expanded almost as much as they could within the rigid walls of national economic separateness. Larger markets, greater opportunities for sales, attracting greater investment and permitting greater growth, were essential to the further development of industry. And upon economic expansion of this sort depended the welfare, the independence, and indeed the survival of Europe.

THE FRENCH AND GERMAN
EXPERIENCES

In order to have a clearer understanding of the varied elements of this general picture of growth, we may look briefly at the economic experiences of the two major countries of Western Europe, France and Germany. Each of these had a characteristic economic situation and problems before the war, and they faced entirely different sorts of problems in the period after 1945. Despite these differences, and despite the contrasting developments, the record of growth has been similar, as indeed it has in the smaller countries, where a similar variety of conditions and problems existed.

France had suffered heavy war damage, though not on the same scale as Italy or Germany. More serious, the French economy and French society in general had a long record of stagnation. The birth-rate was actually declining in the interwar period. Manufactures and agriculture were both protected by high tariffs and import quotas, and in many cases by subsidies and by producers' agreements allotting production and markets. This led to a rather static economy, with restricted competition and relatively little incentive to improve production methods or to experiment with new products. Production costs were made higher by a relatively high minimum wage and by a very elaborate and costly system of social security—a tribute to the political influence of French labor unions. French commerce was to a surprising extent in the hands of very small shopkeepers who were unable to practice mass-marketing procedures. French agriculture was, similarly, mainly in the hands of farmers owning a very few acres (often still divided into small scattered fields, as a legacy of the revolutionary land settlement), who could not afford modern methods of large-scale agriculture. The French currency was exceedingly unstable, which discouraged savings and long-term investment. The French political picture was (as described in Chapter 50) very dark, with endemic colonial problems and unstable ministries. France was faced, more persistently than any other Western European country, with an inclination of its citizens to consume more than they produced—to import more than they exported, so creating a chronic shortage of foreign exchange and putting heavy pressure on the enfeebled franc. On the other hand, France had a large industrial establishment, and its income and standard of living were the highest of any important continental country.

It might have been supposed that France would be the least likely of European countries to move ahead after World War II, let alone to participate in the extraordinary sprint which actually took place.

This supposition, however, was belied in the event. French industrial production precisely tripled between 1946 and 1954—which amounted to an increase of 50 percent over the prewar figure. In the four years following 1954, industrial production increased another 40 percent. French industrial production was increasing faster than that of any major country of Western Europe and considerably faster than that of the United States. The French birth-rate reversed a century-old trend and began to rise. French agricultural production also rose; wheat production was almost 50 percent higher in 1956 than in 1938. Production of sources of energy—coal, hydroelectric power, and oil—was up by well over 50 percent, and consumption of energy by well over 100 percent. Labor productivity—measured by the amount of goods one man can produce in one hour—increased 37 percent from 1939 to 1958. The standard of living, measured in terms of how much goods the individual can afford to buy—increased almost 30 percent during the same period.

In view of the unfavorable circumstances in which the French economy found itself, and its long history of rigidities, this achievement may well rank as a "miracle." To what is it due? Mainly, it may be supposed, to world conditions— the influx of American aid, the rapidly expanding world economy with its increasing markets for French goods and its supplies of capital for French industry, and its infection of confidence among businessmen. It is also due to the skill, industriousness, and technical training of French workmen and businessmen. And the systematic efforts by the French government were important. One of these, the system of "family allocations," which means payment of subsidies for large families, probably contributed to the rise in the birth-rate. The government agricultural policy aimed at, and to some extent achieved, the "consolidation" of holdings, that is, the regrouping of farmers' scattered fields into single units, more efficiently farmed. Government policy also encouraged the increased use of farm machinery—twelve times as many tractors were in use in 1957 as in 1937.

In the field of industry, the most important internal force in industrial growth was the Monnet Plan. This was a plan, drawn up during and after the war, for the re-equipping and expansion of the basic industries of France—fuel, waterpower, steel and other metals, and in particular machinery and machine tools. Government funds, supplemented by Marshall Plan aid, were made available for the modernization of the industries upon which the rest of the economy depended for growth. The consequence was an enormous stimulus to capital production.

The French economy remained curiously disjointed, with many areas of weakness. The record in house-building was very poor. The inflationary thrust remained. The gap between imports and exports remained. The weakness of the franc remained. The backward and intractable little retail merchants remained. The restrictive practices of labor unions and management remained. The inadequate and unfair tax structure remained. But France became nonetheless an economic society not only vastly richer than ever but also vastly more flexible, growing with greater speed, branching out into new fields and new experiments. The contrast between this atmosphere of change and growth and the sluggish rigidity of the interwar years was dramatic.

The situation of Germany in 1945 contrasted very sharply with that of France. Like France, to be sure, Germany had become a mature and highly developed industrial nation. But unlike the French, the German economy had already shown, after World War I and the Great Depression, a striking capacity for growth. In 1945, the economic problems of Germany were not problems of stagnation but rather of destruction.

The total picture of ruin was staggering. Six and a half million Germans were dead, and four million men disabled. This was compensated, in some measure, in West Germany by the arrival of some 12,000,000 refugees from territories occupied by the Soviet or by Czech or Polish forces. The refugees more than made up for West German war losses, but the immediate effect of their presence was total confusion and disorganization. There was no food and no shelter for most of them. Malnutrition, leading to disease, might well have destroyed the German people in 1945–1948 had it not been for the aid brought to Germany by its conquerors.

Twenty percent of all dwellings had been destroyed, and another 20 percent so damaged as to be uninhabitable. This compared to losses of 3 percent in France and 2 percent in Great Britain. In 1946 industrial output in West Germany was about one third of the 1936 level; consumption of almost all goods, including food, was reduced to half the prewar level. Over half the freight cars were destroyed or unusable. The usable productive capacity of West German industry was reduced by 20 percent. The merchant fleet was completely lost. The problem in the western zone of Germany, then, was total reconstruction. This problem was solved, as the different French problem had been solved, with a success that approached the miraculous.

The process of recovery and growth was, however, slow to start. It was greatly retarded by the division of Germany, by the disorganization and demoralization of the population, and by the inflation of the mark. These were gradually rectified. By the middle of 1948, the three western occupation zones (French, American, and British) had been largely reunited into an economic unit, and a new and remarkably stable mark had been introduced. Investment and commerce became possible. United States funds—stimulated by the competition with Russia and the ensuing desire to reconstruct a viable West Germany—had begun to flow. In 1948, however, industrial production in the three western zones was still only about half of what it had been (in the corresponding area) in 1936. In 1950, production reached and passed the prewar figure, and by 1956 had surpassed it in some fields by almost 100 percent. The most basic and important materials, coal and steel, stood in 1957 at 110 percent and 190 percent respectively of the 1938 figure.

The most striking statistics of German recovery are those relating to international trade. The value of exports in 1938 was $114 million; in 1956, $613 million; and it rose even more rapidly after that year.

In almost every field, German growth was equally startling. Merchant marine, textiles, construction, all told a similar story. The ruins, which it seemed could never be rebuilt in the foreseeable future, largely disappeared and were replaced by new factories, office buildings and houses.

By contrast with France, the outstanding characteristic of the German expansion was that it was accompanied by extreme financial stability, a very strong currency, and a high level of exports over imports. Instead of consuming more than they produced, like the French, the Germans produced much more than they consumed, and sold the surplus at a profit. The costs of this policy were high, for the results were achieved by keeping production costs and consequently purchasing power, relatively low. German wages, always lower than French, rose markedly less. Whereas unemployment was negligible in France after the war, it constituted a very serious problem in Germany until 1956, and was still in 1957 running at over half a million, the highest in Europe except for Italy. Because they worked for less return, and because of the labor surplus in Germany, Germans were able to make larger investments in capital goods, and to sell much more abroad, than Frenchmen. This meant that Germany was in a much stronger financial situation than France, but its standard of living was much lower—the income of the average Frenchman in 1956 was $934; that of a German in the same year was $692.

THE PROBLEMS OF EXPANSION

In all the free continental countries, a comparable development took place between 1945 and 1958. In Italy, where the economy grew very little between the wars, industrial production more than doubled between 1938 and 1958. In highly developed Belgium it increased almost 70 percent.

An exception to this record of rapid growth was Great Britain. The British situation in the postwar years was particularly difficult. To a greater extent than the continental countries Britain was faced with the necessity of importing both consumer goods and the raw materials for its industries. A greater measure of control was required in a country which had to export a larger percentage of its products in order to survive at all. Britain's *recovery* was as remarkable as that of the continental countries; its subsequent *growth* was slower than that of most of them. Between 1953 and 1958, French industrial production increased 66 percent and Germany's 50 percent, while Britain's rose only 13 percent. Nevertheless, compared with the record after World War I, and in view of the peculiarities of the British economic position in the world, the success was striking.

The outstanding and peculiar feature of the British situation was its dependence upon investment—that is, the addition of capital to the domestic economy and the acquisition of foreign securities. Two wars and the consequent using up of domestic capital and sale of foreign capital had led to *dis*investment on a large scale. Between 1939 and 1948, almost five and a half billion pounds of national wealth—out of an estimated total of 30 billion—had been lost. A billion pounds' worth of foreign investments had been sold. Like the rest of Europe, Great Britain needed to sell more goods abroad to build up profits to use as capital for new investment, but to do this it needed capital to modernize factories so that it *could* sell abroad.

This dilemma was much more severe in Britain than on the continent, because Britain had fewer resources—food and raw materials—of its own. Britain received something like forty billion dollars in United States and Canadian grants

SECOND STAZIONE TERMINI, ROME. Built 1931–1951. (Italian State Tourist Office)

and loans from 1946 on. With these it was able to rebuild its production and export trade and to double its 1938 rate of investment. But it was not able to move ahead to new growth at the same rate as Germany or France.

The general picture in Western Europe was one of revolutionary growth, with the implication of even larger development in the future. There remained, however, threats and problems.

One problem was regional, and is best illustrated in the case of Italy. Southern Italy had always been the poorhouse of the country. This was due mainly to the more antiquated social system and the much lower level of economic skill and energy of its inhabitants, to lack of capital investment, to the extreme poverty of its land and agriculture. In the period after 1945 a systematic effort was made to overcome the inequality between the progressive north and the backward south. Programs of land reform and improvement and of capital investment were undertaken by a special government agency, the *Casa del Mezzogiorno*. While southern Italy was at last progressing, its economic growth was still slower than that of the north. In other words, the gap in productivity and wealth between the two regions grew wider instead of narrower.

Another, and more serious problem, was the persistence of inflationary pressure. Production kept pace, but barely, with increases in prices and wages. This constant spiralling of costs made the value of money unstable and tended to discourage savings and investment. It also meant that there was a threat of runaway inflation, in which prices would rise faster than the amount of goods available for sale and lead to disastrous reduction in the value of money.

The principal threat to the growth of Europe's economy, in the postwar years came, however, from two possible disasters outside the continent itself: war, or worldwide depression. Europe was no longer strong enough to be able to dominate the world politically or economically, and its growth and welfare were therefore at the mercy of forces over which it had little control.

Despite the problems and the threats, the dynamic economic revival of Europe demonstrated the incredible skill and vitality of its peoples. Twice-battered, they at last resumed the growth which had come to a stop in 1914. They provided themselves with the goods and jobs which softened—though without eliminating—the social cleavages and conflicts of the last two generations. They began to redress the balance between unity and diversity by constructing an international community.

55

POSTWAR REGIMES: THE EAST

In world war II the Russian state and society, instead of collapsing as they had in 1917, stood upright at the end. The country was badly damaged, but Stalin's regime had gained prestige. In East Central Europe, instead of a temporary vacuum in which the peoples could assert themselves, there was a wall of Soviet power. After 1917 Lenin's and Trotsky's hopes for a chain of revolutions had come to nothing; the Russian Bolsheviks had remained isolated in their sanctuary. After 1945 Stalin's old motto, "socialism in one country" was out of date as Russia consolidated a string of satellites in East Central Europe, and China, North Korea, and North Vietnam were captured by Communists. The original sanctuary of Bolshevism was still isolated, but by choice, and it was becoming one of the world's leading urban and industrial societies.

While Stalin lived—until March, 1953—Stalinism, the name given to the crude form of industrialization and dictatorship which had transformed Russia in the 1930's, persisted and was inflexibly forced upon the satellites of East Central Europe. After his death the slight gestures of appeasement which his successors made as they assumed the old dictator's authority and jockeyed for position set up currents of change in the Soviet empire.

STALIN SURVIVES THE WAR

The German drive into Russia in June, 1941, carried the invading armies by December to the outskirts of Moscow. In the north Leningrad was encircled and besieged. In the south the Germans pushed through the Ukraine past Kiev

914

to Rostov on the Don. Russia lost perhaps a million men killed, captured, or missing. Three fourths of the Russian war industries were either taken or endangered. The government was transferred east to Kuibyshev on the Volga, although Stalin stayed in the Kremlin, outwardly imperturbable. December brought Pearl Harbor and the American entry into the war. It also brought temperatures of $-40°$ in the Moscow region, where the German troops were unprepared for winter. The German knockout blow aimed at the capital and the oil fields of the Caucasus had failed, owing to Hitler's decision to press several attacks instead of concentrating on one. Hitler, who had already announced the destruction of the Russian armies, would not order any substantial retreat, but left his troops in encampments —hedgehogs—many of which became islands in the Russian winter counterattack. In the summer of 1942 the renewed German offensive drove to Voronezh and Stalingrad and almost to the Caspian in an effort to squeeze the remaining life out of Russian production of oil, industry, and grain and halt communications with the south, but the large body of Russia still breathed. Stalingrad held out from September, 1942, to February, 1943, in a contest which ended with the encirclement and capture of the German army. American aid began to reach Russia. Many factories were being transported to the region of the Urals. Thereafter, to 1945, Russian counteroffensives slowly pushed back the Germans. The Red Army reached Poland by June, 1944, the date of American and British landings in Normandy, took most of the countries of East Central Europe in the summer and fall of 1944, Austria and Czechoslovakia in the spring of 1945, and—Eisenhower having halted the American advance at the Elbe—Berlin in May, 1945.

At the low point in the war, in 1942, about a third of the Russian population was behind the German lines. A pro-German army of captured Russians led by General Vlasov was organized to serve on the German side. In the Ukraine and the Caucasus it seemed for a time that there might be mass collaboration with the Germans, resulting from nationalism and the grievances of the 1930's. On the whole, however, the Russian population remained loyal and supported the guerrillas behind the German lines. Nazi brutality and exploitation hardened the will to resist. The fighting destroyed more than half of Russia's capacity to produce steel, railroad equipment, pig iron, and coal, together with thousands of tractors and combines and a large portion of the country's livestock. Twenty-five million Russians were deprived of their prewar housing. Perhaps seven million people were killed in the fighting or died of hardships.

Stalin, like the other leaders of the 1930's, had blundered and miscalculated. He had not counted on the swift German victory over continental Europe in 1940. He had been taken by surprise in 1941 in spite of warnings from the Allies. His armies had not been able to meet the Germans on equal terms, and he had made a virtue of necessity and pretended that he had drawn the enemy deep into Russia, like Alexander I or Peter the Great. No one knew at the moment of the German invasion what the morale and competence of the Russian officers would be like after the great purges of the 1930's, or how the soldiers and civilians would respond. But in spite of great confusion and inefficiency the Russians on the whole responded as they had in 1812. The dictatorship, like the autocracy of former times, profited from the general patriotism. Furthermore, the Russian distances, the cold, and the poor roads hampered the finely tuned motors and precision-engineered weapons of the Germans as they had the wagons and horses of Napoleon's day.

Stalin made many capricious decisions and mistakes. He seems, however, to have taken personal charge of the major decisions and, according to the testimony of wartime visitors, to have had a firm grasp both on the larger considerations and on the details. After the first disastrous weeks, when it became clear that the Russian public was not going to take advantage of the war to overturn the Communist regime, Stalin did his best to minimize the past violence of the agricultural collectivization and the purges. Several prominent victims who happened to be still alive were rehabilitated. Stalin also emphasized Russian nationalism and historic Russian traditions in an effort to weld the society together in the midst of its torment. References were made to great generals of czarist days. Officers were given privileges and epaulettes. Stalin himself assumed the title of Marshal. All this was a far cry from the Bolshevik efforts of 1918–1920 to inspire the people with thoughts of the international solidarity of the working class. Stalin disbanded the Comintern in 1943—a move designed to appease his allies—and at the same time (and partly for the same reason) rehabilitated the Orthodox Church. He also encouraged the revival of Pan-Slavism, which like the Orthodox Church might come in handy in the Balkans.

When the war ended in victory, Stalin and the Communist party played down the theme of nationalism and returned to severity in religious affairs. The generals who had become national heroes were pushed into the background. The history of the war was distorted in order to remove any danger to Stalin and to the party from the popularity of the Red Army. The contribution of the Allies to the war effort was minimized. The isolation of Russia from the outside world—the "iron curtain," as Churchill was to call it—was maintained as it had grown up in the 1930's. It became an outstanding part of "Stalinism" in its last years. The Russian people were more than ever asked to make sacrifices so that Russia might build up its productive capacity and maintain its defensive strength. Yet the isolation, and the official propaganda about the danger from outside, increased the tensions in the world and made that danger more real, and therefore made the armaments and heavy industry more urgent. And Russia's greatly expanded influence after the war—in the satellite regimes of East Central Europe and in Asia—made the iron curtain policy more difficult and dangerous. For Russia was no longer truly isolated.

THE PEOPLES' DEMOCRACIES
AND THE IRON CURTAIN

The independent states of East Central Europe began to disappear in the 1930's. In August, 1939, the conditions of 1918–1919 were reversed: instead of the destruction of the three eastern empires, which permitted the peoples of East

Central Europe to determine their own political existence, there appeared the Nazi-Soviet pact, a vise capable of squeezing the life out of their already troubled political existence. This area inhabited by approximately one hundred million people became the jumping-off point for another world war when Britain and France refused to stand aside and let it be reorganized by the two great totalitarian states. When Germany attacked the Soviet Union, East Central Europe became a prize contested between them. One of Hitler's principal objectives had always been control of this area, along with the Ukraine. The defeat of Germany and Italy was at length accomplished; in the ruins of Europe there was little real power to keep Russia back, and the Russian promises of democratic regimes in East Central Europe were not kept.

East Central Europe was conquered by outside forces, but this fact should not obscure the internal conditions which made the Soviet conquest easier. Most of the political regimes had been reactionary and many of them had been discredited by collaboration with the German conquerors. The economic problems of much of East Central Europe had not been attacked with success. At the close of the war there was, perhaps, bound to be some kind of revolution, and there was a possibility that underprivileged peasants and workers would think that Communism stood for land reforms and workers' control of industry. Communists had been associated in people's minds with the exact opposite of the old regimes, and this was what was widely desired. The Russian victory, moreover, would have given Communists prestige even if Britain and the United States had secured the evacuation of Russian troops. Under a system of political freedom in East Central Europe the problems of modernization and social justice would have placed a strain on the political machinery of the states and on the imaginativeness of statesmen—those of the region and those of the great powers.

A second chance for democratic institutions in East Central Europe came only to Finland, Greece, and Austria. In each case there were serious problems. Finland was penalized heavily by the Russians, and made economically dependent to a considerable extent, but stood up to the Russians and to its own domestic Communists and was not made into a satellite. Greece, as already noted, was kept out of Communist hands first by the landing of British troops and then by American military supplies and financial aid, the latter amounting by 1956 to almost two billion dollars. In the 1950's considerable stability was achieved in Greek politics. Despite economic advances there were still serious economic problems, and much remained to be done if Greece was to increase its productivity sufficiently to care for its population. Austria, after ten years of occupation by American, British, French, and Russian forces, was finally permitted to become an independent, neutral state. Austria had to pay large indemnities in goods and money to the Russians. Democratic government was, however, stabilized. The Socialists and the conservative People's party supported by Catholic middle classes and peasantry continued to disagree on fundamental questions, but worked together to restore the economy, of which large segments remained in government hands following their recovery from the Nazis and the Soviets. In contrast to the dismal poverty and instability of the years from 1918 to 1938, remarkable levels of prosperity and growth were achieved after 1945. Austrian recovery, symbolized by the rebuilding of the Vienna Opera House and of the city's great hotels and shopping district, surpassed the grim progress by enforced industrialization and five-year plans in the rest of East Central Europe.

The rest of East Central Europe became part of Stalin's "zone," and in the years after the war it was subjected to his brutal version of progress. Estonia, Latvia, and Lithuania were made into Soviet Republics like White Russia and the Ukraine. The history of the other states followed, with variations, a pattern. There were at first coalition governments in which the Communists, aided in some cases by the presence of the Red Army, held key posts (Interior—controlling police; Defense—controlling the army; Economy—controlling nationalized property and land redistribution). The Communists were prepared to take over the labor movements and, in the process of punishing Nazi collaborators, to catch wealthy bourgeois in their net. Trained in Russia and prepared to seize rather than destroy existing state machinery, the Communist leaders were much more experienced than their elders of 1917. In general, the stage of complete control was reached in 1947 or 1948. Coalition governments on the Popular Front model were abandoned and Peoples' Republics in the Soviet style replaced them, with the Politburos of the local Communist parties in control.

With Eastern Germany and Austria occupied in these years by Soviet troops, the Russians could justify maintenance of forces stationed along their approaches, in such countries as Rumania and Hungary and Poland, as necessary to protect their communication lines. In the presence of Russian troops, socialist and peasant party leaders and other potential competitors of the Communists could not resist. Neither could the Catholic Church, whose leaders Cardinal Wyszynski of Poland, Cardinal Mindszenty of Hungary, and Archbishop Stepinac of Yugoslavia were jailed on charges of treason.

The Peoples' Democracies were not allowed to federate among themselves, but were made members of the Communist Information Bureau (Cominform), which in 1947 took up where the Comintern of former days had left off.

Space does not permit description of many differences in national development, but several were outstanding. In Yugoslavia the Russian-trained partisan leader Tito was able to liberate most of the country from the Germans before the arrival of Russian troops. He was also able to obtain Allied recognition and support, and to eliminate the rival resistance leader General Mihailovic, a Serb whose efforts to build up a strong force had led him to compromise his position by temporizing with the Germans. Marshal Tito became dictator of Yugoslavia without ever passing through the stage of a genuine coalition government. The most that Tito did was to maintain for a time a "national front" in which the Communists had the real control. Albania, aided by the Yugoslav Communists, was also Communist from the beginning. Poland and East Germany had nominal coalition governments for a while, but were really in Communist hands. Rumania and Bulgaria had genuine coalitions of left-wing parties only until 1945 and then passed through a stage of more or less disguised Communist control until 1947, when the non-Communist leaders were placed on trial. The year 1947 also marked the end of the pretense in Poland.

In Czechoslovakia there was a high level of cultural and economic development and a record of successful democratic self-government between the wars. At the close of World War II the Soviet troops withdrew and democratic government resumed under the leadership of President Beneš. In February, 1948, the Communists seized control of the state in a coup which consisted of reshaping the ministry while organizing manifestations in the streets and monopolizing the press and radio. The Communists had infiltrated the Czech army and police. The Communist party was strong, but did not by itself have a majority in the parliament. At the time of the coup Soviet troops in adjoining countries almost surrounded Czechoslovakia's frontiers. It is not certain that they would have intervened if the Czechs had resisted the coup, but neither is it certain that Czechoslovakia could have counted on any aid from the west. Czechoslovakia was rather delicately balanced between east and west because in spite of its democratic traditions, its people were still aware of having been abandoned by the western powers at Munich in the 1930's, and the Slavic Czechs tended to be admirers of things Russian. In the event, the Czech political leaders in 1948 either could not or did not choose to take the risk of resistance. President Beneš had to resign, and the foreign minister Jan Masaryk, son of the founder of the republic, was killed or committed suicide. The Communist Klement Gottwald became president.

Czechoslovakia's neighbors Poland and Hungary had been much less democratic in the period between the wars, but both were noted for their fierce sense of national independence. Despite the fact that the Poles were Slavic, both countries were much less pro-Russian than the Czechs after World War II. But Poland and Hungary were both occupied by Soviet troops guarding communications with East Germany and Austria. Although coalition governments were sponsored by the Russians in both countries, and the peasant parties in both were too strong to be immediately disposed of by the Communists, there was no freedom in Poland or Hungary comparable to that in Czechoslovakia before the Communist coup of 1948.

In East Central Europe there came to be two "iron curtains," one against the west, another between Russia and the satellites, for in spite of its problems, the region was not one with which the Soviet leaders wanted their subjects to make comparisons.

There is no need to dwell upon the political dictatorships of East Central Europe, with their statesmen oriented toward Moscow, their frontier guards and forced-labor camps, their controlled press and radio, and their Marxian catechism in the schools. The larger significance of the experiment which now began was its revolutionary character: not a revolution from below, of peoples, but from above; an attempt to apply the rude Stalinist formula, an attempt to drag these peoples not only into the Soviet orbit, but into the twentieth century, Soviet version.

Between the wars the countries of East Central Europe had failed, for the most part, to solve their old problems of rural overpopulation and industrial underdevelopment. In that brief interlude they had made a start, but Western Europe had failed to appreciate the seriousness of the problem and in Europe's great civil war of 1939–1945 had failed to defend them or safeguard their ties to the west. Now it was Russia's turn to bully them into such progress that their allegiance to the Soviet system might eventually be won.

In comparison with the depression-ridden 1930's, the period which began in 1945 offered the East Central European countries certain economic advantages. In theory they could now work as one great area, with specialization according to the resources and talents of the parts. Russia offered the theoretical prospect of unlimited markets for their products. Now at last mass production could be justified. In practice, however, Russian exploitation and interference drained away all the benefits, so far as the ordinary citizen, irritated but helpless, could see. In the period of relative freedom from 1945 to 1948 all of the countries began economic development programs, but they were handicapped in some cases by huge Soviet reparations and in all cases by postwar shortages and inflation and popular dissatisfactions which the Communists used to justify more rapid nationalization of enterprises. After 1948 the Soviet Union was in complete control and synchronized the five- or six-year plans of all the countries into a program which was supposed by 1955 to increase heavy industry by 130–280 percent (depending on the country), consumer goods industry by 70–173 percent, agricultural output by 50–57 percent, and the standard of living by about 50 percent. This was to be accomplished by an annual investment of about 30 percent of the national income. In 1951, after the outbreak of the Korean War, the Soviet Union increased sharply its demands on the satellites.

In practice it proved impossible to increase agricultural output while investing little or nothing in the farms, enforcing a collectivization which the peasants resisted, and removing a large part of the labor force for work in factories without replacing it with farm machinery. Agricultural production sank, as it had in Russia under the early five-year plans. Industrial production increased remarkably. In general, the national income of the Peoples' Democracies increased by about 6 percent annually as compared with 4.5 percent in the United States in the same period. But this output consisted mainly of heavy machinery—producer goods—rather than consumer goods, which lagged far behind the planned quotas. Shortages of food and housing were severe. The standard of living of even privileged workers and officials was very low. Matters were made worse by the trade agreements and joint companies by which the Soviet Union forced its satellites to deliver to it large quantities of their products at extremely low prices. It is not unfair to say that Russia, while enforcing the sacrifices which paid for modernization in East Central Europe, treated the area as if it were a vast colony.

By 1953 the strain on the economies of the East Central European countries was too serious to be disguised. The populations, instead of being won over to the Soviet brand of socialism, were restless and resentful of foreign and bureaucratic control. They were making progress, but at enormous cost, and their national feelings were being dangerously tried.

Yugoslavia broke with Russia in 1948, long before this stage of intense strain had been reached. The break resulted partly from Soviet exploitation, partly from national pride and irritation at Soviet domineering, and partly from Marshal Tito's refusal to countenance Russia's planting of intelligence agents in the Yugoslav Communist party, army, and secret police. In a word, Tito's rebellion came because of his refusal to allow Yugoslavia's destiny to be decided by the Russian Communist leaders. It also came as a move of self-preservation when Stalin was preparing to replace him and his friends with more subservient men. Marshal Tito refused to submit to discipline from Moscow, and withstood, with American aid, the economic blockade imposed on Yugoslavia by Russia and the other members of the Cominform. Tito's position was not typical of East Central European Communist leaders. He and his party had not been placed in power by the Russians, and had not needed Russian aid in liberating Yugoslavia from the Germans. Any loyalty to Russia which Yugoslav Communists and others felt was distant and theoretical compared to the loyalty inspired by Tito and the other Yugoslav Communist leaders. Yugoslavia was far from Russia, and was not occupied by Soviet troops. "Titoism" was a form of national Communism which (for the moment) was not likely to spread to other parts of East Central Europe.

POSTWAR RUSSIAN SOCIETY

Second only to the drama of Russia's survival against the German wartime drive, and its expansion of influence after the war, was its continued economic and scientific development in the postwar decades. In the early days of the cold war there was a tendency in the western countries to underestimate, at least in public pronouncements, Russia's industrial and scientific capacity. This tendency was perhaps natural in view of the tremendous war damage in Russia and the Allied possession of the atomic bomb. There was also a rather widely held and uncritical assumption that the five-year plans had been a fiasco and that under the Soviet dictatorship technological advance was certain to be slow because of the handcuffing of education and pure science.

The Soviet system had certain advantages in industry and science which in time became apparent. The absence of democratic decisions about the investment of resources in production and research gave the Soviet planners much leeway. They could advance rapidly along selected paths even while depriving the citizens of ordinary comforts. This ability of the Communist party leaders to decide on goals which would increase their own and Russia's power was not unlimited, for they had to keep their ears attuned to public grumbling, but it permitted them just as swiftly to make available, when necessary, consumer goods which they considered desirable—for example radios and television sets. And they were able to concentrate on technological education and on research projects which yielded them the atomic bomb by 1949, the hydrogen bomb by 1953, by the summer and fall of 1957 an intercontinental ballistic missile and the famous *sputniks*, or earth satellites, and by January, 1959, a rocket shot past the moon.

The practice of storming selected heights continued to be applied in the fourth and fifth five-year plans—those of 1946–1950, and 1951–1955. A sixth five-year plan was begun in 1956 but in September, 1957, it was announced that this plan would be discontinued at the end of 1958 in favor of a seven-year plan which would run from 1959 through 1965.

This projected change was part of a reorganization of Soviet industrial management which became law in May, 1957, and was announced as a decentralization from federal ministries to regional councils. Such reorganization was evidence of dissatisfaction with the workings of the Russian economy. Nevertheless, objective students in the west acknowledged that by 1950 Russia had surpassed its prewar output in heavy industry and had passed all other countries except the United States in industrial output. In 1950 Russia still produced only 31 percent as much steel as was produced in the United States, and 23 percent as much electrical power, and 52 percent as much coal. By 1955 Russia and the East Central European Peoples' Democracies still produced little more than half as much of all kinds of goods as the United States, but some observers thought it possible that they would overtake the United States in total output, and perhaps even in per capita output, within the next two decades. The Russians themselves claimed an average annual increase of 11 percent in their national income for the years 1949 to 1956, an acceleration more than twice that of the United States. Objective western observers thought this figure to be exaggerated, but agreed that the Soviet rate of increase was high.

Soviet production of consumer goods continued to be low. Following Stalin's death there was talk of concessions to consumers, but nothing came of it, and the policy of heavy investment in producer goods was reaffirmed. In the 1950's, nevertheless, after production of consumer goods had caught up with prewar standards, life became somewhat easier. Housing remained inadequate, and food was scarce because Soviet agriculture continued to be the weakest link in the Soviet economy, but education and medical care were expanded. It is very difficult to evaluate the real wages—what workers can buy with their pay—of an unfamiliar culture, but it is clear that in terms of actual material rewards the standard of living of Russian workers in the 1950's remained much lower than that of workers in the United States. The same was true of their productivity as measured by output per man-hour, but it was rising steadily. Comparisons of averages are misleading, however, for in those enterprises upon which the Soviet Union's leaders chose to concentrate their efforts—for example in aviation and weapons—they were able to match the accomplishments of the United States.

Soviet agriculture was slow to recover after the war, and may not have reached its prewar output until 1953, the year of Stalin's death. This lag was serious because with the increased population there were more mouths to feed. Soviet agriculture had never been fully socialized, for the characteristic units, the collective farms (*kolkhozy*), were associations of peasants who were allowed to maintain private plots which they worked when not farming as teams in the common fields. After the war the collective farms were reduced in number and increased in size, the better to insure their control by party officials. After Stalin's death substantial concessions were made to agriculture in the form of increased investments in farm machinery, larger payments for crops, and larger money incomes for farmers. These concessions began to increase farm output, and so did a gigantic program of opening new lands to agriculture and the planting of new crops, in particular corn, as in the American Middle West.

There was also much talk of decentralization of planning, and of increasing the initiative of collective farmers, but in practice the party and the state maintained control. Indeed, there were signs that the Soviet leaders intended to work toward the transformation of collective farms into state farms (*sovkhozy*) worked by wage labor. This ending of the compromise in agriculture between the public and the private sectors had several times been discussed and then dropped because of public hostility, but the Soviet leaders continued stubbornly to edge in this direction, which they perhaps regarded as the only acceptable solution to the failure of the collective farms to produce in sufficient quantity in the past three decades.

HOUSE OF GOVERNMENT, MINSK. The architecture of this building in the capital of White Russia, near the Polish border, is decently modern. But the enormous statue of Lenin shows a tendency to confuse mere size with qualitative distinction. (Sovfoto)

Probably the most impressive indication of how Russian society was transformed in those decades is the enormous growth in urban population—from about 18 percent in 1926 (corresponding to the situation in the United States in 1860) to about 33 percent or 56,000,000 people in 1939, and then to 40 percent or about 80,000,000 people in 1953. In the course of this transformation a new "middle class" of managers and professional people grew up and began to provide its children with advantages in education and job placement which made them like privileged groups in other countries. At the same time, however, the great mass of Russians was undoubtedly being trained in the schools and in jobs to live in twentieth-century industrial society. Russian society was settling into sharply distinct classes, but there were still paths upward for the able, and most foreign observers agreed that the society was stable and in no danger of revolution from below. It was impossible to tell exactly what the Russian people thought of the system, but much evidence pointed toward general approval of the regime's social legislation, and acceptance of socialized heavy industry and wholesale trade, coupled with dislike of the personal insecurity of a system which did not provide individuals with lawful safeguards against political persecution, and annoyance with restraints on religion and freedom of expression.

POLITICS AFTER STALIN

Shortly before he died, Stalin enlarged the Politburo of the Central Committee of the Communist Party and changed its name to the Presidium. He was evidently preparing this most powerful group in Russia for some scheme having to do with his succession, and possibly meant to prepared the way with another purge. Stalin died in March, 1953. His most important lieutenants, the rival heirs to his power, announced the establishment of a "collective leadership" and reduced the size of the Presidium which was to be the arena of their struggle.

In this struggle Stalin's lieutenants had their individual strong points in the organizations which they headed. Beria, for example, was head of the secret police. Bulganin, although not a professional soldier, was the head of the army. Malenkov had Stalin's old job as Secretary of the Central Committee of the Communist party and was also premier. It was conceivable that the struggle for control of the Presidium might spread into the Central Committee, or even beyond the party into the police, army, and bureaucracy. Stalin's successors were at pains to prevent this. Their first concern was to keep the party in power in Russia and themselves in control of the party, and to this end they dramatized their collective guardianship of the legacy of Lenin and Stalin.

They had also, however, to defend themselves against each other. Malenkov was forced to give up his party secretaryship shortly after Stalin's death, and Nikita S. Khrushchev obtained it. Beria was executed by the others in July, 1953, if not before. General Zhukov, a hero of World War II, was brought back into the limelight as a supporter, and later a member of the Presidium, to balance with his popularity and influence in the army the disaffected followers of Beria. The latter were purged from key positions. In February, 1955, Malenkov was forced by Khrushchev to resign as premier and make a public confession of his incompetence. Later in the year Molotov, the foreign minister, was forced to confess to ideological shortcomings.

At the Twentieth Party Congress in February, 1956, Khrushchev presented a set of domestic and foreign policies designed to meet the problems of the Soviet Union and assure his own leadership. To this same Congress Khrushchev, in a sensational "Secret Report" which later found its way to the west and was widely published, attacked Stalin for his self-glorification, his personal dictatorship, and his criminal use of terror and purges against innocent party members. Although Khrushchev's control of the party officialdom on the regional and local levels had enabled him to "pack" the Central Committee and had assured him a subservient Party Congress, the "Secret Report" was a dangerous gesture. It was convenient to blame the crimes and follies of the past on Stalin, but there was some risk of arousing discussion of the qualifications of Stalin's heirs, who had been his lieutenants during the period of the crimes.

Khrushchev through the rest of 1956 encountered an unexpected turmoil of discussion at home and abroad both in consequence of his Report and of the "de-Stalinization" which occurred in the satellites and in foreign Communist parties. Matters were made worse by the Polish and Hungarian revolts (described below) against Stalinist and Soviet authority. In 1957, however, he was able to withstand attacks by his enemies in the Central Committee, including a comeback attempt by Malenkov and Molotov. He was also able to call to order the Russian youth and intellectuals who had taken too seriously the liberalization of discussion after the death of Stalin. He was even able to exclude from the Party Presidium Marshal Zhukov, whom many had regarded as the next dictator of Russia. Khrushchev, with his plebeian coarseness, his jokes, his threats, and his deceptive manner of a small-town politician, began to look like Stalin's successor.

THE "POLISH OCTOBER" AND THE HUNGARIAN REVOLUTION

The postwar Soviet empire in Eastern Europe received its first major shock with the defection of Tito in 1948, its second with the death of Stalin in 1953, and its third with the events following Khrushchev's Secret Report in 1956.

Tito's rebellion dramatized by contrast the lack of independence in the other Central European Peoples' Democracies. It also eased the pressure of the Communist bloc on Italy, Greece, and Turkey. Internally the Yugoslavs began to reappraise, not Communism, but the Stalinist version of Communism. There was a rush away from the collective farms, and efforts were made to de-centralize the management of industry. Cut off from its Communist neighbors, Yugoslavia had to readjust its economy, which was still that of an underdeveloped country. American aid was welcomed.

In the immediate aftermath of Stalin's death the Russian leadership tried to give an impression of a new deal both in Russia and the satellites. In Russia the prison labor camps were reduced in size and there was, as already noted, a real effort to repair the disastrous condition of agriculture. In the satellites there were at this time signs that the limits of endurance were being approached. In East Germany in June, 1953, there were revolts which were put down with Russian tanks. After Stalin's death there was a slackening of the emphasis on heavy industry, accompanied by concessions to peasants, wage earners, and consumers. The greatest concessions were made in East Germany, Poland, and Hungary. By late 1954 life was easier in the Peoples' Democracies. But when Khrushchev ousted Malenkov in 1955 there was a reemphasis on heavy industry (whose priority had not been abandoned). In Hungary the change was most noticeable, for the "liberal" Imre Nagy was replaced by the Stalinist Rakosi and the crackdown on free expression was severe. In Poland, on the other hand, only the Stalinist slogans were revived. The Poles did not abandon the slight liberalizations which had come in 1953. In Rumania, Bulgaria, and Czechoslovakia few concessions had been made in 1953 and there was little change in 1955.

On the other hand, Khrushchev's advance toward the Soviet summit brought a dramatic reconciliation with Tito's Yugoslavia. In May, 1955, Khrushchev led a party of Soviet dignitaries to Belgrade. The recognition that Tito had been wronged by Stalin prepared the way for Khrushchev's attack on Stalin in the Secret Report of February, 1956, and for the recognition at the same Twentieth Party Congress that there were "several roads to socialism." By this time Khrushchev had decided upon a program which would permit greater economic specialization in the satellites, and somewhat more political autonomy. At home in Russia there would be emphasis on the imminence of a better standard of living. In the underdeveloped areas of the world there would be military and foreign aid programs, and emphasis on peace. It was asserted that Marxists did not consider war inevitable, and that socialism could be achieved by peaceful means in democratic countries.

This new set of policies, and particularly the "de-Stalinization" which followed the news of Khrushchev's (no longer) Secret Report, led to unexpected ferment in the satellites as well as in Russia itself. In June, 1956, riots against working conditions at Poznan, in Poland, developed into demonstrations against Soviet domination. The demonstrations were suppressed, but in the ensuing trials there was extraordinary freedom of expression. In October, 1956, the Polish Communist party ousted its Stalinist members and restored to leadership Wladyslaw Gomulka, who had been kept in jail by the Stalinists for the past four years. In spite of Soviet threats and a flying visit from Khrushchev, the Poles held firm, removed the Russian watchdog Marshal Rokossovsky from their Politburo and from his command of the Polish armed forces, and freed Cardinal Wyszynski from prison. The Russians hesitated, but then allowed the courageous Poles to get away with it. The "Polish October" was an inspiration to others and an exhibition of remarkable national solidarity. Gomulka, around whom the resistance rallied, was a sincere Communist, and the partisans of Cardinal Wyszynski were very numerous in this Catholic country, but the Poles did not squander their determination in internal quarrels. A remarkable renaissance of free discussion occurred, and Polish intellectuals were able to some extent to renew their ties with the west.

In Hungary the same fundamental economic and national and political reasons for opposition to the Stalinist regime existed as in Poland. On October 23, 1956, Hungarian demands for reform led to public manifestations, attempted repression, and insurrection. Hungarian troops sided with the students and workers and general public in an attempt to drive the Russians from the capital.

During the disorders Imre Nagy, known as a national Communist, became premier and tried to restore peace with promises of democracy in the party, a higher standard of living, and the adjustment of the economy to Hungarian conditions. The disorders continued. Workers' councils were formed in the factories and a general strike took place. The revolution spread through the countryside. Nagy now promised to negotiate with the U.S.S.R. the withdrawal of Soviet troops, and to form a democratic government in which the traditional Peasant and Socialist parties could take part. By the end of October a coalition government had been formed, Cardinal Mindszenty had been freed, and the Soviet troops were withdrawing from Budapest. The Soviet Union, on October 30, announced its intention to treat the Peoples' Democracies as equals and to revise the Warsaw Pact—the eastern counterpart of NATO—so that Soviet troops could be withdrawn from their soil.

In a speech on the next day, October 31, Imre Nagy announced that Hungary would withdraw from the Warsaw Alliance. On November 1, as Socialist and Peasant party newspapers reappeared in the streets of Budapest, Nagy told the Soviet ambassador that Hungary was withdrawing from the Warsaw Alliance. He also proclaimed Hungarian neutrality, and appealed for the protection of the United Nations. On that same day, however, and on the following days, new Soviet troops were entering Hungary and occupying the key roads, railroads, and airports. On November 4 they attacked Budapest. A pro-Soviet government under Janos Kadar was set up. A bloody repression began, against which the Hungarians fought alone with unexampled tenacity which turned into weeks of passive resistance and strikes when they could no longer resist with arms. The west and the United Nations, bemused by the simultaneous Suez crisis and the Anglo-French-Israeli invasion of Egypt, condemned the Soviet Union but did not intervene. Scarcely anyone in the west thought that military action which probably would have started another world war was justified. There were some who asked whether the tragedy could have been forestalled by diplomacy late in October, before the Soviet troops reentered Hungary with the determination to put down the revolution; but no one knew whether the Russian leaders had ever really hesitated. In the end it was clear that they had decided that no regime which passed beyond Communism could be allowed in Hungary.

Meanwhile more than 100,000 Hungarians had taken refuge in the west.

Tito's position had been suddenly highlighted by the explosion: he had endorsed the Soviet intervention, making clear his refusal to countenance Nagy's abandonment of the Communist party's monopoly of political power. In the following year Tito's continued persecution of his heretical lieutenant, Milovan Djilas, reemphasized this position. In Poland the "national" Communist Gomulka had adopted a similar view: his position was much more difficult than Tito's, but few doubted his sincerity. Gomulka's plight, and Poland's, continued in the following years to remind the west, and perhaps the Russians as well, that the division of Europe contained terrible dangers. For what would have happened, and what would happen still, if East Germany revolted against Communist rule as the Hungarians had? Could the people of West Germany stand by while their fellow nationals were suppressed, like the Hungarians? And if West Germany moved to confront the Russians, would they not take Western Europe and the United States into another war?

After the Polish October and the Hungarian Revolution, the form of Soviet control of East Central Europe could not be the same again. Briefly the curtain had been lifted and the anguish, ferment, and development in that broad area had been glimpsed. Russian efforts to direct this development might yet succeed, but for a long time the Russians would be unable to count on the loyalty and military might of this region. To the peoples of the west the spirit of their fellow-Europeans on the other side was heartening, but it was also a reminder that western indifference or illusions about the future could invite disaster.

56

POSTWAR REGIMES:
THE WEST

WORLD WAR II was a catastrophe which killed millions of Europeans, wrecked the economic life of Europe, tore apart its society, and impaired the vigor of the survivors. It might have been expected that the war would be followed by the utter collapse or the thorough remodelling of Western European institutions. But it was not.

Within five years after the war, it had become clear that the peoples west of the Iron Curtain were, so far as institutions went, conservatively disposed. The regimes which took form bore a remarkable resemblance to those of the era before World War I. Only Spain and Portugal, previously equipped with dictatorships and little affected by the war, continued to live under regimes which were not conventional parliamentary democracies. In the countries which escaped invasion—Great Britain, Ireland, Sweden, Switzerland—the prewar constitutions survived intact. In Denmark, the constitutional monarchy had continued to operate under the German occupation and returned to normal after it. The governments of most of the occupied countries had escaped before the German advance and continued to function in exile—this was true of Norway, Greece, the Netherlands, Luxembourg, and Belgium. The exiled governments re-entered the capitals after the Germans left, and took control with remarkably little difficulty. But in the three largest continental countries there were more complicated situations. In West Germany the Nazi state was destroyed altogether and governmental functions taken over by the occupying powers. Constitutional democracy had to be constructed from the ground up. In Italy, on the other hand, the continuity of the state suffered no interruption after the fall of Fascism. The House of Savoy, surviving this vicissitude, restored the pre-fascist state of things, and a legally summoned constituent assembly eventually rewrote the constitution and presided over the transition to a republic. In France, the government of Marshal Pétain, German-dominated and authoritarian, was swept away as France was liberated. Its place was taken by a provisional government which had been formed in London and in the French colonies under the leadership of General Charles de Gaulle. The provisional government took control of the administrative apparatus and called a constituent assembly which wrote the constitution of the Fourth Republic, which differed little from the Third. And in the end, these three countries, like those where no constitutional change was involved, showed that free Europe was faithful to the political ideals and arrangements which had been bequeathed to it by the nineteenth-century liberals.

This tranquil acceptance of the old forms may be attributed partly to the influence of the British and Americans. In Greece and Italy, for example, important local movements fought for social and constitutional revolutions; in the presence of the British and American armies, such movements were frustrated, and essentially conservative regimes subsisted. The survival or restoration of the old forms of government may also be ascribed in part to the role of the Communists. In most underground resistance movements during World War II the Communists formed a conspicuous and energetic part. They were duly rewarded with full political freedom and with office in postwar cabinets. But every western government was increasingly suspicious of them, and as the shape of postwar Communist regimes in the east became clear along with the subservience of western Communists to Russia, even leftist politicians in the west tended to eschew common action with the Communists. The split in the forces which sought a major rebuilding of regimes and social orders helped to salvage the traditional system in the west. In this way Communism became, paradoxically, an agency of conservatism. Finally, constitutional democracy profited from the dismaying results of experiments with other forms. After the horrors of the war, totalitarianism seemed much less attractive than before.

Most regimes, then, retained or revived the traditional forms of parliamentary democracy, and there was no sudden or violent remodeling of western societies or economies. But great changes were nonetheless taking place. In almost every Western European country, very extensive programs of social and economic reform within the old structures were carried out. In all of them, the sphere of government economic action was extended in partnership with private investors. In most of them there was extensive new social legislation and planning for economic development which became part of a new and expanded attitude toward freedom. This reflected in part the price which was paid to Socialist parties and to working class opinion for their acceptance of the old order. It reflected, too, the sudden changes and harsh realities of the war-battered countries.

The remarkable fact was that thirteen years after the end of a devastating war, Western Europe was far more prosperous, stable, and united than on the eve of the war. It had adapted the old forms of constitutional government to the demands of democracy, social security, and an urban society. If its achievements more incomplete and precarious, they were nonetheless proof of continuing vitality and ingenuity.

GREAT BRITAIN'S QUIET REVOLUTION

In Great Britain in 1945, as in 1918, a general election was held on the morrow of the European war. The outcome was dramatic: the Labor party captured 393 seats in the House of Commons, a majority of 186. The Conservative prime minister, Winston Churchill, was obliged to resign, and Clement Attlee, the Labor leader, took his place. Attlee and his principal colleagues were not new to the responsibilities of government. The new foreign minister, Ernest Bevin, and several others, had served for five years in the wartime coalition cabinet. Moreover, the change of government meant no break in the continuity of British foreign policy. But it did mean that there would be a strenuous effort to undertake social reform and to carry out, at long last, the major demands of British socialists.

The "dismissal" (as Churchill bitterly called it) of their wartime hero and his party by the British people reflected dissatisfaction with the Conservatives, who had been in effective control of the government for almost fifteen years. In 1945 the British people voted for new ideas and experiments and social improvements. For the next six years they got them. The enactments of the Labor government contributed to a social revolution, albeit a peaceful and quiet one.

The reforms fell into two main categories, nationalization and welfare legislation. Nationalization was a traditional precept of all socialists and had long been a principal demand of British Laborites. It meant the ownership and operation by public authorities of some of the main industries, and the substitution of "public interest" for the profit motive of private businessmen as the guiding principle of operation. The most important things which the Labor government nationalized were the Bank of England, the railways, the coal mines, public utilities (especially the electrical and gas industries), trucking, and the steel industry. The owners were compensated at approximately the market prices of their holdings. The nationalized industries were organized as boards, or authorities, independent of the cabinet and only indirectly under the control of Parliament. Most of them continued to operate in a fashion not very different from the way they had under private ownership.

In the case of some of these industries, nationalization was neither so revolutionary nor so controversial as might have been supposed. The Bank of England was already in effect a public institution; its changed status was hardly more than a change of title. The railroads and coal mines had been losing money for years, and the Conservatives themselves (as well as the mine owners) were perfectly ready to accept the nationalization. Moreover, the road toward consolidation and control of industry had been opened by the Conservatives in earlier years when they had sponsored state-chartered monopolies for shipping, air transport, radio broadcasting, and other industries.

Welfare legislation affected more people than the nationalizations. Here, too, the area of controversy between the two parties was rather narrow, for the Conservative-led coalition had already mapped out a very large extension of the

British social security program. The Laborites went further, however, and the measures which were eventually enacted were about as complete a system of public welfare measures as could be imagined—the phrase used to describe it, "cradle to grave," was apt. From before birth, when expectant mothers were provided with medical care, special foods, and compensated vacation, until death, when funeral expenses were provided by the state, the individual Briton was insured against every hazard and insecurity possible. The British went in one respect far beyond what any free society had previously ventured: they gave every citizen free medical care. The National Health Act, in 1947, was described by its opponents as "socialized medicine." What it did was to provide that doctors should accept "panels" of patients, for whose treatment they would be paid by the state. Doctors were not required to accept panel patients, and patients could choose their own doctors within certain limits. Their choice was completely free if they wished to pay the usual fees and continue to operate in the usual way. Medicines, appliances like glasses and false teeth, and hospital treatment were all provided free to everyone in Great Britain—including foreigners. The National Health Act was bitterly attacked. Many (though not all) doctors disliked it. The cost was huge, and the burdens to the treasury and the taxpayer were viewed with alarm by some economists. The Labor party, indeed, was split when it became necessary to revise the act by requiring small payments for some medicines and appliances—largely to reduce waste and frivolous use of the service. The Minister of Health, the fiery Welshman, Aneurin Bevan, resigned in protest, and it shortly appeared that his dislike of payments for false teeth was a symptom of his general conviction that the Labor government was far too moderate in its entire program. He and his followers became leaders of a radical group which thereafter for some years declined to cooperate with the rest of the party and denounced its leadership and its program.

But in its main outlines the National Health Act was undoubtedly accepted by most of the nation. Opposition in the medical profession gradually declined, and the extraordinary improvement in the physical condition of the British people, indicated by dramatic declines in infant mortality and tuberculosis, helped to convert conservatives. When the Conservative party took office again in 1951, the National Health Service continued unaltered in its major outlines.

The six years of the Labor government saw a drastic change in the character of British society. The old class structure, better defined and more rigid than in most of Europe, began to break down. The distinction between the working classes and the well-to-do began to diminish, especially with respect to opportunity for advancement and level of income. This was in part the consequence of heavy taxation, and to some extent this taxation was the consequence of the Labor government's expensive welfare program. But to a greater extent the social changes were the result of forces over which the government had little control. Taxes were bound to be high in the postwar age, whatever the nature of the government. Something like four billion dollars was collected and spent by the British government each year after the war. What Labor sought out of doctrine, Conservatives would have had to accept out of necessity.

Taxes levelled large incomes down. Full employment and rising wages levelled them up. The needs of reconstruction, the backed-up demand for consumer goods, the attempt to recapture lost markets, the continuing prosperity of the free world after 1945, all prevented any depression in Great Britain. Wages in general rose faster than prices, which meant that the condition of the working classes improved while that of the middle and upper classes remained relatively straitened.

The most noticeable feature of Great Britain's situation in the decade after World War II was not its quiet social revolution or its socialist experiments, but rather its distressing international economic position. In spite of full employment and rising prices and other earmarks of a boom at home, the British economy was in a difficult and sometimes a perilous situation. The problem was the product of progressive British losses over the decades: loss of exports, resulting from foreign competition, declining efficiency in home industries, and tariffs overseas; and loss of investments abroad, which had been sold in 1914–1918 and further liquidated after 1939 to pay for war materials. These losses meant a loss of income in foreign exchange with which to pay for imports of foods, consumer goods, and raw materials for British industry. By 1945, when British exports declined almost to the vanishing point, the shortage of foreign exchange, particularly dollars, had become acute and threatened to become disastrous.

Several things had to be done, and were done. A loan of $3.75 billion was secured from the United States in 1946, and was later supplemented by American aid under the Marshall Plan. Public money was poured into British industry to pay for re-equipment and modernization. Government assistance of all sorts was extended to exporters. In 1949, with great reluctance, the pound was devalued from about $4 to less than $3. Wartime economic controls were maintained, or even extended, in order to reduce consumption in Great Britain. Reduction of consumption meant fewer imports, and more goods available for export. As a consequence, for many dreary years after the war, rationing continued. This permitted a fair (and adequate) distribution of foodstuffs, but it was aggravating to the populace. Not until after the return of the Conservatives was food rationing finally abandoned, with the end of meat rationing in 1954.

After 1949, despite many ups and downs, the British situation began to improve. By the early 1950's, British exports had surpassed any previous records. Both industry and marketing were more vigorous and better equipped than ever before. The dollar gap was not yet closed; it was kept to a minimum by the surviving controls and compensated by American grants and loans. On occasions in the middle 'fifties, exports actually exceeded imports for a few months. The British economy was a going concern again.

In 1950 the huge majority of the Labor party was greatly reduced although the popular vote for Labor actually rose, in an increasing electorate. In 1951 another general election was fought, and this time won by the Conservatives. Churchill returned to power, and continued as prime minister until he retired in 1955 and was succeeded first by Anthony Eden and later by Harold Macmillan. The general election which followed his retirement increased the Conservative majority, although the two British parties continued to be almost equally divided in the nation.

The Conservative governments in most respects followed the policies of the Laborites. The steel industry, and part of the trucking industry, were denationalized, but few of the basic changes of the period from 1945 to 1951 were reversed. And the revolution which was evening out British class distinctions and tending toward a much greater equality of income proceeded unabated.

These changes did not involve any considerable alterations in the British constitution. The Labor government in 1949 restricted the powers of the House of Lords, unchanged since the Parliament Act of 1911. Since that act, the hereditary Lords could hold up a bill approved by Commons for the length of a single parliamentary session. This power was abolished, after the Lords tried to forestall nationalization of the steel industry. The old forms and pageantry continued, however. In 1953 Queen Elizabeth II was crowned as her predecessors had been crowned in Westminster Abbey, symbolizing the continuity of British institutions. But if the form of the constitution changed little in a generation, some of its substance did. The control of the legislature over the vast and growing administration was made more difficult by the growth in size and functions of the civil service. Cabinet members tended, more and more, to be at the mercy of the subordinates who provided them with information and who, in practice, were responsible for the making of much policy. On the whole, however, despite the vastness of the social changes wrought after 1945, the most extraordinary feature of British history was the persistence of the traditional aspects of its national life.

FROM THE FOURTH TO THE FIFTH FRENCH REPUBLIC

In many respects the experiences of France after World War II contrasted sharply with those of Great Britain. The war had unified and solidified the British nation. It divided the French, as had so many of France's experiences in the previous century and a half. In 1945 diverse tendencies of thought were evident. There were many who longed for a restoration of something like the Third Republic. Others, while deploring the wartime Vichy regime's collaboration with the Nazis, shared its clerical and paternalistic inclinations. There had been, in the wartime Resistance Movement, generous and idealistic hopes for the regeneration of French society. People of all sorts had taken part. The French Communists, especially well organized for underground activity, had lived down their reputation for treasonableness and defeatism earned during the period of the Nazi-Soviet pact. At the close of the war the three greatest Resistance parties, the Catholic *Mouvement Républicain Populaire,* the Socialists, and the Communists drew three fourths of the votes in elections to a constituent assembly, and they appeared to be on the verge of making France over. But it was soon apparent that the traditional France of peasants and small businessmen would again find its voice and that the victorious left-wing coalition could not be held together.

The war had left France in poverty and devastation. Although French battle casualties in 1939–1945 were much smaller than in World War I, the human losses were very great. Over a million and a half Frenchmen were captive in Germany by the end of the war, either as military prisoners, as political victims in concentration camps, or as forced laborers. Physically, France had suffered six years of disrepair aggravated by German plunder, and this had been capped by the destruction which accompanied the Allied invasion. These conditions, following so soon after the horrors of World War I, were a profound shock to the French nation, and their effect was aggravated by the humiliations of 1940 and by the fear that France's primacy among nations was lost beyond recall.

But French economic recovery was rapid and, once reconstruction had been completed, expansion was dramatic. The French economy was more abundantly provided with raw materials and food than the British. Considering the costs of war and the instability of the government, French economic history in the dozen years and more after 1945 verged on the miraculous. The most crucial figure in modern economics is that which represents labor productivity—that is, the amount of goods a man can turn out in one working hour. As remarked in Chapter 54, French productivity rose 37 percent from 1938 to 1948, a rise as great as any in Europe and greater than in most other countries. The French standard of living was higher by 1958 than it had ever been.

There remained, however, grave economic problems in France. The economy was highly regulated and protected, which meant that many inefficient enterprises were kept alive. French exports rarely kept up with rapidly expanding imports which a rich and goods-hungry population insisted on. Moreover, inflation of the franc was caused by the pressure of consumers' demand, which tended to drive up prices, and by the lavishness of government spending. The rising prices caused social distress, particularly to the vast numbers of Frenchmen who had fixed sources of income like veterans' pensions, and to large sections of the wage earners, whose pay increases never caught up with the rising prices. As a result the economic atmosphere in France was one of dizzy but precarious boom.

It was clear that two world wars and the social and political conflicts which attended them had left France with abundant national energy. Its vitality was illustrated in its art and literature, which commanded, as always, the highest respect, and in a purely biological but basic way in a substantial increase in the French birth-rate. But this renewed vitality was not matched by any comparable repair of French political life. The economic successes, intellectual attainments, and rising population were accompanied by a stultified government and parliament and by disasters in the French empire.

The Fourth Republic was born out of the immediate postwar situation. General Charles de Gaulle, who had left France in 1940 and issued a stirring invocation to patriots to continue the struggle against Germany, returned to Paris with the liberating allied armies in 1944, along with a provisional government built up in exile and strengthened from the French internal Resistance. In some ways the de Gaulle regime was a success. It took over the French administration—basically unaltered since before the war—smoothly and efficiently, so that there was no disruption of government services despite the appalling dislocations of war. The Resistance movements, in part strongly Communist and all highly adventurous, were quietly and effectively disbanded as attention was turned to the constituent assembly of 1945 and the making of a new constitution.

But the de Gaulle provisional government and the constituent assembly proved to be merely a preface to a restoration of all the old forms of political life. The elimination of the Resistance as an effective force in public life was followed by the elimination of General de Gaulle himself in January, 1946. The general resigned when he found majority sentiment in the constituent assembly turning against his views, which favored a strong executive. Leaning too far toward the opposite extreme of legislative omnipotence, the assembly was itself repudiated by a referendum a few months later. It was the ghost of the defunct Third Republic, and not the ideas of General de Gaulle, which guided a second constituent assembly as it made the Fourth Republic.

Both under de Gaulle's leadership and under the following ministries, many of whose leaders were familiar from the days of the Third Republic, important social legislation was passed similar to that of the Labor government in Britain. Before the coalition of the M.R.P., Socialists, and Communists broke up, it nationalized some of the basic industries and enterprises, including part of the automobile industry, electricity, coal mines, railways, steamships, air lines, and major banks. In addition, extensive welfare legislation added to the social insurance programs of the 1930's. The immediate postwar era took up where the Popular Front had left off.

The constitution which was finally accepted by the French electorate in the autumn of 1946 closely resembled the constitution of the Third Republic, with certain amendments. The control of the parliament over the ministry was extended. The powers of the president and of the upper house were reduced. Special chambers were added to deal with social and economic problems and with the French colonial empire. The Chamber of Deputies became the National Assembly, symbolizing its increased prestige and power, and the Senate became the Council of the Republic, with lessened authority. The French colonial empire, which had contributed much to the fight against the Germans, was now called the French Union—a term implying a freely associated commonwealth which did not materialize.

The most dramatic feature of the Fourth Republic was the instability of its ministries, most of which were defeated after brief stays in office by adverse votes in the Assembly. This instability was in some ways more apparent than real. To a large extent the real work of governing was done by the administration, the civil servants who formed the permanent staffs of ministries. But the instability was unedifying and inconvenient, and the civil servants were more adept at repeating old practices than at formulating new policies to cope with the problems of the postwar world. It was quite clear that coordinated decisive action was impossible if France was to be periodically without a cabinet and a prime minister.

Under the new constitution of 1946 the same multiplicity of parties as in the Third Republic persisted. Until the spring of 1947 the three powerful parties which had made the constitution and passed the early postwar welfare legislation—the Catholic M.R.P., the Socialists, and the Communists—continued to work together. With the deepening of the cold war in 1947 the Communists were ousted from the ministry. They became a powerful opposition force. At about the same time a "Gaullist" movement which was to persist for several years took shape. It was made up of followers of General de Gaulle, most of them far more reactionary than their leader.

Since the Communists on the left and the Gaullists on the right were in their various ways opponents of the republic's parliamentary regime, the remaining deputies of the center—the so-called Third Force—had to band together if there was to be any parliamentary majority and any legal government. This most of them did in spite of their many party affiliations and differences of opinion. They were obliged, indeed, to keep banding together over and over again in support of various ministerial combinations with the same familiar faces and the same tendency to fall apart at the slightest suggestion of decisive movement in any direction. All they could do was save the republic from its internal opponents, not solve its grave problems, such as tax reform, inflation, the housing shortage, and the progressive disintegration of the colonial empire in a seemingly endless series of hopeless wars which sapped the nation's resources. It was obviously very difficult to agree upon the personnel of a cabinet or a program that would satisfy both the working class Socialists and big business interests, or the Catholic M.R.P. and the anti-clerical Radicals; or the internationalist leftist parties, with their sympathies for colonial aspirations and suppressed peoples, and the chauvinistic, imperialist rightists. These difficulties persisted after the decline of the Gaullist movement in the 1950's and the rise and decline of another right-wing—and more fascistic—faction led by Pierre Poujade. The wonder is that France was governed as well as it was, and in particular that it made the remarkable economic recovery that it did.

In the twelve years of the Fourth Republic, there was only one important effort to build within the constitutional structure a strong government with a popular leader and with definite ideas and policies. This took place in 1954, when the Radical party leader, Pierre Mendès-France, formed a government which promised—and provided—decisive action. Mendès-France was an imaginative statesman who defied classification in the traditional categories of right-center-left. His principal success was to settle the colonial war then raging in Indochina, and prepare the way for a settlement with Tunisia. This he did, with dramatic success, though at the cost of sacrificing French control. He attracted a following of vigorous and able men, predominantly young and original in their views. But Mendès-France was unpopular with the Assembly and even with many of his own party. He was regarded as dangerous, as ambitious, as arrogant, even as "unrepublican," which meant insufficiently solicitous of the power of the Assembly. His opposition to European unity earned him the dislike of many natural allies. His government fell after less than a year.

The second and final effort to adopt strong policies in France came also as the result of colonial troubles. By 1958, nationalist rebels in Algeria had been waging a costly, bloody civil war for many months. The inability of successive ministries to solve this problem had bred in the French army and among many private citizens, especially those resident in Algeria, the conviction that only a change of regime in France itself could bring an end to the struggle and stave off the collapse of the remainder of the French Union and particularly the loss of the Sahara region where oil had recently been found. In May, 1958, the army in Algeria seized control of civil government from the agents of the Republic, and demanded the ending of party government in France and the return of General de Gaulle. Powerless to oppose this military "strike," which threatened to spread to the French homeland, the President and Assembly surrendered to the show of force, and de Gaulle emerged from his twelve-year retirement to take office as prime minister with extraordinary powers. He promised drastic reforms in the political structure of France and its overseas possessions. The first step was taken with the preparation of a new constitution, for a Fifth Republic, intended to strengthen and stabilize the executive power in France and to satisfy the ambitions of colonies by providing them with extensive powers of self-government.

The constitution was submitted for approval to the voters in September, 1958. It was approved, by 80 percent of those who voted in France, and by all the overseas territories except the little African colony of Guinea, which voted for independence instead. The results of the referendum strikingly affirmed the exasperation of the French with the inadequacy of their institutions, and their hope that de Gaulle would remedy the situation. Election of a new national assembly in November and of General de Gaulle as President in December, 1958, set the Fifth French Republic on its way. For the first time since 1851, when Louis Napoleon's dictatorship was set up, France backed a strong leader and looked toward a regime with strong executive authority in the hope of producing a political revival which could match its remarkable economic progress.

THE ITALIAN REPUBLIC

The Italian people, in the years after 1945, installed a stable democratic regime under whose guidance the nation made imposing progress toward prosperity and economic growth. These achievements were reached over singular obstacles. Constitutional government had never operated smoothly nor been very satisfactory in Italy. Democracy, achieved with the universal male suffrage of 1912, had had a brief and turbulent life before Mussolini seized the government in 1922. The long years of Fascism had repressed all dissenting political activity and independent thought; whatever opposition existed had been among exiles or conspirators. World War II brought terrible physical devastation and an extremely confusing and demoralizing political situation in its last years. The static society of Fascism had bred in many quarters a passionate desire for social change. Despite the confusion and the inexperience with responsible government, stability was rapidly achieved. No sudden change took place in the very old-fashioned structure of Italian society, and postwar institutions displayed remarkable fidelity to the traditions of Cavour's Italy.

Mussolini had been disowned by the Fascist Grand Council and dismissed by King Victor Emmanuel III in July, 1943. The Italians had by then suffered an almost unbroken series of defeats, and the Allies had landed on Sicily. Clearly the Fascist decision to enter the war had been a disastrous mistake and public sympathy lay in large part with the enemy and against the German ally. The king appointed as the new premier Marshal Pietro Badoglio, an extremely conservative soldier, and in September, he surrendered to the Allies. The Germans immediately occupied the northern half of the peninsula, including Rome. Mussolini, liberated from his prison by German parachutists, was installed in the north as head of an "Italian Social Republic," which was, however, patently and totally a German puppet regime. The tragic farce of Fascism did not reach its final end until, in April, 1945, as the Germans surrendered in northern Italy, Mussolini was captured and executed by partisans and his mutilated remains hanged from a lamppost in a square in Milan.

In the Allied-occupied areas in the south the king's government was running into grave difficulties. The restoration of political liberty had generated enormous popular enthusiasm and general expectation of the sweeping away of both the political system of Fascism and the social system of aristocrats, landowners, big businessmen, and bosses which had flourished under it. The Resistance Movement, ferocious and popular, was composed in large part of Communists and other social revolutionaries. The pre-Fascist political parties, re-emerging with remarkable speed, demanded a government reflecting popular opinion. Such demands were partly met by a cabinet representing the parties, replacing that of Badoglio, and in June, 1944, the unpopular king turned over his power to his son, Humbert, who became prince regent. Ivanoe Bonomi, who had been prime minister in 1921, resumed the post.

The appointment of an elderly pre-Fascist politician symbolized the extraordinary stability of the party system from constitutional days of a generation earlier, and in the end it was the parties which decided the fate of the nation, prevailing over the ebullient Resistance Movement. The major parties were the following, in approximate order of strength. First in 1945 as it had been in 1922, was the Popolari, the Catholic social party led in earlier days by Don Sturzo and now renamed the Christian Democrats. Originally the Popolari had been a left-wing Catholic party, reflecting the Catholic-socialist program of labor unions and of the encyclicals of Leo XIII. The reorganized Christian Democrats, while retaining a program of social reform and remaining impeccably democratic and staunchly anti-Fascist, now however began to attract the support of conservatives who found both Fascism and the old sort of conservatism represented by Badoglio and the king so discredited as to be politically dead. The Christian Democrats early came to have a mixed following of businessmen, former Fascists, clergy, aristocrats, peasants, working class people, and Catholic intellectuals. It included many who sought to preserve the social order and some who wanted to change it, united by hostility to Marxist socialism and Communism and by devotion to the Church and its interests.

As it had been in 1922, the second largest party was the Socialist. The Socialists were an orthodox Marxist party, heirs of the relatively moderate wing of the pre-1922 party, dedicated to freedom and democracy. Like most progressive parties in the moment of enthusiasm of United Nations victory, they were prepared to cooperate with the Communists. But unlike the French Socialist party, the Italian Socialists did not experience a united revulsion against Communism when its postwar nature came to be revealed by its support of the repressive Soviet policies in Eastern Europe. Instead of breaking with the Communists, as the French and German Socialists did, the Italian party split on the question of cooperation with them. The larger portion, led by Pietro Nenni, remained loyal to the Communists and formed a solid front with them from 1946 on. The smaller part, led by Giuseppe Saragat, broke off in January, 1947, to form an anti-Communist, nonrevolutionary workers party, which generally supported the Christian Democratic government. Both parts lost strength in subsequent elections.

The third party in size was the Communist, and it shortly became the second. Like other European Communist parties, it attracted support by its fierce and gallant struggle against the Nazis, and many people in Italy who were not revolutionary or Marxist voted for it as a matter of course as being the party most likely to undertake aggressive reforms of the antiquated and oppressive social order. The Italian party was the largest in the free world, and continued, despite many shocks and losses, to command a steady electoral strength of about 30 percent of the voters.

There were two smaller groups among the anti-Fascist parties which emerged after Mussolini's fall. One, the Liberal, was by mid-twentieth century standards conservative, standing for free enterprise, private property, and maintenance of the monarchy. The other, the Republican, advocated overthrow of the monarchy and other progressive measures. It was anti-Communist and anti-Fascist, and it attracted the support of many intellectuals, but it never secured a mass electoral following. A third small party, elusively neo-Fascist, was founded after the war. Called "the party of the common man," it had a brief success and then fell into obscurity. Other reactionary or fascist movements proved equally unstable and short-lived.

In November, 1945, Alcide de Gasperi, the vigorous leader of the Christian Democrats, was appointed prime minister of a coalition cabinet composed of the five anti-fascist parties. The political history of Italy in the next three years was largely the story of de Gasperi's widening control of the government, his disbanding of the revolutionary Resistance Movements, his ejection of the Communists and Left Socialists, the writing of a new republican constitution under Christian Democratic auspices, and the preparation of the elections of March, 1948, which saw the party win an absolute majority in the new Chamber of Deputies—the first time in the history of Italy that any single party had won control of the legislature.

These successes were remarkable in view of the diverse character of the Christian Democrats, but the party had a number of assets. It was strongly supported by the United States (which was of vital importance, since the economy of Italy was entirely dependent upon aid from its conqueror). It was even more strongly supported by the Church, whose influence was enormous. It appealed to all conservative opinion as the least revolutionary of the mass parties, and to some progressive opinion as being impeccably democratic and committed to some measure of social reform including division of the lands of the great estates among the peasants who farmed them. At the same time, it was hospitable to private enterprise and was supported by most businessmen as the least dangerous of several unpleasant alternatives. Especially after de Gasperi's retirement, in 1953, there was a tendency for the party to divide into a right, a left, and a center, but his successors as prime minister, Mario Scelba and Antonio Segni, held the Christian Democrats together, and they continued to dominate the Italian government, either alone or in coalition with the Liberals, Republicans, and Right Socialists.

The new constitution, written in 1946–1947, was the work of all parties, but chiefly of the Christian Democrats. It bore a remarkable resemblance to the *Statuto* of 1848. There was a popularly elected Chamber, with a cabinet responsible to it, and a Senate elected by indirect vote, replacing the old House of Lords. The monarchy was replaced (after a referendum in 1946, in which a bare majority of voters chose to oust the House of Savoy) with a president, ornamental rather than powerful. The old system of administrative centralization, one of the principal sources of complaint in the years from 1861 to 1922, was preserved. Provision was made for the establishment of semi-federal, self-governing provinces, but only two were ever set up—in Sicily and in the German-speaking South Tyrol. The largest change from the *Statuto* was the inclusion in the constitution of 1947 of Mussolini's Lateran Treaty with the Pope. Italy's Republic, in contrast to the old constitutional monarchy, was bound to cordial relations with the Church.

The most important facts of Italian history after its devastation and humiliation in World War II were not, however, political, but economic. In Italy, as in Britain and France, remarkable economic progress was achieved, and this accounted in large part for the unexampled stability of the Republic. Despite the war wreckage, Italian production in 1953 had increased by more than half over the 1938 level, and the pace quickened in the next few years. The expanding output was matched by rapid reconstruction of war damage, by an enormous increase in housing, by a rising trade and commerce. By 1958 Italy was not only much richer than it had ever been, but its industry was striking out in new directions, its currency and price levels were steady, and its rate of capital investment extraordinarily high for a country poor in natural resources. The discovery of oil at many points in the country promised the possibility of the growth of an entirely new basic industry.

Problems persisted. The old disparity between the rich, progressive north and the impoverished, backward south was still evident. There was still a shortage of schools. There was still a rapidly increasing population, mainly in the south, which outstripped both employment possibilities and confidence in the future. Although the birth-rate was slowing down, births still outnumbered deaths by almost half a million, annually. Unemployment remained intractably high, at something over two million. Bitter social conflict continued beneath the smooth surface of the Christian Democratic majorities, as the great strength of the Communist party showed in each election. Tension over religious questions recurred, for Italy continued to be at once the most devout and the most anti-clerical of nations, and the privileged position of the Church evoked sporadic complaints.

Despite its problems, however, the record of tranquility and progress in postwar Italy was better than anyone in 1945 would have dared to hope. Despite the survival of an old-fashioned and caste-ridden society, only very gradually and slightly modified by economic change, the restoration of liberty gave rise to displays of Italian creative energies in a most remarkable degree. In the fields of design, of literary and artistic attainment, Italy once again approached a leading position in the world.

GERMANY REBUILT

Italy surprised observers by the rapidity of its recovery and the stability of its institutions; the rebuilding of the German state was an even more striking achievement over even greater odds. Germany was more thoroughly devastated. Its dictatorship, if shorter lived, had been more repressive. Few democratically minded politicians had survived the Nazi whirlwind. Furthermore, the German state had been entirely extinguished and had to be rebuilt from the ground up, and in a nation cut in two by the Iron Curtain.

Despite these appalling handicaps, the West Germans rebuilt their economy with great speed and effect. More than that, they succeeded in constructing in a very few years a form of democratic government which was not only stable but which showed signs of accomplishing what the Weimar Republic had never achieved: an adjustment of the fundaments of liberty and representative institutions to the peculiar traditions and society of the German past. For despite the appalling destruction of the war and occupation, the Germans retained much of their old social patterns and habits, their old institutions, and even their pre-Nazi political party structure. The Germany of 1958 was, *mirabile dictu*, recognizably the child of the Germany of 1914.

West Germany—the German Federal Republic—evolved out of the occupation zones of the American, British, and French armies, and the policies of the Allied authorities helped to shape its character. The Allies had very definite programs. They had prosecuted the policy of "de-nazification"—the elimination of Hitler's supporters from public life and public office. They had, with the Russians, tried, condemned, and in many cases executed high officials of the Nazi regime for "crimes against humanity" and other offenses. They had subjected the depressed natives to an endless flow of propaganda designed to glorify democracy. They had created first local and then provincial governments, democratically chosen, to operate under Allied orders. They had, after more than two years of economic disorder and almost total destitution, succeeded in organizing a sound currency and a reviving trade. All of these measures had their effect, although not always the effect intended. Ordinary Germans, qualified by experience to resist propaganda, often remained unconvinced of their own culpability for the Nazi war crimes, and of the beauties of Allied-advertised democracy; but the foundations for economic revival, and the form of political organization sponsored by the occupiers, formed the basis for further efforts by the Germans themselves.

The area of the three zones was divided into eleven states (*länder*) by the Allies. The state boundaries coincided only vaguely with previous political divisions, but these states came to be the constituent units of the federation. The Allies licensed non-Nazi political parties early in their occupation, and these parties formed the basis of political organizations of the republic. They showed in some respects remarkable parallels to the parties of the Weimar Republic and the empire, but the distribution of electoral strength among them soon came to be entirely novel. Unlike the multi-party system of earlier days, the West German parties, like the Italian parties, soon divided into two major and several minor groups. The largest party, as in Italy, was a Christian party, called the Christian Democratic Union. In West Germany, where the population was about equally divided between Catholic and Protestant, the CDU was less specifically Catholic than its Italian counterpart, but it showed in other ways many of the same qualities: it was devotedly democratic and mildly in favor of social welfare legislation, while remaining hospitable to private enterprise; its economic policies were "orthodox"—that is, low taxes, sound money, and free competition; it was enthusiastic in its support of European "integration," and staunchly friendly to United States policy; it included very diverse elements, labor unionists, peasants, businessmen, aristocrats, and even some extreme reactionaries; it produced a remarkable and much admired leader—in the person of Chancellor Konrad Adenauer, whose commanding eminence helped to harmonize the German tradition of strong-man leadership with the requirements of parliamentary democracy.

THE DIVISION OF GERMANY, 1950

The second major party in Germany was the Social Democratic, which formed the principal opposition and which was the heir of the old Social Democrats of Weimar and imperial days. The Social Democrats of the new Republic presented programs of rather theoretical Marxism, mild opposition to cooperation with the western countries, and demands for negotiations with the Soviets looking toward the reunification of the Germanies. In the first national elections, in 1949, they won 29 percent of the vote (compared to 31 percent for the CDU). They maintained approximately that share in most subsequent elections, while the CDU percentage mounted, to reach, eventually, a majority.

There were several other parties in West Germany, all of which lost strength in subsequent elections. The Communists at first obtained 5.5 percent of the votes. Later the percentage fell, and eventually the party was outlawed and dissolved, having been demonstrably guilty of sabotage and subversion. The other minor parties were all more or less conservative. The largest of them, the Free Democrats, stood at least vaguely for the principles of the old National Liberals. But the Free Democrats split and lost strength over the question of whether to support the CDU in coalition, or to cooperate in opposition with the Social Democrats. More or less reactionary groups, the Germany party, the Refugee party, and others, were unable to secure mass support. Each election showed a stronger tendency toward the creation of a two-party system.

The *länder* had already developed responsible party governments under Allied direction by 1948, and it was their representatives who met by agreement of France, Britain, and the United States, to draw up laws to provide a government for a union of the three zones. The organic law was completed in May of 1949, and approved by the Allies. The first parliament was elected in August of the same year. The capital was located in the small Rhenish university town of Bonn. This peculiar choice, and the fact that the organic laws were not officially called a "constitution," emphasized the provisional character of the regime pending the reunification of Germany and the transfer of the seat of the government to Berlin. But after ten years there was still no likelihood of reunification. The provisional arrangements had become habitual, and crowded Bonn had sprouted parliament buildings, public offices, and embassies.

The Bonn constitution was in many respects similar to that of the Weimar Republic. It provided for a president (elected not by popular vote, as under Weimar, but by a congress of state and federal parliaments) to serve for five years. The legislature consisted of a lower house, the *Bundestag,* popularly elected, to which the chancellor and ministry were responsible, and a federal upper house, the *Bundesrat,* composed of delegates from the states, with limited powers. Very extensive powers were reserved for the states, exclusive only of foreign affairs, customs, currency, and interstate communications. In some respects, however, German federalism tended, as it had in other days, to become more nominal than real.

Under the Bonn regime a rapid economic recovery and expansion took place. This fact no doubt accounted for its stability and for the success of the governing party, the Christian Democratic Union. The word "miracle" is often applied to the German recovery and growth, and considering the destruction and demoralization in 1945, the bustling, expanding, prosperous West Germany of 1958 was indeed miraculous.

In May of 1955, Britain, France, and United States terminated their political control over West Germany, recognized the sovereignty of the Federal Republic, and welcomed it as an equal partner in the North Atlantic Treaty Organization. Its conversion in a decade from a defeated and hated enemy into a friend and ally with an army of its own, epitomized the rapidity not only of Germany's recovery but of its capacity to inspire confidence and respect abroad. There remained, however, problems as yet unsolved, and doubts both within Germany and among its new allies.

For all Germany's wealth, its standard of living remained substantially lower than those of Britain and France and the Scandinavian countries. Unemployment persisted, though decreasing, and the position of the workers was markedly less favorable than in many other western countries. Conversely, the power, influence, and wealth of the factory-owners was greater. The cartels and monopolies had for the most part been dissolved under the Allied occupation, and

New Apartment Houses, Hamburg, Germany. (Photo Viollet)

their former proprietors (mostly Nazi supporters) dispossessed. After the end of the occupation controls, and despite the avowed intention of the Bonn government, the cartels tended to revive; some of the ex-proprietors, like the Krupp family, the great titans of the Essen steel industry, returned to their old positions. Nor was there any certainty that the German people had formed a positive attachment to the political liberties which their conquerors had thrust upon them, nor any real aversion to the dreams of conquest which animated their earlier leaders. Friends of democracy were encouraged to note that the formation of the new army met with reluctance, even hostility, on the part of German public opinion, and to observe the failure of efforts to form neo-Nazi political groups. At the same time, it was noted that the prestige and political power of Chancellor Adenauer amounted almost to that of a dictator.

The most important fact in the history of postwar Germany, aside from its mounting prosperity, remained the division of the country in two. In both the democratic west and the Communist east the division was unanimously deplored. At no time did any German leader so much as hint at acceptance of the division as permanent. Proposals for reunion, and denunciations of those who seem insufficiently zealous for it, formed the stock-in-trade of politicians on both sides of the Iron Curtain. And yet, with the passage of time, a degree of tacit acceptance developed. It became increasingly hard to see what could be done to end it short of a war between the United States and the Soviet Union which would compel one or the other of the great powers to abandon its German client and ally. The economy of each part was organized independently of the other and oriented toward its ideological neighbors. In sundered Berlin, a precarious way of life was slowly worked out. And it was evident that the success of each of the two Germanies in finding friendly support and cooperation among its neighbors, to east and west respectively, was in some measure a consequence of the division. Poles or Frenchmen could accept more easily a Germany which was cut in two and so rendered incapable of renewed aggression. The indispensable loans and grants which the United States had bestowed in West Germany reflected American eagerness to build up the country as a bulwark against attack from the east. In some respects, the division proved a blessing in disguise. Certainly it made possible the organization of Western Europe as a flourishing, cooperative league of democratic states.

In the four great European states west of the Iron Curtain, as in the many lesser ones, the characteristic developments of the postwar years were restitution and progress toward new wealth and social justice under democratic constitutions. It was as if the west had been purged of poisons by the two wars and enabled to resume the forward march which had suffered so fearful an interruption in 1914.

57

EUROPE IN THE
WORLD

THE WORLD WAS SHRINKING. That had become a commonplace, demonstrated in
World War II by the role of transoceanic air power, advertised by statesmen who
found it convenient to hold their meetings in Casablanca, Yalta, San Francisco,
Potsdam. In the fifteen years that followed, jet aircraft and guided missiles and
the dizzy prospect of space travel promised not only a shrunken world but a
shrunken universe.

Upon the diminished surface of the planet the space occupied by the
small subcontinent of Europe was proportionately reduced. As other regions
matured with factories and airplanes and resources of their own, as the United
States and Russia became superpowers and as both China and India seemed to be
candidates for that status, as polar routes opened to unite unlikely destinations,
the position of Europe became progressively less preeminent. Once it had held
the world in fee; now its colonial empires were being lost or transformed into
free associations of equal nations. There was a still more precipitous decline in
its relative military power and diplomatic weight; European governments were no
longer arbiters of world politics. Moral and cultural influence was less easy to
assess, but there was little doubt that Europe's once dominant position in such
realms was changing, merging into a broader and more varied cultural landscape.

Europe's role as the chief architect of world history was coming to an end
in the middle years of the twentieth century. The power and the glory and the
empire were disappearing. But the world had proved a quick pupil of its old
master. The new free countries were still borrowing from the old. The proud
young peoples, lately colonial, were still dependent, intellectually and technically,
upon the rejected mother-countries. Europe had made a world in its own image,

and that world—of nationalisms and regional pacts, of factories and labor unions, of parliaments and printing presses—still paid perfunctory tribute to its maker. Until the transfer of the European heritage to the rest of the world was complete, the European period of world history could not be declared closed. The world's present, like the world's past, was still involved with Europe's condition. As for the future, Europe's part in it would depend upon the persistence in Europeans of the genius which in the past had drawn creative energy from diversity. Europe's role would depend too on its ability to achieve some form of federation—a task at which it had always failed before.

TWILIGHT OF THE EMPIRES

Military power was one symptom of Europe's superior civilization. The technological talent, the organizing skill of Europeans, had enabled them, almost, to conquer the world in modern times. In 1914 the weapons of this arsenal were turned by Europeans against one another, and in the ensuing self-destruction the superior power was lost. After 1918 the peoples of the non-European world became increasingly restive. After 1939, when the great powers once again became embroiled with one another, the colonial peoples began to make good their demands for equality.

But there was more to the revolt of Asia and Africa than the decline of European power. Already before 1914 there had been portents of change—the rise of Japan as a great power, the growing independence of the self-governing British colonies, the Italian defeat in Ethiopia in the 1890's, the stirring of the Arab peoples in the Ottoman empire. Europe had exported to the overseas world ideas of human rights, of nation and class, of economic and scientific progress. And the Europeans had exported to some extent the technical skills which were the secret of their power. Now these exports were turned against the European masters of the colonial empires. In the twentieth century there began to develop on a world scale the same kind of process which Napoleon had experienced at the beginning of the nineteenth. Conquered people disliked subjection at the same time that they were learning to appreciate the reforms which the conqueror had introduced.

Until the end of World War II, the revolt consisted more of omens than of outbreaks. In the previous quarter-century deference to the universal fashion for freedom and self-determination had led some of the European powers to alter their rule over some of the more advanced colonial areas. Salutary concessions—but inadequate to meet the demands of Indian nationalists led by the saintly Mohandas K. Gandhi—were undertaken by the British in their Indian empire. In 1935 Parliament passed the Government of India Act, which reorganized the empire and provided for extensive self-government in the provinces and for a central legislative assembly, partly elected. In many colonies local agencies of self-government or advisory councils with native membership were permitted to assist the European governors. But seldom was European control abandoned. Final authority in India, for example, remained in the cabinet in London. Nor was there much public or effective demand for self-government in most of the colonies. Nationalism could usually be checkmated by the Europeans. As a consequence, it remained for the most part primitive and conspiratorial.

The most important developments in the years between the wars affected areas where there were European populations. Long before 1914 Canada, Australia, and New Zealand had achieved control over most of their internal affairs, and had insisted that they be called "dominions." In 1909 the conquered Boer republics of Transvaal and the Orange Free State had been united to the British colonies in South Africa—Natal and Cape Colony—to form another self-governing dominion, the Union of South Africa. In 1922 the Irish Free State was added to the list. The dominions evolved rapidly into a new and unique constitutional entity in the world. In 1931 the Statute of Westminster, passed by the parliament of the United Kingdom, confirmed their effective independence by providing that no act of the British parliament (and in effect no act of the British government) should be binding on the dominions without their consent. They built up their own diplomatic and military establishments, and defined characteristic foreign policies to a point of independence where the Irish remained neutral throughout World War II. After 1936 the Irish declined to recognize the British sovereign as their ruler, so that even the symbolic link of the Crown disappeared as a necessary element of relations among the dominions. The "British Commonwealth of Nations" was thus an elusive entity, less than a federation, less even than an alliance, consisting of little more than a consultative arrangement buttressed by preferential trade agreements and other economic links and, in some

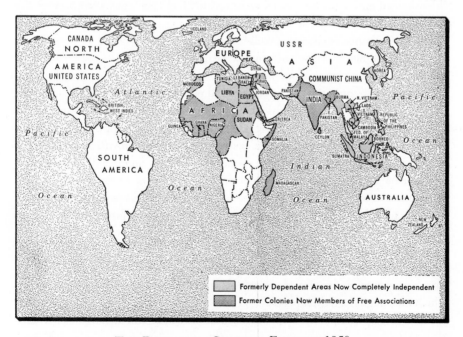

THE DECLINE OF COLONIAL EMPIRES, 1958

cases, by strong sentimental bonds. Despite its singular character, the British Commonwealth was a remarkable achievement, forming a new kind of basis for cooperation among free nations. It was to provide an important model for later emancipations of colonies. The idea of "dominion" status (which in practice meant full self-government), and of gradual evolution toward it, offered in some cases a guide and an inspiration.

Guidance was to be greatly needed. After World War II, colonial empires exploded, owing partly to the experiences of the war itself, and partly to the disorganization and weakness of the colonial powers. The movement began in places like the Dutch East Indies, which had been occupied by the Japanese and where nationalist leaders immediately proclaimed independence when the Japanese surrendered, and then resisted all efforts to restore Dutch control. A very similar situation developed in Indochina. There were successful efforts to overthrow French power in Syria and Lebanon, and an unsuccessful rising in the vast French colony of Madagascar. In the course of the next decade, insurrections took place or threatened in such diverse areas as North Africa, British Guiana, Malaya, and the Gold Coast. In other places, calmer and more gradual demands for self-government spread, as in Nigeria, or French West Africa. It was clear that the revolt against imperialism was worldwide.

The nationalist movements, while very diverse, tended to share certain characteristics. Most of them were led by intellectuals, and most often by European-trained intellectuals. Most of them received the blessing of the Soviet Union, which was in a position to derive enormous benefits from appearing in the guise of protector of suppressed peoples and guide to rapid economic progress. In many cases, particularly in the Arab world, violent complaints about the social and economic privileges of the Europeans were blended with a desire to remake the old-fashioned and oppressive social orders which had been conserved by imperial officials. In almost every case, independence or self-government was presented as a step toward greater economic well-being.

Unfortunately it was difficult for people in the formerly colonial regions to understand the complexities wrought by contact with European civilization. Improvements in sanitation and medicine and public order had upset the millenial patterns of existence. Populations had grown too rapidly for the old agriculture and the traditional occupations. The new enterprises of the colonizers helped, but not enough. Once begun, the race between population growth and economic transformation called for more capital, more enterprises, more skill. These social dislocations spurred nationalist movements. The great libertarian principles learned from the Europeans fortified native intellectuals and political leaders, but the path to independence was mined with possibilities of fanaticism and demagogy, the more so because the process of cutting imperial ties often meant economic dislocation. Competing western and Soviet versions of progress, supplemented by aid and armament programs, gave the politicians of underdeveloped countries a certain room for maneuver but multiplied the traps and pitfalls into which they might lead their peoples.

The imperial powers responded in various ways to the upsurge of nationalism. In general, two sets of alternatives presented themselves. The first was to grant substantial independence, usually attempting to preserve some special connection with the mother-country and to safeguard economic interests and cultural affiliations. This path was followed by the United States with the Philippines, which became an independent republic on July 4, 1946, and later with Puerto Rico, which secured self-government and "dominion status" within the United States customs union in 1950. A similar course was followed by the British, who sought to grant freedom while retaining cooperation within the British Commonwealth. In 1947 Great Britain recognized the independence of India, Pakistan (formed from the Moslem portions of the Indian empire), and Ceylon. The three nations remained Commonwealth members. Burma was granted outright independence in 1948, after rejecting dominion status. In 1957 Ghana, the former Gold Coast, in Africa, gained its independence but remained within the British Commonwealth. Preparations were made for the development of the Central African Federation (Northern and Southern Rhodesia, and Nyasaland) and the British West Indies Federation and Malaya as dominions, and for granting freedom to Nigeria. By 1948 most British colonies of any size had begun to move toward some sort of freedom and self-government, within or without the British Commonwealth.

The second alternative which colonizing powers sometimes adopted was to resist nationalism by force while offering prospects of limited self-rule and "partnership" in a more or less free association. This approach was adopted by the French in Indochina and North Africa, and by the Dutch in the East Indies. After a long and bitter war, the Dutch (under strong pressure from the United Nations and the United States) finally in 1950 recognized the Republic of Indonesia, created out of the Dutch East Indies. In 1954 the last ties of the Republic of Indonesia with the Netherlands were cut. In Indochina the French upon their return in 1945 found a strong nationalist movement, the Vietminh, led by the Communist Ho Chi-Minh. France's preoccupations with the formation of a new government in Paris, coupled with the stubbornness and independent action of military and colonial officials on the spot, led to a disastrous war which complicated France's politics and threatened to wreck its finances and finally led to the humiliating defeat of Dien Bien Phu in 1954. In that year French political control was finally abandoned and Indochina emerged as four troubled sovereign states—Laos, Cambodia, South Viet Nam, and Communist-controlled North Viet Nam.

In North Africa, meanwhile, nationalist movements sought the ejection of French political control from the protectorates of Tunisia and Morocco, and from Algeria, which was regarded as an integral part of France. In the two protectorates, after intrigues which showed again the difficulties of the Paris government in controlling its colonial officials, the reality of independence was conceded in 1954 and 1955 and final recognition granted early in 1956. In Algeria extensive nationalist resistance to the French began in the fall of 1954 and a year later became a full-scale war which required the presence of some 400,000 French troops. Neither side was able to defeat the other, and so much was felt to be at stake that uncertainty about the intentions of the government in Paris led to the overthrow of the Fourth Republic in 1958 (described elsewhere). But the new de Gaulle regime, although its constitution was ratified by a plebiscite in Algeria, had trouble subduing the rebel armies or coming to terms with the nationalist government in exile. The Algerian affair dragged on.

In the surviving portions of the French and Dutch empires, however, a new consciousness of the needs of the situation led to reforms which looked toward the development of free associations with diminishing political control from the motherlands. The Dutch West Indies (Curacao and Guiana) remained loyal, with expanded self-government. In his constitutional referendum of 1958, General de Gaulle challenged nationalist movements in the French empire by offering the colonies a choice of immediate independence or evolution toward partnership with French aid. All of the French colonies except Guinea voted by large majorities for the latter.

Even where the political bonds with the old mother-countries were completely severed, as in Tunisia or Burma, linguistic and economic ties often remained strong. As President Bourguiba of the Tunisian republic was frequently to affirm, free Tunisia was scarcely less dependent upon France for economic and technical assistance, and indeed for cultural inspiration, than colonial Tunisia had been.

The most persistent difficulties developed in countries where European political control had been accompanied by the settlement of considerable numbers of Europeans—in the British East African colony of Kenya, as in Algeria. Here, racial, religious, and social tensions developed in a society where European settlers constituted an economic as well as a political ruling class, and home governments were faced with impassioned pleas for protection against independence movements. The British population, well-established and owners of much of the best land, and much more strenuously pro-British than their co-nationals in London, were confronted with a horrifying native terrorist movement called Mau-Mau, the most extreme and cruel of the many anti-western movements which developed throughout the world. With difficulty Mau-Mau was disarmed and neutralized, but the future of East Africa, with its aggressive white minority and its huge African majority, remained uncertain.

One of the most intractable problems was encountered by the British in Cyprus, with its population of a Greek majority passionately eager for annexation to Greece and a Turkish minority passionately averse to Greek rule. There, no solution seemed feasible. Turks feared and Greeks rejected dominion status, the one because it would place them at the mercy of the Greek majority, the other because they cared only for union to Greece. The obstacles to emancipation were many, but agreement on an independent Cyprus was finally reached in 1959.

The Arab world—the great Moslem region which stretched from the borders of India to the Atlantic and from equatorial Africa to Turkey—presented problems of an especially explosive sort. In the nineteenth century most of it had been in theory part of the disintegrating Ottoman empire. By 1939 it had been divided among Italy (Libya), France (Syria, Lebanon, Tunisia, Algeria, Morocco), Britain (Palestine, Transjordan, Sudan, and a strip of protectorates on the Arabian coast), and nominally independent states under strong British influence (Iraq, Egypt, Saudi Arabia). Egypt, controlling the Suez canal, had always been strategically vital to Britain, and by 1939 the exploitation of oil in the Arabian peninsula and Iraq had added a new dimension of strategic and commercial importance. Even before 1945 there were indications of trouble to come for the western powers. Uprisings in Syria and Lebanon and Iraq indicated a new mood of anti-western nationalism which in time spread to engulf the entire Arab world, forcing out the foreign overlords (in Syria, Lebanon, the Sudan, Libya, Tunisia, and Morocco), challenging them (in Algeria and Aden), or destroying governments and social orders which showed signs of complaisancy toward western influence (in Egypt and Iraq).

The antipathy of Arabs to the dominance of westerners in their affairs was a blending of modern nationalism with ancient religious passions and social and economic appetites. One particular fact enormously sharpened it: the establishment, under British auspices and with United States support, of a Jewish settlement in Palestine. In 1917 the British had promised the creation of a Jewish national homeland in Palestine. Jewish settlers had begun entering the country, which in 1918 came under a British mandate. The flow of settlers greatly increased during and after World War II. From every point of view they were unwelcome to the Arabs, who regarded Palestine as an Arab land.

In 1942 the Jewish leaders announced their demands for an independent Jewish state and thereafter fought fiercely for this goal. The neighboring Arab states announced that further Jewish immigration, and the establishment of a Jewish state, would lead to war. Compromise proposals by the British and the United Nations were rejected by both sides, and in May, 1948, the State of Israel was proclaimed. War with the newly formed Arab League of Lebanon, Transjordan, Syria, Iraq, and Egypt immediately ensued. Before it was ended, six months later, in armistices negotiated by the United Nations, Transjordan had annexed the non-Jewish sections of Palestine (and thereupon changed its name to Jordan), and most of the Arab population of Israel, despoiled of their possessions, had taken flight as refugees. An uneasy truce persisted, accompanied by venomously bad relations and mounting animosities on both sides.

The Arabs were inclined to blame the western powers, particularly Britain and the United States, for the establishment and survival of Israel. This situation gave vigor and popular support to Arab nationalist movements which proclaimed themselves bent on the destruction of Israel and of western influence. Extremist regimes were installed in Syria (1949), Egypt (1953), and Iraq (1958). The Soviet Union, discerning the enormous opportunities for exploiting western embarrassment and securing a foothold in the strategically vital area, backed the nationalists and comforted them with some material aid. The situation exploded in 1956 (see below), and an even more uneasy truce was restored afterward. The position of the western powers remained precarious throughout the Arab world. When Egypt and Syria united to form the United Arab Republic in 1958, the probability of further difficulties increased.

GLOBAL CONFLICT AND COMPROMISE

After World War II there was no longer any doubt about the fact that the theater of the rivalries among the great powers had become worldwide. This change, visible in World War I, extended back to the turn of the century, to the Spanish American and Russo-Japanese Wars. But the difference after World War II was not merely that there had been participants which were not European powers. The great centers of power were now outside of Europe.

After World War II the United States and the Soviet Union seemed at first to have divided the world. Then it became apparent that a giant Chinese state was in formation. India was also advancing toward world power. In the Arab world, there were evolving nations, committed neither to West nor East. In the 1950's Africa's possibilities began to capture the imaginations of educated people everywhere. Meanwhile in the councils of nations the members of the British Commonwealth and the Latin American countries played a role of growing importance, as did many other countries of Africa and Asia. Delegates of Russia and the United States contending in the United Nations Organization had to reckon with the opinions of a multitude of small countries. To the race for scientific and military progress was added a contest for the favor of world opinion.

Europe was still, after World War II, the richest of prizes. Whoever controlled its concentration of resources and skilled, industrious people would do more than improve his military position. Europe, no longer supreme, might still bestow the aspect of empire upon its conqueror. Or Europe, if it could unite and live again as a unit, might itself become a great power in the global balance.

Some leaders, like General de Gaulle at the close of World War II, hoped that the historic European powers such as France might mediate between the United States and the Soviet Union without being committed to either side. It was Europe's fate, however, to become divided into western and eastern zones. In an earlier chapter we have seen this division becoming sharply defined by 1947 and 1948 with the making of Soviet satellites in East Central Europe and with the countermoves of the Truman Doctrine and the Marshall Plan. In 1949 the West German Federal Republic was sponsored by the Allies and the German People's Republic was sponsored by the Russians. In the west the groundwork for NATO was laid when the Atlantic Pact was signed in Washington in 1949.

In the fall of 1949, when the Russians exploded an atomic bomb, the world became aware that the western monopoly of the atomic "deterrent" was ending and that an era of awful nuclear equality was beginning. Europe was now menaced anew, for the enormous Russian ground forces had a new meaning when they were no longer neutralized by an American monopoly of atomic weapons. Western Europe and the United States hastened to build up the NATO shield, but before their plans were completed the year 1949 brought another momentous event. China fell to the Communists and Chiang Kai-shek took refuge on the island of Formosa with the remains of the Chinese Nationalist forces. Suddenly the map of Asia was splashed with red. To the northeast of China since 1948

Korea had remained divided between the northern (Communist) and southern (National) zone. To the south of China since 1946 the former French colony of Indochina had been split by the struggle between French-sponsored and Communist-sponsored forces. Those divisions now became more crucial. Americans fell into disputes and recriminations over responsibility for the "loss" of China. The United Nations was deeply divided between those who wanted China's seat to remain in the hands of the Nationalists (which it did) and those who wished it transferred to the Communist regime.

So in the early 1950's the cold war grew more serious still. In June, 1950, North Korean forces crossed the thirty-eighth parallel and tried to conquer South Korea. In the temporary absence of the Russians, who were boycotting the Security Council, the United Nations supported the South Koreans by sending an international military force. United States troops under the command of General MacArthur were the most numerous part of this force, and were supported by the United States navy. A bitter struggle ensued as Chinese troops came to the aid of the North Koreans. There was real danger that the war would spread into China proper and even into Europe if Russia became directly involved. Meanwhile the French struggle in Indochina continued to be a terrible drain on French resources, and was also capable of becoming a world war if the United States and Red China came to blows.

In Europe there was more need than ever, in view of the American engagement in the Far East, to build up the forces of NATO, where General Eisenhower was in command. Greece and Turkey were invited in 1952 to join NATO. The question of rearming Germany could no longer be avoided. As early as 1950, Churchill had proposed a unified European army. As related in Chapter 54, the French, in order to forestall the building of a specifically German army proposed, also in 1950, an ingenious scheme for a European Defense Community in which German soldiers would be mingled with other European soldiers. In May, 1952, this plan was agreed upon by the foreign ministers of France, Germany, Italy, and the Benelux countries. But the European Defense Community could not be completed until its arrangements were ratified by the parliaments of the countries concerned, and France delayed doing so, for French opinion was deeply divided on the subject. France in 1951 joined with West Germany, Italy, and the Benelux countries to form the European Coal and Steel Community, and there was much painful soul-searching on the subject of "making Europe." But Britain remained aloof from both the Coal and Steel Community and the European Defense Community, and without Britain as a balance against the rearmed Germans the European Defense Force seemed to many Frenchmen to be too hazardous a gamble. Even those Frenchmen who ardently wished for a unified Europe were divided on whether there should first be a European government—a move violently opposed by many Frenchmen—before the formation of a European army, or whether the army could be a reasonable step toward a European government.

To make matters worse, many Britons and Germans (who themselves had no sympathy for the violent Communist opposition to the strengthening of the west) were nonetheless alarmed lest American prosecution of the war in Korea extend the fighting to Europe, reducing it to a radioactive wasteland between the

United States and the Soviet Union. Never before in peacetime had Europe's vulnerability to the outside world been so frightfully real.

Into this atmosphere of trouble and tension came the death of Stalin in March, 1953. For a few days a kind of hush fell over the world, broken only by the funereal chanting of the old dictator's praises by the Communist parties, while everyone else speculated concerning the implications of the death. What ensued was not the unravelling of the Soviet empire—nor any dramatic ending to the cold war, an outcome which only a few hopefuls dared expect. From 1953 to the autumn of 1956 there was, however, a relaxing of international tensions which was variously described as "the thaw" (after a novel by the Russian Ilya Ehrenberg), or "peaceful coexistence" (already a Russian slogan in Stalin's time, and now emphasized by his successors), or "the new course" (of appeasing gestures by the Russian leaders inside and outside the Soviet Union).

The underlying basis for the relaxing of tensions was in part the need of Stalin's successors to consolidate their position. There was also a military side to the relaxation, however. Stalin had emphasized that the world was divided into "two camps" and that those who were not with the Communists were against them, but in practice he had been very cautious. He had advanced the "peaceful coexistence" doctrine because notwithstanding their superior ground forces the Russians were at first made cautious by the west's atomic weapon as well as by their need to reconstruct their own country. The addition of China to the Communist camp, as well as the Soviet development of an atomic bomb, went far toward removing the old fear of "capitalist encirclement" and gave new meaning to "peaceful coexistence." At the same time the west's building of NATO, continued possession of atomic weapons, and probable air superiority still acted as deterrents. Russian production of a hydrogen bomb, announced in 1953, did not change the military equilibrium; it merely indicated that the Soviet Union was keeping up with the United States, which already had the hydrogen bomb.

The principal measures which contributed to a relaxing of tensions between 1953 and 1956 were the armistice in Korea (July, 1953), which stopped the fighting and left the country divided; a cessation on similar terms of hostilities in Indochina (July, 1954), which enabled the French to disengage themselves; and the conclusion of a general peace treaty with Austria (May, 1955), by which the occupying forces withdrew and left Austria neutral and independent. These agreements were of great comfort to the peoples directly concerned, and they considerably lessened the danger of another world war's growing out of the west's clashes with Russia or Communist China. But many serious dangers remained. The fundamental relationship between the two sides in the cold war had not changed. In 1954 the western foreign ministers, and in 1955 Chancellor Adenauer, failed to reach any agreement with the Russians concerning the unification of Germany. The Russians evidently feared that a united Germany would be against them and that withdrawal of their troops from East Germany would make it difficult for them to justify leaving troops in the satellites. The West Germans, British, and French could not accept unification of Germany on terms which would make it possible for the Communists to extend their domination to the whole of this vital territory.

The project of rearming the West Germans as part of a European Defense Community army was killed in August, 1954, when the French parliament refused to ratify it. But there immediately followed a less controversial approach to rearming the Germans. The German Federal Republic joined a so-called West European Union and was allowed to rearm and place its forces under the command of NATO. At the end of 1954 and early in 1955 the Allied occupation of the German Federal Republic was ended and the troops stationed there became troops of West Germany's allies. France did not oppose this more traditional means of arming Germany, since it did not interfere with French sovereignty, and since in any case the French could not have kept the other powers from arming Germany against the Russians. For their part, the Russians responded, in 1955, with the Warsaw Pact and Warsaw Treaty Organization, which integrated the armed forces of Russia and its satellites.

Meanwhile in the wake of the Indochinese settlement a Pacific Charter was signed in September, 1954, proclaiming the rights of the countries of East Asia to self-determination. It was followed by the formation of a Southeast Asia Treaty Organization (SEATO) by which the U.S., Britain, France, Australia, New Zealand, the Philippines, Thailand, and Pakistan promised to consult each other in case of danger. In the Middle East a so-called Baghdad Pact (1955), a defensive alliance of Iraq and Turkey, was later joined by Britain, Pakistan, and Iran, and became known as the Middle East Treaty Organization (METO). Many local considerations played a part in the alignments within the Arab world, and the Baghdad Pact was opposed by other groupings. Nevertheless such treaty organizations formed a part of a global balance of power and European arrangements became, more clearly than ever, merely one part of a worldwide tissue of rivalries and alignments.

In July, 1955, at a "summit" (of executive authority) meeting in Geneva, Switzerland, President Eisenhower, Premier Bulganin, Premier Faure, and Prime Minister Eden aroused the hopes of the world by talking amicably. The world's newspapermen coined a new expression, "the Geneva spirit," which meant relaxation of tension and willingness to negotiate, but in fact nothing concrete came from the Geneva meetings. The most that could be said was that Russian behavior in East Central Europe in 1955 was bearing out the idea that a "new course" was under way. In May, 1955, Khrushchev (rapidly emerging as heir to Stalin's power) had visited Yugoslavia and acknowledged that Tito had been wronged by Stalin. This trip also brought forth the admission that there could be various roads to socialism. These portents of a "new course" continued with Khrushchev's secret attack on Stalin at the Twentieth Party Congress in early 1956, which became known to the outside world and resulted in de-Stalinization movements in the Communist parties of most countries. In keeping with the general atmosphere of international good will, the Cominform was dissolved. In June, 1956, a Poznan rising of Polish workers was followed by trials in which extraordinary freedom of expression was allowed.

But the year 1956 brought a crisis and an awakening on both sides of the iron curtain. The events of the "Polish October" and the Hungarian Revolution have already been described. They were accompanied by the Suez crisis which preoccupied the United Nations and split the NATO powers at the end of October, 1956, at precisely the moment when the Hungarians tried to cease being a Russian satellite.

The Suez crisis arose from Egyptian President Nasser's nationalization of the Suez canal and from the endemic border warfare between Egypt and Israel. Irritated by Nasser's exclusion of their ships from the canal and convinced of Egypt's intention to destroy their state, the Israelis invaded the Sinai Peninsula and moved toward Suez. The British and French, impatient with what they felt was a failure on the part of the United States to understand and defend their interests, went ahead on their own. When Nasser rejected an Anglo-French ultimatum which would have resulted in their occupation of the canal zone, the British and French attacked Egypt. But at this point rude realities of world power dominated the crisis. The General Assembly of the United Nations passed by an overwhelming majority a United States resolution for a ceasefire and withdrawal of the British, French, and Israeli forces. Russia and the United States found themselves working together against the United States' NATO allies who, with Israel, were eventually compelled to withdraw their troops. These events, accompanied by Russian threats to send volunteers to help Egypt, took place at the same time as the terrible Russian repression of Hungary. In the Western European countries sentiments ranging from irritation to fury at the behavior of the United States were accompanied by feelings of impotence, frustration, and anger at the spectacle of Russian brutality in Budapest, unchecked by the United Nations.

The crises of 1956 destroyed illusions, but they revealed, rather than changed, the fundamental facts about Europe's condition. Britain and France were shown to be unable to discipline Nasser. They were still incomparably the stronger; even the small Israeli forces had routed the Egyptians. But Western European superiority to an underdeveloped country was not enough. Not only was Russian power so great that without the support of the United States, Britain and France could not proceed. There was also a new wind blowing out of Asia and Africa, a current of anti-colonialism which entered the halls of the United Nations and came between the Americans and their European allies. In the Suez crisis the Western European states were overwhelmed by considerations of the global balance of power, which made the representatives of the United States remember not only the sanctity of the United Nations but also the desirability of retaining the respect of the Afro-Asian countries not yet committed to the Soviet Union. Thus United States policies in the world at large sometimes worked against the European allies.

The Suez crisis seemed to split the western allies, but in the end the rift was mended and it was proved that even such bitterness as this could not drive them apart. Realism demanded that NATO continue even when the partners disliked one another's behavior. In the larger crisis Russian's treatment of Hungary reminded the west that the relaxations of the Soviet Union's "new course" were very limited indeed. The crisis of 1956 also tested the United Nations, but the verdict was not clear. With American support and Soviet acquiescence, the organization got results at Suez, although many practical problems remained to be solved. On the other hand, in the case of Hungary the U.N., with Soviet opposition, was powerless to do more than investigate and condemn.

Russia, too, had to face realities. The Hungarian Revolution had shown that the military value of Russia's satellites in East Central Europe was highly questionable. (To be sure, the development of nuclear weapons on both sides of the iron curtain had already reduced the military importance of the satellites.) The economic value of the satellites to the Soviets remained, but it was tempered by the necessity, now understood in Moscow, to stop exploiting them so severely. The political value of the satellites in the eyes of the Soviet leadership also probably remained very great. Foreign observers doubted that the Soviet leaders would dare allow a process of unbinding such as that which had occurred in Hungary to take place again lest it damage their prestige and their control of East Germany and suggest a similar process to people within the Soviet Union. In the ensuing campaign to consolidate their hold on the satellites and justify their harshness the Soviet leaders were placed in the embarrassing position of accepting the aid of the Chinese Communists. Even Marshal Tito was given a scare by the Hungarian example of relinquishing the Communist party's monopoly.

After the crisis of 1956 the Soviet Union, like the Western European powers, recovered its equanimity. In November, 1957, the fortieth anniversary of the Bolshevik Revolution was celebrated in the midst of worldwide respect for the Soviet rockets and *sputniks*. Communist orthodoxy, which had seemed to be compromised by Khrushchev's attack on Stalin at the Twentieth Party Congress in 1956, was reaffirmed. The crisis of 1956 had put the "new course" to the test. In retrospect, it was seen to have consisted of modest concessions to farmers and consumers without abandonment of the fundamental emphasis on heavy industry; of modest concessions to freedom of expression without abandonment of Communist supervision; and of modest concessions to phrases like "national communism" and "separate roads to socialism" without abandonment of the Communist monopoly of political power.

There remained noticeable changes since Stalin's day. For one thing, Khrushchev had relaxed Stalin's doctrine of the "two camps" to permit acknowledgment of the existence of uncommitted countries between the capitalist and Communist camps. The Soviet Union had stopped insulting the governments of these countries and had set about winning them by means of foreign aid programs. This form of "peaceful coexistence" continued in the more realistic period after 1956. And there was another form of competition in the United Nations and before world opinion, concerning disarmament. There was genuine worldwide concern over the effects of radiation from nuclear test explosions, and genuine hope that through some system of mutual inspection the danger of surprise nuclear attack could be eliminated. But while world opinion had to be respected, the danger of falling behind in the scientific race was so great that Russia and the United States were still unable, in late 1958, to agree on conditions for controlling the nuclear menace or cooperating to make good the nuclear promise for human betterment. And in Europe, birthplace of modern science and source of many of the persons and principles being used by the Soviet Union and the United States, British, French, and German leaders were reluctant to end the armaments race while their countries were still behind.

EUROPE IN PROSPECT

The decline of colonial empires, the dividing of Europe into zones dependent on outside military protection, seemed like milestones on the track which led to the passing of the European age. In the fifth century of the modern era Europe seemed, like Rome in the fifth century of the Christian era, to be losing its special place of leadership, dissolving into a wider community.

Whether there would be in the future a United Europe capable of playing its part along with the Soviet Union, China, the United States, and the other centers of world power depended in part on outside forces over which the Europeans had little influence. Their efforts to "make Europe" had produced in the west the Council of Europe, the Coal and Steel Community, the Common Market plan, Euratom—projects for peaceful community action, as well as the military cooperation of NATO. Great Britain, with its Commonwealth connections, limited its participation in the new Europe primarily to the military. Germany remained both inside and outside of the new Europe taking shape in the west. In the prospect of a Germany reunified and joined to the west lay, potentially, the key to the disintegration of the Soviet hold on East Central Europe. In a Germany reunified and tied to the east lay, potentially, the key to Soviet domination of the continent. Either way, German reunification might start a new world war. Germany, like Europe, was therefore left divided.

On both sides of the ideological and military frontier in Europe patience and fortitude were the price of continuing peaceful coexistence. Between the two Europes there was taking place a great competition in some ways similar to the Asiatic trial of constructive ingenuity between India and Red China, or to the more highly developed competition between the United States and the Soviet Union. On the eve of the age of nuclear-powered production, Europe waited and worked. Never before had diversity been so sharply defined and so threatening as in the two regions of east and west. Yet the traditions which made for European unity were not all expended. In the west the nineteenth-century legacies of nationalism, conservatism, liberalism, democracy, and socialism still flourished in a Christian setting. All were muted now, in comparison with the fierce challenge from the east or the brutal adolescence of Europe's former colonies. There was a possibility that all of these elements of diversity—of ideals, of language and religion, of the vital force of nationality itself—might be reconciled if Western Europeans could agree on some form of society where the unifying forces might be emphasized and the stimulating diversities tolerated.

In the past, conflict and diversity had been a challenge to creation. Europe had excelled in many things, had gone out to seek the world and had in large measure conquered and inspired it, in the process enabling its own multitudes to begin lifting themselves out of the routines of a primordial existence. But diversity had overbalanced unity. Europe in the midst of these enterprises had fallen into the great twentieth-century wars. Pride of nation and class and race had squandered its inheritance.

Europe's future after World War II depended on more than military and economic recovery. It depended also on recovery of a creative and innovating genius which might transform the old unfinished business into new work worthy of humanity in the twentieth century.

APPENDIX A

LEXICON
OF HISTORICAL
TERMS AND USAGES

THE FOLLOWING are words and phrases frequently used in historical exposition. Although many of them refer to things or persons—such as "constitution" or "noble"—mentioned in the text, the purpose of the list is not to repeat the definitions used in the book; such a catalogue would require another volume. There will be found here only some of the more troublesome words, those which readers may have heard and even themselves used but whose precise meanings sometimes elude them.

ABSOLUTE MONARCHY, ABSOLUTISM. As used in this book, refers to governments of early modern times, in which kings ruled through their officials without having to share the making of law and policy with representative bodies responsible to the people. In theory, absolute monarchs were responsible to God and were required to respect certain traditions.

ARISTOCRAT. Linguistically means a member of a ruling class of warriors, and dates from medieval times when military leadership was associated with a privileged and commanding position in society. An aristocrat in early modern times was usually a person whose privileged position was connected with a title of nobility (conferred by a king) and with ownership of extensive lands. Gradually, as newly enriched officials, and later the merely wealthy, joined the aristocracy, the word lost its precision. Today it is often used merely as a synonym of "upper class."

AUTHORITARIAN. An awkward and unnecessary word frequently used to describe such twentieth-century governments as have imposed strong controls upon the beliefs and actions of their citizens. A powerful government, usually one with a desire to dictate ideas and without any constitutional limitations on the sphere of its power, is described as authoritarian. See TOTALITARIAN.

BALANCE OF POWER. Describes a condition which exists in international affairs when no one country or group of countries is permitted by the others to grow so powerful as to threaten their independent existence. A balance of power emerged with the appearance of separate and competing governments in Europe. The tendency persisted through the centuries and eventually became world-wide. The phrase has been applied to so many different sorts of international situations that it has retained only a very general meaning. It is not a "system" deliberately worked out by statesmen, although statesmen have often sought to "redress the balance of power" by arranging coalitions against aggressors. See pp. 13, 76, and 697.

BOURGEOIS. (Both singular and plural). Originally a person or persons who lived in a *bourg*, a settlement which lay outside the walls and administrative limits of a medieval French city. Taken together, bourgeois were known as the *bourgeoisie*. The German equivalent is *bürger*. Eventually bourgeois came to mean almost anyone who was fairly well off and was not an artisan or laborer, an aristocrat, a churchman, or a peasant. The rough equivalent in English is the phrase "middle-class" (which see).

BUREAUCRACY. A body of officeholders, especially one associated with the king or executive of a government. Bureaucracies played an essential part in the consolidation of the monarchies of early modern times and, more recently, in the growth of socialist or welfare states. Making bureaucracies serve without encroaching upon policy-making authority has been a problem for kings, representative bodies, and modern dictators.

CAESARISM. An epithet derived from ancient history and the regimes of Napoleon I or Napoleon III in France. It connotes a dictatorship based on popular will. It is contrasted to the absolute monarchy of the Old Regime, which was encompassed by presumed laws and traditions regulating the use of royal power and based upon a complicated social structure in which different groups and classes had differently defined rights. In absolute monarchy the source of political power was supposed to be God. In a caesarist regime, the source of political power is the people, whose approval is sought from time to time through plebiscites.

CAPITALISM. Means many things to many people. Most simply it is an economy in which capital—that is, the equipment and resources necessary to produce things—is privately owned by individuals or companies of individuals, and in which an important part of the economic life consists of production for profit through sale in markets. See p. 20.

CIVILIZATION AND CULTURE. "Civilization" comes from the Latin word for city, *civitas*, and suggests the sophisticated life of city-dwellers. "Culture" comes from the Latin word *cultura*, which means tilling or cultivating the soil. Generally speaking, both are used of groups of people, or individuals, characterized by education and training, particularly moral or artistic. Both have come to be used (especially by sociologists and anthropologists) to describe societies, whether they are rich in art or morality or not. A "culture" in this sense usually means certain aspects of a society—certain institutions, beliefs, morals and forms of expression which are shared, and form a pattern which solves persistent human problems. For most historians, however, culture means what it means in ordinary language—the arts and sciences and philosophy, with certain extensions to include economic skills and sometimes religious and moral values. Civilization is used by historians in much the same way as culture—it implies total cultural assets, as in "the civilization of the Renaissance." But "a civilization" also means, to archaeologists and historians, a society (usually a complicated one) which has risen, flourished, and declined.

CLASS. As used by historians and other students of society, a group of people with common or similar traits related to their occupations, social relations, and manner of life. Societies vary in the number of classes they include, in the freedom of movement from one class to another, in the amount and sort of respect shown to the various levels. Philosophies of society vary in the emphasis which they place on the importance of classes. See STRATIFICATION, and p. 425.

COMMUNISM. In all times, a doctrine advocating common ownership of the means of production and more or less equal distribution of the goods produced; since World War I associated in most peoples' minds with the Russian Communist Party and its affiliates in other countries and therefore with Marxian Socialism as interpreted in Russia, and with the practices and aspirations of the Soviet Union and its satellites.

CONSTITUTION. Used in a political sense, a body of laws, traditions, and habits which regulate the allocation of powers among different government officials and determine how these powers shall be used. Constitutional government is usually regarded as the opposite of a "despotism" (which see). A constitution does not imply any particular form of government, but in modern times it has usually suggested rather extensive restrictions on the powers of officials and corresponding protection of individuals and groups from meddling by governments. Constitutions may be uncodified, like the British constitution, which consists of ordinary laws and traditions. More often, at least since the time of the French Revolution, constitutions have been written down.

DEMOCRACY. From two Greek words meaning rule by the common people; semantically it is the alternative to "monarchy" (rule by one man) and "aristocracy" (rule by warriors). The most strict modern definition of democracy is, "the complete and freely exercised rule of all, through voting on issues and for officials, each vote counting equally." But it has connotations which are almost an essential part of its meaning: a measure of freedom—the rights of free speech and free assembly at least; and equality before the law. In common usage it further connotes a measure of social equality. In the last century or so political democracy has almost invariably been organized through representative political institutions and parties.

DESPOT. A ruler who has complete power with no legal limits. Despotism was once perfectly respectable. The Italian republics in the late middle ages often invited despots—usually military men—to take over their affairs in times of crisis. In modern times, "despotism," like "tyranny," came to be associated with oppressive or capricious rule. See also ABSOLUTE MONARCHY.

DIET. One of the words used in Europe to designate an assembly to which is confided power to advise or decide on changes in law, taxation and other subjects. Such assemblies are also known as parliaments (which see), Estates, Cortes, etc. The word "diet" is most common in Germany and Scandinavia. It comes from the same source as the English word "day", and was originally any assembly called to meet on a particular day. Today the word is used (in Germany and Japan, for example) as the name of national representative assemblies. See PARLIAMENT.

EMPEROR. From the Latin for "supreme commander," the word developed by way of Roman generals and rulers, and the medieval Holy Roman Emperors, into a title which implied a collection of sovereign dignities. Peter the Great of Russia and Napoleon in France adopted it. So did others after the death of the Holy Roman Empire in 1806: the Emperor of Austria, the German Emperor, even Queen Victoria, who was proclaimed Empress of India.

ENTAIL. In law, a restriction of inheritance to a certain kind of heir for several generations, or in perpetuity. See, for example, PRIMOGENITURE. An entailed property cannot be disposed of by its holder as he pleases. The landed estates in England tended to remain large because in most cases inheritance was restricted to the oldest son.

DYNASTY. A family, or "House," which possesses hereditary right to reign over a particular territory or group of territories. The adjective "dynastic" usually refers to the politics or diplomacy practiced by the strong monarchs of the sixteenth through the eighteenth centuries.

ENGLAND, GREAT BRITAIN, UNITED KINGDOM. At present the correct name is "The United Kingdom of Great Britain and Northern Ireland." Great Britain is the island formed by England, Scotland and Wales. Wales and England were united in the thirteenth century. Scotland and England had the same ruler from 1603 on, and the governments were merged in 1707 to form the United Kingdom of Great Britain. Ireland, long subject to English kings, was merged with the United Kingdom in 1801, and southern Ireland subtracted from it in 1922. It is inaccurate to speak of the "British government" before 1707 or of the "English government" afterward.

FASCISM. Strictly speaking, the doctrine and movement which controlled the government of Italy under Benito Mussolini from 1922 to 1945, but the word has been applied to Germany under the Nazis from 1933 to 1945 and to similar (usually imitative) movements or parties elsewhere. See TOTALITARIANISM and also pp. 761–763.

FEDERALISM. A condition in which several states exist and operate side by side but have delegated certain of their powers to a common government which is empowered to operate within their territories.

FEUDAL. Relating to "feudalism," a political arrangement by which powers of governing were shared by kings and their vassals. With local variations, feudal arrangements existed throughout much of Europe in the middle ages. The student of modern history does not encounter "feudalism," itself but only some of its remnants, and he should use the word with extreme caution. See pp. 13, 15, 40.

FRANCHISE. Literally, a "freedom," and now often used to mean the grant of a special right, such as a concession to operate an automobile sales agency by a manufacturer. In politics, it has come to mean the right to vote.

GOVERNMENT. Used in two entirely distinct senses in modern history: (1) to mean the sum of officials, agencies, institutions, and procedures by which public affairs are carried on—in this case it is connected with, but not identical with, a STATE (which see); (2) as a synonym for the words "cabinet" and "ministry"—in this sense it means the group of executive heads of government departments (ministers). The first meaning is more common in America; the second is the way the word is used in Europe. See MINISTERIAL RESPONSIBILITY.

HEGEMONY. A jargon word meaning leadership or preponderant influence, usually of one country over others; often loosely used to mean almost the same thing as SUZERAINTY (which see).

IDEOLOGY AND ISM. An ideology is a group of related ideas and attitudes about social or political problems, usually supported by a movement which seeks to win converts to its way of life and its program of action. The expression "-ism" is a rough colloquial equivalent of "ideology," although not all systems of ideas whose name ends in "-ism" are backed by organized movements or characterized by efforts to proselytize. An ideology differs from a simple program for action in being connected with some basic philosophy or notion of values.

INDIVIDUALISM. Usually, a view of society which stresses the value and rights of the individual, particularly his freedom of choice of a career, religious beliefs, mode of life, and (sometimes) political leaders. See also LAISSEZ FAIRE, SOCIAL MOBILITY, and STRATIFICATION.

LAW. A baffling, intricate, and important word. The notion of law is at the root of all political organization and, more broadly, of all relations among individuals and groups. By extreme oversimplification it is possible to say that the word means two things, separate though intertwined: (1) an abstract notion of *rightness* which ought to govern relations between individuals and groups, translated into rules by duly constituted authorities. Some have seen it as divinely inspired, others as inhering in the natural order of things, others as the joint product of the moral ideas of individuals; (2) the rules actually formulated by the law-making authority and enforced on individuals. European languages distinguish the two meanings in the word "law" by separate words—in French, *le droit* for the first, *la loi* for the second.

LEFT. In politics, a conventional manner of referring to relatively radical persons and groups as opposed to the "Right," or relatively conservative persons, and the moderate "Center." The expressions date from the French revolutionary assemblies, in which more radical deputies sat to the left of the presiding officer. The usage persists, often pejorative, although many twentieth century movements like fascism and communism are difficult to classify sensibly as Rightist or Leftist.

LIBERAL. Together with its noun, LIBERALISM, has meant different things to different people at different times. The oldest English use of "liberal" is in the sense of "freeing," as from servitude or ignorance ("liberal education"). It came to be used to describe a political attitude in England in the early nineteeth century. In current United States usage, a liberal is someone of vaguely progressive views. But for the historian the word has a fairly precise meaning: it refers to a particular set of views about society which achieved acceptance and even dominance in some parts of the world in the second half of the nineteenth century and thereafter declined in popularity. For the details of liberal views and programs, see pp. 434–438.

LAISSEZ FAIRE. In French, "you leave it alone"; describes a government policy toward economic matters, advocated by Liberals and others from the mid-eighteenth century, which consisted of a minimum of government regulation.

MERCANTILISM. A set of economic policies and practices which evolved and flourished from the sixteenth through the eighteenth century as statesmen sought ways to unify their states economically and to enrich and strengthen them. See pp. 32–33. NEO-MERCANTILISM refers to roughly similar policies of more recent date, chiefly after 1870.

MIDDLE CLASS. Historically, the people—usually merchants—in the middle between the military aristocracy of great landowners and the peasants. Later, in European usage, the rich and powerful whose wealth derived from business rather than from land. The term is almost meaningless in American usage, since almost everybody considers himself "middle class." See p. 424. At different times the phrase has been used of widely various groups—white-collar workers, shopkeepers, bankers, industrial tycoons, professional men such as lawyers, doctors, and teachers. The only people consistently *excluded* from the middle class in European historical usage have been the nobility, the peasants, and the factory workers. See BOURGEOIS.

MINISTERIAL RESPONSIBILITY. The custom (or constitutional requirement) by which a ministry (cabinet, or government), composed of the heads of the principal government departments and composing the principal policy-making authority, is obliged to resign when the legislature demonstrates loss of confidence in the men or their program. Ministerial responsibility originated in Great Britain and spread to many continental countries in the nineteenth century; it became the standard method for assuring control over the executive authority by the representatives of the voters.

NATIONALITY, NATION, NATIONALISM. Nationality is used to characterize the common quality of a group of people who feel they share a particular kind of bond, usually but not necessarily based on common history, common language, and common culture. See pp. 11, 444. It is necessary to distinguish this idea of nationality based on sentiment and culture from the legal use of the word, which defines it as a common legal citizenship and common allegiance to a government. A nation, in modern usage, means a group of people of the same nationality plus their government. In earlier times, the word had no necessary political content. It meant something like a "tribe." "Nationalism" is a recent word used to describe a growing phenonenon of modern times—an intense loyalty to one's nationality, a loyalty so intense as to lead to a desire to *do something* about one's nationality.

NOBLE. A person enjoying hereditary title and rank, usually accompanied by privileges. The most usual titles of nobility in order of ascending rank: baron; viscount; count (in Britain called earl); marquis; duke. See ARISTOCRAT.

OLD REGIME. An expression used after the French Revolution of 1789 by people wishing to refer to the way things (society, politics) were before the revolution; it came to be used to describe all espects of eighteenth-century France, and by some people to describe the society and politics of Europe in general in the seventeeth and eighteenth centuries.

OLIGARCHY. Literally, "rule by the few"; used to indicate a society dominated (and generally governed) by a ruling group, or to indicate the group itself. The tone is mainly pejorative.

PARLIAMENT. The British assembly has given its name as a generic noun for all national representative assemblies—logically, since in the past hundred and fifty years many legislative assemblies have been fashioned after the British model. Even in France the present-day representative body is unofficially called the *parlement,* although in French history the word meant a very different sort of institution: a law court. The British Parliament originated as a law court (and still sometimes acts as one) but in modern times acquired the functions of making laws and approving taxes, which are the characteristic functions of most modern representative bodies.

PEASANT. Somebody of fairly modest means who earns his living by farming; usually the word suggests a definite connection with a particular piece of land—through ownership, leasing, or some traditional right to its use. The word implies in some measure an inferior social status. In Great Britain, its use disappeared in the nineteenth century. It has never been used to describe farm people in the United States. In its origin it meant merely someone who lived in the country. The French for country is *pays,* for peasant *paysan.*

PRIMOGENITURE. Means approximately "seniority of the first-born," and has been the basis on which the succession to most European thrones has been arranged in modern times. It also has often been the rule governing the transmission of titles of nobility and of private property. Under primogeniture, a king is succeeded by his oldest son; if the oldest son has died but left children, the throne goes to *his* oldest son (rather than to a brother) and so on. In some continental countries the succession was in addition regulated by the Salic Law, which excluded females and their descendants from inheriting thrones. See ENTAIL.

PROLETARIAT. In socialist and, particularly, Marxian theory, a propertyless class of people forced to sell their labor to factory-owners or others who own the means of production. The word was used in Roman times, but in its modern sense is properly applied only to people in an industrial society. It is to be used with caution.

RADICAL. From the Latin *radix,* root (the same source as "radish"). A radical is literally someone who wishes to tear things up by the roots, and since the early nineteenth century the word has been used of anyone who sought drastic changes in the existing order of things. In European history it is, more precisely, the name of a movement which had a fairly definite program; democracy, extensive civil liberties, protection for the underprivileged, protection of private property. European Radicalism may be regarded as an extreme form of Liberalism (which see).

REGIME. Literally, a rule, or set of rules. In continental countries the word is used much as Americans use "constitution," to refer to a *form* of government. Thus, when France changed from liberal monarchy to republic to empire in 1848–1852, it changed regimes. A change in regime is to be distinguished from a change of GOVERNMENT (which see), which means changing the executive leaders of the regime.

REPUBLIC. From the Latin, *res publica,* meaning "public thing" and implying "public welfare." It suggests the participation of the public, or part of it, in selecting a form of government and the governing officials. In practice it has been used in Europe to mean: (1) an elective kingship, associated with some representative institution, as in Poland before 1795; (2) a form of government in which the chief of state is elected, but is not called a king, and in which there is a body representing the public or part of it.

REVOLUTION. In common usage, an abrupt and extensive change or, more precisely, overturn: in opinions, tastes, moral standards, political or economic institutions, or in several of these simultaneously. There is generally an inference of violence in the idea of revolutionary change. The extent of the transformation, its rapidity, and the amount of violence involved have usually been related to the degree to which once-acceptable institutions have become outdated. But no two revolutions are alike except in a most general way.

RIGHT. See LEFT.

SOCIAL. Derived from the Latin word for "companion" and having to do with the association of people and the problems they share. "Social history" is a term used, often vaguely, to describe the study of such matters as education, ways of life, community customs, social classes, and other aspects of group life, as distinguished from the public concerns covered in "political history." In thinking about social history, it is helpful to ask oneself what groups are under discussion and what problems their activities present. See CLASS.

SOCIAL MOBILITY. The movement, or ease of movement, of individuals from one social level (usually the one they were born in) to another. See CLASS.

SOCIALISM. At first (in the early nineteenth century) little more than social concern—that is, solicitude for the underprivileged combined with emphasis on cooperation and distaste for unregulated competition. Later, socialism acquired a more precise meaning—that of a program calling for public ownership (by the state, usually, or by cooperative associations) of the means of production —capital, land, raw materials. See pp. 441–443 and COMMUNISM.

SOVEREIGNTY. Historically, the quality and attribute of sovereigns, which meant total and ultimate authority under God. Today it is generally used in one of two senses: (1) the peculiar quality of "sovereign states," or what are commonly called independent nations, which involves total freedom of action and total freedom from control by any outside government; (2) the location of the ultimate legal authority within a sovereign state. In a democracy, for example, it is usually said that the voters, or "the people," are sovereign. But we still speak of Elizabeth II as a sovereign, even though sovereignty in her kingdom seems to reside in the British voters and not in the queen.

STATE. One of the commonest and most baffling words in modern English. Its meaning depends entirely on the connection in which it is used. It originally meant "condition" and still does in certain uses. Take the sentence, "The building is in a poor state." This might equally well mean that the building is in poor repair or that it is located in some American state, such as Mississippi, with relatively small resources. In medieval times a man's "state" was used to mean his wealth, place in society, or legal status. When a council or assembly was called to advise the government, with representatives of different groups, it was sometimes called an assembly of States (or Estates, which is the same word differently spelled.) The parliament of the Netherlands, for example, is still called the "States General." The highest estate or condition in a kingdom was, of course, the king's, and from this fact we get one of the modern meanings of the word, the idea of the state as the supreme public authority—or all the public authorities taken together. A state in this sense is much like a government, but is more dignified (stately), and more comprehensive. "State" includes territory, which "government" does not, and implies permanent institutions and laws.

STATE SYSTEM. An expression frequently used by historians when they want to refer, without elaborating, to the sum of international relationships (described elsewhere under BALANCE OF POWER) and political institutions of modern Europe.

STRATIFICATION. Literally, making into layers, or *strata*, such as those of the earth's surface studied by geologists; as used by historians and other students of society, stratification is the formation of recognizable social levels, more or less distinct from each other. See CLASS.

SUZERAINTY. A word often loosely used to mean the preponderant influence of one government over a region or of one official within a government. More strictly, it means powers, definite but limited, which some government or sovereign is legally entitled to exercise over another. The most common illustration of suzerainty in the modern world is the relationship of a mother-country to a self-governing overseas territory, in which the former retains—for example—the right to veto laws passed in the latter.

TOTALITARIANISM. The control of every aspect of life—political, economic, cultural, religious—by the state. Such total regulation is associated with the effort to achieve the goals of some IDEOLOGY (which see) and involves penetration of personal and family affairs and the destruction of privacy. It is, therefore, to be regarded as the reverse of INDIVIDUALISM (which see). Fascist Italy, Nazi Germany, and Soviet Russia are usually taken as the principal examples of totalitarianism, and the word is used only to describe phenomena of the twentieth century.

TYRANT. See DESPOT.

VILLAGE. In Europe, "village" has a more exact meaning than in America where it refers to any small collection of dwellings or shops. The European village is a farming community where peasants or other farm workers have their houses and from which they go out daily to work the fields, and is often connected with a manor house and a church. Europeans tended to congregate in villages (rather than living in separated farmhouses) originally for reasons of sociability and defense and because most land was not owned in solid units but allotted to farms in small parcels scattered around the village. The village community sometimes had charge of redistributing the parcels, as they did in Russia. So villages were more than collections of buildings; they were, and often are, the basic social unit and often were institutions with special functions. Not all Europe was organized on the basis of villages. In many Mediterranean areas, especially, farmers lived in towns. Towns differ from villages not so much in being larger as in being market-places and often in having their own defenses and formal governments of their own with chartered liberties. Villages rarely had formal governments, but were most often subject to the jurisdiction of the local manor and its lord, at least until early modern times.

RULERS OF THE PRINCIPAL COUNTRIES SINCE 1500

The kinship of each ruler to his predecessor is indicated.

ENGLAND, GREAT BRITAIN

1485–1509, Henry VII. King of England. Founder of the House of Tudor.

1509–1547, Henry VIII. Son.

1547–1553, Edward VI. Son.

1553–1558, Mary I. Sister.

1558–1603, Elizabeth I. Sister.

1603–1625, James I. King of England and Scotland. Founder of the House of Stuart. Cousin.

1625–1649, Charles I, Son.

Interregnum, 1649–1660. Commonwealth and Protectorate.

1660–1685, Charles II. Son.

1685–1688, James II. Brother.

1689–1702, William III, *and* 1689–1694, Mary II. William was the nephew and his wife the daughter of James II.

1702–1714, Anne, Queen of Great Britain. Sister of Mary.

1714–1727, George I. Founder of the House of Hanover. Cousin.

1727–1760, George II. Son.

1760–1820, George III. Grandson.

1820–1830, George IV. Son.

1830–1837, William IV. Brother.

1837–1901, Victoria. Niece.

1901–1910, Edward VII. Of the House of Saxe-Coburg-Gotha. Son.

1910–1936, George V. Name of dynasty changed to Windsor. Son.

1936 Edward VIII. Son.

1936–1952, George VI. Brother.

1952– Elizabeth II. Daughter.

FRANCE

1498–1515, Louis XII. King of France. Of the House of Valois.
1515–1547, Francis I. Cousin.
1547–1559, Henry II. Son.
1559–1560, Francis II. Son.
1560–1574, Charles IX. Brother.
1574–1589, Henry III. Brother.
1589–1610, Henry IV. Founder of the House of Bourbon. Cousin.
1610–1643, Louis XIII. Son.
1643–1715, Louis XIV. Son.
1715–1774, Louis XV. Great-grandson.
1774–1792, Louis XVI. Grandson.

First Republic, 1792–1804.

1804–1814, Napoleon I. Emperor of the French.
1814–1824, Louis XVIII. King of France. Brother of Louis XVI. (The son of Louis XVI, who died in prison, never reigned, but is counted as Louis XVII).
1824–1830, Charles X. King of France. Brother of Louis XVI and Louis XVIII.
1830–1848, Louis Philippe I. King of the French. Of the House of Bourbon-Orléans. Cousin of Charles X.

Second Republic, 1848–1852.

1852–1870, Napoleon III. Emperor of the French. Nephew of Napoleon I. (The son of Napoleon I, who never reigned, is counted as Napoleon II.)

Third Republic, 1870–1940.
"The French State," under Marshal Pétain, 1940–1944.
Provisional Government of the French Republic, 1944–1946.
Fourth Republic, 1946–1958.
Fifth Republic, 1958–   .

PRUSSIA AND GERMANY SINCE 1619

1619–1640, George William. Elector of Brandenburg. Of the House of Hohenzollern.
1640–1688, Frederick William. "The Great Elector" of Brandenburg. Son.
1688–1713, Frederick III. King in Prussia as Frederick I after 1701. Son.
1713–1740, Frederick William I. Son.
1740–1786, Frederick II, "the Great." Son.
1786–1797, Frederick William II. Nephew.

1797–1840, Frederick William III. Son.
1840–1861, Frederick William IV. Son.
1861–1888, William I. First German Emperor after 1871. Brother.
1888, Frederick III. Son.
1888–1918, William II. Son.

Weimar Republic, 1919–1933.
Dictatorship of Adolf Hitler, 1933–1945.
Under military occupation, 1945–1950.
German Federal Republic (in the west) and German Democratic Republic (in the east), 1950– .

HOLY ROMAN EMPIRE AND AUSTRIA

1493–1519, Maximilian I. Holy Roman Emperor. Of the House of Habsburg.

1519–1556, Charles V. Grandson.

1556–1564, Ferdinand I. Brother.

1564–1576, Maximilian II. Son.

1576–1612, Rudolf II. Son.

1612–1619, Mathias I. Brother.

1619–1637, Ferdinand II. Cousin.

1637–1657, Ferdinand III. Son.

1658–1705, Leopold I. Son.

1705–1711, Joseph I. Son.

1711–1740, Charles VI. Brother.

1740–1780, Maria Theresa. Ruler of the Habsburg domains; married Francis, Duke of Lorraine, who reigned as Holy Roman Emperor 1745–1765. Daughter of Charles VI.

1765–1790, Joseph II. Holy Roman Emperor ruler of Habsburg domains 1780–1790. Founder of the House of Habsburg-Lorraine. Son of Maria Theresa.

1790–1792, Leopold II. Brother.

1792–1806, Francis II. Holy Roman Emperor; Emperor of Austria as Francis I, 1804–1835. Son of Leopold II.

1835–1848, Ferdinand I. Emperor of Austria. Son.

1848–1916, Francis Joseph I. Emperor of Austria and King of Hungary. Nephew.

1916–1918, Charles I. Grand-nephew. In 1918 the territories of the Habsburg Monarchy were divided among the Republic of Austria, Czechoslovakia, Hungary, Poland, Rumania, Yugoslavia, and Italy.

RUSSIA

1462–1505, Ivan III. Grand Duke of Moscow.

1505–1533, Basil III. Son.

1533–1584, Ivan IV. Czar of Russia from 1547. Son.

1584–1598, Theodore I. Son.

1598–1605, Boris Godunov. Brother-in-law.

Time of Troubles, 1604–1613.

1613–1645, Michael I. Founder of the House of Romanov.

1645–1676, Alexis I. Son.

1676–1682, Theodore III. Son.

1682–1696, Ivan V. Co-Czar with Peter I. Brother.

1682–1725, Peter I. "The Great." Took title of Emperor of Russia. Half-brother.

1725–1727, Catherine I. Widow.

1727–1730, Peter II. Grandson of Peter I.

1730–1740, Anna. Niece of Peter I.

1740–1741, Ivan VI. Grand-nephew.

1741–1762, Elizabeth. Daughter of Peter I.

1762, Peter III. Nephew.

1762–1796, Catherine II. "The Great." Widow.

1796–1801, Paul I. Son.

1801–1825, Alexander I. Son.

1825–1855, Nicholas I. Brother.

1855–1881, Alexander II. Son.

1881–1894, Alexander III. Son.

1894–1917, Nicholas II. Son.

Provisional Government, 1917.

Russian Socialist Federated Soviet Republic, 1918.

Union of Soviet Socialist Republics, 1922– .

SPAIN

1479–1516, Ferdinand. King of Aragon:
1474–1504. Isabella. Queen of Castile; married 1469. Took titles of King of Spain (Ferdinand V) and Queen of Spain (Isabella I) in 1479.
1516–1556, Charles I. Reigned as Holy Roman Emperor Charles V, 1519–1556; founder of the House of Habsburg. Grandson.
1556–1598, Philip II. Son.
1598–1621, Philip III. Son.
1621–1665, Philip IV. Son.
1665–1700, Charles II. Son.
1700–1746, Philip V. Founder of the House of Bourbon. Grandnephew.
1746–1759, Ferdinand VI. Son.

1759–1788, Charles III. Brother.
1788–1808, Charles IV. Son.
1808–1813, Joseph Bonaparte. Brother of Napoleon I of France.
1813–1833, Ferdinand VII. Son of Charles IV.
1833–1868, Isabella II. Daughter.

Provisional Government, 1868–1871.

1871–1873, Amadeo I. Of the House of Savoy.
First Republic, 1873–1874.
1875–1885, Alfonso XII. Son of Isabella II.
1902–1931, Alfonso XIII. Son.

Second Republic, 1931–1939.
Dictatorship of Francisco Franco, 1939– .

PIEDMONT AND ITALY SINCE 1831

1831–1849, Charles Albert. King of Sardinia-Piedmont. Of the House of Savoy.
1849–1878, Victor Emmanuel II. Became King of Italy 1861. Son.

1878–1900, Humbert I. Son.
1900–1946, Victor Emmanuel III. Son.
1946, Humbert II. Son.

Republic, 1946–   .

POPES

1492–1503, Alexander VI.
1503, Pius III.
1503–1513, Julius II.
1513–1521, Leo X.
1522–1523, Adrian VI.
1523–1534, Clement VII.
1534–1549, Paul III.
1550–1555, Julius III.
1555, Marcellus II.
1555–1559, Paul IV.
1559–1565, Pius IV.
1566–1572, Pius V.

1572–1585, Gregory XIII.
1585–1590, Sixtus V.
1590–1591, Urban VII.
1591, Gregory XIV.
1591, Innocent IX.
1592–1605, Clement VIII.
1605, Leo XI.
1605–1621, Paul V.
1621–1623, Gregory XV.
1623–1644, Urban VIII.
1644–1655, Innocent X.
1655–1667, Alexander VII.

1667–1669, Clement IX.
1670–1676, Clement X.
1676–1689, Innocent XI.
1689–1691, Alexander VIII.
1691–1700, Innocent XII.
1700–1721, Clement XI.
1721–1724, Innocent XIII.
1724–1730, Benedict XIII.
1730–1740, Clement XII.
1740–1758, Benedict XIV.
1758–1769, Clement XIII.
1769–1774, Clement XIV.

1775–1799, Pius VI.
1800–1823, Pius VII.
1823–1829, Leo XII.
1829–1830, Pius VIII.
1831–1846, Gregory XVI.
1846–1878, Pius IX.
1878–1903, Leo XIII.
1903–1914, Pius X.
1914–1922, Benedict XV.
1922–1939, Pius XI.
1939–1958, Pius XII.
1958–   , John XXIII.

APPENDIX C

A SELECT LIST OF SUGGESTIONS FOR READING AND REFERENCE

INTRODUCTION

Generally useful books grouped according to their subjects are listed in this section.

Dutcher, G. M., and others. *A Guide to Historical Literature*. N.Y., 1931. New edition planned for 1959. The most important one-volume bibliography. Old edition has descriptions of best books in English and of outstanding works in other languages. New edition will have fewer descriptions but many more items about all parts of the world.

Langer, W. L., ed., *Encyclopedia of World History*. Boston, 1952. Lists major events in each country year by year over extended periods. Useful for bird's-eye views and checking on facts.

Encyclopedia of the Social Sciences, 15 vols. N.Y., 1930–1935. Has essays on most important persons and topics encountered in history, economics, political science, sociology, and so on. Try, for example, "History."

Ausubel, H., *The Making of Modern Europe*, 2 vols. N.Y., 1951. Fine collection of periodical articles, most of them interpretive and eye-opening.

Walker, W., *History of the Christian Church*. N.Y., 1918. Still among the best of its kind.

Latourette, K. S., *History of Chrisianity*. N.Y., 1953. By a great authority.

Clough, S. B., *The Economic Development of Western Civilization*. N.Y., 1959. Up-to-date product of many years of research by an outstanding authority.

Clough, S. B., and Cole, C. W., *Economic History of Europe*., 3rd ed. Boston, 1952. Still one of the best.

Heaton, H., *Economic History of Europe*, rev. ed. N.Y., 1948. Like Clough and Cole, one of the best.

Brinton, C., *Ideas and Men*. Englewood Cliffs, N.J., 1950. Most useful brief treatment of intellectual history. The part covering the modern period has been published as a paperback called *The Shaping of the Modern Mind*. N.Y., 1953.

Randall, J. H., *The Making of the Modern Mind*, rev. ed. Boston, 1940. Somewhat more extensive than Brinton, with more attention to formal philosophy.

Baumer, F. L., ed., *Main Currents of Western Thought: Readings in Western European Intellectual History from the Middle Ages to the Present*. N.Y., 1952. Valuable introductions as well as readings.

Russell, B., *A History of Western Philosophy*. N.Y., 1945. A good book for the layman, written by a great English philosopher.

Whitehead, A. N., *Science and the Modern World*. N.Y., 1945. Brilliant lecture series. Earliest chapters the most useful to beginners.

Taylor, F. S., *A Short History of Science and Scientific Thought*. N.Y., 1949. Convenient introduction.

Sabine, G. H., *A History of Political Theory*, rev. ed. N.Y., 1950. An outstanding treatment of the subject.

Gardner's Art through the Ages. Revised under the editorship of Sumner McK. Crosby. N.Y., 1959. Beautifully redone and brought up to date.

Lang, P. H., *Music in Western Civilization*. N.Y., 1941. Probably the most useful general introduction.

Fuller, J. F. C., *A Military History of the Western World*, 3 vols. N.Y., 1954–1956. Provocative, bold.

Petrie, C., *Earlier Diplomatic History, 1492–1713*. N.Y., 1949. *Diplomatic History 1713–1933*. N.Y., 1949. Mainly factual but provide useful coverage.

Albrecht-Carrié, R., *A Diplomatic History of Europe since the Congress of Vienna*. N.Y., 1958. Good, recent text by reliable scholar.

Introduction to Contemporary Civilization in the West, 2 vols. N.Y., 1954. Reading selections of unusual breadth and value, assembled by faculty of Columbia College.

Fox, E. H., ed., *Atlas of European History*. N.Y., 1957.

Hammond's Historical Atlas. Maplewood, N.J., 1957.

Palmer, R. R., ed., *Atlas of World History*. Chicago, 1957.

Shepherd, W. R., *Historical Atlas*. 8th rev. ed. N.Y., 1956.

Whittlesey, D., *Environmental Foundations of European History*. N.Y., 1949.

Barzun, J. and Graff, H., *The Modern Researcher*. N.Y., 1957. Excellent on how to study and write history.

Rowse, A. L., *The Use of History* (Teach Yourself History Library). N.Y., Macmillan, 1946. Useful introduction.

Collingwood, R. G., *The Idea of History*. Oxford England, 1946. Philosophical and historical reflections on the subject of history.

Barraclough, G., *History in a Changing World*. Oxford, England, 1955. Discusses examples of historical interpretation.

Geyl, P., *Debates with Historians*. N.Y., 1958. Discusses some of the great historians.

Berlin, I., *Historical Inevitability*. Oxford, 1955. Brief and analytical.

Nield, J., *A Guide to the Best Historical Novels and Tales*. London, 1929.

PART ONE

The Building of the European States, 1500–1648

The books in this and the following sections are arranged alphabetically by author, to facilitate reference to instructors' suggestions. Nevertheless, it is hoped that the limited length of the list will encourage a birds'-eye view of its contents. In most cases, books are not listed more than once, even when they are relevant to later sections.

Bainton, R. H., *Here I Stand: A Life of Martin Luther*. N.Y., 1950. Very readable biography by an acknowledged authority.

——, *The Age of the Reformation* (Anvil Series). Princeton, 1956. Convenient little paperback, half text, half source readings, by eminent authority. See the following item.

——, *The Reformation of the Sixteenth Century*. Boston, 1952. Excellent account from the Protestant point of view. Extremely readable.

Brandi, K., *The Emperor Charles V*. London, 1939. A standard biography.

Brebner, J. B., *The Explorers of North America, 1492–1806*. N.Y., 1933. Very useful. Paperback reprint available.

Burckhardt, J. C., *Civilization of the Renaissance in Italy* (many editions). A classic.

Butterfield, H., *The Statecraft of Machiavelli*. London, 1940. By a fearless Englishman who has illuminated many crucial topics.

Clark, G. N., *The Seventeenth Century*, 2nd ed. N.Y., 1947. A study, topically organized, of the institutions and characteristics of the age.

Davies, G., *The Early Stuarts, 1603–1660* (Oxford History of England). New ed., Oxford, England, 1949. A standard, scholarly treatment.

Davies, R. T., *The Golden Century of Spain*. London, 1937. A short but authoritative survey of Spanish civilization in the sixteenth century.

Durant, W., *The Renaissance* (Vol. V of *The Story of Civilization*). N.Y., 1953.

Colorful, detailed account by a great popularizer.

Eckhardt, H. von, *Ivan the Terrible*. N.Y., 1949. Laudatory.

Ferguson, W. K., *The Renaissance*. N.Y., 1940. A fine brief introduction.

Ferguson, W. K., *The Renaissance in Historical Thought*. Boston, 1948. An imposing study of what historians have meant by the word "Renaissance," and a criticism of interpretations of the era.

Florinsky, M. T., *Russia: A History and an Interpretation*, 2 vols. N.Y., 1953. Most useful single work in English. Goes from earliest times to the 1917 revolution.

Friedrich, C. J., *The Age of the Baroque, 1610–1660* (Langer series). N.Y., 1952. Synthesis based on recent scholarship.

Geyl, P., *The Revolt of the Netherlands, 1555–1609*. London, 1945.

——, *The Netherlands Divided, 1609–1648*. London, 1936. Outstanding Dutch historian and excellent writer.

Gilmore, M., *The World of Humanism, 1453–1517* (Langer series). N.Y., 1952. Good volume in a good series. Valuable interpretations and bibliographies.

Halecki, O., *Borderlands of Western Civilization: a History of East-Central Europe*. N.Y., 1952. Indispensable, though not easy reading.

Harkness, G., *John Calvin, the Man and his Ethics*. N.Y., 1931. Brief and good.

Hart, H. H., *Sea Road to the Indies*. N.Y., 1950. Portuguese explorations by Vasco da Gama and others.

Haring, C. H., *The Spanish Empire in*

America. N.Y., 1947. Reliable introduction to a vast subject.

Highet, G., *The Classical Tradition: Greek and Roman Influences on Western Literature*. N.Y., 1949. An urbane and well-informed writer treats a great subject.

Hurst, Q., *Henry of Navarre*. N.Y., 1938. Good biography.

Janelle, P., *The Catholic Reformation*. Milwaukee, 1949. Catholic point of view narrated with sympathy.

Kluchevsky, V. O., *A History of Russia*, 5 vols. London, 1911–1931. The great classic, rewarding to consult.

Lamb, H., *The March of Muscovy: Ivan the Terrible and the Growth of the Russian Empire, 1400–1648*. N.Y., 1948. Good popularization.

Lybyer, A. H., *The Government of the Ottoman Empire in the Time of Suleiman the Magnificent*. Cambridge, Mass., 1913. Detailed study of institutions.

Martin, A. W. O. von, *Sociology of the Renaissance*. N.Y., 1941. Useful treatment of a subject which lends itself to controversy.

Mattingly, G., *Renaissance Diplomacy*. Boston, 1955. Excellent, authoritative.

Morison, S. E., *Admiral of the Ocean Sea*, 2 vols. Boston, 1942. Columbus, seen by distinguished American historian and sailor.

Mosse, G. L., *The Reformation*. N.Y., 1952. Very good brief introduction.

Neale, J. E., *Queen Elizabeth*. N.Y., 1934. A biography of the first Elizabeth, and a good picture of sixteenth-century England.

———, *The Age of Catherine de Medici*. London, 1943. The era of the religious wars in France.

Notestein, W., *The English People on the Eve of Colonization, 1603–1630*. N.Y., 1954. Valuable information about life and thought.

Nowell, C. E., *The Great Discoveries*. Ithaca, 1954. Good brief survey of the whole subject.

Ogg, D., *Europe in the Seventeenth Century*, 6th ed., N.Y., 1958. A good general history.

Packard, L. B., *The Commercial Revolu-tion, 1400–1776*. N.Y., 1927. Clarifies a lot of economic history.

Palm, F. C., *Calvinism and the Religious Wars*. N.Y., 1932. Good introduction to a complicated subject.

Parker, T. M., *The English Reformation to 1558* (Home University Library). N.Y., 1950. Brief and good.

Parry, J. H., *Europe and a Wider World, 1415–1715*. London, 1949. Convenient small survey.

Pevsner, Nikolaus, *An Outline of European Architecture*. Hammondsworth, Middlesex, England, 1951. Use for Renaissance and consult for later periods.

Powicke, F. M., *The Reformation in England*. London, 1941. By an acknowledged authority.

Read, C., *The Tudors*. N.Y., 1936. An agreeable and perceptive historical essay.

Renard, G., and Weulersse, G., *Life and Work in Modern Europe*. N.Y., 1926. Still very useful for the early modern period, through the eighteenth century.

Robb, David, *Harper History of Painting*. N.Y., 1951. Use for Renaissance, along with suggestions in previous section.

Rowse, A. L., *The England of Elizabeth: the Structure of Society*. London, 1950. Controversial.

Schevill, F., *A History of Florence*. N.Y., 1936.

———, *The Medici*. N.Y., 1949. Well known special studies of recognized worth.

Tawney, R. H., *Religion and the Rise of Capitalism*. N.Y., Mentor Books, Paperback reprint of well-known essay by English social theorist.

Taylor, H. O., *Thought and Expression in the Sixteenth Century*, rev. ed. N.Y., 1930. Useful, reliable.

Troeltsch, E., *Protestantism and Progress*. N.Y., 1912. By an important German philosopher of religion who was also a pioneer sociologist.

Venturi, Lionello, *Italian Painting*. 3 vols. N.Y., 1950–1952. Good description.

Vernadsky, G., *Kievan Russia*. New Haven, 1948. The latest scholarship.

Weber, M., *The Protestant Ethic and the Spirit of Capitalism*, ed. T. Parsons.

N.Y., 1930. Classic on the influence of Protestantism on capitalism, first published in 1904–1905 by the great German sociologist.

Wedgwood, C. V., *Richelieu and the French Monarchy* (Teach Yourself History series). N.Y., 1949. Well informed and judicious.

———, *The King's Peace, 1637–1641.* N.Y., 1955. Outstanding first volume of a projected history of the Civil War in England.

———, *The Thirty Years War.* London, 1938. Sound scholarship, and reads like a novel.

———, *William the Silent.* New Haven, 1945. Authoritative and interesting.

Whitfield, J. H., *Machiavelli.* Oxford, England, 1947. Sympathetic.

Wittek, P., *The Rise of the Ottoman Empire.* London, 1938. An interpretation of its success.

See also the general works recommended in the introductory section.

PART TWO
The Old Regime, 1648–1789

Ashley, M. P., *Louis XIV and the Greatness of France* (Teach Yourself History series). N.Y., 1947. Convenient and brief.

Barber, E., *The Bourgeoisie in Eighteenth Century France.* Princeton, 1955. Very interesting statement in sociological language.

Becker, C., *The Heavenly City of the Eighteenth Century Philosophers.* New Haven, 1932. Famous lectures, still much discussed.

Beloff, M., *The Age of Absolutism 1660–1815.* London, 1954. Brief and rewarding, but not easy for beginners.

Brinton, C., ed., *The Portable Age of Reason Reader.* N.Y., 1956. Good Enlightenment selections.

Bruford, W. H., *Germany in the Eighteenth Century: the Social Background of the Literary Revival.* N.Y., 1952. Good for sociological and cultural history.

Bruun, G., *The Enlightenment Despots.* N.Y., 1929. Good brief survey.

Buffinton, A. H., *The Second Hundred Years War, 1689–1815.* N.Y., 1929. Anglo-French rivalry.

Butterfield, H., *The Origins of Modern Science, 1300–1800.* N.Y., 1951. A celebrated essay and a good introduction for the layman.

Bury, J. B., *The Idea of Progress: An Inquiry into its Origins and Growth.*

N.Y., 1955. Paperback of old but still useful essay.

Cambridge History of Poland, 2 vols. Cambridge, Eng., 1941–1950. Goes to 1935.

Cassirer, E., *The Philosophy of the Enlightenment.* Boston, 1955. An important book by a great authority. Rather technical for the uninitiated.

Chrimes, S. B., *English Constitutional History,* 2nd ed. N.Y., 1953. Enlightening little survey.

Clark, G. N., *The Later Stuarts, 1600–1714* (Oxford History of England). New ed. Oxford, England, 1949. Important scholarly account.

Cobban, A., *A History of Modern France.* Vol. I. *Old Régime and Revolution, 1715–1799.* Baltimore, Md., 1957. Pelican paperback. Very significant recent history by English authority of high standing.

Cole, C. W., *Colbert and a Century of French Mercantilism.* N.Y., 1939. Fine work of scholarship. Compare with Heckscher (see below).

Dorn, W. L., *Competition for Empire, 1740–1763* (Langer series). N.Y., 1940. One of the best in the series on periods of European history.

Ergang, R. R., *The Potsdam Führer.* N.Y., 1941. About Frederick the Great's father; very useful for Prussian history.

Fay, S. B., *The Rise of Brandenburg-Prussia to 1786*. N.Y., 1937. Much good information in little space.

Firth, C. H., *Oliver Cromwell and the Rule of the Puritans in England*. N.Y., 1900. Old but good.

Fosca, F., *The Eighteenth Century: From Watteau to Tiepolo*. N.Y., 1953. On painting.

Frankel, C., *The Faith of Reason*. N.Y., 1948. Excellent analysis of the Enlightenment by a philosopher.

Gaxotte, P., *Louis XV and His Times*. Philadelphia, 1934. Sympathetic to old regime.

Gershoy, L. *From Despotism to Revolution, 1763–1789* (Langer Series). N.Y., 1944. One of the best in the series on periods of European history.

Gooch, G. P., *English Democratic Ideas in the Seventeenth Century*. Cambridge, England, 1927. Good historian, important subject.

———, *Catherine the Great and Other Studies*. N.Y., 1954.

———, *Frederick the Great, the Ruler, the Writer, the Man*. N.Y., 1947.

———, *Louis XV*. London, 1956. Sound biographical studies.

Goodwin, A., ed., *The European Nobility in the Eighteenth Century*. London, 1953. Very enlightening essays on aristocracies of various countries.

Green, F. C., *Jean-Jacques Rousseau: Critical Study of His Life and Writings*. N.Y., 1955. Best biography of Rousseau.

Guérard, A., *The Life and Death of an Ideal*, new ed. N.Y., 1956. Extremely readable account of Age of Louis XIV and its aftermath.

Hall, A. R., *The Scientific Revolution, 1500–1800: the Formation of the Modern Scientific Attitude*. Boston, 1956. Good, recent.

Havens, G. R., *The Age of Ideas: From Reaction to Revolution in Eighteenth Century France*. N.Y., 1955. Up-to-date essays on various personages.

Hazard, P., *The European Mind, 1680–1715*. London, 1953. One of the principal intellectual histories.

———, *European Thought in the Eighteenth Century*. London, 1954. One of the outstanding intellectual histories.

Heckscher, E. F., *Mercantilism*, 2 vols., revised ed. N.Y., 1955. Classic of its kind. Compare with C. W. Cole (above).

Keir, D. L., *The Constitutional History of Modern Britain, 1485–1937*, 4th ed. London, 1950. Generally useful, and particularly useful for this period.

Kerner, R. J., *The Urge to the Sea: the Course of Russian History*. Berkeley, 1946. Russian expansion.

Konovalov, S., *Russo-Polish Relations: An Historical Survey*. Princeton, 1945.

Lewis, W. H., *The Splendid Century*. N.Y., 1954. About seventeenth-century France.

Mahan, A. T., *The Influence of Sea Power on History, 1660–1783*. Boston, 1890. A classic by an American naval officer.

Manuel, F. E., *The Age of Reason*. Ithaca, 1951. Brief intelligent introduction to eighteenth-century history.

Marriott, J. A., *The Eastern Question: An Historical Study in European Diplomacy*, 4th ed. Oxford, 1940. Important for Eastern Europe and international relations.

Martin, K., *The Rise of French Liberal Thought*, ed. J. P. Mayer. N.Y., 1954. Useful for political and social theories in eighteenth-century France.

Montesquieu, Charles de Secondat, Baron de, *The Spirit of the Laws*, ed. F. Neumann. N.Y., 1949. Introduction by Neumann is an important essay in its own right.

Morley, J., *Diderot and the Encyclopaedists*, rev. ed. London, 1923. Old but still useful.

Mornet, D., *French Thought in the Eighteenth Century*. N.Y., 1929. Small book by great authority.

Morris, C. L., *Maria Theresa, The Last Conservative*. N.Y., 1937. Sympathetic biography.

Namier, L. B., *The Structure of Politics at the Accession of George III*, 2 vols. London, 1929. Important and substantial.

New Cambridge Modern History. Vol.

VI. *The Old Regime, 1713–1763.* Cambridge, England, 1957.

Nussbaum, F. L., *The Triumph of Science and Reason, 1660–1685* (Langer series). N.Y., 1953. Important. Treats all of Europe.

Packard, L. B., *The Age of Louis XIV.* N.Y., 1929. Convenient and brief.

Padover, S. K., *The Revolutionary Emperor, Joseph II.* N.Y., 1934. Sympathetic biography.

Plumb, J. H., *England in the Eighteenth Century.* Harmondsworth, Middlesex, England, 1950. Useful paperback survey; goes to 1815.

Roberts, P., *The Quest for Security, 1715–1740* (Langer series) N.Y., 1947. Synthesis for all Europe.

Robertson, C. G., *Chatham and the British Empire* (Teach Yourself History Library). N.Y., 1948. Brief biography of Pitt.

Robinson, G. T., *Rural Russia under the Old Regime.* N.Y., 1949. Indispensable for serfdom and the peasant question.

Rousseau, J. J., *The Social Contract and Discourses.* N.Y., 1913.

———, *Emile.* (Everyman edition). N.Y., 1955.

Schapiro, J. S., *Condorcet and the Rise of Liberalism.* N.Y., 1934. Helps understand Enlightenment and Revolution.

Schevill, F., *The Great Elector.* Chicago, 1947. About the Hohenzollern who set the pattern of the Prussian state.

Thomson, G. Scott. *Catherine the Great and the Expansion of Russia* (Teach Yourself History series). N.Y., 1950. Brief, readable.

Sée, H., *Economic and Social Conditions in France during the Eighteenth Century.* N.Y., 1927. Best single volume on the subject.

Smith, P., *History of Modern Culture,* Vol. II. N.Y., 1934. Has good brief general statement on Enlightenment, followed by detailed essays on various aspects of eighteenth-century thought.

Sorel, A., *Europe under the Old Regime.* Los Angeles, 1947. Illuminating introduction to a many volumed French classic.

Sumner, B. H., *Peter the Great and the Emergence of Russia* (Teach Yourself History series). N.Y., 1951. Contributes to understanding of other periods as well.

———, *Short History of Russia.* N.Y., 1949. Unusual book, topically arranged.

Tocqueville, A. de, *The Old Regime and the Revolution.* N.Y., 1958. Paperback reprint of classic nineteenth-century analysis of old regime.

Trevelyan, G. M., *The English Revolution, 1688–1689* (Home University Library). London, 1938. One of many good books by a famous English historian.

Vagts, A., *A History of Militarism.* N.Y., 1937. Useful for relationships between warfare and society.

Veale, F. J. P., *Frederick the Great.* London, 1935. A sympathetic biography.

Walizewski, K., *The Romance of an Empress.* N.Y., 1894. About Catherine II of Russia.

Willey, B., *The Seventeenth Century Background.* N.Y., 1958. Essays on famous thinkers: Descartes, Hobbes, and so on.

Williams, B., *The Whig Supremacy, 1714–1760* Oxford, England, 1939. Scholarly account of a period of English history.

Wilson, A. M., *Diderot: the Testing Years, 1713–1759.* N.Y., 1957. An outstanding biographical study.

Wolf, J. B., *The Emergence of the Great Powers, 1685–1715* (Langer series). N.Y., 1951. With Nussbaum (see above) provides synthesis and latest scholarship for Age of Louis XIV in all of Europe.

Young, A., *Travels in France,* ed. C. Maxwell. Cambridge, England, 1929. An English observer describes France on the eve of the Revolution. *See also* the relevant suggestions in previous sections.

PART THREE
Revolutionary and Conservative Europe, 1789–1870

Artz, F. B., *Reaction and Revolution, 1814–1832* (Langer series). N.Y., 1950. Significant synthesis for all Europe.

Ashton, T. S., *The Industrial Revolution, 1760–1830* (Home University Library). N.Y., 1948. Convenient, brief essay.

Babbitt, I., *Rousseau and Romanticism.* N.Y., 1958. Paperback reprint of an unsympathetic analysis.

Barzun, J., *Darwin, Marx, Wagner.* Boston, 1941.

———, *Romanticism and the Modern Ego.* Boston, 1943. Brilliant controversial expositions of much nineteenth-century intellectual history.

Belloc, H., *Danton.* N.Y., 1928. Useful biography.

Berdyaev, N., *The Origin of Russian Communism.* London, England, 1948. A Russian philosopher's fascinating account; contains much information on Russian intellectual history.

Berlin, I., *Karl Marx: His Life and Environment* (Home University Library), 2nd ed. N.Y., 1948. Brilliant brief biography.

Binkley, R. C., *Realism and Nationalism, 1852–1871* (Langer series). N.Y., Harper, 1935. Synthesis for all Europe. Controversial thesis about federalism.

Bowden, W., Karpovich, M., and Usher, A. P., *An Economic History of Europe since 1750.* N.Y., 1937. Generally useful, but especially so for agrarian questions in Eastern Europe.

Brinton, C., *A Decade of Revolution, 1798–1799* (Langer series). N.Y., 1934. Treats all Europe in brilliant interpretive fashion.

———, *The Jacobins.* N.Y., 1930. Best in the subject.

———, *The Lives of Talleyrand.* N.Y., 1936. A sympathetic portrait.

———, *English Political Thought in the Nineteenth Century.* New ed. Cambridge, Harvard University Press, 1949. Valuable.

Brogan, D. W., *The French Nation from Napoleon to Petain, 1814–1940.* N.Y., 1957. By a learned and witty expert. Not always easy reading for beginners.

Bruun, G., *Europe and the French Imperium, 1799–1814* (Langer series). N.Y., 1938. On all Europe, and gives a convenient brief account of Napoleon's career.

———, *Revolution and Reaction 1848–1852* (Anvil). Princeton, 1958. Paperback introduction to the Revolutions of 1848; half text, half documents.

———, *Saint-Just: Apostle of the Terror.* Boston. 1932. Useful brief biography.

Burke, E., *Reflections on the Revolution in France.* (many editions) Classic.

Bury, J. P. T., *France, 1814–1940.* Philadelphia, 1949. Useful brief chapters by a detached and scholarly Englishman.

Carr, E. H., *Studies in Revolution.* London, 1950. Valuable brief essays on various Utopian and Russian socialists.

Caulaincourt, A. A. L. de, *With Napoleon in Russia.* N.Y., 1955. The Emperor's aide and companion.

Clapham, J., *An Economic History of Modern Britain,* 3 vols., 2nd ed. Cambridge, England, 1930–1938. Classic.

Clough, S. B., *France: a History of National Economics.* N.Y., 1939. Valuable for general history as well.

Cobban, A., ed., *The Debate on the French Revolution, 1789–1800.* London, 1950. Seen from across the English Channel.

Darmstaedter, F., *Bismarck and the Creation of the Second Reich.* London, 1948. One of the best in English.

Eyck, E., *Bismarck and the German Empire.* London, 1950. A greatly reduced English version of a standard work in German.

Fisher, H. A. L., *Napoleon* (Home University Library). N.Y., 1945. Good, brief narration.

Flenley, R., *Modern German History*. N.Y., 1953. An attractive and useful history of Germany since the eighteenth century.

Florinsky, M. T., *Russia, a History and an Interpretation*, 2 vols. N.Y., 1953. Probably the most useful general history of Russia in English. Goes to the 1917 Revolution.

Gershoy, L., *The Era of the French Revolution, 1789–1799* (Anvil). Princeton, 1957. Excellent recent paperback; half text, half documents.

Geyl, P., *Napoleon, For and Against*. New Haven, 1949. An unusual and very valuable description of French historians on Napoleon.

Golob, E. O., *The "Isms"! A History and Evaluation*. N.Y., 1954. Social and economic theories clearly explained and bravely evaluated.

Goodwin, A., *The French Revolution*. London, 1953. Good recent short account.

Gottschalk, L. R., *Jean-Paul Marat*. N.Y., 1927. One of many studies by an expert on the Revolution.

Greenlaw, R. W., ed., *The Economic Origins of the French Revolution*. Boston, 1958. Selections from the great historians.

Guérard, A., *Napoleon I, a Great Life in Brief*. N.Y., 1956. Fascinating, brief, and controversial.

———, *Napoleon III, a Great Life in Brief*. N.Y., 1955. Fascinating miniature version of author's longer study of same figure.

Hammond, J. L. and Hammond, B., *The Bleak Age*, rev. ed. Harmondsworth, Middlesex, England, 1947. The seamy side of industrial change.

Hayes, C. J. H., *Essays on Nationalism*. N.Y., 1926. Still an excellent introduction to the subject.

Holborn, H., *The Political Collapse of Europe*. N.Y., 1951. Excellent on the balance of power.

Hook, S., *Marx and the Marxists* (Anvil). Princeton, 1955. Convenient paperback introduction; half text, half documents.

King, B., *A History of Italian Unity*, 2 vols., rev. ed. London, 1924. Long the best account in English.

Kircheisen, F. M., *Napoleon*. N.Y., 1932. Abridgment of a standard work.

Kohn, H., *Basic History of Modern Russia* (Anvil). Princeton, 1957. Convenient paperback; part text, part documents. Most useful on the nineteenth century.

———, *Nationalism, Its Meaning and History*. Princeton, 1955. Convenient paperback; part text, part documents by authority on the subject.

———, ed., *The Mind of Modern Russia*. New Brunswick, 1955. Source readings with valuable introductions.

Laidler, H. W., *Social-Economic Movements* N.Y., 1949. Encyclopedic.

Lefebvre. G., *The Coming of the French Revolution*. N.Y., 1957. Paperback edition of the best book on the subject.

Mack-Smith, D., *Garibaldi*. N.Y., 1956. Good recent account.

Manuel, F. E., *The New World of Henri St.-Simon*. Cambridge, 1956. Outstanding work of intellectual history.

Markham, F. M. H., *Napoleon and the Awakening of Europe* (Teach Yourself History series). N.Y., 1954. A good brief narrative.

Mathiez, A., *The French Revolution*. N.Y., 1928. Brilliant sympathetic account by an admirer of Robespierre. Goes to 9 Thermidor.

Maurois, A., *A History of France*. N.Y., 1956. A good general history.

May, A. J., *The Age of Metternich, 1814–1848*. N.Y., 1933. Useful brief introduction.

Maynard, J., *Russia in Flux*. N.Y., 1949. Essays on the Russian peasant, Russian intellectual history, and the Russian Revolution.

Mazour, A. G., *The First Russian Revolution, 1825*. Berkeley, 1937. First-rate study. Extremely rewarding.

Mill, J. S., *Autobiography*. N.Y., 1944. Classic.

Mumford, L., *Technics and Civilization*.

N.Y., 1934. Unusual appreciation of often neglected material.

Namier, L. B., *1848: the Revolution of the Intellectuals*. London, 1947. Important.

Napoleon I, *Letters*, ed. J. M. Thompson (Everyman edition). N.Y., 1954. A fine collection.

Nicolson, H. *The Congress of Vienna*. N.Y., 1946. Entertaining and valuable.

Packe, M. St. J., *The Bombs of Orsini*. London, England, 1957. A superb biography of a conspirator in the cause of Italian unity and a fine picture of Italy in the years 1830–1850.

Palmer, R. R., *Twelve Who Ruled*. Princeton, 1941. Best book on the Committee of Public Safety and the Reign of Terror.

Pinson, K. S., *Modern Germany, Its History and Civilization*. N.Y., 1954. Good recent text.

Raynal, M., *The Nineteenth Century: Goya to Gauguin*. Geneva, Switzerland, 1951. Beautiful history of painting.

Riasanovsky, N. V., *Russia and the West in the Teaching of the Slavophiles*. Cambridge, 1953. Fine clarification of a much misunderstood subject.

Robertson, C. G., *Bismarck*. London, England, 1918. Old but still one of the best.

Robertson, P., *Revolutions of 1848: A Social History*. Princeton, 1952. Perhaps the most interesting single volume on the subject.

Robinson, G. T., *Rural Russia under the Old Régime,* 2nd ed. N.Y., 1949. Excellent study of serfdom and of relations of peasants and landowners from earliest times to 1917.

Ruggiero, G., *History of European Liberalism*. London, 1927. Standard work on the subject.

Schapiro, J. S., *Liberalism: its Meaning and History* (Anvil). Princeton, 1958. Convenient introductory description accompanied by documents. Paperback.

Shafer, B. C., *Nationalism, Myth and Reality*. N.Y., 1956. A good recent discussion.

Somervell, D. C., *English Thought in the Nineteenth Century*. London, 1929. Convenient little handbook.

Stewart, J. H., *Documentary Survey of the French Revolution*. N.Y., 1951. The best source book, with very useful brief essays on the various periods and topics.

Taylor, A. J. P., *Bismarck, the Man and the Statesman*. N.Y., 1955. Readable, full of risky interpretations.

———, *The Habsburg Monarchy, 1809–1918,* 2nd ed. London, England, 1948. Very useful.

———, *The Struggle for Mastery in Europe, 1848–1918*. Oxford, England, 1954. A controversial recent diplomatic history.

Taylor, P. A. M., ed., *The Industrial Revolution in Britain*. Boston, 1958. Excellent collection of articles expressing various attitudes.

Thompson, J. M., *The French Revolution*. N.Y., 1943. By outstanding English authority.

———, *Napoleon Bonaparte*. N.Y., 1952. One of the best recent biographies.

———, *Robespierre and the French Revolution* (Teach Yourself History Library). N.Y., 1953. Good brief biography.

———, *Leaders of the French Revolution*. Oxford, 1948. Convenient biographical studies.

Thomas, D., *England in the Nineteenth Century, 1815–1914*. Harmondsworth, Middlesex, England, 1950. The most convenient brief history.

Tocqueville, A. de, *The European Revolution and Correspondence with Gobineau*. Edited and translated by John Lukacs (Anchor Original). N.Y., 1959. From De Tocqueville's notes for projected chapters carrying the story through the Revolution to Napoleon.

Viereck, P., *Conservatism from John Adams to Churchill* (Anvil) Princeton, 1956. A general treatment; half text, half documents. Paperback.

Whyte, A. J., *The Evolution of Modern Italy*. Oxford, 1944. Good narrative.

Wilson, E., *To the Finland Station*. Garden City, 1953. Popular history of socialism.

Woodward, E. L., *The Age of Reform* (Oxford History of England). Oxford, 1938. A standard history.

PART FOUR
Plebeian and Imperial Europe, 1870–1914

NOTE: Many of the national and other histories from previous sections carry over into this section. Most of them will not be repeated here.

Adams, W. S., *Edwardian Heritage*. London, England, 1949. A pleasant, if prejudiced, account of the first decade of the twentieth century in England.

Albrecht-Carrié, R., *Italy from Napoleon to Mussolini*. N.Y., 1950. A convenient general survey.

Ausubel, H., *The Late Victorians*. (Anvil). Princeton, 1955. Paperback, with text and documents. A clever and readable analysis.

Brogan, D. W., *France under the Republic (1870–1939)*. N.Y., 1940. A shrewd and sardonic political history, splendidly original.

Bruce, M., *The Shaping of the Modern World, 1870–1914* N.Y., 1958. An extremely detailed textbook of the period, exhaustive and up-to-date, useful for reference. A second value carrying the story to 1939 is projected.

Chapman, G., *The Dreyfus Case: A Reassessment*. N.Y., 1956. A careful reappraisal of the most sensational episode in French history from 1870 to 1914. It reads like a spy story.

Earle, E. M., ed., *Modern France. Problems of the Third and Fourth Republics*. Princeton, 1951. Essays by experts.

Ensor, R. C. K., *England, 1870–1914* (Oxford History of England). Oxford, 1936. A standard work and an admirable general history.

Fay, S. B., *The Origins of the World War*, 2 vols. N.Y., 1932. A standard, but now rather old work. Vol. I is a survey of the diplomacy of the years before 1914. Vol. II is a fascinating, hour-by-hour account of the summer crisis which ended in the outbreak of World War I.

Feis, H., *Europe, The World's Banker, 1870–1914*. New Haven, 1930. A detailed study of the export of capital and of Europe's economic position.

Freud, S., *An Outline of Psychoanalysis*. N.Y., 1949. Important document in twentieth-century intellectual history.

Haimson, L. H., *The Russian Marxists and the Origins of Bolshevism*. Cambridge, 1955. Useful monograph.

Halevy, E., *A History of the English People in the Nineteenth Century, Epilogue (1895–1905; 1905–1915)*. N.Y., 1951. The superb concluding volumes of a monumental work, heavily slanted in the direction of the author's liberal principles.

Hayes, C. J. H., *A Generation of Materialism, 1871–1900* (Langer Series). N.Y., 1941. A brilliant critical study of an age, which may also serve as an excellent textbook for advanced students.

Hobson, J. A., *Imperialism: A Study*. London, 1902. A history-making book, which set forth for the first time the idea that empire-building was the consequence of crass materialistic motives.

Hoskins, H. L., *European Imperialism in Africa*. N. Y., 1930. Brief introductory survey.

Kann, R. A., *The Multinational Empire*, 2 Vols. N.Y., 1950. A detailed study of the structure and nationalities of the Habsburg monarchy.

Kürenberg, J. von, *The Kaiser*. N.Y., 1955. A brilliant and revealing biography of the last German emperor, William II.

Langer, W. L., *The Diplomacy of Imperialism, 1890–1902*, 2nd ed. N.Y., 1951. Has detailed diplomatic history but also discussion of the general subject of imperialism.

Lee, D. E., ed., *The Outbreak of the First World War. Who was Responsible?* Boston, 1958. A convenient little paperback with a collection of points of view of outstanding authorities.

Lenin, V. I., *Imperialism, the Highest Stage of Capitalism*. N.Y., 1939. The basic and original text of the neo-Marxist interpretation of imperialism.

Leo XIII, *The Great Encyclical Letters*. N.Y., 1903. Important to an understanding of Catholic social philosophy.

Lobanov-Rostovsky, A., *Russia and Asia*, rev. ed. Ann Arbor, Michigan, 1951. Useful survey.

May, A., *The Habsburg Monarchy, 1867–1914*. Cambridge, 1951. A convenient and well-written general history.

Moody, J. N., ed., *Church and Society: Catholic Social and Political Thought and Movements, 1789–1950*. N.Y., 1953. Generally useful, but particularly so for the period from 1870 to 1914.

Oliver, R., *Sir Harry Johnston and the Scramble for Africa*. London, 1957. A recent biography of one of the greatest of British empire builders.

Pares, B., *The Fall of the Russian Monarchy*. N.Y., 1939. A detailed narrative by a sympathetic observer.

Pratt, J. T., *The Expansion of Europe into the Far East*. London, 1947. An admirable general account of imperialism in Asia.

Schmitt, B. E., *The Coming of the War, 1914*, 2 vols. N.Y., 1930. A detailed analysis, somewhat more critical of Germany than Fay (see above).

Seton-Watson, H., *The Decline of Imperial Russia, 1855–1914*. N.Y., 1952.

A simplified and controversial, but brief and manageable account.

Sprigge, C., *The Development of Modern Italy*. New Haven, 1944. The clever and intelligible account of a journalist, slanted toward a bleak liberalism.

Staley, E., *War and the Private Investor*. Chicago, 1935. A masterly study of the motives for imperial expansion, which tends to discredit the economic analysis of Hobson and Lenin.

Stavrianos, L. S., *The Balkans since 1453*. N.Y., 1958. With Wolff (see below), with which it differs slightly in coverage, provides best recent information on the subject.

Taylor, A. J. P., *The Struggle for Mastery in Europe, 1848–1918*. N.Y., 1954. A history of international relations which is magnificently written and highly argumentative.

Thomson, D., *Democracy in France: The Third and Fourth Republics*, 2nd ed. London, 1952. Fine analytical study. Not a chronological narrative.

Wallace, D. M., *Russia*. London, various editions from 1877 to 1912. Fascinating descriptions.

Williams, B., *Cecil Rhodes*. London, 1921 (Teach Yourself History series). A good biography of the great British imperialist.

Wolfe, B. D., *Three Who Made a Revolution*. N.Y., 1948. Lenin, Trotsky, and Stalin before the Revolution.

Wolff, R. L., *The Balkans in Our Time*. Cambridge, 1956. One of the best recent surveys. Has valuable section on the area and its history prior to 1939.

PART FIVE

The Forfeiture of World Power, 1914–1939

NOTE: Many of the books in the previous two sections apply here.

Bailey, T. A., *Wilson and the Peacemakers*. N.Y., 1947. Convenient and clarifying.

Birdsall, P., *Versailles Twenty Years After*. N.Y., 1941. A cool and judicious analysis of the peace treaty.

Black, C. E., ed., *Challenge in Eastern Europe*. New Brunswick, N.J., 1954.

Valuable essays by two American authorities, C. E. Black and Henry L. Roberts, as well as by various others including exiles from East Central Europe.

Borkenau, F., *World Communism*. N.Y., 1939. A detailed but readable and rational analysis, by an apostate Communist.

Bowers, C., *My Mission to Spain*. N.Y., 1954. The lively memoirs of the American ambassador to the Spanish Republic. He was frankly and strenuously anti-franquist.

Brenan, G., *The Spanish Labyrinth*. N.Y., 1943. An excellent and relatively detached account of the events that led up to the Spanish Civil War.

Bruun, G., *Clemenceau*. Cambridge, 1943. Fine brief biography.

Bullock, A. C. L., *Hitler: A Study in Tyranny*. London, 1952. The best of the many biographies of Hitler, and one of the best of all recent political biographies.

Carew-Hunt, R. N., *The Theory and Practice of Communism*. N.Y., 1951. A handy and perceptive summary of Communist theory.

Carr., E. H., *A History of Soviet Russia*. 5 Vols. N.Y., 1950–59. A painstaking but exhaustive study of the period to 1926.

Chamberlin, W. H., *The Russian Revolution, 1917–1921*, 2 vols. N.Y., 1935. Most useful narrative history.

Clough, S.B., *The Economic Development of Western Civilization*. N.Y., 1959. See the valuable chapters in Part V.

Craig, G. A., and Gilbert, F., eds., *The Diplomats: 1919–1939*. Princeton, 1953. A monumental collection of biographical essays, some of them excellent.

Cruttwell, C. R. M., *A History of the Great War, 1914–1918*. Oxford, England, 1934. A brief and readable (and very, very British) summary.

Curtiss, J. S., *The Russian Revolution of 1917* (Anvil). Princeton, 1957. Unusually useful paperback introduction; half text, half documents.

Deutscher, I., *The Prophet Armed, Trotsky: 1879–1921*. N.Y., 1954. Very revealing of Trotsky's personality and beliefs.

———, *Stalin: a Political Biography*. N.Y., 1949. Fascinating biography by a scholarly socialist who is emotionally involved, yet objective.

Fainsod, M., *How Russia is Ruled*. Cambridge, Mass., 1953. The Soviet political system described without jargon.

Finer, H., *Mussolini's Italy*. N.Y., 1935. Dated and detailed, but still the best, if not the only, serious study of Fascist Italy.

Fischer, E., *The Passing of the European Age*. Cambridge, 1943. A rather prophetic book.

Gathorne-Hardy, G. M., *A Short History of International Affairs (1920–1939.)* 3rd rev. ed. London, England, 1942. The standard account of the diplomatic history.

Halperin, S.W., *Germany Tried Democracy*. N.Y., 1946. A thorough and finely written account of the Weimar Republic from a strong democratic standpoint.

Harrod, R. F., *The Life of John Maynard Keynes*. N.Y., 1951. A fine biography of the great economist which helps explain the "Keynesian Revolution" and tells about the economic and intellectual tenor of the times.

Hitler, A., *Mein Kampf*. N.Y., 1939. Hitler's tract and autobiography; the fundamental statement of Nazi propaganda and doctrine.

Holborn, H., *The Political Collapse of Europe*. N.Y., 1951. A very brief and readable interpretation of Europe's international problems in the past two hundred years.

Kennan, G. F., *Russia Leaves the War*. N.Y., 1956. A careful study by a famous America diplomat.

Lorwin, V. P., *The French Labor Movement*. Cambridge, 1954. A masterly analysis which includes a cogent summary of events of the interwar years.

Lukacs, J. A., *The Great Powers and Eastern Europe*. N.Y., 1953. A detailed study of the diplomacy concerned with East Central Europe since World War I.

Macdonald, M., *The Republic of Austria, 1918–1934*. N.Y., 1946. A brief survey of the failure of Austrian democracy.

McKay, D. C., *The United States and France*. Cambridge, 1951. Convenient handbook about France as well as about Franco-American relations.

Meinecke, F., *The German Catastrophe*. Cambridge, 1950. A great German historian reviews the record.

Meyer, A. G., *Leninism*. Cambridge, 1957. An excellent study of Lenin's views and policies.

Mowat, C. L., *Britain Between the Wars*. London, 1955. A splendid history, balanced, entertaining, and exhaustive.

Neumann, F. L., *Behemoth: the Structure and Practice of National Socialism 1933–1944*. N.Y., 1944. Difficult but deep and rewarding.

Nicolson, H., *King George V*. London, 1952. A searching and interesting biography of the British monarch who reigned 1910–1936.

———, *Peacemaking 1919*. N.Y., 1939. A brilliant and bitter description of the atmosphere of the Paris Peace Conference by one who participated in it.

Radkey, O. H., *The Agrarian Foes of Bolshevism*. N.Y., 1958. The best book on the Russian Socialist Revolutionaries.

Rauch, G. von, *A History of Soviet Russia*. N.Y., 1957. The views of a German expert.

Roberts, H. L., *Rumania. Political Problems of an Agrarian State*. New Haven, 1951. An admirable survey which provides ample illustration of the paradoxes of Eastern Europe.

Rostow, W. W., *The Dynamics of Soviet Society* (Mentor). N.Y., 1954. One of the most useful books about the Soviet Union; has both historical and analytical chapters.

Salvemini, G., *Under the Axe of Fascism*. N.Y., 1936. A ringing denunciation of Mussolini, which has a good deal of information and insights nowhere else available.

Schwartz, H., *Russia's Soviet Economy*, 2nd ed. Englewood Cliffs, 1954. The best introduction to the subject.

Seton-Watson, H., *Eastern Europe between the Wars, 1918–1941*. Cambridge, England, 1946. By a well-informed Englishman; almost the only book on the whole area.

Shub, D., *Lenin*. N.Y., 1948. A careful, critical biography.

Stavrianos, L. S., *The Balkans since 1453*. N.Y., 1958. With Wolff (see below), with which it differs slightly in coverage, provides best recent information on the subject.

Wheeler-Bennett, J. W., *The Nemesis of Power*. N.Y., 1952. Political role of the German army.

Wiskemann, E., *The Rome-Berlin Axis*. N.Y., 1949. An intriguing study of Italian-German relations which reveals a good deal about the nature of both nations and both dictatorships.

Wolff, R. L., *The Balkans in Our Times*. Cambridge, 1956. One of the best recent surveys. Has valuable section on the area and its history prior to 1939, but is largely devoted to World War II and after.

PART SIX
Divided Europe, Since 1939

Bolles, E. B., *The Big Change in Europe*. N.Y., 1958. A journalist reviews the scene since 1953.

Borkenau, F., *European Communism*. London, 1953. By the well-informed author of the earlier book *World Communism*.

Brady, R., *Crisis in Britain*. Berkeley, 1950. A study of the British Labor government and the problems of Britain's international economic situation.

Campbell, A., *The Heart of Africa*. N.Y., 1954. A study of native problems in awakening Central Africa.

Churchill, W., *The Second World War*, 6 vols. Boston, 1948–1953. Personal, oratorical, and partial, the six volumes are still the best account of the issues and events of World War II.

Clay, L. D., *Decision in Germany*. Garden City, 1950. An account of the crucial period after the end of World War II, by the commander of the American forces in Germany.

Commager, H. S., and others. *Contemporary Civilization*. Chicago, 1959. Convenient survey of contemporary world problems with articles by experts.

Daniel, H., *The Ordeal of the Captive Nations*. N.Y., 1959. Useful popular account of the fall of East Central Europe to the Russians.

Deutscher, I., *Russia in Transition*. N.Y., 1957.

———, *Heretics and Renegades*. London, 1955. Collections of controversial essays by the learned author of *Stalin: A Political Biography*.

Djilas, M., *The New Class*. N.Y., 1957. A Yugoslav Communist in rebellion against communism turned bureaucratic.

Duverger, M., *The French Political System*. Chicago, 1958. Written by recognized French expert just before end of Fourth Republic.

Eichelberger, C. M., *UN: The First Ten Years*. N.Y., 1955. A balance sheet and recommendations.

Farmer, P., *Vichy, Political Dilemma*. N.Y., 1955. One of the most controversial French topics, discussed by an American historian.

Feis, H., *Churchill, Roosevelt, Stalin*. Princeton, 1957. A monumental and impartial account of Big Three relationships.

Fuller, J. F. C., *The Second World War*. N.Y., 1949. A standard account by an able British military analyst.

Gatzke, H. W., *The Present in Perspective*. Chicago, 1957. Convenient survey of world history since World War II.

Hughes, S., *The United States and Italy*. Cambridge, 1953. Valuable for the rebuilding of constitutional government after the fall of the Fascists.

Kennan, G. F., *Russia, the Atom, and the West*. N.Y., 1958. The author of the U.S. "containment" policy reviews the world situation ten years later.

Kertesz, S. D., ed., *The Fate of East-Central Europe*. Notre Dame, 1956. The problems examined by experts on the area.

Kissinger, H. M., *Nuclear Weapons and Foreign Policy*. N.Y., 1957. A discussion of the implications of changes in weapons since World War II.

Lasky, M. J., ed., *The Hungarian Revolution*. N.Y., 1957. A book of documents with useful commentary.

Lochner, L., *The Goebbels Diaries, 1942–1943*. Garden City, 1948. A revelation of the mind of Hitler's right-hand man.

MacLean, F., *The Heretic: The Life and Times of Josip Broz-Tito*. N.Y., 1957.

Mendelssohn, P. de., *Design for Aggression; the inside story of Hitler's War Plans*. N.Y., 1946. A collection of documents and interpretations, based on captured German papers, outlining the cold-blooded war preparations of Hitler.

Nuseibeh, H. Z., *The Ideas of Arab Nationalism*. Ithaca, 1956. An interesting study of one of the world's most explosive forces.

Salvadori, M., *NATO: A Twentieth Century Community of Nations* (Anvil). Princeton, N.J., 1957. A convenient paperback, half text, half documents.

Schoenbrun, D., *As France Goes*. N.Y., 1957. Readable analytical and descriptive chapters by a well-informed reporter.

Seton-Watson, H., *The East European Revolution*. N.Y., 1951. The East Central European countries and their conquest by the U.S.S.R.

Strauz-Hupé, R., and Hazard, H. W., eds., *The Idea of Colonialism*. N.Y., 1958. A collection of essays by experts.

Werth, A., *France 1940–1955*. N.Y., 1956. Detailed history by an unusually well-informed journalist.

Wilmot, C., *The Struggle for Europe*. N.Y., 1952. A controversial account of Anglo-American differences over strategic and political problems, embedded in an excellent narrative account of war and diplomacy.

Wolfe, B. D., *Khrushchev and Stalin's Ghost*. N.Y., 1957. Text of Khrushchev's famous denunciation of Stalin at the 20th Party Congress in 1956, with comments by Mr. Wolfe.

INDEX